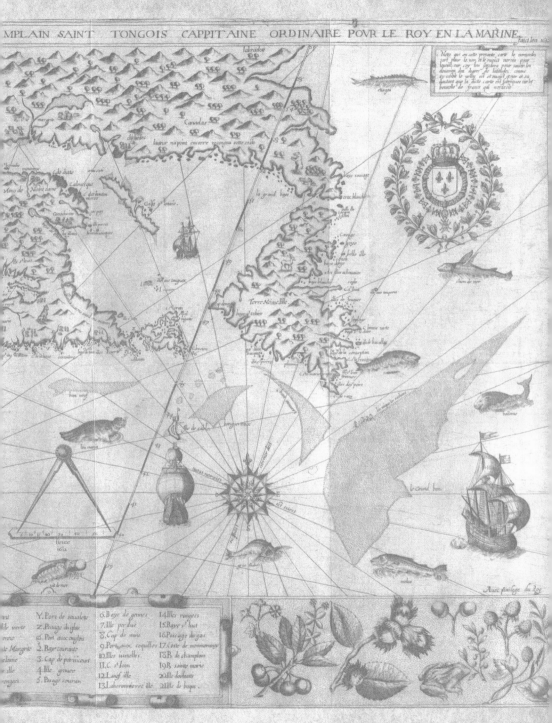

Samuel de Champlain, Map of New France, 1612.

CHAMPLAIN'S DREAM

ALSO BY DAVID HACKETT FISCHER

Liberty and Freedom

Washington's Crossing

Bound Away

The Great Wave

Paul Revere's Ride

Albion's Seed

Growing Old in America

Historians' Fallacies

The Revolution of American Conservatism

CHAMPLAIN'S DREAM

David Hackett Fischer

Alfred A. Knopf Canada

PUBLISHED BY ALFRED A. KNOPF CANADA

Copyright © 2008 David Hackett Fischer

Maps copyright © 2008 Jeff Ward

All rights reserved under International and Pan-American Copyright Conventions. No part of this book may be reproduced in any form or by any electronic or mechanical means, including information storage and retrieval systems, without permission in writing from the publisher, except by a reviewer, who may quote brief passages in a review. Published in 2008 by Alfred A. Knopf Canada, a division of Random House of Canada Limited, and simultaneously in the United States of America by Simon & Schuster, Inc., New York. Distributed by Random House of Canada Limited, Toronto.

Knopf Canada and colophon are trademarks.

www.randomhouse.ca

Library and Archives Canada Cataloguing in Publication

Fischer, David Hackett, 1935–
    Champlain's dream / David Hackett Fischer.

    Includes bibliographical references and index.
    ISBN 978-0-307-39766-9

    1. Champlain, Samuel de, 1567–1635.   2. Explorers—Canada—Biography.
3. Explorers—France—Biography.   4. Canada—Discovery and exploration—
French.   5. Canada—History—To 1763 (New France).   I. Title.
    FC332.F58   2008   971.01'13092   C2008-903173-3

Text design: Jaime Putorti

First Edition

Printed and bound in the United States of America

10 9 8 7 6 5 4 3 2 1

CONTENTS

CHAMPLAIN'S DREAM

INTRODUCTION
In Search of Champlain

His activities, which were revealed mainly through his writings, were always surrounded by a certain degree of mystery.

—Raymonde Litalien, 2004[1]

A N OLD FRENCH engraving survives from the early seventeenth century. It is a battle-print, at first glance like many others in European print shops. We look again, and discover that it shows a battle in North America, fought between Indian nations four centuries ago. The caption reads in old French, "Deffaite des Yroquois au Lac de Champlain," the "Defeat of the Iroquois at Lake Champlain," July 30, 1609.[2]

On one side we see sixty Huron, Algonquin, and Montagnais warriors. On the other are two hundred Iroquois of the Mohawk nation. They meet in an open field beside the lake. The smaller force is attacking boldly, though outnumbered three to one. The Mohawk have sallied from a log fort to meet them. By reputation they are among the most formidable warriors in North America. They have the advantage of numbers and position, and yet the caption tells us that the smaller force won the fight.[3]

The print offers an explanation in the presence of a small figure who stands alone at the center of the battle. His dress reveals that he is a French soldier and a man of rank. He wears half-armor of high quality: a well-fitted cuirass on his upper body, and protective britches of the latest design with light steel plates on his thighs.[4] His helmet is no ordinary *morion,* or crude iron pot of the kind that we associate with Spanish conquistadors and English colonists. It is an elegant example of what the French call a *casque bourgignon,* a Burgundian helmet of distinctive design that was the choice of kings and noblemen— a handsome, high-crowned helmet with a comb and helm forged from a single piece of metal.[5] Above the helmet is a large plume of white feathers called a *panache*—the origin of our modern word. Its color identifies the wearer as a

1

"Deffaite des Yroquois au Lac de Champlain," appeared in his Voyages *(1613). The engraver (probably David Pelletier) introduced small errors, but Marc Lescarbot confirmed the accuracy of Champlain's account from other sources, including one of the arquebusiers (upper center).*

captain in the service of Henri IV, first Bourbon king of France. Its size marks it as a badge of courage worn to make its wearer visible in battle.[6]

This French captain is not a big man. Even with his panache, the Indians appear half a head taller. But he has a striking presence, and in the middle of a wild mêlée he stands still and quiet, firmly in command of himself. His back is straight as a ramrod. His muscular legs are splayed apart and firmly planted to bear the weight of a weapon which he holds at full length. It is not a conventional matchlock, as historians have written, but a complex and very costly *arquebuse à rouet*, a wheel-lock arquebus. It was the first self-igniting shoulder weapon that did not require a burning match, and could fire as many as four balls in a single shot.[7]

The text with this engraving tells us that the French captain has already fired his arquebus and brought down two Mohawk chiefs and a third warrior, who lie on the ground before him. He aims his weapon at a fourth Mohawk, and we see the captain fire again in a cloud of white smoke. On the far side of the battlefield, half-hidden in the American forest, two French *arquebusiers* emerge from the trees. They kneel and fire their weapons into the flank of the dense Iroquois formation.[8]

We look back at the French captain and catch a glimpse of his face. He has a high forehead, arched brows, eyes set wide apart, a straight nose turned up at

This very small image from the Voyages *of 1613 is the only likeness of Champlain that is known to survive from his own time. The original figure is less than one inch high, but its small details reveal many things about the man himself. His great patache was of the sort made by royal* plumassières *at the court of Henry IV. The Burgundian helmet was of a type that appears in equestrian portraits of kings and noblemen. The* arquebuse à rouet *was an advanced model of a very costly weapon. This is the image of an officer of high standing, with the resources of a great state behind him. It is also a self-portrait which offers other clues to the elusive man who drew it.*

the tip, a fashionable mustache, and a beard trimmed like that of his king, Henri IV. The key below the print gives us his name, the "sieur de Champlain."[9]

This small image is the only authentic likeness of Samuel de Champlain that is known to survive from his own time. It is also a self-portrait, and its technique tells us other things about the man who drew it. A French scholar observes that "its style is that of a man of action, direct, natural, naive, biased toward exact description, toward the concrete and the useful." This is art without a hint of artifice. It tells a story in a straightforward way. At the same time, it expresses the artist's pride in his acts, and confidence in his purposes. It also points up a paradox in what we know about him. It describes his actions in detail, but the man himself is covered in armor, and his face is partly hidden by his own hand.[10]

Other images of Champlain would be invented after the fact. Many years later, when he was recognized as the father of New France, he was thought to require a proper portrait. Artists and sculptors were quick to supply a growing market. Few faces in modern history have been reinvented so often and from so little evidence. All these images are fictions. The most widely reproduced was a fraud, detected many years ago and still used more frequently than any other.[11]

Historians also contributed many word-portraits of Champlain, and no two are alike. His biographer Morris Bishop asserted from little evidence that "Champlain was, in fact, a lean ascetic type, dry and dark, probably rather under than over normal size . . . his southern origin is indication enough of dark hair and black eyes." [12] Another biographer, Samuel Eliot Morison, wrote from no evidence whatever: "As one who has lived with Champlain for many years, I may be permitted to give my own idea of him. A well-built man of medium stature, blond and bearded, a natural leader who inspired loyalty and commanded obedience." [13] A third author, Heather Hudak, represented him with bright red hair, a black panache and chartreuse britches. [14] Playwright Michael Hollingsworth described Champlain as prematurely gray, as well he might have been, and an anonymous engraver gave him snow-white hair. Champlain's biographies, like his portraits, show the same wealth of invention and poverty of fact. [15]

Champlain himself was largely responsible for that. He wrote thousands of pages about what he did, but only a few words about who he was. His published works are extraordinary for an extreme reticence about his origins, inner thoughts, private life, and personal feelings. Rarely has an author written so much and revealed so little about himself. These were not casual omissions, but studied silences. Here again, as in the old battle-print, Champlain was hidden by his own hand. He was silent and even secretive about the most fundamental facts of his life. He never mentioned his age. His birth date is uncertain. Little information survives about his family, and not a word about his schooling. He was raised in an age of faith, but we do not know if he was baptized Protestant or Catholic.

After all this uncertainty about the man himself, it is a relief to turn to the record of his acts. Here we have an abundance of evidence, and it makes a drama that is unique in the history of exploration. No other discoverer mastered so many roles over so long a time, and each of them presents a puzzle.

By profession Champlain was a soldier, and he chose to represent himself that way in his self-portrait. He fought in Europe, the Caribbean, and North America, bore the scars of wounds on his face and body, and witnessed atrocities beyond imagining. Like many old soldiers, he took pride in his military service, but he grew weary of war. Always he kept a soldier's creed of honor, courage, and duty, but increasingly did so in the cause of peace. There is a question about how he squared these thoughts.

At the same time, Champlain was a mariner of long experience. He went to sea at an early age, and rose from ship's boy to "admirall" of a colonizing fleet. From 1599 to 1633 he made at least twenty-seven Atlantic crossings and hundreds of other voyages. He never lost a ship under his command, except once when he was a passenger aboard a sinking barque in a heavy gale on a lee shore, with a captain who was unable to act. Champlain seized command, set the mainsail, and deliberately drove her high on a rocky coast in a raging storm—and saved every man aboard. There are interesting questions to be asked about his leadership and astonishing seamanship.[16]

Champlain is best remembered for his role as an explorer. He developed a method of close-in coastal exploration that he called "ferreting," and he used it to study thousands of miles of the American coast from Panama to Labrador. He also explored much of North America through what are now six Canadian provinces and five American states. He was the first European to see much of this countryside, and he enabled us to see it through his eyes. His unique methods raise another question about how he did that work, and with what result.

Champlain also mapped this vast area in yet another role as a cartographer. He put himself in the forefront of geographic knowledge in his era. His many maps and charts set a new standard for accuracy and detail. Experts have studied them with amazement. They wonder how he made maps of such excellence with the crude instruments at his command.[17] He also embellished his maps with handsome drawings. In his own time he was known as an artist. When rival French merchants opposed his appointment to high office, they complained that Champlain was a "mere painter," and therefore unfit for command. In his drawings he left us a visual record of the new world, which alone would make him an important figure. To study the few originals is to discover the skill and refinement of his art. But nearly all his art survives only in crude copies that challenge us to recover the spirit of his work.[18]

Champlain was a prolific writer. He is most accessible to us through his published books, which exceed in quantity and quality the work of every major explorer of North America during his era. A close second was the work of Captain John Smith, but Champlain's published writings were larger in bulk. They covered a broader area, spanned a longer period, and drew deeply on the intellectual currents of his age. The problem is to find the mind behind the prose.

In his books Champlain played a role as a pioneer ethnographer. He left an abundance of first-hand description about many Indian nations in North America. During the late twentieth century some scholars criticized him for ethnocentrism. That judgment is correct in some ways, but Champlain's work remains a major source of sympathetic description. A challenging problem is to sort out truth from error.[19]

He was also a naturalist. Champlain loved plants and animals, gathered information about the flora and fauna of the new world, and studied the climate and resources of the places he visited. He planted experimental gardens in four colonies and did much descriptive writing about the American environment before European settlement, and how it changed.[20]

Especially important to his posterity was Champlain's role as a founder and leader of the first permanent French settlements in North America. A major part of his life was his economic association with many trading companies that paid for New France. This was Champlain's most difficult role, and his least successful. Wealthy investors often defeated him, and many companies failed. But in his stewardship, New France somehow survived three decades of failure—which is not only an unknown but a mystery.

Through those same three decades from 1603 to 1635, Champlain also returned to France in most years. He had another busy career as a courtier and a tireless promoter of his American project. Four people ruled France in that era: Henri IV until 1610, Marie de Medici as queen regent after 1610, Louis XIII from 1617, and Richelieu as "first minister" from 1624. Champlain worked directly with all except the queen regent, argued vigorously for New France, and prodded them so forcefully that one wonders how he stayed out of the Bastille. During that long period, six highborn French noblemen and "princes of the blood" served as lieutenant general or viceroy or "cardinal-admiral" of New France. All but one of them were absentees who never came to America. Each of them without exception chose Champlain to be his chief lieutenant and commander in the new world. He got on with all those very difficult people—another puzzle.

One of Champlain's most important roles was in the peopling of New France. For some reason the French have always been less likely to emigrate than were millions of British, Germans, and other Europeans. And yet in thirty years Champlain did more than any other leader to establish three French-speaking populations and start them growing in North America. In a pivotal moment from 1632 to 1635 when he was acting governor, they suddenly began to expand by sustained natural increase, and they have continued to do so, even to our own time. Champlain had a leading hand in that, and even subsidized marriages and families with his own wealth. Each of these three populations developed its own distinct culture and speechways which made them Québécois, Acadien, and Métis. Today their descendants have multiplied to millions of people. Something of Champlain's time survives in their language and folkways. They are chief among his many legacies.

Champlain also played a role in the religious history of New France. He worked with Protestant ministers, Catholic priests, Recollets, Jesuits, and Capuchins. His Christian faith was deeply important to him, increasingly so as he grew older. But he struggled to reconcile an ideal of tolerance with the reality of an established Church—a problem that he never solved.

If nothing else, his life was a record of stamina with few equals. But always it was more than that. Champlain was a dreamer. He was a man of vision, and like most visionaries he dreamed of many things. Several scholars have written about his dream of finding a passage to China. Others have written of his dream for the colonization in New France. But all these visions were part of a larger dream that has not been studied. This war-weary soldier had a dream of humanity and peace in a world of cruelty and violence. He envisioned a new world as a place where people of different cultures could live together in amity and concord. This became his grand design for North America.

Champlain was not a solitary dreamer. He moved within several circles of French humanists during the late sixteenth and early seventeenth centuries. They are neglected figures of much importance in the history of ideas— bridge-figures who inherited the Renaissance and inspired the Enlightenment. They were not of one mind, but they had large purposes in common. One group of French humanists centered on the person of Henri IV and were guided by his great example. Another was an American circle in Paris who never crossed the Atlantic but were inspired by the idea of the new world. In a third group were many French humanists who came to North America with Champlain—men such as the sieur de Mons and the sieur de Razilly. In the beginning they were his leaders. By the end he became theirs.

Champlain traveled in other circles among the leaders of Indian nations, who also were great dreamers. He knew them intimately, and they live as individuals in the pages of his books. Champlain had a way of getting along with very different people, and he also had the rarest gift of all. In long years of labor, he found a way to convert his dreams into realities. In the face of great obstacles and heavy defeats, he exercised his skills of leadership in extreme conditions. Those of us who are leaders today (which includes most of us in an open society) have something to learn from him about that.

Champlain was a leader, but he was not a saint. We do not need another work of hagiography about him. He was a mortal man of flesh and blood, a very complicated man. He made horrific errors in his career, and some of his mistakes cost other men their lives. He cultivated an easy manner, but sometimes he drove his men so hard that four of them tried to murder him. His quest for amity and concord with the Indians led to wars with the Mohawk and the Onondaga. His private life was deeply troubled, particularly in his relations with women. Champlain lived comfortably as a man among men, but one discovery eluded this great discoverer. He never found the way to a woman's heart. It was not for want of trying. He was strongly attracted to women, but his most extended relationship ended in frustration.

His ideal of humanity was very large, but it was also limited in strange, ironic ways. Champlain embraced the American Indians, but not his own French servants. He had deep flaws and made many enemies, responded badly to criticism, and could be very petty to rivals. But other men who knew this man wrote of him with respect and affection. Even his enemies did so.

Just now, we have an opportunity to study this extraordinary man in a new light. In the early twenty-first century, three nations are celebrating the 400th anniversary of his achievements. Something similar happened in the early twentieth century, for his 300th anniversary. The literature about Champlain is like a century plant. It blooms every hundred years, then fades and blooms again.

At the start of the twentieth century, a very large literature ran heavily to hagiography, and celebrated Champlain as a saintly figure. After 1950 the inevitable reaction set in. Popular debunkers and academic iconoclasts made Champlain a favorite target.[21] These attacks were deepened by a fin-de-siècle attitude called political correctness, with its revulsion against great white men, especially empire-builders, colonial founders, and discoverers.

Incredibly, some apostles of political correctness even tried to ban the word "discovery" itself. Historian Peter Pope met this attitude on the 500th anniversary of John Cabot's northern voyages of discovery. He recalls: "I was asked by a servant of the P.R. industry in June 1996 to summarize Cabot's achievement without using the term discovery. She told me it had been banned. . . . Any talk of 'discovery' is understood as an endorsement of conquest." Pope was ordered to "describe what the Venetian pilot did without using the D-word."[22]

As these attitudes spread widely during the late twentieth century, Champlain began to fade from the historical literature. He all but disappeared from school curricula in France, Canada, and the United States. Many still remember him, but when the subject came up in France, we heard people say, *"Connais pas,* never heard of him." In the United States, one person asked, "Champlain? Why are you writing a book about a lake?" In 1999, Canadian historian W. J. Eccles wrote that "there is no good biography of Champlain." For twenty years from 1987 to 2008, there was no full-scale biography at all.[23]

Since the turn of the twenty-first century, attitudes have been changing yet again. Historians are returning to the study of leaders in general, and to Champlain in particular. With the inspired leadership of Raymonde Litalien and Denis Vaugeois, five volumes of collected essays appeared in Canada, France, and the United States from 2004 to 2007. Together these books prompted more than a hundred new studies of Champlain and his world.[24]

They built on the foundation of a new historiography that had been growing quietly since the 1960s through all the Sturm und Drang of political correctness. Archaeological research has been taking place on an unprecedented scale. A new historical ethnography has deepened our understanding of Champlain's relations with Indians. A major school of Canadian social history led by the great scholarship of Marcel Trudel has wrought a revolution in our knowledge of Champlain's New France. Much important work has happened in demographic and economic history. Geographers led by Conrad Heidenreich have studied his cartography in detail. Archival scholars such as Robert Le Blant have turned up much new material on Champlain and made those findings more accessible to others.

The new scholarship of the early twenty-first century is becoming more mature, more global, more balanced, more empirical, more eclectic, and less ideological than before. A result of this new scholarship has been to undercut the writings of iconoclasts. Two generations ago, the dominant source for Champlain's life was his own writing, which inspired skepticism. Today in every chapter of his life, we can test his own accounts against the evidence of archaeology, archival materials, other narratives, complex chronologies, and interlocking sources in great variety. Many small errors and some larger ones have been found in Champlain's work, but the main lines of his writings have been reinforced by other evidence. An example is René Baudry, who worked with Le Blant to make much new archival material available to others. He writes of Champlain, "It is much to his credit that information from other sources almost always confirms the accuracy of his accounts."[25]

In this recent work, old methods are being used in new ways. One of them is the method of Herodotus, and his idea of history as a genuinely free and open inquiry—the literal Greek meaning of history. Another way forward was the school that taught historians three lessons about their work: "First, go there! Do it! Then write it!" To read Champlain's many books in that spirit, to explore the places that he described, and to follow in his track, is to make an astonishing discovery about our own world. Many of the places that Champlain described in the seventeenth century can still be seen today, not precisely as he saw them, but some of them are remarkably little changed. This is so in large parts of the St. Lawrence Valley and the magnificent Saguenay River. It is so along the Atlantic coast, the Gulf of Maine, the forests and waterways of Canada, the harbors of Acadia, and the coast of Gaspésie. It is so in the United States on Mount Desert Island, the Isles Rangées, the Puffin Islands, and Ticonderoga. It is that way again in the rolling ground of the Onondaga Country, and the natural meadowlands of Cap Tourmente.

Champlain's places of discovery are a world that we may be losing, but they are not yet a world we have lost. It is still possible to explore them by car and plane, by canoe and kayak, by sailboat and zodiac boat, by snowshoe—and some of the best places are accessible only by foot. At all these many sites we can rediscover this great discoverer by going there, and doing it, and traveling through his space in our time.

Other sites in Champlain's life are accessible in a different way. Archaeologists have been hard at work on the sites where he lived and worked. Many traces of what he did have been coming out of the ground in a most extraordinary way. That is so at Sainte-Croix Island, Port-Royal, Quebec, Pentagoet, Cap Tourmente, Ticonderoga, Huronia, and Iroquoia. On the other side of the water, it is the same at Brouage, Crozon, Blavet, Honfleur, Quimper, Fontainebleau, the Marais district of Paris, even the basement of the Louvre. Many of these places that were important to Champlain have preserved much of their character even as the world has changed around them. This book builds on all that physical evidence.

It also seeks a path of understanding between hagiographers on the one hand and iconoclasts on the other. In that regard, one of the most important opportunities of this inquiry is for us to get right with both Champlain and the American Indians.[26] Two generations ago, historians wrote of European saints and Indian savages. In the last generation, too many scholars have been writing about Indian saints and European savages. The opportunity for our generation is to go beyond that calculus of saints and savages altogether, and write about both American Indians and Europeans with maturity, empathy, and understanding. Many historians are now doing that, and this book is another effort in that direction.

After the delusions of political correctness, ideological rage, multiculturalism, postmodernism, historical relativism, and the more extreme forms of academic cynicism, historians today are returning to the foundations of their discipline with a new faith in the possibilities of historical knowledge, and with new results. This inquiry is conceived in that spirit. It begins not with a thesis, or a theory, or an ideology, but with a set of open questions about Champlain. It asks, who was this man? Where did he come from? What did he do? Why did he do it? What difference did he make? Why should we care? The answers to all these questions make a story. It begins where Champlain began, in a small town on the coast of France, looking outward across the Bay of Biscay toward America.

A LEADER IN THE MAKING

1.

A CHILD OF BROUAGE

The Sea as a School

Samuel Champlain, De Brouage

—title page of Champlain's
first published book, 1603[1]

T O TRAVEL THE OLD ROADS on the coast of France, south along the Bay of Biscay, is to find a beautiful and haunted place, full of interest for history-minded people. A few miles below the eighteenth-century navy town of Rochefort, we crossed the sparkling waters of the River Charente on a high-arched modern bridge and entered a region that was like another world. The terrain felt more like a floating island than part of the French mainland. It is very flat and not quite terra firma—a web of waterways and salt marshes, with seabirds swooping overhead and long views of sea and sky. On a sunny spring morning, the fields were green with new growth and the roadsides were brilliant with red poppies.

Near the center of this region, we followed the old D6 road as it veered past a copse of trees. Suddenly we came upon a walled town of very strange appearance. It was the object of our journey, and yet it took us by surprise. Rising before us was an old seaport that lies far from the sea. Its massive stone fortifications were once washed by the tide. Today they are a mile inland, surrounded by pastures and grazing cattle.

Four centuries ago, this little town was an important center of Atlantic trade. In the year 1581, a visitor from the rival port of La Rochelle described it as "without doubt the most beautiful harbor in France," and one of the busiest. Today it is still a place of striking beauty, but its harbor has nearly disappeared. Broad streets that were built for commerce were empty when we walked there, and our footsteps echoed in the silence of an empty town. We climbed its stone battlements and found them carpeted with wild flowers, blooming abundantly in the bright Biscayan sun.

This is the town of Brouage, where Samuel de Champlain lived as a child. Its colorful history was the salty broth in which our hero was cooked.[2]

• • •

In the time of the Romans, the land around the present site of Brouage lay under water, submerged beneath the great gulf of Saintonge. The coast of France was nine miles away, on a ring of rising land to the east. As the gulf receded, it left a muddy mix of water and clay that was called *broue*. The lowlands that emerged from the sea were called *brouage*, which came to mean an area of mudflats and salt marsh.[3]

From an early date, villages began to rise on this new land, and one of them was also called Brouage. It was a small trading town, and its most valuable commodity was salt—a gift of the sea and the sun to the people of this region. Salt was mined from deposits in coastal marshes, and evaporated from brine in open pans. It was vital for the preservation of food, and so much in demand that it was called the "white gold" of medieval Europe. Salt also became important in another way. Monarchs were quick to discover that it could easily be taxed. The result was the hated *gabelle*, the infamous salt tax that became a major source of revenue for the old regime in France, and a leading cause of revolution in 1789.[4]

The salt of this region was known for its color, variety, quality, and price. The Île d'Oléron produced a white salt of great refinement, as "white as snow." Périgord and Limousin yielded salt that was red or gray. Brouage had the most valuable commodity, a black salt that was favored on royal tables after François I made a gift of it to England's Henry VIII. The black salt of Brouage looked very handsome in the beautiful gold salt vessels of the celebrated artist Benvenuto Cellini. In the rank-bound world of early modern Europe, salt became important in yet another way as an emblem of hierarchy. Those of lower rank were said to sit below the salt.[5]

All this was good for business in Brouage, and the salt trade expanded rapidly. As early as the fifteenth century, sailing charts began to mark the harbor of Brouage in red ink as a place of particular importance.[6] Vessels large and small sailed to Brouage from many lands. In 1474, a fleet of twenty-six cogs arrived from the German city of Danzig (now the Polish Gdansk) and loaded salt for the Baltic herring industry.[7] Then came the discovery of the North American fishing grounds, and salt was needed more urgently than ever. In 1525, the Norman port of Le Havre alone sent thirty-five vessels to buy salt at Brouage for the American fisheries. That trade brought great wealth to little ports along the gulf of Saintonge. Their prosperity appears in handsome old buildings that still survive.[8]

Ships that anchored in the harbor of Brouage made room to take on cargoes of salt by dumping piles of ballast stones at the water's edge. In 1555

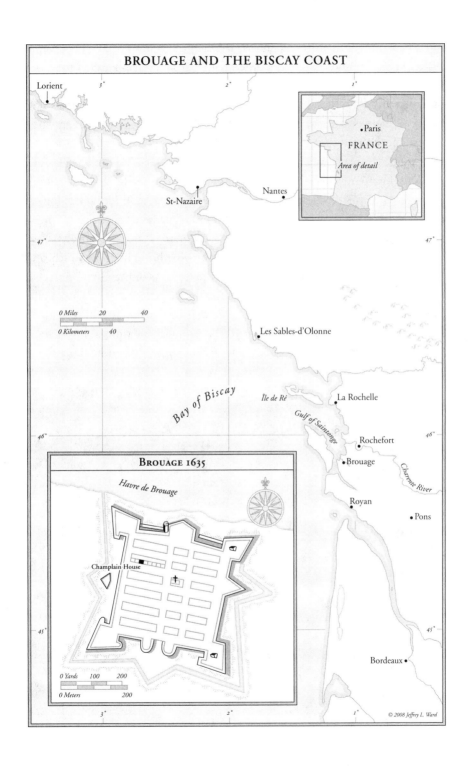

BROUAGE AND THE BISCAY COAST

Lorient

3°

2°

1°

Paris

FRANCE

Area of detail

St-Nazaire

Nantes

47°

47°

0 Miles   20   40

0 Kilometers   40

Les Sables-d'Olonne

Bay of Biscay

Île de Ré

La Rochelle

Gulf of Saintonge

Rochefort

46°

46°

Brouage

Charente River

Royan

Pons

BROUAGE 1635

Havre de Brouage

Champlain House

45°

45°

0 Yards   100   200

0 Meters   200

Bordeaux

3°

2°

1°

© 2008 Jeffrey L. Ward

or thereabout a local entrepreneur named Jacques de Pons decided to rebuild the town on a foundation of discarded ballast stones. People called the place Jacqueville, or Jacopolis-sur-Brouage, or simply Brouage. Charles IX, king of France from 1560 to 1574, dredged a harbor deep enough for large ships. Italian military engineers, the best in the world, constructed ditches, ramparts, and watchtowers.[9]

The new Brouage was designed as a handsome Renaissance *ville carrée*, a perfectly square town just over four hundred yards to a side. It was also built as a *place forte*, fortified against attack by land and sea, with round bastions at every corner, a massive stone gate, and a double wooden drawbridge. The elegant fortifications that stand today were the work of many generations. They were begun before Champlain was born, improved throughout his youth, and massively rebuilt by Cardinal Richelieu in Champlain's old age. Its approaches were expanded by great French military architects.[10]

Champlain witnessed much of this construction in his youth. A detailed manuscript map survives from about 1570, very near the time of his birth. It shows that Brouage was very much a work in progress when he lived there.

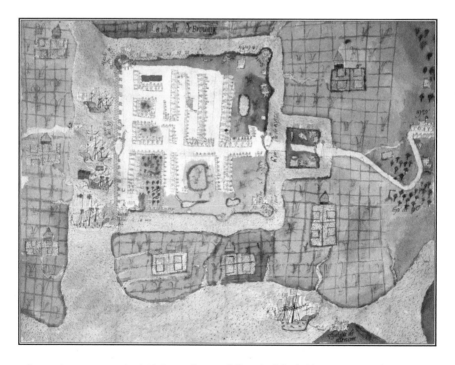

Brouage in a manuscript dated 1570, near the time of Champlain's birth. The town was a work in progress, with half-finished walls and water-logged lots. But its marshes were crowded with saltworks, the harbor teemed with ships, and streets were lined with stone houses. His family's home still stands on the rue Champlain.

Crenellated stone walls had been raised around part of the town; the rest was protected by a wood palisade improvised from old masts and fir planks.[11] The setting was as handsome as it is today, but life was difficult for families who lived there. One visitor wrote in 1581, "This place seems to have been hard-won from the water, which covered the entire place, and even now during the great floods in winter, the streets and the lower floors of the houses are all full of water."[12]

Even so, money could be made in Brouage, and business was booming. By the time of Champlain's birth, the town was packed with people. The land inside the walls was divided into very small building lots, some merely twenty-five-feet wide by a hundred-feet deep with an annual ground rent of 36 livres. On the 1570 map, every street was completely lined with stone-built private houses. Around the town, the surrounding marshes were divided into salt-works, each with its own pans and cottages for the free-spirited *saulniers*, who managed the marshland and brought the salt to town by boat. The map of 1570 shows a harbor crowded with large ships, flying the ensigns of many nations. Historian Natalie Fiquet wrote that the "town's port was large and teeming: Scottish seacoal, Dutch tallow, cordage, herring, dry cod, iron and wood" were exchanged for barge-loads of wine, grain, and especially salt.[13]

Surviving records of trade describe an astonishing range of origins and destinations, even clearance papers from Brouage for Peru in the year 1570. Complex triangular and quadrilateral trades developed. One example was a voyage that began on April 26, 1602. The captain's orders were to sail from Rouen to Brouage, take aboard a cargo of salt, proceed to the Gaspé in America and barter the salt for cod, return to Spain and exchange the cod for a cargo of general merchandise, carry those goods to Marseilles and replace them with Mediterranean freight for Le Havre and Rouen, then back to Brouage once more.[14]

Brouage was a cosmopolitan town. A visitor described it as a "Babel where people speak twenty languages." A few doors away from the home of the Champlain family is a small stone house that was built by a Dutchman. Its stone lintel still bears the inscription that he carved in his native tongue, when young Champlain was living on the same street:

1585
Wol Gode Betrout Die Heft Wolgebout

It might be translated, "He who puts his trust in God has built well," or "*Qui place sa confiance en Dieu a bien construit.*" This near neighbor came from a distant land and spoke a different language, but he worshipped the same God and engaged in the same global commerce.[15]

The new town of Brouage was a bundle of paradoxes. It was a modern *entrepôt* on an ancient foundation, a small town but cosmopolitan, a fortified town but insecure. After the Protestant Reformation it was caught between warring Calvinists and Catholics. Jacques de Pons and his sons chose the Protestant side, as did most of Jacopolis. In 1559, Royal troops seized the town, and many of its inhabitants became Roman Catholic. Eleven years later it was besieged by Protestant troops from La Rochelle, and the strife continued for many years.

Rivalries of trade reinforced conflicts of religion. The people of La Rochelle thought of Brouage as their competitor and seized an opportunity to destroy a rival port. In 1586, the Rochelais sent twenty-one barges filled with sand and rock in an attempt to block the channel that led to Brouage. The port never fully recovered from this blow. Its harbor slowly filled with silt, and the expanding salt marshes that had been the source of the town's prosperity became a factor in its decline. After Cardinal Richelieu defeated the Protestants of La Rochelle in 1628, the Catholic rulers of France made Brouage into a garrison town. They reinforced its walls, and added an arsenal and barracks to control this restless region. Its inhabitants looked with hope to the sea—and with deep suspicion toward their rulers in Paris.[16]

In the midst of this turmoil, Champlain lived his formative years. Like many men of action in the early modern era, the evidence of his early life is lost in obscurity. We have no record of his baptism, perhaps because a fire in the late seventeenth century burned some of the records of Brouage, or because he was

The stone battlements and lanterns of Brouage were begun in Champlain's time and rebuilt by Richelieu and others. Today small canals and ponds are all that remain of its once busy harbor.

baptized in the Protestant Church, or for other reasons as we shall see. We cannot be certain that he was born in Brouage, but he was raised in this town, and he presented himself to the world as "Samuel Champlain, of Brouage." [17]

Champlain was born around the year 1570. A local antiquarian wrote in the nineteenth century that his date of birth was 1567. A modern historian has argued that he was born as late as 1580. A close look at clues that Champlain scattered through his writings (four sets of clues in particular) indicates that the earliest suggested date is improbable and the later date is impossible. The best estimate is about 1570, for reasons discussed in the first appendix to this book. [18]

We know next to nothing about Champlain's mother. Her name later appeared in Samuel de Champlain's marriage contract as Margueritte Le Roy. The local antiquarian wrote that she came from a family of fishermen, but we have no other evidence one way or the other. Margueritte Le Roy had a sister who also lived in Brouage, married a sea captain there, and had relatives in La Rochelle. For many years this was all that historians knew about Margueritte Le Roy Champlain. More recently, American genealogists have turned up information about the Le Roy family in La Rochelle and nearby towns. Some were prosperous lawyers and merchants with country estates and a coat of arms that they shared with other Le Roys in Niort and Poitiers. These Rochelais Le Roys were mostly Huguenots. Many would migrate to the Netherlands, England, and America in the French Protestant diaspora that contributed an important population to the United States. Probably Champlain's mother had relatives in fishing ports and trading towns throughout the region. [19]

Champlain's father left more traces. His name was spelled creatively in several records as Anthoyne Chapellin and in his own legible hand as Anthine Chappelain. Other legal documents called him Anthoine de Complain or Antoine de Champlain. [20] If we study these scattered sources in a systematic way and order them in time, an interesting pattern begins to emerge. They describe the arc of a career that reveals many things about this family. According to the memory of a local scholar, Antoine de Champlain, like Marguerite Le Roy, was descended from families of fishing folk. He earned his living from the sea, and scattered pieces of archival evidence show him working his way up. A document in 1573 identified him as a *pilotte de navires*, a pilot of large ships. *Pilotte* had a particular meaning in the sixteenth century. A maritime historian writes that in this period "all pilots came from the ranks of the able-bodied sailors" and had an elementary education. They learned to manage a ship by long experience before the mast, and they had schooling enough to read and write, and to master the "art of navigation" both at sea and in coastal waters. A pilot was perceived to be an artisan, and he lived "from day to day" on his wages. It was written in the mid-sixteenth century that "most of the pilots are married and they have a house and a wife and children and family, and it takes everything they earn to provide for them." [21]

This appears to have been Antoine Champlain's condition when Samuel Champlain was an infant. In the years that followed, Antoine moved upward from pilot to the rank of master. This advance increased his salary and improved the status of his family. More than that, he became "the administrator of all the economic resources on board the ship, and that gave him extra income. . . . Whoever acceded to the charge of master crossed the frontier that separated salaried workers from those who handled and administered capital." [22]

Then Antoine Champlain moved up again, from master to the rank of captain. A later record identifies him as *capitaine de navires*, a commander of large ships who stood high above the condition of a pilot or master. This title was also a quasi-military rank. A man who held it was expected to lead in time of war or mortal danger. A captain of a large ship was regarded as a man of honor and was treated as a gentleman, even if he came from humble origins. [23] Antoine also went up another step, and received a commission from Henri IV as a naval captain. His son later described him as captain in the King's Marine, and called him Antoine de Complain, with the *particule de noblesse*, a mark of distinction though not usually of nobility.

At the same time Antoine was also getting ahead in yet another way. He became a shipowner, buying small shares in several vessels, as even large investors did, to spread the risk in a dangerous business. This put him on yet another level and took his family to a different place. Owners were the men who hired the crew and employed the officers of their ships. They acquired the cargo and took the lion's share of the profit. Owners were called "ship lords" by seamen and officers. When an owner went to sea, he had the best accommodations on board. The officers deferred to him. Even the captain who had command authority, the master who sailed the ship, and the pilot who was skilled in seamanship and navigation, gave way before a "ship lord." [24]

These few legal documents tell us that Antoine de Champlain succeeded in rising from humble beginnings to high rank in maritime France. He also did well in another way, increasing his income from investments in ships and voyages. Samuel de Champlain always wrote of him with pride and respect. In Brouage, Antoine de Champlain became a man of property. The Champlain family moved to one of the larger houses in the town. They also acquired a second house, and then a third. They were not of the nobility, and their houses

were nothing like the home of Christophe Depoy, sieur d'Aguerres and governor of Brouage, whose estate occupied a corner of the town, with its own gardens, fountains, and a fine view of the harbor.[25] The Champlains were not of
Depoy's rank but they were prosperous and flourishing. Others in the family
were getting ahead in the same way. An uncle from Marseille also rose through
the maritime ranks to become a man of property. Their cousins in La Rochelle
were doing well too. All his life, even in very hard times, Samuel de Champlain had an optimistic way of thinking about the world, an attitude that
comes easily to people whose families have been moving up, especially in their
childhood.

Always at the center of Champlain's life was his Christian faith. It appeared in
his youthful writings as early as 1599, grew stronger through time, and became the passion of his old age. In difficult moments, it was the source of his
inner strength. The roots of Champlain's religion are lost in obscurity. His
Catholic biographer N.-E. Dionne writes, "We know practically nothing of
Champlain's years in one of the most troubled periods in the history of France,
that of the wars of religion." We do not know with certainty if his family was
Protestant or Catholic. The sources are not conclusive, but they offer many
clues.

The first clue appears in his name, and the names of his parents. Samuel de
Champlain was named for a hero of the Old Testament. The biblical Samuel
was the first of the great Hebrew prophets, an upright judge of Israel known
for his stern integrity. Samuel believed deeply in one God and the rule of law.
He fought the Philistines, denounced false priests, and ordered the people of
Israel to "put away strange Gods." He also refused to take bribes, and did not
hesitate to stand against men in power when they went against the law.[26]

Samuel's combination of virtues appealed to Protestants in the sixteenth-
century Reformation. Among English Puritans, one study finds that Samuel
was the third most popular name for boys, exceeded only by John and Joseph.
It was less common in high Anglican households, and rare among Roman
Catholics. Champlain's forename strongly suggests that he was baptized as a
Protestant.[27]

Other clues appear in the names of his parents. Antoine and Margueritte
Champlain were named after Catholic saints. The ascetic St. Anthony and the
martyred St. Margaret were favorite namesakes among Roman Catholics, but
rare among Protestants. Taken together, the evidence of names tells us that
Champlain's grandparents were probably Roman Catholic and baptized their
children in a Catholic church. His parents likely became Protestants before

1570 and baptized their son in a Calvinist meetinghouse, perhaps the Huguenot "temple" that was known to have existed in Brouage at the time of his
birth.[28]

More clues emerge from the history of the region where Champlain was
raised. In the sixteenth century it was one of the most Protestant areas in
France. Most towns granted to Protestants under the Edict of Nantes in 1589
were in the center-west of France, from La Rochelle south to the Gironde estuary.[29] The greatest concentration was in the area around Brouage. After the
revocation of the Edict of Nantes in 1685, the coastal region near Brouage was
said to be almost depopulated by the emigration of Huguenots for Britain and
America. In Brouage today, an old forge still has graffiti that were carved into
its walls by Protestants who were confined there later, when they tried to leave
France in search of soul-freedom.[30]

Other clues to Champlain's faith come from the religion of his extended
family. His uncle was born in Marseille, and is believed to have been a Protestant who converted to Catholicism. His cousin Marie Camaret in La Rochelle
was Protestant. Champlain himself would later marry into a Protestant family
that converted to Catholicism. All this evidence points to the same conclusion: Champlain was probably baptized and raised as a Protestant and later
converted to Catholicism.[31]

At an early age Champlain probably went to an infant school, perhaps several
of them, a common practice in the early modern era. These schools were run
by housewives in their kitchens, especially in Protestant communities where
rates of literacy were higher than among Roman Catholics. The purpose was
to teach the fundamentals of faith, the habits of discipline, and the rudiments
of reading and writing. The housewives catechized the children, kept order
with their pudding sticks, and drilled them on the fundamentals of reading
and ciphering. There Champlain would have learned his letters, possibly as
early as the age of two or three, as was common in households of Protestants
who were Children of the Book.

At a later age, Champlain may also have gone to an academy that existed in
Brouage. On May 5, 1599, the Swiss traveler Thomas Platter visited the town
and wrote a full account of this school. He tells us that it was a place for the
"training and teaching" of "young men of the nobility and other well-born
seigneurs." The school had a rector who received his salary from Henri IV himself, and was equipped with "twenty magnificent horses, all very handsome."
The students attended for two years, and were taught the "exercises and games
of cavaliers," in particular equitation, mounting, jumping, and trick riding.

They also learned to draw, to dance, and play the mandolin. Mainly they received instruction in the arts of war and the use of weapons, which Champlain mastered at an early age. He was an excellent shot with firearms, an expert with the sword, and he could ride. In the afternoons the students learned how to measure distances and lay out the foundations for a fortress. After graduation they went into the army, or into the service of a *grand seigneur*.

A leading French scholar, Jean Glénisson, thinks it "very possible that he attended this institution." Other scholars disagree. Whether Champlain was a student there or not, he clearly learned what the Brouage academy had to teach.[32] He learned to draw a picture, ride a horse, wield a sword, and fire an arquebus. We have no evidence of a mandolin. In legal documents dated March 18, 1615, and again in 1625 and 1626, Champlain was called an *écuyer*, a term of rank which literally meant "a person used to horses," a member of the equestrian class. Later it came to mean a young nobleman before the *adoubement* in which he was dubbed a knight, or more generally an upstanding young gentleman who was not a nobleman. Somehow, Champlain acquired the manners and skills of an écuyer, perhaps in the academy at Brouage.[33]

Young Champlain also learned other lessons from another man who had much to teach him in Brouage. The sieur Charles Leber du Carlo was a friend of the Champlain family and later lived in one of their houses. He was a highly skilled builder of fortifications, an "engineer and geographer to the king," and an expert cartographer. He may have taught young Champlain the art of mapmaking.[34]

In another way, however, Champlain's schooling was very limited. He never received a classical education. Like his contemporary William Shakespeare, he had little Latin and less Greek, and he was not trained in the grammar and rhetoric of classical learning. His writings make a striking contrast with the latinate prose of classically trained writers. But he had a facility with modern languages. Champlain spoke a fluent and muscular French, as strong and colorful as Elizabethan English. Like many men who went to sea in the sixteenth century, he picked up other modern languages. In maturity, he was able to speak English well enough to converse with British seamen on technical subjects. On some of his maps, Champlain mixed French and English inscriptions, and moved easily between them.[35]

Champlain also learned enough Spanish to communicate in that language on his West Indian voyages. His Spanish orthography suggests that he knew it mainly as a spoken language, but he could carry on a conversation with Hispanic speakers in America. He likely had a smattering of other languages, enough to get on with the Dutch, Portuguese, and Basques whom he met in his travels. Long voyages under sail with crews that spoke many tongues made a ship into a language school. Probably that was the way Champlain learned his modern languages.

Champlain's most important school was the sea itself, and his father was his master-teacher. Dionne writes gracefully of Samuel that "his youth appears to have glided quietly away, spent for the most part with his family, and in assisting his father, who was a mariner, in his wanderings upon the sea."[36]

Young Champlain went to sea many times in his childhood and youth. Later in his life he informed the Queen Regent Marie de Medici that he had studied "the art of navigation" from childhood. He remembered, "It is this art which won my love at a very early age, and inspired me to venture nearly all my life on the turbulent waves of the ocean."[37] Just how early Champlain went to sea might be inferred from another brief passage that he wrote near the end of his life. In 1632, he said he had "spent thirty-eight years of my life in making many sea voyages." If we read that passage literally and construct a chronology of his travels after 1594, he must have made "sea voyages" in at least fourteen of his first twenty-four years.[38]

At an early age, Champlain learned the art of pilotage in the modern sense: the skill of sailing in coastal waters. The maritime setting of Brouage was challenging that way. The town was set on a narrow arm of the sea and surrounded on all sides by many shoals and hazards. The tight little harbor of Brouage was often crowded with ocean-going ships and small craft of every size, all bent on their own business in a thriving commercial center. To steer a vessel under sail through the harbor on a busy day was always a challenge.

One can imagine Champlain as a small boy, standing beside his father on the deck of a ship that was underway in Brouage harbor. We might see them studying the flow of tides and currents, feeling the unsteady play of onshore breezes, cocking a weather eye upward at the sky and the sails, watching the movement of shipping, dodging other craft, and carefully avoiding anchored vessels that were shifting on their moorings. All these things had to be done at the same time as they conned their ship through the narrow, twisting channel of Brouage toward the open sea. It was a rigorous school for a bright young lad, with small margin for error.

The tidal waterways from the town led outward to the Bay of Biscay. There young Samuel learned other hard lessons. The prevailing winds came from the west, which meant that he learned to sail on a lee shore. The Bay of Biscay was notorious for sudden squalls and raging storms that could be very dangerous.

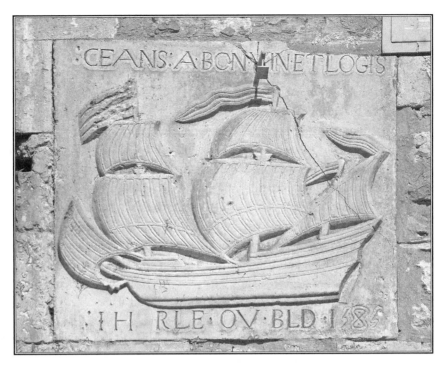

Stone sign for a seaman's inn on the Île d'Oléron near Brouage, 1585. The top line reads, "Within: Good Wine and Lodging." The stylized ship is a moyenne navire of the sort that young Champlain learned to sail with his father in these waters, and later used on most Atlantic crossings.

Sea conditions changed quickly in the bay and could catch an unwary sailor by surprise. A pilot there had to be highly skilled, constantly alert, and very flexible in his responses.

Beyond the Bay of Biscay lay the ocean. Champlain tells us that he made many ocean voyages as a child. As the ship moved out of sight of land, he had yet more skills to learn as a blue-water sailor. In his youth Champlain was probably taught to steer a course by compass and dead reckoning. His father would have instructed him in the use of an astrolabe to estimate the elevation of the sun precisely at noon, which yielded a simple measure of latitude. He would have mastered the use of a backstaffe to observe the angle of elevation for Polaris, the great North Star. It was best done at twilight, when the pole star and the horizon were both visible. It was no small feat to take a sight while standing on a moving deck of a small ship. The horizon itself seemed to rise and fall, and the stars appeared to dance in the sky as the ship rolled and pitched and yawed in a running sea. Then came the computations, with adjustments for the "limb" of the sun, and others for Polaris, which in Champlain's era was not as near true north as today, and had to be corrected by the use of "pointer stars" nearby. Probably he learned this too as a child from his father.

There were other lessons. As Antoine Champlain rose from the rank of pilot to master, captain, and owner, he became responsible for the business side of a voyage. Young Samuel learned about the world of commerce, markets, commodities, and money. He learned to deal with men of business who spoke languages different from his own and absolutely had to be understood. He learned that some were men to be trusted and others were not, and many things hinged on a matter of judgment.

He learned that a voyage could be dangerous in ways that had nothing to do with wind and water. The coastal waters of France were infested with corsairs, pirates, and predators. Even the harbor of Brouage attracted desperate characters. The town map in 1570 showed a gibbet outside the main gate, and it was likely in frequent use. Men at sea learned how to stay out of harm's way as best they could, but when they were in it, they had to be able to defend themselves. A seaman in the sixteenth century was also a man-at-arms. Champlain learned the use of the great guns that every *navire* carried for her own protection. He also had to learn how to deal with irritable passengers and unruly crews, who were often a challenge in unexpected ways. Here was yet another set of skills for Champlain to master. He would have studied these things while he watched his father deal with the routine crises that arise on a wooden ship in an open sea. Champlain had fourteen years of this instruction before he was twenty-four.

He tells us that the sea was deeply interesting to him. The drawings on his maps show us that he was fascinated by ships of all sizes—great galleons, small craft, and anything that floated on the sea. His images of ships were sketched with bold and confident strokes, and were very precise and lovingly detailed. He always had an eye for the beauty of a full-rigged ship at sea, or the sleek lines of a sharp-built *patache*, or the charm of a simple shallop bobbing at anchor in a quiet cove.[39]

Champlain was deeply drawn to the sea, even as he learned how dangerous it could be. Like any experienced seaman, he wrote of the sea with deep respect, for he knew what it could do. His treatise on navigation is full of dire warnings and rueful lessons from hard experience. More than a few passages of his journals describe his encounters with ice and fog in the North Atlantic, rocks and shoals on treacherous coasts, hurricanes in the West Indies, wild nor'easters in the Gulf of Maine, and sou'westers in the Bay of Biscay. He met huge waves on the Grand Bank, and white squalls that suddenly blew up in mid-ocean, out of a clear blue sky. He dealt with tides and currents beyond imagining, and shoal water on the fringes of four continents. In more than a few passages, he marveled that he was still alive when many a good seaman had drowned at sea.

There was always a curious mix of fatalism and instrumentalism in his attitudes. Champlain tells us in his writings that he never learned to swim, which was common among men who kept the sea during the early modern era. It belied a strangely fatalistic attitude that was very distant from our own time. All these attitudes began to form early in his young life, when Champlain went down to the sea in ships, sailing with his father from their home in Brouage, along the coast of France, and into the western ocean. It gave him an education for a life of leadership in the years to come.

2.

TWO MEN OF SAINTONGE
Champlain and the Sieur de Mons

Sieur de Champlain Xainctongeois.

—title page of Champlain's last book,
Les Voyages (1632) [1]

C HAMPLAIN, like most of us, was a man of multiple identities. In his first book, he introduced himself to the world as "Samuel Champlain, De Brouage." Later he described himself in another way as "Champlain Xainctongeois," a man of Saintonge. [2] As he grew older and traveled widely in the world, he increasingly identified himself with the old French region in which he was raised. Here is a paradox of our modern condition, which Champlain helped to create. The more he saw of the world, the stronger was his kinship to what Eudora Welty called the "places of the heart." [3]

Champlain's place was Saintonge. In his time it was the name of a province, a people, a language, a culture, and a way of life. Today, the old province of Saintonge has been replaced by several French departments with administrative names such as Charente-Maritime, but many people who live there still think of themselves as *saintongeais*, and are deeply aware of their culture and history. [4]

The name descended from a Celtic tribe called the Santoni, a fiercely independent people with a strong sense of their own ways. Julius Caesar's legions fought them, and Roman settlers built their villas along the coast of Saintonge. Two millennia later the Roman villas are ruins, but the descendants of the Santoni are still there, clinging stubbornly to their land. They absorbed the Roman population and invented a dialect that combined Celtic, French, and Latin elements in unique ways.

The Santoni had a talent for survival. In the Middle Ages they were assaulted from the sea by the Vikings, and attacked from the land by a multitude of warrior tribes. They took refuge in islands and marshes along the coast, and survived catastrophes that extinguished many other cultures in Europe. [5] A key to their endurance was the Gulf of Saintonge, which two thousand years ago was a huge body of water, much larger than today. Nathalie Fiquet describes it as a great sea, "formed of protruding peninsulas, and sprinkled with islands and islets." It stretched from the present coast to the higher ground of Saint-Sornin and Saint-Agnant, ten miles inland.[6]

Along the coasts and islands of this great gulf, descendants of the Santoni took their living from the sea. The water yielded an abundance of fish and mollusks, and the area is still a major center for France's oyster industry. Marshes around the gulf also supplied salt, the commodity that sustained Champlain's home port of Brouage. The people of coastal Saintonge flourished in many maritime trades. Historian Hubert Deschamps, himself a man of this region, described them as "fishermen, seamen, fishmongers, marsh workers, independent people who love struggle and adventure."[7]

Others lived inland along the river valleys, where fertile fields produced large crops of grain, and pastures supported flocks of sheep. The vineyards of the Charente Valley became the cognac country of France and still supply the world with much of its best brandy.[8] It is a very beautiful landscape. Deschamps wrote lyrically of the "Saintonge of the interior, with its gentle undulations, its fields, its patches of woodland, its vines, its clear rivers, its white villages, a territory humanized through the centuries by a pacific people."[9]

Inland and coastal Saintonge had many differences, but they were part of the same region. They shared a bright and sunny climate, with more hours of sunshine than any other part of France. Most of the region has long views of a large sky. Much of it is near the water, either on the coast or along its rivers. The people of this place speak of the water as the beautiful *robe bleue* that cloaks their homeland. The strong sun, big sky, and flowing waters all lift the spirit in Saintonge, and they have entered into the soul of its population.

Through much of this province and especially along the coast, there is also a comparative abundance of material things. At the end of the sixteenth century a local poet wrote that it was so even for the humble saulniers who earned their living from the salt marshes:

> The marsh worker on his salty plain
> Gets bread, fish, and game without pain.[10]

Peasants in the interior and traders in the towns flourished in other ways—more so in some periods than in others. Even in the late sixteenth and early seventeenth centuries, a time of many troubles in much of western Europe, the governor of Bordeaux reckoned in 1570 that of all the many regions of France, "the most opulent and richest province of the King is that of Saintonge." [11]

With all of these advantages, the people of Saintonge also had their full share of adversity. In the Hundred Years War between England and France (*circa* 1337 to 1453) they suffered much from the ravages of marching armies. It happened again in the wars of religion during the sixteenth century. As in much of Europe, plague and pestilence spread across the countryside, and the farmers of Saintonge experienced shortages during the difficult years of the mid-1590s. [12]

But the troubles of the late sixteenth century were less severe in Saintonge than in other provinces. The cold temperatures of the little ice age caused sea levels to fall a little, which enlarged the productive marshland on the coast of Saintonge. The bounty of the sea and the rivers tended to diminish the hungry seasons that the French called *disettes*, which came each year when the old grain supply ran out, and the new crops were not in. [13]

Military insecurity was also a problem. The peaceable people of coastal Saintonge were often attacked, but they adapted to a dangerous environment and learned to defend themselves. More than one king remitted their taxes because they "always had arms on their shoulders" and knew how to use them in defense of their land. Another official visited the coast of Saintonge in the mid-sixteenth century and was amazed to find an "incredible number of people" living in the marshes. He described them as a strong and sturdy population "hardened to pain, knowing well the movements of the sea and its malign perils and dangers," a people "bellicose, adventurous and skilled in war, both on sea and land," and "valiant and hardy at sea, where they make great voyages." [14]

The people of Saintonge faced their challenges and overcame them without much help from others. They were able to rise above their difficulties by their own effort, and there was a buoyancy in their culture. From their environment and history they developed a sense of themselves that set them apart from other regions of France. Champlain wrote of neighboring Brittany as a foreign country, and that attitude was reciprocated. As late as the sixteenth century, people from other parts of France regarded the Saintongeois as a breed apart. The Parisian writer Theodore de Bèze described them as "a rude people nearly without humanity—pirates and parasites of the sea." [15] It would be more accurate to say that they had a different idea of humanity. A leading historian studied "the regional mentality" of Saintonge, and concluded that one

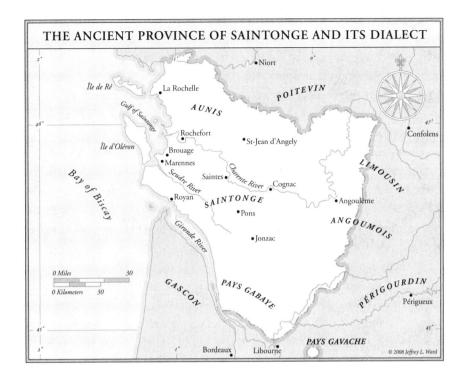

THE ANCIENT PROVINCE OF SAINTONGE AND ITS DIALECT

of its distinctive qualities was "a very strong individualism," a word that has long been a pejorative in other parts of France. He writes that one "searches in vain" for the "communitarian constraints that exist elsewhere" in the nation. This regional mentality had many striking features. They found expression in a unique culture and language that made a difference in Champlain's life.[16]

Through the years, the people of Saintonge developed a language of their own. It was very French, but with a special character. Today linguists in Paris call it the *patois charentais* after the modern departments of Charente and Charente-Maritime. Native speakers think of it not as a *patois* but a language. They still call it the *langue xaintongeaise*, or simply *le parlanjhe*, the speech.[17]

These speechways of Saintonge were shaped by its heritage and its linguistic location, between the dialect-regions of northern and southern France. The langue xaintongeaise combines elements of both French dialects with a vocabulary of its own. The leading example is its word for "snail," which in other parts of France is *escargot*. In Saintonge it is *cagouille*. Throughout this old province, cagouilles are gathered in great abundance and farmed as well. They are highly prized and have a ceremonial function at festivals and harvest rituals. Cagouilles are also cultural symbols of great antiquity. Cathedrals and village churches that date from the eleventh century have cagouilles carved into their medieval stonework. In the modern era the cagouille became the leading emblem of the region, and the people of Saintonge proudly call themselves *cagouillards*. The snail made a perfect symbol of this culture, with its hard shell and soft interior, its slow pace and steady progress, its careful ways and sensitive antennae.[18]

Champlain was a cagouillard and always remained so, even as he traveled far from his native place. When he went to the West Indies and Mexico, he described the flora and fauna of the new world in the old langue xaintongeaise. A French botanist who studied the text of Champlain's report on the West Indies concluded that it could only have been written by a man who was a native of Saintonge in the sixteenth century.[19]

The language of Saintonge was mainly the product of an oral culture, with many special words for people who were important to its transmission, such as *conteur* and *bonconteur*, *conteuse* and *conteusine*, who are skilled at recounting stories and histories in public.[20] It is a language rich in its description of special systems of material production, some of which would be carried to New France. An example is its complex language of dikes and canals that were important to the marshes and salt basins of Saintonge. Especially important to Champlain's new world was the *aboteau, abotiâ, aboitiâ, abouèta,* or *aboiteau*—which described the earthworks and wooden sluices that were used in the managing of the marshes and would become central to the material world of Acadia.[21]

The langue xaintongeaise also offers many clues to the cultural world in which Samuel Champlain was raised. It is a happy language, full of laughter. Children are called *drôles* in Saintonge, and a young girl is a *drôlesse*—without any pejorative connotation, we were assured with the wink of an eye. The people of this region have a highly developed vocabulary of happiness, as in their word *benèze*, for a free and easy, good-natured sort of habitual happiness that is more than merely *heureux*, even as they have that word as well. The two words together become *bienheureux*, which means not only "good-natured" but "blissfully happy." Some of these words appear in metropolitan French, but a person of Saintonge who speaks the parlanjhe of the region is uniquely called a *goulebenèze*, literally, a happy mouth. The word for mouth, *bouche* in standard French, is *goule* in the parlanjhe of Saintonge. Champlain was a *goulebenèze* in every sense, and he had that happy way of speaking. Even late in life, when he was old in years and high in rank, a Montagnais said to him in Canada, "You always say something jolly to cheer us up."[22]

• • •

The proverbs of Saintonge have the same spirit. A favorite saying is "*Qui va chap'tit, va loin*; he who goes gently goes far."[23] A folklorist has written that this maxim is the "motto of the region." Another calls it "the currency of Saintongeais." It became part of Champlain's style of leadership through the course of his career, as we shall see. Other proverbs in this region have similar themes:

> *Bien aise peut éprer; mal aise reste à l'aise.*
> Good nature gets more; bad nature gets nothing.

> *Beunaise se mâche à bout de ne rin faire.*
> A good touch does no harm.

> *Beunaise thiéllés quiavant des sous peur fazir oublier zeu sottise.*
> Very happy are those who have enough *sous* (silver coins) to
>   forget their stupidity.[24]

Another proverb advises: "*In piasit en attire in aute*; to give pleasure is to gain it." The folk wisdom of Saintonge recommends that rule of reciprocity. This is a culture that is comfortable with differences among people. It shows tact for the feelings of others, and a concern for treating them decently. That spirit always suffused Champlain's relations with others.[25]

The Saintongeois are a practical people, very much down to earth. Their proverbs combine large purposes with a spirit of caution and prudence which is common to many rural cultures in France:

> *Avant de feire in fagot, o faut ârgader la riorte.*
> Before starting something, study the means.

> *Pour bin finir, o faut bin commencer.*
> To finish well, start well.

> *Meûx vaut chômer que mal moudre.*
> Better to do nothing than do it badly.

> *Meûx vaut pardre un pain qu'ine faumée.*
> Better to lose the loaf than the oven.

Tache de seug' ton chemin dreit, d'Angoleme à la Rochelle,
   pas d'besoin d'passer prr' Potiers.
To take the best road from Angoulême to La Rochelle,
   there's no need to pass through Poitiers.[26]

Champlain followed these practical maxims all his life. He made a point of preparing carefully, acting prudently in bold ventures, and going directly toward his objective.

The culture of Saintonge also had a strong ethical compass. More than that, it taught that the right way was most successful in the long run. Another proverb was "*Farine dau Yab tourne en bran*; the Devil's flour turns into bran." This mode of thought stressed the importance of doing the right thing in the right way. In the spirit of the region, it is cast not in terms of a moral imperative, but a practical rule of thumb. It is a flexible idea about getting on with others by doing the right thing, rather than a rigid rule of absolute morality.[27]

One of the great classics of French sociology is a study by Maurice Bures called *Le type saintongeois*, first published in 1908 and still in print a century later. It centers on the farmers of the Charente Valley in the late nineteenth century. They were Champlain's country cousins, and they shared a cultural kinship with maritime towns such as Brouage.[28]

Bures found among the inland people the same sunny temperament that he observed throughout the region. He observed that this "amiable Saintonge" had a culture that "encouraged its inhabitants to the love of well-being (*l'amour du bien-être*) and to a peace of the soul (*calme de l'âme*)." But this peace of the soul was combined with a style of life that was lively in body and spirit, "vif d'esprit et de corps." He added that the essence of the Saintonge character was to love joking, good-natured banter, and wordplay.[29]

Bures also found something else in the culture of Saintonge—an outlook essentially "positif," by which he meant a way of thinking that was both positive in its English meaning and also practical. He called it the *sens pratique*, which he thought was one of the strongest qualities of this culture. In practical decisions this spirit was always sheathed in a *fourreau de prudence*, a scabbard of caution.[30]

The people of Saintonge carried these attitudes into their writing. Bures observed that a typical writer of the region tended to be an easygoing storyteller who "does not invent but recounts." He specifically found that pattern in the writings of Samuel de Champlain, and identified him as a leading example of "le type saintongeois." It appeared in Champlain's words and thoughts throughout his life.[31]

These ideas and values developed in Saintonge in large part because of its location, which had a direct impact on Champlain's life. His extended family lived in a broad area of western and southern France. Cousin Marie Cameret and her husband resided in La Rochelle, about twenty-five miles north of Brouage. His maternal uncle Guillaume Hellaine hailed from Marseilles on the Mediterranean coast of France, and was called *le capitaine provençal.*[32]

The environment of Champlain's youth, and the distribution of his extended family, spanned two ecological regions. To the north was an Atlantic world of cool, wet summers that supported a North European farming system. His relatives to the south lived in a Mediterranean region of long, hot summers that sustained a regime of the olive and the vine.

Champlain's family also lived on a borderland between two cultural regions. In the sixteenth century each had its own family of languages, called the *langue d'oc* and the *langue d'oïl*, from their pronunciation of the word for yes. Champlain's cousins in La Rochelle spoke the langue d'oïl. His relatives to the south came from the region of the langue d'oc. Historian Emmanuel Le Roy Ladurie writes that "a literary language developed out of . . . the langue d'oc, very different, despite a common Latin origin, from the langue d'oïl, in use north of the Central Massif."[33]

These speechways were vehicles for different cultures. Le Roy Ladurie explained: "Incompletely unified, the *langue occitane* nevertheless made possible the formation of a vast community of culture which from Languedoc extended nearly to Catalonia, Provence and Gascony, and to the north nearly to Limousin, Auvergne and Dauphiné." He described the process by which the very different *langue d'oïl* also spread among nobility and bourgeoisie in the south during the sixteenth century, so that "those two classes remained more or less bilingual." But the *langue d'oc* persisted in a monolingual way among country people throughout the south in Champlain's lifetime.[34]

Champlain moved back and forth across this linguistic and cultural borderland, as did his Rochelais cousins and his uncle from Provence. He came of age in the midst of a broad diversity of language, culture, religion, and ecology. Raised in the midst of cultural variety, he became comfortable with diversity even within his own family. He was also tolerant of differences among people, deeply interested in the infinite varieties of the human condition, and enormously curious about the world. These attitudes would shape his career. They gave him a broad idea of the human condition, and helped to inspire a dream of humanity that guided him through his life.[35]

Champlain was not alone in the possession of this cultural heritage. Another founder of New France was also a man of Saintonge, and he had similar attitudes, temperament, values, and purposes. He was Pierre Dugua, sieur de Mons. In New France he was Champlain's superior from 1604 to 1606, and a prime mover in the planting of the first permanent French colonies in North America. Like others of the French aristocracy, he was a man of many names and they were spelled in many ways. Sometimes he signed himself by his *nom de famille*, Dugua, which he wrote as one word in a big, bold, rolling, confident script that said much about his character. Often he used his *nom de terre*, which appeared in various forms even on the same page: De Mons, De Monts, De Montz, or simply Montz (his favorite).[36]

No authentic image of De Mons survives. He is not widely remembered in the country of his birth, or in the American nations that he helped to create. A handsome statue of the sieur de Mons, as his biographers now call him, stands high on a grassy hill at Annapolis Royal, overlooking the waters of Port Royal Sound in what is now Nova Scotia. But it is an imaginary likeness and bears the wrong baptismal name on its base.[37]

Historians have judged the sieur de Mons in various ways. For many generations the writing about him was positive but very thin, and he remained in the shadow of his lieutenants. In the early twentieth century more material began to emerge through the efforts of American antiquarian William Inglis Morse, and his stature started to grow. In the mid-twentieth century popular debunkers and academic iconoclasts weighed in. They knew nothing about him, but attacked him viciously. One iconoclast called him "a greedy explorer," selfishly devoted to the "defence of his monopoly," which is a complete miscomprehension of the man and his purposes.[38]

Only at the end of the century did de Mons at last receive his due, in books by Jean Liebel, Guy Binot, and Jean-Yves Grenon. These scholars believe that he was truly the father of New France, and the most important figure in its early history. Jean Liebel calls him the true "fondateur de Québec." Jean Glénisson, a distinguished scholar and another son of Saintonge, writes that "at the moment when all seemed lost for France in America, it was to Pierre Dugua that New France owed her survival."[39]

De Mons and Champlain were both of high importance in the founding of New France, and they reinforced each other. Marcel Trudel writes of de Mons, "Without him, one could assume there would never have been a Champlain."[40] Rival writers in New France, even as they criticized each other, all thought highly of de Mons, and wrote of him with respect and affection. One of them praised his "sturdy loins, in times of difficulty," and wrote in 1609 that de Mons had "done more than all the rest," despite many obstacles in America and France. De Mons was praised for his decency and for a spirit of humanity "that would not have been felt by many others in his position."[41] Champlain added in 1613, "He never wavered in pursuit of his plan, for the desire he had that all things should redound to the good and honor of France."[42]

Champlain and de Mons were linked in many ways. They were raised only a few miles apart. Pierre Dugua is thought to have been baptized about 1558 or 1560, and was at least ten or twelve years older than Champlain. His native place is not known, but probably it was the old village of Le Gua or the small seaport of Royan on the north bank of the Gironde River, near the narrow mouth of its great estuary. Both towns lay only a few miles south of Brouage.

His parents were of the nobility. The title "de Mons" came from a hill that rose above the town of Royan. The crest of that hill, overlooking the River Gironde, was the seat of the family's château. It belonged to Pierre Dugua's grandfather Loubat Dugua, who was also known as the "capitaine du Château de Royan." The old château burned in 1737 and was quickly rebuilt in 1739. The eighteenth-century building still stands today behind the medieval walls that surrounded the old château. It is now a private club in a close-built residential neighborhood. The sieur de Mons probably grew up in his father's house on that hill, near his grandfather's château with its walls and towers. Both buildings had "a magnificent view of ships going and coming in the Gironde estuary."[43]

Pierre Dugua was raised a Huguenot but married a Catholic, Judith Chesnel. Her aristocratic family lived in the Château de Meux near Jonzac, southeast of Royan. Like Champlain, de Mons entered the service of Henri IV as a soldier, and fought in the French wars of religion against the de Guise family. De Mons distinguished himself for "grand courage" and loyalty to the king in heavy fighting for control of Normandy. It was a desperate struggle. In 1589, the Catholic *ligueurs* held every major town in Normandy but two: Caen and Dieppe, where de Mons fought valiantly against them. The citizens of Dieppe elected him one of their captains, and he led them to a great victory.[44]

The sieur de Mons rose rapidly in royal favor, and the king showered honors on him. In January, 1594, Henri IV gave him a pension of 100 écus a month and many offices: Gentleman in Ordinary of the King's Chamber,

Governor of the Château de Madrid, Governor of the Bois de Boulogne, and later Governor of Pons, a Huguenot fortress twenty-five miles inland from Royan.[45] De Mons was said to have the manners of a "grand seigneur" and was known for "his affability, his calm, and his generosity," which "drew sympathy while inspiring respect." He was tolerant of others, in particular those of "the Roman Catholic religion, which was not his own." Most of all he was thought to have a quality of "tact," and a gift for getting people of different beliefs to live and work together, "which was no small thing in that time of religious passions and hatreds."[46]

Like many noble families in this region, de Mons was deeply involved in commerce, and became a wealthy venture capitalist, despite the prohibitions that kept many noblemen out of trade. He sold some of his landed property in the *seigneury* of Puy-du-Fou and obtained a capital of 29,416 écus or 88,248 livres tournois in liquid assets, a large sum by the standards of that age. His purpose was to invest in enterprises "in new lands beyond the sea."[47] To that end he formed an association with Pierre Chauvin, sieur de Tonnetuit, a Protestant and rich bourgeois of Honfleur, and later with Aymar de Chaste. They did well by their investments in the fisheries and fur trade of North America. Some historians have written that de Mons was ruined by the failure of his American investments. This is not correct. For many years he continued to invest actively in American affairs. As late as 1621, he and associates were sending two ships a year to New France, and he became an investor in many trading companies that operated in North America.[48]

At the same time, the sieur de Mons preferred to live the quiet life of a country gentleman, and in a very old-fashioned way. In 1619, he used some of his profits in the American trade to buy a new estate called "d'Ardennes," after the beautiful forest of Ardennes, five miles south of Pons in Saintonge—not to be confused with the Ardennes in Belgium and northeastern France. His house was a medieval château with walls flanked by towers of squared stone, and crowned with crenellated walkways. The main gate was protected by a portcullis and drawbridge, and the house was surrounded by polygonal moats. It had been the seat of a very large seigneury. De Mons bought only part of the property in 1618, and later succeeded in reuniting the entire fiefdom before his death. He made the house into a *maison noble*, and the retreat of a wealthy gentleman who preferred the rural life. There he died on February 22, 1628, and was buried in a small enclosure near the main gate of the Château d'Ardennes.[49]

A friend who knew him well wrote that "the absence of signs of egoism, of greed, of cupidity was remarkable in this man, in whom it was easy to see generosity, benevolence, and sensibility." Another observed that "amiability and good manners came naturally to him. He had no need to intrigue or give himself importance by craft or cunning." His acquaintances added that he was "always the master of himself, calm in all circumstances, never impulsive, [and] he reflected before he acted. His ideas had the merit of being guided by the quality that we call judgment (*bon sens*). They were simple [and] well ordered." [50]

In Champlain and the sieur de Mons, Saintonge produced the two leading founders of New France. Their conduct was always an expression of the culture and values of the region in which they were raised. They had a unique spirit, very different from the Castilians who ruled New Spain, the East Anglian Puritans who dominated New England, the Dutch merchants and patroons of New Netherland, the Cavaliers who ran Virginia, the Quakers of Pennsylvania, the North Britons and Ulster Scots of Backcountry America. All these groups were admirable in many ways, but no two were quite alike. These men of Saintonge, Champlain and the sieur de Mons, shared a distinct regional culture, and they brought a special character to colonial enterprise.

Other Frenchmen also settled in the new world: Normans, Bretons, Percherons, Parisians, Loudonnais, Bordelais, French Basques, and many others. The multiplicity of these groups gave the men of Saintonge another importance. The ancient history of the Santoni, the medieval geography of their region, diversity of their world, and the modern values of their culture helped them to work with others, and gave them strength as mediators among many groups. The spirit of their homeland appeared in the way that Champlain and the sieur de Mons conducted themselves and worked with others.

3.

HENRI IV AND CHAMPLAIN
Monarch, Mentor, Patron, Friend

> His Majesty, to whom I was bound as much by birth as by the pension
> with which he honored me.
>
> —Champlain on his relationship with Henri IV, 1632[1]

> King [and] country . . . God and the world.
>
> —Champlain on his loyalties and large purposes, 1632[2]

IN THE RANK-BOUND WORLD of sixteenth-century France, young Samuel Champlain had a very powerful friend. From an early date, he and his family formed a personal connection with the man who would become Henri IV, king of France from 1589 to 1610. How that relationship began, we do not know. Champlain wrote late in life that he was "obligé . . . de naissance," obligated or bound by birth to the king. It is a curious phrase, and its meaning has never been explained.[3]

Perhaps Champlain meant that his family had long been loyal supporters of Henri IV in a divided France, and they received many rewards for faithful service, which was certainly true. Champlain's father was given a coveted commission as Captain in the Royal Navy of France. His uncle from Marseille received several commissions from the king. His Rochelais first cousin-in-law, Jacques Hersan or Hersaut, was given a special position in the Royal Household, with the wonderful title of "*picqueur de chiens de la Chambre du Roy*; chief whipper of dogs in the royal kennels." It was not the most honorable of royal offices, but it probably paid well and brought other advantages. On legal documents, Jacques Hersan reproduced his royal title with great pride.[4]

The most generous of these royal favors came to young Samuel Champlain himself. From an early date, the king paid him an annual pension. It began by the summer of 1601, perhaps earlier, before Champlain's first voyage to Canada in 1603, and long before any of the major achievements for which we remember him. The pension continued every year until the king's death in 1610, and intermittently thereafter.[5] Henri IV was known to be generous to his

*Henri IV with tousled hair, curly beard, and
the libidinous look of a faun or satyr. The sculptor
has caught his lively intelligence and good humor,
with the brow of a thinker and the eye of a dreamer.
He was the most human of great kings—and one of
the most humane.*

friends, but these many favors to Champlain and his family were acts of extraordinary largesse. One might ask why. What was the origin of this special relationship between a great king, a family of humble origins, and a youth of modest rank? Perhaps Champlain's relatives or even young Champlain himself performed some special service for the king. They might have done so in some moment of danger or desperation, which happened with some frequency in Henri's life.

It is also possible that Champlain and the king had another connection of a different kind. For many years, rumors circulated among historians that Samuel de Champlain was the illegitimate son of a very high-born person in France. Two leading scholars put it into print. The great Canadian historian Marcel Trudel noted that some scholars have "been inclined to see in Champlain . . . the bastard of a great family." A distinguished French historian, Hubert Deschamps, professor in the Institute of Political Studies at the University of Paris, asked if Champlain "was not the illegitimate son of a *grande famille.*" [6] More than that, a report that Champlain was the son of the king himself reached the ears of Algonquin Indians in the St. Lawrence Valley. One of them was alleged to have said that he heard Champlain himself say it was so. The Indians passed on this belief in oral tradition through many generations.[7]

None of these rumors has any probative value. No positive evidence to confirm them has been found by any scholar. The quantum of hard data in support of this hypothesis is approximately zero. But one may ask, could it have happened? Could Champlain have been the illegitimate son of Henri IV? Could such a hypothesis explain some of many anomalies in the life of Champlain? The answer is yes. It could have happened. If so, it would resolve many puzzles in Champlain's life and work.

At the time of Champlain's birth, circa 1570, the future King Henri IV of France was Prince Henri de Béarn and Navarre. The prince was in his late teens. An engraving at that time shows him to have been remarkably mature for his age, and we know that he was sexually active, to say the least. He married his first wife in 1572. In the course of his life, he is known to have had at least fifty-six mistresses of record, and casual liaisons beyond counting. He is also known to have fathered at least eleven illegitimate children by five or more women.[8]

Altogether, Henri IV scattered his seed widely through his kingdom, before and after he came to the throne. During the years from 1568 to 1572, the young prince was often in La Rochelle, where his mother was living at the time, about 25 miles from Brouage. He traveled widely in Saintonge, and was in the right place at the right time to have fathered Samuel by a woman

Henri IV as a triumphant warrior king in black armor and a towering white panache of curled feathers. With a sceptre in one hand and a sword in the other, he called to the French people, "Ralliez vous à mon panache blanc!"

of that region. The infant could have been adopted by a respectable bourgeois family, a common practice for illegitimate children of high-born parents in Champlain's time, as in our own. The rank assumed by the king's many illegitimate children was highly variable, and tended to follow the condition of their mothers.[9]

The hypothesis that Champlain was the illegitimate son of Henri IV could explain why no records of his birth or baptism have ever been found, though many scholars have searched for them. It could account for the anomaly of Champlain's social rank, which has long puzzled historians, and has given rise to a running controversy as to whether Champlain was a nobleman or commoner. Most scholars now agree that his family began in modest circumstances, and yet at an early age young Samuel was called the sieur de Champlain. He rarely wrote his name as "de Champlain," usually as "Champlain." The particule de noblesse and the honorific title of *sieur* were added to his name by others in official documents as early as 1595.[10]

The date and circumstances are important. Champlain did not assume the title of "sieur" and the particule de noblesse for himself late in life, as several historians have mistakenly asserted. They were given to him by others when he was no older than twenty-four or twenty-five. These honorifics did not mean that a person had a title of nobility. They were marks of honor, commonly given to men of high birth, important offices, great achievements, long service, or advanced age. It is interesting that the particule de noblesse came to Champlain before he had done any of the deeds for which he is remembered. An intimate connection with the king could explain why he became the sieur de Champlain at a young age, even though he was not of a noble or wealthy family and had no major achievements to his credit.[11]

It could also account for the royal pension that Champlain received every year from as early as 1601 until the king's death in 1610. And it would help us to understand how and why Champlain had easy access to the person of the king. After returning from his early voyages to the West Indies, and before and after his journeys to Canada, Champlain was able to meet directly with Henri IV. It could help us understand another curious statement by Champlain—that the king made arrangements to keep him "about his person."[12]

And an illegitimate birth might explain Champlain's extreme reticence on the subject of who he was, which was all the more remarkable by contrast with his effusive accounts of what he did. It would give a literal meaning to Champlain's puzzling phrase, "obligé de naissance," bound from birth to Henri IV. All these anomalies in Champlain's life would no longer be strange if he was the illegitimate son of Henri IV. Together they make a long list.

Such a connection would also help us to understand the troubles that came to Champlain after the death of Henri IV: the cold distance of Henri's widow, Marie de Medici; the decision to end Champlain's pension; and the hostility of her servant Cardinal Richelieu, who tried to remove Champlain from his position as lieutenant for New France. It could account for the refusal of those leaders to bestow any honors on Champlain, when others who did much less in New France were given more rewards in the form of titles of nobility, grants of land, and lucrative offices. Many historians have remarked on the refusal of Marie de Medici and Richelieu to honor Champlain, without being able to explain it.

Some of these puzzling anomalies in Champlain's career could be explained in other ways, without assuming that he was the illegitimate son of Henri IV. His developing relationship with the king might be understood as a sequence of contingencies. This alternative hypothesis might begin with the fact that Champlain's family appear to have been loyal supporters of Prince Henri during the most difficult and dangerous years of his life. The center-west of France was his strongest base—especially Saintonge and Aunis. Henri's most loyal supporters were families of modest wealth and middling rank, Protestant in their religion, but not dogmatic or doctrinaire—families such as the Champlains in Brouage; the Le Roys, Hersans, and Camarets in La Rochelle; the Boullés in Paris—all connected to Samuel de Champlain. They and others like them helped Prince Henri and his mother in the hour of their greatest need. When the prince gained the throne, he was generous to these families, as was his nature. He gave them offices, commissions, pensions, and other marks of royal favor.

Then the young Saintongeois began to bring himself to the attention of the king. Suffice to say that Champlain was devoted to the king, loyal to his cause, and quick to seize opportunities to serve him. At the same time, the king himself appears to have taken a liking to this engaging young man and enjoyed having him about. This sequence of events, combined with the chemistry of a great king and the achievements of a personable young man, could explain the connection that developed between them.

Whatever the root of Champlain's special relationship to the king may have been, the fact of its existence is firmly established in the record of his life. Henri's patronage was fundamental to the prosperity of the Champlain family, and it was instrumental in the success of Samuel de Champlain. The king's intervention directly shaped the pivotal events in Champlain's early career, and we shall see that this happened many times.

Henri IV was not only a patron of Samuel de Champlain, but also a model and even a mentor. For this young man and many others, the king's example of leadership was an inspiration, and Henri's values became a creed that Champlain served all his life. To comprehend Champlain, we must understand the character of the king he served so faithfully. Without Henri IV there would have been no Champlain—as we have come to know him.

In the long history of France, Henri IV has a unique place. It has been said that he was "the only king whose memory was cherished by the people." His subjects remembered him as Henri le Grand, Henri the Great. In physical terms he (like Champlain) was not a large man. But there was a greatness in his acts and thoughts, a largeness in his energy and resolve, and an astonishing amplitude in both his virtues and his vices.[13]

The qualities of this king were very different from those of other great figures in the history of France. In his personal style of life, Henri IV was far removed from the formal grandeur of Louis XIV, the imperial splendor of Napoleon, and also from the austere and distant condescension of Charles de Gaulle. The character of Henri IV appeared in the nicknames that his subjects invented for him. They celebrated him as *le roi de coeur*, the king of hearts. Others called him *le passionné*, the passionate one; or *le roi libre*, the free king. The literati liked to write of him as *le vert-galant*, the green gallant—*vert* with its ambiguous connotations of youth, energy, and (in French) promiscuous sexuality; *galant* in its mixed association with courtesy and inconstancy. These sobriquets referred to Henri's public and private life. In his many love affairs Henri IV was indeed *le roi de coeur*, *le roi passionné*, and *le roi libre* all at once, in a sense that had nothing to do with political theory or public policy.[14]

At the same time, Henri's nicknames also described a unique style of kingship that flowed from the heart. Other monarchs cultivated a distance between themselves and their subjects. They used remoteness as an instrument of royal power. Henri went another way. He was known to leave his palace incognito, and mix with his subjects in informal ways. As a leader he was open, informal, warm, free-spirited, brave, witty, clever, generous to friends and enemies alike. He was also thought to be mercurial, fickle, unreliable, and untrustworthy. Another nickname, borrowed from his father, was "Henri l'ondoyant," Henri the Unsteady. His best friends acknowledged his flaws, but his warmth and magnetism drew even his enemies to his service.

Even with this cultivation of intimacy and informality, and in spite of his many vices, there was a common perception of greatness in this man. The strongest evidence appeared in his effect on the conduct of others. Even before he came to the throne, extraordinary things tended to happen when Henri was around: sometimes for better, sometimes for worse. His enemies were deeply alarmed by him and driven to extreme actions. Among his many friends, the king's spirit and vision awakened great enterprises and inspired others to undertake them. Champlain was one of many young Frenchmen who responded to his leadership in that way. "Henri le Grand" was a man who made a difference in other men's lives.

To comprehend Champlain's career, one must understand the character of this great king. As Champlain called himself a man of Saintonge, so Henri was called le Béarnais, the man of Béarn. He came from the mountains of southwestern France, was born in the shadow of the Pyrénées, and brought up in a country château of great antiquity that still survives as his monument. The future king was very much a product of that special place. From infancy he was steeped in the culture of Béarn, which gave meaning to the old German saying that mountains make free. The people of that province were fiercely independent. They preserved their traditional liberties, and stubbornly retained their ancient rights until the Revolution of 1789.[15]

Henri also cherished the language of Béarn, and he learned to speak it as his native tongue. At the age of four he was taken to the French court and presented to Henri II, a formidable character who asked the small boy if he would like to have the king for his father. The child looked to his parents and said in the speech of Béarn, "*Quel es lo seigne pay*; This is my father." The king laughed and asked the child "if he could not be a son, would he be a son-in-law?" The boy answered boldly in his Béarnais dialect, "*Obé!* Yeah!" More impressive than what he said was the way he said it.[16]

The young prince's father, Antoine de Bourbon, came from one of the great noble families of France. He was a brave soldier, but some described him with the same word that others would later use for his son: *ondoyant*, unsteady, unreliable. Henri's mother, Jeanne d'Albret, was made of sterner stuff. She was handsome, headstrong, smart, tough, and extraordinarily able. As heiress to the kingdom of Navarre and the county of Béarn, she held great power in her hands, and she used it to great effect.[17]

Jeanne d'Albret converted to Protestantism, as did many of her subjects in southwestern France. She deliberately kept her son away from Catholic Paris and the Valois court, which she regarded with contempt. She raised him as a Protestant and brought him up to be a young man of broad cultivation and independent spirit. He was trained as a soldier and became highly skilled in the profession of arms. He was also taught by his mother to be a leader. At an early age he was given challenging assignments that required tact, judgment, and a mastery of the intricate politics in Béarn and Navarre. Those skills were soon summoned to a larger stage.[18]

In the year 1559, when Prince Henri of Béarn and Navarre was barely six years old, a bizarre medieval accident transformed the history of modern France. In royal celebrations for the marriage of a princess, King Henri II entered a jousting tournament. He succeeded in smashing his opponent's lance, but a splinter from the shattered weapon pierced the king's eye. The wound festered, and Henri II died suddenly at the peak of his considerable powers.[19] That chance event came at a bad moment. Most people throughout the country shared an ideal of Christian unity: *une foi, une loi, un roi*—one faith, one law, one king, but the reality was very different. The kingdom was divided against itself. The population of France was growing beyond its means. In a time of rapid inflation, extremes of wealth and poverty were increasing, and social orders were moving apart.[20]

The political situation was highly unstable. Authority was divided among kings and nobles, regional *parlements* and estates, autonomous towns and cities, chartered companies and religious institutions. All were deeply jealous of their privileges and united only in their hostility to expanded royal power. Especially hostile to the monarchy were the great noble families, who were rivals for dominion. Bitter conflicts developed between the Catholic House of Guise in the east, the Protestant House of Condé to the west, and the more moderate Houses of Montmorency and Bourbon to the south. All dreamed of succeeding the House of Valois, which had ruled France for three centuries.

These dynastic rivalries were deepened by religious divisions. Most people in France were Roman Catholic in 1559, but Protestants were making converts everywhere, even within leading Catholic families. Adherents of the old church were deeply disturbed by the challenge of a new faith. On both sides, religious leaders aroused feelings of intense fear and hatred.

This was the dangerous moment when Henri II died suddenly from the splintered lance. He was succeeded by his young son Francis II, barely fifteen years old, frail of body and weak of mind. This child-king was dominated by his formidable adolescent wife, sixteen-year-old Mary Queen of Scots, and also by her French relatives in the Catholic house of Guise. They hated Protestants with a passion and chose the path of violent repression. The result was a disaster for France.

Protestant evangelists were rounded up and tried for heresy, which was a capital offense. Catholic judges inflicted barbaric tortures on Protestants who refused to recant. Victims who continued to protest their innocence had their tongues cut out before they were tortured and burned, so they could not preach to the people who gathered to watch their agony. Even these judicial atrocities were not cruel enough to satisfy sadistic crowds, who seized the suffering victims and mutilated them in unspeakable ways. In the streets of Paris, roving gangs of Catholic youths erected images of the Virgin Mary, and passersby who failed to genuflect were assaulted in rituals of bloody violence. The horror of religious persecution came both from the top down and the bottom up.[21]

After eighteen months of growing disorder, young Francis II died in 1560 and was succeeded by his even younger brother Charles IX, who was ten years old. Power passed to his Italian mother, Catherine de Medici, and for a time she ruled the kingdom from a small study in her beautiful château of Chenonceau. In 1562, Catherine tried to restore peace to France by proclaiming limited toleration of dissenters. It was not enough to please Protestants, and too much for Roman Catholics.

A fatal incident followed. On March 1, 1562, a quiet Sunday morning, the militant Catholic duc de Guise was on the road from his estates to court, with a large escort of men-at-arms. As he approached the town of Vassy in Champagne, he heard a bell calling Huguenots to worship in a grange. As the soldiers approached there was an exchange of epithets, then a volley of stones. The duke's men stormed the grange, killed and wounded more than a hundred Protestant men, women, and children, and burned the building.[22]

The result was the first war of religion, which set the pattern for many wars to follow. The Protestant House of Condé raised a Huguenot army, and called for help from English and German Protestants. This Huguenot army began to capture strategic towns throughout the country. The violence was beyond imagining. Catholic atrocities happened in Sens and Tours where two hundred Huguenots were bludgeoned and drowned in the River Loire. Those terrible scenes were followed by a Protestant outrage called the *sauterie* of Montbrison, when Huguenots hurled hundreds of Catholic prisoners from a high tower into fires that were burning below.[23]

The Catholics brought in Swiss and Spanish troops, and won a terrible battle at Dreux, where a surgeon eyewitness estimated that 25,000 were killed on both sides in two hours of fighting. The victorious army moved on to attack the city of Rouen, and sacked it in three days of rapine that left more than a thousand dead in the first of many such scenes. As the Catholic army began yet another siege at Orléans, the Huguenots struck back by killing the duc de Guise—the beginning of many such assassinations by both sides.[24]

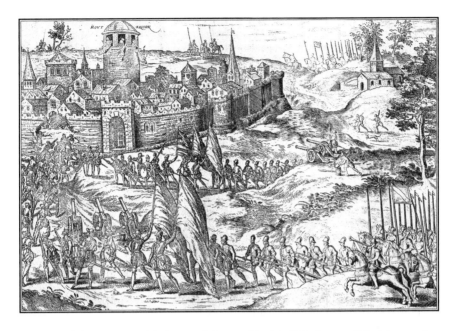

After a Catholic atrocity started the first war of religion on March 1, 1562, the town of Montbrison was the scene of a Protestant crime. Huguenots sacked it in June 1562 and hurled its Catholic defenders from a tower onto spikes and bonfires below.

This first war of religion ended in a shaky truce at Amboise in 1563, but the violence quickly resumed. A new leader of the House of Guise, the cardinal of Lorraine, gained control of King Charles IX and brought Spanish troops into France. Protestants tried to kidnap the Catholic king. This desperate effort failed and started a second civil war in 1567–68, which left a "trail of destruction" across France. The killing continued until the exhausted combatants were too weary to continue. The result was a precarious truce called the Peace of Longjumeau.[25]

That peace also failed, and was followed by a third and even larger religious war in 1568–70. The violence spread to the south and west of France during Champlain's childhood. Some of it rose from angry acts of aggression by French Protestants against Catholics. Much of it came from popular violence by Catholic "confraternities" against Huguenots and anyone who tried to stay neutral. The people of Bordeaux lived in mortal fear of a sadistic gang called the Bande Cardinal, who wore the *bonnet rouge* and tortured, raped, and murdered Huguenots, all in the name of Christ. Some Catholic leaders tried to suppress these atrocities, but others encouraged them.[26]

Saintonge became a theater of war, and Champlain's town of Brouage changed hands many times while he was a child. In 1568 Protestants controlled much of Saintonge and a Huguenot garrison occupied Brouage. The next year, Catholic forces and Italians took the town. The Protestants recovered it in 1570, but it was returned to Catholics by peace treaty and became a base for operations against the Protestant fortress of La Rochelle. Protestants later regained control of Brouage, then lost it again. Warring armies marched and countermarched through Saintonge. They foraged and plundered in a time of famine, plague, and suffering. In the midst of these horrors, Champlain was probably baptized a Protestant, in a world of intense religious hatred and incessant war.[27]

The worst was yet to come. In 1571, Catherine de Medici and Jeanne d'Albret arranged a dynastic marriage between their children, the attractive Catholic Princess Marguerite de Valois and the handsome Protestant Prince Henri de Béarn and Navarre. It was to be a "marriage of two religions," in the hope of lasting peace. A sumptuous wedding was planned for Paris, and Henri rode into town with 1,500 Huguenot leaders. The Catholic nobility turned out in even greater numbers. The ceremony of betrothal took place with outward harmony on August 17, 1572, and the wedding the next day was a brilliant affair. Marguerite de Valois wrote in her splendid memoirs, "I blazed in diamonds." Margot, as she was called, was beautiful, intelligent, and bitterly unhappy. She was reported to be in love with the Catholic duc de Guise, and it is said that she refused to say yes at the wedding until her infuriated brother King Charles IX intervened, and bent her crowned head forward by brute force in an unwilling gesture of assent.[28]

Four days of celebration followed, but behind the scenes the leaders of the House of Guise and the Catholic Church were outraged by the wedding and appalled by the ecumenical spirit that it symbolized. Agents of the English secret service warned Huguenot leaders to be on their guard, and the atmosphere grew heavy with foreboding. On the last day of the marriage festivities, as the great Huguenot leader Admiral Gaspard de Coligny was riding through a Paris street, a shot rang out. This leader of the Protestant cause was severely wounded. But Charles IX promised protection to the Huguenots and they remained in town.[29]

Rumors spread that Protestant assassins were planning to cut the king's throat and seize the throne. A great fear swept through the city of Paris, and the frightened king was caught up in it. On the night of August 23, 1572, Catholic leaders persuaded the terrified monarch to make a preemptive strike against the Huguenots. He agreed. The gates of the city were closed. Boats in

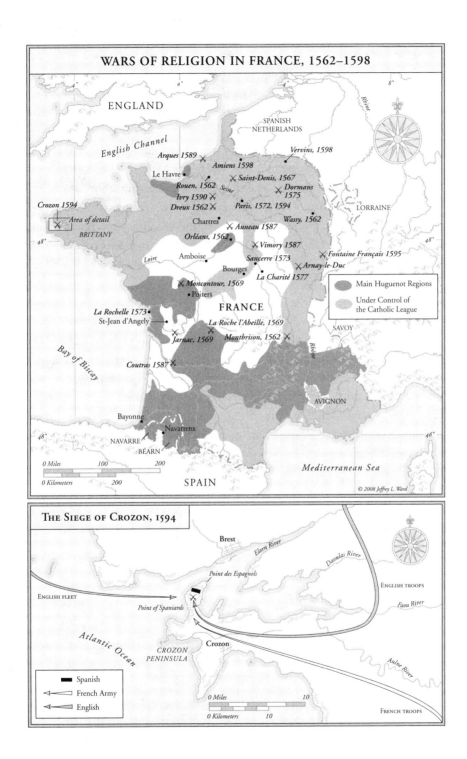

WARS OF RELIGION IN FRANCE, 1562–1598

ENGLAND

SPANISH
NETHERLANDS

English Channel

Rhine

Arques 1589 ✕

Amiens 1598

Vervins, 1598

Le Havre

✕ Saint-Denis, 1567

Rouen, 1562 *Seine*

✕ Dormans
1575

Ivry 1590 ✕

Crozon 1594

Dreux 1562 ✕

Paris, 1572, 1594

LORRAINE

✕ Area of detail

Chartres

Wassy, 1562

BRITTANY

✕ Auneau 1587

Orléans, 1562 ✕

Loire

Amboise

✕ Vimory 1587

✕ Fontaine Français 1595

Sancerre 1573

Bourges

✕ Arnay-le-Duc

La Charité 1577

✕ Moncontour, 1569

• Poiters

FRANCE

SAVOY

La Rochelle 1573 •

St-Jean d'Angely

La Roche l'Abeille, 1569

Bay of Biscay

✕ Jarnac, 1569

Montbrison, 1562 ✕

Rhône

Coutras 1587 ✕

AVIGNON

Bayonne

Navarrens

NAVARRE

BÉARN

Mediterranean Sea

SPAIN

Main Huguenot Regions

Under Control of
the Catholic League

0 Miles   100   200

0 Kilometers   200

© 2008 Jeffrey L. Ward

THE SIEGE OF CROZON, 1594

Brest

Elorn River

Daoulas River

Point des Espagnols

ENGLISH TROOPS

ENGLISH FLEET

Faou River

Point of Spaniards

Atlantic Ocean

CROZON
PENINSULA

Crozon

Aulne River

Spanish

French Army

English

0 Miles   10

FRENCH TROOPS

0 Kilometers   10

the Seine were chained to their moorings, and the Catholic militia of the city was armed. The next night Prince Henri de Béarn and the Protestant duc de Condé were summoned to the king's chamber and arrested. Early in the morning the wounded de Coligny was murdered in his bed. That was the signal for a massacre. Huguenot nobles who had gathered for the wedding of Henri were attacked. Nearly 1,500 were killed, many with their families, in what was to be remembered as the Massacre of St. Bartholomew's Day.[30]

The slaughter spread through the city. Catholics wearing white crosses and armbands turned against Protestant neighbors and murdered three thousand people in a frenzy of fear and rage. Young children were brought into it. Catholic children were given the task of castrating and disemboweling the body of Admiral de Coligny, and dragging the remains through the streets of Paris in a ritual of degradation. Similar scenes spread to the provinces of France.[31]

In the king's chamber, Prince Henri de Béarn and Navarre was given a choice: immediate conversion or instant death. On September 26, 1572, he rejoined the Catholic Church. The Catholics kept him at court in luxurious captivity, closely guarded and carefully watched. The Protestant movement suffered a shattering blow but it survived, and persecution strengthened it. Huguenot armies withdrew into strongholds such as La Rochelle and held their ground. At court, Prince Henri appeared to lose himself in dissipation, but he was biding his time.

An opportunity came after 1574, when Charles IX died and Henri III de Valois came to the throne. A new attempt at coexistence followed. Protestants were granted safe havens. Prince Henri de Béarn and Navarre was allowed to leave the court, and was given the government of Guyenne in southwestern France. Once at large, he abjured Catholicism on June 13, 1576, and went to La Rochelle, where Protestant leaders received him without enthusiasm. Both sides distrusted him.[32]

Henri began to go a third way, looking for a middle path between the contending parties. In Guyenne he cracked down on violence by Protestants and Catholics alike, and recruited an army from men of both faiths. To a Catholic officer he wrote, "those who unswervingly follow their conscience are of my religion, as I am of all who are brave and virtuous."[33]

Extremists on both sides thought this middle way was merely an expedient, and regarded Henri as ondoyant, like his unreliable father. But this was something else. Henri's middle way was not merely a political expedient. It was an act of high principle and Christian faith. The prince said to Protestants and Catholics alike, "We believe in one God, we recognize Jesus Christ, and we draw on the same gospel." He told zealots on both sides that wars of religion were "unworthy among Christians, and specially those who call themselves doctors of the gospel." This idea became an article of Christian faith for him. He deeply believed that nothing could be more un-Christian than the atrocities that had been perpetrated by both sides in the name of Christ. He stood for the unity and pride of France, and for the welfare of its afflicted people.[34]

In Guyenne, people of all faiths began to rally to Henri's cause. He demonstrated a gift of political judgment and a genius for war. Henri created a formidable army with sturdy French infantry and Gascon cavalry. His aide the duc de Sully provided him with the best artillery in Europe. When towns and nobles tried to fight him, he moved against them with courage, energy, and quick decision. He began to expand his control over southwestern France. In war and peace, Prince Henri was a man that other men followed.

Then came another bizarre event. The reigning king of France, Henri III of Valois, began to take notice of the growing popularity of Prince Henri of Béarn and Navarre, as did the leader of the high Catholic party, Henri of Guise. The result was yet another cycle of violence that culminated in the War of the Three Henris, and five more years of strife (1584–89). In this bloody struggle, Prince Henri of Béarn and Navarre skillfully divided Henri of Valois from Henri of Guise. In 1587 he defeated them in open battle. After bitter fighting, two of the three leaders were assassinated. Of the three Henris, only Prince Henri of Béarn and Navarre was left standing. In 1589 he became King Henri IV, the first monarch of a new Bourbon dynasty that would rule France for more than two centuries.

While Samuel Champlain passed from youth to young adulthood, Henri IV began to unite France as it had never been united before. He found himself the Protestant king of a predominantly Catholic people. To the surprise of friends and enemies alike, he decided to convert once again to Catholicism. On Sunday, July 25, 1593, he appeared at the abbey of Saint Denis. In the presence of a huge crowd, Henri knelt before the altar, and swore a vow of obedience to the Church. In the moment of the king's conversion a great flock of doves took flight from the roof of the abbey, which was received as a sign of Providence for the king and his realm.

Many Catholics did not trust Henri IV, and with reason. This was his third conversion to Catholicism, and twice he had returned to his Protestant beliefs. The leaders of the Catholic League alleged that Henri had remarked cynically before the ceremony, "Paris is worth a mass." No evidence exists that he actually said any such thing, which would have been impious, impolitic, and false

On February 27, 1594, Henri IV prepared to take the Catholic city of Paris by storm, but Governor Charles de Cossé-Brissac opened its gates. The triumphant king marched to Notre Dame, took mass in the Cathedral, and the healing began in France.

to his own intentions. Henri IV had larger purposes in mind. He was filled with genuine horror by the wars of religion, which he believed to be deeply inhumane and anti-Christian. He was not a secular man. His object was to recover the true spirit of Christ, to rebuild a broken state, and to unite a divided people. As the leader of that noble cause, the king set a powerful example. On the inspiration of his obeisance at Saint Denis, a large number of Protestants also converted to Catholicism. Among them were many major figures who would loom large in the history of France and New France.[35]

In Saintonge, Samuel Champlain may also have converted to Catholicism at this time. He was certainly a Catholic by 1598, and probably by 1595. He may have become one in 1593, after Henri abjured Protestantism in his dramatic public ceremony.[36] Champlain also followed the example of the king in the substance of his Christian beliefs. Both men had little interest in theology. They disliked doctrinal disputes, despised religious bigotry, and hated religious persecution. They became men of deep and abiding personal faith, and cultivated a spirit of Christian piety. In 1603, it was reported of Henri IV that he "daily grows in piety, acknowledging that he owes everything to God. The Queen says that every morning he prays for half an hour, before speaking to anybody, and does the same at night." [37]

Champlain changed in the same way. As he grew older, he also became more devout. The inventory of his estate included a large collection of religious books, sturdily bound in heavy vellum and designed for daily use. Prominent among them were the *Fleurs des Sainetz*, *La Triple couronne de la bienheureuse Vierge*, a *Chronique et instruction du père Sainct-François*, a collection of *Figures des Pères Hermites*, a handbook on the *Pratique de la Perfection chrestienne*, and other books of that genre. Some of these works celebrated the Virgin Mary and the Catholic saints. Most were guides to practical Christianity. Many offered models of piety, humility, and good works. Champlain detested religious controversy and despised bigotry. Most of all, he hated intolerance as fundamentally un-Christian, even anti-Christian. In their spiritual lives, Henri IV and Champlain matured in similar ways. [38]

Champlain, like Henri IV, also embraced the universal ideal of the Catholic Church, which taught that all people were the children of God, recipients of Christ's mercy, and wards of the universal Church. That religious idea was very different from the Calvinist idea of limited atonement, which held that Christ died only for a small elite. The Catholic idea of a universal religion would be a spiritual key to the kingship of Henri IV, and to Champlain's colonial enterprise in New France.

These men also recognized the urgent importance of religious practice and the significance of sacred ritual. They believed that the observance of religion was vital to the stability of society and the state in the sixteenth century. When Henri came to the throne he carefully performed the public rituals of Christian kingship: visiting the sick, washing the feet of paupers on Maundy Thursday, pardoning criminals on Good Friday, and touching hundreds of sufferers in the healing ceremonies on Easter Sunday. [39]

Henri IV and Champlain lived in an age when western civilization was deeply divided by a common ideal of One True Faith. Many people in the western world shared this obsession, but they did so in different ways. By comparison with other Christians, Henri's and Champlain's way of faith was something special and distinct—even unique to a small circle of leaders in France. It was very much a product of their personal experience and their country's history. Most of all it was a reaction against the cruelty, bloodshed, and oppression of the wars of religion. That experience made Henri IV and Champlain the men they were, and New France the place that it became.

• • •

As king, Henri IV also developed a distinctive style of governance. Here again, Champlain would be deeply influenced by his example. Both men were remarkable for their energy and stamina, and they had an infinite capacity for taking pains. They knew well the importance of tact and generosity in dealing with others. Henri IV wrote, "un Roy pour estre grand ne doit ignorer rien; to be great, a king should not ignore the smallest thing." Champlain led others by the same rule.[40]

By temperament, Henri of Béarn and Champlain of Saintonge were in some ways very different from one another. Henri IV lived for pleasure. He delighted in good food, great wine, and boon companions. Most of all, he loved the company of beautiful women. The pursuit of beauty became an obsession that got in the way of other things, and his closest friends complained to him about it. His faithful supporter Philippe Duplessis wrote, circa 1582, "Sire . . . these open and time-consuming love affairs no longer seem appropriate. It is time for you to begin loving all Christianity, and specially France herself." Henri preferred to love all the ladies of France, seriatim.[41]

Samuel Champlain also enjoyed food and drink, good companions and good times, as did the king. But Champlain was more austere in his private life and he lived by a different creed. Later, those who knew him best in America remarked on his "chastity" in the face of invitations from Indian women who offered themselves to him. In that way Henri IV and Champlain could not have been more different. But in their politics and religious ideas they were very much alike.

Altogether, historians count nine civil wars of religion in France in the years from 1562 to 1598. By comparison, the United States suffered one civil war that lasted four years and its wounds still scar the great republic. The French wars of religion continued for nearly forty years. One scholar reckons the toll at "between two and four million."[42]

Henri IV and Samuel Champlain lived most of their lives in a nation at war with itself. They reacted against the troubles of their age, and learned from them. Both became men of humanity in a world of cruelty and violence. Henri IV worked tirelessly to unite his kingdom, not primarily by force but by persuasion. He appealed to the altruism of his subjects and also to their material interest. He invited all the people of France to share his dream of abundance and prosperity. Every order and estate was offered inducements. Henri began by buying outright the loyalty of former opponents. Enormous sums were paid to Catholic noblemen who agreed to join the king and recognize the House of Bourbon. Some of the largest payments went to the House of Guise.

The duc de Lorraine and the duc de Guise received more than a million écus. Military leaders were paid for their support. The maréchal de Brissac in Paris received 492,800 écus. Maréchal le Châtre, who held the fortresses of Orléans and Bourges, was paid 250,000, and others nearly as much. Henri IV remarked that their loyalty was *pas rendu, vendu*; not given, but bought. But most served the king faithfully.[43]

The cost of this policy was heavy. Henri was severely chastised by other European monarchs, who thought that he set a very bad example by paying his subjects for their loyalty. But Henri told his minister the duc de Sully that it would have cost him ten times as much to do it by the sword, and he was probably right.[44]

Henri's policies impinged directly on the life of Champlain and the community in which he came of age. The town of Brouage came under the control of the Saint-Luc family, a dynasty of Catholic noblemen. After having opposed the Huguenots, François d'Espinay Saint-Luc rallied to Henri IV and was generously rewarded for his loyalty. His family became in effect hereditary governors of the town. In 1596, he was succeeded by Timoléon d'Espinay Saint-Luc, "un esprit plutôt libertin," a libertine who preferred to live at Court. Peace and prosperity returned to Brouage, as to many towns in Saintonge and throughout France. The idea of national unity began to gather strength.[45]

Henri IV also appealed to the material interest of the middle class. He paid large sums of money to Catholic towns for their allegiance and signed treaties of reconciliation that recognized franchises, privileges, and institutions of self-government. Amnesty was granted for past acts. The Catholic Church was established as the religion of the realm, but rights of worship were granted to Protestants. Families who supported the king were rewarded.[46]

Peasants and even day laborers were promised prosperity and abundance. In a conversation with the duc de Savoie, Henri IV is said to have remarked "there will be no laborer in my kingdom who lacks the means to have a chicken in his pot." Others remembered the king as promising "the poorest peasant in the land a chicken in his pot on every Sunday." Henri IV's phrase would reverberate through the ages. The tutors of Louis XIV quoted it to their Royal master, without much effect. In the United States, President Herbert Hoover borrowed the phrase and made a campaign promise of "a chicken in every pot" in the election of 1928.[47]

Henri had a dream of prosperity and abundance for all the people of France. He also became a great builder and vastly improved the city of Paris. Many of the most beloved parts of the city today were his work: the embankments and quais along the river Seine, the graceful Pont Neuf, the gardens of the Tuileries and their linkage to the Louvre, the Champs Elysées, the Place Royale, and the rue Dauphine. A distinctive architecture of brick and stone, the *style Henri IV*, set a tone for Paris. Henri also laid the foundations for a great royal library.[48] The beautiful palace and grounds of Fontainebleau were developed by him, and the royal residences of Monceaux and Saint-Germain were in part his work.

He loved to meet and talk with friends at Fontainebleau, walking with them in the vast wooded park that surrounded the palace, deep in intimate conversation. The king formed the habit of holding his favorite companions by the hand. Other kings created distance as an instrument of power; Henri IV cultivated intimacy. Many people commented on this habit. His biographer David Buisseret believes that it was a cultural style among the *méridoniaux*, the people of southwestern France who had moved into the center of power with the rise of the House of Bourbon.[49]

Henri worked to unite the regions of France in a network of roads and canals. With his chief minister Sully (no friend of Champlain), his projects included canals between the Garonne and the Aude, which promised to link the Bay of Biscay with the waters of the Mediterranean. He maintained a strong army in France, but kept it on a short leash. His soldiers were forbidden to prey upon the civilian population. He told several captains who allowed their troops to pillage the peasantry, "*Qui payera vos pensions, messieurs? Vive Dieu, s'en prendre à mon peuple, c'est s'en prendre à moi!*; Who will pay your pensions, gentlemen? By God, to plunder my people is to plunder me!"[50]

His foreign policy won broad support in France. In the words of a leading French historian, Henri's diplomacy created "a new equilibrium" in the affairs of Europe. He sought to end many years of confrontation between France and Spain, with treaties that were ratified by other European states. Henri IV was a man of large plans, some of them very forward-looking. He envisioned a European Union that could bring an end to violence on that war-ravaged continent. In the late twentieth century he would be rediscovered by French Europeanists as a kindred soul.[51]

This breadth of spirit inspired many young Frenchmen, Catholic as well as Protestant, and they rallied to the causes that Henri le Grand espoused. After a century of violence and cruelty, Henri IV offered an ideal of peace, generosity, and humanity. Champlain was one of many young men of his generation who looked to the king as their model. And for reasons that nobody has been able to explain from the historical record, young Champlain was privileged to know this great king in another way, as a mentor, sponsor, patron, and friend. Whatever its cause, its consequences were a fundamental fact of his life.

4.

A SOLDIER IN BRITTANY

Learning to Lead in the Army, 1594–98

> To Samuel de Champlain, aide to Sieur de Hardy . . . the sum of nine
> écus for a certain secret voyage in which he has made an important ser-
> vice to the King.
>
> —pay records from the Army of Henri IV, Brittany, 1595[1]

E VEN AFTER HENRI IV converted to the Roman Church, a hard core of
leaders in the Catholic League continued to oppose him. As the young
king gained strength, his enemies resolved to stop him by any means.
When all else failed, they took up arms. The result was yet another civil war
in France—the ninth and largest of them all, called the War of the League.
The fighting spread to every part of the kingdom and became a general European war.[2]

Once again the Catholic party invited Spanish and Italian armies into
France, and recruited volunteers from Ireland and other countries. Foreign
troops invaded France from the north, south, and west. A large Spanish force
landed in Brittany and fortified some of its strategic towns. Another Spanish
army crossed the southern Alps and entered Burgundy in 1595. In the northwest, Spanish infantry seized Calais on the English Channel. A mixed force of
Spanish, Italian, and Walloon Catholics under the count de Fuentes, a very
cruel commander, took the town of Amiens the following spring. These foreign armies plundered, raped, and ravaged many parts of France. One of them
advanced nearly to the gates of Paris.[3]

This invasion was a mortal challenge to the monarchy of Henri IV and to
the sovereignty of France. It brought much suffering throughout the country.
The result was an outpouring of patriotism in France. Protestants strongly
supported the king, and this time they were joined by many good Catholics
who were sick of religious strife and appalled by the conduct of the League.
Ordinary people rallied to Henri IV. They turned to him as a leader who could
unite their ravaged country and expel foreign armies that plundered friend
and foe alike.

The king attracted to his cause the best military leaders in the kingdom. The marshals of France, many of them Roman Catholic, strongly supported him against the League. Henri took the field himself and led from the front. He acted with decision, moved with energy, out-generaled his opponents, and his armies began to win. First he dealt with the southern threat. In 1595, he won a brilliant victory at Fontaine-Français and shattered his enemies in the south. He turned to the north and, after a hard siege, recovered the important fortress of La Fère in 1596. On September 15, he liberated the town of Amiens. With each victory his support increased. Then Henri sent an army to the west of France to confront the largest threat to his kingship. The Catholic League had great strength there, and Spanish troops held some of the major seaports in Brittany. The Spanish monarchy poured men and money into the campaign. They built massive fortifications at Crozon in the west of Brittany, and Blavet on the south coast. The forces of Henri IV attacked them in five years of bitter campaigning from 1594 to 1598.[4]

Among the many young Frenchmen who fought for the king in Brittany was Samuel Champlain. He joined the royal army as a volunteer and first appeared on the army's pay records in 1595, serving on the staff of Jean Hardy, an officer in the *logis du Roy*, the service of supply for the royal army. The earliest pay record listed him as a *fourrier*, which historians have understood as quartermaster sergeant (its later meaning). Young Champlain began in the rank of a noncommissioned officer and received the modest but not inconsiderable pay of 33 écus a month.[5]

Champlain was able to make himself useful to senior officers in the logis du Roy. In the Brittany campaign, much of the army's supplies came by water. Champlain knew the business of commerce and he had sailed the waters of western France. His skills were well suited to the difficult task of supplying a sixteenth-century army.[6] He appears to have pleased his superiors, as he rose rapidly in his rank. Within a year he was promoted from fourrier to an "ayde du sieur Hardy." A little later he described himself as a *maréchal des logis*, a commissioned officer in the supply service.[7] Special assignments came to him. In 1595, he received extra pay for a "certain secret voyage in which he had made an important service to the King."[8] Whatever that "secret voyage" and "important service" may have been, the army's paymasters were now referring to him as the sieur de Champlain.[9]

He came to the attention of the highest commanders in the army. Champlain tells us that he served as an aide or staff officer to three of them: Jean d'Aumont, François d'Espinay seigneur de Saint-Luc, and Charles de Cossé-Brissac, a brother-in-law of Saint-Luc. These men were marshals of France, very close to the king. They were in the thick of very heavy fighting throughout the Brittany campaign.[10]

Champlain was in combat too. He was not a man who would have been content to remain in the rear echelon. A sixteenth-century army worked differently that way from a modern force. When a day of battle arrived, aides and staff officers of the logis du Roy put down their pens and picked up their swords. An engraving of a fortified camp that was attacked in a combat zone shows the logis du Roy in the center of the action.[11]

Champlain served in one of the most hard-fought campaigns of the war: the siege of Crozon on the west coast of Brittany. At stake was a strategic peninsula that commanded the entrance to Brest, and control of western rivers. The tip of the peninsula was high ground, with steep rocky cliffs that made it a natural fortress. Today it is a quiet place, with long views across the water toward the French naval base at Brest. In the summer, French families picnic there, and children play among ruined fortifications.

In 1594, the Crozon peninsula was the scene of savage fighting. A very able Spanish officer, Don Juan de Aguila, led 5,000 troops there. His engineers built a massive fort called El Leon, with an outer wall 37-feet thick. Don Juan

In the last war of religion, the high escarpments of the Crozon Peninsula were a key to the port of Brest and control of western Brittany. Here in 1594 French and English troops defeated a Spanish force in heavy fighting. For Champlain, these barren cliffs were bright with laurels.

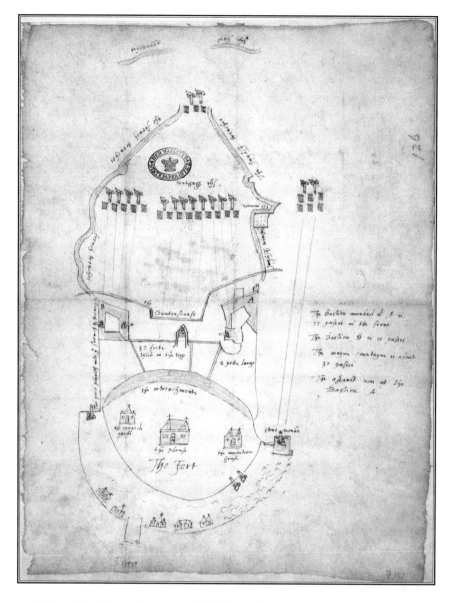

The Spanish fort El Léon at Crozon in a field sketch by English officer John Norreys (1594). After many repulses Martin Frobisher led English troops from the right side of this map and fell with a mortal wound. Champlain and the French attacked from the left, and won the day.

installed a battery that commanded the approaches to Brest, and protected it with a strong force of Spanish infantry.[12]

England's Queen Elizabeth I sent a strong force to support the army of Henri IV in a combined operation against the Spanish at Crozon. A hard campaign followed, in which Champlain saw action. The French army was commanded by his own superior, Marshal Jean d'Aumont. The English fleet of eleven ships was led by the great Elizabethan explorer Martin Frobisher.

The allied forces tried to take the Spanish fort by storm, and were thrown back several times with heavy losses. An attempt was made to tunnel under the wall of the fort and destroy it with a mine. On November 7, the mine was exploded and opened a small breach. English and French troops rushed in, led by Frobisher and d'Aumont, perhaps with his aides at his side. Champlain was said to have conducted himself with great gallantry.[13]

The 400 Spanish defenders fought with dogged courage. They retreated to the edge of the cliffs behind them, and resisted nearly to the last man. The British leader wrote that they "never asked for mercy, so all were put to the sword." After the battle five or six Spanish soldiers were found alive in the rocks below. They were taken prisoner and returned with honor to their Spanish commander, who hanged them for not having fought to the death. The French, in tribute to the courage of the defenders, called the place the Pointe des Espagnols. It still bears that name.[14]

The fighting in Brittany continued for five years. Two of Champlain's commanders were killed in action: Marshall d'Aumont in the summer of 1595, and Marshall Saint-Luc at Amiens to the north. Champlain soldiered through the entire campaign.[15] In 1597, he appeared in army records as "capitaine d'une compagnie," a line officer with command responsibility for troops in the garrison of Quimper, a fortified river town in southwestern Brittany, midway between Brest and Blavet.[16]

In the course of his service, Champlain rose steadily in rank and responsibility. He went from being a volunteer to a noncommissioned officer, became an aide to a supply officer, was soon an officer himself entrusted with a secret mission in the king's service, then an aide to the highest ranking marshals in the royal army, and finally got his own command. It was exactly the same sequence that would later occur in his American career. Some of his opportunities might have come from the king himself. Royal favor may have opened doors for this promising young man; but merit took him through them.

For Champlain, the royal army in Brittany became a school of leadership. He learned about fidelity to comrades, obedience to superiors, responsibility for others, loyalty to a cause, and endurance in a long struggle. That experience taught him to master himself, which was the first step in learning to lead others. He also learned the importance of strength, stamina, and steadfast purpose. A good captain, he wrote, "must be hardy and active," and "untiring at his work."[17] Most of all he learned about courage, honor, and duty. Many years later he wrote that a "captain must give proof of a manly courage, and even in the face of death make light of this, and issuing his orders in a calm voice incite each to be courageous and to do everything to clear the danger." [18]

Champlain was learning other things as well. Some of the men who soldiered with him in Brittany had long experience of America. Among them was the English commander at the siege of Crozon, Martin Frobisher. He was older than Champlain but they had much in common. Both were men at arms and men of the sea. Both were employed in the 1590s on secret missions for their monarchs. Both fought at Crozon.[19] They may have had opportunities to meet when Frobisher worked with the French commander, Jean d'Aumont, and Champlain was on d'Aumont's staff. They probably fought together in the final assault at El Leon, when the English and the French charged side by side across a narrow causeway into the Spanish fort. Frobisher was shot in the leg and mortally wounded.[20]

These two men could have met and talked together in the course of the Crozon campaign. They also had something else in common. Both shared an interest in the exploration of North America. In later years, Champlain called his comrade in arms "Messire Martin Forbichet" in a familiar way, as if he had made his acquaintance. He knew much about Frobisher's three northern voyages to America in search of gold, a passage to China, and sites for settlement. Frobisher failed in all of those purposes, but his adventures were mentioned by Champlain as part of his inspiration for a vision of New France in North America.[21]

For Henri IV, the crisis of the religious wars came in 1598, and some of the decisive events happened in Brittany. After the Spanish defeat at Crozon, the Breton armies of the Catholic League were broken in other engagements. As the fighting came to an end, the king began to wage peace with the same relentless determination that he had shown in the war. It was done in his inimitable way, with a combination of coercion and conciliation. The last chief of the defeated League, the Catholic duc de Mercoeur, was invited to surrender, and required to gave his daughter in marriage to the king's illegitimate son César, the duc de Vendôme.

Peter de l'Estoile, a Paris diarist, told a revealing story about the victorious king and the defeated duke. "The composition was advantageous and honorable," l'Estoile wrote, ". . . the final clause of the treaty was the marriage of the King's son César to the Duke's daughter." L'Estoile added, "This involved an exchange between the king and Madame [the Duchess de Mercoeur], who found His Majesty fixing little César's hair. . . . She asked him, laughing, if it was possible that a great King could be a good barber. To which he replied in a flash, 'Why not, Cousin? I'm barber to the whole World. Didn't you see what a good job I did a few days back, on M. de Mercoeur your husband?' " [22]

Henri moved quickly to consolidate his victory in Brittany. On April 13, 1598, he hammered out a solution to the religious question in the Edict of Nantes. Protestant and Catholic leaders in France accepted a compromise that was offered to them: an officially Catholic state with toleration of Protestant dissent, and much latitude for local hegemonies. It was a complex agreement, with 92 general articles plus 56 secret provisions which mostly exempted individual towns and leaders from the general terms. Two royal warrants also gave large sums to Huguenot towns for "heavy expenses," and annual pay to Huguenot troops. Some Catholics and Calvinists were unhappy with this middle way, but it began to work. [23]

The following month, the king achieved another settlement, which brought peace to Europe. In May of 1598, many French and Spanish leaders met together in the town of Vervins and signed a formal treaty between their countries. This "Peace of Vervins" is little remembered today, but it was a pivotal event in early modern history. In most parts of France it ended forty years of savage religious war, and began a period of internal peace. Philip of Spain agreed to withdraw his troops from French soil. Portuguese and Italian forces departed with the Spanish armies, as did Catholic volunteers from Ireland and Scotland. [24]

The Peace of Vervins was also a European event. Major parts of it were ratified by rulers in other states. Elizabeth of England and leaders of the Low Countries all became formal parties to the peace in various ways. The main agreement at Vervins was followed by other treaties between England and Spain, France and Savoy, and also Spain and the Netherlands. Catholic kings in France and Spain, and Protestant leaders in England and the Netherlands grudgingly accepted an idea of coexistence. It was all very fragile, but it survived through the reign of Henri IV. [25]

The king's biographer David Buisseret writes that "the year 1598 was for Henri an *annus mirabilis*, when Mercoeur ended his stubborn resistance, the Protestants accepted an edict of compromise, and an honorable peace was concluded with Spain." For the first time in many years, the king of France became the master of all his territory. The country rallied to the support of a triumphant young king and his dream of France, as a place of peace and plurality. Henri's vision was of a country bound together by a tolerance of diversity and a mutual respect for its differences. Many came to share that vision in 1598.

The war ended in the Treaty of Vervins (1598). Philip II of Spain recognized Henri IV as king, and withdrew his armies. This victory for France led to peace in Europe, and opened North America to French and English enterprise. Here a young and virile Henri IV bows gracefully to unhappy Spanish leaders.

With Henri's leadership the divided people of France were beginning to think of themselves as a united nation.[26]

The Peace of Vervins also proved to be a pivotal event in American history. The end of hostilities with Spain opened opportunities in the New World for France, England, and the Netherlands. Many historians believe that the negotiations at Vervins included a secret understanding about America. Henri IV and Philip II are thought to have recognized "*lignes d'amitié*; lines of amity" in the Atlantic, which regulated conflict among the major European powers.

No documents to that effect have been found in the treaty of Vervins or in the papers of the men who negotiated it. A very able French historian, Eric Thierry, doubts that a ligne d'amitié was drawn in any formal way as part of the negotiations at Vervins. He is probably correct, but something else appears to have happened there, and it made a difference in Champlain's career.

European rulers had already drawn many lines on maps of the Atlantic Ocean, before and after the treaty of Vervins. On May 4, 1493, Pope Alexander VI issued a papal bull that established a "line of demarcation," running north and south one hundred leagues west of the Azores. All undiscovered lands to the east were decreed to belong to Portugal, and all to the west to Spain. The Portuguese were not happy about that, and a treaty at Tordesillas substituted another line, 370 leagues (1,110 nautical miles) west of the Cape Verde Islands, which gave Portugal a stronger title to Brazil. Other states rejected the treaty entirely. In 1598, Henri IV put Spanish leaders on notice that he would not be bound by old agreements that carved up the world between Spain and Portugal. He wanted a more open system.[27]

After 1598, another set of lines came to be recognized informally by Henri's successors in France. In 1634, Louis XIII of France wrote of a "ligne d'Amitié et d'Alliance," drawn "a few years ago" (*depuis quelques années*). Sometimes they were called "les lignes d'enclos et d'amitié." Louis XIII seems to have believed that one of these lines ran from north to south at "the meridian" of 18 degrees west longitude, which passed through the town of Ferro [Hierro], on the far southwestern island of the Canary Islands. Another line ran east to west on the Tropic of Cancer, which passed between Florida and Cuba in America, and midway between the Canaries and the Cape Verde Islands off the coast of Africa. North and east of these lines, hostile acts between French and Spanish vessels were prohibited. But south and west of the ligne d'amitié that rule did not apply.[28]

No definitive written text appears to have existed. As a consequence, French rulers after Henri IV drew lines of amity in different places. Marie de Medici, Queen Regent of France after Henri IV's death, thought that the north-south line lay further west, through the longitude of the Azores, not the Canaries. But she agreed that the east-west line was the Tropic of Cancer.

Wherever the lines were drawn, the rulers of France and England recognized the principle of amity to the north and east, and an open field for rivalry to the south and west. In 1611, Marie de Medici wrote to James I of England, "all acts of hostility that are committed beyond the Azores, or below the tropic of Cancer are not subject to complaints and restitution." She added, "the strongest in those quarters are masters there."[29]

The English shared the same idea and summarized it in a brutal phrase: "no peace beyond the line." Historian Carl Bridenbaugh writes that this maxim guided the official acts and private conduct of the English, French, Dutch, and Spanish in the Antilles throughout the seventeenth century.[30]

Henri IV went further and warned Spanish rulers that he did not accept their hegemony in the new world. He clearly intended to challenge it—by peaceful means if possible, but by war if necessary. After 1598, he encouraged French settlement in Brazil and French trade in the West Indies, and he proclaimed a rule of retaliation against Spanish ships that attacked the French in those waters.[31] Immediately after the Peace of Vervins, Henri IV also made clear to other rulers that he meant to exercise sovereignty in the region of

North America that was widely recognized as New France on European globes. The French claimed their title by right of discovery in the voyages of Jacques Cartier and others. Henri understood New France in a typically spacious and large-spirited way. He set its southern boundaries at the 40th parallel, approximately the latitude of Philadelphia. Above that line he claimed the coast and interior of America as French territory.[32]

This activity was linked to another major purpose that Henri IV began to pursue more actively after 1598. He had long been interested in many parts of America, and often thought of himself as following François I, who had sponsored the voyages of Cartier and other French explorers. As early as the 1570s before he came to the throne, Henri had supported French colonization in parts of South America.[33] In August 1588, he corresponded with Sir Francis Drake, his "most affectionate and best friend," about opportunities in the new world. These early discussions were mostly questions, not assertions.[34]

After taking the throne, he grew more seriously interested in his determination to make France a global power, and very active in promoting settlement in New France. He also tried to create a strong French navy, which had scarcely existed in his youth. Before Henri's reign the navy of France was described by a French historian as "totally unable to intervene against corsairs or pirates." It was incapable even of delivering a French diplomat abroad. In 1579, the government of France had to ask a Venetian warship to carry a French ambassador to Constantinople.[35] A leading French naval historian, Étienne Taillemite, writes that the weakness of the navy compelled French merchants to arm their ships as if they were men of war. Every French seaman who ventured abroad had to be a fighter.[36]

Henri did not succeed in his effort to build a powerful navy. Not until the reign of Louis XIII and the rule of Richelieu would French naval power begin to develop. But he had more success in promoting French exploration abroad. He visited the maritime provinces of France and met with men who kept the sea. In 1601 he was at Calais in the north; in 1602, he went to Saint-Jean-de-Luz in the far south. During the year that followed, he was in Rouen, Le Havre, Dieppe, Dives, and Caën. Some of these events were state visits. Others were inquiries of another kind. In the early years of his reign, the king liked to travel incognito, dressed in the tattered clothing that he often preferred. He sought out salty fishermen in waterfront taverns and talked directly to them without revealing his identity.[37]

His purposes did not center on a single continent or ocean. He strongly supported Arctic exploration and chartered a North Pole Company to seek a northwest or northeast passage. This group did not find a route to Asia but it developed a whaling industry in the Arctic Ocean, near Greenland and Spitzbergen.[38] The king also encouraged French voyages from Normandy to the Cape of Good Hope. In 1604, he tried to found a French East Indian Company on the Dutch and English models, with little success. The first merchant who led the company died suddenly and the enterprise faltered. It was a story often repeated in French overseas exploration. Henry tried again, but met strong opposition at home and abroad, not least from his own minister the duc de Sully, who was thought to be in the pocket of Dutch interests. The East Indian project had no driver except the king himself. It collapsed with his death and was not revived for many years.[39]

Even so, individual French seamen boldly explored the world. In 1586, a captain from Dieppe, Jean Sauvage, went in search of a northeast passage. He doubled the North Cape of Norway and got as far as Archangel, which was opened to western trade by Boris Gudonov. In Saint-Malo, another small group of merchants founded a French Asia company and sent out ships in 1601. One vessel reached Madagascar and was wrecked on the Maldive Islands in the Indian Ocean. Another called at Ceylon, continued on to Sumatra, and returned to Europe after many adventures, only to be captured by a Dutch ship off Cape Finisterre in Spain. Henri's interest was truly global. Few parts of the world did not attract his interest.[40]

Henri IV made a major effort to support a French presence in North America, and kept working at it in the face of many difficulties. Historian Bernard Barbiche writes that the king pursued his goal "with a remarkable perseverance that none of his predecessors had shown in overcoming obstacles" and it was Henri himself who "finally succeeded in establishing a durable French presence in Canada."[41]

As in many other projects, the king was very clear about what he was trying to do. His primary purpose was to promote colonization in New France. In letters patent for settlement in America, the king ordered that land should be granted to people of merit in "fiefs, seigneuries, châtellenies, comtés, vicomtés, baronies and other dignities relating to us." He had a vision of an ideal society on a feudal and monarchical model, a better version of the world he knew. It was to have an elaborate social hierarchy of descending ranks, all rooted in the soil. He intended that this society should be ruled from the top down, by a nobility of merit and virtue. Henri also wanted New France to be open to Protestants and Catholics, bound by their faith in the same God, and their allegiance to the same crown. The colony was to have a mixed economy, but without free trade. The king awarded monopolies of fisheries and the fur trade to individuals and groups who were useful to his purposes.[42]

Henri IV was himself the driver, an "ardent partisan of French expansion overseas," in the words of Bernard Barbiche, and "the colonial policy of France under his reign had been his work." It was very different from the policies of his successors. Under Louis XIII and Louis XIV, the drivers were the great ministers of state, Richelieu and Colbert. The kings approved, but they were not personally occupied in colonizing projects. In the reign of Henri IV the king himself was the prime mover, against heavy resistance from leading ministers in his own court.

His very powerful minister, the duc de Sully, strongly disapproved of colonial enterprises. He was of the opinion that colonies abroad required an effort "disproportionate to the natural capacity and intelligence of the French people, who," he said, "I regretfully realize have neither the foresight nor the perseverance that are necessary."[43] He also thought that colonies drew effort away from the most important sources of wealth in France. In his *Economies Royales* (1638), Sully argued that "farming and herding are the two breasts from which France is fed," not the mines and treasures of Peru.[44]

Sully specially disliked North America, arguing that "great riches are never to be found in places above forty degrees" of latitude. He not only opposed Henri's plans for New France but did what he could to disrupt them. Sully controlled the purse strings in the French government and spent nothing on Canada, "not so much as a single *denier*," in the words of one French historian. Sully insisted that colonization should draw nothing from the royal treasury, and demanded that it be supported entirely by private capital. He worked with rival commercial groups to undercut the men that the king had chosen to take the lead in New France. Sully may have been in league with Dutch merchants, perhaps even in their pockets. It was surprising that the king put up with it, but they were old comrades and agreed on other things.[45]

The men who founded New France knew their enemies, and they understood the vital role of Henri in their enterprise. Many years later Samuel de Champlain wrote about it in his *Voyages de la Nouvelle France* (1632), with words of praise, fondness, and gratitude for "Henri the great of happy memory who had great affection for this design."[46]

Champlain's "design" grew from Henri's vision of New France. Both men had much in common that way. Both reacted against the horrors they had witnessed during the wars of religion. Both dreamed of a Nouvelle France in North America that combined the best of the old world as they understood it, with an expansive idea of humanity that embraced people different from ourselves. Some dark spirits who are writing history today laugh cynically at such a thought. But these extraordinary Frenchmen who lived four centuries ago had witnessed some of the worst cruelties that human beings have inflicted on one another. They also knew something else about our condition that others never learned. They had witnessed the good and noble things that people do in bad times, which gave them hope for a better world to come.

5

A SPY IN NEW SPAIN

On His Majesty's Secret Service, 1599–1601

> The King [of Spain] . . . at the commencement of his conquests, established the inquisition among them and enslaved them or put them to death in such great numbers that the mere account of it arouses compassion for them.
>
> —Champlain on the Indians in New Spain.[1]

T HE YEAR WAS 1598. In Brittany the war was over, and the young captain from Saintonge found himself "without any charge or employment," in his own words.[2] Champlain was at Blavet, a seaport on the south coast of Brittany. Today it is called Port-Louis, a very attractive stone-built town that still preserves many old buildings and parts of a massive fortress that the Spanish army built during the War of the Catholic League.[3]

The Spanish garrison was still there, preparing to return home under the terms of the Treaty of Vervins. During the war, Champlain had been sent with a detachment of French troops to keep an eye on them. From the waterfront, he looked across a broad estuary with two passages to the sea. The *passe du sud* pointed south across the Bay of Biscay toward Spain. The *passe de l'ouest* opened to the west toward America. Behind him was a dark and ruined countryside, ravaged by decades of religious strife. Before him stretched the open sea and a bright new world of boundless opportunity.[4]

In that setting, this restless young man made a plan for himself. It centered on a vision of America. Champlain had heard much about the new world. In Brouage and Brittany he had met men who had been there, and they must have spun many a yarn for an eager listener. He was aware of the king's expanding interest in America. Champlain wanted to know more. The question was where to begin.

As he studied the problem on the waterfront at Blavet, one possibility was to take the passe de l'ouest, and follow Jacques Cartier and Martin Frobisher to the higher latitudes of North America. Many people had searched there for a northwest passage to China, but nobody had been able to find it. After a century of heavy traffic by fishermen and fur traders, much of that vast area remained to be explored.

Another option was the passe du sud. Champlain could go that way, toward the American regions where Spaniards and Portuguese had built their empires. The kings of France and Spain had agreed to a comprehensive peace in 1598, the first in many years. It was a moment when a well-connected Frenchman might visit the Spanish dominions in America in hope of learning from their imperial experience.

Champlain weighed those choices, and decided to take the passe du sud. He wrote, "I resolved, so as not to remain idle, to find means to make a voyage to Spain, and being there to acquire and cultivate acquaintances, so that by their favor and intervention I could find a way to get aboard one of the ships in the fleet that the King of Spain sends to the West Indies every year." [5] He was very clear about his goal, which was "to make inquiries into particulars of which no Frenchmen had been able to gain knowledge, because they had no free access there, in order to make a true report of them to His Majesty on my

The fortress of Blavet (now Port-Louis) on the south coast of Brittany was built in part by Spanish troops during the wars of religion. After the war in 1598, Champlain was there without employment. Looking outward to the sea he formed a plan for himself in the New World— a Frenchman's American dream.

In 1598, the brooding fortress at Blavet and its setting on the sea symbolized a dramatic contrast in Champlain's thinking. Behind him was an old world ravaged by forty years of religious war. Before him was a bright new world of boundless opportunity.

return." One wonders if Henri IV himself might have had a hand in this plan. Champlain had already been employed on at least one secret mission on His Majesty's service. Perhaps the king gave him this new assignment, but Champlain tells us that it was his own idea.[6]

Whatever the origin, it was a bold plan and very dangerous. Even after the crowned heads of France and Spain had made peace, old enmities were slow to fade. The hard men who ran the Spanish empire in America were far from Madrid, and some were farther from God. The penalty for entering New Spain without permission was death. Champlain himself wrote that interlopers were executed there. Others were sent to the galleys and chained to an oar, or locked away in tropical dungeons, which was a death sentence by another name. And all that was merely for trespassing. The punishment for espionage was worse than death. But Champlain was not deterred by danger. He found it a positive attraction.

The only question in his mind was about how to get started. How could he obtain an open invitation to visit a closed empire? Champlain knew that Spanish leaders were chronically short of ships and seamen, and were compelled to employ foreigners from other Catholic countries. Sometimes these arrangements were made with official sanction. More often they were private deals that were not reported to the imperial bureaucracy in Seville.[7]

In the summer of 1598, such an opportunity suddenly presented itself. The Treaty of Vervins called for the return of all Spanish troops from French soil, and one of the largest garrisons was at Blavet. Both sides agreed that these soldiers should be repatriated by sea, but the Spanish rulers lacked the ships to carry them. To bring the troops home, they proposed to charter several French vessels. One available ship was the *Saint-Julien*, a big navire of 500 tons. Her commander happened to be Champlain's uncle.[8]

He was a fabulous character, with a life so complex that more than one historian has wondered if several men shared the same name. In the sixteenth century, his name was written many ways, a common practice in that era. In French records he appears as Guillaume Allène, or Guillaume Helaine, or Guillaume Elene. In Spanish archives he turns up as Guillermón Elena, or Guillermo Elena. On the waterfronts of many countries, he was known as "le capitaine Provençal," from his reputed birthplace in Marseilles. Captain Provençal moved frequently from port to port and made a prosperous living from the sea. He sailed under many flags, and some were flags of convenience. At one stage in his career, he won notoriety as a corsair, ranging the sea and raiding the coast of England. At other times he served as a commissioned officer in France's *armées de mer* and received marks of royal favor from Henri IV. He also won an appointment as a Pilot-General in the Spanish Marine. On another venture he gained entry to Portuguese Brazil in a ship hopefully named *L'Espérance*, and he also traded on the coast of Africa. His religious affiliations were variable. At one time he appeared as a Huguenot; at another, as a Catholic. Through it all, he became a man of wealth, with commercial property in Spain and a country estate in France near La Rochelle.[9]

For a time Captain Provençal lived in Brouage, where he married the sister of Samuel Champlain's mother. Young Samuel wrote with family pride that his uncle was "considered one of France's first-rate seamen." Captain Provençal, for his part, responded with feelings of affection for his nephew and took an active interest in his career.[10]

On one of his many adventures, Captain Provençal had acquired a one-eighth share of a large French vessel called the *Saint-Julien* (*San Julian* to the Spanish). She was old and not in the best repair. Probably her hold still stank of fish, for she had long been in the Newfoundland trade. For several years she had been out of service and even out of the water, sitting high and dry on stocks in a French port. Some doubted that she was seaworthy, but Champlain described her as a "strongly-built ship and a good sailor." [11]

Her principal owner was Julien de Montigny de la Hottière, a French nobleman of flexible politics, who had been a leader of the Catholic Party in Brittany and later a supporter of the new Bourbon regime in France. He was well connected, and had access to both Phillip II of Spain and Henri IV in France. Governor de la Hottière moved easily across national and religious lines, and held offices of trust in both countries—which made him an ideal candidate for the Blavet mission.[12]

In 1598, he and Captain Provençal received a lucrative offer to carry Spanish troops home from France, with the blessing of both governments. Young Champlain may have helped to make the arrangement. In the last days of the Breton campaign he was working on the staff of Maréchal Brissac, who had been commissioned to supervise the return of the Spanish troops.[13]

Captain Provençal outfitted the ship *Saint-Julien* and brought her to Blavet, where a Franco-Spanish fleet was assembling. In overall command was a Captain General of Spain, Pedro de Zubiaur, a rough character renowned for his exploits as a corsair against the English.[14] Along the way, Captain General Zubiaur had been an associate of Champlain's uncle Captain Provençal. In Blavet, the two men became partners in side-investments of dubious legality, loading aboard their ships private cargoes of valuable commodities such as wine and silk.[15]

Saint-Julien was duly chartered to join Zubiaur's Spanish squadron for the voyage from Brittany to Spain. Captain Provençal was in a position to help his nephew and he invited Champlain to come along. The young man leaped at the chance. Champlain's status aboard the ship was not clear. He held no formal rank, except that of gentleman. Perhaps he went along as his uncle's assistant, or companion. Champlain tells us only, "*je m'embarquay avec luy*; I embarked with him," a phrase that hints at his own agency and a personal connection.[16]

At Blavet, *Saint-Julien* took aboard a large number of Spanish soldiers with their artillery. She was one of eighteen ships in the squadron, all crowded with men. On August 23, 1598, they sailed from Brittany, outward bound through the passage du sud for Cadiz on the southwest coast of Spain.[17]

The journey began with a fair wind, and promised to be an easy passage in pleasant summer weather. But in the sixteenth century, any voyage could turn dangerous in unexpected ways. As they sailed south across the Bay of Biscay, a pestilence began to spread through the crowded ships. Zubiaur reported to his superiors, "With my own hands, I threw into the sea the corpse of an Irish gentleman who died aboard my flagship." So many others fell ill that the Spanish commander converted one vessel into a hospital ship, and the victims were quarantined aboard her.[18]

As they struggled with this ordeal, the fleet approached Cape Finisterre on the northwest tip of Spain. Here the waters of the Bay of Biscay met the currents of the Atlantic Ocean, with abrupt changes in sea-temperature. Suddenly they found themselves in thick fog on a lee shore, with rocky shoals around them. Champlain recalled: "All our vessels scattered, and our flagship was nearly lost, having touched upon a rock and taken aboard much water."[19]

At last the fog lifted and the ships began to find each other. They steered for Vigo Bay and anchored for ten days while repairs were made to the flagship. Zubiaur ruthlessly ordered the hospital ship to be burned and sunk (*brûlé et coulé*) to stop the contagion. One wonders what happened to the sick and dying. When that brutal work was done, the fleet got underway. They sailed south along the Atlantic coast of Spain and Portugal, doubled Cape Saint Vincent at the southwest corner of Iberia, and turned east toward their destination. On September 14, 1598, *Saint-Julien* dropped anchor in the clear waters of Cadiz Bay.[20]

Saint-Julien remained there for about a month, and Champlain seized the opportunity to explore the town of Cadiz, a vital center of Spain's American trade. Cadiz was then an island at the end of a long peninsula. It had been attacked by Sir Francis Drake in 1587, and was heavily fortified with massive walls and towers.[21]

Champlain went ashore, and described his visit in the language of espionage, as "reconnoitering" Cadiz. He later made a careful sketch of the town, with particular attention to its fortifications. As he walked its streets, Champlain found a very mixed population. One street, still called the Calle de Bretonnes, was a gathering place for seamen and merchants from Brittany. He would have met many people who could tell him about the Spanish empire. Throughout his career, Champlain gathered knowledge in every way he could—working from his observations and information that others gave him.[22]

After a month at Cadiz, *Saint-Julien* was ordered to shift her mooring across Cadiz Bay to the sprawling river town of Sanlucar de Barrameda. This was the place where Spain's American treasure fleets assembled for their annual voyage to America. It was also where they returned, in armadas of as many as a hundred ships or more, laden with wealth from the new world.[23]

Once again, while his ship was in the harbor, Champlain made the best of his time by "reconnoitering" another strategic Spanish town and studying its defenses. He found much of interest in Sanlucar. It was vital to imperial communications with America, as a port of entry for the fabulous city of Seville, fifty miles upstream on the Guadalquivir River. From Sanlucar to Seville, the banks of that busy waterway were lined with shipyards, chandleries, warehouses, taverns, brothels, and all the industries of maritime trade.

Seville itself was a great city in 1599, one of the largest and fastest-growing urban places in Iberia, with a population of perhaps 150,000 souls. It was also the commercial center of the Spanish empire. While Champlain was there in 1598, construction began on a new home for the Casa de Contratación, a powerful institution that regulated Spain's imperial trade. The city was also known for the strength of its medieval towers and walls, and for the majesty of its Alcàzar, which had been the home of King Ferdinand and his queen, Isabella. It was renowned for the beauty of its Moorish palaces and gardens, and the creativity of its culture. The painter Velasquez was born there in 1599, and Murillo a few years later.

Champlain went ashore and studied the city. He was no casual tourist who went wandering through its ancient streets. Later he made small bird's-eye sketches from the same oblique perspective that would be favored by intelligence analysts from the sixteenth to the twenty-first century. His drawings showed the location of city walls, the construction of towers, the placement of gates, and the height of crenellated battlements. Champlain appears to have done all these things in a discreet way, without arousing the suspicion of Spanish authorities, who were constantly on the *qui vive* for inquisitive strangers.[24]

While Champlain studied the fortified cities that controlled the commerce of the Spanish empire, *Saint-Julien* lay restlessly at her mooring in the Guadalquivir River. She remained there for three months, longer than Champlain had anticipated. He and his uncle were looking for another job, and hoped that their ship might be chartered yet again for the annual treasure fleet to America. That arrangement would have given Champlain a chance to visit a large part of the Spanish empire.

But the treasure fleet was delayed that year. In the summer of 1598, a dispatch vessel arrived at Cadiz with a report that the English Earl of Cumberland had attacked the island of Puerto Rico. This was no small raid. The Earl of Cumberland led a force of 600 freebooters in twenty privately armed ships. They had sacked the capital of San Juan, spread out through the big island, and gathered up anything of value that they could carry away.[25]

This assault was a major threat to the Spanish empire. Puerto Rico lay athwart the main lines of trade from Spain to America, and the fall of San Juan threatened major arteries of communication. Spanish leaders acted quickly. They postponed the sailing of the treasure fleet, and mobilized the resources of the empire to recover Puerto Rico. As part of that great effort, Captain-General Zubiaur was instructed to extend the charters of the French ships from Blavet, and to prepare his squadron for a voyage to Puerto Rico. It was to be a large operation. Zubiaur's ships were to be joined by a second squadron from the Azores and a third from Lisbon, with more ships from Cadiz, Seville, and Sanlucar.[26]

Saint-Julien and her French crew were hired for that task, with Captain Provençal as master. Both General Zubiaur and Captain Provençal were thought to be especially well qualified for the mission by their experience of fighting English corsairs. Young Champlain welcomed this unexpected opportunity, which promised to give him another way of reaching the Spanish colonies in America.[27]

As these plans were maturing in the late fall, another dispatch boat arrived in Sanlucar with yet more news. The English at Puerto Rico had been defeated, not by Spanish forces but by tropical disease. In the summer and early fall, the Earl of Cumberland and most English survivors had abandoned Puerto Rico and sailed away.[28] In Spain, plans changed yet again. The special expedition to recover Puerto Rico was cancelled. General Zubiaur was given a new assignment in the Mediterranean, and he invited his friend Captain Provençal to join him. Champlain heard the news with a sinking heart. He despaired of seeing New Spain and wrote of his "great regret at seeing myself frustrated of my hope." [29]

Meanwhile, Spanish authorities also decided that the treasure fleet could safely sail to America, and they put it under the command of an able officer with much experience of the new world, Don Francisco Coloma. It would be his third treasure fleet, more than any other officer in Spain. Once again the Spanish leaders were short of large ships with trained crews. Don Francisco proposed to charter *Saint-Julien* with her French seamen. As Captain Provençal himself would not be able to make the voyage, he wanted to put the ship under experienced Spanish officers and assigned a Spanish master, Captain Jeronomino de Vallebrera.[30]

Champlain tells us that he and Captain Provençal had a meeting with Don Francisco. One might imagine the scene: an austere Spanish chamber with stark white walls. In the center would have been a massive oak table, covered with maps of the new world, charts of the open sea, and dispatches from America. Don Francisco himself was a leader of great dignity and courtesy. He would have been dressed in black with a pristine white ruff. He liked to wear a single decoration suspended by a gold chain from his neck: an eight-pointed Maltese cross that identified him as a Chevalier in the Order of the Knights of Malta. The eight points symbolized the beatitudes of the Sermon on the Mount. It was a proud emblem of honor, courage, and Catholic faith.[31]

Enter two Frenchmen: weatherbeaten old Captain Provençal, brightly dressed in the colorful clothing called *bizarria* that were much loved by seamen of every nation, and a step behind was, his young nephew Samuel de Champlain.[32] After an elaborate exchange of courtesies, Don Francisco offered terms for the charter of the *Saint-Julien*, which now became *San Julian*. Captain Provençal agreed on one condition. He explained that he was "engaged by General Zubiaur to serve elsewhere and unable to make the voyage," and asked if his young kinsman might remain aboard the ship "to keep an eye on her, *pour esgard à iceluy.*"[33]

Don Francisco agreed, and an arrangement was made to the benefit of all parties. By its terms, the Spanish leader added a large vessel to his fleet. The owners received 500 crowns a month for the charter of their ship. Captain Provençal put aboard a trusted young kinsman who could look after his interests. And Champlain was able to visit Spanish America with the protection of the fleet commander. The young Frenchman wrote that Don Francisco "freely granted me" permission to make the voyage, "with evidence of being well pleased, promising me his favor and assistance, which he has not denied me upon occasions."[34]

A mutuality of material interest made such an agreement possible. So also did the personal qualities of these men. Don Francisco was a courtier and a gentleman, renowned for his exquisite manners. His letters suggest qualities of intelligence, cultivation, decency, and sympathy for others. Young Champlain was by all accounts a serious and large-spirited young man, very engaging in his Saintonge manners and happily endowed with an easy gift for getting on with others. He was able to work with Catholics and Calvinists, merchants and priests, scholars and soldiers, French corsairs and Spanish Dons.

The arrangement was a private understanding. The parties appear not to have consulted the Casa de Contratación, and nothing has yet been found in Spanish records of the voyage that mentions Champlain by name. This was an informal agreement, like many others in the Spanish fleet. *San Julian* alone was later reported to have had no fewer than six "clandestine" Spanish and Italian passengers aboard, not counting Champlain and his personal servant.[35]

Champlain's name did not appear on surviving lists of the ship's officers. He was not formally recognized as a supercargo, or as the owner's legal representative with powers of attorney. Champlain explained his role in another way. "My uncle . . . committed to me a responsibility to watch over the said vessel, which I accepted very willingly." Historian François-Marc Gagnon explains that "the responsibility given to Champlain was one of surveillance, rather than command." In that anomalous role, Champlain returned to his berth aboard *San Julian* and prepared to sail. He wrote happily, "I had occasion to rejoice, seeing my hopes revive."[36]

On February 3, 1599, the Spanish fleet weighed anchor at Sanlucar de Barrameda and crossed the bar at the river's mouth, outward bound for America. The ships made a magnificent sight as they sailed into the deep blue water of the open sea. The great galleons were bright in their brilliant paintwork of scarlet and saffron, the national colors of Spain. Blazoned on high bulwarks were rows of red and yellow shields, shining in the light. From mastheads flew Spanish flags, royal standards, imperial ensigns with the double eagles of the House of Hapsburg, the broad pennants of admirals and generals, and the long pennants of each ship. Behind the galleons came large merchantmen such as *San Julian*. Each large ship was accompanied by a small tender that Champlain called a patache. *San Julian*'s patache was a little vessel called *Sandoval*.[37]

In open water, the Spanish pilots set a course with a favoring breeze behind them. Aboard each ship, helmsmen on the *puente*, or steering deck, strained against the heavy *cana*, or tiller, as sailing masters carefully trimmed their billowing sails to catch every knot of speed. Working at the rails were experienced Spanish navigators who well understood the winds and currents of their "ocean sea," as they called it in a proprietary way. They thought of the Atlantic as a private lake, and guarded their knowledge as a state secret, which it was.[38]

Champlain watched these Spanish seamen at work and was amazed by their skill. He paid close attention as the fleet set its course and steered along a rhumb line south-southwest from Sanlucar, running before a remarkably "steady and very sharp wind" nearly eight hundred miles down the coast of Africa, on a course for the Canary Islands. The prevailing winds and currents gave them a quick passage. After six days, by Champlain's reckoning, lookouts in the rigging sang out that the islands were in sight.[39]

The Spanish navigators passed through the Canaries and searched carefully for seamarks in what they called *le goulphe de las damas*, Ladies' Gulf. They watched the wind with close attention, for they were approaching a pivot point in their voyage. Beyond the islands they picked up the strong trade winds that blew steadily in that latitude. Once again the helmsmen shifted their heavy tillers, and seamen hauled away on sheets and braces. The great galleons turned downwind in unison and settled on a new course, sailing due west toward the setting sun.[40]

A Spanish navigator using an astrolabe to find his latitude from a fix on the sun at noon. In 1599, Champlain sailed to America with these men, and learned much from their experience about seamanship and navigation in the North Atlantic.

Once more Champlain marveled at the steady wind astern, *vente en pouppe*, that swept them across the ocean toward the West Indies. Every day precisely at noon, the navigators shot a daily sunline with their circular astrolabes. At dusk when the line of the horizon could still be seen, and stars began to appear in the northern sky, they brought out their cross staffes and calculated the elevation of Polaris. They used these methods to find the sixteenth parallel, which was the latitude of a small West Indian island that Christopher Columbus had named Deseade, the Desired One. It is now La Désirade, a French possession five miles east of Guadeloupe.[41]

That was their destination, and after six weeks at sea they made their landfall exactly on course. Lookouts high in the rigging would have been the first to see the distinctive high headland of Deseade, visible from a great distance at sea. Champlain sketched the island and noted that Spanish navigators had long used it as a landmark for their voyages to the West Indies. He studied these highly skilled men, and learned from them to navigate the North Atlantic.[42]

At Deseade, the ships parted company and sailed in different directions. Don Francisco Coloma was worried about Puerto Rico. He was under orders to land a new garrison of four hundred men as quickly as possible. Most of his fleet sailed there directly without making the customary stop for water at Guadeloupe. *San Julian* went a different way. Don Francisco reported that the battered old ship had begun to leak early in the voyage, and at a dangerous rate. The crew was barely able to keep up with the pumps. Perhaps her seams had opened, or fastenings had worked loose, or rot had got into her planking. Whatever the cause, the Spanish commander reported he was "a hundred times" on the verge of ordering *San Julian* to be abandoned.[43] After the fleet turned north toward Puerto Rico, Champlain tells us, his ship stopped at Guadeloupe and anchored in a harbor he called Nacou, today's Grande Bay. The leaking ship was probably ordered there so that her bottom could be inspected and repairs made. Working alongside was her small tender, the patache *Sandoval*.[44]

While they were at Guadeloupe the crews rowed ashore for water and fresh fruit. Champlain went with them and explored the island, which he described as "very mountainous, full of trees, and inhabited by savages." He wrote, "As we landed, we saw more than three hundred savages, who fled into the mountains, without our being able to overtake a single one of them, they being more nimble in running."[45]

Champlain had no designs upon them. He merely wanted to meet and talk. Here again he was fascinated by the variety of humanity in the world and by the diversity of their ways. But the Indians of Guadaloupe had met Europeans with other purposes in mind, and they ran for their lives. It must have made a striking scene on that beautiful beach at Guadeloupe. Young Champlain splashed ashore, perhaps with a sword at his side, and he walked toward a crowd of curious Indians. They watched him from a distance, then turned and ran toward the mountains. Champlain hitched up his sword and struggled after them through the sand, while his companions on the beach roared with laughter.[46]

This comic scene touched a matter of serious importance in Champlain's life. It was the first sign of a continuing theme in his career: a deep interest in native Americans. He always regarded them as human beings like himself, and remarked on their intelligence. Often he commented on their physique and appearance, which was much superior to European contemporaries. Champlain was interested in the Indians for themselves and also for what they could teach him about the new world. He always tried to learn from them, mostly about humanity itself. That attitude first appeared in 1599, in this comic scene on a beach in Gaudeloupe, but it was a very serious business, and it continued all his life.[47]

• • •

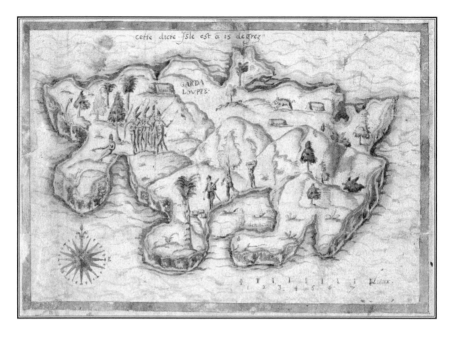

In 1599, Champlain landed on the island of Guadeloupe, saw American Indians for the first time, and was consumed with curiosity. He approached in amity, but they fled into the hills. This watercolor by Champlain himself shows that moment, which marked the beginning of his lifelong interest in native Americans.

While Champlain tried in vain to make contact with the Indians, the crews of *San Julian* and her tender *Sandoval* replenished their water and provisions. It is probable that some hasty repairs were made, and the two ships got underway for Puerto Rico. They sailed together as far as the Virgin Islands. Perhaps at that point it was clear that *San Julian* could reach Puerto Rico without assistance, and *Sandoval* departed on a special mission of high priority in the Spanish empire. Every year the Spanish treasure fleet sent a small vessel five hundred miles south to the Isla de Margarita off the coast of Venezuela.[48]

"Margarita" is the Latin word for pearl. The island was a great center for pearl fishing in the Spanish empire. Champlain tells us that he got permission to make this side voyage aboard *Sandoval*, which allowed him to visit another part of the empire and observe an important source of its wealth. Little *Sandoval* made a swift passage southward across the Caribbean Sea from the Virgin Islands to the coast of South America, and arrived safely. Champlain studied Margarita with great attention and made an accurate map of the island. He also wrote a detailed description of the pearl fisheries. Every day he observed that three hundred canoes put to sea, carrying slaves who were compelled to make "free dives" in deep water, with small baskets under their arms.

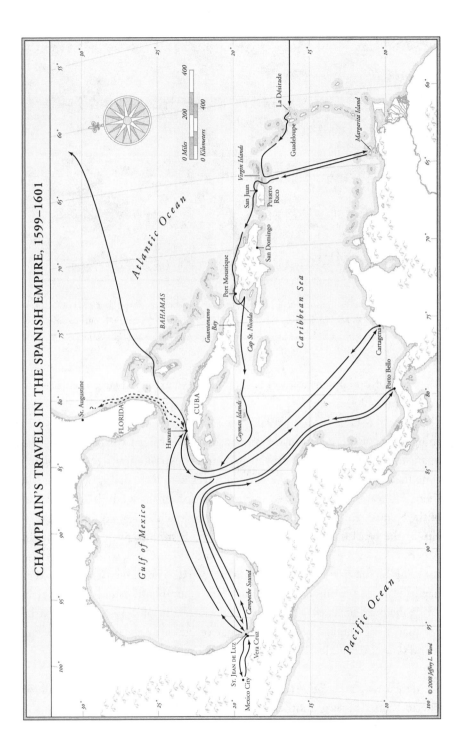

CHAMPLAIN'S TRAVELS IN THE SPANISH EMPIRE, 1599–1601

© 2008 Jeffrey L. Ward

Champlain sailed south to Margarita Island, center of the pearl fisheries in the Spanish empire. He observed the exploitation of Indian and African slaves who were forced to dive for pearls. His Brief Discours *included many paintings of Spanish cruelty to American Indians, which shocked and offended him.*

They brought up oysters and other mollusks, and extracted large quantities of pearls, some of great size.[49]

The pearl fisheries were a brutal business. The "free dives" were the only free thing about this cruel industry. Indian divers had been conscripted by the Spanish, and were soon destroyed by ruthless exploitation. In Champlain's time they were replaced by the African slaves who were diving when he was there. He was deeply interested in the condition of these ethnic underclasses of the Spanish empire, and his concern increased with every contact. The cruelty of the pearl fisheries inspired one of the first antislavery movements in America, led by the Spanish monk Bartolomé de Las Casas, who described the suffering of the pearl slaves in harrowing detail. The industry was also very harsh in its environmental impact. When Champlain visited Margarita in 1599, the pearl fisheries were already in decline. One of its historians has written that it was the first recorded instance of "resource declines in any of the world's marine fisheries, brought about by intensive harvesting."[50]

At Margarita Island, *Sandoval* took aboard her precious cargo and set sail for Puerto Rico. This was another long voyage of five hundred miles across the Caribbean, routine in the life of the Spanish empire and vital to its prosperity. Every year the annual crop of pearls from Margarita was carried in small fast-sailing vessels to expert pearl merchants in San Juan and Santo Domingo. They sorted and graded the pearls for shipment in the annual treasure fleet.[51]

Sandoval made the voyage successfully, and anchored in the harbor of San Juan among the great galleons of Don Francisco's fleet. "The harbor is very good," Champlain observed, "and sheltered from all winds except the northeast, which blows straight into it," as is still the case.[52] He was shocked by the condition of the town. It had been wrecked by the Earl of Cumberland's freebooters, in an orgy of senseless destruction. The English had anchored down the coast, attacked in the night, surprised the defenders, destroyed the fortress of San Juan, and removed its cannon. Champlain noted that "most of the houses were burned, and not four persons were to be found, except a few negroes who told us that the merchants had mostly been carried away as prisoners by the English treasure fleet, and the rest had fled into the mountains, fearing the return of the English." The raiders had taken most things of value, and filled twelve ships with booty. They left behind big piles of sugar, ginger, cassia, molasses, and hides, rotting in the tropical climate.[53]

Champlain found that the reconstruction of San Juan had already begun. It was a remarkable effort that demonstrated the energy and resources of the Spanish empire at its peak. Don Francisco replaced the garrison at San Juan with four hundred troops, and rearmed the fort with forty-seven bronze cannon that had been in Blavet. The Spanish authorities also sent another 300 men from Santo Domingo (today's Hispaniola) to Puerto Rico, with orders to rebuild the ruined fortress of San Juan. Champlain noted that most of the workers were Indians, and others were African. Once again he sought them out and talked with them.[54]

Champlain was able to explore parts of the big island. He wrote, "Puerto Rico is very agreeable, however a little mountainous," and drew a charming small map of the island.[55] He was deeply impressed by the magnificent forests, and the profusion of species that he had never seen before. To explore Puerto Rico's El Yunque Forest today, with its towering trees and wild *impatiens* blooming brilliantly in the half-light underneath the dense canopy, is to share Champlain's impression. He made many drawings of plants and animals, noting that they were from direct observation. Among Champlain's many wonders was a "tree called *sombrade* [from the Spanish *sombra*, shade], the tops of whose branches, as it grows, drooping to the earth take root immediately and produce other branches which fall over and take root in the same way. I have seen one of these trees of such an extent that it covered a league and a quarter." Champlain also described dense old Mangrove swamps, which are still to be seen in the same condition on the coast of Puerto Rico between San Juan and the old settlement of Loiza Aldea to the east. He was observing the wonders of a new world for himself.[56]

While Champlain studied the scenery in Puerto Rico, Don Francisco Coloma divided his fleet into three squadrons and sent them in different directions. The commander himself took one squadron to Cartagena (in today's Colombia), and sent another to Panama. A third squadron, commanded by Joannes de Urdayre received orders for Vera Cruz in Mexico. It included three large ships, among them *San Julian*. Each galleon had a smaller tender. Once again *San Julian* was assigned *Sandoval*.[57]

Urdayre's squadron departed from San Juan and sailed westward along the north coast of Puerto Rico. Their destination was the island of San Domingo.[58] They followed the north coast of San Domingo and put in at the harbors of Puerto Plata, Manzanello, Port Moustique, Monte Christi Bay, and Cap St. Nicolas. Champlain made sketches of the towns and their fortifications.[59] This coast was the northern edge of the Caribbean, often visited by interlopers from England, France, and the Low Countries. Some were pirates who came to fight and steal. Others were merchants who wished to trade. Many were freebooters who combined both roles. Their ships were built for speed and rigged in ways that allowed them to point close into the wind, or to run freely before it. They were nimble, heavily armed, very fast, and not easy to catch. Urdayre's squadron was ordered to clear the north coast of the Caribbean of these unwelcome visitors. The Spanish were very cruel to interlopers. Those who were caught were tortured, executed, or sent to the galleys, from which few returned. So brutal was the treatment of galley slaves in that cruel era that some were compelled to wear pear-shaped wooden gags to muffle their cries when they were whipped.

At Port Moustique, now a very beautiful bay on the coast of Haiti, the Spanish ships caught two small French vessels from Dieppe. Their crews fled ashore and disappeared into the forest, all but one unfortunate seaman who was too lame to run. The Spaniards persuaded him to tell what he knew, and he spoke of "thirteen large ships, French, English and Flemish, fitted out half for war, half for trading," lying at anchor beyond Cap St. Nicolas on the west coast of what is now Haiti. The Spanish commander, although outnumbered two to one, did not hesitate. Urdayre ordered his three large ships and four pataches to attack. They sailed quickly around Cap St. Nicolas and found the interlopers in a bay behind the cape. A wind was blowing from the shore, and the Spanish squadron was unable to enter the bay. Urdayre anchored for the night and planned to attack in the morning. During the night he sent soldiers ashore to block the flight of their crews.[60]

The interlopers did not wait to be attacked. At dawn they seized the initiative, and sailed boldly through the Spanish squadron while it lay at anchor. Spanish crews worked frantically to get underway, cutting their anchor cables with axes—but too late. The interlopers passed quickly between the great Spanish ships, which could bring only a few of their guns to bear. Once at sea, in Champlain's words, they "took the wind of us," seized the weather gage, and sailed blithely away, leaving the great Spanish ships lumbering after them against the wind. Even then, the interlopers were not done. They confused the Spanish by yet another stratagem. A small vessel, with all sail set, was sent directly through the Spanish fleet. Champlain wrote, "many cannon shots were fired at it, but it kept going before the wind. Finally two small Spanish pataches came alongside and found that nobody was on board. The superstitious sailors refused to board it, saying that the little vessel was "steered by the Devil." Champlain wrote that it "gave all something to laugh about," except Commodore Urdayre, who was not amused. He blamed two junior officers and punished them severely. Champlain blamed Commodore Urdayre and the senior Spanish officers. He was more sympathetic to the interlopers, even as he stood on a Spanish deck.[61]

Champlain was deeply interested in the condition of African slaves and Indians on San Domingo. Once again, as at Guadeloupe and Puerto Rico and the Isla de Margarita, he was drawn to them. In Puerto Plata and perhaps at Gonaives or Cap St. Nicolas he appears to have found a way to make contact with African slaves, and to meet with Caribbean Indians. He talked with them and wrote that they were "a good natured people (*gens de bonne nature*), and very friendly to the French nation, with whom they traffic as often as they can, but this is without knowledge of the Spaniards."[62]

Champlain also studied the Spanish system of security against interlopers on Santo Domingo, and discovered a secret network of coast watchers, African slaves who watched for foreign vessels, with a promise of emancipation if they discovered an intruder. Champlain reported, "These negroes will go a hundred and fifty leagues on foot, night and day, to give such notice and acquire their liberty."[63]

Commodore Urdayre's Spanish squadron departed from Santo Domingo with *San Julian*, and sailed south and west on a course for Vera Cruz. Champlain wrote that they "coasted the island of Cuba on the south side, where the land is rather high," and he made an accurate description of that arid shore, with the Sierra Maestra rising behind it.[64] They sailed past the pale green waters of Guantanamo Bay and continued due west through "some small islands called the Caymans." They stopped there for a day, and once again Champlain managed to explore two of them. He accurately described the flora and fauna, and was fascinated by the enormous flocks of birds, and the big iguanas that are still in residence.[65]

From the Caymans they continued west across the Sound of Campeche toward the coast of Mexico. Their course took them through a tricky channel, edged with dangerous shoals. "The leadline must always be in hand, when passing through this channel," Champlain wrote. One of their small pataches foundered there, "without our being able to learn the cause." In mid-passage, Champlain wrote, his ship lay to for a few hours and the crew went fishing. They brought up large quantities of a beautiful fish he had never seen before, "the size of a dory, of a red color and very good if eaten fresh." This was an accurate description of the red snapper that abound in these waters. Champlain greatly admired its flavor. He noted that this fish was not suited for salting and keeping, but it brought fresh food for the crew, always important to the health and spirits of the ship's company. He observed that experienced Spanish captains were careful to seize opportunities for fresh water, fruit, vegetables, meat, and fish. From much experience they were more successful than north Europeans in controlling dietary illnesses such as scurvy, which they called the English or Dutch disease. Here again, Champlain learned from them, and acted on their example throughout his career.[66]

After a voyage of eight days, they reached the coast of Mexico and steered for the port of St. Jean de Luz.[67] It was an extraordinary place, an island about half a mile off the coast, also known as San Juan de Ulúa. In Champlain's time it was, in his words, "the first port of New Spain, where the king's galleons gathered every year to carry their cargos of silver and gold, pearls and precious stones and cochineal."[68]

The site was chosen for security rather than convenience. It was surrounded by shoals, and very difficult to approach by land or sea. Spanish authorities turned the entire island into a fortress. Treasure galleons moored directly to heavy bronze rings set in massive stone walls—not a comfortable berth. Champlain wrote, "The ships are so crowded together that when the wind comes from the north, the most dangerous quarter, the vessels grind against one another, though they are moored fore and aft." Around the fort a seaborne town grew up, with strange houses rising on piles above the shallows.[69]

On the mainland, fifteen miles along the coast, was Vera Cruz, the terminus of a great road that led to Mexico City about two hundred miles distant. Champlain wanted very much to go there. An opportunity presented itself when Commodore Urdayre sent two officers to Mexico City with orders to arrange the shipment of silver to the squadron. The commander of this mission was Captain Jeronomino de Vallebrera, master of *San Julian*. Champlain tells us that Urdayre gave him permission to go along, and he remained "an entire month in Mexico." Spanish documents confirmed the journey as 39 days long, without mentioning Champlain.[70]

Champlain was fascinated by what he saw of Mexico. Nearly half of his written account is devoted to this trip. His journey took him through dense tropical forests near the coast, "filled with the most beautiful trees that one could hope to imagine," and birds of bright plumage. The road continued through "great plains, stretching as far as the eye can see, and covered with immense herds of horses, mules, oxen, cattle, sheep and goats, which have pastures always fresh in every season, there being no winter." He marveled at the fertility of the Mexican soil, which yielded two crops of grain each year, and orchards that were "never bare of fruit." He saw grapes as big as plums, and other fruits and vegetables in proportion. Altogether, he wrote, "it is not possible to see or to desire a more beautiful country."[71]

Much of Champlain's account was devoted to the flora, which fascinated him. He described accurately the major fruits and vegetables and field crops. Still more amazing to him were the fauna. He could scarcely believe the strange creatures that he observed: rattlesnakes, fireflies, hermit crabs, llamas from Peru, crocodiles thirty feet long "and very dangerous," and turtles "of marvellous size, such that two horses would have enough to do to drag one of them."[72]

Like many naturalists of his era, Champlain was interested in describing "true wonders" that he discovered. Always there was a tension between what was true and what was wonderful. Behind his approach was an expanding interest in truth-seeking and truth-telling—an attitude that was fundamental to the history of science in Champlain's generation. We may observe this search for true wonders at work when Champlain heard reports in Mexico of dragons of strange shape, having a head like an eagle, wings like a bat, a body like a lizard, large feet, and a scaly tail. He carefully reported what he had heard, but made clear that he had not seen it with his own eyes.[73] In the same spirit he also described the legendary Quezal bird, which was said to have no feet at all, and spent all its life flying. Champlain wrote cautiously, "I have only seen one, which our general bought for 150 crowns." He was aware that Mexican entrepreneurs had a flourishing business in amputating the feet from dead birds and selling the remains to credulous visitors. Champlain hedged his account of these true wonders, as he would later do in Canada, but he reported what he heard.[74]

As Champlain made his way into the highlands of Mexico, he found that the natural wonders of the countryside were nothing compared with the marvels of Mexico City, "which I had not believed could be so superbly built of handsome temples and fine houses." He had no idea of its size before he saw it, and estimated the population at 12,000 or 15,000 Spaniards plus six times that number of Indians—about 100,000 altogether.

As his travels continued, Champlain became more sympathetic to the native people of Mexico. He described them as fully equal to Europeans in intellect, and wrote that they "are of a melancholy disposition, but nevertheless have a very quick intelligence."[75] He was appalled by the treatment they received from Spanish conquerors. Champlain noted a widespread pattern of tyranny, cruelty, and exploitation throughout the Spanish dominions. He reported that the silver mines of Mexico were worked by forced labor, as were the pearl fisheries, the construction of cities, the manning of galleys, and many industries. Champlain attributed this regime directly to the king of Spain, who "reserved the right of employing in them a great number of slaves, to get from the mines, for his profit, as much as they can; and he draws besides the tenth part of all that lessees get, so that these mines can produce a very good revenue to the king of Spain."[76]

Champlain was even more horrified by the system of religious tyranny that the Spanish imposed upon the Indians. He wrote that the king of Spain, "at the commencement of his conquests, had established the Inquisition among them, and enslaved them or put them cruelly to death in such great numbers, that the mere account of it arouses compassion."[77] Champlain strongly favored the spread of Christianity in the new world, but not by cruelty and violence. He reported that the Indians were so outraged by their treatment that they made war against the Spaniards, and killed and ate them. So strong was the resistance of the Indians that "the Spaniards were constrained to take away the Inquisition, and allow them more personal liberty, granting them a milder and more tolerable rule of life."

But even in this more moderate regime, Champlain reported that Indians who did not attend mass were beaten severely by Catholic priests and given "thirty or forty blows with a stick outside the church before all the people. This is the system adopted to keep them in the faith, in which they live partly from fear of being beaten." Champlain's horror at this system appeared not only in his text but also in his vivid illustrations of Indians being burned by Catholic inquisitors and beaten at the church door for not attending mass.[78]

Champlain's account of Mexico contained many errors. Some things were kept secret from him. He could not discover the location of the silver mines and was not allowed to go near them. He did not understand the source of cochineal, an enormously valuable scarlet dye that was guarded as a state secret in Spanish America. Champlain mistakenly believed that it came from a plant; perhaps he was deliberately misled by Spanish informants. He also confused cacao with the maguey, or agave. But altogether he was a very keen observer, and what he saw had a deep impact on his thinking. Champlain's visit to New Spain would be fundamental to his career in New France.[79] It turned his thoughts to another idea of empire, where Indians and Europeans could live together in a different spirit.

After returning from Mexico, Champlain's squadron remained for a time at St. Jean de Luz. He reported that he seized another opportunity and "embarked in a patache that was going to Porto Bello, 400 or 500 leagues distant," near the Isthmus of Panama. "I found a very bad land indeed," he wrote, "this place of Porto Bello being the most evil and unhealthy residence in the world." He described a climate of constant rain and extreme heat, and a country so unhealthy that the "greater part of the newly arrived soldiers or sailors die." He noted the excellent harbor, guarded by two strong castles, but also reported a way to attack it by an unguarded approach.[80]

Champlain was interested in the Isthmus of Panama, but it appears from his account that he did not explore it. Perhaps he was forbidden to do so. Gold and silver from Peru and Bolivia were brought by sea to the Pacific coast of Panama, and then carried by mule across the Isthmus to Porto Bello. Champlain observed, "If an enemy of the king of Spain held the said Porto Bello, he could prevent anything from leaving Peru, except with great difficulty and risk, and with more expense than profit."[81]

Champlain was quick to see the potential for a canal across the Isthmus, and a passage to the "South Sea." He reckoned that the canal needed only to be four leagues in length to connect two rivers. He underestimated the distance and made an error in his account, writing that one of these rivers flowed through Porto Bello when in fact it went through Colon. Otherwise, his description was accurate.[82]

Champlain's patache hastened back to St. Jean de Luz, where the great ships in the squadron were careened on the shore, and their hulls were repaired in preparation for the long voyage home. This was a heavy labor for hard-worked crews, who had to unload each ship, work her ashore, and haul her on her beam ends with block and tackle until her bottom was exposed. Then came the work of scraping and cleaning the hull to remove the heavy growth of weed and barnacles that reduced the ship's speed and threatened the integrity of her planking. Champlain wrote that the work was finished in fifteen days and Commodore Urdayre's squadron made ready to sail for Havana, where the treasure ships assembled for their return to Spain.[83]

It was well that the Spaniards had repaired their ships. As they made their way into the Caribbean Sea, they ran headlong into a huge storm such as Champlain had never met before. "A hurricane from the north caught us with such fury, that we were all lost," he wrote. The *San Julian* began to leak again, more dangerously than ever. "Our ship made so much water, that we thought we could not escape this peril," Champlain remembered. "If we took half an hour's rest, without pumping out the water, we were obliged to work for two hours without ceasing."[84]

The ships lost sight of each other, and *San Julian*'s pilot had no idea where he was. Luckily they met a small vessel and were warned that they were sailing into danger. It was a miraculous deliverance. "Had we not met with a patache which set us on our course again," Champlain wrote, "we should have gone to our destruction on the coast of Campeche . . . our pilot had completely lost his reckoning, but by God's grace who sent this patache across our path, we made our way to Havana."[85] There they found Don Francisco Coloma, who had arrived safely with his galleons from Cartagena by July 27. The storm-beaten ships of Urdayre's squadron straggled into Havana harbor during the days of August.[86]

At this point, Champlain's narrative became very thin and incomplete. After the hurricane, by his own account, he was in Spanish territory from August of 1599 to the spring of 1601. His *Brief Discours* covers this period of twenty-one months in only three pages. By comparison, he gave thirty-six pages to his travels from January to August in 1599—a period of seven months. His sketchy account of the later period was rushed and grossly incomplete. Unlike the bulk of his *Brief Discours*, these last three pages do not match information from other sources. We know from documents in Spanish archives that Don Francisco Coloma surveyed the battered *San Julian*, judged her to be unfit for sea, and sold her in Havana. Her officers were reassigned to other vessels in the

En route from Mexico to Cuba, Champlain's fleet was nearly destroyed by a hurricane, and almost wrecked on the treacherous coast of Campeche. His shattered ship, the San Julian, *barely survived, and was condemned in Havana, but Champlain's sense of mission grew stronger with every test.*

fleet. Champlain's narrative makes no reference to *San Julian's* fate, and mentions no other ship by name.[87] He does tell us that he made another voyage from Havana to Cartegena in South America, with a passport from Coloma, who allowed him free access to that magnificent port. He was there a month and a half, and returned to Cuba in December 1599. "I returned to Havana to find our general [Coloma], who gave me a very good reception, for having viewed by his *commandement* the places where I had been."[88]

Champlain tells us that he remained in Cuba for another four months, explored the island, and admired the town and harbor of Havana, "one of the finest I have seen in all the Indies." He studied its fortifications and the great iron chain across the narrow entrance to keep enemies at bay. Once again he was deeply interested in Indians and African slaves, and described in brutal detail the slave *rancheros* who hunted livestock with hooked lances, hamstrung the animals, skinned their hides, and left the carcasses to be eaten by wild dogs. It was another dark image of life in the Spanish empire.[89]

That period of four months in Cuba took him to the spring of 1600. Some scholars suggest that he visited Florida. Champlain added a brief account of its resources, terrain, soil, and vegetation in only a few sentences, but they were accurate and very revealing of his own purposes. Champlain described Florida as "one of the best countries that could have been desired, for it is very fertile if it were cultivated, but the king of Spain takes no account of it because there are in it no mines of gold and silver." As always he studied the new world mainly as a place for permanent settlement, and he was contemptuous of Spanish purposes. He was also deeply interested in the Indians of Florida, and wrote of the "great numbers of savages who make war against the Spaniards." He described the fort at St. Augustine, and his description of natural features had the feel of an eyewitness account.[90]

In the spring of 1600, Champlain tells us, "the whole fleet of the Indies" gathered in Havana's huge harbor "from all parts" of the Spanish empire. He sailed home with it, probably leaving in the same season. He reported an uneventful trip, north through the strait between Florida and Cuba, past the Bahamas, where he mistook the long mass of Andros Island for San Domingo. They sailed north with the prevailing winds to the latitude of Bermuda (about 32 degrees), then east at about 39 degrees to the Azores, with their high sugarloaf peaks that are visible for many miles at sea. He marveled at the storms around Bermuda, with "waves as high as mountains," and was fascinated by the flying fish and their enemies the sharks. They steered for home through waters infested with privateers, and captured two English ships, "fitted out for war." At last they arrived in Cadiz Bay, probably on August 11, 1600.[91]

Champlain went to visit his uncle Captain Provençal, who was living at Cadiz in the "purple house" of a friend named Antonio de Villa. The old Captain was very ill, and Champlain decided to move in and look after him. Captain Provençal's commercial affairs were in disarray, and he asked his nephew to take them in hand. It was a big job. Official papers in Spanish archives give us some idea of what Champlain had to deal with. There was the matter of a trading ship of 150 tons and "merchandise from the vessel" that had been left with associates at the village of San Sebastian, near Vizcaya on the northeastern coast of Spain, very far from Cadiz in the extreme southwest.[92]

Captain Provençal thought he was owed money by Spanish officials for the charter of San Julian, and for the cargo and supplies that had been in her hold. There were investments in various parts of Spain, and real estate in France as well. It was all a great tangle. Champlain probably had to travel on many commercial errands. He was still at this task on June 26, 1601, when Captain Provençal lay on his deathbed. The dying man summoned a large circle of friends and neighbors, and dictated a new will that made Champlain his heir.

The will was drawn in Spanish, and recorded under the name of Guillermon Elena. It left a large estate to Champlain. The tone of the document tells us much about them both. The dying man wrote, "I say that I have very much love and bequeath to the Frenchman, Samuel Zamplen [sic], born at Brouage in the province with the name Santonze, that he is my heir, for much good work he did for me in my illness, and he came when I needed him." The captain added that he made Champlain his heir "also for the great love I feel for being married to his aunt, his mother's sister and also for other reasons and for the just respect I have for him; this moves me to prove for all of these reasons of my own free will and in the greatest way that I can give, and I know that I do thank him with a donation of as much as is necessary for the said Samuel Zamplen."

A week after the will was signed, Captain Provençal died. By his order the estate passed immediately to Champlain. No inventory or other probate record has been found, but it appears to have been large. The will was drawn under a Spanish law for estates worth more than five hundred times the average income of a laborer in Spain. The dying man swore that "this donation exceeds the quantity mentioned of 500 salaries." Champlain inherited a landed estate near La Rochelle, "land enough to plant an orchard," fields, vineyards, houses, and warehouses, along with all its "roads and exits, uses, customs and servants." He also inherited commercial property in Spain and a ship of 150 tons, along with cash, investments, and merchandise. The generosity of his uncle made Champlain master of a landed estate, and holder of much other property.[93]

While Champlain was in Cadiz, he began to draft a "Brief Discours" on his travels in the Spanish empire. It was written for a single reader, Henri IV. In a later work, he wrote of his relationship to "the late King Henry le Grand, of happy memory, who ordered me to make the most exact researches and discoveries that I found possible."[94]

Champlain probably had not been able to keep a journal or consult maps and charts during his travels—understandably so, given the sensitive nature of his mission. As he wrote, the facts were beginning to blur in his memory. He rarely referred to calendar dates, but constructed a rough and often inaccurate chronology, reckoned by the passage of days and weeks. The circumstances in which he was working may explain the character of the document, which was very rough and uneven. Its early sections were more finished and polished. The latter parts of the text bore the marks of haste, heavy pressure, and frequent distraction. The last three pages were very thin, and filled with gaps and errors. Always Champlain combined his own observations with reports from other sources, a method that he would use throughout his career. He always tried to work from first-hand observation, but did not hesitate to use other material when only that was available. The purpose of his mission appeared in patterns of description. He carefully observed the military condition of New Spain, described its major fortifications, and noted the vulnerability of towns in Panama. Overall he found great strength in the defenses of New Spain, and very little opportunity for France.[95] He also painted images of New Spain as a system of violence and exploitation and in that way an example of how not to run an empire.

After a draft of this document was in hand, Champlain returned to France and went directly to Henri IV. Once again he appears to have had no difficulty getting access to the king. "I went to court," Champlain later wrote, "having just arrived from the West Indies, where I had been nearly two and a half years, after the Spaniards had left Blavet, and made peace in France." Champlain presented the king with his *Brief Discours* as a book-length intelligence report, with many maps and illustrations. The king appears to have been very pleased. He granted Champlain an annual pension and ordered him to remain at court.[96]

Champlain himself wrote later that he felt bound by "His Majesty's orders, to whom I was under an obligation not only by birth but also by a pension wherewith he honored me as a means to keep me about his person." At this point Champlain began to receive a regular pension from Henri IV for faithful service.[97] The patronage of the king had an impact on Champlain's material condition. He had already inherited a sizable estate from his uncle, and at some point he also acquired title to several houses in Brouage from his family. His pension from the king also gave him an annual income. Altogether, Samuel de Champlain had become a man of means by about the age of thirty. Later in his life he mentioned this condition of independence in his writings. Of his relations with merchants and major investors in New France, he wrote in 1632, "I am not dependent on them." He was able to act as his own master, subject only to God and the king, and to the fulfillment of obligations that he had freely chosen to accept. He began to live his life in that spirit.[98]

Independence gave Champlain a new range of choices. If he wished, he could retire to his estate near La Rochelle, settle down, raise a family, and live the quiet life of a country gentleman. He might also become a courtier in the king's daily service. Or he could go another way, toward a career of exploration and discovery in the new world. He could do these things on his own terms. Champlain was now his own master, free to follow his dreams.

EXPLORER OF ACADIA

6.

GEOGRAPHER IN THE LOUVRE
A Design for New France, 1602

> To plan such designs in table talk, to speak from the imagination of dis-
> tant places . . . that is not the way to carry out with honor the work of
> discovery. One must first consider maturely the matters that present
> themselves in such undertakings, and talk with those . . . who know
> the dangers.
>
> —Champlain on his grand design [1]

I T WAS THE WINTER OF 1602–03. Champlain was in Paris at the court of
Henri IV. It was an interesting place for an ambitious young man to be.
"People of all conditions went there," writes Philippe Erlanger, "gentlemen, clergy, captains, cadets eager to make their fortunes. The court was their
Eldorado. Here one gained positions, pensions, and commands. Here a royal
smile sufficed to change one's destiny. Here one found also the great model: it
was necessary to walk, to dance, to talk as at the court." [2]

Others went to court for another purpose, which reveals the distance between their world and ours. They wished only to serve their king. Erlanger
quotes Henri's court poet, François de Malherbe, who observed: "Good subjects are to their Prince as good servants are to their masters. They love what he
loves, desire what he desires, share his sadness and his joy, and in general accommodate the movements of their spirit to those of his passion." [3]

Those many motives—ambitious and altruistic, selfless and self-serving—
drew young Samuel Champlain to the court of Henri IV. It was an institution
of astonishing complexity. Sometimes it was called the Royal Household and
always it had something of a domestic air. But it was also the seat of power in
France, and the center of its civilization. In the year 1602, more than 1,500
people "of rank" belonged to the royal household, not counting 1,400 soldiers
of the king's guard, and menial servants beyond reckoning. [4]

All this humanity crowded into the buildings of the Louvre, a sprawling
compound in Paris between the rue Saint-Honoré and the river Seine. Its architecture was another of the king's passions, and its buildings were in a state

On return from Spain, Champlain reported to the king, received an annual pension, and was ordered to remain at Court. It was a school of manners for a young adventurer. Upstairs in the Louvre, the King endured boring rituals such as this banquet. Below stairs, he and Champlain worked with experts on cartography and navigation.

of perpetual reconstruction. Ancient walls rang with the hammers of artisans who were endlessly at work on Henri IV's projects. In 1594, he had ordered them to build a huge addition to the Louvre, a great gallery that ran along the river from the Pont des Arts to the Pont Royal. Altogether it cost him the immense sum of eight million livres. The king laughed about the money: "People say I am miserly, but I do three things that are unrestrained by avarice: I make war, I make love, and I build!" [5]

The Grande Galerie was fifteen years in construction. Its upper floor was a magnificent open space that extended the full length of the building. There the king liked to walk among his subjects. Below were a mezzanine with elegant shops, a ground floor with studios for artists and musicians, and a vaulted basement with quarters for the palace guard. By 1603, Henri's Grande Galerie was only half completed. The long hall was filled with craftsmen and laborers, toiling among crowds of elegant noblemen, painted ladies, high clergy in robes of red and purple, musketeers in uniforms of blue and white, scholars in black gowns, servants in livery, opulent merchants, and impoverished petitioners of every rank. In the reign of Henri IV, the Louvre was a place of beauty and refinement. It was also ugly, smelly, noisy, and filthy. Most of all, it teemed with life and throbbed with energy.[6]

Officers of the royal court held many levers of power in their hands. Even in a monarchy that aspired to absolute dominion, authority was distributed more broadly than one might imagine. The most worthy proposal had to win the support of many people if it was to succeed. The opposition of one powerful person could stop it, and there were many such people here. They could make all the difference for a young man with large plans in mind.

In 1602, the court included four hundred clergy who served the king in his role as *rex sacerdos*, the ruler-priest who was the sacred leader of France and a living symbol of divine favor. The clergy had a public role of profound importance in early modern Europe. Nothing could be done without them. Champlain was quick to understand that these men were vital to his purposes, and he was careful to cultivate Catholics and Protestants alike.[7]

Equally important were the high nobility. Hundreds of noblemen lived at court and served Henri in his role as *rex princeps*, head of state. They conducted the elaborate rituals that were fundamental to the legitimacy of the new Bourbon dynasty. At the same time, the ceremonial life of the court converted a fractious nobility into a mannered aristocracy. It bound these restless men to the king's will.[8]

Other nobles in large number assisted the king as *rex gubernator,* head of government. They were the royal ministers, councillors, and superintendents who attended to the administration of the kingdom. Some of the most able people were governors of provinces and commanders of fortresses, men with much experience in managing institutions. Among them were the sieur de Chaste and the sieur de Mons, who shared Champlain's purposes.

Among the most powerful men at court were soldiers who served the king as *rex dux*, commander-in-chief of his armed forces. Henri IV was highly successful in binding the military leaders of France to his person—which was fundamental to the survival of his new dynasty. Young Champlain knew some of these men. He had served on the staff of at least three marshals of France and soldiered with them in Brittany. They could help with his career—and did so.

More numerous at court than the clergy and nobility were men and women of the third estate. In the field of medicine, Henri IV kept eighty royal physicians around him, an entire medical faculty. More than a few were specialists in the venereal diseases that afflicted the vert-galant and his mistresses. Others of the third estate were experts in the arts that added to the *douceur de vie* which Henri le grand greatly enjoyed. He mustered platoons of painters, companies of sculptors, and battalions of musicians. He gave employment to gifted chefs, both the Italians who served the Medici women at court, and French *cuisiniers* in the tradition of the great Taillevent, who had invented the first French *haute cuisine*. Royal *couturiers* created the constant whirl of fashion that became part of the complex rhythms of modernity.[9] Royal *parfumeurs* improved the aroma of the court, even of the king himself, who was not noted for hygiene (veteran courtiers approached him upwind). Another corps of royal *plumassiers* supplied the white-feathered panaches that became emblems of the new Bourbon dynasty.[10]

Some of the most interesting people at court were scholars and scientists. The king recruited experts in many fields and gave them apartments in the basement of the Louvre, where they worked at projects of strategic importance. Among them were the gunsmiths who invented a new and very efficient flintlock musket in these years. It would become the standard infantry weapon in Europe for many generations.

Others were professional geographers. Henri IV was fascinated by maps, globes, and the new cartography. He sponsored a great atlas called the *Théâtre Français*, which carefully mapped every province in the kingdom for the first time. The king also founded a geographic and hydrographic museum that boasted six huge maps of France, the continents, and the oceans. He created a center in the Louvre below the Grande Galerie, for the development of skills that would be useful in exploration, discovery, and colonization around the world. Experts in astronomy, surveying, cartography, navigation, and geography worked there.[11]

One of them was Samuel de Champlain. He was not a casual visitor at court but a pensioner of the Crown with a particular job. A close acquaintance described him as *géographe du roi*, one of many geographers employed by Henri IV in the basement of the Louvre.[12] The role of geographer was more than a job for Champlain. It was a calling that he had chosen for himself. He was fascinated by the New World, all the more so after his adventures in the Spanish empire. But what he had seen of the West Indies and Mexico made him less interested in those regions as a field for French ambition. He had witnessed at first hand the appalling inhumanity to American Indians and cruelty to African slaves in New Spain. He knew that sustained effort by France in that part of the New World would lead to incessant strife—and he had seen too much of that at home.

In Oronce Fine's "Current and Complete Description of the World" (Paris, 1536), the earth became an image of the human heart and a symbol of the sacré coeur. *This linkage of science to humanism and Christianity was central to Champlain's thinking. The map shows that the least known of its inhabited continents was North America.*

• • •

In Paris, Champlain's thoughts turned to North America, and especially to the vast region above the fortieth parallel that had been labeled "Nova Francia" on maps since the voyages of Jacques Cartier. Here French activity could expand without a head-on collision with Spain and Portugal. The English and Dutch were moving into it, and each of their voyages was a warning, but France had a claim that was recognized by other nations. Champlain was keenly aware of the king's interest in Nova Francia. He knew that Henri IV was determined to convert that geographical expression into an actual country called La Nouvelle France.

Champlain learned of many projects, past and future. With the king's encouragement, he made it his business to learn more. From 1601 to 1603, he visited French seaports and gathered information from Norman and Breton fishermen who were active in America. He may have spent some time in

Champlain's task was to study North America. Among his best sources were French Basques who made annual whaling voyages to seasonal stations such as this one in Red Bay, Labrador, during the 16th century. They traded with the natives in a pidgin speech that combined Basque and Indian languages.

Dieppe with *armateurs*, the ships' chandlers who outfitted ships for voyages to the new world. These men had long memories of earlier ventures.[13] He also talked with French seamen who had been sailing to North America since the early sixteenth century, perhaps earlier. Champlain believed that "it was the Bretons and Normands who in 1504 were the first among Christians to discover the grand banks of the codfish and the islands of Newfoundland."[14]

Men of Brouage and La Rochelle were also very active in the American trade. Champlain's own family had been in the business. As early as 1570, his affluent uncle Guillaume Allène had sent the ship *Espérance* to Newfoundland with a captain and pilot from Saintonge. Allène's vessel was big enough to carry twelve "pieces of artillery" and was heavily manned with a crew who could defend themselves in dangerous seas. The voyage was financed by an international partnership of merchants from La Rochelle in France and Bristol in England. Allène's voyage showed the scale and sophistication of French enterprise in North America during the sixteenth century.[15]

Every year, even during the worst of the religious wars, hundreds of French fishing vessels made summer voyages from Dieppe, Saint-Malo, Honfleur, Le Havre, La Rochelle, and many other ports. These fishermen worked along the coasts of America from Labrador to Nantucket. They arrived in late spring, stayed a few months, and sailed home in late summer before the autumn storms on the North Atlantic. A few wintered among the Indians, not always by choice. In 1602, a crew from Honfleur found three fishermen in the St. Lawrence Valley who had been marooned by a skipper from Saint-Malo. Others chose freely to live among the Indians, learned their ways, and formed unions with native women. These French seamen gained much knowledge of America.[16]

Some of Champlain's best sources were Basque whalers and fishermen—French Basques and Spanish Basques as he called them. Their whaling stations dotted the American coast from Labrador to the Gulf of Maine for many years. They developed the technology of whale hunting and invented the light and graceful whaleboats that would be used for many centuries.[17] Later, Champlain got to know a Basque named Captain Savalette, a "fine old seaman" who hailed from the French port of Saint-Jean-de-Luz. They first met in 1607, on Savalette's forty-second voyage to North America. He had been making annual Atlantic crossings for many years—eighty-three of them since 1565, before Champlain was born. Captain Savalette and his crew of sixteen men worked near Canso in what is now Nova Scotia, operating out of a little fishing cove that Champlain later named in his honor. The work was perilous, but highly profitable. In a good year they took home 100,000 big cod, which brought as much as five crowns apiece on the Paris market.[18]

Through the sixteenth century, the Basques also traded with Indians, who wanted iron pots, copper pans, steel knives, metal arrowheads, and woolen tex-

Basques invented this 16th-century whaleboat, found intact by underwater archaeology off Labrador. Champlain thought that they were the best whalers in the world and learned much from them.

tiles such as red blankets from Catalonia.[19] In return, the Basques wanted furs. So strong was the European demand that the rate of exchange for a fine beaver pelt rose from one knife to eighty knives in the course of Captain Savalette's career. Europeans also traded for products of the forest: sassafras was valued as a medicinal tea, and ginseng as a sexual restorative. By 1600, Native Americans had become aggressive entrepreneurs. Some Indians got the jump on competitors by acquiring European shallops and meeting European vessels at sea—a maritime equivalent of forestalling the market.[20]

A complex web of cultural relations had developed between Europeans and American Indians long before Champlain came to the new world. The northern coast acquired a unique trading language, a pidgin speech borrowed from many tongues. Much of it was Basque and Algonquian. A startling example is the word *Iroquois*. Linguists conclude that it was a complex coinage in the pidgin speech of the North American coast—a French understanding of an Algonquian version of two Basque words that meant "killer people." The term was well established when Champlain became the first to publish it in 1603.[21]

In the midst of this flourishing Atlantic trade, many French colonies had been planted during the sixteenth century. Every one of them failed. More than a few were epic disasters. Champlain was dismayed to discover that "so many navigations and explorations had been undertaken in vain, with so much labor and expense."[22] He studied their history with close attention. Why had they gone wrong? What errors had been made? How could one learn from that experience?

His inquiry was a search for the cause of past failure, in the hope of future success. Mainly he was interested in the choices that leaders had made. Four of these failed ventures shaped his thinking in fundamental ways. Among them were efforts by Jacques Cartier in Canada (1534–43), Jean Ribault and René Goulaine de Laudonnière in Florida (1562–67), the marquis de la Roche on Sable Island (1597–1602), and Pierre de Chauvin at Tadoussac (1599–1600). Each of them taught Champlain a lesson about how not to found a colony.

Champlain was especially interested in the career of Jacques Cartier, a seaman of Saint-Malo whose voyages laid the foundation for French claims in North America. Champlain read Cartier's journals with respect and thought that he was "very knowledgeable and experienced in seamanship, as much as anyone in his time."[23] In 1534 Cartier crossed the Atlantic in the amazing time of two

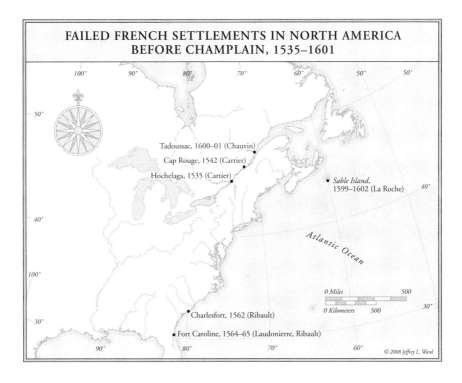

**FAILED FRENCH SETTLEMENTS IN NORTH AMERICA
BEFORE CHAMPLAIN, 1535–1601**

Tadoussac, 1600–01 (Chauvin)

Cap Rouge, 1542 (Cartier)

Hochelaga, 1535 (Cartier)

Sable Island,
1599–1602 (La Roche)

Atlantic Ocean

0 Miles   500

0 Kilometers   500

Charlesfort, 1562 (Ribault)

Fort Caroline, 1564–65 (Laudonierre, Ribault)

© 2008 Jeffrey L. Ward

weeks and six days from France to Newfoundland. He explored the coast and
entered the estuary of the St. Lawrence River. On the Gaspé Peninsula he
found a summer camp of two hundred Laurentian Iroquois who had come
down the river to catch tinker mackerel. Cartier treated the Indians brutally,
kidnapped several, and took them captive to France.[24]

Cartier made a second voyage in 1535. He sailed up the St. Lawrence River
to Tadoussac, and continued to Île d'Orléans, Cap-Rouge, and the site of
present-day Quebec. He sailed on, to the head of navigation on the river,
where he found the large Indian town of Hochelaga near what is now Montreal. His men built a fort there, wintered over, and suffered severely from
scurvy. The Indians gave them a remedy from the leaves of a tree they called
annedda, but Cartier was shaken severely by that experience and returned to
France. Once again he kidnapped Indians, including Donaconna, a powerful
leader of the Laurentian Iroquois, and carried him and his sons back to France
against their will. They were never seen again in Canada.[25]

A third mission followed in 1542, led by Cartier and Jean François de la
Roque, seigneur de Roberval. They came to Canada with three ships, and
planted a settlement on Cap Rouge, near Quebec, where Cartier and Roberval

thought they had discovered diamonds and gold. It turned out to be quartz and iron pyrites, and the disappointment gave rise to a French proverb, "false as a diamond from Canada." The Laurentian Iroquois mistrusted the French, in large part because of Cartier's cruel treatment of them. He and his men lied repeatedly to the Indians, kidnapped at least ten of them, and gained an evil reputation in America as "wonderful thieves" who would "steal everything they can carry off."[26]

In the summer of 1543, the two leaders Cartier and Roberval abandoned their own colony and returned to France, leaving thirty settlers without a leader. Champlain was taken aback by their behavior, and wrote sadly, "Little by little this enterprise dwindled to nothing for the lack of necessary attention." Thereafter, François I died in 1547, Cartier perished of the plague in 1557, and Roberval was killed in the wars of religion. French colonizing in the St. Lawrence Valley was abandoned for many years.[27]

Champlain asked himself why Jacques Cartier's voyages did not lead to a permanent French settlement. He answered that Cartier himself had caused the failure by losing faith in his own enterprise: he "was so dissatisfied with this voyage and with the great ravages of scurvy, whereof most of his men died, that, when spring came, he returned to France very sad and grieved at this loss."[28] Champlain observed that Cartier mistakenly thought that the "mal de scorbut" was a "mal de terre" in North America. He came to the false conclusion that "the air was contrary to our constitution," and gave it up. "And so," Champlain wrote, Cartier lost heart and "the enterprise was fruit-less." Here was the reason. "To tell the truth," Champlain continued, "those who are in charge of explorations are often the very people who cause a laud-able project to be abandoned . . . that is why this undertaking failed." Cartier also alienated the Indians by treating them in a brutal and treacherous way—another fatal mistake.[29]

Champlain also studied the calamitous history of French colonizing ventures in Florida, where Jean Ribault had led two ships to the St. Johns River and built a settlement in 1562. Champlain's short history of this venture became another catalogue of fatal errors. The leaders did not bring enough provisions and failed to clear lands for planting. Discipline collapsed. When an officer or-dered a man hanged for "some slight offence," others rose in rebellion. Some built a small barque and tried to sail home, but they had nothing to eat and were reduced to cannibalism. Champlain concluded that the venture had been "badly directed in every way."[30]

Another effort followed in 1564, under Captain René Laudonnière and Ribault. Here again Champlain found "grave defects and shortcomings" in their leadership. They brought "provisions for only ten months" and tried to clear land for tillage, but were unable to bring in a crop in time to help. Food ran out, and the colonists lived on roots that they found in the forest. There was much "disorder and disobedience," in Champlain's words.[31] Ribault de-cided to attack the Spaniards, against the advice of other leaders. Champlain observed: "It is a stubborn man's trait to wish always to have his own way without consultation."[32] The Spanish struck back with great cruelty, crushed the settlement, and executed some of the settlers. In an escalating cycle of vio-lence and retribution, the French settlement collapsed. Here again Champlain thought the cause of failure was erratic leadership and a failure to prepare.[33]

The worst of these disasters was the failed French colony at Sable Island on the outer edge of the fishing banks. After the Peace of Vervins, Henri IV spon-sored colonizing ventures by an eccentric character with the exotic name of Troilus du Mesgòuez, marquis de la Roche-Helgomarche. In 1597, La Roche sent a fishing expedition to Sable Island. The voyage appears to have been a commercial success. The following year, Henri IV gave La Roche letters patent to plant a colony in North America. The king later contributed 12,000 écus to the enterprise.

The project instantly ran into difficulty. Few people volunteered for the expedition—a persistent problem in French colonization. La Roche was forced to conscript beggars and vagabonds. He persuaded Royal officials to sell him criminals who had been condemned to death and were given the choice of America or execution.

La Roche hired a captain named Thomas Chéf-d'Hostel and ordered him to land the colonists on Sable Island. A worse location could scarcely be imagined. It was a desolate crescent of sand on the outer edge of the Grand Banks, a hundred miles from the coast, swept by fierce gales and shrouded in dense Atlantic fog.[34] In 1599, La Roche's sixty colonists were put ashore with a leader named Commandant Querbonyer and a small party of soldiers to keep order. La Roche supplied materials for shelters and a storehouse, stayed for a short time, and then sailed home.[35] He promised to send supply ships every year, and kept his word in 1600 and 1601. The ships returned on schedule, but the colony did not flourish, and La Roche lost support in France. In 1602 the settlers rose in mutiny, murdered the officers in their sleep, and looted the storehouse. La Roche learned what had happened from passing fishermen, and suspended the annual supply ship. The colonists lived precariously on fish, seals, and wild cattle left on the island by a Spanish ship. Sable Island lacked wood or stone, and the settlers were soon living "like foxes underground." As supplies dwindled they made war on one another. In a few years, most were dead. A ship found eleven survivors with gaunt faces, matted hair, and sealskin suits and took them back to France.[36]

La Roche was thought to be "a man of the best intentions," but among all the many colonial disasters in North America, Sable Island was one of the worst. Champlain studied its history and concluded that the enterprise had two fatal flaws, one in America and the other in Europe. He believed that the marquis de la Roche had chosen a bad site because he had "no knowledge of the land" and "did not have the place explored and examined carefully by someone with experience." At the same time he was unable to protect his base in France. Champlain noted that "envious people" intrigued against the colony, turned the king against the enterprise, and destroyed "the good will felt by his Majesty." It was a lesson he would not forget.[37]

Champlain also studied yet another recent failure. It had been led by Pierre de Chauvin, sieur de Tonnetuit, a Huguenot from Dieppe and a successful fur trader in the St. Lawrence Valley. Champlain described him as "a man very expert in navigation, and a captain who had served the king in past wars."[38] In 1599, Henri IV commissioned Chauvin to plant a colony in the St. Lawrence

Valley, with a monopoly of the fur trade for ten years. The following year he assembled a fleet of four ships. Sailing with him as an observer was a nobleman from Saintonge, Pierre Dugua, sieur de Mons. The result was yet another disaster, which Champlain attributed to errors of judgment by Chauvin himself. The first mistake was in the recruitment of settlers and leaders. Chauvin insisted that "there would be none but Calvinist ministers," but the settlers were Catholic. The result was deep division and constant strife.[39]

That mistake in France was compounded by others in America. The most serious error in Champlain's opinion was in the choice of a site. The sieur de Mons wanted to move further up the St. Lawrence River, but Chauvin insisted on settling downstream at the Saguenay River, a major center for the fur trade. Champlain wrote that the location was "one of the most disagreeable and barren in the whole country." It was also one of the coldest. "The cold is so great," he added, that "if there is an ounce of cold forty leagues up the river, there will be a pound of it here."[40]

The colonists were not given supplies to see them through the winter, which Champlain found to be a common failing in early settlements. Worst of all, the leaders departed before winter set in, and left sixteen colonists living under the same roof, "with a few commodities." The settlers ran out of food, and suffered terribly from illness. Only five survived the winter, by abandoning the colony and living on the charity of the Indians.[41]

Champlain concluded that the cause of all these problems was a total failure of leadership, government, and discipline. He wrote that Chauvin's colony was "like the Court of King Pétaud," referring to an old French folk saying about "the court of King Pétaud, where everyone is master." The name Pétaud derived from *peto*, or beggar. Champlain added, "idleness and laziness along with diseases that seized them unawares, reduced them to such desperate straits that they were forced to give themselves up to the Indians who charitably took them in."[42]

This failed colony had one constructive result. Its leaders brought two young Montagnais Indians back to France. They were not kidnapped, but came willingly with the support of their chiefs to learn French and study the culture. They were treated well and survived the illnesses of the old world. Later they would return to North America with consequences of high importance for New France, as we shall see.

From this long record of failure, Champlain drew many lessons. First was the necessity of detailed planning. In the ventures that failed he found too little serious preparation, "too much table talk," and too many fantastic schemes. "Filling the mind with illusions," he concluded, "is not the way to carry out with honor the work of exploration."[43]

A second lesson was the importance of careful exploration before settlement. He wrote, "it is of little use to run to distant lands and go to inhabit them, without first exploring them and living there at least an entire year, to learn about the quality of the land and the diversity of the seasons, in order afterward to lay the foundation of a colony." Champlain observed, "Most colonizers and travellers do not do this, and are content to see the coasts and the elevations of the lands in passing, without staying there." He believed that only the evidence of first-hand experience could be trusted. In particular, it is a common mistake "to believe that everything follows the rule that exists in the latitude of the places where they live, and it is in this that they find themselves greatly mistaken."[44]

A third lesson was about order and authority. These many French disasters persuaded Champlain that a successful colony must have unity and strict discipline. The Florida fiascos were evidence that leaders must work together and harmonize their purposes. The disaster at Tadoussac showed clearly that they must establish a system of firm and just authority. Champlain was not a believer in what we understand as liberty or equality. He believed in order and subordination, and he drew the same conclusion from the disorders in France during the sixteenth century.

There were logistical lessons as well. To maintain order and peace in colonies, an ample supply of food was an important key. Nearly all of the failed colonies had suffered from a shortage of provisions. This problem required capital, foresight, and very careful planning.

Religious policy was another issue. Champlain concluded from the wreck of the Chauvin settlement that religion in the colony should be modeled on Henry IV's solution for France. He believed that New France should have one official religion, and it should be Roman Catholic but it should extend toleration to other faiths. He strongly opposed persecution and sectarian strife.

And he was very mindful of the Indians. The experiences of Cartier, Roberval, Laudonnière, Ribault, and Chauvin all demonstrated that the indigenous people must be treated with humanity and respect. A major effort should be made to establish a rapport by straight words and equitable dealing.

Finally it was clear to Champlain that colonies often failed because of events at home. He noted that "envious people" in France intrigued against colonial ventures. The trouble came from rival merchants, competing seaports, jealous courtiers, and representatives of foreign powers. The most pow-

New France had enemies at Court. Most powerful was the duc de Sully, the King's chief minister, who insisted that nothing good could come from settlements above the 40th parallel (the latitude of Philadelphia). Witnesses testified that Sully took Dutch bribes to oppose French colonies.

erful opponent of settlement in New France was the king's chief minister, the duc de Sully, who thought that colonies were a distraction from business at home, and tried to turn the king against them. De Mons and Champlain believed that Sully had been bribed by Dutch merchants, but his dislike of New France rose fundamentally from an idea of national interest. There was a debate in France during the reign of Henri IV between leaders who favored domestic reform and others who supported expansion abroad. It was similar in some ways to the debates in Victorian England between imperialists and Little Englanders, and to struggles in the United States over foreign policy in the twentieth century.

In each of these conflicts there was also a middle way. Centrists and moderates favored a mediating position: a forward foreign policy and progressive reform at home. This was the policy of British leaders such as Pitt the Elder and Winston Churchill, and Americans including Theodore Roosevelt, Franklin Roosevelt, Harry Truman, and the "wise men" in the United States during the mid-twentieth century. It was also the choice of Henri IV in France. In 1602, he favored reform at home and expansion abroad, and believed that each of these two policies could reinforce the other.

Champlain also believed that a key to success in America was a continued effort to rally support in France, particularly at the court of Henri IV, where the good will of the king was absolutely necessary to the enterprise. He wrote that "kings are often deceived by those in whom they have confidence." Much of his career was an ongoing effort to promote a new France in the old world.[45]

• • •

FRENCH PORTS AND AMERICAN FISHERIES, 1600–1635

Severn

London

• Bristol

Thames

ENGLAND

Dover •

Dunkirk

Calais

Étaples •

SPANISH
NETHERLANDS

Plymouth •

Dartmouth •

English Channel

Tréport

50°

50°

Cherbourg •

Fécamp •

Dieppe

Le Havre
de Grace

• Rouen

Caen •

Honfleur

Seine

Granville

NORMANDY

Paris •

St-Brieuc

St-Malo •

Roscof •

Brest •

BRITTANY

48°

48°

Crozon —

Quimper •

Tours •

Loire

FRANCE

Blavet (Port-Louis) —

• Nantes

VENDÉE

Les Sables-d'Olonne •

Île de Ré

• La Rochelle

46°

46°

Oléron →

Charente

SAINTONGE

Brouage •

Gironde

Bay of Biscay

44°

44°

BASQUE
COUNTRY

Montpellier •

• Bordeaux

Bayonne •

Béziers •

St-Jean-de-Luz •

Marseille •

SPAIN

Mediterranean Sea

42°

42°

SHARE OF FISHING VOYAGES TO NORTH AMERICA

- 40-50%
- 20-25%
- ca. 5%

0 Miles   100   200

0 Kilometers   100   200

In 1602, an opportunity suddenly came to the friends of New France. That year, Chauvin forfeited his monopoly of fur trading in the St. Lawrence. Orders were issued from court in 1602, commanding two eminent figures to take the problem in hand. One of these men was the sieur de la Cour, president of the Parlement of Normandy. The other was the sieur de Chaste, Vice Admiral of the Navy, and an officer of high distinction. The two Royal Commissioners proposed to authorize two trading ventures: one for the merchants of Rouen in Normandy; the other for traders from Saint-Malo. In return for special trading privileges, each group was required to contribute one-third of the cost of founding a permanent colony in New France.

The king agreed, and appointed Aymar de Chaste as overall commander of the entire enterprise.[46] Today he is largely forgotten—the most obscure of all the major figures in the founding of New France. He did not come to America and was in command of the colonial enterprise for a very short period, but he played a pivotal role in the history of New France and in the career of Samuel Champlain.

The sieur de Chaste was a soldier, a seaman, a chevalier, and knight-commander of the Order of Malta. He had faithfully served Catherine de Medici, led a military expedition to the Azores, and became governor of the town and fortress of Dieppe. In the wars of religion he played a major part. After the death of Henri III in 1589, de Chaste opened the gates of Dieppe to Henri IV and helped to bring moderate Catholic leaders to the support of the young king. Champlain described him as a "most honorable man, a good Catholic, a great servant of the king," who "worthily and faithfully served his Majesty on many important occasions." Others spoke of him in the same way.[47]

In 1602–03, de Chaste was near the end of his career. In the twilight of his life, he was deeply interested in founding a French colony in America, and he thought more of the future than of the past. He had a clear vision of New France as a place of harmony and prosperity, and also proposed to make it self-supporting, even a source of revenue for the Crown. Champlain wrote that "though his head was covered with as many grey hairs as years, he still wished to leave to posterity a charitable example by this project, and even to go there himself and devote the rest of his years to the service of God and his King."

The king was happy to give him a commission as ruler of New France. De Chaste also received a charter that gave him a monopoly of trade and colonization (but not fishing) in America from the latitude of 46 degrees north (Cape Breton), to 40 degrees north (Philadelphia). De Chaste was everybody's

A. S.Iaques.   C. S.Remy.   E. Tour de Male,   G. Porte de la poiſſonnerie,   I. Tour Iumelle,   L. Les rampars,   N. La Faloiſe,   P. Champ du pardon,   R. Arque riuiere,
B. L'hoſtel de Ville.   D.Tour du Polet.   F. Porte Sailly.   H. Porte Goſlin.   K. Le Chaſteau.   M. Gueulle du hautte.   O. Neu-uille,   Q. La gettee.   3 b ij

In 1602–03, Dieppe became a center of effort for New France. Leadership passed to the very able Aymar de Chaste, governor of that walled seaport. Champlain went there to work with chandlers and merchants who had much experience of North America.

choice for the job and he brought many strengths to the American project. He was well connected at court and had the respect of Henri IV and his Council. He was a good Catholic, in high standing with leaders of the church.

Most important were his close relations with merchants in the American trade. De Chaste put together a partnership of investors in northern France. Several noble families bought in. At the core of the group were leading merchants in the prosperous seaports of Normandy. They agreed to accept "certain conditions" that differed from other investments by these hard-headed businessmen. De Chaste persuaded them not only to fit out vessels for "the execution of a business enterprise" but also to "explore and colonize the country."[48]

When Champlain learned of this new project, he was quick to approach de Chaste. The two men appear to have met before. Their paths may have crossed in the army during the war in Brittany. Probably they met in Dieppe when de Chaste was governor of that town, and Champlain was working with its ship

chandlers. Champlain tells us that they met again at court in 1602, and thereafter he "went to see Commander de Chaste from time to time."

Champlain probably gave de Chaste a manuscript of his *Brief Discours* on
the West Indies and New Spain—in all likelihood the copy that found its way
from Dieppe to the John Carter Brown Library in Providence, Rhode Island.
De Chaste spoke of his project. As they talked together about America, they
discovered many purposes in common. Both men shared a way of thinking
about religion and politics, exploration and colonization, France and the
world. In Champlain's words, the commander "did me the favor of communicating something of his plans," and "believing I could be of help with his design, he asked me if I would like to make the voyage, to see the country and
what the entrepreneurs might accomplish there." [49]

Champlain leaped at the invitation. "I told him that I was at his disposal,"
he wrote. But there was a problem. As a pensioner of the king, Champlain was
not at liberty to take another job without orders from His Majesty. He suggested that "if Commander de Chaste could speak with the king about it, and
if it should be the king's command," then he would very much like to go. [50] De
Chaste had a word with the king, and all obstacles were removed. His Majesty
not only approved, but commanded Champlain to make the voyage, and ordered that he make a "faithful report" directly to the king himself. The royal
secretary, Louis Potier de Gesvres, gave Champlain a letter that was addressed
to senior leaders of the expedition, ordering them in the king's name "to receive Champlain aboard ship, and allow him to see and explore as much as
possible of those places, and to assist in every possible way." [51]

And so the elements came together. Aymar de Chaste, the forgotten
founder, was a leader with a large spirit who won the respect and affection of
all who knew him. Champlain was the junior partner, but with the ear of the
king and his strong support. Henri IV was the royal patron who contributed
his own broad vision, energy, and resolve. As a group, these men framed a
great enterprise that combined exploration, trade, and settlement. The goal
was to increase the power and prosperity of France, to spread the Christian
faith, to learn more about the world, and to bring together its many people in
a spirit of humanity.

7.

TADOUSSAC
The Great Tabagie, 1603

> The chance diplomatic meeting [at Tadoussac] was an historic event of
> high importance. . . . It established the foundation for the Amerindian
> policy of France in this region.
>
> —Alain Beaulieu[1]

WITH THE KING'S LETTER in hand, Champlain left the court and made his way to the port of Honfleur, near the mouth of the River Seine. He walked along old stone quays through crowds of weather-beaten seamen, merchants, prostitutes, and all the teeming humanity who worked along the busy waterfront. He was looking for his ship, and at last he found her—a small storm-beaten navire with the happy name of *Bonne-Renommée*, "Good Renown."[2]

Champlain also found her commander, Captain François Gravé, sieur du Pont. He was a fabulous character, much loved for his large spirit by men who sailed with him, and greatly feared by those who ran afoul of his temper. His shipmates called him Pont-Gravé, and so shall we. He loved good company, great food, and the fiery *calvados* of his beloved Brittany, which he was famed for drinking straight, and he suffered the consequences in a painful gout that troubled him for years. Pont-Gravé was a jolly giant of a man, a "loud, hearty, back-slapping fellow" with a deep booming voice that could be heard above a howling gale. He was a native son of Saint-Malo, born and raised in that rough-and-tumble seaport, baptized in its Cathedral-Church, and fiercely proud of his Breton heritage. At sea, when he met a fishing boat of familiar appearance, he would climb the rigging and shout *Malouins!* Then he would sing a joyous song of Brittany at the top of his lungs.[3]

One historian has called him the Falstaff of New France. In many a biography he has played that role, a Falstaff to Champlain's Prince Hal. But Pont-Gravé was much more than that. His family was of wealth and eminence in Saint-Malo. The king was told that the leading *homme de créance*, or man of

In 1603, little Honfleur at the mouth of the river Seine became the leading port of embarcation for New France. Some of its old streets around its inner basin are much the same as in Champlain's time.

credit, in the town was Pont-Gravé's cousin Thomas Gravé.[4] Pont-Gravé was himself a courageous seaman and a major figure in the colonization of New France. In 1603, he was forty-three years old, about ten years older than Champlain, and a seaman of long experience in the North Atlantic. Recently he had commanded a ship in Chauvin's ill-fated expedition and had warned against its errors, but nobody listened until it was too late. Champlain hoped to learn from him. He wrote that Pont-Gravé was a man "very skilled in sea voyages, having made many of them."[5]

The two men met and Champlain presented the king's letter, which made clear his role in the expedition. He was not to be in the chain of command. Champlain was to go along as an observer, but no ordinary observer. His assignment was to report directly to the king. This might have made trouble with many commanders, but Champlain was open and candid, Pont-Gravé was good-natured, and the two men took a liking to each other. They became shipmates and fast friends. Pont-Gravé was senior in age, rank, and service. He became a mentor to Champlain, and taught the young man the lessons of experience in the hard school of the North Atlantic. "As for the sieur du Pont," Champlain wrote, "I was his friend, and his years would lead me to respect him as I would my father."[6]

• • •

At Honfleur, Champlain also met two interesting people who would join the voyage. They were Montagnais Indians, "young men of rank in their own country" who were homeward bound after a year in Europe. Pont-Gravé, on his last voyage to Canada, had persuaded their elders to send them to France, so that they could see the country and learn the language. The hope was that they would return to America and work as interpreters or mediators between two cultures. Their stay in France had been a brilliant success. They were invited to court and met Henri IV, who was kind and welcoming. The great houses of France were open to them, and they were received as "Indian princes." They formed a high respect for the people of France, and spoke warmly of their reception—a fact of much importance for the history of Canada, as we shall see.[7]

The sponsor and leader of this enterprise was Aymar de Chaste. He was very able and highly esteemed, but he was elderly and not in good health. He decided to remain in France so that he could attend to the tangled affairs of the company. De Chaste worked well with his investors. He pushed ahead with preparations and raised money enough for three ships of modest size. *Bonne-Renommée*, the flagship, was a vessel of 120 or 150 tons, and about ninety feet long overall, including her great *poulaine*, or prow, which projected forward under the bowsprit. She was said to be a sturdy seaboat, and was well equipped by the merchants of Honfleur. Sailing with her were two smaller vessels. *La Françoise*, 100 tons, was outfitted by the merchants of Rouen. A third vessel of unknown name and tonnage belonged to Jean Sarcel de Prévert of Saint-Malo.[8]

From the start, this expedition had the double purpose of trade and exploration. Its leaders meant to make a profit in fishing and the fur trade, which was vital to the enterprise. Given the state of the royal treasury, Henri IV and his ministers had insisted that Champlain's grand design for New France must pay its own way. De Chaste raised capital for the voyage among merchants and "gentilhommes" in Honfleur, Saint-Malo, Dieppe, Le Havre, and probably other towns. The commercial risk was thought to be very great. A measure of danger, in the judgment of hard-headed businessmen who had much experience of America, was the price of insurance: 35 percent. But de Chaste promised his investors a return on their investment, and they trusted his judgment.[9]

Trade was necessary to the voyage, but its primary purpose was to study the possibility of settlement in New France. The object was not to plant a colony, but to prepare for colonization in the near future. To that end, the instructions from Aymar de Chaste and the king were to establish good relations with the Indians, to explore the great rivers of Canada, to examine sites for a permanent colony, and to return in six months.[10]

For purposes of exploration, the ships also carried at least two vessels of middling size. Champlain called them *moyenne barques*, and reckoned their size at about 12 or 15 tons. Also aboard were small, open-hulled shallops of five or seven tons, which would be useful for exploring and making charts. They were prefabricated in sections for assembly in America.[11]

The ships got underway on March 15, 1603, the Ides of March, not the most propitious day to start a dangerous voyage, or the best season to brave the ocean sea. It was late winter on the North Atlantic, a time of cyclonic sou'westers on the coast of Europe, violent nor'easters in America, and floating icebergs in between. But Pont-Gravé and his officers were in a hurry to get away. In the tight little port of Honfleur they hoisted sail, left their moorings, and threaded their way through the shifting sand banks of the Seine toward the open sea.

As they left the mouth of the river, the wind turned against them, and they were forced to anchor in the roadstead of Le Havre on the north bank. The next day the winds were favorable, and they started again, steering southwest past the Channel Islands of Guernsey and Alderney. By the evening of March 19 they were off Ushant, the westernmost point of France. Europe was behind them and ahead lay the great western ocean—always a moment of exhilaration for a blue-water sailor.

Two days later the mood changed when they sighted a strange ship hull-down on the horizon. More ships hove into view, seven in all, steering toward them on the steady bearing that warns a wary seaman of a collision course. In that era, one never knew what to expect from strange ships off the coast of France. A constant menace were pirates, sea rovers, and freebooters who flew many flags or none at all. The ships drew closer and cleared for action. Champlain recognized them as Flemish vessels, homeward bound from a long trading voyage to the East Indies. The two squadrons passed in peace, to their mutual relief.[12]

Bonne-Renommée and her consorts continued on their way, and made good progress in a week of clear weather and steady sailing. Then the wind shifted, the sea began to rise and the sky turned dark. Suddenly they found themselves in a sou'wester of terrific violence, blowing directly into their faces. In deep green seas, Champlain's ship rolled and pitched and yawed with such force that no fires were possible, and the crew had nothing warm to eat or drink.

The storm continued for seventeen days and, as Champlain remembered, "we rather lost than gained ground." Everyone was chilled to the bone, and many were filled with terror.[13]

At last, on the eighteenth day, "the weather began to improve, and the sea became more calm, to the contentment of all." They continued on their course for two weeks. The water turned warm as they crossed the gulf stream, then cold again as they entered the Labrador current. On April 28, they met an iceberg that towered above their ship. The next day they passed an ice floe twenty miles long, and "an infinite number of smaller ones, which hindered our passage." The pilot reckoned their latitude at 45 degrees, 40 minutes, north latitude, and they could not find a way through the ice.

They turned south, and at 44 degrees "found passage" to the west, which brought them to "the bank" as they called it, the Grand Bank south of Newfoundland. They sailed west and ran into thick fog. In the dark silence of a foggy night they began to hear a distant sound, which suddenly they recognized as the crash of waves breaking on a coast. The alarm was given and the crew rushed on deck. Topmen raced up the shrouds. As the sound of the surf grew louder, the pilot threw over the helm. Eager hands hauled on braces, and slowly the ship came about, canvas beating in the wind. At last the sails began to fill again, and they sailed away from the surf in the nick of time. Next morning the fog lifted, and they found that they were just off the rocky cliffs of Cape St. Mary's, jutting south from Newfoundland's Avalon Peninsula. They had come to the edge of disaster—a lesson that Champlain would long remember.[14]

After that first landfall, they still had a long passage ahead of them through the coastal waters of North America. They were ten days getting past Newfoundland and were "overtaken" by another hard gale, a classic American nor'easter by Champlain's account. At last they reached Cabot Strait, sixty miles wide, between Newfoundland and Cape Breton Island. Little *Bonne-Renommée* sailed through that huge passage and entered the Gulf of St. Lawrence, an inland sea of enormous size. The pilot gave orders to come right and they set a course west-northwest across the gulf, dodging more ice floes. Champlain was astonished by the magnitude of this new world. Even by comparison with the Caribbean and the Spanish Main, the coast of North America was on an immense scale.

At last they entered the "River of Canada" as Champlain called it, today's St. Lawrence. It too was large beyond imagining. The mouth of the river was a hundred miles wide. It was divided by the great tongue of Anticosti Island, 122 miles long, the home of huge white polar bears of legendary ferocity who attacked humans on sight. European seamen and American Indians alike gave Anticosti Island a wide berth. Onward they sailed along the south bank of the estuary, past the great sea-carved stone arches of "Île Percée" that made it an important seamark. They passed the Gaspé Peninsula with its mountains that surprised Champlain by their height, four thousand feet above the sea.

They were another week sailing up the great St. Lawrence River. In the last week of May, they reached the mouth of the Saguenay River and dropped anchor in the tight little harbor of Tadoussac. The date was May 26, 1603. It had been a crossing of ten weeks, with many desperate moments. But by comparison with others, Champlain remembered it as a "happy voyage." Perhaps it was Pont-Gravé and the Montagnais princes who helped to make it so.[15]

In Tadoussac harbor Champlain and Pont-Gravé thought about contacting the Indians. The next day, an opportunity presented itself entirely by chance. Just before the French arrived, many Indians had gathered on the other side of the Saguenay River, only a few miles from Tadoussac. They built a summer camp of bark lodges at St. Matthew's Point, today's Pointe aux Alouettes.[16]

It was a huge assembly. Champlain counted more than two hundred large canoes and reckoned that a thousand Indians were there. They were of many nations. Among them were several groups of Montagnais, who call themselves

The Île Percée, on the eastern end of the Gaspé Peninsula, was a giant rock of red sandstone, a quarter mile long and 300 feet high. Famed for its enormous sea-carved arches (now reduced to one), it served Champlain and his captains as an aid to navigation.

Tadoussac's small circular harbor had long been a center of trade in the lower St. Lawrence River.
Theodore de Bry's print (1592), shows a canoe and whaling vessel of 50 or 60 tons. The whale is a white beluga
with a rounded head and no dorsal fin, so it can break the winter ice. A pod still lives in these waters.

Innu today (not to be confused with the Inuit to the north). The hosts were
the Tadoussac Montagnais, who lived nearby. The Bersiamite Montagnais
came up from the lower St. Lawrence, and the Attikamègue Montagnais journeyed down the river from Quebec. The Porc-épic were from the Saguenay
Valley.[17] Also present were Algonquin nations from the Ottawa River to the far
northwest and Etchemin from as far south as the Penobscot River, in what is
now the state of Maine. They had come together to celebrate a victory over
their common enemy, the Iroquois.[18]

   Champlain and Pont-Gravé acted quickly. They and the two Montagnais
interpreters climbed into a shallop, sailed across the windswept Saguenay
River, and went into the huge Indian camp. It was a lively scene: billowing
clouds of white smoke rising above the lodges, a swirl of color and movement
in the camp, crowds of young braves and beautifully dressed Indian maidens
mixing with each other, gangs of children and packs of dogs dashing to and

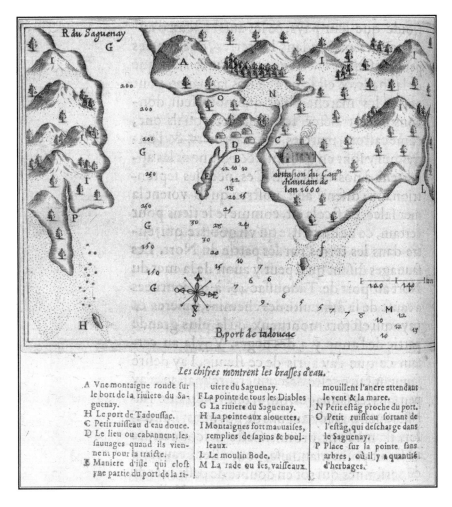

Champlain's very accurate chart of Tadoussac and the mouth of the Saguenay River, with St. Matthew's Point (Pointe aux Alouettes) to the West. Note the depth of the river: 250 French fathoms, or 1500 feet. On shore are Indian bark houses and the ruins of Chauvin's failed colony.

fro. The Indian drums were beating in celebration. More than a hundred fresh Iroquois scalps were on display. Wounded Iroquois captives were tightly bound to stakes, and their torture had already begun. Blood dripped from what remained of slashed and shattered fingers, as they stoically awaited their fate.

The two French leaders came ashore with their young Montagnais companions and walked boldly into the camp. They showed not the slightest sign of fear or hostility—a demeanor that was very different from that of many Europeans. Probably they were wearing half-armor and gleaming steel helmets, adorned with the white plumes of their Bourbon king, but without firearms—different again from others in similar circumstances.[19]

Pont-Gravé, Champlain, and the Montagnais were taken to a chief they called Anadabijou. They found him in a big bark lodge sixty or seventy paces long, holding a *tabagie*, a tobacco-feast for "eighty or one hundred companions." Champlain described these leaders as *sagamores*, and Anadabijou of the Tadoussac Montagnais as the "grand sagamore" who presided over the gathering as the host.[20]

Anadabijou welcomed the French "according to the custom of the country," and invited them to sit in a place of honor. When all were seated, an expectant silence followed. Then one of the two Montagnais who had been to France rose and began to speak. He described the castles and cities he had seen, spoke warmly of his meeting with Henri IV, and talked at length of his good treatment by the people in France. Champlain remembered that the young Indian was heard "with the greatest possible silence." When he finished, the grand sagamore smoked a long pipe, passed it to the other sagamores and to Pont-Gravé, and began to speak "with great gravity." He said that "in truth they ought to be very glad to have His Majesty for their great friend." The Indians "all answered in one voice, *ho, ho, ho*, which is to say, yes, yes."

Anadabijou paused, then spoke again. He said to the Indian nations that it would be well if "His Majesty [the king of France] should people their land, and make war on their enemies, and there was no nation in the world to which they wished more good than to the French." Champlain wrote that the sagamore "gave them all to understand the advantage and profit they might receive from His Majesty."[21]

After the speeches, the Indians returned to their feast and invited the French to join in. The kettles were filled with "the flesh of moose" which Champlain found very much like beef. There was also the meat of bear, seal, beaver, and "great quantities of wild fowl." Then a round of ceremonies began. Champlain watched in fascination as a warrior rose to his feet, picked up a dog, "and went leaping about the kettles from one end of the lodge to the other." When he came in front of the Anadabijou, he hurled the dog violently to the ground. Then all in one voice cried "*ho, ho, ho!*" Other warriors did the same. After the feast the Indians began a triumphant scalp dance, "taking in their hands as a mark of rejoicing the scalps of their enemies." The dancing continued into the night, then all retired.[22]

At first light, the grand sagamore emerged from his lodge and ran shouting through the sleeping camp. Anadabijou cried in a loud voice that they should break camp, go to Tadoussac, and visit their friends the French. Champlain watched as "every man pulled down his *cabanne* in less than no time at all." He noted that "the great sagamore himself was the first to pick up his canoe and carry it to the water, and he embarked with his wife and children with a quantity of furs." Champlain was quick to observe that rank and power worked differently among the Indians.[23]

The French watched in amazement as two hundred canoes went into the water, and began to move across the turbulent open water of the Saguenay River toward Tadoussac at astonishing speed. Champlain wrote, "our shallop was well manned, but their canoes went much faster." He was fascinated by the birchbark canoes, so light that a single man could carry them on land, and yet so strong and buoyant that they could carry many men, or a cargo of a thousand pounds.[24]

The canoes converged on Tadoussac harbor where *Bonne-Renommée* lay at anchor. The Indians went ashore, built a new camp and began another celebration. Champlain had never seen anything like it. "After they had made good cheer," he wrote, "the Algoumequins [Algonquin], one of the three nations, went out of their lodges and withdrew by themselves in an open place. They placed all their women and girls side by side, and themselves stood behind, all singing and dancing in unison."

Champlain delighted in their singing and dancing. He wrote: "They do not stir from one spot when they dance, but make certain gestures and motions of the body, first lifting up one foot, and then the other, and stamping on the ground." "Suddenly," he continued, "all the women and girls began to take off their deerskin robes and stripped themselves stark naked, revealing their private parts, and wearing nothing but ornaments of beads and braided cords of dyed porcupine quills in many colors." Champlain described the beauty of these girls and young women, their supple bodies undulating before him. "All these people are well proportioned in body, without any deformity," he observed. "They are agile, and the women are well shaped, filled out and plump, of a swarthy color." When the song was done, the Indian warriors turned toward the naked women and shouted "*ho, Ho, HO!*" The dancers demurely put on their robes, did their dance again, and "let fall their robes as before."[25]

After the Algonquin women finished their dance, a sagamore of the Algonquin, who was called Bessouat or Tessouat, rose and said: "See how we rejoice in the victory we have won over our enemies. You must do the same, and we will be content." Once more the Indians shouted. Then Anadabijou and all the Montagnais and Etchemin rose and stripped themselves naked except for a small piece of deerskin over their genitals. Each took up something of value to

them, jewelry or tomahawks, kettles, pieces of meat, and gave it to the Algonquin.[26]

After more dances and celebrations the Indians retired to their lodges.
Champlain delighted in their company. He was fascinated by their character
and culture, and quick to perceive its complexity. "All these people are of a joyous humor, and they laugh frequently," he wrote, "and yet they are somewhat
saturnine." By "saturnine" he meant that they had an undertone of melancholy. That tension deeply interested him, and he reflected much on it. He
also listened closely to their speeches, probably with the two young Montagnais translating in his ear. "They speak very deliberately," Champlain wrote,
"as though they would make themselves well understood, and stopping suddenly, reflect for a good while, and then begin to speak again."[27]

Champlain was curious about the Indians, and happy to be among them.
That attitude was reciprocated, but feelings were very complex. In the midst of
much warmth, there was also a wariness on all sides. Both groups remained on
their guard toward each other, and with good reason. But together they began
to build a relationship that would be one of the longest and strongest on record between Europeans and Native Americans.

Here was a moment of high importance in the history of North America.
Nobody had planned these events, but both French and Indian leaders were
quick to see an opportunity. The Great Tabagie marked the beginning of an alliance between the founders of New France and three Indian nations. Each entered willingly into the relationship and gained something of value in return.
The Indians acquired a potential ally against their mortal enemies, the Iroquois. The French won support for settlement, exploration, and trade. The alliance that formed here would remain strong for many years because it rested
on a mutuality of material interest.[28]

The leaders who had met at Pointe aux Alouettes also did something else.
They gave a tone to the alliance. Pont-Gravé, Champlain, Anadabijou, the sagamores, and most of all the two young Montagnais who had been to Paris did
that together. They treated each other with dignity, forbearance, and respect.
They began to build an atmosphere of trust that was fundamental to relations
between Europeans and Indians. They also kept it growing. When trust grew
strong, many things were possible. When trust was lost, it was rarely regained.
This meeting was important for that spirit, as well as for its substance. It
marked the beginning of a relationship that was unique in the long history of
European colonization in America. Something of its spirit has endured in
Canada between Europeans and Indians even to our own time—an extraordinary achievement.[29]

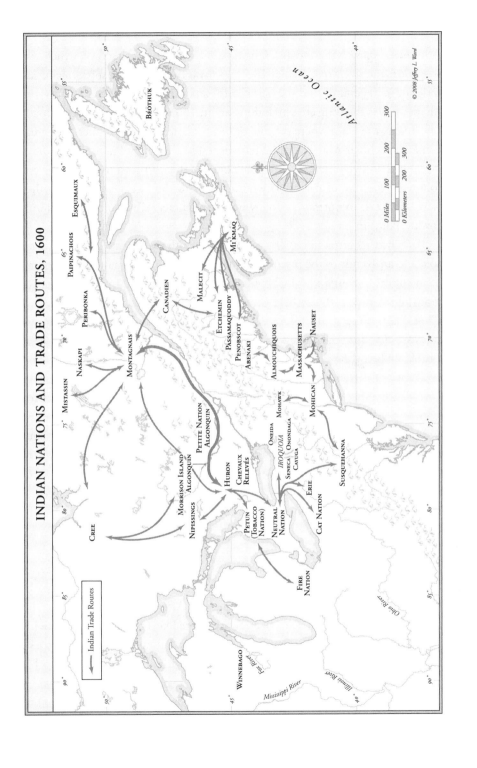

INDIAN NATIONS AND TRADE ROUTES, 1600

Indian Trade Routes

© 2008 Jeffrey L. Ward

BÉOTHUK

ESQUIMAUX

PAPINACHOIS

PERIBONKA

MI'KMAQ

NASKAPI

MALECIT

CANADIEN

ETCHEMIN

MISTASSIN

PASSAMAQUODDY

PENOBSCOT

MONTAGNAIS

ABENAKI

ALMOUCHIQUOIS

NAUSET

MASSACHUSETTS

PETITE NATION
ALGONQUIN

MOHICAN

MOHAWK

ONEIDA

CREE

MORRISON ISLAND
ALGONQUIN

HURON

CHEVAUX
RELEVÉS

IROQUOIA

ONONDAGA

SENECA

CAYUGA

SUSQUEHANNA

NIPISSINGS

ERIE

PETUN
(TOBACCO
NATION)

NEUTRAL
NATION

CAT NATION

FIRE
NATION

WINNEBAGO

Ohio River

Fox River

Illinois River

Mississippi River

Atlantic Ocean

0 Miles 100 200 300

0 Kilometers 200 300

• • •

After meeting with the Indians, Champlain turned to another task, which was to explore the rivers of Canada. The object was to seek the most promising arteries of trade, and to find the best site for a permanent settlement. His starting point was the little cove at Tadoussac. In 1603, it was truly the crossroads of Canada, the place where two major lines of communication met. The great Canadian scholar Marcel Trudel has suggested that New France might have developed on two different axes. One ran from the northeast to the southwest, following the line of the St. Lawrence River to the Great Lakes. The other went southeast to northwest, following the Saguenay River and its tributaries toward Hudson Bay.[30]

Each had its attractions. The St. Lawrence offered advantages of climate, soil, and an avenue to the interior of a continent. The Saguenay was the source of the most lustrous and valuable furs, which came from animals in colder regions of the north. It also held the promise of a northwest passage to Asia.[31] Champlain wanted to explore them both. The mission commander, Pont-Gravé, ordered the carpenters to fit out one of the small vessels that had been carried on board *Bonne-Renommée*, a barque of about 12 to 15 tons. It was no small labor to assemble that vessel, caulk her seams, put her in the water, ship a rudder, step her masts, reeve the rigging, bend the sails, and prepare her for a voyage. While the artisans were hard at work, Champlain was also very busy. This restless young man rarely sat in idleness. He began by studying the land around Tadoussac. Working ashore, Champlain searched for the remains of earlier visitors. He found the house that Chauvin had built in 1600 and other remnants of that ill-fated colony. And he also discovered traces of three French sailors who wintered there after they had been marooned by their Malouin captain.

Champlain made a chart of Tadoussac harbor. He sketched the shoreline in meticulous detail and checked his accuracy by using his compasses to make careful cross-bearings. Then he surveyed the waters of the harbor itself, working with a lead line from the bow of a shallop. After he finished his chart, he began to survey the Saguenay River. It was more like a fjord than a river, with rocky hills and rugged mountains on both sides, falling steeply to the water's edge. Probably he began by taking soundings with a small lead line. To his amazement he could not find the bottom. He got out *Bonne-Renommée's* dipsey lead, which had hundreds of fathoms of line. With that equipment in hand, Champlain and his crew began to sound the depths of the Saguenay River, which was a mile wide at its mouth. The French seamen who were swinging the heavy lead sang out that the water was 250 fathoms deep—1,500 feet! Champlain discovered that the mouth of the Saguenay River had a "*pro-fondeur incroyable*, truly an incredible depth."[32] He was also astonished by the very cold temperature of the river water that flowed from the frozen north. The current was so strong that even "at three-quarter tide running into the river, it is still flowing out."

The deep cold water of the Saguenay supported an abundance of marine life. It was home to a large pod of handsome small white Beluga whales. They had been there long before Champlain's time. For many generations, Basque ships came to hunt them, but these beautiful white creatures are still there today—swimming with exquisite grace, like spirits from another planet. They were yet another wonder of this astonishing new world.[33]

Champlain finished a chart for the mouth of the Saguenay River, and on June 12, 1603, he began to work his way upstream. Altogether he spent a week on the river, and went "twelve or fifteen leagues," halfway to the great waterfall of Chicoutimi. Champlain described the Saguenay as a *belle rivière*, but the countryside did not attract him. He wrote, "The whole region as far as I could see was nothing but rocky mountains, mostly covered with fir, cypress and birch, a most unpleasant land." The waters from the north made it one of the coldest places in the St. Lawrence Valley. "In short," Champlain noted of its banks, "these are true deserts, unfit for animals or birds."[34]

Champlain concluded that the lower Saguenay was not suitable for permanent settlement, but he wanted to learn more about it as an artery of trade, and perhaps a route to the northwest passage. He hoped to follow the river to its source, but his Montagnais allies were not happy about that idea. They told him in no uncertain terms that he should go no farther up the Saguenay. "I often desired to explore it," Champlain wrote later, "but have been unable to do so without the natives, who have been unwilling that I or any of our people should do so."[35]

The Montagnais functioned as middlemen in a lucrative fur trade, acquiring thick subarctic pelts from northern nations that Champlain called the Peribonka, Mistassini, and Ashuapmouchouan. The Montagnais bought their furs and sold them to Europeans and other Indian nations at Tadoussac. This trade was their leading source of income, and they did not permit other traders—Indian or European—to go up the Saguenay on pain of death. Control of this artery was vital to their prosperity. Other Indian nations did the same thing: the Attikamèques in the valley of the Saint-Maurice River, the Nipissing further northwest, and the Huron in their hinterland to the west.[36]

Champlain was careful not to challenge the Montagnais on this issue. His success with the Indians arose from a sensitivity to their vital interests, and he took great care not to trespass upon them. But the Montagnais also understood his interest in the Saguenay, and they were willing to talk in general terms about the country to the north. They also appear to have had no objection to Champlain's survey of the lower Saguenay.[37]

In Champlain's explorations he always worked with the Indians, quizzing them about the country, carefully recording their reports, and noting clearly what he had not seen with his own eyes. He learned much from them, listened with a critical ear, and asked them to sketch maps with charcoal on pieces of white birch. He learned carefully from their knowledge, and the information proved to be highly accurate. They told him about the waterfall at Chicoutimi, the head of navigation on the Saguenay, and many other falls and rivers upstream. The Montagnais informed Champlain of other Indian nations far to the north who lived within sight of a great salt sea. He wrote, "If this be so, it is some gulf of this our [Atlantic] sea, which overflows in the north into the midst of the continent, and indeed it can be nothing else."[38]

Champlain instantly recognized the Indians' great salt sea as Hudson Bay. He knew that the English had already been there, searching for a route to China. In a week or two on the Saguenay, he had gained a remarkably accurate idea of the country that lay eight hundred miles north of the St. Lawrence Valley. He sketched it from the descriptions of the Indians, being careful to note that he had not seen it himself.

After his week on the lower Saguenay, Champlain returned to Tadoussac. The river barque was ready, and it was time to explore the St. Lawrence River. Pont-Gravé decided to lead this journey himself, with Champlain at his side. The primary purpose was to find sites for settlement, and to learn about the territory that lay to the west. Champlain's assignment was to chart the river. He tells us that he brought lead lines, a compass, and what was probably a small traveling astrolabe for calculating latitude. The barque also carried skiffs that held seven or eight people and were useful for exploring shallows and small streams.[39]

They were not the first Europeans to study the St. Lawrence Valley. Later, Champlain would come upon the chimneys of Cartier's habitation. He found rotting wooden crosses and traces of other European visitors. But Champlain went about his exploration more systematically than his predecessors had done. This was a major expedition, carefully planned and fully equipped, with ample provisions for more than two months on the river.

It was also a reconnaissance in force by a large party of armed Frenchmen with Indian guides, commanded by Pont-Gravé but increasingly guided by

Champlain. They were heading into dangerous territory, close to Iroquois country. Champlain hoped to meet them. Ever the optimist, he was eager to "make friends with the Iroquois." But always the realist, he understood that any friend of the Algonquin and Montagnais might be taken as an enemy by the Iroquois. The French went in peace with Indian guides but prepared to defend themselves if attacked.[40]

On June 18, 1603, they left Tadoussac harbor, and made a slow passage up the St. Lawrence with the current and westerly winds against them. For many miles the riverbanks were disappointing to them. "All this coast is nothing but mountains both on the south side and the north, most of it like the Saguenay coast," he wrote.[41]

On Sunday June 22, they reached the Île d'Orléans, named by Jacques Cartier, and found it "very pleasant and level." On the mainland, near its western end they came upon a waterfall 265-feet high which still bears the name that Champlain gave it, Montmorency Falls, after the admiral of France in 1603. Beyond the island, they anchored at the place the Indians called Kebec, an Algonquian word that meant the narrowing of the river, less than a cannon-shot wide. On the north shore Champlain described "a very high mountain which slopes down on both sides," and "all the rest a level country, with good land covered with trees and vines." He wrote, "If this soil were cultivated, it would be as good as ours" in France. Here at the narrowing of the river, Champlain found the site for his settlement.[42]

The next day they sailed beyond Quebec. The great river broadened again, as much as five miles wide, and, he wrote, "the country grows finer and finer." They anchored thirty miles beyond Quebec on the south shore. Champlain went ashore, dug into the ground, and found it to be soft, friable, rich, and black. He wrote, "The soil was better than in any place I had seen . . . if it were well tilled it would yield a great increase."[43]

As they sailed upriver, the countryside kept improving. "The farther we went, the finer the ground," Champlain wrote. The land was laced with many small rivers and streams. Ninety miles beyond Quebec they came to the broad mouth of the Saint-Maurice River, which was divided in three parts by small islands. They called it Trois-Rivières, the name it bears today. Champlain attempted to explore the Saint-Maurice in a skiff, but he got only about two leagues and was stopped by rapids. The Indian guides told him that the headwaters of the Saint-Maurice were close to the Saguenay. Champlain immediately recognized the importance of this river as a place of trade with northern nations.[44] He also noted something else about Trois-Rivières. "The climate begins to be somewhat different . . . inasmuch as the trees are more forward there than in any place I had hitherto seen." As they sailed upstream, they were moving steadily southwest. The distances made a difference in their latitude.[45]

Champlain continued up the great river and came to a lake twenty miles long and seven miles wide, and beyond it another very large stream that the Indians called the River of the Iroquois. The Indians explained that it flowed from two very large lakes to the south. They spoke of another great river beyond the lakes, which flowed in the opposite direction, toward "Florida." They were describing Lake Champlain, Lake George, and the Hudson River. Once again Champlain quickly formed an accurate idea of the country many miles to the south, mostly from conversations with the Indians.[46]

They resumed their journey upriver and soon found themselves among islands, rapids, and shallows. The current became so strong that the barque could no longer move forward. Champlain and five sailors took the skiff, but met "an infinite number of small rocks level with the water," and could not get through, even when the sailors were ordered into the water to free the boat. Champlain wrote that only a canoe "passed easily." He anchored near a large island on the northern shore. Behind it was a height that Cartier had named "Mont Réal," from which the city of Montreal takes its name.[47]

Champlain went on by foot and canoe and came to massive rapids. "I never saw any torrent of water pour over with such force as this does, though it is not very high, being in some places only one or two fathoms, and at most three. It descends as it were step by step, and wherever it falls from some small height, it boils up extraordinarily, owing to the force and speed of the water as it passes through the said rapid."[48]

This was the head of navigation on the St. Lawrence River in 1603. "It was beyond the power of man to pass with any boat, however small it may be," he wrote. They continued on foot to the end of the rapids, through "very open woods," where "one may easily carry one's weapons."[49] Champlain appears to have used his astrolabe to take a noon sight on the sun, which yielded an estimate of latitude, "45 degrees and some minutes." The latitude of downtown Montreal is 45 degrees, 30 minutes. By comparison, the north side of the St. Lawrence estuary is 50 degrees at its mouth, a difference of three hundred nautical miles in latitude. In this countryside from Quebec to Montreal, with its "milder and more equable" climate, Champlain believed he had found not merely the site for a settlement, but the seat of a nation.[50]

Champlain quizzed the Indians on what lay beyond the great rapids. They described the river in detail and told him about the Great Lakes, Niagara Falls, and the Detroit River, and said that they themselves had passed no farther.

Once again, Champlain's conversations with the Indians gave him a remarkably clear idea of the Great Lakes. From two weeks of exploration, and much conversation with the Indians, he had formed an accurate image of North America from Hudson Bay to the Hudson River, and from the St. Lawrence to the Great Lakes.[51]

Champlain had found much of what he was after, and he was eager to report to the king. On July 4, 1603, they set off downstream. With the current and the wind behind them, they made a fast passage. At the Île d'Orléans they stopped to visit with a party of Algonquins, who told Champlain about the Ottawa River and beyond it another huge sea with sweet water, which we know as Lake Huron. Other Indians told him about rivers to the south of the lakes, in the country of the Iroquois, which was good land for corn and other crops that did not grow farther north. The Algonquins spoke also of another nation called the "good Iroquois," who had their own homeland to the west and access to a mine of pure copper. Some spoke of a great salt sea far to the west, which Champlain took to be the Pacific Ocean.[52]

On July 11, they were back in Tadoussac where *Bonne-Renommée* was waiting for them. They still had another month for exploration and decided to spend it on the Atlantic coast of the Gaspé Peninsula. Champlain met the Malouin trader Prévert, who told him of a "very high mountain, jutting somewhat into the sea" with deposits of copper, and of another mine further south with iron and silver.[53] Then they sailed for home and made a quick passage, with the prevailing westerlies and the gulf stream pushing them swiftly across the Atlantic. They reached Le Havre in fifteen days from the Grand Bank.[54]

It was a successful mission in every way. The backers made money from their fish and fur, which had been traded at Tadoussac by others in the expedition. One scholar reckons that they realized a net return of 30 to 40 percent on their investment, after all expenses were paid.[55] Pont-Gravé and Champlain brought a new level of refinement to the exploration of the coast, the Saguenay, and the St. Lawrence Valley. They had made contact with the Indians, and the tone was good. As time passed, the importance of the tabagie at Tadoussac steadily increased. That chance meeting supported Champlain's grand design. It sustained his vision of a new world where different nations could dwell in peace. Champlain was officially present only as an observer, but he demonstrated a gift for getting along with others. This pivotal event also brought out a recurrent theme in his life and work. The tabagie at Tadoussac came as a sudden opportunity. He acted quickly and was prepared to make the most of it. This was an attitude that he called *prévoyant*, a word that has no English equivalent. It was not a gift of prophecy, but the power of a prepared mind to act upon chance events in a world of deep uncertainty.

Champlain, like Churchill, was "confident that history would be kind" to him, for he intended to write it himself. After he returned to France, he published a book on what he had seen. Probably he drafted it on the voyage home, for it went to press very soon after he got back. The censors licensed publication on November 15, 1603, just eight weeks after his ship reached Le Havre.

Champlain's manuscript was published by Claude de Monstr'oeil, bookseller to the University of Paris and proprietor of a fashionable bookstore "in the Court of the palace, at the sign of Jesus." Four centuries later, the book is still in print and sells well in both French and English editions. It remains an enduring classic of early North American history.[56]

Perhaps the publisher chose its sensational double title, *Des Sauvages, ou, Voyage de Samuel Champlain, De Brouage*. Part of Champlain's purpose was to describe the "true wonders" of the new world. He described the grandeur of the great "River of Canada," the depth of the Saguenay, the height of the Montmorency Falls, and the roaring rapids of Lachine. He repeated Indians' accounts of the cataract at Niagara, published the first reports of the Great Lakes, and described the dimensions of the great American forest that was larger than the entire continent of Europe. He searched for words to describe the grandeur of American distances, the beauty of the countryside, and the drama of its seasons.

In all these wonders Champlain saw evidence of God's Providence. He believed that to reveal them to others was to honor God and his works. Many discoverers had the same feeling, and most things that Champlain did in his life were instruments of that driving purpose. Some modern critics have read his book as a promotional tract, but it was more than that. Champlain meant to awaken in others the passion that he felt for exploration of the world and to engage them in his *grand dessein*, his vision for New France.

The book centered on his account of the American Indians. In that respect, its title has misled modern readers. Many people today have understood its operative word *sauvages* as having the same meaning as "savages" in modern French and English. In modern usage "savage" means people who are primitive, uncivilized, coarse, simple-minded, barbaric, brutal, violent, vicious, treacherous, ferocious, and inferior to civilized people.

Champlain called the people of North America "les sauvages," but not in

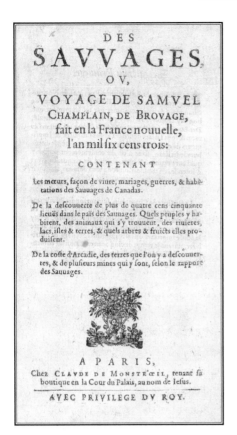

Champlain's first book, Des Sauvages, ou, Voyage de Samuel Champlain *(1603), combines a story of his visit with a survey of "mores, manner of life, marriages, wars, and habitations of the Sauvages of the Canadas." By* sauvage *or* salvage *(from the Latin* silva*) he meant forest dwellers—an ecological idea, not racial. He was strongly attracted to the Indians, and they to him.*

that sense. In old French and early English, "sauvage" or "savage" was sometimes written *salvage*, a clue to its original meaning. It derived from the Latin *silva*, for a forest or a woodland. In the seventeenth century "sauvage" preserved this meaning, and was used to describe wild things that lived in the forest. When Champlain used the term "sauvages," he meant forest-dwellers. It is interesting that he applied this word to North American Indians but did not often use it for the people of the West Indies. He called them *Indiens*, people of the Indies, not "sauvages," or people of the forest, unless they lived in woods as they did on Guadeloupe.[57]

When Champlain wrote about "les sauvages," he did not mean an inferior race of people. There was nothing racist in his thinking, nothing invidious about the intellectual capacity of the people it described. The modern idea of race developed after Champlain's era. In French and English, the full-fledged ideology of race did not emerge until the nineteenth century, with writers such as Joseph Arthur Gobineau and his contemporaries.

Champlain regarded American Indians as fully equal to Europeans in intelligence and judgment, and he was much impressed by their qualities of mind. He wrote, "I assure you that many of them have excellent judgment, and respond very well to any question that one puts to them."[58] Once he wrote, "Should their spirit not grasp the usage of our arts, sciences and trades, their children who are young could do so."[59] Champlain was not alone in this way of thinking. Other French humanists of the period, such as the historian Marc Lescarbot, had the same high respect for the Indians, and wrote: "They have courage, fidelity, generosity, and humanity, and their hospitality is so innate and so praiseworthy that they receive among them every man who is not an enemy. They are not simpletons."[60]

Champlain (and most of his contemporaries) also celebrated the physical condition of Native Americans. He observed that their limbs were straight, their muscles strong, their teeth were perfectly straight and white, their health seemed better, and they made a dramatic contrast with Europeans. Champlain empathized deeply with the Indians. He understood the difficult conditions of their lives, especially in the cruel Canadian winters. "All these people sometimes suffer so great extremity, on account of the great cold and snow."[61]

Even as Champlain wrote of the Indians with sympathy and respect, he thought that some of their customs were inferior to the practices of civilized nations. He talked with the sagamore Anadabijou about their values and beliefs, and his judgments were complex. He concluded that Indians worshiped one Great Spirit, believed in the immortality of the soul, and had an idea of the Devil. But he regarded them as a people who had never been brought to the true faith. He tried to persuade the sagamore that the Christian faith and the Catholic religion were more true and more universal, apparently with no success.[62]

The sagamore told him "they do not make much use of religious ceremonies," but "everyone prayed in his heart as he thought good." Champlain wrote: "That is why I believe they have no law among them, nor know what it is to worship and pray to God, and that most of them live like brute beasts; and I think they would speedily be brought to be good Christians if their country were colonized, which they desire for the most part." He deeply believed that the Indians were lost souls, with no hope of redemption until they were taught the true faith. But in other ways he regarded them as equal in mind and spirit to Europeans.[63]

Champlain was very curious about Indian ideas of law, and judged that in a European sense, "they are for the most part a people who have no law." He meant that they lived by a primitive system of customary law, and an ethic of *lex talionis*, the rule of retaliation.[64] He described the sadistic tortures that they inflicted on captives, and wrote: "They have one evil in them, which is that they are given to revenge, and are great liars, a people in whom it is not well to put confidence, except with reason and with force at hand. They promise much and perform little."[65]

He also studied the structure of authority among the Indians, and observed that the chiefs had very little power or authority over others. Champlain noted repeatedly that chiefs would express strong opinions, but the Indians would act and judge for themselves.[66] Most of all he thought that the Indians were too free. "Sauvage" for him also meant living in a condition of complete liberty. He had a language to describe an excess of liberty—*libertinage*, as in our libertine, and license. He described their sexual freedom, but noted that when an Indian girl takes many lovers and keeps company with whomever she likes, she was engaging in a form of courtship and marriage, and that by that method she selects a partner who pleases her most for her husband and they live together to the end of their lives.[67] In these ways Champlain's judgments of the Indians were negative, but they coexisted with many positive assessments. He took pleasure in the discovery of humanity with all its infinite variety.

In 1615, Champlain wrote of "the passion that I have always had for discoveries in New France." He described how that passion led him to "travel through this land by means of the rivers, lakes and streams of which there are many, to gain a complete knowledge ("parfaicte cognoissance"). And also it led him to meet and know ("recognoistre") the people who live there and "lead them to the knowledge ('cognoissance') of God."[68]

In his thoughts and acts we always find a consuming curiosity about the world. Here was a spirit that was sweeping the western world in the sixteenth century. Part of it was linked to the Protestant Reformation and the Catholic Counter-Reformation, and to a search for the spirit of God in the natural world. Another part of it flowed from the Renaissance and its hunger for knowledge. It inspired a fascination with *scientia*, not the modern idea of science but its epistemic ancestor, which was a broader idea of ordered knowledge. With it came an idea of disciplined inquiry, a systematic spirit of observation, a love of study, and a deep belief that knowledge would be immediately useful and beneficial. These values expressed themselves in another quality of Champlain's book: its exhilaration in the act of discovery, not in the sense of being the first to find something, but in the pleasure of revealing it to

René Descartes (1596–1650), in a portrait by Franz Hals. This kindred soul explored the inner mind in the same spirit that Champlain studied the outer world. Both shared a passion for knowledge and reason. Each was a seeker for God's truth in the world.

others. Like many others of his age, Champlain used every discipline and art and science within reach. His most important instrument was the printing press.

In some ways Champlain's thought was similar to that of his younger contemporary René Descartes. Both were of the *haute bourgeoisie* of France. Both, in Champlain's phrase, were men of "pious habits, and inspired with a great zeal and love for the Honour of God." Descartes' meditations were dedicated to proving the existence of God and the immortality of the soul. Both men believed in the Devil as a malevolent demon who was alive in the universe. The horrors of their own time convinced them that evil was something real in the world, something that must be fought and conquered. Both had been in military service, and that experience made them men of peace. They had seen much of war, and witnessed its horror and cruelty and destruction. But they also believed that some things were worse than war, and the worst thing was the triumph of evil in the world.[69]

Both believed that truth and knowledge could overcome evil. They delighted in inquiry, devoted themselves to reason, and pursued science ("scientia") in the large sense of knowledge and truth. Champlain and Descartes believed in absolute truth and despised skepticism, cynicism, obscurantism, and the vices of learning. In their writing, they both cultivated a language that was simple, direct, precise, and very clear. They lived in the light, and shared an idea of enlightenment.

Most of all Champlain and Descartes were men of humanity. They believed that all people in the world were God's children and that each possessed an immortal soul. This recognition of common humanity in the people of America and Europe—and all the world—lay at the heart of Champlain's dream. It was also the center of his vision of a new world. Part of it grew from the idea of a truly Catholic Church, in the best and most literal sense of catholic, as reaching out to all humanity. And another part came from the large spirit of the Renaissance.

This principle of humanism was not an idea of liberty or equality. Those words rarely appeared in Champlain's writings, and never with an ideological meaning. Like most Europeans of his age, he believed in a hierarchy of orders and estates. But he also believed that, by God's will, people of all nations should be treated with respect.

Many of Champlain's French associates shared this way of thinking: Protestants such as the sieur de Mons, and Catholics such as Lescarbot. Here again, as in many other ways, these men were profoundly influenced by the example of Henri IV. This circle of French humanists were pivotal figures in more ways than one. In the history of Europe they transformed the purpose of the Renaissance into the program of the Enlightenment. In America they also played a vital role. After many failures of French colonization in the sixteenth century, they were the first to succeed. They planted the seed of New France, and bent the sapling to the pattern of its growth. Their history bears witness to the importance of small beginnings in the history of great nations.

Michel Montaigne (1533–92) was a generation older than Champlain and in the same humanist tradition. A moderate Catholic who supported Henri IV and shared a spirit of tolerance, he wrote, "Everyone calls barbarity what he is not accustomed to." These French humanists played a vital role in modern history. They inherited the Renaissance and inspired the Enlightenment.

8.

SAINTE-CROIX
Champlain's Worst Mistake, 1604–05

It was not easy to know this place without having wintered
here. . . . There are six months of winter in this country.

—Samuel de Champlain, 1605 [1]

WHEN CHAMPLAIN AND HIS FRIENDS got back to France in the late
summer of 1603, they were shocked to learn that their leader,
Aymar de Chaste, was dead. His sudden loss was a shattering blow.
Champlain wrote, "It grieved me greatly, as I realized that anyone else would
have difficulty in undertaking this enterprise, and not being thwarted, unless
it was a nobleman whose authority could overcome the envy of others." [2]

Champlain went directly to court and once again he had no trouble getting
direct access to Henri IV. He met several times with the king, gave him a manuscript map of New France, and delivered a "very special account which I
drew up for him." [3] The two men talked about a grand dessein for America.
"He was very pleased," Champlain wrote, "promising not to give up this dessein, but to have it pursued and supported." [4]

Perhaps they also talked about a new leader. No one could replace Aymar
de Chaste, but someone had to succeed him—and quickly. The North American initiative had been without a driver in France for five months. To find a
person with the necessary qualifications was not an easy task. He had to be a
nobleman who could command respect, a gentleman who could attract support, a friend of the king with full access at court, a man of wealth who could
work with investors, a man trained to arms and the sea, a leader of experience
and maturity, a competent administrator, and most of all, a man of vision for
New France.

That long list of qualities meant a short list of candidates. The search came
down to one man: Pierre Dugua sieur de Mons, who was qualified in every
important way. He was a nobleman of ancient family, a soldier who had fought
bravely for the king, an officeholder with much administrative experience, and

An imagined image of Pierre Dugua, sieur de Mons. He was yet another leader in this circle of soldiers who supported Henri IV, fought for peace and toleration in France, and shared a vision of a New France in North America.

a man of wealth who could work with investors. He was a Protestant with a Catholic wife, and he had a spirit of tolerance. His Saintonge manners helped him get on with others. He had been to America on Chauvin's ill-fated voyage, and knew the problems and opportunities in New France. Most important, as the king observed, the sieur de Mons was a man of "great prudence," with much "knowledge and experience."[5]

He was very close to Henri IV. Since 1594, he had been a "Gentleman of the King's Chamber," one of about twenty noblemen who were authorized to enter even the most private rooms, where they functioned as chamberlains. De Mons was often at court, and went with the king as he shuttled between his palaces at the Louvre in Paris, Fontainebleau in its great forest to the south, and Saint-Germain-en-Laye to the west.[6]

At court in the fall of 1603, de Mons and Champlain used their access to Henri IV to promote the American project. De Mons made a report to the king on the fertility of the soil in New France. Champlain did a presentation on "the means of discovering the passage to China." He argued that the waterways of New France might make a convenient middle route to Asia, "without the inconvenience of the northern icebergs, or the heat of the torrid zone, through which our seamen pass twice in going and twice in returning, with incredible labors and perils."[7]

De Mons and Champlain also worked with what might be called an American circle at Court. Three men were at its center. All were a generation older than Champlain. Pierre Jeannin was Intendant of Finances and president of the Parlement of Burgundy. Nicolas Brûlart, marquis de Sillery, was a great jurist, soon to be chancellor of France. Champlain's former commander, Charles II de Cossé-Brissac was a marshal of France and governor of Brittany. These men were trusted members of the king's inner council. They held many offices in his government, and wielded great influence at court. All were men of learning, with a global outlook and a particular interest in the new world. These French humanists were caught up in the intellectual currents of their age. They shared the spirit of Champlain's dream, and supported his project for New France.[8]

While Champlain and the sieur de Mons worked with these men in France, they also discussed sites for settlement in North America. On this question they were not of one mind. Champlain was drawn to the St. Lawrence Valley by the magnitude of the great river and the abundance of its fur trade. He observed that to advance up the river was to move south to a warmer climate and more fertile ground. Reports from the Indians about big bodies of water to the west also held the promise of a route to China.

The sieur de Mons saw the strength of these arguments, but he favored another place. His painful experience of Chauvin's voyage to Tadoussac had, in Champlain's words, "taken away any desire to enter the great river St. Lawrence, having on that voyage seen only a forbidding country."[9] De Mons wanted to find a site further south along the American coast, "to enjoy a softer and more agreeable climate." He was drawn to a coastal region that had the same latitude as Saintonge, warmer winters than Tadoussac, more fertile soil than the St. Lawrence Valley, and a very beautiful name. It was called La Cadie, l'Acadie—or in English, Acadia.[10]

The name had first appeared on American maps early in the sixteenth century. Historians are of two minds about its origin. One story links it to the Greek Arkadia through Giovanni da Verrazzano, the Florentine navigator who sailed the coast of North America, and gave the name of Arcadia or Acadia to what is now North Carolina, for its handsome trees. Samuel Eliot Morison made a study of the name. He found that it first referred to the Carolinas, and was slowly moved northeast, "by the whims of successive cartographers."[11]

Another story holds that l'Acadie was an Indian word. In Algonquian languages, "cadie" is a suffix that means place, in combinations such as Tracadie, or Shubenacadie. Many "cadies" and "quoddys" are to be found in the place

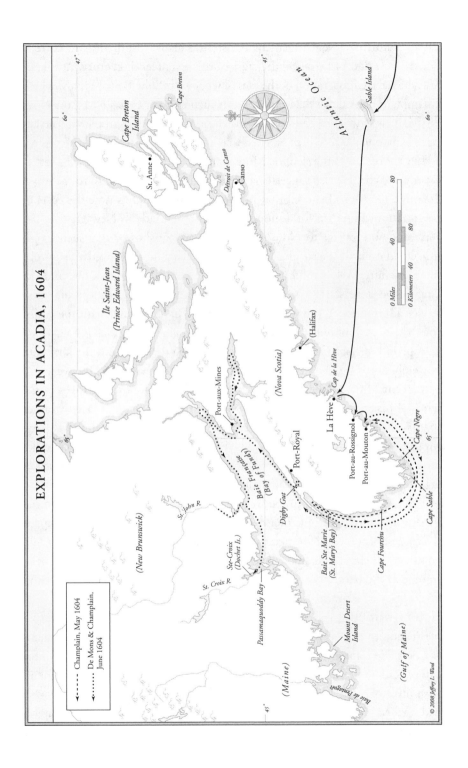

EXPLORATIONS IN ACADIA, 1604

names of northern New England and eastern Canada.[12] Both ideas are correct, but the first had priority. By the start of the seventeenth century, Acadia or l'Acadie referred to land on both sides of what we call the Bay of Fundy, which Champlain named the Baie Françoise. It included the coasts of today's Nova Scotia, New Brunswick, and part of downeast Maine. An example was the Lavasseur map in 1601, which labelled that area as the "coste de Cadie."[13]

In October 1603 the sieur de Mons went to the king and proposed a settlement in Acadia. He also suggested a way to pay for it without cost to the Royal Treasury. De Mons believed that private investors could assume the costs of colonization, in return for a monopoly of the fur trade in New France. The very profitable voyage to Tadoussac earlier that year showed that such a venture could even yield a surplus for the Crown. That idea removed a major obstacle at court. Sully would not have to pay a sou from the treasury, and the king was very pleased. On October 31, 1603, de Mons received a commission as vice admiral for "all the seas, coasts, islands, harbors, and maritime countries which are found in the said province and region of Acadia."[14]

A period of hard bargaining followed between de Mons and the king. On November 6, 1603, de Mons submitted "Seven Articles for the Discovery and Settlement of the Coast and Lands of Acadia," and proposed changes in the terms of his appointment. He asked "very humbly" to be made viceroy rather than vice admiral of New France. Henri IV refused, on the ground that de Mons was not a "prince of the blood." But he agreed to raise de Mons to the rank of lieutenant general, with quasi-regal powers that allowed him to act as if he were viceroy in North America.[15]

De Mons also wanted to report directly to the King's Council, where the American circle was strong. Henri agreed but added one exception, perhaps at the request of lobbyists for merchants. He required that legal questions should go first to officials in the financial center of Rouen. That decision would make trouble in the years to come. It gave investors an advantage, as de Mons and Champlain were aware; but they could not resist the king.[16]

There were other issues. De Mons, thinking of Sully's opposition, requested permission to take artisans to New France and also to recruit vagabonds and convicts. He wanted authority to impose fines on illegal traders, and asked for a direct order to build fortresses in America—probably to strengthen his hand with investors. The king approved, and added a request of his own. Reports had reached him that copper had been found in Acadia. He asked for a careful search of mines and minerals, and that was agreed. On November 8, 1603, the king signed a commission to his "dear and well beloved sieur de Mons, as lieutenant general for the country of Acadia."[17]

• • •

For the sieur de Mons, Champlain, and their friends, Acadia was not merely a place. It was an idea, and even an emotion. They thought of it as a place of natural abundance, with many resources in fish, fur, timber, and soil—a place where people could live comfortably. More than that, they also envisioned Acadia as a place where Catholics and Protestants could live in harmony—a vision that came from the king himself. Henri IV ordered de Mons in no uncertain terms to "colonize the country on condition of establishing there the Catholic, Apostolic and Roman religion, permitting each person to practice his own religion." This policy for America followed Henri IV's solution for France.[18]

De Mons and Champlain also thought of Acadia as a region where Euro-

Henri IV's grant of absolute powers and a trading monopoly to the sieur de Mons, Dec. 18, 1603. After the fiasco at Sable Island, the king insisted that French colonization in North America must pay its own way. It never succeeded in doing so.

pean settlers and American Indians could live side by side in a manner very different from what Champlain had observed in New Spain. These French humanists did not wish to make the Indians into a servile work force, or drive them from their land. They respected the humanity of the Indians even in their "savage state," without "faith or law or authority," *ni foi, ni loi, ni roi,* as Champlain put it. They hoped to convert the Indians to Christianity, and to coexist with them.

These men were not utopians. They had no hope of a heavenly city on this earth. Forty years of civil war and religious strife had made them realists. But the horrors they had seen also gave them a sense of urgency about higher ideas of humanity and toleration. It was a generational phenomenon. Like later generations of American founders who witnessed the atrocities in eighteenth-century warfare, and also like the "wise men" of the mid-twentieth century who had survived two world wars, the earlier generation of de Mons and Champlain combined realism and idealism in their vision of a better world.[19]

Before these men could erect a colony in Acadia, they had to build a base in France. They knew that the king would give them strong moral support, little material assistance, and no money. The sieur de Mons faced a major problem that way. The king's grant of a trading monopoly did not sit well with other French merchants. In Brittany the provincial Estates continued to demand full "liberté de trafic du Canada." In Normandy the Parlement at Rouen refused even to register the Royal grant.

Henri IV was quick to intervene. He made very clear to the men of Rouen that the project for New France was vital to the "advancement of Our Power and Authority," and a monopoly of the fur trade was its necessary instrument. The king informed the merchants who claimed liberty of trade that they had full liberty to join the company of monsieur de Mons.[20] Many did so. De Mons succeeded in raising a capital of 90,000 livres from investors in four commercial centers: Rouen, Saint-Malo, La Rochelle and Saint-Jean-de-Luz. All contributed to the company and were encouraged to send their ships to New France. At the end of the first year, profits were to be reinvested in colonization. Thereafter, dividends would be paid to the investors. A large sum of capital was paid into the venture, and the future of the De Mons Company looked very bright.[21]

In the early months of 1604, the sieur de Mons began to organize an expedition. One of the first people he invited was Champlain, who wrote, "The sieur de Mons asked if I would agree to make this voyage with him." Champlain was quick to accept, but as the king's servant and pensioner, once again he could do so only by royal leave. "I agreed to his request," he said, "provided that I had the approval of His Majesty." Champlain went to see the king again and wrote, "He gave me permission" on one condition, "that I should always make him a faithful report of everything I saw and discovered." [22]

As often in his life, Champlain's status was not clearly defined, which appears to have been the way he liked it, as it gave him larger possibilities. As before, he was not an officer in the chain of command, but he had the rank of a gentleman, with a pension from the Crown and orders to report directly to Henri IV on all that he saw and discovered. Champlain always acknowledged the authority of the sieur de Mons as commander of the expedition and was completely loyal to him. At the same time he served his own purposes, with the sanction of the king himself.

The next step was to recruit colonists. No roster has survived, but many individuals can be identified by name, rank, or occupation. They made a model of diversity in early modern France. The leaders were "several noblemen," and "a large number of gentlemen, of whom not a few were of noble birth," in Champlain's phrase. Nine of these gentleman-adventurers can be identified by name, all with the honorary title of "sieur." Among them were the sieur de Mons, commander of the expedition, traveling with his able secretary Jean Ralluau, his servant Artus Daniel, and his bodyguard François Addenin, who may have been selected by Henri IV and was described "carrying arms under his charge for the service of his Majesty." [23]

Another nobleman was Jean de Biencourt, sieur de Poutrincourt. He came from Picardy and he liked to say that he was going "for pleasure," but he was also in search of a site in America "to which he might retire with his household, his wife and children." Poutrincourt was a nobleman and a gentleman, "well-educated in the classics, a competent musician, and a brave soldier." His companions took pleasure in his company. [24]

Others of high rank were identified as the sieurs d'Orville, de Genestou, de Sourin, de Beaumont, La Motte Bourgjoli, Fougeray de Vitré, and Pierre du Bosc-Douyn, called du Boullay, a senior captain in the Régiment de Poutrincourt. Little is known of these men beyond their garbled names and titles. None were mentioned for any special skill. Most were men of independent means who came as volunteers for what promised to be a great adventure. They were given special accommodations, as suited their station. [25]

Below these gentlemen were men of middling rank, recruited for their skills. At least seven were mariners with long experience at sea. The commander afloat, and first lieutenant of the sieur de Mons ashore, was François

Gravé, sieur du Pont, as he was recorded in the port records of Honfleur. We have already met him as Champlain's shipmate Pont-Gravé. He was greatly respected for his knowledge of the North Atlantic. Under him were Captain Timothée le Barbier of Le Havre, Captain Nicolas Morel of Dieppe, Captain Guillaume Foulques, and also Master Guillaume Duglas and Master Cramolet. These men appeared in the records of many voyages to America.[26] Others with professional expertise included Pierre Angibault, sieur de Champdoré, a skilled shipwright and amateur pilot. Henri, sieur de Beaufort, was an affluent young apothecary, the son of a prominent Paris merchant. None of these men were nobles, but they were addressed as sieur.[27]

Champlain tells us that the sieur de Mons also recruited "about 120 workers," men who worked with their hands. There were several surgeons, who labored with their hands and were not quite gentlemen, as apothecaries and physicians were thought to be. Others included housewrights, master carpenters, sawyers, masons, blacksmiths, gunners, armorers, and locksmiths (*serruriers*) who were expert in the repair of gunlocks. At the king's request, the sieur de Mons employed two master miners named Maître Simon and Maître Jacques, who were identified as coming from Slavonia in southeastern Europe.

Jean Biencourt de Poutrincourt was a Catholic nobleman from Picardy who fought against Henri IV until the king's conversion, then joined him. He envisioned Acadia as his own feudal utopia, but he was also a humanist, classicist, mathematician, and musician. Some believe that this is his image; others think it is his cousin's. It represents the dress and appearance of these men.

Perhaps they were Croatian Catholics. Their task was to search for mineral deposits.[28]

There were also a large number of semiskilled artisans, unskilled laborers, and boys as young as ten and twelve. Only a few appeared by name in the notarial records of Le Havre and Honfleur. One of them was Anthoine Lemaire, aged nineteen, a plasterer of houses.[29] Some may have been convicts and paupers whom de Mons had permission to recruit, perhaps from prison-cells where they were offered the choice of a ship or a scaffold.[30] Several groups tended to live and eat apart from the others. A detachment of Swiss soldiers came along. They were the leading mercenaries of their era, highly respected for discipline and widely used to protect princes from their own people. They were probably recruited to keep order among artisans and workers. The soldiers lived in special quarters between the officers and "other ranks." Their commander may have been the veteran Captain du Boullay.[31]

A party of seamen (*matelots*) also clubbed together as shipmates and messmates. Most of them sailed back to France at the end of the first summer, but at least twelve remained in the colony through the winter to sail its barques and shallops. Another interesting group were professional hunters, probably recruited from gamekeepers on country estates in France. They appear to have been very independent. They preferred to spend as much time as possible in the open air, ranging across the countryside.

One very interesting member of the expedition was recruited for the purpose of communicating with the American Indians. His name was Mathieu Da Costa, or De Coste in French documents which described him as a "nègre" or "naigre" of African origin who "spoke the languages of Acadia." One wonders how he learned them. His name suggested that he had been baptized in Portugal or Spain or perhaps the Cape Verde Islands. Somehow Da Costa had found his way to Acadia, perhaps on a Portuguese or Basque or Spanish ship. He may have been shipwrecked on the coast, or jumped ship, or marooned by an angry captain in North America. However it happened, Mathieu Da Costa appears to have been an African who lived for a time among the Indians of Acadia and learned to speak their Algonquian languages. His services were much sought by merchants in the American trade. On at least one occasion he appears to have been kidnapped by Dutch corsairs. The sieur de Mons was able to hire him, and later became involved in litigation with other men who wanted Da Costa's skills.[32]

Another purpose was represented by three men of the cloth who were specially recruited, perhaps on orders from the king. One was a young Catholic priest, Nicolas Aubry, of a "good family" in Paris. He came along despite the strong opposition of his parents, who were frantic with anxiety. They followed him to Honfleur in a desperate effort to persuade him not to go.[33] With Father Aubry was another Catholic priest whom Champlain called "le curé," and a Protestant pastor called "le ministre." Their names have not been found.[34]

A spirit of toleration was fully embraced by the leaders of the expedition, both Protestants such as sieur de Mons and Catholics such as Champlain. They shared the king's religious policy, which combined Catholicism as the es-

tablished religion with toleration for Protestant dissenters. Unhappily that
spirit was not shared by the curé and the minister. From the start they raged
against each other, and even came to blows, much to the disgust of others in
the expedition, who showed more of the Christian spirit than either of these
two *religieux*.

This expedition consisted entirely of men and boys. No women were
aboard, no families or farmers. That fact makes very clear the purpose of this
mission. Its object was not to plant a permanent settlement with a population
that could grow by natural increase, but rather to build an *avant-poste*, an outpost of empire in North America. The sieur de Mons intended to construct an
advanced base in the center of Acadia, analogous to a space station in our
time, a safe and secure platform, strong enough to defend itself against the
possibility of attack by Spanish or English raiders. Its function was to provide
a base for exploring missions, to map the coast, and find sites for colonies
where French families might settle and start small populations growing.

All these adventurers gathered in the Norman seaports of Honfleur and Le
Havre, and crowded aboard two ships. One of them again was *La Bonne-
Renommée*, 120 tons burthen, under three experienced seamen: Pont-Gravé as
her commander, Captain Nicolas Morel of Honfleur as master, and Guillaume
Duglas as pilot.[35] The other vessel was *Don de Dieu* (Gift of God), 150 tons
burthen, and a hundred feet long. She was the "amiral" or flagship of the expedition. On board were sieur de Mons as her commander, Captain Timothée
le Barbier of Le Havre, her master, Louis Coman as pilot, and Champlain.[36]

These ships were very small by comparison with ocean-going vessels of later
generations, but they were large by the standards of their time. The *Don de
Dieu* was described as "one of the largest Norman ships that went every year to
the Newfoundland cod fisheries."[37] Their holds were packed with absolutely
everything that life required, as if they were going to the moon. There were
tons of provisions: casks of red wine, hard cider, and water; barrels of salt pork,
herring and cod, sacks of grain, dried vegetables and fruits, live sheep, swine,
and chickens. They carried building supplies, prefabricated housing, sawn timbers, windows and doors, and everything that a shipwright would need to repair a vessel or build a new one. Also aboard were prefabricated parts for
several shallops and skiffs. Perhaps sailing in company with the larger vessels
was a 40-foot patache of 17 or 18 tons.[38]

After much labor and tedious paperwork, some of which still survives, the
expedition was ready. On April 7, 1604, the *Don de Dieu* left her mooring in
Le Havre. Pont-Gravé followed in *Bonne-Renommée* on April 10. The two

A Mi'kmaq petroglyph of an early European ship with a high poop, carved into the rocks of Kejimkujik Park, Nova Scotia. This Indian nation was familiar with Europeans long before Champlain. A leader, Membertou, acquired his own French shallop, painted its sails with his totem, and traded with fishermen far out at sea.

ships sailed independently with orders to meet at the fishing harbor of Canso on the northeastern tip of what is now Nova Scotia.[39] Their departure had the air of a great occasion. They sailed as the king's ships, and flew the naval ensign of France with the royal standard of Henri IV. Salutes were fired in their honor from other vessels and forts at Le Havre. Other French ships deferred to them. One man wrote, "It is a custom at sea for a merchant ship meeting a king's ship such as ours, to come under her lee, and to sail parallel to her but at an angle, and also to dip her ensigns."[40]

Don de Dieu was a fast sailor. Once at sea she made excellent time, but it was a lively passage and probably hard on landsmen who had never been afloat. They had favorable winds from the east in the North Atlantic, a rare occurrence in early spring, and went spanking along with a following sea and waves so high that they smashed the stern gallery of the flagship. We are told that "a carpenter was carried overboard by a wave," but he "held fast to a line that happened to be hanging down the ship's side." One can only imagine conditions on the lower decks, which were crowded with frightened animals and seasick passengers.[41]

As they approached the new world, the ships began to meet floating ice in their path. The sieur de Mons ordered the *Don de Dieu* to steer a more southerly course, toward the lower coast of Acadia. They were moving very fast, and the pilot had more than the usual difficulty in calculating their position. On May 1, they were amazed to see the low sandy beaches of Sable Island on the outer edge of the great fishing banks. It was a surprise to the navigators, as they were only three weeks out of Le Havre, and their reckoning was off the mark. Champlain wrote that they were nearly wrecked on that unfortunate island, which was littered with the bones of broken ships.[42]

With luck they got clear and sailed onward to the coast of Acadia. On May 8, 1604, they sighted a headland with cliffs more than a hundred feet high.

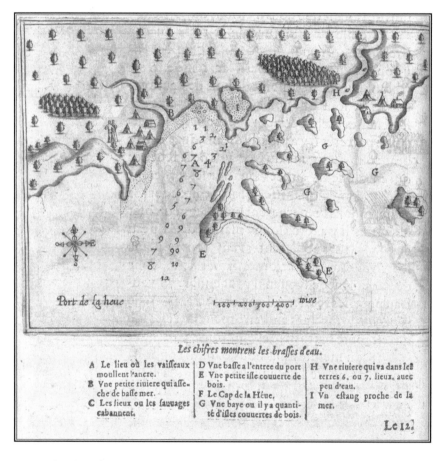

*Champlain's chart of Port de la Hève (now LaHave), a handsome harbor on the Atlantic coast.
It was the first place where he and de Mons came ashore in Acadia, May 8, 1604. Note the Indian and
European houses, side by side.*

Champlain called it Cap de la Hève, after a French landmark near Le Havre with the same name and similar appearance. It marked the start of Champlain's long career as an inventor of names for the land of North America. Many are still in use. Most of his early names were French. Later, as he began to work with Indian guides, they drew from native languages.[43]

The *Don de Dieu* entered a long bay and dropped anchor. The date was May 8, 1604, and they had made a very fast crossing. Champlain wrote, "The weather was so favorable that we were only a month to Cap de la Hève." The average speed of *Don de Dieu* was about five knots, with daily runs that would have been above eight knots—faster than some transatlantic convoys in the Second World War.[44]

The passengers and crew were happy to go ashore on terra firma, and thanked God that they were still alive. Champlain got a small skiff and surveyed the bay with great care. He sounded its depth, calculated the latitude, measured compass variation, and made a very accurate chart.[45] On both sides of the bay he mapped two large Indian camps where the Mi'kmaq (he called them Souriquois) came every summer to fish along the coast. They returned to their forest hunting grounds in the winter. A web of Indian paths bore witness to the importance of this place, and old burial grounds testified to its long use.[46]

The Mi'kmaq had met many Europeans on the coast long before Champlain and the sieur de Mons arrived. Their legends recorded memories and dreams of earlier contact. One was clearly an account of Vikings. Another was recorded as the dream of a young Mi'kmaq woman who one morning looked out to sea and saw a "little island" which had "drifted near to the land" with "trees on it and branches to the trees on which a number of bears as they supposed were crawling about." The Mi'kmaq seized their bows and spears and went to shoot the bears, and were amazed to discover that "these supposed bears were men, and that some of them were lowering down into the water a very singularly constructed canoe, into which several of them jumped and paddled ashore." Among them was a man dressed in white who "came towards them making signs of friendship, raising his hand towards heaven, and addressing them in an earnest way, but in a language which they could not understand." The young woman described the other men as dressed in skins, which suggested that they were Basques. European accounts of the fishing coast noted that Basques wore "good garments of skins," and that they were on the coast of Acadia long before Champlain arrived.

The Atlantic coast of North America was already a busy place in 1604, with much traffic by seaborne Indians, European fishermen, Basque whaling ships, and trading vessels of many nationalities. By every account, the Mi'kmaq welcomed the French, and offered to help them.[47]

The harbor at La Hève was an attractive site for settlement but in 1604 it seemed dangerously exposed to seaborne predators of many nations. The French stayed four days and moved on, running south along the coast in search of opportunities.

On May 12 they sailed about twenty-five miles to another harbor, now called Liverpool. Here they surprised a small French trading vessel of about 50 tons called *La Levrette* (Greyhound). Her captain, Jean de Rossignol of Le Havre, was busily bartering furs from the Indians. He claimed to have a license from the French admiralty, but it was only for trade on the coast of Florida. The sieur de Mons told him that he was in violation of the king's patent, and probably offered terms, but Rossignol was defiant. De Mons seized the ship and made the captain a prisoner for return to France. Champlain mapped the harbor and named it Port au Rossignol.[48]

A memory of this event survives in the oral traditions of the Mi'kmaq people of Bear River Reserve. It was recorded in the early twentieth century by a Métis guide named Henry Peters. "Well," said he, speaking of Champlain's vessel, "they came into Liverpool one time and there was a ship there that wasn't supposed to be. They boarded the ship, and there was just the mate and cook on board. Well, they had to tell where the captain and the crew were. They were upriver trading with the Indians, which they didn't have permission from the governor to do. Well, when the traders came down the river they waylaid them and took the canoes of fur and the crew. They thought they got them all. Rossignol was the captain and that's where Lake Rossignol, the largest lake in Nova Scotia, got its name." Peters remembered that two of Rossignol's seamen were named Peter and Charles. They slipped over the side of their canoe, and "swam to shore underwater to keep them from being shot. So where were they to go? They went back up the river to Kedgie."[49]

This was a Mi'kmaq community on islands in Lake Rossignol. Peters recalled that each Mi'kmaq family had its own island. The two European seamen took Indian wives, but no islands were left for them, so they settled on the lakeshore, at places that came to be called Peter's Point and Charles Point. Henry Peters himself was descended from the seaman named Peter, and learned the story from his father, who had heard it from his father. It describes a process by which a unique population began to grow in Acadia as early as

1604—a mix of Indians, French, English, Scottish, Basques, Portuguese, and Africans.[50]

After this affair, the sieur de Mons and Champlain sailed on, with little *Levrette* in company and master Rossignol an angry prisoner below. They went about ten miles along the Atlantic coast of Acadia and entered another very beautiful bay with open cleared land. Champlain named it Port au Mouton after a sheep that fell overboard, and was "eaten as a fair prize." It was an inviting place, with fresh water, game, and birds. De Mons decided to bring his men ashore and give them a rest from their seaboard routine. He ordered them to make camp at Port au Mouton on high ground between the bay and two

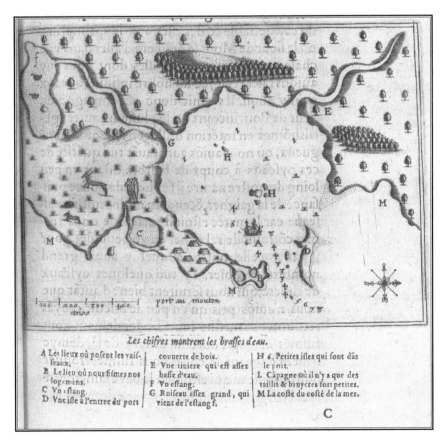

port au mouton

Les chifres montrent les braſſes d'eau.

A Les lieux où poſent les vaiſ-
ſeaux.
B Le lieu où nous fiſmes nos
logemens.
C Vn eſtang.
D Vne iſle à l'entrée du port

couuerte de bois.
E Vne riuiere qui eſt aſſez
baſſe d'eau.
F Vn eſtang.
G Ruiſſeau aſſez grand, qui
vient de l'eſtang f.

H 6. Petites iſles qui ſont d'ãs
le port.
L Cãpagne où il n'y a que des
taillis & bruyeres fort petites.
M La coſte du coſté de la mer.

C

Port au Mouton (pronounced Matoon *in Nova Scotia) was named by Champlain after a sheep fell overboard and drowned there. De Mons led his men ashore, and they built their own shelters, "each according to his fancy," while Champlain went exploring.*

fresh water lakes. The men improvised their own cabins "Indian fashion," or "according to their fantasy," in Champlain's words.[51]

The sieur de Mons decided to stay there for several weeks with *Don de Dieu* and *Levrette* moored in the bay, while he ordered two smaller craft to explore the coast in opposite directions. A shallop with Indian guides was sent northeast in search of Pont-Gravé and *Bonne-Renommée*, which carried many of the expedition's supplies. At the same time, de Mons asked Champlain to take command of a small barque of eight tons. Champlain's orders were to proceed with Jean Ralluau, the secretary of the expedition, and maître Simon, one of the Balkan miners. They were told to search the "coasts, ports and harbors" and find "where our vessels might proceed in safety."[52]

Champlain left on May 19, 1604, and found himself on a dangerous Atlantic coast with many capes, rocks, and treacherous shoals that extended far from shore. He had to stand well out into the ocean to keep clear of them, then work his way back, chart the coast, and set maître Simon ashore to search for mineral deposits, while he and Jean Ralluau examined the soil for its fertility. Then he returned to the sea, dodged sunken obstructions that could sink his boat, and repeated the operation at the next cove. It was slow and tricky work, with rough seas, rip tides, and strong currents.[53]

By this laborious method Champlain followed the deep-indented Atlantic coast of Acadia, and found more than ten coves and bays in a stretch of forty miles. At last he came to Cape Sable, an island that marked the extreme southeastern tip of Acadia. Near it Champlain found a haven "where vessels can anchor without the least fear of danger." It was a promising place for a fort and trading post.

Then he rounded the southern end of Acadia and came upon islands with an unimaginable abundance of nesting birds. Champlain named one of them Isle aux Cormorans "because of the infinite number of these birds of whose eggs we took a barrel full." On another island he found birds he called *tangueux*, probably gannets, and wrote that "we killed them easily with a stick." On two other islands, he wrote, "the abundance of birds of different kinds is so great that no one would believe it possible unless he had seen it: such as cormorants, ducks of three kinds, snow geese, murres, wild geese, puffins, snipe, fish-hawks and other birds of prey, sea-gulls, curlews, turnstones, divers, loons, eiders, ravens, cranes and other kinds unknown to me which make their nests there."[54]

The beaches of these islands were also "completely covered with seals, whereof we took as many as we wished," and he discovered a taste for seal meat, which with a marinade makes very good eating. In the face of this vast abundance of life, the first thought of these hungry men was to kill as many as possible for pleasure and the pot, then gorge themselves, kill again, and eat once more.[55]

Champlain and his crew sailed on, along the short southern coast of Acadia, and found more harbors. They took a close look at Cap Fourchu (which resembled the tongs of a *fourchette*, or fork), and Champlain studied an attractive harbor that is now the port of Yarmouth. Nearby, maître Simon found what might have been mines of iron and silver. Then they turned north and entered the long inlet of St. Mary Bay, where Champlain discovered an attractive site for settlement with open meadows and "soil among the best I've ever seen." He named it Port Sainte-Marguerite. Maître Simon also thought he had found a deposit of iron and silver.[56]

They could go no farther. With provisions running low, Champlain came about, and returned the way he had come. On the Atlantic coast he was overtaken by a wild gale, and saved his barque only by running her ashore in a safe place. After the storm passed, they sailed on and reached Port-au-Mouton the next day. Champlain wrote, "The sieur de Mons was expecting us from day to day, not knowing what to think of our delay except that some accident must have happened."[57]

Champlain had acquitted himself well in his first independent command. It was no small feat to navigate so difficult a coast with twelve men in a small barque. He had followed de Mons' instructions to the letter. The sieur de Ralluau (a skilled seaman himself) appears to have made a favorable report, and Champlain was given more responsibility.[58]

De Mons wanted to examine the coast of Acadia himself, on both sides of the Baie Françoise, now the Bay of Fundy. He put the gentleman-adventurers aboard the *Don de Dieu*, while he and Champlain took a small shallop and worked closely together, exploring promising parts of the coast.[59] They moved quickly around the southern end of Acadia, following the route that Champlain had explored. De Mons wanted to have another look at the long stretch of water that is now called St. Mary Bay, probably because of the report from maître Simon about deposits of iron and silver there. They found little in the way of minerals, and "no place where we might fortify ourselves."[60]

They sailed out of St. Mary Bay and headed northeast up the much larger Baie Françoise in search of good sites. Two leagues along the coast, they turned into a narrow opening between high headlands, and found themselves on a magnificent sheet of water, almost like an inland sea. Champlain wrote, "we entered one of the most beautiful harbors I have seen on all these coasts, which could safely hold 2,000 ships." They named it Port-Royal—today's Annapolis Basin.[61] To enter it from the sea today is to share his sense of wonder and discovery.

The land attracted them as much as the harbor. Champlain added: "From the mouth of the river to the point we reached are many prairies or meadows but these are flooded at high tide, and numbers of small creeks that cross from one side and another. . . . The place was the most proper and pleasant for a settlement that we had seen."[62]

They might have planted their settlement there, but de Mons wanted to explore the rest of the Baie Française before he made a decision. Thinking perhaps of the king's interest in mines they sailed up the bay to another large basin where minerals were said to have been found. They went ashore, did some prospecting, and came upon some hopeful traces of copper, and they called the place Port-des-Mines, today's Minas Basin.[63]

Champlain and de Mons continued around the head of the bay and were astonished by its prodigious tides, among the highest in the world. They began to explore its western shore, moving very quickly now. On June 24, they came to "one of the largest and deepest rivers we had yet seen," and named it the rivière Saint-Jean "because that was the day when we arrived." They entered the river and were startled to discover a reversing falls, which changed direction when the incoming tide submerged the rapids, as it does today. They waited for the tide to change, and sailed through the falls on the incoming tide. Upstream they found another broad bay, and they could go no farther. Indians told them that the St. John River offered an avenue to the St. Lawrence Valley with only a short portage. On the coast to the north, they also found a fine harbor, today's handsome city of Saint John, New Brunswick.[64]

From the St. John River they headed south through so many islands that they were unable to count them. They were traveling with Indian guides, and named a large island Grand Manan, after the Algonquian word for island.[65] They came to Passamaquoddy Bay, entered a broad estuary and followed it upstream to a beautiful place where three rivers came together in the shape of a crucifix, and just below, a handsome wooded island of about five acres which they called "Isle Sainte-Croix," Holy Cross Island.

It caught Champlain's eye as "easy to fortify." He was deeply mindful of defense, not primarily against Indians but Europeans. Champlain keenly remembered the fate of Laudonnière's colony in Florida, destroyed by a Spanish commander who ordered his men to murder the French colonists in cold

Les chifres montrent les brasses d'eau.

A Trois isles qui sont par de-
   la le saut.
B Montaignes qui paroissent
   par dessus les terres deux
   lieues au su de la riuiere.
C Le saut de la riuiere.
D Basses quand la mer est per-
   due, ou vaisseaux peuuent
   eschouer.
E Cabanne où se fortifient les
   sauuages.

F Vne pointe de cailloux, où y
   a vne croix.
G Vne isle qui est a l'entree
   de la riuiere.
H Petit ruisseau qui vient
   d'vn petit estang.
I Bras de mer qui asseche de
   basse mer.
L Deux petits islets de rocher.
M Vn petit estang.

N Deux Ruisseaux.
O Basses fort dangereuses le
   long de la coste qui asse-
   chent de basse mer.
P Chemin par où les sauuages
   portent leurs canaux quand
   ils veulent passer le sault.
Q Le lieu où peuuent mouiller l'ancre où la riuiere a
   grand cours.

The St. John River, in what is now New Brunswick, was named by Champlain for Saint John's Day, June 24, 1604, when he went there and made this map. He was interested in its reversing falls (C) and its river valley, which was joined by a portage to the St. Lawrence. The Indian fort (E) later became a French and English post.

blood. In 1604, the French leaders in Acadia were determined that they would not be caught in the same way.

Sainte-Croix was a natural fortress, "eight or nine hundred paces in circumference." On three sides it had granite cliffs twenty to thirty feet high, so steep as to be virtually impassable. On the fourth side of the island, facing downstream, they found a small crescent beach of sand and clay, guarded by granite

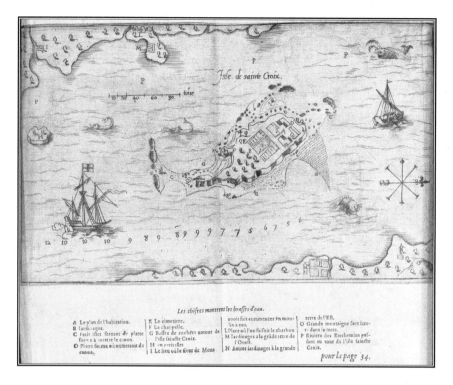

Sainte-Croix Island was occupied by the French in June 1604. It lay in a river of the same name that is now the boundary between the United States and Canada. Champlain's shallop is anchored upstream of the island and a three-masted patache is moored below.

rocky outcrops called "nubbles," which could bear the weight of ramparts and cannon.[66]

The island was attractive in other ways. In June it looked lush and very fertile. Champlain and the sieur de Mons explored the banks of both its rivers, and found good ground for farming, with flowing streams of fresh water, excellent sites for mills with a good head of water, and an abundance of timber. Upstream they found deposits of copper ore, sand, clay, and building-stone. The river teemed with alewives, bass, and shad. At low tide, Champlain found "plenty of shellfish such as clams, mussels, sea-urchins and sea-snails, which were of great benefit to everyone."[67]

And so it was decided. This would be their first settlement. After a long search, de Mons and Champlain made a quick judgment. They must have been very tired, and they had an anxious eye on the calendar. It was the last week in June when they arrived at Sainte-Croix Island. Spring had gone, and something had to be done.[68]

The settlers swarmed ashore, and were immediately assaulted by an enemy they had not met before. Champlain described them as "mosquitoes which are little flies," and "several of our men had their faces so swollen by their bites that they could scarcely see." New Englanders and New Brunswickers will recognize them as the dreaded black flies, clouds of tiny carnivores that are often at their worst in late June.[69]

The other French ships soon came up the river—*Don de Dieu* with little

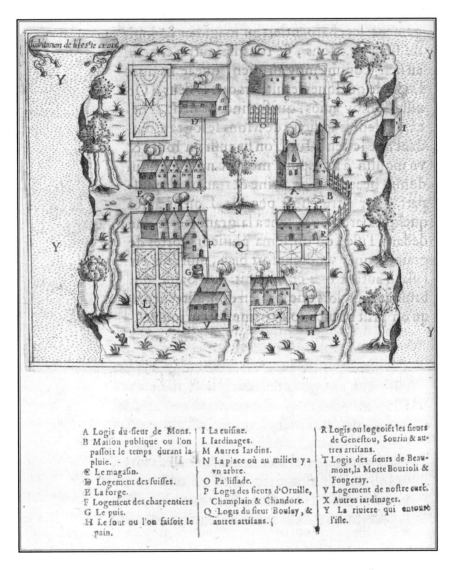

Champlain's plan of settlement on Sainte-Croix Island. The elegant house of de Mons is to the right of the tree. To the north are the storehouse and barracks for the Swiss soldiers. To the south are houses for gentlemen and bunkhouses for artisans and laborers.

Levrette, and several shallops. A few days later a small *barque du port* of about 8 tons arrived. She had been sent by Pont-Gravé from Canso on the Atlantic coast, where he was gathering a cargo of fish and furs. On board were the masters of Basque ships arrested by Pont-Gravé for illegal trading. The sieur de Mons "treated them humanely, *les receut humainement*," in Champlain's phrase, and he ordered their return to France.[70]

On Sainte-Croix their first task was to fortify the island. Champlain wrote, "We began to erect a barricade on a small islet, a little apart from it, and this served as a platform for mounting our cannon." Today it is still called Cannon Nubble, and it appears very much as Champlain described it. The battery faced downriver toward the open sea, where they felt the greatest danger. Its guns controlled the entire width of the river, and a deep anchorage where Champlain found sixty feet of water, enough for large ocean-going ships to ride safely at their moorings. After the battery was in place, a palisade was built across the exposed southern end of the island, and within a few days the settlement was declared to be in "a state of defense."[71]

Then the sieur de Mons laid out the settlement. He ordered that the woods on the island should be cut down, "save the trees along the shore," and one large tree was left standing in what appears to have been a small village square. A very handsome house was erected for the governor, made of "fair sawn timber, with the banner of France overhead." It had an elegant hipped Mansard roof and "artistic and beautiful woodwork." A fireplace was built with beautiful yellow bricks that had been brought from France, as were the timbers, heavy doors, and casement windows. The colonists also built a big storehouse, the largest and most important structure on the island, for its provisions were "the safety and life of each." It had a stone foundation, a deep cellar, and was "built likewise of fair timber, covered with shingles."[72]

A covered gallery went up, "wherein we spent our time when it rained," and also a bakehouse, cookhouse, blacksmith's shop, and carpenter's house. The dwellings followed, "each working at his own." The gentlemen and servants put up their own small tenements. Champlain wrote, "I worked at mine, which I built with the aid of some servants of the sieur d'Orville and myself." Artisans and laborers constructed bunkhouses for themselves, and the Swiss soldiers had barracks. An oven was added, and a hand mill, and an attempt was made at digging a well, but it appears not to have been very successful. On the shore opposite the island, an Indian village sprang up and the French built them a chapel "in the Indian manner."[73]

Fields were planted on the mainland and a large garden on the island.

Champlain wrote that the seeds "came up very well" except on the island, where "the soil was dry and sandy, and everything was scorched when the sun shone." They had trouble watering the seedlings, which required "great pains." [74]

Much archaeology has been done on this island from the eighteenth century to the twenty-first. In general these projects have confirmed the accuracy of Champlain's written account. An engraving of the settlement in Champlain's *Voyages* depicts a more idealized image, but it is also accurate in its main lines. [75]

In September, the sieur de Mons ordered the *Don de Dieu* and *Levrette* back to France, and seventy-nine men prepared to stay the winter, with de Mons in command and Champlain at his side. The latitude of Sainte-Croix Island was about the same as Saintonge, and the French expected that the winter would be similar as well. To their shock, the first snow fell in the first week of October. By January three feet of snow were on the ground, and a cruel wind howled down the river. Temperatures plummeted and the winter bitter cold for many long months. [76] The Sainte-Croix River froze during the first week of December. The movement of the tide broke the heavy ice into jagged pieces that froze again in an impenetrable tangle of slabs and blocks. The men on Sainte-Croix Island could not cross the river by foot or boat, and were isolated from the mainland. Their cider and wines froze solid, except for some fortified Spanish wine. They had no source of water except melted snow, and soon they were short of firewood as well. Their diet of dried provisions and salt meat was miserable. Men began to grow weak from malnutrition, and symptoms of scurvy began to appear among them.

In mid-winter the *habitants* started to die, many in severe pain. Of the seventy-nine French colonists who wintered on the island, Champlain tells us, thirty-five died and twenty more were "very near it." Here again, the evidence of archaeology has confirmed Champlain's account. The bodies were buried in graves so shallow that the skeletons began to emerge from the ground. For many years, the Indians called this haunted place Bone Island. [77]

The French surgeons were baffled by these deaths. They performed careful autopsies on the victims in hope of finding the cause. Champlain wrote, "We opened several of them to determine the cause of their illness." In the twentieth century, archaeologists found the body of a settler on whom an autopsy was performed—the earliest evidence of a European autopsy in North America. Once more, the evidence of archaeology confirmed the accuracy of Cham-

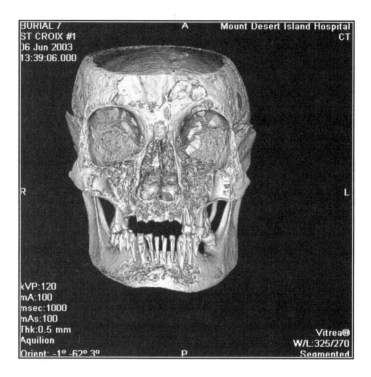

This skull of a French settler was found on Sainte-Croix Island by archaeologists. He died of scurvy in 1604, and an autopsy was performed by a skilled French surgeon who sought to understand the cause of death. This CT scan confirms the account in Champlain's Voyages.

plain's account. Forensic pathologists examined the remains in 2003, and were impressed by the professional skill of the French surgeons. But the autopsies gave the colonists no way of understanding what was happening to them.[78]

Champlain believed that scurvy was a dietary disease and he attributed its cause to an excess of salt provisions and a shortage of fresh food. Not until the twentieth century would the absence of vitamin C be identified as the cause, but even before the settlement on Sainte-Croix Island, ships' doctors on long voyages were beginning to find a cure. As early as 1602–03 a writer named François Pyrard reported outbreaks of scurvy on ships bound for the East Indies, and concluded that "there is no better or more certain remedy than oranges or citrons." Champlain heard about this finding. He wrote that "the Flemish" had found "a very strange remedy, which might be of service to us, but we have never ascertained the character of it."[79]

Champlain observed that Indians survived the winter without scurvy and concluded that another remedy was fresh-killed meat. A Jesuit priest who talked with the survivors reported: "Of all the men of sieur de Mons who wintered first at Sainte-Croix, only eleven remained in good health. These were the hunters who much preferred the chase to the air of the fireside, running actively to lying passively in bed, setting traps in the snow for wild game to sitting around the fire, talking of Paris and its great chefs."[80]

In late March the river thawed. The sieur de Mons and Champlain obtained a supply of fresh meat from the Indians, and the French settlers began to recover, before the greening of the forest plants.[81] But when spring finally came to Sainte-Croix Island, only eleven of seventy-nine settlers were in good health. Most were dead. They had made a calamitous choice of site, without studying the island carefully enough to realize that it had no reliable source of water and fuel. They did not think that communications with the mainland might be difficult in the winter, or that relations with the Indians would be vital to their survival. Both de Mons and Champlain had read about earlier colonies that had been planted on islands, and had been cut off from assistance, with disastrous results. In 1560, French Admiral Nicolas Durand de Villegaignon had founded a French settlement on a small island in the Bay of Rio de Janeiro, and it had failed. Something similar had happened on Sable Island.[82]

The choice of Sainte-Croix appears to have been a decision that de Mons and Champlain made together. There were no recriminations. Both men learned from their terrible mistake, and moved on. They were determined to persevere—but in another place.

9.

NORUMBEGA

Three Captains, Three Results, 1604–06

> This would be the last French exploration along that coast; the history
> of New France in this region reached its end; that of New England had
> its beginning.
>
> —Marcel Trudel[1]

I N THE SUMMER OF 1604, while the settlement was rising on Sainte-Croix
Island, Champlain received another assignment. The sieur de Mons asked
him "to explore the length of the coast of Norumbega," which we know
as Maine. France and England both claimed that region, as far south as the
Delaware Valley. Its destiny would be decided by three French voyages between 1604 and 1606. Champlain sailed on them all, but each had a different
commander. He led the first, de Mons the second, and Poutrincourt the last.
These leaders worked at the same task, with different results.[2]

On the first voyage, Champlain's orders were to find sites for settlement in
a warmer climate. He was given a highly specialized vessel called a patache,
which a French text defined in 1628 as "a small warship designed for the surveillance of coasts." Champlain wrote that she was a keel-built ship of "17 or
18 tons," probably with a length of about forty feet and a draft of five feet. She
was fully decked over and designed for voyages in dangerous seas, unlike the
smaller open-hulled shallops that he used in more protected waters.[3]

Champlain's chart of Sainte-Croix Island has drawings of both these types:
a small bluff-bowed shallop above the settlement, and below, a trim little vessel that may have been his patache. She was built man-of-war fashion with a
sharp prow, long lines that held the promise of speed, a high forecastle and a
raised poop with a battery of small swivel-mounted falconets. Her mastheads
were crowned by large crows' nests. She flew a large French marine ensign,
which represented another purpose: to show the flag on a contested coast.[4]

Champlain's sketch shows three masts and a very interesting rig. The foremast carried a lugsail that he called a *bourcet* on a yard that crossed the foremast at an oblique angle. The mainmast was rigged with a large square-rigged

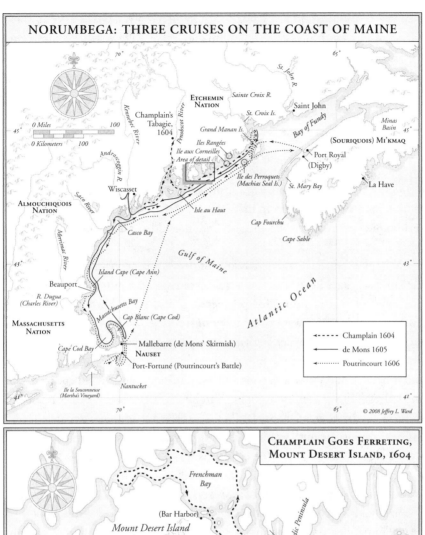

NORUMBEGA: THREE CRUISES ON THE COAST OF MAINE

St. John R.

ETCHEMIN
NATION

Sainte Croix R.

St. Croix Is.

Saint John

Kennebec River

Champlain's
Tabagie,
1604

Penobscot River

Grand Manan Is.

Bay of Fundy

Minas
Basin

(SOURIQUOIS) MI'KMAQ

Iles Rangées
Ile aux Corneilles
Area of detail

Port Royal
(Digby)

Androscoggin R.

Ile des Perroquets
(Machias Seal Is.)

St. Mary Bay

La Have

Saco River

Wiscasset

ALMOUCHIQUOIS
NATION

Isle au Haut

Cap Fourchu

Merrimac River

Casco Bay

Cape Sable

Gulf of Maine

Island Cape (Cape Ann)

Beauport

R. Dugua
(Charles River)

Massachusetts Bay

Atlantic Ocean

MASSACHUSETTS
NATION

Cap Blanc (Cape Cod)

Mallebarre (de Mons' Skirmish)

Cape Cod Bay

NAUSET

Port-Fortuné (Poutrincourt's Battle)

Ile la Souconneuse
(Martha's Vineyard)

Nantucket

- - ◄- - - Champlain 1604
──────── de Mons 1605
········◄······· Poutrincourt 1606

© 2008 Jeffrey L. Ward

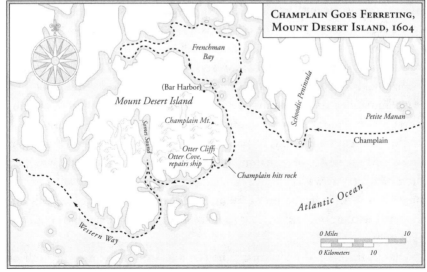

CHAMPLAIN GOES FERRETING,
MOUNT DESERT ISLAND, 1604

Frenchman
Bay

Schoodic Peninsula

(Bar Harbor)

Mount Desert Island

Petite Manan

Champlain Mt.

Champlain

Somes Sound

Otter Cliffs
Otter Cove,
repairs ship

Champlain hits rock

Atlantic Ocean

Western Way

0 Miles   10

0 Kilometers   10

sail, and possibly a topsail. A small mizzen added a triangular lateen. These sails could be used in different combinations that were vital to Champlain's work. The lateen and lugsail could be close-hauled, allowing a vessel to sail very close to the wind. The mainsail and lugsail could be used to run before the wind. In light airs, all sails could be set to capture the slightest whisper of a variable breeze. It was a versatile rig, much favored by explorers.[5]

A patache was well suited to his method of close-in exploration in a vessel that "*furette par tout*; ferrets everywhere." On his coastal voyages, Champlain wasted no time and passed rapidly over stretches of coast that offered nothing of interest. He sought out the promising places, explored them with close attention, and surveyed them in meticulous detail. It was dangerous work on a rockbound coast with strong currents and huge tides, but Champlain found it "very agreeable."[6]

Champlain's patache carried a crew of twelve seamen (matelots). On long exploring voyages he also took several servants, and a gunner, a carpenter, a locksmith, a master-miner for prospecting, and several arquebusiers. Also aboard for this cruise were two Etchemin Indians "as guides on a coast that they knew well." Altogether, perhaps twenty men crowded aboard the patache. The hold was packed with a month's supplies—biscuit, peas, flour, salt meat and fish, wine and water, weapons and ammunition, lumber and cordage, sails and spares.[7] The Etchemin brought a birchbark canoe, and Champlain added skiffs for surveying.[8] On September 2, 1604, Champlain departed from Sainte-Croix Island and dropped down the river. He was happy to be at sea in a good ship, indulging what he called his "passion for discovery." To read his account is to feel that there was nothing in the world that he would rather be doing—another reason why he was so good at it.[9]

He quickly discovered that the coast of Maine could be a hard school for a new commander. At the mouth of the Sainte-Croix River, he found Poutrincourt's vessels lying at anchor and unable to sail for France "on account of bad weather and contrary winds"—probably a nor'easter of the sort that often blows hard on this coast. Champlain anchored and waited for the weather. Three days later he was on his way and enjoyed clear sailing—for all of two or three leagues. Then he ran into a rolling fogbank of a kind that suddenly appears on the coast of Maine. It was so thick that Poutrincourt's ships vanished from sight.

Champlain pressed on through the fog and stood out into the Gulf of Maine to get clear of the coast. He was a bold explorer, but prudent in the way he managed risk. He made frequent use of the lead line, and discovered "sandbanks, shoals, and rocks in some places projecting more than four leagues out to sea."[10] With more sea room, Champlain steered southwest on the outer side of "a great number of islands." He gave them names with the help of his Indian guides. A cluster of rocky islets were called the Isles aux Perroquets after a large colony of Atlantic puffins—thousands of wonderful birds with glossy black coats, white pigeon breasts, hooded eyes, and big red and yellow parrot beaks. Today these rocks are called Machias-Seal Island and claimed by two nations. The puffin colony is still there—much reduced, but the only rightful owners.[11]

Champlain sailed on, past another group of islands with their seaward faces all in a row. He called them the Isles Rangées, the Ordered Islands. Next to them is Roque Island, one of the most beautiful on the Maine coast, with a crescent beach of white sand and blue-green water inside a perfect half-moon cove.[12] Further south, he steered closer to the mainland, studied the rocky coast of Schoodic Peninsula and found "many harbors that are beautiful, but not good for settlement."[13] Champlain did not tarry in these places. He rounded Schoodic Point, crossed the handsome sheet of water now called Frenchman Bay, and "on this same day," September 5, 1604, "passed very near an island which was four or five leagues long." It was an extraordinary sight: an island twelve miles in diameter with many mountains, "very high and cleft in places," and peaks as high as 1,500 feet above the water. At first sight Champlain counted "seven or eight mountains, one alongside the other," and then many more came into view, twenty-seven peaks in all. He noted: "The tops of most of them are bare of trees, because there is nothing but rocks. The woods consist only of pines, firs, and birches."[14]

Champlain named this place l'Isle des Monts-Déserts, today's Mount Desert Island. He often used the adjective *désert* in his writings to describe an uninhabitable wilderness that he regarded as "*terre fort mal plaisante*; a very unpleasant place." Champlain's idea of natural beauty was a garden rather than a wilderness—an attitude different from our own. But then again his "désert" described the bare mountaintops, and not the island. Champlain was fascinated by this place, as many visitors have been through the centuries.[15]

On the afternoon of September 5, 1604, he approached from the east and sailed north to the head of Frenchman Bay, far enough to discover that Mount Desert was an island, separated from the mainland by "less than a hundred paces." All earlier charts had shown it as a peninsula. He was the first to map it for what it was.[16]

At the head of Frenchman Bay, Champlain came about and sailed down the rocky eastern coast of Mount Desert Island, ferreting in his usual way, very close to the shore. The hour was late and the sun was low in the western sky.

The east side of Mount Desert Island lay in the shadow of its mountains. Champlain tells us that since early dawn they had sailed twenty-five leagues.[17] It had been a long day, and the lookouts may have been less alert than usual, or more alert to other things. Perhaps they were studying the dramatic scenery of the island as they sailed past a ridge now appropriately named Champlain Mountain. They may have noticed the falcons that breed on its steep seaward cliffs and are sometimes seen swooping overhead at incredible speed, so nimble in the air that they pass food in mid-flight. Just to the south, these Frenchmen might have seen families of sleek otters playing in the sea near what is now called Otter Point.[18]

As Champlain ferreted along that spectacular coast, he felt a sudden jolt and heard the painful grinding sound that sailors dread. His patache had run on a granite ledge and slipped off again with a hole in her wooden bottom. Champlain wrote, "We were almost lost on a little rock, level with the surface of the water." Islanders have long surmised that he hit an infamous ledge off Otter Point that has long taken a toll of local traffic. At low water, it is visible with the sea breaking over it; at high tide it lurks below the surface for unwary mariners.[19] The blow was a heavy one, and the patache began to sink. The crew must have pumped and bailed while Champlain looked for a place of refuge. Just beyond Otter Point he came to an inlet called Otter Cove, with a broad tidal flat of rounded pebbles that the English call a shingle beach. As the tide flowed out, Otter Cove was a perfect place to careen his vessel. They brought her in with the high tide, and eased her gently on her side as the water ebbed. Champlain and his carpenter splashed through pools of water, studied the ship's bottom, and found a hole near her keel. Luckily the keel itself and the rudder were undamaged.[20]

While some of the crew made repairs, others probably foraged on the shore for something to eat. There were birds to shoot, shellfish to gather from tidal pools, and berries in profusion. Today a small stand of wild chokecherry trees stands near the tide line on Otter Cove. In late August and early September they bear abundant fruit, which several generations of this historian's family have happily harvested. Champlain made a point of supplementing his crew's rations with fresh food wherever he could find it.

The next day, September 6, 1604, the patache floated on the rising tide, and Champlain resumed his voyage. He sailed southwest, around the bottom of Mount Desert Island, past the present site of Seal Harbor, where summer cottagers in 1904 erected a small monument of granite and bronze in his honor. Champlain continued about two leagues and "caught sight of smoke in a cove which was at the foot of the mountains above mentioned." This would have been Somes Sound with mountains on both sides, and the safe havens of today's Northeast Harbor and Southwest Harbor on either side of its entrance.

Several Indians came out in their canoes and studied Champlain's patache, but were careful to keep a musket shot away. Champlain sent his Indian companions to "assure them of our friendship," but "the fear they had of us made them turn back."[21] Champlain implies that he spent that day and another night near the island. Probably he explored Somes Sound, which some describe as one of the few fjords on the western side of the Atlantic Ocean. Had he done so, he would have seen crystal-clear mountain streams tumbling from steep mountainsides into the deep water. One of them, now called Man O'War Brook, was a perfect place for a ship to come alongside and fill her water-casks.[22]

The following morning, September 7, Champlain was still at Mount Desert Island when the Indians returned in their canoes. They came alongside his patache, talked with Champlain's Indian companions, and exchanged presents: Indian fish and beaver for French biscuit and "sundry other trifles." The Indians offered to take Champlain to their chief, named Bessabez, on a river they called Pentegouet, now the Penobscot. Off they went through the Western Way, into Penobscot Bay. Champlain wrote, "Almost midway between them, out to sea lies another high and striking island." He called it Isle au Haut, which it remains today.[23]

The scenery was spectacular as he sailed into Penobscot Bay, with Deer Island and Castine to his east, Islesboro to the west, North Haven and Vinalhaven dead ahead. Champlain was working without a chart, and he tells us that he threaded his way through many rocks and shoals, "lead line in hand." He delighted in the beauty of the place. "Entering the river," he wrote, "one sees fine islands, which are very pleasant on account of their beautiful meadows, *belles prairies*." Here again he was more apt to comment on the beauty of open land than dense forest.[24]

Champlain called it the Norumbega River. He sailed north through its magnificent narrows, with high wooded headlands on both banks towering above his patache. He admired the present site of Bucksport, sailed on as far as the water could float his patache, and came to a big waterfall, two hundred paces wide and seven to eight feet high. He had reached the head of navigation on the Penobscot River in what is now the center of Bangor, Maine.[25] "Below the fall," he wrote, "the river is beautiful, and unobstructed as far as the place where we anchored. I landed to see the country." He went hunting, probably with his Indian guides, and "found the part I visited most pleasant and agreeable." Near the river, he found a fine grove of old oaks where "one would think the oaks had been planted there for pleasure." It is now Bangor's Oak Street, a neighborhood severely blighted by urban renewal, and a sad commentary on our stewardship of this very beautiful place.[26]

Indians began to gather, and Champlain's guides told them that the French came in peace. More Indians arrived, a band of thirty and then the sagamore Bessabez, a leading presence in the region. He would later become well known to other Europeans, who variously called him Betsabes or Bashaba, and they were very much impressed. A Jesuit missionary met him in 1611 and described him as a "man of great discretion and prudence." He added, "I must confess we often see in these 'sauvages' natural and graceful qualities, which will make anyone but a shameless person blush, when they compare them to the greater part of the French who come over here."[27]

The Indians also held Bessabez in high esteem. Champlain observed that when he arrived "they all began to sing, dance and leap, until he had landed." Then they sat in a circle "according to their custom, when they wished to make a speech or hold a festival."[28] Another group arrived with a chief named Cabahis and "twenty or thirty of his companions." They "kept by themselves" and sat apart from the Indians who followed Bessabez. Clearly there had been trouble between them, but they joined in welcoming Champlain. "All were much pleased to see us," he wrote, "inasmuch as it was the first time they had ever beheld Christians."[29]

The meeting place was a stretch of level ground where the Kenduskeag River joins the Penobscot. Champlain came forward with two Frenchmen and two Indian interpreters. Unlike other French explorers, he made a point of approaching the Indians with only a small party, so as not to seem threatening. Champlain acted with extraordinary boldness, but made clear that he came in peace. In his usual way, he quietly prepared for the possibility of trouble. "I ordered the crew of our patache to draw near the Indians," he wrote, "and to hold their weapons in readiness to do their duty in case they perceived any movement of these people against us." But the weapons were kept out of sight, and there was no sign of hostility on either side.[30]

His approach won respect and trust. Bessabez beckoned to Champlain and his companions, and "bade us sit down." They began the long ritual of a tabagie, and started to smoke together, "as they usually do before beginning their speeches." Gifts of American venison and waterfowl were exchanged for French biscuits and peas. Then they began to talk. Champlain spoke through an interpreter. He said that he wished to visit the people of this beautiful country, and to be in amity with them, and to promote peace between them and their enemies the Souriquois and Canadiens. He also hoped "to settle in their country and show them how to cultivate it, so that they might not lead a life as miserable as theirs."[31]

Bessabez made a graceful reply. He said they were "well content" with what Champlain had said and that "no greater benefit could come to them than to have our friendship." The Indian leader added that he wanted the French to live in his country, and his people wished to live in peace with their Indian enemies, so that they could hunt the beaver more than they had done before and exchange pelts for useful things. After the speeches, Champlain made presents of "hatchets, rosaries, caps, knives, and other little things." The remainder of the day was given to song and dance and good food (*bonne chère*).

The celebration continued through the night. Champlain appears to have had an important asset in these meetings—a remarkable gift of social stamina. When dawn came, the Indians and French bartered beaver skins and trade goods in a spirit of amity and peace, with the promise of serious commerce to follow. Then they parted. Champlain wrote that Bessabez and his companions went in their direction, and "we in ours, well pleased to have made the acquaintance of these people."[32]

The next day, Champlain took out his instruments and reckoned the latitude at 45 degrees, 25 minutes north. He was about thirty-seven miles off the mark, not bad for a hard-partying navigator with a traveling astrolabe.[33] Then he was off again in his patache, sailing down the Penobscot River with the sagamore Cabahis aboard as his guest. They went twelve leagues to a "little river," probably the Passagassawakeag River near today's town of Belfast, with a handsome shoreline and long views across a broad bay.[34]

Champlain quizzed Cabahis about a mythical place in the interior called Norumbega, which a European traveler had reported to be a city of gold. Probably the word came from the Wabenaki *nolumbeka* for a mix of rapids and quiet water, of which there are plenty on the upper Penobscot, but no city and no gold. Champlain was quick to dismiss that report as a fable. Gold was not his object in North America.[35] He was more interested in the rivers themselves. The Indians told him of portages from the head of the Penobscot to a tributary of the St. Lawrence River. Champlain also asked about the next big river to the south, which the Indians called Qui-ni-be-quy, today's majestic Kennebec, which also had a short portage to the St. Lawrence. These conversations gave him a clear idea of the region.[36]

At the present site of Belfast, Champlain parted company with Cabahis and continued down the Penobscot River, which broadened into a great bay. He passed the high ground called the mountains of Bedabedec, today's Camden Hills, anchored perhaps in Camden Harbor, and sailed on to what is now the town of Rockland.[37] Then he turned south along the coast, heading for the Kennebec River. He went about ten leagues, but the wind was against him, the weather turned foul, and his supplies were running low. It was time to turn around. Champlain wrote, "In consideration of the scantiness of our provisions, we decided to return to our settlement [at Sainte-Croix] and to wait until the following year, when we hoped to come back and explore more fully." On September 23, he ordered the helmsman to come about and head for home. They made good time, running downwind along the coast with the prevailing westerlies behind them—the origin of the expression "down east" in Maine. On October 2, 1604, one month to the day after his departure, Champlain was back at Sainte-Croix Island.[38]

Champlain had failed to find a site for settlement, but in other ways his cruise was a great success. His meeting with the Indians at Kenduskeag was an important event in the history of this region. Once again, Champlain and other groups of Indians led by Bessabez and Cabahis built a firm foundation for friendship on a basis of mutual interest and reciprocal trust. The result, as at Tadoussac, was another enduring Franco-Indian alliance. It began on the banks of the Penobscot River in 1604 and continued for the better part of two centuries. Champlain had a genius for this work and a rare gift for getting on with others. He had a straight-up soldier's manner, and Indian warriors genuinely liked and respected him. He did not approve of their religion or their law, and probably he let them know that. But always he treated them with respect and they worked together to reconcile vital interests.[39]

Unhappily, others did not do it that way. Eight months later, after the hard winter at Sainte-Croix Island, another coastal voyage followed in the spring of 1605. This time the sieur de Mons went along "in search of a more suitable site for settlement, and one where the climate was milder." De Mons decided to command the mission himself, with Champlain at his side. He brought "several gentleman-adventurers" of "high rank," and others to a total of about thirty souls. All squeezed into a vessel similar to Champlain's patache, with provisions for six weeks.

With them were two Indian translators. One was an Etchemin trader named Panounias, who could speak with the northern Indians. The other was his Almouchiquois wife, who could talk with nations to the south. We do not know her name, but this woman of Panounias must have been an extraordinary person. She was the only female whom Champlain mentioned as going

with him on an explor-
ing voyage, and he
wrote of her with re-
spect. Later, he embel-
lished one of his maps
with an Almouchiquois
woman of striking grace
and beauty. One won-
ders if she might have
been the woman of Pa-
nounias.[40]

From the start,
Champlain and the
sieur de Mons differed
on the plan for this
cruise. Champlain pro-
posed to sail directly to
the Kennebec and start
ferreting where the last

An Etchemin warrior appeared on the title page of Champlain's Voyages *in 1619. It might have been the warrior Panounias, who sailed with Champlain as an interpreter.*

voyage had stopped. But the sieur de Mons wished to see the northern coast, and his will was done. Champlain was a loyal subordinate to his commander, but an undercurrent of frustration flows through his written account.

These two good friends had different styles of leadership. Champlain ran a taut ship, centered his missions rigorously on the task at hand, and pushed hard to his objective. The sieur de Mons was an excellent leader in other ways, much liked by those who served with him. He appears to have been more re-laxed and easygoing. Under his command, they sailed slowly down the coast, lingering at attractive islands that could serve no serious purpose. They visited an island called Head Harbor, a curious place with an inner basin so tight that down-east sailors still call it the Cow's Yard.[41] Champlain noted that the island was inhabited only by "a great multitude of crows." The gentleman-adventurers amused themselves by slaughtering large numbers of them, and de Mons allowed them to remain several days for the sport. Champlain named it Île aux Corneilles, or Crow Island.[42]

From there they sailed to Mount Desert Island. Champlain, on his last visit, had found its terrain and soil to be unpromising, and its location offered no access to the interior. But the sieur de Mons wanted to study it, and per-haps the restless gentleman-adventurers wished to see the sights.[43] They stayed several days at Mount Desert, then sailed to Penobscot Bay and crossed its

*Champlain's image of this handsome
Almouchiquois woman might have been
the woman of Panounias, who sailed
with him on the coast of Maine, the
only female he mentioned as coming on
his exploring voyages. She appears on his*
Carte Géographique, *1612. Her image
is also on the title page of the* Voyages
in 1619.

broad mouth. Three Indians came out in a canoe from the cape now called
Owl's Head, and said that their chief would like to meet the French. Some
"conversation" ensued, but no meeting and no tabagie— a common pattern
on voyages commanded by the sieur de Mons.

Suddenly de Mons noticed the time. He had taken two weeks to reach the
Penobscot River, which was only two days' sail from Sainte-Croix. A third of
his provisions were gone, and he had not covered the ground of the last cruise.
Abruptly he picked up the pace. They left Owl's Head on July 1, 1605, and
made twenty-five leagues in one day to the Kennebec River.[44] Here at last they
reached the place where the last voyage had ended, and Champlain's narrative
became more detailed. He explored the mouth of the Kennebec, and charted
its islands and channels. They met two canoes of Indians who were hunting
swans and geese. The French asked the woman of Panounias to "explain the
reason of our coming."[45]

The Indians offered to take them upstream to meet their chief and led them
through an astonishing maze of meandering channels that connect three major
rivers in mid-coast Maine: the Kennebec (by the modern town of Bath), the

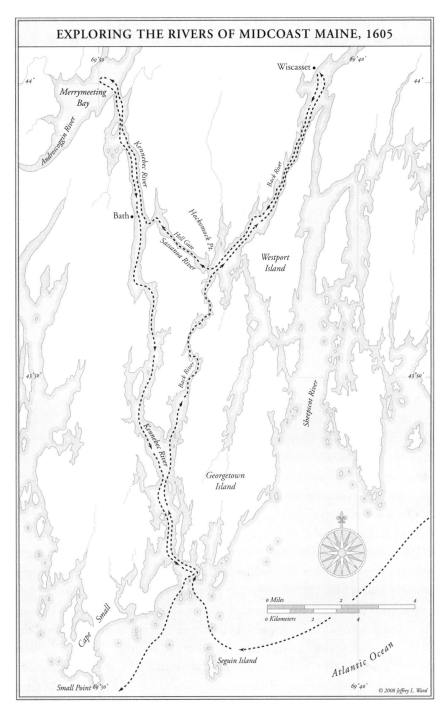

EXPLORING THE RIVERS OF MIDCOAST MAINE, 1605

Wiscasset

Merrymeeting Bay

Androscoggin River

Kennebec River

Back River

Bath

Hockomock Pt.

Hell Gate

Sassanoa River

Westport Island

Back River

Sheepscot River

Kennebec River

Georgetown Island

Cape Small

Seguin Island

Atlantic Ocean

Small Point

0 Miles   2   4
0 Kilometers   2   4

© 2008 Jeffrey L. Ward

The track of Champlain and the sieur de Mons, July 1–8, 1605.

Sheepscot to the east (Wiscasset), and the Androscoggin River to the west (Brunswick). The Indians led the French eastward from the Kennebec through a passage called the Back River, which was easy for a canoe but difficult for a patache.[46] They emerged on the Sheepscot River near Wiscasset, and a sagamore they called Manthoumermer came to greet them in a canoe. The woman of Panounias talked with him, and the sagamore "made a speech, in which he expressed pleasure at seeing us, desired to have an alliance with us," and promised to send word to Indian leaders named Marchin and Sasinou, whom he called "chief of the Kennebec."

The sieur de Mons responded with small gifts of hardtack and dried peas, but again there was no tabagie or extended discussion. De Mons did not go ashore as Champlain liked to do. He remained aboard his ship while the Indians came alongside. He seemed uncomfortable in their presence and remained at a distance, unlike Champlain who moved easily among them.[47]

The Indian guides led the French back through an even more difficult passage to the Kennebec River and what is now Merrymeeting Bay. They were to meet the river chiefs Marchin and Sasinou, but Indian leaders did not show up. Things were not going well with the Indians, and the guides gave them no explanation. De Mons was unable to establish a rapport with them or build a basis for friendship.[48]

He turned away, sailed down the Kennebec to its mouth, and turned southeast along the coast to "a broad bay in which lie a great many islands," today's Casco Bay. Champlain wrote that from a vantage point off the coast, "one sees high mountains to the west," the White Mountains in New Hampshire. They put in for the night near the present site of Portland. In the morning they continued south, exploring the coast.

On September 10, they came to a bay and small river that Champlain called Choüacoet, today's Saco. The French crossed the river bar, anchored in a deep pool, and Champlain watched with interest as "many Indians came toward us on the bank of the river and began to dance." A few hours later their chief Honemechin, arrived with two canoes "and went circling round and round our vessel." Champlain wrote that he was "good-looking, young and active," but the French were not able to communicate with him. He was of the Almouchiquois nation, and Champlain observed that their language "differs entirely from that of the Souriquois and Etchemins." Their Etchemin guide Panounias "could understand only certain words," and the Almouchiquois woman of Panounias had suddenly disappeared. Champlain does not explain why. Perhaps some misfortune befell this woman, sailing as she was in a small vessel with thirty Frenchmen who were many months from home. Possibly she

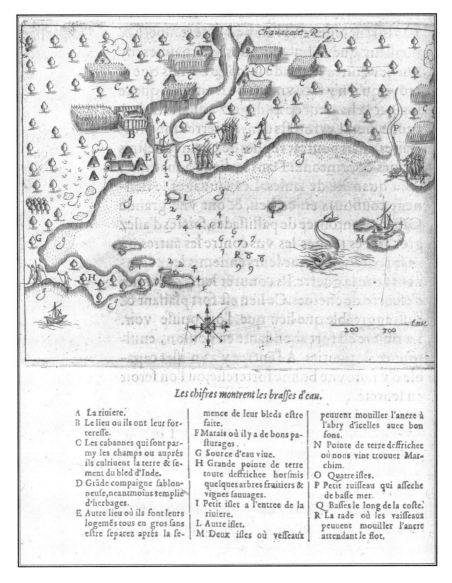

Les chifres montrent les braſſes d'eau.

A La riuiere.
B Le lieu ou ils ont leur for-
   tereſſe.
C Les cabannes qui ſont par-
   my les champs ou auprés
   ils cultiuent la terre & ſe-
   ment du bled d'Inde.
D Gräde compaigne ſablon-
   neuſe,neantmoins remplie
   d'herbages.
E Autre lieu où ils ſont leurs
   logemês tous en gros ſans
   eſtre ſeparez aprés la ſe-

mence de leur bleds eſtre
faite.
F Marais où il y a de bons pa-
   ſturages.
G Source d'eau viue.
H Grande pointe de terre
   toute deffrichee horſmis
   quelquesarbres fruitiers &
   vignes ſauuages.
I Petit iſlet a l'entree de la
   riuiere.
L Autre iſlet.
M Deux iſles où veſſeaux

peuuent mouiller l'ancre à
l'abry d'icelles auec bon
fons.
N Pointe de terre deffrichee
   où nous vint trouuer Mar-
   chim.
O Quatre iſles.
P Petit ruiſſeau qui aſſeche
   de baſſe mer.
Q Baſſes le long de la coſte.
R La rade où les vaiſſeaux
   peuuent mouiller l'ancre
   attendant le flot.

Champlain's map of the Chouacoit (Saco) River. Here the French met the Almouchiquois, a densely settled farming people. The French were unable to talk with them. De Mons was not comfortable with the Indians and moved on. There was no tabagie on the Saco River, as on the Saguenay, St. Lawrence, and Penobscot.

was weary of the voyage, or wished to visit with her own people. Whatever the reason, she was gone—and just when a translation was most needed.[49]

The Saco Indians were different from the nations to the north and east. The name Almouchiquois was not their own. It came from hunting and gathering neighbors to the north, and appears to have meant something like "dogs who raise corn." Champlain wrote, "they till and cultivate the land, a practice we had not seen previously." He went ashore and admired fields clean of weeds, with corn planted in small hills three feet apart, and bush beans that twined around the corn, with squash, pumpkins and tobacco. For tools they used "an instrument of a very hard wood in the shape of a spade," and the shells of horseshoe crabs.[50]

Champlain also described their "fixed abodes" and stocks of surplus food. He found large stores of nuts that had been harvested the previous year, and vines with "very fine berries." He observed: "The Indians remain permanently in this place, and have a large wigwam surrounded by palisades on a high bluff. This place is very pleasant and as attractive a spot as one can see everywhere." But the French could not communicate with them. They were unable to make any alliance with the Saco Indians.[51]

The French continued south to a "baye longue" between two capes and a long stretch of sand beaches on the present coast of New Hampshire.[52] At the end of the day they rounded the southern "Island Cape," which is today's Cape Ann. In the gathering darkness they found no anchorage, and kept on through the night under short sail. The next morning they found themselves in Massachusetts Bay, near the present site of Boston. The Indians were welcoming and wanted to trade. The sieur de Mons remained aboard ship and sent Champlain ashore to talk with the Indians. Champlain gave "each a knife," which "caused them to dance better than ever."[53]

Champlain tried to communicate with them, and with signs and sketches he began to have success. He took a piece of charcoal and drew a sketch of the Long Bay and Cape Ann. With gestures he asked the Indians "to show me how the coast trended." They took the same piece of charcoal and sketched "another bay which they represented as very large. Here they placed six pebbles at equal intervals giving me to understand each marked a chief and a people," all of the Massachusetts nation. The Indians drew a large stream and small inlet, which are today's Charles River and Boston's Back Bay.[54]

Champlain continued to communicate with the Indians by sign language for several hours. He took a professional interest in their boats, observing that Indians south of Cape Ann used *pirogues*, or dugouts, made from solid tree trunks by "burning and scraping with stones, which they use in place of knives." Champlain appears to have tried his hand at steering a dugout, and found it "very liable to upset unless one is very skilled." One imagines him struggling to stay upright as the Indians looked on with amusement.[55]

A good feeling was beginning to grow, but de Mons decided to move on. They sailed seven or eight leagues, anchored near an island in Massachusetts

Bay, and saw "many columns of smoke along the coast and many Indians who came running to see us." Champlain was surprised by their numbers and observed, "These places are more populous than the others we have seen." The French sent a canoe with small gifts of knives and biscuits, but Champlain wrote sadly, "We could not learn the name of their chief because we did not understand their language." [56]

The following day, July 17, they left Massachusetts Bay without making effective contact. Champlain's account betrayed an air of growing frustration. They sailed south to Scituate, and on to Brant Point, where more Indians in dugout canoes came to greet them. Champlain wrote that they showed "great signs of joy." A chief appeared and Champlain understood his name as Honabetha: "We received the chief very kindly and gave him good food." He reciprocated with "little squashes as big as your fist, which we ate as a salad like cucumbers and they were very good." After that exchange, communications failed yet again. [57] The next day they sailed around a "long cape" now called the Gurnet and entered Plymouth Bay. Once again Champlain remarked on the large number of wigwams and gardens. They passed big Indian dugouts that were returning from cod fishing off the coast. The Indians caught them easily on bone hooks tied with hemp. Here again Champlain wrote that many Indians "treated us kindly," but they did not meet at length and could not talk together. [58]

The French headed south toward the great sandy peninsula that they named White Cape; we call it Cape Cod. Champlain described the waters of its bay as very clear, and the cape itself as covered with beautiful woods, "very delightful and pleasant to the eye." [59] The next day, July 20, they sailed around the outer banks of the cape, facing the Atlantic Ocean. Near its elbow, they came to "a bay with wigwams bordering it all around." They entered a small harbor and found it "a very dangerous port on account of shoals and sandbanks, where we saw breakers on every side," and a treacherous bar at the harbor's mouth. Champlain named it Mallebarre, Bad Bar. It is today's Nauset.

Champlain wrote that Indian "men and women came at us from all sides dancing." He observed: "All these Indians from the Island Cape (Cape Ann) southward wear no skins or furs except very rarely; their clothes are made from grass and hemp, and barely cover their bodies and come down only to their thighs. The men and women have their privy parts covered by a small skin . . . the rest of the body is naked." He thought that they were a beautiful people, and well groomed: "I saw, among other things, a girl with her hair quite neatly done up by means of a skin dyed red and trimmed on the upper part with little shell beads." [60]

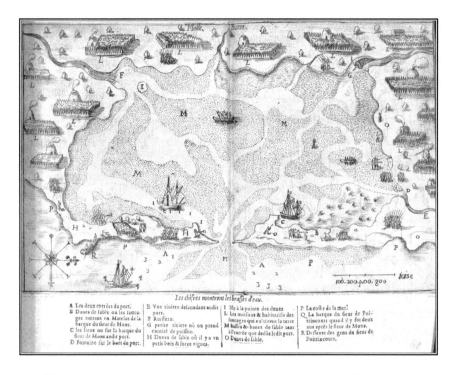

Mallebarre, now Nauset harbor on Cape Cod. Here again, de Mons was unable to establish a rapport with the Indians. Discomfort gave rise to suspicion, which grew into hostility. Fighting broke out between the French and Indians, and appears on this chart.

The next day, the sieur de Mons "resolved to go and inspect their settlement, and nine or ten of us accompanied him with our arms," in a manner very different from Champlain's way. De Mons and his men-at-arms marched about a league along the coast through fields planted in corn which was in flower, about five and a half feet high. The fields were very fertile, and full of tobacco, beans, and squash in great variety. The French helped themselves to the crops without asking permission.[61] Perhaps at the urging of de Mons, Champlain asked the Indians by sign language if they had much snow in the winter. The Indians explained by gestures that "the harbor never froze over" and "snow fell to a depth of about a foot." Champlain noted: "We were unable to ascertain whether the snow lasted a long time. I consider however that the country is temperate and the winter not severe." The sieur de Mons and his men began to talk among themselves, and "the question was opened whether settlement of Acadia should not begin somewhere to the South."[62]

At first the Indians had been friendly, but now the tone began to change.

The French had come armed as if for war. They took the Indians' crops without asking and behaved as if they owned the country. Distrust began to grow. On July 23, 1605, a watering party of French sailors went ashore with large metal pots that were very attractive to the Indians. As the French began to fill them, an Indian ran forward and "snatched one by force." A sailor gave chase but could not catch him. Other Indians came forward in what the French thought a menacing way. The sailors turned and sprinted toward their ship, "shouting to fire our muskets at the Indians who gathered in large numbers." Several Indians were visiting aboard the French ship. They "hurled themselves into the sea," and swam for their lives. The French seized one of them and made him a captive. On the beach, the Indians turned against the sailor whose kettle they had taken, shot a volley of arrows, brought him down, and "finished him with their knives." [63]

Champlain was aboard the ship. He rallied the crew and "made haste to go ashore," weapons in hand. To save the watering party, they laid down covering fire at the Indians. Champlain aimed his weapon and fired. It exploded in his hands and he wrote that it "nearly killed me." The Indians, "hearing this fusillade, again took to flight." The French ran in pursuit but found "no likelihood of catching them, for they are as swift afoot as horses." The watering party was rescued and the dead sailor was buried. He had been a carpenter from Saint-Malo.[64]

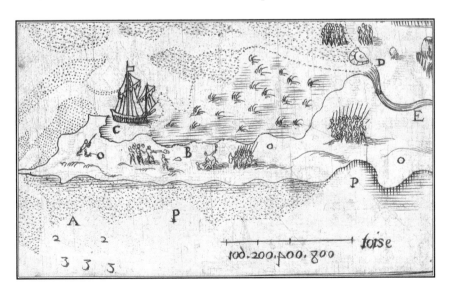

Detail of the fight between de Mons' men and the Nauset Indians on Cape Cod. Here Indian warriors killed a French carpenter. Champlain led an armed party in a vain attempt to rescue him, as other Indians arrived in strength. The Fench vessel is a two-masted barque.

The Indians gathered in the distance, and the French raised their weapons, but the sieur de Mons "ordered them not to fire, as the murderers had fled." He also ordered the release of their Indian captive as "he was not to blame."[65] With difficulty de Mons was able to control his men, but here again he could not communicate with the Indians. Anger and distrust continued to grow on both sides. Even Champlain was caught up in it. He wrote, "One must be on one's guard against these people and mistrust them." It was a sad day for the French leaders. They mourned the loss of their comrade. Another casualty was Champlain's dream of harmony with the Indians, which failed totally at Mallebarre.[66]

The Indians were now openly hostile, and made clear that the French should go. On July 25, 1605, de Mons ordered his men to get underway. They sailed out to sea, keeping well clear of Massachusetts, as signal fires behind them began to send columns of smoke along the coast. They stopped at Saco and again at Kennebec, hoping to find Chief Sassinou, but again he did not appear. They met another Indian named Anassou, bartered furs with him, and they were able to communicate. He brought more bad tidings. Champlain wrote: "He told us that ten leagues from [the Kennebec] there was a ship engaged in the fishery, and that those on board under cover of friendship had killed five Indians from this river. From his description we judged that they were English." This was George Weymouth's English ship *Archangel.* The five Indians had not been killed, but kidnapped with their weapons and canoes.[67]

The Indians of New England were now on their guard, and with reason. On another voyage to Maine by Martin Pring in 1603, the English brought "two excellent mastiffs." An English explorer wrote, "When we would be rid of the savages' company, we would let loose the mastiffs and suddenly with outcries they would flee away." All this opened an opportunity for the French if they could distinguish themselves from the English, but the misadventure at Mallebarre had blurred that difference.[68]

De Mons and his weary men made their way back to Sainte-Croix Island. They had achieved none of their goals. The sieur de Mons, for all his spirit of humanity, had not been able to work well with the Indians. He had found several sites for settlement, but the Indians turned against him. Many factors were involved: the language barrier and English predators, to name but two. Another major problem was de Mons' approach to the Indians. He was insecure among them. To the natives, his distance and discomfort appeared hostile and threatening—more so than he intended. An attitude of humanity alone was not enough.

• • •

A third French voyage to Norumbega followed in 1606, with the sieur de Poutrincourt in command. He was a nobleman of high rank, a soldier of proven courage, a Catholic of deep piety, and a gentleman who treated others with kindness. But he had a weakness as a leader. At critical moments his men did not follow him and refused to obey his orders. It had happened in the fall of 1604 when he commanded the company's ships on a voyage home to France. They had a rough passage, and in the English Channel were almost wrecked on the Casquets. Poutrincourt ordered the crew to help him "shift the sails." They refused. A friend of Poutrincourt wrote that "only two or three of them did so." [69]

It happened again in September 1606, when Poutrincourt led the third voyage along the coast of New England, once again in search of sites for settlement. He proposed to use a barque of the same size as before, but she was not in good repair. Others warned that the barque was unseaworthy, but Poutrincourt was not one for waiting. He decided to make repairs underway and took along the shipwright Champdoré, several artisans, a "store of planks," and a shallop. [70]

Without listening to advice, Poutrincourt decided he would sail westnorthwest from Port-Royal to Sainte-Croix Island, and then work his way south. Champlain thought it was "not a wise decision." He suggested, "It would have been more to the purpose, in my opinion, to cross from where we were to Mallebarre, by the route which we knew, and then to employ the time in exploring to the 40th degree or farther south, revisiting on our return the entire coast at our leisure." But Poutrincourt's plan prevailed. [71] They sailed on September 5, 1606, and got off to a very slow start. Several stops were needed to repair the leaking barque, and Poutrincourt made a long diversion to Sainte-Croix. They were sixteen days getting to Saco. Champlain wrote, "We lost much time in going over again the discoveries that the sieur de Mons had made." [72]

At Saco, Poutrincourt brought together three powerful Indian leaders: the Souriquois chief Messamouet, and the Almouchiquois chiefs Onemechin and Marchin. They had long been blood enemies, and Champlain thought it was not a good idea. When these wily old foes met, the French lost control of events. Messamouet made a speech appealing for peace, and then continued the hostilities in a war of gifts. [73] With a dramatic flourish he threw trade goods worth more than 300 crowns into Onemechin's canoe. Onemechin gave in return gifts of corn, squash, and beans, which Messamouet openly despised as not of equal value. Onemechin released a Souriquois prisoner, but gave the captive to Poutrincourt and not to Messamouet. That gift was taken as an insult, in the way it was given. Tone and gesture were of high importance in that world. The chiefs were now angrier than ever, and they parted with a determination to make war. Champlain watched it go wrong, but Poutrincourt insisted that he alone could speak for the French. Perhaps Champlain could have done no better, but an opportunity was lost.[74]

After that meeting the French departed, sailing southwest to the Island Cape (Cape Ann), and entered an excellent harbor that they called Beauport. It is the site of Gloucester, Massachusetts. Hundreds of Indians gathered and appeared friendly, but things went wrong again. French presents were spurned. An Indian with a wounded foot refused treatment by the French, with expressions of distrust. The French gave a gift of grape juice and the Indians spat it out "thinking . . . that it was poison."[75]

The next day some of the French crew were doing laundry ashore, while others were mending their leaky barque. Poutrincourt caught sight of "a great many Indians" in the woods with weapons in hands. They appeared to be sneaking toward the French who were washing clothes, "with the intention

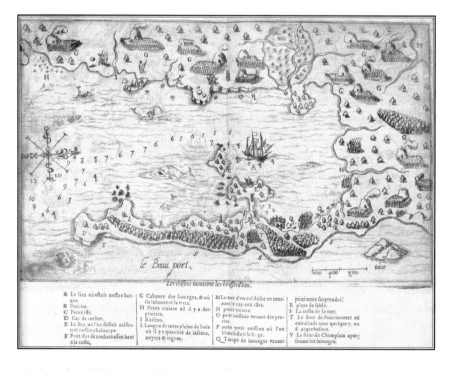

In September 1606, Poutrincourt led a third cruise. They found a handsome harbor and called it Beauport (now Gloucester, Massachusetts). Hundreds of Indians gathered, and Champlain began to make contact, but Poutrincourt approached with arquebusiers, and Indians fled, "fearing some bad turn." The French departed in haste.

of doing us some injury." Champlain ran alone to intercept them. They received him well, and began to dance. He asked them to dance some more, which they did, putting their arms inside a circle, and tensions diminished. Suddenly the Indians saw Poutrincourt marching toward them with a file of musketeers, and "withdrew in all directions, being apprehensive lest some bad turn should be done to them." Here were two French approaches to the Indians. Champlain's worked; Poutrincourt's failed. Tensions began to rise again.[76] The French learned that a hundred canoes were approaching with six hundred men. Poutrincourt ordered a hasty departure. They put out to sea, and sailed all night. By dawn they were in Cape Cod Bay, where they explored the inner cape, and Champlain admired the cultivated landscape of cornfields, meadows, beautiful beaches, small coves, and fine stands of trees.[77] They found "a good safe harbor," with "plenty of oysters of very good quality," and named it Port-aux-Huistres. It is today's Wellfleet, and the oysters are still of "very good quality."

After a brief visit they left the bay, rounded Cape Cod, and sailed south along its Atlantic coast to its outer elbow. There they found a harbor called Port-Fortuné, now Stage Harbor in the town of Chatham. The harbor mouth was barely deep enough to float their ship. They scraped bottom on a shoal and damaged their rudder, but they found their way to an anchorage. Champlain was impressed by the density of Indian settlement and deeply interested in their way of life. "Regarding their polity, government and religious belief," he wrote, "they have chiefs whom they obey in regard to matters of warfare but not in anything else. The chiefs work, and assume no higher rank than their companions. Each possesses only sufficient land for his own support."[78]

Champlain thought that the region was very suitable for a colony, but trouble developed with the Indians. Poutrincourt decided to stay a while. He showed no sign of leaving and appeared to be settling in. The French built an oven on the beach, gathered firewood without permission, and began to bake bread. In the harbor, shipwright Champdoré repaired the damaged rudder while Champlain surveyed the anchorage and made a chart. Each day Poutrincourt went ashore with a heavily armed party of ten or fifteen musketeers and marched through the countryside. He entered Indian villages and "passed among their wigwams, where there were a number of women, and gave them bracelets and rings."[79]

The French began to notice columns of white smoke rising on the coast. Champlain wrote: "Some eight or nine days later, on the sieur de Poutrincourt's going out walking as he had done before, we observed that the Indians were taking down their wigwams and sending their wives and children into

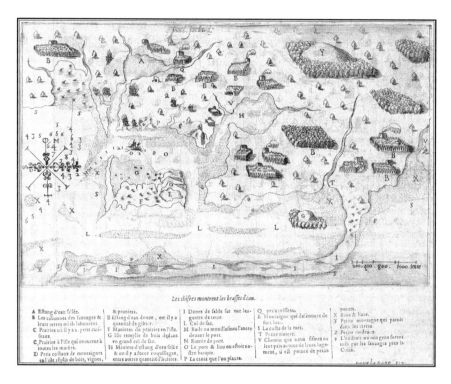

*Poutrincourt sailed south to Cape Cod and entered Port Fortune (now Stage Harbor in the town of Chatham).
Here Champlain made another chart and mapped the many Indian settlements, but more trouble followed.*

the woods, along with provisions and other necessaries of life. . . . That made us suspect some evil design."[80] Every day Poutrincourt continued to march his musketeers four to five leagues through the Indian settlements. As tensions continued to rise, he sent two men ahead with swords drawn, and instructed them to engage in mock swordplay, a source of puzzlement to the Indians. He also ordered demonstrations of musketry and showed that bullets could penetrate a log. All this was meant to overawe the Indians. It succeeded only in alarming them. Champlain noted that "when passing near us they trembled for fear lest we should harm them."[81]

On October 14, 1606, Poutrincourt came ashore yet again. This time he erected a cross, which the Indians perceived as a symbol of possession. He put up crosses frequently without asking. Champlain did so less often, usually by permission, and he invited Indians to participate. Tensions were mounting dangerously. Poutrincourt issued standing orders that "all things should be in readiness" to repel an attack, and all the French should come aboard the barque at night. Once again his men refused to obey him. A party of four remained on the beach, tending the oven. Three defied Poutrincourt's orders to return aboard. Two others also disobeyed their commander and left the ship to join the beach party. Champlain was shocked by their defiance, "despite remonstrances made to them on the risks they were running and the disobedience they were showing to their chief." [82]

Early the next morning, October 15, 1606, a scouting party of Indians crept up to the French on the beach, found most of them asleep and one tending the fire. "Seeing them in this condition," Champlain wrote, "Indians to the number of 400 came quietly over the little hill" and attacked the Frenchmen. They "shot such a salvo of arrows at them as to give them no chance. All the men were hit by arrows. They struggled to their feet and retreated toward the barque, shouting 'Help! Help! They are killing us!'" [83]

Two Frenchmen died on the beach, and a third in the water. A fourth was mortally wounded, and a fifth struggled out to the barque with an arrow in his chest. A sentry on the barque shouted, "To arms! To arms! They are killing our men." The crew boiled out of the hold, and fifteen or sixteen went ashore in the shallop. Their leaders were Champlain, Robert Gravé, Daniel Hay, the apothecary Hébert, the surgeon, a trumpeter, Poutrincourt himself, and his son Biencourt de Poutrincourt. [84]

The Indians fled. Champlain wrote, "All we could do was carry off the bodies and bury them near the cross." One of the dead Frenchmen was found with a small dog on his back, both shot by the same arrow. The dead Frenchmen were laid into the ground with their shirts for winding sheets. During the burial, the Indians "did dance and howl a-far off." [85] The French went back to their vessels, and three hours later the Indians returned. The French fired at them. Champlain wrote: "Whenever they heard the report they threw themselves flat on the ground to avoid the charge. In derision they pulled down the cross, and dug up the bodies, which displeased us greatly and made us go after them a second time." The bodies were reburied and Indians dug them up again, and "turning their backs toward the ship, they threw sand with their two hands betwixt their buttocks in derision, howling like wolves." There was desperate talk of seizing captives and binding them with chains of rosary beads! The French baited a trap, but the Indians were old hands at this game. They trapped the French instead, and killed several more of them.

Finally, on October 16, 1606, Poutrincourt ordered his men to weigh anchor and they sailed away, steering south toward Nantucket Sound. Once out of sight from the land, he ordered a change of course and they headed north. Trouble continued to dog them, and they suffered more misadventures at sea. Their shallop bucked and surged at the end of a towline, and smashed

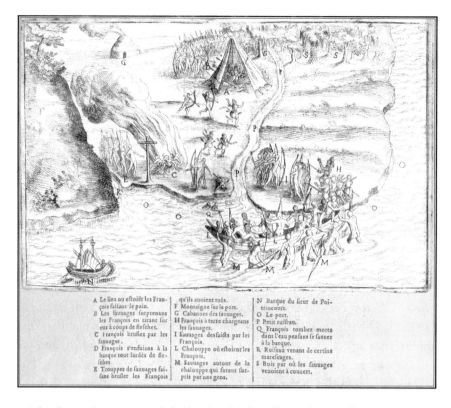

A Le lieu ou eſtoiēt les François faiſans le pain.
B Les ſauuages ſurprenans
  les François en tirant ſur
  eux à coups de fleſches.
C François bruſlez par les
  ſauuages.
D François s'enfuians à la
  barque tout lardés de fie-
  ſches.
E Trouppes de ſauuages faiſans bruſler les François

qu'ils auoient tués.
F Montaigne ſur le port.
G Cabannes des ſauuages.
H François à terre chargeans
  les ſauuages.
I Sauuages desfaicts par les
  François.
L Chalouppe où eſtoient les
  François.
M Sauuages autour de la
  chalouppe qui furent ſur-
  pris par nos gens,

N Barque du ſieur de Poi-
  trincourt.
O Le port.
P Petit ruiſſeau.
Q François tombez morts
  dans l'eau penſans ſe ſauuer
  à la barque.
R Ruiſſeau venant de certins
  mareſcages.
S Bois par où les ſauuages
  venoient à couuert.

At Port Fortune, Poutrincourt marched soldiers through Indian villages, took crops without permission, and
raised a cross without leave, and the Indians were not happy. Poutrincourt responded with a show of force,
which provoked an attack on October 15, 1606. The French lost many men—and a region of North America.

the rudder of the barque. Champdoré managed another miraculous repair at
sea, and they got back to Port-Royal.

Here were three voyages by three French leaders, with three very different results. Champlain, de Mons, and Poutrincourt had many of the same values
and purposes. All shared a genuine ideal of humanity, and wanted very much
to establish good relations with the natives. But when they actually met the
Indians, they conducted themselves in different ways.

Champlain's first voyage to Norumbega in 1604 repeated the success at
Tadoussac in 1603. He approached the Indians with only a few men, and
made no display of weapons (though his men were armed and ready on their
ship). He sat down with the Indians in another tabagie, took an interest in
their ways, honored their customs, and treated them with respect. They re-

After the voyages of de Mons and Poutrincourt, the French turned north to Acadia and the British became more active to south. Bartholomew Gosnold (in this de Bry engraving) explored the coast and planted a post on Cutty-hunk Island in 1602. Thirty British settlements followed by 1625, and Norumbega became New England.

sponded in the same spirit, with warmth and trust that grew on both sides. Together they formed an alliance that lasted for many years.

De Mons' results in 1605 were mixed at best: a slow beginning, lack of focus, failed communications, and loss of rapport with the Indians. There were no tabagies or other meetings. He kept his distance and seemed unsure of the Indians. They perceived his distance as arrogance and his insecurity as enmity. The result was growing fear and hostility that compounded on itself. It ended in a needless fight.

Poutrincourt's relations with the Indians were a disaster. He could not control his men and alienated the Indian nations of Norumbega. He was fearful of them and insensitive to their feelings. Poutrincourt went among the Indians heavily armed, marched his men across their lands without warning, took crops from their fields without permission, and erected crosses that were perceived as emblems of possession. The Indians became deeply distrustful of his intentions. As things began to go wrong, Poutrincourt responded with a stronger show of force. He ordered his men to unsheathe their swords and fire their weapons in a demonstration of power. The Indians were terrified of him, literally trembling with fear. They sent away their women and children, and suddenly attacked. The result was a total rupture of relations.

These failures put an end to French colonization south of the Penobscot River and marked the beginning of English hegemony in this region. But with Champlain's success north of the Penobscot, a new leader emerged in New France. His way of working with the Indians made the difference.

10.

PORT-ROYAL

A Model Colony Fails at Home, 1605–07

> These people called savages . . . are men like ourselves. . . . They have
> courage, fidelity, generosity, humanity, and their hospitality is so innate
> and praiseworthy that they receive among them every man who is not
> an enemy. They are not simpletons like many people over here; they
> speak with much judgment and good sense.
>
> —Marc Lescarbot on the Indians of Acadia [1]

IN THE SPRING OF 1605, the sieur de Mons decided to move his settlement
from Sainte-Croix Island. The new site was Port-Royal, near the present
town of Annapolis Royal in Nova Scotia. It was (and is) a beautiful setting, with a magnificent harbor. The soil in this part of Acadia is fertile, and
the winters are more temperate than on Sainte-Croix Island. One French visitor wrote, "No earthly paradise could be more agreeable than this place." [2]

Most important, the Indians were friendly. The Mi'kmaq (Champlain's
Souriquois) wanted close trading relations and an alliance against their enemies. They welcomed the French settlers, wanted them to found a colony
there, and gave much vital assistance. One settler wrote, "We were not, as it
were, marooned on an island, as was M. de Villegagnon in Brazil, for this nation loves the French, and would if necessary take up arms, one and all, to aid
them." [3]

Once de Mons made his decision to resettle at Port-Royal, his small band
of colonists went to work with a will. "The time being short," Champlain
wrote, "we fitted out two barques, which we loaded with the woodwork of the
Sainte Croix, to transport it to Port-Royal twenty-five leagues distant." Every
structure was dismantled except the storehouse, which was too big to move.
Many trips were needed to carry the buildings across the bay. [4]

The sieur de Mons stayed in Port-Royal until "everything had been set in
order," and then he hurried home to France. The colony had powerful enemies
at court, and rival merchants were challenging his monopoly. His own investors were growing restless. After the winter at Sainte-Croix, the tropics seemed

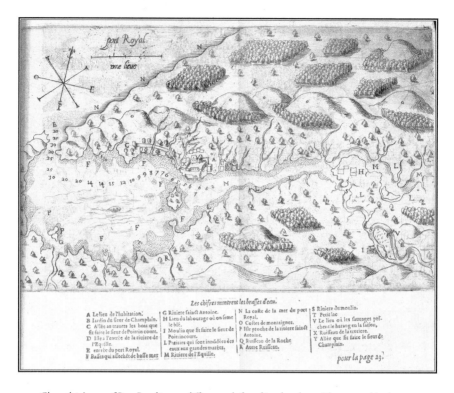

Champlain's map of Port-Royal is on a different scale from his other charts. The protected harbor was fifteen miles long, the soil was more fertile, the climate was less severe than Sainte-Croix, and the Mi'kmaq nation very welcoming.

more attractive for settlement. In the summer of 1605, Henri IV was thinking seriously about planting a French colony between Portuguese Brazil and New Spain. He appointed a soldier named Daniel de la Revardière to be lieutenant general for the territory from the Amazon to Trinidad.[5]

New France was in danger at home, and de Mons needed to "obtain from His Majesty what was necessary for his enterprise." To that end, he carried back many gifts in the hope of reviving the king's interest in North America. The most striking present was a big birchbark canoe, thirty feet long and stained bright red. It was launched on the River Seine by returning sailors, who paddled past the Louvre at "an incredible speed," much to the pleasure of the king and the delight of the little Dauphin, four years old, who would become Louis XIII. Other presents included a baby moose (six months old and already "as big as a horse"), a caribou (the first recorded use of that word), a muskrat (*rat musqué*, they called it), a huge set of moose antlers, a living hummingbird, a collection of dead birds, plus bows and arrows, Indian portraits, and other marvels for the royal collection.[6]

Before he left Acadia, the sieur de Mons appointed an acting lieutenant to govern Acadia in his absence. His first choice had been the sieur d'Orville, a French nobleman who was still suffering the effects of scurvy and unable to serve. Next in line was Pont-Gravé, who took the job.[7] Champlain could have gone home with de Mons, but he wanted to stay at Port-Royal in the hope of "making new discoveries towards Florida." The sieur de Mons "highly approved," and Champlain received many privileges as well as strong support for his explorations.[8]

The settlement of Port-Royal rapidly took form. Champlain made a sketch and described its plan as a tight rectangle, sixty feet long and forty-eight feet wide. He called it the fort. These men were always thinking of military defense—not against Indians but European attackers. Their experience of incessant war at home inspired a habitual sense of insecurity.[9] The settlement at Port-Royal resembled a fortified farming hamlet in France. It stood on the crest of a low hill, completely enclosed by outer walls nearly two hundred feet in circumference. At one corner of the rectangle, the builders added a projecting bastion with four guns that commanded the anchorage and covered two walls of the fort. At another corner, a log platform of similar design protected the gate and a third wall.[10]

The interior was carefully planned to maintain social rank and internal order. Standing alone at the northern corner of the fort was an elegant little house with a high-hipped roof and "handsome woodwork." This was the same building that had been prefabricated in France, and erected for the sieur de Mons on Sainte-Croix Island. At Port-Royal it became the residence of Pont-Gravé and Champlain. These old friends lived comfortably together, and their harmony set a tone for the settlement.

Next to their house on the northwestern side was a row of smaller dwellings for officers of rank. The Catholic priest and Protestant pastor lived there, the surgeon Deschamps, and the skilled shipwright Champdoré. On the southwest was a dormitory for artisans.[11] To the southeast was the bakery, kitchen, blacksmith shop, and a "maisonette" for small boats and rigging. Probably some of the laborers and servants slept in the kitchen, bakery and smithy, which would have been warm in the winter. On the northeast side was the vital *magasin*, a storehouse with a "very fine cellar, five or six feet deep" that held the colony's stock of wine, cider, grain, and other provisions. The end closest to the commander's house may have served as an armory and barracks

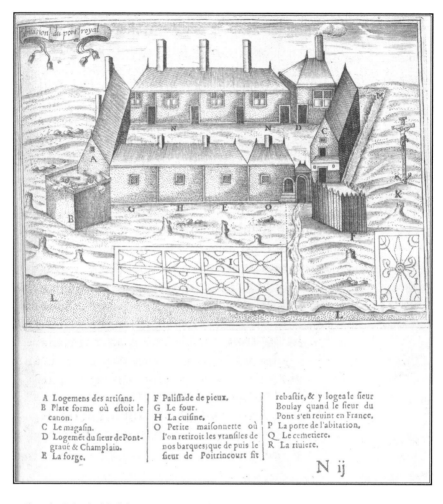

A Logemens des artifans.
B Plate forme où eſtoit le
    canon.
C Le magaſin.
D Logemét du ſieur de Pont-
    graué & Champlain.
E La forge.

F Paliſſade de pieux.
G Le four.
H La cuiſine.
O Petite maiſonnette où
    l'on retiroit les vtanſiles de
    nos barques;que de puis le
    ſieur de Poitrincourt ſit

rebaſtir, & y logea le ſieur
Boulay quand le ſieur du
Pont s'en reuint en France.
P La porte de l'abitation.
Q Le cemetiere.
R La riuiere.

N ij

Champlain's sketch of the habitation at Port-Royal, ca. 1605–06, shows a fortified settlement surrounded by fertile gardens on rising ground above the harbor. It was a highly successful colony—until its funding failed in France.

for the small detachment of Swiss soldiers who were billeted between officers and "other ranks," much like marines aboard warships.[12]

Pont-Gravé kept the colonists at work on the settlement, urging them to make the fort weather-tight before winter. He was a driver, but not unpopular with the men. They admired his large spirit even as they feared his temper. Lescarbot wrote, "M. du Pont was not a man to sit still, nor allow his people to remain idle."[13] After the buildings went up, the colonists cleared the outer grounds and created something like a protective *glacis* around the fort.

A year later, a visitor described Port-Royal as "almost wholly surrounded by meadows."[14]

Champlain and Pont-Gravé began to make gardens outside the fort. They encouraged all the colonists to till individual plots for their own gain. Champlain himself loved gardening and worked with his servants to prepare the ground. His purpose was to experiment with various crops, as he did wherever he went in New France. At Port-Royal, he tells us, he "sowed there some seeds which throve well; and . . . took therein particular pleasure, although beforehand it had entailed a great deal of labor."

Champlain surrounded his garden with "channels full of water, wherein I placed some very fine trout; and through it flowed three brooks of very clear running water, from which the greater part of the settlement was supplied. I constructed near the seashore a little sluiceway, to draw off the water whenever I desired." His servants added "a small reservoir to hold salt-water fish, which we took out as we required them."[15]

He made a particular effort to attract birds into his garden, and they swarmed around him. He wrote happily, "The little birds thereabouts received pleasure from this; for they gathered in great numbers, and warbled and chirped so pleasantly that I do not think I ever heard the like." Near his garden, stream, and fishpond, Champlain constructed a small "cabinet" or gazebo where he could work at his maps and papers or talk with Pont-Gravé and his friends. "We often resorted there to pass the time," he recalled.[16]

One day Champlain and Pont-Gravé were discussing the king's interest in minerals. A Breton seaman named Prévert had earlier reported a deposit of copper at the Port of Mines. Champlain and the sieur de Mons had made a quick search the year before, without success. In the fall of 1605, Pont-Gravé agreed that Champlain might have a look, with maître Jacques, one of the miners from Slavonia.[17]

They took a barque across the Baie Française to the Saint John River, in search of the Etchemin sagamore Secoudon, Champlain's friend and Prévert's guide. "Having found him," Champlain wrote, "I begged him to come with us. He willingly agreed, and showed us the way." Together they went to the Port of Mines and found "several small pieces of copper as thick as a *sou*, embedded in grayish and red rocks." Maître Jacques also discovered veins of "rose copper." Its exceptional purity was a sign of large deposits, but the tide covered the site twice a day. While the miner was chipping away with his hammer, Champlain went out of his way to meet Indian leaders, and cultivated relationships by working with them. That constant effort was important to his success.[18]

When Champlain returned to Port-Royal, where forty-five settlers were preparing for the winter, he was shocked to discover that some of them were already showing symptoms of scurvy. Everyone remembered the horror of the past year and looked ahead with deep foreboding. Fortunately, the first snow did not fall until December 20, two months later than at Sainte-Croix. Small floes of ice came down the river past the Port-Royal settlement, but to their relief, "the winter was not so severe as it had been the year before, nor was the snow as deep, or of as long duration."[19]

The settlement had a sufficiency of grain and dried provisions, and this time Champlain got fresh game from the Indians. But as the winter wore on, scurvy began to spread again. The toll was not as terrible as at Sainte-Croix, but still very cruel. Of forty-five colonists, twelve died from this dread disease. Five more fell very ill, and recovered only in the spring.[20]

Still, something had diminished the mortality rate from the year before. It might have been a late winter and an early spring. The Indians had good hunting and brought an abundance of fresh meat to Port-Royal. They helped in another way too. Lescarbot later wrote that they "took in one of our men, who lived with them for some six weeks in their fashion, without salt, bread, or wine, sleeping on the ground in skins, and that too in time of snow. More-over they took greater care of him, as also of others who often went with them, than of themselves, saying that if any of these died, his death would be laid at their door." Probably they also had antiscorbutic plants and herbal remedies.[21]

When spring arrived in 1606, supply ships were expected from France. They did not appear, and the settlers at Port-Royal began to run short of pro-visions. The wine gave out first, and other stocks fell short. The first month of summer came and went without any news from home. By mid-July Pont-Gravé and Champlain feared that they had barely enough food to reach the fishing coast where they could find a passage home. The settlement had two barques. The colonists crowded aboard these small vessels, all except two in-trepid Frenchmen who agreed to stay behind as caretakers of the fort.

On July 17, 1606, the settlers departed for Canso on the Atlantic coast, where they hoped to find fishermen who could help them. The first night they anchored for some reason in Long Island Strait, an entry into Baie Sainte-Marie, south of Port-Royal. It was not a wise decision. When the tide began to run, an anchor cable parted on one shallop, and they were lucky to survive. They got clear of the shore and ran into a sharp squall. High seas smashed their rudder irons. Only one man could put it right—the shipwright Champdoré, who "cleverly mended the rudder."

They sailed on, still far from Canso and very near starvation. They were on the edge of despair, when suddenly a sail appeared. She was French, and they were hailed by the familiar voice of Jean Ralluau, Mons' secretary. He reported that a supply ship had at last reached Canso with abundant provisions, fifty colonists, and a new governor with instructions to "remain in the country."

The sieur de Mons was still their leader, but he had decided to remain in France to rally support at court and work with his investors. He ordered Pont-Gravé to run commercial operations on the fishing coast, and sent out Poutrincourt as governor of Port-Royal. We have met him as commander of an ill-fated exploring mission on the coast of Norumbega.

Poutrincourt was an interesting man. He was the fourth son of an ancient noble family from Picardy in the north of France, with close connections to the Catholic House of Guise, and a record of long service to the Valois kings through the better part of three centuries.[22] His family had suffered severely in the wars of religion. Poutrincourt's two older brothers were killed in 1562 and 1569. His sister Jeanne became lady-in-waiting to Mary Queen of Scots, and was caught up in that tragedy. Poutrincourt himself fought against Henri IV, but when the new king converted to Catholicism, Poutrincourt broke with the Catholic League, and was rewarded with many offices.

In 1605 Poutrincourt was forty-eight years old. He had inherited the seigneury of Marcilly-sur-Seine, and the barony of Saint-Just on the River Marne in Champagne, but had trouble managing his property. He was also a man of broad interests and large spirit, a man of the Renaissance, a humanist with an interest in literature and the arts. Music was his passion; he was an active composer of secular and sacred works.[23]

Traveling with Poutrincourt was another extraordinary character—Marc Lescarbot, his lawyer, literary companion, and family friend. Lescarbot tells us that he had suffered a wrong at the hands of corrupt judges in Paris and decided to "flee" to Acadia as a place of refuge for those who "love justice, and hate iniquity." He was another Renaissance man—a living example of its ideal of the *uomo universale*, the universal man. Lescarbot was a poet, playwright, historian, and man of learning, steeped in humanistic values and widely read in Latin, Greek, Hebrew, Italian, and his native French. His first love was classical literature, and his dream was to emulate its glories in the modern era.[24]

Poutrincourt and Lescarbot joined the circle of humanists who had founded New France. They had much in common with de Mons and

Champlain—a passion for knowledge, a curiosity about the new world, an interest in the Indians, a vision of enlightened enterprise, a dream of humanity, a hunger for peace, a loyalty to the large spirit of Henri IV, and an abiding hope for a greater France in North America. They also enlarged this circle by contributing their own purposes, which were not the same as those of de Mons and Champlain. Like others in New France, they were dreamers too, but they dreamed of other things.

Lescarbot was drawn to Acadia as a field for literature. With much encouragement from Poutrincourt and the sieur de Mons, he hoped to be the Virgil of this colonizing venture, and sought to compose an Acadian *Aeneid* in modern poetry and prose. When he went to join his ship, he withdrew from the others, "keeping at times a little apart from the company," and wrote a long poem called "Adieu à la France." It cleverly combined deep nostalgia for the old world with high anticipation for the new—the mood of many immigrants to American shores. Lescarbot had it printed in La Rochelle and remembered with pride that it was received with "much applause." [25]

Poutrincourt had yet another vision of Acadia. He hoped to found a feudal utopia in the new world, which he and his family could rule in a benevolent way, for the good of the whole. Poutrincourt asked the sieur de Mons for a grant of land at Port-Royal, proposing "to live there, and to establish his family and his fortune, and the name of God above all." De Mons agreed, and on February 25, 1606, Henri IV granted Poutrincourt "the seigneury of Port-Royal and adjacent lands." In return, he was required to plant a colony within two years. [26]

Poutrincourt recruited about fifty colonists. Half of them can be identified by name or occupation. Once again they were highly stratified by social rank, as in France itself. At the top were a tight circle of family and friends: Poutrincourt himself, his son Charles de Poutrincourt de Biencourt, and their cousins from the barony of Saint-Just in Champagne; Claude Turgis de Sainte-Étienne et de la Tour, and his son Charles de Saint-Étienne de la Tour, who would become leading figures in the history of Acadia. Also in that circle was Poutrincourt's cousin-german from Paris, Louis Hébert, a master of pharmacy who came from a family of prosperous merchant-apothecaries and spice dealers. [27]

Other gentlemen and officers included Jean Ralluau, secretary to sieur de Mons. Also welcomed to the expedition was Robert Gravé, son of Champlain's friend Pont-Gravé. This young man was "favoured with a splendid physique, good looks, and an alert, practical intelligence." He was a free spirit who went his own way and quarreled with Poutrincourt, but in the end they got along. [28]

Three officers chose to remain from the year before: Samuel Champlain, the shipwright Pierre Angibault called Champdoré, and the sieur de Boullay, a captain in Poutrincourt's regiment.[29]

These men of rank had a large number of servants who were rarely mentioned by name. Poutrincourt had a valet named Estienne. Champlain had several "lackeys." He scarcely ever referred to them by name—a common attitude among gentlemen-humanists in the early modern era.

Below the gentlemen were skilled artisans who worked with their hands, such as the surgeon Estienne and the locksmith Jean Duval. Poutrincourt also enlisted many young journeymen. At least three journeyman carpenters received contracts and three journeyman woodcutters signed on for one year and were paid 100 livres.[30] At the bottom were the unskilled laborers. Lescarbot regarded them as a wild bunch. "I do not wish to rank all of them in this category," he wrote, "for some among them were quiet and respectful." But many were turbulent characters. At La Rochelle before they sailed, Lescarbot remembered, "Our workmen, who received twenty sous per day, played marvelous pranks in the Saint Nicolas Quarter where they lodged . . . some were made prisoners and kept in the town hall until departure."[31]

Even in a small ship or a close-built colony, a great distance separated the gentlemen from other men. Marc Lescarbot's classical humanism embraced the Indians, but not these lowest orders of Frenchmen. "The common people is a queer beast," he wrote in a casual way that denied their humanity and individuality in a single phrase. "In this connection," he added, "I remember the so-called Peasants' War, in the midst of which I once found myself when I was in Quercy. It was the most bizarre thing in the world to see this clutter of folk all wearing wooden shoes, whence they had got the name of Clackers, because their shoes, hobnailed behind and before, went clack at every step. This motley mob would hear of neither rhyme nor reason. Everybody was master."

The gentlemen of New France had no sympathy for "clackers," and none at all for democracy or equality. They were quicker to recognize the humanity of the Indians than that of their own servants and laborers—an attitude that Champlain shared.[32]

This hierarchy of orders and estates was transplanted to Acadia, but not without change. Some men of humble rank rose rapidly in the new world. Daniel Hay, a carpenter, won honor through repeated acts of valor. Lescarbot celebrated him as a man "whose pleasure it is to display his courage among the dangers of the deep." Champlain praised his bravery and presence of mind. He appears to have been a natural leader, and began to be treated with respect by gentlemen who might not have deigned to notice him in Europe. Another example was François Addenin, "servant to sieur de Mons," a soldier who was sent as his bodyguard. He won a reputation as the most skilled hunter in the settlement, and was welcomed to the tables of gentlemen. We shall meet him again.[33] The experience of these men brought out a paradox in New France, which was at once highly stratified and highly mobile. Clear lines were drawn between social orders, but men such as Daniel Hay and François Addenin were able to cross the lines more easily than in the old country.[34]

There were no European women in Acadia from 1604 through 1607. Their absence was much regretted. Lescarbot told a story about an attempt that had been made to settle Cape Breton. The managers had "sent some cows two years and a half ago, but for want of some village housewife who understood taking care of them, they let the greater part die in giving birth to their calves. Which shows how necessary is a woman in a house."

Lescarbot missed the company of women, as did many of his companions. Others were of a contrary mind and didn't miss them at all. These early settlements attracted more than a few misogynists. Lescarbot was not among them: "I cannot understand why so many men slight them, even though they cannot get on without them. As for myself, I shall always believe that in any settlement whatsoever, nothing can be accomplished without the company of women. Without them, life is sad, sickness comes, and we die without their aid and comfort. This is why I despise those woman-haters (*mysogames*) who wish them all sorts of harm, which I hope will overtake that lunatic . . . who said that woman is a necessary evil, since there is no blessing in the world to be compared to her."[35]

On July 27, 1606, Poutrincourt brought his fifty male colonists ashore at Port-Royal. He met with those who had stayed the winter, and spoke of his purposes. He explained his vision of Acadia as a self-sustaining agricultural colony, and he began to work toward that end. Large grain fields were cleared along the river on rich alluvial soil. On a small stream near a waterfall he built a water-powered grain mill with a proper grindstone that must have been brought from France. It was thought to be the first water mill in this country. An old grindstone in the park at Fort Anne today is said to be the original wheel.[36]

He also planted orchards, "perhaps the first fruit trees in a region that was to become famous for its apples." Poutrincourt brought over so many animals that his ship *Jonas* became a veritable ark. He introduced a small herd of cattle, but, as Lescarbot lamented, they did not flourish, perhaps indeed for the want of skilled dairywomen. Poutrincourt also brought swine, which increased and multiplied, as did pigeons and poultry. A solitary sheep was allowed to live in the courtyard of the fort, and was sheared for its wool. Other unintended animals in this menagerie were the rats that traveled in the hold of Poutrincourt's ship and found their way ashore. The result was a plague of rats, a problem in many early colonies. The worst sufferers were the Mi'kmaq, when the rats moved into Indian villages and consumed their small stock of supplies.[37]

Poutrincourt gave Port-Royal a different tone from other feudal utopias in America, which were strongly collectivist. He was persuaded to follow the example of Champlain and Pont-Gravé, and encouraged his colonists to work both for the colony and for themselves. The result was a system of mixed enterprise. The men were asked to work at collective tasks for a small part of each day. Together they dug ditches and moats around the fort to strengthen its defenses and to improve its cleanliness. A well was also dug in the middle of the courtyard and lined with bricks burned of "Port-Royal clay."[38]

This collective labor was limited to two or three hours. The rest of the day, the leaders urged the men to work at their own gardens. Lescarbot set them an example by tilling his own plot, as Champlain had done the year before. Lescarbot wrote, "I can say without lying that never before had I worked so hard as the days of summer were very short. I had often in the spring continued by moonlight."[39]

The settlement at Port-Royal had a dual character. Poutrincourt and Lescarbot made it a feudal seigneury, subject to the king of France. One of their first acts was to mount the arms of France and the king above the gate, along with the heraldry of the sieur de Mons and the sieur de Poutrincourt. At the same time, these French leaders were quick to discover that settlers were more productive when they worked for their own gain. These two ideals, feudal and entrepreneurial, coexisted at Port-Royal.

French artisans and workmen brought many skills to Port-Royal, as Lescarbot records. "We had numerous joiners, carpenters, masons, stone-cutters, locksmiths, ironworkers, tailors, woodsawyers, sailors, etc., who worked at their trades." The pace of work was relaxed, and food was abundant. Lescarbot recalled that the men spent much of their time "gathering mussels . . . found in great numbers at low tide in front of the fort, or a species of lobster, or crab, which abound beneath the rocks of Port-Royal, or clams [he called them cockles] which grow beneath the mud in all parts of the beach of the harbor. All these were gathered without either boat or net."[40]

Fish was available in quantity. Lescarbot remembered that "when the Indians camped near us had made a catch of any sturgeon, salmon, or smaller fish, or of any beaver, moose, caribou, or other animals . . . they gave us the half thereof, and frequently put up the remainder to public sale, and anyone who wished bartered bread for it."[41] A barter economy developed rapidly, and a spirit of improvisation was encouraged. "Some of the masons and stone-cutters tried their hand at baking, and made us as good bread as that of Paris. . . . No one lacked bread, and each had three half-pints of wine a day." In 1606, they ran low on wine and Poutrincourt was forced to reduce the daily ration to one pint of wine a day. "Yet even so an extra supply was frequently served out."[42]

The abundance of supplies was partly the product of individual effort and partly the result of careful planning in France by the sieur de Mons, who had enlisted the aid of merchants in La Rochelle. Lescarbot, for one, was apprecia-tive. "We owe much praise to the said M. de Mons and his partners, Messrs. Macquin and Georges of Rochelle, who made such honorable provision for us. For our rations we had peas, beans, rice, prunes, raisins, dried cod and salt meat, besides oil and butter." Fuel was not a problem. "Our wood-sawyers sev-eral times made us a great quantity of charcoal."[43]

In the late summer and fall of 1606, as we have seen, Poutrincourt and Champlain went exploring on the coast of Norumbega. The rest remained at Port-Royal under Lescarbot's authority. He kept the peace, worked well with the Indians, supported the spiritual life of the colony, and spent much of his time at his writing desk.

On November 16, 1606, the sieur de Poutrincourt and Champlain limped back into Port-Royal in a battered barque with a broken rudder and three men wounded from their bloody encounter with the hostile Indians of Cape Cod.[44] They were amazed to be welcomed by Marc Lescarbot with a theatrical enter-tainment, an elaborate masque that he had written specially for the occasion. It was staged on the water at Port-Royal with music, verse, costumes, and spe-cial decorations on the fort. French workers wore Indian clothing. The real Indians attended, some afloat in their canoes; more than a few were probably wearing articles of European dress that they had acquired in trade.[45]

Lescarbot called this spectacle *Le Théâtre de Neptune*. It had a cast of eleven actors: the Sea God Neptune, six Tritons, and four Frenchmen dressed as In-dians, plus at least one trumpet and drum. Poutrincourt and Champlain were asked to take seats in their barque, while a shallop approached, bearing Nep-tune in a regal blue robe, wearing a crown and carrying a trident. He greeted the sieur de Poutrincourt with a poem of praise for his courage.

Marc Lescarbot's masque, The Theatre of Neptune, *was performed on November 16, 1606, to welcome Poutrincourt's return to the colony. The drawing is by artist-historian C. W. Jeffreys.*

> Hail to you, Sagamos, rest and stay awhile!
> Come listen to a God who welcomes with a smile! . . .

Neptune and his Tritons took turns reciting many lines of Lescarbot's classical verse, punctuated by trumpet and drum, and leavened by Parisian jests that mocked the manners and speech of French colonists who came from the provinces to the south and west. The masque reached its climax in a panegyric to the sieur de Poutrincourt:

> Go then with happiness and follow on the way
> Wherever fortune leads you since I foresee the day,
> When a prosperous domain you will prepare for France
> In this fair new world, and the future will enhance
> The glory of De Mons, so too, your name shall ring
> Immortal in the reign of Henry—your great and puissant king.

This was the first recorded theatrical production performed in New France. Historian Marcel Trudel quoted a comment by an anonymous contemporary of Champlain: "When the French founded a colony, the first thing they built was a theater; the English, a counting house; the Spanish, a convent."[46]

This masque was not the first European theatrical production in North America, as has often been claimed. Spaniards had performed at least three dramas before *The Theatre of Neptune*—at Florida as early as 1567, Cuba in 1590, and New Mexico in 1598. No texts have survived, but the theatrical in New Mexico was described as "written by a Spanish soldier in celebration of their conquests."[47] Marc Lescarbot's *Theatre of Neptune* is all the more interesting by its contrast with that earlier work. It is not in any way a celebration of military conquest. Poutrincourt and the French settlers are welcomed by four Indians who "render homage" to the sacred *fleur de lys* of the French, and hope for the establishment of "all that is good and peaceful." After the welcoming speeches, the Indians are welcomed in their turn to the French habitation and they all break bread together.[48] The play proclaims the excellence of French culture, but treats Indians with respect, celebrates an entirely peaceful encounter, and ends with Indians and Europeans dwelling together in peace.[49]

Music and celebration had a prominent place in the life of Port-Royal. To Lescarbot's masque, Poutrincourt also added his own entertainments. He was a gifted musician who, in the words of one historian, "seriously contends for the title of North America's first composer."[50] He also wrote religious and secular pieces for production in Port-Royal. Lescarbot wrote, "I remember that on a Sunday afternoon, the 14th of [January 1607], we amused ourselves by singing music along the banks of the Rivière l'Équille, now called Dauphin River, and that during this same month we paid visit to the cornfields, two leagues from our fort, and dined joyously in the sunshine."[51]

The settlers observed saints' days and royal birthdays with musical events. In the spring of 1607, they learned that the queen had given birth to a second son, "Monseigneur le duc d'Orléans," a large title for a newborn baby. His arrival greatly cheered the men of Port-Royal. The birth of a second son meant that their good king Henri IV had two sons who could inherit the throne, and his subjects had brighter hopes for peace and stability in France. Champlain wrote that the news brought "great rejoicing (*rejiouissance*)." Lescarbot recalled their celebrations. "We made bonfires in honour of the birth of my lord the Duke of Orléans, and began afresh to make our cannon and falconets thunder, with good store of musketry, though not until after we had sung a Te Deum for the occasion."[52]

•   •   •

The leaders of this French colony were devoted to the idea of living well in L'Acadie. When winter came in 1606–07, Champlain added his own contribution. He explained: "We spent this winter very pleasantly, and had good fare by means of an Ordre de Bon Temps, which I established and which everybody found beneficial to his health, and more profitable than all the varieties of medicines that we might have used."[53]

In a happy turn of phrase, Champlain's English-speaking editors W. F. Ganong and H. P. Biggar translated the "Ordre de Bon Temps" as the Order of Good Cheer, and so it has remained in anglophone Canada. Champlain himself thought of it as an order in the sense of a medal or decoration. "This order," he wrote, "consisted of a chain which we used to place with certain small ceremonies around the neck of one of our company, commissioning him to go hunting that day. The next day it was conferred on another, and so on in succession. All competed with one another to do it best and to bring back the finest game. We did not come off badly, nor did the sauvages who were with us."[54]

Lescarbot confirmed Champlain's invention of this order, and added more detail. "To this Order," he wrote, "each man of the said table was appointed

Champlain founded the Ordre de Bon Temps, a dining society, at Port-Royal. This reconstruction by C. W. Jeffreys closely follows accounts by Champlain and Lescarbot.

Chief Steward in his turn, which came round once a fortnight. Now this person had the duty of taking care that we were all well and honorably provided for. This was so well carried out that, though the epicures of Paris often tell us that we had no *Rue aux Ours* over there, as a rule we made as good cheer as we could have in this same *Rue aux Ours* and at less cost," than on that Paris Street famed for its cooked meats.[55]

He continued: "There was no one who, two days before his turn came, failed to go hunting or fishing, and to bring back some delicacy in addition to our ordinary fare. So well was this carried out that never at breakfast did we lack some savory meat of flesh or fish, and still less at our midday or evening meals; for that was our chief banquet, at which the ruler of the feast or chief butler [*architriclin*], whom the savages call Atoctegic, having had everything prepared by the cook, marched in, napkin on shoulder, wand of office in hand, and around his neck the collar of the Order, which was worth more than four crowns; after him, all the members of the Order, each carrying a dish. The same was repeated at dessert, though not always with so much pomp. And at night, before giving thanks to God, he handed over to his successor the collar of the Order, with a cup of wine, and they drank to each other."[56]

So enthused was Lescarbot that he added more detail. "I have already said that we had abundance of game, such as ducks, bustards, grey and white geese, partridges, larks, and other birds; moreover, moose, caribou, beaver, otter, bear, rabbits, wildcats (or leopards), raccoons, and other animals such as the savages caught, whereof we made dishes well worth those of the cook-shop in the *Rue aux Ours*, and far more; for of all our meats none is so tender as moose-meat (whereof we also made excellent pasties), and nothing so delicate as beaver's tail. Yea, sometimes we had half-a-dozen sturgeon at once, which the savages brought us, part of which we bought, and allowed them to sell the remainder publicly and to barter it for bread, of which our men had abundance. As for the ordinary rations brought from France, they were distributed equally to great and small alike; and, as we have said, the wine was served in like manner."[57]

Champlain intended his Order of Good Cheer to be something more than merely a dining society. He believed that scurvy could be kept at bay by a diet of fresh meat and that health could be improved by exercise and entertainment. The Order of Good Cheer also promoted comity among the leaders of the colony, and encouraged an idea of service and mutual support. Altogether, it was a brilliant success.[58]

Most of its members can be identified. At the head of the table was Poutrincourt, "commandant" of the colony. Others included his son Biencourt and cousins Charles and Claude de la Tour, Captain Boullay, surgeon Estienne, apothecary Hébert, nobleman Fougeray de Vitré, Robert du Pont-Gravé, son of Champlain's old friend, Daniel Hay, Marc Lescarbot, and Champlain. Also a member was François Addenin, one of the best shots in the settlement, who supplied the table "abundantly with gamebirds."[59]

The "lower orders" of French colonists were not invited, but Indians were very much a part of these events. "At these proceedings," Lescarbot wrote, "we always had twenty or thirty sauvages, men, women, girls and children, who looked on at our manner of service. Bread was given to them gratis as one would do to the poor. As for sagamore Membertou and other chiefs who came from time to time, they sat at table, eating and drinking like ourselves. And we were glad to see them while, on the contrary, their absence saddened us, as happened three or four times when they all went away to the places wherein they knew that there was hunting."[60]

A key to Port-Royal's success was the relationship between the French and the Acadian Indians, who were four nations by Champlain's reckoning, and six by ours today. Champlain and Lescarbot referred to them as *Souriquois* (now the Mi'kmaq), mostly on the east coast of the Bay of Fundy, the *Etchemin* (now Maliseet, Penobscot, and Passamaquoddy) on the west coast, *Abenaquioit* (now Abenaki or Wabenaki) inland to the west, and the *Canadien*, who lived north of Acadia and south of the St. Lawrence River. The *Canadien* were probably a southern branch of the people who were called Montagnais by Champlain. These nations were primarily hunters and gatherers, but they were not primitive, as too often they have been made to appear. They were highly skilled traders, and thought of themselves as superior to the farming nations to the south and west. All spoke Algonquian languages, but in different dialects. All were enemies of the hated Iroquois, but they also fought each other. They hoped that the French would be trading partners and allies in their incessant wars. Champlain tried to keep peace among them.[61]

The French deliberately settled very near the Indians and were comfortable in their presence. In a country of enormous size, they did not attempt to drive the Indians off the land or to push them away. To the contrary, French leaders of Port-Royal invited Mi'kmaq sagamores to share their table, and to eat and drink with them as equals on a regular basis. The Mi'kmaq in turn welcomed the French as neighbors. Each side invited the other to tabagies, as Champlain had done at Tadoussac and again on the Penobscot River. In these festivals, the French were quick to adopt Indian customs of evening feasts, with speeches and dancing, and smoking together. The Mi'kmaq sponsored some of these gatherings, and the French reciprocated. It was very different from the English in Massachusetts and Virginia, who settled apart from the Indians, kept them at a distance, annexed large tracts of land, and cultivated an attitude of distrust and contempt.

The French also sent young gentlemen of the highest rank in the colony to live among the Indians, master their languages, and learn their ways. Three in particular did so in Acadia. One was Poutrincourt's son Charles de Biencourt, fifteen years old in 1606, and his young cousin Charles La Tour, aged about fourteen. A third was Pont-Gravé's son Robert, who was about the same age.[62] They leaped at the opportunity. Biencourt and La Tour learned the languages of the Souriquois and the Etchemin. Gravé became fluent in the Etchemin tongue. All of them learned much more besides. As M. A. MacDonald writes, "the French boys" began to "acquire woodcraft, visiting the Indian camps and taking easily to Indian ways." She tells us that they learned how to build a birchbark canoe, and steer it without splash or ripple. They learned to glide through the forest without a sound, and mastered "the wide-swinging snow-shoe stride, tracking moose through deep snows, learning to keep all senses alert, to be aware of everything—wind direction, broken twigs, shades of expression on a human face." All three became leaders of French settlement in Acadia. They moved easily among Indian and French cultures, and understood the customs of the country.[63]

Champlain also fostered Indian relations in another way. More than any other high leader in New France, he sought out Indians in their own territory, and visited them with only one or two companions. He formed enduring relationships with many native leaders. Among his friends were Secoudon the sagamore of the St. John Valley, Bessabez in the Penobscot Valley, Sasinou in the Quinibequi country (Kennebec today), and many more.[64]

The most important of these relationships was with the Souriquois sagamore Membertou, who lived close to Port-Royal. Some scholars have tried to minimize his role and have accused Champlain of exaggerating his position, but Lescarbot and the missionaries had the same judgment of his importance. Nearly all wrote that he was a man of great influence, the leader of a group of four hundred Indians, and builder of "a town surrounded by high palisades." Jesuit Father Pierre Biard met him and described him as "the greatest, most renowned and most formidable savage within the memory of man: of a splendid physique, taller and larger-limbed than is usual among them, bearded like a Frenchman, though scarcely any of the others have hair upon the chin; grave and reserved; feeling a proper sense of dignity for his position as a commander."[65] He appeared before the French in a "beautiful otter robe" that was much coveted by French leaders and added greatly to his gravitas. Membertou combined many roles as warrior, magistrate, healer, and soothsayer. He was also a shaman or *aoutmoin*—a prophet, healer, and medicine man. His biographer writes that "the prestige of *aoutmoin* reinforced that of the *sagamo* and gave him a special authority in the councils." At the same time Membertou was a leader in trade and acquired his own European shallop, which he decorated with his own totems and used to sail the coast of Acadia.[66] He sailed far out to sea, met approaching ships, and offered Indian goods at high prices—forestalling the coastal markets.

When the French arrived, Membertou was elderly but fit and very strong. Lescarbot, never at his best with numbers, reckoned his age as "at least 100," and he had a son aged sixty, "though even now he does not look more than fifty years old."[67] The French were amazed by the keenness of Membertou's senses. One morning, he shouted to the French that a sail was heading toward Port-Royal. "All ran to see, but none was found with such good sight as he," Lescarbot remembered. "We soon saw [that it was] a small merchant vessel."[68]

Lescarbot, Poutrincourt, and Champlain held Membertou in high respect,

This "Gourd of Membertou" was elaborately carved to symbolize an alliance between the Mi'kmaq sagamore Membertou and the French. It also bears the arms of the Robin family, who helped to fund Port-Royal and sent several men to Acadia.

but they understood him in different ways. Lescarbot was mainly interested in writing a work of literature that celebrated the humanity of the American Indians. "From a human point of view at least," he wrote, "the savages were more humane and more honorable than many of those who bear the name of Christians."[69] He applied that idea to Membertou and made him the model of a noble savage who led his people with wisdom. "He has under him a number of families whom he rules, not with as much authority as our king has over his subjects, but by his ability to harangue, to give counsel, to lead into war, and to give justice to those who received injury." Lescarbot added, "He does not impose taxes on them, but if there is a hunt, he gets a share without taking part in it. It is true that sometimes he is given presents of beaver pelts and other things when he is employed to heal the sick or exorcise demons, or to reveal the future or those who are absent. . . . Membertou is the one who has practised these arts among his people. He has done it so well that his reputation is very high among the other sagamores in the land."[70]

Poutrincourt approached the Indians in another spirit. He "regarded as the chief end of his journey thither to bring about the salvation of these poor, savage and barbarous tribes." To that purpose, he saw in Membertou a way of converting the "savages of Acadia" to Christianity, and persuaded him to be baptized along with his family. Poutrincourt himself served as the sponsor and chose Christian names for each convert. Membertou and his wife and eldest son were named Henri, Marie, and Louis after the first family of France. Other members of Membertou's family were christened with the names of French noblemen.[71]

Poutrincourt also tried to suppress Indian rituals of death and burial, with no success whatever. Membertou insisted on practicing two religions at the same time. Without abandoning his own original faith, he took up Christianity with the proverbial zeal of the convert and proposed to "make war on all who refused to become Christians." The French urged him to make converts by persuasion rather than by the sword, for they had seen too much of that at home.[72]

Champlain thought of Membertou in a third way. He recognized Membertou's many virtues, and found him to be honorable and trustworthy in his dealings with friends, neighbors, and guests. But he tried to understand the Indian leader in his own terms. He understood that Membertou lived by ethics very different from those of the French. In a wilderness that was ruled by fang and claw, he kept the hard code that the Romans called lex talionis, the rule of justice by retaliation, often by sudden raids and surprise attacks. Champlain wrote that in war Membertou "had a reputation of being the worst and most treacherous of all his nation."[73] In the summer of 1607, for example, Membertou led his people to war against the Saco Indians. Champlain observed that "this entire war was solely about a member of Membertou's nation who had been killed at Norumbega."[74] After the body of the slain kinsman was recovered, Membertou arranged an elaborate funeral. The friends and family of the murdered man painted their faces black, "which is their manner of mourning," Champlain observed. The body was arrayed in red cloth that Champlain supplied. Instead of trying to suppress the Mi'kmaq burial customs as Poutrincourt did, Champlain supported them.[75]

These very different ways of thinking about the American Indians met and mixed among the French humanists who settled at Port-Royal.[76]

As the winter of 1606–07 came to an end, the men of Port-Royal made ready for another planting season. One imagines them toiling around the fire at night, mending their tools, sharpening blades, and replacing handles. Once again the leaders urged every man in the settlement to cultivate his own garden. They encouraged a spirit of rivalry that spurred them on to greater effort. "Near the end of March," Lescarbot recorded, "the best-disposed among us set themselves who should best till, with a pride of ownership and achievement, and a feeling that they were working for themselves that spurred them to greater labor."[77]

The seeds sprouted quickly, and the French were astonished by the results of their labor. "When each of us had finished his sowing," Lescarbot continued, "it was a marvelous pleasure to see them grow and increase day by day, and still a greater contentment to make abundant use of them. . . . This commencement of good hope made us almost forget our native country." They also went to work on the fishing in the same spirit, and "were yet more astonished by the abundance of their catch. . . . The fish began to seek the fresh water and to come in such abundance into our brooks that we knew not what to do with them."[78]

On May 24, 1607, the habitants of Port-Royal saw a sail coming up the great sound. It proved to be a small barque du port of about six or seven tons, flying a French ensign. In command was a young captain of Saint-Malo named Chevalier.[79] He brought letters from the sieur de Mons, and they were heavy with bad news. The colonists were shocked to learn that the company had failed. It had been brought down by many blows. Individual investors had been cheating the company; they sent their own ships to trade for fish and furs, and kept the profits for themselves. Then came the crowning blow. The Royal council found that de Mons had failed to meet the conditions of his patent, and they terminated his monopoly of the fur trade. Without it, the company was no longer able to support a colony in Acadia. With much sadness, the sieur de Mons ordered Poutrincourt to abandon Acadia and bring the settlers back to France.[80]

Some habitants of Port-Royal were delighted to go home, but the leaders did not want to leave quickly. The crops were coming splendidly, and the sieur de Poutrincourt wanted to see the result. Champlain's work of surveying and mapmaking was unfinished. Others believed that they could obtain furs and fish sufficient to help the sieur de Mons weather a financial crisis. They decided to remain in Acadia for another three months, and make the most of the time.[81]

In July, another message arrived from France. It was Ralluau again, with more peremptory orders to return home. A ship had been sent for that purpose, the ill-named *Jonas*, and she was waiting at Ingonish on Cape Breton. The settlers closed up the colony, and went aboard the company's vessels. Most sailed in two barques on July 30, 1607, but still the leaders were reluctant to depart. Poutrincourt wanted to stay for a few more weeks until the first grain crops ripened. They also wanted to say farewell to Membertou, who had been away leading a war party against the Almouchiquois at Saco.[82]

On August 10, 1607, Membertou returned in triumph. The next day, the French harvested some grain from their fields, put it aboard their small shallop, and made ready to depart. Membertou and the Indians were sorry to see them go. There were tears and lamentations. The Indians promised to protect the settlement, which they did with complete fidelity. The French leaders sailed on August 11, and met the ship *Jonas* at Canso for the voyage home.[83] The habitants left with a sense of pride and achievement. They had nothing but praise for their leaders. Although Poutrincourt had not done well in command of exploring expeditions, he was more successful in command of a fortified post among Indians who repeatedly demonstrated their friendship.

Champdoré brought from Acadia a beautiful blue amethyst, which he had cut in two pieces, and "gave half to M. de Mons and the other to M. de Poutrincourt," as a token of esteem. The two men had the stones handsomely set, and presented them to the king and the queen as glowing symbols of New France, and of the "beautiful things that lie hidden in these countries, knowledge of which has not yet been given to us." The leaders believed that something had gone profoundly right at Port-Royal—with the Indians, with one

another, and with the place itself. They thought of Port-Royal as an ideal settlement, and held it up as "a successful model, well suited to conditions in
North America." The leaders were determined to try again, and plant another
settlement that might endure. But first they had some urgent business in
France.[84]

FOUNDER OF QUEBEC

11.

QUEBEC

The First Permanent Colony, 1608–09

> Those who know the least shout the loudest.
>
> —Champlain, 1607[1]

IN THE AUTUMN OF 1607, Champlain sailed home to France in the battered barque *Jonas* with the sieur de Poutrincourt, Marc Lescarbot, the Port-Royal colonists, and a young Indian convert. It was a miserable crossing in a crowded ship, with short rations and a fragrant cargo of 100,000 codfish. Foul winds forced them into the port of Roscoff on the west coast of Brittany, where, by Lescarbot's account, they "remained two and a half days to recuperate." They went ashore to recover their land legs, and Champlain took delight in the Indian's discovery of Europe. The lad was "astonished to see the buildings, spires, and windmills of France" and amazed by "the women whom he had never seen dressed in our manner."[2]

When the wind turned fair, they went aboard and sailed east to Saint-Malo. There the passengers scattered in various directions. Poutrincourt and Lescarbot took the Indian boy to court and presented him to Henri IV as evidence that the natives were converting to Christianity. They also offered the first crops of corn, wheat, rye, barley, and oats from Port-Royal as proof of the colony's success as an agricultural settlement. With his usual flourish, Poutrincourt gave the king five young Canada geese (*outardes*) that he had raised from hatchlings aboard ship. Those indestructible birds were soon swimming in the pools of Fontainebleau.

The king was gracious to the young Indian and pleased with the gifts, but he was keenly aware that the De Mons Company had failed and its colony had been abandoned. Once again, after so much effort, no French settlements survived in North America. In the gardens of Fontainebleau, the honk of Canada geese made a mocking chorus on the fate of New France.[3]

Champlain was not part of that scene. For the first time, he did not go directly to court. He was deeply troubled by the failure of the De Mons Company and wanted to know why it had happened. In a phrase of Winston

After the failure of Port-Royal and the collapse of its funding, Poutrincourt returned to France, met Henri IV, and made him a present of Canada geese. In the gardens and pools of Fontainebleau, the cry of geese made a mocking chorus in what appeared to be the tragedy of New France.

Churchill's, who knew a thing or two about leadership in large causes, Champlain was always "Lord Root-of-the-Matter." Before he met the king he turned in another direction and moved straight to the heart of the problem. "I went to find the sieur de Mons," Champlain wrote, "and found him living on a pleasant street in Paris, happily called rue Beaurepaire." Champlain greeted his friend, and spoke of the "things I had seen since his departure."[4]

He also presented "a map and drawings of the coasts and ports" in Acadia. This may have been the map now in the Library of Congress, which bears Champlain's signature with the date 1607. It is the only manuscript map known to come directly from his hand—a miracle of survival, and a superb work of cartographic art.[5] De Mons must have examined it with great interest. Historian David Buisseret suggests that its quality comes clear when we compare the "sober work of Champlain" with Captain John Smith's map of New England (1614)—also a very good piece of work but in a different way. In Buisseret's phrase, Champlain's map seeks "simply to set out the main geographical features," and also gives much attention to the Indians. His chart work is meticulous in its detail, and could only come from "a series of observations made from a small boat, working along the coast." Smith's map by com-

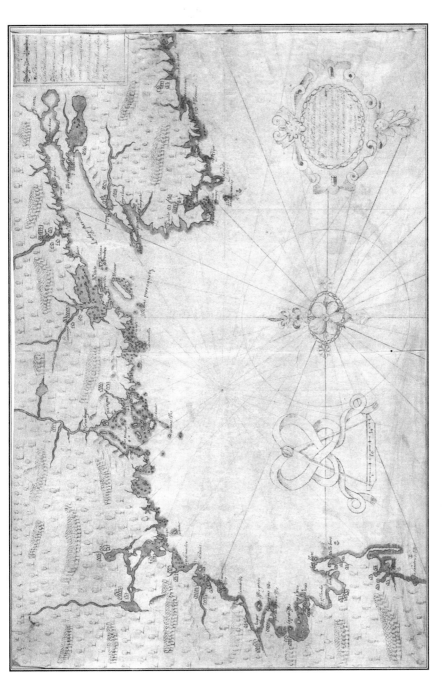

Champlain's manuscript map of New France (1607–08) is a work of meticulous detail for coasts that he explored in Acadia and Norumbega, but less so for Cape Cod and beyond. His map is attentive to the land itself and the towns of the Indians, with no symbols of imperial dominion, and nothing of self-advertising.

By comparison, John Smith's map of New England (1614) is roughly right in its main lines, but sketchy and careless in detail. It is inattentive to the Indians and imposes emblems of British sovereignty on the land with an English armada on the sea. The dominant element is a self-promoting portrait of John Smith.

parison is finely engraved but frequently inaccurate in detail. It gives little attention to the Indians. The dominant features are a large portrait of Smith himself and the arms of England. Buisseret observes that Smith "seems determined to impose his presence on the land about to be seized."[6] Champlain's work was very advanced in its cartography. He used new mathematical work of Guillaume de Nautonier on compass declination to orient his map and its elements, with somewhat mixed results but to a very high standard of accuracy and integrity. The sieur de Mons would have studied the map in two ways— for what it displayed of the American coast, and also for what it revealed of its maker. It may have made a difference in the events that followed.[7]

After the two men discussed the map, de Mons told Champlain what had happened to the investment company—and it made a long litany of woe. One ironic factor in its demise was a change of fashion in Paris hats. Feathers were out; beavers were in. Demand for beaver pelts of high quality was insatiable in Europe, and it was growing at a great pace. Also in favor were lustrous furs

The beaver was second only to the cod in the economy of New France. Philosophes were fascinated by these appealing animals and celebrated their busy lives, collective labor, and social ethic. A happy example is this image from Henri Chatelaine's "Carte très curieuse" (1719).

from higher latitudes of North America: marten, lynx, white fox, and the beautiful black otter. The best source was the St. Lawrence Valley, where furs could be bought for a small fraction of their Paris price. Ironically, the increasing value of American furs made big trouble for the settlement of New France. Many merchants wanted a share of this lucrative trade and they joined forces to break the monopoly of the sieur de Mons. Champlain was told that "the Bretons, the Basques, the La Rochelle and Normandy people were renewing their complaints, and getting the ear of those who were ready to show them favor." In Paris, the powerful Hatters' Association joined in. Some of its members complained that a monopoly in America would drive up the price of furs. Others hoped to be monopolists themselves.[8]

These rivals had deep pockets, and money changed hands in the dark corridors of the Louvre. "At Court," Champlain wrote, "people were not wanting who promised for a sum of money to annul the commission of the sieur de Mons." He added that "in a short time his Majesty's patent was revoked for a certain sum which a certain person received without his said Majesty knowing anything about it."[9]

De Mons knew the identity of this "certain person." Once again it was his old rival, the duc de Sully. In a court case, de Mons later testified that the "monopoly of ten years was revoked by the king around the fourth year [1607] be-

PERRUQUES et COIFFURES au 17ᵐᵉ S.

gentilhomme en 1605
recueil de Gaignières

d'apres une gravure ancienne
1610

vers 1596 d'ap. une gravure ancienne

Vers 1630 d'ap. Ab. Bosse
Bib. nat. estampes

The whirl of fashion in Paris hats created an insatiable demand for beaver pelts and made big trouble for de Mons and Champlain. Hatmakers, fur merchants, and their friends at court broke the trading monopolies that paid for the colonization of New France.

cause it was wanted by monsieur le duc de Sully, at the request of several hatters in the city of Paris." [10] In 1607, Sully was at the peak of his career as the king's most powerful minister. While in office, he also built a very large private fortune. Much of it was the gift of a grateful monarch, but the Paris hatters pitched in. [11] Sully appears to have been corrupt in an honorable way, a man of principle who practiced what in America would later be called "honest graft." He accepted bribes only for actions that he believed to be good for the king and the country. [12] Sully had never been a friend of colonization and often argued that "lands beyond the seas can only entail considerable cost while being only of slight or extremely little use." His repeated view was that nothing could come from American colonies above the fortieth parallel (the latitude of Philadelphia). [13]

Sully had long wished to put an end to French settlement in North America, but knowing the king's feeling, he bided his time. In 1607, he saw an opportunity. On the fishing coast, agents of the sieur de Mons had seized French vessels in a high-handed way. The result was a wave of anger in French seaports, and a tangle of litigation. For every ship that was seized, many others defied the monopoly with impunity. In 1607, Champlain estimated that eighty ships were trading illegally for furs in the St. Lawrence. Most were owned in France; some were Dutch ships with French pilots. The monopoly was not working, and it caused deep resentment. [14]

The sieur de Mons also had another problem. He was losing his investors. They had not received the dividends they had been promised after the first year, and they balked at the costs of colonization that they were expected to bear. Champlain later observed that de Mons had spent more than 100,000 livres to found the settlements at Sainte-Croix and Port-Royal, with very little to show for it. Sainte-Croix had failed as a colony, with heavy loss of life. Port-Royal had failed as an investment. Both settlements lay at a long distance from the most profitable centers of the fur trade. Even some of de Mons' leading investors, led by a truculent merchant of Rouen named Daniel Boyer, sent their own traders to Canada in violation of the monopoly. [15]

With this dismal record in hand, Sully persuaded the Royal Council that the sieur de Mons had not met the terms of his commission, and argued that the monopoly should be revoked. The council showed sympathy for de Mons, and authorized him to receive 6,000 livres in cash payments "from the ships that went out to trade in furs," as compensation for his loss. But when de Mons tried to collect the money, hostile courts in Saint-Malo and other towns told him he had the wrong names, or the defendants had disappeared, or the suits were invalid for technical reasons. It proved impossible to collect so much as a sou from these slippery *contrebandiers*, as they were called.[16] Champlain remarked, "To find out who had been trading, and what amount should be levied on more than eighty vessels that frequented those coasts . . . was like trying to drink the sea!"[17]

All these blows did heavy damage to the company of de Mons, and were a severe setback for the grand design that he shared with Champlain. Some people would have given up, and de Mons came close to that decision in the fall of 1607. Champlain wrote that the "sieur de Mons spoke . . . several times about his intentions." It must have been a painful subject, but they kept talking, and de Mons decided to try one more time. In Champlain's words, he resolved "to continue such a noble and worthy enterprise, notwithstanding the pain and labor it had cost him."[18]

De Mons also made another decision. To protect the enterprise at home, he had to stay in France. Someone else would have to take the lead in America, but whom should he choose? The senior men were not quite right for the job. Pont-Gravé was a great seaman and a good trader, but he was not in good health and his behavior was increasingly erratic. Poutrincourt had his own purpose in seeking to found a feudal utopia in Acadia, and he had failed as a leader on the coast of Norumbega. A third candidate came to mind. The sieur de Mons had watched Champlain in 1604 and 1605, when the two men had worked closely together. Champlain had done well in independent commands, better than his superiors in the same role. Others were beginning to notice his gift of leadership. One of them was Marc Lescarbot, who wrote a sonnet to Champlain about it:

> And if you accomplish your beautiful enterprize,
> One cannot estimate how much glory will one day
> Accrue to your name, which already each person prizes.[19]

There was one problem. Champlain was not a nobleman, and great enterprises in France were rarely led by commoners. But the more de Mons thought about it, the more he believed that Champlain would be the best choice. In the fall of 1607 he asked his younger friend to take command in New France. Here was an important opening for Champlain and his grand design. It was a major opportunity, but full of risk. Every French colony without exception had failed in North America. Even so, Champlain believed that he could succeed. He accepted the offer of de Mons, but on one condition. The two of them had to win back the king's support for New France. In truth it could work in no other way.[20]

• • •

With Champlain's encouragement, the sieur de Mons returned to court in the winter of 1607–08, and launched a campaign for the king's ear. He made a strong appeal for a permanent colony and for the return of a trading monopoly to support it. He and Champlain added a new argument, and recent events supported them. While the French were failing to make good their claim in North America, the English were moving rapidly. In 1607, investors in London had founded colonies at Jamestown in Virginia, and Sagadahoc in Maine, which was within the territory claimed as New France. If these initiatives succeeded, France would be in danger of forfeiting its claims in North America. Were that to happen, merchants in Rouen and Paris would have no share of the fur trade whatever. Demands of French investors for free trade, low taxes, and no spending for colonies could only end in new monopolies for England and the Netherlands, from which the French would be excluded. Champlain felt deep contempt for these shortsighted businessmen. He declared, "These envious folk were clamoring not for their own advantage, but their own ruin."[21]

The king was persuaded. He was also moved by reports from Poutrincourt about the success of agriculture at Port-Royal and the progress of Christianity in New France. On January 7, 1608, Henri IV issued a new decree. On the basis of "information that has been given to us by those who have come from New France, regarding the good quality and fertility of lands in that country, and that the inhabitants thereof are disposed to receive the knowledge of God, we have resolved to continue the settlement which has already begun there."

The king overruled Sully and the council. He supported "the offer made to us by the sieur de Mons, Gentleman-in-Ordinary of our chamber, and our Lieutenant-General in that Country, to undertake the said settlement if we grant him the means and possibility of bearing the expense." To that end, Henri IV further decreed that "none of our subjects but [de Mons] himself shall be permitted to barter in furs and other merchandise for the period of one year only."[22] It was one of the king's typical compromises. The sieur de Mons would receive his new monopoly but only for twelve months to help him start again. Thereafter the king favored open trade. It was a slender reed for so large a mission, but de Mons and Champlain were ready to act.

The next step was to raise the money—no small task. De Mons used a combination of coercion and persuasion. In Rouen he employed a respected merchant named Lucas Le Gendre to be his "procureur général," with full power to prosecute French traders without a license. De Mons brought suit against some of them and won enough judgments to prove that he could enforce his powers. During the next year, any Frenchman in the fur trade would have to do business with de Mons.[23]

Then de Mons went to the Atlantic seaports and made agreements with individual merchants who were his friends. In the Basque country, a small group agreed to send a large ship from Saint-Jean-de-Luz with a license from de Mons. He visited Saint-Malo and signed similar agreements with five merchants. Other arrangements were made in Dieppe, Le Havre, Honfleur, Rouen, La Rochelle, and Paris. A common provision was that a quarter of the profit should go to the De Mons Company.[24]

Altogether more than twenty-one vessels are known to have cleared from French ports for "Canada" in the spring of 1608, not counting many others that were bound for the fisheries of "Terre Neuve." Many of the trading voyages appear to have been under some sort of agreement with the sieur de Mons. This method of mobilizing capital was different from what had been done for the Acadian voyages in 1603–05. In place of a corporate system with three major centers, this new initiative was an improvised web of agreements with individual merchants. More than forty have been identified by name. All these arrangements required major effort on the part of the sieur de Mons.[25] Unlike the Acadian venture, this new mission was built on promissory notes, and colonizing expenses were met with borrowed money. The credit of the company was not strong. Much of the borrowing was done by individuals on their own credit, with interest charges in the range of 25 to 50 percent.[26]

As these precarious financial agreements began to fall into place, Champlain and the sieur de Mons had a hard choice to make. Where should they plant the next settlement? After the brutal winter on Sainte-Croix Island in 1604, the sieur de Mons still "hoped to go farther south to found a healthier and more temperate colony." Champlain wanted to go north and settle on the St. Lawrence River.[27] The two friends agreed to "meet in council," and Champlain organized his thoughts carefully, as was his habit. He gathered evidence about the St. Lawrence Valley and framed an argument on "why it was more convenient and useful to establish a settlement there." First on his list was the problem of security from attack by European powers, in light of recent English and Dutch activity. He predicted that Acadia would be "difficult to hold because of the infinite number of its harbors which could only be guarded by large forces." The St. Lawrence Valley, on the other hand, could be controlled at a few choke points along the river.[28]

Champlain also favored the St. Lawrence for another reason. It was closer

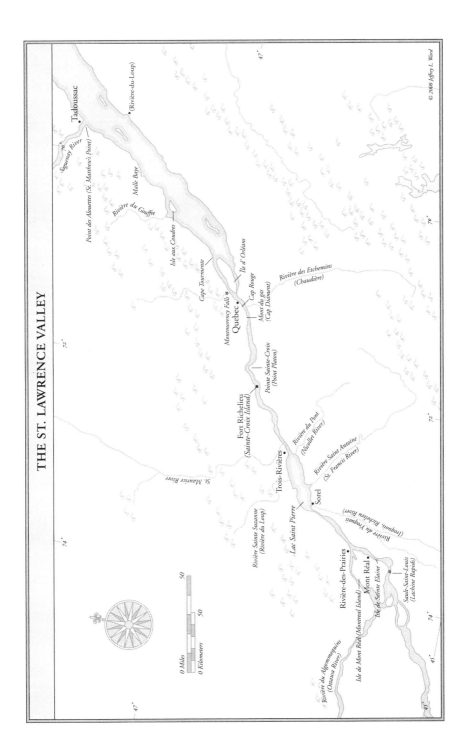

THE ST. LAWRENCE VALLEY

Tadoussac

Saguenay River

Point des Alouettes (St. Matthew's Point)

Malle Baye

Rivière du Gouffre

Isle aux Coudres

Cape Tourmente

Ile d' Orléans

Cap Rouge

Rivière des Etchemins
(Chaudière)

Montmorency Falls

Quebec

Mont du gas
(Cap Diamant)

Pointe Sainte-Croix
(Point Platon)

Fort Richelieu
(Sainte-Croix Island)

Rivière du Pont
(Nicolet River)

Trois-Rivières

Rivière Saint Antoine
(St. Francis River)

St. Maurice River

Sorel

Rivière du Yroquois
(Iroquois, Richelieu River)

Rivière Sainte Suzanne
(Rivière du Loup)

Lac Saint Pierre

Rivière-des-Prairies

Mont Réal

Isle de Sainte Elaine

Rivière du Algomnequins
(Ottawa River)

Isle de Mont Réal (Montreal Island)

Saut-Saint-Louis
(Lachine Rapids)

(Rivière-du-Loup)

© 2008 Jeffrey L. Ward

0 Miles   50

0 Kilometers   50

47°

47°

47°

74°

72°

72°

70°

45°

45°

74°

to the heart of the fur trade and "commerce could be carried on by means of the great river." He was thinking of its many Indian nations with trading networks of their own. By contrast, he wrote, Acadia "was sparsely populated by sauvages, who on account of their small numbers cannot penetrate from these regions into the interior where sedentary people live, as one could by the river St. Lawrence." He was planning a large trade over long distances between small numbers of Frenchmen and many Indian nations, all working together without coercion in an open relationship for mutual gain. This vision of New France was very different from that of New Spain or New England.[29]

To all this reasoning Champlain added the argument that more souls were to be saved in the St. Lawrence Valley. He argued that the Indian nations of that region were receptive to French colonists and the land was suitable to settlement. And especially important in Champlain's thinking was the promise of a passage to Asia, through the St. Lawrence Valley and the great lakes to the west.[30]

The sieur de Mons perceived the strength of Champlain's reasoning but persisted in his own purposes. The result was another compromise. The company would send three ships in the spring of 1608: two to found a permanent settlement in the St. Lawrence Valley and a third to revive the settlement in Acadia. Champlain wrote that de Mons "resolved to do that, and to this end he spoke about it to His Majesty, who agreed."[31]

As mission commander, Champlain received the title of "lieutenant for the country of New France." His orders were to negotiate a "treaty of amity" with the Indian nations, to plant a permanent settlement, and "to lay the foundation of a permanent edifice for the glory of God and the renown of the French people." After many failures, permanence became an important purpose.[32]

For the first time in his colonizing career, Champlain was in command. His mentor, Pont-Gravé, would go in a secondary role, with instructions to trade in Tadoussac harbor and return in the fall with furs and fish that might pay the costs of colonization. In 1603, Pont-Gravé had been commander and Champlain was his subordinate. Now, five years later, their roles were reversed. It is a tribute to both men that they made it work. A division of labor was agreed between them. Pont-Gravé would look after the fur trade; Champlain would plant a permanent settlement.[33]

In the early weeks of 1608, Champlain and the sieur de Mons recruited their colonists. The Acadian expeditions of 1604 and 1606 had drawn from the top and bottom of French society. Champlain's colonists in 1608 came more from the middle. There were few noblemen and gentlemen-adventurers. The leaders of this expedition were experienced seamen with long service as ships' officers: Champlain, Pont-Gravé, and Captain Guillaume Le Testu. Historian John Dickinson observes that their colony was run on the model of a ship, following the customs of the sea—a pattern different from Port-Royal.[34]

Most of the settlers were skilled artisans and laborers in the building trades. Contracts survive for woodcutters, sawyers, carpenters, masons, smiths, laborers, and a surgeon. Champlain also hired a gardener named Martin Béguin. These men agreed to stay two years for annual salaries that ranged from 150 livres for skilled artisans to 65 livres for laborers. About half these men were able to sign their contracts—a larger proportion of literacy than in the population of France in 1608.[35]

Several youngsters came along, and two of them would loom large in the history of New France: Étienne Brûlé and Nicolas Marsolet. No contracts survive for them. They may have come as *engagés*, or indentured servants. Champlain also had personal servants on most of his voyages from 1599 to 1635. He rarely referred to them by name, merely as anonymous lackeys (*laquais*). Once again this French expedition had no women, a surprising omission for a settlement that was to be permanent. Also, there were no Swiss soldiers, perhaps for reasons of economy.[36]

And no clergy came, which was a surprise. Everyone agreed that a major purpose of the colony was to aid in the conversion of American Indians to Christianity. That idea appeared in Champlain's arguments, in the representations of the sieur de Mons, and in the king's commission. But how could the work of conversion be done? Which religious order would be invited to participate? Who would pay? On these issues, there was no agreement.

The leaders of the last venture remembered the unhappy experiment with religious toleration in Acadia, which had led to constant strife between a Catholic priest and the Protestant pastor. Champlain wrote sadly, "Two contrary religions are never very fruitful to God's glory among the infidels." Something similar had happened when toleration was tried in Maryland, Rhode Island, and Eleutheria Island during the early seventeenth century.[37]

Champlain and the sieur de Mons agreed that something else should be done. At the urging of Henri IV they decided to approach the Jesuits. De Mons went to see the king's Jesuit confessor, Father Pierre Coton. Henri wanted the Jesuits to work in New France and promised 2,000 livres to support them. A devout Catholic woman of great wealth, Madame de Guercheville, also gave the Jesuits a larger sum of 3,600 livres for missions in America. The sieur de Mons tried to persuade Coton to commit that money to missions in the St. Lawrence Valley, but they could not agree on terms. Champlain was asked to join the discussion, with no better success. He and de

Mons decided to go without priests or chaplains. It was an ominous start for any venture in an age of faith.[38]

Early in the spring of 1608, the sieur de Mons and Champlain moved to the port of Honfleur on the river Seine. They chartered at least three ships.[39] Champlain's flagship was a large vessel, probably of 150 or 200 tons to judge by her cargo. Her captain was Guillaume Le Testu of Le Havre. The name of the vessel has not been found. A few seasons earlier Le Testu had been master of the ship *Fleur-de-Lys*; perhaps she was Champlain's ship. The vessel was heavily laden with settlers, materials, supplies, and all "things necessary and proper for a settlement," in Champlain's phrase.[40]

The other vessels were very small. One was the *Lévrier* [41] of only 80 tons, with Nicolas Marion (or Marien) as master and Pont-Gravé as commander. She carried some supplies for the settlement but was meant mainly to serve as a trading vessel in Tadoussac.[42] A third vessel was chartered for a different mission. Her captain was Champlain's friend the shipwright Champdoré. His orders were to sail to Port-Royal, resettle Acadia, explore the coast, and renew alliances with Indian nations.[43]

The small size of these vessels and the heavy borrowing at high interest were evidence of financial weakness in the De Mons Company. This mission was hanging by a thread. Money problems may also have been responsible for a late start. Champlain preferred to sail in March, but he appears to have met many delays in gathering men and material.[44] Pont-Gravé sailed first on April 5, 1608. Champlain followed on April 13, very late in the season. He had lost a month of good weather, but the Atlantic passage was quick and uneventful. Champlain crossed the Grand Bank on May 15. Two weeks later he reached Isle Percée, a huge red sandstone rock 290 feet high and 1,500 feet long, with two natural stone arches. Even the aids to navigation were gigantic in this vast new world.[45]

Champlain continued up the St. Lawrence River and arrived at Tadoussac on June 3, 1608. There he found several ships, and they posed a major challenge to his leadership. Pont-Gravé had arrived earlier and found a Basque whaler anchored in the harbor. Her captain was buying furs from the Indians without a license. He was probably Martin Darretche, from a prominent French Basque family who worked out of Saint-Jean-de-Luz.[46]

Pont-Gravé told the Basques that they were in violation of a royal command. Darretche may have tangled with him before, as Basques and Malouins had long been rivals on the North American coast. Both were apt to fight first and ask questions later.[47] The Basques were armed to the teeth and were determined to defend themselves, especially when challenged by a man of Saint-Malo. Pont-Gravé brought out the king's commission, and the Basques ran out their guns. According to Champlain, Pont-Gravé attacked first and the Basques "defended themselves very well." They brought "all of their cannon to bear" and in the first exchange of fire, Pont-Gravé fell severely wounded. Three of his men were also hit, and one of them died. The Basque traders boarded the French ship, made Pont-Gravé their prisoner, seized "all his cannon and arms," and promised to return them when they were ready to go home.[48]

Then Champlain arrived. He was very angry, both with the Basques and with Pont-Gravé. Later he wrote, "I was much annoyed at the brewing of a quarrel we could well have done without." The Basques warned him that he could enter the harbor "only by force." Champlain lacked the strength to impose his will by force of arms. He proposed a parley, and the Basque leaders agreed to talk.[49]

As they spoke, Captain Darretche began to have second thoughts about the use of force against men who carried the king's commission. The Basques knew well that Henri IV moved swiftly to punish armed resistance against his authority, even as he offered generous rewards for loyalty. The Basques had been able to defeat the first French ship, but here was a second, and a third was close behind. Champlain continued his negotiations with patience and forbearance. "After a good deal of discussion," he wrote, "I made peace between Pont-Gravé and [Darretche]." The Basques confessed to "a conviction of having done wrong." They appear to have been worried mainly that "they should not be allowed to fish for whale," which was not forbidden by de Mons' commission. Champlain proposed a compromise. They were allowed to continue whaling, and perhaps to barter with the Indians under something like a license. Champlain also promised that he and Pont-Gravé would "undertake nothing against them while they were in New France." In turn the Basques swore that they would "undertake nothing against Pont-Gravé nor against the king's interest, nor that of the sieur de Mons." All parties agreed that outstanding issues should go to courts in France, where "justice should be done."[50] The warring parties laid down their arms, signed a written agreement, and began to live together in peace. Champlain was good at this work of reconciliation. He had a genuine gift for peacemaking through a combination of firmness and restraint, and he used it many times in his career.

After peace was made with the Basques, Champlain anchored his ship beside them in the small circle of Tadoussac harbor. He tells us that he "set the carpenters to work," fitting out a *petit barque* of 12 or 14 tons that had been carried out from France for the purpose of exploring the St. Lawrence River. While he waited, Champlain met with the Montagnais Indians, who remembered him from his last visit in 1603. They traded American furs for French manufactures, and Champlain asked about the country north of Tadoussac. Once again, the Montagnais did not want him to go there, but allowed him to explore the lower reaches of the Saguenay River. He may have gone as far as Chicoutimi Falls, about a hundred miles upstream, and confirmed his earlier judgment that the valley was not a site for settlement. "All the land I saw there," he wrote, "was nothing but mountains and rocky promontories, for the most part covered with spruce and birch." [51]

While Champlain was searching the Saguenay to the north and Pont-Gravé was recovering from his wounds, their friend Champdoré led the third vessel on a southern voyage to the coast of Acadia. He visited Port-Royal, received a warm welcome from Membertou, chief of the Mi'kmaq, and found the settlement still intact. The Indians had guarded the buildings and tended the gardens and fields, which were flourishing. Membertou had harvested six or seven barrels of grain, and gave some of them to the French. [52]

The French leaders encouraged individual colonists to settle in Acadia with small proprietary grants, in an attempt to maintain their claims and keep the English at bay. Some of these settlements failed, but even the failures left behind a few Frenchmen who occupied the buildings, intermarried with Indians, and remained on the coast. In 1610, a French ship visited Sainte-Croix Island and found "a certain Frenchman . . . living with an Indian girl." [53]

Champdoré sailed across the Bay of Fundy and cruised the coast as far south as the "land of the Almouchiquois." There he worked to reconcile the Almouchiquois, Etchemin, and Souriquois with one another. The idea that the French sought to rule by pitting one group of Indians against another is not correct for the early seventeenth century. De Mons, Champlain, and Champdoré all believed that peace among the Indians was fundamental to their purposes.

On the coast of Maine, Champdoré also met a new generation of Indian leaders, in particular the Penobscot sagamore Asticou, "a man of weight and fine presence" who summered on Mount Desert Island. Here again, the French and the Penobscot Indians built good relations that endured in a remarkable way. Asticou's memory is still green on Mount Desert Island, where even today Indians, islanders, cottagers, and tourists continue to meet and trade every summer on the campus of Bar Harbor's College of the Atlantic, in the spirit of Asticou and Champdoré. [54]

• • •

In the last week of June, 1608, Champlain ended his work on the Saguenay and prepared to sail up the St. Lawrence Valley in search of a permanent site. His river barque was finally ready on June 31, and he set off that very day to explore the great river. He did not sail in midstream as others might have done, but preferred to study the banks and tributaries with close attention. This method called for great skill and constant vigilance. It put his vessel at risk among the submerged rocks and shifting shoals of the river. He loved to go ferreting on an unfamiliar shore—sounding, sketching, entering every major stream, going ashore, studying the soil, collecting flora and fauna. The tone of Champlain's account reveals the pleasure that he took in this happy work.

He also took delight in naming every prominent landmark along the river, often in colorful ways. On this trip, he named one tributary the Rivière du Gouffre, Whirlpool River, for its dangerous currents. He called another prominent landmark Cap Tourmente because of his struggle against its tricky winds and currents. His names are still to be found on the land in Canada and the United States.

For many miles beyond Tadoussac the countryside did not attract him as a place of settlement. "All the coast," he wrote, "both on the north and south sides, from Tadoussac to the Isle d'Orléans, is hilly country and very poor, with nothing but pine, spruce and birch, and very ugly rocks, amongst which, in most places, one cannot penetrate." Today, visitors find this terrain very attractive, but Champlain had different aesthetic ideas—and another purpose.[55]

When he came to the Île d'Orléans, about a hundred miles upriver from Tadoussac, he examined its shoreline closely and charted its very dangerous shoal water. Then he went ashore to explore the island itself, and admired its clear fertile meadows and open woodland, with "many fine oaks and nut trees," and "vines and other trees such as we have in France." Here was a very promising site for a large settlement.[56]

At the eastern end of the island he went ashore near the great waterfall that he had earlier named after Admiral Montmorency of France, who had supported him. Champlain climbed to the top of the falls, walked inland on land that was "level and pleasant to see," and found "a lake some ten leagues in the interior." From that elevation, he wrote that "one can see high mountains which seem to be fifteen or twenty leagues away."[57] Champlain returned to his boat and headed upstream, noting that the land had changed its character. "Here begins the fine good country of the great river, distant 120 leagues from its mouth."[58]

• • •

On July 3, Champlain and his men went another mile up the river past the Île d'Orléans, and reached the place that the Indians called Kebec, the narrowing of the waters. He had been there five years previously. This time he judged it by far the best place for permanent settlement. The strength of its position caught a soldier's eye. The high rocky promontory commanded the full width of the river. A strong fort could control traffic through the St. Lawrence Valley.

Below the promontory was a level area, perfect for a trading settlement. It is now the lower town of Vieux-Québec. Champlain found it covered by a thick stand of nut trees, with an odor that reminded him of French walnuts. The settlers came ashore and immediately began the heavy work of clearing

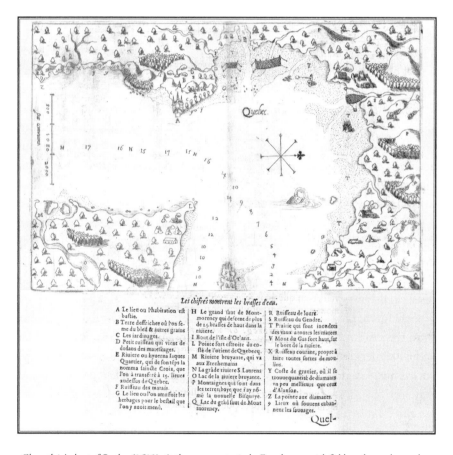

Champlain's chart of Quebec (1613). At the upper center is the French town with fields to the north, meadows to the west, and fish weirs on the St. Charles River to the east. Across the St. Lawrence River is the Indian town at Levis, and the Rivière des Etchemins, which led to Norumbega. Downstream is the Île d'Orleans.

the land. Champlain divided his workers into several parties: one group cut down the trees; another sawed the logs into planks; a third dug cellars and ditches. A fourth had the easiest duty, sailing from Quebec to Tadoussac and back again many times with supplies.[59]

The first priority was to build a secure storehouse, which was done promptly "by the diligence of every one." The storehouse had two purposes: to serve the needs of trade and to hold provisions for the winter. As always, Champlain insisted on an abundance of food stocks, remembering the disasters that had destroyed many French settlements.[60] Then they went to work on the building that Champlain called the *habitation*. It was different from the design of Acadia, where the settlement took the form of a quadrilateral fort. In Quebec, Champlain put up three interconnected buildings. One was for the artisans. Another, on the south side, looking out over the river, was the residence of Champlain. A third was for a forge and workshops. To the west was the storehouse with its deep cellar. In the courtyard he placed a dovecote with the escutcheon of the sieur de Mons and probably the king's arms.[61] Each part of the habitation was a large structure of two stories. On one of buildings, Champlain put a great symbolic sundial as an emblem of light, time, symmetry, and order. He also raised the flag of France on a staff high above the roof. It caught the strong winds on the river, and flew bravely over the busy settlement.[62]

The habitation was designed to withstand a siege. The entire complex was surrounded by a palisade (unfinished until 1610), with a ditch fifteen feet wide and six feet deep that could only be crossed by a drawbridge. The ditch was enfiladed by cannon mounted on triangular bastions. Historian Marcel Trudel writes that Champlain "reproduced in miniature a European fortress." The strength of the fortress also demonstrated his resolve to build a permanent settlement and hold it against any enemy.[63]

Around the settlement at Quebec, Champlain also ordered his workers to plant gardens. He had done it in every settlement: first on Sainte-Croix Island, once more at Port-Royal, and now in Quebec. "While the carpenters, sawyers and other laborers worked on our quarters," Champlain wrote, "I put the rest to work clearing land around the settlement in order to make gardens in which to sow grain and seeds to see how everything would succeed. The soil appeared to be very good."[64]

His published engravings show the plan of the gardens. Here again, as in Champlain's other experiments, the plantings were done not in functional hills or rows but in elaborate designs that resembled the formal gardens of France. Champlain's drawing of the settlement showed six garden plots, and

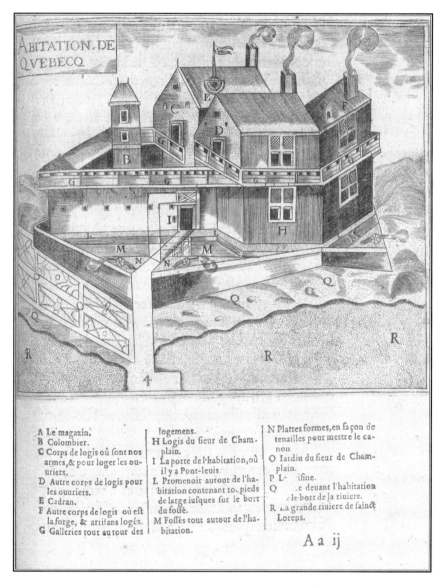

ABITATION. DE QVEBECQ

A Le magazin.
B Colombier.
C Corps de logis où sont nos armes, & pour loger les ouuriers.
D Autre corps de logis pour les ouuriers.
E Cadran.
F Autre corps de logis où est la forge, & artisans logés.
G Galleries tout autour des logemens.
H Logis du sieur de Champlain.
I La porte de l'habitation, où il y a Pont-leuis.
L Promenoir autour de l'habitation contenant 10. pieds de large iusques sur le bort du fossé.
M Fossés tout autour de l'habitation.
N Plattes formes, en façon de tenailles pour mettre le canon.
O Iardin du sieur de Champlain.
P L- ifine.
Q _e deuant l'habitation _le bort de la riuiere.
R La grande riuiere de sainct Lorens.

A a ij

The first habitation at Quebec (1608–10), with its fortress, warehouse (A), barracks (C, D, F), and Champlain's quarters (H). Above are a dove cote (B), sundial (E), and a flag with the lilies of Henri IV's Bourbon dynasty. On the water's edge is a quay (4), and Champlain's garden (0).

there were likely more. He was still planting in the fall. "On the first of October," he wrote, "I had some wheat sown and on the fifteenth some rye." He noted that the killing frosts came early, with a mild "white frost" on October 3. Even so, he kept on sowing. "On the 24th [of October]," he wrote, "had some native vines planted and they prospered extremely well." [65]

Champlain was much interested in native plants and made a list of the more attractive varieties: "nut trees, cherry trees, plum trees, vines, raspberries, strawberries, gooseberries, red currants and several small fruits which are quite good." Among the others were blueberries, which caught his eye. He wrote, "There are also several sorts of useful herbs and roots." Champlain was quick to discover the botanical expertise of the Indians and sought to learn from them. He also introduced many seeds and plants from France. Grains were tried in great variety, especially wheat and rye. Fall and spring sowings both succeeded at Quebec.[66]

Champlain also introduced flowers, and was especially fond of roses. He was very much the driver of French gardening in America. The men who did the work did not share his passion. Often he complained of his gardens that "after I left the settlement to come back to France, they were all ruined for want of care, which distressed me very much."[67] Champlain's gardens were not only useful and ornamental. They were also symbols of sovereignty and order. Champlain made an association between *l'estate* and *l'état*, the garden and the state.[68]

Champlain was racing the calendar and he drove his men very hard. The labor was heavy and unremitting. The food was not good, and the men began to grow restless and unhappy. In late summer and fall of 1608, four of them turned against Champlain. Their leader was Jean Duval, a skilled locksmith with a special expertise in the repair of gunlocks, and access to weapons. He had been in trouble before. On Poutrincourt's southern cruise to Nauset in 1606, it was Duval who had refused to obey a direct order to remain aboard ship, and slept on the beach with his friends. All had been killed except Duval, the sole survivor.[69]

At Quebec, Duval enlisted three workers in a conspiracy. They made a plan to murder Champlain. The four men decided that it had to be done by deep stealth and extreme secrecy—a testament to Champlain's strength and alertness. Probably he always carried arms, and knew how to use them. The conspirators agreed that he had to be killed, but they could not decide how to do it. They met together in the dark, and debated whether to poison him, blow him up with a bomb, strangle him in his bed, or sound an alarm and shoot him from ambush as he emerged from his quarters.[70] Once Champlain was dead, they planned to take over the colony, and seek an alliance with the Basques, or even with Spain. The ringleaders found broad support among other workers at Quebec. Even one of Champlain's personal servants joined the conspiracy—evidence perhaps of resentment to Champlain's driving leadership at this stage of his career. They set a date, and all were made to swear a solemn oath of secrecy, on penalty of death by many dagger-thrusts.[71]

Just before the fatal day, a river barque arrived from Tadoussac and began to unload its cargo. Its commander, Captain Guillaume Le Testu, was a "very prudent man," in Champlain's phrase, and much respected by others. An artisan in the settlement, a locksmith named Natel, approached Captain Le Testu and warned him of the plot. The captain went at once to Champlain and found him laying out his gardens, completely absorbed in the task at hand. The two men walked alone into the woods, and Champlain learned what was afoot.

He moved very quickly. First he spoke secretly with the informer Natel, who was shaking with fear. Natel was offered full pardon if he revealed the identity of the leaders. He named four men. Champlain laid a cunning trap for them. He arranged that a young seaman should invite the ringleaders onto Le Testu's ship, with a promise of two bottles of alcohol. The conspirators went aboard and instantly were seized by Champlain and Le Testu's loyal crew. All were clapped in irons.

Then Champlain went ashore. It was ten o'clock at night and pitch-dark. He summoned everyone in the colony. Standing with him in the shadows were the captain and some of Le Testu's men, all heavily armed. A faint light glinted on their weapons. Champlain told the colonists that Duval and the ringleaders had been put in irons. He gave each man a choice: pardon if he spoke the truth; death if he did not. Every man confessed and testified against the leaders. Champlain carried the four conspirators to Tadoussac and returned with Pont-Gravé (now nearly healed from his wounds) and more men who were also well armed. He convened a tribunal of four officers: Champlain himself, Pont-Gravé, Le Testu, and the surgeon Bonnerme. All were men with long experience of discipline at sea.[72]

They constituted a formal court, and a public trial followed, with depositions in great detail. The men of Quebec testified against the conspirators. Under the accumulating weight of evidence, Duval also made a confession and begged for mercy. For him, there would be none. The tribunal sentenced Duval to death, and Champlain ordered his immediate execution. Jean Duval was hanged, strangled, and beheaded. His severed head was mounted on a pike in Quebec as a grim warning to others.[73]

The three other ringleaders were also sentenced to death, but at Champlain's recommendation the tribunal ordered that they should be taken to France in chains and their sentence should be reviewed by the king's courts. On September 19, Pont-Gravé carried them home, and much later they were pardoned—a common pattern under Henri IV. Champlain had faced a mortal threat to the colony. He moved against it with energy and dispatch, but also with restraint. He executed one man, sent three to France, pardoned all the rest of the habitants, and regained their loyalty. Afterward Champlain wrote that all the others conducted themselves properly and did their duty. He won them to his leadership by a combination of strength, resolve, and restraint that held the colony together.[74]

Mutinies happened frequently in early French colonies and destroyed several of them, as in the murder of La Pierria at Charlesfort, the attack on Laudonnière at Fort Caroline in Florida, and the repeated revolts on Sable Island off the Grand Bank. Champlain, unlike earlier leaders, was able to suppress the rising before it happened, and dealt with it in a way that his men accepted as legitimate. This mortal challenge made the colony stronger—and Champlain, too.[75]

In the late summer, Indians visited Quebec and talked with Champlain. Most were Montagnais, and Champlain took a deep interest in them. "I studied their customs very particularly," he wrote.[76] He knew that the Montagnais were a hunting and gathering people—and thought that they were the most skillful hunters he had ever met. They were also expert traders, and constructed complex networks of exchange. He admired them as a handsome people, "well-proportioned in body, without deformity and agile." He found the women very attractive, "well-formed, plump, of a dusky hue on account of certain pigments with which they rub themselves, which make them look olive-colored."[77]

Algonquins also began to appear—many nations who lived along the upper St. Lawrence River from Quebec to the Great Lakes. Among them was the son of Iroquet, a leader of the Petite-Nation who lived far to the west, near Georgian Bay on the shore of Lake Huron. These nations, Algonquin and Montagnais, had "long been at war" with their ancient Iroquois enemies, especially the Mohawk, the easternmost of the Iroquois nations. Nobody could remember when this fighting had begun. It started long before the Europeans arrived. But with the expansion of the fur trade, these wars were growing more violent. The result was a cycle of violence and vengeance that kept all parties at war. The Algonquin and Montagnais wanted Champlain to join them in fighting the Mohawk.[78]

Champlain welcomed them all to Quebec, and gave them a "kind reception," in the words of one Algonquin sagamore. They began to build alliances, French and Indians together, but with different purposes in mind. The Mon-

Champlain sketched this Montagnais warrior, wife, and baby. He admired this "great nation," as expert hunters and skilled traders in highly developed networks. They thought themselves superior to farming Indians, whom they called "dogs who raise corn."

tagnais and Algonquins wanted Champlain to join them in defeating their mortal foes the Mohawk. The French commander agreed, and said that he "wished to help them against their enemies," but with a different purpose in mind. His object was to bring peace to the St. Lawrence Valley. He hoped to break the cycle by striking forcefully against the Iroquois, whom he regarded as the aggressors. The plan was not to destroy their power; it was to raise the price of raiding in the St. Lawrence Valley. During the summer and fall of 1608, they made an alliance with different goals in mind. It was a fateful agreement.[79]

While Champlain was meeting with the Indians, the seasons were changing rapidly. Winter came early to Quebec in 1608. On November 18, the settlement was lashed by "a great gale," and a "heavy fall of snow."[80] It was the harbinger of a long winter that nearly destroyed the colony. The months from

October to December were bad enough, with fierce winds, wet weather, and high water. Then the weather turned bitter cold and very dry—the cruelest combination. Houses were without the insulation that snow provided. Communications became difficult. Thick ice choked the rivers, and snow paths failed to form on the ground. Without deep snow, the hunting of large animals became difficult.

All of this was very hard on the French settlers and much harder on the hunting Indians. When the fall of 1608 approached, the Montagnais moved to Quebec, as they did every year. Champlain observed that they lived on the edge of subsistence and had a complex annual rhythm in their hunting and fishing. They came to the narrows of Quebec to fish for eels that began to come up the river in great numbers from about September 15, and continued to run abundantly to mid-October. "During this time," Champlain wrote, "the natives all live upon this manna and dry some for the winter to last till the month of February." They were a vital source of food.[81]

After the eel-run, the Montagnais went hunting for beaver from late October to December. Then in the coldest months they hunted large game such as moose, which were more easily caught when the snow was deep.[82] Champlain greatly respected the skill of the Montagnais, and their mastery of the environment in which they lived. He was interested in their warm and handsome clothing. "In winter," he wrote, "they are clad in good furs, such as the skins of moose, otter, beaver, bear, seal, deer, and more, which they have in great quantity." He was fascinated by their snowshoes. "When the snow is deep," he wrote, "they make a kind of racquet, two or three times as large as those in France, and tie them to their feet, and in this way they walk over the snow without sinking; otherwise they could not hunt or walk in many places."[83]

When the Montagnais had good luck in all of their successive hunts, they could eat through a long North American winter. But the failure of even one hunt meant a time of hunger. The failure of several hunts could cause starvation. The Montagnais had no reserves of food, unlike the Huron and Iroquois, who were highly successful farmers and produced surpluses from their fields.[84] Champlain urged the Montagnais to take up farming—not in the European way, but on the model of their Indian neighbors. "The soil is very good and suitable for cultivation," he wrote, "if they were willing to take the trouble to sow Indian corn, as do all their neighbors, the Algonquin, Huron, and Iroquois," who "are free from such cruel attacks of famine," and "live prosperously in comparison with the Montagnais, Canadien and Souriquois."[85]

In the fall of 1608, Champlain worried about the Montagnais, and watched as something terrible began to happen to them. All of their hunts ran short.

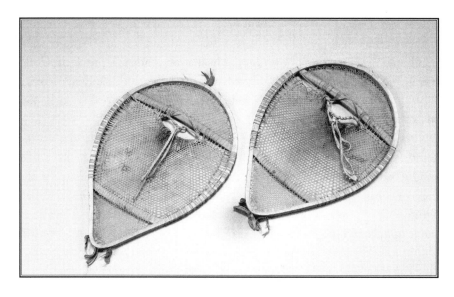

These small snowshoes were made for a Montagnais child. Champlain was fascinated by this hunting nation's adaptation to a hard environment, but he was deeply saddened by its extreme suffering in 1608–09, when the winter hunts failed.

The eel season was shorter than usual. The beaver hunt failed mainly because of a very wet fall. In high water the hunters could not get to the beaver lodges. The Montagnais reported to Champlain that "they did not take many beavers because the waters were too high, on account of the rivers overflowing."

The wet fall was followed by a long dry winter with very little snow. The moose hunt failed—the third hunting failure in a row for the Montagnais. Champlain observed: "All these tribes suffer so much from hunger that sometimes they are obliged to live on certain shell-fish, and to eat their dogs and skins with which they clothed themselves."[86] The crisis came in February of 1609. Montagnais families began to appear on the south side of the St. Lawrence, across from Champlain's habitation. The river was high and the current strong, and great floes of ice were tumbling downriver. The Montagnais called to the French for assistance, and in desperation launched their canoes into the turbulent stream. Their fragile vessels were caught by the ice, and "broken into a thousand pieces." The French watched as men, women, and children, weakened from hunger, fell into the water, clinging to ice floes. Suddenly the current drove the ice ashore and they leaped to safety. Champlain wrote that "they came to our settlement so emaciated and worn out that they look like skeletons."[87]

He gave them bread and beans, and bark to build their huts. Some were so hungry that they seized the rotten carcasses of a dog and a sow that the French had set out as carrion, and ate the putrid flesh half cooked. "When they have food," he wrote, "they lay nothing by, but eat and make good cheer continuously day and night, and after that they starve to death." He observed the misery of the Montagnais with great sadness, and their swings from exaltation to deep depression and despair. The instability of their life and chronic insecurity took a terrible toll. Champlain wrote that they were in "great dread of their enemies," and hardly ever slept quietly. They were "afflicted by terrible dreams that haunted them." [88]

As the winter grew worse, the French also began to suffer. They had plenty of bread and beans and some supplies of salted fish and meat, but not much else. In late November, the French settlers began to fall ill with severe symptoms that Champlain described as "dysentery." The Indians were also afflicted. Champlain wrote, "in my opinion," it came from "having eaten badly cooked eels." So severe was this "dysentery" that it killed many Frenchmen, including the locksmith Natel, who had saved Champlain's life. [89]

In midwinter, the survivors came down with scurvy. For three months, they had some success in keeping it at bay, perhaps by hunting and fishing in late fall and early winter, which brought supplies of fresh meat that many explorers have found to possess antiscorbutic properties, and possibly by eating roots and husks that offered a source of vitamin C. But in February they began to run out of whatever had protected them. Champlain wrote that "the scurvy began very late in February, and lasted till the middle of April." It took a terrible toll. Champlain ordered the surgeon Bonnerme to do autopsies, "to see if they were affected like those in other settlements. The same conditions were found." Then the surgeon himself fell severely ill, and died of the same cause. Champlain wrote, "All this gave us much trouble, on account of the difficulty we had in nursing the sick." Altogether seven Frenchmen died of scurvy, and thirteen of dysentery. [90]

After four months of suffering, spring at last arrived. A harbinger was the first run of fish in the St. Lawrence River. Vast numbers of shad swam upstream—more than anyone could possibly eat, and the French discovered a culinary delight in a vast abundance of shad roe, with a bit of French bacon for flavor. The last pockets of snow melted away, and the countryside turned green again. Only a small remnant of the colonists came through the winter. Champlain wrote that of twenty-eight habitants, eight remained alive, and "half of the living were very ill." But the settlement at Quebec had survived—to face another challenge.

12.

IROQUOIA

At War With the Mohawk, 1609–10

> They were sick and tired of the wars they have had with one another for
> more than fifty years. . . . They have spoken to me about it many times,
> and have often asked my advice, which was that they should make
> peace with one another, and we would assist them.
>
> —Champlain on Indian Wars[1]

O N JUNE 5, 1609, Champlain's Indian allies reported a sail on the St.
Lawrence River, heading upstream toward Quebec. The settlers ran
to the water's edge and saw a small shallop with a big French ensign
flying bravely from her masthead. She worked her way past the Île d'Orléans,
turned inward to the landing, and a young French captain sprang ashore. He
introduced himself as the sieur Claude Godet des Maretz, a high-spirited nobleman from the province of Perche, and another son-in-law of the prolific
Pont-Gravé. With him were master Pierre Chauvin de la Pierre, pilot Jean
Routier, and a crew of French matelots, who began to unload provisions.[2]

The handful of survivors rejoiced in their arrival. They were relieved to hear
that Pont-Gravé was in Tadoussac, with men and supplies to replace their
heavy losses through the winter. "This news made me happy," Champlain
wrote with his usual understatement. "It brought the relief that we had hoped."
Instantly he flew into action. Godet des Maretz was asked to take over as acting commander at Quebec. Champlain commandeered the shallop and sailed
downstream as fast as the wind and current could carry him.[3]

In Tadoussac harbor he met Pont-Gravé and heard the latest news from
France. It was very mixed. As expected, the company's one-year monopoly of
the fur trade had not been renewed and a swarm of free traders was expected
on the river. The investors had raised money for supplies and settlers, but only
enough to increase the population at Quebec to sixteen for the next winter, a
dangerously small number. The sieur de Mons also sent a small detachment of
soldiers to keep order in the settlement.[4]

Then came the bad news. Pont-Gravé delivered a private letter from de

Mons. Champlain tore open the seal and was shocked to read its tidings. He was to be relieved of command! De Mons ordered him to return to France in the fall of 1609 and report on Quebec. Pont-Gravé was instructed to work at Tadoussac through the summer, and take command in Quebec through the following winter. The letter fell on Champlain like a blow. What did it mean? After Duval's conspiracy and the execution of the ringleader, had de Mons lost confidence in his young lieutenant? Or did he merely mean to rotate his leaders and give him a well-earned leave? Either way, Champlain was to be replaced.[5]

Other leaders would have been shattered by this news. Some might have resigned on the spot, but Champlain responded in a different way. He was still in command, and could not return to France until the trading ships went home at the end of the summer. In the meantime he decided to center his thoughts on the next several months.

Champlain had a very large purpose in mind. During the winter, when the settlement at Quebec was near collapse, he had made an ambitious plan for the next season. A major threat to his design for New France was incessant warfare among Indian nations in the St. Lawrence Valley. Much of it pitted the Iroquois League, and especially the Mohawk nation, against the Algonquin and Montagnais to the north, the Huron to the west, and the Etchemin to the east.[6] The consequences of this endemic warfare were profoundly hostile to Champlain's vision for North America. As long as it continued, there could be no peace in the St. Lawrence Valley, no security for trade, and no hope for his dream of American Indians and Europeans living together in peace.

Champlain proposed to deal with the problem in several ways. He believed that a major cause of war was fear, and his remedy was to seek peace through diplomacy. To that end he built alliances among the Montagnais, Algonquin, and Huron, and other nations in Acadia and Norumbega. But a major problem remained with the Iroquois League, the Mohawk in particular. One historian of the Iroquois observes that by the start of the seventeenth century they were "at odds with all their neighbors—Algonquin and Huron to the north, Mahican on the east, and Susquehannock to the south." Many Indian nations in the northeast were at war with some of their neighbors; the Iroquois were at war with nearly all of theirs. They had a reputation for skill in war, among many warrior nations. And they were also known for cruelty, in a very cruel world.[7]

In 1608, Champlain had promised to aid the Indian nations of the St. Lawrence Valley when they were attacked by the Iroquois. At the same time, he was aware that the Iroquois were victims as well as aggressors, and he

Champlain's sketch of an Indian ally "showing the dress of these people when going to war," and the "way they arm themselves," with a bow in one hand and a war club in the other. He often showed Indian women with paddle and papoose, and wrote that Algonquins and Montagnais "both great nations," appeared much the same that way.

sent peace feelers to them through a captive woman of the Mohawk nation whom he had protected in Quebec with that purpose in mind. These overtures went nowhere. Mohawk war parties continued to attack the St. Lawrence Indians.[8]

By the spring of 1609, Champlain had come to the conclusion that peace could be achieved only by concerted military action against the Mohawk. He did not intend a war of conquest. Rather, he was thinking of one or two sharp blows by a coalition of Montagnais, Algonquin, and Huron, with French support. The object was to deter Mohawk attacks by raising the cost of raiding to the north. In that way Champlain hoped to break the cycle of violence and bring peace to the great valley.[9]

At the same time, Champlain also hoped to expand trading relations with many Indian nations, not primarily for trade itself but for a larger purpose. He thought of trade as an instrument of peace. American Indians also shared that belief. Ethnographer Bruce Trigger writes that "in historical times, all neighboring tribes either were at war or traded with one another." Historian William Fenton quotes an Indian who said, "Trade and peace we take to be the same thing." [10]

Champlain was determined to move forward with this plan in the spring of 1609, despite his heavy losses. After a cruel winter, he commanded a grand total of four able-bodied survivors in Quebec, but Pont-Gravé had brought more men. When the two French leaders met at Tadoussac on June 7, Champlain laid out a bold plan for "certain explorations in the interior," and made clear his intention to enter "the Iroquois country," with "our allies the Montagnais." Both men knew that this plan would mean a fight with some of the most formidable warriors in North America. It was an act of breathtaking audacity, considering the small size of Champlain's force. But what Champlain lacked in mass, he made up in acceleration. He also had the arquebus, and the Mohawk did not. The sieur de Mons had sent him a few good men who were trained in the use of that difficult weapon. Champlain also had many Indian allies, with hundreds of warriors.

Pont-Gravé listened to the proposal and gave his full support. These two old shipmates were always able to work together. They agreed that Champlain would take a shallop and twenty men—a large number for exploration, but very small for a military campaign against the Mohawk nation. He would gain the numbers that he needed from Indian allies in the St. Lawrence Valley. [11] Champlain hurried back to the shallop. "I left Tadoussac at once," he wrote, "and went back to Quebec." For two weeks the crew of the shallop were busy ferrying men and supplies for the settlement and for the mission to the country of the Iroquois. [12]

On June 18, 1609, all was ready. Champlain left Quebec with his twenty men, and pointed the bow of his shallop upstream. A large body of Montagnais warriors followed in their canoes. From the start he combined boldness with prudence—the secret of his long career. "As for the river," he wrote, "it is dangerous in many places, on account of the shoals and rocks which lie in it." The shallop sailed slowly against the strong spring current, and he kept leadsmen constantly at work, sounding the depth of the river. Champlain probably rigged a crow's nest for himself and studied the river with close attention. He discovered its main channel on the south side, about a mile from shore. [13]

The great river never ceased to fascinate Champlain. Beyond the narrows of Quebec, he wrote, "it begins to broaden, in some places to a league or a league and a half [three to five miles] across. The banks of the river were very handsome . . . the countryside becomes more and more beautiful as you advance . . . covered with great high forests." He sampled the soil and found it

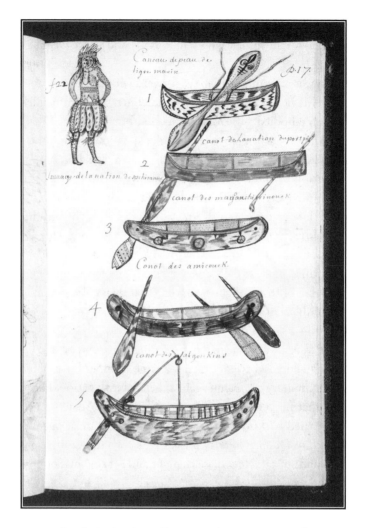

Indian canoes were adapted to local conditions. This seventeenth-century manuscript shows an Inuit sealskin kayak with a covered deck, and birchbark canoes of the Montagnais (lower St. Lawrence), Têtes-de-Boule (St. Maurice River), Amiakoues (Ottawa), and Algonquin (upper St. Lawrence). The Iroquois made big, heavy elm canoes.

deep, soft, and fertile. When he worked ashore, some of the crew went fishing and caught "great varieties of fish, both those we have in France, and others we do not have." The best were saved as specimens for the king's collection. The rest went into the pot.[14]

Thirty miles upstream from Quebec, Champlain came to a place that he called Sainte-Croix, and he found two or three hundred Indians, mostly Huron and Algonquin of the Petite-Nation, who were coming down the river to meet him. They were interested in Champlain, and were thinking about the possibility of going with him to the "country of the Iroquois," but they were not sure about this extraordinary Frenchman, and they wanted to know more.[15]

Champlain went ashore and presented himself to two leading chiefs: Iroquet of the Algonquin Petite-Nation and Ochasteguin of the Arendarhonon Huron. What followed was a meeting that combined spontaneity and ritual in high degree. The French and Indian leaders exchanged visits and smoked ceremonial pipes together. Champlain explained his plan to enter the Iroquois country, and left the two Indian leaders to talk it over. They did so, and returned his visit. The two Algonquin and Huron leaders came out to Champlain's shallop in the river and climbed aboard, while hundreds of Indian warriors gathered along the water's edge and watched intently. Many had never seen a European before.[16]

On board the shallop, more words were spoken. The two chiefs brought out their pipes again and began "smoking and meditating" in silence. Suddenly they stood up, turned to the warriors on the riverbank, and shouted that Champlain had come to help them against their blood-enemies. The chiefs proposed that everyone should sail downstream to Quebec.

The Indians wanted very much to observe Champlain himself and judge the strength of his vital spirit, which the Huron called *orenda*. They believed that all natural things had orenda in different degrees. It was a form of spiritual power that could be used for good and evil. Good hunters had strong orenda, more so than the animals they killed. Great warriors had very strong orenda. An important question for Iroquet and Ochasteguin was about the quality of Champlain's orenda. Was it strong? Was it good?[17]

The chiefs made a surprising request. They asked Champlain to order the firing of arquebuses. It was done, and the Indians responded with "loud shouts of astonishment." One ethnohistorian has written of the Indian belief that "*orenda* can reside in an object, and clearly guns had power."[18] After the firing of the weapons, Champlain made a speech, urging the Indians to observe that he and his companions came as warriors, not traders. They brought weapons, not trade goods. With a broad gesture of hospitality, he invited all the Indians to visit Quebec as his guest. It was an act of extravagant generosity—and a splendid display of orenda.[19]

All parties quickly agreed, and off they went downstream to Quebec. Together they made a brave sight on the beautiful river: Champlain and the French in their shallop with their arquebuses, burnished armor, plumed helmets, feathered hats, bright ensigns, streaming banners, and all the panoply of European warfare. Around them were Indians of many nations, three or four hundred Montagnais, Algonquin, and Huron in an armada of more than a hundred war canoes. Some of the canoes were stained in bright colors. Others were marked with vivid symbols of enemies killed and scalped.[20]

When they reached Quebec, Champlain sent an urgent message to Pont-Gravé at Tadoussac, urging him to come quickly with all the strength he could muster and as much food as he could spare. A few days later Pont-Gravé appeared with two shallops "filled with men." Everyone joined in a large feast and five or six days of ritual dancing. Every element of this event was a test of Champlain's orenda. He and Pont-Gravé were well aware that rituals were centrally important in these affairs, so they stinted at nothing. The tone of Champlain's account suggests that these two gregarious French leaders vastly enjoyed themselves and delighted in the bonhomie of their Indian allies.[21]

After the dancing was done, the French and Indians departed together from Quebec on June 28, 1609. Two French shallops were now filled with heavily armed men, and many canoes were crowded with hundreds of Indian warriors. Champlain was pleased with the numbers, but he worried about the calendar. Time was getting away from him. By July 1, they were only thirty miles upstream at the place called Sainte-Croix. Pont-Gravé could not stay much longer. He was running a trading post at Tadoussac, and Quebec had to be protected. At Sainte-Croix the French leaders had a conference. They agreed that Pont-Gravé should go back to Tadoussac, and some of the soldiers should return to Quebec.[22]

Champlain continued with the Indians and twelve Frenchmen. On July 3, they passed Trois-Rivières, "a very beautiful country," and sailed on to Lac Saint-Pierre, twenty miles long and nine miles wide, with beautiful meadows that held more game and fish than any other part of the great valley. They were in a no man's land between the Iroquois and the northern nations, a place "where no Indians live, by reason of the wars."[23] By July 5 or 6, they reached the mouth of what Champlain called the Rivière du Yroquois, today's Richelieu River. Here they stopped for two days and refreshed themselves with venison, birds, and fish that the Indians gave the French as gifts. While they rested they began to reflect on the difficulties that lay ahead for them. Champlain and his allies were about to enter "the country of the Iroquois."[24] They were marching on the Mohawks, one of the most powerful of the Iroquois people, and "keepers of the eastern door" to Iroquoia. Their territory ran as far east as the Hudson River and the lakes above it. In the Iroquois League the Mohawk were the "eldest brother," first among equals. The unwritten laws of

Iroquoia gave them a special place of honor. They were also among the most successful fighters in North America.[25]

As Champlain's companions absorbed these thoughts, some of them suddenly remembered urgent reasons why they had to be somewhere else. Champlain wrote that "only one part resolved to continue with me, and the others returned to their own country with their wives and the trade goods they had bartered." He had started with three or four hundred warriors and more than a hundred canoes. Within a few days, only sixty men remained in twenty-four canoes. Champlain was undaunted. Without hesitation he led his small force forward from the St. Lawrence Valley, and sailed up the river of the Iroquois. He wrote, "No Christians but ourselves had ever penetrated this place."[26]

The river of the Iroquois was handsome but hard going for the French shallop. All hands had to row against the current. They went thirty miles and came to a lake (today's Chambly Basin). Beyond it Champlain was surprised to meet rapids that the shallop could not pass. He wrote, "We trusted to the assurances of the Indians that the way was easy." So it was for canoes, but not for the larger French vessel.[27]

Champlain thought for a moment about abandoning the mission, but he was determined to see it through. The shallop would have to be left behind. The only way forward was to join the Indians in their canoes, and some of the

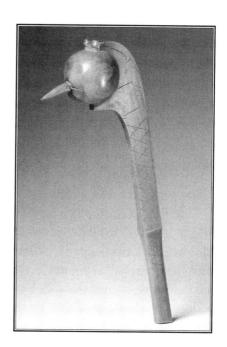

This Iroquois club of fire-tempered hardwood was called by the French a casse-tête, *skull smasher. It was a weapon of war, and an instrument of execution by a single stunning blow called the* coup de grâce, *which was sometimes an act of mercy to a captive in this violent world.*

French had no stomach for that. Champlain ordered them back to Quebec where he hoped "with God's grace, I should see them again." He wrote, "I took with me two men who were eager to go." One of them was probably François Addenin, a veteran soldier who had been sent by the king as a bodyguard for the sieur de Mons in Acadia. He had remained with Champlain at Port-Royal. Addenin was a soldier of long experience, a crack shot, and the most skillful hunter in the French colony.[28]

Champlain turned to the Indians and told them that "with two others I would go on the war path with them in their canoes; for I wished to show them that for myself I would not fail to keep my word to them, even if I went alone." They were pleased with his spirit and "promised to show him fine things." Champlain was about to challenge hundreds of Mohawk warriors on their own turf, with only sixty Indians and two Frenchmen at his side. It was a courageous decision. Others would have called it foolhardy to the point of madness. Champlain was usually very prudent, but he was capable of risking everything at a critical moment. A factor in his thinking may have been his recall by the sieur de Mons. This could be his last chance.

Champlain and his allies made a portage of about a mile around the rapids on the Richelieu River, and came to pine-covered Sainte Thérèse Island. Now they were well into Iroquois country, and the Mohawk were renowned for having "always sentinels along the approaches taken by their enemies." [29] The allies changed their method of advance. At the end of each day, they built a semicircular fort on the edge of the river. Some took bark from trees to make wigwams, while others felled big trees to make an abatis of tangled branches around their camp, leaving only the riverbank open as a line of retreat. Champlain observed that the Indians were able to complete a forest fort in less than two hours, and they did it so well that "500 of their enemies would have had difficulty in driving them out without losing many men." They sent forward a party of three canoes and nine men to search four or six miles ahead. The scouts found nothing, and all retired for the night.[30]

This was one of the first occasions when a European soldier traveled with a large Indian war party in North America. Champlain studied their ways. He was impressed by the skill with which they improvised forts, but he was troubled by their lack of attention to patrols. He urged them to place sentinels at listening posts, "to keep watch as they had seen us do every night." The Indians explained patiently that they had different customs. Their parties normally divided into three groups: one for hunting, another always under arms, and a third scouting ahead for signs "by which the chiefs of one nation reveal themselves to another." [31]

On July 14, 1609, they reached the large lake from which the river flowed. Champlain exercised his right to name it Lake Champlain on his map, as he and his two French companions may have been the first Europeans to see it.[32] The Indians had not exaggerated its size and beauty. Champlain reckoned its length at 80 to 100 leagues, and later corrected his estimate to 50 or 60 land leagues, which is roughly right. Lake Champlain is 125 miles long.[33] He was fascinated by its fine woods, beautiful islands, open meadows, and vast abundance of "game stags, fallow deer, fawns, roebuck, bears and other animals" that swam from the mainland to the islands. Champlain observed that one reason for this plenty was that no Indians lived there, "on account of their wars." He explored both sides of the lake, saw the Green Mountains of Vermont to the east, and to the west sighted the Adirondacks, which are visible from the eastern shore. With delight he studied the flora and fauna of this very beautiful region. On all his many maps, this lake was the only place where he put his name on the land.[34]

Champlain was able to spend two weeks studying the lake because the Indians suddenly changed the pace of their advance. They began to move very slowly, probably because of the phases of the moon. They had reached the lake one day before a full moon, which would have made them highly visible on the surface of the water to enemies who were hidden in the woods. While the moon was full and bright, they remained in the upper reaches of the lake and on its eastern shore. At last, on July 26, the moon was reduced to a small crescent and the nights were dark again. Champlain's explorations were interrupted by his Indian allies, who told him that it was time to move forward. The Indians reckoned that they were "within two or three days' journey of the enemy's homeland."[35]

They changed their routine again and began to advance only at night, all in a body except their scouts. As dawn approached they retreated into deep woods, rested without a fire, and ate only cold corncakes and water. They consulted with their wizards (*pilotois* or *ostemoy*, Champlain called them) and modeled their attack with small sticks in the ground. All warriors engaged in these discussions, and they rehearsed the attack again and again. Champlain was impressed by their planning. He wrote: "They arrange themselves in the order which they had seen these sticks. Then they mix themselves up, and again put themselves in proper order, repeating this two or three times, and go back to camp, without any need of a sergeant to make them keep their ranks, which they are quite able to maintain without getting into confusion. Such is the method they observe on the warpath." Each night the Indians were quickly

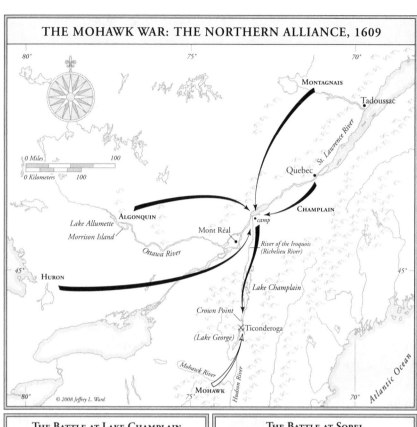

THE MOHAWK WAR: THE NORTHERN ALLIANCE, 1609

80° 75° 70°

MONTAGNAIS

Tadoussac

St. Lawrence River

0 Miles 100
0 Kilometers 100

Quebec

ALGONQUIN CHAMPLAIN
Lake Allumette
Morrison Island
Mont Réal
•camp
45° Ottawa River River of the Iroquois (Richelieu River) 45°

HURON

Lake Champlain

Crown Point

✕Ticonderoga
(Lake George)

Mohawk River Hudson River

MOHAWK

Atlantic Ocean

80° © 2008 Jeffrey L. Ward 75° 70°

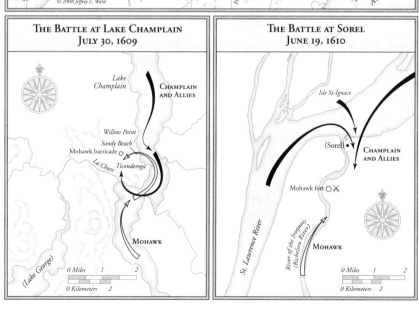

THE BATTLE AT LAKE CHAMPLAIN
JULY 30, 1609

Lake Champlain CHAMPLAIN AND ALLIES

Willow Point
Sandy Beach
Mohawk barricade ○
La Chute Ticonderoga

MOHAWK

(Lake George)

0 Miles 1 2
0 Kilometers 2

THE BATTLE AT SOREL
JUNE 19, 1610

Isle St-Ignace

(Sorel) • CHAMPLAIN AND ALLIES

Mohawk fort ○✕

St. Lawrence River River of the Iroquois (Richelieu River)

MOHAWK

0 Miles 1 2
0 Kilometers 2

on the trail again. Champlain was impressed by their expertise in woodcraft and their uncanny skill as trackers.[36]

In these hidden camps, tension began to mount as they moved deeper into Mohawk country. The Indians looked for signs from their medicine men, who performed many rituals and "superstitious ceremonies in order to know what was to happen to them." They also studied their dreams, which they regarded as an ultimate reality. Again and again, they asked Champlain if he "had dreams, and had seen their enemies in them." Champlain's answer was always the same. "I would tell them, that I had not, but nevertheless continued to inspire them with courage and good hope."[37]

The next night they made another hard journey, and as dawn approached they made secret camp deep in dense woodland. After the fortifications were complete, Champlain made his rounds, always on the alert. About ten or eleven o'clock in the morning he took a rest and fell asleep on the forest floor. When he awoke, the Indians asked him again if he had dreamed. Champlain said yes, and they gathered around, eager for a sign. He told them: "I dreamed that I saw in the lake near a mountain, our enemies the Iroquois drowning before our eyes. I wanted to rescue them, but our Indian allies told me that we should let them all die, for they were worth nothing." The Indians recognized the place in Champlain's dream as a site that lay just ahead, and they were much relieved. He wrote, "This gave them such confidence that they no longer had any doubt as to the good fortune awaiting them." To Champlain's Indian allies, dreams not only revealed the future. They controlled it. The next night the allies moved forward in a new spirit.[38]

The date was July 29, 1609. When evening came they broke camp, moved silently to the edge of the lake, and put their canoes in the water. Champlain admired the Indians for their astonishing control of sound. They paddled "without making any noise," not the smallest splash or the slightest touch of a paddle against a canoe. Sixty Indians and three Frenchmen glided like spirits across the still waters of the silent lake. The night was dark but very clear, and the stars were bright in the northern sky. Champlain looked upward at the constellations rotating around Polaris and reckoned the time at ten o'clock. They were coming near the southern end of the lake, deep in Mohawk country. On their right they passed a low peninsula with willow trees, and a sandy beach below a steep eroded bank. Beyond the beach Champlain saw a promontory projecting into the water. He called it a *cap*, which in his old French meant "a point of land often elevated."[39]

In the distance, silhouetted against a star-filled sky, Champlain was astonished to see the mountain of his dream. His Indian allies knew it well. The Iroquois called it "the meeting place of two waters," *tekontaró:ken* or, to European ears, Ticonderoga. The name came from two big and very beautiful lakes. Lake George to the south and west was two hundred feet above Lake Champlain, and drained into it from a height greater than Niagara Falls. The water flowed downward through a run of falls and rapids which the French called a *chute*, and entered Lake Champlain at Ticonderoga.[40] For many generations, Ticonderoga was one of the great strategic places in North America. It was the key to a long chain of lakes and rivers that ran from the St. Lawrence to the Hudson.[41] For the Mohawk, it was also a sacred and magical place. They believed that the promontory with its high limestone face and rocky caves was inhabited by spirits. The sandy beach to the north near Willow Point was thought to be visited by invisible artisans who lived at the bottom of Lake Champlain and brought up fragments of stone arrowheads and spear points, which they left as gifts for the Mohawk, who in turn left gifts of tobacco. Many stone shards can still be found there today.[42]

In the night of July 29, Champlain and his allies approached this fabled place in their canoes. As they rounded the promontory of Ticonderoga, their bow paddlers saw shadows stirring on the water ahead of them. They stared intently into the darkness, and the shadows began to assume an earthly form. They were boats of strange appearance, larger than northern birchbark canoes, and filled with men. The Indians instantly identified them. Mohawk![43]

Each group sighted the other at about the same time, and both were taken by surprise. "At the extremity of the cape," Champlain wrote, "we met the Iroquois. . . . Both they and we commenced to make loud cries, and each warrior made ready his arms." Both sides turned away and moved in opposite directions. "We retreated into the middle of the lake," Champlain wrote. The northern Indians had an advantage on the water. Their birchbark canoes were nimble, and very fast. The Mohawk boats were made of thick elm bark, often from a single tree. They were big and strong, but slow and clumsy. The Montagnais, Algonquin, and Huron could control the terms of engagement on the lake.[44]

The Mohawk chose not to challenge them afloat, and turned toward the land, which they knew very well. They came ashore on a sand beach between the promontory of Ticonderoga and Willow Point to the north, where a fringe of willow trees still flourishes near the water's edge. They pulled their boats close together, then climbed a low bank and gathered in an area of cleared ground with the forest just beyond. On the edge of the forest they began to fell trees and made a fort or barricade. In this work they were as skillful as Champlain's allies and, in his words, "fortified themselves very well."[45]

Champlain and his allies remained afloat on the lake and lashed their canoes together with poles so as not to become separated in the night. To his surprise a parley took place in the darkness. The Montagnais, Algonquin, and Huron sent two canoes "to learn from the enemy if they wished to fight." The Mohawk replied that "they had no other desire, but for the moment nothing could be seen and it was necessary to wait for daylight to distinguish each other." They proposed that, "as soon as the sun should rise, they would attack us." "To this," Champlain wrote, "our Indians agreed."[46]

"We were on the water," he wrote, "within bow-shot of their barricades." Songs and cries pierced the night. The Mohawk shouted insults at their enemies. "Our side was not lacking in repartee," Champlain recalled, "telling them that they would see feats of weaponry that they had never known before, and a great deal of other talk such as is usual at the siege of a city."[47]

As dawn approached, both sides prepared for battle.[48] In the darkness before first light Champlain's Indian allies paddled around the promontory and landed in a secluded spot where they were not under observation. "My companions and I were always kept carefully out of sight, lying flat in the canoes," he wrote. His Indian allies sent scouts ahead to watch the Mohawk fort. The rest assembled in their fighting formation, and moved forward toward the Mohawk barricade.

The three Frenchmen remained carefully hidden behind them. Each prepared his weapon, a short-barreled, shoulder-fired arquebus à rouet, Champlain's highly developed wheel lock weapon that did not require a smouldering matchlock, which might have betrayed their position. Champlain loaded four balls in the barrel of his arquebus. It was a dangerous thing to do. On Cape Cod in 1605, Champlain's weapon had exploded in his hands and nearly killed him. But overloading was highly effective in close combat, and he accepted the risk.[49]

A few Montagnais warriors crept close to the Iroquois barricade, using their highly developed hunting skills. At first light a Mohawk scout emerged from the fort, and looked warily around. A Montagnais archer drew his bow, and the scout fell silently to the ground, probably transfixed by an arrow through his throat.[50] The Mohawk warriors mustered quickly and came out of the fort, many of them wearing wooden armor that was proof against stone arrowheads. Both forces assembled in close formation on opposite sides of a clearing between the water and the woods.[51]

A Huron warrior girded for war. Champlain wrote that they and the Iroquois wore armor and carried shields of "wood woven with cotton thread, as proof against their arrows." They fought in close order—until they met Champlain and his arquebusiers in 1609. The battle at Lake Champlain wrought a revolution in Indian warfare.

Champlain peered through the ranks of his allies and studied the Mohawk as they emerged from their barricade. He counted two hundred warriors, "strong and robust men in their appearance," and he watched as "they advanced slowly to meet us with a gravity and assurance that I greatly admired." The Mohawk were in tight ranks—a disciplined close-order forest-phalanx that had defeated many foes. Their wooden armor and shields covered their bodies. In the lead were two Mohawk leaders, each wearing three high feathers above their heads. Champlain's Indians told him that the men with the big feathers were chiefs, and "I was to do what I could to kill them." [52]

Champlain's Indian allies were now about two hundred yards from the Mohawk, and began to move forward also in close formation. Once again Champlain was kept in a position behind them, where he could not be seen by the other side. The other two Frenchmen, on Champlain's orders, slipped silently into the forest and crept forward around the right flank of the Mohawk. Their orders were to stay out of sight until Champlain discharged his weapon. Then they were to advance and fire into the flank of the Mohawk formation.

Champlain remained hidden as his Indian allies advanced. When they were about fifty yards from their enemy, Champlain remembered that they "began to call to me with loud cries." Suddenly they divided in two parts, and Champlain was revealed to the Mohawk. He strode forward alone, twenty yards to the front of his friends and about thirty yards from the enemy. Champlain's burnished steel cuirass and helmet glittered in the golden light of the morning sun.

The Mohawk stopped in amazement and studied this astonishing figure who had suddenly appeared before them, as if he had risen out of the ground. They observed him for a moment that must have seemed an eternity. Then a Mohawk leader raised his bow. Champlain tells us, "I put my arquebus against my cheek and aimed straight at one of the chiefs." As the Indians drew their bowstrings, Champlain fired. There was a mighty crash and a cloud of white smoke. Two Mohawk chiefs fell dead, and another warrior was mortally wounded—three men brought down by one shot. Champlain's Indian allies raised a great shout, so loud that "one could not have heard the thunder." [53]

The Mohawk were stunned. Champlain wrote that they "were much astonished that two men should have been killed so quickly, even though they were provided with shields made of cotton thread woven together and wood which was proof against their arrows. This greatly frightened them." Even so, the Mohawk fought back bravely. Both sides fired clouds of arrows and Champlain reloaded his weapon. As he did so, his two French companions emerged on the edge of the forest. They appear to have been veteran soldiers—skilled arquebusiers, and highly disciplined men. Using the trees for cover, they knelt side by side, steadied their weapons, and took aim. Champlain wrote, "As I was reloading my arquebus, one of my companions fired a shot from the woods." This second blow was delivered into the flank of the Mohawk formation and it had a devastating effect. A third chief went down. The tight Mohawk formation shuddered in a strange way and suddenly came apart. Champlain wrote, "It astonished them so much that, seeing their chiefs dead, they lost courage, took to their heels, and abandoned the field and their fort, fleeing into the depth of the forest." Champlain led his Indian allies in a headlong charge. "I pursued them, and laid low still more of them," he wrote.

These Mohawk warriors, famed for valor in battle, were shattered by that sudden turn of events. It was a victory for the Montagnais, Algonquin, and Huron allies. Champlain noted, "Our Indians also killed several, and took ten or twelve prisoners. The remainder fled with the wounded." Altogether the Mohawk were thought to have lost about fifty warriors. On the other side, Champlain and his arquebusiers were unscathed. His Indian allies suffered "fifteen or sixteen arrow wounds, which soon healed." [54]

Champlain may have been the first European to join a battle between two North American Indian armies. What he observed was very different from what he expected. In 1609, these northern Indians fought major engagements in tight formations. They wore hardwood armor and carried shields, which Champlain observed to be highly effective against stone-age spears and arrows. In those massed battles, casualties were not heavy.

All that changed when Champlain and his two arquebusiers went into action. Wooden armor and shields offered no protection against firearms, and the close formation of the Mohawk made them vulnerable to French marksmen with quadruple-loaded weapons. In this battle, Europeans fought in open order and used forest cover effectively. The Indians fought in close formation. In the face of a new reality, the Indians learned quickly, and changed to what would later be called a "skulking way of war." This was a pivotal event in the history of Indian warfare.

After the battle, Champlain's allies looted the Mohawk camp, and took "a large quantity of Indian corn and meal belonging to the enemy, as well as their shields, which [the Mohawk] left behind, the better to run." Then there was the ritual feast, with singing and dancing to propitiate the spirits of the living and the dead. [55]

While the Indians conducted their sacred ceremonies, Champlain returned to his role as explorer. He got out his astrolabe and calculated the latitude of the battlefield at 43 degrees and several minutes. [56] His allies had told him of the chute where water flowed from Lake George into Lake Champlain. [57] It was very near the battlefield, and he seized the opportunity to go there. In only a few hours, he followed the shore of the lake, found the chute, and explored part of it. [58]

Indians also told him of a mighty river beyond the lakes, flowing to the south. Champlain quizzed the Mohawk captives "with the help of some Algonquin interpreters who knew the Iroquoian language." The prisoners said that they could reach that river by canoe in two days. [59] By coincidence in that high summer of 1609, while Champlain was moving south on the lake that bears his name, the English seaman Henry Hudson was sailing north on the river named in his honor. Hudson reached the present sites of Albany and Troy on September 19, 1609. These two great explorers came within a few miles and a few months of meeting each other on the ground between Lake Champlain, Lake George, and the Hudson River.[60]

All this exploring, looting, and feasting was crowded into a few busy hours after the battle. Champlain and his allies wanted to be away as quickly as possible, knowing that the Mohawk could muster a much larger force against them. Three hours after the battle, the victors climbed into their canoes and departed at high speed with their Mohawk captives securely bound.[61] They went about sixteen miles from the battlefield, heading north on the lake toward the river of the Iroquois that would carry them home. As night fell, they made camp, probably on the eastern shore of the lake where they would be safe from pursuit. The victors turned to their captives and began a "harangue," in Champlain's word, about the cruelty of the Iroquois toward their prisoners. They made it clear that the same fate was in store for them, and ordered one of their captives to sing. Champlain remembered that "it was a very sad song."[62]

Everyone knew what was coming. A fire was built and Champlain watched in horror as many warriors came forward and claimed the victor's role of torturer. He wrote: "Each took a brand and burned this poor wretch a little at a time, so as to make him suffer more torment. They stopped from time to time, and threw water on his back. Then they tore out his nails and applied fire to the tips of his fingers and his penis. After that, they scalped him, slowly poured very hot gum on the crown of his head, pierced his arms near the wrists, and with sticks they tried to pull out his sinews by brute force. When they could not get them out, they cut them off. This poor wretch uttered strange cries, and I felt pity to see him treated in this way. Still he bore it so firmly that sometimes one would have said that he felt scarcely any pain."[63]

The Indians invited Champlain to join in. He refused. "We do not commit such cruelties," he responded, but "if they wished me to shoot him with the arquebus I would be willing to do so. They said no, that he would not feel pain. I went away from them as if angry to see them practice so much cruelty on his body. When they saw that I was not pleased, they called me back, and told me to shoot him with my arquebus. I did so without his perceiving anything, and with one shot caused him to escape all the tortures he would have suffered, rather than see him brutally treated."[64]

Even that was not the end of it. Champlain wrote: "When he was dead they were not satisfied. They opened his body and threw his entrails into the lake. After that they cut off his head, arms and legs, which they scattered about, but they kept the scalp, which they flayed, as they did with the scalps of all the others whom they had killed in their attack. They committed another atrocity,

Champlain sketched this scene of Indian torture (1619). Women appear among the torturers, and he observed they were the most ingenious in their cruelty. He tried in vain to stop torture and wrote that Indian nations had no true system of law—only a customary lex talionis, which punished a wrongful act by a greater wrong.

which was to cut his heart in several pieces and to give it to his brother to eat, and to other companions who were prisoners. They took it and put in their mouths but would not swallow it. Some of the Algonquin Indians who were guarding the prisoners made them spit it out and throw it into the water. This is how these people act with regard to those whom they capture in war. . . . When this execution was over, we set out upon our return with the rest of the prisoners, who went along continually singing, without any expectation other than to be tortured." [65]

Torture and cannibalism of captives was an ancient custom among these nations. Not all Indians in the northeast practiced it. Acadian nations did not usually treat warrior-captives that way. But the evidence of archaeology indicates that the Iroquois and their northern neighbors had used torture for centuries. Scholars have explained this ancient custom as a ceremony or ritual, rooted in cultural practice and religious belief. Everyone was required to play a role: the audience, the torturers, and most of all the victim, who was expected to endure his torment with courage, dignity, and stoic calm. Many did so with amazing strength and resolve. [66]

Champlain understood this ritual atrocity better than some ethnographers have done, and he refused to accept any part of it. He hated Indian torture. It offended his deepest ideals and created a major obstacle to his grand design. He observed that the explicit purpose of torture was to commit an act of vengeance and retribution, designed to exceed the horror of tortures past.[67] This was the foundation of Champlain's judgment that the Indians had no law. He meant that their conception of justice was to punish a wrong by a greater wrong. That way of thinking was very different from an idea of law and justice as the rule of right.

He also recognized that Indian torture was also rational and functional in a very dark way. In the warrior cultures of North America, the continuing practice of torture was a way of guaranteeing a state of perpetual war. It meant that the work of retribution would always need to be done, and warriors would be needed to do it. For Champlain it was utterly destructive of peace and universal justice.

After the torture, Champlain and his allies resumed their journey, heading north on the river of the Iroquois. He wrote that they moved with "such speed that each day we made twenty-five or thirty leagues," at least fifty or sixty miles.[68] The Indians were driven by their fear, which appears to have been deepened by the torture of their captive. In the dark nights along the lake, the torturers dreamed terrible dreams. Then in the morning they acted upon them. Champlain wrote: "When we reached the entrance to the river of the Iroquois, some of the Indians dreamed that their enemies were pursuing them. This dream made them shift their camp, and they spent the entire night among the high bulrushes in Lac Saint-Pierre, because of the fear that they had of their enemies."[69]

At last they made their way down the Rivière des Iroquois and reached the St. Lawrence. The Algonquin and Huron warriors went west to their country with some of the captives. Champlain and the Montagnais turned east, running down the river. They made incredibly good time, and reached Quebec in two days. The Montagnais insisted that Champlain go with them to their villages for more ceremonies of another kind. They decorated the scalps of their victims and put them on sticks in their canoes. As they approached their villages, singing a victory song, Champlain watched as the Montagnais women "stripped themselves quite naked, and threw themselves into the water, swam out to the canoes, took the scalps of their enemies which were at the end of long sticks in the bows of the canoes." The women hung the scalps around their necks, "as if they had been precious chains, and they sang and danced." They made Champlain a present of a scalp and a pair of shields, "to show the king." Champlain wrote with a hint of shame, "to please them I said I would." [70]

Once back in Quebec, Champlain obeyed his orders from the sieur de Mons, and made ready to pass his command to Pont-Gravé and return to France. But a problem arose. Pont-Gravé was not in good health, and too ill to spend the winter in America. Together he and Champlain decided to leave two officers in command at Quebec: Captain Pierre Chauvin de la Pierre, a seaman and soldier of Dieppe, was to remain until the sieur de Mons could "give orders on the subject." With him was another very able young nobleman, Jean de Godet du Parc. [71]

Champlain left the colony in their good hands and departed for home. He made a fast eastward crossing, and reached France by October. Henri IV and the sieur de Mons were both at the palace of Fontainebleau, fifty miles southeast of Paris. Champlain instantly "took post" there, in his phrase, and was admitted to the presence of the king. As always, he had quick access to the Crown. "I at once waited upon His Majesty, to whom I told the story of my expedition wherein he took pleasure and satisfaction." Champlain presented the king with gifts that were fit for a monarch. He brought a pair of scarlet tanagers, beautiful little birds with spectacular red and black plumage. He also gave the king a belt of porcupine quills, "very well woven, according to the fashion of the country, which His Majesty liked very much." [72]

Equally successful was Champlain's report of his adventures. The king offered encouragement and strong support. At Fontainebleau, Champlain began to flourish in another role, as a promoter of New France. He had a flair for that task, and a skill at the brutal blood sport of court politics. At the same time, he had a talent for reaching others through his maps and books. Champlain did not think in our terms of manipulating images, mainly because his generation did not separate images from objects. His efforts at promotion centered on the substance of the thing, not its shadow. His world was very distant from ours that way. [73]

At Fontainebleau Champlain also talked with the sieur de Mons. If there was any lingering concern about the younger man's leadership, it left no traces in the record. Champlain wrote: "I informed him in detail of all that had taken place in the winter, and also the new explorations. And I spoke of hope for the future, touching the promises of the natives called Ochateguins [Huron]." Champlain called them the "good Iroquois." "The other Iroquois, their enemies, live farther south," he explained. "The former understand and do not differ much in language from the people recently discovered, and who hitherto had been unknown to us."[74]

After their audience at Fontainebleau, Champlain and de Mons hastened to meet their investors at Rouen. They talked with two leading backers, le sieur Collier and Lucas Le Gendre, "in order to consider what they were to do the following year." The meeting went well. Champlain tells us that both investors continued to support the settlement of Quebec and the exploration of the country. They also approved the alliance with the Huron, and supported Champlain's promise "to assist them in their wars." They agreed that Le Gendre would "take charge of the purchase of goods and provisions, and of the hiring of ships, men and other things necessary for the voyage."[75]

Then de Mons and Champlain went back to Paris, where they tried to obtain a monopoly of the fur trade "in the parts newly discovered by us." On this question the king's judgment went against them—one of the few instances when that happened.[76] De Mons decided to stay at court and keep trying. "Although he saw it was hopeless to obtain this commission, he did not cease to pursue his project, from his desire for the welfare and honor of France." Champlain also noted: "During this time the sieur de Mons had not yet informed me of his wishes concerning myself. . . . He left the entire question a matter of my choice." Once more Champlain would continue as commandant in Quebec.[77]

Champlain remained in France for six months. In the spring of 1610, he returned quickly to New France, eager to pursue his plans there. He sailed from Honfleur in early March, and reached Tadoussac by April 26. There he found other ships that had arrived at the start of the season. With the new system of free trade, Basque, Norman, and Breton trading ships were lying at anchor in the little harbor, and Tadoussac was full of activity. The Montagnais were there in strength and in good health. The winter had been mild, with little ice in the harbor. Old men told him that such a thing had not been seen for sixty years.[78]

Champlain hurried upriver to Quebec. He met the leaders Pierre Chauvin de la Pierre and young Jean de Godet du Parc, who are little remembered in the history of Quebec but were vital to its survival. They told him that the entire garrison was well, and "only a few had been slightly ill." Champlain wrote, "Having fresh meat, one's health is as good there as in France."[79]

Soon after Champlain arrived at Quebec a war party of sixty Montagnais appeared. They reported that many Basques and "Mistigoches" (Malouins and Normans) had said they would join them on the warpath.

"What do you think of that?" the Montagnais asked. "Do they speak the truth?"

"No," said Champlain. "I know well what they have at heart. They say this only to get your goods."

"You speak the truth," the Montagnais replied. "They are women, who wish only to make war on our beavers."[80]

Champlain assured the Montagnais that he would join them in a second campaign against their enemies the Iroquois as he had done before, and he asked something in return. He reminded the Montagnais that they had promised to help him explore the rivers to the north and west as far as the large sea, which we know as Hudson Bay. He also made another agreement with the Algonquin and Huron: that he would help them in their wars if they would take him to their own country and to the great lake beyond (Lake Huron), and show him copper mines and other things they had mentioned. "Hence," Champlain wrote, "I had two strings to my bow; if one failed, the other might stay taut."[81]

Champlain left Quebec on June 14. He had gone about forty miles up the river when he met a canoe with an Algonquin and a Montagnais who were looking for him. They urged him to push on as quickly as possible. Two hundred warriors were already waiting at the River of the Iroquois, and two hundred more would be coming.[82] He moved on to Trois-Rivières where he found the Montagnais waiting for him. The date was June 19, 1610, a moonless period when Indian attacks were likely to happen.[83]

Suddenly a canoe approached at high speed. The paddlers shouted that the Algonquin and Huron had already arrived, and moved up the river of the Iroquois without waiting for the rest. They had run into a Mohawk war party of about a hundred men, who had "barricaded themselves well," near the River of the Iroquois. A battle was in progress and the message was urgent: come quickly.

The Indians begged Champlain and the French to come with them. Champlain agreed, and climbed into a canoe with four French arquebusiers.[84] They went about a mile, then hauled their canoes on the bank and gathered up their weapons. Some carried bows and arrows. Others had clubs and spears that Champlain described as swords fixed to long handles. They plunged into the forest and moved very quickly. Champlain and his four Frenchmen were wearing breastplates, backplates, and helmets. They could not keep up, and the Indians disappeared ahead. Champlain tried to follow their track, and often went astray. He and his French soldiers struggled through thick woods, marsh, and swamp, knee deep in water, weighed down with "a pikeman's corselet

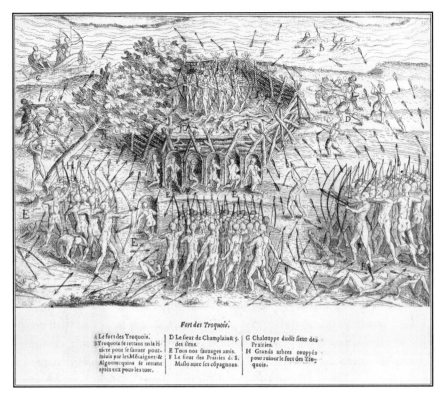

Fort des Troquois.

A Le fort des Yroquois.   D Le sieur de Champlain& s.   G Chalouppe dudit sieur des
B Yroquois se iettans en la ri-   des siens.   Prairies.
uiere pour se sauuer pour-   E Tous nos sauuages amis.   H Grands arbres couppés
suiuis par les Mōtaignet &   F Le sieur des Prairies de S.   pour ruiner le fort des Yro-
Algoumequins se iettant   Maslo auec ses cōpagnons.   quois.
apres eux pour les tuer.

Champlain's second battle with the Mohawk, June 19, 1610, on the Iroquois River (now the Richelieu River),
in the city of Sorel. He and his allies attacked a log fort and killed nearly all defenders. This victory brought
seventeen years of peace between the French and the Mohawk. He is marked by the letter D, with five
arquebusiers.

which bothered us greatly." They were assaulted by "hosts of mosquitoes, a strange sight, so thick that we could barely draw breath, so severely did they persecute us." [85]

The French lost the trail, then found two Indians and called out to them. Farther on, they met an Algonquin chief. He urged them to make haste. The Algonquin and Montagnais had tried to force the Mohawk barricade and had been repulsed. Some of the bravest Montagnais warriors had been killed and wounded. "You are our only hope," they told Champlain. [86]

The French went another quarter mile and began to hear "howls and shouts of both parties, flinging insults at one another, and continually skirmishing while waiting for us to come up." At last they reached the battlefield in deep woods on the bank of the River of the Iroquois, about three miles from the St. Lawrence River. Champlain wrote, "As soon as the Indians saw us they began to shout." [87]

He ordered his four arquebusiers to stay with him, and they reconnoitered the Mohawk barricade, which was "made of strong trees, placed one upon the other, in a circle, which is the ordinary form of their forts." The Montagnais and Algonquins also approached the barricade. Champlain and his men began to fire through the branches of the barricade, but "we could not see them as they could see us." As Champlain fired his first shot, he was hit by a Mohawk arrow that split the tip of his ear and pierced the side of his neck, barely missing his carotid artery by a fraction of an inch. He was lucky it did not kill him.

Champlain tells us that he "seized the arrow which was still in my neck and pulled it out." Even as he did so in the heat of battle, he admired the craftsmanship of the Iroquois arrowhead. "The point was tipped with a very sharp bit of stone," he wrote, but added, "my wound did not interfere with my duty, and our Indian allies also did theirs." Once again he admired the courage of his Mohawk opponents. "The enemy fought well," he observed, "so much so that one could see arrows flying on all sides as thick as hail." [88]

The French arquebusiers began to take a toll. They triple-loaded their weapons, rested them on the logs of the barricade, and fired carefully at close range. Champlain observed that the Mohawk in the fort were "astonished at the reports of our arquebuses," and "frightened at the execution done by the bullets, having seen many of their companions fall dead and wounded, thinking these shots to be irresistible." When they heard the report of a firearm, the Mohawk threw themselves on the ground, then rose again, and kept fighting. "We hardly missed a shot, and fired two or three balls each time," Champlain wrote.[89]

The arquebusiers began to run low on ammunition. Champlain turned to his Indian allies and told them that they must take the fort by storm—using their shields to get close enough to put ropes around the upright posts that held the barricade together. Champlain also urged the Indians to cut down several large trees near the barricade, "in order to make them fall on the enemy and crush the walls of the fort." Others were instructed to use their shields to protect the axmen, "all of which they carried out very promptly." [90]

Just as they were about to assault the fort, more Frenchmen arrived from the barques on the river three miles away, with weapons and ammunition. They had heard the arquebusades, and some of them hurried to the sound of the battle. In the lead was a trader named Des Prairies, "a young man full of courage," in Champlain's words, who "said to those who had stayed behind that it was disgraceful of them to see me fighting in this way with savages without going to my aid, and as for himself he held his honor too high for anyone to reproach him with such a thing." [91]

Champlain advised the Indians to stop work on the barricade. The French reinforcements began firing into it and brought down more Mohawk. Then Champlain and the Indians moved forward with arquebusiers on their flanks, and made a breach in the barricade. Champlain shouted a command: "*Ne tirez plus!* Cease fire!" In a moment twenty or thirty Indians and Frenchmen leaped into the breach "without meeting much resistance." In this way, he wrote, "by God's grace victory was won."[92]

A few Mohawks tried to get away, but "they did not get far," Champlain wrote, "for they were laid low by those about the barricade, and any who escaped were drowned in the river." Nearly the entire Mohawk force of about a hundred warriors was killed, except fifteen unfortunates who were taken alive. Of the Montagnais and the Algonquin, three were dead and fifty wounded. Champlain and the French arquebusiers suffered two men wounded, including their commander. The French traders appear to have been unscathed.[93] To the disgust of those who had done the fighting, more French traders arrived, "just in time to carry off the booty, which was not much." They found "only a few beaver skins of the dead, covered with blood, which the Indians did not take the trouble to pick up, and made sport of those who did so."[94]

Champlain went aboard a shallop in the river and had his wounds dressed by a French surgeon named de Boyer. His neck and ear were severely scarred. For the next twenty-five years, the Indians of the St. Lawrence Valley recognized the scar on his ear and touched it as if it were a talisman. After the two victories over the Mohawk, Champlain became a mythic figure among them. The victorious Montagnais and Algonquin "went home singing." With them went their captives, tightly bound. Everyone knew what was in store. Champlain intervened, and asked the Indians to give him a Mohawk prisoner, which they did. Champlain wrote, "It was no small service I did him." By degrees, Champlain allowed his captive more liberty in hope of gaining an emissary for peace, but he "escaped out of fear and terror."

Two days after the battle, the Indians began to torture their captives by fire and water, burning them with birchbark torches. Champlain wrote that the victims, "feeling the fire, would utter such loud cries, that it was awful to hear." Then the torturers would "throw water over their bodies to make them suffer more," and went to work with the torches again, "in such a way that the skin would fall from their bodies, and the captors would continue with loud shouts and whoops, dancing about, until these poor wretches fell dead."[95]

Some of the captives were kept alive so that they could be tortured by wives and daughters. Champlain observed that the women "greatly surpass the man

in cruelty, for by their cunning they invent more cruel torments, and take delight in them. Thus they cause the captives to end their lives in deepest suffering." After these events the victors went to an island in the St. Lawrence River
and feasted for three days. The Huron, Algonquin, and Montagnais celebrated
their victory. The French and Indians exchanged young men to learn languages, and then they parted.[96]

Many historians have criticized Champlain for going to war with the Iroquois.
Some have written that he started hostilities which would continue for two
centuries. In the late twentieth century, ethnohistorians studied this question
in a new spirit and came to a different conclusion. Most agreed that Champlain did not start these wars. The fighting had been going on between the
Mohawk and their neighbors to the north long before he arrived.

Further, Iroquois ethnologist William N. Fenton writes, "Nineteenth-
century historians to the contrary, this incident did not precipitate a hundred
years of Mohawk vengeance against New France."[97] It put a stop to major
fighting between the Mohawk and the French for a generation. An ethnologist
of the Huron agrees. Bruce Trigger writes of the two battles: "This was the last
time that the Mohawks were a serious threat along the St. Lawrence River
until the 1630s. Having suffered serious losses in two successive encounters,
they avoided armed Frenchmen."[98]

Champlain's two campaigns in 1609 and 1610 cost the Mohawk between
150 and 250 warriors. Their total population was between 5,000 and 8,000,
of whom less than a quarter were warriors, perhaps 1,000 to 2,000 men. They
probably lost between 10 and 20 percent of their fighting strength at a time
when they were also waging war against Indian nations to the south and east.
Small wonder that they steered clear of another collision with the French for
many years.[99]

After the battles at Ticonderoga and the Rivière des Iroquois, the Mohawk
made several peace overtures to the French. Champlain tried similar approaches to them, but he could not find a way to make lasting peace with the
Iroquois without alienating the Montagnais, Algonquin, and Huron. Even so,
he hoped for a modus vivendi between the French and the Mohawk, and he
achieved it. A very fragile quasi-peace was won by force of arms, and it continued for a generation, until 1634. The leaders who followed Champlain in Paris
and Quebec were unable to keep it going. They used too much force, or
too little. Champlain's policy was a middle way of peace through the carefully
calibrated use of limited force. We are only beginning to understand how
he did it.

13.

MARIE DE MEDICI

Starting Over in France, 1610–11

> I was deeply afflicted to hear such evil news. . . . All this, I say, put new life into me.
>
> —Samuel de Champlain, 1610[1]

IT WAS THE SUMMER OF 1610 in the St. Lawrence Valley. Champlain was hard at work in Quebec, and things were going well for him. As always, his top priority was to build relations with the Indian nations, especially the Montagnais, Algonquin, and Huron. It was an unceasing effort. Even as he extended the hand of fellowship, and they did the same to him, he and the Indian leaders were always aware that things could go wrong in a moment. A single troublemaker, French or Indian, could destroy years of patient labor. But in 1610 the alliances were strong, the Mohawk were quiet after two defeats, and peace prevailed through much of the valley.

At the same time Champlain was working at another task—the improvement of fortifications in Quebec, against the danger of attack by European enemies. The English had recently planted settlements in Virginia and Maine. Champlain kept a close eye on their activities. Illegal traders were also multiplying on the St. Lawrence River. Some of their vessels were more heavily armed than the ships that flew the king's standard. With all these groups in mind, Champlain put his men to work in Quebec, building a sturdy palisade, digging a deeper ditch, constructing a new drawbridge, reinforcing the batteries, and repairing the magazine. The colony was slowly gaining strength—its best protection against predators.

Important as these projects may have been, Champlain's most pressing task was to prepare the settlement for the winter. In the spring he had ordered his small band of colonists to plant large gardens, and by the summer they were "well provided with kitchen vegetables of all sorts." He also asked them to work on grain fields, and noted the progress of "very fine Indian corn, with wheat, rye and barley, which had been sown with vines" planted during his winter's stay. Champlain was hopeful that the settlement could become self-sufficient in the near future, and it was moving in that direction. Altogether the future looked bright for New France during the summer of 1610, brighter than ever before.[2]

Then, in an instant, everything changed. A ship arrived from France and it brought shattering news. The king was dead! Henri IV had been murdered, cut down at the peak of his power by a religious fanatic who hated his policy of toleration. Champlain's first response was disbelief. He absolutely refused to believe that such a thing could happen. More accounts arrived, with many rumors and alarms. Still he was in denial. "For me," he wrote, "it was very difficult to believe them on account of the different versions that were told, and they did not have much appearance of truth."[3]

But slowly the truth came clear, and it was a heavy blow. With the thrust of an insane assassin's knife, France had lost one of her greatest kings. Champlain had also lost his patron, protector, mentor, and friend. The king had been his strongest supporter and suddenly he was gone. "I was deeply afflicted to hear such evil news," Champlain wrote. Many people shared his grief in France and in Quebec. He sadly recalled that "all these reports brought great sorrow to true Frenchmen who were then in those parts."[4]

Even more troubling than the event itself was uncertainty about what might follow. After so many civil wars in France, nobody knew what would come next, and many feared the worst. A letter arrived from the sieur de Mons, urging Champlain to return immediately to France and help with problems at home.[5]

Champlain quickly settled his business in Quebec and once again appointed a very able successor to run the colony. Jean de Godet du Parc was the amiable young nobleman who had been tested as commander during the winter of 1609–10. His kinsmen had long been active in America, and he supported the grand design. With du Parc, sixteen habitants promised to stay the winter of 1609–10. Champlain swore them to their duty in a solemn ritual of honor that was important to these men. On August 8, 1610, he left Quebec and hurried down the river to Tadoussac. Five days later he was aboard a ship and homeward-bound for France.[6]

It was a slow passage of seven weeks, with contrary winds. In midocean the ship collided with a sleeping whale. The hull suffered no serious damage, but the whale was terribly wounded. Great gouts of bright red blood stained the sea around the ship. It seemed a dark omen to these deeply troubled men. They sailed on, in a mood of grim foreboding.[7] At last, on September 27, 1610, Champlain's ship reached the coast of France, and he came ashore at Honfleur. The half year that followed was one of the darkest periods in his life. He wrote very little about it in any of his books. That long silence cloaked a time of struggle and uncertainty, with many setbacks in France and America.[8]

In Paris, Henri IV had indeed been assassinated. Many attempts had been made on the king's life and on May 4, 1610, one of them at last succeeded. The killer was a schoolmaster named Ravaillac, a religious fanatic and an academic lunatic who had been crazed with rage against the king's edicts of toleration, and was consumed with fury in the frustration of a failed career.

When news of the murder reached the court, Queen Marie de Medici collapsed in tears and cried out, "The king is dead!" At her side the Lord Chancellor, Nicolas Brûlart, the marquis de Sillery, gently corrected her. "Forgive me, Majesty," he said. "The king is alive." He gestured toward her small son, the dauphin, who in that dark moment became Louis XIII of France.[9]

The heir apparent was still a child, nine years old. His foreign-born mother was proclaimed queen regent, and she became the ruler of France until her son came of age. Marie de Medici was thirty-seven years old in 1610, and a woman of surpassing beauty. In appearance she was more like her Austrian mother than her Italian father. She was very fair, with bright blond hair and perfect skin. Her refined features and Rubenesque form were much to the taste of her time. A French admirer wrote that her breasts were exceptionally "beautiful and well shaped," and she displayed them at every opportunity, even in a set of

In 1610, Louis XIII became child-king of France at the age of nine, with his mother as Queen-Regent. In this portrait by Frans Pourbus, his eyes are watchful, distant, and deeply suspicious, as well he might have been, in a Franco-Italian court that was more dangerous than the American forest.

Rubens, The Felicity of the Regency of Marie de Medici *(1625), one of twenty-four adulatory paintings ordered by the Queen. It symbolized her regency in a scale of justice and a shower of gold, which was far from the fact. Her corrupt Italian friends provoked a revolution. They were killed, and she was banished by her own son. Champlain lost his job but was quick to get it back.*

twenty-four huge canvases that Rubens himself was ordered to paint of her life. Her face was described as bewitching, and it was said that her mouth "supplemented the devastation that was caused by her eyes." Many observers wrote of Marie de Medici as one of the most exquisite women of her era. She used her beauty as an instrument of power and moved quickly to consolidate her position as ruler of France.[10]

The queen regent continued many of Henri IV's ministers in power—Brûlart and Sully in particular—and she supported most of his domestic policies. One of her first acts was to reconfirm her husband's Edict of Nantes, with its two principles of supremacy for the Roman Catholic Church and tolerance for Protestants throughout the realm.[11]

On foreign relations she went a different way. Marie de Medici moved closer to the papacy and strengthened ties with Spain. She surrounded herself with a circle of Italian friends and gave great weight to their counsel, especially the advice of her foster sister Leonora Galigaï Concini and her husband, Concino Concini. The Concinis were deeply resented at the French court, and the queen herself was perceived as a foreigner, in part because she never mastered French. Her letters were written in a unique language, part French and part Italian, with a bizarre orthography of her own invention.[12]

Marie de Medici showed no sympathy for Henri IV's grand dessein in Europe, and she had little interest in America. In 1610, she informed the Protestant sieur de Mons that he could no longer be "a member of our chamber" at Fontainebleau. His dismissal was a heavy blow, not so much for de Mons himself as for the cause of New France.[13]

Champlain went to court, but had no access to the queen. Some people there also attempted to end Champlain's pension of 600 livres a year, which had been granted originally by Henri IV. Later Champlain wrote that he met "all kinds of jealousies and attempts at alteration from certain ill-disposed persons." He never named them, but we know that some were merchants in the American trade who wanted free access to Canadian furs or a monopoly for themselves. Others opposed American ventures in general, as Sully had done in the court of Henri IV. More than a few were personal enemies of the prince de Condé. Sully was still in this group, and would be so even after his fall from power in 1611. The queen's Italian advisors had no liking for an expansive New France in North America. English and Spanish agents were everywhere. The clergy was an unstable cluster of contending groups. The court itself was a cockpit of rivalry among honor-obsessed nobles, who were rivals for the ear of the queen and for the favor of her son, the young king.[14]

The problems that Champlain faced in the court of the queen regent were similar in one way to those he had met in the councils of American Indians. To form an alliance with one group was to make an enemy of another. In both worlds, people cultivated elaborate rituals of politesse, but behind a screen of courtesy they fought constantly with one another in combats of unimaginable cruelty. In Champlain's two worlds, some of the most dangerous people wore diamonds and brocade.

It was a time of crisis for Champlain's cause, and the future of New France was very much in doubt. Many such moments came to Champlain in the course of his long and troubled career. Any one of them could have been fatal for his purposes. His responses were always the same. Opposition spurred Champlain to press onward. Danger awakened him to greater efforts. Defeat increased his determination to try again. He wrote later, "All this, I say, put new life into me, as it were, and redoubled my courage for the continuance of my labors in the exploration of New France." [15]

At court, Champlain appears to have made no immediate effort to approach the queen directly. Instead he worked at cultivating relationships with three of the most powerful "Lords of the Court," as he called them. One of these men was his former commanding officer Charles de Cossé, maréchal de Brissac, whom Henri IV had raised to high rank in 1594. Champlain consulted him on American affairs, and gained his help and advice at court. [16]

Once again, Champlain also sought out Pierre Jeannin, the respected president of the parlement in Burgundy. He had held high office under Henri IV as councillor and comptroller general of the king's finances. Champlain called him "monsieur le président Jeannin," and wrote that he was "a man who wished to see good enterprises flourish." He was a man of learning and a humanist with a thirst for knowledge. In 1609, Lescarbot dedicated his history of New France to Jeannin, and celebrated him as a man who "loves great undertakings by sea and ocean." In the words of historian W. L. Grant, Jeannin became a "special patron of geographers and explorers"—and of Champlain in particular. [17]

Champlain's most powerful friend and advisor was Lord Chancellor Nicolas Brûlart, the marquis de Sillery, a man who tried to keep the peace at court and was held in high esteem for his wisdom and judgment. Champlain often consulted him on American affairs. He frequently appeared in the writings of Lescarbot and Champlain as a faithful friend of New France. [18]

In Paris from 1610 to 1611, Champlain also made an effort to build a strong base at court by another method. At the same time that he cultivated relations with members of the high nobility, he formed alliances with officials and administrators who ran the daily business of the state. Historian Victor Tapié writes that in the regency of Marie de Medici, "governmental methods and procedures remained as they were under the late king. With few exceptions, the personnel and the entire administration were the same, and a corps of royal officials continued to manage the business of government, but without the close direction that they had received from Henri IV." This in some ways increased their power, and Champlain was keenly aware that they could make all the difference between success and failure for his plans.

In 1610, Champlain suddenly decided to take a wife, and his choice tells us something about his purposes. She was Hélène Boullé, the daughter of Nicolas

Boullé. Her father was a Protestant who appears to have converted to Catholicism, a man of the high bourgeoisie in Paris, with a job at the very heart of the royal regime. He was referred to as monsieur le Contrôleur Boullé. His offices were variously called *huissier des finances du roi*, or *huissier collecteur des finances*, or *secrétaire de la Chambre du Roi*. At court, a huissier was an officer of rank, charged with carrying out executive decisions of the monarch. He was a man at the center of power in France. That position brought him wealth and influence, which was cemented by the marriages of his children. One of his daughters, Margaret Boullé, married Charles Deslandes, secretary to the prince de Condé, and linked the family to one of the most powerful men in France.[19]

Champlain was already a friend of the family. He had known Nicolas Boullé since the days of his military service in Brittany. Hélène Boullé's brother Eustache had been his companion in Acadia, and served with him in the St. Lawrence Valley.[20] Together these men arranged a marriage, with an elaborate contract and a generous dowry. Nicolas Boullé offered 6,000 livres, of which 4,500 was to be paid at the start. Champlain agreed in return to pay 1,800 livres a year for his wife's support when he was out of the country.

Champlain was about forty years old in 1610; Hélène Boullé was barely twelve. She was so young that all of the contracting parties agreed that the marriage could not be consummated for two years. Hélène would continue to live in her parents' home through that period and move to her husband's home when she was fourteen.[21]

It was done in haste. The marriage contract was arranged on December 27, 1610, and required that the bride and groom were to "take each other in lawful wedlock within the briefest space of time possible." The wedding followed three days later on December 30, 1610, in the church of Saint-Germain l'Auxerrois, which still stands in Paris facing the east end of the Louvre. It had been the parish church of Henri IV. The documents were signed by the king's notaries and record keepers. We know from the list of witnesses that the ceremony was attended by many of the dead king's personal attendants. His physician, apothecaries, and councillors were on the list. The sieur de Mons and leading Paris merchants were also present.[22]

This union cemented an alliance between Champlain and administrative figures at court. It also connected him with investors and financiers in the city of Paris. They could be a counterweight to merchants in the western seaports of Normandy and Brittany who might be unhappy with a commercial venture that was controlled by a colonizer. The marriage promised to help Champlain's grand design in many ways.

Everyone appears to have been delighted, with one exception. The bride was bitterly unhappy. Even at the age of twelve, this spirited and headstrong young person was in a fury about her fate. Champlain showed no apparent concern for the feelings of the child who was forced to marry him against her will.

In Paris, while Champlain was working to strengthen his connections with court officials such as Nicolas Boullé, he also turned in another direction. During the regency of Marie de Medici, leaders of the Catholic Church were gaining power and influence in France. It was clear that Champlain had to win their approval for his project in America. He launched another campaign to rally support within the Church and its religious orders. This was uphill work. In Paris, clergy of all denominations looked unfavorably on a colony that had operated without a spiritual leader for several years. An expanding circle of Catholic leaders also wanted to banish all Protestants from New France, a move that would have excluded many seamen and settlers.

Champlain went to work and tried to build support among the lords spiritual of France: the cardinals and bishops, as well as the clergy, the heads of religious orders, and Catholic laymen. That effort began in 1610–11, and it was not an easy task. The complex structure of the Catholic Church in France presented a challenge. A great danger was fragmentation of effort and scattering of scarce resources.[23]

A case in point was an affair that started in 1610. It involved a small group of Jesuits and one of the most beautiful women in France. Henri IV had expelled the Jesuits in 1594, but they had survived in some provinces, and in 1603 the king relented. He formed a friendship with Pierre Coton, a very able Jesuit priest who became his confessor. Henri allowed the Jesuits to return, on condition that they must be native-born Frenchmen and swear an oath of loyalty to the Crown. It was part of a larger campaign by the king and later the queen regent to make peace with the major Catholic orders, and to encourage them to function in France, in the hope that "all nature's difference, might keep nature's peace." Among the beneficiaries were Augustinians, Jesuits, Capuchins, and Franciscans such as the Récollet fathers. Most of these groups would play important roles in New France.[24]

In France the Jesuits made connections with the high aristocracy. Prominent among their supporters was an extraordinary figure who never came to America but played a role in its history. She was Antoinette de Pons, the marquise de Guercheville, a young widow who was renowned for her formidable intellect, great wealth, deep piety, and a sensual beauty that drove some men

Antoinette de Pons, marquise de Guercheville (1570–1632) was a woman of piety, wealth, and beauty—hotly pursued by Henri IV, but never caught. She devoted herself to Jesuit missions and became proprietress of Acadia. Champlain begged her to support a common effort in New France—another of his many failures.

mad with desire. Some of the stories about her might have been written by Rabelais.[25]

One of these tales had involved King Henri IV himself, who was fascinated by Madame de Guercheville. She spurned his advances and retreated from the court to her château at La Roche-Guyon on the river Seine, thirty miles west of Paris. The king organized a hunting party near her château and sent a gentleman of the court to ask the marquise if he could spend the night. She replied that the king did her great honor and she would do her best to receive him. For the occasion she ordered a magnificent supper, illuminated her château with torches in every window, put on a beautiful gown covered with diamonds, and prepared to receive the king.[26]

Henri rode in from his hunt in high anticipation, and Madame de Guercheville came out to greet him, preceded by pages with torches, and surrounded by ladies and gentlemen of the neighborhood. The king found her "more beautiful than ever, in the shadows of the night, and the dancing light of flambeaux and her diamonds." He said to her, "Is this really you, and am I the king you so dislike?" To his delight, she led him directly to her bedroom, opened the door, and then withdrew. The king thought she was going to arrange an intimate feast for them both. Then he heard her in the courtyard below, calling for her carriage. The king went running down the stairs after her and cried, "*Quoi, madame?* Am I driving you out of your own house?" She answered with great firmness, "Sire, a king should be master wherever he is. But as for me, I like to keep some little power in whatever poor places I find myself." Without waiting for his reply, she climbed into her carriage and rode off to spend the night with a lady in the neighborhood. It was said that the king formed a high respect for her in the years that followed.[27]

The passion that Madame de Guercheville denied to the king was lavished upon the Church, and still more on the Society of Jesus and its many missions. Her religious advisor was a young Jesuit priest, Father Énemond Massé, a friend of Pierre Coton. After the death of Henri IV, she became the patroness and sponsor of Jesuit missions. Her particular interest turned to the conversion of the American Indians. A Jesuit scholar wrote that "the only difficulty . . . was to restrain her zeal within reasonable bounds." She enlisted the queen regent and the marquise de Verneuil to her cause. The queen authorized 2,000 crowns, much of it raised by subscription from royal princesses and the ladies of Paris and Rouen.[28]

With Madame de Guercheville's sponsorship and the support of the queen regent, in 1610, two Jesuit priests, Massé and Pierre Biard, were recruited to found a mission in America. Two Huguenot merchants of Dieppe, Du Jardin and Du Quesne, were hired to fit out a ship, but when they discovered that they were to carry two Jesuits, they refused to participate. The Jesuit leaders went to Madame de Guercheville. She bought the ship and supported the mission at a cost of 5,700 livres.[29]

The venture combined two purposes: piety and profit. The Jesuit contract authorized the priests to operate a fur trade from their missions, and Madame de Guercheville insisted that all profits should revert to the mission. The idea was to create what has been called an "Acadian Paraguay" in the Gulf of Maine, comparable to the South American country that was run by the Jesuits for many generations. The two Jesuit fathers, Massé and Biard, sailed for America on January 26, 1611, and suffered terribly on a long winter voyage. These were the first Black Robes in New France. The colony was called Saint-Sauveur, and it was planted on Mount Desert Island, perhaps at a beautiful and sheltered place on the western side of Somes Sound which is still called Jesuit Point.[30]

Madame de Guercheville also worked with the sieur de Poutrincourt and his son Biencourt de Poutrincourt for a time, but fell out with them over a question of land titles in America. She received an enormous grant of land in Acadia, as far south as Florida. Alarmed English leaders ordered its removal. Two years later, this French Jesuit colony was attacked and destroyed by an English force from Jamestown in Virginia. The English commander, Samuel Argall, had orders to evict the French, burn their settlements, and enforce England's claim to what is now the coast of Maine.[31]

Champlain regarded these events with dismay. A very large sum had been lavished on the Jesuit colony at Saint-Sauveur, and it was a total loss. Champlain went to Father Coton two or three times, and urged him to join a common effort for a colony centered on the St. Lawrence River rather than in southern Acadia. The two men were unable to agree on terms. They differed over money, but even more over control. Champlain wrote that Coton wanted terms which "could not have been to the advantage of the sieur de Mons, and this was the reason why nothing was done, in spite of all I could urge upon this father." He wrote that this enterprise was thwarted by many misfortunes which could well have been avoided at the start if Madame de Guercheville had given 3,600 livres to the sieur de Mons, who wished to have the settlement at Quebec. The lost colony of Saint-Sauveur on Mount Desert Island never revived. Its history revealed the troubles that afflicted New France and Champlain in the regency of Marie de Medici after the death of Henri IV.[32]

In all these ways, Champlain struggled through the dark years from 1610 to 1612. Lacking direct access to the queen regent, he had succeeded in organizing several centers of support: from his old American circle, from friends in the city, and from an expanding network of royal officials at court. But he had failed with the religious orders and their patroness, Madame de Guercheville.

Still, he kept at it. His elaborate efforts to broaden the base of his American project were shaped by the structure of power in France. By comparison with the empire of New Spain, French colonies in America began as experiments in mixed enterprise. Champlain needed the support of the Crown, the Catholic Church, its monastic orders, great nobles, ministers, court officials, provincial parlements, towns, courts of law, merchants, commercial companies, lawyers, and others. A major difficulty from the start was the division of power in France, fragmentation of control, and tangled lines of authority. Even in small matters he had to win the backing of many people at home. And at the same time, he kept an eye on events in North America. In the early months of 1611 Champlain turned again in that direction.

14.

TRANSATLANTIC TRIALS

Champlain's Shuttle Diplomacy, 1611–15

> He left to me the task of finding the ways and means of keeping New
> France and laid upon me the entire responsibility for it.
>
> —Samuel de Champlain on de Mons, 1611[1]

WHILE CHAMPLAIN STRUGGLED in France, the infant settlement at Quebec was surrounded by danger. Every Canadian winter was a mortal challenge to its habitants. Every spring brought more traders and fishermen who saw the habitants as rivals and their leaders as regulators. Merchant-capitalists regarded a permanent settlement as a folly. English neighbors perceived it as a threat.

Even to its friends, the future of Quebec seemed very doubtful in 1611. Little was known about the interior of New France. It was laced with great waterways, but where did they lead? It was blessed with resources, but how could they be exploited? It was inhabited by many Indian nations who outnumbered the small European settlements, but to become a friend of one was to make an enemy of another.

It was typical of Champlain to seek a solution in growth. His primary purpose was to broaden the base of support for New France on both sides of the Atlantic. In America he planned to enlarge the base for New France by building more alliances with Indian nations to the west. He was thinking in particular of the Huron nation, whom he called the Good Iroquois, and also of the many Algonquin nations northwest of Montreal. Everything hinged on communication. To help with that task Champlain recruited more young men for his "corps of interpreters," both Indians and Europeans. One of them was a Huron named Savignon, who had spent a year in France. Another was a Frenchman named Nicolas de Vignau, who had been sent to live among the northern Indians.[2]

• • •

To succeed with these plans, Champlain was compelled to shuttle back and forth across the ocean, moving rapidly from one opportunity to the next. It was a hard trial for transatlantic leadership. The growing number of his Atlantic crossings was a measure of the magnitude of his leadership. Their timing was another sign of stress. Increasingly he had to make his voyages in difficult seasons of the year, even in midwinter.

In February, 1611, Champlain organized a voyage with the help of Thomas and Lucas Le Gendre, merchants of Rouen with long experience in overseas trade and a strong relationship with the sieur de Mons. They were silent supporters of New France. Without them, Champlain could not have functioned in these lean years. Thomas Le Gendre capitalized the voyage as a trading venture, and "came himself to Honfleur, to oversee the outfitting of the voyage." Somehow Champlain also recruited "several artisans" for Quebec, and purchased supplies for another precarious year.[3]

He sailed from Honfleur on March 1, 1611. It was one of his earliest crossings—a winter passage on the stormy North Atlantic, and it nearly killed him. At sea his little ship met heavy winter gales that forced him north of his usual track. Champlain wrote that "contrary winds from the south-southwest and west-northwest . . . drove us as far as latitude 42 degrees, without being able to make a southing." One can only imagine what life was like on his small vessel, rising and plunging in dark gray seas with white water streaming from her deck. Champlain wrote that they were able to advance only with "much pain and labor, by going from one tack and another in order to take our direct line."[4]

When they were within eighty leagues of the Grand Bank, they met thick fog and mountains of floating ice. Several times they came close to collision with icebergs. Champlain reckoned their height at 180 to 240 feet, three times higher than the mastheads of his ship, and these mountains of ice were moving at high speed before the wind. As they dodged among the biggest bergs, small fields of floe-ice crunched dangerously beneath the ship. They crossed the Grand Bank, but Champlain found that winds and currents had set them still farther north. They could not get below 44 degrees, 30 minutes.[5]

So cold was the North Atlantic, that even in the latitude of today's Halifax, Champlain found himself on the edge of a "great bank of ice that extended as far as the eye could see."[6] Soon they were surrounded by it. Night came with rain, snow, and wind so strong that the ship "could hardly carry our mainsail." With great effort, they worked their way south and got clear of the pack ice, only to enter another ice field surrounded by "thousands of ice floes on all sides." Champlain wrote, "More than a score of times we thought we should not escape with our lives."[7]

"The cold was so great," he recalled, "that all of the ship's running rigging was frozen and covered with big icicles, so that we could not manoeuvre or even stand on the ship's deck."[8] At one point they struck their sails and drifted with the ice. In the night they hoisted sail again but could find no passage, and the ice was closing in. They tried to force their way. Seamen in the forward part of the ship worked with iron bars and long poles to ward off the most dangerous floes. Time and again, new ice appeared in their path. It was now the last week of April, and they had been nearly two months on the North Atlantic. In thick fog, Champlain wrote, "We tacked a hundred times from side to side, and many times thought we were lost."[9]

Then suddenly the fog lifted. "When we looked about us," Champlain remembered, "we saw that we were enclosed within a small pond, less than a league and a half in circumference." In the distance they sighted land, which Champlain recognized as Cape Breton. At last they left the ice behind, and reached Tadoussac on May 13, 1611, after eleven weeks at sea. It was one of Champlain's hardest crossings.[10]

As Champlain sailed up the St. Lawrence River, he was surprised to find "the whole country almost covered with snow" even in mid-May. It had been one of the coldest winters on record. He found the Indians in a desperate state, particularly the Montagnais, who came to meet Champlain's ship, with "only a few articles which they wished to barter merely in order to get food."[11]

Champlain gave them food and hurried on. His purpose was to sail up the St. Lawrence River to the great rapids beyond Montreal, where he hoped to "meet the Algonquins and other nations who had promised . . . to be there with the young lad" he had given them. The lad was Étienne Brûlé, who had been sent to live among the Indians and to discover what lay to the west and north. They had agreed to meet on May 20. Champlain was consumed with curiosity "to learn from him what he had seen while wintering in the interior."[12]

So eager was Champlain that he left his ship at Tadoussac to buy furs from the Indians, and sailed upriver in a battered barque that was barely seaworthy. Halfway to Quebec, the leaky boat took on much water and was in danger of foundering. He reached Quebec just in time. Champlain was happy to find that the settlement had survived the winter with no losses. Commandant Jean Godet du Parc and his sixteen companions were "all very well, without any sickness," a credit to du Parc's leadership. Once again this able and self-effacing young nobleman had held the colony together. The habitants told Champlain that they had enjoyed good hunting through the winter. He took their experience as further proof that fresh meat prevented scurvy.[13]

Champlain pushed forward with the repair of his boat. When the work was done he was off again, driving his men up the river. They reached the Great Rapids beyond what is now Montreal by May 28, eight days late for a prearranged meeting with the Indians, and found nobody there.[14] In their absence, Champlain came upon a battered canoe. With two men he used it to explore the riverbanks below the rapids. He was searching for a "site of settlement" near the head of navigation on the St. Lawrence River. Champlain examined the banks for eight leagues and studied the high hill that Cartier had named Le Mont Réal. Finally he found a stretch of level land a league downstream near a small tributary called the Rivière Saint-Pierre. It included more than sixty arpents that had been cleared long ago for cornfields and were now open meadow, mixed with young trees. Champlain was told that "formerly the Indians had cultivated these lands, but they abandoned them on account of the frequent wars which they carried on there."[15] He studied the land with a soldier's eye and thought that a large area could be moated and fortified. Champlain named it la Place Royale and set his men to leveling the ground. He built a small house and a masonry wall ten yards long, "to see how it would last during the winter when the waters came down." Then he planted his usual test gardens, "one in the meadows and the other in the woods," and sowed an abundance of seeds. He was happy to observe that they "came up quickly and in perfect condition."[16]

Champlain mapped the area with much attention to the river, its islands, and the terrain. On the north bank of the river he literally put Cartier's name "Montréal" on the map—its first published appearance.[17] An attractive island in the river was three-quarters of a league in circumference, with "space to build a good strong town." He named it Isle Sainte-Hélène, probably in honor of his reluctant bride.[18] Champlain and his men were surprised by the fertility of the land. Everywhere they found wildlife in unimaginable numbers. They came upon an island covered with "so many herons that the air was completely filled with them."[19]

Above Montreal were the rapids, a roaring cataract of white water. He described one stretch of "seven or eight waterfalls" that "descend from ledge to ledge, and the smallest of them is three feet high. . . . Part of it is completely white with foam that marked the most fearful place. The roar is so loud that one would have said it was thunder, as the air rang with the sound of these cataracts."[20] It was a place of beauty and danger. While Champlain was there, an impetuous young Frenchman named Louis and two Indians tried to run the rapids in a canoe. They capsized, and two of the three were drowned. Champlain and the sole survivor went searching for their bodies: "When he showed me the spot," Champlain wrote, "my hair stood on end to see so terrifying a place." He described the rapids as *fort dangereux, effroyable, espouvantable*— very dangerous, frightful, terrifying. It was a language of fear that rarely appeared in his writings. So violent were the rapids that the Frenchman's body was never found. Champlain named this place the *Grand Sault Saint-Louis*, perhaps to commemorate the Frenchman who died there. Today they are called the Lachine Rapids, an ironic echo of Champlain's search for a passage to China.[21]

On June 1, 1611, while Champlain was busily exploring the river above Montreal, Pont-Gravé arrived from Tadoussac in search of trade. He had crossed the Atlantic after Champlain, and was followed by fur traders in unexpected numbers. By June 12, thirteen barques and pataches were moored below the rapids. The next day, the Huron began to arrive, two hundred warriors led by three chiefs who were friends of Champlain. He went to greet them in a canoe, and they responded with loud shouts of celebration. The French replied by firing their weapons in a *feu de joie* that alarmed the Huron, some of whom had never seen a gun.

Champlain brought forward Savignon, who spoke well of his reception in France. The Huron produced Étienne Brûlé, who was dressed as an Indian, and had learned to speak the Huron and Algonquian languages.[22] The following day, the Indians invited Champlain and Brûlé to meet with them. The Huron insisted that they come alone—another sign of the special relationship that Champlain had formed with them. The Indians said that they wished to make a "close alliance" with Champlain, but they were not happy to find so many traders on the river, and "saw clearly that it was only a love of gain and avarice that brought these people together." The Huron feared that these mercenary Frenchmen "would do them harm."[23] Champlain defended the traders, and assured the Indians, "we all served the same king." After much discussion, the Huron made Champlain a princely gift of a hundred fine beaver pelts, and Champlain responded with presents of his own. He talked with them about the river's source, and they told him of "many things, both of the rivers, falls, lakes and lands, and of the nations living there." Four Hurons said that they had seen a sea far from their own country, but there were many enemies in between, and the country was difficult. Champlain wrote: "They spoke to me of these things in great detail, showing me by drawings all the places they had vis-

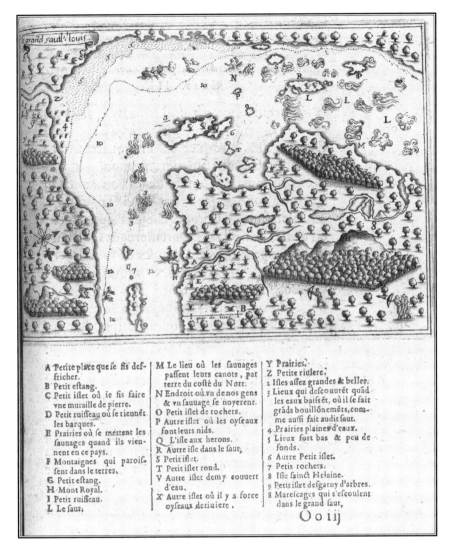

A Petite place que ie fis def-
fricher.
B Petit eftang.
C Petit iflet où ie fis faire
vne muraille de pierre.
D Petit ruiffeau où fe tiennét
les barques.
E Prairies où fe mettent les
fauuages quand ils vien-
nent en ce pays.
F Montaignes qui paroif-
fent dans le terres.
G Petit eftang.
H Mont Royal.
I Petit ruiffeau.
L Le faut.

M Le lieu où les fauuages
paffent leurs canots, par
terre du cofté du Nort.
N Endroit où vn de nos gens
& vn fauuage fe noyerent.
O Petit iflet de rochers.
P Autre iflet où les oyfeaux
font leurs nids.
Q L'ifle aux herons.
R Autre ifle dans le faut.
S Petit iflet.
T Petit iflet rond.
V Autre iflet demy couuert
d'eau.
X Autre iflet où il y a force
oyfeaux deriuiere.

Y Prairies.
Z Petite riuiere.
2 Ifles affez grandes & belles.
3 Lieux qui defcouurét quäd
les eaux baiffét, où il fe fait
gräds bouillônemêts, com-
me auffi fait audit faut.
4 Prairies plaines d'eaux.
5 Lieux fort bas & peu de
fonds.
6 Autre Petit iflet.
7 Petis rochers.
8 Ifle fainct Helaine.
9 Petit iflet defgarny d'arbres.
8 Marefcages qui s'efcoulent
dans le grand faut.

O o iij

The head of navigation on the St. Lawrence River were these roaring rapids, which Champlain called
le grand sault St. Louis. *Stripped to his shirt, he ran them in a birch canoe with skilled Huron paddlers and*
barely survived. Near the falls he met many Indian nations in tabagies, and framed a web of western alliances.

ited, taking pleasure in telling me about them. And as for myself, I was not
weary of listening to them."[24]

The next night the Huron summoned Champlain again and he found them
all in council. They explained their custom of nocturnal councils, "for at night
we thought only of listening," and they told Champlain that they wanted to
"tell me their desire in secret." Once again they said that they were "afraid

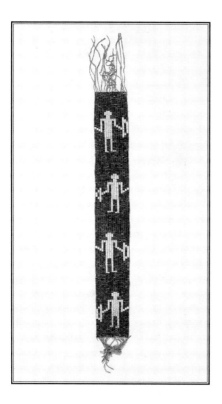

This finely woven wampum belt represented four Huron chiefs or clans, who presented it to Champlain in 1611 as an emblem of their esteem and a token of alliance. He in turn gave it to the King, and it survives today in the royal collections of France.

of the other vessels on the river" and "displeased at seeing so many Frenchmen who were not very friendly towards one another." They added that they "much mistrusted" the many traders. The Huron gave Champlain more gifts and asked him to come to their country. They talked together through the night.[25]

In the morning, the Huron withdrew another eight leagues, increasing their distance from the French traders, and once more they invited Champlain to visit them alone. This time they discussed the possibility of an alliance against the Iroquois. Champlain observed the complexity of their feelings and the autonomy of individual warriors. One of the Huron had been tortured by the Iroquois and wanted revenge. The chiefs did not support him, but could not restrain him. Champlain promised help if they were attacked but he also expressed a strong wish for peace, which they also shared.[26]

After the meeting Champlain asked the Huron to take him back to his vessel below the rapids. They agreed and brought eight canoes to run the rapids, much to Champlain's alarm. He did not want to do it but felt he could not back away without forfeiting the respect of the Indians. He wrote, "They stripped naked, but left me in my shirt, for it often happens that some are lost running the rapids." The Huron advised everyone to "keep close to one another in order to give prompt help." They told Champlain: "If unfortunately my canoe should upset, since I did not know how to swim, I ought under no circumstances to let go, but to keep hold of the small pieces of wood (thwarts) in the center of the canoe; for they would easily rescue me."

Champlain was a man of courage, but he confessed that he was terrified by that roaring cataract. He told his readers, "I assure you that even the bravest people in the world who have not seen nor passed this place in small boats such as theirs, could not do so without apprehension."[27] With a show of outward calm and inner terror he hitched up his shirt and climbed into his canoe. It was one of the great rides of his life. The rushing water seized the boat and swept it forward through massive boulders that could have crushed it in an instant. The fragile craft bucked and twisted in the roaring river, and many times Champlain thought they were lost. But the Indian paddlers brought him through and he was astonished at their skill. "These nations are so clever at shooting rapids, that this is easy for them," he wrote. "I ran this one with them, a thing I had never done before, nor had any other Christian, except my young man [Brûlé]."[28]

The Huron went on their way and Champlain remained at the rapids to meet the Algonquin who arrived on July 12. Another large celebration followed, with yet more tabagies. Champlain worked to build an alliance with them. Once again he was planning for the long run. More young lads were exchanged by the French and the Algonquin, so as to learn each other's customs. After much discussion, the meetings came to an end.[29]

Champlain headed quickly down the river for Quebec. He made thirty leagues to Trois-Rivières on the first day, and reached Quebec on July 19. Champlain remained only one day at Quebec but made the most of it. He inspected the settlement, "ordered repairs made," and planned other improvements. Thinking always of the world as a garden, he found a moment to plant roses in Quebec. He was also planning new possibilities for commerce, and carried home some split oak to be tested in France for wainscoting and window frames. Champlain hoped that the American forest might yield an export commodity.[30] All this activity was the work of a single crowded day. Champlain wrote that he "gave directions about the things at our settlement, according to the charge given me by the Sieur de Monts." He departed as suddenly as he arrived, and sailed away for France in a Rochelais vessel. They reached La Rochelle on September 10, 1611.[31]

• • •

From La Rochelle, Champlain went to visit the sieur de Mons at his château near Pons in Saintonge. De Mons had very bad news. His investors had informed him that they were "unwilling to continue the partnership," because the lost monopoly of the fur trade appeared to be irrecoverable. He had bought them out with his own money. There was also some other "unexpected and important business," probably a reversal in his private affairs.

On top of that, de Mons had lost his access to the throne. Marie de Medici continued to make clear that he was not wanted in her presence. This Protestant friend and companion of Henri IV was no longer welcome in the Catholic court of the queen regent. De Mons said sadly that where New France was concerned, he was no longer permitted "to prosecute the matter at Court." Champlain's old patron promised that he would continue to help behind the scenes as a silent partner, friend, and adviser, and this Protestant angel for New France did just that. But he told Champlain that he must relinquish the role of leadership for the enterprise of New France.

Both men agreed that the project should be managed by someone else, preferably a Catholic, who would be more acceptable to the queen regent. The sieur de Mons turned to his younger friend, and in Champlain's words, "he left to me the task of finding the ways and means of keeping New France," and "laid upon me the entire responsibility for it." De Mons advised Champlain to go back to court and "put this business in order." [32]

With a heavy heart, Champlain left his friend and headed for court. He set off on the long journey, traveling by horseback on the rough country roads of France. Fate seemed to be conspiring against him. Along the way, he wrote, "my wretched horse fell on me, and nearly killed me; this fall delayed me for a long time." [33]

As soon as he was able to travel, Champlain was on the road again, thinking about the task ahead. Marie de Medici's court was dominated by great noblemen and he was a commoner. Champlain decided to begin by approaching the three members of his American circle once more. They had been helping him for several years. He tells us that he went to M. le President Jeannin, and gave him a "mémoire," summarizing recent events in New France, stressing his expanding alliances with the Huron and the western Algonquin nations. Once again Champlain argued for the importance of American enterprise. Jeannin responded positively. Champlain wrote, "he approved my project and encouraged me in its pursuit." Jeannin was a man who could make a difference at court. Even the queen deferred to him, and the merchants treated him with respect.[34]

Champlain tells us that he also went to see other powerful "Lords of the Court" whom he did not name. One of the most helpful people was the sieur de Beaulieu, a royal councillor, almoner, and chaplain in ordinary to young King Louis XIII. With Beaulieu's help, Champlain moved closer to the boy-king himself and made an effort to befriend the young lad by friendly attention, small acts of kindness, and gifts from New France.[35]

He also talked with his advisers about the most pressing problem, which was to secure an income for New France, to overcome rivalries of merchant-investors and attract them to the support of the colony. Champlain and his friends at court worked out an ingenious solution to this problem. As historian Gustave Lanctot writes, it was Champlain himself who "conceived the notion of putting the scheme into the hands of some illustrious person, whose influence would greatly outweigh that of the selfish 'merchandisers.'" He and his advisers decided to recruit a prince of the blood, a great nobleman related to the ruling Bourbon dynasty, and in the line of succession to the throne. He would be invited to rule over New France and regulate its trade with an authority that merchants would not be able to challenge.[36]

An eligible candidate was Charles de Bourbon, comte de Soissons, governor of Normandy and Dauphiné. He was deeply interested in America. Champlain approached him through the sieur de Beaulieu, and asked if he would be willing to serve the cause of New France by becoming its titular head. Soissons was indeed willing. One by one, Champlain and his friends enlisted the support of the most powerful noblemen at court. Then he submitted a proposal to "the King in Council," and on October 8, 1612, young Louis XIII granted a royal commission to the comte de Soissons as governor of New France. Soissons instantly appointed Champlain as his lieutenant. Everything was arranged—and disaster struck yet again. The comte de Soissons fell ill and died suddenly, perhaps of smallpox, on November 12, 1612, after little more than a month in office.[37]

Champlain turned quickly to another prince of the blood, Henri de Bourbon, prince de Condé and duc d'Enghien, a nephew of Soissons and cousin to the young King Louis XIII. Condé was twenty-four years old in 1612 and very popular among a large circle of friends, but he was a difficult character and something of a rebel against members of his own royal family. Champlain and his advisers agreed that Condé could replace Soissons, and approaches were made to him. The prince de Condé had extravagant tastes, and a very expen-

At Champlain's urging, and with much help from his American circle at Court, this "prince of the blood" became viceroy of New France, and its lord protector. He never came to America, and quickly appointed Champlain his chief lieutenant, as did every viceroy who preceded or followed him, to the year 1635.

sive hobby of collecting highbred horses. He hoped that New France would be a source of income. Others at court may have wished that an involvement in America might keep him out of trouble in France.[38]

Condé drove a hard bargain. He demanded and received the title of Viceroy of New France—literally vice-king for North America. Champlain had another object in mind. He sought to obtain authority for a prince of the blood to act as ruler of New France with full powers to license all trade in that dominion, in hope of securing an income for the colony. He tells us that he "presented to His Majesty and to the Lords of his Council, a petition with articles praying that it would please him to issue articles and regulations for the control of this matter." The young king agreed, and the queen regent did not object. Letters patent were issued on November 22, 1612, appointing Condé as viceroy with authority to license trade in the St. Lawrence Valley for a period of twelve years.[39]

Soissons and Condé were the first of many viceroys of New France who followed one another in swift succession. Most were kinsmen of the king; all bought and sold their offices in France. None went to Canada in the early seventeenth century. They had little knowledge of the huge area that they claimed to rule. The prince de Condé had no intention of living in America. On the same day that his letters of appointment came through, he appointed Champlain as his "lieutenant pour la Nouvelle-France," with very broad powers to run New France. Champlain accepted quickly, and extended thanks to Condé for "having supported us against all kinds of jealousies and challenges from ill-disposed people."

Champlain immediately asked leaders in the seaports of western France to recognize Condé's viceregal authority over New France. Angry protests came from the parlement in Rouen and from the merchants of Saint-Malo, who brought suit for free trade. The king compelled the parlement to drop its opposition, and ordered the Malouins to withdraw their suit. Unable to attack a prince of the blood, their wrath fell on Champlain. They presented memorials against him, urging Condé that Champlain was a "mere painter who went to Canada out of curiosity and discovered nothing; to send him out again would only contribute to his own glory and drain the royal treasury."[40]

Condé stood by his lieutenant, and even expanded his powers. Lanctot writes that Condé gave Champlain "quasi-absolute authority throughout the whole country with power to establish settlements, promote land explorations and finally, to set up a financial and commercial association."[41] In turn, Champlain worked closely with the viceroy and defended him against many attacks. Champlain wrote, "These things hindered me greatly, and forced me to make three journeys to Rouen with orders from His Majesty." He published the king's commission in all the ports of Normandy. But it was one thing to gain a judgment in France, and another to enforce it in America.[42]

Champlain wrote that during these disputes it was not possible for him to do anything for the habitation at Quebec. The little settlement suffered, but it survived, and Champlain tried to stay in touch with events there.[43] He also continued to work at exploration, even from a distance. In Paris, Champlain had conversations with Nicolas de Vignau, his young interpreter who had lived among the Algonquin. Vignau had returned to France, and he told Champlain that "the mer du nord" or northern sea could be reached in seventeen days from Sault-Saint-Louis by ascending the Ottawa River to a great lake which emptied into it. Champlain was dubious. He had formed a rough idea of the distances from his conversations with the Montagnais. As he thought about it, he began to distrust Vignau.[44] He discussed Vignau's report with his friends at court, Marshall Brissac, Chancellor Sillery, and President Jeannin. They advised Champlain that he "must go and see the thing himself."[45]

With that mission in mind, Champlain decided to return to America in the late winter of 1613. On March 6, Champlain and Pont-Gravé sailed from

Honfleur for New France. They reached the coast of Cape Breton by April 21, and made good time up the St. Lawrence River. As they approached Tadoussac, the Montagnais Indians "ran to their canoes and came to meet us." Champlain contrived an experiment to study their reactions. "As soon as they came on board our ship they peered into each one's face, and as I was not in sight, they asked, where was Monsieur de Champlain?" He kept his distance and was disguised. Then "one old Indian came to the corner where I was walking up and down," and "taking me by the ear (for they suspected who I was) . . . saw the scar of the arrow wound which I had received at the defeat of the Iroquois. Then he cried out, and all the rest after him, with great demonstrations of joy, saying 'your men are waiting for you.'"[46]

It had been another hard winter for the Montagnais. Champlain found them "so thin and ghastly that I did not recognize them." He continued sadly, "As they approached they began to cry out for bread, saying they were famished." Some of the French were dressing three geese and two rabbits and threw the entrails on deck. The Indians "like hungry beasts devoured them, contents and all." Then they squatted down, "scraping off with their fingernails the tallow with which our ship had been greased and devoured it greedily." Once again he helped them through a hard season.[47]

Champlain sailed on to Tadoussac harbor, where they dropped anchor on April 29, 1613. There he ran into another kind of trouble from unlicensed traders. Soon after he arrived, other trading ships began to appear. A vessel from Rouen came up on the same tide, and the next day, April 30, two more ships arrived from Saint-Malo. They had sailed before the King's Commission had been published in France and were not aware of its terms. Champlain went aboard the ships and explained the situation. He wrote, "I read the King's Commission and the injunction against violating it with the penalties therein set forth." The Malouins replied that "being subjects and loyal servants of His Majesty they would obey his commands." Champlain appears to have worked out an accommodation with the two Malouin captains, the sieur de la Mainerie and the sieur de La Tremblaye, and they found a peaceful solution. "After that," he wrote, "I had His Majesty's Arms and Commissions publicly posted up in the harbor, so that no one might pretend cause of ignorance."

Champlain had a different sort of problem with some of the French captains. Complaints were brought to him about traders "who abused the Indians and treated them badly." Here again Champlain worked not only to promote trade, but also to protect the Indians from unscrupulous traders. He was particularly anxious to stop any commerce in alcohol or firearms.[48]

While Champlain was sorting out these questions, the carpenters were outfitting two shallops for travel on the river. On May 2, the boats were ready and Champlain took one of them heading upstream toward Quebec. He started in bad weather and ran into a severe storm on the river. The wind was so violent that the shallop was dismasted—another desperate moment that brought him near death. "Had not God saved us," he wrote, "we should all have been lost, as happened before our eyes to a shallop of Saint-Malo on its way to the island of Orléans." They replaced the mast with a jury-rig, and reached Quebec on May 7.[49]

Champlain found the settlers "in good health, having been in no wise indisposed." They reported that the winter had been mild and the river had not frozen. Spring was well advanced, "the trees were beginning to put forth their leaves, and the fields were turning bright with flowers.[50] He remained at Quebec for a week. Then on the thirteenth he was off to the rapids at Montreal, where he arrived on the twenty-first. A trading barque was already there, bartering with small parties of Algonquin who were carrying their weapons and shields of wood and moose-hide. The Indians were cordial to Champlain, but reported trouble with the western Iroquois and also complained that many traders were not treating them well.[51]

He promised to assist them against the Iroquois, but told them that first he wanted to pass through their country on a voyage of exploration to the northwest. He asked them to help with three canoes and three guides. The Algonquin were not forthcoming. After much effort and many presents, Champlain was able to get two canoes and a single guide.[52]

It meant a dangerously small expedition, but Champlain was determined to push forward into the interior of the country. He planned to go up the St. Lawrence River to the "River of the Algonquins," today's Ottawa River, and to follow it to the northwest. Again he met the young interpreter Vignau, who repeated his story that he had been to Hudson Bay and back in seventeen days, and had seen the remains of a British ship there. Champlain had read an account of Henry Hudson's voyage of 1612, published that year in Amsterdam. He knew that Hudson's men had sailed into the great bay that bore his name, had wintered as far south as 53 degrees of north latitude, and had lost some ships there. But it was a very long way from Montreal. Champlain was suspicious of young Vignau's account, and told him bluntly that "if he was telling a lie he was putting a rope around his neck." The young Frenchman swore it was true.[53]

On May 27, 1613, Champlain and Vignau set off from Montreal with another interpreter named Thomas, an Algonquin guide, and two more Frenchmen. Their canoes rode low in the water, heavily laden with provisions, weapons, trade goods, and the tools of exploration. It was slow going, and the weather turned against them. They were a full day traveling from Île Sainte-Hélène to the great rapids, and then portaged around the rapids—which was "no small labor," Champlain wrote. Above the rapids they entered the great Lake of the Two Mountains, where the Ottawa River flowed in from the north. The countryside was beautiful and fertile, but there was a sense of danger in it. Onondaga and Oneida war parties were active in this region. Every night Champlain and his companions made camp on a defensible island, built a barricade, and kept a strong watch until morning. Those precautions added greatly to the time and labor of their journey.

From the lake they turned north into the Ottawa River. Champlain took a sun line and estimated their latitude at 45 degrees 18 minutes, which was remarkably accurate. It told Champlain that the "North Sea" or Hudson Bay was at least five hundred miles away in a direct line, and farther by river. Clearly Vignau's estimate of time and distance was wrong.[54]

As they moved northwest on the Ottawa River they met many more rapids and passed some of them by "hard paddling," others by portage. In a few places the banks of the river were so rugged that they could advance only by "tracking" or dragging their canoes by "cords" through the turbulent water. This was dangerous work. Champlain was tracking his canoe with a cord wrapped tightly round his hand. Suddenly the current caught his boat and spun it into deep water. Champlain fell between two rocks. The canoe pulled at the cord with a force so strong that, in his words, it nearly cut off his hand. "I cried aloud to God and began to pull my canoe toward me, when it was sent back to me by an eddy such as occurs in these rapids. . . . I nearly lost my life," he wrote, "and having escaped, I gave praise to God, beseeching him to preserve us."[55]

The other Frenchmen suffered terribly and "several times were nearly lost" as they slowly learned the art of white-water canoeing with the "dexterity . . . needed to pass these rapids, in order to avoid the eddies and shoals that occur in them." Champlain observed, "This the Indians do with the very greatest skill, seeking byways and safe passages which they recognize at a glance."[56]

The next day they passed through a lake and met fifteen canoes of an Algonquin nation that Champlain called the Quenongebin. He wrote that they were "astonished to see me in that country with so few Frenchmen and only one Indian." They saluted each other "after the manner of the country," and Champlain invited them to stop and talk. He told them that he wished to push on through their country to meet other Indian nations. They strongly

CHAMPLAIN'S EXPLORATION OF THE OTTAWA VALLEY, 1613

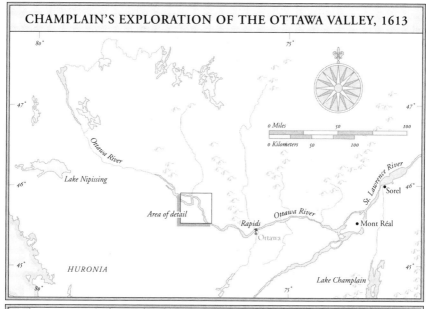

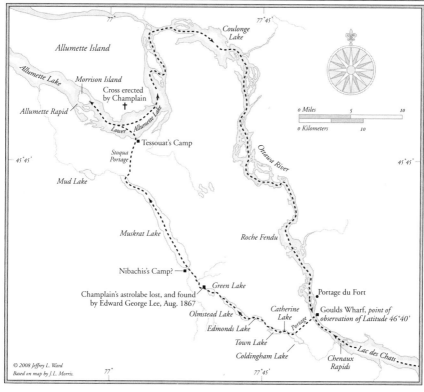

discouraged him, saying that the country became even more difficult. He asked for a guide and offered to give them a Frenchman as a hostage in return. They agreed. Many things were being settled at the same time in this brief exchange.[57]

Champlain's party pressed on and came to another river, "very beautiful and wide," with banks covered with "fine open woods." Upstream were an Algonquin people known as the Ouescharini. He called them the Petite nation. The French continued on, through many rapids and falls, and found themselves in a very beautiful lake many miles long, the lac des Chats. Here he met a nation he called "Matou-Ouescarini," today's Madawaska nation. He was amazed by huge stands of cedar, but noted that the lake was surrounded by pines that had been "all burned down by the Indians."[58]

On the advice of their guides, Champlain and his men left the Ottawa River and followed another line of advance through a chain of lakes with very hard portages. On one of these portages, while they were struggling through a tangle of fallen timber and "suffering more from the mosquitoes than their loads," Champlain lost his small traveling astrolabe. It would be found in 1867 near Green Lake in Ontario. Today it is preserved as a national treasure in the Canadian Museum of Civilization on the banks of the river that Champlain explored on this journey in 1613.[59]

They paddled on to Muskrat Lake, where they met yet another Algonquin nation, with a chief named Nibachis, who was "astonished that we had been able to pass the rapids and bad trails." He said to his companions, "They must have fallen from the clouds," for "he did not know how we had been able to get through, when those who live in the country had great difficulty in coming along such difficult trails." Nibachis had heard of Champlain, and he said that the journey convinced him "I was everything the other Indians had told him." Here was more evidence that Champlain's reputation was spreading rapidly from one Indian nation to another. His reputation traveled even more widely in North America than did the man himself.[60]

Champlain told Nibachis through an interpreter that he was "in the country to assist them in their wars," and that he "wished to push on to see other chiefs for the same purpose." They agreed to help, and gave Champlain and his men some food. They smoked tobacco and made an alliance. After this tabagie, Nibachis led Champlain across Muskrat Lake, and then by easy beaten trails to a much larger body of water that today is called Allumette Lake.[61]

Here lived a great Algonquin war chief named Tessoüat, whose fame rivaled that of Champlain in the St. Lawrence Valley. They had first met in the tabagie at Tadoussac in 1603, and Champlain wrote that Tessoüat was "astonished to

Champlain used this small brass traveling astrolabe (dated 1603) to calculate his latitude by a noon sun-sight. It was suspended from a plumb line to measure the angle of elevation. In 1613, he lost it in the Ottawa Valley. It was found by a farmboy in 1867, with a rusty chain, bowls in copper cases, and two silver goblets with coats of arms that were melted and sold.

see me, telling us that he thought I was a ghost and that he could not believe his eyes." The old chief took him to today's Morrison Island in the middle of Allumette Lake. Lacking his astrolabe, Champlain reckoned its latitude at 47 degrees with less than his usual accuracy. It is in fact 45:48 degrees north. One wonders how he could have reckoned it at all, perhaps by an improvised instrument of wood and string.[62]

Champlain asked Tessoüat why they lived on such poor soil when fertile ground lay to the south. He said they were safe here. Champlain told them that he planned to build a fort and plough the land near Montreal, below the great rapids on the St. Lawrence. "When they heard this," he wrote, "they gave a great shout of approval" and said they would come and live nearby, thinking "their enemies would do them no harm whilst we were with them." Tessoüat welcomed Champlain with still another tabagie on Morrison Island. They had a great feast, and then the young warriors withdrew and the older men smoked tobacco for a long time. Champlain told them he wanted to visit another nation called the Nebicerini (or Nipissing) who lived on today's Lake Nipissing, and asked for the use of four canoes. The island Indians said the Nebicerini were a nation of wizards who killed people with magic, and Champlain would not be safe among them. Champlain persisted, pointing to his interpreter and saying that Nicolas de Vignau had been there.

To his amazement the Indians responded with an explosion of anger. Tessoüat called Vignau a liar to his face and said, "If you visited those tribes it was in your sleep, and every night you slept beside me and my children." They refused to allow Champlain to go farther, allegedly for his own protection, and offered to deal with Vignau themselves. "Give him to us," Tessoüat said, "and we promise he will tell no more lies." Champlain protected Vignau, gave up his plan to go farther, and prepared to return south. Before he left, Champlain erected a cross of white cedar with the arms of France and asked the Algonquin to protect it. On June 10, he started home again with an escort of Tessoüat and his sons and warriors, who were suddenly friendly again. One suspects that the Indians were protecting the sources of their fur trade, much as other nations had done. Champlain was careful not to challenge them.[63]

On June 17, he and his party were back at the falls near Montreal. Champlain confronted Vignau and demanded an explanation. The young Frenchman confessed that he had never been to the northern sea, and had lied about it so that he would be taken back. He asked Champlain "to leave him in the country among the Indians." Champlain asked some of the Indians to take him in, but wrote that "none of the Indians would have him, in spite of my request, and we left him in God's keeping." Vignau walked off into the forest, and Champlain never saw him again. Perhaps he formed a union with an Indian woman, or possibly he became a solitary trader. He may have been killed by the Indians, who hated a liar more than a murderer. His fate is unknown.[64]

Champlain never reached Hudson Bay, but on his long journey he succeeded in exploring the Ottawa Valley and made alliances with many Algonquin nations. He returned to Quebec, but could stay only briefly. It was time to go home and deal with problems and intrigues on the other side of the Atlantic. He sailed from Tadoussac on August 8, 1613, and reached France on September 26, in time to resume his labors there.

Within a few weeks of his return, Champlain had formed a new investment group called La Compagnie du Canada. He worked hard to bring together merchants of La Rochelle, Rouen, and Saint-Malo as investors in a single company, each town holding one-third of the shares. The object was to unite three leading centers in a single venture, all licensed by the viceroy. Champlain organized a meeting on November 13, 1613, and men from Rouen and Saint-Malo were present. Among the drivers were merchants of three families: Le Gendre, Porée, and Boyer. They agreed to the proposal, and saved a third of the shares for the men of La Rochelle.[65]

The company was formally founded on November 20, 1613, with Condé's active sponsorship. The investors were granted a monopoly of the fur trade in the St. Lawrence Valley to Quebec and beyond, for a period of eleven years. In return, the company agreed to contribute 1,000 crowns each year, and transport at least six families of settlers every season, which pleased Champlain. It also promised to make an annual gift to the viceroy of a highbred horse worth a thousand écus, an arrangement that greatly gratified the prince.[66]

The company appeared to work for a time, but at the last minute the merchants of La Rochelle withdrew, and somehow they persuaded the prince to give them a special "passport" to send their own trading vessel to the St. Lawrence. One wonders how many blooded horses that arrangement may have cost. In that act, Condé broke the monopoly of Champlain's company, fueled intense animosities between the trading towns, and gave rise to twenty years of litigation. Undeterred, Champlain went to Rouen to meet his business partners, and left them "well pleased with the mission." The merchants of Rouen pledged to support settlers and to keep them in provisions.[67]

The prime mover was Champlain himself. The leading historian of trading companies in New France calls this new group "Champlain's Company." Champlain himself was careful to call it the Compagnie de Condé. It represented a change of leadership. The sieur de Mons continued as an investor, but not as an officer of the company. After ten years of faithful leadership he moved to the periphery and Champlain replaced him at the center. Under the auspices of the new viceroy, Champlain became the leader of the colonizing effort in New France, and would continue in that role for twenty-two years, from 1613 until his death in 1635.[68]

While working with his investors, Champlain somehow found the time to finish another book called *Les voyages du Sieur de Champlain, Xaintongeois, capitaine ordinaire pour le Roy, en la marine.* It bore the date of 1613 and was published by Jean Berjon, at the sign of the Flying Horse on the rue St. Jean de Beauvais in Paris. It was a work of extraordinary quality and detail, both in its text and in its maps. Champlain included thirteen very accurate charts of harbors and coasts in North America, based on his meticulous surveys and drawn with his own hand.[69]

He also published three larger maps of New France. One of them was called a "Carte Géographique de la Nouvelle France (1612)," a long narrow map that centered on the St. Lawrence Valley. The cartography was not his best, but the plate was a superb work of art—the most beautiful and visually appealing of all his maps. Its object was to attract interest in the colony and its native inhabitants, with very handsome engravings of the Indians, the flora and fauna. Most of all, it was meant to draw and hold the attention of the queen regent, young Louis XIII, and their ministers. The royal arms were added, not on the land but on the sea. The map appears on the front endpaper of this book.[70]

Two other Champlain maps of this period (1611–13) were interesting in

Champlain's Voyages *(1613) were issued in two books bound as one. This was his handsomest work, with fourteen maps and much of his best surviving art. The work described his travels (and travails) in America and France from 1604 to 1611. It was dedicated to the young King and the difficult Queen Regent.*

other ways. They are less striking as works of art, but more developed as works of cartographic science. They are two different states of the same base-map, and to study them together is to see how Champlain's cartographic knowledge was growing. The first state of this map was begun in 1611 with the collaboration of David Pelletier, a highly skilled engraver, and finished in 1612. It has a rectolinear projection centered on the 45th parallel of latitude. After it was done, Champlain returned to America and explored the Ottawa River. He also saw a newly published work called *Tabula Nautica* by Hessel Gerritsz, which showed the explorations of Henry Hudson in northern waters and Hudson Bay. On the basis of this new information, Champlain revised his earlier map. The result added more information about North America and made an important point about the possibility of a northwest passage.[71] In all these works, writes a student of Champlain's cartography, "the input of effort and outpouring of information is astonishing in itself, but the real miracle of Champlain's work is its quality and originality." He dedicated his books and maps to the young King Louis XIII and the Queen Regent. He desperately needed their help.[72]

• • •

In 1614, thinking partly of their concerns, Champlain returned to the old problem of religion in New France, and searched for a new solution. He decided to recruit some "good friars" to "plant the faith" in Canada, or at least to do what was possible in the way of their vocation. The way he went about it is very revealing—both of the man himself and of the enormous problems that he faced.[73]

He consulted with his friend Louis Hoüel, the king's secretary and controller general of the salt works at Brouage. Hoüel was "a man of pious habits, and inspired with a great zeal and love for the Honour of God." He had a particular fondness for the "good fathers of the Récollets," a Franciscan order that had been founded in Spain as early as 1484, and been admitted to France in 1592. Hoüel urged Champlain to take a few Récollets to New France, offered to support them from his own pocket, and promised to find other donors.[74]

This proposed solution created problems within the Roman Catholic hierarchy. The Récollet fathers were reluctant to act without a commission of the Pope, and the Papal Nuncio Roberto Ubaldini refused to help. In another amazing scene, Champlain went to an assembly of all the French cardinals and bishops, who had gathered in Paris for the meeting of the Estates General in 1614. His talks with them were a great success. The French prelates gave Champlain their full support, and even contributed 1,500 livres to support the mission.[75]

Champlain at last was having some success in building a broad base at home for his purposes in North America. During the difficult period from 1610 to 1614, he had gathered a powerful group of supporters at court, and worked closely with them. At the same time, he also founded a new investment company to replace that of the sieur de Mons. And he established close relations with Catholic leaders and the Récollets, while keeping on good terms with Jesuits and other groups.

Although things were going better for Champlain in his public affairs, he suffered a calamity in his private life. His marriage came apart. Hélène Boullé Champlain was by all accounts a beautiful, intelligent, and high-spirited young girl. When they married in 1610, Champlain was more than three times her age, and they had little in common. She was a young, city-bred Parisienne of affluent family; he was a middle-aged, battle-scarred soldier and seaman of modest provincial origins. She longed to be among family and friends; he enjoyed the company of Indians, soldiers, and seamen. She lived

Champlain's Geographic Map of New France in Its True Meridian *survives in two printers' states. This, the first of them, shows the results of his explorations through 1611.*

among the ceremonies of the court; he was away for long periods, often living among the Indians.

Another divisive issue may have been the religion that they had in common. Both appear to have been catechized as Protestants and become devout Catholics. Each of them embraced their Catholic faith with a fervor that may have kept them from embracing each other. They drew a veil of silence over their marriage, and we shall never know the secrets of their life together. But two facts were clear enough. Champlain was devoted to his young wife but from a distance. And Hélène Boullé was deeply unhappy.

In August of 1613, when Champlain returned to France, Hélène's parents ordered her to move in with her husband as the prenuptial contract had re-

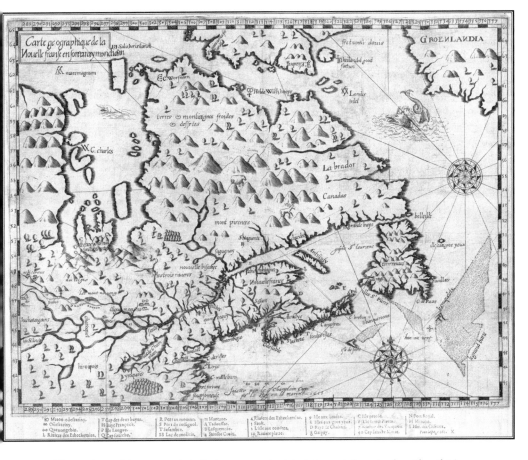

The second state of the same map is similar in most ways, but it includes new information from Champlain's travels in 1612, and also from a new Dutch account of Henry Hudson's voyage to the north. In this revision one sees Champlain's passion for truth and his hunger for new knowledge.

quired. During the weeks that followed Hélène rebelled. According to the testimony of Hélène's parents, things began to go wrong in the fall. The breaking point came on January 4, 1614, when Hélène suddenly fled from her husband's house. Nobody could find her. Her parents were frantic with anger, worry, and embarrassment. They raged against Hélène for the "atrocious and scandalous injury" that she had done to the "honor and good name" of her family. On January 10, 1614, her parents called in two notaries and disinherited her.[76]

Somehow her husband and parents tracked her down. Hélène was convinced or compelled to return to her husband, and a reconciliation of sorts followed. They lived in the same house, but there were no children, and one wonders if they were living as man and wife. Champlain, for his part, declared on his deathbed that Hélène was the only woman he ever loved.[77] She became a dutiful consort to her husband and made a determined effort to support him. She would go to Canada with him of her own free will, and stayed with him there for five years. She helped promote his cause in France. Little evidence survives about the interior of this marriage. Scraps of material suggest that it grew very cold around the year 1614, warmed about five years later, and grew colder again in the late 1620s. But even when they lived together, it was one of the most difficult of all triangles: a younger woman, an older man, and a grand design.

15.

HURONIA

A Year Among the Indians, 1615–16

> It is not the act of a warrior, as you call yourself, to behave cruelly
> toward women who have no other defence than their tears, and
> who . . . one should treat with humanity.
>
> —Champlain to Iroquet, war chief of the Algonquin Petite-Nation, 1615[1]

A S SPRING APPROACHED IN 1615, Champlain was anxious to leave for America. At the end of February, he left Paris for Rouen and met his merchant-partners. The meetings went well. Old investors rallied to the enterprise, and new ones came forward.[2]

Champlain asked the merchants to support a few missionaries in Canada and wrote that "our associates were well pleased with this." On the last day of winter, March 20, 1615, he organized yet another meeting in Rouen, so that the venture capitalists could meet the Récollet fathers. Each group was vital to the success of New France, but together they made a difficult combination. One part of the problem was the eternal tension between God and mammon. Another was the continuing strife between Protestant investors and Catholic clergy.[3]

Other leaders might have kept these groups apart. Champlain brought them together in the same room. He was effective in the role of intermediary, conciliator, and what the French call a *porte-parole*.[4] "We sojourned together for some time," Champlain later recalled. The Récollet fathers grew more enthusiastic for their mission. The venture capitalists promised to "assist the said fathers to the utmost" and offered "to keep them in provisions."[5]

In early April Champlain led the Récollets and some of the merchants down the river Seine from Rouen to Honfleur, where a great ship was loading for New France. In that small but busy port, Champlain had raised enough money to charter the *Saint-Étienne*, a large navire of 350 tons. She was a good ship and a fast sailor. Once again her captain was Champlain's old friend and shipmate Pont-Gravé.[6]

• • •

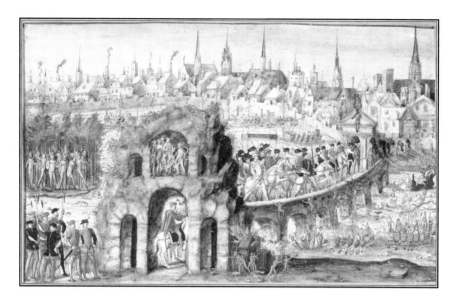

Rouen in 1550. This city on the lower Seine was the center of commerce and capital in Normandy. Champlain often met with his investors here and had much business before its courts. He suffered many defeats at the hands of monied men who regarded his dream as a drain on their capital—which it was.

In Honfleur, Champlain recalled, "we remained some days, waiting for our vessel to be fitted out, and laden with the necessary things for so long a voyage." Mountains of provisions and trading goods on the quayside were carried aboard the *Saint-Étienne* and stowed below. More investors signed on, and the crew was rounded out with seamen from the port of Le Havre, across the Seine.[7]

These rough seafaring men were a vital part of colonial enterprise, but they are often anonymous in its history. At Honfleur Champlain turned his attention to them in a new way. He encouraged the Récollet fathers to look after their spiritual condition. In Champlain's words, each seaman and soldier was invited "to examine his soul, to cleanse himself of his sins, to receive the sacrament and put himself in a state of grace so as to become afterward more free (*plus libre*) in his own conscience and in God's keeping, when he exposed himself to the mercy of the waves in a great and dangerous sea."[8]

Here we see the continuing growth of Champlain's Christian faith—and its special character. There was little theology in his thinking and no ecclesiology at all, but much of Christian piety. In the best spirit of the universal Catholic Church, Champlain's piety reached out to embrace all humanity—an attitude very different from that of the Calvinists who founded New England and New

Netherland. Champlain believed that Christianity made men more free, "plus libre" in his phrase. He was thinking of grace as liberation from sin, and of Christianity as the freedom to be one with Christ in communion with other free souls. These ideas were growing more important in his own life, and in the history of New France.[9]

While Champlain looked to the spiritual condition of his migratory flock, he also tended to the expedition's material needs. One of his last tasks was to load shallops aboard his ship, and to acquire several midsized shallow-draft vessels, designed for exploration and trade on the St. Lawrence River. Champlain called them his barques. They were larger than a shallop and smaller than an ocean-going navire. One wonders how he got them to America. Were they knocked down in the hold or nested together on the weather deck of the *Saint-Étienne?* Such techniques worked better for small shallops than for middling barques. Did they come at the end of a towline? A long tow was dangerous in a following sea. Or did his moyennes barques sail independently? Perhaps the *Saint-Étienne* led them in convoy across the ocean, like a mother duck with her straggling brood. Whatever the method, Champlain was delighted with the result. His versatile moyennes barques were vital to the life of New France.[10]

At last the work was done. Passengers and crew approached the moment of departure, when a seaman's pulse begins to race and even landsmen share the excitement of a fresh start. On April 24, 1615, Champlain and Captain Pont-Gravé came aboard the *Saint-Étienne.* The Récollet fathers blessed the ship and all who sailed in her. Deckhands hauled in the long, heavy anchor cable until it was "up and down." On command the ship's anchor came "aweigh" from the bottom. Topmen raced aloft, and released the billowing sails from their gaskets. On the weather deck, hands went to braces, and the sails began to fill. The wind and tide carried the ship away from her mooring. As she gathered steerage way the pilot guided her safely out of Honfleur's tight little harbor into the brown current of the Seine, and turned her prow toward the deep blue water of the North Atlantic.

It was a late crossing, and a lucky one. In fine spring weather, the *Saint-Étienne* spread her sails before a "very favorable wind," and they went flying across the western ocean. The timing of the voyage made a difference. Champlain noted with relief, "We made the voyage without meeting any ice, or other hazards, thanks be to God, and in a short time arrived at the place called Tadoussac on the 25th day of May." Allowing for the long passage up the St. Lawrence River, which often took ten days or more, the ocean crossing to the

Grand Banks must have lasted no more than twenty days. It was a passage of surprising speed for an east-west voyage, and a tribute to the seamanship of her commanders.

Between the two of them, Pont-Gravé and Champlain had made more than fifty crossings of the North Atlantic, and they never lost a large ship at sea. A lucky voyage was one thing. A long run of lucky voyages was quite another, and it had deep meaning for men who went down to the sea in ships. With every voyage, Champlain was gaining a reputation as a fortunate commander. Seafaring men are superstitious that way. They know what a rogue wave can do, or a white squall that could strike without warning and blow a navire as big as the *Saint-Étienne* on her beam-end.

In their day and ours, sailors who survive those events come to believe in fortune as a driving force in their dangerous world. They observe from experience that some people have good fortune and others do not. They also think that fortune is a fickle goddess, and make every effort to propitiate her. Even in our own time, seamen with postgraduate degrees in science will go out of their way to avoid starting a long voyage on a Friday. Modern naval officers trained to reason and empiricism make a habit of never setting their caps upside down, in fear that they might fill with water and sink. They like to sail with lucky captains and dread a leader who is thought to be a Jonah.

In the early modern era, it was not quite the same. A deep belief in fortune (which we possess) coexisted with a spirit of fatalism that is alien to our world. Champlain and many mariners never learned to swim, even though they lived their lives on the water. In the seventeenth century most European seamen seemed to believe that they were destined by fate and fortune to float or sink, and there was nothing much that they could do about it. In the sixteenth and seventeenth centuries those feelings were deepened by a religious belief that a man's fortune was not a matter of random chance—not a throw of the dice or a turn of the wheel. It was a sign of divine purpose. A verse in Tyndale's Bible summarized that idea in a sentence: "The Lord was with Joseph, and he was a luckie felowe." [11]

Champlain shared that way of thinking. So did his shipmates, from the grizzled captain to the greenest hand. He tells us that when the *Saint-Étienne* dropped anchor at Tadoussac on May 25, 1615, the first act of all these men was to fall on their knees and "offer thanks to God" for their good fortune, and for having guided us so seasonably to this haven of safety." The men who sailed with Champlain on yet another fortunate voyage were coming to believe that the Lord was with their leader. Like Joseph, he was a "luckie felowe." [12]

In 1615, Champlain brought four Récollet missionaries to New France. They were followed by Gabriel Sagard, who lived among the Huron (1623–24) and published his Long Voyage to the Land of the Hurons in 1632. Its title page combines icons of his Franciscan order with images of Huronia. The text borrows from Champlain, and adds excellent ethnography and a Huron glossary. His Histoire du Canada (1635) includes Huron sheet music and more details of Champlain's life.

• • •

In Tadoussac harbor, the ship's carpenters aboard the *Saint-Étienne* went to work on Champlain's flotilla of river craft. Masts were stepped and rigged for sails. Locust tholepins were driven into gunwales and adjusted for oars and sweeps. Merchants checked inventories of trade goods. The holy fathers polished their communion silver and made preparations for their mission to the Indians. Champlain adjusted his instruments. All were eager to be on their way.

The first boats were ready on May 27. That very day, Champlain and the Récollets departed, heading upriver from Tadoussac to Quebec. The journey took nearly a week against the winds and currents on the St. Lawrence River. They arrived on June 2 and found the settlement in better condition than they had expected. Champlain wrote that the Récollet fathers "were greatly encouraged to find a place that was completely different from what they had imagined." [13]

Good as it may have been, Champlain was never satisfied. He assembled the habitants and ordered them to make it better. As always, he was full of energy and purpose, and he imposed his will on the settlement. This was not an open system. Champlain conscripted the labor of the habitants for what he believed to be the general good. He ordered some to clear land. Others were told to build a new residence for the Récollet fathers, with a chapel where they could celebrate mass.[14]

When these projects were well begun, Champlain was off again, sailing upstream from Quebec. With him went Pont-Gravé, several Récollet fathers, a party of soldiers, and the seamen who worked the boat. The Récollets were amazed by the scale of the river, and overwhelmed by the beauty of the countryside. Champlain wrote of the "delight of our Fathers" on seeing "the extent of so grand a river, filled with many beautiful islands, and bordered by the banks of a fertile land."[15]

They continued to their destination, a large island that is now part of the city of Montreal. Just beyond was the head of navigation on the river—the wild rapids that Champlain had run in his shirt.[16] Below the island was the Rivière-des-Prairies. Its open meadows became a meeting place for Europeans and Indians of many nations. Champlain and his party came ashore and found that a crowd was already waiting for them. They were Huron, Algonquin, and others. All greeted the French warmly, Champlain especially. "As soon as I reached the rapids," he wrote, "I visited among these people, who wanted very much to see us, and were joyous at our return." He recorded the surprise of the Récollet fathers, who were astonished to meet "a very large number of strong and hardy men, who made clear that their spirit was not as savage as their customs."[17]

This gathering, warm as it may have been, was a collision of cross-purposes. The Indians had a particular object in mind. They complained that their ancient foes "were continually along their trading paths, and prevented them from passing." This time they were not speaking of the Mohawk, who had stopped their northern attacks after Champlain's campaigns against them. These raids came from central Iroquoia. The Onondaga and Oneida nations were plundering fur routes along the upper St. Lawrence Valley and the Ottawa River. The Huron and the Algonquin were deeply concerned about security in their own country.[18]

Champlain discussed the subject with Pont-Gravé, and they agreed that "it was very necessary to assist them, both to engage them the more to love us, and also to provide the means of furthering my enterprises and discoveries, which apparently could only be carried out with their help, and also because this would be to them a kind of pathway and preparation for coming to Christianity." They were convinced that another quick campaign against the central Iroquois was a path to peace in New France, as it had been with the Mohawk five years before.[19]

At the Rivière-des-Prairies Champlain convened a tabagie: "We summoned them all to an assembly," he wrote, "in order to explain our intentions." Working through an Indian interpreter, Champlain explained that he hoped to go beyond the Sault-Saint-Louis and visit the western nations. He wanted to "examine their territory" and explore the way to the "western sea." Once again he offered to "help them with their wars."[20]

Champlain and the Indian leaders discussed these questions. They agreed to send a strong force against the central Iroquois. It would be a grand alliance of Indian nations in the St. Lawrence Valley, with others near the Great Lakes and even beyond. The Indian leaders at the assembly promised to muster 2,500 warriors. Champlain offered to go back to Quebec and return with as many Frenchmen as possible.

They also discussed strategy and tactics, on which the Indians and Champlain had different ideas. He wrote, "I began to explain the means we must employ fighting." The speech does not survive, but to judge from words and acts that followed, he proposed a bold campaign against one of the large fortified towns in the very center of Iroquoia. Champlain had in mind a punitive expedition, executed with great power and speed. He favored campaigns of rapid movement with strong concentration of force. The object was to strike a hard blow against an important target, take a heavy toll of their warriors, and make a quick retreat. This was not a war of conquest or extermination. Champlain's purpose, whenever he took up arms, was never to make war on women, children, and the elderly. He warred only against warriors. The object was to deter future attacks and to create a foundation from which peace could grow.

His Indian allies were thinking in other terms: not a punitive expedition in the European sense, but a revenge raid to retaliate for old losses, and a mourning raid to replace them with new captives. Their differences with Champlain did not emerge at the tabagie. The emphasis was on combined effort, and all agreed on the main lines of the campaign.

The Indians were eager to get started, but Champlain pointed out that the expedition "could not take less than three or four months," and he had to go back to Quebec and settle some "essential matters." He promised to return in four or five days.[21] Champlain sailed quickly down the river to Quebec on June 26 and found that all was well. Two Récollet fathers, John and Pacifique, had fitted out the chapel and celebrated Holy Mass on Sunday, June 25, which Champlain believed to be the first there.[22] Unhappily, a third Récollet, Father Joseph Le Caron, had gone up-country with twelve Frenchmen. "This news troubled me a little," Champlain wrote. He had hoped to take the men on his expedition. "I could have ordered many things for the voyage which now I was not able to do, because of the small number of men, and also because not more than four or five knew how to handle firearms."[23]

Undeterred, Champlain left Quebec on Tuesday, July 4, and hurried up the river to the rapids for his rendezvous with the Indians. He was late, and they were gone. After two weeks with no sign of him, the Indians had despaired of his arrival and departed for their homes. A rumor spread that he had been killed by the Iroquois.

Champlain arrived just after they had gone and went racing after them. He took his servant, an interpreter, and ten Indian paddlers in two big canoes. They left the Rivière-des-Prairies and went up the river, determined to go forward with his expedition. It was a hard journey. From the great rapids of the St. Lawrence River to Huronia, the distance was nearly five hundred miles upstream against the current and prevailing wind, with many painful portages. They did it in twenty-three days, the Indians bending over their paddles and singing their rhythmic canoe songs, as their glistening blades flashed in the bright summer light.[24]

For the first part of the journey, Champlain followed the line of his earlier travels in 1613–14. Then he detoured far to the north to keep clear of the western Iroquois and especially the Onondaga, whose war parties were much feared. Beyond Morrison Island, Champlain's party left the Ottawa River and entered "an ill-favored region full of pines, birches, and a few oaks, very rocky, and in many places rather hilly." They were crossing the Laurentian shield of Canada, which Champlain described as "a wilderness, being barren and uninhabited," full of "rocks and mountains and not ten arpents of arable land." But even in this "frightful and abandoned land," Champlain found an abundance of sorts—a "grand quantity of blueberries," *blüets* as he called them, "in such plenty that it is marvelous."[25]

Along the way he met many Indian nations, talked with them, and encouraged alliances with the French. He visited again with the Morrison Island Algonquin, whom he knew well. In another poor region, he met a group called the Otaguottouemin, who lived by hunting, fishing, and harvesting a huge abundance of blueberries, which they dried and ate through the winter.[26]

Champlain portaged around several rapids to Lake Nipissing, where the nation of that name gave him "a very kind reception." Then he went yet another thirty leagues to the French River and made his way to Lake Huron, which he called the Lake of the Attigouautan, after the Bear clan of the Huron nation. He traveled forty-five leagues along its shore, marveling at its size. He called it *la mer douce*, the sweet-water sea. It was a disappointment to him that way, as he was he searching for salt water that promised a route to China. But he felt better when he caught lake trout that were four and a half feet long. The pike were of the same size, and the sturgeon reached as much as nine feet, "a very large fish and marvelously good eating." [27]

Near the lake he came to yet another Indian nation called the Cheveux-Relevés or High Hairs, with pierced nostrils and ears fringed with beads. Their hair was "raised very high, and arranged and combed better than our courtiers." Champlain became especially fond of the Cheveux-Relevés and delighted in their ways. He gave their senior chief a metal hatchet and quizzed him about his country, "which he drew for me on a piece of bark." [28]

From Lake Huron, Champlain crossed Georgian Bay and entered the country of Huronia. Measured against the vast distances of Canada, it appears very small on a map of this great nation, but Champlain explored it on foot and had a different impression. "The whole country which I visited on foot extends for some twenty to thirty leagues," he wrote, "and is very fine." He reckoned that it had an area of about forty by sixty miles, roughly 2,400 square miles. Champlain calculated the latitude of Huronia at approximately 44 degrees, well south of the lower St. Lawrence Valley. Its growing season was long enough to produce abundant crops of corn, and he was impressed by the quality of its soil. "This country is very fair and fertile," he wrote, and he took pleasure in traveling through it. [29]

If he was surprised by the extent of Huronia, Champlain was amazed by its population. He described the land as "a well cleared country" and "well peopled with a countless number of souls." He tried to count them and came to a rough estimate of thirty thousand inhabitants. [30] He was astonished by the number of towns, and still more by their size and strength. The town of Carhagouha (not the largest) impressed him with its massive triple palisade, thirty-five feet tall, as high as a four-storey building. [31]

The Huron villages were surrounded by big cornfields, some larger than a thousand acres. He found bumper crops in the fields, much of them nearly ripe in mid-August. The production of corn exceeded consumption. Champlain observed that the Huron raised crops for export to other Indian nations. He wrote, "They are covered in the pelts of deer and beaver, which they ac-

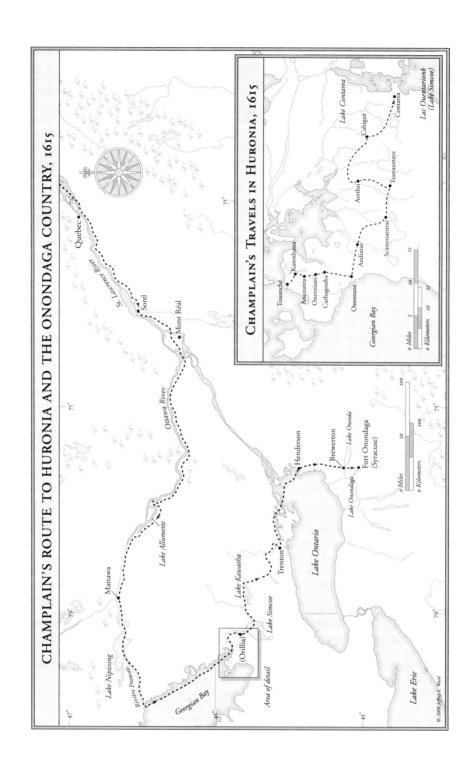

CHAMPLAIN'S ROUTE TO HURONIA AND THE ONONDAGA COUNTRY, 1615

CHAMPLAIN'S TRAVELS IN HURONIA, 1615

Lac Ouentaronk
(Lake Simcoe)

Contarea

Lake Contarea

Cahigué

Teanaustaye

Arethsi

Scanonaenrat

Touanché

Karenhassa

Anonatea

Onentisati

Carhagouha

Andiatae

Ossossane

Georgian Bay

0 Miles   5   10   15

0 Kilometers   5   10   15

Quebec

St. Laurence River

Sorel

Mont Réal

Ottawa River

Mattawa

Lake Nipissing

Rivière Français

Lake Allumette

Georgian Bay

(Orillia)

Area of detail

Lake Simcoe

Lake Kawatha

Trenton

Henderson

Brewerton

Lake Oneida

Fort Onondaga
(Syracuse)

Lake Onondaga

Lake Ontario

Lake Erie

0 Miles   50   100

0 Kilometers   50   100

© 2008 Jeffrey L. Ward

quired from Algonquins and Nippissing for Indian corn and meal." Huronia became the breadbasket of other Indian nations. It also produced an abundance of squashes and sunflowers, plums and small apples, raspberries, strawberries, and nuts.[32]

Champlain tells us that he visited most of Huronia's major towns and many of its villages in a systematic way. He became increasingly aware of the open structure of politics in Indian cultures. Each Huron village had separate sets of leaders for every clan that lived there. Champlain met with many of these men. It was an extraordinary effort in frontier diplomacy that consumed much of the month of August. In the end, it may have had two consequences, one of them unintended. Champlain broadened his own base of support among the Huron, but at a price. In the process, he may have weakened the already limited authority of the most eminent leaders in Huronia. That problem would come to haunt him in the weeks to follow.[33]

On August 17, 1615, Champlain reached the town of Cahiagué, "the chief village of the country," larger than Carhagouha. Here the warriors of Huronia were asked to gather for the campaign against the central Iroquois. He wrote: "I was received with great joy and gratitude by all the natives of the country, who had abandoned their project, thinking that they would never see me again, and that the Iroquois had captured me. This was the cause of the great delay which had happened in this expedition."[34]

It was agreed that they would make a long march from Huronia into the center of Iroquoia and launch a bold attack on a major town of the Onondaga nation, which Champlain called Entouhonoron or Antouhonoron. These people had been raiding to the north across Lake Ontario, which he knew as the Lake of the Entouhonoron, the Lake of the Onondaga.[35]

While Champlain waited for the war parties to gather, he explored the town of Cahiagué. It was an extraordinary place. He counted two hundred large lodges, with a population in the range of three thousand to perhaps six thousand people. It was protected by a massive palisade with seven rows of posts. The strength of its defenses was a measure of the scale of fighting between the Huron and the Iroquois.[36]

By the last week of August the Huron warriors had assembled. They set off on September 1, passing from Cahiagué to the land near the attractive modern town of Orillia between Lake Couchiching and Lake Simcoe, where they paused for the Algonquin war parties to join them. Champlain's visits had borne fruit. The Algonquin Petite nation turned out in force, with their war chief Iroquet. So did the Morrison Island Algonquin and their chief Tessoüat. Other nations also came forward.[37]

The Huron and Algonquin hoped that yet another major Indian nation would join them from the southern side of Iroquoia. These were the Susquehannock, who lived in what is now Maryland, Pennsylvania, and southern New York. The Iroquois were at war with them as well. The Susquehannock were allies of the Huron and had heard good things about the French. They had captured three Dutch traders who were with the Iroquois and let them go, thinking they were Frenchmen. They offered to join the attack on the central Iroquois with five hundred men. The Huron told Champlain that the Susquehannock were good fighters, but they could be reached only by a long detour around the country of the Seneca. The Huron decided to send a delegation of twelve of their best warriors. Champlain's *truchement*, his interpreter Étienne Brûlé, asked to go along, and it was agreed.[38]

On September 1, the main force of Huron and Algonquin warriors was at last ready, and off they went together. Champlain had between ten and thirteen French arquebusiers; the Indians mustered at least five hundred warriors, probably more.[39] The size of the expedition is not clear, but it was large enough to cause a major problem of logistics. Champlain wrote, "we advanced by short stages, hunting continually." He described a hunt by "400 or 500" Indians, who formed a line and drove the deer onto points of land surrounded by lakes and rivers. The deer threw themselves into the water and were killed with sword blades attached to long poles. Champlain wrote, "I took a peculiar pleasure in watching them hunt in this manner, noting their skill."[40]

The French joined the hunt with their firearms, and caused an accident. An arquebusier aimed at a stag and wounded an Indian warrior, which threatened to disrupt the expedition. Indians did not believe in accidents. Champlain wrote that "a great clamor arose." It was settled with presents to the wounded man and his family, "the ordinary method of allaying and ending quarrels."[41]

It was a very long distance from Cahiagué to the center of Iroquoia, a journey of forty days from their departure on September 1. Most of it was done by canoe. Indian guides led them through a long chain of lakes with short portages: today's Cranberry, Balsam, Cameron, Sturgeon, Pigeon, Buckhorn, Deer, Clear, and Rice lakes, and the Otonabee and Trent rivers. That route took them south from Huronia to the northeast shore of today's Lake Ontario.[42]

There they launched their canoes and set out across the northeastern corner of Lake Ontario, by way of islands that gave them passages of no more than seven miles in open water. This ingenious route brought them to the eastern shore of Lake Ontario, south of today's Sacket's Harbor, below a cape called Pointe à la Traverse. The Indians carefully hid their canoes in deep woods, which was vital to the success of their mission. If they lost their canoes they would be trapped in enemy country. The canoes were cached with great skill.[43]

On October 5 or thereabouts, they started on the last leg of their long journey. Champlain wrote that they went due south by foot along a "sandy beach," across "many small streams and two little rivers" that flowed into Lake Ontario. As always, Champlain studied the region, and wrote that the countryside was "very agreeable and handsome," with many ponds and prairies, and "an endless variety of game." He admired the "beautiful woods" with their "great number of chestnut trees (*chastiaigners*), and sampled the abundant chestnuts, and found them to be good eating (*de bon goust*)." With Champlain in command, even a military campaign had a way of becoming a triumphant *tour gastronomique*.[44]

They followed the coast of Lake Ontario to its southeastern corner. Here, very near the present Selkirk Shores State Park, they crossed the Salmon River (more good eating), and turned away from the lakeshore into the forest. They made another long march along the line of today's New York Highway 11 and Interstate Route 81, into the heart of Iroquoia. It was a dangerous place for them. This part of the journey took four days to go about forty miles, over several large creeks and the Oneida River, which they crossed near the present town of Brewerton. They were marching through the country of the Oneida to the land of the Onondaga nation.[45]

When they entered the Onondaga country, Champlain's Indian allies changed their march discipline. They began to move forward in silence and great stealth. In deep woods, their scouts surprised a small Onondaga party of three men, four women, and four children who were "going to catch fish." They were taken prisoner and brought to the main body. An Algonquin warrior of the Petite nation ran up, seized a woman, and cut off her finger, "for a beginning of their usual torture."

Champlain rushed to her defense. "I came at once," he wrote, "and reprimanded the chief," who was his friend Iroquet. Champlain was very angry. He said to Iroquet, "This is not the act of a warrior, as he calls himself, to behave cruelly toward women who have no other defence but tears, and whom by reason of their weakness and helplessness we should treat with humanity." Those were his words: *on doibt traicter humainement*. He told Iroquet that the torture of women would be judged as coming from a "base and brutal disposition," and if any more of this cruelty followed, the French would not assist them in their war. Iroquet replied that the enemies did the same to them, but if it was displeasing to Champlain, nothing more would be done to the women. He promised to torture only the men.[46]

But that response was not the end of it. According to a later account by Jesuit father Paul Le Jeune, another Algonquin warrior of the Morrison Island nation heard Champlain's words and was enraged by the interference of this meddlesome Frenchman. He turned defiantly on Champlain and said, "See what I shall do, since you speak of it." He seized an Iroquois infant who had been nursing at the breast of its mother, took it by the foot, and smashed its head against a rock or a tree. The French were appalled by the murder of this innocent baby—and still more by the way that "these proud spirits (*ces superbes*) spoke to a captain who had arms in hand." The alliance between the French and the Indians threatened to fly apart—in the middle of Iroquoia.[47]

Then suddenly another crisis came upon them. The scouts at the head of the column came in sight of their target—a large fortified town of the Onondaga nation. It lay on a good-sized stream that flowed into the southern end of Lake Onondaga in what is now the city of Syracuse, New York.[48] Champlain had already worked out a careful plan of attack. He proposed that his arquebusiers remain out of sight and wait for a battle to develop. When the Onondaga warriors emerged from the fort, the French would intervene at the critical moment, some of them from the flanks, as they had done twice against the Mohawk.

At first contact with the enemy the plan came apart. As his Indian allies came within sight of the fort, a small group of Onondaga warriors rushed out to fight them. Some of the allies raced forward in quest of captives. The operation dissolved into a chaos of small fights, and the Iroquois began to get the upper hand. Champlain watched with concern as more Indians from both sides joined the fight and the tide of battle turned against his allies. He called to his arquebusiers and led them forward. They opened fire, and the Onondaga recoiled in shock. Champlain thought that many of them had never seen European soldiers armed with "thundersticks."

The Onondaga retreated into the fort with their dead and wounded. Champlain also fell back, with wounded Indians whom he had rescued from the field. He was in a state of fury. To protect a few impetuous warriors, he had lost the vital element of tactical surprise that had worked so well against the Mohawk. He remembered that he used "hard and unpleasant words" and warned the Indian war chiefs that "if every thing went according to caprice . . . evil alone would result, to their loss and ruin."[49]

• • •

Champlain studied the Onondaga town, which was more a castle than a fort. It was surrounded by four massive palisades of heavy interlocked timbers thirty feet high. On the top were galleries or parapets protected by double timbers that were proof against French musketry. The castle had an ample supply of water, and a system of gutters and waterspouts that could be used to put out fires along its wooden walls. Altogether Champlain thought that the Onondaga fort was stronger than the towns of the Huron.

Champlain invited his Indian allies to a council of war and recommended a new plan. Drawing on his experience of European siegecraft, he proposed that they construct a "siege engine" called a *cavalier*. This was a protected platform on stilts, higher than the palisades, with loopholes for firearms. Then he suggested that they build large shielded enclosures called *mantelets*, and use them to approach the palisades and set the walls ablaze.

It was agreed. With incredible speed the Indians and the French built a big cavalier. Two hundred men pushed it forward, within a "pike's length," about sixteen feet, of the palisade. From its high platform, French arquebusiers began to fire into the town, loading their weapons with three or four balls at each discharge. They had an abundance of ammunition, and they raked the interior of the crowded Onondaga fort for three hours, inflicting heavy losses on the defenders. Champlain wrote, "Those on the Cavalier killed and maimed many of them." [50]

Champlain started the next maneuver. Other Indians came forward under cover of the mantelets. They piled kindling against the palisades and started fires. But they did it on a side of the fort where the wind was against them, and the defenders used their gutters to pour water on the flames. The attackers ran short of kindling, the fires went out, and the frustrated attackers emerged from their mantelets. They fired arrows that had little effect, screaming defiance at the enemy. Champlain wrote, "One could not make oneself heard, which troubled me greatly. In vain I shouted in their ears. . . . They heard nothing, on account of the great noise they were making." [51]

Champlain observed that the Onondaga "took advantage of our confusion" and returned in strength to their ramparts. The defenders aimed great numbers of arrows at their attackers. The French fired back and inflicted severe losses, but more Onondaga warriors replaced their fallen comrades. Champlain wrote that the arrows "fell upon us like hail." Two of the three leading Huron chiefs were wounded. Then Champlain went down, hit by several arrows. One penetrated an unprotected spot on his leg. Another went into his knee. He fell to the ground, unable to walk, and wrote that the wound caused

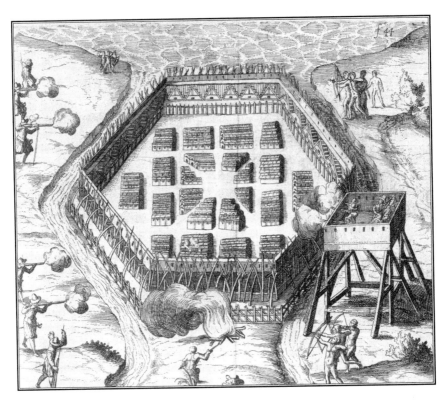

Champlain's sketch of his attack on the Onondaga fort in 1615, at Lake Onondaga. He tried to capture it with a European siege engine called a "cavalier," while his allies tried to burn the palisade. Champlain thought the attack a failure, but Indians on both sides judged it a highly successful revenge raid. It led to a long period of peace.

"extreme pain." Despite his injury, he believed that victory was in reach and urged his allies to "turn against the enemy again." The Indians refused. Champlain said, "My discourses availed as little as if I had been silent." He observed that "the chiefs have no absolute control over their men, who follow their own wishes and act as their fancy suggests, which is the cause of their confusion and spoils all their enterprises."[52]

The Indians fell back from the fort, but under heavy pressure from Champlain, they agreed to wait four or five days in hope that the Susquehannock might join them. The next day a great wind came up, and Champlain saw another opportunity to burn the wooden castle. Once again the Indians did not agree, and "would do nothing." They continued in their camp around the fort for a few days, waiting for word of the Susquehannock. Onondaga war parties came out of the fort and small skirmishes took place. Champlain wrote that the Onondaga again got the upper hand in these engagements, and withdrew only when Champlain sent forward his arquebusiers, "which the enemy greatly feared and dreaded." [53]

Finally, on October 16, the Huron and Algonquin would wait no longer for the Susquehannock, and decided to go home. Champlain, for all his frustration, sympathized with them. "They must be excused," he wrote, "for they are not trained soldiers (*gens de guerre*) and moreover they do not submit to discipline or correction, and do only what they think right." The siege of the Onondaga fort was at an end. [54]

Champlain judged the battle by the measure of his intention, and believed that he had been defeated. His object had been to capture the Onondaga "castle," and in this he failed completely. He succeeded only in charring a small part of the outer palisade, did no damage to its structure, and was compelled to retreat. Champlain always wrote of this battle as a defeat, and he regarded the entire mission as a failure. For many years most scholars, including this historian, shared that view. Marcel Trudel went further and concluded that the assault on the fort was not merely a defeat but a disaster for New France. He believed that it marked the beginning of the great expansion in Iroquois power. [55]

More recently, historical ethnographers have approached the same question in a different way. Working from their familiarity with Indian cultures, they studied the campaign by the standards of Indian warfare and came to a surprising conclusion. Bruce Trigger, a leading ethnohistorian of the Huron, found that "none of the Indians involved regarded the campaign of 1615 as a defeat for Champlain or his allies." After this battle and the two fights against the Mohawk, Trigger observed that the Iroquois Five nations "did not wish to fight the French." He added: "The question that must be asked is why, after the French had played a leading role in killing about 160 Mohawks in 1609 and 1610, and attacking the Oneida [Onondaga] settlement in 1615, these tribes were not more vindictive."

Trigger's answer was complex, involving relations between the Iroquois and the Dutch, and other opportunities to the south and west. An important factor was the high cost to the Iroquois of hostilities against the French. In the attack on the Onondaga castle, Champlain's arquebusiers killed and wounded many Indian defenders of the fort. We have no count of casualties, but the firing was heavy and prolonged, the range was point-blank, and the cost must have been severe to this small Iroquois nation. Champlain's allies withdrew successfully with few losses of their own. Trigger concluded that Indians on both sides regarded such an attack as a success. [56]

An ethnohistorian of the St. Lawrence Indians agreed with Trigger. José António Brandao also wrote that the campaign succeeded by the standards of Indian warfare. The attackers made a bold march into the heartland of the Iroquois League, launched a major assault on one of its most formidable strongholds, and inflicted heavy casualties on Onondaga warriors who had been raiding the St. Lawrence Valley. From the perspective of Indian culture, the attack was brilliantly effective as a revenge-raid, and it appears to have been regarded that way by Indians of many nations.

Brandao observed that it was also a success when measured against another of Champlain's larger purposes, which was to deter Iroquois attacks to the north. After his campaign, "none of these groups, nor the [Iroquois] confederacy as a whole, was eager to wage war against the new French settlers and their native allies. Instead, the Iroquois tried to make peace with their native foes." He added, "Even though he had aided the Algonquins, Hurons and Montagnais against the Iroquois, Champlain did not appear to rule out the hope of peace among these groups. Indeed, at first Champlain looked favorably on peace efforts between the Iroquois and his native allies." [57]

William Fenton, an ethnohistorian of the Iroquois, also agreed with Trigger and Brandao. He wrote that after the battle of the Onondaga fort, Iroquois raids to the north were much reduced. For twenty years, the Onondaga and Mohawk were careful not to fight the French. Fenton observes that major Iroquois hostilities did not revive until 1640, by his reckoning. Champlain's campaign against the Onondaga was a successful example of limited war for purposes of peace and stability. [58]

After the battle, Champlain was immobilized by his wounds. His Indian allies took command and organized the withdrawal with practiced skill. The Onondaga came after them, urgently seeking prisoners for their own ceremonies of revenge. They got none. Champlain wrote, "The enemy followed us about half a league, but at a distance, to try to capture some of those who formed the rear-guard, but their efforts proved vain, and they withdrew." Champlain was much impressed by the conduct of the withdrawal, which showed a discipline that had been lacking in the attack. He wrote of his allies that "they conduct their retreats very securely, putting the wounded and the elderly in the middle, and strong forces on the front, flanks and rear, without breaking ranks until they reach a place of safety."

Even so, it was a terrible ordeal, especially for Champlain himself. They had to march seventy-five miles to their canoes. Champlain was unable to walk, as were "many of their wounded." To leave them behind was to condemn them to death by the unspeakable agony of Iroquois torture—and also to forfeit the victory of a revenge-raid. The Indians improvised large baskets, or *paniers*, as Champlain described them. The wounded warriors were put into the baskets and "bound in such a manner that it was impossible to move any more than a little child in its swaddling clothes." The paniers were strapped to the backs of very strong Indians who carried them to safety.[59]

"It caused the wounded great and extreme pain," Champlain later testified. "I can say this indeed with truth from my own case, having been carried for several days because I was unable to stand, chiefly because of the arrow in my knee. Never did I find myself in such a hell as during this time, for the pain I suffered from the wound in my knee was nothing in comparison with what I endured tied and bound on the back of one of our Indians. This made me lose patience, and as soon as I was able to stand, I got out of this prison or more accurately this hell that I was in."[60]

If the wounded were "greatly fatigued," so were their carriers. Able-bodied Indians took turns, and the way was long and hard. On October 18, just after the withdrawal began, they were overtaken by heavy snow, hail, and "a strong wind which caused us much trouble." The Indians kept on with a stoic determination that Champlain admired. At last they reached Lake Ontario, and found their canoes still safely hidden.

Champlain asked to be taken back to Quebec, which the Indians had promised to do after the campaign. But the chiefs did not agree. Four individual Indians came forward and offered to take Champlain and his French arquebusiers to their settlement. The warriors did so in defiance of their chiefs and "of their own accord, for as I have said before, the chiefs have no authority over their companions." But they needed canoes, and the Indian leaders insisted that there were none to spare. Champlain was very unhappy. The Indians were breaking a promise, and he was "badly equipped for spending the winter with them." Gradually it dawned on him that the Indians had a complex purpose in mind. "I perceived that their plan was to detain me with my comrades in their country, both for their safety and out of fear of their enemies." His allies worried that a small party might be intercepted by the Iroquois, with fatal results for the alliance. Further, they wanted Champlain to be part of their "councils and assemblies, and to join in decisions about what might be done for the future against their enemies."[61]

It was soon clear that protests had no effect. Champlain wrote, "Not being able to do anything, I had to resign myself to be patient." He decided to make the best of his situation and use the time to observe the ways of the Huron and their neighbors: "During the winter season, which lasted four months, I had leisure enough to study their country, their manners, customs, modes of life, the form of their assemblies, and other things which I should like to describe." [62]

An ethnohistorian, Elisabeth Tooker, compared Champlain's studies of the Huron with those of the Jesuits who followed him. She observed that the Jesuits were men of great learning who described the religion of the Huron in depth but were superficial on other aspects of their culture. Champlain's studies were in her judgment "less cultivated but not less precise." He had less interest in Huron religion but was "more attentive to other aspects of culture neglected by the Jesuits, in particular the life cycle, inheritance, and modes of subsistence." He studied them as a participant-observer, "a man among men, who took part in military expeditions, hunted big game with them, and later wrote of his experiences." [63]

The Huron treated Champlain very well. The chief named Atironta (Champlain called him Darontal) gave Champlain his cabin, with abundant supplies and furniture. He was invited to join a great deer hunt, which Champlain called their "noblest sport." He hunted with the men of the nation as they drove the deer into an enclosure 1,500 paces on a side, made of wooden stakes eight or nine feet high. The Indians imitated wolf cries, drove the animals into the trap, and killed 120 deer. He was astounded by the skill of the Indian hunters, by their success in working together, and by their very elaborate forms of organization. [64]

Champlain also studied the flora and fauna of Huronia. Like many hunters, he loved animals, birds, and plants. While on a hunt, he wrote: "[I observed] a certain bird which seemed to me peculiar, with a beak almost like that of a parrot, as big as a hen, yellow all over, except for its red head and blue wings, which made short successive flights like a partridge. My desire to kill it made me chase it from tree to tree for a very long time, until it flew away in good earnest."

He tried to retrace his steps but could not find the Huron hunting party, and soon he was completely lost in a trackless forest. He had no compass or map, and for three days no sun. But he was armed, and killed a few birds, and cooked them over a fire. Finally he found his way. Champlain did not tell us how, but he appears to have adopted the old Indian method of following watercourses downstream, which took him to a lake where he was able to locate the hunting party. The Huron were appalled, and required him always to take a compass and a skilled Indian guide, "who knew so well how to

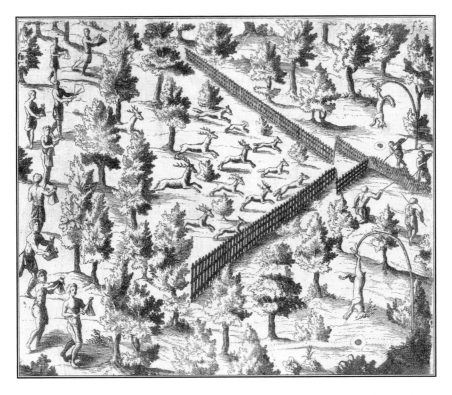

The Huron invited Champlain to join their communal deer hunts in October 1615. He sketched their skillful methods of driving large numbers of deer into pens and trapping others with snares. He respected their skill as hunters and their mastery of collective effort.

find a place whence he had set out, that it was a strange and marvelous thing to see."[65]

Champlain was amazed by the stamina of the Indian hunters. On the return to their villages, he carried a weight of twenty pounds, which with his other equipment soon exhausted him, and probably did nothing good for his wounded knee. He observed that the Huron carried loads of a hundred pounds without apparent strain over very long distances and at a rapid pace. Few Europeans matched their powers of endurance.[66]

Champlain traveled widely in Huronia. He described the larger region as "almost an island which the great River of St. Lawrence surrounds, passing through several lakes of great size on the shore of which live many nations speaking different languages, having fixed places of residence, given to cultivation of the earth, but with different manners and customs, and some better than others." [67]

Champlain also visited other nations nearby. He especially liked to stay with the Cheveux-Relevés, who were among his favorites of all the many Indian nations. He visited the western Algonquin, and persuaded the Huron to take him to the Petun or Tobacco nation. Champlain also wanted to make a journey to the Neutral nation, as they were called, but the Huron did not agree. Perhaps they worried that a French alliance with the Neutral might weaken their position and even open negotiations with the Iroquois. Possibly they feared that some mishap might befall Champlain. Whatever the reason, the Huron kept him away from the Neutral nation. Blocked in that way, Champlain went in the opposite direction. He visited the Nipissing and built another alliance.

One day Champlain came back from a visit to the Nipissing and found big trouble among his allies. The Petite nation of the Algonquin and their chief Iroquet were wintering with the Huron as was their custom, and exchanging furs for food. The Huron had given them an Iroquois captive, "expecting that Iroquet would exercise on this prisoner the vengeance customary among them." Iroquet took a liking to the captive, found him to be a good hunter, treated him as a son, and set him at liberty.

The Huron were very angry, and sent a warrior to kill the prisoner, which was done in the presence of the headmen of the Algonquin Petite nation, who were doubly outraged by the murder and the breach of manners, and killed the killer. Now it was the turn of the Huron to be insulted. They took up arms, surrounded the Algonquin village, and attacked. Iroquet was wounded by two arrows, and his lodges were looted. The Algonquin were greatly outnumbered and agreed to pay fifty wampum belts, a hundred fathoms of wampum, many axes and kettles, and two female prisoners. It was a great price to pay, and it brought no peace. The two nations were full of rage against each other, each nourishing a sense of injustice.

At that point two Hurons from Cahiagué asked Champlain to intervene and reconcile the angry parties. Champlain acted quickly and with great tact. He sent his interpreter, probably Thomas Godefroy, to collect the facts, being careful "not to go myself, so as not to give suspicion to either party." Then he brought together the "leading chiefs" and "elder men" of both sides, and they agreed to accept Champlain's role as arbitrator. He told them that "the best course was for all to make peace and remain friends," and that they had dealt with each other in ways "unworthy of reasonable men, but should rather be left to brute beasts." Peace was restored.[68]

In a village that he called Carmaron, Champlain had another encounter. He was sleeping in a crowded lodge and found himself assaulted by fleas, "which were in great number and a torment to us." Champlain rose from his bed in the middle of the night and walked outside into the darkness of the sleeping village. In Huronia, young women and men did that for a very different purpose—not to escape the fleas but to catch a mate. They made a custom of midnight trysts, which were an important part of trial marriages in their culture. It was thought perfectly proper for nubile young women to have experimental unions with many men, sometimes twenty or more, before settling down with one of them. This was a rational custom of what might be called informed choice, but it was very far from Champlain's folkways.

As he walked alone in the sleeping village, a young woman approached and offered herself to him. Probably she assumed that he was abroad for that reason. Why else would a single man be wandering alone through a Huron village in the middle of the night? Champlain was shocked. "I declined with thanks," he said, "sending her away with gentle remonstrances," and he returned to the fleas.

In this encounter, the young Indian woman was keeping one code, and Champlain another. One wonders which of them was more surprised. Many young Frenchmen were delighted to embrace these bold and free young women. Others went a different way—Catholic priests, Indian shamans, and Champlain. He was a soldier and a man of the world who acted like a holy man. It was so unusual that Indians and Europeans talked about him with amazement and admiration in his lifetime and afterward. Among the Indians, his abstinence added to his orenda, or spiritual power.[69]

Champlain's impression of the Huron was in many ways very positive. He greatly admired their agriculture and huge fisheries, marveled at their skill in hunting, and came to form high respect for their woodcraft. As before with many other nations, he found these Indians to be the equal of Europeans in their intelligence, and superior in physical strength and the proportion of their bodies. He thought that they excelled Europeans in courage and stamina. "All of these people," he wrote, "are of a very cheerful disposition although many among them are of a sad and saturnine complexion. They are well proportioned in body; the men big and well shaped, as also the women and girls are

Champlain's sketch of a Huron girl adorned with strings of wampum. He wrote that they were "well shaped, strong, and robust . . . many pleasing and pretty in figure, complexion, and face, everything in proportion." He wrote, "After night comes, the young women run about from one lodge to another, as do the young men who possess them when it seems good to both, but with no violence, leaving the choice entirely to the young woman."

pleasing and pretty, both in figures, faces and complexion. . . . Some of the women are very powerful and of extraordinary height."[70]

In Champlain's thinking, the many good qualities of American Indians were countered by three great negatives: *ni foi, ni loi, ni roi;* no faith, no law, no king. He and other French leaders in his circle believed that the Indians had souls, which were denied by some Europeans. Champlain agreed with his good friend Paul Le Jeune who wrote: "I believe that all souls are made of the same stock, and they do not differ substantially. . . . Their soul is a naturally fertile soil, but it is loaded down with all the evils that a land abandoned since the birth of the world can produce." Champlain believed that the Indians had nothing like the universal faith of the Christian religion.[71] He added, "It is a great misfortune that so many poor creatures should live and die without any knowledge of God, and even without any religion or law, whether divine, political or civil."[72] He was interested in their beliefs, studied their ideas of spirits, and talked with their shamans. From this he concluded that in a Christian sense, "they adore and believe in no God nor in any such thing, but live like brute beasts (*bestes bruttes*)."[73]

Linked to the absence of faith and universal religion, in his sense, was the absence of law. "As for their laws," he wrote, "I did not see that they have any, nor anything approaching them; as indeed is the case, inasmuch as there is no correction, punishment or censure of evil-doers except by way of revenge, rendering evil for evil, not as a matter of law but through passion, engendering wars and quarrels which exist among them most of the time."[74] He understood their custom as lex talionis, the law of retaliation, which punished one wrong by the commission of another. In Champlain's thinking, this rule of conduct was not truly an idea of law, which for him was a principle of right, grounded in an idea of universal justice and equity: *lex equitatis*.

In the absence of what he believed to be *loi et foi*, true law and true faith, Champlain regarded the ethics of Indian culture as primitive and inhumane. The leading example was the treatment of prisoners, who were condemned to suffer unimaginably in horrible rituals of sadistic savagery. Some of these helpless victims had done nothing wrong, and yet were wronged themselves in retribution for similar acts that had been committed by others. Champlain regarded this custom of lex talionis as one that betrayed the absence of true law, which rested on an idea of universal right—not a wrong for a wrong.[75]

Champlain also believed that the culture of North American Indians lacked the authority of kingship and the discipline of subordination. He disapproved of the way that Indian children were raised, with a latitude of indulgent liberty that created young people "so bad and perverse in disposition that they often strike their mothers, and some of the more ill-tempered strike their fathers when they have gained strength and power, that is, if father or mother do something they dislike, which is a kind of curse that God sends them."[76]

He also disapproved of the way Indian warriors treated women and compelled them to "serve as mules." And "as to the men," he wrote, "they do nothing but hunt deer and other animals, fish, build lodges and go on the war path. Having done this, they visit other nations to trade and exchange, and on their return do not cease from feasting and dancing, with which they entertain one another, and afterwards they go to sleep, which is their finest exertion."[77]

In the late twentieth century, some ethnographers have severely chastised Champlain for these attitudes. They have criticized him for being uncomprehending of Indian culture, and ethnocentric in his judgments. It is true that Champlain had a strong and abiding Christian faith, a deep belief in an idea of law as the rule of universal right, and an allegiance to kingship and subordination. At the same time, he was deeply interested in the ways of the Indians, lived with them for long periods, traveled with them, and fought beside them in three campaigns. He knew intimately the Etchemin and Mi'kmaq, Montagnais and Algonquin, Huron, and many other Indian nations. He understood their complex politics and their way of war.

There were limits to his understanding. He was not fluent in Indian languages and worked through interpreters on important occasions, though he could communicate directly in pidgin speech, as he often did. His understanding of Indian groups was incomplete and sometimes erroneous. But he deeply respected the Indians, admired their character, and wrote that "their spirit was not as savage as their customs." Champlain also believed that Indians could become Christians and learn to live by an idea of law as universal right. At the same time they would remain Indians, and their unique culture should preserve its integrity. Champlain believed that people are capable of complex identities. He knew that it was possible to be Huron and Christian at the same time. Also he thought it was possible for the French to be faithful to their ways and respectful of others.

Here again, in Champlain's winter among the Huron we see his grand design for New France, as a vision of Indians and French living close to one another, preserving the best of their cultures, guided by principles of universal faith, and respectful of universal law. Champlain was indeed ethnocentric in some of his attitudes, but his thinking was more generous and large-spirited than some of the judgments that have been made against him.

CHAMPLAIN'S NATIVE BROUAGE, IN THE PROVINCE OF SAINTONGE

Samuel Champlain (1570?–1635) was raised in the flourishing small seaport of Brouage, seen here in an aerial photograph. Today it lies more than a mile inland from the Gulf of Saintonge, with the Bay of Biscay and the Atlantic Ocean in the distance. In Champlain's youth, the busy town was crowded with people from many nations. He grew accustomed to diversity and was consumed with curiosity about the world. The sea became his school, and his father (a ship captain) was his teacher. The surrounding province of Saintonge was a borderland between different French regions, economies, cultures, and languages. It produced leaders such as Champlain and the sieur de Mons who learned to work with others unlike themselves. (A1)

THE WARS OF RELIGION IN FRANCE, 1562–1598

François Dubois, "Massacre of Saint Bartholomew's Day," is a chronicle of horror in Champlain's world. In one day, August 24, 1572, Catholics killed thousands of Protestants in Paris. France suffered nine civil wars of religion in four decades, with deaths reckoned in millions and atrocities beyond description. In that era of cruelty and violence, Henri IV (1553–1610) became king of France in 1589. Baptized a Protestant, he converted to Catholicism (three times), defeated his many rivals in heavy fighting, united the people of France, and in 1598 established a new regime that was dedicated to humanity, peace, and tolerance. Champlain became a soldier in the royal army, served in the largest religious war, and made Henri's purposes his own. (A2)

FROBISHER AND CHAMPLAIN

In 1594, Champlain soldiered with Martin Frobisher, an English seaman with a reputation for courage and cruelty. They had a common interest in the exploration of America, but did it in very different ways. This portrait shows Frobisher with the world at his elbow, pointing a pistol toward the artist, who gave his subject a hard eye and an angry look. (A3)

TWO APPROACHES TO AMERICA

Frobisher treated the Indians with brutality. In 1577, he trapped and killed many Inuits, seized an older woman, and stripped off her clothing "to see if she were cloven footed." He did not think of her as a human being. John White's scene of this "Skirmish at Bloody Point" was a celebration of violence. Champlain's approach would be far removed from Frobisher's. (A4)

CHAMPLAIN'S MISSION TO NEW SPAIN

After the wars of religion, Champlain visited New Spain in 1599. This image from Georg Hoefnagel's *Civitates Orbis Terrarum* shows his Spanish shipmates—seamen in bright clothing called bizarria, soldiers with weapons in hand, an owner paying wages, and highly skilled officers who taught Champlain much about navigation and the new world. (A5)

CHAMPLAIN'S DRAWINGS OF SPANISH BRUTALITY TO THE INDIANS

In New Spain, Champlain was deeply interested in American Indians and African slaves. He talked with them at every opportunity and was shocked by Spanish cruelty and exploitation. For his report to the king, he painted this image of Indians burned alive by the Inquisition. (A6)

CHAMPLAIN'S OUTRAGE AT RELIGIOUS CRUELTY

Another of Champlain's paintings showed Indians being beaten for not attending Mass. This pious French Catholic was most deeply offended by atrocities committed in the name of Christ by Spanish priests with the blessing of the Church. (A7)

THE LOUVRE'S GRAND GALERIE

On his return to France in 1601, Champlain reported to the king and received a pension "to keep me near his person." He worked in the basement of the Louvre, which Henri IV made into a Center of Study by scientists, humanists, artisans, and cartographers. A friend described Champlain as a "royal geographer," one of many in the Louvre. (A8)

A BALL IN THE COURT OF HENRI IV

For Champlain the court was also a school of manners, where he studied the art of pleasing others. Some of his most important work for America was done as a courtier in France, where he became highly skilled at the art of politics in a complex monarchy. (A9)

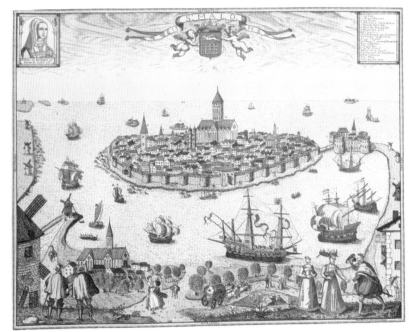

CATHOLIC ST. MALO WITH ITS GREAT CATHEDRAL

In 1602–03, Champlain's interest began to center on North America. He visited the Breton port of St. Malo, and worked closely with Malouin captains such as François Gravé, sieur DuPont (Pont-Gravé to his friends), who had much experience of the new world. (A10)

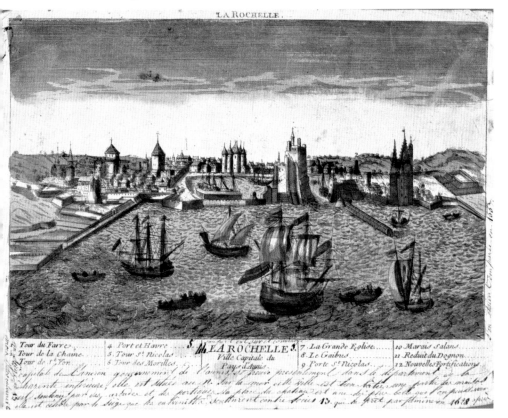

THE PROTESTANT FORTRESS OF LA ROCHELLE

Champlain worked with the Protestant merchants of La Rochelle and Catholics in Honfleur and Dieppe, who had a long acquaintance with North America. He began to develop a "grand dessein" for New France in a spirit of tolerance and humanity similar to the policies of Henri IV and different from Catholic New Spain and Calvinist New England. (A11)

THE MARINERS MIRROVR

Wherin may playnly be seen the courses, heights, distances, depths, soundings, flouds and ebs, risings of lands, rocks, sands and shoalds, with the marks for th'entrings of the Harbouroughs, Havens and Ports of the greatest part of Europe: their seueral traficks and commodities. Together w.th the Rules and instruments of NAVIGATION.

First made & set fourth in diuers exact Sea-Charts, by that famous Nauigator LVKE WAGENAER of Enchuisen And now fitted with necessarie additions for the use of Englishmen by ANTHONY ASHLEY.

Herin also may be understood the exploits lately atchiued by the right Honorable the L. Admiral of England with his Ma.ties Nauและ.some former seruices don by this worthy Knight S.r FRANCIS DRAKE.

TREATISES ON NAVIGATION IN CHAMPLAIN'S ERA

Champlain also worked with ships' chandlers in Dieppe. He mastered the science of navigation and studied works such as Wagenaer's *Mariner's Mirrour* in its first English edition (1588?), and Pedro de Medina's *Regimiento de Navegacion* (1543, 1595). Champlain also wrote his own treatise about the duty of a mariner and the art of leadership in large causes (1632). (A12)

BUILDER OF NEW FRANCE

16.

THE COURT OF LOUIS XIII
Another New Master, 1616–19

> When the head is sick, the members cannot be in good health.
>
> —Samuel Champlain, ca. 1616 [1]

O N AUGUST 3, 1616, Champlain and Pont-Gravé sailed down the St. Lawrence River, homeward bound for France. They were blessed with fine weather and made a happy crossing in thirty days from Tadoussac to Honfleur. On arrival, their mood suddenly changed. They were astonished to hear that the viceroy of New France was a prisoner in the Bastille.[2] The prince de Condé had been arrested on the orders of the queen regent herself, for the capital crimes of treason, rebellion, and *lèse majesté*. Champlain was deeply alarmed for the viceroy, and also for the fate of New France. He wrote, "The detention of My Lord the Prince led me to think that our rivals (*nos envieux*) would not be slow in spewing out their poison, for when the head is sick, the members cannot be in good health."[3]

Champlain recalled that "from this moment, affairs changed their complexion." The man who arrested Condé replaced him as viceroy of New France. He was Pons de Lauzière, marquis de Thémines de Cardillac, marshal of France. His appointment as viceroy was confirmed by the queen regent on October 25. Events were moving rapidly at court, and they were deeply threatening to Champlain's design. One of his rivals approached Thémines and asked to be the viceroy's lieutenant for New France. We do not know his name. Champlain contemptuously referred to him only as a "certain personage," and tells us that he offered a bribe to Thémines, promising to treble the viceroy's annual income by extorting large sums from merchants who wished to trade in New France. Whoever this "certain personage" may have been, he was successful, and the queen appointed him lieutenant for New France. Suddenly Champlain was unemployed.[4]

He responded as he always did when the grand design was in danger. Champlain fought back with every resource at his command, and recruited others to help. Condé, from his luxurious cell in the Bastille, brought a series of lawsuits against the new viceroy. The duc de Montmorency also filed a suit for his own outstanding claims. Maréchal de Thémines found himself in a tangle of litigation, with two princes of the blood against him.[5]

These contending parties were soon caught up in a larger and more dangerous game. Champlain began to discover what had been happening in France during his absence. In 1615, while he had been in Huronia, Marie de Medici had grown deeply unpopular in France. She sought a Spanish alliance by proposing to marry her son and daughter to the children of Philip III in Spain. Many people in France disliked these policies, and they detested the queen's close circle of Italian friends at court. Especially hated were her Italian intimates, Concino and Leonora Concini, whose corruption had become an open scandal. It was one thing for the wealth of the kingdom to flow into French pockets, but quite another when it passed to foreigners.

Anger grew rapidly throughout the country in 1615 and 1616. Marie de Medici felt that power was slipping away, and she specially feared the prince de Condé. After the death of her younger son, Condé stood second in line to inherit the throne. He despised the corrupt circle around the queen. Others rallied to him, and he raised an army in the countryside. Once again the kingdom of France teetered on the brink of civil war. Fighting actually began in 1615 when Condé's supporters took possession of the town of Méry in Champagne. In a battle that followed, allies of Champlain's viceroy killed Champlain's friend the sieur de Poutrincourt, proprietor of Port-Royal in Acadia. He was mourned by many Frenchmen, who blamed their hated Italian queen regent for provoking the trouble.[6]

In the summer of 1616, Condé rode into Paris to attend the Royal Council and was received with rejoicing by the people of the city. Nobles left the court and flocked to his mansion. In Richelieu's words, the Louvre became a solitude, and "Condé's house became what the Louvre had been."[7] Marie de Medici gave way to panic. On September 1, 1616, she ordered that Condé be arrested and confined in the Bastille. The princesse de Condé, an appealing figure, insisted on joining her husband in prison and gave birth to a stillborn child—further outraging the country.[8]

Marie de Medici chose the path of repression. At the urging of her French adviser Armand Jean de Plessis Richelieu, Bishop of Luçon, she assumed more powers and gave greater favors to her Italian circle, the Concinis in particular. She banished from court the most respected French ministers of Henri IV. Among the victims of her wrath were Champlain's strong supporters Chancellor Brûlart-Sillery and President Jeannin, who had been very close to Henri IV and had supported Champlain and his design for New France. Sillery's office was of such a nature that the queen regent could not remove him. She could only order him from her presence, but he was still around. Her ill-considered action increased her isolation.[9]

Then, writes historian Victor Tapié, "a new character appeared on the stage—the King." Louis XIII was nearly sixteen years old, no longer a child. He was very frail, often in ill health, and suffered from many ailments, including the tuberculosis that would kill him at the age of forty-three. He had a dark, restless spirit and an explosive temper. His mother had left his upbringing in the hands of a governess, Madame de Monglat. His father, Henri IV, regarded him with profound disappointment and instructed his caregiver to "beat the Dauphin as often as possible," to make a man of him.[10]

In his childhood Louis XIII had been kept on the fringe of power, but after the death of his father he had been anointed king, and in 1616 he was coming of age. He hated his mother's Italian friends, and strongly sympathized with his father's faithful servants, in particular Chancellor Sillery, a man of exceptional character and intellect. After the queen banished Sillery from court, he visited the young king to say farewell. It was an emotional scene. Many others observed that the young king wept. The queen appeared not to notice her son's distress.

Louis XIII by Philippe de Champaigne is an image of a young, sickly, and deeply troubled king who looked old beyond his years. He aspired to the title of Louis Le Juste, but also to absolute dominion. He tried to help Champlain, but they had different ideas about New France.

The king's adviser, Charles d'Albert de Luynes, urged him to assert himself and save the country from the Concini. Suddenly the king began to act. He recalled his father's old ministers and ordered the arrest of the queen's favorite, Concino Concini, on a charge of embezzlement. The king's guards were instructed to seize Concini at court and kill him if he fought back. Concini was apprehended on the bridge of the Louvre. He resisted, and was instantly put to the sword. His wife, Leonora Galigaï Concini, was imprisoned, accused of witchcraft and executed. The queen regent feared for her life, but her son the young king showed her more pity than she had shown to him. He allowed her to retreat to a château at Blois, where she raged against the ingratitude of children. With her in this domestic exile went her French adviser Richelieu. His career was thought to be over. The event was nothing less than a coup d'état. It ended the regency of Marie de Medici, removed her closest advisers, and installed the young king in her place.

With young Louis XIII now in power, France took a long step on the road to royal absolutism. He would have a turbulent reign. The king himself was a deeply troubled young man and his private life was in disorder. He was thought to be bisexual in a strongly heterosexual world, and he surrounded himself with beautiful young creatures of doubtful gender who came and went in rapid succession. Some of these royal favorites tried to turn their intimacy into power. There were reports of a homosexual affair between the king and François de Barradat, who would be banished from the court for political intrigue and perhaps other things. He was replaced by Claude de Saint-Simon and then fifteen-year-old Henri d'Effiat, the marquis de Cinq Mars, a bold young man who dared to challenge the greatest ministers in the kingdom. The king also had mistresses and a very complicated platonic triangle involving the beautiful Marie de Hautefort. Young Louis XIII was unstable in these relationships. He trusted few people and was withdrawn, silent, and dangerously "secretive." He turned on people who thought they were his friends. It was said that he sometimes ordered the arrest of former associates "without warning or outward emotion, and a touch of cruelty."[11]

Through it all, the king tried to steer a middle course for France. In his religious policy, Louis XIII continued his father's Edict of Nantes and supported toleration of Protestant worship, but he also formed a closer connection with Catholic leaders. Protestant churches were ordered to return lands and buildings to the Catholic Church, which increased its wealth and power. The young king also changed his mother's foreign policy. He sought to expand the power of France through the world—an opportunity for Champlain.

•   •   •

In the midst of all this turmoil, Champlain regained his job. He never explained how it happened. Suddenly his rival appears to have resigned the office of lieutenant for Quebec, perhaps in fear of his life. The viceroy, Thémines, appointed Champlain to his old position as lieutenant in New France. Confirmation by the king followed speedily on January 17, 1617.[12]

For Champlain one problem was solved, but many others remained. He was deeply worried about conditions in Canada, and even more concerned about support for his project at court. To judge from his writings, he was most troubled by his financial backers. The monied men of Rouen were growing restless. They had invested in Champlain's company in the hope of gaining a monopoly of the fur trade in New France, and had done well in 1615 and 1616.[13]

Most of these investors had never shared Champlain's dream for North America. They supported exploration, which promised to enlarge the fur trade, but they were not enthusiastic about colonization, which entailed heavy costs and threatened to disrupt their business. Champlain insisted that settlements were vital to the success of commerce in the long run, but business leaders were more concerned about the short run. He complained to the investors about "the small results they had shown in forwarding the growth of the settlement," and warned that "nothing was more likely to break up the company," unless more families were sent out "to put the land in cultivation."[14]

The investors also worried about the strife at court, which created a climate of uncertainty that was not good for business. They were not happy to learn that they might be liable for large sums to three viceroys at once: Condé under their old contract, and Thémines under the new arrangement, with other claims for compensation still outstanding from the duc de Montmorency. The investors were also supporting the Récollet fathers as well as the habitants at Quebec. The cost of Champlain's design kept rising. And if all that were not enough, merchant capitalists in La Rochelle, Saint-Malo, and other towns were renewing their appeals for liberty of commerce.[15]

Champlain was losing patience with court intrigues and litigation, and wrote, "Let us leave them to their pleading, and go and make ready our ships."[16] In the early winter months of 1617, he found an opportunity for a quick voyage to New France. He traveled from Paris to Honfleur, where a ship was waiting. Even before he could sail, yet another attempt was made to remove him from his office as the king's lieutenant in New France. This time it came from Daniel Boyer, a merchant associated with the Rouen Company. Champlain described him as a malicious enemy and *grand chicaneur*.[17]

Just as Champlain was about to sail, Boyer appeared in Honfleur. Claiming to represent the entire company, he reported that the parlement had issued an order that required that "their lordships the Prince de Condé, Montmorency, and Thémines, without prejudice to their rights, should be debarred from receiving any part of the money to which they could lay claim." Therefore, said Boyer, the associates of the company could not pay Champlain as their deputy on pain of a heavy fine for violating a court order. As they could not pay him, Champlain could "no longer claim the honor of functioning as lieutenant of my Lord the Prince."[18]

Champlain was infuriated. He had been appointed by three viceroys and confirmed by the king. His title to the job was clear, and debt litigation had nothing to do with it. Further, Boyer claimed to act in the name of a company that Champlain had founded. "Here was my reward from these gentlemen," he said. They had done very well by their investments, and now they were trying to eliminate him in hope of squeezing a few more livres out of the fur trade. The more Champlain thought about it, the more angry he became. He turned the full force of his rage against Boyer. "All this was no concern of mine," he said, and he sent Boyer on his way, maybe at the point of a sword. When the other partners heard about it, they "shifted the responsibility to Boyer, saying that what he had done was without authorization." Once again, Champlain had survived.[19]

Champlain sailed from Honfleur on March 11, 1617, aboard the *Saint-Étienne*, commanded by his friend Captain Morel, a good seaman and an old hand in the North American trade.[20] It would be a very short stay in New France. Champlain reached Tadoussac on June 14, and he was back in Paris by July 22, when he signed a legal document. He must have left Quebec no later than the first week in July, which means that he was in New France for a few weeks at most.[21]

Short as it was, Champlain turned his visit to a constructive purpose. He took with him Pont-Gravé as "conducteur en chef" of trading operations, plus three Récollet fathers, Joseph Le Caron, Denis Jamet, and Paul Huet.[22] Most important, he brought out the first French family to settle permanently in Quebec and support themselves by farming. The head of the family was an old friend, Louis Hébert, the young Parisian apothecary who had sailed with Champlain on exploring voyages and helped start the first settlements in Acadia. The Hébert family lived near the Louvre and were part of the American circle there. They were connected by marriage to Jean de Biencourt de Poutrincourt, and by friendship to the sieur de Mons and Champlain.[23]

Young Hébert had experienced New France first hand. In 1616, Champlain convinced him to settle at Quebec, with a contract from the company and a large grant of land. Hébert decided to emigrate with his entire family: his wife, Marie Rollet, and three children—Anne, a teenager; Guillemette, about eleven years old; and Guillaume, still very small. Also with him were his brother-in-law Claude Rollet and a servant named Henri Choppard.[24]

When the Héberts arrived at Honfleur to begin their journey, they were shocked to learn that the company would not honor its contract. One suspects the grand chicaneur Daniel Boyer was at work again, with a faction in the company that strongly opposed colonization. The Hébert family had sold their property in Paris and could not return. A bitter compromise was forced upon them. Hébert would receive only half the land and money that he had been promised, and the company would continue to charge interest of 20 percent even on what he had not been given! They also required that Hébert, his wife, and servant would have to work for the company in the fur trade. Altogether the conduct of the company to the Héberts was even more cruel and faithless than it had been to Champlain.[25]

But Louis Hébert was another man with a dream—a true believer in the idea of New France. He agreed to emigrate even on very unfavorable terms, confident that he could improve his condition in America. In Quebec, Champlain did all in his power to help the Héberts. He ordered employees of the company to work for the Hébert family and build them a sturdy stone house. For many years the Hébert home was the only private family residence in Quebec. With great labor the Héberts established a working farm, tilled it without a plough, and raised food enough to feed themselves and others at Quebec. Hébert also contributed his skill as an apothecary, treating Europeans and Indians equally. Like Champlain, he respected the Indians, welcomed them to his home, and treated them fairly. They in turn regarded him and his family with great affection.

Champlain also helped the family acquire more land along the St. Charles River. They became major landowners, and Louis Hébert began to appear in the records as the sieur de Hébert. Two daughters married Frenchmen in Quebec, and the family began to multiply. The family became an important presence in New France; the Récollet fathers wrote much about them, as did the Jesuits and Champlain. They played a major role in the survival of Quebec through its early years and brought an urgently needed element of stability and order to the new settlement.

Their example was also important to Champlain in another way. The success of their farm demonstrated that his dream of a self-supporting French population was practicable in America. But the Héberts were unique: the only firmly established farming family for many years. They demonstrated that it was possible, but also very difficult.[26] In 1617, between fifty and sixty French were reported to be living in Quebec, mostly traders and seamen. Nearly all were men and boys who had no intention of settling permanently. Quebec was more like a military post or transitory work camp than an established community.

But there were some elements of stability. The Récollet fathers became an important presence in New France. These devoted friars came to carry the gospel to the Indians. They also worked among French seamen and traders, and built a small chapel at Tadoussac, where large ships anchored for the season. There were also three Récollets in Quebec and one in Huronia. They went to work with a will, and appear to have made themselves useful and well liked by the French and the Indians.[27]

For the coming winter in Quebec, Champlain once again chose as commander Jean Godet du Parc, the young nobleman from Perche. He had wintered at Quebec in 1609–10 and had been put in command during the following winter. By all accounts he was able, experienced, and trustworthy. The settlement was in very good hands.[28]

On this quick trip in 1617, Champlain did not have time to go up the river. When he wrote about this short visit, he said that "nothing happened worthy of note." He meant that he was unable to go exploring, or meet with the Indians—things he loved to do. But he was deeply worried about events in France, and felt an urgency to get back.[29]

Champlain returned to Paris in July and joined his wife, Hélène Boullé, in their home on the rue St. Germain de l'Auxerrois. Together they worked at repairing their troubled marriage. On July 22, 1617, they went together to a leading firm of notaries and signed a contract with a young woman of good family, arranging for her to be a lady's maid and companion to Hélène. It was a routine legal transaction, very spare in its details, but it tells us something about all the parties. The maid's name was Isabel Terrier, daughter of a merchant named Richard Terrier. Champlain and Hélène both signed the contract, and it is interesting to see how the notaries described them. Champlain was no longer merely the "sieur de Champlain," but the "noble homme Samuel de Champlain, Captain in Ordinary to the King in the Western Navy." Hélène was elevated to "the demoiselle, Madame Eslayne Boullé, his wife." With each successive legal document, Samuel Champlain and his wife appeared to be of higher rank.

Richard Terrier and his daughter Isabel agreed that she would serve four years, and Isabel's father warranted that she was "honest and of good character." Her new master and mistress promised to pay a salary of thirty livres tournois each year, and to advance money to outfit her according to her station. Samuel Champlain and Hélène Boullé were working together at the daily business of life. They were spending more time with each other, but still there were no children.[30]

In Paris Champlain went to work organizing a new base of support for New France. Troubles continued with Daniel Boyer and the merchants of Rouen, and resentments were growing among investors in Saint-Malo, and La Rochelle as well. Champlain dealt with these problems by turning to financial leaders in Paris. He approached the Chamber of Commerce in that city, and submitted a letter to "Gentlemen of the Chamber." In twenty paragraphs he made an argument for the economic promise of North America. It highlighted the importance of the new world for the kingdom of France and for individual investors. The tone of the document was different from Champlain's other promotional writings. It was an appeal to reason, with much discussion and hard evidence of "certain facts," specific numbers, and precise estimates of profit, but always for what Champlain called "the honor and glory of God, the increase of this realm, and the establishment of a great and permanent trade."[31]

First on Champlain's long list of investment opportunities were the cod fisheries, which he estimated to yield a gross profit of a million livres annually. Champlain reckoned that between 800 and 1,000 French vessels were annually engaged in the North American cod fisheries every year, which was probably accurate, and the number was growing. Champlain asserted that returns of equal value could be found in other fisheries for salmon, sea sturgeon, sea trout, herrings, sardines, eels, and other fish. He reviewed the profits of the whaling industry in oil and bone, and the value of walrus tusks for ivory ("better than elephant's teeth") and the vast abundance of seals, which together were worth nearly as much as the cod fisheries.[32]

Next, Champlain described American forests, with many varieties of trees of "marvelous height" that were suitable for shipbuilding. He had brought home small amounts of sawn oak which were excellent for window frames and wainscoting, white pine that were perfect for masts, conifers in great variety that were good for pitch, tar, and turpentine, and other trees that were suitable for potash. For each product, he estimated the value of an annual crop. He told the Chamber of Commerce about mines that held no promise of gold but were rich in iron, copper, and other minerals. And he mentioned quarries that yielded building stone of the highest quality.

Champlain discussed the trade in furs, beaver pelts, moose hides, deerskin, and buffalo robes. He mentioned the abundance of hemp in America, of a "quality and texture in no way inferior to ours," and wrote of the possibilities for agriculture, field crops, vines, fruit trees, and herds of cattle on grazing land. Finally, Champlain also described the great rivers and lakes of North America, and wrote hopefully of finding a "short route to China" by way of the St. Lawrence River, noting that he had been working for sixteen years with "little assistance." He said that he needed help to plant permanent colonies, and asked the Chamber of Commerce to come to his support, as he made his case to the king.

The appeal worked. The Chamber of Commerce agreed to do as he asked. Its officers sent a very strong letter of support to the king on February 9, 1618. They asked Louis XIII to provide Champlain with the means to establish three hundred families in New France. Champlain informed the members of the Royal Council of what the chamber had done, and prepared an address for the king himself.[33]

Champlain had nothing like the direct access to the throne that he had enjoyed in the reign of Henri IV. He carefully prepared another letter, and addressed it directly "To the King and the Lords of His Council." Its central argument was different from his appeal to the Chamber of Commerce. He began by reminding them of the work that he had done as an explorer, "both in the discoveries of New France and of various nations and peoples whom he has brought to our knowledge, who have never been discovered before but by him."[34] He told them what had come from these discoveries: information about passages to the "north and south seas," and the promise of "reaching easily to the kingdom of China and the East Indies." He spoke of the "planting there of divine worship, by the efforts of the Récollet friars," and he informed them of the "abundance of merchandise that could be drawn from the countryside every year, through the diligence of workers who might go there."[35]

He reminded them of the great stake that France had in North America, where "more than a thousand vessels go each season for fishing and whaling fisheries," and he asked him to think how much would be lost "if this country would be given up and abandoned to the English and Dutch," who were "jealous of our prosperity and would seize upon it and enjoy the fruits of our labors"—as indeed they had already done by burning the settlements of the Jesuits on Mount Desert Island and destroying the colony of Poutrincourt in Acadia, and attacking fishing boats in the north.[36]

Champlain made frequent reference to what had been done and could be done "for the Glory of God" and "the honor of His Majesty." He made an argument with changes in emphasis that reflected the king's interests. The first purpose was the establishment of Christianity "among an infinite number of souls." The second was for the king to become "master and lord of a country nearly 1,800 leagues in length," and he described its beauty and abundance in lyrical terms.[37] A third purpose was to find a passage to China and the East Indies by way of the St. Lawrence, which he had already ascended to a distance of more than four hundred leagues, and beyond that was a great lake more than three hundred leagues in length. He observed that the king could derive a great and notable profit from the "taxes and duties on merchandise from China and the East Indies—I value more than ten times greater than all those levied in France.[38]

At the center of this great empire, Champlain proposed to build a capital town "as large as Saint-Denis," and "if it please God and the King," to call it Ludovica, or Louistown. In it he wanted to erect a great church called the Church of the Redeemer, to commemorate the conversion of the people in this country. On the high ground above Quebec, Champlain proposed that a great fortress should be constructed to control the river, and he planned another town on the opposite shore of the river. To that end he asked for more Récollet friars (the propagation of the faith was again first on the list), and three hundred French families to populate the country, with a military force of three hundred men. Champlain estimated the cost of provisioning this population at 15,000 livres a year for three years. Thereafter he hoped that it could support itself. Mindful of the king's deep concern about corruption, he proposed that the baron de Roussillon, one of the commissioners of the Chamber of Commerce, should be appointed manager of funds. None of it would be handled by Champlain himself.[39]

It was an extraordinarily bold statement, carefully crafted for Louis XIII, and it succeeded completely. The king and his council agreed with enthusiasm. On March 12, Louis XIII signed a letter recognizing the authority of Champlain in command in New France, and ordering his subjects to help implement the plan. "*Chers and bien aimez*," it began. "Dearly beloved, on information that has been given to us, that heretofore there has been bad management in the establishment of families and workmen who have been brought to Quebec and other places in New France, we write this letter to you, to declare to you our wish that things might go better in the future, and to make known to you that it is our pleasure that you should assist the sieur de Champlain as far as you can conveniently do so, with the things requisite and necessary for executing the commands that he has received from us . . . and to carry on all work that he shall judge necessary for establishing the colonies that we wish to plant in the said country, in the interest of our service and for the advantage of our subjects." [40]

The king added another phrase that Champlain might have preferred to do without: "All those things were to be done without allowing the said exploration and colonization to disturb or hinder your factors, clerks and agents in the business of the fur trade, in any manner and fashion whatsoever, during the period which we have allowed you." The letter ended with a royal commandment to all concerned: "In this do not fail. For such is our pleasure. Given at Paris, the 12th day of March, 1618." [41]

It was a triumph of court politics. In a systematic campaign, Champlain had shifted his base and broadened it. He gained the strong support of the Paris Chamber of Commerce, the Royal Council, and most important the king himself. It was an extraordinary and hard-won achievement. In a moment of crisis, Champlain had found an opportunity—and made the most of it.

Acting with astounding speed, within a few days of the king's letters Champlain decided to make another quick trip across the Atlantic. On March 22, 1618, he and his brother-in-law Eustace Boullé left Paris for Honfleur, "our usual place of embarkation." They were delayed there for two months. Champlain attributed the problem to "contrary winds," and he did not entirely mean the weather. Ill winds of another sort were blowing in the trading towns. Whatever the problem, it was sorted out in about sixty days. They sailed on May 24, 1618, aboard a *grand vaisseau* of the Company of New France, a vessel commanded by Pont-Gravé, who was also responsible for the commercial part of the voyage. [42]

They made a quick crossing and anchored at Tadoussac on St. John's Day, June 24, 1618. Everything was done in haste. Champlain and Pont-Gravé went immediately up the St. Lawrence River in a *petite barque de port* of 10 or 12 tons and reached Quebec on June 27. There they remained for a week. Champlain met and talked with the Récollet fathers and found them flourishing. He also visited with the Héberts and was delighted with the condition of their farm. "I inspected everything," Champlain wrote, "the cultivated land which I found sown and filled with fine grain, the gardens full of all kinds of plants such as cabbages, radishes, cucumbers, melons, peas and beans, and vegetables as fine and as well forward as in France."[43]

Champlain remained in Quebec a little more than a week and then continued upriver to Trois-Rivières, reaching that place in two days on July 5. He was concerned about relations between the French and Indians, which had begun to fray while he was gone, particularly in regard to questions of law, order, and justice.[44] It was a problem of great difficulty. The French colony was surrounded by much larger populations of Indians. Leaders on both sides wanted to maintain good relations. It was hard to do so among the European residents, who included many troubled characters. It was harder among the Indians, who gave great latitude to individual acts, and it was hardest when these two turbulent groups met and mixed.

Champlain met such a problem on this trip. It centered on the murder of two Frenchmen in 1616. One victim was a locksmith; the other, a seaman named Charles Pillet. This very tangled case filled many pages in Champlain's published *Voyages*. "Regarding the account of the affair," he wrote, "it is almost impossible to extract the truth." The incident began when one of the two Frenchmen quarreled with a Montagnais Indian. "Through some jealousy," the Frenchman "beat the said savage," and "invited others to beat him severely." There was broad agreement that the Indian had been "ill-treated."

The Montagnais warrior watched for an opportunity to take revenge. With a comrade he enticed the Frenchman and a friend into the woods. The two Indians murdered the Frenchmen, tried to disguise their deaths as a boating accident, lashed the bodies together, weighted them with heavy stones, and threw them into the water.[45] They reckoned without the river, which swept up the bodies and washed them on the shore, where they were discovered with clear marks of the crime. The event caused anger on both sides, and trouble began to grow among the Montagnais and the French.[46] Each feared the wrath of the other, and both were "seized with mistrust." So strong were these emotions that French and Indian leaders feared that a war could break out—even "perpetual warfare."[47]

Indian leaders sought to settle the problem by offering reparations, as was their custom. This solution was not acceptable to the French, whose ideas of justice required punishment of the guilty. The murderers were persuaded by other Montagnais to seek a third solution. They surrendered themselves to the French, hoping to confess and receive pardon for the crime. But when one of the murderers entered the French settlement he was arrested, the drawbridge was raised, and the French flew to arms. Some demanded instant execution. Others urged restraint. The Indians surrounded the settlement in great numbers, and tensions rose very high. Then Récollet father Joseph intervened. He recommended that the murderers not be punished immediately but that they should await "the return of the vessels from France, so that following the advice of the captains and others, they could reach a definitive judgment, and with more authority."[48]

At that point, Champlain arrived. He made clear his feeling that murder could not go unpunished without inviting more violence in the future. But he also knew that very different ideas of justice prevailed among French and Indians. A European-style execution of the murderers could start a sequence of escalating acts of retribution that could lead to war.[49]

Champlain proceeded with caution, and with close attention to detail. First he tried to discover the facts of the case. Then he convened a council of elders, consulted with the reverend fathers, met at length with Montagnais leaders, and discussed the case with other Indian nations. An important part of his method was to listen and consult at length. He invited ideas from all sides, and many suggestions were made. At one point the leaders of other Indian nations proposed that they themselves should execute the murderers, which would have started a full-scale war in the St. Lawrence Valley.[50]

Champlain chose another solution: "We all decided that it was agreed that the savages should feel the enormity of the murder, and yet not to proceed to an execution." With the helpful advice of the Récollet fathers, he went a different way: the chief murderer would be required to acknowledge his guilt, and would be returned to his people. Guarantees of good behavior should be given by his nation, and by his own father. Two of his sons would be surrendered as hostages, and put in the custody of the Récollet fathers, who would offer them instruction in the Christian religion and the French language. By this means, wrote Champlain, "we decided to settle this matter amicably, and to pass things over quietly."[51]

The tangled case of the Montagnais murderers brought out Champlain's idea of multiethnic justice that was fundamental to his grand design. He faced many difficult problems of order and justice in New France. By trial and error, he found ways to resolve many of them in this same spirit. He rejected the ancient idea of justice as the rule of retribution, which had adherents on all sides. He also rejected the European idea of trial and execution for a murder (which was unacceptable to many Indian nations). And he could not accept the Indian custom of settling murders merely by reparation (which was unacceptable to Europeans). In place of these different ideas of justice, he led others in the invention of another set of principles that combined equity and balance with humanity and restraint. He insisted that murder must be punished, but he favored the rule of moderation, and diminished the rigor of customary law on all sides. Most important, he searched for a way to keep the peace, establish a rule of law, and create a standard of justice that all could accept.

On July 5, 1618, Champlain sailed upstream to Trois-Rivières and found a great gathering of Indians who were eager to talk. He wrote that "All the savages of my acquaintance, and with whom in their own country I had become intimate, were awaiting me with impatience and came to meet me, and as though very pleased and happy to see me again, embracing me one after another with demonstrations of great joy." [52]

They asked "if I would again assist them in their wars against their enemies, as I had done in the past and I had promised them; by which enemies they are cruelly troubled and harassed." At Trois-Rivières he also met "several different nations of Indians not known to the French or to the Indians at our habitation." They also asked the French to "help them in their wars." [53] This was a difficult problem for Champlain. He observed that "there is not a single tribe that lives at peace except the Neutral Nation." Champlain wanted to have alliances with as many Indian nations as possible, but primarily for the sake of peace. He was willing to lead punitive expeditions against aggressors, but his strategic goal was to stop the killing. This war-weary old soldier hoped for a new world that would be at peace with itself. [54]

The tabagies at Trois-Rivières ended on July 14, 1618. That day Champlain went to Quebec, where he took leave of the Récollets. He embarked twelve days later with the Récollet fathers Paul and Pacifique, who had wintered there for three years, "in order that they might report both what they had seen in the said country and what could be done there." They were in Tadoussac on July 27, sailed for France on July 30, and reached Honfleur on August 28, 1618, "with a favorable wind, to everybody's satisfaction." [55]

In Paris, Champlain moved his household to the faubourg Saint-Germain-des-Prés, rue de Vaugirard, parish of Saint-Sulpice. It was a neighborhood much favored by courtiers and the king's ministers, very near the palace of Saint-Germain, which was one of the king's favorite residences, and the birthplace of the dauphin, the future Louis XIV. [56]

Champlain spent much of his time at court. He went to work again, returning to the perennial problem of building support for New France. He did it in several ways at once, always with the object of reaching the king, and keeping America in his thoughts. While Champlain was at court, New France began to appear in court entertainments, in which Louis XIII took a great in-

Abraham Bosse's genre scene of the "galerie du palais" shows fashionable "courtisans" at a stall that sold ribbons, gloves, lace, and fans, while a "cavalier" browses in a bookstall such as those of Jean Berjon and Claude Collet, who sold Champlain's works "at the palace," and helped him to promote the cause of New France.

terest. The court ballet was an elaborate art form, developed in Italy during the Renaissance. It became very fashionable in France, and it was written that "the art of the dance [itself] is perfectly French." [57]

A leading French scholar, François Moureau, has described it as a form of *belle danse* as distinct from *danse de bal.* The *ballet du cour* required a full orchestra with winds and brass, in addition to the traditional twenty-four violins of the king. It used complex scenery and gave much attention to creative costume-design, in which Italians had long been masters.

The center of these productions was the king himself. Louis XIII made the court ballet his hobby. He participated actively as a composer, designer, and dancer. He never played himself but usually appeared in other allegorical roles, such as Apollo, "or as the sun," as later did his son, Louis XIV. [58] Many of the high nobility followed his lead, and joined with professional dancers in these spectacles. Great nobles competed with one another for royal favor by dancing "before the king in ballets heroic, allegoric and farcical." [59]

Champlain did not appear as a character in these ballets. One scholar has

In the reign of Louis XIII, the humanity of American Indians became a dramatic theme in elegant court ballets.
The King himself produced these spectacles, and often appeared as Apollo or the Sun, shining above all the people
of the world. Nobles and courtiers performed them with the help of professional dancers.

written that "none of the founders of New France appear there," but Indians were very prominent. These works were marked by "the presence of a new exoticism, that of America, at the center of a form that was ritualized and politicized."[60] Moureau writes, "If one analyzed this repertory over a long period, which runs from the last decade of the reign of Henri IV to the death of his successor (1643), for half a century the American thread is clearly visible in the fabric of the spectacle."[61]

The interpretation of the Indians changed in an interesting way. In the late sixteenth century, they appeared in court ballets mostly as stylized figures from New Spain and Brazil. During the reign of Louis XIII, they became more prominent and more North American. The Court Ballets were advertisements for New France and its native people. In this effort, the king himself, the high nobility, choreographers, and set designers dramatized Champlain's grand design.

Champlain also tried to win a large public to the cause of New France by publishing another volume of his *Voyages*, with striking illustrations of many tribes of North American Indians. While he had been at sea in 1618, Champlain had used the time to draft another book about New France. It was finished in the fall, and published as *Voyages et descouvertures faites en la Nouvelle France, depuis l'année 1615.* As with all Champlain's books, this one was written for a very special purpose and it was addressed mainly to a single reader, Louis XIII, who held the success of New France in his hands. Champlain dedicated his book to the king, with gratitude for his past support and an appeal for his continued sponsorship of New France.

It was an honest book, entirely open in its promotional purposes, straightforward in its history, and candid in its account of problems in the colony. Champlain wrote that the king's subjects had been working hard in the new world, "so that Your Majesty may be declared the lawful Lord of our labors, and of the good that shall result therefrom, not only because the land belongs to you, but also because you have protected us against so many kinds of persons who had no other design than by troubling us, to hinder the success of so sacred an undertaking."[62]

Champlain appealed to the king's interest in the Indians, and described them in very sympathetic ways. He wrote in the preface that his last books had given more attention to the land and its exploration. This one centered on "manners and mode of life of the Indians, narrated with many particulars of such a nature as to satisfy an inquiring mind."[63] The book was an argument that France should "send out people and colonies to instruct them in the knowledge of God, the glory and the triumphs of Your Majesty, so that with French speech they may also acquire a French heart and spirit."[64] For that attitude, some ethnographers have condemned Champlain. But the Indians understood and respected this extraordinary man, even as they preferred to keep their own beliefs.

Much of the work was about religion, the missionary activities of the Récollets, and the progress of the Christianity in the new world. Champlain also wrote about the problems of founding a colony in America, and was painfully honest about the battle at the Onondaga fort. He also wrote plainly about the difficulties of reconciling large purposes in New France with the very different goals of merchants in France.[65]

Champlain's book circulated as a manuscript at court. It was read and approved by members of the Royal Council, and published by the king's printer, Claude Collet, in the palace at the "Galerie des Prisonniers," with the "privilege of the King." The date of publication by royal license was May 18, 1619.

Other good things happened as Champlain's star rose at court. On Christmas Eve, December 24, 1618, the author received a welcome present from His

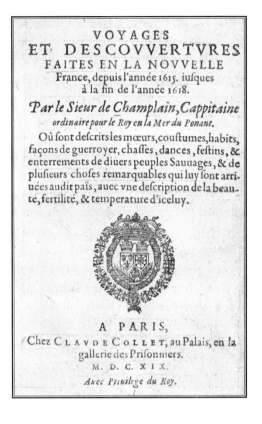

Majesty, a pension for 600 livres a year. Three weeks later, January 14, 1619, Champlain also received the unpaid balance of his wife's dowry, another 1,500 livres from her father, Nicolas Boullé, secretary of the king's chamber. It was yet another sign of how the winds were blowing. Champlain's long campaign to win the support of Louis XIII was producing results.

This success at court did not help Champlain with his investors in the west of France. Champlain was having more trouble with the old company, especially with the merchants in Rouen. As he had pointed out in his new book, their goals were fundamentally opposed to the founding purpose of New France. Champlain noted that some merchants "aimed only at their private gain." [66] He wrote that he had "no other purpose than to see the country inhabited by industrious people, for the clearing of land," so that the colony could support itself. He had seen too much hunger and even starvation when the ships were late in the spring, particularly "when the ships had been nearly two months behind their usual date, and there had been almost a tumult and revolt." [67]

Champlain and the merchants differed not merely in their purposes, but also in the time frame of their thinking. Merchants planned very precisely one season at a time. They complained that "affairs in France were so unsettled that although they had gone to great expense they held no position of security to themselves, since they had seen what had happened in the case of the sieur de Mons." They were very intolerant of political uncertainty and had little interest in planning for the long run.[68] They also sought to lower the costs of their operations, in hope of increasing their returns. They felt that colonizing ventures added heavy expenses. But that was only part of the problem. Champlain knew that they were also "afraid of something more serious, if the country became inhabited their power would wane," and "a little later they would be driven away by those whom they had installed at great cost."[69]

In New France itself, a different sort of conflict rose between the company's employees and Champlain's colonists such as the Hébert family, who complained of exploitation, and justly so. This animosity became a major discouragement to migration and a friction-point between colonizers and investors. Yet another problem was religion. Some of the investors in the western towns were Protestant. As Champlain noted, "they had anything at heart rather than that [the Catholic religion] should be established there, but they agreed to maintain friars because they knew it was His Majesty's desire."[70]

Champlain tried to work with the investors. He thought they had an agreement for the number of new colonists "besides those already there." On December 21, 1618, he drew up an *aide-mémoire* in elaborate detail: eighty people to be brought to Quebec and maintained there for the year 1619, with clothing, bedding, weapons, tools, two tons of lime, 10,000 curved roof tiles or 20,000 flat, ten thousand bricks, livestock including bulls, heifers and sheep; seeds and other supplies; weapons and officers to control arms and ammunition, and on top of everything else a dinner service for the leaders with thirty-six table settings. The document was signed by investors Le Gendre, Vermulles, Bellois, Dustrelot, and also Pierre Dugua. The sieur de Mons was becoming more visible in his continuing support of the grand design for New France, as Louis XIII warmed to the enterprise.[71]

Unhappily, the support that Champlain received from several merchants was strongly opposed by others. In the spring of 1619, Champlain's agreement with the merchants came apart, just as he was preparing to move his wife and their servants to America for an extended stay. Hélène had at last agreed to accompany her husband. Together they went to Honfleur and prepared to board a ship for America. They were stopped by agents of the company and told that the directors would not allow Champlain to be in command of its ships or the colony. He wrote that the prime mover was again his enemy Daniel Boyer, who had persuaded the merchants that Champlain was unfit to lead the colony. They insisted that the "sieur de Pont must remain in command over the people of their settlement." Champlain would be allowed to serve only as an explorer, mapmaker, and artist.[72]

Champlain refused to agree. He took his family to Rouen, and met with the merchants. "I showed them the articles," he wrote, and he insisted that "as the Lieutenant to the Prince I had the right of command over the settlement, and over all the men who might be there, save and except only the store where their head clerk was."[73] The merchants were defiant. Champlain showed them the king's letter. To Champlain's amazement they refused again, and the ship sailed without him.[74]

With his family Champlain returned to Paris. While his wife and servants unpacked, he went directly to the Royal Council and reported that the merchants of Rouen had defied a direct order from the king himself. The council gave complete support to Champlain. They confirmed him as lieutenant for New France, and expanded his powers to include full command "at Quebec and in other parts of New France."[75]

Now the merchants were in trouble. Louis XIII did not take kindly to subjects who defied his royal will. This was a capital crime, and the punishment was to be broken on the wheel before a howling mob in Paris. The directors of the company were quick to reverse themselves, and laid the blame entirely on Daniel Boyer. Suddenly Champlain was acceptable to them as commandant in Quebec. It was too late to sail in 1619, but he began to make preparations for the following year. He did not ask the merchants for their support. Champlain demanded it in the name of the king and they obeyed. Once more, Helen Boullé and the servants began to pack.[76]

17.

A FRAMEWORK FOR NEW FRANCE
Two Models, 1620–24

> CHAMPLAIN . . . It is my pleasure to write you this letter, to assure
> you that I shall be very agreeable to the service that you will render me,
> especially if you keep the country in obedience to me, making the peo-
> ple there live as closely in conformity with the laws of my kingdom as
> you can.
>
> —Louis XIII to Champlain, May 7, 1620[1]

> We must give fortune a trial sometimes. . . . With the assistance of the
> people of these lands, one should be able to do something worthy of
> record.
>
> —Samuel Champlain, ca. 1620[2]

IN THE YEAR 1619 the destiny of New France lay in the hands of two people. One was Samuel Champlain, now in middle age and a veteran of
long service in America. The other was King Louis XIII, aged eighteen
and already with nine years on the throne of France. Each had a vision of the
new world. Champlain and his American circle shared a dream of humanity
and peace, in an age of cruelty and violence. The king and his ministers served
an ideal of order and justice, under the absolute authority of an all-powerful
monarch who claimed the name of Louis le Juste. Together, these leaders
framed a set of institutions for New France.[3]

In the fall of that year, Louis XIII and his advisers took up the problem of
organizing their disordered American dominion. The king himself began that
process by making peace in his own family. On October 20, he ordered his
cousin the prince de Condé to be released from prison after three years' confinement. On November 9, Condé was received at Chantilly. In a formal ceremony he swore an oath of obedience, and the king solemnly proclaimed his
innocence. All of Condé's many privileges were restored, including his former
office as viceroy for New France. He was granted 3,000 livres, and gave half

Henry, second duc de Montmorency at Dampville, succeeded Condé as viceroy of New France from 1620 to 1625, and was one of the most able men in that office. He shared Champlain's purposes, resisted the absolutism of Richelieu and Louis XIII, supported the rights of parlements, and was executed for treason in 1632, at the age of 38.

the money to the Récollet friars for their work in America. Everybody was happy except the man who had put him in the Bastille and taken his job. The maréchal de Thémines was dismissed as viceroy.[4]

Condé had lost interest in New France, and he sold the office to his brother-in-law for 30,000 livres. The new viceroy was Henri de Montmorency, duc of Damville and Montmorency, governor of Languedoc, and admiral of France. He came from one of the ancient noble families of France and was described as "brave, rich, gallant, and liberal," in the old sense of liberal as generous and large-spirited. Montmorency was much admired for his style. It was said that he danced well, looked splendid on a horse, and had "the most agreeable manners in the world." He was also intelligent and well informed about world affairs. In his office as admiral, Montmorency took a serious interest in commerce and colonies as a way of strengthening the maritime power of France. He was sympathetic to Champlain's large purposes.[5]

Champlain thought it an excellent appointment and believed that "everything would be better managed for the honor of God, the service of the King, and the good of the Country." Champlain himself may have helped to arrange it, working with another powerful man at court, the sieur de Villemenon, intendant of the French Admiralty in 1620 and a key figure in the events that followed.[6] Immediately after Montmorency became viceroy of New France, he

made two appointments. On March 8, 1620, he chose Champlain as his lieutenant for New France, and commandant in Quebec. At Villemenon's urging,
he also created a new office of intendant for New France.

The office of intendant was becoming very important in France by 1620. The
word itself has no English equivalent and is inadequately translated as "steward" in bilingual dictionaries. French intendants functioned as instruments of
royal absolutism. They were responsible for seeing that the wishes of the king
and his council were carried out. They kept higher authorities informed about
the performance of officials, the enforcement of edicts, the review of accounts,
and the supervision of administration. Intendants were not what we would
call line officers; they were not in the chain of command, but they had great
influence.[7]

Champlain understood the importance of intendants, and was quick to see
that they could be useful for the purposes of his grand design. Rather than
thinking of them as rivals or threats, Champlain perceived them as potential
allies, and he formed a good working relationship with men such as Villemenon. Here again, he was very flexible and highly skilled at the art of working within the developing institutions of royal absolutism in France.

On March 12, the job of intendant in New France went to Jean-Jacques
Dolu, a man of strength and presence who was highly placed as one of the
king's advisers, and also as *grand audiencier* (chief usher) at court. Champlain
and Dolu appear to have known each other, and got on well. Dolu supported
Champlain's vision and strengthened his powers as commandant. Champlain
in turn was careful to respect Dolu. They began to work comfortably together
even before their appointments were confirmed by the king.[8]

An early test of their relationship came in the spring of 1620. Champlain
went to Honfleur and made arrangements for the dispatch of two ships to
New France. Once again he met strong opposition from the merchants of the
old company of Rouen and Saint-Malo. Champlain wrote that "there was still
some dispute about the command I was to exercise in the country." After a
confrontation that he described as a bit of a *brouillerie*, or free-for-all, he called
for help. The new intendant Dolu came quickly to his support and told the
merchants in no uncertain terms that the king himself intended Champlain to
have "entire and absolute command over the entire settlement and everything
in it, except what concerned the storehouse for their goods." He added a stern
warning that "if their men were unwilling to obey the wishes of his Majesty,"
Champlain had full authority and power to "arrest their ship."[9]

The merchants continued to protest, and took their case to other officers at the Admiralty. They got nowhere, and Louis XIII himself intervened. Champlain wrote that the merchants finally "listened to reason." They had succeeded only in diminishing their credit with the king and his ministers, who increasingly regarded their resistance as an act of lèse majesté. The merchants of Rouen were allowed to send trading ships to New France for one more year, but the days of their company were numbered.[10]

Champlain returned to North America in 1620 with greater powers than ever before. He held the rank of captain in the king's navy, the office of lieutenant to the absentee viceroy of New France, and the role of commandant in Quebec. He had the full cooperation of the intendant, the confidence of the viceroy, and the active support of Louis XIII himself, who sent him on his way with a personal letter. The king wrote carefully: "I shall be very agreeable to the service that you will render to me on this occasion, especially if you keep the country in obedience to me, making the people there live as closely in conformity with the laws of my kingdom as you can."[11] It was a strong expression of support, but also a statement of purpose that was not the same as Champlain's. The king instructed Champlain to impose a top-down system of absolute authority over the Indians, which he was unable to do and unwilling to attempt. Always he made a point of working with the Indians in another way.

Armed with his new powers, Champlain sailed from Honfleur in May 1620, aboard the ship *Saint-Étienne*. Traveling with him for the first time was his wife, Hélène, with her companion and maid, Isabelle Terrier, a retinue of household servants, and Champlain's manservant, a young man who would later be sent to live among the Indians and learn their language. Champlain called them his family, and it was a large one. But there were no children.[12]

Also aboard were three Récollet friars in their brown Franciscan robes, led by Georges le Baillif, a man of noble birth who had been strongly recommended by the viceroy and was "highly regarded by the king." Others who came out to Quebec were Intendant Dolu himself and an officer named Baptiste Guers, who functioned in yet another royal office as *commissionnaire* to the viceroy, the intendant, and Champlain. There was also a small detachment of the king's soldiers—only a handful, but sufficient to show the flag, patrol the river, man the guns at Quebec, guard the commandant's habitation, and keep order in the settlement. Champlain was their commander. They were merely a corporal's guard, but he assumed yet another title: Lieutenant General for New France.[13]

Saint-Étienne left Honfleur very late in the season, on May 8, 1620. Champlain wrote that they had a rough passage in stormy seas, and his family "suf-

The Gust of Wind, *by Willem van der Valde, typical of conditions that Champlain met on many Atlantic crossings, and especially on the rough voyage in 1620 when his wife, Hélène, and their household came to America.*

fered much discomfort." They reached Gaspé after about seven weeks on June 24 and sailed up the St. Lawrence River toward Tadoussac, keeping very close to the south shore.[14] Champlain was concerned about his wife's safety, and took many precautions on this voyage. Illegal traders were on the river in fast-sailing, heavily armed vessels, and some were selling arms to the Indians. Not knowing who might be lurking in Tadoussac, Champlain took his ship into a secluded cove called Moulin-Baude two miles downriver, and dropped anchor on July 7. He made sure that Tadoussac harbor was safe, then brought *Saint-Étienne* in. "All praised God," he wrote, "to find ourselves safely at our journey's end, and I most of all on account of my family."[15]

On July 11, 1620, Champlain and his party transferred to a small barque and continued up the St. Lawrence River to Quebec. The arrival was carefully staged as a piece of political theater. He sent ahead a vessel filled with supplies for the settlement and brought another boatload of provisions, which guaranteed a warm welcome from the hungry habitants. Then he came ashore in high state, led a procession to the chapel, and once again "gave thanks to God." The next morning, a Récollet father sang a mass and delivered a "sermon of exhortation." He reminded the congregation of their obligation to "devote themselves to the service of His Majesty and the seigneur de Montmorency." Champlain noted that the sermon ended in a declaration that "everyone must act in obedience to my commands, according to his Majesty's Patents, as bestowed upon His Grace the Viceroy and given to me as his lieutenant."

After the sermon, the new commandant summoned the entire population of Quebec. "I assembled all the people," he wrote, "and commanded Commissioner Guers to read aloud the King's commission to the Viceroy, and that of his Grace the Viceroy." All this was done "so that no one could plead ignorance." When the reading was complete, the settlers were invited to cry "Vive le Roi," and cannon were fired as "an expression of joy." Champlain concluded: "Thus I took possession of the habitation and the country, in the name of My Lord the Viceroy." He also asked Commissioner Guers to write an account of the ceremonies, "for use when and where required." [16]

One of its most important uses was to reassure Champlain's superiors in Paris. He was carefully staging ceremonies that were fundamental to the regime in France. The complex ritual of masses and sermons joined the sanctity of the church to the prerogatives of the state. Other rituals in the order of procession and acts of obeisance enacted the concept of order as a hierarchy of estates in which everyone was assigned a place. They linked power to authority, and authority to legitimacy, through the solemn recitation of patents and edicts and royal commands, not by Champlain himself but by a royal commissioner. These rituals were combined with the discharge of cannon, and a parade of soldiers in the king's uniform that combined the lilies of France, the cross of Jesus, the arms of the Bourbon dynasty, and the royal cipher of Louis XIII. The habitants themselves played a part in a ritual of consent. They were put on notice that if authority failed, power would be backed by force. The results were evident in the flow of events. Champlain faced no recurrence of the mutiny that had threatened his life at Quebec in 1608, although rebellions happened frequently in other French and English colonies. [17]

After the ceremonies, Champlain ordered an inspection of the colony. He sent Commissioner Guers and six men upriver to Trois-Rivières, "to learn what was going on in those parts." Others went downstream on the same errand. They spread the news of Champlain's arrival and extended his authority through the valley of the great river.

While that was happening, Champlain himself inspected the settlement of Quebec. On a stormy day he slogged through muddy pathways from one wretched shanty to the next and was appalled by what he found. In his words, the settlement was "in a desolate and ruinous condition." The roofs were leaking and "the rain was coming in everywhere, and the wind blew in through all the seams in the planks." Worse, he found that "the storehouse was on the edge of falling down, the courtyard was filthy and disgusting, and one of the dwellings had collapsed." [18]

Champlain attributed this state of things to failures of leadership. "As to the settlement," he wrote, "it was in a very wretched state owing to the fact that the workmen had been taken off to build a dwelling for the Récollet Fathers about half a league distant on the banks of the River St. Charles, and also two other dwellings, one for the said Hébert at his farm, and one near the settlement, for the locksmith and his baker, who could not be accommodated in the precinct of the dwellings." Champlain added that he felt not anger, but "pity" for the colonists.[19]

One can only imagine what the feelings of his wife, Hélène, must have been. This beautiful young woman had been raised in an opulent Paris household, and at the court of the king himself. She was asked to live in a hovel that would have been thought unfit for animals in her world. Her reaction was perhaps reflected in the tone of Champlain's account, which had a sense of urgency about it. "I set the men to work at once, both stone masons and carpenters, and in a short time a building was habitable for us."[20]

Champlain was also shocked to discover that the settlement was indefensible against attack. English and Dutch ships had been prowling the coast. Some of them were heavily armed, with crews that outnumbered the entire French population of Quebec. "We can hold our ground only by force," he warned. He was thinking of attacks not only by other European powers but also by pirates and predators who flourished in American waters. At the same time, Champlain was concerned about the Indians. Some of the Montagnais were beginning to show signs of distance and even hostility in a manner very different from their earlier attitudes. He wrote, "Some people think that we are too strong for anyone to venture to attack us in this situation." Champlain warned that this was a dangerous assumption: "Mistrust is the mother of security."[21]

On written instructions from the king and the viceroy, which he had helped to draft, Champlain ordered the workers in the colony to build a new fort, large enough to shelter the entire population of Quebec "in a very good situation, on a mountain that commanded the channel of the St. Lawrence River." He called it Fort St. Louis.

The partners of the trading company were not pleased with this project, which they regarded as a distraction from their commercial purposes, and a heavy expense. Champlain, for his part, complained of their greed and folly, and their habit of planning for the short run. "It is not always best to follow the feelings of people who think only of momentary gain," he wrote. "It is necessary to think farther ahead."[22] He worked on a different timescale from the merchant-adventurers, who centered their thoughts on immediate returns. He

This lead and tin writing set was found on the site of Champlain's habitation, and might have been used by him. It includes a quill holder, ink well, and sand dish (for drying the ink) and a box for pencils, a penknife, letter opener, sticks of sealing wax, and small seals. It is in the Interpretation Center, Place Royale, Quebec.

also had a different way of reckoning profit and loss, not merely in monetary terms but by the test of material progress toward a larger goal.[23]

Through the first year, Champlain kept some of his laborers at work on the fortification of Quebec and ordered others to repair the storehouse. Here again he was planning for the long run. These buildings were not temporary structures. For the storehouse he found a local source of "excellent limestone" and erected a solid building that was meant to last for centuries. Champlain's design for the storehouse was also an instrument of control. He added an outside entrance to the cellar, "closing up a trap-door that was in our warehouse, through which some persons often went to drink our liquors without any compunction."[24]

Some of the dwellings were also built of stone, as was the farm of the Hébert family. Champlain meant to encourage as many people as possible to live on the land. Twelve years after settlement, Quebec was still dependent on food from France. He intended to change all that by using public resources to promote private effort in agriculture, with small farmers producing for their own gain. Like other French leaders, he did not favor communal farming, which had been tried without success in the early years of Jamestown and Plymouth.

• • •

Hélène was a strong presence in the small colony. Her husband tells us that she chose to come to America of her own free will. On arrival they were met by a small boat under the command of her brother Captain Eustache Boullé, who had been in the country for two years. He had expected to greet the commandant and was amazed to discover that Hélène too was on board. Champlain wrote that Boullé "was utterly astonished to see his sister, and to learn that she herself had made up her mind to cross a sea so dangerous, and was greatly pleased, and she and I still more so." [25]

The tone of the marriage had changed very much for the better. Hélène was now twenty-two years old. As befitting her husband's station, she had come with many servants and a well-dressed lady-in-waiting, Isabel Terrier, to keep her company. With Champlain's manservants, they made a *ménage* of more than half a dozen people. This was the first time that a commandant of Quebec had maintained something like a domestic establishment in New France. Its presence changed the character of the settlement. [26]

Hélène had a great impact in Quebec, and she was long remembered by Indians and Europeans alike. The Indians were not prepared for her. In Acadia, Lescarbot wrote that male settlers had told the Indians that the ladies of France wore beards and mustaches. Then Hélène arrived, and the Indians were overwhelmed by her beauty, youth, grace, and refinement, as indeed were the French habitants. Francis Parkman wrote: "Madame de Champlain was still very young. If the Ursuline Tradition is to be trusted, the Indians [were] amazed at her beauty, and touched by her gentleness." [27]

She was also very bright. Like her husband she was filled with curiosity about this strange new world of North America, and she became deeply interested in the Indians. After settling in, Hélène studied the Algonquian languages of the St. Lawrence Valley, and learned them well enough to teach Indian children. Indian women also gathered around her. She nursed them through their illnesses, comforted them in their troubles, and talked to them of her Christian faith.

A happy story has come down to us about her work with them. It was recounted in the nineteenth century by N.-E. Dionne, who wrote that it had been "the fashion of the time for a lady of quality to wear . . . a small mirror, and the youthful Hélène observed the custom." The Indian women were fascinated by the mirror, which she wore on a chain around her neck. They gathered round and studied their reflection. One of the women asked why she could see her own reflection so close to Hélène's breasts. Hélène replied, "because you are so near my heart." One Indian remarked, "A lady so handsome, who cures our diseases, and loves us to so great an extent as to bear our image near her breast, must be superior to a human being." [28]

This "pretty story of the mirror, *jolie histoire du miroir*," as one scholar calls it, was passed down by the Ursuline sisters who later lived with Hélène in France and knew her well. We have no reason to doubt its authenticity. It helps us to understand this remarkable young woman and her complex relationship with her husband. Since the discovery of documents about their troubled early years together, historians have tended to bring out the worst in the relationship and to extend it over the entire span of the marriage. An historical novelist has built a breathless two-volume work of romantic fiction on that assumption without a shred of evidence. Other sources strongly suggest that the marriage improved with time and maturity. Despite Champlain's many Atlantic crossings, the couple managed to spend most of their time together. Historian Marcel Trudel calculated that in their three hundred months of married life (actually 255 months from December 1610 to December 1635, not including the initial separation), they spent more than 181 months living together. [29]

When they were apart, business records indicate that Hélène supported Champlain's work, managed his investments in commercial companies, defended his interests, and championed his grand design. We have very little information about her, but every piece of evidence for the later years of their marriage, and especially in the period from 1618 to 1633, indicates that they grew closer to one another than historians have assumed from their early troubles. Champlain and his wife lived and worked harmoniously together in Quebec. They shared an interest in the Indians, a spirit of humanity, and a growing piety. She also appears to have won the affection of Indians and habitants in Quebec, and especially the Hébert family, who asked her to be godmother for their children.

Another person who strongly supported Champlain in Quebec was the intendant, Jean-Jacques Dolu. The viceroy and the king had ordered him to go with Champlain, live in Quebec, observe closely, and report on conditions in the colony. Champlain wrote that Dolu's primary task in New France was "to introduce good order (*bon règlement*) there," and he noted that the intendant "busied himself in it with entire devotion, burning with zeal to do something for the advancement of the glory of God and of the country, and to put our company into a better condition of prosperity than it had been." [30]

They seem to have got on very well in America, as they had in France. Champlain wrote, for example, "I saw him on this subject and made him understand the situation, and gave him notes for his instruction." Dolu returned to France in the late summer of 1620 and made his report. Early the next spring, the first ships of the season brought a bag of mail for Champlain, with letters from Viceroy Montmorency and the king himself. Dolu had delivered his evaluation. In the words of one historian it was a "damning report" on conditions in the colony but with high praise for Champlain. The letters that followed from the king were very positive, and Viceroy Montmorency doubled Champlain's salary.[31]

While the weather was still warm in 1620, Champlain began to prepare for the winter. He always remembered the colonies that had failed because they ran short of food, and he himself had lived through the agony of scurvy at Sainte-Croix, Port-Royal, and Quebec. He was determined that it would not happen again. "I took stock of the provisions," he wrote, "so as to make them last till the return of the vessels [in the spring]."[32]

The ships had brought from France a large supply of food, more than enough to support the entire population for a year. He reckoned the population that would winter over at "sixty persons all told, men, women, friars and children." As winter came, he made a point of keeping them all occupied and well fed. When spring arrived in 1621, he wrote, "Everyone was in good health, save one man who was killed by the fall of a tree, which crushed his skull."[33] Nobody died of scurvy or any other illness—a great achievement for an infant colony in the seventeenth century. Thereafter, under Champlain's command there would be no major problem with scurvy, except a small outbreak at Trois-Rivières in 1634–35. The habitants of Quebec began to receive more varied provisions from France. Champlain wrote that one vessel brought "some puncheons of cider, biscuits, peas and dried plums."[34] Spruce beer, which has antiscorbutic properties, may have helped, but the only remedy mentioned explicitly by Champlain was fresh meat.[35]

Constant labor was required to get provisions from France, to barter with the Indians, and to extract a flow of food from farms in the colony. The French learned from the Indians how to hunt in the winter before the animals went away to bear their young, and struggled to master the intricate techniques of eeling in the fall. The cruelest season was always the early spring before the relief ships arrived, often not until June or even later.[36] One year, for example, the supply ships were very late, and Champlain had only enough flour and cider to last until June 10. After it ran out, the colonists survived on *migan*, made from Indian corn and fish. The ships finally reached Quebec on July 10, a month after the provisions were gone. Hunger continued to be a problem in a land of plenty, but Champlain succeeded in preventing the worst ravages of malnutrition with much help from the Indians.[37]

Quebec was a raw and very rough frontier settlement. Merchants in trading companies and captains of ships in the St. Lawrence River cared little for the authority of a distant Crown. The king's officers were unable to keep the peace along the full length of the great river. As in many new colonies, there was much crime—even assault and murder—and a growing concern among the habitants about the problems of order.

On August 18, 1621. Champlain and Father Le Bailiff called a general assembly of Frenchmen in Quebec, about sixty men altogether. Most of the colonists turned out, except officers of the trading company who stubbornly refused to acknowledge Champlain's authority. This was not the first such assembly in Quebec. An earlier one had convened in 1616, but it had been organized by the Récollets and concerned itself mainly with religious questions.[38] This one was a secular event led by the "principal French inhabitants," who came together to "advise on the most proper means" to deal with "the ruin and desolation of all this country." [39]

These gatherings were nothing like lawmaking assemblies in English colonies. The people of Quebec worked within the French tradition of the *cahier général de doléances*, a meeting to draw up a petition of grievances. The assembled group elected Le Bailiff as their deputy and resolved to send him to the king and the viceroy with a list of their complaints. In the manner of a cahier, it began with professions of faith and loyalty to the king. The petitions celebrated the country and its prospects for growth but expressed deep unhappiness about the lack of law, order, and security. They asked for a judicial system that would put an end to "robberies, murders, assassinations, lechery, and blasphemy." They were worried about the English and the Iroquois, and wanted a strong fort with a garrison of fifty soldiers. And they asked that Champlain be given more money. They requested that Protestants should be kept out of the colony, a judgment that differed from the attitude of tolerance that Champlain favored. And they asked that schools be founded for Indian and French children. Altogether they demanded more control from above, not less as in the British colonies.

Le Baillif carried this petition to France, and the king in Council responded positively to the complaints. He ordered changes in the trading companies, supported the Récollets, strongly backed Champlain, gave him more money as the habitants had asked, and ordered the recruitment of families for New France. But he did not endorse the idea of assemblies and deputies for Quebec. No reference to this assembly appeared in any of Champlain's writings. It is interesting that Champlain supported the assembly in Quebec but gave it no recognition in France. If he included it in any of his books, it was removed by censors in Paris. This early assembly was soon forgotten, except in the writings of some of the Récollet fathers and in the few manuscripts that found their way to the Bibliothèque Nationale in Paris.[40]

The assembly in Quebec was an advisory body of principal inhabitants. They met on the invitation of leaders to present grievances and submit a petition to the king, the viceroy, and the governor of Quebec. Even so, such meetings were not welcome in France. This was the road not taken in Quebec.

In 1621, Champlain also issued laws for New France, which appear to have been primarily of his own devising. He proclaimed them only in response to what he took to be urgent problems. He was, for example, troubled by two families who had been in New France for two years: one headed by a butcher, the other by a needle maker. They had settled on the land with the understanding that they would farm it. Champlain sent a commissioner to "examine what they had done." He learned they "had not cleared a single yard of land, but simply gave themselves to hunting, fishing, sleeping and getting drunk in company with those who gave them the means to do so." He decided to banish them from the colony. "I sent them back as useless creatures who cost more than they were worth," he said.[41]

After the fact, Champlain issued edicts to legitimate his act. "To avoid troublesome disputes and keep all parties to their duty," he wrote, "I thought right to make certain ordinances, which I caused to be published on the twelfth of September."[42] Historian John Dickinson observed that this "first Canadian legislation" was not enacted by an assembly or even by a council. It was framed by the will and judgment of one man. Scholars believe that Champlain issued other ordinances to regulate prices, proclaim holy days, prohibit the sale of liquor to the Indians, and preserve peace within the colonies. But no texts have as yet been found.[43]

To proclaim a law was one thing; to enforce it was quite another. Champlain had to maintain order among a turbulent set of colonists and neighbors in a disorderly and sometimes violent world. He had to keep peace between Catholics and Protestants, Indians and Europeans, soldiers and civilians, seamen and shopkeepers, farmers and traders, rival companies and royal officials. He had a distinctive way of dealing with these questions. When he faced a fundamental threat such as Duval's conspiracy, the 1608 attempt to kill Champlain and seize the colony, he acted decisively and did not hesitate to use force when he thought it necessary. But in nearly all cases, Champlain preferred to reject force as a solution. He began by introducing a tone of reason, and sought the path of peace. First, he asked questions about what had actually happened, listened carefully to answers, and consulted with others in difficult cases. Then he tried to identify vital issues that could not be compromised without damage to the colony or to his larger purposes. Within that framework he tended to become a mediator in an effort to reconcile rival interests, resolve conflicts of principle, and harmonize different ideas of ethics and justice in a way that all parties could regard as just.

The religious life of the colony continued to be a cause of friction. During the reign of Henri IV, as we have seen, the sieur de Mons and Champlain had adopted the king's solution for New France: an established Catholic Church and a toleration of Protestants. They encouraged religious diversity and brought a Protestant minister as well as Catholic priests to Sainte-Croix and Port-Royal. That experiment was not successful.

The death of Henri IV had brought a change of policies in France and America. Marie de Medici and Louis XIII both maintained the Edict of Nantes, but gave more support to the Catholic Church and showed less tolerance of Protestants. Some of their ministers actively discouraged the presence of Protestants in New France. Yet many French merchants and seamen were Huguenots. This friction increased when Viceroy Montmorency brought in the Compagnie de Caën, led by Guillaume and Émery de Caën. Guillaume was Protestant and Émery was Catholic. Their traders and seamen were also of both faiths.

Champlain received strict instructions from France about Guillaume de Caën: "As to the exercise of his religion I was to tell him that he was not to practice it either on land or on sea, and as to anything further I was to use my own judgment." [44] Aboard ship in the St. Lawrence, de Caën was "accustomed to have his [Protestant] prayers in his cabin, at the stern of the vessel, while the Catholics were at their devotions in the bow." In de Caën's absence, his Catholic lieutenant Raymond de Ralde assumed command and insisted that the Catholics should "do their praying in the cabin, and the so-called Reformers should be in their proper place, and do theirs in the bow." Champlain wrote that "on this point a great dispute arose." It was settled only with the intervention of the Récollet fathers, who helped Champlain to keep the peace. [45]

Later the same issue exploded again. A Jesuit priest complained to Champlain that Protestant sailors "paid no attention to the restrictions," and sang their psalms in such a way that "all the Indians could hear them from the shore." Champlain allowed the sailors to keep singing. "There is no use talking to them," he wrote wisely. "It is their great zeal for their faith that impels them."[46]

Champlain always sought a solution to these problems in the spirit of Henri IV. He maintained the Catholic Church as an establishment but protected the right of Protestants to worship. He also worked out a series of flexible compromises that allowed both groups freedom of conscience, but asked them to exercise those rights in ways that did not offend others.

Other issues tested the limits of liberty of expression in New France, and Champlain responded in an unexpected way. He ordered the burning of a book in Quebec. It was called the *Anti-Coton*, an attack on Father Pierre Coton, the Jesuit confessor and friend of Henri IV, and an acquaintance of Champlain. The author suggested that the Jesuits, and Coton in particular, had a hand in the murder of Henri IV. His book passed from "room to room" and was reported to have been widely read in the settlement. Catholic priests demanded that the book be suppressed. Champlain ordered that it be burned. His primary motive was to keep the peace and to discourage attacks on others, rather than to repress heresy or punish dissent. But whatever the cause, the result set a precedent for restraints on liberty of speech and press in Quebec. In time these restrictions would multiply. The habitants of Canada were not encouraged to think of themselves as free people. In New France, limits on liberty and freedom were imposed by the will and judgment of an absolute ruler who was accountable only to another absolute ruler in Paris.

If liberty means the right to speak and worship freely, and if freedom means the right to vote and to trial by one's peers, there was little liberty or freedom in Quebec. Its denial severely diminished the growth of New France. Had French authorities actively encouraged dissenters to settle in the new world, the history of North America might have been very different. The colonies of New France would have been more disorderly but also more dynamic, and much quicker to grow. But this was another road not taken in the history of New France.[47]

While Champlain dealt with these difficult problems, he also continued his policy in regard to the Indians. His approach was fundamentally different from that of the founders of New Spain and New England, and also from that of earlier French leaders such as Cartier. He never wanted to conquer or enslave the Indians, and never imagined that he could control them. Always he regarded them as people who were fully equal to Europeans in powers of mind, and thought them superior in some ways. There was much about their culture that he did not like. Champlain often repeated his belief that the North American Indians had neither faith nor law. But he admired their many strengths, treated them with respect, tried to learn from them—and they reciprocated.

How did he do it? First, he spent time with them, sitting in councils, listening to speeches, inquiring about their customs, asking them to map the country on sheets of bark. Champlain wanted to learn what they knew. He also had a keen sense of their vital interests, and tried to construct alliances from which all parties had much to gain. Between 1620 and 1624, he also sent more young men to live among the Indians. Nicolas Marsolet went to the Montagnais in the Saguenay country; young Jean Nicollet and Jean Richer lived among the Nipissing. Brûlé and Du Vernay worked in Huronia, and Olivier Le Tardif dwelled among the Algonquin, to mention only a few. At one feast alone, the Algonquin nations of the upper St. Lawrence and Ottawa rivers agreed to take eleven Frenchmen, each with his own Indian minder.[48]

There were many strains in these relations. In 1620, Champlain had a major problem with the Montagnais. From his earliest meeting in 1603, and for many years thereafter, they had been allies. But when Champlain returned to the colony in 1620 after a two-year absence, he perceived clear signs of growing distance, and even hostility. A major problem was trade in the lower St. Lawrence Valley. The Montagnais wanted to trade with ships of many nations. Champlain wrote, "We prevent other vessels from trading with them, and though on the other hand we give them the best possible treatment, this is the friendship they show us." His first efforts at dealing with the problem were ill conceived. Champlain himself wrote that he "came down on them sharply."[49] The Montagnais were furious, and relations went from bad to worse. Champlain wrote: "We have no worse enemies than these Indians; for they say that if they were to kill off our men, other vessels would come, the owners of which would be greatly pleased, and that they would themselves be much better off than they are, owing to getting goods more cheaply from the Rochelais or the Basques. Among the Indians, the Montagnais are the only ones who talk in this fashion."[50]

Relations sank so low, Champlain tells us, that some Montagnais began to plan a surprise attack on Quebec and Tadoussac, an event that would have changed the history of New France in a fundamental way. Somehow he dealt with it. He wrote only that "measures were taken" to nip the plan in the bud.[51] Champlain immediately went to work repairing relations with the Montagnais. He gave them more trade privileges and better terms than interlopers could match. He also invited some of them to settle on cleared land and to add a little farming to their hunting and gathering economy. Champlain believed that part of the problem of the Montagnais was their extreme vulnerability to famine. They were a hunting and gathering people who maintained very little by way of food stocks. In their approach to survival, they were very different from other Indian nations such as the Huron and Iroquois and Saco, and others to the south.

Much of the Montagnais territory in the Saguenay Valley did not lend itself to agriculture. There was better land near Quebec on the southwestern range of their country. Champlain offered them seed stock and the use of open fields that the French had cleared. He told them if they could bring the land under cultivation, they could gather a crop of corn for their use, and "if they did so we would regard them as brothers." Champlain did not wish to turn them entirely from hunting to farming, but to create a mixed economy of the sort that many Indian nations practiced in North America. His object was to improve their condition, encourage them to lay up something for the winter, and help them escape the terrible periods of hunger and starvation that he had witnessed.[52]

In the spring of 1622, Champlain supported a Montagnais captain he called Miristou, whose father had followed Anadabijou as a powerful chief. Champlain wrote that Miristou "had a very strong and special liking for the French" and "was ambitious of commanding and being the head of the band as his father had been." Champlain helped Miristou gain power. In turn, Miristou paid him 105 beaver skins, and Champlain spent them to put on a great feast for the Montagnais. As a leader of his people, Miristou worked with Champlain to improve relations.[53]

Champlain tried throughout this period to make peace with the Iroquois, and with much success. He urged the Algonquin and Montagnais to "live at peace" with the Mohawk, and offered to help them. Some Indian leaders said they were "sick and tired of the wars they had, which lasted over fifty years," since the mid-sixteenth century. "Their fathers had never been disposed to enter into a treaty, owing to the desire they had to wreak vengeance for the murder of relatives and friends who had been killed."[54]

Champlain kept talking, and persuaded his Indian allies to send a peace mission to the Mohawk. A delegation of very brave Montagnais warriors went into Iroquois country, and they were well received. On June 6, 1622, two Mohawks came to talk with the St. Lawrence nations at Trois-Rivières and met Champlain at an Indian camp near Quebec. There was feasting and dancing.

After he returned to Quebec, Champlain received a visit from the Iroquois ne-
gotiators, who had come "*en pourparlers de paix*; for peace negotiations." The
Mohawk dined with the French and Indian leaders, danced together once
more, and Champlain gave them another feast. It was all very hopeful. "Thus
we made good progress," Champlain wrote. "*Voilà un bon acheminement.*"[55]

But it would be the old story yet again. Many people of all nations wanted
peace but a single person could start a war. Such a man was a Montagnais warrior called Simon by the French. Champlain wrote that "he seemed to have a
kind of craze, a thing to which they are often subject, principally when against
the will of all the captains and companions, they wish to make war against
their enemies the Iroquois."[56] Just as peace talks were making progress, Simon
announced that he would launch his own personal war on the entire Iroquois
confederacy. The Montagnais leaders could not control him, and they asked
Champlain to intervene and "cure him of his frenzy." Champlain tried to reason with him, but Simon said that Iroquois were "worthless, that they were
worse than dogs, and that the idea had consequently taken hold of him that
he would never be satisfied until he had the head of one of them, and so he
was resolved to go with three others on the warpath." Champlain concluded
that "he was obstinate and no remonstrance could move him," so he dealt with
him in another way. "I used threats to deter him," Champlain said, and "he
went off to his cabin in a meditative mood." Whatever Champlain's threat may
have been, it worked. Simon decided on reflection not to go to war against the
Iroquois, and the chiefs thanked Champlain for what he had done.[57]

Three months later, a Montagnais peace mission went to the Iroquois, who
"gave them a hearty welcome." But Simon tagged along, and Champlain wrote
that on the way home "this perfidious, treacherous and evil man murdered an
Iroquois in cold blood." The Montagnais delegation "had much difficulty in
making amends for the crime." Champlain commented, "One rogue (*coquin*)
can wreck all sorts of good enterprises."[58] But both sides genuinely wanted
peace, and the Iroquois judged that the man who had killed their companion
had "acted from his own malice," without the support of his nation. They sent
six people to confirm a peace with "all the Indians." Champlain helped with
this difficult peacemaking, and it succeeded in a limited way. A peace began to
operate in 1624, more as a modus vivendi than a formal agreement. But it
held for nearly a decade.[59]

It was a constant struggle to keep the peace in the St. Lawrence Valley.
Small skirmishes between Indian nations sometimes threatened to explode
into full-scale war. One such incident occurred when the Huron complained
that some of the Algonquin had treated them badly, closing some routes to

them, levying tolls on their goods, "and not content with that, robbed them into the bargain." With Champlain's encouragement, the nations came together near Quebec, "held an assembly of their own," and "on all these matters . . . were brought into agreement." With much trial and many errors, Champlain and Indian leaders created conditions for a peace among the Indian nations in the St. Lawrence Valley for many years.[60]

At the same time Champlain pursued his vision for the French settlement at Quebec. The project closest to his heart was the development of agriculture, in the hope of making Quebec self-supporting, as he was confident it could be. He encouraged the planting of fields and gardens and orchards, and gave close attention to their progress. He imported plants and seeds from Europe and studied the native flora with close attention. Every spring, as soon as the fields thawed, he began sowing. Champlain delighted in the natural world and kept a botanical calendar of spring events.[61] In the fall he experimented with winter crops of grain. He wrote in 1622, "I spent the time in preparing the gardens for autumn sowing, so as to see what would come of it in the spring, and took a singular pleasure in the work."[62]

Champlain sought to bring more land into cultivation. In 1624, he and Guillaume de Caën visited the Île d'Orléans just below Quebec, and planned to begin farming there. Farther downstream Champlain saw another opportunity at Cap Tourmente, where natural meadows produced large crops of hay. The critical limit on animal husbandry in North America was the quantity of fodder that was needed to sustain animals through the winter. Champlain and de Caën studied the meadows at Cap Tourmente, and concluded that it was "a good place for pasturing cattle." They began to harvest hay for the colony and planned a settlement there to raise livestock.[63] Champlain built roads and paths around Quebec, including "a small road to Fort St. Louis," completed by November 29, 1623. Another road, "both for men and beasts," ran along the St. Charles River. "I employed all hands," he wrote, "and so well did they do their work that it was soon finished."[64]

In Quebec itself Champlain started his most ambitious project. The habitation was falling apart again, as it did every year. Champlain wrote, "The opinion was that it would take less time to build a new one than annually to be repairing the old one." He drew up plans for a new structure "thirty-six yards in length, with two wings of twenty yards in each side and four small towers at the four corners of the structure, a ravine in front, commanding the river, the whole encircled by ditches and a drawbridge."[65]

Champlain's second habitation was begun in 1624, severely damaged by British invaders, and rebuilt in 1633. These solid stone foundations supported handsome round towers. The evidence of archaeology confirms Champlain's written accounts in this and many other details.

During the fall of 1623 he began to gather materials: "a quantity of lime made, trees cut down, stone brought in, and materials generally prepared for the mason work, carpentry and heating." He put eighteen men to work, and wrote that, "with this small number we managed to accomplish a great deal." Carpenters made windows and doors, and cut thirty-five beams and fifteen hundred boards for the buildings, with framing timbers for the roof.[66] In the spring of 1624, the heavy work of construction began. On May 6, 1624, the masons began to lay stone for the foundation. Champlain wrote, "I placed a stone on which were engraved the arms of the King and those of my lord de Montmorency, with the date and my name in writing as Lieutenant."[67]

There were many setbacks. On May 20, a violent gale blew the roof off Fort St. Louis and destroyed a gable of Hébert's stone farmhouse. Champlain ordered his workmen to repair the damage, which delayed his other projects. But by the end of May, the first story of the new habitation was rising, with doors and windows in place and joists laid for the second floor. Work continued through the summer, and by early August construction was "well advanced." Most of this work was done under the orders of Champlain himself; very little was undertaken by private enterprise.[68]

As the month of September approached, Champlain had a hard choice to make. Should he stay for another winter, or return to France? After four years in Quebec, his wife was growing restless and wanted to go home. Champlain tells us only that he decided to go back to France with his family, "having now wintered in the country nearly five years, during which time we were ill-supplied with fresh provisions and with other things very sparingly."⁶⁹ He left with many projects underway, and some very near completion. The handsome new habitation was almost done. Champlain tells us that he "left the new buildings in a forward state, built up to fourteen feet in height, with fifty-two yards of wall made, with some joists on the first floor, and with all the other beams ready to put in place; with boards sawn for the roof; most of the wood dressed and piled up for the framework of the roof of the dwelling, and all the windows made, as well as most of the doors, so that all that was needed was to put them in." He added, "I left two kilns full of quicklime, with stone drawn on the spot, and all that was left to do in order to have the whole wall erected, as to build up seven or eight feet, a thing that could be done in a fortnight, the materials being at hand."

Champlain also ordered the work to continue on the fort. "I requested them to collect fascines and other things for finishing the fort," he wrote, "although in my own mind I felt pretty sure that they would do nothing of the sort, since they had the greatest dislike of the work, notwithstanding that the safety and preservation of the country depended on it, a thing they either could not or would not comprehend." Champlain left behind Émery de Caën, Catholic nephew of Guillaume de Caën, to continue the work and "to command in my absence at Quebec." The resident population had risen to sixty people.⁷⁰

On August 21, 1624, Champlain sailed from Tadoussac to Miscou Island on the fishing coast. With his family aboard, he decided to wait for Pont-Gravé and other fishermen to finish their work, so that they could all sail in company. Pont-Gravé finally completed his catch on September 6. That night they sailed in a fleet of four ships: one with Champlain, Hélène, and Guillaume de Caën on board, another commanded by La Ralde, a third by Pont-Gravé, and a fourth small *patache d'avis* of 45 to 50 tons, commanded by one of the Cananée family, which sent several captains into the American trade.⁷¹

It was well that they sought safety in numbers. The Peace of Vervins was wearing thin, and the French government was unable to protect even its coastal waters. Champlain's four ships sailed in convoy across the Atlantic and crossed soundings near Britain on September 27, 1624. That day Captain Cananée's small patache parted company, under orders to sail to Bordeaux with dispatches. Later Champlain learned that she was captured on the coast of Brittany by Islamic pirates, "who carried off the men they found on board and made slaves of them." Captain Cananée died in captivity, the fate of many Christian seamen in that era.[72] Champlain himself had a bad moment when he sighted a strange vessel. His fleet of armed merchantmen gave chase but could not catch her. On October 1, they entered the port of Dieppe, "praising God for having brought us to a safe harbor."[73]

18.

THE CARDINAL'S RING
Richelieu's Hundred Associates, 1625–27

The Sieur de Champlain shall . . . bring into subjection, submission and obedience, all the peoples of the said country.

—Orders from the duc de Ventadour and Cardinal Richelieu, 1625[1]

The Sieur de Champlain . . . was one of the few men capable of living among the Savages as he had done. . . . In all the years he had dwelled among these native people, he had never been suspected of any dishonesty.

—Gabriel Sagard on Champlain, 1636[2]

CHAMPLAIN remained at Dieppe for a few days and then went to Paris with his wife and servants, and *tout mon train*, as he put it. He traveled in high state, as suited a man of consequence. In the city, Champlain moved again to a house on the rue Saintonge in the fashionable Marais-Temple district near the Place Royale, not far from the Louvre. His new home was close to his wife's family and suggests a concern for her feelings. He also sold his uncle's country estate near La Rochelle, perhaps to pay for it.[3]

While his family settled in, he went to the palace at Saint-Germain "to see the King and my Lord of Montmorency, the Viceroy of New France." The meetings were a success. Champlain wrote: the viceroy "presented me to His Majesty, to whom I gave an account of my voyage, as I did to several gentlemen of the Council, to whom I had the honor of being known."[4]

Champlain discovered a major change among the councillors who were closest to the king. For many years, some of the strongest men around the throne had been supporters of the design for New France. A leader of this American circle was Nicolas Brûlart, marquis de Sillery, the long-serving chancellor of France. With him was his son Brûlart Puysieulx, secretary of state for foreign affairs. Both men had encouraged Champlain in the reign of Henri IV. They helped him again during the regency of Marie de Medici and in the early years of Louis XIII. But after 1620, the Brûlarts were called "the greybeards" by the younger generation who hoped to succeed them. In 1621 they lost their offices and were replaced by ambitious but undistinguished placeholders.[5]

The king searched for a statesman of higher ability and at last he found his man. Armand Jean du Plessis de Richelieu was thirty-six years old at the time. He was born in Paris, the youngest son of a mid-ranking noble family from Poitou. At his christening, his parents raised a banner above his crib: "*Regi Armandus*, Armand for the king." His grandmother taught him to calculate the worth of people by counting the number of quarterings in their coat of arms. Those attitudes shaped his character in a fundamental way.[6]

Richelieu's father was a soldier and a holder of high office who had died in the wars of religion with his affairs in disorder. One of the family's most valuable assets was the bishopric of Luçon. Their claim was challenged by the clergy. To serve the urgent needs of the family, Richelieu was sent into the Catholic Church and nominated Bishop of Luçon at the age of twenty-one.[7] Richelieu took his vows without enthusiasm. Though he wrote on religious subjects, he was worldly in his outlook. All his life he was close to his beautiful niece Marie-Madeleine de Vignerot du Pont Courlay, madame de Combalet, the future duchesse d'Aiguillon. She was his companion for many years, and her likeness was carved into Richelieu's tombstone. Some historians have suspected that Richelieu "indulged in relations that were not only amorous but incestuous," but he was always discreet. It was said that "he loved women, and feared scandal."[8]

He became a dutiful son of the church, but Richelieu was passionately drawn to the pursuit of politics. He sat in the Estates General in 1614, joined the circle around Marie de Medici, rose and fell with her, was banished from court by the king, and then brought back to restore relations with his mother. In 1620, Richelieu's star began to rise again. Louis XIII asked the Pope to make him a cardinal, which was done in 1622. He joined the Royal Council on April 29, 1624, and within a year, Cardinal Richelieu became the king's "first minister." He served in that capacity until his death in 1642.

Richelieu had a genius for power and influence. "Listen well, and speak little," he liked to say.[9] Rivals were ruthlessly pushed aside; one of his strongest challengers found himself arrested on the king's orders. At the same time, he was very corrupt and used his public offices to build one of the largest fortunes in France.[10] Everyone at court feared this extraordinary man, with his piercing brown eyes that seemed to see everything and reveal nothing. Dressed in brilliant red robes with pristine white collars, adorned with a blue silk ribbon and a Maltese Cross of diamonds and gold, he became one of the most striking fig-

Cardinal Richelieu, after Philippe de Champaigne's portrait in 1636. This much-hated man believed that leaders are not bound by ordinary rules. He was intelligent, watchful, silent, cruel, and relentless in his service of raison d'état. *Richelieu tried to turn New France away from the purposes of Henri IV and Champlain, with mixed results.*

ures at court. Often in his company was his mentor and friend Père Joseph, a Capuchin monk in sandals and gray robe—the original *éminence grise* behind Richelieu's *éminence rouge.*[11]

Richelieu was a man of intelligence and complexity, a bundle of paradoxes. He became a man of great wealth but lived a very frugal life. He insisted that "all things must be done according to reason," but he was swayed by intense emotions, and in moments of high tension he "gave way to tears" that embarrassed him. He studied humanity with a clinical eye, but was more comfortable in the company of cats. This saturnine figure was said to prefer the feline to the human species.[12]

Always he acted on an ethical imperative that was distant from the ways of Champlain and his humanist circle. On the great question of means and ends, the heritage of Christianity is divided. On one side is Christ's golden rule of always treating others as one would wish to be treated. On the other is the idea of a higher law that releases privileged people from lower ones. It is akin to St. Paul's ethical rule that "unto the just, all things are just." Champlain and the sieur de Mons came down on one side of this great question; Richelieu on the other. The cardinal believed that higher ends sanctified any means. More than that, he worked out a code of conduct for public office which was in many ways the inversion of private morality. He believed that for kings and great ministers, deception was a duty and cruelty a virtue. On the subject of deception he wrote, "To know how to deceive is the knowledge of kings." He added in one of his many *maximes d'état*, "One may employ any means against one's enemies." [13]

In regard to cruelty he went further and declared: "Harshness towards individuals who flout the laws and commands of state is for the public good; no greater crime against the public interest is possible than to show leniency to those who violate it." Rarely was Richelieu accused of leniency. In his hubris, he was alleged to have said, "Give me six lines written by the hand of the most honest man, and I will find something there to hang him." [14]

Richelieu not only practiced this inverted code but also preached it to others in high places. Many European rulers were persuaded by his thinking, which became one of the defining features of Europe's *ancien régime*. This philosophy of ruthlessness appeared to get results. It could be brutally effective in the short run, but the idea that the end justified any means had an ironic way of failing at the very end. Richelieu used it to build an absolute monarchy in France, but it fatally injured the legitimacy of that regime. In the fullness of his power, he was feared and obeyed; but by the end he was hated and despised. One historian has written that Richelieu's death in 1642 was "greeted throughout France with scarcely controlled feelings of relief and joy, sentiments which, according to observers were shared by his employer, Louis XIII himself." [15]

The king accused Richelieu of believing in nothing, which was not the case. The cardinal believed in kingship—in the absolute authority of a strong monarch, the hierarchy of an established church, the force of an omnipotent state, and the superiority of an ancient nobility over other mortals. He believed in the state and lived by his rule of *raison d'état*, which descended from Cicero's *ratio res publicae*. Richelieu replaced the public interest with the power of the state, another raw imperative that he served all his life. He believed in order and thought of it as hierarchy and hegemony. In his writings, Victor Tapié found that "one particular word occurs over and over again—disorder, *dérèglement*," as representing everything he was against. [16]

Richelieu hedged those purposes with one constraint. Unlike many leaders who lived for power and dominion, Richelieu had no love of war. Like Champlain, he had witnessed the horror of war, and had counted its cost in blood, treasure, and most of all disorder. He knew what war could do, but most of all he hated its uncertainties. As he expressed it, "war is one of the scourges with which it has pleased God to afflict men." [17]

For all these qualities, historians have celebrated and condemned Richelieu in equal measure. He succeeded in building a strong monarchical state and he worked to integrate a nation, but he did so by methods that separated the state from the nation and turned one against the other. In a letter to Louis XIII he wrote: "I promised Your Majesty to employ all my industry and all the authority which it pleased you to grant me to ruin the Huguenot party, to abase the pride of the great nobles, to reduce all your subjects to the obedience that they owe you, and to restore your name among foreign nations to the position it should rightly hold." Even within his beloved France, he made entire orders and denominations of humanity into his bitter enemies.[18]

In his effort to strengthen the state and the monarchy, Richelieu was deeply hostile to the high nobility, and especially to princes of the blood who regarded the state with suspicion and the monarch as their equal. These free spirits also had an idea of their own liberties and fiercely defended the rights of provincial assemblies. One of the most able and outspoken of them was the viceroy of New France, Henri II, duc de Montmorency, who placed the law above the king and sometimes put regional parlements above the monarchical state. Richelieu regarded him with suspicion—and more than a little jealousy. The cardinal came from the lesser nobility; Montmorency had the rank, manners, and bearing that Richelieu could never hope to match, and was also a close companion of the king.[19]

As Richelieu moved to the center of power, Montmorency withdrew. He gave more attention to his role as governor of Languedoc, in defense of its ancient liberties. In the fall and winter of 1624–25, Montmorency decided to give up his job as viceroy of New France. He was sick of strife and litigation with investors. Champlain tells us that "the troubles that sprang from this source were in part the cause of my lord Montmorency's resignation." But only in part. Another factor was the rise of Richelieu.[20] Even as Montmorency gave up the office he was careful to keep it in the family, and sold it for 100,000 livres to his nephew.[21] The new viceroy was Henri de Lévis, duc de Ventadour, prince de Maubuisson, and comte de la Voulte. He also came from the high nobility, but had a different character and did not pose a threat to Richelieu. Ventadour, as we shall call him, was twenty-eight years old in 1625 and he had just come into his inheritance on the death of his father in December, 1624. He had been trained as a soldier and had fought in campaigns against the Huguenots, but his great passion was religion. Ventadour was devoted to the Roman Catholic Church.[22]

The quality of Ventadour's faith appeared in the condition of his marriage.

A few months before his father's death, he took the hand of Marie Liesse de Luxembourg, heiress to one of the largest fortunes in France. They knew each other very well, having grown up in the same household where Marie Liesse had been raised by Ventadour's mother. They were engaged to be married when she was eight years old and he was twenty-three. On their wedding day four years later she was a child bride, less than half her husband's age.

Their marriage was similar in some ways to that of Samuel Champlain and Hélène Boullé. The duke and duchess of Ventadour had no children. Their marriage appears never to have been consummated. Both husband and wife were very devout, so much so that in 1629 they mutually agreed to separate and lead lives of chastity and Christian devotion. Marie Liesse entered a convent, Carmel d'Avignon. Ventadour founded a holy society called the Compagnie du Saint-Sacrament. He summarized its purposes in half a sentence: "to cover the land of France with a flowering of good works." In 1643, he would be ordained a priest.[23]

Ventadour agreed to become viceroy of New France for a religious purpose. His central goal was to spread "the Catholic Apostolic and Roman Faith and Religion" among the American Indians and Europeans in the new world.[24] He strongly supported the Récollet fathers, and at the urging of his spiritual adviser, Father Philibert Noyrot, he also encouraged the Jesuits to work in New France. In January, 1625, three more Jesuit fathers and two brothers went to Quebec.[25]

One of Ventadour's first acts as viceroy was to confirm Champlain as his chief lieutenant in New France, with a commission dated February 15, 1625. In doing so he followed every previous viceroy and general of New France since 1604. The sieur de Mons, the comte de Soissons, the prince of Condé, the marquis de Thémines, and the duc de Montmorency all had chosen Champlain as their lieutenant and had come to think of him as their indispensable man in New France.[26]

Ventadour went further. He avowed his "entire confidence" in Champlain, and praised him for his "intelligence and judgment, capacity, practical skill and experience," as well as for his "good diligence, and the knowledge that he possesses of the country, arising from the various navigations, voyages and visits that he has made there."[27] He gave Champlain more authority than before, with full power to appoint and replace military officers in the ranks of captain and ensign, "on our behalf, as may be required." Champlain acted quickly and awarded a captain's commission to his able young brother-in-law, Eustache de Boullé, who had much experience of New France and had worked closely with Champlain. He also selected an ensign named Destouches, of a naval family prominent in the Old Regime.[28]

When the viceroy gave Champlain his commission, he added a personal request. In Champlain's words, Ventadour asked that "for this year [1625] I should remain near to him, in order to instruct him in the affairs of the said country, and to give order to some of my own affairs in Paris." Champlain was happy to agree, and the center of his activity shifted to the Hôtel de Ventadour, the duke's mansion in Paris.[29]

The most urgent problem was that of the commercial companies. There were now two of them.[30] One was the old Company of Rouen and Saint-Malo. The other was the new Company de Caën, based in Dieppe, Paris, and Orleans. Only a few men (Ézechiel de Caën for one) belonged to both. The two groups differed in their origins but shared the same interest in extracting quick profits from a monopoly of the fur trade. Neither was happy with Champlain's relentless effort to expand permanent settlements at their expense. Some leaders complained that the colonizing effort was doomed to fail. Others feared that it might succeed and that colonists would become competitors.

Several leading investors continued to be very hostile to Champlain in a personal way. Chief among them was a faction within the old company led by his enemy Daniel Boyer, together with Boyer's Dutch kinsman Corneille de Bellois, a Flemish merchant named Louis Vermuelen, and another investor named Mathieu Duisterlo, who was identified as German. These merchants came from other countries and had no loyalty to France. They cared nothing for the founding of French colonies in North America. Their only purpose was to buy beaver pelts and sell them at a profit. They thought that Champlain's grand design was bad for business and resented his victories even more than his defeats.[31] While Champlain was in New France between 1620 and 1624, these conflicts had grown more intense. Boyer's friends were highly litigious. Both companies and the viceroy were caught in a tangle of lawsuits. It seemed that the only people in France who consistently made money out of America were the lawyers.

In 1625, the duc de Ventadour summoned the leaders of both companies to the Hôtel de Ventadour in the hope of achieving "a friendly understanding between the two parties." His gesture was in vain. Champlain wrote that the meetings were marked by a "good deal of contention." Champlain and Ventadour tried to buy out the old company, and offered its shareholders a payment of 37 percent on their capital of 60,000 livres if they would withdraw from the fur trade and surrender all other claims. They refused, and rejected every effort by Champlain and the viceroy to intervene.[32]

Ventadour and Champlain referred the dispute to the court of Admiralty. The old shareholders tried to block the proceedings, and the viceroy took the matter directly to the Royal Council. With the leadership of Richelieu, the council acted decisively. In the name of the king, it ordered the old shareholders to accept a payment of 40 percent on their capital, and withdraw forthwith from trade in the St. Lawrence Valley. In 1626 the Company of Rouen and Saint-Malo ceased to take an active role in New France.[33]

The Company de Caën was offered a monopoly of the fur trade on condition that it appoint Catholics to command its ships. This was agreed. The fisheries remained open to all comers. Fishermen were also allowed to take up to twelve beaver pelts for each vessel, but they had to sell them to agents of the Company de Caën at a fixed price. On these terms, it was hoped that trade and colonization could revive.[34]

No sooner had the problem of the quarreling companies been resolved than more trouble landed on the viceroy's desk. In the late summer and fall of 1625, letters began to arrive from Jesuits and Récollets in New France. They testified that conditions in the colony had sadly declined in the year since Champlain had left. These accounts had a broad reach. Jesuit father Philibert Noyrot returned to France and made similar reports to many people at court, where his judgment carried great weight. Jesuit Charles Lalemant also sent letters to Champlain and the heads of both religious orders. Récollet father Joseph Le Caron wrote an address directly to the king and had it printed in Paris.[35]

These writers all agreed that many things were going wrong in Quebec. Some of it was the eternal complaint about the winters in New France. Lalemant wrote, "Our Frenchmen have even told me that they dragged their maypole over the snow on the first day of May." The fathers warned that the settlers were desperately short of food, and that "nothing is to be hoped" from the Indians in the way of provisions. The colony was shrinking. Champlain had left sixty habitants in the late summer of 1624–25. In his absence, that number fell to fifty-two over the winter of 1624–25, and forty-three in 1625–26.[36]

The fathers also described growing tensions between the French and the Indians. The missionaries were having trouble reaching the natives, and some Indian interpreters were reluctant to help them. Letters from both the Jesuits and Récollets showed increasing hostility to the Indians. The fathers complained that they were not treated with respect, and that the Indians "consider the French to be less intelligent than they." One wrote of their missions that "the promise of success is not yet very great, so crude and almost bestial are the natives."[37]

Father Lalemant was very negative about the people he had come to convert. He wrote that they "commit all kinds of shameless acts, without disgrace or attempts at concealment" and "as to cleanliness among them, that never enters into the question; they are very dirty." Most of all he complained that they were violent and cruel, and could not be trusted. They even "kill their fathers and mothers when they are so old that they can walk no longer."[38] These letters expressed growing fear of the Indians. "There is no security for our lives among these savages," Lalemant wrote. "If a Frenchman has in some way offended them, they take revenge by killing the first one they meet. . . . If during the night they dream they must kill a Frenchman, woe to the first one whom they meet alone."[39]

This fear and hatred of the Indians never appeared in Champlain's writings, nor was it widely evident when he was present in New France and running the colony. Sometimes he was very displeased with particular acts by individual Indians, and with some of the Montagnais in particular, but he had nothing like this general attitude of terror, hysteria, and loathing toward the native people. The letters that came from Quebec in Champlain's absence were graphic evidence of his impact when he was present in the colony.

The bulk of these letters also complained about something else—the misconduct of the French merchants. Missionaries of both orders were very angry with the de Caën company, especially with Émery de Caën, who had briefly replaced Champlain as commander in Quebec, and his cousin Guillaume de Caën, who commanded the company's ships in the St. Lawrence. Jesuits and Récollets reported that Protestant leaders of the company refused to accommodate them. According to an account by Father Lalemant, when the Jesuits arrived, Émery de Caën told them "it was impossible to give us lodging in the settlement or at the fort, and we must either return to France or withdraw to the Récollet fathers." The Récollets took them in and they survived, but in a state of fury against the merchants.[40]

The Récollets added another complaint that de Caën was not providing for the security of the colony. Le Caron wrote that Champlain's fort had been grossly neglected. He reported that it was guarded by two poor women and its only sentinels were two chickens. On top of everything else, trade was not flourishing under the de Caëns. Lalemant wrote, "An old man told me that he had seen as many as twenty ships in the port of Tadoussac, but now since this business has been granted to the [de Caën] association, which today has a monopoly over all others, we see here not more than two ships which belong to it, and that only once a year."[41]

Récollet father Joseph Le Caron agreed with his Jesuit colleagues and urged sweeping reforms. His memorial was a broad indictment of the Company de Caën and its leaders in Quebec. Le Caron wrote that it was "impossible to establish the Catholic faith when the colony is run by Protestants." He urged that the viceroy should live in Quebec, and that only Catholics should be allowed to come to Canada, or venture into the interior. Further, Le Caron thought that the de Caën company had failed to meet its responsibilities and should forfeit its monopoly. He urged that markets should be as open as in France, and that a system of "free" trade be established—for everyone but Huguenots.[42] There was an air of desperation in these letters. Lalemant begged Champlain to come quickly. He wrote, "We are awaiting your arrival, to determine what will be well to do."[43]

This chorus of complaint from Quebec was clearly heard in Paris. In the spring of 1626, Vendatour asked Champlain to return quickly to New France and "take up his residence at Quebec."[44] The viceroy's instructions repeated the imperial phrases of Louis XIII, and echoed the state-building purposes of Cardinal Richelieu. Further, at Quebec, "and other places which the said sieur de Champlain shall consider suitable," he was "to order the construction and building of such forts and fortresses as he shall judge useful and necessary."[45]

Champlain hurried to the port of Dieppe and went to work with the leaders of the Company de Caën. Together they outfitted five vessels for New France. Champlain went aboard the ship *Catherine* with Récollet father Le Caron and Captain Raymond de La Ralde, a Catholic who was commissioned as admiral of the fleet. A second vessel, *La Flèque*, was commanded by Émery de Caën. The Jesuits chartered a small vessel of 80 tons called *Alouette* to bring their strength to seven members of their order in the colony, with twenty workmen. Two other unnamed vessels of 200 and 120 tons completed the expedition.[46]

Champlain's ship weighed anchor on April 15, 1626, and tacked to and fro in the roadstead of Dieppe waiting for the other ships. On April 24, they finally departed together for New France. Increasingly ships were sailing in convoy, and with good reason. International tensions were rising, and conditions were growing more dangerous on the Atlantic. On April 27, they sighted a strange sail that Champlain took to be a corsair or a smuggler. As a captain in the king's marine, he ordered the entire convoy to give chase. Champlain wrote that they "pursued it for some three hours; but as it sailed better than we did, we gave up the chase and came about" and steadied on a course for America.[47]

It was a slow passage. Large convoys meant longer voyages, as the ships were forced to keep company with the slowest sailor, and time was lost when they separated in the night. On May 23 they ran into a great storm that lasted two days. Little *Alouette* disappeared with the Jesuits aboard, and Champlain feared the worst. But she miraculously survived and made her own way to America. The ships were at sea for more than two months and six days, "delayed as we were by bad weather."[48]

At last, on July 5, Champlain reached Quebec. He was happy to find the habitants in good health, but was shocked to discover that "not a thing had been done" to finish the buildings since he left two years before.[49] With the new arrivals aboard his ships, Champlain counted fifty-five people in the settlement, of whom twenty-four were laborers on the company's payroll. He set them to work on the fort and the dwellings. The Company de Caën resisted and once again refused to keep its contractual promise. Champlain wrote: "They should have given me ten men to work at His Majesty's fort. Even though the Sieur de Caën and all of his associates signed an agreement to do so, and although his Majesty and the Viceroy desired it, still they oppose it, and hinder it to the utmost of their power . . . as long as trading goes on, that is enough for them."[50]

But this time Champlain prevailed, and the laborers went to work for him. Once the buildings were on their way to improvement, he turned to another purpose. An important goal was to make the settlement self-sustaining, at least for its own food. The Île d'Orléans near Quebec looked to be a good site, with fertile soil and ample water. It offered an abundance of good farmland, but Champlain had a shortage of farmers at Quebec in 1626. The settlement of the Île d'Orléans would have to await a larger flow of migration.

In the meantime he gave his attention once again to Cap Tourmente on the north side of the St. Lawrence River, thirty miles downstream from Quebec. Here was a perfect place to raise cattle, with open grassland that did not require the enormous labor of land clearing.[51] In 1623, Champlain had visited Cap Tourmente with the sieur de Caën, and both men thought it was "a very fine place" for farming, with "everything that one might desire for that purpose." Later that year, the meadow grass began to be harvested and large quantities of hay were carried to Quebec. When Champlain returned to Canada in 1626, one of his first acts was to go to the meadows near Cap Tourmente and choose a site for a settlement. He picked a place on a small creek where pinnaces and shallops could land at high tide, with the meadows nearby, a great growth of trees, and an abundance of snow geese.[52]

Champlain moved decisively with all his resources. "I resolved to build as soon as possible," he wrote. "Although we were then in July, I nevertheless decided to employ the greater part of all the workers in Quebec." The farm at Cap Tourmente was called into being by Champlain and the leaders of the colony. No major decision was left to the will of any individual except himself. Like much of the culture of Quebec—and unlike Acadia, the fishing coast and the western frontier—the building of the settlement was highly ordered and controlled from the top down. But Champlain tried to run its daily operations by private enterprise as he had done many times before.[53]

Champlain ordered his workers to build "a dwelling, a stable sixty feet long, and more than 20 feet wide, and two other cottages each eighteen by fifteen feet, constructed of wood and clay after the fashion of those in the villages of Normandy." The evidence of modern archaeology confirms the accuracy of Champlain's description and adds depth to his brief passage. Excavations by Canadian archaeologists have discovered that the farm buildings at Cap Tour-

Champlain constructed this farm at the natural meadows on Cap Tourmente in 1626. Artist Francis Back based this reconstruction on the work of Jacques Guimont and a team of archaeologists sponsored by Parcs Canada, 1992–93. Here again archaeology confirms the accuracy of Champlain's texts, and deepens our historical knowledge.

mente were indeed built on the model of Norman peasant architecture, in an old tradition of half-timbered clay construction, just as Champlain wrote. Wooden posts were set in clay, about a yard apart. Between the posts, walls were made of densely packed, or "puddled," clay. This ancient method was neolithic in its origin, widely used in Belgium and Normandy but uncommon in the south of France. Here again, in the years of Champlain's lieutenancy, we find a strong connection between the culture of Quebec and that of north-western France.[54]

The farm buildings at Cap Tourmente were not as strongly built as their Norman models: the walls were about eight inches thick, compared with fifteen or twenty inches in the north of France. The dwellings were low and dark, with small windows covered by translucent oiled paper. Archaeologists were puzzled by a lack of evidence of stone fireplaces; probably the interiors were heated with clay fireplaces. The buildings were grouped together to form a small village, to which the Récollets later added a chapel. By September of 1626, the farm was habitable.

To run the farm, Champlain sent farmer Nicolas Pivert with his wife, Marguerite Lesage, and their young niece, a "petite fille." To help them he added five workers and entrusted them with cattle that had been brought from France. Champlain also sent provisions that had been shipped in graystone pottery crocks of Norman design. Archaeologists have found much evidence of what they ate. They raised Indian corn and enjoyed a mixed diet of fresh beef and pork, fish from the river and geese and ducks from the marshes, as well as beans and other dried provisions from France. It was a diverse diet, and a key to the survival of the colony. Champlain was always very mindful of food, which he recognized as essential to the morale of the habitants. The traces of food that archaeologists have found at the farm could have made a fine Norman cassoulet. One might imagine Champlain on his visits sitting down to such a dish, with good bread and a sturdy wine. In its regard for gastronomy, this was a very French colony.[55]

Champlain watched over the farm through the winter and was happy that the workers survived in good health. In the spring he sent more than half of the workers to finish the buildings at the cape and to help bring in hay for the following winter—which was essential to the survival of livestock in North America—and the farm began to flourish.[56]

Champlain also ordered the workers to fortify the farm and erect a strong palisade, "not only against the Indians, but principally against the enemies from Europe." It was needed. Two drovers that he sent to help with the cattle were attacked and killed by a renegade Montagnais raiding party. This incident "distressed me greatly," Champlain wrote. He went to the scene and found that the drovers had been murdered "as they lay asleep, about half a league from our habitation." He was shocked by the gratuitous violence of the assault. "We went to get the bodies, which had been dragged into the river in order that they might be carried away by the tide. . . . Their skulls had been smashed by blows with axes, and there were many other wounds by swords and knives."[57]

The French were angry and frightened. Some wanted to kill several Montagnais in retaliation. In Spanish, English, and Dutch settlements, a policy of retribution was adopted more frequently than any other. Champlain rejected it out of hand. He declared: "As to taking vengeance upon a number who were not guilty, there would be no sense [raison] in that. It would be a declaration of open war, and would ruin the country."

Instead he invited all the Montagnais captains to a meeting. He showed them the bodies of the murdered Frenchmen, and told them that these acts were wrong and unacceptable. He asked them to join in a search for a solution that all could accept as just. Some of the Montagnais inspected the bodies and tried to blame the Iroquois. Champlain would have none of that, and he made clear that the murders were clearly the work of Montagnais. Much earnest discussion followed. Champlain persuaded the captains to agree that the killings were in truth the work of Montagnais men, but they insisted that they had no idea who the murderers might have been. Champlain also refused to accept that judgment and pointed out that it did not respond to the problem at hand. He reasoned with them: if peace were to prevail on the St. Lawrence River, justice had to be done in a way that all the people of the valley could accept as legitimate. More discussion followed, and at last a solution was found. The Montagnais captains agreed that they would deliver several of their own children to Champlain as hostages for the keeping of peace. This was done. The hostages were treated with humanity, the killing stopped, and Champlain slowly began to rebuild trust between the French and the Montagnais. It was an achievement much valued in both nations.[58]

Afterward, in the winter of 1627–28, a group of Montagnais came to Champlain and said that they wished "to join with us in a closer friendship than ever before, and to remove any distrust of them we could possibly have." To cement that relationship they had decided to entrust the French with three young girls, aged eleven, twelve, and fifteen. Champlain wrote that he was "greatly astonished by the offer" and by the request of the Montagnais to "have them instructed and treated like those of our own nation, and to have them marry if that seemed right to us."

After much reflection, Champlain agreed to take them in. Some writers have been suspicious, but the clergy watched carefully and testified that nothing was amiss. Champlain named the girls Faith, Hope, and Charity. The Récollet missionary Gabriel Sagard wrote that they were instructed for two years in religion and in "the small skills of young women." Champlain added that they learned "needlework both plain and fancy, which they did very well, besides which they were very civilized." Sagard reported that "these *bonnes filles* honored Champlain as their father and he treated them as his daughters." Amity between the French and the Montagnais was much restored.[59]

At the same time Champlain also renewed his efforts to improve relations with the Iroquois. In August a canoe arrived from the "River of the Iroquois, with news that they had killed five Dutchmen, who had previously been their friends and allies." The Iroquois had also gone to war against the Mohicans to the south, and small parties were skirmishing with the Algonquin, Montagnais, Huron, and the Neutral to the north and west. Champlain dealt indirectly with this problem by rescuing two Iroquois captives from torture and death. He kept one a prisoner and made sure he was treated humanely. The other was sent home as a gesture of good will. And in the spring of 1627, Champlain dispatched a French emissary to the Iroquois on a mission of peace. Slowly relations with the Iroquois did get better. Attacks diminished in the St. Lawrence Valley.[60]

Champlain also tried to maintain his policy of religious tolerance within the colony, a task that in some ways was more difficult than keeping the peace with his Indian neighbors. Jesuit priests and Récollet brothers demanded that Protestants be excluded from Quebec. In the summer of 1626, Jesuit father Philibert Noyrot was ordered to carry that request back to France, where he was very well connected at court. When Noyrot met with Cardinal Richelieu and the king, he tried to convince them that Henri IV's Edict of Nantes, which had guaranteed Protestants the freedom to practice their religion, should be revoked in New France, and that only Catholics should be allowed to settle there. But what, then, was to be done about the many Protestant seamen and traders in Quebec?[61]

Champlain, Ventadour, Richelieu, and Louis XIII were not of one mind on this contentious question. The king favored toleration. He strongly supported his father's policy in the Edict of Nantes, prohibited general attacks on Protestants at court, and was very close to Protestants in his household, such as his *valet de chambre* Beringhen and his physician Héroard. He insisted that Protestants should be loyal to the Crown and required them to grant toleration to Catholics in Huguenot towns. In the same spirit, he protected the right of Protestants to worship freely throughout his realm, including New France.[62]

Ventadour did not support toleration. As viceroy he tried to forbid Protestant worship in New France, and issued orders to ship captains in 1626 that Protestant seamen could sing their Huguenot hymns and psalms on ships at sea, but not in the St. Lawrence River. Clearly he meant New France to be an entirely Catholic colony.[63]

Richelieu took a third position. He subordinated religious questions to the raison d'état. In 1627 he was largely responsible for letters patent to the Company of Canada, which required that it "populate the colony with native-born French Catholics." But he insisted that the colonies in America would be governed by all the laws of France, which included the Edict of Nantes and protected Huguenot seamen and traders.[64]

Champlain's views were complex. His own Catholicism was growing stronger, so much so that he began to refer to Protestantism as a *"religion prétendue réformée*; a religion that claims to be reformed." With the sieur de Mons and Henri IV, he had always agreed that the Catholic Church should be fully established in the New France, and that all missionary work with the Indians would be done by Catholics, but he also believed that Huguenots should be allowed into the colony and fully protected in their right to worship privately in their own way. But Champlain also had to follow contradictory instructions from Louis XIII, Ventadour, and Richelieu.[65]

He solved the problem by quiet compromise. A test case arose in 1626 when the ship *Catherine* anchored in the St. Lawrence River with a mostly Protestant crew and Raymond de La Ralde, who was staunchly Catholic (and also strongly anti-Jesuit), as its captain. Ralde mustered his crew and told them that the viceroy "did not wish them to sing their psalms in the Great River, as they had done at sea." Champlain was aboard at the time. He wrote that the men "began to murmur and say that they ought not to be deprived of that liberty."[66] After much conversation, he found a middle way. "Finally," he wrote, "it was agreed that they should not sing their psalms, but they should assemble for prayer, since near two-thirds of them were Huguenots."[67] Champlain commented, "and so out of bad debt one gets what one can." That was his policy: a compromise that kept the peace in the colony, and allowed Catholics and Huguenots to coexist. It preserved a spirit of toleration and humanity that was fundamental to his grand design.[68]

• • •

While Champlain was at work in Quebec, more reports from the Jesuits and Récollets reached Cardinal Richelieu and persuaded him that sweeping changes were necessary in the commerce of New France. In October, 1626, the cardinal decided to take personal control. He added to his many powers a new office as "grandmaster, chief, and general superintendent of the Navigation and Commerce of France." By the spring of the following year, Ventadour was out as viceroy, and Richelieu replaced him as the man in charge of New France.[69]

The cardinal wasted no time. First, he dealt summarily with the persistent problem of the rival trading companies. In the spring of 1627, the Company de Caën lost its monopoly and trading privileges in New France. It was replaced by an entirely new company that Richelieu created. He named it the Compagnie de la Nouvelle France. It was also called the Compagnie du Canada but came to be more generally known as the Compagnie des Cent-Associés, the Hundred Associates, after the number of its stockholders.[70]

The Company of the Hundred Associates began with a capital of 300,000 livres. Richelieu required each investor to pay in 3,000 livres, and all profits would be reserved by the company for three years. On the list of the hundred stockholders dated January 14, 1628, Richelieu appeared as number 1. Samuel de Champlain was number 52. As he was in Quebec at the time, his wife, Hélène, paid his capital of 3,000 livres in full—another sign that she now strongly supported his endeavors. Many investors were Royal Councillors and

The seal of Richelieu's Company of New France (the Hundred Associates). The obverse shows a figure holding a crucifix and the lilies of France, with the motto "me donavit Ludovicus Decimus Tertius, 1627; Louis XIII gave me, 1627." The reverse shows a ship and a seaman's prayer: "in mari viae tuae; in the sea your way [to salvation]."

holders of high office at court. Others were merchants and financiers—a few from Rouen and Bordeaux, and many from Paris. Several members were Champlain's friends who came to New France: Charles Daniel, Isaac de Razilly, Charles Saint-Étienne de la Tour. The mercantile families who had dominated the earlier companies were excluded: there were no Boyers from Rouen and no de Caëns from Dieppe. Altogether the company was closely controlled by Richelieu, and could also be called the cardinal's ring.[71]

The entire colony of New France was made a fief of the company. It claimed a vast territory in North America from Florida to the Arctic Circle. The company was required to support settlement on a larger scale than ever before. It was run by Richelieu himself with a board of twelve directors. Half were court officials; the rest were merchants, mostly from Paris. Champlain, Razilly, and Daniel did not sit on the board.[72]

In a few months, Richelieu had put New France on a stronger material base than ever before. At the same time, Champlain had invigorated the settlement of Quebec. He had repaired the buildings in the town, rebuilt the fort, and led the settlement toward self-sufficiency. He had improved relations among the clergy, traders, and habitants. He aligned his actions with the new policies of Cardinal Richelieu. Most important, he stopped a threatening decline in relations with the Indians and restored amity with the Huron, the Algonquin, and many of the Montagnais, while he also made peace with the Iroquois.

Champlain had made real progress on many fronts, but in other ways the tiny settlement remained fragile. Its population was very small and in most years grew scarcely at all. In the winter of 1627–28, Champlain wrote that "55 people, men, women and children depended on the habitation for subsistence, not including the native inhabitants."[73] Other European settlements, by comparison, were expanding rapidly. By 1628, the Dutch had 270 colonists in New Netherland. The English Pilgrims at Plymouth were 300 strong in 1629. A census of Virginia counted 1,275 English settlers and 22 Africans in 1624. Massachusetts had 506 English Puritans in 1630. New France had dangerous neighbors, and tensions were building.

19.

NEW FRANCE LOST
The British Conquest, 1628–29

> The advice I give to all adventurers is this: seek a place where you can
> sleep in safety.
>
> —Champlain, *Voyages*, 1632 [1]

I N 1625, France and England went to war. It had been a long time coming.
Since the death of Henri IV, the monarchs of England, Spain, and France
had been striving with one another in rivalries of high complexity. Each
country was ruled by an ambitious king and an able minister: Charles I and
the Duke of Buckingham, Philip IV and the Count-Duke Olivares, Louis XIII
and Cardinal Richelieu. [2]

Their goals were similar: absolute authority at home, a strong hand in Europe, and an expanding empire in America. But ambitions exceeded resources,
and they all were weary of incessant war, especially the French. In 1624, Louis
XIII proposed an Anglo-French alliance, and he suggested that it be cemented
by the marriage of his sister Henrietta Maria to England's Charles I, with a
dowry of 2,400,000 livres. Charles agreed, and the wedding followed in May,
1625. It brought a bright hope of lasting peace between England and France,
but the marriage itself made the alliance more difficult. Henrietta Maria was
devoted to her Catholic faith, and the English people were strongly Protestant
in 1625. She was bitterly unhappy, and the marriage was riven by quarrels. At
one point the queen was so overcome with fury at her exile in London that she
rammed her arm through a glass window. All hope of harmony collapsed in
the bloody aftermath. On top of that, half the dowry had not been paid, and
Charles urgently needed the money. [3]

These troubles were reinforced by turmoil in France over the Huguenots
of La Rochelle, who made their city into a fortress—a Protestant state within
the state. Louis XIII regarded them as disobedient subjects and attacked.
Charles I supported them, and two angry royal brothers-in-law went to war. A
large British force came to the aid of the Huguenots and was defeated in heavy
fighting at the Isle of Ré.

INDIAN FESTIVALS AND ALLIANCES

On Champlain's first visit to New France (1603), he and Pont-Gravé walked boldly into a camp of a thousand Indians on the Saguenay River, joined a tabagie or tobacco feast, and made an alliance that lasted two centuries. He did it again with Penobscots, Mi'kmaq, Huron, Algonquins, and many other nations. In some ways, these scenes resembled George Catlin's later painting of this festival among the Mandan nation, who lived near the Great Lakes in Champlain's era, and later moved west to the Great Plains. (B1)

SAINT CROIX

Sainte-Croix Island in this aerial photo of 2004 is remarkably similar to Champlain's map of 1604. The sieur de Mons and Champlain planted their first colony here, with disastrous results during the terrible winter of 1604–05. It is in the Saint Croix river, part of the present boundary between the United States and Canada. (B2)

PORT-ROYAL

In 1605 the French moved from Sainte-Croix to Port-Royal, now Annapolis Royal in Nova Scotia. It flourished in America with strong support from the Mi'kmaq nation, but it failed in France when the Council ended its monopoly in 1607. Francis Back's drawing rests on much contemporary evidence and archaeology. (B3)

MI'KMAQ WARRIORS

The seventeenth-century *Codex Canadiensis* of Louis Nicolas shows a seaborne war party of Champlain's Souriquois or Mi'kmaqs on its way to fight hereditary enemies across the Gulf of Maine. Champlain worked to end incessant violence among the maritime Indian nations. (B4)

INDIAN FISHERMEN AT WORK.

Indians of the St. Lawrence and Acadia were skilled watermen. The *Codex Canadiensis* of Louis Nicolas shows them at work. The bowman uses a flute to please the Spirit and summon the fish, while the sternman works with a weighted net and spear. Their catch included sturgeon, salmon, carp, flounder, mackerel, bass, and shad. (B5)

FUR-TRADING IN QUEBEC

Champlain's Second Habitation at Québec, 1624–35, stood in today's Place Royale. This scene by Francis Back, derived from Champlain's accounts and archaeology, shows a busy trading day. Hurons arrive (left), while Algonquins gather in the background, and a perfectly coiffed Cheveux-Relevé departs (right front). Champlain in his favorite red suit talks with a truchement and Montagnais, while other Indians move freely through his habitation. (B6)

THREE RULERS IN CHAMPLAIN'S FRANCE

Champlain kept his American dream alive under three very different French rulers. He flourished with the support of Henri IV (1589–1610), survived the enmity of Marie de Medici (1610–1617), and won over young Louis XIII (1617–1635). It is a marvel to see how he managed it. Rubens shows the Queen taking the Orb from the King in one hand, while she grasps the Dauphin in the other. Is she helping him up, or holding him down? (B7)

CHAMPLAIN'S AMERICAN CIRCLE AT COURT

At court, three powerful men helped Champlain during the regency of Marie de Medici and youth of Louis XIII. Charles II de Cossé-Brissac (top left) was a Maréchal of France, and Champlain's former commander. Pierre Jeannin (1540–1622)(left) was president of the Dijon parlement, and royal councillor. Nicolas Brulart de Sillery (1544–1624) was Lord Chancellor of France. All supported Champlain's Grand Design. (B8)

RICHELIEU AND CHAMPLAIN

Cardinal Richelieu (1585–1642) was chief minister under Louis XIII, architect of French absolutism, and ruler of its colonies. His ruthless *realpolitik* was far removed from the spirit of Champlain's dream. The two men worked together but never got on. Their troubled history was a conflict of two ethics. This triple portrait by Philippe de Champaigne suggests something of the cardinal's complexity. (B9)

CHAMPLAIN'S LAST LABOR

In 1635, a stroke left Champlain paralyzed but keen of mind. He prepared for death with his accustomed *prévoyance,* and studied works such as *The Pious Learning of the Christian Poet* (1600), with its poem about "contemplation of death" by a "wise and well-versed navigator." In his last months, Champlain dictated a will and testament in which he left much of his estate to support New France, subsidize settler marriages, and help his Indian godson. Even on his deathbed he served his dream of humanity and peace. (B10)

"Charles I as Garter Knight," a portrait by Anthony Van Dyke, 1632. This English king aspired to absolutism on the French model. He tried to rule his restless people without a Parliament, and involved them in unsuccessful wars with France, Scotland, and Ireland. He also authorized British mercenaries to seize New France.

La Rochelle proved too strong for the French to take by assault. Richelieu decided to starve it into submission and gave the war his own brutal touch. The town was besieged, and Rochelais who tried to escape were driven back inside the walls or summarily hanged, even women and children. The population of La Rochelle fell from 27,000 to 8,000 starving people. Finally, that small remnant surrendered, and Louis XIII entered the gates in triumph on November 1, 1628. He destroyed its fortifications, banished a few leaders, and pardoned the rest. The largest churches became Catholic, but Protestants were allowed to worship under the Edict of Nantes.[4]

Richelieu and Louis XIII had succeeded in defeating the "Huguenot state within a state," but at heavy cost. The Anglo-French war spread to America. Charles I and his ministers resolved to destroy the settlements of New France and seize the Atlantic fisheries. But the English king lacked money for a proper military force. He attacked New France with mercenary bands of ill-disciplined freebooters who went to war on speculation and were paid by plunder.

Charles authorized two families of Scottish lairds, the Alexanders of Stirling and the Stewarts of Ochiltree, to seize Acadia. James Stewart attacked with two large ships and a pinnace. In a small cove he found a Basque fisherman named Michel Dihourse, of Saint-Jean-de-Luz, drying his cod. Stewart seized the ship and its catch, and plundered the Basque crew. Then he built a fort, using the guns he had taken from the Basques, and announced that no Frenchman could fish or trade on the coast without paying ten percent of his goods. Those who refused would lose their ships and their liberty.[5]

Henrietta Maria with her "pet dwarf" Sir Jeffrey Hudson, 1633. This beautiful sister of Louis XIII became the wife of Charles I. The wedding was meant to cement an alliance, but she hated Protestant England, the dowry was not paid, and war followed between two infuriated brothers-in-law. Quebec was seized and Champlain captured.

In 1627 yet another set of mercenaries appeared on this crowded stage. They were a family of entrepreneurs with a Scottish name, English origins, and a French residence. The family patriarch was Gervase (or Jarvis) Kirke, a merchant who was born in Derbyshire, traded in London, and lived in Dieppe among a colony of Scottish adventurers on the rue Écosse. There he married Elizabeth Gowding (or Goudon), daughter of another merchant in that busy town. They had five sons: David, Louis, Thomas, John, and James (or Jarvis), all born and raised in Dieppe. Together the family ran a flourishing international business with one base in England, another in France, and a web of partnerships on both sides of the law.[6]

The Kirkes received a commission from Charles I to seize French shipping in the St. Lawrence River. In 1628 they sent out an expedition and began to intercept French vessels bound for Quebec. The commander was David Kirke. Champlain called him the General, but he was not a soldier or seaman. David Kirke was a businessman. A Huguenot who knew him well said that he was "a wine merchant in Bordeaux and Cognac, ignorant of the sea, knowing nothing of navigation, having made only two voyages." Serving under him were his brothers, "Vice Admiral" Thomas Kirke and "Captain" Louis Kirke. Their pilot was a fugitive French Huguenot, Captain Jacques Michel, who knew the coast of New France and had scores to settle with Catholic leaders after the siege of La Rochelle.[7]

When war began, Richelieu's Company of the Hundred Associates was preparing to dispatch a very large convoy to New France. Its directors asked for a delay until their ships could be protected. Richelieu refused. With little knowledge of the danger but much confidence in his own judgment, he rejected the warnings of informed advisers and insisted that the ships must sail. On January 28, 1628, a royal proclamation ordered them to depart for Quebec forthwith.[8]

The company directors obeyed, much against their better judgment. Everything went wrong, as they feared. In the uncertainty of war, the Hundred Associates were unable to raise capital. The best they could do was 56,000 livres, not nearly enough. Richelieu insisted again, and their only recourse was to borrow 164,720 livres at ruinous rates of interest. Without the money in hand, they outfitted the largest expedition that had been sent to New France. At the Cardinal's demand, the company gambled everything on this enterprise.

It began by sending a single ship with food and supplies that were urgently needed in Quebec. Then it dispatched four large merchant vessels: *Estourneau*, *Magdaleine*, *Suzanne*, and another of unknown name. A small barque was separately chartered by Jesuit father Philibert Noyrot. On board these vessels were two other Jesuits, Charles Lalemant and François Ragueneau, with two Récollets, Daniel Doursier and François Girard de Binville. Altogether the ships carried four hundred people, mostly colonists. The company made a major effort to recruit families, with some success. It was the largest group of French settlers that had been sent to America.

In command was Admiral Claude Roquemont de Brison, a founding member of the Company of the Hundred Associates. He had been selected by Richelieu and was the very model of the cardinal's idea of a leader. Roquemont was a highborn nobleman, a devout Catholic churchman, a strong supporter of Royal absolutism, and an obedient servant of the cardinal. He was an officer of proven courage, but man of little intellect and less judgment. He knew nothing of New France and was unfamiliar with its waters.[9]

After many delays, the convoy sailed from Dieppe on April 28, 1628. It was a troubled voyage from the start. The fleet ran into a major storm. Then it was menaced by two ships with crews from La Rochelle who were eager to attack Richelieu's fleet with the same ruthless determination that he had brought against their city. The convoy escaped. After seven weeks at sea, it reached the uninhabited waste of Anticosti Island at the mouth of the St. Lawrence River, where Roquement erected a cross among the seals and polar bears. They sailed south to the Gaspé coast, and Roquemont learned from fishermen that a squadron of powerful British ships had taken possession of Tadoussac and were seizing French vessels in the river.

These Britons were the Kirke brothers and they were out in force. While the French ships had been preparing to sail, the Kirkes had arrived on the coast of North America with a formidable fleet of three or four big ships, all heavily armed and filled with large crews of men at arms. They began by seizing French fishing vessels at Miscou Island in the Bay of Chaleur, south of the Gaspé Peninsula. The Kirkes also captured a large Basque trading ship and intercepted the first provision ship that the Hundred Associates sent out that year, with supplies for the settlers of Quebec. Now with six ships, the Kirkes sailed up the St. Lawrence River and anchored in Tadoussac harbor.[10]

In Quebec, Champlain and the French settlers were desperately short of food. Dry rations always ran low in the late spring, and by June they were nearly gone. Champlain wrote: "All our provisions were exhausted, excepting some four or five barrels of quite bad biscuit, which was not much, and some peas and beans, to which we were now reduced without any other commodities."

Their supply ships were overdue, and they did not know why. Was it trouble in Europe? Politics at home? Weather on the North Atlantic? Every morning they looked anxiously down the great river in hope of sighting a sail, but there was nothing. Champlain remembered, "We were waiting for news from day to day, not knowing what to think."[11]

The settlers had left their river barques at Tadoussac, as was the custom. Champlain retained only a small shallop at Quebec. It was not caulked or seaworthy, and he wrote that Quebec "was without a single sailor, or any man with knowledge enough to fit out and navigate a vessel."[12] He asked a Montagnais, whom the French called La Fourière, to go down the river in search of news. On June 18, La Fourière returned and said that "he had not heard of any vessels having arrived off the coast."[13]

On July 9, two men arrived on foot from Tadoussac. They brought news that lifted hearts in Quebec. Six vessels had anchored there together, "an extraordinary thing for a trading voyage," Champlain wrote. Who were they? Several parties of Indians came with contradictory stories. They recognized one man aboard the ships. He was Jacques Michel, a Frenchman and a Huguenot. But whose side was he on? Champlain ordered a young interpreter "of the Greek nation" to disguise himself as an Indian, go down the river by canoe, and discover who these visitors might be.[14]

The Greek interpreter set off with two Indians. An hour later he was back with another canoe carrying a wounded Frenchman named Foucher, who had been taking supplies to the farm at Cap Tourmente. Close behind was Father Joseph, who came running to Quebec along the riverbank. They had a grim story to tell.[15]

Father Joseph had gone from Quebec on a routine mission to administer the sacraments to the French workers at the farm on Cap Tourmente, thirty miles down the river. He had gone only a short distance when two canoes of Montagnais came paddling upstream at "incredible speed." The Montagnais shouted, "*A terre! A terre! Sauvez-vous!* Get ashore! Save yourselves!" They explained, "The English have arrived at Tadoussac, and went this morning to ravage and burn Cap Tourmente."[16]

Then Father Joseph came upon a drifting canoe with Foucher "stretched out full-length in the bottom, half dead from the bad treatment by the English," his mustaches severely singed by fire. In a panic Father Joseph left him there, afloat in the river. He and his paddlers hurried ashore, hid their canoe in the woods, and ran overland to Quebec.[17]

Champlain began to piece together the story. The big ships at Tadoussac were British. Their commander David Kirke had sent fifty men, heavily armed, upstream to Cap Tourmente, where they attacked the defenseless French settlement and captured the workers who lived there: four men, a woman and a little girl. In a carnival of sadistic violence, the raiders killed some of the animals in the pasture, locked others in their stables, and set the buildings on fire. One can imagine the screams of the terrified animals, the shock of the French farmers, and the terror of the child.

The raiders then burned two houses into which Foucher had retreated, laid waste to the fields, and "destroyed everything they could, even to the caps worn by the little girl." Somehow Foucher got away, severely injured, and he did not know what had happened to the other French people at the farm. The English raiders failed in their primary task; six cattle escaped. The Montagnais caught five and ate them. Champlain sent a boat to the cape to see if anything had been left. The French found one lonely cow wandering in the woods.[18]

Champlain was saddened by the destruction of the farm and deeply shocked by something worse. Foucher reported that several Montagnais warriors had joined the British, guiding them to the farm and "helping them to kill our cattle and pillage the houses of our people, just as if they had been our enemies." Only a few Montagnais actually assisted the raiders, but many knew what was happening and said nothing to Champlain. This was an ominous development. If he lost the support of his Indian allies, the future of New France was bleak and his vision was merely a chimera.[19]

Early in the morning of July 9, a strange pinnace silently approached Quebec. Fifteen or sixteen armed men came ashore and marched on the settlement, "thinking to surprise our men in their beds." By pretending to be friends, they were able to capture four Québécois. The alarm was sounded, and the habitants mustered at the fort. Champlain wrote: "Being now only too sure that the enemy was at hand, I set all hands to work making entrenchments around the habitation, and barricades on the ramparts of the fort which were not completed. . . . I assigned the men to the places." The garrison went on high alert.[20]

The next day the French saw a small shallop on the river, moving toward the houses of the Jesuit fathers at St. Charles, near Quebec. Champlain sent men with arquebuses into the woods to stop them and discovered that they were "our own people." In the boat were the forlorn French prisoners who had been taken at Cap Tourmente: farmer Privert, with his wife and his little niece. Also with them were six Basque captives who had been seized by the British. They carried a letter from David Kirke, addressed to Samuel de Champlain.[21]

Kirke announced that he had a commission from the king of England to take possession of New France, and that eighteen ships of war had been sent from England on that errand. His claim was roughly correct, counting the vessels of Alexander and Stewart that had been sent to Acadia. Kirke informed Champlain that he had seized the post at Miscou Island and had taken all the French pinnaces and shallops on that coast, as well as those at Tadoussac. He announced that he had captured a vessel of the French company with supplies for Quebec and had destroyed the farm at Cap Tourmente, "for I know that when you are short of food and supplies, I will gain more easily what I desire, which is to have your settlement." The rest of the letter offered easy terms and menacing threats.[22]

Champlain responded in his accustomed way. First, he ordered the letter to be read aloud "in the presence of the sieur du Pont and myself, and several other principals of our habitation, whom I had ordered to assemble for the reading, and to advise on how we should respond." They talked together. Champlain listened carefully, then spoke. He urged that they should call the British bluff and if necessary they must fight. They agreed, and stood by him. Champlain said, "We concluded that . . . if he wanted to see us closer at hand he ought to come here and not menace us at such a distance."

Champlain sent a reply of elaborate courtesy and complete defiance. It began by praising the king of England and his officers as gentlemen of courage and generosity, and explained that "were we to surrender a fort and settlement, conditioned as we now are, we should not be worthy of the name of men in the presence of *our* King." He told Kirke that the French had lost little at Cap Tourmente and had "grain, Indian corn, peas and beans, not to mention what this country produces." Champlain warned, "honor demands that we fight to the death." He invited the British commander to visit Quebec, and added, "I am confident" that on seeing and reconnoitering it, you will judge it not so easy of access as perhaps someone has led you to believe, nor its defenders to be persons destitute of courage to defend it." He concluded, "We are now waiting from hour to hour to receive you, and to resist if we can, the claims that you have on these places, from which I remain, Sir, your affectionate servant, CHAMPLAIN."[23]

The Basques carried Champlain's letter down the river to David Kirke. According to Champlain, Kirke "made enquiries of the Basques," then decided to "assemble all the men in his vessels, and notably his officers, to whom he read the letter." These British leaders were businessmen, not soldiers. They met in council and decided not to attack. Champlain's bluff had worked. He wrote that the Kirkes believed "we were better supplied with provisions and ammunition than we were."[24]

In fact, Champlain had only about fifty pounds of gunpowder and "very little in the way of fuse or other supplies." Even if the British did not attack, he could barely hold Quebec, for his garrison had very little to eat, only seven ounces of peas a day. "If they had pushed on," he recalled, "it would have been very hard for us to resist them because of the wretched condition that we were in." Champlain later commented, "All of this shows that on such occasions it is a good thing to put on a bold appearance."[25]

David Kirke knew much about Champlain's condition, but he was an entrepreneur, more interested in profit than glory. Champlain's Fort St. Louis on the heights above Quebec was a formidable position. Further, this determined Frenchman believed deeply in a cause, and he did not make his choices by a calculation of profit and loss, which to a businessman made him dangerously unpredictable. The Kirkes had already realized a large return by the plunder of ships and supplies, and they had seized many valuable cargoes of furs and fish. He ordered his men to burn the French barques that were too small to sail across the ocean. Then the Kirkes weighed anchor and sailed down the river, with the intention of returning the next year.[26]

While these events were happening up the river, the newly arrived convoy of French ships lay at anchor downstream. The company's admiral, Roquemont de Brison, appears to have called a council. He knew that a strong British force was upstream at Tadoussac, but he was also aware that the French settlers at Quebec were in urgent need of supplies.

Roquement and his officers made a brave but brainless decision. They decided to sail upriver to Quebec under cover of fog, hoping that the British ships would not see them. If need be, they would fight their way through, a foolish choice for a commodore in command of four armed merchantmen with women and children on board. He did not know the river, and a much more powerful British force was blocking the way. It was a desperate decision, but they made it with courage, advancing, as Sagard wrote, "*entre la crainte et l'espérance*; between fear and hope." They also sent a small shallop ahead, with ten men under the command of junior officer Thierry Desdames. His orders were to discover if Quebec was still in French hands.[27]

The French and British vessels got underway at about the same time, the French sailing upstream from Gaspé with the four large merchantmen, and the English coming down from Tadoussac with their five or six large ships, plus the smaller French pinnace that they had captured. The British vessels were armed as men-of-war, with larger crews, bigger batteries, and heavier weight of metal. The two fleets sighted each other on July 17, in the St. Lawrence River, downstream from the present site of Rimouski. With much luck and more fog on the river, the French might have succeeded in getting through, for the great river was more than thirty miles wide at that point. But the English were alert and they discovered the French with great "diligence," as their enemies observed.[28]

The English ships were upstream and had the advantage of the current, the riverine equivalent of the weather gage, which in the days of sail brought an important advantage in control. The prevailing wind was in their favor as well, blowing from the west behind their backs, and the French were unable to maneuver and slow to close the distance.[29] Aboard the English flagship, David Kirke and the French Huguenot pilot, Captain Michel, decided to remain at extreme range, beyond the reach of the French guns, and "batter them with the cannon," in which they had the advantage.[30]

The English ships anchored fore and aft to maintain their position in the current, brought their broadsides to bear on the French fleet, and opened fire. Richelieu's admiral put his ships in a position where they were within reach of the enemy's guns, but the English were out of range. The French commander remained in that position for fourteen or fifteen hours. By one count more than twelve hundred shots were fired by both sides, and the heavier English guns began to strike home. The French took casualties, including Admiral Roquemont himself. There were no reports of British losses—evidence that the battle was indeed fought beyond the range of most French guns.[31]

The French resisted stubbornly in this very one-sided engagement, but after fifteen hours they ran low on ammunition. In desperation they fired whatever they could find, even the weights on their lead lines. Then, one by one, their guns fell silent. Unable to continue the fight against an enemy who had the advantage of strength, numbers and position, the French surrendered. All major ships of the Hundred Associates and their long-awaited cargo were lost, and the four hundred souls aboard were taken prisoner.

The British acted with humanity. They promised to protect the virtue of the women and girls, agreed to treat the priests with respect, and received the officers with honor. Also, they provided shipping to carry the passengers and crew home to France—all but the leaders, who were held for ransom by the Kirkes, always looking for a chance to turn a profit.[32]

One little French barque got away. Later Champlain was told by Indians of what he called the Canadien nation that "a small French vessel coming up while it was going on, and not wishing to take part in it, made its escape, partly by rowing and partly by sailing; and it was learned that it was the vessel of the Jesuit father Noyrot, who had separated a good while before from the sieur de Roquement." Champlain observed that "they could easily have run up to Quebec to help us; as it was, they returned to France."[33]

After the battle, the Kirkes spent ten days at Gaspé refitting their ships. They had failed to take Quebec, but they succeeded in their other purposes and realized a very large profit on their investment in war. Altogether they captured eighteen vessels in the coastal waters of New France and burned another dozen that they were unable to carry away. They had spared two ships "to take the French families, crews, women and children back to France. The largest colonizing effort by the Hundred Associates had ended in a complete loss.[34]

The Kirkes returned in triumph to England with many large prizes and much plunder, including 138 cannon, large quantities of supplies, and trade goods. It was a highly successful business venture. The choices they made throughout the expedition, especially the choice to turn away from Quebec and attack the French ships down the river, had the effect of minimizing losses and maximizing profits, at considerable cost to the imperial purposes of England.[35] Even so, David Kirke would be knighted by Charles I, and his coat of arms was augmented by a canton with the arms of French commander Claude de Roquement—the lion "couchant and collared with a chain, prostrating himself to the mercy of his vanquisher." In 2003 archaeologists in Newfoundland discovered a gold seal bearing Kirke's new arms and the emblem of a flaming heart.[36]

While the French and the English squadrons were meeting in battle, the small French shallop got past the enemy force, and hugged the riverbank in a patch of fog. The crew dragged the boat ashore until the British were gone, then continued upstream to Quebec.

The arms of David Kirke, British conqueror of Quebec. In 2003 archaeologists in Newfoundland found three very small enameled gold seals. Charles I added a rectangle to them, with the arms of French Admiral de Rocquement, whose fleet Kirke captured in battle on the St. Lawrence River in 1628.

They found the French commandant in a towering rage. Champlain was under heavy strain. He furiously upbraided the young captain of the shallop, and told him he should have sailed downriver to find out who won the battle. The officer replied that he had no orders to do so. Champlain complained that the arrival of eleven men only increased the number of mouths to feed from their dwindling supply of peas. It was a rare moment when Champlain lost control of himself, and treated a junior officer with cruelty and injustice. But he recovered his self-discipline and wrote, "There was no remedy for it; I gave them the same ration as everyone else."[37]

What followed was a year of agony for Champlain and the habitants of Quebec. Approximately seventy-three people had been living there in the winter of 1627–28. About fifty-six lived in the habitation, of whom eighteen were laborers. Another six lived at the Hébert-Couillard farm, three with the Récollets, and eight in the Jesuit compound at St. Charles. In the summer another six or eight had returned from the farm on Cap Tourmente, and eleven arrived in the shallop that so displeased Champlain. With various interpreters, traders, waifs, and strays, the population of Quebec was probably between ninety and a hundred souls in the winter of 1628–29.[38]

Champlain had little food for them. They still had a supply of dried peas and beans, enough for a ration of seven ounces a day, "and so we had to go through a very wretched time." Even in the previous summer, Champlain wrote, "we were eating our peas very sparingly, which diminished our strength greatly, most of our men becoming feeble and sickly."[39] He put the entire colony on short rations and took the smallest share for himself. The opposite had been done in other starving colonies. At Virginia in its first terrible year, the leaders took the lion's share, and most survived the winter. Colonists of lower rank at Jamestown received much less, and most of them died. In Quebec, Champlain wrote, the smallest share went to "those who were with me in the fort, we being the worst provided of all in every respect."[40]

Champlain looked for other ways of stretching the rations by grinding peas into meal. He tried it first with wooden mortars, but it was slow work. He asked the artisans if they could make a millstone. They found suitable materials, shaped the stones, and set them up. "The necessity we were in," Champlain wrote, "thus caused us to devise what in the previous twenty years had been considered impossible. The mill was finished with diligence, and each man brought his week's allowance of peas . . . from which he got good pease-meal, which made our soup stronger, and did us much good, and put us again in a little better condition than before."[41]

In the fall came the season of eel fishing, "which helped us considerably,"

Champlain wrote. The French had still not mastered the art of eeling, which often was done in the dark, by two Indians in a canoe—one holding a torch to attract the eels, and the other spearing them with a long weapon much like a harpoon, or a whaler's lance. The Montagnais were "skillful fishers" of eels, but they guarded the secrets of their fishing. Champlain wrote that they "gave us few and sold them very dear, our men giving their coats and other possessions for fish. We bought 1200 with goods from the storehouse, giving new beaver-skins in exchange . . . ten eels for one beaver. . . . These were distributed to all, but it did not amount to much."[42]

When the season of winter hunting arrived, some of the Indians helped them, in particular the Montagnais captain Chomina, who supported his friend Champlain. Other Indians brought in "a few moose, although only a small number for so many persons." Champlain sent out French hunters, who killed a very large moose but kept most of it themselves, "devouring it like ravenous wolves." Champlain reproached them for their selfishness and did not let them go hunting again.[43]

In the cold months of 1628–29, the people of Quebec were growing weak with hunger. On top of everything else, the winter was long and hard. The habitants had to bear the heavy labor of cutting firewood and hauling it more than a mile. It made for "fatiguing work all the winter," but they stayed warm through the coldest part of the year, and scurvy did not return.[44]

By the spring their meager supply of vegetables was almost depleted, and no word had reached the starving settlement from France. Champlain wrote of "children crying with hunger." The habitants lacked bread, wine, salt, butter—and hope. They had dry provisions for only a month, and Champlain was deeply worried. "All this caused me great anxiety," he wrote.[45]

They had to live by hunting and gathering. Champlain urged his companions to devote themselves to fishing. He wrote that "the others did their best to catch fish, but owing to the lack of nets, lines, and hooks, we could not do much." He added, "Powder for hunting was so precious that I preferred to suffer rather than use what little we had, which was between thirty and forty pounds, and that of very poor quality.[46] Our only recourse, though a miserable one, was to go in search of herbs and roots," Champlain recalled. "While awaiting the harvest we went every day to look for roots for food, which was very fatiguing." They searched the forest for anything that could sustain life. "We had to go six and seven leagues to get them at a cost of great trouble and patience, and without finding enough to live on." Still, they harvested plants and roots such as solomon's seal, clintonia borealis, and bulbs of wild lilies.[47]

Starvation proved a great stimulus to agriculture in Quebec. They had enough seeds to sow crops both at the Hébert farm and the Jesuit garden. By the spring of 1629, many fields were cultivated around the settlement. The Jesuits tilled their own fields, but Champlain wrote that they "had only enough cleared land in seed to support themselves and their servants, to the number of twelve." Even so, they gave Indian corn and turnips to the habitants, and shared enough food to sustain the children in the settlement.[48] The Récollet fathers had more land in crops, and they were only four in number. Champlain wrote, "They promised us that if they had more from their four or five arpents of land sown with several sorts of grain, vegetables, roots and garden herbs, they would give us some." There were several small Montagnais farms near the settlement. One of them was tilled by the Indian convert La Nasse, who had a cabin near the Jesuits, and he helped too.[49]

The Hébert-Couillard farm was also beginning to become productive. The widow Hébert and her son-in-law "had between six and seven acres sown," mostly in "peas and other grains." They produced enough to meet their own needs and supply a small surplus of seven barrels of peas and barley for the settlement. In the summer, they also contributed each week a small basin of barley, peas, and Indian corn, "about nine ounces and a half of weight, which was a very small quantity among so many persons." It was mixed into a "potage of farina," half peas, half barley, mixed with roots that they found in the woods, and flavored with forest herbs, "which helped a little." Even on the edge of starvation, these French habitants gave some attention to gastronomy. The Héberts held back part of the produce to feed their family and Champlain looked the other way. He wrote, "I pretended not to see what was going on, though I was enduring considerable privation."[50]

The French habitants had garden plots as well. Champlain was very active in promoting them, and it is interesting to see how he went about it. In this, as in other realms, he tried to encourage individual enterprise, and understood that confiscation and forced labor would be counterproductive. He encouraged people throughout the colony to raise crops for themselves, and asked them to contribute their surplus to others. In this period of adversity he was developing an agricultural base for Quebec, by an open method of mixed enterprise, which was more successful than the conscription and collective labor that prevailed in other colonies. It was also more effective than laissez-faire.[51]

In this desperate moment, the Indians supported the French in a very substantial way. Champlain had asked the Huron to take in twenty Frenchmen "so as to lighten our burden." They agreed, and fed them through the winter and the spring of 1628–29.[52] The Huron also gave Father Brébeuf fifty pounds of cornmeal for the colony. The Récollet fathers added two sacks of corn meal from the Huron, and Pont-Gravé traded for another.[53] In midsummer, the Huron sent the Frenchmen back to Quebec. On July 17, 1629, Champlain wrote, "Our men from the Huron country came in twelve canoes."[54]

There was no food for them in the settlement. Champlain turned to another Indian nation and sent them "to the settlement of the Abenaki to live on their Indian corn till spring." He dispatched others to the Etchemin in the south, and a few to the nation he called the Canadien in Gaspésie. On June 15, Thierry Desdames took the shallop downriver to Gaspé, met Juan Chou, a captain of the Canadien Indians, who "did their best to welcome them" and promised that "in case our ships did not arrive, we would want nothing that their hunting could provide." Chou also gave the French a barrel and a half of salt, and offered to take "twenty of our companions and distribute them among his own people to spend the winter, where they would be secure against hunger, at a cost of two beaver skins per person." Champlain wrote that the Canadien strongly supported the French, and "had a great aversion to our enemies."[55]

The Montagnais were divided. Their leader Choumina and his brother tried to help. Champlain wrote that Choumina "offered to go to the coast of the Etchemins where the English live, to barter for powder. Choumina also asked that a Frenchman who lived two day's journey inland from that coast to be given to him [as a companion], which request was granted in order to try every possible expedient for holding our ground." He started July 8, left the great river, and went some distance into the Etchemin country, but "found the water so low that they were obliged to return."[56]

Champlain charged these French emissaries with another assignment. Even in deep adversity, he continued to gather knowledge about the new world. He could not leave the settlement with so many uncertainties and hardships there. Instead, he sent interpreters in many directions to gather information on the countryside, study the rivers and waterways, and get to know the "peoples and nations inhabiting those regions, and their modes of life."[57]

While Champlain was struggling with these problems in the late spring of 1629, the English returned.[58] The Kirke brothers, all five of them this time, arrived at Gaspé on June 15, 1629. Their attack in 1628 had whetted the appetites of British entrepreneurs. The wealth of the fur trade and fisheries was vastly attractive, and the small settlements of New France seemed ripe for the plucking. To that end, William Alexander and a group of Scottish investors had joined the Kirkes to form the Company of Adventurers to Canada, also called the English and Scottish Company. In February of 1629, Charles I gave them a monopoly of the fur trade in the St. Lawrence Valley and adjacent places. They also received a commission to destroy all French settlements.[59]

This time they were stronger than before. Two fleets came to North America. Alexander led one to Acadia; the other under David Kirke sailed to the St. Lawrence. They intercepted the small French vessel that Champlain had sent in search of aid. The Kirkes learned in detail about the condition of Quebec, and its shortage of food and ammunition. There could be no bluff this time.

On the morning of July 19, 1629, Champlain's servant went out of the fort to gather a breakfast of roots and berries. At about ten o'clock he came running back and said that English vessels were behind Point Lévis, a league away from the settlement. Champlain mustered his men and "put in order the little we had to prevent a surprise at the fort and the habitation." The Jesuits and Récollets "came as fast as they could on hearing the news."

Champlain convened a council of "those I judged proper to advise as to what we should do in this extremity." After a short discussion, "it was agreed that considering that we were powerless, without provisions, powder or matches, and destitute of help, it was impossible to hold out, and that we must therefore seek the most advantageous terms that we were able to get."[60]

When the tide came in, the English crossed to Quebec and sent a boat with a white flag to seek a parley. Champlain hoisted a flag on the fort to let them know that they could approach. An English gentleman with impeccable manners came ashore and handed Champlain a letter from the Kirke brothers—Louis Kirke who had come to take command of the fort, and Captain Thomas Kirke, his brother and "vice admiral" on the river. Their letter was drafted with exquisite courtesy. It began by reminding Champlain of his correspondence the year before, and reported that David Kirke "has instructed us to assure you of his friendship, as we assure you of ours." They added with an air of regret that they knew well the "extreme destitution in which you are with respect to everything." The Kirkes invited Champlain to "place the fort and habitation in our hands," and assured him of "the best treatment for yourself and your people, and also of as honorable and reasonable a settlement as you could desire." There was no threat, no abuse, no expression of hostility or contempt.[61]

Champlain responded with the same courtesy. "Gentlemen," he wrote, circumstances "have put it out of our power to prevent the carrying out of your design," but he added "Your claims . . . will only be realized now on condition

Champlain's surrender of Quebec to Louis Kirke, July 19, 1629. In the foreground is a British mercenary with a boarding pike. An elderly but very fit Champlain is immaculate in black velvet, white lace, slashed sleeves, and a scarlet sash. The habitants salute their defiant leader, who promised to recover the colony.

of your carrying into effect the offer you made to us, of terms which we will communicate very shortly." In the meantime, he insisted that the English should not come ashore "until everything has been resolved between us, which will be for tomorrow." [62]

Champlain did not wait for terms to be offered. He drafted them himself.

First on his list was that Kirke should produce his commission as proof that their campaign was an act of legitimate warfare. He also asked that a ship be assigned to take all the people of Quebec (nearly a hundred persons) back to their country, including the Jesuits and Récollets, and two of the native Montagnais girls who "were given to me two years ago." Third, he asked that the French "be allowed to leave with weapons and baggage and other articles of every kind, and that in exchange for furs a sufficiency of provisions be given to us; and no violence towards anyone."[63]

The Kirkes granted most of Champlain's demands. They promised to produce their Royal commission in Tadoussac, offered passage to England and then to France, and allowed the officers to keep their arms, clothes, and furs. Others were given their clothing and one beaver pelt; but the fathers were allowed only their "cassocks and their books." Only one of Champlain's requests was refused, but it was one that he cared deeply about. He was denied permission to take his adopted Indian children to France.[64]

Champlain and his officers discussed the terms and decided to accept them as "the best to be done in these extremities." On July 20, the English sailed up to Quebec in three vessels, a flyboat and two pinnaces, with twenty-two guns and 150 men. Champlain went aboard the flyboat and talked with Louis Kirke about his Indian girls. Champlain made clear that his relationship with them was paternal and that the girls wanted very much to go to France. "I managed to dispel the doubts that Captain Louis [Kirke] had entertained on the subject, so that he granted me permission to take them away, at which the girls greatly rejoiced."[65]

Then Louis Kirke came ashore with his men, and in Champlain's words "acquitted himself of the duty like a man of character." He insisted that Champlain should retain his quarters, and sent English guards to protect the chapel, the Jesuits, and the Récollets. Champlain requested that the fathers be allowed to say a mass, and Kirke agreed. Champlain asked for an inventory of all that was in the fort and the habitation, and Kirke agreed once again. The inventory survives and gives us a clue to the armament of Quebec, which made it a place of considerable strength, but with only forty pounds of powder, not enough to stand a siege. Kirke offered his provisions to the hungry people of Quebec.[66]

Four Frenchmen joined the Kirkes, and their conduct was very different. Le Baillif, a former clerk of the Company de Caëns who had been dismissed for bad conduct, turned his coat and joined the British. Champlain wrote that he was "without either faith or morals, though he calls himself a Catholic. . . . We had every kind of courtesy from the English, but from this wretch only injury."[67] Another turncoat was Pierre Raye, a wagon maker of Paris and "one of the most perfidious traitors and scoundrels of the lot." And two interpreters, Étienne Brûlé and Nicolas Marsolet, also went to work for the British, much to Champlain's fury.[68]

The next day Louis Kirke ordered his drummers to beat assembly for his men. He went to the fort and hoisted the flag of England. The scarlet cross of St. George on its white field caught the wind on the river and flew above the ramparts of Quebec. The English fired salutes from the ships in the river and from the ramparts about the town.[69]

Some of the French habitants did not want to leave Quebec. The Héberts and the Couillards, who had land, wished to stay in America, even under English rule. Champlain wrote: "Louis Kirke was courteous, and, although the son of a Scot who had married in Dieppe, he was French in disposition and always had a liking for the French nation. He wished as much as possible to help the French families and others from France to remain, liking their conversation and finding their manners "more agreeable than those of the English, to whom his nature seemed averse."[70]

Kirke promised the French habitants that they could keep their land and houses and remain in them, and would be "as free to do so as they had been under the French." He promised that they could trade with the Indians, and if they were not happy they could return to France.[71] "They asked my advice," Champlain wrote. He told them that he hoped that the French would resume possession "through the grace of God," and advised them to stay for a year. They responded that they would do as he suggested. With that decision a strong French presence continued in Quebec, even as the English took control.[72]

Champlain was treated with courtesy by Louis Kirke, and he was allowed to live undisturbed in his quarters at the fort. But it was an agony for him to watch the English conquest of Canada.[73] Finally he could bear it no longer, and he asked Louis Kirke: "Let me go down to [Tadoussac], and await there the departure of the vessels, passing my time with the General [David Kirke] who was there." It was agreed. Champlain's personal belongings were put aboard the English flyboat.[74]

In Tadoussac, Champlain found that the Kirkes were present in great strength, far beyond the resources that the French had been able to muster in America. In addition to the three small vessels that had come up the river to Quebec, the Kirkes had five large ships of 300 or 400 tons, "very well equipped with cannon, powder, balls and devices for throwing fire," and about six hundred men.[75]

Thomas Kirke turned him over to David Kirke, who gave the French commander "a very kind reception." They reviewed the surrender that had been negotiated in Quebec. There was trouble on only one point. To Champlain's surprise he was again refused permission to take his Indian wards to France. One of them, Faith, had chosen to stay with her people in America and that had been arranged. The other two, Hope and Charity, wanted very much to visit France. But Nicolas Marsolet tried to stop them. He wanted to have the girls for himself and told David Kirke that the Montagnais people did not wish them to leave for France. Champlain and the girls themselves called Marsolet a liar.

It came to a head when the Kirkes invited the British captains, Champlain, Marsolet, and the girls all to dine at the same table. The girls were so unhappy that they refused to eat or drink. Hope attacked Marsolet, calling him a traitor, and accused him of trying to seduce her. She turned toward him and said, "If you come near me again, I shall plunge a knife into your breast, though I should die for it a moment after." Charity joined in and said to Marsolet, "If I had your heart in my hands, I should eat it more readily and with greater spirit than I should eat any of the meats on that table."

David Kirke did not know whom to believe, and was afraid of displeasing the Montagnais. He ordered the Indian girls to remain in America, despite their tears and pleading. They attacked Marsolet with the "courage of Amazons" and said that they would follow Champlain to France if they had to do it in a canoe. But David Kirke was adamant, and the girls were forbidden to go.[76]

In other respects Champlain was treated very well. He was careful never to aid his British captors in any way, or to recognize the legitimacy of their conquest. But in personal terms he and David Kirke got along. In one amazing scene, the captive and captor went hunting together. "We passed the time with the General hunting," Champlain wrote, "game in that season being abundant and consisting principally of larks, plovers, curlews and sandpipers, of which more than twenty thousand were killed." They were shooting for the pot, to feed the many French captives and British seamen for whom they were responsible. But these two gentlemen of the old regime were also shooting for pleasure.[77] After the hunt, they went fishing together with the Indians, "for salmon and trout which they brought us in very good quantity, and for smelts, which were caught in nets, and other fish, all very excellent."[78]

In the course of their conversations, Champlain told the "general" of some news from France. "I informed him that Émery de Caën had assured me positively that peace had been made, having learned it from persons worthy of credit as he was leaving La Rochelle." If true, the Kirkes' conquest of Quebec was unlawful. David Kirke was contemptuous of this report. "Has he the articles?" he insisted.

"No," Champlain replied.

"Then," said Kirke, "it is only an idle rumor."[79] But Champlain had put David Kirke on notice. If these persistent reports of peace were true, the conquest of New France was an illegal act. It could not stand, and Champlain was determined to undo it.

20.

NEW FRANCE REGAINED
Champlain's Greatest Test, 1629–32

> From the time the English took possession of Quebec, the days seemed
> like months to me.
>
> —Samuel de Champlain, *Voyages*, 1632[1]

I N THE FALL OF 1629 the Kirkes prepared to sail home to Britain. David
Kirke ordered his ships to be careened. In the tight little harbor at Tadoussac, their bottoms were cleaned, tarred, and tallowed. With some prod-
ding from Champlain, he sent more supplies to Quebec, sufficient to see the
habitants through a long winter. The river barque also carried Champlain's two
Indian girls, Hope and Charity, back to their Montagnais people. Champlain's
brother-in-law, Eustache Boullé, gave them rosaries. Champlain told them
that the French would be back, and made arrangements for them to be taken
into the Hébert household, if they wished. On September 14, 1629, Champlain watched as Guillaume Couillard and the girls sailed up the river to Quebec. It was a moment of sad parting.[2]

On the same day, the Kirkes weighed anchor at Tadoussac and sailed down
the St. Lawrence River, homeward bound for England. Champlain noticed
that they were in a state of "considerable apprehension." Indians had reported
a French fleet of "ten well-armed vessels" on the coast near Gaspé. David
Kirke insisted that he was "not afraid of them in the least," but Champlain observed that he steered very close to the coast of Anticosti Island, fourteen
leagues north of Gaspé, "so as not to be noticed," and so he got safely to sea.[3]

They were leaving much later in the season than Champlain's normal practice. Just off the American coast they ran into autumn storms. Champlain
wrote, "We were kept back by very bad weather accompanied with fogs till we
reached the Grand Banks." Sickness spread through the crowded British ships.
"On the way across," he noted, "eleven of Kirke's men died of dysentery."[4]

On October 16, 1629, the Kirkes crossed soundings on the coast of England, and ran into the west-country port of Plymouth. Champlain immediately asked for news and was told that the war was over. More than that,

England and France had signed a peace treaty six months earlier, in the town of Suze (Susa to the English). By its terms, all conquests or seizures made after the peace had to be returned. The effective date of the treaty was April 24, 1629, nearly three months before the fall of Quebec in July.

Champlain was delighted. David Kirke was in a fury, "greatly angered by the news." He had seized twenty-one fishing vessels, some of them after several people had told him the war was over, thereby making him liable for damages. He was still holding French leaders and priests for ransom. Kirke's actions had been outside the law, and even against it.[5]

David Kirke promptly left Plymouth for Dover, the English port closest to France. He released his captives and made arrangements to send them home as quickly as possible. It was not an act of kindness. Kirke wanted to get these troublesome Frenchmen out of the country before proceedings could be brought against him in an English court. Most of them seemed happy to go home, with one exception. Champlain refused to leave England until he could determine the status of New France. He was humiliated by its loss and outraged by the way it had happened. Under the terms of the Treaty of Susa, which had the force of law in both countries, Quebec rightfully belonged to France, and England was required to return it. But Champlain knew that it was one thing to have a title, and another to gain possession.[6]

Others in his position would have sailed home to France and put the problem in the laps of Cardinal Richelieu and the king, but that was not Champlain's way. Having lost Quebec, he felt a personal responsibility to get it back again. Acting on his own initiative, he went to work in Dover, documenting what had happened. First he compiled a record of the Kirkes' acts. He probably consulted with his fellow prisoners and collected testimony before they left England. Then he dispatched letters and documents in several directions. One set went to France, addressed to M. de Lauson, Superintendent of Affairs in New France under the Company of the Hundred Associates. Champlain enclosed "an account of all that had taken place" and asked that copies be forwarded to Cardinal Richelieu and the king, with an appeal that Louis XIII might send letters to the French ambassador in London, "recommending this matter to his special attention."[7]

Then, while his fellow travelers were en route from Dover to France, Champlain headed in the opposite direction. He made his way to London by sea, sailing from Dover to the River Thames, then to Gravesend and the London docks, where he arrived on October 29. The next day he went to see the French ambassador, the marquis de Châteauneuf, a splendid character who embodied the virtues of the Old Regime. Even the English highly respected him. The marquis received Champlain with grace and exquisite courtesy. Champlain told him the whole story and gave him another set of his documents. Later he recalled: "I related all the reasons for our voyage, and how we had been seized two [actually three] months after the peace, namely on the 20th of July, through lack of provisions, munitions of war, and assistance. After having endured many privations for a year and a half, we had to go into the woods to dig roots to sustain life; although I kept only sixteen persons at the fort and habitation, the greater part of my companions having been sent to live with the Indians, so as to avoid severe famine." [8]

Champlain spoke not only of Quebec but also of Acadia and other parts of New France that English freebooters had occupied while the Kirkes were in the St. Lawrence. Champlain had put his cartographic skill to work and he presented a detailed map of the entire area, mainly "to show to the English the discoveries that we had made and the possession we had taken in that country of New France before the English, who had only followed in our tracks." His map showed the full extent of British seizures at Quebec, Cap Tourmente, Tadoussac, Gaspé, Cape Breton, Miscou, Acadia, and the small French trading post at Pentagoet, now the town of Castine in Maine.[9] Champlain also documented the damage that had been done to French trade and fisheries, and gave the ambassador copies of the surrender of Quebec. He made very clear that these events had happened after the end of the war, and even after reports of the peace had reached America.[10]

Champlain added a complaint about another issue that offended him in a personal way. The English had attempted to abolish the place names that the French had given to the American land. With great indignation, he wrote that the English had "within two or three years, imposed on parts of La Nouvelle France such names as New England and New Scotland." This insult infuriated Champlain more than any material injury that les Anglais and les Écossais had done him. "They took this notion into their heads very late in the day," he wrote. "They ought to act reasonably and not change names already given." It was a point of honor among cartographers.[11]

The French ambassador listened to Champlain with close attention and acted quickly. "Having heard my story," Champlain wrote, "the ambassador resolved to speak of it with the king [of England]." He obtained an audience and presented some of Champlain's original documents. One of them has been found in British archives. King Charles I received the ambassador with respect and even with sympathy. To Champlain's surprise he accepted full responsibility for what had happened in New France, and agreed that the colony rightfully belonged to Louis XIII. According to the marquis de Châteauneuf, the English king "gave all good hope that the place would be restored to us, together with all the furs and merchandise that he had ordered to be taken from us." Champlain had high praise for the ambassador and wrote that "he applied himself to the business in a very praiseworthy manner, hoping to get the Council to issue an order for the restitution of the colony and the property seized there." [12]

Champlain expected that the matter would be settled quickly and waited in London for instructions from his superiors in France. But nothing happened. Weeks passed without a word from Louis XIII, or Richelieu, or any French minister in Paris. Champlain was baffled, mainly because he appears not to have known about another major problem that stood in the way of a solution. Charles I had a major grievance of his own against France. When he married Louis XIII's sister Henrietta Maria, he had been promised a dowry of 2,400,000 livres. Six years later, only half of it had been paid, and Charles desperately needed the money. Unknown to Champlain, he had promised secretly to return New France on one condition—full payment of the dowry. [13]

In Paris the king and his ministers were slow to respond for one simple reason. They did not have the money. More weeks went by. Champlain remained in London at the ambassador's request, with growing irritation. He wrote, "I was nearly five weeks in close touch with the ambassador, awaiting news from France all the time, marking how little diligence they showed in sending anyone over, or in advising me of what they wanted to be done." [14]

The month of November neared its end, and the English weather was growing cold and gray. The days dragged on and Champlain grew weary of waiting in London with no word from his own government. Finally, in the last week of the month, he decided to head for France and seek out the king and Richelieu. Champlain was an old hand at court politics. Before he left London he was careful to ask the marquis de Châteauneuf for permission to depart. "I asked the ambassador whether he any longer wanted my services, because I wanted to return to France," Champlain noted. "He granted me permission, gave me a letter to my Lord the Cardinal and assured me that the King of England and his council had promised to restore the place [New France]." [15]

Champlain tells us that he left London for France on November 30, 1629. It was a difficult trip, with ill winds in the English Channel and misadventures on the road. [16] Champlain made his way to his home in Paris, almost as a stranger. He had been gone for more than three years and he was returning in deep adversity. The fall of Quebec was the worst defeat of his career. He was out of a job and short of money. Just when it seemed that nothing more could go wrong, he suffered another heavy blow. His marriage came apart. Hélène Boullé, his beautiful young wife, told her husband that she no longer wished to live with him. Divorce was out of the question in Catholic France. She requested her husband's permission to enter a convent. He appears to have asked her to stay with him. From what little we know they may have agreed to live separately in the same house. It must have been an agony for both of them. Hélène never traveled with Champlain again, and she did not return to Canada. In Quebec she was sorely missed by Indians and Europeans alike, but New France was not for her. She turned away from her husband and retreated into a life of religious devotion for the rest of her years.

We shall never know the full story of this marriage, beyond the fact of its troubled start, happier middle years, and final failure. These two extraordinary people were both attractive to others who knew them, yet they were unable to find happiness with one another. This was perhaps one more part of what Champlain meant when he wrote in 1632, "From the time the English took possession of Quebec, the days seemed like months to me." [17]

Somehow Champlain found the resources to go on. His Christian faith was a source of strength to him. So also was his grand design. Even in his suffering, Champlain resolved to keep striving for his dream.[18] In Paris he took up the cause of New France once more, and moved straight to the heart of the problem. "I went to pay my respects to his Majesty, my Lord Cardinal, and Messieurs the Associates," he wrote. The loss of Quebec was not held against him, and he was able to get access to the king. As he had done so often in the past, he began to build a new base for his project. In the winter of 1629–30, he cultivated yet another circle of friends, and soon found supporters who were close to Louis XIII. They were younger men, a generation removed from the American circle who had helped him before but now were gone from the scene. Like the older group, they had powerful friends at court. One of them was André Daniel, a physician highly connected in Paris, with an active interest in New France. He was a major investor and a leader of the Hundred Associates, with many personal ties to America. His brother Captain Charles Daniel had made many voyages to the new world, and Father Antoine Daniel was a Jesuit missionary who would later be martyred in New France.[19]

With the support of these men and others like them, Champlain was able to gain the ear of the king and the attention of Cardinal Richelieu. "I gave full particulars of my voyage," he wrote, "and explained what was necessary for them to do with reference to matters in England, and also in regard to other things for the benefit and advantage of New France." [20] He urged them to hasten the restitution of New France before it was lost forever. They responded positively. "Some time after my arrival at Paris," Champlain recalled, "they despatched the sieur [André] Daniel to London, to see the French ambassador, with letters from his Majesty calling upon the King of England to restore the fort and habitation of Quebec, and other ports and harbors which he had seized on the coasts of Acadia, after peace had been made." [21]

Daniel carried five memoranda that he and Champlain had prepared together, and they had some success, particularly in regard to Quebec. Charles I and his council met, and "made an order that the fort and habitation should be given back into the hands of His Majesty [Louis XIII], or those empowered by him." But Champlain was quick to note what others had missed: the English response "made no mention of the coasts of Acadia." He informed the French ambassador of the omission, and the marquis asked Louis XIII if "his Majesty would be satisfied with the offer." Acadia was added to the list. [22]

Champlain also met with the directors of the Company of the Hundred Associates, who had little capital left and very large debts. They petitioned Louis XIII "to let them have six of his ships with four pataches, which they would fit out to go to the great river St. Lawrence, to resume possession of the fort and habitation of Quebec." Champlain wrote that the fleet was "equipped and fitted out with all that was necessary." It looked very promising. [23]

Then suddenly everything stopped again. The king and Richelieu turned their attention to another pressing problem: a war in Italy. Completely absorbed by events in Europe and chronically short of money, they put aside the problem of New France yet again. Champlain wrote, "His Majesty, who had the wars in Italy on his hands, was unable to return an answer to the King of England, and monsieur the Ambassador was kept waiting for His Majesty's dispatch." [24]

Champlain was filled with frustration about the loss of New France and gave vent to his feelings in documents that found their way into print. They could not have made pleasant reading at court. Champlain repeated his account of the English seizures in New France and asked: "What is the explanation of their having taking possession of our places so easily? It is because the King has not, up to the present, attached importance to these matters; but the just complaints made to him are now producing a resolve on his part to recover the territory encroached upon by the English, and the thing will be done whenever, and as often as, His Majesty may desire." [25]

It was dangerous to speak such words in the era of Louis XIII, and still more so to write them. Champlain was on the brink of lèse majesté, for which the penalties were severe. But he got away with it, perhaps because the king and his chief minister were too busy to notice.

Champlain also turned to another problem. The Hundred Associates were almost at the end of their resources. They had spent 270,000 livres and only 30,000 remained. The directors somehow borrowed another 40,000 livres, and in 1630 they outfitted a fleet to take colonists to New France. The king ordered the chevalier de Montigny and five captains to recover Quebec, and to return Champlain as commandant.[26]

According to Champlain, "the English took alarm at the armament of these vessels." Louis XIII gave them satisfaction "by dealing with the matter in a friendly way." The king of England again promised to restore what had been taken after the peace. The king of France countermanded his own orders. Neither the French warships nor the transports were permitted to sail for America. The voyage was canceled. It was yet another huge loss for the company, its third major failure in a row.[27]

Champlain renewed his appeals to Louis XIII in a powerful submission that amplified his earlier arguments. He wrote of the riches and the grandeur of the land, the opportunity for commerce and wealth, the possibility of a northern route to China. He included the old spiritual imperative of "infinite numbers of natives; *nombre infiny de peuples sauvages* who might be brought to Christ." Champlain added new arguments for French colonization, and a new imperative for French settlers to cultivate the land, so that they could feed themselves without needing supplies from home. Champlain's arguments prevailed. Louis XIII was persuaded to resume discussions with Charles I and to do something about the dowry.

Champlain's years in France from 1629 to 1632 were in some ways the most productive of his life, despite his many troubles. He played a major role in keeping the issue of New France alive, urging the king, the cardinal, and the Royal Council to work for its recovery. He collaborated closely with the directors of the Hundred Associates and helped reorganize it into a network of subsidiary companies. He formed new and very strong alliances with the next generation of young leaders such as the Daniel family.

For Champlain himself, these years were full of achievement in other ways as well. He wrote his biggest and most important book, called *Voyages de la Nouvelle France*, and published it in 1632. In modern reprint editions it fills two or three volumes. It reached an expanding public with some success, and Champlain's publisher, Claude Collet, brought out a second edition.

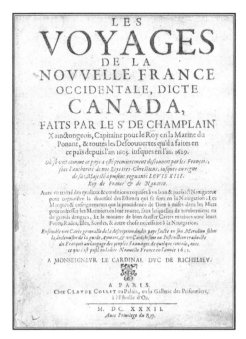

LES
VOYAGES
DE LA
NOVVELLE FRANCE
OCCIDENTALE, DICTE
CANADA,
FAITS PAR LE S⁰ DE CHAMPLAIN
Xainctongeois, Capitaine pour le Roy en la Marine du
Ponant, & toutes les Descouuertes qu'il a faites en
ce païs depuis l'an 1603. iusques en l'an 1629.

Champlain's Voyages de la Nouvelle France Occidentale, dicte Canada *(1632), his fourth and largest book, was dedicated to Cardinal Richelieu. It was part of a successful campaign to recover New France. Early in 1633, Richelieu appointed Champlain his lieutenant for Quebec and the St. Lawrence, with the utmost reluctance.*

Champlain published the book with one major purpose in mind: to promote his grand design for New France in the court of Louis XIII. The *Voyages* were dedicated to Cardinal Richelieu. Another major goal was to establish the legitimacy of France's claims to North America. It was also a tale of troubles, many of them caused by the lack of strong and stable support from chartered companies, and from the court. This was dangerous ground. Champlain made his case mainly by discussing particular problems in close detail, rather than by general indictments or personal attacks. The *Voyages* documented Champlain's long record of his service, with detailed accounts of all his major voyages from 1603 to 1629, his labors during the reign of Henri IV, the regency of Catherine de Medici, and the reign of Louis XIII. The book was also a promotional tract for North America. It was a work of description, and an argument for the importance of discovery and colonization in New France. Champlain also described the American Indians in great detail. Most of his writing was very sympathetic to them and showed a sustained interest in their culture. He stressed the importance of converting the Indians to Christianity, celebrated their intelligence, and validated the Indians as human beings. Here again, a central part of his vision was an expansive idea of humanity that embraced the people of Europe and America. His book was a sustained appeal for that principle.

Champlain promoted his project for New France through other publications as well. Pieces on his grand design appeared in that magazine of news and opinion, *Le Mercure François*, especially after Richelieu intervened and chose for its editor Father Joseph, the cardinal's éminence grise. Some of these promotional pieces were written by Champlain, and others were submitted anonymously, with his active encouragement.[28]

In 1632, Champlain also published a map of New France which many cartographers recognize as his best. It had a different character and purpose from the work he had done before. Most of his earlier cartography produced charts, intended as aids to navigation, with much information about coasts and harbors, rocks and shoals, depth of water, and other directions for seamen. The great map of 1632 had some of those elements. The Grand Bank and Green Bank and the Banquereaux were clearly indicated in the Atlantic Ocean, with extraordinary precision. The map includes a navigator's scale framed by a pair of dividers, indicators of latitude and longitude, and two examples of a compass rose, each with thirty-two radiating rhumb lines. But in this work Champlain was not thinking primarily of navigation. Coastal features are only approximate here, and less accurate in shape and scale than in his earlier work.

This itinerant map seller, in a ceramic figurine by Johann Joachim Kaendler (circa 1764), suggests the reach of Champlain's cartography to an expanding public. His map of 1632 supported French claims to North America. It had an impact in London and also in Paris, where the major obstacles lay. The map appears on the back endpapers of this volume.

Examples are Cape Cod, Mount Desert Island, the Sainte-Croix River in Maine, Sable Island, and Halifax harbor.

This work was a map rather than a chart, centering more on the land than the sea. It carefully marked places where the French had lived in North America from 1603 to 1629. Settlements were carefully named, accurately placed and marked by the maritime ensign of France. Missions, both Jesuit and Récollet, were also marked by a cross.

The map showed the names that were put on the land by French explorers, mostly by Champlain himself. The entire region of settlement was called by the single name of La Nouvelle France. It is interesting that Champlain no longer used the words Acadie or Norumbega. Gaspé and Cape Breton referred only to points of land, not to regions. The primary object of the map was to display the integrity and unity of New France. That name appeared twice: once on the Gaspé Peninsula, and again in larger letters on the huge regions to the west as far as the Great Lakes. All of this vast territory was claimed for France, and the royal arms of Louis XIII were displayed above it with the lilies of France, the Crown, and the cross of the Order of Malta—symbols of Bourbon sovereignty, French nationality, and the Roman Catholic faith.

Another layer of detail, very dense and carefully done, gave the location of Indian nations. Champlain's legend explained that he was showing the nations of forest-dwelling people—many of whom were unknown to the larger world before he had met them and made alliances.[29] To reinforce this visual display of French claims, Champlain added a very full gazetteer that was published at the same time. This map of 1632 was probably very similar to an earlier one that he made in 1629 and gave to the French ambassador in London, for use in negotiations with British rulers.[30]

Finally, in 1632, Champlain's labor achieved its intended result. After much delay, Louis XIII agreed to pay the balance of Henrietta Maria's dowry with interest: the very large sum of 1.8 million livres. After long negotiation, Charles agreed to restore New France. Both monarchs promised to stop doing what they should not have started to do in the first place. Each also agreed to keep treaty obligations that they had already broken. These terms were ratified by the Treaty of Saint-Germain-en-Laye in 1632.

While the two kings were moving toward a diplomatic solution, the Company of the Hundred Associates had been changing its operations in a fundamental way. After three ruinous failures in 1620, 1629, and 1630, the directors tried a new approach. They decided to sponsor a web of subsidiary companies, so that subcontractors could undertake smaller ventures with limited goals.

The subject was the same: to recover control of New France. This approach was different: it leveraged the company's capital, broadened its investor base, created drivers for particular ventures, and gave them a stake in the outcome.[31]

One of the first of these ventures was an attempt to reinforce an unexpected success by Champlain's friend Captain Charles Daniel. In the spring of 1629, after the Peace of Susa and before the fall of Quebec, Daniel had been sent to New France by the Company of the Hundred Associates, with dispatches and supplies for Champlain. He sailed from La Rochelle on June 26, reached the Grand Banks, and was caught in dense fog. The ships lost sight of each other and Daniel sailed on alone. He met a small ship flying an English flag at the mainmast. Daniel boarded her, reported that their nations were at peace, and allowed her to continue to her destination, which was Plymouth Colony with a cargo of English cattle and other freight.[32]

Captain Daniel continued to Cape Breton in August 1629, stopping at Grand Cibou (now Bras d'Or Bay) and Port-aux-Baleines (now Baleine Cove) just west of Cape Breton. There he found a ship from Bordeaux and learned that another group of British mercenaries, led by Sir James Stewart, had seized a French fishing vessel, confiscated her catch, and robbed her crew—another illegal act after the Peace of Susa. Stewart had built a fort at Port-aux-Baleines and forbade any Frenchman to trade on the coast without paying a 10 percent fee of furs for permission to trade.[33]

Daniel was outraged by this "usurpation of territory belonging to the King, my master," and took it upon himself to evict the Scots. On Sept. 18, 1629, at about two o'clock in the afternoon, fifty-three Frenchmen landed at Port-aux-Baleines and advanced on the British fort with orders to "attack at different points and make plentiful use of grenades, fire-pots, and other fireworks." Daniel himself led the assault on the main gate, and personally seized the British commander. The defenders replied with a few rounds of musketry, and were overwhelmed. After a token resistance they raised a white flag and begged for "life and quarter." Down came the "standards of the English king, and up went the lilies of France.[34]

In the fort Daniel freed a French fishing captain named René Cochran from the port of Brest, who had been held as a hostage until the owner of his vessel paid a ransom. Daniel loaded all the provisions, munitions, and weapons aboard a Spanish caravel that was aground near the fort. Then he ordered the Scottish fort to be demolished. All the usable material was carried to Cibou, and Daniel put fifty British captives to work building a new fort called Fort Sainte-Anne. He raised a habitation and chapel, filled the storehouse with a plentiful supply of provisions and munitions, and set up the arms of the king and "my lord the Cardinal." Other refugees from Quebec made their way to the settlement, including the Jesuit fathers Vimond and Vieuxpont. A garrison of forty Frenchmen prepared to spend the winter of 1629–30 there, under the command of the sieur Claude de Beauvais. Then Daniel sailed home with his captives, landed them at Falmouth in England with their personal belongings, and took their commander to France, "awaiting the instructions of my lord the Cardinal." The liberation of New France from England had begun by force of arms well before the Treaty of Saint-Germain-en-Laye.[35]

When Daniel returned to Paris, Champlain worked with him to send reports to the king, Richelieu, and other high officials. In 1631, the Hundred Associates created a subordinate company in Normandy to reinforce Fort Sainte-Anne and plant a settlement on Cape Breton Island.[36] This small effort did not succeed. A larger company was formed in Dieppe by Captain Charles Daniel of Dieppe and merchant-hatters in Paris to revive the fur trade.[37] The Hundred Associates sponsored another special voyage to Fort Sainte-Anne and Cape Breton in 1632. Its purpose was to strengthen the French presence on the fishing coast, and to prepare the way for the recovery of New France by controlling the approaches to the St. Lawrence River. Two leading historians of New France, Lucien Campeau and Marcel Trudel, believe that Champlain sailed with it and returned quickly to France in the late summer or fall.[38]

He strengthened the small French post at Sainte-Anne, a strategic site on the peninsula of Cape Breton with a protected harbor on the south side of the great gulf of the St. Lawrence. We are told that Champlain "worked there to put the fort in a better state," so that this settlement could be used as an alternate site, "in case the company of the Hundred Associates would not be able to recover Quebec."[39]

A second French effort developed at the same time. It began with a small success at a small French trading post at Cape Sable Island off the southeastern tip of what is now Nova Scotia. There a little band of French traders had survived the onslaught of the British mercenaries in 1628–29. They held the last remaining fort in New France, and their leader Charles de Saint-Étienne de la Tour was hanging on by his fingernails. To help him, the Hundred Associates sponsored a new subsidiary company in the southeast of France. Some of the investors were Basques, the central figure was Jean Tuffet, a merchant-adventurer of Bordeaux and a director of the Company of the Hundred Associates. He fitted out several ships to sail from Bordeaux for Cape Sable. The commander was Captain Bernard Marot, a Basque seaman from Saint-Jean-de-Luz. The ships carried three Récollet fathers, "workers and artisans," and supplies for the beleaguered settlement at Cape Sable. They arrived in time to save the settlement with provisions, arms, and men. Champlain wrote that young La Tour was delighted with this support, which he had scarcely dared to hope for." [40]

The ships landed their cargo and laborers, who began to rebuild the small colony. The French at Cape Sable were in an expansive mood, and decided to plant another trading post across the Bay of Fundy at the Saint John River, near the modern city of Saint John in New Brunswick. It is a dramatic spot, where the river curves between high headlands and joins the sea. At a spectacular bend in the river, its strong current meets the great tides of the Bay of Fundy to create the reversing falls that fascinated Champlain and still attract a flow of tourists. [41] This new French settlement was also a success. It was founded primarily for a flourishing trade in moosehides, beaver pelts, and sea otter skins, which were sold through a consortium of merchants in the Cardinal's Ring. The Hundred Associates were beginning to revive as a network of small sub-companies and small ventures. [42]

Champlain had a hand in these events as a friend of Charles Daniel and associate of Charles de La Tour. In 1632, La Tour returned briefly to Paris. He made a great splash in the city, arriving with a party of Indian warriors, French traders, and their mixed offspring. La Tour lived on the rue Quincampoix in the financial district of Paris. One street away on the rue St. Martin were the offices of the Hundred Associates. There La Tour and Champlain worked together. In the winter of 1632–33, Nova Scotia historian M. A. MacDonald writes that these two men "were sure to have renewed their acquaintance, spending absorbed hours talking over affairs in New France, to which both would return the next Spring." [43]

In this period, the Hundred Associates also sponsored a third subsidiary venture, and once again Champlain was a part of it. The object was to plant yet another small trading post and settlement at another strategic place on the fishing coast. The island of Miscou lay in the Bay of Chaleur, south of Gaspé Peninsula and northwest of Cape Breton. A fort there could control the approaches to the St. Lawrence estuary and much of the Atlantic coast. The French had operated a seasonal fishing station on Miscou since 1622, and had stayed the winter as early as 1626. It was the first permanent settlement on the fishing coast. But in July1628, Miscou had been captured and looted by David Kirke. The French wanted it back. [44]

In 1632, while Champlain was in Paris, the Hundred Associates took an interest in Miscou, and sponsored a colonizing and commercial effort in the Bay of Chaleur and the Isle of Miscou. It authorized a subsidiary called the Company Cheffault-Rozée, with a capital of 100,000 livres. One third of the capital was contributed by the Hundred Associates. The rest was raised from individual entrepreneurs.[45] Champlain himself became an active investor in the Company Cheffault-Rozée and paid 900 livres of his own money to develop the Miscou settlement. Here was an entirely new role for him. He participated not in the hope of realizing a profit, but with the intention of supporting an initiative that might help to recover New France. It worked. In 1632, the French successfully resettled Miscou, and Champlain's friend and assistant Thierry Desdames became its commandant for many years.[46] Champlain appears to have realized no monetary return from his capital investment, but Miscou Island became French again.[47]

These successes encouraged the Hundred Associates to think seriously about the recovery of Quebec. They turned to the de Caën family, who were still trading and fishing in troubled American waters. Protestant merchant Guillaume de Caën was the key figure. Richelieu was more comfortable working with Guillaume's Catholic brother Émery. On March 4, 1632, Émery de Caën was asked to visit Quebec and see if it could be returned to French control. If so, he was authorized to take possession as acting commandant. He sailed for Quebec with the sieur Charles du Plessis-Bochart and Jesuit Father Paul Le Jeune.

On arrival, Émery de Caën found British traders still firmly in control of the fort and the settlement, and busily trading with the Indians. On June 29, 1632, de Caën and Father Le Jeune came ashore and boldly demanded that the occupiers should leave forthwith. The British delayed for a few days, and at last on July 13 they handed over the keys to Émery de Caën and departed. The colony was back under French control.[48]

The choice of a permanent leader for Quebec remained an open question. Richelieu was not pleased with Champlain. Perhaps the cardinal blamed him for the loss of the colony, though most people did not hold Champlain responsible, and it was amazing that he had held out as long as he did. Richelieu himself was more culpable for having interfered with the company at the critical moment and sending its largest fleet to destruction. Champlain's open criticism of the cardinal and the king might have been another cause of Richelieu's coolness. In negotiations with England, the relentless pressure that Champlain brought to bear at court must have been resented. Whatever the reason, Richelieu resolved in 1632 not to send Champlain to Quebec.

Many other people wanted the job. The merchant Guillaume de Caën had powerful friends in the Council of State, and they intervened in his support. He was a very able man, and his family had much experience of New France, but his Protestant religion made him unacceptable. Émery de Caën, although a Catholic, was not a strong candidate. The Caëns proposed du Plessis-Bochart, a good Catholic, but Richelieu had another idea. The Cardinal's Ring was operating again. Richelieu decided to appoint his cousin Captain Isaac de Razilly. A commission was actually sent to Razilly with the name left blank.

It would have made a strong appointment. Razilly was an officer of ability, deeply interested in New France. Champlain had great respect for him. But to Richelieu's surprise, Razilly refused the job. He returned the blank commission, with the message that he would be happy to serve under anyone whom it pleased the king to appoint. He is alleged to have added that he would prefer to serve as a lieutenant to Samuel Champlain, "because he is more competent in colonial affairs." [49]

Richelieu yielded to that advice. After long delay and at the last possible moment, he reluctantly appointed Champlain to the top job in New France, with the title of lieutenant to the cardinal. It was not the title that Champlain wanted, and it did not come in the way he hoped. But once again Champlain was in command at Quebec. [50]

FATHER OF
FRENCH CANADA

21.

REALIZING THE DREAM

Champlain as Acting Governor, 1632–35

> When the French were absent, the earth was no longer the earth, the river was no longer the river, the sky was no longer the sky. But on the return of the sieur de Champlain everything was as before; the earth was again the earth; the river was again the river, and the sky was again the sky.
>
> —A Huron captain on Champlain's leadership, 1633[1]

> The wise conduct and prudence of Monsieur de Champlain, Governor of Quebec and the St. Lawrence River, honors us with his good will, holding everyone to the path of duty.
>
> —A Jesuit missionary on Champlain's leadership, 1634[2]

I N THE OLD PORT OF DIEPPE, on March 23, 1633, three small French ships prepared to sail on a very large mission. Their orders were to recover the lost colony of New France and rebuild its ruined capital at Quebec. Nobody knew what to expect. Were the English conquerors still there? Would they fight? The French ships were armed with thirty-two guns and a small force of the king's musketeers and pikemen, but their instructions were to avoid battle if possible. This was not a military expedition. It was a colonizing voyage, and the ships were crowded with passengers.[3]

In the flagship *Saint-Pierre*, 150 tons, Captain Pierre Grégoire took aboard 82 souls. Among them were four Jesuit priests, at least one married woman, and two girls aged six and thirteen.[4] Captain Pierre de Nesle's *Saint-Jean* (160 tons) carried 75 men. Many were artisans and workmen. Captain Michel Morieu's *Don-de-Dieu*, 90 tons, had 40 souls aboard. Altogether the three ships carried 197 people. About 150 were *hivernants* who had promised to stay through the next Canadian winter.[5]

The mission commander was Samuel de Champlain, now with an extraordinary array of titles and powers. He carried the King's Commission as Captain in the Royal Navy, and another as Lieutenant General in New France. Cardinal Richelieu had appointed him "Lieutenant" for "the St. Lawrence Valley." Directors of the Company of the Hundred Associates had made him their chief representative in North America. He was also *général de la flotte*, or commodore of their ships for the crossing, commander of the troops who sailed with him, chief judge and lawgiver for Quebec, and administrator of the colony. All these powers were gathered in a single hand. In 1633 Champlain was the absolute ruler of his domain, subject only to the will of Louis XIII and Cardinal Richelieu.

But there were limits to his authority, especially where Richelieu was concerned. He had not wanted to appoint Champlain, and he gave clear signals of distrust. One factor may have been the memory of Champlain's association with Henri IV. Another might have been a lingering suspicion of Protestant origins. A third was the matter of rank. Champlain had no quarterings of nobility on his escutcheon—at least none without the bar sinister of illegitimate birth. He was not a Knight of Malta. But perhaps what rankled Richelieu most were the qualities of Champlain's character. He was always obedient to his superiors, but his deepest loyalty was to his design for New France. Whatever the reason, Richelieu limited Champlain's authority to the rank of lieutenant for the St. Lawrence Valley, and denied him the official title of governor. The cardinal was careful to proclaim his own authority and to restrain his subordinates, especially when the leash was 3,000 miles long.

Those who knew Champlain and sailed with him to America had a different understanding of the man and his role. Even when the title of governor was officially denied by Richelieu, the people of Quebec gave it to him anyway. They called him their governor, often "our governor," even "my governor." The Indians of the St. Lawrence Valley went further. In 1633, they called him "the Captain of the French," all the French. Europeans of other nations treated Champlain with deference and respect when they met him in America. So did the people of New France. Clerics and laymen, habitants and seamen, Québécois and Acadians, fishermen and interpreters recognized this man as their leader.[6]

By mid-March preparations for the voyage were complete. Prominent French leaders descended on Dieppe to see the ships off. Major investors and directors of the Company of the Hundred Associates arrived for a last round of meetings with Champlain. Father Barthélemy Jacquinot, head of the Jesuit Order in France, came to the harbor himself and led the blessing of the ships. The departure was something new in Champlain's experience—a national event. In France this display of interest in North America was unprecedented. More than a few French leaders did not discover the importance of their American colony until the English tried to take it away from them.

Another factor was the recent publication of Champlain's *Voyages*, his largest and most important work. It made a splash when it came off the press in 1632. So also did his magnificent maps. Champlain was a tireless promoter of New France, and he was quick to discover the expanding power of the periodical press. The sailing of the ships was covered by the Paris gazettes in 1633, especially by the *Mercure François*. Champlain later published a long account of the voyage anonymously in the *Mercure*, a major piece of writing that was missed by the editors of his works.[7]

At last, on the morning of March 23, the ships were ready. On board the flagship *Saint-Pierre*, Champlain nodded to the master and pilot. On command, master-gunners fired a salute that echoed across the anchorage. Seamen in gaudy dress hauled in the slippery anchor-cable, dripping with green weed. Topmen ran aloft and released the great sails from their gaskets. The canvas caught the wind, and filled with the happy thump that warms a sailor's heart. On steering decks, burly helmsmen threw their weight against the long tillers, and guided the ships through the harbor.

It must have been a happy moment for Champlain. He was going to sea again, doing what he loved to do more than anything in the world. As the three ships cleared the harbor and turned together into the English Channel, he would have felt the wind on his cheek and smelled the salt in his nostrils. Flocks of white gulls soared free around him, and black cormorants raced straight and low across the water. In that moment he must have shared the feeling of release that any blue-water sailor will recognize.

The wind was fair for America, and westward they went with white bow waves streaming beneath sharp-pointed prows. They sailed along the emerald coast of England, passed Torbay in a fresh breeze, left the Isles of Scilly behind, and settled on a course for the new world. Overhead the flags of France snapped and fluttered on their halyards—the beautiful marine ensign with its white cross on a blue field, and the Bourbon banner with its gilded lilies on a white cloth. Perhaps the mastheads of the *Saint-Pierre* also flew Cardinal Richelieu's standard, and the house flag of the Hundred Associates, as well as Champlain's broad pennant as général de la flotte.

This was his twenty-seventh Atlantic crossing, and Champlain was the most experienced navigator in the fleet. His expertise gave him yet another responsibility for guiding the ships across the ocean. All his skill would be needed on this voyage. Trouble began as they left the English Channel in what the sailor-poet John Masefield called "the mad March days." On the morning of March 30, lookouts reported that little *Don-de-Dieu* had vanished in the night. Champlain shortened sail and found her again. He ordered all his ships to hoist lanterns in the night and instructed them to keep beacon-fires burning in iron cressets above their high stern rails.[8]

The three ships pressed on together with all sail set, and made very good time. By April 12, they were a thousand miles at sea. Then, inevitably, the Atlantic weather changed. The sky turned dark, and seamen were ordered aloft to take in topsails, just in the nick of time. On a pitch-black night the little ships ran into a mid-ocean storm of terrific violence, with strong head winds, high seas, a clatter of hail, sheets of driving rain, and the crash of thunder. All around them, the horizon was filled with great flashes of lightning that reflected on the wet sails and rigging. Champlain wrote that "in the darkness of the night, everything appeared to be on fire." It was a stunning sight, and even he was shaken by it after all his many years at sea.[9]

The storm passed quickly, and the next day they found themselves in fair weather. All hands thanked God for their delivery. The ships set their topsails and ran before a favorable wind. Champlain reckoned his latitude by noon sunlines and the elevation of Polaris in the evening. He also studied his seamarks, and by April 24 he knew they were in American waters very near the Grand Bank. Here they met another hazard. The three small ships sailed into huge banks of rolling fog so thick that Champlain wrote that they "could see nearly nothing." He ordered out the deep-sea lead, and on April 26, 1633, the leadsmen found bottom at 45 fathoms, or 270 feet. The lead brought up a few bits of sand and shell embedded in a pocket of tallow on its hollow bottom. A skilled Atlantic seaman could learn much from these telltale signs by sight and smell, and even taste. Champlain studied the evidence and reckoned from long experience that they were twelve leagues on the Grand Bank in the latitude of 45 degrees 30 minutes. Even in the fog he was able to identify his position with uncanny accuracy. They were exactly on course after five weeks at sea.

In the fog the flagship lost touch with the *Saint-Jean*. Champlain was confident that she would find her way toward the funnel-shaped estuary of the St. Lawrence River, as indeed she did, and the ships found each other the next day. Champlain led his ships safely through Cabot Strait to the protected waters of Cape Breton, where a sub-company of the Hundred Associates had built Fort St. Anne. Champlain had probably been there the year before and was well acquainted with its commander, the sieur de Mercier. As the ships approached, they hoisted a secret signal and the French fort replied with a sign of its own. Champlain's little squadron entered the harbor to a tumultuous welcome. He had completed another Atlantic voyage and preserved his perfect record. In twenty-seven ocean crossings he had never lost a major ship under his command.[10]

• • •

From Fort Sainte-Anne the French ships sailed up the St. Lawrence River to Tadoussac, and found two English ships anchored there. Each carried thirty-eight guns, enough to over-match Champlain's entire fleet in weight of metal. But the English were not there to fight. They were traders and had nearly filled their holds with cargoes of fish and fur. Champlain engaged them in an amicable discussion, and they departed in peace.[11]

Champlain hurried up the river to Quebec in high uncertainty, and arrived on May 22. He was delighted to discover that the English were gone, and that the French habitants had recovered control of the settlement. They were few in number, but full of enthusiasm, and they turned out to welcome him in high style. Prominent among them were a party of Jesuit fathers who had come in 1632. Father Le Jeune wrote, "We were in doubt if Monsieur de Champlain would come, or someone else on the part of the gentlemen of the Company of New France, or sieur Guillaume de Caën." He tells us that they prayed to God for Champlain. Then the ships arrived and Champlain it was. The habitants were overjoyed. One of them wrote, "all at once Champlain had come." Le Jeune remembered that "it was for us one of the good days of the year; we were full of strong hopes after so many storms."[12]

The vessels were welcomed with a salute of three guns, and Champlain answered with three more, in billowing clouds of white smoke that rolled across the river. A boat splashed into the water, and Champlain was rowed ashore with "a squad of French soldiers, armed with pikes and muskets." They paraded through the settlement, entered the fort, and the soldiers summoned the habitants with a roll of drums. Champlain assembled all the people, and read his dual commission as Lord Lieutenant to Richelieu and representative of the Company of the Hundred Associates. The habitants listened attentively. After much strife surrounding the old companies, they were greatly relieved by the terms of Champlain's commission, and his "orders from Monsieur le Cardinal," which "ended the dispute in favor of the Company of New France."[13]

The commercial affairs of the settlement were still in the hands of Émery de Caën, an old rival and distant friend. He stepped forward and with a gesture of deference handed the keys of the settlement to an intermediary, the sieur Du Plessis-Bochart, who in turn presented them to Champlain. It was a symbol of the transfer of power from the old Company de Caën to the new Company of the Hundred Associates. Everything was done with ritual acts of fealty and obeisance.[14]

• • •

Champlain's second habitation, as reconstructed by him in 1633–35. This drawing, based on archaeological research, shows its defenses, the battery that controlled the narrows of the river and five outbuildings and small farms. An even stronger fortress was built on the heights above.

Then the hard work began. Champlain looked about and found once again that much of the town was a ruin. The old habitation where Champlain and Hélène had lived together in their happiest years was a tangle of broken stone and charred timber. The English had burned it, and the fort was also a wreck. Nothing had been built since Champlain had left four years before. In the absence of authority, Quebec had become a wide-open frontier town. In the filthy streets Champlain found a scattering of fur traders who were a law unto themselves—English, French, and Indian alike. Only one French family was living there—the long-suffering Héberts, still working the farm that Champlain had given them. They loved the land but lived in daily fear of violence by Indians and Europeans alike. The Héberts were delighted to see Champlain, and hopeful that he would restore order.

Champlain had only a handful of pikemen and musketeers, but disciplined troops with a determined leader swiftly worked their will upon the settlement.

He did it with a grace that made it look easy, which it was not, as the tragic history of many a colony made clear. In 1633 Champlain's energy seemed undiminished, even after thirty years of labor in New France. He mustered the men of the colony and set them to work rebuilding the settlement. The most urgent task was to make the colony defensible. The fort was a ruin—looted, burned, and struck by lightning. Champlain repaired its broken palisade, rebuilt its eroded ramparts, reinforced gates, and added platforms for great guns that commanded the river. In the town below, no weather-tight building remained to shelter the company's supplies. Champlain repaired a structure to serve as a storehouse, restored shops for artisans, and renovated living quarters for servants and soldiers. Within the fort he constructed a seat of royal government. The king's arms went up on the building, and once again the flag of Bourbon France was hoisted above the rooftops of the little town. His habitation became a North American echo of the French court, perhaps more in the spirit of Henri IV than Louis XIII.

Champlain also built a new chapel for Quebec and named it Notre-Dame-de-la-Recouvrance, Our Lady of the Recovery, to honor the restoration of New France. Champlain ordered the Angelus to be sounded three times a day, morning, noon, and night. He actively encouraged worship, and the chapel became an important center for the life of the settlement; Quebec's Notre-Dame Cathedral stands today near the same site.[15]

The result was a full-scale revival of religion at Quebec during the winter and spring of 1633–34. This was a common occurrence in European colonies during the seventeenth century. Something similar happened in English settlements at Jamestown and Boston, but it took different forms in Catholic and Protestant colonies. Among Protestant populations, revivals centered on conversion experiences. The Catholic revival in Quebec appeared in exercises of piety. Father Le Jeune reported many acts of "extraordinary devotion in soldiers and artisans, such as are the greater part of our Frenchmen here."

Jesuit rings were given to Indian converts by Father Paul Le Jeune, head of the order in New France. The emblem of the order was a crucifix with the initials IHS, which stood for Jesu Hominum Salvator, *Jesus the Savior, and also for Constantine's* In Hoc Signo. *They also became an article of trade.*

Some made barefoot pilgrimages in deep snow. Le Jeune wrote of one peni-
tent who "came on last Shrove Tuesday [1634], with bare head and feet over
the snow and ice from Quebec all the way to our Chapel, that is a good half
league, fasting the same day, to fulfill a vow made to Our Lord; and all this was
done without any other witnesses than God and our fathers." Other habitants
practiced "abstinence and fasting." One "took the discipline more than thirty
times." A third devoted a tithe of his profits to "works of piety." Le Jeune observed the revival with gratification, and attributed much of it to Champlain's
example. The Jesuit father concluded that "the winter in New France is not so
severe that some flowers of Paradise may not be gathered here." [16]

While Champlain's habitation was under construction, he moved in with the
Jesuit fathers. The mission of these Black Robes in New France had not been
Champlain's idea. He favored the Franciscan piety of the brown-robed Récollets, much as Cardinal Richelieu had preferred the gray-gowned Capuchins.
The Jesuits in New France had been sponsored by the relentless Madame de
Guercheville, who applied her wealth and beauty to their cause. In Quebec,
their presence was resented by some habitants and would continue to be controversial among Catholics even to our own time. But Champlain got on well
with them, and especially with Father Paul Le Jeune, a former Protestant who
had converted to Catholicism.

Le Jeune told a happy story that is a clue to their relationship. On May 29,
Champlain attended Mass in the chapel of the Jesuit fathers, and afterward
was invited to dine with them. Le Jeune remembered that "as luck would have
it, an Indian friend of the mission" had given them "a choice piece of bear
meat, which we served to Champlain. Having tasted it he began to laugh and
said to me, 'If they knew in France that we were eating bear, they would turn
their faces away from our breath, and yet you see how good and delicate the
meat is.'" [17]

In that snatch of conversation we hear Champlain's laughter, feel his easy
way with others, and see his pleasure in bountiful food, abundant drink, good
company, and cheerful conversation. Here again, we observe his happy gift for
working with people whose purposes were different from his own. In his advice to leaders, Champlain recommended an "affable manner" as an act of policy. But for him it was not a mask. Champlain genuinely delighted in the
company of others, and they delighted in him. [18]

Le Jeune and Champlain became fast friends. Both men were probably catechized as Protestants, converted to Catholicism, and embraced that faith with
a whole heart. Although their goals for New France were not the same, they

RELATION

DE CE QVI S'EST PASSE'
EN LA
NOVVELLE FRANCE
EN L'ANNE'E 1636.

Enuoyée au
R. PERE PROVINCIAL
de la Compagnie de IESVS
en la Prouince de France.

*Par le P. Paul le Ieune de la mesme Compagnie,
Superieur de la Residence de Kébec.*

A PARIS,
Chez SEBASTIEN CRAMOISY Imprimeur
ordinaire du Roy, ruë sainct Iacques,
aux Cicognes.

M. DC. XXXVII.
AVEC PRIVILEGE DV ROY.

*A major source for Champlain and New France are the Jesuit Relations, especially those that Father
Paul Le Jeune sent home every year. They tell us how Champlain succeeded in realizing his dream
of New France during his last years there.*

worked together to strengthen the colony and to improve relations between church and state in Quebec. Champlain also encouraged the Jesuits to found a seminary for the training of priests. It opened in 1635, the first college in the English colonies. Within two years it was called the Collège de Québec.[19]

With Champlain's support, the Jesuits became an active presence in the colony. They met the immigrant ships that began to arrive from France. The Jesuit fathers rowed out to vessels in the river, climbed the high companion ladders in their billowing black robes, and performed mass on the weather deck, with their communion silver sparkling in the bright Canadian light. Once they brought a choir of seven Indian boys who sang the Paternoster in their own language, to Champlain's delight and everyone's pleasure.[20]

After the fort was repaired, Champlain invited the Jesuits to dine in his quarters, which they did frequently. Le Jeune recalled that "the fort . . . seemed like a well-ordered Academy. Monsieur Champlain has someone read at his table in the morning from some good historians, and in the evening from the lives of the saints."[21] The tone of the settlement was transformed by Champlain's spirit. Le Jeune wrote, "We have passed this year in great peace and on very good terms with our French [habitants]." He attributed that success to "the wise conduct and prudence of Monsieur de Champlain, governor of Quebec of the Saint Lawrence River, who honors us with his good will, holding everyone to the path of duty. In a word we have reason to console ourselves when we see a chief so zealous for the glory of our Lord, and for the welfare of these gentlemen."[22]

Another of Champlain's many responsibilities was to control the river. Illegal traders continued to appear in the St. Lawrence. Champlain complained again and again that they used any means to make a profit, and gave no thought to the future. These interlopers offered firearms and alcohol to the Indians, and threatened to burn Indian settlements that traded with the French. As the flow of French shipping increased in the St. Lawrence Valley, the company ordered its captains to attack unlicensed traders when they had the power to do so. In 1634, an English ship was captured after a battle in the river.

Champlain lacked the strength to remove interlopers from the lower reaches of the river. He decided to deal with the problem in another way, by building a new fort and trading post on the small, rocky island of Sainte-Croix, in the St. Lawrence River near the present village of Deschambault, fifteen leagues upstream from Quebec. The channel was narrow there, and, in Champlain's words, the fort "held the entire river in check." Its guns kept the English from coming upstream, and Champlain erected a trading post there to provide opportunities for commerce with the licensed traders. Later he changed its name from Sainte-Croix to Richelieu Island, in hope of improving relations with the cardinal. In 1633 Champlain was often on the water, visiting the island, supervising construction, talking with the garrison, and meeting with the Indians. This policy of controlling choke points on the river met with mixed results, but it helped Champlain to keep the peace along the river.[23]

Champlain's next task was, yet again, to repair relations with the Indians. When he arrived in Quebec, scattered acts of violence were increasing dangerously between Indians and French. The English conquest had done real damage that way. The Indians could not understand why a kingdom as great as France could be defeated by a small force of freebooters. Some Indians felt abandoned by the French. Others thought that the French could not be trusted as allies or even as trading partners. A few saw them as ripe for the plucking.

On May 30, 1633, an Algonquin warrior killed a Frenchman. The murderer was caught and confined in chains at the French fort in Quebec. Then on July 2, another Frenchman was murdered by an Indian of the Petite-Nation as he was washing his clothes in a stream near the settlement. The killer tried to disguise his crime as the work of the Iroquois. When Champlain and Indian leaders discovered the truth, the murderer was captured and taken to the fort. French leaders asked what should be done with him. Champlain posed the question in another way. What sort of justice would satisfy both the Indians and the French? It was a problem that Champlain had dealt with several times before, always in the same spirit, but each time with more refinement.

Long discussions followed between Champlain and large assemblies of Indians, mostly about standards of justice. The Indians made several proposals. Some suggested that they should kill an Indian who was related to the murderer. Champlain refused, and said to them, "Your law is much more brutal than ours. It would kill another innocent person and allow the criminal to go free." [24] Montagnais leaders proposed that their nation should give Champlain several children as hostages. They took two small children by the hand, laid them at his feet, and said to him: "We give them to you. Do whatever you wish." Champlain had done something like this before, but this time he said no. "Innocent children cannot carry the guilt of the murderer," he explained. "I desire no further hostage than the guilty one to be in my hands—a perfidious traitor, with no more courage or friendship than a tiger." [25] Champlain proposed that only the perpetrator should be punished, and in a way that all nations could recognize as just. The killer remained in a condition of "open confinement," so that his wife and others of his nation could visit him. How it ended is not known. The murderer was still in that condition when the only account was written. But Champlain succeeded in finding a path of coexistence among the French, the Algonquin, and Montagnais, both in what was done and in how they did it. As always, he kept working to restore the rule of law in the St. Lawrence Valley on that basis.[26]

Another incident happened on May 23, 1633, when the French at Quebec were visited by twelve or fourteen canoes of the Nipissing nation, whom the French called the nation des Sorciers. The Indians were fascinated by the exercises of a young French drummer boy. One pressed too close, and the drummer accidentally hit him in the head with a drumstick. The wound bled abundantly, and the Indians asked for justice, which in their nation called for the payment of presents. Champlain answered that justice would be done in a different way and he ordered the French drummer boy to be whipped. As the "switches were being made ready," the Indians rushed forward to protect the French lad. One Nipissing stripped himself naked, and threw his blanket over the French boy and said, "If you wish to beat someone, beat me, but do not beat him." The drummer was spared a beating, and Champlain himself got a lesson in humanity.[27]

Champlain's task of restoring relations was compounded by the cultural complexity of the St. Lawrence Valley. Each Indian nation presented a different challenge. Champlain had to find solutions that worked for the Montagnais, for the many Algonquin groups, the Huron, and especially the Iroquois. His first step was to expand communications. Champlain's main recourse was, as always, to listen and talk. He had a smattering of Indian languages, not enough to speak directly on sensitive questions. Most of his communications had to happen through interpreters.

Some of Champlain's old corps of French interpreters were still living in the St. Lawrence Valley. When the English had arrived, several interpreters had gone to live among the Indians. Others chose to work for the conquerors. Champlain had made these men what they were and he was appalled by what some of them became. He had come to detest Étienne Brûlé, and disliked Marsolet for having lent aid and comfort to British mercenaries. After 1633, he worked more closely with other interpreters who were held in high respect. Everyone thought well of Olivier le Tardif, who became fluent in Montagnais, Algonquian, and Huron, and was also perceived as an *honneste homme*. The Indians held him in high esteem. He often appeared at Champlain's side and became a major figure in New France.[28]

Within the settlement of Quebec, Champlain worked at changing attitudes of the new habitants toward the Indians. With his example, relations between the French settlers and American Indians began to improve. Le Jeune supported Champlain, shared the same humanism, and greatly admired the style and character of the Indians. He remarked on the grace and dignity of "un sauvage de bonne façon." Once, upon observing an Indian family passing his residence he wrote: "This family has something inexpressibly noble about it. If they were dressed *à la française*, they would yield nothing to our gentilhommes." Le Jeune added: "They will feed you without asking anything of you if they think you have nothing. But if they see that you have something, and they want it, they will not stop asking you for it until you have given it." [29] The Indians were permitted to move freely in and out of buildings, "according to their custom," Le Jeune wrote. "They enter everywhere without saying a word, or without any greeting. Their houses are not closed; all can enter who will." Here again, Champlain had set an example. Others followed his lead, and relations improved in a reciprocal way. [30]

On May 24, 1633, two days after Champlain had returned to Quebec, eighteen large canoes filled with Indians led by the Montagnais leader Capitanal came to visit him. Champlain met with them and made a speech through his interpreter, Olivier le Tardif. He reminded them of the alliance that he had made with their forbears in the first tabagie on St. Matthew's Point exactly thirty years before. He recalled how he and Capitanal's father had fought side by side against the Iroquois in battles where Capitanal's father had been killed and Champlain wounded.

Champlain told the Montagnais of his dream that their children might intermarry and live together as one people. Gesturing to the fort and settlement, he said, "When that great house is built, our young men will marry your daughters, and henceforth we shall be one people." [31] These words flowed from his heart, and the Indians were moved by his spirit. [32] Father Le Jeune was present at this meeting and wrote an account of it. He observed that the Indians "listened very attentively" to Champlain and "appeared to be in deep thought," as did one of their leaders, "drawing from his stomach this aspiration from time to time: *Ham! Ham! Ham!*, as if approving." [33]

Champlain spoke of the trade that had grown between the Montagnais and the British, and warned them that freebooters were "thieves who had come to pillage the French." He told the Indians about the treaty between the monarchs of England and France, and urged the Montagnais to "consider well what they were doing; these robbers were only birds of passage, while the French would remain in the country as it belonged to them."

After Champlain finished, the Montagnais leader Capitanal rose. Father Le Jeune was amazed to hear him speak "with a keenness and delicacy of rhetoric that might have come from the schools of Aristotle or Cicero." Capitanal said that Champlain spoke the truth, and for thirty years had lived the ideas that he espoused. The Indian leader said he had heard his father speak highly of Champlain, and they had learned that the French were different from the English. Capitanal promised that he would "not go to the English; I will tell my men they should not go there." He explained that his powers were limited. "I promise you that neither I myself nor they who have any sense will do that; but if there is some young man who jumps over there without being seen, I shall not know what to do; you know well that youth can not be restrained." [34]

A particular problem was trade in alcohol. "Since the English have introduced them to this drink," Champlain wrote, "it has caused many quarrels, fighting, smashing their cabins . . . and trouble throughout the country." He prohibited traders from giving wine and spirits to the Indians, on pain of severe corporal punishment and flogging. Together Champlain and Capitanal endeavored to stop trade with English interlopers, and to shut down the trade in alcohol. They both knew the limits of their power, but these men did what they could, and they did it together. [35]

As relations with the Montagnais began to improve, the Algonquins presented another challenge. On May 24, 1633, two days after Champlain reached Quebec, a large delegation of Algonquin Indians came down the river in a fleet of canoes. Champlain suspected that they might go on to the English, who had three vessels at Tadoussac and "a barque far up the river." He went to their camp, and met with the Indian leaders, and more important, he listened as few Europeans did. Then he spoke of his vision for the Indians and New France. Unlike the conquistadors of New Spain, Champlain did not wish to make them into a force of servile workers. Unlike the founders of New England, he did not want to keep the Indians at a distance or drive them from their own lands. He urged the Indians to move closer to Quebec, and shared with them his vision of Europeans and North Americans, living side by side in peace.

After his conversations with the Montagnais and the Algonquin, Champlain also met with the Huron, and worked to restore relations with them. This was a very difficult task. Twenty years earlier, Champlain had been close to the Huron, and lived in their villages through a North American winter. But they had grown apart. Some of the Huron felt that Champlain had abandoned them. Still, in 1633 they remembered him with affection and respect. When they heard that Champlain had returned, a large party of Huron came down the river to see this man who had become a legend in their own culture. On July 28, between 500 and 600 Huron visited Quebec in hundreds of large canoes. They came ashore and built a camp on the edge of the river.[36]

It was an amazing sight. Le Jeune was an eyewitness, and he reported: "I could scarcely tell you how the people of this nation wear their hair. Each follows his own fancy. Some wear it long and hanging over to one side like women, and short and tied up on the other, so skillfully that one ear is concealed and the other uncovered. Some of them are shaven just where others wear a long moustache. I have seen some who have a large strip, closely shaved, extended across the head, passing from the crown to the middle of the forehead. Others wear in the same place a sort of queue which stands out because they have shaved all around it."[37]

The next day the Huron held a council of sixty leaders, sitting on the ground, with each village and clan grouped together. Father Le Jeune was struck by their dignity. He wrote: "I have been told that Louis XI once held his council of war in the country, having for his throne or chair only a piece of wood, or fallen tree. . . . This is the picture of the Council of the Hurons."[38] Champlain was invited to join them, and the Jesuits were allowed to sit in. A Huron leader rose and said that they had come "to see their friends and brothers the French," and offered presents to "the captain of the French, the sieur de Champlain." They gave him three large bundles of beaver robes. Other Indians joined in expressing their support. One of their captains rose and said, "All the people rejoiced in the return of the sieur de Champlain and they all have come to warm themselves by his fire." Then the Huron gave him more bundles of beaver robes.[39]

Champlain rose and said that he "wished very much to have them as his brothers, that he recognized old men with whom he had gone to war against the Iroquois." The Huron warmed to his remarks. Then two Huron captains rose, and Father Le Jeune listened in astonishment as "they vied with each other trying to honor sieur de Champlain." One said: "When the French were absent, the earth was no longer the earth, the river was no longer the river, the sky was no longer the sky. But on the return of the sieur de Champlain everything was as before; the earth was again the earth; the river was again the river, and the sky was again the sky."[40] The other celebrated Champlain as a warrior, and said that the sieur de Champlain was frightful (*effroyable*) in his looks; that when he went into battle, "a glance from his eye struck terror into the hearts of the enemies."[41]

The discussion turned to the Jesuit fathers. Champlain urged the Huron to accept them in their villages, and he dictated the arrangements both to the Huron and the Jesuits. Both accepted his judgment, even though it was in some ways against their own. In 1633, Champlain was truly ruling over the St. Lawrence Valley.

After the Huron council, the Jesuits invited Champlain and the captains of French ships on the river to visit their chapel and receive indulgences, and another side of Champlain's character appeared. The Huron followed him to the chapel, so many that there was no room for them in the small building. One Huron put his head through a window to see what was happening. Father Le Jeune wrote that Champlain, "enjoying their wonder, gave one of them a piece of lemon peel." The Indian tasted it and cried, "How good it is!" He asked what it was. Champlain said with a laugh, "it is the rind of a French pumpkin." Others came for a taste "saying they would like to taste them, so they could tell about them in their country. Soon all joined Champlain in his laughter." Le Jeune wrote, "You can judge for yourself how the room began to laugh!" [42]

Relationships with the Iroquois remained a problem. All the major Indian nations of the St. Lawrence Valley asked the French for help against them. On November 13, 1632, Father Le Jeune had been startled by a visit of a Montagnais leader in a state of extreme agitation. Le Jeune wrote: "Manitougache, our guest and neighbor, came to tell us that a great many Hiroquois [sic] had been seen near Kebec. All the Montagnais trembled with fear. He asked if his wife and children could not come and lodge with us. We answered him that he and his sons would be very welcome, but that girls and women were not permitted to sleep in our houses, indeed, they never entered them in France." He "sent his whole party, all the young people, to cabins in the neighborhood of Quebec, where they were told that some arquebusiers would be sent to protect them." The Algonquin and Huron made similar requests of Champlain. Twenty years after his campaigns against the Mohawk and the Onondaga, warfare was increasing once again between the Iroquois and the Indian nations who lived and traded on the river. [43]

On June 2, 1633, Mohawk warriors ambushed a party of Frenchmen near the site of Trois-Rivières. It was a brutal affair. The French were going up the river in a barque and a small shallop. The current was strong and several men went ashore to tow the shallop along the bank. As they reached a point of land, a war party of thirty or forty Iroquois sprang an ambush and attacked with great fury. Other Iroquois tried to board the shallop from their war canoes. The larger barque came to the rescue, and French arquebusiers presented their weapons. The Iroquois were driven off, but not before they had killed two or three Frenchmen, wounded three or four more, scalped their victims and retreated with cries of triumph.[44]

Here was Champlain's most intractable problem: the reviving hostility of these formidable warriors. Champlain had tried many times to make peace with the Iroquois. For many years from 1609 to 1628 he had succeeded, when the Iroquois were engaged in wars to the south. An informal peace was agreed, but the English conquest had disrupted this understanding. The Mohawk turned north again, and rivalries for the fur trade were intense. Peace initiatives had failed, and Champlain lacked the military strength to deal with them. What to do?

In 1633 and again in 1634, Champlain laid out his thoughts in letters to Cardinal Richelieu. On August 15, 1633, he explained that the Iroquois had gained control of a large part of the countryside south of the St. Lawrence River, and held "more than 400 leagues in subjection." In that area, he reported, the rivers and trails were not open to the French and their Indian allies. "It will be necessary sooner or later to prevent them from making trouble for people who wish to come and go freely on the lakes and rivers, and trade peacefully with the French."[45]

Champlain told Richelieu that this goal could be achieved only by force of arms, but not by a conventional European army. He proposed to form a special sort of military unit, adapted to conditions in the new world. First it would be very small, carefully selected, trained for operations among the Indians, and highly mobile in the American forest. "To make ourselves masters of these people [the Iroquois]," he wrote, "it is necessary to have one hundred picked men of courage, well mannered, quiet, disciplined, accustomed to fatigue, and able to accommodate themselves to the customs of the Indians in the matter of food and drink."[46]

Champlain designed this new force in great detail. He requested permission to recruit "eighty men armed with *carbines* of three or four feet [in length], and the caliber of a musket, highly skilled in their use." Another ten men would be "trained in the use of two-handed swords and armed with pistolets"; four artificers skilled in the use of mines and petards for breaking down palisades; ten halberdiers and ten "strong and robust" pikemen trained in the use of that weapon; four carpenters and four locksmiths (skilled in the repair of gun locks); and two surgeons each armed with pistols. He proposed that all of these men would also be armed with cutlasses ("short but very sharp"). The entire force was to wear uniforms of chamois or well-cured leather of a faded color. They were to be protected by helmets and half armor of light steel that would offer protection from arrows.[47]

It is interesting to see the combination of qualities that Champlain had in mind for these men. They were to be highly efficient, capable of swift movement, and inured to hardship. They were also to be young men of manners, discipline, and restraint, who could adapt to the ways of the Indians and live and work with them in harmony. Champlain intended this small French force to operate in alliance with much larger numbers of 3,000 or 4,000 Indian allies, from the nations of the St. Lawrence Valley. He requested as well that the French supply the Indians with 1,000 hatchets and 4,000 iron arrowheads.[48] His purpose was clear. When the Iroquois attacked the French and the Indians of the St. Lawrence Valley, he proposed to muster a combined force of French troops and Indian warriors. His intention was to strike quickly, with a large and highly mobile expedition that would advance quickly into the heart of Iroquoia, attack one or more of their major villages, withdraw in about twelve days, and raise the cost of aggression.[49]

Champlain was not interested in imposing French conquest on North America by brute force, or in building a sedentary empire in the British fashion. His object was to live among the Indians and work with them to create a lasting basis for peace, and to enforce it by joint effort where necessary by quick, strong and decisive measures, followed by conciliation. His letter to Richelieu laid out this strategy and an operational plan. Whether it would have worked against the Iroquois is another question. They were formidable opponents, highly skilled in the warfare that Champlain proposed to wage against them.

His plan required the active support of Cardinal Richelieu, and that support was not forthcoming. Champlain may have made a major tactical mistake in developing his thoughts not only in letters to the cardinal himself but also in a "relation" that was published in the *Mercure François*. Considerable skepticism may have arisen in Paris about Champlain's proposal to take the field himself at the age of sixty-three. The cardinal had no knowledge of North America, and nothing of Champlain's long experience of warfare in the new world. Whatever the reason, Richelieu did not act on Champlain's advice, and may not even have replied to it. Once again it cost France dearly. After Champlain's death, the Iroquois became more aggressive against the French, and a large force of conventional infantry would be sent to America with instructions to impose order by a more heavy-handed application of *force majeure*. It would be less effective than Champlain's more adroit approach.

• • •

While governing in Quebec, Champlain made every effort to improve relations with Cardinal Richelieu and the Crown. This was not easily done. The cardinal was absorbed in European affairs. Richelieu wanted to create a world empire for France, and his attention wandered from one project to another. He acquired the West Indian islands of Martinique and Guadeloupe, and was interested in South Asia and the East Indies. Canada was also on the cardinal's list, but rarely at the top. Champlain wrote a series of letters to Richelieu, which survived in the archives of the Ministry of Foreign Affairs in Paris. Every year, Champlain made an annual ritual of fealty to his superior. He wrote little about himself, but much about the importance of New France. He described the magnitude of "this land more than 1500 leagues in longitude, lying between the same parallels of latitude as our own France." He celebrated the St. Lawrence River, "one of the most beautiful rivers in the world, with many tributaries, some more than 400 leagues." He spoke warmly of the native people in their great variety, "some of them sedentary in towns and villages built of wood, like the Moscovites," others nomadic hunters and fishermen, "all wishing to have a number of French and religious fathers for instruction in our faith." [50]

He wrote of the beauty of the countryside and the bounty of its arable land, its great open spaces and immense forests, its abundance of animals and fish, its rich deposits of copper, iron, silver, and other minerals. Each letter was a promotional tract and more—a testament that came from the heart, about a country that he loved as dearly as France itself. [51]

These annual letters were also warnings to Richelieu not to lose sight of New France among his other projects. "I pray you will pardon my zeal," Champlain wrote, "if I say that after your fame has spread throughout the East, you should end by compelling its recognition in the West." Champlain warned that a great French empire could be lost to the Iroquois and the English and the Flemings (as he called the Dutch), who were enemies of New France. Already the Iroquois had gained control of many rivers, and were threatening an advance to the heart of New France. Again and again, Champlain argued that in this moment of small beginnings, an even smaller force could settle the fate of a great continent. Champlain impressed upon Richelieu that with a little effort at the right moment, they could "expel our enemies both English and Flemings," and "force them to withdraw to the coast," and within a year that force could encourage the spread of "order, religion, and commerce." He reckoned that the cost was small, and the enterprise "the most noble that can be imagined." [52]

There was no reply. A year later, on August 18, 1634, Champlain wrote again. He reported that many artisans and families had arrived, and that the effort of the Hundred Associates had given him new courage. He mentioned that he had named a river after Richelieu, and also an island fifteen leagues above Quebec, on which he had built a fort to control movement on the great river. Once again he asked for 120 men.[53]

These annual letters from Quebec must have been tiresome for Richelieu to receive. Perhaps he never even read them. He did not like to be hectored by his inferiors, particularly by this troublesome old commoner who was driven by a dream. If he replied at all, no letter has survived. When the cardinal's thoughts turned to colonies in this period, he gave more attention to Guadeloupe than Quebec, more to Martinique than Acadia, more to North Africa than North America, more to the Indian Ocean than the Atlantic. For the Catholics of New France the cardinal's inattention must have appeared a form of punishment. For the Calvinists of New England, it might have seemed a gift of Providence.[54]

22.

THE PEOPLING OF QUEBEC
The Pivotal Moment, 1632–35

Enfin des colons! At last, the colonists!

—Marcel Trudel on the years 1633–36 [1]

WHEN CHAMPLAIN returned to Quebec as governor in 1633, he found seventy-seven people living there. Their numbers were smaller than the eighty suffering souls who had settled on Sainte-Croix Island in 1604 three decades earlier. The peopling of New France had been his goal from the start, but for thirty years Champlain and other leaders made little progress. The French population of North America ebbed and flowed at low levels, with no sustained growth and scarcely any natural increase.

For three decades most French inhabitants of North America were birds of passage—solitary males who stayed briefly and moved on. In the year 1632, when Jesuit father Paul Le Jeune arrived in Quebec, he reported that only one French family was living there. [2] This was the Hébert-Couillard household, the extended family that Champlain had helped to establish in 1617. Hébert had died in the winter of 1626 after a fall on the ice. His widow, Marie Rollet, remarried and remained in Quebec. Their daughter Guillemette Hébert married an illiterate ship's carpenter named Guillaume Couillard, and by 1632 she had given birth to four daughters: Louise, then aged 8; Marguerite, 7; Elizabeth, 2, and Marie, 6 months. [3] Father Le Jeune visited their home, "the oldest house in the country," and wrote, "God is blessing them every day; he has given them very beautiful children, their cattle are in fine condition, and their land produces good grain." [4]

The Héberts and Couillards showed what could be done, but they had suffered much through the years. Commercial companies had cruelly exploited them. An Indian had killed one of their workers. French and English predators had looted their property. By 1632, the Hébert-Couillard family had lost heart, and Father Le Jeune was dismayed to learn that they had decided to give up and go home. "They were seeking some way of returning to France," he

A hopeful sketch of Quebec as St. Matthew's shining city on a hill, with many spires and crucifixes. In the foreground are symbols of agriculture, commerce on the river, and industry on the water's edge, where a small barque with a dangerously high poop is taking shape.

wrote.[5] Then, when the Héberts and Couillards learned that the French were coming back to Quebec, "they began to regain courage, and when they saw our ships coming in with the white flags on their masts, they knew not how to express their joy."[6]

In the spring of 1633, Champlain arrived with three ships and about 150 settlers. That event proved to be a pivotal moment in the peopling of Quebec. They were followed in 1634 by four ships with two hundred colonists, and in 1635 by six vessels with three hundred more immigrants. These thirteen shiploads of settlers marked the true beginning of a sustainable French population that was able to reproduce itself in Quebec.[7]

Its rate of growth was still painfully slow. Between 1633 and 1636, as many as half of these new immigrants returned to France. Even so, the number of hivernants who wintered in Quebec increased from 77 in 1632–33, to 227 in 1633–34, and about 400 in 1635–36.[8] Once started, this new trend continued for many years. A thousand immigrants arrived between 1636 and 1640; 3,500 more from 1640 to 1659; and 9,000 from 1660 to 1699. The "take-off" came during the years of Champlain's governorship from 1633

Champlain's dream of a self-sustaining French population in Quebec hinged on women such as this young Canadienne, with her pretty face, sturdy forearms, white cap, black shawl, and gleaming crucifix: an image of beauty, industry, virtue, grace, and piety.

to 1635, a moment of "deep change," when one change-regime yielded to another.[9]

The vital factor was the growing proportion of French immigrants who were women and girls. In the autumn of 1632 Father Le Jeune counted five French females in Quebec, all in the Hébert-Couillard household. By 1636, according to historian Marcel Trudel's count, at least sixty-five women were living in Quebec plus seventy-eight children.[10]

As more women settled in the colony, other trends appeared. The proportion of single females who found husbands was very high, higher than in France. Their age at first marriage was low, far below European levels: before 1660 most Quebec brides married in their teens and had many children. In families that remained intact through the wife's childbearing years, the *average* number of babies born alive was between eight and nine. Mortality of infants was high, but fertility was much higher. This dynamic population began to double every twenty-five years and it kept on doubling at that rate for many generations. From these small beginnings in the years from 1633 to 1635, the European population of Quebec grew at an extraordinary rate. It might be observed of New France, as of New England, that the only biblical commandment these Christians consistently obeyed was to increase and multiply.[11]

The result was a genetic pattern in Quebec that astonished the demographers who studied it. The French population of Quebec and its kin in North America now number in the millions. One careful study of this large population finds that it grew from a small genetic base. More than two-thirds are descendants of 1,100 French women who came to Quebec between 1630 and 1680.[12]

Champlain's role was critically important. He actively promoted the peopling of Quebec in a spirit that was very different from that of other French leaders. He did all in his power to encourage it. Other leaders were more interested in regulating it. Cardinal Richelieu's Hundred Associates had been ordered in letters patent to "populate the country with native-born French Catholics." This was the wish of the Royal Council and Richelieu himself. Champlain favored a more open policy.

A case in point was his relationship with the family of Abraham Martin, called Maître Abraham, l'Écossais.[13] He was a seaman and fisherman of Scottish origin who turned up in the port of Dieppe. There he married a French woman named Marguerite Langlois before 1619, and they came to New France perhaps in the following year. Martin worked as a seaman and fisherman on the St. Lawrence River, rose to the rank of pilot and master of a company barque, and built a house in Quebec.[14] A child was born and baptized Eustache Martin, son of "sieur Martin (Abraham) and Marguerite Langlois his wife" on October 24, 1621. Eustache is sometimes celebrated as "the first French baby born in America," certainly the first recorded baptism in New France. The name suggests that the godfather may have been Champlain's brother-in-law, Eustache Boullé, who was then in Quebec with his sister Hélène Boullé and Champlain. They did all in their power to support Abraham and Marguerite and their growing brood.[15]

The Martin family lived in Quebec until the British conquest in 1629, when they returned to Dieppe. They remained there until 1632 and came back later that year or the next. Once more Abraham Martin went to work on the river. He and Marguerite had at least three sons who died without issue, and six daughters who married and produced many children. Large numbers of the French-speaking population of Quebec are descended from the daughters of Marguerite Langlois and Abraham Martin, l'Écossais.[16]

Later in life, Abraham Martin continued to do his best to populate Quebec. In 1649, at the age of sixty-four, he got himself into trouble for fornication with a "jeune voleuse," a juvenile delinquent who was sixteen years old. Historians observe that this episode did nothing to damage Maître Abraham's reputation in New France. He did well as the master of a river barque, flourished in the fisheries, and remained an honored member of the community.[17]

Champlain welcomed the Martin family, strongly supported them, and rejoiced in their fecundity. Abraham Martin received a grant of twelve arpents of land near Quebec in 1635, and later twenty arpents more from "friends." Champlain himself dipped into his own wealth and bequeathed to Martin a sum of 1,200 livres to clear land and settle his offspring near Quebec.[18] A persistent legend in Quebec tells us that Martin owned part of the high ground above the town, and that the Plains of Abraham took its name from him. Some historians believe that this legend is founded in fact; others dispute it.[19] Beyond doubt, Champlain made a major effort to settle Abraham Martin's family on the land above the town, surveyed the land with his own hand, built a fourteen-foot roadway up the hill, and helped Martin settle his children on the land.[20] Champlain was happy to have a mixed French and Scottish family in Quebec. Thanks to the strong genes of Abraham l'Écossais, the fecundity of Marguerite Langlois, and the tolerant spirit of Samuel Champlain, many French-speaking Québécois today have an ancestral right to wear the kilt and sporran.

Another example of Champlain's role in the peopling of Quebec followed in 1634. The largest single addition to the population of the colony in this period was the extended family of Robert Giffard de Moncel, a close friend of Champlain. Giffard was an apothecary and master surgeon, a man of wealth and rank from Perche, southeast of Normandy. He came to New France as a ship's surgeon in 1621 or 1622 and liked what he saw. Giffard shared Champlain's dream of New France and his vision of humanity in relations with the Indians. He sought to marry an Indian woman and settle permanently in America. She accepted his proposal, but her nation rejected him, and he went home to France.[21]

The dream still haunted Giffard, and in 1627 he returned to Quebec and built a cabin at La Canardière near Beauport, a few miles below Quebec. When British freebooters captured New France, they made Giffard their prisoner and stole his property. He made his way home to France and with Champlain's support asked the Company of the Hundred Associates to compensate him with a grant of land. They gave him a large holding on both banks of the Beauport River near the site of his old cabin. In turn Giffard undertook to bring colonists at his own expense and settle them on the land. Champlain helped with the arrangements in much the same way that he had helped the Hébert-Couillard and Martin families.[22]

In 1634 Giffard came to America with his French wife, Marie Renouard, who was eight months pregnant. A week after their arrival she gave birth to a healthy daughter, and both survived. Giffard used his wealth to recruit a large party of relatives and servants. Altogether he brought forty-two people to New France in that year: ten men, eight women and twenty-four children, mostly from Perche. Another large group followed in 1635, and more thereafter. A census in 1666 found twenty-nine families and 184 people living on or near Giffard's land, and they were multiplying at a mighty rate. Giffard himself was the driver, and Champlain was an enabler who helped in many ways, and in the face of many setbacks.[23]

The beginning of sustained population growth in Quebec was fundamental to Champlain's grand design, and an artifact of his intention. Its success, after many years of failed effort, came as a great relief to him. In 1634 he wrote to Richelieu, "Seeing so many artisans and families who have migrated this year gives me new courage."[24] At the same time Champlain's leadership gave those French families the courage to go forward on their errand into the new world. The immigrants and their progeny regarded him as their patron and protector. A nineteenth-century descendant wrote that Champlain was "the providential man in whom was placed the confidence of all the families" who came to Quebec in the years from 1633 to 1635.[25]

In these pivotal years, Champlain also had an impact on the development of the seigneurial system, which began to expand in Quebec during his governorship. It was designed to work as an engine of population growth. Champlain himself got it started in 1623 when he arranged a grant of land for Louis Hébert just outside Quebec and ordered workers in the colony to build a family home and farm. Champlain had also arranged for the seigneurial grant of the Île d'Orléans to Émery de Caën and his family.[26]

After Champlain's return in 1633, a general pattern of seigneurial grants became the standard way of organizing the land in New France. It was a system of elegant simplicity, centered at first on the St. Lawrence River. Each grant was defined by a survey line, commonly at right angles to the St. Lawrence, and also to other rivers and streams near Quebec and later Montreal. The result was a riparian pattern of landholding that was crisp and very clean. It was more orderly than the metes and bounds of Virginia, which created a pattern of landholdings like a crazy quilt; and it was more adaptable to the terrain than the rectangles which New Englanders spread west across the continent.[27]

No original document has been found that established the seigneurial system in a definitive way. A pivotal moment was the grant of the seigneury of Beauport to Robert Giffard de Moncel on January 15, 1634, when Champlain was governor.[28] From that moment, the system began to spread rapidly. Seigneurs received land and feudal privileges in return for a commitment to bring colonists to Canada at their expense. Quebec from the start acquired a nobility, or more accurately a landed gentry, under the auspices of the Company of the Hundred Associates. Later the Crown granted seigneuries mainly to nobles, but this was not a high nobility. With a few exceptions such as the Sillery family, it did not include families from the top ranks of the French nobility. There were no princes of the blood in Quebec, and nothing like the great ducal families whose châteaux dominated the French countryside and whose *hôtels* lined the Champs d'Élysées. Even so, an elite of feudal seigneurs became firmly established in New France. Below the seigneurs were sous-seigneurs and habitants working long narrow strips of fertile land that ran back from the river. Beneath them were the engagés, servants and a few slaves. The result was a truncated stratification system, but stratified nonetheless. It was "a society built on networks of kinship and patronage." It began to flourish in Champlain's time, with his encouragement.[29]

And it kept on growing. Even today, four centuries later, this system of land use can still be observed in many parts of the St. Lawrence Valley. Visitors to the city of Quebec can see it by making a short drive across a modern bridge that leads to the Île d'Orléans. Here one still finds the long riparian strips, with old houses of modest size, and small stone-built parish churches. The seigneurs of New France did not as a rule build great châteaux in splendid isolation; they lived modestly and farmed the land beside their tenants.

Another place to observe the remains of this old seigneurial system is on the south bank of the St. Lawrence River from Rivière-du-Loup downstream toward Rimouski. Here again one still finds the long narrow fields sretching back at right angles to the river. On a ridge of high ground parallel to the shoreline, the old houses still stand today, lovingly preserved with colorful paintwork that vividly displays their distinctive architecture.

The same riparian system of land grants also appeared along the larger tributaries of the St. Lawrence. These patterns later spread south along the Richelieu River toward Lake Champlain, and some of these seigneuries continued to exist under the laws of the state of New York until 1854. It was also established in parts of what is now New Brunswick, and traces of it still appear in the state of Maine. On the eastern side of Mount Desert Island, traces can be seen at Hulls Cove in an estate called Cover Farm, with its long strip of land running back from the Frenchman Bay. Cover Farm was the seat of a

seigneury given to a Gascon adventurer named Antoine de La Mothe Cadillac, seigneur de Douaquet et des Monts Déserts. Later the seigneurie passed to
Cadillac's granddaughter, a formidable woman named Maria Theresa de Grégoire, who, with the help of the marquis de Lafayette, convinced the General
Court of Massachusetts to accept her claim. The deeds for the homes of this
historian's family on Mount Desert Island descend from that old French seigneury.[30]

As this system of land use began to develop in New France, something else
started to happen in that same pivotal moment. A distinctive culture began to
grow in Quebec. It was a creation of French immigrants, and of Champlain
himself, and it began to emerge in the critical period from 1633 to 1635. This
new culture developed from the interplay of a new environment and old folkways that the newcomers had carried from France. This hybrid was very much
a product of an historical moment in the seventeenth century. Timing made a
difference, and its place of origin was important too—not France in general,
but particular regions within that kingdom.

In the critical period from 1633 to 1635, immigrant ships to Quebec came
mostly from Norman ports. The largest number of settlers were from Normandy itself. Their proportion has been estimated variously at between 18 and
31 percent of the whole. Perche, inland from Normandy, supplied another
4 percent, probably more. The Île de France, east of Normandy in the valley of
the Seine, contributed 15 percent. Picardy and Champagne added 5 percent;
Brittany, 3.5 percent; Maine, 3 percent; and the Loire Valley, about 7 percent.
Altogether, about 60 percent of colonists in the St. Lawrence Valley came from
these provinces in northern and western France, mostly between the valleys
of the Seine and Loire.[31]

They were joined by a smaller but important flow of migration from another region—four provinces in the west-center of France, which supplied
about 30 percent of Quebec's founders, of whom about 17 percent were from
Aunis and Champlain's Saintonge, 11 percent from neighboring Poitou, and
2 percent from Angoumois. All the other provinces of France together added
only about 10 percent to Quebec's colonizing families.[32]

These patterns of regional origin appeared in the first large stream of migration during the years from 1632 to 1636. Once started they continued in what
scholars call a pattern of chain-migration—families, friends, and neighbors
who followed others they knew to America. The primary area of recruitment
was a triangle that extended from the seaports of Dieppe and Honfleur inland
to Paris, a hundred miles from the sea. The secondary area ran along the Bay

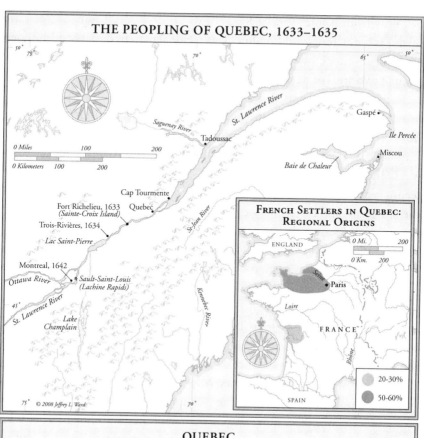

THE PEOPLING OF QUEBEC, 1633–1635

50°
78°
70°
65°
50°

St. Lawrence River

Saguenay River

Tadoussac

Gaspé

Ile Percée

Miscou

Baie de Chaleur

0 Miles 100 200

0 Kilometers 100 200

Cap Tourmente

Fort Richelieu, 1633
(Sainte-Croix Island)   Quebec

Trois-Rivières, 1634

Lac Saint-Pierre

St-Jean River

Montreal, 1642

Ottawa River   Sault-Saint-Louis
(Lachine Rapids)

St. Lawrence River

45°

Lake
Champlain

Kennebec River

75°   © 2008 Jeffrey L. Ward   70°

FRENCH SETTLERS IN QUEBEC: REGIONAL ORIGINS

ENGLAND

0 Mi. 200

0 Km. 200

Seine

Paris

Loire

FRANCE

Rhône

SPAIN

20-30%

50-60%

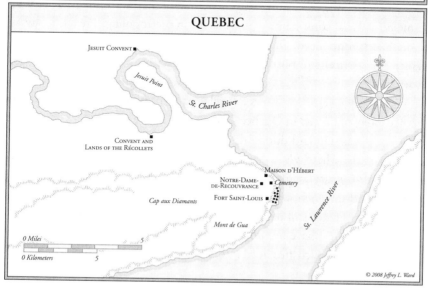

QUEBEC

JESUIT CONVENT

Jesuit Point

St. Charles River

CONVENT AND
LANDS OF THE RÉCOLLETS

MAISON D'HÉBERT

NOTRE-DAME-
DE-RECOUVRANCE   Cemetery

Cap aux Diamants   FORT SAINT-LOUIS

St. Lawrence River

Mont de Gua

0 Miles 5

0 Kilometers 5

© 2008 Jeffrey L. Ward

of Biscay from Nantes and La Rochelle to Brouage and Royan, and reached inland as far as Tours and Loudon. This regional pattern developed from networks of investors, captains, outfitters, acquaintances and friends of Champlain in two areas of western France.

It is a surprise to find that two other coastal regions of France were not prominent in these migrations to Quebec. Not so many immigrants came from the ports of Brittany or from southwestern maritime towns such as Saint-Jean-de-Luz. These other places had important American connections in other ways. They were major centers for the North Atlantic fisheries in the seventeenth century, but they did not contribute to the peopling of Quebec as did the northwest and the center west. To repeat, this pattern began to appear in the period of Champlain's leadership, from 1633 to 1635.

The importance of these regional origins was evident in the culture that began to develop in Quebec during Champlain's era. One of the best ways to study its history is through its language.[33] In the eighteenth and early nineteenth century, visitors such as John Lambert (1809) observed that the Quebec speech had a distinct character. Linguists later studied this dialect in detail and found a close kinship to archaic patterns of speech in northwestern France during the early seventeenth century. Marker vowels are similar, and different from metropolitan French today. For example, *e* went to *a*, and *a* to *o*, and *oi* to *e* (*froid* became *fret*). Long vowels were (and are) diphthongs, as *père* became *pèire*. Final consonants that are silent in metropolitan French today are sometimes pronounced, and archaic suffixes such as *eux* in *obstineux* (obstinant) and *téteux* (stubborn) or *niaiseux* (irritating) persisted in the new world.

Vocabulary of Quebec shows a similar pattern. Blueberries are *myrtilles* in France today but *bluets* in Quebec, as they were in the writings of Champlain. That usage was standard during the early seventeenth century, but is now archaic in Paris, where *bluets* have become French cornflowers. Many other seventeenth-century words from Champlain's era have disappeared in France and persisted in Quebec. Linguistic rituals of courtesy and deference from early modern France still have an echo in Quebec. *Mon oncle* (my uncle) and *ma tante* (my aunt) have become single words. People speak of *mon mononcle* and *ma matante*, which are elided into the affectionate rhythms of *momononcle* and *mamatante*.

The founders of Quebec came by sea from maritime towns, and the language of their descendants still has a nautical flavor that derives from the maritime coast of western France in the seventeenth century. Today a Québécoise will *débarquer*, or disembark from her car, as if she were stepping ashore from Champlain's ship. When a Québécois is fed up with something, he may say *j'ai mon voyage*.

This phenomenon is called colonial lag, and it appeared in many settler societies, but lag was only part of the process. Quebec was also very dynamic, and the pattern of creative dynamism began to appear in Champlain's era. Examples are its creative borrowings from Indian languages for place names such as Canada and Quebec, and for flora and fauna: *achigan* for black bass, *atoca* for cranberry (*canneberge* in France), *ouananiche* for a freshwater salmon, *ouaouaron* for a bull frog, *orignal* for moose, and *caribou* for a genus of large deer. The first recorded use of "caribou" appeared in Champlain's *Voyages*. Everyday objects have Indian names: *boucane* for smoke, *cacaoui* for an older woman, *mocassin* for a soft shoe, *micouène* for a wooden spoon.

Often, colonial persistence and dynamic creativity are combined, as in Quebec's unique language of cursing, which draws on the rituals of the old Catholic mass. In a moment of fury a Québécois may say *câlice* (chalice) or *tabarnak* (tabernacle). This language of cursing of Quebec is very old and was common in Champlain's France. But it is also very creative, and has been continuously reinvented even to our own time.[34]

The culture of Quebec is a bundle of historical paradoxes. To listen to the speechways of Quebec in the twenty-first century is to hear an echo of Champlain's world. It is also to observe a process of preservation and dynamism that began in Champlain's era, and is the most fundamental key to understanding his legacy in North America.[35]

As it was with language, so it would be with other aspects of culture. The same complex patterns of persistence and change also appeared in the vernacular architecture of Quebec, which have long preserved something of Champlain's era and of French regional origins even as it adapted to a new world. Architectural historians have found that the buildings of Quebec derived from the provinces of northwestern France during the mid-seventeenth century, with modifications for the American environment. The early houses that survive in Quebec today tend to be of stone, usually fieldstone, with chimneys of French brick, and they show a strong Norman influence. One common form is a rectangular house with a steeply pitched four-sided, double-hipped roof, chimneys enclosed in gable ends, and simple doors beneath stone lintels, flanked by small French casement windows.[36]

The linkages were often very specific. In Beauport and its vicinity, where Robert Gifford had his seigneury, old houses follow the vernacular architec-

The vernacular architecture of Quebec took form by 1635 and persisted for many generations. It derived from building ways of Normandy, Perche, and other provinces in northwestern France, with many creative adaptations to climate and environment.

ture of Perche. Here one still finds fieldstone houses that are long and low, with a stone stair, elongated roof, triangular pitches, central chimneys, and distinctive small structures attached to the main building.[37] In Quebec and Trois-Rivières, patterns of vernacular architecture had stronger associations with Normandy, as in the restored manor of Niverville, near the city of Quebec. The buildings of Quebec show a distinctive pattern of persistence and change that began to develop four centuries ago.

From 1632 to 1635, as the population in Quebec began to grow, its seigneuries were established, and a distinctive culture began to crystallize, the religious institutions of Quebec underwent a renewal. From 1604 to 1633, the clergy of New France had had a very mixed character: a scattering of Catholic priests, a Protestant minister, and lay preachers on ships in the river. In 1615, with the encouragement of Catholic hierarchy, Champlain turned to the Récollets. The first missionaries of that Franciscan order arrived in that year, three of them together. In total, sixteen Récollets came to New France between 1615 and 1629. Jesuits began to arrive in 1625—three priests and two brothers. The two orders worked side by side until the English conquest, when they were all sent back to France. Champlain had been comfortable with religious diversity, but Richelieu was not. In 1632, the Cardinal forbade the Récollets to operate in New France, and gave his support to the Jesuits, who quickly became dominant in Quebec In 1632, Father Paul Le Jeune arrived as superior, and the Jesuit presence grew very rapidly in the pivotal period from 1633 to 1635. Six Jesuit priests were working in the colony during the winter of 1633–34, fifteen by the winter of 1635–36. They began to operate missions from Cape Breton to Lake Huron. Champlain would have favored a more open system in which tolerance could flourish, but he yielded to Richelieu as he had to do. He supported the Jesuits, helped their missions, and became a very close friend of Father Le Jeune and other priests. He also supported two churches in Quebec, Notre-Dame-de-la-Recouvrance for the habitants, and Notre-Dame-des-Anges for the Jesuits and their Indian converts.[38]

In the three years of Champlain's governorship, these new trends were very powerful. The peopling of the colony began to grow apace, and the land began to be carved into seigneuries. A Quebec culture began to spread across the colony, and Jesuit missions multiplied. These processes put the colony on a firm foundation but a heavy price was paid, mostly by the Indians.

With the establishment of a larger and rapidly growing European population, epidemic disease began to spread through the St. Lawrence Valley. Historians have found references to earlier local epidemics in the region as early as the mid-sixteenth century. Jacques Cartier wrote of an epidemic in 1535–36 among the Laurentian Iroquois people who lived at Stadacona near the site of Montreal. It may have spread from Cartier's ships.[39]

Champlain mentioned a sickness that appeared among the Algonquins at Tadoussac in 1603 and killed one of their leaders and many of their companions. The same thing happened in Acadia, where a missionary wrote in 1616 that the Mi'kmaqs were ravaged by disease after the French arrived and traded with them. It may have happened yet again in Huronia after Champlain's stay there in 1615–16. Jesuit sources report that the Huron accused missionaries of poisoning them and making them ill. Some evidence suggests that the Huron displaced to the north to get clear of epidemics. But most of these infections appear not to have been widespread.[40]

That pattern changed in 1634. In July of that year, Jesuits in Huronia reported a series of deadly epidemics on a new scale. Yet another epidemic followed in the fall of 1636 to the spring of 1637, and altogether at least four contagions spread between 1634 and 1640. The Huron suffered terribly. Huronia was vulnerable because of its dense population, but diseases also began to spread among many other Indian nations during the 1630s. Algonquins returning from the land of the Abenaki reported a *variole* that was very danger-ous, and many thousands of Indians died.[41]

Scholars have speculated on the cause of these epidemics and have tried to identify the diseases that caused massive loss of life among the Indians, but comparatively little mortality among Europeans. Specific diagnoses are much in doubt, but one conclusion is clear. This was a new period of deadly polydemics that were lethal to Indian populations, while Europeans grew ill but recovered. Something had happened to the structures and composition of these populations. One possibility is that growing numbers of children in Quebec turned the colony into an incubator for childhood diseases that were endemic in Europe but became epidemic in America and shattered Indian na-tions. In short, here was another pattern of deep change in Indian populations at a moment when one regime yielded to another. The pivot point appeared *circa* 1634. Just as the French population began its rapid increase, the Indian population started to decline in one of the cruelest events in modern history. Champlain did not live long enough to see what was happening. It would have broken his heart.

But at the same time there were other great transformations in the peopling of New France, and some were more mixed and hopeful for Europeans and Indians alike. Many Indian nations suffered severely, but most of them sur-vived. And in the midst of heavy mortality, other new Franco-Indian nations and cultures were born. One them appeared on the western frontier, and an-other to the east in Acadia. There again, Champlain had yet another role to play.

23.

THE CRADLE OF ACADIA
Champlain and Razilly, 1632–35

The settlers whom Razilly placed here were the ancestors of the Acadian people, to whom this place should be endeared as the cradle of their race in America.

—William Ganong on Acadia [1]

W HILE QUEBEC began to grow in a new way, something similar happened in another part of New France. After three decades of struggle and frustration, settlements suddenly started to multiply in Acadia. We have followed the troubled history of that region from the moment when the sieur de Mons and Champlain planted the first settlement on Sainte-Croix Island in 1604. It was abandoned in 1605, refounded at Port-Royal, abandoned again in 1607, revived by Poutrincourt in 1610, burned by English raiders in 1613, rebuilt by Poutrincourt in 1614, abandoned for another site in 1618, occupied once more by the French in 1623, and seized by Scottish adventurers in 1629. Through all these events, a few Frenchmen remained in Acadia. Some formed unions with Indian women and made a precarious living from the fur trade, but nobody had been able to found a French settlement that took root and grew of itself.[2]

The critical moment came in 1632 when, at Champlain's prompting, Acadia was added to the list of territories that England was obliged to return to France. The Hundred Associates quickly sponsored four subsidiary companies to support trading forts at strategic places along the coast. None were primarily colonizing ventures. That task went to a fifth subsidiary, the largest of them all, called the Compagnie de Razilly.[3] Its leader, Isaac de Razilly, was one of the most able yet least remembered leaders in the drama of New France. He was a good friend of Champlain. They shared the same large purposes for North America and adopted similar policies. In difficult times they strongly supported each other, and they achieved similar results.

Isaac de Razilly was thirty-nine years old in 1632, a battle-scarred naval officer with a patch over one eye and a hard look in the other. His noble family had an ancient seat in Touraine forty miles inland from La Rochelle, and was well connected at court—Cardinal Richelieu was a cousin. Razilly was raised to the profession of arms, and became a captain in the king's marine. He won fame in five campaigns against the corsairs of Morocco, fighting with such ferocity that he was called the Loup de Mer, the seawolf of France. At the age of eighteen he became a Knight of Malta—a high distinction in that honor-bound world.[4]

Razilly was also a devout Catholic. In 1625, he commanded a squadron at the siege of Protestant La Rochelle, won a battle against a relieving English force at the Isle of Ré, and lost an eye when a captured Huguenot ship blew up in his face.[5] While Razilly was convalescing from his wounds, Richelieu consulted him on maritime affairs. Razilly was a man of many gifts, with a statesman's vision and a scholar's way with ideas. His naval service gave him a global perspective and an interest in colonies. As early as 1612, he and his brothers had tried to found a Capuchin mission near the Amazon River. When it failed, they turned to North America and began to work with Champlain.[6]

In 1626, Cardinal Richelieu asked Razilly to draft an aide-mémoire on colonies. The result was a document of great importance to the history of New France. Razilly made a strong argument for the role of colonies to the destiny of nations. He envisioned a global empire for France, with African fortresses at Guinea and Senegal, trading factories in South Asia and the East Indies, outposts in South America, and a major colony in North America. For New France he urged a new company with a capital of 300,000 livres, new settlements with 4,000 colonists, and military forces strong enough to expel British settlers north of Cape Hatteras in North Carolina.[7]

Razilly's document had a major impact. Some of its language appeared in the charters that created the Company of One Hundred Associates. He and Champlain became members within five days of one another in 1628. They invested in its subsidiary ventures and actively supported each other in a common cause, even as they led different parts of it.[8] Razilly persuaded Richelieu to send Champlain to Quebec as acting governor. Without his support Champlain would not have had the job at all.[9] In turn Champlain supported Razilly's plans for Acadia and wrote in glowing terms of "Monsieur the Commander de Razilly, who has all the requisite qualities of a good and perfect sea captain being prudent, wise and industrious, and possessed by a holy desire to increase the glory of God and to carry his courage to the country of New France." Champlain predicted that his friend would "raise the standard of Jesus Christ and make the Lilies flourish there."[10]

Champlain also assisted Razilly in another way, as one of the few seamen

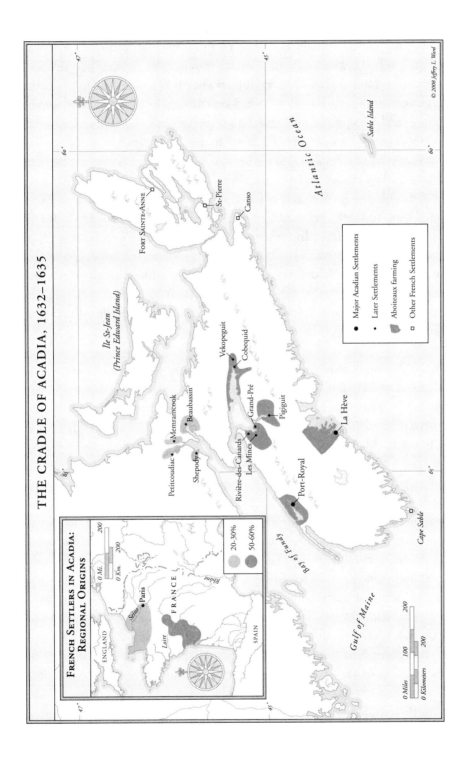

THE CRADLE OF ACADIA, 1632–1635

© 2008 Jeffrey L. Ward

Major Acadian Settlements •
Later Settlements ·
Aboiteaux farming
Other French Settlements □

Atlantic Ocean

Sable Island

Fort Sainte-Anne

St-Pierre

Canso

Île St-Jean
(Prince Edward Island)

Vekopeguit

Cobequid

Memramcook

Beaubassin

Grand-Pré

Pigiguit

Petitcoudiac

Shepody

Rivière-des-Canards

Les Mines

La Hève

Port-Royal

Bay of Fundy

Gulf of Maine

Cape Sable

FRENCH SETTLERS IN ACADIA: REGIONAL ORIGINS

ENGLAND

FRANCE

Paris

Seine

Loire

Rhône

SPAIN

20–30%
50–60%

0 Mi.   200
0 Km.   200

0 Miles   100   200
0 Kilometers   200

who had explored virtually every harbor and inlet on Acadia's long indented coast. He had also studied the natural resources of Acadia, planted test-gardens, and found places of extraordinary fertility that could indeed make the lilies flourish there. To travel in Nova Scotia during the growing season is to be impressed by its pockets of rich farmland and flourishing field crops, which are more abundant than New England's in the same latitude. Champlain had studied Acadia's great stands of timber and its unrivaled fisheries. Like Razilly he also had an eye for beauty in the land.[11]

Champlain especially favored two sites for settlement. One was a very handsome and well-protected harbor on the east coast, which he named La Hève, today's La Have. The other was Port-Royal on the west coast, with its great sheet of sheltered water inside the narrow entrance called Digby Gut today. Both places had protected harbors, defensible ground, sweetwater streams, abundant timber, fertile soil, and natural beauty. Many a good site was to be found along the coast of Acadia, but La Hève and Port-Royal were Champlain's favorites. They moved to the top of Razilly's list.

In 1632, while Champlain was planning a return to Quebec, Razilly raised a capital of 150,000 livres for Acadia. It was very much a family venture. Richelieu himself contributed 10,000 livres and a fully equipped French warship called *L'Espérance-en-Dieu.* Her captain was another Razilly cousin, Charles de Menou, sieur d'Aulnay, who would become a major figure in Acadia. Another large vessel was commanded by Razilly's brother Claude de Launay-Rasilly [sic].[12]

Razilly made his plans for Acadia in much the same way that Champlain operated in the St. Lawrence Valley. Their purpose was the same: to plant a population that could sustain itself. Both found capital enough for a fleet of three immigrant ships in the first year. They planned to send other fleets in the next four years. Razilly selected a group of able leaders from his own rank and region. Some were of the nobility, as was d'Aulnay. Others were men of commerce such as Nicolas Denys, a man of modest origins and much ability who came from Razilly's native province. He would be a major asset.[13]

Altogether Razilly recruited three hundred settlers. Like Champlain he selected them carefully. A Paris gazette described them as "hommes d'élite." They were men with many skills that would be useful in the building of a colony. Both leaders were mindful of religion. Where Champlain decided to go with the Jesuits, Razilly recruited three Capuchin fathers of the order that he and Richelieu specially favored.[14]

Again like Champlain, Razilly made a particular effort to recruit families.

For both men, this was the hardest part of their task and the most vital to the peopling of a colony. French families showed great reluctance to emigrate, unlike those from Britain, Germany, and other European countries. The anomaly of French attitudes toward emigration has never been explained. With great effort, Razilly found twelve or fifteen French families for his first voyage in 1632—not many, but enough to start a population growing.[15]

In one respect Champlain and Razilly did things differently. The settlers of Quebec came from French provinces north of the Loire, especially from Normandy. They sailed in three ships from the Norman port of Dieppe, with others following from Honfleur and Le Havre. Razilly's colonists for Acadia came from provinces south of the Loire in the west-center of France. They sailed from the ports of Auray and La Rochelle on the Bay of Biscay.

Razilly's fleet was the first to sail, late in the season of 1632. On September 8, 1632, they reached their destination and his colonists came ashore on the Atlantic coast of what is now Nova Scotia, in the beautiful harbor of La Hève. It was, and is, a very attractive place. At the mouth of the harbor was an island that the colonists called the Isle aux Framboises, "its top being nothing but raspberry bushes." The island was said to be "completely covered with pigeons." Thousands of them fattened on the raspberries, and the settlers fed on the pigeons.[16]

On one side of the harbor was a spectacular headland of yellow clay a hundred feet high. At first light of day it gleamed like gold, and they called it Cap Doré. Inside the entrance was a beautiful basin, big enough to hold many ships. A handsome river flowed into it through large groves of oaks and elms. There were open meadows, marshes, and "fine and good lands" with soil of deep fertility.[17]

To the settlers, Acadia seemed a place of unimaginable abundance. On both banks of the river they found "an infinity of scallops like those of Mont St. Michel and Saint Jacques." In the waters off the coast they discovered "lobsters as big as little children," with fore-claws that could hold a pint of good French wine. Salmon and shad swarmed in the river. There were large numbers of deer and moose, birds beyond imagining, wild blueberries and strawberries.[18]

Even in this earthly paradise, Razilly's first concern (like that of Champlain for Quebec) was military security against European rivals. At La Hève he built a strong battery on what is still called Fort Point. At the same time he constructed a chapel for the Capuchin fathers and encouraged them to open the first boarding school in New France. Children of both French colonists and

Mi'kmaq families were invited to study together. Again like Champlain, Razilly made a sustained effort to establish good relations with the Indians, encouraged them to settle close by, opened the colony to them, and treated them with humanity.[19]

The French had been slow getting started and arrived very late in the season. They suffered through a hard winter, but Razilly took precautions against scurvy that he may have learned from Champlain's experience of Indian remedies. All the colonists survived. Some returned to France, but it was a healthy settlement. Its population began to grow by natural increase, slowly at first, but with gathering momentum.

Once begun, the flow of colonists continued the next year, mostly in ships sailing from La Rochelle and other ports in west-central France. On January 24, 1633, d'Aulnay returned to France, recruited more colonists, and sailed back again on March 12 in "a vessel filled with men, provisions, munitions, and other supplies that the company sent to Commander de Razilly."[20] In 1634, Isaac de Razilly's brother Claude de Launay-Razilly combined with Jean Ordonnier, a bourgeois of Paris, to found another group sponsored by the Hundred Associates, which they called a "Society for the Peopling of Acadia." Through their cousin Cardinal Richelieu they petitioned the king for five of His Majesty's ships to be used for trade and fishing. On their outward-bound voyage from France, they carried supplies and settlers to Acadia. Richelieu himself took an active role in recruiting investors for the society of Razilly and Cordonnier, "to support the enterprise that they have made to populate the settlements of Port-Royal and La Hève on the coast of Acadia."[21]

After the French colony at La Hève was well on its way, Razilly turned to another task. A few Scottish Freebooters were still living at Port-Royal on the other side of Acadia, and some of them were acting as if they meant to stay. Their leader, Andrew Forrester, was a violent, cruel, and angry man who had defied orders from his king to abandon the colony. He led a party of Scots in a surprise attack on the French trading post at Fort Sainte-Marie, across the Bay of Fundy on the Saint John River. Forrester entered the French fort with professions of peace, made prisoners of the habitants, clapped them in irons, tortured one of them to find things of value, stole their furs, food, and trade goods, pulled down a Catholic cross, removed the royal arms of Louis XIII, and returned to Port-Royal. He put his French captives aboard a passing New England pinnace and ordered the captain to maroon them on a barren island in Penobscot Bay—a sentence to death by starvation. The New England captain released them instead near the Saint John River, and they found their way back to Cape Sable on the southeast coast with a report of their cruel treatment.[22]

Forrester had crossed the line between freebooting and piracy, and the French went after him. Razilly mustered his men and led them ashore at Port-Royal. Forrester was overmatched, and asked for terms that he had denied to others. Razilly acted with wisdom and restraint. After a parley, he offered the Scots transportation to Britain and payment for their possessions, if they surrendered the fort intact. They were very quick to agree.[23]

Razilly occupied Port-Royal, and ordered some of his colonists to take possession of the old French settlement under the command of René Le Coq de la Saussaye, an old hand on the Acadian coast. They restored relations with the Mi'kmaq and a fur trade began to revive in 1633. A few of the Scots chose to remain with the French and were made welcome. They began to mix with French families in Port-Royal to form a hybrid culture that still exists in Nova Scotia, even as its proportions have changed. Here again Razilly was much like Champlain in his tolerance of diversity, as long as he had unity of command.[24]

In 1634, Razilly sent a long letter to Marc Lescarbot, describing in detail the success of his small colony at Port-Royal. He had spent his own wealth lavishly to supply the settlers with food from France and had brought over "cattle, pigs, goats and poultry," which were doing well. He planted vegetables and kitchen gardens. Razilly told Lescarbot that the tools and building supplies had cost many thousands of livres, but that "a miserly man could never found a successful settlement." His hope was to "give his wealth to such a cause if he could establish a place for the poor people of France in the abundance of the new world.[25]

Razilly also devoted himself to the economic development of his colony, with mixed results. He encouraged Nicolas Denys to organize a timber operation near La Hève, with workers cutting oak, squaring it into timbers and preparing it for export to France when the immigrant ships sailed home. Denys also founded a fishing settlement near La Hève at Port-Rossignol.[26]

At Canso, in northeastern Acadia, Razilly built another fortified trading post called Fort Saint-Francis. Its purpose was to organize the fur trade. Here he faced a challenge to his leadership. While Razilly's men were building the fort, they were attacked by a French fishing captain named Jean Thomas, who traded wine for furs from the Mi'kmaq Indians—a lucrative business, but illegal. Thomas had a license from Cardinal Richelieu to operate on the Grand Bank but he was expressly forbidden to trade in furs or to sell wine to the Indians. He led a party of Mi'kmaq warriors in an assault on Fort Saint-Francis. The French commander was wounded and the post was looted. Razilly responded much as Champlain had done when faced with a rebellion in Quebec. He gathered his strength, moved quickly with all the strength at his command, arrested Thomas, and sent him in irons to La Rochelle.[27]

In three years, Razilly had succeeded in the same way that Champlain had done at Quebec. He had reclaimed the heartland of Acadia for France, removed British freebooters, established settlements at La Hève on the east coast and Port-Royal on the west, with a trading post at Canso, and he started a population growing. More French families arrived each year. The economy was developing, and good relations were established with the Mi'kmaq Indians.

Just as everything was going so well, Razilly died very suddenly in November 1635, at the age of forty-eight and the peak of his powers. It was a heavy loss for New France. He was mourned by those who knew him for his strength, integrity, and humanity. In Acadia his death was an especially heavy blow— heavier than anyone could have known at the time. But Razilly had laid a firm foundation.

Razilly's cousin d'Aulnay became commander of the colony. He encouraged many settlers to move from La Hève to Port-Royal. That larger site became the center of the colony. By 1644, according to a memorandum from d'Aulnay, the habitants of Port-Royal numbered two hundred men, including soldiers, laborers and other artisans, plus Capuchins, women, and children who were not enumerated. D'Aulnay reported that more than twenty French households had migrated intact and many more begun to form in Acadia. He also noted that his count also did not include "enfants sauvages" who were taken into the French settlement. More than a few Frenchmen in that settlement made unions with Indian women. The Razillys in Acadia, again like Champlain in Quebec, encouraged *métissage*.[28]

Nicolas Denys visited Port-Royal in 1653, and reported, "All the inhabitants there are the ones that M. le Commandeur de Razilly had brought from France to La Hève" in 1632. They had continued to move from La Hève to Port-Royal after Razilly's death in 1635. Denys observed, "Since that time they have multiplied much at Port-Royal, where they have a great number of cattle and swine."[29] In 1671 a census found 227 children in sixty-three households at Port-Royal alone. These families founded many settlements along the coast. A study of Acadian parishes in the early eighteenth century found that migrants to La Hève accounted for two-thirds of the entire Acadian population. The same evidence also showed an astonishing concentration of French family names. In the census of 1671, Acadians had a total of only fifty-three French names. That concentration persisted for many generations. In the mid-twentieth century, yet another census found that 86 percent of 34,000 French Acadians, had only seventy-six family names as late as the year 1938. Scholars have compared those two lists and they have found that fully two-thirds of twentieth-century Acadian names appeared in the census of 1671. Geneviève Massignon observes that "the cradle of the Acadian population was Port-Royal," which in turn derived from the migration that began at La Hève in 1632.[30]

Where did Acadia's founding families come from? Many studies have found a pattern, based on choices that Razilly and Champlain had made about the recruitment of colonists and the charter of their ships from 1632 to 1635. As we have seen, most immigrants to the St. Lawrence Valley came from Normandy, Perche, the Île de France, and other western provinces north of the Loire River. These provinces together supplied more than 51 percent of the colonists in Quebec, and less than 25 percent in Acadia. A different pattern appeared in Acadia. Colonists from Touraine, Poitou, Saintonge, Aunis, and other provinces in the center-west of France accounted for more than 51 percent of the Acadian population, but less than 25 percent in Quebec. Brittany was a small but important element in both populations, about 4 percent each. Very few immigrants came to either place from the north, the east, the southeast, or far southwest of France. English, Scots, Irish, Portuguese, and Basques, all mixed, added at least 7 percent of Acadian population.[31]

A distinctive French dialect took root in Acadia, and it was a clue to the importance of founding events in the era of Razilly and Champlain. Acadian speech derived in part from the patois of Poitou, Saintonge, Aunis, Anjou, and Touraine. To speakers of metropolitan French today, Acadian dialect sounds quaint and old-fashioned—and so it is in some ways. But it was another instance of that American paradox—stubbornly archaic in some ways, strongly inventive in others. Acadian pronunciation is so distinct that speakers of standard French sometimes have difficulty understanding what is said.

One defining feature is familiar to us all. Acadians were apt to drop an initial vowel, and add a *j*-sound before a second vowel. Thus *Acadien* became *Cadjin* or *Cadjen* in Canada, and later *Cajun* or *parler le cajun* in Louisiana. In the same way, *bon dieu* (Good God) became *bon djeu*, and *braguette* (trousers) is *brajette*. The letter *r* has a way of disappearing in the last syllable: *libre* is *libe*, and *arbre* is *arbe*. In many words an initial *c* or *q* or *t* is sounded like a sneeze:

queue becomes *tcheue*, the imperative *tiens!* (hold on! or stop!) is *tchin!*; *cuillère* is *tchuillère* and *quelque chose* becomes *tchecu'chouse*.[32]

Some Acadien pronunciations derived directly from regional origins of the founding families in the 1630s. Linguist Yves Cormier estimates that 55 percent of Acadianisms of French origin are regional words, and 45 percent are archaic words peculiar to their period of origin in the seventeenth century. Among Acadian words of regional origin, more than half are from the center-west of France, about 15 or 20 percent from Normandy and the northwest, fewer than 15 percent from other parts of France.[33]

The vocabulary of Acadia also had many nautical terms, as in *amarrer* (to moor) for "tie," or *piquer* (to get a fish) for "open." This was an industrious culture that valued honest toil. The praise word *vaillant* meant "brave, busy, and industrious." It was a raw and muscular language. A metropolitan French baby will *pleurer* (cry); an Acadian baby will *horler* (howl). To disturb somebody in France is to *déranger;* in Acadia it is to *boloxer*. To have a difficulty is not, as in French, *avoir de la difficulté* but *avoir de la misère*. Acadian *vêtements* (clothing) are *hardes*; *aussi* is *itou*; *et* is *pis* (from et puis); *se dépêcher* (to hurry) is *se haler*, literally to haul oneself.[34]

Acadian speechways were also very inventive in the creation of new expressions for unfamiliar objects in a new world. The slender bright green glasswort that grows on northern beaches was called *tétine-de-souris*, literally, a mouse tit. Later, the Académie française did not approve and made it *salicorne d'Europe*. A cranberry is a *canneberge* in France; in Acadia it is a *pomme de pré* (literally a saltmarsh apple); in Quebec it is the Indian *atoca*. The hearty Acadian diet required new words for its cuisine: *fricot* for a wonderfully thick stew of meat, potatoes, onions, carrots, and lumps of dough; *poutine râpée* for a heavy ball of chopped potatoes with a piece of pork at the core. Some words appear in both Quebec and Acadian dialects, but these two distinct speechways came from different parts of France in the same period, 1632–35.[35]

The French-speaking families of Acadia rapidly outstripped the land available at Port-Royal, and began to found other settlements along the coast at Grand-Pré (today an Acadian shrine), at Pigiguit (today's Windsor), and at Cobeguit (Truro). Other Acadian settlements were planted at Beaubassin, Petitcousdiac, and Memramcook at the head of the Bay of Fundy. Some of the most enduring were to the south at Sainte-Anne's on St. Mary's Bay, Pobompoup (Pubnico), and other sites along the south-western coast of Nova Scotia which are still strongly francophone today. On the opposite side of the Bay of Fundy, settlements were planted near the present city of Saint John in New Brunswick. Other Acadian descendants later moved to settlements in Maine at Madawaska, Caribou, Presqu'isle, Saint-Francis, Saint-Luce, and Saint-Joseph.

From an early date, Acadians in many of these places worked their land in a very distinctive way. They created grain fields by building dykes around marshes on tidal rivers and freshwater streams. The dyking of fertile marshlands in Acadia developed in the 1630s and was well advanced by 1650.[36] An early reference to this practice was at Port-La-Tour, near Cape Sable. There the Récollet fathers had a mission, and one of them kept a garden of about half an acre, "on excellent fertile land . . . formerly a marsh or meadow, still called French meadow." This marsh soil was extraordinarily productive. The younger La Tour did the same thing, and planted a garden where "the land is very flat near the bottom of the bay," with similar success. The date was approximately 1630.[37]

The draining of marshlands multiplied along both coasts of Acadia in the mid-1630s. It was so important that Isaac de Razilly's brother Claude de Launay-Razilly recruited five *saulniers*, or marshworkers, for service in Acadia. These men signed a contract in March, 1636, at the Three Kings Tavern in La Rochelle.[38] In France they had been specialists in ditching and dyking tidal marshes for the salt industry. In 1632 Razilly had already recruited some of these skilled workers to make salt in Acadia for the fishing industry. Once there, they discovered the fertility of deep topsoil in the tidal marshes, and began to make salt marshes into arable fields. He also brought saulniers from Touraine, where they were well practiced in the dyking of freshwater marshes.[39]

The marshlands of Acadia were used in two ways: sometimes for the evaporation of salt from seawater, as in the area around Brouage in France, but mostly for the draining of cropland. The work of draining the land was heavy, but so also was the labor of clearing the forest for fields. Within a generation of settlement, these dykes had become very extensive. Denis commented on "the great extent of meadows which the sea used to cover and which sieur Aulnay had drained."[40] Visitors remarked on the size of "rich but hard-won grain fields behind the dykes.[41] The French families of Acadia won this land from the sea by their unceasing labor, and they became strongly attached to it. They developed a different attitude from other colonists in North America, who favored extensive agriculture, mining the soil, and moving on to new land when it wore out. The Acadians gained a reputation for clinging stubbornly to the land when others tried to remove them.

• • •

Acadians also adopted a distinctive building style for their small settlements. Here again we find evidence that this unique culture began to take form in the time of Razilly and Champlain. As in many colonies, the earliest buildings were rough impermanent *poteaux-en-terre* (post-in-ground) structures, with one or two rooms, clay chimneys, and thatched roofs. These houses were adapted in various ways to the cold northern climate. One account describes beds that were boarded all round, for warmth and privacy.

Permanent buildings evolved from these crude structures. In a timber-rich environment, a common design was the *maison de charpente*, a rectangular, single-pitched, post-and-beam house, with a heavy frame, carefully mortised, pegged, or dove-tailed together. It could have as many as three or four rooms, with a cellar below, and an attic above called a *garconnière*, where the boys slept. Walls and roofs were made of horizontal boards, insulated with birchbark, and covered with weather-tight wooden shingles.[42] Other Acadian house-types varied in the construction of walls. A *maison pièce-sur-pièce* (piece-on-piece house) was made of large square timbers laid one above another and mortised into vertical posts. The *maison de madrier*, or plank house, had walls of vertical planks pegged tightly together. The very common *maison de torchis* was a post-and-beam house with the spaces between walls filled with various mixtures of clay, oat-straw, chopped hay, moss, or hair, stiffened with horizontal wood poles called *palots* or *palissons*. As late as 1687–88, most Port-Royal houses were small maisons de torchis. Even the governor lived in a plank house.[43]

The Acadians also developed a unique political tradition. Unlike the habitants of Quebec, the people of Acadia adopted a customary practice of local self-government. Historian Peter Moogk writes, "Only in Acadia was there a form of village self-government provided by elders." He thinks that this exception was "due to the French government's indifference to what happened in Acadia."[44]

That "attitude of indifference" might explain how this practice could persist, but not why it emerged in the first place. Clearly it came from the interplay of a cultural heritage with a new environment. The people of some provinces in southwestern France during the early seventeenth century still maintained parliamentary bodies that preserved traditional legislative powers of self-government, long after the parlements of northern France had become administrative and judicial bodies. The Acadians brought something of that heritage to North America. And in a new environment they found opportunities for economic development that required collective effort in the construc-

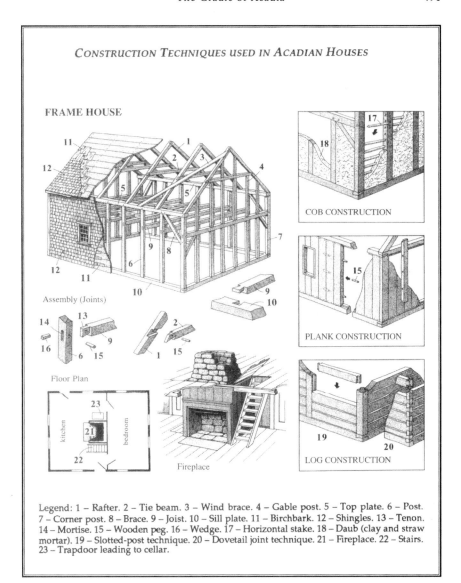

CONSTRUCTION TECHNIQUES USED IN ACADIAN HOUSES

FRAME HOUSE

COB CONSTRUCTION

Assembly (Joints)

PLANK CONSTRUCTION

Floor Plan

kitchen

bedroom

LOG CONSTRUCTION

Fireplace

Legend: 1 – Rafter. 2 – Tie beam. 3 – Wind brace. 4 – Gable post. 5 – Top plate. 6 – Post. 7 – Corner post. 8 – Brace. 9 – Joist. 10 – Sill plate. 11 – Birchbark. 12 – Shingles. 13 – Tenon. 14 – Mortise. 15 – Wooden peg. 16 – Wedge. 17 – Horizontal stake. 18 – Daub (clay and straw mortar). 19 – Slotted-post technique. 20 – Dovetail joint technique. 21 – Fireplace. 22 – Stairs. 23 – Trapdoor leading to cellar.

The buildings in Acadia followed house plans in west-central France, with many major changes in materials that were abundant in the American environment. This drawing by Bernard and Ronnie Gilles LeBlanc analyzes four house types that were expressions of a unique French culture that took root in Acadia ca. 1632–35.

tion of dykes and aboiteaux. These complex hydraulic systems required constant maintenance and regulation. The people of Acadia responded by developing political systems of self-government and maintaining them for many generations. The land system of Acadia reinforced a heritage of local self-government.[45]

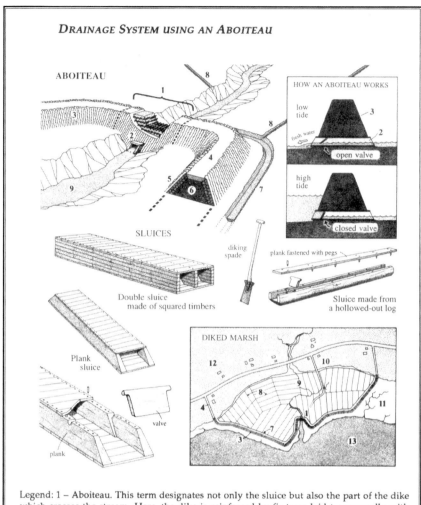

DRAINAGE SYSTEM USING AN ABOITEAU

ABOITEAU

HOW AN ABOITEAU WORKS

low tide

fresh water

open valve

high tide

closed valve

SLUICES

diking spade

plank fastened with pegs

Double sluice made of squared timbers

Sluice made from a hollowed-out log

Plank sluice

valve

plank

DIKED MARSH

Legend: 1 – Aboiteau. This term designates not only the sluice but also the part of the dike which crosses the stream. Here, the dike is reinforced by fir trees laid transversally with alternate layers of clay soil. 2 – Sluice. 3 – Levee or dike. 4 – Road or path along the top of the dike. 5 – Dike facing made of sod. 6 – Earthen core (made of soil dug from the marshlands). 7 – *Contre-ceinture*. 8 – Drainage ditch. 9 – Stream. 10 – Road leading into the marshlands. 11 – Salt marsh. 12 – Dwellings on higher terrain. 13 – River or bay.

The aboiteaux, or earth and timber dykes of Acadia, were another important adaptation of coastal and river marsh cultures in Saintonge and Touraine to the American environment. They became a major part of the material base of Acadian culture, society, and politics. Their structure and function are analyzed in this excellent drawing by Bernard and Ronnie Gilles LeBlanc.

The collective building of dykes to reclaim tidal marshes for cultivation and maintenance of the embankments also encouraged interfamilial cooperation among the Acadians. Spontaneous self-organized economic cooperation with other families was less common in the St. Lawrence Valley. In French-speaking settlements throughout Quebec, "the priest provided social leadership and the parish provided the framework for community life. It was not a framework that people created for themselves, and it was always subject to external authority."[46]

Acadians rapidly acquired a reputation for self-government and community building. One governor of New France complained that Acadians were "demi-républicains," and very different from the stereotypical *moutons* (sheep) of Quebec and the *loups* (wolves) of Montreal. For their stubborn determination to keep their own ways, the Acadians were called "*les entêtés*," hardheads—stubborn, obstinate, difficult, and very strong—a race of survivors. Acadians took that name to themselves as a badge of honor. They also gained a reputation in New France as a distinct people, deeply attached to their land, and strong in their determination to endure.[47]

The distinct culture that began to develop among the Acadians from a very early date was not a unitary thing. On the coast of Acadia there were a multiplicity of small settlements, which tended to be diverse in ecology, ethnicity, religion, culture, and language. Here again we find variations in speechways. A distinctive dialect is spoken around St. Mary's Bay, with its flourishing institutions and its own college. In the late twentieth century, a popular song in Canada by the band nostalgically called Grand Dérangement ("Great Displacement") was titled "L'homme à point d'accent" ("The man with no accent"). It is sung in the dialect of St. Mary's Bay French. Across the Bay of Fundy in New Brunswick and Maine, there are other speechways.

The later history of these diverse cultures is a complex subject. Control of Acadia changed many times. It was French until 1629, British from 1629 to 1632, French from 1632 to 1654, British from 1654 to 1670, French from 1670 to 1710, British from 1710 to 1740; and in the 1740s and 1750s a battleground where the French and Abenaki were pitted against the British and other Indian nations. In 1755 a British governor in Nova Scotia, Colonel Charles Lawrence, proclaimed that all families who refused to take an oath of allegiance to the British crown would be required to leave Acadia. About 6,000 Acadians were expelled, mostly to colonies in the British empire. Others found their way to France, Louisiana, and other nations. Many lost their lives. But many Acadians did not leave. They disappeared into the woods and remained there. Others later came back in large numbers. Altogether, perhaps as many as one-third to one-half returned to Acadia. Even to this day French continues to be spoken along the southwest coast of Nova Scotia.

After that great dispersion, Acadian families continued to multiply remarkably throughout the world. In the United States alone, the census of

1990 reported that 668,000 people identified themselves as wholly or partly of "Acadian" or "Cajun" origin. Comparable estimates for Canada and other countries would certainly bring the numbers above a million. Most of these self-identified Acadians or Cajuns in the Acadian diaspora are descended from Razilly's colonists who migrated to La Hève and Port-Royal.[48]

That process of population growth began in the years 1632–35, when Champlain was acting governor in Quebec and Isaac de Razilly was governor of Acadia, and it was largely due to their leadership. They worked in harmony together, and brought a period of order and stability to these colonies. After their deaths the next generation of leaders were not of the same character, and in Acadia they started another French civil war. But Champlain and Razilly kept the peace in New France during a critical period.

They also got along with the Indians. A leading scholar of Acadia, Andrew Hill Clark, wrote of a "harmonious modus vivendi" between French Acadians and Mi'kmaq that began in the early seventeenth century and continued for many generations. Clark observed that "an almost symbiotic relationship of mutual tolerance and support grew up between the two cultures." It went back to the founding of Port-Royal in 1605 and was sustained by French humanists who included Champlain, de Mons, Poutrincourt, and Razilly. The French of Acadia differed in many ways from their cousins in Quebec, but they shared a common spirit in the way that they cooperated with the native populations. Here again the visions of Champlain and Razilly became a living reality.[49]

24.

TROIS-RIVIÈRES

New Ways in the West, 1634–35

> Our young men will marry your daughters, and henceforth we shall be one people.
>
> —Champlain's prophecy to the Montagnais, 1633[1]

> They cherish freedom as they cherish life.
>
> —an account of the Métis People, 1856[2]

I N THE SUMMER OF 1634 Champlain launched another project in the St. Lawrence Valley. He planned to establish a chain of fortified posts to the west, strong enough to control the flow of traffic on the river. They were also to be trading posts, missionary stations, and permanent homes for adventurous young Frenchmen who would explore the country and live among the Indians.

He began by building a fort seventy-three miles upstream from Quebec at the mouth of the Rivière Saint-Maurice, which flowed into the St. Lawrence through three channels and was called Trois-Rivières. It was a strategic spot. The Saint-Maurice entered the St. Lawrence from the north; twelve miles away the Rivière des Iroquois joined the St. Lawrence from the south. Three major arteries came together in this part of the valley. One purpose of the settlement at Trois-Rivières was to control movement from the Iroquois country. Another was to provide a trading center for Indian nations to the north and west.[3]

On July 1, Champlain sent a barque under the command of the sieur de La Violette with orders to build a fort and trading post there. Little is known of La Violette, not even his full name. He is thought to have been an employee of the Hundred Associates. From the job that Champlain gave him, one might guess that he had a military background. La Violette brought a detachment of soldiers and a party of artisans and laborers to construct the fort. A fictional statue of La Violette with the face of historian Benjamin Sulte marks the approximate spot.[4]

Later in the summer of 1634, Champlain himself visited the site and appears to have supervised the building of a log fort with barracks, a magazine, a storehouse, and homes for French habitants. The settlement was protected by a strong palisade. Cannon were emplaced to control the approaches to the fort and movement on the rivers. La Violette remained as commandant from July 4, 1634, to August 15, 1636.[5]

Trois-Rivières rapidly became an important place for trade with Indians of many nations, who exchanged furs and pelts for European goods. Two interpreters, Jacques Hertel and Jean Godefroy, settled there, and many others soon made it their home. So also did Jesuit father Jacques Buteux, who built a mission and a chapel. Houses multiplied within the palisade and soon spread beyond it. By 1666, almost as many French families would be living at Trois-Rivières as in the town of Quebec.[6]

This small settlement quickly acquired another importance. A new culture began to form there, on what was then the western frontier of New France. Its creators were young men and women, French and Indian together, who improvised new ways of life from the meeting of their cultures. Once again Champlain played the seminal role. He had already set this cultural process in motion when he sent French youths to live among the Indians and learn their customs. At the same time, he and Indian leaders sent their youths to France on similar errands.

He called these young people "truchements," or interpreters. It was an exotic word in French, borrowed from the Turkish *tergiman* and Arabic *targuman* on another cultural frontier, where Christians, Turks, and Arabs had met during the crusades. Champlain used the word in its literal meaning, but he thought of his truchements as more than merely translators. The interpreters were instructed to explore the country, live among Indian nations, master native languages, promote trade, build alliances, observe carefully, and report on what they saw.[7]

Champlain was not the first French leader to follow this practice. In 1602, Pont-Gravé recruited two Montagnais "princes," took them to France, and brought them back to play a central role as interpreters in the great tabagie of 1603. Champlain followed this example, but on a much larger scale and with a broader purpose. He recruited an entire corps of truchements. Dozens of these young people can be identified by name, and many more appear anonymously in the records. They were vitally important to his grand design.[8]

Each of Champlain's interpreters had a story to tell. Some lived briefly among the Indians and returned to European ways. Others liked the life of the Indians, took Indian women as consorts, and formed close ties to Indian com-

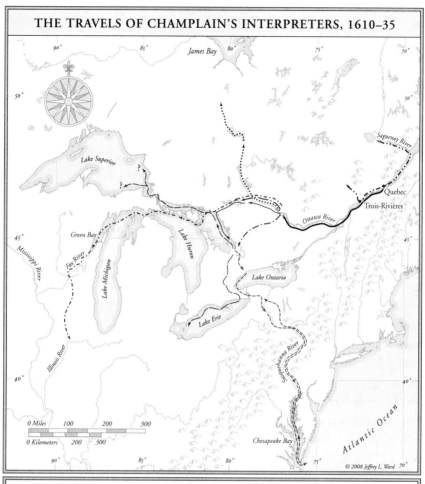

THE TRAVELS OF CHAMPLAIN'S INTERPRETERS, 1610–35

James Bay

Saguenay River

Lake Superior

Quebec

Trois-Rivières

Ottawa River

Green Bay

Lake Michigan

Lake Huron

Mississippi River

Fox River

Lake Ontario

Lake Erie

Illinois River

Susquehanna River

Atlantic Ocean

Chesapeake Bay

0 Miles 100 200 300

0 Kilometers 200 300

© 2008 Jeffrey L. Ward

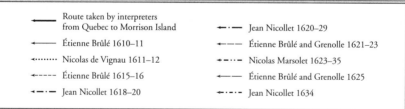

——— Route taken by interpreters from Quebec to Morrison Island	◄—·— Jean Nicollet 1620–29
◄——— Étienne Brûlé 1610–11	◄——— Étienne Brûlé and Grenolle 1621–23
◄········ Nicolas de Vignau 1611–12	◄—·—· Nicolas Marsolet 1623–35
◄----- Étienne Brûlé 1615–16	◄——— Étienne Brûlé and Grenolle 1625
◄—·— Jean Nicollet 1618–20	◄—··— Jean Nicollet 1634

munities. Most went back and forth. In many different ways they all contributed to the growth of hybrid cultures that were part-European, part-Indian, and entirely American. This was the new world that found its first home at Trois-Rivières.

Even as Champlain set this process in motion, he was not entirely happy with its results. Some of these young people troubled him. In his words, more than a few of them began to "live licentiously and freely, after the English fashion," in what he called *la vie angloise*. Others acquired complex loyalties, and Champlain believed that some had no loyalties at all. Indian leaders shared his mixed feelings about several of these young people.[9]

He was concerned about two men in particular, Étienne Brûlé and Nicolas Marsolet. Their story began in June, 1610, with an understanding between Champlain and a young French lad who has appeared several times in our story. Brûlé (or Bruslé) was born around 1592, perhaps in Champigny-sur-Marne, southeast of Paris, where his brother was a wine producer. Probably he came to Quebec with Champlain in 1608, at the age of sixteen. He must have been an engaging youth—bright and lively, with extraordinary initiative. He spent some time among the Montagnais and in 1610 asked if he could also "go with the Algonquins and learn their language." Champlain made the arrangements. He later recalled: "I went to see chief Iroquet, who was very friendly to me, and asked him if he would take this lad home with him to spend the winter in his country, and to bring him back in the spring. He promised to do so, and to treat him like his own son, saying he was much pleased."[10]

It was an elaborate three-cornered arrangement between the French and two Indian nations. Iroquet was an Algonquin leader of the Petite nation, who wintered with his people near Huronia. He had close ties to the Huron leader Ochasteguin and his Arendahuronon people. Iroquet and Ochasteguin agreed to take in Brûlé, and made one request in turn. They asked Champlain to take a young Huron to France, teach him the ways of the French, and bring him home again. Champlain wrote that this young Indian, named Savignon, "was of the nation of Ochasteguin and it was done." Brûlé departed in the care of two Indian leaders, with elaborate instructions from Champlain to learn the Huron language, explore the country, establish good relations with all Indian nations, and report in one year's time. Amazingly he did it all, and learned Algonquian to boot.[11]

Exactly one year later, on June 13, 1611, Champlain returned. We might imagine the scene: French leaders with their burnished helmets, gleaming cuirasses, arquebuses, flags, and feathers; the Huron and Algonquin in vivid face paint, buckskins, bows, arrows, beadwork, and more feathers. Champlain was astonished to see his young Parisian lad looking very comfortable in a deerskin shirt, and chatting with the Huron and Algonquin in their own languages. Champlain urged him to continue among the Indians so that he could fully master their "mode of life." [12]

After that meeting, Champlain appears to have lost contact with Brûlé for several years. They met again at Huronia in 1615. Brûlé told Champlain that he had traveled widely through North America. With another French interpreter named Grenolle, he followed the north shore of what they called the "mer douce," the sweetwater sea—today's Lake Huron—as far as the great rapids of Sault Ste. Marie, where the waters of another *grand lac* (Lake Superior) entered Lake Huron. Brûlé saw at least four of the Great Lakes on his travels, possibly all five. In 1615 Brûlé went on yet another long mission with twelve Huron warriors. Their orders were to travel around the western side of the Seneca country and make contact with the Susquehanna Indians. Brûlé set off as Champlain requested, and vanished into the vast American forest. The French thought he had died in the wilderness. Three years later he suddenly reappeared in the St. Lawrence Valley. The year was 1618, and Brûlé seemed in no hurry to meet Champlain. The French leader had to demand a meeting. Brûlé said that he and his Huron companions had covered an immense territory. They probably explored the Ohio Valley, the Potomac River, Chesapeake Bay, and the Susquehanna country. On their way back, they ran into a Seneca war party, and Brûlé was taken prisoner. Some of the Seneca began to torture him but others intervened. He was released with a promise that he would try to establish relations with the French, which some of the Iroquois very much desired.[13]

Even after the experience of capture and torture, Brûlé wanted to return to Indian country. Champlain wrote: "He took leave of me to go back to the Indians, whose acquaintance and affinity he had acquired in his voyages and discoveries. . . . I encouraged him to keep to this good intention." [14] Brûlé remained among the Huron for several years and became active in the fur trade. Some time during that period, things started to go wrong for him. In 1621, Champlain heard reports from missionaries about "the bad life that most of the Frenchmen had led in the country of the Hurons." In particular, he was told that "the interpreter Brûlé" was "very vicious and addicted to women," and that he took bribes from traders. Champlain's attitude toward his protégé began to change.[15]

In 1621 Brûlé appeared in Quebec again with four hundred beaver pelts, which he sold at a profit. He sailed back to France in 1622, returned to Canada in 1623, traded actively between Huronia and Quebec, and in 1626 returned again to Paris, where he married a French woman. His skills as an interpreter and his knowledge of North America were much in demand. The company of the Hundred Associates employed him on generous terms, but on his way back to New France with a Huron companion he was captured by the British and taken to London. There Brûlé agreed to join the Kirkes in 1628 against his own compatriots.[16]

Champlain was shocked, all the more so because something similar happened with another interpreter, Nicolas Marsolet. As early as 1613, Champlain had recruited Marsolet from a village near Rouen, brought him to New France, set him to work in the Saguenay Valley, and called him the "Montagnais interpreter." This young man also learned other Indian languages, but mainly he worked as a trader at Tadoussac. Marsolet came to know the Saguenay River as well as any European, and Champlain gave him positions of responsibility there in 1623–24. Like Brûlé, he moved deep into the country of the Indian nations, and also traveled back and forth across the Atlantic. Marsolet was in Paris on March 24, 1627, and back in Canada later that year.[17] Then came the Kirke brothers, and the conquest of Quebec in 1629. Marsolet turned his coat, and began to work for British employers.[18]

Champlain was appalled by the treachery of his interpreters. On August 1, 1629, he met Brûlé and Marsolet at Tadoussac and hard words were exchanged. "I remonstrated on their faithlessness to their King and to their Country," Champlain wrote. He accused them of abandoning their Catholic faith and said: "You remain without religion, eating meat on Friday and Saturday, and you are living freely in unrestrained debauchery and libertinism. . . . You are losing your honor; you will be pointed at with scorn on all sides."[19]

The two interpreters said that they had been forced to work for the British. Champlain refused to believe a word of it and answered, "You say that they gave each of you a hundred pistoles and a certain amount of trade, and . . . on these terms [you] promised them complete fidelity." He warned them: "Remember that God will punish you if you do not mend your ways. You have no relative or friend who will not tell you the same thing; it is they rather who will be most eager to bring you to justice. If you knew that what you are doing is displeasing to God and to mankind, you would detest yourselves."

The more they talked, the angrier Champlain became. "To think of you," he said, "brought up from early boyhood in these parts, turning round now and selling those who put bread in your mouths! Do you think you will be esteemed by this nation? Be assured you will not, for they only make use of you from necessity." [20] Brûlé and Marsolet replied: "We know quite well that if they had us in France they would hang us; we are very sorry for that, but the thing is done; we have mixed the cup and we must drink it, and make up our minds never to return to France; we shall manage to live notwithstanding."

Champlain broke decisively with them. By the time he came back to Quebec in 1632–33, Brûlé had retreated to the Huron country and ran into more trouble there. Social historians think that his relations with Huron women became increasingly disruptive. Economic historians believe that Brûlé trespassed on Huron trading networks. Political historians suspect that he may have betrayed the Huron to the Iroquois, as he had sold out the French to the British. It is possible that all these things happened. Whatever the cause, the Huron turned against Brûlé and ordered him to leave their country. But he had nowhere else to go. The Kirkes were gone, and the French despised him as a traitor. The nearest thing that Brûlé had to a home was Huronia, but now he was unwelcome there as well. Finally, in June, 1633, after much agonized discussion, the Huron were driven to a desperate measure. They killed him and then told Champlain what they had done. He is thought to have been the only Frenchman that the Huron ever killed.[21] The French leader said that he understood and that their action would not be held against them. In the end, nobody wanted Étienne Brûlé. This very gifted young man who moved so easily in many cultures was ultimately rejected by all.[22]

Marsolet had a different fate. For a time he also got on the wrong side of the French. Jesuit father Paul Le Jeune wrote angrily, "In all the years we have been in this country no one has been able to learn anything from the interpreter named Marsolet, who, for excuse, said that he would never teach the Savage tongue to anyone."[23] But Marsolet dealt with his difficulties by continuing to work as an agent among the Montagnais. He acquired his own boat, traded in furs with much success, and his profits brought him wealth and respectability. He came to be called "the little king of Tadoussac." After Champlain's death, Marsolet settled down, married a French wife, raised a family of ten children, acquired a seigneury from the Company of the Hundred Associates, and accumulated land and offices. He lived to the ripe age of ninety and died in 1677, a respected citizen of New France.

After his troubles with Brûlé and Marsolet, Champlain gave more attention to qualities of character in his interpreters. The result was a second generation of these young men, and some of them were very different from the first. Two men in particular were outstanding in that regard. Both began their American careers as assistant clerks for commercial companies in Quebec. They lived among the Indians and learned several languages. During the 1620s they began to work with Champlain, shared his large purposes, and had a long reach in the history of New France.

Olivier Le Tardif (or Letardif, as he wrote his name) was born about 1604 in Brittany, where he was baptized in the bishopric of Saint Brieuc, and he moved to Normandy. Champlain called him "Olivier le Tardif de Honfleur," and may have recruited him in that Norman port. He was in Quebec as early as 1621, perhaps earlier, working as an under-clerk for the Company de Caën. As a young man he traded actively with the Indians of the St. Lawrence Valley, lived among them, and learned their languages with remarkable success. Champlain began to refer to him as "Olivier le truchement" and wrote that he became as "skilled in the languages of the Montagnais and Algonquin as in those of the Huron," an extraordinary achievement.[24]

People who worked with Le Tardif spoke highly of his ability and integrity. Pont-Gravé knew him well and wrote that "Olivier traded with the savages and . . . acquitted himself of his duties like a man of character." Champlain praised him as a "very fit person" in character and ability. The Jesuit father Le Jeune called him "le sieur Olivier, truchement, *honneste homme*, and well suited to this country." Le Tardif was described as "always pious and devout." He gave strong support to Indian missions, encouraged the baptism of Indians and was godfather to many of them. The Indians held him in high esteem, and he remained very close to them. Like Champlain, he adopted three Indian children, raised them as his own, and helped them marry well.[25]

After the English conquest, Le Tardif left New France with Champlain and returned with him in 1633. He often appeared at Champlain's side and worked closely with him as an interpreter in some of the most important meetings with the Indians from 1633 to 1635.[26] After Champlain's death, Le Tardif became a leading figure in New France. He rose steadily in the Company of the Hundred Associates, from *sous-commis* to *premier commis*, and then to *commis général*, and oversaw its affairs in the St. Lawrence Valley. He acquired seigneuries on the St. Lawrence River, became a developer of the Île d'Orléans, and married Louise Couillard, who connected him to the first family in New France. There would be a second wife and five children. Today his descendants include a progeny of Tardifs and Le Tardifs in Canada and the United States.[27]

A leader in Champlain's second wave was his greatest interpreter, a man of extraordinary character and achievement. Jean Nicollet de Belleborne was a native of Normandy, born around 1598 in modest circumstances near the port of Cherbourg. His father was a royal courier who carried the mail between Cherbourg and Paris. Young Nicollet came to New France by 1619 as a trader for the old Company of Rouen and Saint-Malo.[28] He was sent to winter with the Algonquin Indians on Allumette Island in the Ottawa River, a difficult assignment. Nicollet did well. He stayed two years as "the only Frenchman" in that place, learned the language and customs of the Allumette Algonquin, and explored the country. Unlike Brûlé, he impressed Indians and Europeans alike by his strength of character. The Algonquin accepted him in their lodges, admitted him to their councils, and were said to have made him one of their chiefs.[29]

After 1620, Nicollet moved to the Nipissing nation, who lived on the lake of the same name. Altogether he was with them for "eight or nine years," built a trading post, went into business "fishing and trading for himself," and returned to Quebec each year with his furs. He explored large areas of the western country and visited many Indian nations who lived between Huronia and Hudson Bay.[30] While Nicollet was among the Nipissing, he lived with an Indian woman and had at least one child—a daughter named Madeleine-Euphrosine. Later he brought her to Quebec, where she married two Frenchmen in succession and had nine children or more.[31]

During the British conquest of New France from 1629 to 1632, Nicollet disappeared from Quebec and lived among the Indians on the western frontier. At least part of that time he was with the Huron, and learned their language. When Émery de Caën and a small party of French traders came back to Quebec in 1632, Nicollet returned and offered to help restore trade between the Indians and the French. Then Champlain and his immigrants reached Quebec in the spring of 1633. Soon after he arrived, Champlain heard that a large party of Nipissing in forty canoes had come to Sainte-Croix Island, the island of commerce in the St. Lawrence River upstream from Quebec. They were led by a "French interpreter" who must have been Jean Nicollet.[32]

Champlain tells us that he "went immediately to Sainte Croix" on June 20, 1633, and met Nicollet that very day. The two men began to talk.[33] Together they planned a major expedition beyond the western frontier of New France. A Jesuit father who knew them well, Barthélemy Vimont, wrote that Nicollet was "delegated to a journey to the people called the Gens de Mer," the People of the Sea who lived beyond the sweetwater sea.[34]

The mission was conceived in the same spirit as Champlain's early voyages. One purpose was to explore the country that lay west of New France and to study the quality of its land. Another was to map the rivers and lakes. Watercourses were of great interest to Champlain, and the French leaders shared the stubborn dream of Lachine—a route to China through North America. In 1633, the French knew very little about the Great Lakes. Champlain had knowledge of Lake Huron, Lake Ontario, and Lake Erie, but not enough to map them accurately. He knew of another huge lake to the northwest, and was aware that a torrent of water flowed from this grand lac (now Lake Superior) to the mer douce of Lake Huron, through two leagues of falls and rapids. Champlain called them the Sault de Gaston; we know them as the Sault Ste. Marie. The Indians told Champlain that to cross the two great lakes was a journey of thirty days by canoe. He wanted to know more about their size and shape, and what lay beyond.[35]

The Indians spoke to Champlain of a distant nation called the Puan, who lived beyond the great lakes, and also were reported to have traveled farther west to the coast of a big salt sea. Nicollet was instructed to seek them out and to meet other nations along the way. Champlain was interested in extending alliances and expanding the fur trade. As always, he also wished to encourage peaceful relations between Indian allies and nations to the west.[36]

In the summer of 1633, Nicollet departed from Quebec for Huronia, where he picked up an escort of seven warriors. It was a very long journey. They followed the north shore of Lake Huron as it curved toward an intersection with Lake Superior and Lake Michigan. After he reached the end of Lake Huron, his route is not clear. He could have gone northwest along the rapids of the Sault Ste. Marie to the north shore of Lake Superior, Champlain's "grand lac."[37] It is more than likely (though less than certain) that he went another way. Nicollet probably crossed the narrow northwestern neck of Lake Huron, found a way through the straits of Mackinac, and reached the northern and western coast of Lake Michigan. A short journey along the lakeshore would have brought him to Green Bay and the home of the Winnebago nation, who were probably the Jesuits' Ouinipigous. Nicollet wrote that "the Ouinipigous had an unknown language, neither Algonquin nor Huron." The Winnebago spoke a Siouian tongue—a family of Indian languages different from those to the east. All of these linguistic clues reveal that Nicollet and his Huron guides reached what is now Green Bay, Wisconsin.[38]

Nicollet and his companions came ashore at Green Bay, placed two poles in the ground, and put gifts on them to indicate they had come in peace. Two Hurons were sent ahead to announce that a Frenchman was coming in a spirit of amity, and a huge crowd gathered. Nicollet had Champlain's sense of an occasion. According to a Jesuit who read the journal that Nicollet wrote about his trip, he put on a "grand robe of China damask, all covered with flowers and

Jean Nicollet, greatest of Champlain's interpreters, lived among the Algonquin and Huron, was sent by Champlain beyond the Great Lakes, and reached the Fox and Illinois Rivers in the Mississippi Valley. This image shows his visit to the Winnebago nation. He is remembered through much of the American middle west.

birds of many colors." In each hand he carried a pistol, and fired both of them in the air. We are told that "the women and children fled at the sight of a man who carried thunder in both hands." A throng of between 4,000 and 5,000 warriors received him, and chiefs invited him to a series of feasts. At one meal alone they served an entrée of "six-score beavers." With high ceremony, the Huron warriors and their French interpreter made peace with these nations.[39]

After that meeting, Nicollet is said to have explored the country to the west. Perhaps the Indians told him of rivers that flowed to the west, and he may have gone in search of them. The Fox and Illinois Rivers are not far from Green Bay. He was very close to the tributaries of the Mississippi, but never found that great waterway. Even so, he had explored a large part of North America, and was the first European to see much of it. Each of these epic journeys inspired others on the frontier of New France, and more interpreters followed in his tracks.

Nicollet and his Huron guides started the long journey home, and reached Quebec in 1634. He probably reported to Champlain, but no record of that meeting exists. The original of Nicollet's journal has disappeared but it was read by Jesuit fathers Paul Le Jeune and Vimont. Portions of it appear in the *Jesuit Relations*.

After his return in 1634, Nicollet made several short trips and helped Jesuit missionaries to find their way up the Ottawa River. He decided to settle down, sought a position with the Company of the Hundred Associates, and appears to have set himself up as a trader at Trois-Rivières. He married the daughter of Guillemette Hébert and Guillaume Couillard, and had a son and a daughter, in addition to at least one Indian daughter. By his marriage he also became the brother-in-law of Olivier Le Tardif. The two men were close friends and co-owners of a seigneury.

By all accounts Nicollet was a sterling character. A spirit of selfless humanity ran deep in him, and it was the cause of his death. In 1642, while visiting Quebec, Nicollet received a message that a Huron party had taken an Iroquois captive and were preparing to torture him to death at Trois-Rivières. Nicollet rushed to the assistance of an Indian he did not know. He took a shallop and raced up the St. Lawrence River with all sail set. They ran into a sudden gust of wind and Nicollet's boat capsized. This man who had explored many great lakes and rivers of North America was unable to swim, and he drowned at the age of forty-four. The Jesuits wrote that Jean Nicollet was "equally and singularly loved" by both the French and Indians. He shared Champlain's dream and enlarged it by his spirit.

Altogether, Champlain sent several dozen French interpreters to live among the Indian nations, and he also worked with many Indian translators. He was always looking for bright young men who could be recruited for these purposes. In the year 1629 alone, eleven interpreters worked for Champlain in Quebec, and fourteen were employed by the Hundred Associates. He met ships from France, and searched for "some of those people from our settlement whom I sent with the natives into the interior."[40]

They tended to be restless young men from seaport towns and commercial cities of France. Many appear briefly in Champlain's writings and the records of the colony. It is interesting to observe their origins and the course of their careers as Champlain sent them to live among the Montagnais, Algonquin, Huron, Nipissing, and many other Indian nations.[41]

One of them, whom Champlain called "Bouvier's young lad," began as an apprentice working for the captain of a patache on the St. Lawrence River. In 1611 he became an interpreter with the Huron, living and trading with them.[42] Jacques Hertel de la Fresnière migrated as soldier to Quebec around 1626. He went to live among the Algonquin, became an interpreter for Champlain and the Jesuits, then acquired land and raised a family in Trois-Rivières.[43] Jean-Paul Godefroy, who may have been the "Jean Paul" that Champlain mentioned in 1623, was a young man of good family in Paris, where his father held high offices at Court. He worked as an interpreter for the trading companies at Trois-Rivières and later became a ship's captain, entrepreneur, and in 1648 a member of the Council at Quebec.[44]

There were many more. Thomas Godefroy was an interpreter to the Algonquin and Huron.[45] François Marguerie worked among the western Indians and settled in Trois-Rivières.[46] Jean Richer came from Dieppe and went as an interpreter to the Nipissing and Algonquin.[47] Jean Manet lived among the Nipissing.[48] One of those two men might have been Champlain's "Gross Jean de Dieppe," or perhaps he was a third interpreter. Another named Grenolle appeared in New France in 1623 as an "apprentice interpreter" to the Huron and the Pétun. He was a companion of Brûlé on his journey to Sault Ste. Marie and Lake Superior and later visited the Neutral nation and the Pétun. Another interpreter, La Valleé, also went to the Neutral nation and the Pétun people.[49] Many of these interpreters made their homes in Trois-Rivières.[50]

Leaders who recruited these autonomous young men also tried to restrain them, but could not control them. Their numbers began to grow. Champlain's dozens of interpreters and traders were followed by hundreds of free spirits who left the settlements of New France and went to trade among the Indians. They began to be called *coureurs de bois*, and French officials did not approve of their ways. In 1672, Intendant Talon wrote that they disrupted the agriculture of New France, shattered families, and created disorder. He tried to limit their numbers, with no success. In 1679, Intendant Duchesneau wrote a scathing report, and estimated the number of coureurs de bois at between 500 and 600, not counting others who were leaving "every day" for the woods. A year later he reckoned their numbers had grown to 800, out of a total population of 9,700 in New France. "There is at least one coureur de bois in every family," he wrote.[51]

The coureurs de bois differed much from one another, but all were part of a great historical process that had a long reach in time and space. In the seventeenth century they advanced beyond the eastern woodlands to the great plains and the mountains in the middle of the continent. They followed the western rivers into the Mississippi Valley as far south as Louisiana, always in pursuit of furs and skins, which they gained by trading, hunting, and trapping. In the interior parts of North America, their small camps and trading posts grew into towns and later great cities that honor their memory. They became iconic figures in the cultural identity of North America and were living examples of the mixing and merging of people, in the spirit of Champlain's dream. At the same time they became symbols of other ideas that Champlain did not share—of liberty and freedom on the western frontier.

French officials tried to limit the flow of these free spirits by a system of licenses called *congés*, which literally meant permissions to leave the settlements of New France. But the numbers kept growing. At Montreal and Detroit alone, 2,431 traders were licensed in 1777, according to records. Many more went west without asking anyone's lease. One estimate reckoned that more than 5,000 coureurs de bois were functioning in North America during the late eighteenth century. French merchants organized this trade. A proprietor who had capital enough to invest in trading goods and supplies was called a *bourgeois*. He in turn hired workers who were called *voyageurs*. The voyageurs were divided into several types. Seasonal workers who returned every year to New France were called *mangeurs de lard*, pork eaters. Others who went farther into the west and stayed for more than a single season were called *hivernants*, the men who wintered in the wilderness. The culture of the fur trade was dominated by these voyageurs.

One traveler, Alexander Ross, met an old voyageur and recorded his memories. "I have now been forty-two years in this country," the voyageur recalled. "For twenty-four I was a light canoeman; I required but little sleep, but sometimes got less than I required. No portage was too long for me; all portages were alike. My end of the canoe never touched the ground till I saw the end of it. Fifty songs a day were nothing to me. I could carry, paddle, walk, and sing with any man I ever saw. . . . over rapids, over cascades, over chutes, all were the same to me. No water, no weather, ever stopped the paddle or the song. I have had twelve wives in the country, and was once possessed of fifty horses and six running dogs trimmed in the first style. . . . No bourgeois had better dressed wives than I; no Indian chief finer horses; no white man better harnesses or swifter dogs. . . . There is no life so happy as a voyageur's life; none so independent; no place where a man enjoys so much variety and freedom as in the Indian country. Huzza, Huzza pour le pays sauvage!"

"After this cri de joie," Ross added, "he sat down in the boat and we could not help admiring the wild enthusiasm of the old Frenchman. He had boasted and excited himself till he was out of breath and then sighed with regret that he could no longer enjoy the scenes of his past life."[52]

These voyageurs drew upon European and Indian ways to create new cultures in America. They invented new vocabularies by a creative process of cultural fusion, and coined new terms to describe the new world, its inhabitants, and its flora and fauna. The expression "Mush!" as a command of dogsled drivers, comes from the French *Marche!* for "Walk on."[53] The place name "Ozarks" derives from the French *Aux Arcs*, which was a slang word among voyageurs for the place of the Arkansas Indians, whose name in turn was an Indian slang word for the people who called themselves Quapaw and lived near the Arkansas River.[54]

This process of linguistic mixing produced not only new words but new languages. French and Indians invented hybrid contact-languages, part European and part Native American. Early hybrids emerged on the fishing coast in the form of pidgin speech, which was nobody's native tongue. Pidgins are improvised contact languages with simplified grammar and vocabulary.

Other Franco-Indian contact languages developed in a form very different from pidgin speech. An example is *Michif*, or *Métif*, a combination of French and Cree, with elements of English, Assiniboine, and Ojibway. It emerged by the early nineteenth century on the western prairies of Canada and the United States. Michif was not a pidgin language, nor was it what linguists call a creole language (a pidgin that becomes a native tongue), which also has simplified rules of grammar and syntax. Informed observers have noted: "The Michif language is unusual among contact languages, in that rather than choosing to simplify its grammar, it chose the most complex and demanding elements of the chief languages that went into it. French noun phrases retain their lexical grammar and adjective agreement; Cree verbs retain their polysynthetic structure." Linguists conclude from this pattern that "people who devised Michif were fully fluent in both French and Cree," and they invented a new language by combining some of the most complex elements in several others.[55]

This mixing of language developed from a mixing of people. Champlain's interpreters, the coureurs de bois and voyageurs formed families of combined Indian and French ancestry. These unions multiplied rapidly in the early and mid-seventeenth century. Some were made by Frenchmen of high rank. A leading example was the Baron de Saint-Castin, who came to Quebec with the Carignan-Salières regiment in 1665 and married an Indian woman whom he called Marie-Mathilde Madokawando. Her father was an Abenaki sachem, and she was described as "a beautiful and accomplished woman." The baron made his home close to his Indian relations. Some of his many children and grandchildren married other Indians; others were wed to French nobility. There were many similar stories of mixed unions in the La Tour family of Acadia; the Denys family on the fishing coast; and the Le Tardif, Nicollet, and Prévost families in Quebec, to mention but a few. These mixed marriages were actively encouraged by French leaders and were blessed by the Catholic clergy. French Catholic leaders after Samuel Champlain were more tolerant of marriages with Indians than of unions with Protestants. A Mohawk whom they called the "Flemish bastard" was denounced as "the monstrous offspring of a Dutch heretic father and a Pagan woman." The "pagan woman" was not a problem for them, but they were incensed by the fact that his father was Calvinist.[56]

Champlain actively encouraged the intermixing of French and Indians. Within his lifetime, the children of these mixed unions began to be called "Métis," a term that was recorded as early as 1615. By the late eighteenth century, that word also acquired another meaning. It referred to an entire population of French-Indian descent.[57] In the nineteenth century it began to be used in a third way to describe communities and cultures. A scholar who has studied narratives of western travel, reports, "During the 1820s, Englishmen and Americans travelling into the Great Lakes fur-trade universe discovered to their surprise that they had entered a foreign country."[58]

In that region "Métis" became a term of pride. Métis writer Duke Redbird observes: "The Métis are the only ethnic group indigenous to the continent. All races, including Indian and Inuit, came from elsewhere."[59] Where Métis formed communities, as they did in both Canada and the United States, they also created societies in new forms, with distinct patterns of stratification, family life, material culture, and architecture. In the nineteenth century some Métis communities were nomadic wagon trains that followed the buffalo and were guided by leaders with flag signals. Others were circles of small cabins built around a large central building for meeting and dancing. Music and dance combined Indian and European forms in creative combinations. Their dress ran to highly patterned and richly decorated buckskin coats and leggings, blanket coats for men; and black dresses with bright shawls and sashes for women.[60] Creative political systems were invented, as open and free as those of the Indians, but with a chief called *le gouverneur* and elected leaders called *les soldats*. This culture was marked by a very strong sense of liberty and freedom. American Indians sometimes called the Métis people *otipemisiwak*. Jennifer Brown explains that this complex Indian term "means 'free people' or 'their own boss,' and is a Cree rendering of *gens libres*." It is a word drawn from the old French fur trade for engagés who served their time and went free. This idea of a people living in freedom was applied to entire mixed populations on the frontier of New France.[61] Ross wrote on his travels: "While enjoying a sort of licentious freedom they are generous, warm-hearted and brave. . . . Feeling their own strength, from being constantly armed and free from control, they despise all others; but above all they are marvelously tenacious of their own original habits. They cherish freedom as they cherish life."[62]

In the year 2001, the Canadian Census reported that 292,310 people in Canada identified themselves as Métis, and there are many more in the United States. These self-identified Métis have founded associations in every Canadian province and five American states. And yet they are only a fraction of North Americans who have both Indian and European ancestors. Demographers have reckoned that more than 750,000 Canadians are descended from Métis. Even those estimates do not come close to the full extent of intermixing. In 1970, a Canadian biologist reckoned that 40 percent of Canadian families had both Indians and Europeans in their family trees, which would yield eight million people of mixed ancestry in 1970, and twelve million in 2005. DNA analysis might soon be able to test the accuracy of these estimates.[63]

Other North Americans in even greater number have a cultural identity with Champlain's interpreters, coureurs de bois, voyageurs, and Métis. A web survey turns up a large number of organizations who claim that heritage in our own time. That tradition is flourishing in the twenty-first century. It rose from Étienne Brûlé, Nicolas Marsolet, Olivier Le Tardif, Jean Nicollet, and behind them all was Samuel Champlain, four centuries ago.

Champlain thus had a pivotal role in founding three different francophone cultures in North America: Quebeçois, Acadian, and Métis. One could also add a fourth culture on the fishing coast, with early settlements at Miscou, the Bay of Chaleur, Cape Breton, and Placentia Bay in Newfoundland.

Each derived from different parts of France, and developed a distinct population, language, and material culture through a complex process of persistence and change. All of them began to crystallize in a pivotal moment of deep change, circa 1632–1635. Champlain played a seminal role in every one of them. In that special sense he can truly be called the father of French Canada.

25.

CHAMPLAIN'S LAST LABOR
The End as a Beginning, 1635

> I did not lack materials. . . . Truly he led a life of great justice and
> equity.
>
> —Paul Le Jeune, on his funeral oration for Samuel de Champlain, 1636 [1]

I T WAS OCTOBER, 1635, and another glorious fall had come to the St. Lawrence Valley. The air was crisp and very clear. In the strong autumn light
the great river turned deep blue and sparkled like a stream of liquid sap-
phire as it flowed to the sea. On its banks the forest was ablaze with scarlet
swamp maples, yellow birch and hickory, russet oaks, golden tamaracks, and
dazzling orange sugar trees. To this display, the French habitants had added
new colors of their own creation: the vivid green of expanding pastures and
meadows, and gleaming whitewashed cottages that were multiplying on the
land.

In the autumn of 1635 the future of New France seemed as bright as the
colors of its countryside—brighter than ever before. Its right to exist was recognized by other Atlantic powers. In France itself, the colony was supported
by Louis XIII and Cardinal Richelieu. The Company of the Hundred Associates was flourishing with its many subsidiaries. The fur trade was highly profitable, and the French fisheries were larger in 1635 than ever before, or since. [2]
Agriculture was taking root in seigneuries along the St. Lawrence Valley and
behind the aboiteaux of Acadia. Settlements were spreading east on the fishing
coast, south along the coast of Acadia, and west into the interior of North
America. In 1635, the French habitants were at peace with all Indian nations
except the Iroquois.

In Quebec, Samuel Champlain regarded this record with satisfaction, as
well he might have done. More any other individual, he had made it happen.
Through the last three years he had ruled the colony wisely and well. In 1633
and 1634, he had traveled up and down the St. Lawrence Valley from Tadoussac to Trois-Rivières. He had made his presence felt in the missions of the
Gaspésie, in the new fishing settlements at Cape Breton, and among his

truchements and traders to the west. In his advancing years he was loved by those who knew him in New France: habitants, missionaries, and traders. The Indians held him in high regard. They respected him as a warrior, valued him as a peacemaker, and most of all, they trusted his word. As Gabriel Sagard had written, "In all the years he had dwelled among these native people, he had never been suspected of any dishonesty."[3]

But after many years of labor, Champlain was growing weary. His spirit was strong, but his physical strength was beginning to ebb. During the spring and summer of 1635, he appears to have made no journeys on the river—a major change for him. A steady flow of correspondence from Jesuit missionaries throughout New France reported that Champlain was active in his oversight from Gaspé to the Great Lakes. But he was more sedentary than ever before and rarely left the settlement at Quebec. Everyone knew he was not well. Reports filtered back to France, and leaders there began to think about a successor.[4]

Then, in mid-October Champlain suffered a stroke. Its effects were severe. He lost the use of his legs and was unable to rise without assistance. He was carried to his bed, and the paralysis spread to his upper limbs. One report described his condition as including a *perclus de bras*, a crippling of the arms. For ten weeks Champlain remained a prisoner of his infirmity, locked within an immobile body and unable to move by himself.[5] His servant Jean Poisson tended him, as did the Jesuit fathers and others in the colony.[6]

Champlain fought against his affliction. His vital organs continued to function, and his mind remained active. He tried to attend to his official business, but the documents were drafted by other hands. Some were signed by Champlain, with help from friends who guided his fingers across the page. His painful signature was mute evidence of his infirmity.

Even as he lay paralyzed in his bed, Champlain embarked on one final project. In his last months on this earth, he dedicated himself to a spiritual quest with the same restless energy he had brought to his worldly pursuits. In his accustomed way, he had already begun to prepare for this last labor. Jesuit father Le Jeune wrote that "he was not taken unaware in the account which he had to render unto God."[7] Champlain's faith had been growing through the years. He had gathered a library of devotional volumes: the *Fleurs des sainctz*, the *Pratique de la perfection chrestienne*, the *Triple couronne de la bienheureuse Vierge*, the *Chroniques et instruction du père Sainct-François*. Probably he and the Jesuit fathers read these books together. In that age of faith many Christians found deep solace in confessions of faith and acts of devotion.[8]

In his last months Champlain renewed his faith in an extraordinary way. He began by making a confession. His friend Le Jeune tells us that it was no ordinary effort. Champlain "prepared a general confession of his entire life, which he made with great contrition." His confessor was Jesuit father Charles Lalement. The two men had become good friends. We are told that "the father comforted him throughout his malady, which lasted two and a half months, and did not leave him until his death."[9]

People close to Champlain were awed by the intensity of his faith. Some began to understand for the first time the strength of spiritual striving that had driven him through his career. "At his death, he crowned his virtues with sentiments of piety so lofty that he astonished us all," Father Le Jeune wrote. "What tears flowed from his eyes! How ardent were his affections for the service of God!"[10]

In that soaring faith and zeal for God's work, Champlain returned yet again to his dream for New France, and to his grand design. He did so on his deathbed in a spirit of Christian *caritas* for the French habitants and Indian friends who came to visit him. Father Le Jeune wrote of his last days: "How great was his love for the families here! He kept saying that it was necessary to assist them with all power for the good of the country (*le bien du Pays*), and to support them and give them solace in every possible way." He turned to his confessor and said "he would do it himself if God gave him health."[11]

Through the bright October days Champlain hoped for a recovery, but his condition did not improve. As he lay abed the seasons were changing, and so was his mood. Every year, North America has two autumns. The first is October's glorious fall. The second is what Herman Melville called the "damp November of the soul," when the incandescent colors fade and the world turns drab and gray. Earth and water, sea and air, mist and rain, dormant trees and living creatures all became different shades of gray. In Quebec a cold wind stripped the dead leaves from the trees, and dark branches rose like twisted fingers toward a leaden sky. Overhead, low scudding clouds oppressed the spirit, and a cold light etched the surface of the St. Lawrence River with silver lines that chilled the soul.

In mid-November, Champlain decided that the time had come to make his will. He summoned his friends and associates, and eleven of them gathered around his bed to serve as witnesses. They made a cross-section of New France. Some were highborn French aristocrats of the old *noblesse d'épée*. At his bedside was Marc-Antoine Bras-de-Fer de Châteaufort, a nobleman and Knight Chevalier of Malta. He had come to Quebec in 1634 as Champlain's lieutenant—and Richelieu's informant. Champlain had won him over, and by 1635 they were fast friends.[12] Others were of the *noblesse de robe*, such as Champlain's kindred spirit François Derré de Gand, a member of the Hundred Associates and the company's commissioner general of Quebec. In the colony Derré de Gand was known as a pious and charitable man who "sought God in the spirit of truth."[13]

Several men at Champlain's bedside were of a new seigneurial class that was emerging in Quebec with his patronage. Robert Giffard de Moncel was there, the wealthy gentleman from Perche who shared Champlain's dream, invested heavily in New France, and brought many settlers from his province at his own expense. There was Olivier Le Tardif, who looked after the company's trade and became Champlain's most trusted interpreter and companion in his meetings with the Indians. Guillaume Couillard stood beside them. This very able man had come from Saint-Malo to New France as an illiterate ship's carpenter. He married Guillemette Hébert, sired a large family, and rose to high rank in the colony. These men all received large seigneuries, high offices, and titles of nobility. Champlain had helped them rise; now they came to him.[14]

Others in Champlain's chamber were men of humble rank. Three were recent immigrants who had come to Quebec in 1635. We scarcely know their names: Pierre Goblet, D. Rousseau, and Boulard. Probably they worked as servants in Champlain's habitation and helped to look after him.[15] In close attendance was Champlain's valet, Jean Poisson, who would later found an important family in Quebec.[16]

Also present was an Indian boy, a young Montagnais who had become Champlain's godson—one of many young Indian boys and girls he had looked after. This lad had lost his parents at an early age. A warrior was about to kill him—a common fate of unwanted orphans in that cruel world. Another Montagnais intervened and carried him to the Jesuits, who gave him a home and named him Fortuné. Champlain took a liking to him, became his godfather, and christened him Bonaventure. That name had many meanings. It honored a great Franciscan saint who combined piety with a passion for learning. Champlain also chose it with a flash of humor that was typical of him. At sea a *bonaventure* was the French name for a very short mizzen mast, stepped abaft a tall mainmast—in much the same way that this young Indian lad tagged along behind the governor. He was living in his house, much as Champlain's three Montagnais girls, Faith, Hope, and Charity had done.[17]

Another witness was Jacques De Laville, a sturdy old soldier who became the official *greffier*, or registrar, of Quebec, and joined the bedside group in an official capacity. His task was to record and certify Champlain's testament.[18]

Champlain dictated his will to this gathering, and all the witnesses added their names except Couillard, who signed by mark.

As always, Champlain had several purposes in mind when he made his will. It was first a testament of Christian faith. He began with the usual phrases but gave them a touch of his own. "Considering that nothing is so uncertain as the hour of death," he wrote in his prevoyant way, "and not wishing to be surprised without declaring my last wishes, I leave this present script so that they will be manifest and made known to everyone." [19] Yet another confession of faith followed: "Now my God, summoned to your presence and all your celestial court, I proclaim that I wish to live and die in the faith and religion that is Catholic, Apostolic, and Roman, and to receive all the sacraments of which I am capable." Champlain forgave all those who had sinned against him, and asked God to pardon his own sins. "You have given me a rational soul, O my God, and I return it to your hands, begging you to dispose of it for your glory."

Then Champlain gave away his worldly goods, and in a most extraordinary way. He was a man of substantial means—not wealthy by the standards of his world or ours, but he had amassed considerable property in the course of his life. As part of his will he made individual bequests in cash, which alone totaled nearly 10,000 French livres, a sum roughly equal to 50,000 silver *thalers*, or dollars, in 1635 values. [20] Lacking an inventory of Champlain's wealth, it is impossible to know the full value of his estate, but it was much larger than his cash bequests. He had made commercial investments in the Company of the Hundred Associates and other ventures. At various times he had owned real estate in Paris, Brouage, and La Rochelle. His wife's dowry had been large. Her inheritance had been restored, and her assets probably exceeded his own. She had dedicated some of them to his cause while he was in America. [21]

Champlain disposed of his personal wealth in a highly purposeful way. Even as he lay on his deathbed, he still actively pursued his great project for New France. Most of his bequests were instruments of that purpose. One major goal was to strengthen its institutions, and especially the Church of Notre-Dame-de-la-Recouvrance. Champlain began his benefactions by announcing in his own inimitable way, "I desire now, O my God, that the most holy Virgin your mother should inherit everything that I possess here in personal property, gold, and silver." The language was a little confused on the Trinity, but it was crystal clear on Champlain's earthly intent. He explained that everything not otherwise committed was to go to "the Chapel devoted to her name and commonly called Notre-Dame de Recouverance," with exceptions for which "I ask her permission to dispose in favor of certain individuals." Champlain specified particular sums for furnishings, altars, tapestries, and other decorations in the chapel. Clearly he intended the chapel to become a church, and even a cathedral as the colony grew larger. Another large sum was given to the mission of the Jesuits in Quebec, on condition that they would pray for Champlain and sing a mass for the repose of his soul every year, on the anniversary of his death. Its purpose was also to strengthen the Society of Jesus in New France.

Many individual bequests followed, always with the same large purpose in mind. Champlain deliberately used his will to promote the growth of the French population at Quebec. He gave much of his money to individual French families who had put their roots into the American soil, and were beginning to increase and multiply. Among the leading beneficiaries were the family of his Scottish friend Abraham Martin l'Écossais, and his French wife, Marguerite Langlois. Champlain was very fond of them both and delighted in their daughters. The Martin family received his largest individual bequests, totaling about 1,200 livres.[22] Abraham and his wife were given 600 livres expressly to pay the cost of "clearing land in this country of New France." Perhaps Champlain had in mind the ground above and behind the lower town of Quebec, part of which is still known as the Plains of Abraham.

Champlain also used his wealth to subsidize the peopling of the land in very specific ways. Another sum of 600 livres went to the Martin family for their daughter Marguerite, "to aid her to marry in this country of New France a man who must be resident of the said country, *and not otherwise.*" Similar bequests were given to four families in Quebec—the Couillards, Giffards, Piverts, and Héberts. Champlain's purpose was clearly to encourage the habitants of New France to increase and multiply.

Another interesting pattern in Champlain's bequests was his support of exploration and discovery. He bequeathed his copper astrolabe, compasses, and other navigational instruments to a man who would use them, Father Charles Lalement, his confessor, who was interested in exploration and the tradition of Jesuit science. Like Champlain, the object of his scientific inquiries was to study God's way in the world. Along with Champlain's scientific instruments, Father Lalement also received a painting of the Crucifixion. Champlain expected the good father to combine Christian faith and empirical science in the way he had done.

Other bequests were offered in the spirit of Christian charity. Champlain's valet, Jean Poisson, received some of his best clothing, including a red and gray jacket. The Indian godson, Bonaventure, received a suit of fine English cloth, in the same bright red color. The will tells us that one of Champlain's favorite color was red. Other large sums were directed toward religious institutions for the poor in Paris.

Yet another purpose of the will was to express Champlain's love for his wife, Hélène. He left her all his property in France, naming his cousin in La Rochelle, Marie Camaret, residual legatee if his widow was unable to inherit. Champlain also bequeathed to his wife two prized possessions, his Agnus Dei, a wax medallion of the Lamb of God, made with the dust of martyrs' bones, and a gold ring with "something like a diamond," perhaps a piece of Canadian crystal. He also gave Hélène a bundle of fine gray fox furs that she loved.

Champlain asked Father Lalement and Derré de Gand to collect his papers and deliver them to his wife. For historians, this was the most valuable part of the estate. From the language of the will, Champlain understood their importance, but others apparently did not. His papers have disappeared. Perhaps some day they might turn up in a French attic, but the odds are not encouraging. Champlain's manuscripts are very rare today.

Champlain made all these arrangements in the document that he dictated on November 17, 1635, with the help of his companions, friends, and servants in Quebec. He signed it with their assistance. Now he could do nothing on his own. On December 2, he decided that he was no longer able to function as governor, and on that date he yielded some of the duties of his office to his pious and upright friend François Derré de Gand. Here again Champlain's choice reveals his values and purposes.[23]

As Champlain continued in his bed, the North American seasons changed yet again. Winter came to Quebec, and the first snow fell on the settlement. The world turned white and clean. The quiet air smelled wondrously fresh, and the fallen snow was pure and pristine. After the snow, the sky turned a pale ethereal blue, and the temperature began to fall. In Champlain's chamber, the casement windows were etched in frost. The fire in the hearth flared and faded, and the candles guttered in the wintry drafts that swept the room. Champlain's spirit was slipping away, and the Jesuits in black robes kept a vigil beside him.

On Christmas Eve the people of Quebec held a joyous celebration of their Savior's birth. A midnight mass was sung in the church of Notre-Dame-de-la-Recouvrance. At Fort Saint-Louis on the hill, a crash of cannon marked the birth of Christ with a feu de joie.[24] It was one of the last earthly sounds that Champlain heard. On Christmas Day, as Father Lalement prayed at his side, Champlain drew his last breath and died peacefully in his bed. Father Le Jeune recorded the moment. "On the twenty-fifth of December," he wrote, "the day of the birth of our Savior upon earth, Monsieur de Champlain, our Governor was reborn in heaven. The least we were able to say is that his death was full of blessings." [25]

Father Le Jeune saw the day and manner of Champlain's passing as a mark of Providence. He added, "I believe that God has shown him this favor in consideration for the good things he has obtained for New France." The good father also believed that the last struggle of Champlain on his deathbed was a prophecy. "One day," the Jesuit predicted, "God will be loved and served by all our French, and known and adored by all our Indians." Champlain had shown the way, not by words but by acts. "Truly he led a life of great justice and equity, and with a perfect fidelity to his King and to the gentlemen of the Company: but at his death he crowned his virtues with a piety so great that he astonished us all." [26]

In Quebec the entire population turned out to honor him. They walked together in a procession through the settlement: Jesuits in their black robes, soldiers in the king's uniform of white and blue and gold; seamen in their bizarria, officers in brilliant finery, feudal seigneurs in feathered hats, and hundreds of French habitants—bundled against the bracing cold in their caps and capes and wooden shoes. The Indians were there, wrapped in lustrous furs. They marked his passing with genuine grief. A delegation of Huron later arrived with a large gift of wampum to console the French people of Quebec on their loss. Their myths and legends kept his memory green for many generations.

Champlain was buried in a small private grave while a chapel was constructed next to the Church of Notre-Dame-de-la-Recouvrance. Five years later the buildings were burned, perhaps by an arsonist. The congregation rebuilt the church, and the resting place of Champlain's body remains in doubt. The Church sextons believe that his bones remain in a crypt below the beautiful cathedral that stands there today, but nobody knows for sure. The mystery of Champlain's tomb has inspired a large literature in Quebec, and many scholars have tried to solve it without success. It is one of the persistent puzzles of Quebec's history. But one fact is clear. Wherever Champlain's remains may be, they have become part of the soil of New France. [27]

In old France Champlain's wife accepted his will. She withdrew into a convent and became an Ursuline nun, Hélène de Saint-Augustin. Later she founded an Ursuline convent in Meaux, not far from Paris, and lived there until her death in 1654. [28] Champlain's testament was challenged by his Protestant relatives in La Rochelle. His first cousin Marie Camaret went to court and sought to break the will, insisting that it was contrary to the terms of his marriage settlement (which in fact it was). She also argued speciously that "it was difficult to suppose that Champlain had chosen the Virgin Mary as his heir," which he did not do. Her argument suggests that Cousin Marie was staunchly Protestant and not sympathetic to the sanctity of the Holy Virgin. She also appears to have been desperate for his money. She or her lawyer twisted the language of the will in an effort to prove that Champlain was not of sound mind. The Parlement of Paris accepted their appeal, if not their arguments, and annulled the will. One suspects that some of Champlain's benefactions may have been distributed in Quebec before the lawyers went to work in France, probably even before the will was made, but the disposition of Champlain's many bequests remains unclear.[29]

Even before Champlain's death was known in Paris, Cardinal Richelieu had decided to remove him from office. The decision was made before January 15, 1636, probably earlier. The replacement was Charles Hualt de Montmagny, a nobleman in the cardinal's circle, a soldier who had won a reputation for courage, a lay churchman, and a Knight of Malta. Richelieu greatly favored that small fraternity of high Catholic noblemen who wore the Maltese Cross. He sought to place its members in command of the expanding French empire throughout the Mediterranean, Africa, Asia, and America. This was actually done in New France. Historian Marcel Trudel writes, "In the St. Lawrence, from 1636 and for many years, all superior authority was in the hands of Chevaliers of Malta." That small elite of Catholic noblemen combined rigid authority and strict discipline with devotion to an absolute monarch, obedience to the princes of the Church, and loyalty to Cardinal Richelieu. Champlain had never been admitted to their order.[30] The sieur de Montmagny was by all accounts a decent, colorless, and unimaginative man. He governed New France for twelve years, built a massive stone fortress at Quebec, broke with Champlain's Indian policy, and involved the colony in bloody Indian wars. Today he is forgotten.[31]

When Montmagny was sent to replace Champlain, historians have noted that he "brought not even a word of thanks from King or Cardinal to his predecessor, news of whose death had not reached Paris when he sailed." After thirty years of faithful service, Champlain received no major honors in France. Richelieu had always been cool to him. Louis XIII and the cardinal recognized his usefulness and employed him for their purposes, but they did not reward him for his service. Richelieu and his successors distributed patents of nobility to many settlers in Canada, but not to Champlain. They gave the formal title of governor to many forgotten functionaries, but denied it to Champlain even as he assumed all of the duties of that office. They created many seigneuries in the St. Lawrence Valley with large tracts of land. Champlain never received a grant, or any of the ceremonial sinecures of large profit and little labor that multiplied in the old regime. Historians have often remarked on this failure of Louis XIII and Richelieu to honor Champlain. The Boston historian Samuel Eliot Morison adds with a flash of republican fury, "What a perfect example of the ingratitude of princes!" [32]

True enough, but another cause also operated here, and it flowed from Champlain's choices. At court he used his influence for his cause, and not for himself. Through many years of striving, Champlain asked much for New France and little for his own advantage. He fought to keep his pension, which was important to his project in many ways. Like most great workers he kept his focus on the work itself, and not on its rewards. For such a man in such a cause, the absence of honors became an honor in itself.

Honors came in other ways. At his funeral ceremonies in Quebec, people who knew him spoke from the heart about his greatness and their grief. They talked most eloquently not of the things that Champlain had done, but of the way in which he did them. They celebrated his record of achievement, but mostly they remembered the manner in which he treated others and served purposes that were larger than himself. Most of all, they praised him as a principled leader, and celebrated the principles themselves.

In Quebec, the eulogy for Champlain was given by his good friend and close companion, Father Paul Le Jeune, Jesuit Superior in New France. He wrote, "I did not lack materials." Le Jeune praised Champlain's moral qualities. He described his *foi* and *piété*, faith and piety "so lofty as to astonish us all." He spoke of Champlain's integrity and reputation, his sense of justice and equity, and celebrated his qualities of loyalty and fidelity, *loyauté* and *fidélité parfaite*. And he praised Champlain's sense of duty, *devoir*. Others, and Champlain himself, wrote of his concern for *humanité*, and of his regard for *renommée*. Most of these words from seventeenth-century French have cognates in modern English, and we tend to assume that they carried the same meaning for Champlain as they do for us. Not so. At Quebec in 1635, these words conveyed thoughts that were different from ours.

Foi et piété, faith and piety, sustained him in a special way. Champlain's faith was not at all like that of English Puritans of Massachusetts Bay, who were driven by an ethic of striving to prove that they were God's elect in a world where most people were condemned to depravity and damnation. Champlain's faith was Roman Catholic, not in the sense of emphasizing a particular denomination of Christianity, but in the original and literal meaning of catholic as encompassing all humanity. His aspiration to this large ideal of catholicism was Champlain's driving passion. He believed that all people and all things were of God and revealed His divine purposes. This idea lay at the root of Champlain's insatiable curiosity about the world—a form of faith and piety that was very different from most other people in his time, and many in our own.

Loyauté had complex meanings in Champlain's world. French dictionaries on historical principles tell us that it meant the quality of caring for others. It also meant honest dealing with other people, and it had connotations of equity, decency, and humanity. Some French dictionaries translate the English word "fairness" as "loyauté." "Loyauté" in Champlain's lexicon had all of these connotations.

Devoir was also prominent in Champlain's thought and the thoughts of others about him. In the early seventeenth century, "devoir" denoted a strong sense of duty and service, and preserved its ancient meaning of obligations among unequals. It was also used as a plural noun, with several layers of meaning. On one level it meant a set of moral obligations. On another it described an entire "code of obligation." On yet a third it referred to rituals of obeisance in a hierarchical society. A man in Champlain's world was expected to "présenter ses devoirs" to those above him, and to receive with grace "les devoirs" of those below.[33]

Humanité was a word that also appeared in the writings of Champlain. It signified that all people in the world are God's creatures, endowed with immortal souls and powers of reason. In Champlain's understanding, it was a Christian ideal that embraced all humankind. This altruism was shared by others in his circle of French humanists, especially his mentors Henri IV and the sieur de Mons. Many of his companions in North America shared it too: Pont-Gravé, Lescarbot, Razilly, Hébert, Giffard, the Récollets, the Jesuits, and others. This idea arose from the deepest wellsprings of their Christian faith. In our secular world, Champlain's Christian faith has been perceived as ethnocentric by secular ethnographers. But it was precisely that faith which inspired the principles of humanism and humanity on which modern ethnography rests.

Renommée was another word that has changed its meaning from Champlain's world to our own. Its most literal equivalent in English is "renown" or "good reputation." He sailed to America in one ship named *Renommée* and another that was called *Bonne-Renommée*. Some scholars have taken this quality to represent a concern for "fame" in the early modern era. An iconic emblem often appeared in that era, of fame and renown as an angel on a cloud blowing a trumpet. Champlain shared a pursuit of reputation, and it was urgently important to him. But he thought about it in a way that belonged more to his age than our own. It was related to honor, which then referred not to reputation in our sense, but to a way of living one's life that was worthy of honor.

This way of thinking was far removed from our own view of reputation as an "image" to be cultivated by "public relations." *Bonne renommée* at the time was not about images of things. People then did not have our highly developed sense of images as things in their own right, which have an existence apart from the object they purport to represent. Champlain sought to do acts worthy of renown. He was also driven by a dream of contributing to the honor and reputation of France. He wrote rarely of his own *renommée* but often of the *renommée* of France and New France as a leading purpose of his grand design. In all those ways, his thinking about reputation was profoundly different from that of spin-doctors and image-mongers in our time.

People have tended to associate Champlain's thought with ours, and to understand him as a modern man who contributed to the making of our contemporary world. In some ways that is true, but he was a man of his own time, and his mind worked differently from ours. He lacked the sense of individualism and individual autonomy that is so strong in North American culture today. Champlain believed that individuals were literally members of a larger entity—much as arms and legs are members of body and cannot exist apart. This idea was at the heart of his ideas of "loyauté" and "devoir."

Champlain did not share our passion for liberty and freedom, which was already highly developed among the founders of English colonies before 1635. He wrote less often of liberty than of its corruptions, for which he had a highly developed vocabulary that we do not use. He wrote of some Frenchmen and Indians as living in a state that he called *libertinage* and *license*, which was in his thinking the vice of liberty and the anarchy of selfishness, egoism, personal autonomy, and individual self-seeking. He called it *la vie angloise* and thought of it as licentiousness. Ideals of discipline, authority, order, and devotion to others were always important to him.

There was nothing of equality, democracy, or republicanism in Champlain's thinking. Champlain was raised in a European world where everyone had a rank and station. Like most of his European contemporaries, he was a confirmed monarchist. More than that, he firmly believed that hierarchy and hegemony were fundamental to order, which he valued in an era of violence and deep disorder.

Champlain's ideals were distant from ours in many ways, but some of our most cherished values have grown from his. We share his belief in principled action, even if our principles are not the same. Many of us are raised to his ideal of responsibility and leadership in a large cause, even as the causes have changed. We have inherited his idea of humanity even as we have transformed it in many ways. And we are dreamers too, nearly all of us.

CONCLUSION

A Leader's Long Reach

> Would to God that all the French who first came to this country had
> been like him; we should not so often have to blush for them before our
> savages.
>
> –A French missionary on Champlain [1]

I N THE YEAR 1832, an Indian warrior dictated a volume of his memoirs. He was Mà-Ka-Tai-Me-She-Kià-Kiàk, war chief of the Sac and Fox nations. English-speaking people knew him as Black Hawk. They held him in respect, even as they fought him in a struggle called the Black Hawk War, where Abraham Lincoln had his first experience of leadership.[2] After the last campaign, Black Hawk asked a Métis interpreter named Antoine LeClaire to have "a history of his life written." An enterprising Yankee journalist published it as *The Autobiography of Black Hawk* in 1833. Two centuries later it is still in print.[3]

The author dedicated his book to the general who had defeated him, in the hope that he "might never experience the humility that the power of the American government has reduced me to." He explained, "This is the wish of him who in his native forests, was once as proud and bold as yourself." The book was a warning to leaders of all nations, against the folly of false pride and blind prejudice.[4]

Black Hawk also wanted to share his memory of leaders who had avoided those errors, and he began the book with a story about two of them. One was his ancestor Na-Nà-Ma-Kee who lived "in the vicinity of Montreal" during the seventeenth century and became a war chief of his people. The other was a Frenchman who appeared in the St. Lawrence Valley at the same time.[5]

The story began one night when Na-Nà-Ma-Kee had a dream. The Great Spirit appeared to him and said that "at the end of four years," he would "see a white man." Na-Nà-Ma-Kee prepared himself for that event. For many months he blackened his face, ate only at sunset, and continued dreaming whenever he slept. Then the Great Spirit came again and told him to make a

In the nineteenth century, Black Hawk, war chief of the Sac and Fox nations, vividly remembered Champlain through the oral traditions of his people. He began his autobiography with an account of Champlain and his own ancestor Na-Nà-Ma-Kee, as exemplars of wise and humane leadership.

long journey. Na-Nà-Ma-Kee and his two brothers traveled five days down the St. Lawrence River, "in a direction to the left of the sun rising."

At the end of their journey they met a white man, the first they had seen. He "took Na-Nà-Ma-Kee by the hand and welcomed him into his tent." He said that he was "the son of the King of France" and that he also had been dreaming for many years. The Great Spirit had directed him to sail across the sea to a new world, where he would meet a nation "who had never seen a white man," and they would live together as if they were members of one family. The white man said that he had shared this dream with his father, the King of France, who "laughed at him and called him a Ma-she-na," but he insisted on coming to America, where the Spirit had directed him.

This white man was a "great and brave general," but he came in peace. He brought trade goods but gave them to Na-Nà-Ma-Kee as gifts. They spoke different languages, but understood each other and made a bond. Then the white man departed, promising to meet again at the same place, "after the twelfth moon." A year later he returned, just as he had promised. He was a man who kept his word. Na-Nà-Ma-Kee and the white war chief began a regular exchange of goods and purposes. The white man behaved honorably, and they became allies for many years.

After many years the white man stopped coming. The French said he was dead. Na-Nà-Ma-Kee also died, and his people were attacked by other white men. They moved west beyond the Great Lakes to Wisconsin, then south to Iowa, and east again to a village in the Illinois country. Black Hawk said, "At this village I was born, being a regular descendant of the first chief Na-Nà-Ma-Kee." He also became a war chief, but the more he fought with others, the more he remembered the example of Na-Nà-Ma-Kee and the great white general who regarded other nations as their kin.

Black Hawk did not recall the name of this white man who lived long ago, but he was able to describe him in detail. Only one historical figure matched his description: Samuel Champlain. Black Hawk wanted his readers to remember this leader, who was unlike so many others. The memory had been preserved among the Sac and Fox nation, and carried more than a thousand miles from the St. Lawrence Valley to what is now the United States. In 1832 Black Hawk had it recorded on paper, in the hope that we might remember this story of Indian and European leaders who met in peace, and shared their dreams, and lived together.[6]

Many stories have been told about first encounters between American Indians and Europeans. Few of them are about harmony and peace. The more one reads of these accounts, the more one learns that something extraordinary happened in New France during the early seventeenth century—something different from what took place in New Spain, New England, and New Netherlands. Scholars of many nations agree that the founders of New France were able to maintain good relations with American Indians more effectively than any other colonizing power.[7] This was not a simple contrast between all the French on one hand, and all the Spanish or English or Dutch on the other. Some Spaniards and Englishmen got on well with the Indians. Bartolemé de Las Casas and his Dominicans did so in New Spain, as did John Eliot and Roger Williams in New England.[8] And other Frenchmen were very cruel. Jacques Cartier was welcomed by Indians of the St. Lawrence Valley in 1534. He repaid them by seizing their children and carrying them to France against their will. On his second voyage in 1535 Cartier kidnapped five Indians, including a chief, and their families never saw them again.[9]

But in the next century, something remarkable happened when a small group of French explorers landed among the Montagnais at Tadoussac in 1603. It happened again when they met the Penobscots at Kenduskeag in 1604, and once more when they settled among the Mi'kmaq of Acadia in 1605. The story was the same when these Frenchmen came among the Abenaki of Maine, the Canadien of Gaspésie, the Algonquin in the upper St. Lawrence Valley, the Huron near the Great Lakes, the Susquehannock to the south, the Winnebago in the west, and other nations. The only exceptions were their troubles with some of the Iroquois—some of the time.

These Frenchmen did not try to conquer the Indians and compel them to work, as in New Spain. They did not abuse them as in Virginia, or drive them away as in New England. In the region that they began to call Canada, from 1603 to 1635, small colonies of Frenchmen and large Indian nations lived close to one another in a spirit of *amité* and *concorde*. They formed a mutual respect for each other's vital interests, and built a relationship of trust that endured for many years.

How did that happen? The search for an answer leads to small groups of leaders in many nations, and to one French leader in particular—the only man who was at the center of events in New France through the pivotal period from 1603 to 1635. Samuel de Champlain was able to maintain close relations with many Indian nations while he founded permanent European colonies in the new world. He lived among the Indians and spent much of his time with them, while he also helped to establish three francophone populations and cultures—Québécois, Acadien, and Métis. They were very small in Champlain's lifetime, but by the end of his life all of them had taken root and were growing in a sustained way. From those small beginnings, millions of people in North America trace their descent today, and they still preserve something of their origins in the way that they talk, think, and act. The most important fact about Champlain is not that he did any one of these things, but that he did all of them together. And it was done through the span of three decades, in the face of many failures and defeats.

How did he do it? The first answer is that he did not act alone. Champlain always worked closely with others—Europeans and American Indians alike. He moved in a world of many circles, and worked with people who were unable to work with one another. Champlain could do that because he was genuinely interested in others and comfortable with their diversity. His origins made him so. As a child in Brouage he had lived in the presence of diversity

through his early years. As a youth in Saintonge, he had grown up in a borderland between different cultures and regions. The folkways of this province had
long been adapted to that environment, and they served him well through his
career.

Something else shaped him too. He came to maturity in a time of cruel and
bitter conflict: forty years of religious strife, nine civil wars in France, and millions of deaths. As a soldier he had witnessed atrocities beyond description.
After that experience, this war-weary soldier dreamed of a new world where
people lived at peace with others unlike themselves. After a long and terrible
war, he traveled through the Spanish empire on a mission for his king. There
he had another shaping experience when he met American Indians and African slaves. Champlain was genuinely shocked by the abuse that had been visited upon them, and he painted images of their suffering for his king.

In a world of cruelty and violence, Champlain was heir to an ethical tradition that had deep roots in the teachings of Christ. As a child he learned the
Protestant paradox of God's omnipotence and human responsibility. In later
life, he became a Catholic, and believed deeply in its idea of a universal Church
that was open to all humanity. He shared the large spirit of French Christian
humanists who took the world for their province and regarded all God's children as their kin. They were students of the world, with a passion for the pursuit of knowledge, as a way of understanding God's purposes.

Champlain shared this way of thinking with many others in his time. In
France he belonged to several circles of French humanists. They are important
and neglected figures in modern history—men who inherited the Renaissance
and inspired the Enlightenment. They kept the vital impulse of humanism
alive in a dark and difficult time. In that way they were world figures of high
importance, and Champlain had an important place among them.

In France from 1585 to 1610 these humanist circles formed around King
Henri IV, and were inspired by his large ideas of peace and tolerance. Several
circles centered their thoughts on North America. Champlain worked closely
with three generations of French humanists who shared that impulse. He
sought the advice of an older generation of Aymar De Chaste, Dugua de
Mons, Pierre Jeannin, Cossé Brissac, and the elder Brulart-Sillery. Closer to
him in age was a middle generation of Marc Lescarbot. He also worked with a
younger generation who included Isaac de Razilly, Charles de La Tour, and
others. There were also several circles of Catholic humanists: Jesuits led by
Paul Le Jeune and Récollets such as Theodat Sagard.

In America, some of Champlain's most interesting circles formed among
Indian leaders. He worked with Membertou in Acadia, Bessabez in Norum-

bega, Anadabijou of the Tadoussac Montagnais, Iroquet of the Algonquin Petite nation, Ochasteguin of the Arendarhonon Huron, and many more. Dozens of Indians are mentioned by name in Champlain's *Voyages*, and often described at length. He wrote of them as individuals, almost always with respect and affection.

These Indian leaders, like Na-Nà-Ma-Kee's ancestor, had their own visions and dreams. Their nations had long been at war with one another. That incessant strife had been reinforced by the coming of the Europeans. The result was a surge of violence that compounded on itself. Many Indians told Champlain that they were sick of war and wanted to find a way to end it. They were hard and practical men. But like the French leaders, they were men of vision who dreamed of a better world.

And yet, visions and dreams were not enough. We have seen that the sieur de Mons and Poutrincourt shared Champlain's ideal of humanity and peace. But when these three men took turns leading expeditions south along the coast of Norembega, only Champlain succeeded in establishing good relations with the Indians. De Mons and Poutrincourt tried and failed. Even as they sought peace, they lost control of events and found themselves caught in an escalating cycle of fear and suspicion that ended in violence.

Champlain added another vital element to the purposes that these men shared. He was able to convert a dream into reality. By trial and error he learned how to lead men in large causes—and to do so in difficult circumstances, sometimes against desperate odds. It was typical of Champlain that he studied the problem of leadership with the same care that he brought to other questions. In 1632 he wrote a little book called *Traitté de la marine, et du devoir d'un bon marinier*, a Treatise on Marine Affairs, and the Duty of a Good Mariner."[10] It is also a treatise on leadership. Most of it was about mastering skills in a rigorous way and doing small things with great care.[11] Much of it was on the qualities that a leader must have if he wishes to succeed, and some of it remains remarkably fresh and urgent after four centuries.

Champlain argued that a leader must be prévoyant, a word that has no exact equivalent in modern English. His idea of prévoyance was different from foresight in its common meaning. It is not a power to foresee the future. To the contrary, prevoyance was the ability to prepare for the unexpected in a world of danger and uncertainty. It was about learning to make sound judgments on the basis of imperfect knowledge. Mainly it is about taking a broad view in projects of large purpose, and about thinking for the long run. All these elements were important parts of Champlain's leadership—so much so that this idea of prevoyance appeared even in the first sentence of his will and testament.[12]

Champlain's idea of leadership was also an ethical idea. "Above all," he wrote, a good leader "keeps his word in any agreement; for anyone who does not keep his word is looked upon as a coward, and forfeits his honor and reputation, however valiant a fighter he may be, and no confidence is ever placed in him."[13] He believed that leadership was about treating other people with humanity. He wrote that a leader "should be liberal according to his opportunities, and courteous even to his enemies, granting them all the rights to which they are entitled. Moreover, he should not practice cruelty or vengeance, like those who are accustomed to inhumane acts, and show themselves to be barbarians (*barbares*) rather than Christians, but if on the contrary he makes use of his success with courtesy and moderation, he will be esteemed by all, even by his enemies, who will pay him all honor and respect."[14]

Champlain's greatest achievement was not his career as an explorer, or his success as a founder of colonies. His largest contribution was the success of his principled leadership in the cause of humanity. That is what made him a world figure in modern history. It is his legacy to us all.

MEMORIES OF CHAMPLAIN
Images and Interpretations, 1608–2008

> Let the past show us its physiognomies. Yes! It's time for statues! The
> books have spoken. Let the chisel do its work!
>
> —Benjamin Sulte, 1884[1]

I N FOUR CENTURIES, many claims have been made on the memory of Samuel de Champlain. To search library catalogues under his name is to find hundreds of books and articles in French and English. To scan the web for "Champlain" is to turn up six million Google pages, mostly on the man himself and things that were named for him. The books include many volumes for young readers (some very charming), a scattering of mystery novels and Harlequin romances (some incredibly bizarre), occasional works of poetry and drama, promotional literature, books of religious devotion, editions of Champlain's works, monographs in many disciplines, and many major works of historical scholarship. Taken together, sixteen generations of scribbling about Champlain appear at first sight to confirm the old cliché that every generation writes its own history. This endless whirl of interpretation might also seem to support arguments for the relativity of historical knowledge.

But to look again is to find another pattern that is more interesting, and less clearly understood. Scholars do not merely rewrite history. They revise and improve it. They add new discoveries, correct old errors, deepen understanding, and enlarge the spirit of inquiry. Every serious book about Champlain, however flawed, has contributed something to what we know about the man himself, his world, and our own. To study this literature is to find a continuing growth of historical knowledge, through many generations of research.[2]

Champlain's French Contemporaries: Lescarbot and Others

The first published historical writings about Champlain were written by men who served with him in New France. The most prolific author was Marc Lescarbot (1560/70?–1641), a gifted writer with a classical education. He was a lawyer in Paris who had trouble in the courts and came to Acadia in 1606 "to flee a corrupt world." Lescarbot was in New France for only a year, then returned to Paris in 1607 and published an *Histoire de la Nouvelle-France* in 1609. The book was a success, with an English translation in the same year, another in German, and four French editions by 1618. It was followed by other works, among them *La Conversion des sauvages* (1610) and *Relation dernière de ce qui s'est passé au voyage du sieur de Poutrincourt en la Nouvelle France depuis 20 mois ença* (1612).[3]

Lescarbot's early writings about Champlain were positive, even adulatory. While they were working together in New France, Lescarbot wrote a sonnet celebrating Champlain's leadership in his "belle entreprise":

TO SAMUEL CHAMPLAIN
Sonnet

CHAMPLAIN, I have long seen that your leisure
Is employed persistently and without respite . . .
And if you accomplish your beautiful enterprise,
One cannot estimate how much glory will one day
Accrue to your name which already everyone prizes.[4]

But then they had a falling out. In one brief passage of his *History of New France*, Lescarbot mocked Champlain for "credulity" in writing about the Indian spirit Gougou as the Devil himself. He also plagiarized Champlain's *Des Sauvages* and, in the words of one editor, "made a sad hash of it."[5] Champlain in his next book mocked Lescarbot, writing that the farthest his critic had traveled in New France was to cross the Bay of Fundy to Sainte-Croix. This response outraged Lescarbot. In later editions of his work, he removed some favorable references to Champlain and sniped at him in small ways. It was a petty authors' quarrel, unworthy of these two large-spirited men.[6]

But even as that feud continued, later editions of Lescarbot's history drew on new sources. He confirmed the accuracy of Champlain's accounts of the disaster at Sainte-Croix, the happy story of Port-Royal, the founding of Quebec, and explorations of North America. Lescarbot supported Champlain's claim to have founded the Ordre de Bon Temps. From his own sources, he corroborated Champlain's account of Duval's conspiracy and the battle on Lake Champlain in 1609, even to the incredible first shot.

Lescarbot also substantiated Champlain's account of events in France, including his relations with Henri IV, the sieur de Mons, President Jeannin and the American circle, the struggles with the trading companies, and politics at court. Even after their quarrel, both men were devoted to the cause of New France. They shared many of the same humanistic values, and wrote of the Indians with deep interest and respect. In all these ways, Lescarbot documented Champlain's grand design for New France, and confirmed the main lines of its history.[7]

Other French contemporaries also wrote secular accounts of Champlain's activities. Some were primary documents such as Charles Daniel's *Voyage à la Nouvelle France* (1619). Others were secondary works, including Pierre Victor Palma Cayet's *Chronologie septenaire* (1605) and Jacques-Auguste de Thou's *Histoire universelle depuis 1543 jusq'en 1607*. De Thou copied freely from Champlain and Lescarbot, and wrote that he much preferred Champlain's work. The most important journal of the period, *Le Mercure François*, published pieces on New France, and anonymous works by Champlain himself. All confirmed the main lines of Champlain's *Voyages* and enlarged upon them.[8]

Indian Memories of Champlain

Native Americans also held Champlain in high esteem. In general the Huron cherished the memory of his acts and made a legend of his virtues. In the spring of 1636, they called at Quebec to express their sadness on his death and "made some presents to cause 'our French' to dry their tears and more easily swallow the sorrow that they had suffered on the death of Monsieur de Champlain."[9] As we have noted, Champlain also became a legendary figure in Algonquian oral traditions such as Na-Nà-Ma-Kee's tale, which was preserved among the Fox and Sac nations in the Mississippi Valley. Stories were passed down by the Mi'kmaq in eastern Nova Scotia.[10] Montagnais oral traditions preserved the memory of good relations with French settlers and the "chief of the French" in the early years, followed by growing trouble in later generations, such as in the memory of Na-Nà-Ma-Kee.[11]

An exception to this pattern was noted by Father Paul Le Jeune, who wrote that "a certain Algonquin, a very evil man, reported to [the Huron] last year that the late monsieur de Champlain, of happy memory, had told a captain of the Montagnais, just before giving up his soul, that he would take away with him the whole country of the Huron." This story blamed Champlain's spirit for having started the epidemics that ravaged the Indian nations of the St. Lawrence Valley. The account was attributed to Indian sorcerers, and to one man in particular—a Huron of the northern Attignawantan called Captain Aenon, who took the lead in torturing Iroquois captives and was thought "chiefly responsible" for the murder of Étienne Brûlé. But in general, Champlain's reputation remained high among the Indian nations after his death.[12]

The Jesuit Relations: "Monsieur de Champlain of happy memory"

Every year the Jesuit fathers in New France were required to make full reports to their superiors. These extraordinary documents were published in Paris and have been reissued in two major scholarly editions. Today they are a treasure for historians. The Jesuits made frequent reference to Champlain during his lifetime and for many years afterward. The fullest accounts were those of Father Paul Le Jeune, head of the Jesuit mission during Champlain's acting governorship. They could not have been more positive. Le Jeune described Champlain's breadth of achievement, his success in working with the Indians, his devotion to the welfare of New France, his lack of self-seeking, his selfless support for settler-families, and his high standing among them. Most of all, the Jesuits celebrated Champlain's faith and piety. They also portrayed a leader of great ability.

When Jesuit missionaries in the Huron country learned of Champlain's death in 1635, they responded by renewing their vows in thanks to God for the gift of his leadership. Father Le Mercier wrote, "We could not do too much for a person of his merit, who had done and suffered so much for New France, for the welfare of which he seemed to have sacrificed all his means, yea, even his own life. . . . His memory will be forever honorable."[13]

For many years, the Jesuits held up their memory of Champlain as an example for leaders who followed. Their interpretation made a striking contrast to their judgments on other lay leaders in New France. One declared, "Would to God that all the French who first came to this country had been like him; we should not so often have to blush for them before our Indians."[14]

The *Jesuit Relations* started the hagiography of Champlain. Secular historians have mocked this hagiographic tradition, but they are its unwitting heirs. A Dominican scholar, David Knowles, studied Champlain's Catholic contemporaries, the Bollandists who compiled the *Acta Sanctorum,* and the Maurists who gathered the patristic texts. He found that these great hagiographers were pioneers of critical scholarship in their attempts to distinguish true saints from imposters, and genuine miracles from bogus claims. That combination of Christian faith and rigorous scholarship was strong among the Jesuits, who were good scholars and great admirers of Champlain. They constructed an interpretation that would persist through many generations.[15]

Récollet Historians: Sagard and Le Clercq

The Récollet brothers also wrote histories of New France. The best known was Gabriel Sagard (born circa 1590–05), a lay brother in this Franciscan order who took the name of Théodat (God-given). Sagard was a delightful character. He loved all humanity except an Englishman, cherished God's animal creatures, and made a pet of a baby muskrat that lived in the folds of his Franciscan robe. In the spring of 1623 he came to Canada and lived among the Huron as a missionary. The following year he visited the lower St. Lawrence Valley and got to know the Montagnais and Mi'kmaq. Then he went back to France and published two books. The first was called *Le grand voyage du pays des Hurons* (1632). The second, an expansion of the first, was his *Histoire du Canada* (1636).[16]

Sagard was an excellent naturalist, a gifted linguist, and a very good ethnographer. He studied Indian languages before he came to America, observed the customs of the Huron with keen attention and warm affection, described their culture, and even recorded their music. He did not write in the secular spirit of a modern anthropologist but studied the native people of North America as a way of understanding God's purposes in the world. Sagard was a man of faith, and his primary purpose was to convert the Hurons to Christianity. He also worked within a strong moral philosophy, and noted the vices of the Huron—sadistic cruelty to enemies, the practice of torture and cannibalism, and incessant gambling, even with their wives as stakes. At the same time he observed their virtues as a people who were "faithful to their oaths" and had "a punctilious sense of justice" within the framework of their own culture.[17]

Sagard's most enduring contribution was the extraordinary depth of his descriptions of the Huron people—their country and culture, economy and polity, society and history. He plagiarized freely from Champlain without credit, made a few sparse but very favorable references to him, and contributed bits and pieces of information about him. But in general he amplified Champlain's account of Huronia and highly praised his character.

Another Récollet historian, two generations after Sagard, was Christian Le Clercq (1641–post-1700), a missionary who worked in Gaspésie and Acadia from 1675 to 1687. He published books on the history of missionary enterprise in New France and on his own work among the Indians of Gaspé.[18] Le Clercq talked with many people who knew Champlain. He praised his "untiring" devotion to the founding of New France and the care with which he "forgot nothing to sustain his enterprise, in spite of all obstacles which he met at every step." Le Clercq also spoke highly of Champlain's attempts to settle French families in Quebec, his attention to the Indians, and his support of Récollet missions. The villains of Le Clercq's account were the trading companies. He wrote, "Monsieur de Champlain, who had himself first formed that Company, had tried in vain during his stay in France to open their eyes and to appeal to honor and conscience."[19] Le Clercq made a contribution by his access to the records of the Récollets, and by publishing manuscript material from their archives. He made errors on events before he came to New France, but added useful information from his own experience. On the subject of Champlain the judgments of these Récollet writers were as positive as those of the Jesuits, even though the two orders differed on other subjects.[20]

Champlain in the Age of Reason: Charlevoix

In the eighteenth century, writers who were part of the Enlightenment brought a new perspective to the study of Champlain. A pivotal figure was Pierre-François-Xavier de Charlevoix (1682–1761), a Jesuit scholar of noble birth who had a broad interest in world history. In 1704, while still a student at the College Louis-le-Grand in Paris, he acted as a dormitory prefect for Voltaire, who remembered him as a great scholar and a good man, though "a bit longwinded." The next year he taught at the Jesuit College in Quebec, traveled widely through the colony, returned to France and began to write global history, with three volumes on the history of Jesuits in Japan.[21]

In 1722 Charlevoix was sent back to New France with instructions to explore the continent and find a passage to Asia. The result was one of the epic journeys in American history. With two canoes and eight voyageurs he went up the St. Lawrence Valley to the Great Lakes, then down the Mississippi to Louisiana. He made his way east to Florida, was shipwrecked in the Keys, returned to New Orleans in a row boat, traveled through the Caribbean, and finally sailed home to France. Charlevoix failed to find a way to China, but he wrote a classic travel book, followed by a history of New France, and other studies of Haiti and the Jesuit regime in Paraguay.[22]

The first chapters of Charlevoix's *Travels* were a running commentary on Champlain's works, with much attention to their accounts of Indian ways, and their descriptions of flora and fauna. Charlevoix praised him as the founder of Quebec, and condemned the weakness and irresolution of his successors. He was very positive about Champlain, writing that "he won the goodwill of all, and spared himself in nothing [and] daily invented something new for the public good."[23]

Charlevoix himself had faced many of Champlain's challenges. Working from his own experience and from historical records, he was the first writer to bring out the full range of Champlain's activities and the power of his mind: "He had good sense, much penetration, very upright views, and no man was ever more skilled in adopting a course in the most complicated affairs." Charlevoix wrote: "What all admired most in him was his constancy in following up his enterprises; his firmness in the greatest dangers; a courage proof against the most unforeseen reverses and disappointments; ardent and disinterested patriotism; a heart tender and compassionate for the unhappy, and more attentive to the interests of his friends than his own; a high sense of honor, and great probity. . . . We find in him a faithful and sincere historian, an attentively observant traveler, a judicious writer, a good mathematician, and an able mariner. But what crowns all these good qualities is the fact that in his life, as well as in his writings, he shows himself always a truly Christian man."[24]

Charlevoix defended Champlain against Lescarbot, but praised both men for their humanity toward the Indians. He criticized Champlain for his campaigns against the Iroquois, with whom he "unfortunately embroiled himself on behalf of his allies." But he added, "We must . . . do Mr. de Champlain the justice to say, that his intention was solely to humble the Iroquois, in order to succeed in uniting all the nations of Canada to our alliance by a solid peace, and that it is not his fault if circumstances which he could not foresee turned events quite differently from what he had believed." Charlevoix noted that hostilities between the Iroquois and their northern neighbors had been endemic before Champlain arrived, but he observed that Champlain involved himself in this long war in ways "that did not serve our true interests." He also criticized Champlain for allowing men such as Brûlé to move freely among the Indians.[25]

On balance he concluded, "We cannot too greatly admire the courage of Mr. de Champlain, who could not take a step without meeting fresh obstacles, who expended his own energies without ever dreaming of seeking any real personal advantage, and who never renounced an enterprise, for which he had constantly to endure the caprices of some, and the opposition of others." Charlevoix concluded that Champlain was "beyond contradiction, a man of merit, and may well be called THE FATHER OF NEW FRANCE." This may have been the first use of that phrase.[26]

The Philosophes on Champlain: Colden, Diderot, and d'Alembert

Charlevoix's writings had a great impact on men of the Enlightenment throughout the western world. One example was the work of an Anglo-American *philosophe* in New York, Cadwallader Colden, who wrote about Champlain in exactly the same spirit as Charlevoix. Colden got a few of his facts wrong. He wrote inaccurately of "the French, who settled Canada under Mr. Champlain, their first governor in the year 1603." He called Champlain's Indian allies the Adirondacks, and wrote that "Mr. Champlain, desiring to give his Allies proof of his Love and the Valour of the French nation, put himself at the Head of a Body of Adirondacks, and passed with them into Coirlars Lake [sic], which from this time on the French have called by Mr. Champlain's name." [27] Colden described the battle at the lake in 1609 in great detail from Champlain's own writings, which he appeared to know well. Like Charlevoix he chastised Champlain for what he had done. "Thus began a War and hatred between the French and the Five Nations, which have cost the French much blood, and more than once had like to have occasioned the entire destruction of the colony." [28]

The same memories of Champlain appeared in writings by French leaders of the enlightenment; they celebrated him and established his reputation as the founder of Quebec. In 1751 Denis Diderot and Jean d'Alembert identified him that way in their great *Encyclopédie*. They wrote, "It is to the Sieur de Champlain, a gentleman of Saintonge, that the French owe the first establishment in Quebec. He founded it in 1608 and died there in 1635, after twenty-seven years of labor." They also drew on Champlain's works of travel, botany, natural history, and ethnography. A vital part of the Enlightenment was this expanding interest in cultures and environments throughout the world, which derived in part from Champlain. [29]

An Image for an Age of Reason: Champlain as a Man of the Enlightenment

In the Archives nationales du Québec, there is an old sketch of Champlain. It is what artists call a *sanguine*, a drawing made with a crayon of red ocher that was much favored by Watteau, Boucher, and other artists in the eighteenth century. Champlain's features are very clear and consistent with the small self-portrait in his own works: a high forehead and arched brows, eyes set widely apart, a fine-boned and slightly aquiline nose, pursed lips, a thin mustache, and a close trimmed beard. The hair is neatly back-combed, and the expression on the face is pleasant and engaging, with the hint of a smile. The gaze is open and direct, with a quality of candor in the classical sense. This is the image of a "gentleman of Saintonge," as Diderot and d'Alembert called him, who is at ease with others and at peace with himself, a man of reason, observation, benevolence, and enlightenment. The drawing gives much attention to Champlain's costume. He wears a soldier's half-armor, an officer's broad sash, and a gentleman's laced collar. The drawing is of unknown provenance and uncertain date, but whatever its origin, it is true to interpretations of Champlain in the Enlightenment. [30]

Quebec's Progressive Whig Historian: Garneau's Liberal Catholic Champlain

After the second British conquest of New France in 1759–60, the memory of its founders tended to fade for a generation or two. Comparatively few references to Champlain appeared in the period from 1760 to 1815. But in the nineteenth century, interest began to revive. The leader was one of Canada's greatest historians, François-Xavier Garneau (1800–1866). He came from a family with

This anonymous sanguine of Samuel Champlain, of uncertain date and origin, matches the interpretations of 18th-century philosophes.

deep roots in Quebec and briefly attended its schools, but was largely self-taught. As a young man he became bilingual, traveled widely in the United States, England, and France, and moved easily in the cultural milieu of three nations. In his travels he met many young nationalists; a Polish leader in France had a particular impact. He adopted liberal and Catholic views, and returned to Canada with a deep attachment to its history. His goal was to combine the heritage of Quebec with an ideal of a Canadian nationalism that could unite its French and English inhabitants.

Garneau's greatest work was his *History of Canada*, published in four small volumes (1845–52), and reprinted in many editions. It is a major work, remarkable for its command of primary sources, breadth of thought, accuracy of detail, and maturity of judgment. Garneau wrote as a Catholic and a Liberal in the nineteenth-century sense. His works were similar in outlook to the books of George Bancroft in the United States, and Thomas Babington Macaulay in Britain. Like these Whig historians, Garneau thought of history in teleological terms as the progress of liberty, freedom, democracy, and national self-determination. The result was another great work of Whig historiography, and a monument of Canadian literature.[31]

Garneau took a liking to Champlain and recognized him as the most important figure in the founding of New France. He associated him with Henri IV. "In losing Henry IV two years after the founding of Québec," Garneau wrote, "he lost a friend and mentor [*bon maître*] whom he had served faithfully, and who had been of great assistance to him." Garneau described Champlain's work in detail, observing that he was important not merely for the things he did but for the way he did them. Garneau's Champlain was himself a proto-whig, a man of reason, experience, liberality, and large purposes who had been endowed with a "judgment sound and penetrating [*jugement droit et pénétrant*], and a practical genius [*génie pratique*)], Champlain was able to conceive and follow without ever swerving an extended and complicated plan for thirty years of effort to found Canada [*établir le Canada*] which proved his perseverance and his strength of character." He assured to France the possession of immense countries "without the help of almost any soldiers, by the sole means of missionaries and alliances with the indigenous people."[32]

Garneau defended Champlain from Charlevoix's criticism that he was responsible for hostilities with the Iroquois, and for the destruction of the Huron nation. Not so, Garneau insisted:

"He had been blamed for having declared war against the Iroquois, but the war already existed between them and other nations in Canada. He never ceased his efforts to maintain them in peace."[33] Garneau also believed that the destruction of the Huron was the result of changes in French policy after Champlain: "His death was a great loss for the Huron, who had great confidence in him." Garneau's Champlain was a man of large spirit: "One finds him a faithful author, a judicious and attentive observer, whose works are filled with detail on the customs of the indigenous people and the geography of the country." He was also a liberal supporter of toleration and even freedom of conscience, a vision of a union of the Canadas.[34] Altogether Garneau's Champlain was a truly heroic character, and looked the part. From sources that he did not identify Garneau wrote, "Champlain had a handsome appearance, a noble and military bearing, a vigorous constitution which gave him the strength to resist physical stress, and a spirit that he sustained throughout a hard life.[35]

The Canadian response to Garneau's great work was mostly very positive. The book went through several French editions, and in 1860 Andrew Bell published it in English, informing his readers that he had tried to do a "moderately *free* rather than a slavishly *literal* translation" which was "shaped, to some extent, to meet the reasonable expectations (but not to flatter the prejudices) of Anglo-Canadian readers." Bell's translation gave little attention to Champlain's Catholic faith, which was muted into a vaguely "religious turn of mind." Bell's Champlain "effected the exaltation of New France" by "equitable diplomacy and Christianising influences," more than by a close connection to the Catholic Church.[36]

In Quebec, other reactions to Garneau's history went the opposite way. Conservative Catholic clerics in Quebec liked its literary strength, but criticized Garneau's interpretation of Champlain as a liberal Catholic, and rejected his vision of Canada as a bilingual nation. Garneau himself was called a Liberal (which he was) and a Protestant freethinker (which he was not). After Garneau's death, Catholic conservatives writers worked with members of Garneau's family to revise his work. Subsequent editions made the book less liberal, more conservative, and more supportive of the clerical establishment in Quebec. Marcel Trudel remembered: "We were referred to the work of François-Xavier Garneau as to a bible. As late as 1935 you didn't speak of New France in classical colleges without citing Garneau." But Trudel also recalled that "this veneration resulted in a falsified edition of Garneau's work." In 1913 Garneau's grandson made many changes and marked them with brackets. Yet another revised edition in 1944 kept the changes but removed the brackets. Through it all, Garneau became a major figure in Canadian culture. Today his home is maintained in Quebec as a living shrine.[37]

Parkman's Medieval Champlain

While Garneau's liberal whig history had a major impact in Canada, a very different book on Champlain was published in the United States by Francis Parkman (1823–1893). He called it *Pioneers of France in the New World*, the first in a series of nine volumes called "France in America." Parkman was a gentleman-scholar of independent means, and this great historical project was his life's work. He prepared himself by traveling widely in his youth through New England, New York, and Canada, visiting the scenes of the history that he meant to write. His youthful rambles in New England and Canada had made him "familiar with most of the localities of the narrative." He was deeply interested in American Indians, and after going west to study them he wrote a book about his experiences called *The Oregon Trail*.[38]

His first volume on New France was written during the American Civil War and dedicated to three kinsmen who had been "slain in battle." Parkman wrote that the history of New France was about "the attempt of Feudalism, Monarchy and Rome to master a continent where, at this hour, half a million of bayonets are vindicating the ascendancy of a regulated freedom."[39] This Boston-born Anglo-Saxon Protestant was a conservative Whig who believed strongly in ideals of freedom and republicanism, but those large principles were bounded by a narrow arrogance of race, class, gender, nation, religion, and place. He hated slavery but showed no sympathy for the enslaved. He celebrated liberty but opposed the great liberal reforms of his day, and wrote polemics against women's suffrage. Race was central to his thinking. He observed the American Indians in the years of their decline and despised them as a "fickle and bloodthirsty race."[40]

Parkman's national stereotypes also appeared in his contempt for the institutions of France. But he greatly admired individual Frenchmen, and most of all Champlain. Two-thirds of the first volume in his great work was called "Champlain and His Associates." Parkman extolled Champlain for his selfless and "untiring" devotion to the cause of New France. "His books mark the man," Parkman wrote of Champlain, "all for his theme and his purpose, nothing for himself." He celebrated the character and achievements of Champlain, and wrote that he had been "fittingly called the father of New France. In him were embodied her religious zeal and romantic spirit of adventure."[41]

Parkman raised Champlain to the stature of a world figure, but his understanding of the man was fundamentally misconceived. He thought of the French leader as a living anachronism, and wrote that "Champlain belonged rather to the Middle Age than to the seventeenth century . . . a true hero, after the chivalrous medieval type. His character was dashed largely with the spirit of romance." From Lescarbot he took the false theme of Champlain's credulity and reinforced it. "Though earnest, sagacious and penetrating, he leaned to the marvelous," the historian wrote, and he judged Champlain as "prone to overstep the bounds of reason and invade the domain of fancy. Hence the erratic character of some of his exploits."[42] Parkman interpreted Champlain's entire career in these terms, celebrated the medieval virtues of a "faithful soldier," and wrote: "A soldier from his youth, in an age of unbridled license, his life answered to his maxims." But he also judged Champlain severely for his attacks on the Iroquois, and suggested that he prepared the way for the conquest of a medieval and feudal New France by modern and progressive forces in New England.[43]

All this was deeply mistaken. Champlain was a man of his own age, not at all medieval. Parkman's work was marred by major interpretive error, but it was important in another way. He created the most visually striking images of Champlain, ironically so. Parkman himself was nearly blind and said that his physical and mental condition "never permitted reading . . . continuously for more than five minutes, and often has not permitted it at all." He could write only a few words a day, with his pen guided by wires across the page. But he saw his subject clearly in the mind's eye, and this blind bard of Boston wrote some of the most vivid prose that any historian has put on paper.[44]

Parkman also drew on another strength in his command of sources. He worked carefully from primary materials—the published writings of Champlain in their original editions, the manuscript of the *Brief Discours*, the works of Lescarbot, LeClercq, Sagard, and the *Jesuit Relations*. He employed a researcher in French archives, and manuscripts came to him from friends, colleagues, and collectors.[45] Large lacunae appeared on many subjects, especially economics, and there were many errors of detail. But he applied to his sources his gift of creative imagination. Ethnohistorians in the late twentieth century noted a surprising strength. Even as his work was marred by strong racist judgments on Indians, ethnographer Bruce Trigger observed that Parkman was the first general historian who understood the differences among Indian nations.

In the United States, anglophone scholars were drawn to the subject of Champlain by Parkman's prose. In France and Quebec, others responded with deep and justified resentment against Parkman's contempt for their culture and history. But here again, Parkman's work inspired both groups to write their own correctives. His great contribution was to dramatize his subject in ways that attracted others to it.

The Abbé Ferland's Filial Champlain: A Faithful Son of the Church

While Francis Parkman was toiling away in his Boston study, a circle of clerical scholars were writing on Champlain in Quebec. Chief among them was the Abbé J. B. A. Ferland, who published a major two-volume work called a *Cours d'histoire du Canada* (1861–65). It was a serious and substantive work, informed by a broad reading in the history of the French and British colonies, which he knew well.

Ferland thought of New France as "above all a missionary colony" whose primary purpose was to bring Christianity to the Indians. He believed that it succeeded in this divine mission, which was still ongoing at the time he was writing. He himself promoted a new surge of Catholic missionary activity in the 1860s, from Ontario to the Pacific. Ferland was very sympathetic to the Indians and attentive to the diversity of their cultures. He wrote that they could be "monsters of barbarity," but he respected their pride, their strength, and their devotion to their own ways. It troubled him not at all that the Indians refused to become French—an attitude similar to Champlain's. "Well," Ferland wrote, "although they did not adopt the customs of the French, they became excellent Christians!" He believed that "life in the bush maintains them in their attachment to the Catholic faith and the purity of their morals. The less frequent their contacts with civilization, the more they keep to the dignity of nature and innocence of life which belong to Christ's true disciplines." [46]

This approach gave Champlain a new role. In Ferland's judgment, his most important contribution was to assist French missionaries in America. Ferland agreed with many others that Champlain's greatest error was his decision to attack the Iroquois: "The attack of the French against one of the Five Nations was probably the beginning, the cause of hostility which . . . stopped the progress of the colony and indeed nearly killed it in its infancy." But in general Ferland celebrated Champlain for "establishing the small colony on the only solid foundations of a state: religion and honor." [47]

The Abbé Laverdière's Great Project of Champlain Scholarship

A landmark in the historiography of Champlain was the first publication of a major modern edition of his works in 1870. The editor was the Abbé Charles-Honoré Laverdière, a professor of history and librarian at the Séminaire de Québec. In the 1850s, Laverdière had begun to gather unpublished materials on the early history of Canada. He also edited an historical journal for young people and called it *L'Abeille* (*The Bee*). His office became a hive of historical activity.

In 1859, an English translation of Champlain's *Brief Discours* on his voyage to New Spain had been published by the Hakluyt Society, with a brief biography that was judged "by no means remarkable for accuracy." [48] Clerical leaders in Quebec decided that the time had come to publish

Champlain's works in a French edition, with editorial notes that supported their interpretations. In 1864, Laverdière took on the job, with strong support from clerical administrators, who gave him a house, a staff, and the resources of the seminary. Laverdière made rapid progress, and finished his huge task five years later. The manuscript was sent to a printer and set in type.[49]

Just before the work was to be published, a fire destroyed the printing plant and melted the type, which had all been set—a scholar's worst mightmare. But the author and his publisher were undeterred. A single set of proofs survived. From it they reset the book and printed it as the "second edition," though there was no first. The entire set appeared in 1870, under the patronage of Laval University. It is a magnificent specimen of the printer's art, beautifully set in monotype, and a monument of scholarship.[50]

Laverdière shared the conservative clerical memory of Champlain, tempered by a strong hostility to the Jesuit order. He was a great historian, devoted to scholarship and to the accuracy of his work. He corrected printers' errors and garbled passages that abound in Champlain's books, and subsequent editors have accepted his judgment in many cases. He also added notes and appendices that are still very valuable today. Some francophone historians still prefer Laverdière's texts, and every serious scholar of Champlain will always consult them.

Laverdière greatly stimulated serious study of Champlain by making his major texts more accessible than ever before. In 1908, as heroic sculptures of Champlain were rising in many cities, the Abbé Gosselin wrote that Laverdière's volumes were "the real monument in honour of Champlain."[51]

Images of Champlain for a Catholic Revival

Clerical interpretations inspired a new image of Champlain. In 1854, a French lithograph was brought to Quebec, and registered as an authentic image of "Samuel de Champlain, governor general of Canada." It was a formal portrait, attributed to Louis-César-Joseph Ducornet (1806–1856), an artist renowned in France for his physical disability, and for the quality of his work, which triumphed over it. Ducornet had been born without arms. He worked by gripping a brush in his mouth or holding it between his toes. He specialized in devotional images and individual portraits of extraordinary detail.[52]

This lithograph of Champlain was brought to Quebec by Pierre-Louis Morin, a designer and entrepreneur who claimed that it was the work of Ducornet. It represented Champlain in middle age. He appeared overweight and out of shape, with heavy jowls and a double chin. The features had a tentative expression, an air of passivity, and even a feeling of timidity. The hair and beard were impeccable and the dress was immaculate: a dark doublet cut to the latest fashion, with sleeves slashed to reveal a shirt of lustrous silk that shimmered in the light. In the background was a heavy Renaissance curtain, drawn back to reveal a distant scene of Quebec.[53]

Altogether this image was very surprising for a man of Champlain's recorded acts. The face lacked strength, character, and authority. He looked less like a soldier, seaman, or explorer, and more like a man in a sedentary occupation—perhaps a merchant or minor public official. But Morin testified to its authenticity, and the engraving began to be reproduced in Canada, the United States, and France. The image matched the interpretation of the Abbé Ferland, who had represented Champlain as a pious son of the Church whose role had been to support the missionaries whom Catholic historians represented as the true founders of New France. It was also consistent with Laverdière's idea of Champlain. One version of this engraving appeared as the frontispiece to Laverdière's great work.[54]

It also inspired many copies. The painter Théophile Hamel did a handsome oil painting, which was made into a steel-plate engraving by artist J. A. O'Neil. Champlain's face was much improved. Hamel and O'Neil elongated the head, removed the jowls, erased the double chin, refined the features, and created a more attractive portrait of Champlain that was an image of strength and authority. By the end of the nineteenth century the Ducornet-Morin engraving of Champlain and its variants were widely accepted as authentic, and became the conventional image of Champlain.[55]

But after 1900, two scholars in Canada and the United States began to study the Ducornet engraving and its provenance. Both came to the same conclusion: this was not an image of Champlain at all. Worse, it was not merely an error but a fraud. This was the finding of Victor-Hugo Paltsits, chief of manuscripts and the American History Division at the New York Public Library. Paltsits discovered evidence that the image was a deliberate counterfeit, concocted by a ring of French artists, bibliophiles, publishers, and literati—among them George-Barthélemi Faribault and publisher Léopold Massard.[56]

A Canadian scholar, H. P. Biggar, dug deeper and identified the source of the image. It had been copied from a portrait of Michel Particelli, an Italian courtier who became a superintendent of finance in France during the reigns of Louis XIII and Louis XIV. Particelli was reported to be a corrupt and despicable character. One court memoir described him as a "gross and vicious spiritual swine." The portrait had been painted in 1654 by Balthazar Moncornet of another man who was very different from Champlain.[57]

To an historian, the most astonishing part of the story followed after the fraud was discovered. The false portrait continued to be reproduced even more widely than before. Scholars who knew it to be a forgery published it over and over again in their works without any warning to the reader that it was false. Denis Martin writes that "among the most important historians of New France, only Marcel Trudel seems to have avoided the pitfall of the false portrait of Champlain."[58] The indefatigable Champlain Society has published an essay on its website, reproducing the Ducornet engraving and its variants with a stern warning: "These pictures are NOT Champlain."[59] But in

This image of Champlain began as a fraud by French promoters who reproduced a 17th-century painting of a corrupt and hated courtier and sold it in 1854 as a portrait of Champlain. Its tone matched an interpretation of Champlain as a pious son of the Church. This version, one of many, was published in good faith by the Abbé Laverdière as the frontispiece of his great Oeuvres de Champlain *(1870).*

vain. As recently as 2007, the false portrait was represented as genuine in publications by major institutions in Canada, Europe, and the United States. In the twenty-first century, the fraudulent Champlain is reproduced on the web more frequently than ever.[60]

Dionne's Paternal Champlain: Founder of Quebec, Father of New France

In 1891, a new biography of Champlain appeared in Quebec. The author was Narcisse-Eutrope Dionne (1848–1917). Trained as a physician, he became a distinguished historian, an eminent scholar, and provincial archivist of Quebec. In the judgment of Marcel Trudel, Dionne became the leader of a generation of Canadian scholars who "advanced historical methodology." He was careful with his sources and meticulous in his facts. At the same time, Dionne celebrated Champlain as a paragon of Catholic faith and virtue, a man "impossible to overpraise." The book was revised in 1926, and reissued in 1962 in an abridged English translation.[61] Other biographies followed quickly in the same vein. Leading works were by Abbé Henri-Raymond Casgrain in Quebec and Gabriel Gravier, who published in France. Gravier summarized his interpretation in two concluding sentences: "The name of Samuel de Champlain is inscribed in letters of gold on the frontispiece of the history of Canada. . . . He had been faithful to his God, his country, his work, and fundamentally, it is with good cause that he is called the First of Canadians."[62]

Benjamin Sulte's Plebian Champlain: A Rough-Hewn Man of the People

A new idea of Champlain appeared in the writing of Benjamin Sulte (1841–1923), a self-taught man of modest origins from Trois-Rivières, who fought against the Fenians, became a civil servant in Ottawa, and was a highly productive historian. His *Histoire des Canadiens français* in eight volumes (1882–84) was an extraordinary achievement by a prolific writer who is said to have published 3,500 articles in his career. History was Sulte's life work and his great passion. "I wrote for the fun of it," he said, "and made no money from any of it."[63]

Sulte took an important step forward in his writing. He moved beyond an idea of an history of Canada to write a massive history of Canadians. He was part of a world movement in historical writing. A kindred spirit was John Bach McMaster, whose *History of the People of the United States* began to appear in 1883.[64] These scholars were passionate nationalists who thought of the nation not as a territory or a state, but as a people and a popular culture. Sulte celebrated the people of Canada and fiercely attacked historians in France, England, and the United States—especially Francis Parkman, whom he despised. But like Parkman he also thought in racial terms. A student of his career observed that he "uses the terms 'people' and 'race' interchangeably." He celebrated the French Canadians as a race, and thought of Indians as racially inferior, and "hardly more civilized than animals." At the same time he was a liberal anti-clericalist, hostile to the Jesuits and Catholic clergy, who sought power for the Church. Most of all, he was an outspoken agrarian, who thundered against commercial exploitation, and celebrated honest Canadian farmers and tillers of the soil.[65]

Sulte brought all these passions to bear on the life of Samuel Champlain and created a new idea of him. He made Champlain his hero, and hoped that Canadian poets also would "study this great man's career and celebrate his work." Sulte described him as an honest, generous, disinterested man, who "died a victim of the egoism of the merchants and the pettiness of the Court." In the many pages of Sulte's work, Champlain was a man who opposed "mercantile interests" and worked to bring farmers to New France and establish an agrarian base for a new and more virtuous society.

*This coarse image of Champlain as a plebian figure
was engraved by French artist Eugène Ronjat and
was used by Benjamin Sulte in his new interpretation
of Champlain as a rough-hewn man of the people,
circa 1882–1884.*

"Our forefathers were farmers," Sulte wrote, and he thought of Champlain as their leader and patron.[66] Sulte believed that the settlers of Sainte-Croix had failed because "most of them knew only city life; they were unable to fend for themselves; they were totally lacking in the initiative prevalent among rural people. It was a different matter when later Champlain was able to recruit farmers for the soil of Lower Canada! The resources of the country were available to these men of experience and good will; they took advantage of them; the Canadian spirit was in these men."[67]

Altogether, Sulte thought of Champlain as a "patriot of the highest rank," which in his thinking meant a man who served the welfare of ordinary French people in America. Sulte outraged conservatives of many stripes—businessmen, politicians of the right, and especially the clergy of Quebec, who preached and wrote against him. But his thinking was widely shared by others in his generation. His understanding of Champlain caught on, and his vision of a history for the people began to grow. Sulte and MacMaster were mocked by scholars of the old school, but they made a major contribution. Marcel Trudel wrote: "People derided Sulte, but he represents an important stage, because his work marks the advent of ordinary people—*le petit peuple*—as a subject for historians."[68]

In 1870 the French artist Eugène Ronjat produced a new image of Champlain that perfectly matched Sulte's plebian interpretation. The artist began with the fraudulent Ducornet-Morin engraving and rearranged its features. He enlarged the jowls and thickened the double chin. The features became more heavy and fleshy. The face bore marks of hard experience, and a scar ran downward from the mouth across the lower cheek. The bridge of the nose appeared to have be broken and badly healed. The eyes were large, sad, weary, and distant. It was the image of a man who had risen from poverty, identified with the people, experienced their suffering, shared their hopes, and known their sorrows. Ronjat's engraving was reproduced in Benjamin Sulte's *Histoire des Canadiens français*.

Canadian Anglophones: An Imperial Champlain

A very different Champlain emerged in the late nineteenth century, mainly from the work of English-speaking Canadians. A central figure was Sir Edmund Byron Walker (1848–1924), an eminent Victorian with a long white beard. He began as the son of English immigrant-farmers in Ontario. "I was taught," he wrote, "to appreciate that the truth regarding nature was a divine thing, and that we must learn it so far as was possible." His schooling ended at the age of twelve and he went to work as a clerk in a Hamilton bank, became its president, accumulated a large fortune, and devoted his wealth to the pursuit of the learning in Canada. A patron of the sciences and arts, Walker studied the Burgess Shale fossils, founded the Toronto Art Gallery, promoted the Canadian Group of Seven, supported classical music in Canada, and helped make the University of Toronto the great university that it is today. In 1905 he founded an organization to gather documents in Canadian history, and called it the Champlain Society.[69]

The society's first major publication was an edition of Champlain's books, maps, engravings, and some of his manuscripts. The editor was Henry Percival Biggar (1872–1938), who was born in Carrying Place, Ontario, studied at the University of Toronto and Oxford, and became chief archivist for Canada in Europe. The object was to create a definitive bilingual edition with accurate texts in old French and modern English.[70] In general the editors and translators did a careful job of establishing authentic French texts. With some exceptions they produced accurate translations, but notes and commentaries have been superseded by subsequent research.[71] The Champlain Society also published more than ninety volumes of primary material, including bilingual editions of major primary sources for Champlain's era.[72]

Another scholar in this circle was William Francis Ganong (1864–1941). His Loyalist forbears had moved from New York to New Brunswick, and he preserved their strong sense of attachment to the British Empire. Ganong was a scientist who trained at the universities of New Brunswick, Harvard, and Munich and went on to become professor of Botany at Smith College in 1894. His hobby was the history of New Brunswick and Nova Scotia, and he applied his scientific discipline to the research, traveling through the region by canoe and on foot, interviewing Mi'kmaq and Maliseet informants, doing archaeological and documentary research in an empirical spirit. The result was a careful history of Champlain and the French settlement on Sainte-Croix, still in print and very useful.[73] Ganong celebrated Champlain's role as the founder of a bicultural New France that became part of Canada within the British Empire. He caught the mood of this interpretation when he wrote that Champlain's career was part of the "expansion of two of the most virile races of Europe into the wonderful New World."[74]

Hero-Images of Champlain: The Monumental Man, 1898–1925

This spirit flourished in Canada during the years from 1898 to 1925. Champlain became an heroic figure with many faces: a cultural hero for people of French identity throughout the world, a national hero for Canada, an imperial hero for the British Empire, and a Pan-American hero for admirers in the United States. A triggering event was the 300th anniversary of the founding of New France, which began to be celebrated as early as 1870 and continued for fifty years into the 1920s.

The most striking expression of these proud attitudes were monuments of Champlain in many cities and towns. They were ornate structures of bronze and stone—large full-length figures,

A new interpretation of Champlain as a powerful and energetic colonial leader appeared in this monument by French sculptor Paul Chevré, erected on Quebec's Dufferin Terrace in 1898.

mounted on massive pedestals and set in prominent places—altogether, seven major monuments and many smaller ones.

One of most important was erected at Quebec in 1898: a statue more than four meters high, atop a massive pedestal. It stands in a dramatic spot on the Dufferin Terrace near the Château Frontenac, high above the old town, with a long view down the St. Lawrence River. Champlain appears to be striding forward into a wind that catches the folds of his clothing and blows it back against his muscular frame. French sculptor Paul Chevré invented a very masculine image, far removed from Ducornet's engraving. Champlain's body has the strength of youth, and his face has the character of maturity. He wears a handsome doublet, broad breeches, and high-topped seven-league boots. Strapped to his side is his heavy sword, sheathed in its scabbard but ready for use. He has swept off his broad-brimmed hat with its great panache, in what historians have variously interpreted as a salute to the city of Quebec or to the land of Canada. In his other hand he holds a roll of papers, which might be his commission from the old world or his plans for the new. This is a portrait of Champlain as a great founder and a formidable leader.[75]

Other monuments stressed different aspects of Champlain's life and work. In the maritime city of Saint John, New Brunswick, sculptor Hamilton MacCarthy created a full-length bronze monument to commemorate Champlain's first visit on St. John's Day, June 24, 1605. It is an image of Champlain as an explorer, holding one of his maps. For the tercentenary, a huge celebration was staged on the same day in 1905, with a reenactment, speeches, and parades. The monument itself was finally completed on June 24, 1910. One observer wrote that Champlain "was perched at a less lofty height than in Quebec city, but he appeared more dynamic, pointing toward the horizon, like a guide or a visionary."[76]

On July 4, 1907, another monument to Champlain was erected in the United States, in the small town of Champlain, New York, on the border with Canada. This community had been settled by a francophone population from Quebec. Its Catholic priest, Father François-Xavier Chagnon, was the driving spirit. He raised $4,800, mainly from French Canadian immigrants throughout the United States. Patrice Groulx writes that "all of Franco-America was asked to contribute by its clergy and national societies." The bronze monument was erected between the Catholic and Presbyterian churches within what Groulx calls "the symbolic perimeter of francophone Catholicism." It still stands as a symbol of national pride in the history of Quebec, the heritage of New France and the values that Champlain personified.

At the same time it was very much a product of the pluralist culture of the United States, where many different ethnic and national groups met. In that setting, many people became even more conscious of their own national origins than they had been in the nations whence they came. And something else happened as well. When one ethnic group celebrated its heritage with pride, Americans of other ethnic groups rallied to their support, and even joined the celebration, as on St. Patrick's Day when most Americans become a little bit Irish. So it was on July 4, 1907, when the English-speaking citizens of Champlain, New York, turned out and joined their francophone neighbors to honor a French Catholic hero. In that act they became a little bit French themselves in their cultural affiliation—a great unwritten theme in America, where historians and journalists tend to exaggerate the horrors of nativism, and ignore a larger and happier and more important countertheme.[77]

The largest monument of the tercentenary was erected in another part of the United States at Crown Point, New York. It is a heavy granite structure that still looms high above a steep bank overlooking Lake Champlain. It was built upon an error, and marks the spot where Champlain did not fight his battle against the Mohawk, despite fierce local claims. The monument was sponsored by a New York tercentenary commission. The Canadian government was invited to be a cosponsor but declined. In France another group was formed under the leadership of respected historian Gabriel Honotaux. Its purpose was to celebrate the spirit of France in the United States. A subscription was raised to pay for a bas-relief by the renowned sculptor Auguste Rodin. Titled "La France," it was mounted at the base of the monument. Above the image of France is a sculpture of Champlain as the heroic discoverer, gazing at the lake that bears his name. New Yorkers added a functional purpose. They designed the monument to double as a lighthouse for the assistance of mariners who ventured down the great lake at night, as Champlain had done.[78]

Another tercentenary statue of Champlain also went up at Plattsburgh, New York. It is unusual among Champlain monuments. Sculptor Carl Augustus Heber represented Champlain as a soldier wearing a cuirass and carrying an arquebus—one of the few monuments that showed him arrayed for battle. It was dedicated on July 5–6, 1912, with much ceremony, as a symbol of peace and Franco-American unity.

The Canadian capital city of Ottawa erected yet another very large monument to Champlain that still dominates the skyline of the city. It was the work of Hamilton MacCarthy, who had already done the monument at Saint John. For Ottawa he made a change. Champlain is holding an astrolabe at full length above his head. It was meant to be a triumphant celebration of Champlain's career as a navigator and the astrolabe was held high so that members of the Canadian Parliament could see it from their building as they embarked on projects of political navigation. It is not the most hopeful symbol, as astrolabes were normally suspended from a ring, and Champlain is holding his navigational instrument upside down.

MacCarthy modeled the face of Champlain on the features of the historian Benjamin Sulte.

Another monumental theme appeared in Carl Augustus Heber's sculpture, dedicated at Plattsburgh, New York, in 1912. It is one of the few monuments that shows Champlain as a soldier in armor and helmet, carrying an arquebus and arrayed for battle.

The project was supported by both anglophone and francophone Canadians and was meant to be a symbol of national unity. It was dedicated on May 27, 1915, after the First World War had begun. In Quebec that great struggle was widely regarded as an imperial venture for the greater glory of Britain, and many French Canadians chose not to serve. That attitude infuriated English-speaking Canadians, who believed that France was fighting for her survival. They could not understand why French Canadians would not support their own *patrie*. The dedication of the Champlain monument in Ottawa was diminished by those tensions. Patrice Groulx writes, "If the Royal Society and political leaders wanted to make Champlain a unifying symbol, they missed their mark." To broaden the appeal, another figure was added to the base in 1917—an Algonquin guide. Champlain remained the dominant figure, but the addition of an allegorical Indian gave it yet another layer of symbolism.[79]

In 1925, one of the most elaborate Champlain monuments was erected in Orillia, a small town in the region he had known as Huronia. It had become a summer community where affluent Canadians built summer cottages. A monument was proposed in 1913, but the war delayed its completion until 1925. The sponsors selected a British sculptor, Vernon March. He created a narrative monument with many figures representing the history of the region: Indians, traders, missionaries, and above all the heroic statue of Champlain. It told the story of New France and Canada as an interplay of many actors.

In this same period from 1890 to 1929, smaller monuments honored Champlain's friends and companions. The sieur de Mons was given a monument in Annapolis Royal, and La Violette at Trois-Rivières. Nearly nothing was known of La Violette beyond a reference to his name in Champlain's *Voyages*. This project was the work of Trois-Rivière's own historian Benjamin Sulte and his

For a monument in Ottawa, Hamilton MacCarthey sculpted Champlain as an explorer and navigator with an astrolabe in hand. Perhaps it was meant to inspire Canadian legislators, who could see it from the Parliament buildings. But Champlain is holding his instrument upside down. One wonders if the artist was making a political statement.

friend, the sculptor Louis Hébert. Sulte wrote: "The face of the person is unknown to us. Here, I will use my imagination. Lively eyes, thin cheeks accentuated aquiline nose, a thin mustache, light imperial beard, and the head set squarely on the shoulders in the attitude of a man on the lookout. A slight air of a musketeer." [80] This became a formula for the founders of Canada, who began to look like fraternal twins. Sulte offered the rationale of a scholar without a source: "When documents are unavailable," he wrote, "it is customary to rely on things of the time and to convey our thought through forms that do not contradict the facts as a whole." [81]

Champlain and the Cataclysms of the Twentieth Century

In the early twentieth century, authors in America and Europe began to give more attention to the inner life of Champlain. This was not easily done. Champlain's writings centered more on his acts than on his thoughts or feelings, and his biographers rarely wrote of him in an intimate way. Even so, twentieth-century writers became more attentive to his personality and searched Champlain's writings in a new spirit, looking for clues to the man himself. They did so in conversation with the scholars of the nineteenth century—Garneau, Parkman, Sulte, Dionne, and others.

The new generation of scholars in the twentieth century were equally positive about Champlain, but they wrote about him with a different purpose and in a different historical context. The two leading examples were men who had served in the world wars and saw Champlain as a kindred spirit, who lived in an earlier age of conflict and cruelty comparable to their own time. From their experience they greatly admired his strength of character and the way that he conducted himself in an era of extreme violence and disorder.

Constantin-Weyer's Champlain: A Portrait in Patience

In France, a leader of this literary generation was Maurice Constantin-Weyer (1881–1964). He was born to a "good family" of Bourbonne-les-Bains, and educated at the Lycée Henri IV. In 1904 he emigrated to Manitoba, where he lived in the French settlement of Saint-Claude, and worked as a rancher, hunter, trapper, horse-dealer, and journalist. He married a Métisse in 1910 and fathered three children. In 1914, he returned to France, fought on the western front and near east, received the Médaille Militaire and Légion d'Honneur, suffered fifty-three wounds, and left the army as an 80 percent invalid. He became a successful writer and won the Prix Goncourt in 1928 for his novel *Un homme se penche sur son passé (A Man Considers His Past)*. Constantin-Weyer published forty-six books, many on Canadian themes. His purpose was to engage the history of Canada in the literature of France.[82]

In 1931, Constantin-Weyer brought out a short biography of Champlain in a series called "Les grandes figures coloniales." It was done in a hurry, one of four books he published that year, and it was dedicated to young Canadians, particularly those educated in the universities of Laval and Montréal, as "the heirs of French thought." Constantin-Weyer opened his book with a preface on Francis Parkman, "le grand historien américain." He challenged Parkman's thesis that the conflict between France and England in North America was an epic struggle between "feudalism, monarchy and Rome" on one side, and the cause of liberty and republicanism on the other. In particular, he took issue with Parkman's claim that the moral advantage lay on the side of English-speaking people. Constantin-Weyer observed that the democracy of the English-speaking people became a tyranny of the majority. He argued that in the United States, a republic that loved liberty had destroyed many indigenous nations of America for its own gain.

His book was an argument that a higher ethic appeared in New France and that Champlain was its personification. Constantin-Weyer wrote that Champlain's relations with the Indians and "the simple grandeur of that life, entirely consecrated to the King and the Faith (*au Roi et à la Foi*) [was] a better response than any other argument to the assertions of Francis Parkman."[83] The book was about Champlain's devotion to his grand dessein, and his perseverance through thirty years of hardship, frustration, suffering, and defeat. It was also about Champlain's concern for the Indians, his fidelity to French habitants, and his combination of "courage and humanity." Most of all Constantin-Weyer admired Champlain's ability to persist in the face of adversity, and wrote that Champlain "suffered fatigue, pain and sickness not only without complaint, but even with a smile!" He painted a word-portrait of Champlain as a saint for a secular age: "A saint, I say to you," he wrote, "and the proof is that he has the greatest virtue of the saints: patience."[84] Altogether, Constantine-Weyer interpreted the life and work of Champlain as evidence of moral strength in French culture. The author added with pride: "*Voilà qui est français! Voilà aussi qui est chrétien!* That's what it means to be French! That's also what it means to be Christian!" He emphasized that others who are not French or Christian had much to learn from such a model.[85]

Bishop's Champlain: The Life of Fortitude

A kindred interpretation appeared in another biography of Champlain by an American, Morris Gilbert Bishop (1893–1973). Bishop was a soldier in three wars. He served with the cavalry on the Mexican Border, the infantry in the First World War, and psychological warfare in the Second World War. He was also a businessman (advertising), a public servant (the American Relief Administration in Finland), a literary figure (frequently writing for the *New Yorker*), and a professor of Romance Literature at Cornell. Like many of his generation, Bishop was raised to high moral purposes in the reign of Queen Victoria and experienced at first hand the horror of total war in the twentieth century. He was a tough-minded idealist, all the more so because of the realities of his age.

Bishop's most substantial book was his biography of Samuel de Champlain. Mainly he sought to answer one question: "What manner of man was he?" Bishop answered: "The passion of his mind was exploration, discovery. He was possessed of the old *libido sciendi*, the lust of knowing. His lust turned to the great unknown of his time, the white void on sailors' maps."[86] Most of all, Bishop admired Champlain for his moral qualities. "He was a good man," Bishop wrote. "He had the qualities necessary for the adventurer: toughness, tenacity, foresight, courage. But it was the natural virtue of his spirit that little by little impressed itself on the hard fur-traders and on the perfidious Indians. Not many of the great conquerors of our continent have been eminently good men. . . . The reader of Champlain's works, the student of his life, must feel himself constantly in touch with a man to whom good was a reality; one who believed in the goodness of God's purpose, and who sought to realize it in the welfare of his fellow men."[87]

Bishop was quick to note Champlain's flaws, but saw them as linked to his strengths. "He had the faults of the idealist," Bishop wrote. "He stood a little apart from men. He was not sly enough to overreach the sly . . . he dreamed too far ahead. This was his passion. His character was fit for the fulfillment of his passion." Bishop returned again and again to one great strength: "the mark of his character, as it had been developed through war, adventure, and privation, was fortitude." Bishop explained: "Fortitude is, I think, the strength to endure for a purpose. Champlain possessed this strength. When others complained, he did his work. When others turned back, he persevered; when others died, he lived. His strength was physical, for only a man of extraordinary toughness could have survived his trials. His strength was also mental, for his whole long life was a battle against faint hearts, the mean-spirited, the avaricious, the sensual." Altogether Bishop concluded, "the life of fortitude is a noble thing to contemplate." He thought of Champlain as a model for others who live in troubled times.[88]

Deschamps' Champlain: A Humane Imperialist

Another interpretation in the mid-twentieth century came from a French leader and scholar of great distinction. Hubert Deschamps was himself a son of Saintonge, born at Royan in 1900 to a prosperous middle class family. During the First World War he served in the French navy; he then went to the École Coloniale and was sent to Madagascar as a district officer, or in his words *roi de la Brousse*, a king of the bush.[89] A democratic socialist, he joined Léon Blum's Popular Front in 1936, became an aide to the Premier, and was later appointed governor of three colonies in Djibouti, Côte d'Ivoire, and Senegal. Deschamps continued to hold office under the Vichy government from 1939 to 1943, though he was not of its politics, until the Gaullists removed him from office. He changed careers, and became the first professor of African history at the Sorbonne. A superb French stylist, he published thirty books, mostly on exploration, African politics, and colonial administration.[90]

Deschamps had a great love for the African people. He favored the intermixing of Africans and Europeans, and practiced what he preached in a complicated personal life with two wives and many mistresses from both cultures. A keen student of history, he discovered a kindred spirit in his fellow son of Saintonge, Samuel de Champlain. In 1951, Deschamps published a one-volume anthology of Champlain's works with the Presses Universitaires de France.[91] A long introduction offered a new interpretation of Champlain by a man who had witnessed the worst of the twentieth century and remained an idealist. In an essay of luminous intelligence, Deschamps analyzed Champlain's career as one colonial governor on the work of another. He thought of Champlain as "one of the most illustrious sons of Saintonge" and a leading model of *"colonisation humaine."* [92]

The Debunkers' Champlain: Imposter, Liar, Fraud, Fantasist

After the celebration of Champlain's personal qualities by so many generations of writers, a reaction inevitably followed. The mid-twentieth century was an age of irreverence, and in 1922 Americans coined a new word for its attitude toward history. They called it "debunking," after Henry Ford's half-remembered axiom that "history is bunk." For debunkers, things were never what they seemed to be. Reality was the underlying fact, and truth was "the lowdown" in more senses than one. Idealists of all varieties were suspect. Debunking was often done in good humor, almost as an intellectual prank, and with a knowing smile. Debunkers delighted in reviling leaders who had been heroes and saints to earlier generations. Champlain made a perfect target.

A leading example was a little book by Florian de la Horbe, *L'incroyable secret de Champlain.* The author, a French essayist and novelist, took his point of departure from Champlain's obscure origins. He claimed that Champlain was an imposter. He was really Guy Elder de la Fontenelle, "a renowned ruffian who was sentenced to be broken on the wheel, and who is presumed to have escaped this punishment and turned up again as an honest man, under the name of Champlain." [93]

Could it be true? Many things might have happened in the past, but not this hypothesis. Florian de la Horbe's *incroyable secret* was unbelievable in more ways than one. Marcel Trudel wrote that it was "nothing more than a very inferior *roman policier*," a crime fiction story that began with the mystery of Champlain's origins and was developed as history "after the manner of Alexandre Dumas." It was a classic example of the debunking impulse, and it represented a leading genre of debunkery—part fact, all fiction.

Much debunking was done in good humor, but some of it had a hard edge and a nasty bite. In Canada, Jean Bruchési published an essay in 1950 called "Champlain a-t-il menti?" Had he lied? Was he a liar? Bruchési strongly suggested that much of what Champlain wrote was false and even fraudulent—that he lied when he claimed military service in Brittany, lied again about many of his activities, lied once more when he claimed to have been captain of the *Saint-Julien*, never made a voyage to the West Indies, and used Captain Provençal's logbooks "to write under his own name, an account of a voyage that he did not make." All this was offered not as a set of firm conclusions, but a cunning set of strong suggestions. Nearly all of the suggestions were on one side of the question, and very hostile to the document and Champlain. [94]

Bruchési's debunking essay was followed by others. Claude de Bonnault, a prominent Canadian archivist, adopted some of Bruchési's suggestions and added arguments that Champlain was never in Blavet, that he invented the story of Captain Provençal, and that he was not in the West Indies at all. Bonnault topped it off with a conspiracy theory that the *Brief Discours* was concocted in 1612 to support the comte de Soissons and prince de Condé against the queen's Spanish party in France, and to support rapprochement with England. Bonnault concluded that the entire *Brief Discours* was an "histoire fantaisiste," a mere fantasy. Neither of these essays was supported by evidence, and both would be proven false by the research that they inspired. The debunkers themselves turned out to be the fantasists. It was a strange phenomenon, but in the mid-twentieth century, many people wanted desperately to disbelieve. [95]

The Growth of Professional Scholarship

Other tendencies were moving in a different direction. Through that troubled era, the study of history developed as a professional discipline in universities and other institutions. That trend began at a surprisingly late date. During the nineteenth century, history had been taught in American colleges mainly as a branch of moral philosophy, often in a single course of that name, taught by the college president to all students in their senior year.[96]

History as an autonomous academic discipline developed at the same time as did economics, anthropology, biochemistry, and many others. They became academic departments and acquired the full apparatus of a learned discipline during the late nineteenth and early twentieth centuries. Once begun, the profession of history developed rapidly. Today it is one of the largest academic disciplines, and also the most eclectic. It has an active interface with most other disciplines in a university. History is not only a discipline in its own right. It is also a method of inquiry in other disciplines. Today, much academic historical scholarship happens outside history departments. Increasingly it is difficult to tell what academic department a work of history comes from. The expanding eclecticism of history is its saving grace. In the twentieth century this eclectic spirit brought an extraordinary outpouring of historical knowledge, not only in academic history but in archival scholarship, archaeology, and other fields. That pattern clearly appears in scholarship on Champlain.

Professional Archivists and Champlain: Robert Le Blant's Discoveries

Some of the most important work was done by professional archivists, in finding, preserving, and making primary sources more generally available. A major difficulty for students of Champlain was the loss of manuscripts. Champlain tried to preserve his papers, and Lescarbot used them for his history. On his deathbed, Champlain asked that they be sent to his wife in France, and they disappeared. The records of the Company of New France also vanished. They are believed to have been destroyed by the Communards of 1871 who hauled them out of the Châtelet and made a bonfire in the streets of Paris.[97]

Other manuscripts survived in the archives of French ministries. Materials relating to North America in the early seventeenth century were copied by the Library of Congress, mostly from the major French ministries: Colonies, Marine, and Foreign Affairs. They were very useful for this inquiry. Canadian archivists have also made a major effort to find manuscripts in public archives, with much success. Early leaders were H. P. Biggar, who worked in British and French archives; Claude de Bonnault, an archivist trained at the French École des Chartes, and more recently Raymonde Litalien, who has played a major role in supporting the history of New France. In many years of labor, Canadian archivists began by compiling inventories, then ordered manual transcriptions in the early twentieth century. After 1945, massive microfilm projects copied more than 2.5 million pages of records on New France. In 1988, the emphasis began to shift toward digital databases and electronic texts. Since 1999 these materials have been coming online in websites sponsored by Library and Archives Canada in Ottawa and its office in Paris.[98]

An effort of another kind has been made by a very able French archivist who had a particular interest in Champlain. Robert Le Blant was a lawyer, jurist, councillor of the French Court of Appeal at Douai in the north of France, and a highly skilled archivist who knew well the complex ways of French legal and archival institutions. He searched many French provincial and national archives, and found a trove of materials that had eluded earlier students of Champlain. Le Blant published his findings in historical journals, and also in a larger work called *Nouveaux documents sur Champlain et son époque*, edited with René Baudry. The first volume, covering the period from 1560 to 1622, was printed by the Public Archives of Canada, as it then was, in 1967. A second volume, from 1622 to 1635, was promised but not published. A careful bibliography of Le Blant's work by M. A. MacDonald surveys a large body of primary scholarship that is indispensable for any serious student of Champlain.[99]

Documentary Historians and Champlain's World: Lucien Campeau

Working closely with archivists were other scholars who might be called documentary historians. Many have worked under the auspices of the Champlain Society and have prepared scholarly editions of major texts for the early history of New France. The society's work continues, and the first volume of a new translation of Champlain's works is promised for 2008, under an editorial team headed by Conrad Heidenreich.

The another example of documentary history in the late twentieth century is the work of Lucien Campeau (circa 1915–2003), a Jesuit scholar who was trained at the Gregorian University in Rome and taught at the Université de Montréal. Campeau devoted his energy to a great historical project that he called *Monumenta Novae Franciae*. Conceived as a subseries of the Jesuits' *Monumenta Historica Societatis Jesu*, Campeau's project was to publish all major documents relating to the Jesuits in Canada and Acadia, with another series to follow for the Illinois country and Louisiana. He intended it to supersede a large bilingual collection of the *Jesuit Relations* edited by the American historian Reuben Gold Thwaites.

Campeau made two organizing decisions that expanded the scope of his project but limited its use. Roughly 80 percent of his documents had never been published before. He decided to publish them only in their original languages. His fourth volume, for example, includes 178 documents, of which more than 100 are in Latin, eight in Italian, and the rest in French. They are sources of importance—and frustration—for modern users who are not trained in Church Latin. Campeau's volumes reproduce large quantities of material on the history of New France, but they were dated in their historiography and marked by expressions of strong identity to the Jesuits and bitter hostility to their enemies. At the same time, the documents are accompanied by helpful introductions, notes, and "notices biographiques," which have been separately published as a *Biographical Dictionary for the Jesuit Mission*. Altogether, for all their flaws, they are a major contribution.[100]

Archaeology: Material Traces of Champlain's Life

Historical archaeology, which made great strides in the twentieth century, has contributed in a major way to our knowledge of Champlain and his world. The first amateur archaeology in this field was done as early as 1797 at Sainte-Croix Island.[101] Other amateur projects followed in the nineteenth century, and much professional work in the twentieth century. A major center is Quebec, where the Ministry of Cultural Affairs has sponsored archaeological research in the city of Quebec and throughout the province, with results that have been published in more than a hundred volumes of research reports. One of the most useful for students of Champlain is volume 58, *L'Habitation de Champlain*, by François Niellon and Marcel Mousett (1981). It established the sequence of buildings on that site, uncovered much evidence of their architecture, and found many artifacts, including what may have been Champlain's writing set, his sword, and much more. This work also confirmed the accuracy of Champlain's written accounts, and went far beyond them in documenting his material life. Other volumes in the same series have studied the origins of "la vie québécoise" and the material culture of American Indians in the same era. Many artifacts that came out of the ground are on display today in the cultural center at Place Royale in the old town of Québec.[102]

Several other archaeological projects have had an impact on our knowledge of Champlain's career. A careful excavation at Cap Tourmente established the history of Champlain's farm. A project of Indian archaeology in New York state made clear that Champlain's expedition in 1615 was mounted against the Onondaga nation near Syracuse and not at Oneida sites to the east, as historians had mistakenly believed. Underwater archaeology on the fishing coast found much evidence of that era, including early Basque whaleboats and many material remains. Excavations on Sainte-Croix Island turned up evidence of the ravages of scurvy and the remains of its victims, exactly as Champlain described, and give his description a new depth of meaning. Field archaeology in Nova Scotia supplied evidence of life at Port-Royal including land management and agriculture, systems of stratification and material culture. At Castine in Maine another archaeological project excavated the history of a French trading post. Maritime archaeology in the West Indies yielded much evidence about the Spanish empire at the time of Champlain's visit, and much detail about the ships he sailed. In France archaeological work has continued at the home of the Champlain family in Brouage, which is now open to the public as a visitor center. Archaeology in this historical period has proven to be a versatile tool and an important source of knowledge that interlocks with documentary materials.[103]

Prosopographers and Champlain

In the mid-twentieth century, another major contribution was a large project in what the Greeks called prosopography, or collective biography. A successful Canadian businessman, James Nicholson, left a bequest to the University of Toronto for a Canadian counterpart to the British Dictionary of National Biography. The result was the *Dictionary of Canadian Biography/ Dictionnaire Biographique du Canada*, founded to provide critical biographies of major figures in Canadian history. Begun in 1959, the project expanded two years later into a joint Anglo-French enterprise directed by George Brown and Marcel Trudel. Historians were mobilized, and volume I appeared in 1966. The first series, for individuals who died before 1901, was completed in 1990. A second series followed for Canadians who lived in the twentieth century and was complete through 1920 at the time of this writing.

The *DCB/DBC* is an invaluable aid for any project in Canadian history. By comparison with the first British *Dictionary of National Biography*, and the original *Dictionary of American Biography*, the *DCB/DBC* is superior in coverage, documentation, and quality of writing. The Canadian project was also made more accessible than its British and American counterparts, a testament to the large purposes of its organizers. Sets were donated to schools throughout the country. The entire text was digitized and also made available on line without charge to all who wish to use it—a pattern very different from more proprietary practices in the United States and the United Kingdom.

The *DCB/DBC* has become an indispensable work for every period of Canadian history to the early twentieth century, especially for Champlain's time. Much of the first volume is about his contemporaries. A particular strength of the *DCB/DBC* is the large number of biographies of Indians, including many who Champlain knew. Volume I also gives much attention to Champlain's habitants, traders, interpreters, and seamen. For many of them, the biographies in the *DCB/DBC* are the only ones available. In interpretative terms, a major contribution of this great project is to make clear that Champlain rarely worked alone. His way of working with others appears more clearly in this large project of collective biography than in any other source.

Maritime History: Morison's Champlain

In the mid-twentieth century, highly specialized professional historians studied Champlain's career in different ways. Many approaches emerged from the diversity of scholarship. One of these areas was maritime history, a special sub-discipline with organizations such as the Hakluyt Society, journals such as *American Neptune* and the *Mariner's Mirror*, and scholars such as Robert Albion at Princeton, Frederic Lane at Johns Hopkins, and Samuel Eliot Morison at Harvard.

Morison was Boston-born and bred, a professional historian who taught at Oxford and Harvard and wrote history as literature for a large reading public, on the inspiration of his hero Francis Parkman. Morison was an extraordinary character, a cantankerous Yankee and a great scholar who did important work on the early American republic, the founding of Massachusetts, and the history of Harvard College. His deepest love was maritime history, which absorbed the last forty years of a long career. Among his major works were a great biography of Christopher Columbus, a maritime history of Massachusetts, and the official history of the United States Navy during the Second World War in fifteen volumes. He taught the history of exploration and discovery at Harvard, often with Champlain's maps in hand.[104]

Morison summered on Mount Desert Island all his life, and sailed that beautiful coast. Even when he reached the rank of rear admiral, he preferred to call himself a sailor, and liked nothing better than to cruise the coast of Maine in his old wooden yawl, following in the wake of Champlain. Morison studied Champlain's voyages for many years, and published a full-scale biography in 1972.[105]

It is a lively book, the product of long reflection. Morison was mainly interested in Champlain as a seaman and explorer. He followed every voyage in the Gulf of Maine "from Pemaquid to Port Royal," as he said. Later he traced Champlain's other voyages by air, in a small private plane. He wrote that his purpose was to celebrate great discoveries, "to honor one of the greatest pioneers, explorers and colonists of all time." From his own experience, he especially admired Champlain's seamanship, gave close attention to Champlain's "Traitté de la Marine," and retranslated parts of it as a guide to practical seamanship for young sailors. He was also interested in Champlain as a great captain, "a natural leader who inspired loyalty and commanded obedience."[106]

Morison had a sailor's keen awareness of contingency and he posed a set of counterfactual questions in his biography. What if Champlain had sailed another two hundred miles on his New England voyages in 1604–06 and reached Manhattan Island and its great river before the Dutch? What if the sieur de Mons had found his southern site for settlement before the founding of Jamestown? What if Poutrincourt's party had not provoked the Indians to violence at Nauset in 1605? Morison suggested that the history of North America and the world might have been very different if those events had happened in another way.

Morison's biography was thin on other aspects of Champlain's career. It was one of his last books and not as well documented as his best work, but within its unique frame it was a contribution to our understanding of Champlain as a seaman.

Historical Geography: Heidenreich's Champlain as Cartographer and Scientist

Another major contribution came from a distinguished Canadian scholar, Conrad Heidenreich, a geographer trained at both the University of Toronto and McMaster University, and founder of the Geography Department at York University, where he began to teach in 1962. His published works are models of interdisciplinary study in history, the natural sciences, social sciences, and humanities. Among them is a prize-winning history and geography of the Huron nation during the early seventeenth century. For students of Champlain it is doubly useful as a very close and detailed discussion of the Huron, and also for its careful assessment of Champlain as an observer. Heidenreich found some errors in Champlain's account of the Huron economy, religion, politics, and society, but concluded that he was "an accurate observer of geographical detail and most material aspects of Huron culture." He wrote that "his view of the Huron and other groups is essentially sympathetic, accounting for the excellent rapport he established with them." [107]

Also of high importance was a monograph by Heidenreich on Champlain as a cartographer. It is a work of meticulous scholarship that carefully reconstructs Champlain's travels, compares his maps with modern terrain studies, estimates the accuracy of his work, and observes that "by and large his observations are extremely accurate, and when one takes into account the enormous area covered by him are nothing less than phenomenal." Heidenreich assessed the quality of Champlain's maps and concluded that "Champlain emerges as the first scientific, or at least modern cartographer of Canada. His written observations and maps are so much better than earlier ones that a comparison is not really possible." Heidenreich added that "with some justification the large 1612 and 1632 maps may be called the 'mother maps' of Canadian cartography." [108]

Another perspective on Champlain's career appeared in published work by historians of surveying. One scholar of this subject, Paul La Chance, wrote that Champlain was not merely the "fondateur du Québec." He was also "*le père des arpenteurs-géomètres du Canada*, the father of Canadian surveyors." This interpretation appeared in a treatise by Don W. Thomson, *Men and Meridians: The History of Surveying and Mapping in Canada* (1966). It adds material not available elsewhere on Champlain's role as a pioneering surveyor of New France, and develops yet another dimension of a busy life. [109]

Other scholars in the burgeoning field of environmental history have studied Champlain as an ecologist. One of the first was Carl Sauer, a geographer and ecologist at Berkeley, who gave Champlain high marks for his ethnography and ecology. Chandra Mukerji, a scholar at the University of California at San Diego, studied Champlain's interest in nature and horticulture and found a close connection between these two subjects in his thinking. [110]

The New Social History: Trudel's Champlain

A major approach developed from the new social history of the 1960s. This was not merely a new subdiscipline of history, but the discipline itself in a new form. It developed simultaneously in Britain, the United States, Canada, and especially France, where a group of gifted scholars founded a new journal called *Annales* in 1929. The leaders were Marc Bloch and Lucien Febvre in the first generation, Fernand Braudel in the second, and Emmanuel Le Roy Ladurie in the third. Their ideal was an "histoire totale" of all people everywhere. Their protagonists were often not individuals but societies, economies, and cultures. Much of their work centered on the history of *structures* and *conjunctures* (long trends or processes); they were less interested in the study of events, *histoire événementielle*, as they called it.

The new social history developed in many different forms. In Britain it was linked to issues of social class. In the United States, it gave more attention to race and gender. In Canada, social historians were very eclectic, and their work was among the best in the world. The leader was Marcel Trudel, a truly great and highly prolific historian. He was born in 1915 at the small country village of Saint-Narcisse-de-Champlain north of Trois-Rivières, one of eleven children. After the death of his mother, he was raised by his relatives in a very large extended family and educated in religious schools. "In my student days," he remembered, "the nuns of Quebec City's Hôtel-Dieu were still singing an annual mass for the Hundred Associates of 1627. . . . I myself as a youth, and even in recent years, lived under institutions established during the French Regime." [111]

Trudel was raised in a culture of discipline, piety, and authority. He rebeled against it, and his early writings were about Pascal and Voltaire. In 1939 he won a scholarship to study in Paris, but the war intervened, and he went instead to Harvard. He explored the United States, wrote a novel, and decided that history was the path for him. Trudel taught at Université Laval, joined the *Mouvement laïque de langue française*, and sought the "entire laicization of society" and the growth of a pluralist society. In Quebec he was bitterly attacked, even by a close friend from the pulpit in his own parish. After that, he wrote, "I left the church, and at the same time I left the Church." [112] At Laval, he was passed over for promotion, and decided to leave the university. All his books and papers were burned in a mysterious fire. Offers came from many Canadian universities and he went to anglophone Carleton. Trudel wrote at the age of forty-eight, "I was beginning anew with a wonderful enthusiasm, in an atmosphere of freedom such as I had never known." [113]

Trudel wrote in a large spirit, and published more than forty volumes, mostly on the history of New France from 1524 to 1760. Trudel's scholarship was scientific, empirical, meticulous, distinguished by a quality of craftmanship and careful research. Marcel Gagnon observed that Trudel achieved an "authenticity that was probably without equal in French Canada." [114] His major project is an *Histoire de la Nouvelle-France*, of which five volumes have appeared. It has an extraordinary mastery of sources, and a depth of detailed description and analysis that is unrivaled in any other work. Altogether, it is one of the masterworks of modern history in any language. [115]

Among many other works, Trudel also published a book on Champlain, a collection of documents with an important interpretative essay. He also contributed a brief sketch on Champlain to the *Dictionary of Canadian Biography*. [116] Where Parkman had thought of Champlain as a medieval man, Trudel saw him as a man caught up in the intellectual currents of his own time, and in the commercial revolution of the early modern era. Trudel argued that Champlain opposed the fur traders' idea of a *colonie comptoir*, a colony that was a trading post, and had a larger vision of a *colonie commerciale*, which was stable and "well populated" with a rounded economy that would ensure a permanent commerce with France. "This," wrote Trudel, "was the entire drama of his life." [117]

Trudel was critical of Champlain and other Catholic leaders of New France in another way, for not doing more to promote Protestant settlement in New France, which "would have totally altered the history of Protestantism in America; French Protestantism would have had a dominant and long lasting influence here." [118] But mainly Trudel's Champlain was "a man of ever-reviving plans," who despite many defeats succeeded in founding three permanent French settlements in America. Trudel's short biography concluded: "At the starting point of the uninterrupted history of Canada we find Champlain. He was at its origin by his own choice, and because of the principles in which he believed. In him we must salute the founder of Canada." Trudel's entire corpus of work is our leading history of that great process. [119]

The New Demographic History

Another advance came with the invention of historical demography. The leaders were French scholars at the Institut national d'études démographiques in Paris. There Louis Henry and others invented a rigorous new method for the study of populations before modern vital registration systems. It is called family reconstitution, and it laboriously reconstructs the demographic history of individual families from fragmentary records of baptism, marriage, and burial in the early modern era.[120]

One of its first successes was in the history of New France, where Catholic clergy kept meticulous parish records, and genealogists such as Cyprien Tanguey gathered materials of exceptional strength. In Canada these sources were combined with rigorous methods of family reconstitution to produce some of the best historical demography in the world. A pioneering work appeared in 1954, when Jacques Henripin applied the methods of Louis Henry to Canada, and studied 570 families in Quebec during the seventeenth century. With great care Henripin measured their astonishing fertility. He found that early Québécois families that remained intact to the mother's age of fifty produced an average of nine children and the population had a doubling time of less than twenty years by natural increase.[121]

In 1966, Hubert Charbonneau and a team of Canadian historical demographers established a Programme de recherche en démographie historique at the Université de Montréal. They launched a larger reconstitution project on the entire population of Quebec to 1850, based on parish registers, genealogical materials, and census data that had been refined by Trudel and others. This great labor produced a study of unrivaled depth, rigor, and comprehension. It found that as many as eight million people of French-Québécois ancestry were living in North America during the early twenty-first century. They descended from a very small population of 1,425 women who crossed the Atlantic between 1608 and 1680, and perhaps 1,800 men. An even smaller number of forbears produced an Acadian population that has spread throughout the world, and other interesting patterns apppeared for Métis populations.[122]

This demographic research, when combined with the new social history of Trudel and with sources on Champlain, locates an inflection point for sustained population growth in Quebec and Acadia during the years from 1632 to 1635—a moment of deep change between two change-regimes. All this work gives new significance to the role of Champlain, and to his choices in that critical period of deep change.

Economic and Econometric History: From Biggar to Innis and Egnal

In the twentieth century, new research in economic history also enlarged our understanding of Champlain and his world. The early work was descriptive and institutional, and the best of it is still very useful. A leading example is H. P. Biggar's study of trading companies in New France. On the basis of primary research, Biggar credited Champlain with playing the central role in the economic development of New France from 1608 to 1635, by strongly supporting commercial companies, developing a sound economic policy, and framing an Indian policy that worked. Biggar wrote, "It was the failure of his successors to adopt this policy which brought such ruin and disaster on the colony in later years."[123]

In the mid-twentieth century, as the discipline of economics became more theoretical, a great Canadian scholar, Harold Innis, took the lead in developing a new theory of early modern economic growth which has come to be called the staple model. He and his followers hypothesized that when factors of production such as labor and capital shifted to a resource-rich environment, marginal returns rose and productivity increased without change in technology. A fisherman who moved from European waters to the Grand Bank suddenly became much more productive, by reason of the greater abundance of larger fish. The same thing happened in extractive industries such as furs and forest products. Innis's staple model has since been applied throughout the world and is critically important in econometric history, as explaining a transitional stage of economic growth in the early modern era.[124]

The staple theory helps us to understand how the economy of New France grew, and why it did not grow more rapidly. The fur trade and fishing industries were so profitable that for two centuries they drew capital away from other patterns of investment that yielded less in the short term but much more in the long run. A new generation of theory-driven econometric history gives us a better way of understanding Champlain's economic policies and acts. And Champlain's career in turn helps us to understand how this process of staple-growth developed through the acts and choices of individual people. Other opportunities exist for the study of Champlain's experiments in mixed enterprise, which took him beyond practices in his era, and also beyond the constraints of neo-classical economic theory in our own time.[125]

Images: A Streamlined Champlain as a Symbol of Economic Development

In 1958, Canadians observed yet another anniversary, the 350th birthday of Quebec, by creating a new image of Champlain. It appeared on a postage stamp designed specially for the occasion by an artist with a sense of humor. An imagined face of Champlain appears from a new angle. He is seen in profile. The features are consistent with earlier images and once again follow the formula of Benjamin Sulte: "lively eyes, thin cheeks, accentuated aquiline nose, a thin mustache, light imperial beard, and the head set squarely on the shoulders in the attitude of a man on the lookout. A slight air of a musketeer, in short."

But this time that image is drawn in a different spirit. The founder's profile is streamlined, with a bold simplicity of line that was typical of mid-twentieth century design. Much of the face is drawn with a few flowing curves. The curve of the brow and the aquiline nose make a single line. This streamlined Champlain is looking toward the modern city of Quebec, with its tall buildings and the Château Frontenac rising high above his own Old Town. In the foreground a passenger ship sails down the river, which is now part of the great St. Lawrence Seaway, begun in 1954 and completed in the spring of 1959. Champlain in his seventeenth century dress studies this twentieth century scene with a look of satisfaction. The interplay of past and present makes a charming, witty, and very gallic *drôlerie historique*.

Marxist and Neo-Marxist History: Hunt to Delâge

In the twentieth century, Marxists have contributed much important scholarship to our understanding of Champlain. Marx and Engels themselves were interested in applying their models to early stages of history, and studied Lewis Henry Morgan's great work on the Iroquois with close attention.[126] In the troubled years of the 1930s, Marxist historiography grew rapidly in North America. An important and provocative book appeared in George Hunt's *The Wars of the Iroquois*, an exercise in historical materialism. It argued that the power of the Iroquois derived from their central position in trading relationships among European and Indian nations, and that their wars were driven by economic determinants. This thesis received much criticism from non-Marxists for its reductive model and its determinism, which in some forms made individuals into the objects of history, rather than its agents. But the best Marxist scholarship was careful in its chronology, precise in its causal models, and it deepened understanding of structure and process even for historians who did not share its ideological assumptions.[127]

In the late twentieth century, an academic movement called neo-Marxism gathered strength throughout the world. One of the best scholars of this school is the Canadian social scientist Denys Delâge. In 1985, he published a major work called *Le pays renversé: Amérindiens et Européens en Amérique du Nordest, 1600–1664*. It has been translated by Jane Brierley as *Bitter Feast: Amerindians and Europeans in Northeastern North America*.[128] This work is Marxist in its historical materialism, its model of historical stages, and its attention to systems of production. It is neo-Marxist in its attempt to integrate a materialist model with cultural history and in its efforts to combine a concern for individual actors with its attention to structure and process. Delâge summarized his frame in a sentence: "The race to accumulate capital drove European ships to the shores of northeastern North America, bringing into conflict two civilizations—one on the brink of the Industrial Revolution, the other still in the Stone Age."[129]

Delâge gave much attention to individual acts and choices, especially those of Champlain. He wrote: "Champlain, more than anyone, understood that simply being a trader was not enough when engaging in the fur trade. Amerindian mores must be taken into account. This is the secret of his success—not just the force of his personality, but his ability to organize the fur trade in ways that were compatible to the two economies." He also recognized that the Indians played equally

Denys Delâge constructed a neo-Marxist interpretation of Champlain as important for structuring the fur trade, and as a French leader who "would travel seated in the middle of a canoe manned by Amerindians," and could not have functioned without them. Both themes were captured in this image.

vital roles: "Champlain would travel seated in the middle of a canoe manned by Amerindians. . . . Without the Amerindians, neither Champlain nor the Jesuits would have been able to draw maps of northeastern North America." But at the same time he reminded the reader, "It is not so much the political acts of their leaders that interest us as the transition of these social groups to capitalism."[130]

Delâge was careful with his evidence and attentive to fact, but I would tend to disagree on one issue of interpretation. He observes that the early French settlers and Indians of Acadia and the St. Lawrence Valley lived close together, "traded, made treaties, and intermarried," but he believes that "the relationship between First Nations and the French was based on a serious misunderstanding." Here was the Marxist theme of "false consciousness" for historical actors who were in denial of the Dialectic. Another interpretation is a better fit for the evidence. The alliance of Champlain and the Indians rested on a solid basis of material interest, in terms of military security, trading networks, and political coalitions. One might ask, what choices would have served them better? These were highly intelligent people on both sides, and they had a deep understanding of their alliances in both their costs and benefits. Others will disagree.[131]

The New Ethnohistory: Bruce Trigger

While Trudel, the historical demographers, economic historians, and the new Marxists were at work on their projects, another important field for Champlain scholarship was rapidly developing. Historical ethnography emerged from the interplay of many academic disciplines. It transformed our knowledge of native culture in North America and had a major impact on Champlain studies.

Among its leaders was Bruce Trigger, an archaeologist and anthropologist at McGill University. His idea of ethnohistory was a step forward in two ways at once. It expanded historical methods in anthropology, and applied ethnographic methods to history.[132] Trigger's *The Children of Aataentsic* recast the history of an Indian nation in its own terms rather than those of Europeans. In that effort it brought a new depth of understanding to the history of the Huron in particular and American Indians in general, in large part by studying them as agents rather than objects of historical processes. Trigger found that Huron history had been dynamic before European contact, that it must be understood in terms of relations within and among indigenous populations, and that "Huron culture flourished as a result of European contact as long as the Huron people were not dominated by Europeans." The book was less successful in its interpretation of the French, and denied to European actors the empathy and empirical understanding that it demanded for the Indians. Even so Trigger's work on Huron remains a landmark of historical ethnography and a major contribution to the history of an indigenous nation.[133]

Academic Iconoclasts: Trigger Once More

In the 1960s and 1970s, a new generation of academic historians came of age. They were very diverse in their interests but shared an historical moment that framed their thought and set them apart from generations that preceded and followed. Many worked in the new social and cultural history, particularly in the study of race, class, gender, and ethnicity, and they greatly expanded the discipline of history in those dimensions. They tended to move toward the political left, even the far left; and they matured at a time when North American governments and electorates were shifting to the right. Their early work was positive in tone. The Civil Rights movement and liberal governments in the early sixties gave them much encouragement. But then came Vietnam, Watergate, and the world events of 1968, which many on the academic left remembered as a revolution that failed. In North America, historians of the left became deeply alienated from their own societies and institutions, and were filled with rage and bitterness.

The result was the growth of iconoclastic writing about American culture and American leaders. In scholarship on Champlain, the strongest iconoclastic voice was that of Bruce Trigger. In 1971 he brought out an article called "Champlain Judged by His Indian Policy: A Different View of Early Canadian History," and followed with a larger work, *Natives and Newcomers: Canada's "Heroic Age" Reconsidered*.[134] Trigger argued persuasively that much writing in early American history had been ignorant and contemptuous of Indians, and he made a strong plea for an integration of historical and ethnographic approaches. Many historians were with him on that. But then he turned to the history of the French in America and dismissed out of hand much of what had been published on the subject. Trigger wrote that virtually all "biographies of Champlain, even recent ones, were mere hagiography." Among them he included the work of Dionne, Bishop, Morison, Trudel, and many others. He launched a sweeping and highly personal attack on Champlain, reversing the judgments that most scholars had made before him.

Trigger allowed that Champlain was "obviously brave and adventurous, and apparently well-suited to win the support of Indian trading partners by accompanying them on their expeditions against their enemies." But overall he was severely hostile to Champlain and described him as "insecure," "ambitious," and "cynical." Where most historians had been impressed by Champlain's humanity, decency, and devotion to a large cause, Trigger asserted that "he came to regard the Indians and even most Europeans with whom he had dealings, less as individuals than as means whereby he could advance his own career." Further, Trigger asserted that Champlain was "extremely ethnocentric and inflexible," that he cared little for the Indians, completely misunderstood their culture, and abused them, especially after 1612.[135]

This indictment of Champlain appeared briefly in the *Children of Aataentsic* and at greater length in *Natives and Newcomers*. Large parts of both works were correct and important. Trigger was right to argue that interactions between Indians and Europeans were fundamental to the history of New France and had been much misunderstood. He was right again to insist that scholars should write about that process in an evenhanded way, and study Indians with understanding and respect. He was also correct in asserting that European traders had been neglected figures in the early history of New France.

But he was mistaken about Champlain and other French leaders. Trigger made no sustained effort to understand these men in their own terms. His reading of Champlain's writings was so hostile that it led to major inaccuracy, which in some cases reversed the meaning of what was actually written. Trigger violated his own ethnographic rules by treating Champlain, the Récollets, and other Frenchmen with the same contempt and misunderstanding that he complained about when it was directed to the Indians. The way forward is to apply the large spirit of Trigger's best work on the Huron to all the people and cultures who met in North America, including the Europeans.[136]

Popular Iconoclasts and the Revival of Empathy

The iconoclastic impulse of the late twentieth century also appeared in popular culture and mass media, where it became even more negative and cynical than in academe. On the subject of Champlain, a startling example came from René Lévesque, the leader of Quebec's separatist movement, who mounted an assault on the founder of Quebec. Lévesque wrote contemptuously in 1986,

"Champlain? Not very stimulating, the old founding father. His wife seems to have been a lot more fun. Poor guy, always stuck with the building of his habitation at Quebec with the English overrunning it time and again, and all the while there was lovely Hélène living it up in those far away places perhaps giving secret rendezvous to a certain young soldier from Gascony, or to Athos with the velvet eyes, or to that Jesuit so quick to hoist up his skirts, Aramis by name." [137]

Never mind the fact that the English overran Champlain's Quebec only once, and he got it back again. Never mind that La Belle Hélène was on her way to a convent. Never mind the facts at all. For René Lévesque, history appears to have been a pastiche of Rabelais, Dumas, and Balzac's *Droll Stories*. His assault on Champlain was an extraordinary statement, coming as it did from a leader of the Parti Québécois. Anglophone Canadian Joe Armstrong commented, "With this lack of pride in the French heritage, no wonder the revolution failed." [138] Worse was to come in the popular writings of Pierre Berton, who called Champlain an "assassin," and accused him of murdering "unsuspecting Indians" in a complete reversal of his relations with his Indian neighbors. Lévesque had merely accused Champlain of being a bore. Berton insisted that he was a criminal. [139]

Iconoclasts will always be with us, but in the early twenty-first century their influence is waning. A new and more balanced mood is evident in popular writing about Champlain. An example is a wonderful book for children by Caroline Montel-Glénisson, called *Champlain au Canada: les aventures d'un gentilhomme explorateur*. It is cast as a story about Champlain for young readers, told by Guillaume Couillard who came to Canada in 1613, married Guillemette, daughter of the Hébert family. Champlain appears as a leader who was one of the people in Quebec. The violence and cruelty of the new world are made very clear. But Champlain appears as an engaging and very attractive figure, often surrounded by small children both Indian and European, as in fact he was. Charming illustrations by Michel Glénisson show him playing with children, working in his garden with children, ice-fishing with children. In many other scenes we see Champlain moving easily with the Indians, missionaries, traders, and people of all descriptions. The theme is Champlain's humane spirit. The tone is irreverent and affectionate—a touch of the iconoclastic mood is combined with empathy and respect—a happy synthesis of older approaches with an impulse that was entirely new. [140] The same approach appears in Caroline Montel-Glénisson's *Champlain, La découverte du Canada* (2004), a brief biography for mature readers, with the same qualities of balance, insight, and empathy.

The Stirring of a New Spirit: The 400th Anniversary

In the early years of the twenty-first century, interest in Samuel de Champlain began to revive very rapidly. A stimulus was the 400th anniversary of the founding of New France, celebrated at Sainte-Croix Island in 2004, Acadia in 2005, Quebec in 2008, and the United States in 2009. The 400th anniversary has a different spirit from the monumental work inspired by the tercentenary. In the early twenty-first century, a new trend began to appear. After a period when political correctness, multiculturalism, postmodernism, relativism, and ideological rage were in fashion, scholars in many disciplines have rediscovered empirical possibilities in a different mood. Many examples appeared in new writing on Champlain, the founding of New France, and the interplay of Indian and European cultures in the new world. In the period from 2004 to 2007, historians from many nations published six volumes of new essays on Champlain and his world, with more than 100 articles, many of excellent quality. [141]

This effort was led by two French Canadian historians, Raymonde Litalien and Denis Vaugeois. In 2004, they published *Champlain: la naissance de l'Amérique française* (*Champlain: The*

Birth of French America), a major work with many important essays on Champlain and his age. This book is full of clues about new directions for historical scholarship in the twenty-first century. We see in it the growth of a new global history and a revival of empirical work, after the relativism and postmodernism of the late twentieth century. New digital tools extend the historian's reach and tighten his grasp. Among the results are new projects of primary synthesis (that is, broad works written from primary materials). This new scholarship makes more intensive use of images and artifacts, not merely as illustrations but as texts. In a process of fusion, it links separate sub-fields and combines strengths. The results are presented in braided narratives rather than analytic monographs, which combine story telling and problem solving in ways that realize the episetemic power of historical approaches. There is also a shift from ideological polemics to more open-ended inquiries, and a growing maturity of historical judgment. In writings on Champlain, this new generation of scholarship is beginning to get the balance right between European and American Indians.

One of the most hopeful new tendencies is the effort to study the past in its own terms and at the same time link it with the present. Only a generation ago, scholars held these two purposes to be mutually exclusive and came down on one side or another. Some insisted that any attempt to think of the present while studying the past is "unhistorical." Others condemned that idea as academic antiquarianism. Scholars in the twenty-first century are finding a middle way, and they have opened new possibilities that we are only beginning to discover. In all these ways, the central theme is the growth of historical knowledge in the human sciences, and a larger idea of humanity, in the spirit of Champlain himself.

CHAMPLAIN'S BIRTH DATE

A persistent problem for students of Champlain is his date of birth. We have no formal record of his baptism and no firm evidence of his age at any moment in his life. He never told the reader how old he was in his writings, nor did anyone who knew him. In the early modern era, this was also the case for Columbus, Cabot, Verrazzano, and Cartier, to name but a few. These men were born before laws that required registration of vital events. Church records were often incomplete, lost or destroyed, especially in France during the wars of religion and the revolutions that followed. Champlain's native town of Brouage changed hands in the strife between Protestants and Catholics during the sixteenth century; town records that survived the fighting were destroyed by an arsonist before 1690.

It is unlikely that a birth record will ever be found for Champlain. More probable is a chance discovery of some reference to his age in a primary source, but nothing of that sort has turned up to the date of this writing.[1]

In the absence of firm evidence, scholars have suggested three birth dates for Champlain. The first appeared in Pierre Damien Rainguet's *Biographie saintongeaise ou dictionnaire historique de tous les personnages* (Saintes, 1851), which tells us that *"ce navigateur célèbre naquit à Brouage d'une famille de pêcheurs, en 1567*; this famous navigator was born at Brouage of a family of fishing folk, in 1567." Rainguet himself was a public official, a notary, and a prolific writer who lived at Saint-Fort-sur-Gironde, approximately thirty miles south of Champlain's birthplace. He devoted his life to the history of his region and knew its records and local lore. But scholars have found errors in his work, and he gave no source or citation. Another historian has written in frustration, "We have no means of knowing whether the editor had access to material since lost, or whether he was merely guessing."[2]

In the 1860s, a very able French Canadian scholar and editor of Champlain's works, the Abbé C.-H. Laverdière, tested the accuracy of Rainguet's estimate by comparing it with two passages in Champlain's writings. One was Champlain's statement that he had been maréchal des logis for several years in the army of Brittany under the maréchal d'Aumont, who died in August, 1595. Laverdière wrote that this rank was "a post of confidence, given only to a person of some experience," and he believed that Champlain would have had to be about twenty-five when he was appointed, perhaps in 1592. On that assumption, Laverdière calculated that Champlain must have been born around the year 1567.

Laverdière made a mistake in understanding Champlain to say that he had served several years under d'Aumont, who died in 1595. Champlain wrote that he had served several (*quelques*) years under d'Aumont, St. Luc, and also Brissac, who survived the war. It ended in 1598, when Champlain was still in service. One cannot subtract several years from d'Aumont's death date, as Laverdière did, to reach a conclusion that Champlain was serving as an aide from as early as 1592. The earliest date that can be supported by the evidence is 1594. Therefore Laverdière's inference of a birth date in 1567 may by its own assumptions be several years too early.[3]

Laverdière also made another test against a passage in which Champlain wrote of his colleague François Gravé, sieur du Pont (also called Pont-Gravé or Du Pont Gravé) in 1619, *"son âge me le ferait respecter comme mon père*; his age would lead me to respect him as my father." Laverdière reckoned that Pont-Gravé must have been "at least ten or twelve years older" than Champlain, and he quoted Gabriel Sagard as saying that Pont-Gravé was about sixty-five years old in 1619, which yielded a birth date of 1554 or 1555. Assuming twelve years between the two men, Champlain would have been born about 1567. On the basis of that reasoning, Laverdière concluded that a birth date of 1567 would have been "not far from the truth."[4]

Laverdière's judgment was widely accepted in the nineteenth century. Champlain's birth date was identified as 1567 on monuments in France and in Canada. Biographers, editors and reference works adopted it. Bishop spoke for many scholars when he wrote, "on the whole, 1567 seems about right."[5]

Other scholars went a different way, and a second estimate emerged in the late nineteenth and early twentieth centuries. The Canadian biographer Narcisse-Eutrope Dionne wrote without explanation in 1891 that "*l'immortel fondateur de Québec y vit le jour, vers l'année 1570*; the immortal founder of Quebec was born there around the year 1570." One of the most influential Canadian historians of the twentieth century agreed. Marcel Trudel wrote: "*On calcule généralement qu'il est né vers 1570, sinon en 1567*; the usual calculation is that he was born around 1570, if not in 1567." Others began to adopt the judgment of "vers 1570." As late as 1972, the American historian Samuel Eliot Morison accepted this conclusion, and wrote in his clipped Boston English that Champlain was born "about 1570, natal day unknown and year doubtful." This estimate has been repeated in many other works.[6]

In 1978, yet another birth date was proposed by Jean Liebel, a French historian and biographer of Champlain's associate Pierre Dugua, sieur de Mons. In the course of his research, Liebel discovered a new piece of evidence that was relevant to this question. In the records of the cathedral-church at Saint-Malo, he found the baptismal record of François Gravé du Pont, dated November 27, 1560, which made him a little younger than other scholars had believed. Sagard had guessed that Pont-Gravé had been baptized in 1559 or the year before; Laverdière reckoned that his date of birth was between 1555 and 1557. Liebel's discovery shifted a benchmark that scholars had used to estimate Champlain's age.

Liebel published an article, arguing that if Champlain respected Gravé du Pont "as a father," there must have been "at least twenty years" between their ages, not twelve as Laverdière had reckoned. On the basis of that assumption and the new evidence of Pont Gravé's baptismal date, he concluded that Champlain was born in 1580.[7]

There are several difficulties here. For one, Liebel's discovery moved Gravé du Pont's baptism by between one and six years, but he used it to move Champlain's birth date by ten or thirteen years. For another, Liebel had an "axe to grind," as a Yankee would say. He believed that the subject of his biography, Pierre Dugua, sieur de Mons, had received too little credit for the founding of Quebec, and Champlain had been given too much. Liebel took particular exception to the idea often engraved on monuments in Canada, that Champlain was "the founder of Quebec." He insisted that the title properly belonged to his hero, de Mons, who gave Champlain the means, the men, the material and the provisions to construct the habitation at Quebec.[8]

In making his case Liebel wrote: "The word 'founder' that one sees in our own time, so often following his name implies a man not only rich and powerful, but also aged. . . . The grades, titles and qualities with which one had bestowed on Champlain after his death were totally excessive if one had no reason to suppose an age in proportion to them." He concluded that in 1608, the year when Quebec was founded, Champlain was 28, not 38 or 41.[9]

Whatever Liebel's purposes may have been, the validity of his historical argument is an empirical question, and the accuracy of his statements is a separate issue from his motives for making them. After Liebel's article appeared in 1978, several French and Canadian scholars were quick to accept it. In a collection of essays on Champlain, published in 2004, most writers who discussed the subject of Champlain's birth agreed with Liebel. Nathalie Fiquet wrote that "the theory that he was born around 1580 seems to best correspond to the image conveyed by his writings." Other scholars agreed that the evidence "would make Champlain's birthdate around 1580."[10] But is Liebel's thesis consistent with the evidence? Let us look again at the sources. Although Champlain never mentioned his age or his date of birth, at least four sets of clues appear in his writings and other documents.

The first clue comes from Champlain's army service records. This evidence appears not only in Champlain's *Brief Discours* as Liebel asserts, but also in pay records of the army, which Robert Le Blant and René Baudry have found and published. In the year 1595, they tell us, Champlain received pay as a *fourier*, a quartermaster officer, in the months of March and April. By the end of that year, he was identified as the "*ayde du Sieur Hardy, marschal de logis de l'armee du roy*; assistant to the sieur Hardy, marshall of lodgings in the king's army." The paymaster's records show that he received extra money in 1595 for a "certain secret voyage in which he made an important service to the King." He also had been present at the siege of Crozon in 1594, and distinguished himself in that bloody assault sufficiently to have been mentioned in the history of that battle. In 1597 he also appears in military records as "captaine d'une compagnie" of troops at Quimper, a garrison town in southern Brittany midway between Brest and Blavet, where he is also known to have served in those years.[11]

Moreover, throughout the period from 1595 to 1597, army records referred to him in all but one instance as the "Sieur de Champlain." He was given a title of respect and a particule de noblesse. These distinctions did not necessarily imply nobility, but they were reserved for officers of rank, and gentlemen in positions of honor and trust.

To conclude that Champlain was born in 1580 is to assert that in the midst of a war he was given offices of trust and distinctions of honor at the age of fourteen or fifteen. It might have been so for members of the royal family, or princes of the blood, or sons of great noble families, but Champlain was not of that rank. And this was active duty in time of war. It is reasonable to think that he was older than fourteen or fifteen—perhaps in his early twenties, when he served in positions of high responsibility with the army of Brittany in 1595–97, such as a captain in command of a company. This would indicate a birth year around 1570, plus or minus several years.

A second set of clues appears in several statements that Champlain made about the years that he spent at sea. One of these passages appeared in a dedicatory letter to the queen regent in 1613. Writing of "the art of navigation," Champlain declared, "It is this art which won my love at a very early age, and inspired me to venture nearly all my life on the turbulent waves of the ocean."[12] This passage becomes significant in relation to another preface to Champlain's *Traitté de la marine et du devoir d'un bon marinier* in 1632. Champlain wrote of "having spent thirty-eight years of my life in making many sea voyages."[13]

It is a simple statement, but what exactly did he mean? One could understand him in at least three ways. Perhaps Champlain meant to say that he had logged the equivalent of thirty-eight years of what the navy calls sea duty; but this is impossible. To survey his many voyages, as in Appendix B below, is to discover that for all his many voyages, the total time actually spent at sea did not come even close to thirty-eight years. Clearly, this was not what he had in mind.

Or he may have meant that he had been going to sea for a period of thirty-eight years from the date of his statement. That is the way Liebel read this passage, and he takes it to mean that Champlain began to go to sea in 1594, which would have made a total of thirty-eight years by 1632, when this passage was published. Liebel's interpretation runs into several difficulties. First, Champlain told us that he had gone to sea at an earlier age. Second, it is not what Champlain actually wrote. He did not state that he had been going to sea for a period of thirty-eight years, but that he had spent or passed (*passé*) thirty-eight years in making sea voyages. The difference between these two statements becomes important when we remember that in the period from 1594 to 1632, Champlain spent many years ashore, sometimes two or three years at a time. When we construct a chronology of his voyages, we find that he was at sea in twenty-two years out of thirty-four between 1598 and 1632. To reach his total of thirty-eight years at sea he would have had to make voyages in at least sixteen years before 1597.

To reach a total of thirty-eight years, Liebel's thesis that Champlain was born in 1580 would have required Champlain to have made sea voyages in sixteen of the seventeen years from 1580 to 1597, which is highly improbable. An inescapable conclusion is that Champlain began his sea voyages before 1580. If Champlain's statements about his years at sea were correct, Liebel's estimate of his birth date must be mistaken.

There is also another problem in Liebel's thesis. Let us consider Champlain's statement that he had been drawn to "the art of navigation" at a "very early age," and had ventured, as he wrote, "nearly all of my life on the turbulent waves of the ocean." From this statement it is reasonable to think that Champlain's voyages did not begin in the year 1594 as Liebel argues, but much earlier when as a boy Champlain was sailing with his father, who was an experienced pilot and probably his teacher. Historians in Brouage believe that Champlain also spent some of his early years ashore, perhaps attending an academy in the town.

If Champlain had been born in 1570, he would have had to have been at sea in sixteen of his first twenty-seven years from 1570 to 1597, and this would have allowed him to have spent his infancy in his mother's arms and some years in school. A birth date of 1570 fits this frame better than does a birth date of 1580. It is also consistent with the literal meaning of Champlain's statement about his thirty-eight years of sea voyages and his interest in the art of navigation at a very early age. To study this evidence is to find that Liebel's thesis requires us to believe that Champlain began his sea voyages at the age of one.

Then there is a third clue that was discussed by Laverdière in 1870 and became the basis of Liebel's argument. This is Champlain's statement that when he thought of Pont-Gravé he thought of him as a father because of his age.[14] Most scholars accept Liebel's discovery that Pont-Gravé was baptized on November 27, 1560, but there is a problem of interpretation here. How large an age-difference was necessary for Champlain to think of Pont-Gravé as a father? Liebel's answer is at least twenty years. Laverdière believed that ten or twelve years could have done it.

In the United States Navy, during and after the Second World War, young seamen and midshipmen tended to think in paternal terms of chief petty officers or commissioned officers who were often much less than twenty years their senior. Officers in turn called enlisted men "son," even when their ages were less than a decade apart. A published example appears in a memoir of John A. Williamson, a lieutenant aboard USS *English*, a destroyer escort that sank six Japanese submarines in twelve days. Halfway through that campaign, Williamson was on his way to the wardroom for that elixir of the old Navy, a cup of coffee, when a "young seaman" came up to him:

"Lieutenant Williamson," he said, "can I have a word with you? . . . Are we really sinking those submarines, sir?"

"Yes, we really are," said the lieutenant.

"Sir, how do you feel about killing all those men?"

Williamson recalled, "I had no good answer, but I didn't let him know that." Instead, he said, "Son, war is killing. The more of the enemy we kill, and the more of the enemy we can kill, and the more of his ships we can sink, the sooner it will be over. . . . We are in a war that we must win, for to lose it would be far worse."

Later Williamson commented, "My young inquisitor seemed relieved. At least he thanked me. But somehow when I reached the wardroom, that cup of coffee didn't taste as good as I thought it would."

The "young seaman" in this story would probably have been no younger than seventeen, plus or minus a year. Lieutenant Williamson was twenty-five or twenty-six. They were nine years apart, and yet they spoke literally as if they were father and son.[15]

In short, Liebel is certainly correct about the age of Pont-Gravé. His discovery of the baptismal record is a useful contribution. But Laverdière was correct about the difference in age that might have sustained a feeling of paternal respect. Ten years could have done it, or even less depending on the circumstances. We have no hard evidence here to settle this question, which will always remain a matter of interpretation. Suffice to say that Champlain's statement is consistent with the possibility that only ten years separated them.

We also have a fourth clue, which rules out the possibility of a birth date much earlier than 1570. In 1634 Champlain wrote to Richelieu, suggesting that he himself should lead a punitive expedition against the Iroquois. Bishop writes: "Make every allowance for a valiant old gentleman's sense of well-being; he could still not be over seventy. That gives us 1564 as the earliest possible date."[16]

In short we have four suggested birth dates for Champlain in the secondary literature. They yield the following age patterns through his life cycle:

Scholar	BORN 1564 Bishop	BORN 1567 Rainguet	BORN 1570 Dionne, Trudel	BORN 1580 Liebel
Age first at sea	17	14	11	1
Army 1594–97	30–33	27–30	24–27	14–17
Indies 1599–1601	35–37	32–34	29–31	19–21
Tadoussac 1603	39	36	33	23
Ste.-Croix 1604	40	37	34	24
Quebec 1608	44	41	38	28
Marriage 1610	46	43	40	30
Death 1635	71	68	65	55
Pont-Gravé's age	+4	+7	+10	+20

In my judgment, a date of birth around 1570 is most probable. The earliest recorded estimate of 1567 could also be correct. A birth date as early as 1564 is at the outer limit of possibility and highly improbable. A date of 1580 is beyond that limit and impossible. I conclude that Champlain was born around the year 1570, plus or minus several years.

CHAMPLAIN'S VOYAGES

A Chronology

YOUTH

1570–94   Many voyages with his father, a pilot and captain

BRITTANY

1594–98   Campaigns in Brittany; secret missions and at least one voyage for the king

SPAIN AND HISPANIC AMERICA

1598   Blavet (now Port-Louis), to Cadiz, Spain, in *Saint-Julien*

1598–09   Cadiz to Sanlucar to Seville to Sanlucar

1599   Sanlucar to Guadeloupe in *San Julian*

           Guadeloupe to Virgin Islands, in *San Julian*

           Virgin Islands to Margarita, in patache *Sandoval*

           Margarita to Puerto Rico, in patache *Sandoval*

           Puerto Rico to Haiti in *San Julian*

           Haiti to Mexico in *San Julian*

           Mexico to Panama

           Panama to Mexico

           Mexico to Cuba in *San Julian*

           Cuba to Cartagena

           Cartagena to Cuba

1600   Cuba to Florida and return?

           Cuba to Spain by way of Bermuda and the Azores

1600–01   In Cadiz with his uncle

1601   Cadiz to France?

1602–03   In France, visiting family in Brouage; studying with geographers in Paris; working
           with ships' chandlers at Dieppe; visiting other ports and places

TADOUSSAC, 1603

1603   *March 15* Departs Honfleur in *Bonne-Renommée* with *Françoise*

              May 26 Arrives Tadoussac Harbor

              May 27 Tabagie at St. Mathew's Point (Pointe aux Alouettes)

              May 28–June 9 Meetings with Montagnais, Etchemin and Algonquin at
              Tadoussac

              June 11–17 Explores lower Saguenay River

              June 18–July 11 Explores upper St. Lawrence River from Tadoussac to the Great
              Rapids near Montreal

              July 15–19 Explores lower St. Lawrence River from Tadoussac to Gaspé and re-
              turn

              July 20–August 3 Explores upper St. Lawrence River

              August 16–September 20 Tadoussac to Honfleur in *Bonne-Renommée*

FRANCE, 1603–04

1603   *September 20* Arrives Honfleur in *Bonne-Renommée*

              November 15 Receives license to publish his first book, *Des Sauvages*

              September–April Working in France

ACADIA AND NORUMBEGA, 1604–05

1604   *April 7–May 8* Sails from Honfleur (Normandy) to La Hève (Acadia) in *Don-de-*
              Dieu with de Mons, Pont-Gravé, and Poutrincourt

              May 13–June ? Explores coast of Acadia from Port Mouton to St. Mary's Bay, his
              first independent command in New France

              June 16–24 Explores coast of Acadia to the Bay of Fundy with de Mons in com-
              mand; finds sites for colonies at Cape Sable, St. Mary's Bay, Port Royal, Sainte-
              Croix, Saint John

              July–September Working on Sainte-Croix Island; exploring Sainte-Croix River

              August 31 Poutrincourt leaves Sainte-Croix for France in *Don-de-Dieu*

              September 2–October 2 Explores coast of Maine from Sainte-Croix to Penobscot
              and mouth of the Kennebec River; his second independent command

              October 2 Returns to Sainte-Croix Island

              Winter at Sainte-Croix Island

PORT-ROYAL, 1605–07

1605   *March 15–April 10* Explores the coast and islands of Acadia, Pont-Gravé in com-
              mand and Champdoré as pilot; ends in wreck of their barque near Port-Royal;
              Champlain saves all passengers and the crew

June 18–August 3 Explores coast of New England to Cape Cod with de Mons in command

July 23 Fight with Indians at Mallebarre (Nauset on Cape Cod)

August–September Helps move the colony from Sainte-Croix to Port-Royal

November–December? Voyage from Port-Royal to Saint John River and the Port-aux-Mines in search of copper deposits

1605–06   *Winter* at Port-Royal (now Annapolis Royal, Nova Scotia)

1606   *Spring* Explores coast of Acadia with Pont-Gravé in command

July 26 Poutrincourt arrives, takes command at Port-Royal

September 5–November 14 Explores coast of New England with Poutrincourt in command

October 15–16 Fight with Indians at Misfortune Harbor (Stage Harbor, Cape Cod)

1606–07   *Winter* at Port-Royal

1607   *July* Colonists ordered by de Mons to return to France

August 11–September 2 Sails from Port Royal to Canso

September 3–30 Sails from Port-Royal to Saint-Malo in ship *Jonas*

FRANCE, 1607–08

1607   *September 30* Arrives Saint-Malo

Meets with De Mons and the king

1607–08   *Winter* in France, completes manuscript map of 1607 (now in Library of Congress)

1608   Offered command of a new settlement at Quebec

April 13–June 3 Sails from Honfleur to Tadoussac Roads in *Don-de-Dieu*

QUEBEC, 1608–09

1608   *June 3–29* Explores Saguenay River and lower St. Lawrence River

June 30 Sails upriver from Tadoussac

July 3 Founding of Quebec

July 4 Begins construction of storehouse and first habitation

July "Some days after" July 3, Jean Duval's conspiracy to kill Champlain is discovered; conspirators are arrested; Duval is executed; other leaders sent to France in chains

September 18 Pont-Gravé sails for France; Champlain remains in command of 28 hivernants

September–October Montagnais and French work together at eel fishing

November 18 First heavy snow

1608–09	Very hard winter, two or three fathoms of ice and snow on the river; many Montagnais die; only eight of twenty-eight French survive
1609	*June 5* Supplies and men arrive from France
	June 7 Champlain sails from Quebec to Tadoussac; receives letter from De Mons, recalling him to France
	June 18 Champlain explores upper St. Lawrence Valley; meets Indians; plans campaign against Mohawks
	June 28 Leaves Quebec with Montagnais
	July 3–12 Rendezvous with Algonquin and Huron; enters River of the Iroquois
	July 12–29 Leaves rapids on the Iroquois River for Lake Champlain and explores the lake and Vermont shore while waiting for the dark of the moon
	July 30 Champlain and allies win battle with Mohawk; afterward he explores the chute from Lake George
	July 30–August Returns to Quebec
	August Visits with Montagnais in Tadoussac and Algonquins in Quebec
	September 1 Leaves Quebec for Tadoussac, homeward bound
	September 5–October 10 Sails from Tadoussac to Île Percée, Le Conquet, Honfleur

FRANCE, 1609–10

1609	*October 10* Arrives Honfleur
	October Takes post to Fontainebleau; meets de Mons and Henri IV
	November De Mons and Champlain meet investors in Rouen, work closely with Lucas Le Gendre to plan next expedition
	December–February With de Mons in Paris
	February 28 To Rouen and Honfleur; recruits artisans, settlers
1610	*March 7* Sails from Honfleur; Champlain taken ill; returns to Le Havre
	March 15 His ship returns to Honfleur to shift ballast
	April 8 Sails from Honfleur in the ship *Loyale*; Pont-Gravé in command

QUEBEC, 1610

1610	*April 26* Arrives in Tadoussac, New France, after a passage of 18 days
	April 28 Sails from Tadoussac for Quebec; finds all well
	May 18 Meets with Montagnais and others; plans another campaign
	June 14 Leaves Quebec to meet Montagnais, Algonquin, and Huron; Iroquois at Trois-Rivières
	June 19 Leaves Trois-Rivières for River of the Iroquois
	June 19 Arrives at river, told that his allies had surrounded Mohawks in a barri-

cade at what is now Sorel. Champlain and arquebusiers engage; nearly all Mohawk are killed or captured; ends major hostilities with Mohawk for 20 years

July Champlain meets with Iroquet; arranges for Étienne Brûlé to live among the Algonquin Petite-Nation and Iroquois

July–August Champlain returns to Quebec, learns that Henri IV was assassinated on May 14; letter from de Mons urges Champlain to return to France at once

August 8 Leaves Quebec for Tadoussac and France

FRANCE, 1610–11

1610   *September 27* Arrives in Honfleur after a slow crossing of 50 days

              December 30 Marries Hélène Boullé in Paris

QUEBEC, 1611

1611   *March 1* Departs from Honfleur for America

              May 13–17 Arrives Tadoussac; sails for Quebec in a leaky barque

              May 21 Arrives Quebec; repairs boat; departs on exploring voyage

              May 28 At Great Rapids near Montreal

              June Explores St. Lawrence

              June 1–13 Selects site for future settlement of today's Montreal; plants test gardens

              June 13–July 18 Meets Hurons, Algonquins, and has reunion with Étienne Brûlé; explores upper St. Lawrence

              July 18 Returns to Quebec; repairs settlement, plants roses

              July 20–3 Sails to Tadoussac

              August 11 Departs for France

FRANCE, 1611–13

1611   *September 10* Arrives La Rochelle; visits de Mons in Saintonge

              September Starts for court; "nearly killed" when horse falls on him; meets de Mons at Fontainebleau; consults President Jeannin, Chancellor Brûlart, and Marshal Brissac on how to support New France; they recommend a noble protector; Champlain gets help of sieur de Beaulieu, chaplain to Louis XIII

1612   *September 27* Through Beaulieu, Champlain approaches the comte de Soissons and asks him to be governor of New France; he agrees

              October 12 Soissons, cousin of Louis XIII, appointed lieutenant general and governor of New France, with vice-regal powers

              October 15 Soissons appoints Champlain his lieutenant in New France

              November 1 Soissons dies suddenly; approaches are made to prince de Condé

November 22 Condé appointed viceroy of New France; makes Champlain his lieutenant

1613   *January 9* Champlain publishes *Les Voyages* and second general map

January–February Champlain and Condé meet opposition from merchants; Champlain makes three journeys to Rouen; prepares an expedition of three ships from Rouen and one from Saint-Malo with men and supplies for Quebec

March 6 Departs from Honfleur in a ship commanded by Pont-Gravé

April 10 Sights Grand Bank; goes fishing; survives severe storm

QUEBEC, 1613

1613   *April 29* Arrives Tadoussac after a crossing of 54 days; Montagnais recognize Champlain by his wound-scars, welcome him

May 2–7 Sails to Quebec; finds settlers in good health and fields "bright with flowers"

May 13–27 Sails to Great Rapids; meets Algonquin, who report more trouble with central Iroquois

May 29–June 17 Explores the Ottawa River, to Morrison Island and Allumette rapids; meets Indian nations and makes alliances; returns to Great Rapids on the St. Lawrence; more meetings with Indians; and arrangements for interpreters

June 27 Departs Rapids and sails downriver

July 6 Reaches Tadoussac; waits for ship and good weather to sail home

August 8 Departs from Tadoussac for Île Percée on a Malouin ship

August 18 Leaves Île Percée at Gaspé for Grand Bank

August 28 On the Grand Bank; "caught as many fish as we wished"

FRANCE, 1613–15

1613   *September 26* Arrives Saint-Malo; meets with merchants there and invites them to form a new company with merchants of Rouen

November 15 New Company of Canada formed in Rouen; sometimes called Compagnie de Champlain; he calls it Compagnie de Condé

1614   *January–September* Works with Louis Hoüel, king's secretary, to recruit Récollets for New France; also meets with Robert Ubaldini, Papal Nuncio in France to the same end

October 27 Meets with all French cardinals and bishops, who have come to Paris for the Estates General; all support Champlain's plan to recruit missionaries, and contribute 1500 livres themselves

November Champlain at Fontainebleau; makes a presentation on New France at court; establishes rapport with Louis XIII

1615   *February 28* Goes from Paris to Rouen to meet investors in the company and introduces them to Récollets; more investors support the company; establishes good relations with Condé.

March 20 Champlain, Récollets, and investors go to Honfleur

April 24 Departs Honfleur in *Saint-Étienne* with Pont-Gravé

QUEBEC, 1615–16

1615   *May 25* Arrives off Tadoussac after a crossing of 31 days

May 27 Champlain and Récollets sail to Quebec; land cleared and quarters built for a mission; Récollets establish themselves

June 8–9 Champlain and Récollets sail up the river to the Great Rapids

June 23 Mass said at Rivière-des-Prairies before many Indians

June 26 Champlain returns to Quebec

July 4 Champlain sets off upriver for a journey to Huronia and campaign against the central Iroquois

July 9 Departs Rivière-des-Prairies for Huronia; explores upper St. Lawrence; takes northern route to avoid Iroquois war parties; visits many Indian nations along the way

July 26 Visits with Nipissing nation

July 28? Visits Cheveux-Relevés

HURONIA, 1615–16

1615   *August 1* Enters and explores Huronia

August 17 Meets Huron warriors in Cahiagué

September 1 Étienne Brûlé and 12 Huron depart on mission to Susquehannock nation

September–October Organizes campaign against the Onondaga

October 9–16 Fight at Onondaga Fort (in today's Syracuse, N.Y.)

October 18 Heavy fall of snow slows retreat to Huronia

October 28 Deer hunting in Huronia to December 4

December 23 Arrives at Cahigué, Huronia; lives with Huron through the winter

1616   *January* Meets Father Le Caron at Carhagouha

January 4 Visits with Algonquin Petite-Nation

January 17 Visits Petun nation; also Cheveux-Relevés and Nipissing

February 15 At Cahiagué mediating between Huron and Petite-Nation

May 20 Leaves Huronia for Great Rapids of the St. Lawrence River

July 1 Reaches Great Rapids; leaves for Quebec

July 11 Returns to Quebec

July 20 Goes to Tadoussac

August 3 Sails from Tadoussac to Honfleur

FRANCE, 1616–17

1616   *September 10* Arrives at Honfleur

           October 25 Thémines appointed viceroy; Champlain loses lieutenancy

           Fall? Publishes map of New France

1617   *January 17* Champlain confirmed as lieutenant to Thémines

           March 7? Sails from Honfleur for Quebec in *Saint-Étienne*

QUEBEC, 1617

1617   *June 14* Arrives at Tadoussac, sails to Quebec for a very brief visit; by July 20 is back in France

FRANCE, 1617–18

1617   *July 22* Samuel and Hélène Champlain sign a contract with Isabelle Terrier, in Paris, evidence that Champlain remained in Quebec for no more than a few weeks

1618   *February 9* Champlain presents a major plan for the development of New France to the Paris Chamber of Commerce and on this day joins in a proposal to the king

           March 12 Louis XIII agrees to the proposal

           May 24 Champlain arrives in Tadoussac

QUEBEC, 1618

1618   *June 24* Champlain arrives in Tadoussac?

           June–July Champlain is at Quebec

           July 26 Champlain sails from Tadoussac for Honfleur

FRANCE, 1618–20

1618   *August 28* Champlain returns to Honfleur

           December 21 Champlain wins agreement from investors to support eighty settlers in Quebec

           December 24 Louis XIII grants Champlain a pension of 600 livres

1619   Company directors forbid Champlain to sail for New France in their ship; the king intervenes, but too late for this season

           May 18 Champlain licensed to publish *Voyages . . . depuis l'année 1615*

1620   *February 25* Condé sells office of viceroy to Montmorency

            March 8 Montmorency appoints Champlain his lieutenant

            May 7 Louis XIII confirms Champlain's commission as lieutenant

            Spring Sails to Canada in *Saint-Étienne* with Hélène

QUEBEC, 1620–24

1620   *July 7* Champlain arrives at Moulin Baude one league from Tadoussac

            July 11 Sails from Tadoussac to Quebec

            Summer Champlain orders repair and rebuilding of Quebec; construction of Fort
            St. Louis

            November Viceroy Montmorency authorizes fifteen-year monopoly on trade to
            New France to the Compagnie de Caën

            December–March Quebec colonists survive winter with only one accidental death;
            Hélène Desportes born in Quebec

1621   *February 2* Dolu makes positive report to Montmorency, who renews his appoint-
            ment

            May 7 Royal Council rules that the old and new Compagnies de Caën share mo-
            nopoly and the costs of settlement

            June Pont-Gravé's ship for the old company arrives at Tadoussac; de Caën seizes it;
            Champlain restores order; ship is returned

            August 18 Assembly of settlers meets to draw up a cahier général de doléances for
            the king; they strongly support Champlain's policies; king responds favorably; in-
            creases Champlain's pension

            September 12 Champlain issues laws for Quebec

1622   *Spring* Champlain encourages farming by Montagnais near Quebec

            April 1 Royal Council confirms rights of new Compagnie de Caën

            June 6ff Champlain sponsors peace talks with Iroquois

            December 24 Council regulates relations between old and new companies

1623   *July 23* Champlain meets with Huron and Algonquin at Trois-Rivières

            July–August Champlain adjudicates murder case with Indians

            August Farm planned at Cap Tourmente

            November Road built to Fort St. Louis

            Winter Hauling timbers for fort and storehouse in Quebec; Champlain plans a
            new habitation

1624   *April 29* In France, Richelieu is appointed to Royal Council; within a year he be-
            comes "chief minister" to Louis XIII

            April–July Champlain and Indian leaders try to restrain Simon, insane Monta-
            gnais who murders an Iroquois; peace with Iroquois preserved

            May 1 Excavation begins for new habitation at Quebec

May 6 First stone laid

June–August Much trade and many meetings with Montagnais, Algonquin, and Huron

August 15 Champlain, wife, and servants leave Quebec for Tadoussac

August 24 They leave Tadoussac for Gaspé to form a convoy

September 6? Convoy of four ships sails for France

FRANCE, 1624–26

1624	*October 1* Champlain and family return to Dieppe
	October Champlain goes to Paris; thence to Saint-Germain to meet with Montmorency, the king, and Royal Council, "to whom I gave an account."
	Fall In Paris, meets with old and new shareholders; Montmorency sells office of viceroy to Ventadour
1625	*February 15* Ventadour commissions Champlain as lieutenant in New France
	Spring+ Champlain works with Ventadour in his Paris mansion
	Summer+ Negative reports of New France from Jesuits and Récollets
	December 29 Champlain sells part of estate from his uncle
1626	*March 10* Ventadour grants lands in New France to Jesuits
	April 15 Champlain sails from Dieppe with five ships

QUEBEC, 1626–29

1626	*June 29* Arrives Tadoussac, after a crossing of sixty-eight days
	July 5 Arrives Quebec
	July–August Expands farm at Cap Tourmente
	October Richelieu takes control of commerce, colonies, maritime affairs
1626–27	*November 21–April* Long hard winter in Quebec
1627	*Spring* Ventadour ceases to be viceroy; powers assumed by Richelieu
	April 29 Compagnie de Caën replaced by the Company of New France (Cent-Associés); Richelieu is first associate; Champlain joins as fifty-second associate; capital share of 3,000 livres paid by his wife
	July 14ff Tabagies with Huron at Trois-Rivières; Champlain urges peace with Iroquois
	October 7 Meeting with Indian "captains" about murder of two Frenchmen
1627–28	*November–April* Another very hard winter
1628	*February 2* Champlain presented with three Montagnais girls whom he names Faith, Hope, and Charity, aged 11, 12, and 15.

Spring Charles I authorizes British mercenaries to seize New France; The Kirke family seizes ships in the St. Lawrence and the fishing coast; Scottish groups seize Acadia

Spring The Cent-Associés equips a very large fleet of merchantmen with colonists for New France. The directors do not want to send it fearing capture by the British forces. Richelieu insists it must sail; the result is disaster

Spring Champlain expands farming in Quebec; works closely with Indians; sponsors missions

July Kirkes burn and destroy the farm at Cap Tourmente

July 9 Champlain learns of English warships at Tadoussac

July 10 Kirkes appear at Quebec and demand its surrender. Champlain refuses and prepares to fight; the Kirkes retreat and seek to starve the French into submission

July 17–18 The great fleet of the Hundred Associates is captured by the Kirkes

August Kirkes return to England with much plunder; no help comes from France

1628–29   *November–April* A third very hard winter in Quebec with grave shortages of food; the Huron, Algonquin, Canadien, Etchemin, and some Montagnais help by taking in Frenchmen and bringing food to the settlement; there is much hunger but no scurvy and no starvation

1629   *Spring* No help comes from France; Champlain continues to send habitants and workers to live with Huron, Algonquin, Canadien, Etchemin, and other nations; others live precariously by farming, hunting, and gathering

April 24 Treaty of Susa ends war between England and France; terms include return of property seized after the peace

June 25 Kirkes' warships arrive in the lower St. Lawrence

July 19 Kirkes demand surrender of Quebec; Champlain nearly out of food and ammunition; proposes terms

July 20 Champlain surrenders Quebec; habitants treated humanely; some choose to remain in Quebec on Champlain's advice with a guarantee of their property

July 24 Champlain taken to Tadoussac by Kirkes

September 14 Champlain carried to England by Kirkes

ENGLAND, 1629

1629   *October 27* Champlain arrives in Dover; learns of the peace treaty

October 29 Champlain refuses repatriation to France; goes to London, meets with French Ambassador to demand return of New France because its seizure was unlawful after the Peace of Susa

November English agree in principle but refuse to return the colony until Louis XIII pays dowry promised for marriage of his sister Henrietta Maria

FRANCE, 1629–32

1629	*November 30* Champlain makes a voyage from England to France
	December He urges the king, Richelieu, and Hundred Associates to hurry the return of New France
1630	*Spring* More appeals and protests to French leaders
	April Louis XIII demands restitution of New France from England
	September 27 Champlain sells two houses in Brouage
1631	*July* Charles orders Kirkes to return Quebec
	August Champlain insists on return of Acadia and other parts of New France
1632	*February 13* Mutual division of property between Champlain and Hélène Boullé
	March 29 Treaty of Saint-Germain-en-Laye restores Quebec to France; England agrees to evacuate Acadia, and all of New France; Louis XIII agrees to pay his sister's dowry
	Spring? Champlain publishes *Les Voyages de la Nouvelle France Occidentale*
	April 20 Richelieu appoints Isaac de Razilly as his lieutenant for New France; he refuses to serve, insisting that Champlain is better qualified

CAPE BRETON, 1632

1632	Champlain may have made a voyage from France to St. Anne, Cape Breton; this voyage was not included by Laverdière, Dionne, Biggar, Morison, and other biographers; it is believed to have happened by Campeau and Trudel; the exact date is unknown, and evidence is less than conclusive, but two leading historians of New France are convinced that it happened, and the inferences from other documents support this probability

FRANCE, 1632–33

1633	*March 1* Richelieu reluctantly appoints Champlain his lieutenant for New France
	March 23 Champlain leaves Dieppe for New France with three ships: *Saint-Pierre* (flag), *Don-de-Dieu*, and *Saint-Jean*, with 150 colonists.

CANADA, 1633–35

1633	*May 22* Champlain takes possession of Quebec
	Spring Begins construction of Notre-Dame-de-Recouvrance
	Summer Renews alliances with Montagnais, Algonquin, Huron
	August 13 Champlain sends report to Richelieu seeking to limit English trade, and to form a military force strong enough to keep the peace; Richelieu does not respond; both problems grow

1634   *Spring* Establishes forts and trading posts on Sainte-Croix and Richelieu islands
              in the St. Lawrence

              Summer Establishes new settlement at Trois-Rivières; Champlain makes voyages
              between Quebec and Trois-Rivières

              August 18 Champlain sends another report to Richelieu who again makes no re-
              sponse and does not act

1635   *Spring* Champlain in declining health

              October Suffers massive stroke and paralysis

              November 17 Signs his will and testament

              December 25 Dies in Quebec on Christmas Day

TOTAL VOYAGES

From 1599 to 1635, Champlain probably made twenty-seven Atlantic crossings in thirty-seven
years. He also made many coastal and river voyages in Europe, the Caribbean, and North American waters. This does not include other voyages made in his military service, and earlier voyages as
a child aboard his father's ships. Morison's count is mistaken.[1]

APPENDIX   C

CHAMPLAIN'S *BRIEF DISCOURS*
Problems of Accuracy and Authenticity

For half a century, scholars in six countries have debated the accuracy and authenticity of Champlain's *Brief Discours,* a report about his travels in the Spanish Empire from 1598 to 1601. At issue
is not only the document itself, but the character of Champlain and our judgment of his life and
work.

The *Brief Discours* is problematic in many ways, not least because Champlain did not publish
it in his own time. At least three early manuscript copies survive. None are in Champlain's hand,
but all bear his name on the first page. The most complete manuscript is in the John Carter Brown
Library at Brown University in Providence, Rhode Island. Its provenance is a saga in its own right.
In 1884, an agent for the library bought the manuscript from a respected dealer, the Librairie
Maisonneuve in Paris, which had acquired it from the estate of P. J. Féret, a collector in Dieppe
who was a collateral descendant of Aymar de Chaste, governor of Dieppe, supporter of New
France, and friend of Champlain in the years 1602–03. De Chaste or his family are thought to
have deposited this copy for a time in the custody of the Couvent des Minimes in Dieppe. We
have a chain of custody that reaches back to Champlain himself.

Another manuscript copy—less complete, and variant in detail—is in the library of the University of Bologna, and appears to be approximately contemporary with the Brown manuscript. A

third copy has been found in the Archivio di Stato at Turin. Their dates are uncertain and their provenance is unclear. All three copies are incomplete, with breaks in the text and references to missing illustrations, but the Brown text includes more material than any other, with sixty-two illustrations, plans, and charts. Some scholars believe that the Brown manuscript may have been the original, but each copy has elements that are missing in the other two, and textual analysis turns up strong evidence that all three copies derive from an original that has not yet been found. It might have gone to Henri IV, or remained with Champlain. These are the conclusions of a careful study of the three manuscripts by Laura Giraudo, an historian at the University of Milan.[1]

Published Editions and Editorial Judgments

The *Brief Discours* was first printed not in its original French but in a high-quality English translation by Alice Wilmere and Norton Shaw for the Hakluyt Society in 1859. The first French edition was published in 1870, as part of Charles-Honoré Laverdière's excellent collection of the *Oeuvres de Champlain*. A third text was published in the Champlain Society's bilingual edition of Champlain's works, with a French text collated from the Brown manuscript, and an English translation by a team of editors including H. P. Biggar, H. H. Langton, W. F. Ganong, and J. Home Cameron.

The editors of all three printed editions discovered many inaccuracies in the *Brief Discours*. They added copious notes on "confusions of dates," errors in spelling, mistakes of geography, garbled names, and mistakes in descriptions of events, flora, and fauna. But all the editors accepted the manuscript as authentic, agreed that Champlain was its author, and believed that he actually made a voyage through Spanish America, more or less as described in the *Discours*.[2]

Judgments of Early Biographers

Before 1950, Champlain's French Canadian biographers also generally agreed that the *Brief Discours* was authentic, and in most cases accepted it as literal fact. This was so especially for N-E. Dionne, Gabriel Gravier, and H. R. Casgrain.[3]

Anglophone biographers took a different view. Francis Parkman wrote: "At Dieppe there is a curious old manuscript, in clear, decisive and somewhat formal handwriting of the sixteenth century, garnished with 61 colored pictures, in a style of art which a child of ten might emulate. . . . Here too are descriptions of natural objects, each with its own illustrative sketch, some drawn from life and some from memory—as, for example, a chameleon with two legs; others from hearsay, among which is a portrait of the griffin said to haunt certain districts of Mexico—a monster with the wings of a bat, the head of an eagle, and the tail of an alligator. This is Champlain's journal."

Parkman greatly admired Champlain, and believed that the *Brief Discours* was authentic, but he read it as a work of fantasy, and studied it as a clue to the character of "a true hero, after the chivalrous medieval type" and a personality "dashed largely with the spirit of romance." Parkman explained: "Though earnest, sagacious, and penetrating, he leaned to the marvelous; and the faith which was the life of his hard career was somewhat prone to overstep the bounds of reason and invade the domain of fancy. Hence the erratic character of some of his exploits, and hence his simple faith in the Mexican griffin." This was a misunderstanding of Champlain, who was very far from being a medieval man. But at the same time, Parkman was the first reader to observe that the flaws and inaccuracies in the *Brief Discours* are evidence of its authenticity.[4]

Another anglophone biographer was Morris Bishop, author of *Champlain: The Life of Fortitude* (1948) and a professor of romance languages at Cornell University. He decided to check the *Brief Discours* against Spanish records in the Archivo General de Indias in Seville, the first scholar to do so. Bishop hired a researcher, who reported that he "failed to reveal Champlain's name on the manifests of Don Francisco Coloma's convoy of 1599, or any mention of him in accessory documents." Bishop wondered if he might have used a false name. "He must have made the journey," he wrote, "for he could have copied his errors nowhere." Bishop was very conscious of inaccuracies in the work, but like Parkman took them as evidence of its authenticity. He too thought that the errors were clues to the character of the author.[5]

The First Attacks on the Brief Discours

After Morris Bishop's book appeared in 1948, three iconoclastic writers in Canada and France saw an opportunity to attack Champlain by impugning the accuracy of the *Brief Discours*. All assumed that he had written it, and attacked his veracity in a general way.

In 1950, Canadian writer Jean Bruchési published an article with the sensational title, "*Champlain a-t-il menti?* Did Champlain Lie?" Bruchési suggested that Champlain falsified the record of his military service in Brittany, falsely claimed to have been captain of the *San Julien*, never made a voyage to the West Indies, and used Captain Provençal's logbooks "to write under his own name, an account of a voyage that he did not make."[6] This criticism was offered as a hypothesis, not as a firm conclusion. But nearly all the hypothesizing was on one side of the question, and was severely hostile both to the document and to Champlain.

Much of this thesis was quickly proven to be false. Champlain's military service was confirmed by Robert Le Blant's research and by documents published in 1967. And even a cursory reading of the *Brief Discours* shows that Champlain never claimed to be captain of the *San Julien*. Even so, the charge in Bruchési's title, that Champlain was a liar, traveled farther than the corrections, and was repeated by others.

Canadian archivist Claude Bonnault adopted Bruchési's hypothesis and added his own arguments that Champlain was never in Blavet, that he had invented the story of Captain Provençal, and that he was not in the West Indies at all; Bonnault topped it off with a conspiracy theory that the *Brief Discours* may have been concocted in 1612 as a political document to support the comte de Soissons and the prince de Condé against the queen's Spanish party in France, and to support a rapprochement with England. He concluded that the entire *Brief Discours* was an "histoire fantaisiste," and false in the first degree—a willful and premeditated falsehood by Champlain for his own gain. This argument, coming from a prominent Canadian archivist, had a long reach.[7]

These judgments were amplified by Hubert Deschamps, editor of another edition Champlain's works, *Les voyages de Samuel de Champlain, saintongeais* (1951). Deschamps was no iconoclast. In many ways he admired Champlain, and celebrated his career in New France. But he rejected the *Brief Discours* as a fraud. On the basis of Bruchési's work, he wrote, "This voyage appears most doubtful; probably it was only a compilation of accounts by other voyagers."[8]

A Botanist Finds Evidence of Authenticity

Not everyone was convinced that Champlain was a liar. Bruchési's attack inspired another critique that yielded an opposite conclusion. In 1951, a distinguished French botanist, Jacques Rousseau, studied the botanical descriptions that made up a quarter of the *Brief Discours*. He approached the work in a scientific spirit and analyzed its wealth of botanical information. Rousseau found some of it to be very confused and clearly mistaken. He came to believe that it was written by a "voyageur de passage," who was passing quickly through a country he did not know, obliged to make conjectures, and forced to trust too much to memory. But Rousseau concluded that the errors in the work were themselves evidence of its authenticity. He found that the botanical descriptions, despite their imperfections, "were made directly from nature" and could only have been made by a Frenchman who "actually made a voyage in the Antilles and Mexico," and who had come from Saintonge, for he "used many *Saintongeais* terms." In short, Rousseau's botanical analysis identified many inaccuracies in the *Brief Discours* but confirmed its authenticity and found strong internal evidence that Champlain himself was the author.[9]

A Mixed Verdict: Vigneras

Yet another scholar launched a search of Spanish records, and reached a different result. L. A. Vigneras spent many months in the Archivo General de Indias at Seville and the Archivo de Simanca. In 1957, he published his findings in an article that is an important, detailed, and fair-minded critique of high value to any serious student of Champlain. Like Bishop's researcher, Vigneras was unable to find any explicit reference to Champlain in records of the Spanish treasure fleets from 1599 to 1601. He documented many errors of fact, dates, times, and confusions of chronology in the *Brief Discours*, but also confirmed the substantive accuracy of large parts of the work and concluded that whoever wrote them was an actual eyewitness to many of the events and scenes in the work.

Specifically, Vigneras confirmed the accuracy of the first parts of the *Brief Discours* about the Treaty of Vervins, the charter of Captain Provençal's ship, and its voyage from Blavet to Spain. He corroborated many movements of the *San Julien* just as Champlain described them, confirmed Champlain's statement that each galleon was assigned a patache, and that the *San Julien* was paired with the patache *Sandoval*, which was sent to collect pearls at Margarita Island.[10] But Vigneras believed that Champlain's accounts of his visit to Guadeloupe, the trip to Margarita Island, and his claim to have visited Mexico City and Portobello were impossible or very doubtful.

Altogether, Vigneras felt unable to confirm or deny the accuracy of the *Brief Discours*. In a mixed and tentative conclusion, he suggested that Champlain might have made the voyage as a clandestine passenger, or might have based his narrative on interviews with others who had actually been to the West Indies and Mexico. Vigneras appealed for further research, restraint in judgment, and respect for the memory of Champlain, who should not be condemned for "a possible error of youth."[11]

The Discours *Defended: Bishop, Morison, and Trudel*

In response to these various critiques, other writers defended Champlain. Morris Bishop wrote a measured reply to Bruchési, Bonnault, Vigneras, and others, referring to them as "some Canadian historians who have been treating the Father of Canada most unfilially, giving him, in fact the lie." Bishop noted that all of them, even the most hostile, had "greatly enlarged our knowledge" in substantive ways. Bruchési discovered that Guillermo Eleno was the same man as Captain Provençal. Bonnault found the Turin manuscript of the *Brief Discours*. Vigneras first reported the Bologna manuscript and found much new information in Spanish archives.

But Bishop observed that the critics of Champlain had made errors of their own, and were unable to resolve the central questions for a Champlain biographer. Did he make the journey himself? Did he represent the experience of others as his own? Did he lie? Bishop argued that these questions should be answered not only from an analysis of the *Brief Discours* itself but also from "our experience of life, our knowledge of men and their behavior." Bishop wrote that Champlain was not only an honest man but one who "always regarded the lie with horror." He offered examples, and added: "For Champlain, as for the Indians, the lie was the worst of offenses. In my study of Champlain, I have never caught him in a lie. Inadvertences, certainly; errors, often; lapses of memory, commonly. But never an outright lie. Add to this the universal chorus of his contemporaries, who acclaim his rectitude, conscience, uprightness of spirit." Bishop added an argument that Champlain had little to gain and much to lose from creating a "clumsy, dangerous falsification." On this basis, he ended with a firm conclusion: "Champlain did not lie." Bishop's essay was graceful, witty, and wise, but it lacked a foundation in empirical fact and had no effect on the iconoclasts, whom he called the "misocamplanites." [12]

Another line of defense appeared in Samuel Eliot Morison's biography of Champlain. Morison had an intimate knowledge of the waters of the West Indies and North America. He formed a high respect for Champlain's veracity, and wrote with disdain of the critics: "Vigneras finds so many inaccuracies in the *Brief Discours* as to suggest that Champlain never left Spain and composed it ashore by picking the brains of sailors! That hypothesis to my mind is refuted by the quality of the colored sketches which (excepting some of the bird's eye views of towns) could not possibly have been copied from existing books, and are obviously from the same hand as those of Champlain's books on Canada. I conclude that, as a Frenchman in a ticklish situation (the Inquisition was already well established in Mexico and his very presence there was illegal) he dared not take notes or make sketches, but wrote his text and painted the illustrations from memory after his return to France. That would explain his sometimes mixing up characteristics of two different plants in one painting. The style of Champlain's work is evidently based on that of Théodore de Bry, some of whose illustrated works on the New World came out early enough to have been seen, or even owned, by him." [13]

A third defence appears in the judgment of Marcel Trudel. The first volume of Trudel's excellent *Histoire de la Nouvelle-France* includes a brief but balanced discussion that takes seriously the problems that critics found in the text of the *Brief Discours*, but argues that the drawings are probably Champlain's work. He suggests ways in which the inaccuracies can be understood without condemning the text or the author in a rounded way. [14]

Attacks Repeated and Amplified: Liebel and Codignola

In Canada and France, attacks on the *Brief Discours* continued during the late twentieth century. An interpretation hostile to Champlain appeared in the work of Jean Liebel, a Saintongeais historian who published an important biography of Pierre Dugua, sieur de Mons, with much new and useful evidence, and argued that Champlain's importance had been exaggerated at the expense of de Mons. He severely condemned the *Brief Discours* as a work "of doubtful origin, published long after the death of Champlain," and full of "numerous errors and improbabilities which lead one to think that it was surely not written by Champlain." He argued that Champlain "would not have allowed himself to mislead the reader with falsehoods as gross as those of the *Brief Discours*; this was an honnête homme." [15]

Yet another critic extended Liebel's argument in a new direction. Luca Codignola, an Italian scholar of Canadian studies, published two essays that argued that Champlain did in fact visit the

Indies before 1601, but condemned the *Brief Discours* as an account of a "prétendu voyage" that is "completely useless," and "full of all sorts of errors." Codignola suggested that the *Discours* was not the work of Champlain at all, but a forgery commissioned by a collector of "exotic memorabilia," perhaps the "most celebrated among passionate collectors in Champlain's epoque, the scholar and savant Nicolas-Claude Fabri de Peiresc." Codignola observed that his idea was only "in the domain of speculation."

There is no evidence to support this hypothesis, and indeed much to contradict it. Peiresc left a large body of papers that made no reference to the *Brief Discours*. He was respected as a scrupulously honest and honorable man. The provenance of the Dieppe manuscript falsified this interpretation, but its effect was to reinforce the mood of skepticism about the *Brief Discours* and Champlain himself, which was growing in the late twentieth century.[16]

New Archival Material: Armstrong

More positive was the response of Joe C. W. Armstrong in his *Champlain*, which first published an important piece of new evidence: the last will and covenant of Champlain's uncle Captain Provençal in Cadiz, written on June 26, 1601. This document had been in the collection of the Archivo Historico Provincial in Cadiz, and a copy was given to the National Archives of Canada, now Library and Archives Canada, in Ottawa in 1975. It proved that Champlain was present on that occasion and that he signed the document as "Champlain." The Spanish "public writer" named Marcos Rivera who drafted the document wrote Champlain's name as "Samuel Zamplen," a variant that may help to explain why no reference has been found to Champlain in Spanish archives.[17]

This discovery clearly established the nature of the relationship between Champlain and his uncle, which had been challenged by several iconoclasts. It confirmed Champlain's account of it, described the movements of the *San Julien* in 1598–99, placed Champlain in Cadiz for an extended period during the spring of 1601, and explained why he was there, looking after his uncle. The will named Champlain as sole heir to a large estate in Spain and France.[18] Armstrong also made another contribution. He studied Champlain's references to Florida and suggested that he made a clandestine visit to Florida during the last part of his visit to the New Spain. He concluded: "It is reasonable to assume that Champlain was a bona fide explorer of the Florida coast." Altogether, Armstrong published a major new piece of supporting evidence for Champlain's *Brief Discours*.[19]

New Archival Material: Giraudo

Two research projects by Laura Giraudo were also positive in their result. In the first, she made a rigorous comparative study of the three manuscript copies of the *Brief Discours* and found that copyists were responsible for some of the errors that had been attributed to Champlain. Giraudo also published a second essay that reported a further round of research in Spanish archives: once more in the Archivo General de Indias in Seville (which Vigneras had searched); and for the first time the Archivo Ducal de Medina Sidonia (which Vigneras had not been allowed to use). She also found no explicit reference to Champlain's presence in the Spanish treasure fleet, but she turned up evidence that corroborated Champlain on the movements of the treasure ships themselves, the role of Pedro de Zubiaur and Francisco Coloma, the contracts with Champlain's Uncle Provençal, the charter of *San Julian*, the route from Spain to America, events in Puerto Rico, the movements of the *San Julian* from San Juan to Santo Domingo and Vera Cruz, and events along the way. She also found evidence that supported the possibility of Champlain's visit to Mexico City, found supporting evidence for the voyage of the *San Julian* from Mexico to Cuba, and documented other events that Champlain observed in the Caribbean and the return to Spain. Giraudo concluded that the probability that Champlain was a clandestine passenger in the *San Julian* "appears more and more likely." She also believed that further research in Spanish archives could be still more fruitful.[20]

Positive Assessments and Mature Judgments: Gagnon and Glénisson

An important contribution of another kind was made by François-Marc Gagnon. It was an *explication de texte*, a critique of critics. Gagnon found more errors in the works of Bruchési, Bonnault, and Vigneras. He also began to explore possibilities for reconciling the testimony of Champlain with documentary evidence from materials in other sources, especially the Spanish archives. This approach suggested an important and useful way forward in Champlain studies.[21]

Yet another contribution appeared in 2004. Raymonde Litalien published an interview with a highly respected French scholar, Jean Glénisson, who was asked his opinion of the *Brief Discours*. "In my view," he answered, "there is absolutely no reason to doubt the authenticity of Champlain's voyage to Spanish America." Glénisson observed that Champlain "did not have permission to divulge information he had gathered on his trip, because the Spanish were very discreet about their wealthy colonies in America. The *Brief Discours* given to Henri IV was therefore clandestine. It greatly resembles an espionage report." Glénisson went on to note that Champlain confirmed the fact that he made the journey and referred to it "a number of times" in other works and in a request that he made to Louis XIII in 1630. Moreover, the contents of his report were consistent with those writings in substantive ways.[22]

The Approach in this Volume

After this long controversy, how do we judge the *Brief Discours*? The first step is to ask what sort of text it was. As Morison and Glénisson pointed out, it was not a journal or diary or logbook. Also, it was not called a *Voyage of Champlain*, but rather a *Brief Discours* on "the most remarkable things that Samuel Champlain of Brouage observed in the West Indies." It was also an espionage report, written for presentation to Henri IV.[23]

Further, we should also ask how the *Brief Discours* was compiled. An important clue is its chronology. Champlain's *Discours* and Spanish records used different ways of timekeeping. The Spanish record-keepers worked from documents and used calendar dates. Champlain worked from memory and reckoned time not by fixed dates but by intervals of weeks and months. He rarely referred to the calendar, and then only with vague references and never exact dates. In the absence of a log or journal, reliance on memory led to many errors, and also caused bias in time estimates. Throughout the *Brief Discours* Champlain tended to overestimate the length of time intervals in the past, a clear pattern of memory distortion. For example, he remembered the passage from Blavet to Vigo Bay as lasting eleven days; Spanish records showed that the voyage lasted five days. This sort of error occurred frequently in the manuscript. Champlain was unable to keep notes or diaries or records of any kind, and the entire work was drafted after his return from America. Here is more evidence that he was a clandestine passenger, as were at least six people aboard the *San Julian*.

With these patterns in mind, we might approach Champlain's manuscript in a constructively critical spirit. We might begin by comparing Champlain's *Brief Discours* with other evidence. To do so is to find and correct many errors of dating and mistakes of other kinds. But instead of merely compiling a list of discrepancies as hostile critics did, a more useful step is to try to reconstruct Champlain's travels in the West Indies in a coherent way that reconciles the main lines of his account with the evidence of other sources. The result of that effort appears in chapter 5 above. "A Spy in New Spain" is that sort of reconstruction, cast in the form of a narrative, with issues of interpretation discussed and documented in the notes, and historiography in this appendix.

When that work was done, it was clear that the *Brief Discours* is frequently inaccurate but entirely authentic, and its main lines are consistent with evidence found by other scholars in Spanish archives. The *Brief Discours* is precisely what it purports to be: a manuscript by Samuel Champlain, a Frenchman of Saintonge, who made a report for his king of "the most remarkable things" he observed with his own eyes in Spanish America.

The next step is to look at it yet again and ask what this document has to tell us about Champlain himself. The answer is that it is an important and revealing source. The *Brief Discours* is informative about his purposes and the process of his development. We find in it a consuming curiosity about the world, a fascination with other people, a strong interest in the native people of America and in African slaves, and an attitude of sympathy and respect. Champlain was a man of deep and abiding Christian faith. He was appalled by the cruelty of the Spanish conquest, horrified by the behavior of some Spanish clergy, and shocked by atrocities committed in the name of Christ. We see Champlain's developing interest in settling close to native people, and his indifference to the pursuit of gold, silver, pearls, and precious gems. We also see his humane spirit and his ethical purpose in the world. In short the *Brief Discours* is not only an authentic work, but also a vitally important key to an understanding of Champlain himself.

APPENDIX D

CHAMPLAIN'S PUBLISHED WRITINGS
A Question of Authorship

Several writers have called into question the authenticity of Champlain's voyages, and in particular his last book, *Les Voyages de la Nouvelle France . . .* (Paris, 1632). The Abbé Laverdière believed that Jesuits changed the text of this work, removed references to the Recollets, and added a celebration of their own order. "Not only had someone reviewed or even made alterations to the text of Champlain," he complained, "but we can be certain that this work was done either by a Jesuit or by a friend of the members of that order." [1]

Other historians have disagreed. Biggar wrote: "As to the theory which has been advanced that the Jesuits had a hand in the production of this edition, I cannot find any grounds for accepting it. The few mistakes cited by the Abbé Laverdière are apt to occur in any large work of this kind and are doubtless chiefly printer's errors." Biggar believed that Champlain himself curtailed passages to the Récollets for two reasons. He was giving a résumé of his earlier works, and also he "no longer bore towards them the same friendly feelings as formerly, as a consequence of the conduct of Récollet father Georges in 1621 when Champlain thought that he had sent forged letters to the King."[2]

Biggar concluded that the 1632 edition reflected the judgment of Champlain himself, and that its strength and importance flowed from Champlain's high integrity. "Champlain's writings," Biggar wrote, "are a source of the first value and however much one may regret the years he passes over in silence, yet this very loss enhances the value of the remainder by proving that it contains nothing but what was actually seen or experienced by himself."[3]

Secular scholars in the twentieth century have also doubted the authenticity of a pietistic tone that grew strong in Champlain's later works. But his unpublished writings and his essays in the *Mercure François* showed the same interpretive patterns as the *Voyages*. One prime example is the manuscript text of his will. It is a stronger statement of Champlain's growing faith than any published work that might have been altered by Jesuits or others.

A third line of criticism in the late twentieth century came from iconoclasts who argued that Champlain's published works were shameless acts of self-promotion. How can we assess these and other lines of criticism, as well as the works themselves? The first step is to consider the purpose of these works. If we study the unpublished "Brief Discours" of 1601 and four major volumes that Champlain published in 1603, 1613, 1619, and 1632, we find several patterns. All Champlain's publications were works of promotion, but not self-promotion. Their primary purpose was to promote a grand design for New France, more than to advertise Champlain himself. In that respect we might compare them with the works of Captain John Smith, who embellished his maps and books with a large self-portrait. Nothing like that appears in Champlain. As many scholars have noted, Champlain is also very taciturn about himself, his thoughts, and his feelings. This is not the style of a self-promoter. He is also very candid about failures and errors—for example, the decision to settle Sainte-Croix Island.

Another clue appears in the rhythm and timing of these publications. These works were written and published at pivotal moments when the future of New France was hanging very much in the balance: the winter of 1603–04, the winter of 1612–13, the winter and spring of 1618–19, and the winter and spring of 1631–32. In moments of particular danger and opportunity, all of them promoted Champlain's grand dessein, his great vision for New France.

Further, Champlain's promotional efforts centered on the French court and particularly on the monarch. His major books are dedicated to figures who were in a positions of power: Charles de Montmorency (admiral of France in 1603, and uncle of the future viceroy); Marie de Medici, the queen regent in 1612–13; the young King Louis XIII, who was taking power in 1618–19; and Cardinal Richelieu in 1631–32.

The works changed not because the Jesuits were rewriting the later ones, but because Champlain was trying to reach powerful people who had different values and purposes. His books combined two themes. One was a theme of continuity in steadfast support for the grand design. The other was a theme of change in tone and substance, from attention to the values of Henri IV in the *Brief Discours* (1601) and *Des Sauvages* (1603) to concern for the attitudes of Marie de Medici in the *Voyages* of 1613. Later works gave more attention to the purposes of Louis XIII in the *Voyages* of 1619, and Richelieu in the *Voyages* of 1632. These promotional efforts were successful. They helped Champlain to sustain his great project.

On the question of accuracy, Champlain's published works all contain small errors, misstatements of fact, and confusions of dates. In moments of crisis they were rushed to the press, and have the appearance of haste in their composition. Some parts were clearly based on logs and journals. Biggar believed: "He must have kept a diary, and in several places the existence of some such source is betrayed. Thus at the end of the last chapter of the first part of the edition of 1613, there is an account of what occurred almost every day during the month of September 1607. This could not have been given unless he kept a diary of what took place." Biggar observes that "a very faithful journal of observations was made" in that part of the book. In other passages, Champlain was writing from memory and errors crept in, as in the *Brief Discours*. But always Champlain was trying to be careful with his facts and usually tells us about his sources. Biggar found that Champlain "does little more than describe events of which he himself was an eyewitness and in which he usually took a very prominent part." When he had a different source, he was usually careful to inform the reader, or add a disclaimer.[4]

In our own time, it is increasingly possible to test the accuracy of much of Champlain's *Voyages* against other sources in great variety. For the voyage in 1603 we have interlocking documentation from port records, the letters and edicts of Henri IV, and interviews later conducted by Marc Lescarbot for his history of New France. For the explorations of the Acadian coast in 1604, we have oral history from the Mi'kmaq which is consistent with French records. For the settlements at Sainte-Croix Island and Quebec, we have an extraordinary abundance of archaeological evidence. For the Port-Royal Colony, Marc Lescarbot confirmed the accuracy of Champlain's texts in every important way, even when the two authors had turned against each other. Lescarbot did the same for the military campaign against the Mohawk. The more research is undertaken, the more corroboratory evidence we find for events in France, England, and America. The writings of Recollets and Jesuits, and pieces published in the *Mercure François* confirm the accuracy of Champlain's voyages at almost every point where they can be compared. Increasingly, state papers and documents have been found to do the same. This evidence frequently corrects small mistakes in dates (a confusion of months was a common problem). Champlain also had strong biases and powerful purposes. But these are the writings of an honest and honorable man.

APPENDIX E

CHAMPLAIN'S *TRAITTÉ DE LA MARINE*
An Essay on Leadership

Near the end of his life, Champlain wrote a small treatise explicitly on the subject of how he went about the task of leading others. He published it with his last volume of *Voyages* in 1632 as a long appendix, but it is really a separate work with its own title page and theme. He called it a *Traitté de la marine, et du devoir d'un bon mariner*, a *Treatise on Maritime Affairs, and the Duty of a Good Mariner*. It is most accessible in the bilingual text edited by H. P. Biggar in his edition of Champlain's major works.[1]

Scholars have studied it in different ways. Morris Bishop, a scholar of French literature, read it as "Champlain's most important literary achievement," in which he made his "only effort to rise

above the day-to-day journal, and create a work of conscious literary art." Bishop thought of it as
a work of "self-revelation" in which the "good navigator" is "the man he aspired to be." [2] Joe Armstrong, a Canadian businessman and map collector, interpreted it as a work "full of confidence, life
and buoyancy of language," and a key to "his contribution as a geographer, naturalist, and cartographer. [3] Samuel Eliot Morison, a maritime historian and small boat sailor, studied it as "a seaman's
manual on the handling and navigation of ships." Morison was specially impressed by Champlain's
"feel for the sea," and translated excerpts for the instruction of young sailors in every generation. [4]

The book belonged to a very large literature on seamanship and navigation in Champlain's era.
He lived at a time when the art of navigation became a science. Its most important contribution
was not any particular discovery, but the invention of a process by which discoveries are made and
shared with others. To that end, its most useful instrument was not a ship or cross-staff or astrolabe, but a printing press. Historian D. W. Waters has identified 203 treatises on navigation that
were printed by Portuguese, Spanish, French, Dutch, and English authors before 1640. [5] Some of
these books were technical manuals on the tools of navigation. Others were textbooks on mathe-
matics, or monographs on astronomy, or workbooks on logarithms, trigonometry, spherical geom-
etry, cartography, and various special subjects. Chief among them was Pedro de Medina's *Arte de
navegar* (Seville, 1545), an excellent manual on methods of finding latitude from the sun and stars,
with a very accurate table of the sun's declination. It was translated by John Frampton as *The Arte
of navigation. . . . made by Master Peter de Medina* (London, 1581). It also appeared in French, Italian, and Dutch editions, and was widely used throughout the world. The Dutch explorer William
Barents carried Medina's *Arte de navegar* on his last arctic voyage, and his copy was found in the
nineteenth century, preserved in polar ice. Frobisher and Drake also used Medina's book, and
Champlain read it closely. [6]

Other navigation books took the form of what would be called today Sailing Directions, or
Pilots. Among the most important of that genre was Lucas Janszoon Wagenaer, *T'eerste Deel Vande
Spieghel der Zeevaerdt vandde Navigatie der Westersche Zee*, "The First Part of the Mirror of the Navigation for Sailing the Western Sea." [7] It was translated into English as *The Mariner's Mirror*. The
title pages of the Dutch and English editions both show a group of seamen and scholars studying
a globe which is also a spherical mirror that reflected the images of the men who sailed it.

A third genre was favored by English explorers who created discursive dictionaries of navigation terms. The leading examples were two books by Captain John Smith of Jamestown fame.
Smith's first volume, in the words of its modern editor, is "little more than an omnium gatherum
of names for the appurtenances and people that make up a ship and her crew." His second is basi-
cally the same sort of work as the first, much enlarged. Other works of a similar nature included
John Davis, *The Seaman's Secrets*, in Albert Hastings Markham, ed., *The Voyages and Works of John
Davis, the Navigator*; and also in Sir Henry Mainwaring's "The Seaman's Dictionary," in G. E.
Mainwaring and W. G. Perrin, eds., *The Life and Works of Sir Henry Mainwaring* (vols. 54 and 56).
None are like Champlain's *Traitté*. [8]

Champlain read these works in a professional way and wrote of "the special pleasure" he had
derived from "the perusal of books on this subject." But he wanted to write another kind of book
"for those who may be curious to learn more especially on those matters of which I have not found
an account elsewhere." [9]

To study these other works and then to read Champlain's *Traitté* is to discover that his book
had a special character that set it apart from the field. By comparison, Champlain's *Traitté de la
marine* stands out as a book about how to lead men in extreme conditions, on dangerous ventures

"into distant and unknown regions." More than that, it became a treatise on leadership, based on many years of personal experience.

Champlain began by addressing the reader as a comrade or colleague, *amy lecteur*, in an amiable tone that was fundamental to his style of leadership. He tells us that he had spent thirty-eight years making sea voyages, and had run many risks and been in many dangers, "from which God had preserved me." He wrote of the pleasure that he found in his work, "having always been fond of making voyages to distant and unknown regions, and wherein I had great enjoyment principally in relation to navigation, learning by experience and by the teaching of many good navigators, as well as through the special pleasure I have described from reading books on the subject." His purpose, he wrote, was to compose for his own satisfaction, a little treatise "on the qualities one should possess" to be a good mariner and an effective leader.[10]

Religion, Morality and Self-Discipline

For Champlain, the first requirement of a good leader was to be "above all a good, God-fearing man." This phrase had several meanings for him. It meant "not allowing God's name to be blasphemed, always to have prayers morning and night, and if possible to take along a man of the Church or of a religious order to help the soldiers and seamen and take their confessions and keep them in fear of God."[11]

He believed that leadership also entailed a quality of trustworthiness. "Above all," Champlain wrote, a good leader "keeps his word in any agreement; for anyone who does not keep his word is looked upon as a coward, and forfeits his honor and reputation, however valiant a fighter he may be, and no confidence is ever placed in him." He is always faithful and loyal to his men, and looks after them. "Before sailing it is necessary to have everything requisite for giving necessary aid to the men."[12]

Champlain also thought that a good leader required strength, stamina, discipline—and most of all sobriety. A commander, in his judgment, "should live plainly, and accustom himself to hard conditions" and "not be delicate in his eating or drinking, adapting to places in which he finds himself." He should be "robust and alert," with good sea legs, (*le pied marin*, literally, "sea foot"). He must be "inured to hardship and heavy labor, so that whatever happens he may be able to stay on deck, and in a strong voice give orders to each one as to what to do." Most of all, "he should not allow himself to be overcome by wine; for when a captain or a seaman is a drunkard, it is not good to entrust him with command or control, for accidents are likely to happen while he is sleeping like a pig, or has lost all judgment and reason."[13]

Ways of Working with Others

Also important was the way one treated others. Champlain wrote that a good leader should be "pleasant and affable in his conversation, absolute in his orders, and he should not talk too familiarly with his companions, except those who share in command. Otherwise a feeling of contempt for him might arise over time." He works alongside his men but remains clearly in command. "Sometimes he must not be above lending a hand to work himself, in order to make the sailors more prompt in their vigilance and to prevent confusion."

Always he should be strict, but kind: "A good leader should severely chastise malefactors, and make much of good men, being kind to them and gratifying them with some gesture, praising them and not neglecting others, so as not to give occasion for envy, which is often the source of bad feeling, much like a gangrene that little by little corrupts and destroys the body. Want of early attention to this sometimes leads to conspiracies, divisions and factions, which often cause the most promising enterprises to fail." [14]

Champlain believed that a good leader must seek to learn from others: "A wise and vigilant captain should take into consideration everything that makes for his advantage and get the opinion of the most experienced men, so as to carry it out with the means he judges to be necessary and advantageous." [15] He added: "A sage and cautious mariner ought not to trust too much in his own judgment when in an urgent need to take some important step, or deviate from a position, or change a dangerous course. He should take counsel of those who he knows to be the most wise, notably ancient navigators who have had most experience with the fortunes of the sea, and have escaped dangers and perils." Champlain advised a commander: "Let him weigh well the reasons that they advance, for it is not often that one head holds everything." But he added that after a leader consults with others, he must make the major decisions, and once a decision is made, "he should be the only one to speak, lest differing orders in doubtful situations cause the execution of one maneuver instead of another." [16]

Prudence and Prévoyance, Especially in Bold Enterprises

A good leader is prudent, Champlain said, especially in bold enterprises. He "should be wary, and hold back rather than run too many risks, whether in sighting land, particularly in foggy weather when he will bring his vessel to, or stand off [as] in the fog or darkness nobody is a pilot." He "must not carry too much sail with the idea of driving ahead; this often dismasts the ship. . . . The prudent seaman ought to be just as apprehensive of other difficulties that may occur as [of mistakes] in respect to his reckoning." [17]

A good leader must always be alert, he wrote, and must insist on alertness in others. He needs to be especially alert "if he is finding himself in ordinary perils, be it by accident, or sometimes through ignorance or rashness, as when you run before a wind inshore, or doggedly try to double a cape, or steer a dangerous course at night among sandbanks, shoals, reefs, islands, rocks, or ice." [18] At sea, Champlain recommended, a leader "should make the day his night, and be awake the greater part of the night, always sleep in his clothes, so as to be promptly on hand." He should get his sleep "more in the daytime than the night."

Champlain wrote that a good leader must be prévoyant. This quality was not a power to know the future in advance, but a determination to prepare for the unexpected in the future by remembering the past. A prévoyant leader plans ahead, and takes precautions. He should "be careful to take soundings off all coasts, roadsteads." He should have a good memory for recognizing landfalls, capes, mountains and coastlines, tidal currents and their bearings, wherever he has been." [19]

A prévoyant commander "should not be slow in striking sail, when he sees a great wind gathering on the horizon." He "should take care when a storm arrives, that the ship is lying to, to take down the small spars, to lower yards and have them made fast, as well as all the other rigging, to have the guns run in, so that in a rough sea they would not be under strain and break their tackle." [20]

Courage and Resolve

Champlain's good leader was a man of courage, ready to fight if attacked, and he should be an example to his men in battle. Champlain detested war, but he believed that some evils were worse than war, and a man of peace must be ready to fight. He wrote: "When ill-fortune brings you to such a pass it is necessary to display manly courage, to make light of death even as it confronts you, and with a steady voice and a cheerful resolution urge everyone to take heart and do what must be done to escape danger, and thus to dispel fear from the most cowardly bosoms, for when they find themselves in a hazardous situation, everyone looks to the man who is thought to have experience. . . . If he is seen to blanch and give orders in a shaky and uncertain voice, all the others lose courage and it is often that ships are lost in places from which they might have escaped, if they had seen their captain brave and resolute, issuing his commands boldly with authority." In battle, "the commander must always be on the alert, sometimes in one place, sometimes in another, so as to encourage every man in doing his duty." [21]

Champlain learned early in life that courage was required of a leader. The French had many words for this quality, and each of them had a different meaning. *Courage*, from *coeur*, was a quality of the heart. It meant an inner depth of physical or moral courage. *Bravoure*, bravery, was an outer display: a crying child is told to be brave, and is taught to act bravely. But that posture could be carried to excess and become *bravade*, or bravado. *Galanterie*, gallantry, was the ability to show manners and courtesy and grace under pressure. To do something with *élan* was to do it with dash and flair. To be *intrépide* was to act as if one had no fear. To show *effronterie* was to put up a bold front. *Défiance* was being on one's guard. In all these ways, Champlain wrote, a leader should show courage in the face of danger, resolve in adversity, and magnanimity in victory.

Humanity, Honesty, and Honor

Champlain insisted that a good leader must treat enemies, friends, and strangers with humanity. He wrote that a principled leader "should be liberal according to his opportunities, and courteous to defeated enemies, granting them all the rights of belligerents. Moreover, he should not practice cruelty or vengeance, like those who are accustomed to inhumane acts, and show themselves to be savages (*barbares*) rather then Christians, but if on the contrary he makes use of his victory with courtesy and moderation, he will be esteemed by all, even his enemies who will pay him all honor and respect." [22]

Most of all, a good leader is honest and honorable. Champlain's long career of exploration and discovery may be thought of as a moral navigation. He always steered his course by a constellation of values that would shine more brightly against the darkness, violence, and cruelty that surrounded him in an age of religious war and political strife.

At the center of this constellation was one very bright star, which Champlain called by a single old-fashioned word. It was absolutely fundamental to Champlain's sense of himself. In his last years, he wrote simply, "*Ie suis honneste homme*. I am an honest man." [23] He spelled it in the old-fashioned way that was close to its simple Latin root, *honestas*, but there was nothing simple about its meaning. In French it inspired a vocabulary of related words: *honneste, honnête, honnêteté*. As in English it meant speaking truthfully, not only in a sense of telling no lies, but also with a broader sense of speaking candidly. Honesty was also a form of conduct. It meant acting fairly and reasonably, and not taking advantage of another person. "Honnête" also had another meaning in Champlain's French. "Honnête homme" is defined in *Le Grand Robert* as an *homme du monde, agréable et distingué par les manières comme par l'esprit*; a man of the world, agreeable and distinguished by his manners as well as by his spirit.[24]

This quality had a special prominence in the thinking of Champlain's younger French contemporaries. Blaise Pascal (1623–1662) wrote of another in his *Pensées*, "He is an honnête homme; only this universal quality pleases me." Another French writer explained, *"L'honnête homme est à sa place partout*; the honest man is at home everywhere." He acquits himself in everything with a superiority that has no technique or artifice about it, but is always natural and easy.

An honnête homme was also a man of *honneur*, an even more complex idea. On one level, "honneur" meant a pride of reputation for doing the right thing in the right way. But more than that, it spoke of a person of any rank or gender who always tried to act in such a way as to deserve a reputation for doing the right thing. Most of all, it was an idea of integrity of such strength that one always tried to act in an upright way, even though one often fell short. To study Champlain's *Voyages* with this treatise in mind is to discover the integrity of this ethical ideal, and the strength of his determination to serve it.

A P P E N D I X   F

ANOTHER SELF-PORTRAIT?

In addition to the small self-portrait in Champlain's "Defeat of the Iroquois" from 1609, a few other sketches also appear in engravings for his books. One such image appears in his drawing of the attack on the Iroquois forest fort at Sorel in 1610. It is a figure, very similar to eight other French arquebusiers and is labeled as Champlain, but it is so small and crude that it reveals nothing beyond what can be seen in the "Defeat of the Iroquois." A third engraving, an illustration of the attack on the Onondaga town in 1615, shows twelve small French figures. One of them presumably is Champlain, but which? All are equally indistinct.

Other images appear on Champlain's maps. Two in particular have been discussed by Marcel Trudel. These are round faces, set within a compass rose on Champlain's maps of 1612 and 1632. Trudel suggests that they may reveal to us the face of Champlain in his maturity. Other scholars disagree. François Marc Gagnon and Denis Martin note that many cartographers decorated their maps with round "sun-faces," which were highly conventional on seventeenth-century maps.[1]

One other full-face sketch has passed unnoticed by his biographers. It appears on the only manuscript map that survives from Champlain's hand and with a signature: his "Descr[i]psion des costs p[or]ts, rades, Illes de la novvele france . . ." It is dated 1606 and corrected to 1607 by a heavier hand, and is in the map division of the Library of Congress, where it is cherished as one of the great treasures of that collection. It is very handsome in the original manuscript. Most reproductions distort its color and do not bring out the fine detail of the drawings.

In an elaborate border around the map's cartouche, Champlain added two good-humored sketches of a beardless young man, and a wild-haired and bearded older man. They are very small cartoons, and their purpose is not clear. Perhaps they are merely meant to be abstract images of youth and age. They might also be something more and other than that. One wonders if the younger figure is a self-portrait of the artist in his youth. The other face might perhaps represent an older man of some importance in his life. It could possibly represent the sieur de Mons. If so, this would be our only representation of him.

The hypothesis that the young man is a self-portrait of Champlain meets two difficulties. The figures are stylized in bizarre ways; and in 1609, Champlain wore a beard and represented himself as a man of mature years. The youthful, beardless face in the map cartouche was drawn only one or two years earlier. But these are not conventional images, like the sun-faces that appear on his other maps. They have very distinct features, and appear to be representative images. But who do they represent? Here is a question for further study.[2]

APPENDIX   G

CHAMPLAIN'S SUPERIORS
Viceroys and Generals of New France

From 1604 to 1635, New France was under the authority of a vice-regal ruler who reported directly to the king. With one exception (the sieur de Mons), all these men were absentee rulers who remained in France and governed through a "lieutenant." To fill that office, all of them sooner or later chose Champlain.

Historians have regarded the post of viceroy as a sinecure of small importance in the history of New France. One scholar borrowed the language of Merovingian France, and called them *vice-rois fainéants*, "do-nothing" viceroys. Champlain took another view. He believed that they could be very useful in promoting the colony at home, and he encouraged them to take an active role. Every one of them did so except Soissons, who was viceroy for only a few weeks. All the others made a contribution in one way or another.

Here was yet another role that Champlain played behind the scenes. It required tact, wisdom, and a highly developed political intelligence. The viceroys came mostly from a narrow circle, but they were very diverse in their character, purposes and principles. Champlain got along with nearly all of them, adjusting his tactics in many ways but always preserving his large purpose. If he worked for all these viceroys, they also worked for him and aided his grand design.

Most of the viceroys have been omitted from the *Dictionary of Canadian Biography*. A brief survey might bring out another narrative line in Champlain's career. He was able to find his footing again and again. He established a working relationship with all except Richelieu. In the midst of many changes, here was an important continuity in the early history of New France.

DE MONS (var. Monts, Montz), Pierre Dugua, sieur de Mons (1558?–1628), born to an aristocratic family in Saintonge, raised a Protestant, a soldier for Henri IV, he became a gentleman of the king's chamber with a large pension, and governor of Pons. De Mons visited New France with Chauvin in 1600. In 1603 the king granted him a monopoly of the fur trade and authority to found a permanent settlement. He was given the rank of lieutenant general for New France. He requested the title of viceroy and was refused, but received vice-regal powers with direct access to the king and his council.

De Mons was the first successful colonizer of New France. He came to America in 1604–05, the only vice-regal figure to do so, and founded settlements at Sainte-Croix and Port-Royal, invited Champlain as geographer, and gave him more responsibility. De Mons had trouble establishing a rapport with the Indians, but he set an example for humane and principled leadership. In France he also founded a commercial company in 1603 but lost his monopoly in 1606, and ordered his settlers to return to France in 1607. In 1607 he raised money for the founding of Quebec and chose Champlain to be his lieutenant there.

After the death of Henri IV in 1610, de Mons was banished from the presence of the queen regent, and he asked Champlain to take the lead at court. De Mons continued to support New France behind the scenes, aided Champlain against his rivals, contributed to the colony, and sent out commercial voyages for many years. Champlain and Lescarbot and all who knew him held de Mons in the highest respect. He was a major figure in the founding of New France.[1]

SOISSONS, Charles de Bourbon, comte de Soissons (1566–1612), was a prince of the blood, the son of Louis de Bourbon, first prince de Condé, and Françoise d'Orléans, cousin-german of Henri IV and cousin of Louis XIII, not his uncle as others have written. Champlain and his advisers at court recruited Soissons through intermediaries, as a way of finding a protector for New France. In consequence, Soissons succeeded the sieur de Mons with the title of Lieutenant General and Viceroy on October 8, 1612. He was granted a monopoly of trade in the St. Lawrence Valley for a term of twelve years. One of his first acts was to appoint Champlain as his lieutenant on October 25, 1612, and he began to help Champlain at court. They were just beginning to work well together when Soissons fell ill and died very suddenly, after serving only three weeks. Champlain, whose commission lasted merely fifteen days, wrote that his death was "greatly regretted."[2]

CONDÉ, Henri de Bourbon, prince de Condé (1588–1646) was also a prince of the blood, the son of Henri, first prince de Condé and Charlotte-Catherine de La Trémouille. He was baptized a Protestant and raised a Roman Catholic. In 1609 he married Marguerite de Montmorency and became the father of the "Grand Condé," with whom he is sometimes confused. He was described by a writer in the *Mercure François* as having a "vivacity of spirit" and an extraordinary "knowledge of languages and many sciences." Champlain had a connection with him through marriage. Hélène Boullé, Champlain's wife, was a sister-in-law of Charles Deslandes, secretary to the prince de Condé, after Deslandes married Marguerite Boullé. In 1612, following the death of his cousin Soissons, Condé bought the office of lieutenant general, admiral, and now viceroy of New France, and acquired a monopoly of trade in the St. Lawrence River and its tributaries for twelve years. His pay included a fine horse worth 1,000 écus, or 3,000 livres. Condé immediately appointed Champlain as his lieutenant on November 22, 1612. The two men worked well together. From 1612 to 1615, Condé played an active role in granting passports for trade in New France, brought a flow of income to the colony, helped the Récollet missionaries to establish themselves, and gave strong support and protection to Champlain. But in 1615, Condé led a party in opposition to the queen regent, Marie de Medici, and her Catholic circle. The following year, he was arrested on her orders, and imprisoned in the Bastille and then at Vincennes.[3]

THÉMINES, Pons de Lauzières, Marquis de Thémines de Cardillac (1552–1627), a courtier who served the queen regent, Marie de Medici, and was made by her a maréchal of France at the age of sixty-four (1616). On the queen regent's order, he arrested Condé in the Louvre and took him to the Bastille in 1616. In the same year (on October 25) Thémines received another reward from the queen regent, who made him viceroy of New France while Condé was in the Bastille. The appointment was rapidly confirmed on November 24, 1616, with the same pay of 1,000 écus or 3,000 livres. The queen also appointed a friend of Thémines to replace Champlain as lieutenant for New France. Champlain fought back. Thémines soon fell out with his lieutenant over the spoils of their offices. Thémines removed him and on January 15, 1617, made Champlain his lieutenant for New France. The two men worked effectively together. Their relations were complex. In a document of the Royal Council dated July 18, 1619, when Condé was still in prison, Champlain was described as serving simultaneously as lieutenant to both Thémines and Condé. He was able to work with two bitter enemies at the same time. Thémines helped Champlain to submit the program of 1618 and worked until the following year when Condé was released from prison at Vincennes. Thémines was dismissed as viceroy, and Condé recovered the office, held it briefly from 1619 to 1620, worked with Champlain on mounting the expedition to New France in 1620, then sold the office of viceroy to his brother-in-law the duc de Montmorency for 30,000 livres.[4]

MONTMORENCY, Henri, the second duc de Montmorency et de Dampville (1594–1632), was the son of Henri, first duc de Montmorency, and Louise de Bourbon en Budos, and brother-in-law of the prince de Condé. He succeeded his uncle, Charles, duc de Dampville, as admiral of France. On February 25, 1620, he received letters patent as viceroy of New France. Twelve days later, on March 8, 1620, he chose Champlain as his lieutenant. Montmorency was one of the most able of all the viceroys of New France, an experienced leader in colonial and maritime affairs. As viceroy, Montmorency restructured the commerce of New France, established the post of intendant, helped provide funds for fortifications, and supported a chapel and residence for the Récollets. Some scholars date the origin of the seigneurial system in New France from a grant of Cap Tourmente and the Île d'Orleans to Guillaume de Caën, January 3, 1624. Montmorency gave strong support to Champlain, increased his powers and his pay, and protected New France at home. The success of Champlain's leadership from 1620 to 1624 was made possible by his good relations with this viceroy. In 1625, after a tenure of five years, Montmorency resigned his office. He was a strong defender of the traditional rights of the parlements and provinces. Later, Montmorency supported a political movement in Languedoc that the king perceived as treason. Richelieu may also have feared Montmorency as a rival, despite a show of support. In 1632 Montmorency was arrested and executed for treason at the age of 38.[5] He was always a faithful friend of Champlain and New France.

VENTADOUR, Henri de Lévis, duc de Ventadour, var. Vantadour (1596–1680), was the son of Anne de Lévis, duc de Ventadour, and Marguerite de Montmorency, and the nephew of the previous viceroy. In the spring of 1625, Ventadour purchased the office of viceroy from his uncle the duc de Montmorency for 100,000 livres. Ventadour was drawn to the office by his deep religious feeling, and a determination to spread the Christian faith in America. Immediately after his commission as viceroy, his first act was to commission Champlain as his lieutenant. They worked closely together in Ventadour's Paris mansion. Champlain supported the missionary work that Ventadour desired, and the new viceroy backed Champlain's plans and purposes. A difference arose between them over Ventadour's wish to exclude Protestants from New France. Champlain continued to support Henri IV's solution. He supported a Catholic establishment, but wanted to allow Protestants to live and trade in the colony. The men were able to continue working together even though they were not of one mind on that question.[6]

RICHELIEU, Armand-Jean du Plessis, bishop of Luçon, cardinal of the Roman Catholic Church, duc de Richelieu and de Fronsac (1585–1642), was born into the lesser nobility, the son of François du Plessis, sieur de Richelieu, and Suzanne de La Porte. His older brother was killed in a duel by the marquis de Thémines in 1619. He entered the church and became bishop of Luçon to serve his family's interests; was helped at court by Madame de Guercheville; became first minister of state under the queen regent and went with her when she was banished from court; and helped to reconcile the queen and her son Louis XIII. For that service he was made cardinal in 1622 and member of the King's Council in 1624. Four months later he became head of the council and chief minister. Richelieu took maritime and colonial affairs into his own hands, and in 1626 the king made him chief and superintendent of navigation and commerce of France. He founded the Company of the Hundred Associates, put his kinsman Isaac de Razilly in charge of Acadia, and grudgingly accepted Champlain as his lieutenant for Quebec and the St. Lawrence Valley. Richelieu brought energy and power to New France. He insisted that it should be always in his hands, but it was not always in his thoughts, and the quality of his decisions was very mixed. He mustered resources for a major colonizing effort by the Hundred Associates, but against much informed advice insisted that a large fleet should sail for New France when a more powerful British fleet was in the St. Lawrence. The entire French expedition was lost, and the Hundred Associates were nearly bankrupted. Richelieu selected leaders in the colony for their rank, religion, and personal loyalty rather than experience and ability. He gave Champlain no support in the critical years from 1633 to 1635.[7]

TRADING COMPANIES AND MONOPOLIES IN NEW FRANCE, 1588–1635

Before 1636, New France was financed through the agency of commercial companies. Strictly speaking they were not private companies but arms of the state. The public-private distinction as we know it did not emerge until the eighteenth century. These companies were created and regulated by the Crown, but were required to raise their own capital and to subsidize colonization, often much against their will. They sought to raise money by licensing trade under grants of monopoly from the Crown.

The Cartier Monopoly, 1588

In 1587, Stephen Chaton, sieur de la Jannaye, and Jacques Nouel petitioned King Henri III for a monopoly of the fur trade in New France. Both were captains in the French Navy and nephews of Jacques Cartier. They pointed out that Jacques Cartier and his heirs were still owed a sum of 1,600 livres. A royal commission confirmed their claim. In January, 1588, they received a monopoly on fur trade and mining in New France for twelve years, and authorization to transport sixty convicts to New France and start a settlement. The monopoly was instantly attacked by traders and fishermen and was revoked for all but mining rights. Nothing appears to have come of this colonizing effort.

La Roche's Monopoly, 1598

In 1577, Troïlus du Mesgoùez, seigneur de La Roche-Helgomarche, marquis de Coëtarmoal, vicomte de Carenten and Saint-Lô, received from Henri III authorization to "conquer and take various lands and countries newly discovered and occupied by barbarous people." He was authorized to be viceroy and feudal proprietor of all lands that he was able to seize, and to rule them as his personal possession. Nothing came of this grant, but its spirit reveals an attitude toward the new world far removed from that of Champlain and his circle. La Roche, as he was called, was himself captured in the French wars of religion and held a prisoner of the Catholic League from 1589 to 1596. In 1598 Henri IV gave La Roche new powers as lieutenant general for "Canada . . . and adjacent lands" and granted him a monopoly of trade. The king himself contributed 12,000 écus. The result was one of the worst disasters in the history of European colonization.

Chauvin's Monopoly, 1599–1603

In 1599, part of La Roche's monopoly passed to Pierre Chauvin, sieur de Tonnetuit, a Calvinist merchant born in Dieppe and resident in Honfleur. In 1599 he petitioned the king for a monopoly of the fur trade in a territory that stretched a hundred leagues along the St. Lawrence River. The monopoly was granted for ten years, on condition that Chauvin would transport fifty settlers a year, five hundred altogether. He sent ships to Tadoussac in 1600, traded profitably for furs, left sixteen settlers to their own devices and returned home. Champlain believed that Chauvin's proposal was a fraud, and that he had no interest in colonization. In any case he failed to meet his commitments. His monopoly of the fur trade, which had been granted for ten years, was withdrawn after three years, partly as a response to protests from rival merchants in Saint-Malo, Dieppe, and La Rochelle. Chauvin died in 1603.

Aymar de Chaste's Monopoly, 1603

In 1603, Chauvin's monopoly passed to Aymar de Chaste. This admirable man was governor of Dieppe, well connected at court, and respected by those who knew him. He organized a successful group of investors in Dieppe, Rouen, and Saint-Malo. Together they funded a voyage of reconnaissance with Pont-Gravé in command. Champlain went along as geographer, explorer, cartographer, and observer for the king. De Chaste, in bad health, remained in France. This voyage to Tadoussac in 1603 was successful in every way. It identified sites for settlement, established good relations with the Indians of the St. Lawrence Valley, and turned a profit that has been estimated at 40 percent of its capital. De Chaste died before the voyagers returned, and the company ended with his demise.

De Mons' First Monopoly and the Company of Rouen, 1603–08

In 1603, the sieur de Mons received a ten-year monopoly on trade in New France from the fortieth to the forty-sixth parallel, with a requirement to plant a colony of fifty settlers. He founded the Compagnie de Rouen, also called the Compagnie de Mons. In February 1604, merchants invested 90,000 livres in five "portions." Two portions were reserved for merchants of Saint-Malo; two for La Rochelle and Saint-Jean-de-Luz, and one for Rouen. The investors agreed to send out two trading vessels from Saint-Malo, a trading and whaling ship from Saint-Jean-de-Luz; and two colonizing vessels from Le Havre or Honfleur. Two colonies were founded, at Sainte-Croix Island in 1604–05 and Port-Royal in 1605–07. The monopoly was strongly opposed at court by Sully and rival interests. It was revoked in 1607, and the settlements were abandoned. A period of free trade followed from 1607 to 1608.

De Mons' Second Monopoly and the De Mons Company, 1608–09

On the urging of de Mons and Champlain, Henri IV revived de Mons' monopoly in 1607, but only for a period of one year, with a requirement to plant settlements in New France. The investment company was recognized in Rouen, and de Mons raised money by individual agreements and loans. This company succeeded in founding the first permanent settlement at Quebec, with Champlain as commandant. The monopoly expired in 1609, and another period of free trade followed from 1609 to 1612.

Soissons' Monopoly, 1612

On September 27, 1612, Soissons received a monopoly of trade for twelve years. It ended abruptly with his death in 1612 before a company could be organized. Trade was in the hands of merchants in the towns of Rouen, Dieppe, Honfleur, Saint-Malo, and La Rochelle.

Condé's Monopoly and the Company of Rouen and Saint-Malo, 1613–20

This new venture followed the failure of the last. It was organized on November 15, 1613, and was variously called Condé's Company by Champlain, and Champlain's Company by historians. People at the time spoke of it as the Company of Rouen and Saint-Malo. It operated under a new monopoly of trade in the St. Lawrence Valley, which had been granted to Condé as viceroy and assigned by him to this company for a period of eleven years. The investors agreed to obey the viceroy, support Champlain, and transport six families of settlers. None of these promises were kept, and the company failed.

Montmorency's Monopoly and the old Company de Caën, 1620–1625

On November 8, 1620, this new group was formed. At first it was called the Montmorency Company, and later the Compagnie de Caën. It received a monopoly on the fur trade from the forty-eighth to the fifty-second parallel for a period of eleven years, later extended to fifteen years. The company was required to pay Champlain's salary and support his family. It agreed to establish six Récollet missionaries and promised to settle six families in New France. The capital stock of the company was divided in 1621, with seven twelfths for the Compagnie de Caën and five twelfths for members of the old Compagnie of Rouen and Saint-Malo.

Ventadour's Monopoly and the new Compagnie de Caën, 1626–27

This was a reconstitution of the old Compagnie de Caën under the authority of the new viceroy, Ventadour. The merchants of Rouen and Saint-Malo were ordered to surrender their share of the company for a lump-sum payment equal to 40 per cent of their stake. In 1627 it came to an end through the efforts of Cardinal Richelieu, who took control of New France and organized a new company.

The Company of New France, 1627–1632

This new body was also variously called the Compagnie des Cent-Associés (Company of the Hundred Associates) or Richelieu's Company. It was founded by Cardinal Richelieu on April 29, 1627, and received a royal charter in May 1628. The first name on the list of a hundred shareholders was that of Richelieu himself. Each was required to pay 3,000 livres. It received a monopoly on the marketing of Canadian furs in Europe and undertook to colonize New France.

Richelieu caused a disaster when he ordered the directors of the company to send out a large convoy of ships with four hundred people aboard, despite a war with England and warnings that British ships were on the coast. The directors acted against their best judgment, and the French ships were intercepted in the St. Lawrence River. All but one small vessel were captured. The company lost its entire investment and was driven to the edge of bankruptcy. The settlement of Quebec received no supplies or support from Richelieu or the company for two years. Champlain and the French colonists were driven to the edge of starvation and forced to surrender to small forces of British freebooters, along with most of New France.

Richelieu and Ventadour caused more trouble by seeking a policy of religious conformity in New France. The bylaws of Richelieu's company required that habitants should be native-born French subjects of the Catholic faith. At first that policy of uniformity was not enforced. Champlain did all in his power to preserve a measure of tolerance for Protestants in the St. Lawrence Valley, while supporting a Catholic establishment under the terms of the Edict of Nantes. But religious conformity slowly prevailed and it was a calamity for New France. Permanent English and French settlements began in America within a year, between1607and 1608. By 1760 the more open and diverse English colonies had a population of 1.6 million. New France, with its national and religious restrictions, had a population of 60,000.

Subsidiaries of the Company of New France, 1632–35

The Hundred Associates recovered control of New France after the Treaty of Saint-Germain-en-Laye, March 23, 1632. The company, desperately short of capital, began to organize subsidiary companies and partnerships that were separately capitalized. They were variously called *compagnies particulières* or *compagnies sous-contractantes*. Among the most important in the period from 1630 to 1635 were the following subsidiaries:

The Company of Bordeaux, 1630, was formed by a consortium of six of the Hundred Associates. It supported the trading forts of the La Tours on Cape Sable and at the mouth of the Saint John River.

The Company Tuffet succeeded the Bordeaux Company.

The Company of Normandy was founded in 1631 for the support of the settlement at Fort Ste. Anne on Cape Breton. Champlain may have made a voyage there in 1632.

The Company Desportes de Lignières took its name from its leader Pierre Desportes de Lignières, one of the Hundred Associates. It succeeded the Company of Normandy and continued to support settlement and trade on Cape Breton.

The Company Cheffault-Rozée in 1632 raised a capital of 100,000 livres for settlements and trading posts on Miscou Island, in the Baie des Chaleurs, and in the lower St. Lawrence Valley. Champlain himself was an investor.

The Company Razilly, 1632, led by Isaac de Razilly and supported by Champlain, was authorized to raise capital for the colonization of Acadia, first at La Hève, then at Port-Royal. Under Razilly's inspired leadership it succeeded in establishing the nucleus of the Acadian population in the years from 1632 to Razilly's death in 1635.

The Company of Beaupré under the Hundred Associates acquired title to the seigneury of the Isle d'Orléans and the Côte de Beaupré, on the north bank of the St. Lawrence River, downstream from Quebec.

Other companies followed after Champlain's death in 1635, with seigneurial grants and rights to fishing and navigation in the St. Lawrence Valley and other parts of New France.[1]

APPENDIX I

INDIAN NATIONS IN CHAMPLAIN'S WORLD, 1603–35

A NOTE ON LANGUAGE

Throughout this book Indians are called Indians, a choice that after a generation of political correctness, requires an explanation. A few years ago I was invited to the Newberry Library in Chicago, to meet leaders from many Indian nations throughout the United States. They had requested a meeting with historians to discuss problems of concern in the literature of American history. In the course of our conversations, I asked what they would prefer to be called. The answers were the same, from Apaches in the southwest to Wampanoags in the northeast. Without exception they wanted to be called by the name of their own nations. I asked what word we should use to refer to all of them together, and they said that "Indian" was as good as any other, and better than some. They used it with pride, and it is adopted here. The pattern of usage is now changing. In the United States, "Indian" is returning to favor without pejorative connotation. In Canada, "first nations" is still preferred, but "Amerindiens" is frequently used. Champlain called the indigenous people of the West Indies "Indiens," and those of eastern woodlands of North America "Sauvages," which in the usage of his age meant native forest dwellers. Champlain always wrote of major groups as "nations," never as tribes. That usage is preferred by many Indians and is adopted here.

The many nations of eastern North America were rapidly forming confederacies when Champlain arrived, a process that had been underway for a long period before European contact.

No definitive taxonomy exists for the Indian nations that Champlain knew. Many lists have been compiled, and no two are the same. Most attempts begin with language groups, and then subdivide them into nations, of which there were many. Every nation had its own name for itself, and also the names it was given by Indian neighbors and Europeans. Many nations also acquired names in Spanish, Portuguese, Basque, Breton, Dutch, French, and English. (See Sources, pp. 613–14.)

INUIT LANGUAGE GROUP

Inuit nations were Esquimaux to the French, Eskimo to English speakers. They lived in Labrador and the subarctic region of Canada.

BÉOTHUK LANGUAGE GROUP

Béothuk or Terre Neuve or Newfoundland Indians, after the island where they lived.

NORTHERN INDIANS

The Naskapis, Mistassins, Peribonka, and Ashuamouchuan were hunting nations who lived many days journey north of the Saguenay River. They lived on rivers of similar names that flowed into Lake St. John and Lake Mistassini, and some could "see the salt sea" of Hudson Bay. Champlain knew them through their Montagnais trading partners to the south.[1]

ALGONQUIAN LANGUAGE GROUPS (VAR. ALGONKIAN)

Among scholars, Algonquian or Algonkian refers to the larger language groups. Algonquin, or Algonkin, denotes some of the nations who spoke Algonquian languages.

Montagnais or Innu

Today this nation calls itself Innu, not to be confused with Inuit. The French called them Montagnais, or mountain dwellers. They were a hunting people with many subgroups, which included:

> Papinachois
> Kakouchaki (Porcupine)
> Attikameque (White Fish)
> Chicoutimi
> Tadoussac
> Nekubaniste
> Chomonchouaniste
> Outabitibec

Algonquin

(Algoumekins to the French; Algonkin to English; they call themselves Anishinabe, the humans) (DC)

Andataouat, Outaouac, or Ottawas
Cheveux Relevés to the French; High Hairs to the English (CWB, CM)

Ouescharini or Weskarini
Petite-Nation Algonquin to Champlain and French (CM)

Kichesperini, Algonquin of the Island; Champlain knew their headman Tessouat
Allumette to the French; Morrison Island Algonquin to the English (DC)

Kinouchepirini, Muskrat Lake Algonquin
Champlain met their headman Nibachis

Onontchataronon, Iroquet's Algonquin
Atontrataronnon to the Huron, with whom they wintered; Champlain worked
with their headman Iroquet (CWB, DC, CH)

Matouweskarini
Madawaska River Algonquin

Bastisquan Algonquin (CWB's map of 1612) lived east of the Ottawa River near
the St. Maurice River; Champlain named them for their headman Batiscan. Some
ethnographers believe they were Montagnais (DC)

Otagouttouenmin, Kotakoutouemi, Mataouchkairini and Ounchatarounounga
were hunting people north of the Kischesperini (DC)

Sagnitaouigama, Sagaigunini lived north of the Huron on Georgian Bay

Attikameks (Têtes de Boule) lived on the upper St. Maurice River

Northwestern Algonquian-speaking Nations who were not Algonquin

Epicerini; Called sorcerers by their Algonquin neighbors, who regarded them as a
people apart. They were Nipissing to Champlain, who visited them near the lake
of the same name. They spoke an Algonquian language but were distinct from Algonquin nations (M, CH, DC)

Abitibi, who lived around Lake Abitibi, south of James Bay (DC)

Temiskaming, who lived around Lake Temiskaming, south of Lake Atibibi

Suk and Renard to French; Sac and Fox to English. They were Na-Nà-Ma-Kee's
people who lived "near Montreal" and later moved west and south

Cree
    O'pimittish Ininiwac (Gens de Terre)
    Kilistinon

Ojibwa (Chippewa)
    Mississague (Oumisagi)
    Nocquet (Nokes)
    Pauoitigoueieuhak (Sauleurs)

Roquai
Mantoue
Outchibous (O'chiiboy, Chippewa)

Eastern Algonquian-speaking Nations

Eastern Wabenaki or Abenaki Confederacy (FMW)
Etchemin (Champlain's Estechemins)
Passamaquoddy
Penobscot
Malicite (Maliseet)
Abenaki

Mi'kmaq Confederacy
Souriquois to French, Micmac to English
A Confederacy with seven subgroups (FMW)

Canadaquoa (Canadaquois; Canadien) (CWB) [2]

Southern Algonquian-speaking Nations

Almouchiquois or Saco (CM)

Penacook-Western Wabenaki Confederacy (FMW)
Penacook
Western Abenakis
Pawtucket (Wamesit)

Massachusett-Coastal Indian Confederacy (KJB)
Massachusetts
Pokanokets (Wampanoag)
Nauset (Cape Indians)
Narragansett

Mountain Indians
Mahigan to the French; Mohican to the English (FMW)
Wappinger

Mohegan-Pequot-River Indian Confederacy (FMW)
Mohegan-Pequot
Nehantic
Nipmuck
Podunk
Tunxis
Nanatuck

IROQUOIAN LANGUAGE GROUPS included three large confederations: the Iroquois, Huron, the Neutral Nation, and many other nations.

THE IROQUOIS LEAGUE

They called themselves Hodenosaunee, People of the Long House. The French called them Yroquois, Hroquois or Iroquois, which was in its origin a Basque-Montagnais-French pidgin word. English called them the Five Nations in the seventeenth and early eighteenth centuries.

> Agniehrononnon (Agniers in French, Mohawk in English; Champlain called them Yroquois and used the word both for the Mohawk and the larger league)
>
> Oneiochronnon (Onneiouts in French, Oneida in English; Champlain called them Entohonorons after the Huron word for them)
>
> Onontagereronnon (Onontagués in French, Onondaga in English; Champlain called them Entohonorons from the Huron)
>
> Ouioenrthonnon (Cayuga in English; Champlain called them Entohonorons from the Huron)
>
> Sonnontouan (Seneca in English, Tsonnontouans in French; Champlain called them Chouontouarpuon or Sonontoerrhonons after the Huron)[3]

The Huron Confederacy

The name by which they are most often called is from the French *hure*, for the hair of a wild boar. Champlain called them Ochateguins from the Bear Clan below (CM). They called themselves by many names. Some took the name of Ouendat, Wendat (Islanders). Most referred to themselves by the names of their Clans or Phrartries, of which there were as many as five or more (T749):

> Attigouautan (CWB 3:55) or Attignawantan (People of the Bear) (T, CM);
>
> Atinouaentans may have been the same or a sub group (CWB);
>
> Arendarhonon (People of the Rock) (T30);
>
> Attigneenongnahac (People of the Barking Dogs) (T30);
>
> Tahontaenrat (People of the Deer) (T30);
>
> Ataronchronon (People of the Marshes) (T30).

The Neutral Confederacy

Champlain called them Les Neutres. The Huron spoke of them as the Attiwandarons, "people of a slightly different language." The Iroquois were said to call them Atirhagenrat, or Adirondacks, a name they also used for other Iroquoian-speaking people. Champlain wrote: "The Neutral nation is one which holds itself aloof from all the others, and carries on no war except with the Assistaqueronons. It is very large, having 40 very populous villages"[4] (CWB 6:249). Like the Huron and Iroquois they were a confederacy of nations:

> Onguiarahronon or people of the Ongniarah (Niagara) River, the leading nation, which were called the "Neutrals proper" (GKW 6)

Wenrohronon or Wenroes, who lived near Iroquoia in what is now New York

Aondironon, who lived near the Huron in what is now southern Ontario

Attiouendarankhronon, who lived west of the Niagara River and north of Lake Erie

The nations of this confederacy were attacked and destroyed by the Iroquois after the death of Champlain (GKW).

Western Iroquoian-speaking Nations

Eriehronnen (Erie in English)

Khionontateronnon (Tobacco in English, Petun in French)

Nation de Chat (the Cat Nation in English) (SP 16/53)

Mascoutens (Nation de Feu in French; Fire People to the English (SC 16/53; CM 326M)

Southern Irooquoian-speaking Nations

Andastes, called Andastoéronons by the Hurons, Carantouanais by the French and Susquehannocks or Susquehannah to the English (T 504)

SIOUAN-SPEAKING NATIONS

Winnebago, who lived in what is now Wisconsin. Champlain's interpreter met them and called them Oinipigous, as did the Jesuits. They may have been the nation that Champlain called Puan. The French were quick to discover that they spoke a different language.

SOURCES

CWB	H. P. Biggar, ed., *The Works of Samuel de Champlain*, 6 vols. and a portfolio of maps and drawings (CWB) (Toronto, 1922–36, reprinted 1971).
CCE	Champlain's ethnographic map, "Le Canada faict par Sr de Champlain, 1616." It survives in an unfinished printer's proof perhaps engraved for Champlain's *Voyages et descouvertures* (1619) but not published in it. Copies survive in the John Carter Brown Library, Brown University, Providence, Rhode Island; and in the National Library of Russia. The plate appears to have been acquired by mapmaker Pierre Du Val, who reused it in 1653 with additions and corrections.
KJB	Kathleen J. Bragdon, *Native People of Southern New England* (Norman, Okla., 1996), 243.
DC	Daniel Clément, ed., *The Algonquins* (Hull, 1996).
RCH	R. Cole Harris, *Historical Atlas of Canada* (Toronto, 1987).
CH	Conrad Heidenreich, *Huronia* (Toronto, 1971), map 24.

CM   Christian Morissonneau, in Litalien and Vaugeois, *Champlain: The Birth of French America* (Montreal, 2004), 162.

HSR   Howard S. Russell, *Indian New England before the Mayflower* (Hanover, 1980) 19–29.

T   Bruce G. Trigger, *Children of Aataentsic* (Montreal, 1976, 1987).

FMW   Frederick M. Wiseman, *The Voice of the Dawn: An Autohistory of the Abenaki Nation.*

GKW   Gordon K. Wright, *The Neutral Nations* (Rochester, N.Y., 1963).

APPENDIX J

THE BATTLE WITH THE MOHAWK IN 1609
Where Did It Happen?

Historians have long debated the location of the battle at Lake Champlain in 1609. Most scholars agree that it could have happened only in one of two places, and monuments have been erected at both spots. One of them is Crown Point; the other is Ticonderoga.

The evidence to settle this dispute comes in two forms: cartography and chronology in Champlain's accounts. In his 1632 map, Champlain explicitly identified the "place on Lake Champlain where the Iroquois were defeated." It bears the number 65 in his key and is located between Lake George and Lake Champlain. On this map, Champlain's sketch of Lake Champlain clearly shows the promontory of Ticonderoga, and Willow Point to the north. His marker 65 is placed between those two points at an indentation that has been called Sandy Beach.[1]

The second piece of evidence is the chronology of Champlain's account. He wrote that after the battle he visited the chute that flowed from Lake George to Lake Champlain, and he explored it at least as far as the lowest falls, "un saut d'eau que ie vis, a waterfall that I saw."[2] Champlain also stated that he had only three hours after the battle to go exploring, before his allies headed home. This was his only visit to the area. The distance by canoe from the sandy beach around the promontory at Ticonderoga and into the chute is about 1.8 miles. In the summer of 2007, four of us paddled this route in two canoes (Nick Westbrook, Ann McCarty, my wife, and I). It took us about 45 minutes to go that distance in one direction. Champlain's round trip from the Sandy Beach to the outlet of the chute would have been about 3.6 miles. He could easily have done the round trip on the lake in an hour and a half, with time enough to paddle or walk up the chute to the lowest rapids, and to return within three hours.

The same test of time and distance rules out Crown Point as the site of the battle. The distance by canoe from Crown Point (Fort St. Frédéric) to the chute is approximately twelve miles. A round trip of twenty-four miles from Crown Point to the chute and back would have taken Champlain six hours at a minimum. Certainly it could not have been done in three hours. If Champlain's narrative is correct, Crown Point could not have been the site of the battle. Only a site near Ticonderoga is consistent with his account. In short, Champlain's map of 1632 and his written account both clearly support Ticonderoga as the site and rule out Crown Point. No evidence of that sort exists on the other side of the question.

On both sides, other arguments have been made in terms of Champlain's description of the terrain. Each site could qualify as a promontory or cape. Each had steep, eroded banks and a sandy beach on part of its shoreline, with level ground and a forest beyond. In my judgment arguments in these terms are inconclusive, but the evidence of Champlain's map of 1632 and the chronology in his narrative are decisive in favor of Ticonderoga.

The Crown Point hypothesis first appeared in Laverdière's and Biggar's editions of Champlain's works. Both were highly skilled editors and scholars, but neither appears to have visited Lake Champlain, and their thesis was asserted with no evidence. Other historians followed them into error. The case for Crown Point was made by the New York Tricentennial Commission, Guy Omeron Coolidge, and Joe Armstrong. Arguments for the Ticonderoga site have been developed by S. H. P. Pell, Morison, Trudel, and other scholars.[3]

APPENDIX K

THE ATTACK ON THE IROQUOIS FORT IN 1615
Which Fort? What Nation?

Where was the Iroquois fort that Champlain attacked in 1615? Which Iroquois nation was he fighting? This question has given rise to a controversy that has continued through two centuries.

Champlain's accounts of the battle are unclear on both issues. He called the enemy that he was attacking the Entohonorons, which was his understanding of their name in the Huron language. Experts on Iroquoian languages conclude that this word might have applied to the Oneida or Onondaga nation, or even the Cayuga. It does not clearly identify any one of these three Iroquois nations.

The precise location of the battleground would solve the problem, but on this question historians have disagreed. Most scholars are of one mind in tracing Champlain's route from Huronia to the Iroquois country, as far as the town of Brewerton at the outlet of Lake Oneida. They also agree that the fort was on a lake nearby with small streams on either side of it. But which lake, and where exactly? Local historians who know the ground have made claims for many sites in upstate New York. At issue here is not only the location of the fort but also the identity of the Iroquois nation that occupied it.

In the mid-nineteenth century, E. B. O'Callaghan, Francis Parkman, and the Abbé Laverdière believed that the fort stood on Lake Canandaigua, twenty-five miles south of Rochester, New York. This site was in the far west of Iroquoia, the homeland of the Seneca nation, "keepers of the western door" of the confederacy. On further examination, this location was inconsistent with

Champlain's account of his route. The distances were too great given the time available, and no positive evidence of any kind has been found to support it. Parkman abandoned this idea in later editions of his work.[1] Other historians have put in a claim for Lake Cayuga and argued that Champlain was attacking the Iroquois nation of the same name. But this also would have required an impossibly long march to the west, and no evidence supports it.

A third thesis came from antiquarians John S. Clark and Lambertus Ledyard, who argued that Champlain attacked an Oneida town on Nichols Pond, in Fenner, Madison County, New York, twenty miles southeast of Syracuse. On that site, amateur archaeologists found Indian artifacts that persuaded many scholars in the mid-twentieth century. As late as 1972, most students of Champlain believed this was the site, and that Champlain was fighting the Oneida Nation. Samuel Eliot Morison strongly supported this interpretation.[2]

Professional archaeologists William Ritchie and Peter Pratt excavated the site and found the remains of a precontact Oneida village there, but they concluded that it had been abandoned a century before Champlain's attack. They also discovered that the palisade on this site did not match Champlain's description of the fort he attacked, and Nichols Pond was for many centuries (and is today) more a swamp than a lake. We walked the terrain in the summer of 2007 and found that it does not match Champlain's account.[3]

Pratt, the leading expert on this question, concludes from many years of study that Champlain's fort stood at the south end of Lake Onondaga on a site presently occupied by the Carousel Shopping Mall in the city of Syracuse, New York. I visited the site in 2007 and observed that the location and the terrain matches descriptions in Champlain's accounts. The ground has been much disturbed by development, but many Indian artifacts were found there. That evidence supports the presence of a large Onondaga fort in Champlain's era. Tests of time and distance confirm that the location of this site fits the chronology of Champlain's narrative in those terms. Many ethnohistorians now agree. Other sites have also been suggested on the north and east sides of Lake Onondaga, but they are problematic in other ways, by dates of occupation, terrain, and watercourses.[4]

In light of present evidence, the most probable location of the fort was between two streams on the south end of Lake Onondaga. Champlain was attacking one of the principal towns of the Onondaga nation, who had been very active in raiding fur-trading routes to the north.

APPENDIX   L

CHAMPLAIN'S FAVORED FIREARM
The Arquebuse à Rouet

What European firearms did Champlain employ in his American campaigns? Many historians have written that Champlain used a matchlock, or a "matchlock musket," in his major American engagements, ca. 1609–15.[1] Close inquiry yields a different conclusion. Champlain's texts and engravings, inventories of weapons in Quebec, and expert studies of the weapons themselves make clear that Champlain was using an *arquebuse à rouet* in his major engagements. This was not a matchlock but a wheel-lock. It was developed in the sixteenth century to correct some of the matchlock's major problems.

In a matchlock, the smoldering end of a slow-burning cord was lowered into a pan of powder, and fired the charge. A wheel lock operated in a different way. The mechanism had a rough steel wheel which, when turned against a flint, sent a shower of sparks into priming powder, much like a modern cigarette lighter. Sometimes the wheel was a rough mineral that revolved against a steel platen, with the same result. This was the first self-igniting shoulder-fired weapon.

The advantages of a wheel lock were many. A slow-burning match cord was difficult to ignite and keep burning, especially in combat. Wet weather or even dampness and high humidity could render it useless. Once the cord was lighted, a matchlock was dangerous in another way, as the burning cord could ignite other powder in the vicinity. In battle, a matchlock with a lighted cord made surprise difficult, as its smoke and odor could alert others and betray the user's position.

The wheel lock, or *rouet*, may have been invented by Johann Kiefuss in Germany in 1517. It solved some those problems but created others in their place. It was a complex and fragile mechanism that required frequent maintenance and careful handling. It was also very costly—twice the cost of a matchlock—and could not be produced on a large scale.

To solve those problems, other inventions followed. In the late sixteenth century, gunsmiths developed a new lock called a snaphance. A flint was fixed on a spring-mounted arm. When the trigger released the arm, the spring drove it forward with a snap against a metal plate and sent sparks flying into a separate priming pan.

The principle of the snaphance in turn was simplified by the invention of the flintlock, which combined the metal platen and the priming pan cover in one piece. It was invented by one of Henri IV's expert gunsmiths, Marin le Bourgeois, who had his workshop in the basement of Louvre, and was in use by 1612. A flintlock was much cheaper to make, easier to maintain, and comparatively simple to use. In 1639–42, the average value of an arquebus à rouet was 80 livres; flintlock muskets were valued at 6 livres.

Champlain stated repeatedly that he and other Frenchmen with him used an arquebus, but what sort of arquebus? Russel Bouchard, an expert on firearms in New France, studied Champlain's engravings, and concluded that he used an arquebuse à rouet, with a wheel lock. There is no sign of a match in Champlain's engravings of his weapons, which look very much like a wheel lock. Inventories of weapons at Quebec refer explicitly to the presence of "harquebuses à rouet."

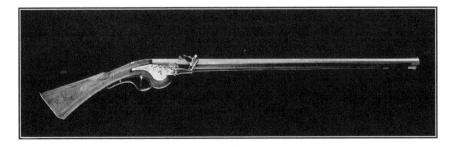

In 1609–10, Champlain fought the Mohawk with this arquebuse à rouet, a wheel lock weapon that did not require a burning match. It was also an arquebuse de chasse, a weapon light enough to be fired from the shoulder without a fork. A matchlock would have been very difficult to use at Lake Champlain, perhaps impossible.

*Historians mistakenly assume that Champlain used this weapon, a matchlock that required a burning
cord and was so heavy that it could not be presented without a fork to support its barrel.
This would not have worked well for him at Lake Champlain, given his tactics.*

So also do probate records for the colony. Patterns of use changed after 1615. By 1619, the new flintlock muskets were becoming the weapon of choice in New France. A Quebec inventory in that year listed four "harquebuses à rouet" and forty "mousquets avec leurs bandoliers." The proportion of muskets continued to increase in this period.[2]

Champlain's weapons were also distinctive in another way. Many early models of an arquebus were heavy weapons. Some were mounted on a cart and fired a ball of three ounces. Others were carried by individual soldiers, but could be fired only with a fork or crutch supporting the barrel. This early model was called an *arquebuse à croc*, after the crutch that was needed to steady the weapon. By Champlain's time, the wheel lock was combined with lighter weapons and shorter barrels, which could be fired from the shoulder without a fork. This lighter arquebus was developed for hunting and adopted by Champlain for use in America. It was between 32 and 52 inches long. It could be loaded with several one-ounce balls, which were lethal against large animals and men who were not wearing metal armor. These weapons were reported by contemporary writers to weigh in the range of 8.5 to 15 pounds, less than an arquebuse à croc. M. A. O. Paulin-Desormeaux, in his treatise on these weapons, called them the arquebuse de chasse, a hunting weapon. Champlain's chosen weapon combined the characteristics of an arquebuse à rouet and an arquebuse de chasse.[3]

The technology that produced the arquebuse à rouet also led to the development of wheel-lock pistols, which were larger than modern handguns but small enough to be hidden in clothing. They became an assassin's weapon, and were quickly put to that use. In 1584 a wheel-lock pistol was employed to kill William the Silent in the Netherlands and to murder Protestant leaders in France.[4]

In short, Champlain fought at Lake Champlain, and probably at the Rivière des Iroquois and the Onondaga Village, with an arquebuse à rouet that was fired by a wheel lock. It was light enough and short enough to be used as a shoulder weapon, but its barrel was forged with sufficient strength to allow triple or quadruple loading. This weapon did not require a slow match or a fork, which made it much easier to use in the field. The absence of a burning slow match helped Champlain to achieve surprise at Lake Champlain, and his independence of a fork permitted him to move more easily on the battlefield in all his engagements. The outcome of these battles, especially the first, might have been very different without the advantages of this highly developed, complex, and costly weapon.

APPENDIX   M

CHAMPLAIN'S SHIPS AND BOATS

In more than forty years afloat, Champlain worked with ships and boats in great variety. He described them very briefly, usually in terms of tonnage and ship-types. His language of description is not self-evident to modern readers and problematic even to experts in the field. Notes and translations on ship types in the Biggar edition of Champlain's works are frequently inaccurate, and even the sailor-historian Samuel Eliot Morison was mistaken on this subject.

Champlain's ships were the products of a revolution in maritime technology during the early modern era. In his time, ships could move people and goods with more speed and efficiency than overland transportation, which had improved little since the Romans. Until the nineteenth century, water was more "permeable" than land, as today air is more permeable than water.[1]

The improvement of ships made it so. They were complex artifacts, the most highly developed industrial products of their age. Champlain's ships were machines designed to convert the energy of winds and currents into motion. They were also homes for their crews, sometimes for months or years at a time. They were mobile warehouses for supplies, platforms for guns, tools of science, instruments of power, emblems of authority, and dynamic symbols of an expansive western culture that was spreading rapidly through the world. The characteristics of these ships created Champlain's opportunities, and also set his limits. To understand them, let us begin with his terms of description: first the problem of tonnage, and then the problem of ship-types and their properties.

TONNAGE for Champlain, was primarily a measure of volume, not weight. It was an estimate of a ship's capacity, in terms of the number of very large casks of wine or water, called tuns, that she could carry. This was an absurd way to measure a ship, but it was widely adopted because it was convenient to tax collectors and had long been used. In the ancient world, Cicero spoke of a "2,000 jar ship." In medieval Europe, the unit of measurement changed from pottery jars to wooden "tuns."[2]

By Champlain's time this method was widely used throughout Europe, but the standard definition of a tun varied from one country to another, and also from one province and seaport to the next. In England a measurement-tun had a standard capacity of 252 gallons, and when full of water weighed 2,240 pounds, the origin of the English "long ton," which became the basis of maritime measurement rather than the short ton of 2,000 pounds.[3]

In France, a standard *tonneau de mer* was equal to "four *barriques bordelaises*" of wine or water, which together equaled about 480 pots, and a pot was about .498164 of an English Exchequer gallon. French *tonneaux de mer* by that measure were approximately 239 English gallons, which made them about 5 per cent smaller than an English long tun.[4]

In Spain after 1590, the official unit of measure was the *tonel macho* or *tonel de Vizcaya*, which was "equivalent to the French sea ton (*tonneau de mer*) used in Bordeaux." It was 1.2 times larger than the earlier *tonelada* or *tonel de Andalusia*.[5]

In ships of identical dimensions, the slightly larger size of an English ton yielded an estimate of total tonnage that was smaller by about 5 percent than did a French tonneau de mer or a Spanish tonel macho. But these variations were smaller than the range of error in actual measurements.

This idea of tonnage was called "tons burden," because it measured not the ship itself, but the volume of what a ship could carry. All Champlain's tonnage estimates were tons burden. This measure of "tunnage" as units of volume should not be confused with other measures of weight that developed later, such as "displacement tons." This was the Archimedean idea that a ship's tonnage should be the weight of water displaced by the ship. Displacement tonnage became the standard measure for warships in the twentieth century. For the same vessel, tons displacement came to a much larger number than tons burden, which Champlain used.

By Champlain's era, most western states had settled on conventional ways of calculating tonnage by an equation from the length of keel, internal breadth, and interior depth of a vessel. In England, the number of tuns burden that a ship could take aboard was estimated by multiplying length of keel, times breadth, times depth, and dividing by 100.

$$Tb = \frac{KBD}{100}$$

The relationship between tonnage and dimensions such as length, breadth and depth was highly variable, mainly because of differences in design and construction from one ship-type to another. But rough estimates were made for specific classes of ships and boats, on the basis of actual measurement and prevailing patterns of proportion. Let us review them in order of size.

LARGE FULL-RIGGED SHIPS (350–1,000 tons burden) included vessels that Champlain and his contemporaries called *navires, naos, hourques, felibotes, flutes,* and *galleons.* One of his largest vessels was his uncle's *Saint-Julien.* By Champlain's reckoning and Spanish accounts, her size was estimated at 500 tons burden. He described her as a "grand navire," a great ship. In Spanish records she was variously called a *nao* or *felibote* or *hourque.*

A *grand navire* was a generic noun for any large ocean-going vessel, usually a merchantman, and was also called a *navire de commerce.* One French treatise defined a navire as "un vaisseau rond et de hauts bords tels que sont ceux de l'océan, a round ship with high sides, such as those of ocean-going vessels." These "round ships" were powered entirely by sail, unlike other "long ships" that used sails and oars.

A nao was a Portuguese term (*nef* or *nau* in French) for a full-rigged round ship, with large square-rigged sails on two or three masts, sometimes with a lateen-rigged mizzen and a smaller mast called a *bonaventure* abaft the mizzen.

A hourque (or hulk) denoted a large ship with a distinctive hull type, designed for maximum cargo volume, broad in the beam, with a rounded bow and stern, a comparatively flat bottom, high sides curved out and then in again, in a pattern that sailors called "tumble-home." They were constructed in northern Europe, on the model of large freight-carrying Dutch canal boats.

A felibote (Spanish) or flibot (French) or "flyboat," in one of its early meanings, was, as defined by R. M. Nance, "an enlarged, ship-rigged barge, contrived to carry as much merchandise as possible with the smallest possible crew." Hourques and felibotes as large as 600 tons were not uncommon in Champlain's era. They were reputed to be crudely constructed and slow sailors. Champlain described the *Saint-Julien* as "un fort navire et bon de voile, a staunch ship and a good sailor." If so, she was exceptional for her class. In service she was unsound and leaked so badly that several times she was close to foundering. From the proportions of other ships in her era, we might guess that her deck length was about 100–120 feet, and her beam about 36–40 feet.[6] Later, as we shall see, flyboats were given another and entirely different meaning: small fast-sailing vessels, often heavily armed for their size.

The *galleon* was another type of large ship that Champlain knew well. He sailed in company with these great ships during his visit to the Spanish empire, from 1598 to 1601. Their design evolved through time. In the mid-sixteenth century, galleons tended to be ships of moderate size, often about 200 tons, with high forecastles and sterncastles. They grew rapidly larger. The Spanish Armada in 1588 included three Portuguese galleons of 1,000 tons, and six Spanish galleons of 800 tons, which were among the largest ships of their time in the western world. By Champlain's time they had changed again. In the early seventeenth century, they tended to stabilize in the range of 400–600 tons burden, with a deck-length of about 100–120 feet (120–140 feet overall including her prow but not her bowsprit), a beam of about 30–35 feet, and a ratio of about 1:3.5 to 1:4 compared with merchantmen such as the *Saint-Julien*, which would have been closer to 1:3.

By Champlain's time the high forecastle had been cut down, and the sterncastle was higher

The Spanish galleon was a product of long development in the 16th and 17th centuries.
This was the type that Champlain would have known in 1599—smaller than the biggest galleons
in the Armada of 1588, but very capacious. The foremast was canted forward, and the mainmast
was raked aft. The high poop gave a platform for fighting.

This navire (from Champlain's 1612 map) was typical of vessels he used in North American trade—a midsized merchantman with square-rigged courses and topsails, a martingale beneath the bowsprit, and a lateen-rigged mizzen or bonaventure aft. They were not fast ships, but they were sturdy and seaworthy. Champlain never lost one.

than before. The foremast was canted forward, the main mast was nearly vertical, and a small mizzen was raked slightly to the stern. The big foremasts and mainmasts were surmounted by topmasts and sometimes topgallant masts. A spritsail on the bowsprit and lateen (or latine) on the mizzen were used for trim and balance, to make the helmsman's work easier. There were no jibs, but extra sails called bonnets could be rigged in light breezes.

These galleons carried battery of great guns on two or even three gun decks, and were crowded with men. Altogether they were highly refined ships, the product of long experience. Their officers in Spanish treasure fleets were highly skilled navigators. Champlain learned much from these ships, and from the men who sailed them.[7]

The *vaisseau des indes*, which the English called an East Indiaman, was another specialized type of large navire that developed in the early seventeenth century. This was a hybrid design: a large and very capacious merchantman designed for voyages as long as two or three years. She was built as stoutly as a man of war, heavily armed, and broad at the waterline to bear the weight of guns and cargo. Examples were two Norman ships owned by merchants of Rouen and Dieppe, which were sent to the East Indies and provisioned for two and a half years. One was *Le Montmorency*, 450 tons, 22 guns, and a crew of 126 men and boys. The other was *L'Espérance*, 400 tons, 26 guns, and a crew of 126. The officers and crew in these East Indiamen also sailed on American voyages in smaller ships. Robert Gravé, Claude du Boullay, Claude de Godet, and sieur des Maretz were all as familiar with the East Indies as with the waters of New France. But they used different ship-types when they moved from one theater to another. The vaisseau des Indes rarely appeared in North American waters, where voyages were shorter, capital was scarce, rivers and ports were shallow, security was less of a problem, and speed was more important than strength or endurance.

MID-SIZED SHIPS OF 100–350 tons were the result. These were Champlain's "navires de moyen calibre." Nearly all his Atlantic crossings were made in them. A great many mid-sized navires appear in his published *Voyages*. Most were in the range of 100–200 tons burden. Champlain's crossings in 1603 and 1604 were made in *La Bonne-Renommée*, which was variously rated at 100–120 tons, with a length of about 90 feet overall including her long prow. In 1605, he sailed in *Don-de-Dieu*, which was estimated at 120–160 tons, with an overall length of about 100 feet. His largest ship in the North Atlantic was the *Saint-Étienne*, 350 tons, which he used in 1615 and again in 1620.[8]

These mid-sized navires tended to be longer in relation to their tonnage than grand navires such as the *Saint-Julien*, a proportion that gave them more speed. With good weather and fair winds, they were capable of sustained runs of eight knots, which meant, for shorter periods, speeds of ten knots or a little more.[9]

They were rigged in various ways. A manuscript by Jacques de Vaulx, a pilot from Le Havre, described them in detail. Most appear to have been three-masted and ship-rigged, like their larger cousins. Their fore and main masts were square-rigged, sometimes with topsails and sometimes not, but rarely with the topgallants that were beginning to appear aboard larger vessels. They carried a spritsail on a yard under the high-angled bowsprit, and a lateen sail on a mizzen or a bonaventure. The spritsail was square-rigged, but could be close-hauled so tight as to be nearly fore-and-aft. Maritime paintings of the seventeenth century often show spritsails braced that way, at angles that seem improbable to modern sailors, but may well have been correct. The purpose of the spritsail and the mizzen lateen was to trim or balance the ship, more than to add driving power. When properly trimmed, the ship could ride more easily, and helmsmen had an easier time. In light winds the main sails could be rigged with extra sails called bonnets to port and starboard, "when chased by an enemy." This combination of hull-type and rigging plan created an extraordinarily safe and stable vessel—one reason why Champlain never lost a navire.[10]

Mid-sized navires were armed with a main battery of ten guns in *Don-de-Dieu* and *Saint-Pierre*, twelve in *Saint-Jean*, and sixteen "pieces of cannon in battery" in the navire *Marguerite* in 1629.[11] This armament was more than enough to keep corsairs at bay and drive off small predators. This type of mid-sized *navire* was the mainstay of maritime commerce in New France. Champlain often sailed alone in one of them across the North Atlantic in peacetime, but in time of war convoys were the rule.

Another type of mid-sized ship, called a *heus* in the records of Normandy, was built in shipyards near the mouth of the River Seine. They were rigged in a different fashion from what were called *navires communs*. They were two-masted vessels with the mainmast forward, a lugsail, and a large lateen. They tended to be on the small side, perhaps 60–80 tons. Some examples of them appear as embellishments on Champlain's maps. He called them *barques*, one of many applications of that generic term.[12]

The port records of Normandy also refer to a third type of mid-sized ship called the *roberge*, or *navire roberge* in primary sources of the period, or in later sources *rombarge*. These vessels were long and narrow, designed to be propelled by sails and oars. They had as many as three masts, and all were rigged with large lateen sails. They also had a single bank of oars, and were similar to sailing galleys such as the *barca longa* that had developed in the Mediterranean. Specifications for one *roberge* survive in Norman port records for 1576. She was a vessel of 80 tons. Her keel was 45 feet long, her overall length 92 feet, and she had a draft of 11 feet. Her ratio of length to breadth was probably 5:1.[13] The navire roberge did not appear in New France, but Norman port records show that merchants sent them on trading voyages to the Mediterranean and Africa.

SMALL OCEAN-GOING VESSELS, 20–100 tons, included two types that were important in New France and frequently mentioned in Champlain's writings. Most common were vessels that he called *barques*. They are not to be confused with European barques or American "barks" of the nineteenth and twentieth centuries, which were defined by their rig: usually two square-rigged masts, and a third that was fore- and-aft rigged. These later barques were as large as full-rigged ships, and were much used in the nineteenth century for reasons of economy and versatility.

In the early seventeenth century, French barques were another sort of vessel altogether. Randall Cotgrave's *Dictionarie of the French and English Tongues* (1611) offered a translation of a barque as "little ship, great boat." Champlain wrote frequently of barques in both senses. Sometimes he had in mind a little ship of 30–100 tons. In other passages he was describing a great boat of 6–20 tons that could be carried aboard a ship.

Ocean-going barques tended to be broad of beam in proportion to their length—they were described as "blunt" and "stubby." One example, built in 1590, was a barque of 35 tons burden, with a keel length of 35 feet, a breadth of 14 feet, and a hold 6 feet deep. She had a standard three-masted rig, with square courses, topsails, a mizzen sail (perhaps lateen), and bonnets for square sails. They were the first ships to be built in New France and the British colonies.[14]

Ocean-going barques as small as 30 tons were often three-masted, with fore and main masts square-rigged with courses and topsails, a lateen on the mizzen, and bonnets for the square sails. One example appears at anchor in Champlain's chart of Beauport (now Gloucester, Massachusetts). She was three-masted, with a martingale below a high bowsprit, single square-rigged sails on the fore and main, and a lateen on a small mizzen. A very similar English vessel was the barque *Kathryn*, 35 tons burden, with two decks, a raised forecastle and a raised poop. Other French barques were two-masted and rigged in many ways. Many carried a *bourcet*, or lugsail, on the foremast (see below for an explanation), or two lugsails on the fore- and mainmasts as their only rig.[15]

The port records of Normandy show that barques as small as 20 tons burden were sent on long ocean voyages to North America, and even to the East Indies. On long voyages they sailed in the company of larger vessels. Many were lost at sea or wrecked on foreign shores. It was said that the outer banks of Sable Island on the Grand Bank were littered with the bones of French barques.

But Champlain never lost a barque. The only exception was an occasion when he was sailing as a passenger in a barque with Pont-Gravé as captain and Champdoré as master. This was a barque of 17 of 18 tons. Pont-Gravé suffered a "mal de coeur," probably a heart attack. He lay below in his berth, refused to relinquish command, and ordered Champdoré to get underway in wind, rain, and fog. It was a crazy thing to do, but Champdoré obeyed. He ordered the "anchor raised and lugsail spread to the wind," and tried desperately to get clear of a lee shore. The vessel was caught by the wind and tidal currents, and was driven onto the rocks in a heavy surf. Champlain rushed on deck, took command, and ordered the mainsail to be set, in hope of driving the doomed barque higher on the rocks so that the crew could get ashore. It was a desperate act, but it worked. The vessel was smashed but every soul on board survived, and most of her supplies were saved. Indians came in their canoes, and took the crew and cargo back to port. Champlain's account of this misadventure reveals much about the barque, her rig, and her sailing properties.[16]

A second type of small ocean-going vessel in New France was called a *patache* by Champlain. English seamen called them pinnaces. Champlain's pataches and his barques had a similar range of tonnage. He described "pataches of forty tons and six cannon each," and others as small as seventeen or eighteen tons.[17] Pataches were designed for purposes different from barques, and the two vessels had distinct hull-types. Barques were meant to be small freighters or transports, and were built to carry goods and people in an efficient way. Pataches were built for exploration, discovery, and reconnaissance. In 1628, one French maritime treatise defined a patache as "a small warship designed for the surveillance of coasts."[18] "They were built for speed, constructed man-of-war fashion, and strongly armed in proportion to their size. In France and Spain they were also used as dis-

The patache was a purpose-built vessel for reconnaissance, surveys, and exploration. She was a small man-o-war, lean and heavily sparred, ideal for surveys and exploration, designed for sailing into harm's way, and rapidly out again. An example appears in Champlain's map of Sainte-Croix Island.

patch boats, which Champlain called a *patache d'avis*. Spanish treasure fleets also employed them as tenders to larger vessels. Champlain wrote that every galleon had its patache.

In 1604, Champlain was given a patache for his exploration of the Maine coast. He described her as a small keel-built ship with a draft of five feet, and a burthen of seventeen or eighteen tons. Her length was probably about thirty-five or forty feet, her beam eight or nine feet. She was fully decked over and designed for voyages in dangerous seas—unlike the open-hulled shallops that Champlain used in more protected waters.

Champlain's chart of Sainte-Croix Island includes a drawing of a lean mid-sized vessel that may have been his patache. She was built man-of-war fashion with a sharp prow, long lines that held the promise of speed, and a raised poop with a battery of small swivel-mounted brass falconets. Her mastheads were topped by large crow's nests.[19]

Champlain mentioned a third type of ocean-going vessel, which he called a *flibot*, a flyboat. He described one example as "nearly a hundred tons, with ten cannon" and a crew of about 75 men," and distinguished her from a "pataches of forty tons and six cannon." But this was an English vessel, more nearly the size of a navire."[20]

SMALL COASTAL AND RIVER SAILING CRAFT were vital to the life of New France. Here again Champlain used two principal types of vessels: the *moyenne* (middling) *barque* and the *chaloupe* or shallop. They were of similar size, ranging from 2–3 tons to as many 12–16 tons burden. Many were 6–8 tons. Champlain described one example as a small *barque du port* of 5–8 tons, and another as a barque moyenne of 10–13 or thirteen tons. Barques were decked over, with a few dry berthing spaces below in a weathertight hold. Shallops were open-hulled, and offered no protection against wind or weather.

Barques were the workhorses of New France. Normally, navires of 100–200 tons anchored at Tadoussac, and transferred their cargo to barques, which carried them up the river. Champlain used these vessels to haul freight cargo on the St. Lawrence River and the coast of Acadia, and to move trade goods upriver to the head of navigation. He also employed barques to carry prefabricated houses to Port-Royal, cattle to the farm at Cap Tourmente, building supplies to Trois-Rivières, and trade goods to Montreal.[21]

Champlain's open chaloupes, or shallops, were small enough to be built in sections or carried across the Atlantic *en fagot*, in bundles of pieces. They had one or two masts, each with a single sail. Rails were fitted with hard locust thole pins for oars or sweeps, which were used frequently on the river. They were shallow boats without a deep keel, often rigged with leeboards, and were at risk of capsizing in a sudden squall. One such accident on the St. Lawrence River took the life of Champlain's interpreter Jean Nicollet.

Shallops were constructed with different hull-types. One common form was the Biscayan shallop, or the Basque shallop. It was a sharp-built, doubled-ended craft and was used as a whaleboat by Basques. A plan of such a *chaloupe biscayenne* is in the collection of the Fine Arts Museums of San Francisco.[22] Accounts survive of Biscay shallops on the coast of New France, some of them owned by Indians, who probably acquired them from Basque whalers.

Other shallops were more bowl-shaped with rounded bows, molded sides and tumblehome. Several examples appear as illustrations in Champlain's maps and charts. They were rigged in various ways: single-masted or double-masted with square sails, or sometimes gaff-rigged, or carrying a spritsail, or with something like what was called a leg-o-mutton rig on Chesapeake Bay log canoes in the author's youth.[23]

VERY SMALL CRAFT: ESQUIFFES AND CANOTS (SKIFFS AND CANOES) Champlain also worked with very small boats in rivers and harbors. He made frequent use of *esquiffes*, translated through this book as skiffs. A skiff was commonly defined as a boat carried by a ship. Champlain often carried them aboard his navires and barques. In one scene on the St. Lawrence River near Montreal, he described his skiff as "a very small light boat," but big enough to hold four matelots bending over their oars, a fifth at the tiller, and two officers aboard.[24] He used skiffs to survey harbors, which might have required half a dozen hands—to work the boat, swing the lead line, and take cross-bearings that were the key to the accuracy of his charts, and note the location of each sounding on a log and draft-chart. From those descriptions Champlain's skiff was more like a ship's jolly boat or a captain's gig or an admiral's barge, clinker-built with overlapping strakes, rounded bows and molded sides, rather than a painter's skiff today, which is often a very small flat-bottomed slab-sided rowboat that would be overcrowded with three people aboard.

Larger vessels were called *bateaux* or *batteaux*. They loomed large in the history of rivers and lakes throughout North America. They tended to be flat open boats, powered by oars, sweeps, and sails, and were used for many purposes, but Champlain rarely mentioned them.

By Champlain's time, Basque whalers in New France had invented the beautiful and very light whaleboat, double-ended with incredibly thin strakes, which oarsmen could send skimming across the water. They were not invented by Nantucket Yankees. French and Spanish Basques developed them from Biscayan shallops, called *chalupas* in Basque. They were framed from naturally curved oak and planked with very thin oak strakes, clinker-built above the waterline and carvel-built below to reduce drag and increase speed. They could carry a crew of seven or eight. These chalupas were in use on the coast of Labrador and the lower St. Lawrence River by 1600. Maritime archaeologists from Red Bay, Labrador have recovered early examples, remarkably intact.[25]

Fishermen on the Grand Bank also developed their distinctive fishing boats, which were much bigger than the later dories, designed for a crew of half a dozen men, each with two compartments or working spaces called a *rum*, one for the man and one for his catch. The boats were big enough to hold 500 or 600 large cod or halibut. They were heavy, sturdy keel-boats with floor-timbers called *varengues* that were three inches thick, and high sides crowned by a gunwale two inches square. They were built for an era of vast abundance in the codfisheries, and after Champlain's era were replaced by smaller dories.[26]

SMALL CRAFT of American Indians fascinated Champlain. He used them frequently, studied their construction, and described their characteristics in his *Voyages*. They existed in great variety, and might be divided into three types: *canaux* or canoes, *pirogues* or dugouts, and skin boats of various kinds.

Birchbark canoes were the boat of choice in the St. Lawrence Valley. Champlain delighted in them. He described them as "eight or nine yards long, about a yard or a yard and a half wide in the middle, tapering off towards the two ends. They are very liable to upset if one does not know how to manage them, and are made of birch-bark, strengthened inside by small ribs of white cedar very neatly arranged, and are so light that one man can easily carry one. Each of them can carry the weight of a hogshead (400–700 quarts)." [27] On one trip Champlain traveled with a servant, an interpreter, and ten Indians in two canoes. [28] The design of birchbark canoes varied from one Indian nation to another. They were built with astonishing speed, and in a variety of sizes. In general they were light, nimble, stable in the hands of a skilled paddler, and very fast. [29]

Elmbark canoes were used to the south of the St. Lawrence River by woodland Indians who lacked a large supply of canoe birch. The Iroquois made their boats out of elm, often from the bark of a single tree. They were big and strong, but slow and clumsy. The differences between elmbark and birchbark canoes had an impact on the battle between the Mohawk and Champlain's Indian allies at Lake Champlain. An example of an Iroquoian elm boat survives today at the Peabody-Essex Museum in Salem, adorned with diagonal red stripes, in a motif that was repeated on paddles and fishing equipment. [30]

Pirogues or dugouts were used by Indian nations to the south, from Cape Ann in Massachusetts to Florida. Champlain took a professional interest in these small craft. He observed that Indians south of Cape Ann used pirogues made from solid tree trunks by "burning and scraping with stones, which they use in place of knives." Champlain tried his hand at steering them and found that, like birchbark canoes, they were also "very liable to upset unless one is very skilled." [31] Pirogues were ancient watercraft, widely used throughout the world. Some were surprisingly light and maneuverable, much more so than modern versions. A very early example was found by archaeologists, perfectly preserved in an old bog within the city of Paris. It is thought to be more than 6,000 years old, and can be seen in the basement of the Musée Carnavalet in Paris. It is incredibly light, and beautifully carved, with long and very lean lines and would have been very fast in the water.

Kayaks were widely used by Indians north of the St. Lawrence Valley. Early designs in the east were remarkably similar to modern kayaks in appearance, construction, and use. [32]

Coracles were observed by Champlain's interpreters who went west into the interior of North America. They were made of moose hides or buffalo skins sewn together and secured over a frame of saplings. Some had the proportions of a canoe. On the prairies, they were rounded and called bull boats. Bull boats were rarely more than five feet in diameter, mostly too small to carry a person. They were used by swimmers to ferry goods across a pond or river. [33]

APPENDIX N

CHAMPLAIN'S WEIGHTS AND MEASURES

Champlain and his contemporaries frequently used many different units of measurement. They derived from a customary system of weights and measures, and the customs were complex. Some units referred to objects that were variable in themselves: a grain of barley, or a king's foot. Marcel Trudel found one measure of length that was "the height of a white horse's belly."[1] Many units varied from one jurisdiction to another and from one commodity to the next. Champlain tended to record units as they were given to him by others. The result in New France was a gathering of weights and measures from many sources: Indian, English, Spanish, and Dutch, as well as French.

Indian Units of Distance and Time

Champlain frequently recorded Indian units of measurement, which referred to relations in the natural world. Champlain followed the Indians when he reckoned long distances over water in days of travel by canoe. Intermediate distances on land were reckoned in days of travel by foot. Long periods of time were counted in numbers of moons; and directions were recorded in reference to the rising or setting sun.

Measures of Length: French and English

Most of Champlain's European measures of length derived from the customs of the kingdom of France, where they were specified by "the royal measure":

> *Graine d'orge*, a grain of barley, was equal to one-half of a *ligne*, or line.
>
> *Ligne* (line) was one-twelfth of a *pouce*.
>
> *Pouce*, was literally a big toe in the seventeenth century, similar to an English inch but slightly larger; by the king's measure, the king's big toe was standardized at 1.06575 English inches.
>
> *Pied du roi*, the royal foot, was twelve pouces, a little larger than an English foot, just as a *pouce* was larger than an inch: 1.06575 English feet, or 12.789 English inches.
>
> *Pas*, or pace, was the length of a footstep, three *pieds du roi* in most parts of New France but 3.5 *pieds du roi* in Martinique.
>
> *Aune* (ell) equaled 3 *pieds du roi* and 8 *pouces*.
>
> *Toise* was six *pieds du roi*, or 6.3945 English feet, or 1.949 meters. This was the mason's *toise*. The carpenter's *toise* was 5.5 *pieds du roi*.
>
> *Perche* was three *toises*, 18 *pieds du roi*, or 19.1835 English feet, or 5.847 meters, or 1.162 English rods. This was the *perche de Paris*. A *perche royale et forestière* was 22 *pieds du roi*. A *perche moyenne* was 20 *pieds du roi*.
>
> *Arpent*, was 10 perches, or 58.47 meters, variously reckoned at 191.8 or 192 English feet. This was the linear *arpent*, as distinct from the *arpent superficiel*, a measure of area, below.

Measures of Distance

Lieues, or leagues, were Champlain's most common measure of distance, and also the most variable.

Nautical *lieues* were 3 nautical miles, or three minutes of latitude, or 18,228 English feet, or 3.452 English statute miles. It is the origin of the "three-mile limit." An English statute mile is 5,280 English feet; a nautical mile is 6,076.11549 English feet or 1,852 meters, or exactly 1 minute, which is 1/60 of a degree of latitude. Each degree of latitude is equal to 60 nautical miles, or twenty nautical leagues.

Spanish *lieues* or leagues were 3.428 nautical miles. A degree of latitude was roughly equal to 17.5 Spanish leagues.[2] This was Champlain's conventional measure of maritime distances.

Common *lieues* or *leagues* in French usage were of two types. A common land league was 84 linear *arpents*, or 16,128 English feet, or 3.05 English statute miles, or 2.654 English nautical miles. C. E. Heidenreich makes it 2.43 statute miles.[3]

Lieue de poste was 2.13 statute miles, commonly used by Champlain for overland distances. His inland leagues averaged 2.1 statute miles.

Petites lieues were 2.03 statute miles.

In practice, leagues tended to be elastic in Champlain's usage. Scholars have attempted to measure their actual length in particular instances, with various results. W. F. Ganong reckoned Champlain's leagues at "about two and a half of our geographical miles." S. E. Morison measured Champlain's leagues on his charts and found that they varied by about 10 percent, mostly between 2.2 and 2.7 nautical miles.[4]

Heidenreich found that Champlain's leagues differed on land and water. He observed that Champlain's maps contain bar scales reckoning 17.5 leagues as equal to one degree of latitude. The only league that matches this measure is the Spanish league. Heidenreich found that most of Champlain's estimates of distance in open water were consistent with this number, about 3.5 statute miles. But on land and interior waterways Champlain's leagues were approximately 2.1–2.3 English miles per league in 62 measurements compiled by Heidenreich. In overland journeys he also used the postal league. In coastal waters, Champlain's leagues were highly variable.[5] Heidenreich's estimates are based on the largest samples.

Measures of Area

pouce carré, comparable to a square inch.

pied carré, equals 144 *pouces carrés*, comparable to a square foot.

toise carrée, equals 36 *pieds carrés*.

perche carrée, equals 9 *toises carrées*.

arpent, equals 100 *perches carrées*, or 5/6 of an English acre.

lieue carrée equals 7,056 *arpents*.

By comparison:

> An English acre equals 120 *perches carreés*. *Arpents* and acres are not the same. A hectare equals 2.47 English acres.

Measures of Depth

> *Brasse* was Champlain's most common way of reckoning depth. It was similar to an English fathom, but not the same. To be precise, a French *brasse* was six pieds du roi, or 1.06575 English fathoms, which equaled six English feet. Champlain's *brasse* was 6.6 percent larger than an English fathom.

Measures of Weight

> *once*, comparable to an English ounce, avoirdupois.

> *livre* equals 16 *onces*, comparable to an English pound.

> *quintal* equals 100 livres, comparable to an English hundredweight.

> *short ton* equals 2,000 livres; not to be confused with nautical tonnage in its various meanings, for which see Appendix M, Champlain's ships and small craft.

Measures of Wet Volume

> *roquille* equals an English gill, 4 ounces liquid measure, or one half of an English cup.

> *demiard* equals two roquilles or half a chopine, 8 ounces.

> *chopine*, about the same as an English pint, equals two demiards or half a French *pinte*.

> *pinte*, about the same as an English quart, equals two chopines, or half a pot.

> *pot*, a basic unit, 2.2648 litres, or approximately half (49.8164%) of an English exchequer gallon of 1601.

> *barrique*, usually 110 pots, but sometimes 120 *pots*, or even as many as 180 pots.

> *pipe*, 220 pots.

> *tonneau de Bordeaux* (*tonneaux de mer*), 440 pots, or two pipes, or four barriques.

> *tonneau de vin*, about 440 pots.

French merchants used many specialized cask-measures, for particular purposes:

> *velte*, 4 pots.

> *ancre,* 32 pots, was a cask used only for brandy, 7.45 or 7.61 litres.

> *baril* or *barril*, variously given as 35 to 40 pots, or 55 pots.

> *quart* about 80 pots, a *quart français* has nothing to do with an English quart.

poinçon, 93 pots, similar to an English puncheon.

muid, about 140 pots, similar to an English hogshead.

tonneau d'Orléans, about 280 pots.

Measures of Dry Volume

litron half a quart.

quart equals to 2 litrons.

boisseau (bushel) equals 4 quarts.

minot equals three boisseaux.

setier equals 4 minots, or 12 boisseaux.

muid equals 12 setiers.

pipe equals 1.5 muids.

These measures varied from one commodity to another. They tended to be gross weight. The net weight equaled the gross weight minus the *tare* which was the weight of the container.

Measures of Bulk in Commercial Transactions

These units varied by commodity.

Beaver pelts were measured by the *ballot* or bale, which normally weighed 120 livres.

Bois de brûler, or firewood was reckoned by the *corde*, which was a stack of wood, four feet wide, four feet deep and four feet high and eight feet long, similar to the English cord, but reckoned in French pieds du roi, which made a *corde française*, 6.575 percent larger in each of its three linear dimensions; thus 21.05034 percent larger in cubic volume than an English cord.

Bacon was sold in *ancres du lard*, of 70 livres and up.

Cereals: a minot of grain could be 37 litres or 1.05 bushels.

Salt (*sel*) was sold by the *barrique de sel*, which was equal to 6 minots.

Peas (*pois*) and small beans (but not *fèves*) were sold by the *poinçon de pois*, equal to 9 minots.

Flour (*farine*) was sold in *barils de farine*, 180 livres and up.

Sugar (*sucre*) was sold in *barriques de sucre*, up to 1000 livres.

Cod and other fish were sold *à la poignée*, or by the handful. Larger quantities were sold *au cent*, but this "hundred of cod" was 132 codfish; a *quarteron* of that unit was 33 cod.

CHAMPLAIN'S MONEY

Monetary systems in Champlain's era were in some ways more complex than those of our own time. Most national economies had two sets of monetary units: money of account, and money of exchange. Money of account did not commonly exist in the form of hard coin. In early modern England, for example, pounds sterling did not exist as actual coins. They were accounting terms, used to reckon values in sterling accounts. English money of exchange included actual golden guineas, silver shillings, copper pennies and other coins. In our own time, ironically, pounds sterling (20 shillings) are now a money of exchange, and guineas (21 shillings) have become a pretentious money of account, used for calculating the cost of Rolls Royce automobiles, tickets to Oxford Commemoration Balls, and bills from Harley Street physicians. They were actually paid in pounds.[1]

The French monetary system was similar, but not the same. In 1602, French money of account was fixed thus:

> Twelve *deniers* equaled one *sou*.
> Twenty *sous* equaled one *livre tournois*.
> Three *livres tournois* (comparable to English pounds) equalled one *écu*.

Deniers were roughly comparable to English pennies (twelve to a shilling); sous to English shillings (twenty to a pound), and livres to English pounds, and écus to three English pounds. The value of these monetary units varied by region. For example, one *livre parisis* equaled twenty-five sous. But *livres tournois* (twenty sous) were increasingly standard in Champlain's world. French money of exchange (hard coins that actually circulated) included billon, copper, silver, and later gold, coins. Billon was a base alloy of tin, copper, and silver, meant to resemble silver. Denominations of hard coin circulating in New France included:

billon	*douzain* = 12 deniers	
copper	*double tournois* = 2 deniers (4 deniers in New France)	
	liard = 3 deniers	
	demi-sou = 6 deniers	
	sou = 12 deniers	
	douzain = 12 deniers (revalued to 15 in 1640)	
	deux sols = 24 deniers	
silver	*mousquetaire* = 20 deniers	
	quatre sols = 32 deniers	
	six sols = 48 deniers, 1/20 écu	
	douze sols = 96 deniers; 1/10 écu	
	vingt-quatre sols = 192 deniers; 1/5 écu	

petit écu or half *écu blanc* = 1/2 crown, 2.5 shillings

écu or *trois livres* = 1 crown, 5 shillings

gold   *demi-Louis d'or* = approximately 3 écus

Louis d'or = a little more than 6 écus

The coins most commonly found at archaeological sites in Quebec have been the copper double tournois, the copper douzain, the billon douzain, the copper liard, and the silver quatre sols.

What were these monetary units worth in the values of our own time? This question is impossible to answer in any meaningful way by a single estimate, because the value of many commodities changed in different ways, and monetary units have fluctuated in relation to one another. Market-basket price-indicator series have been constructed with limited success. A better answer might be given in terms of wages. On the voyage that founded Quebec in 1608, "Gentlemen" were paid 500 livres tournois for two years. Skilled locksmiths received 120 livres tournois for two years' service. Gardener Martin Beguin was paid 90 livres tournois for the same two-year period, and laborers Clément Morel and Guillaume Morel got 75 livres tournois. All these salaries were for two years' service in addition to food and lodging.[2]

CHAMPLAIN'S CALENDARS

During Champlain's lifetime two different calendars were in active use. Champlain used the newer and more accurate Gregorian calendar, which was adopted by Catholic France in 1582 in place of the older Julian calendar. Protestant countries continued to use the Julian calendar, mainly because the newer one was associated with the Roman Catholic Church. Dutch Calvinists did not shift until 1700. England and its American colonies continued to use the Julian calendar until 1752.[1]

In Champlain's era, Julian dates were ten days behind, and the new year began on March 25. The Gregorian calendar corrected that accumulated error, and began the year on January 1. Gregorian dates were marked as New Style (N.S.) in England and *stille nouveau* (S.N.) in French. Julian dates were identified as Old Style (O.S.) or *stille vieux* (S.V.).

These different usages caused discrepancies in the dating of documents during Champlain's lifetime. French Catholic writers used the Gregorian calendar; English writers employed the Julian calendar. Documents that passed across these national and religious lines were double-dated. An example is David Kirke's letter to Champlain demanding the surrender of Quebec. Kirke's dateline was "18. Juillet 1628. Stille vieux, ce 8. de Juillet stille nouveau." He had it backward.[2]

A further complication arose from the old French custom of numbering the months by their place in the old Julian calendar, which began the year in March. The last four months of the year were referred to by the numbers in their original Latin: September was 7bre; October became 8bre; November was 9bre; and December was Xbre. To add another element of complexity, this Julian custom continued in France and New France long after the adoption of the Gregorian calendar, which shifted the first month from March to January and made September the 9th month, October the 10th month, November the 11th month, and December the 12th month. The names of the months remained the same and still do, a relic of the Julian calendar in our own time.

Customary units of time coexisted with these calendars in New France. In Quebec a short unit of time was called the *pipe*, which was the time it took to smoke a pipe full of tobacco. It also became a measure of distance. The eminent historian Marcel Trudel remembers hearing of a village that it was "three pipes away."

NOTES

INTRODUCTION

1. Raymonde Litalien, "Historiography of Samuel Champlain," in Litalien and Denis Vaugeois, eds., *Champlain: The Birth of French America* (Montreal, 2004), 12. This volume is an English translation of Raymonde Litalien and Denis Vaugeois, eds., *Champlain: la naissance de l'Amérique française* (Sillery, Québec, 2004).

2. Samuel de Champlain, *Les Voyages faits au Grand Fleuve Sainct Laurens par le sieur de Champlain Capitaine ordinaire pour le Roy en al marine, depuis, l'année 1608 iusques en 1612* (Paris, 1613): translated and republished in Henry Percival Biggar, ed., *The Works of Samuel de Champlain, 6* vols. and a portfolio of maps and drawings (CWB) (Toronto, 1922–36, reprinted 1971) 2: 1–236; the self-portrait appears on plate V, "Deffaite des Yroquois au Lac de Champlain," CWB 2:100–01.

3. The naked warriors are an inaccuracy. Champlain tells us in the accompanying text that the Indians wore hardwood armor tied together with hemp or cotton. Probably this error was introduced by engraver who might have followed conventional images of American Indians by Theodor de Bry and other European artists. Several scholars have written that the trees which appear to be palms may be an error of the same sort. But historians at Fort Ticonderoga believe that they may have been an attempt to represent clumps of willow trees, which still stand at that place on the shore of Lake Champlain.

4. E. Ewart Oakeshott, *The Sword in the Age of Chivalry* (New York, 1964); Harold Peterson, *Arms and Armor in Colonial America, 1526–1783* (New York, 1956).

5. Stephen Bull, *An Historical Guide to Armes and Armour* (New York, 1991); Charles ffoulkes, *The Armourer and his Craft* (London, 1912), a great classic.

6. The white panache that Henri IV wore at the head of his army appears in an engraving of his entry into Paris, March 1594, in the Bibliothèque nationale de France. His elaborately curled court panache is in a formal portrait, "Henri IV, école française, ca. 1595," Château de Versailles. For an essay on the word itself see Alain Rey et al., eds., *Dictionnaire historique de la langue française* 3 vols. (Paris, 2006) 2: 2542–43; s.v. "panache."

7. On the arquebus, a leading work is M. A. O. Paulin-Desormeaux, *Nouveau manuel complet de l'armurier du fourbisseur et de l'arquebusier,* nouvelle édition, 2 vols. (Paris, 1852, rpt. Paris, 1977) 1:11–14; copy in the author's collection. On Champlain's use of the *arquebuse à rouet* see Russel Bouchard, *Les armes à feu en Nouvelle France* (Sillery, Québec, 1999), 102-06. Champlain appears to be carrying a light arquebus that Paulin-Desormeaux calls a *fusil de chasse*, a hunting weapon; ibid., 1:184-93; for a more extended discussion, see below, chapter 12, and Appendix L.

8. CWB 2: 1-236; The self-portrait appears on plate V, "Deffaite des Yroquois au Lac de Champlain," 101.

9. Ibid.

10. François-Marc Gagnon, "Champlain: Painter?" in Litalien and Vaugeois, eds. *Champlain*, 302–11.

11. For discussion, see "Memories of Champlain," below, and Appendix F.

12. Morris Bishop, *Champlain: The Life of Fortitude* (New York, 1948), 7.

13. Samuel Eliot Morison, *Samuel de Champlain; Father of New France* (New York, 1972), 22.

14. Heather Hudak, *Samuel de Champlain* (Discovering Canada) (Calgary, 2005), cover.

15. [Michael Hollingsworth], "The History of the Village of the Small Huts (n.p., 1985), 24; www.videocas/com/pdfs/nfchamplain.

16. Samuel Eliot Morison, *Samuel de Champlain, Father of New France* (New York, 1972), xiii.

17. C. E. Heidenreich, *Explorations and Mapping of Samuel de Champlain* (Toronto, 1976).

18. Allan Forbes and Paul Cadman, *France and New England*, 3 vols. (Boston, 1925–29).

19. For a positive judgment of Champlain, see Carl O. Sauer, *Seventeenth Century America* (Berkeley: Turtle Island Foundation, 1980); for a more negative interpretation, see Bruce Trigger, *The Children of Aataentsic: A History of the Huron People to 1660* (Montreal, 1976, 1987); and Trigger, *Natives and Newcomers: Canada's "Heroic Age" Reconsidered* (Montreal, Kingston, 1985). Sauer was a geographer at Berkeley; Trigger was for many years an anthropologist and archaeologist at McGill University.

20. Chandra Mukarjee, "Champlain as Gardener," unpublished lecture, College of the Atlantic, 2005.

21. For the historiography of Champlain see "Memories of Champlain," below.

22. Peter E. Pope, *The Many Landfalls of John Cabot* (Toronto, 1997), 165, 225n.

23. W. J. Eccles, "Samuel de Champlain," *American National Biography* (New York, 1999), s.v., "Champlain."

24. Raymonde Litalien and Denis Vaugeois, eds., *Champlain: la naissance de l'Amérique française* (Sillery, Québec, 2004); it was followed by an English translation as *Champlain: The Birth of French America* (Montreal, 2004); Mickaël Augeron and Dominique Guillemet, *Champlain, ou les portes du nouveau monde: cinq siècles d'échanges entre le Centre-Ouest français et l'Amérique du Nord, XVIe–XXe siècles* (Geste, 2004); Annie Blondel-Loisel and Raymonde Litalien, in collaboration with Jean Paul Barbiche and Claude Briot, *De la Seine au Saint Laurent avec Champlain* (Paris, 2005); Bertrand Guillet and Louise Pothier, eds., *France/Nouvelle France: naissance d'un peuple français en Amérique* (Montreal and Paris, 2005); James Kelly and Barbara Clarke Smith eds., *Jamestown-Quebec-Santa Fe; Three North American Beginnings* (Washington and New York, 2007).

25. Robert le Blant and René Baudry, *Nouveaux documents sur Champlain et son époque*, vol. 1 (1560–1662) (Ottawa, 1967), xii, xxiv.

26. Indian is the term of choice throughout this book. In meetings at the Newberry Library with Indian leaders from many parts of the United States, I asked them what they wished to be called. Invariably they wanted to be known by the name of their own nation. I asked what word we should use for all of them together. They said that Indian was as good as any other. They used it with pride. After much experiment with other clumsy terms, Indian sounds better and better. See also Appendix I below.

1. A CHILD OF BROUAGE

1. Samuel Champlain, *Des Savvages, ov, Voyage de Samvel Champlain, De Brouage, fait en la France nouvelle, l'an mil six cents trois* (Paris, 1603); in CWB 1:83; an excellent modern edi-

tion, *Des Sauvages* by Alain Beaulieu and Réal Ouellet, was published in Montreal in 1993 and is very helpful for its learned commentary.

2. Lancelot Voisin, sieur de la Popelinière, *L'histoire de France enrichie des plus notables occur-rances*, 2 vols. (La Rochelle, 1581); as quoted in Eliane Vigé and Jimmy Vigé, *Brouage, ville d'histoire et place forte* (Saint-Jean-d'Angély, 1989), 12; and Nathalie Fiquet, "Brouage in the Time of Champlain: A New Town Open to the World," in Raymonde Litalien and Denis Vaugeois, eds., *Champlain: The Birth of French America* (Montreal, 2004), 39.

3. The term derived from *broue*, a word in the *langue saintongeaise* related to the French *boue*, a muddy mix of water and clay. See "Le grand lexique du patois charentais," *Xaintonge* hors serie 1 (2003) 48, s.v. "broue: boue"; and Alain Rey et al., *Le Grand Robert de la langue fran-çaise*, nouvelle édition augmentée, 6 vols. (Paris, 2001) 1:1576, s.v. "boue"; for the etymol-ogy of *brouage* in the *langue d'oïl*, see Nicolas Chéreau, *Visite historique de Brouage* (La Mothe-Achard, 2003), 1.

4. Eliane Vigé and Jimmy Vigé, *Brouage: capitale du sel et patrie de Champlain* (Bordessoules, 1990); Marcel Delafosse and Claude Laveau, *Le commerce du sel de Brouage aux XVIIe et XVIIIe siècles: Cahiers des Annales* 17 (Paris, 1960) centers on the economic history of salt in the early modern era; Micheline Huvet-Martinet, *L'aventure du sel* (Rennes, 1995) is by an expert on the fiscal history of salt; J. F. Bergier, *Une histoire du sel* (Paris, 1982) is strong on iconography.

5. On the colors of salt, see Marc Séguin, *Histoire de l'Aunis et de la Saintonge* (Ligugé, 2005), 108.

6. Examples include the Gap Portolano in the Archives of the Département des Hautes-Alpes, and the Dijon Portolano in the Bibliothèque municipale de Dijon. Both are of doubtful date; see Tony Campbell, "Census of Pre-Sixteenth-Century Portolan Charts," *Imago Mundi* 38 (1986), 67–94. See also Nathalie Fiquet and François-Yves Le Blanc, *Brouage, ville royale, et les villages du golfe de Saintonge* (Chauray-Niort, 1997), 25; and Nathalie Fiquet, "Brouage in the Time of Champlain; A New Town Open to the World," in Litalien and Vaugeois, eds., *Champlain*, 35, 33–42.

7. Nathalie Fiquet, "Brouage in the Time of Champlain," 33–42; Séguin, *Aunis et Saintonge*, 92–96.

8. Delafosse and Laveau, *Le commerce du sel de Brouage*, 13–26; Michael Mollat du Jourin, "Les marais salants charentais: carrefour du commerce international (XIIe–XVIe siècles)," *Annales de l'université francophone d'été Saintonge-Québec* (1979).

9. Alice Drouin, *Les marais salants en Aunis et Saintonge jusqu'en 1789* (Royan, 1999); Bernard Callame and Isabelle Delavaud, *Brouage et son marais: pour une meilleure connaissance des marais littoraux en Charente-Maritime* (Saintes, 1996); citing L. Papy, "Brouage et ses marais," *Revue géographique des Pyrénées et du Sud-Ouest* 6 (1935), 281–323.

10. Nathalie Fiquet and François-Yves Le Blanc, *Les Arsenaux de Richelieu: Brouage, Brest, Le Havre, vers l'arsenal idéal* (Brouage, 2003), 25–27.

11. Plan of Brouage, c. 1570, manuscript in the Public Record Office, now the British National Archives, Kew and London. For a detailed discussion, see Fiquet and Le Blanc, *Brouage, ville royale*, 76–78.

12. The historian La Popelinière wrote in 1581: "C'est une petite ville nommée Jacopolis du nom de son fondateur qui vers 1555 y fit édifier les premières maisons et distribua les places pour y bastir ce qui ce fit à grande difficulté . . . étant tout ce rivage un marais . . . tellement ce lieu semble avoir été conquis sur l'eau, qui paravant couvrait toute la place, et encore de

présent, en hiver durant les grandes marées, les rues et bas de maisons sont tous plein d'eau." *Histoire de France enrichie,* 439 verso.

13. Fiquet, "Brouage au Temps de Champlain," 36, 39; my translation here. Other contemporary accounts of its commerce include la Popelinière, *Histoire de France enrichie*; Nicolas Alain, *De Santonum regione et illustrioribus familiis* (Bordeaux, 1598).

14. Robert Le Blant and René Baudry, eds., *Nouveaux documents sur Champlain et son époque,* xxvi (Rouen, La Rochelle, Brouage, Gaspé, Spain, Marseilles, Le Havre, and home again in a hexagonal Atlantic and Mediterranean trade of high complexity); Fiquet, "Brouage in the Time of Champlain," 33–41.

15. Photo by Judith Fischer, June, 2006; with thanks to my brother Miles Pennington Fischer for help with the Dutch translation.

16. Fiquet, "Brouage in the Time of Champlain," 39.

17. A.-L. Leymarie, "Inédit sur le fondateur de Québec," *Nova Francia* 1 (1925) 80–85; Marcel Trudel, *Histoire de la Nouvelle France* (Montreal, 1963–1979) 1:253.

18. For a discussion of the evidence, see Appendix A, "Champlain's Birth Date."

19. For Champlain's marriage contract, see Champlain, CWB 2: 315–17; Narcisse-Eutrope Dionne, *Samuel de Champlain, fondateur de Québec et père de la Nouvelle-France* (Quebec, 1891, 1926) 1:399–403; for the new work by American genealogists, see Newbold Le Roy 3rd and Scott C. Steward, *The Le Roy Family in America, 1753–2003* (Boston and Laconia, 2003), ix; I am grateful to Scott Steward for this information, and for a copy of the book.

20. For Champlain's father, see Champlain, CWB 2: 315–17; Dionne, *Samuel de Champlain,* 1:399–403; Le Roy 3rd and Steward, *The Le Roy Family in America*; and also "Vente d'une moitié de navire par Antoine Chappelain, Dec. 23, 1573," Le Blant and Baudry, eds., *Nouveaux documents,* 1: xxv, 10–11. The editors observe that "very probably if not with absolute certainty" Antoine Chappelain was Champlain's father. Guillaume Allène married Guillemette Gousse in 1563, and they were still married in 1579. Was she the stepsister of Margueritte Le Roy, or had one or another of them married before, or did Allène remarry? Pauline Arsenault, "Acadia in Champlain's New France: From Arcadia to China," in Litalien and Vaugeois, eds., *Champlain,* 120; Le Blant and Baudry, *Nouveaux documents,* 1:2, 12–13.

21. Pablo E. Pérez-Mallaína, *Spain's Men of the Sea: Daily Life on the Indies Fleets in the Sixteenth Century* (Baltimore, 1998), 35–36, 39–41, 122–23.

22. Ibid., 122–24, 87–92, 177–78.

23. Ibid., 82–83, 92–95, 100.

24. "Vente d'une moitié de navire" in Le Blant and Baudry, eds., *Nouveaux documents* 1: 10–11.

25. This house was "sise derrière l'église rue Saint-Jean (actuelle rue du Port)"; "situated behind the church on rue Saint-Jean (now rue du Port)," and was ceded to Du Carlo in 1616; for the mansion of Christophe Depoy, see Vigé and Vigé, *Brouage: ville d'histoire et place forte,* 292–93.

26. 1 Samuel: 7–8; King James version.

27. Several scholars date the "Hebrew invasion" of "font names" from the publication of the Geneva Bible in a compact quarto edition in 1560. See David Hackett Fischer, "Forenames and the Family in New England: An Exercise in Historical Onomastics," in Robert M. Taylor, Jr. and Ralph J. Crandall, eds., *Generations and Change: Genealogical Perspectives in Social History* (Macon, Ga., Mercer University Press, 1986), 215–41.

28. The learned Abbé Laverdière, a great Champlain scholar, came to the same conclusion. He observed that the parents' "deux noms" were "tout à fait catholiques" ("both the parents' names were entirely Catholic") and that the son's Protestant name suggested that "le père et la mère de Champlain avaient dû apostasier" (the father and mother must have renounced their faith). This historian agrees on all except "apostasier." Cf. C.-H. Laverdière, *Oeuvres de Champlain,* publiées sous le patronage de l'Université Laval (Quebec, 1870) 1:xi (in my five-volume edition).

29. Leonce Anquez, *Histoire des assemblées politiques des réformés de France* (Paris, 1959), 162–65; these generalizations exclude towns controlled by individual Protestant nobles.

30. For Protestants in Poitou and Saintonge see *Guide du Protestantisme Charentais* (La Mothe-Achard, 2006), 19.

31. "Vente par Jacques Hersan et Marie Cameret à Samuel de Champlain, de la moitié d'une maison, à Brouage, Feb. 23, 1620," Le Blant and Baudry, eds., *Nouveaux documents* 1:170; Marcel Delafosse, "L'oncle de Champlain," *RHAF* 12 (1958), 208–16; L.-A. Vigneras, "Encore le capitaine provençal," *RHAF* 13 (1959–60), 544–49.

32. Thomas Platter, *Le Voyage de Thomas Platter,* ed. Emmanuel Le Roy Ladurie (Paris: Fayard, 2000), 50, 573–77; Jean Glénisson, "Interview," Litalien and Vaugeois, eds., *Champlain,* 282; Nathalie Fiquet disagrees, writing that "it is unlikely that Samuel was taught in an academy (reserved exclusively for the nobility)," but Platter observed explicitly that youths not of the nobility also attended the Brouage academy. Cf. Fiquet, "Brouage in the Time of Champlain," 37.

33. See Trudel, *Histoire de la Nouvelle-France,* 1: 256; *Le Grand Robert,* s.v. "écuyer." In medieval France, an *écuyer* had been something else, a squire who carried the weapons of a *chevalier,* and looked after the horses.

34. Glénisson, "Interview," 282; and Fiquet, "Brouage in the Time of Champlain," 37, both drawing from Vigé and Vigé, *Brouage, capitale du sel.*

35. For example, on his map of 1612, he noted in English, "The Bay where Hudson did winter." Samuel E. Morison, *Samuel de Champlain: Father of New France* (New York, 1972), 133.

36. Dionne, *Samuel de Champlain,* 1.

37. Champlain to Marie de Medici, Queen Regent of France, 1632, in *The Voyages of the Sieur de Champlain of Saintonge. . . .* (Paris, 1613), preface; CWB 1:209–10.

38. Ibid. For the other phrase, "après avoir passé trente huict ans de mon âge à faire plusieurs voyages sur mer," see Champlain, *Traitté de la Marine et du Devoir d'Un Bon Marinier,* (*Treatise on Marine Affairs, and the Duty of a Good Mariner*) (Paris, 1632); CWB 6:255. See also Appendix C.

39. For Champlain's ship-types see Appendix M.

2. TWO MEN OF SAINTONGE

1. Henry Percival Biggar, ed., *The Works of Samuel de Champlain,* 6 vols. and a portfolio of maps and drawings (CWB), (Toronto, 1922–36, reprinted 1971) 3:231–34.

2. Cf. Champlain's name on three title pages: "Samuel Champlain, De Brouage," in *Les Sauvages* (1603); "Sieur de Champlain Xaintongeois," in *Les Voyages* (1613); "Sr. de Champlain Xainctongeois" in *Les Voyages* (1632); CWB 1:81–83, 202–07; 3:231–34.

3. Champlain's biographers have not explored the importance of Saintonge in his life. Samuel Eliot Morison (*Samuel de Champlain: Father of New France*) and Narcisse-Eutrope Dionne

(*Champlain, Fondateur de Québec et Père de la Nouvelle France*) make only a brief mention of the province; Morris Bishop (*Champlain: The Life of Fortitude*) and Joe Armstrong (*Champlain*) made no reference at all. One finds two classes of exceptions. The first are historians who lived in Saintonge such as Hubert Deschamps, Jean Glénisson, and Nathalie Fiquet. The others are French Canadian descendants of immigrants from Saintonge, such as the genealogist Jacques Saintonge.

 4. Marc Seguin's excellent *Histoire de l'Aunis et de la Saintonge: le début des temps modernes, 1480–1610* (Poitou, 2005) is a recent contribution to a large literature, with a good bibliography. It is part of a series published under the direction of Jean Glénisson. For the persistence of old identities today see the lively popular journal called *Xaintonge*, which has been published in Saint-Jean-d'Angély since 1997.

 5. Julius Caesar, *The Gallic Wars*, Loeb edition (London, 1970) book I, 10–11; book VII, 75. For ancient sources and numismatic evidence of the Santoni see www:cgb.fr/monnaies/vso/v15/gb.

 6. Nathalie Fiquet, "Brouage in the Time of Champlain," in Raymonde Litalien and Denis Vaugeois, eds., *Champlain: The Birth of French America* (Montreal, 2004), 33; see also Maxime le Grelle, *Brouage Québec: foi de pionniers* (Saint-Jean-d'Angély, 1980), 11.

 7. Hubert Deschamps, *Les voyages de Samuel de Champlain Saintongeais, père du Canada* (Paris, 1952), 3.

 8. Hugh Johnson, *The World Atlas of Wine* (New York, 1971, 1977), 258–59.

 9. Ibid.

10. Mage de Fiefmelin, *Les Oeuvres du Sieur Fiefmelin*, 44, quoted in Seguin, *Histoire de l'Aunis et de la Saintonge*, 104.

11. Seguin, *Histoire de l'Aunis et de la Saintonge*, 104, citing municipal archives of Bordeaux, ms. 776, 881 (14 July 1570).

12. For the Hundred Years War, I follow the traditional dates of Édouard Perroy and Kenneth Fowler. See Édouard Perroy, *The Hundred Years War*, introduction by David C. Douglas (1945; New York, 1965), 322; Kenneth Fowler, *The Hundred Years War* (London, 1971), 1. For trends in climate and the economy see Emmanuel Le Roy Ladurie, *Times of Feast, Times of Famine: A History of Climate since the Year 1000* (New York, 1971), 21, 67, 348–50; David Hackett Fischer, *The Great Wave: Price Revolutions and the Rhythm of History* (1996), 4th printing (New York, 2006), 65–102; for the local impact of these large movements, see Seguin, *Histoire de l'Aunis et de la Saintonge*, 334–37 (1573–93), and 383–84 (1594–95).

13. Seguin writes of coastal Saintonge, "La mer offre ses ressources alimentaires qui rendent sans les disettes exceptionnelles." On *disettes*, see Fischer, *Great Wave*, 31, 53, 77; and for *disettes* in Saintonge, see Seguin, *Histoire de l'Aunis et de la Saintonge*, 104, 334–37 (1573–74), and 383–84 (1594–95).

14. Seguin, *Histoire de l'Aunis et de la Saintonge*, 102, 103.

15. Fiquet, "Brouage in the Time of Champlain," 34.

16. Seguin, *Histoire de l'Aunis et de la Saintonge*, 73; for the semantic history of "individualism" in France, see an excellent and pathbreaking study by Steven Lukes, *Individualism* (New York, 1973), 3–16.

17. Georges Musset, Marcel Pellisson, and Charles Vigon, *Glossaire des patois et des parlers de l'Aunis et de la Saintonge* 2 vols. (La Rochelle, 1922); a new dictionary has been in process of publication since 2003, *Le grand lexique du patois charentais*, in six livrets by the editors of the journal *Xaintonge*, hors série 1–6 (May 2003–December 2006).

18. An entire issue of the journal *Xaintonge* 2 (Oct.–Nov. 1997) 1–32, is devoted to the subject of "La Cagouille: l'emblême des Charentais," with essays on "Légendes et croyances," "Coutumes et traditions de la race Cagouillarde," and "Des Cagouilles sur les églises."

19. Jacques Rousseau, "Samuel de Champlain, botaniste mexicain et antillais," *Les Cahiers des Dix* 16 (1951) 39–61.

20. *Le grand lexique du patois charentais* 2: 35.

21. Other examples include *acheneaux* for canals, and *clairs* for shallow places in the marshes.

22. "Tu nous dis tousiours quelque chose de gaillard pour nous resiouyr; si sela arriuoit nous serions bien-heureux." Le Jeune, "Relation" (1633), *Jesuit Relations* 5:211; Bishop, *Champlain*, 337.

23. It has been translated from the parlanjhe into standard French as "qui va doucement, va sûrement," which is not at all the same thought.

24. "Patoiser dans les Règles," "Proverbes Charentais," http://membres.lycos.fr/xaintong/lang .htm; J. L. Buetas, "Patoiser dans les règles," (2007) 9–15.

25. "Patois Charentais," Société d'Ethnologie et de Folklore du Centre-Ouest http://www .cths.fr/FICHES/Fisches_Societes/S_309.shtm; "Lexique du patois Charentais," [http:// membres.lycos.fr/xaintong/lexique.htm; http://membres.lycos.fr/xaintong/patois.htm.

26. Ibid.

27. Ibid.

28. Maurice Bures, *Le type saintongeais* (1908, Paris, 1991), especially chapters 3 and 4, "La Saintonge dans le passé," and "Le type social," pp. 47–72. This book centers on the response to "la crise phylloxérique," which did grave injury to the vineyards of Saintonge, until revived with plant stocks from America—a return for the contribution of Saintonge to the new world.

29. Bures, 70, 57–59.

30. Ibid., 57, 65–72.

31. Ibid., 69.

32. Biggar, CWB 1:4.

33. Emmanuel Le Roy Ladurie, *Histoire du Languedoc* (Paris, 1962; 6th edition, 2000), 28–29, 8–9, 41–45, 59–60.

34. Ibid. Like Champlain in another era, the cultural experience of Emmanuel Le Roy Ladurie carried him back and forth across the great cultural regions of France. He stayed with us on one of his many visits to America. In his company, we observed the same intense curiosity about other cultures and the same tolerance of diversity that appeared in Champlain.

35. Historians have written about Champlain's religion in these terms, but religion was only one of many dimensions of diversity in his formative years: a diversity of region, language, culture, and environment.

36. Contemporaries referred to him in many different ways. Champlain wrote his friend's *nom de terre* as De Monts; royal documents addressed him as De Montz. His *nom de baptême* was also spelled in different ways: Dugua, Du Gua, Du Gas, Du Guast. His very able biographer Jean-Yves Grenon calls him Pierre Dugua De Mons, and reports that "the spelling 'Dugua de Mons' is favoured by people of Royan and the Saintonge area today." Cf. Grenon, *Pierre Dugua de Mons: Founder of Acadie (1604–05); Co-founder of Quebec (1608)* (Annapolis Royal, 1997, 1999, 2000), 2.

37. Jean Liebel, *Pierre Dugua, sieur de Mons, fondateur de Québec* (Paris, 1999), 35.

38. William Inglis Morse, *Pierre Dugua, sieur de Mons; Records: Colonial and 'Saintongeois'* (London, 1939).

39. Jean Glénisson, *La France d'Amérique* (Paris, 1994); quoted in Jean-Yves Grenon, *Pierre Dugua de Mons: Founder of Acadie*, 1; Jean Liebel, *Pierre Dugua, sieur de Mons, fondateur de Québec* (Paris, 1999); Guy Binot, *Pierre Dugua de Mons, Gentilhomme Royannais, Premier Colonisateur du Canada, Lieutenant Général de la Nouvelle-France de 1603 à 1612* (Royan, 2004); Marie Claude Bouchet, *Pierre Dugua de Mons* (Royan, 2000); for other interpretations see Bruce G. Trigger, *Natives and Newcomers: Canada's "Heroic Age" Reconsidered* (Montreal and Kingston, 1985), 172–77, 306–12, which describes and dismisses de Mons as merely a "trader."

40. Morse, ed., *Pierre Dugua, sieur de Mons;* Grenon, *Pierre Dugua de Mons, Founder of Acadie;* Liebel, *Pierre Dugua sieur de Mons, fondateur de Québec;* Binot, *Pierre Dugua de Mons, Gentilhomme Royannais*, 1.

41. Lescarbot, *History of New France*, 3 vols. (Toronto, 1907) 2:250, 277.

42. Quoted in Grenon, *Pierre Dugua de Mons, Founder of Acadie*, 13–14.

43. Grenon, *Pierre Dugua de Mons, Founder of Acadie*, 1–3; Morse, ed., *Pierre Dugua, sieur de Mons;* Liebel, *Pierre Dugua, sieur de Mons;* M. G. Rodrigues, *Le père du Canada: Pierre Dugua* (1994), not seen. Marcel Trudel, *Histoire de la Nouvelle-France,* vol. 1: *Les vaines tentatives 1524–1603* (Montreal, 1963).

44. Liebel, *Pierre Dugua, sieur de Mons*, 37.

45. CWB 2: 215; 3:319.

46. Liebel, *Pierre Dugua, sieur de Mons*, 8; also helpful in correcting much confusion about the origins of his family.

47. Ibid., 8, 61; Le Blant and Baudry, eds., *Nouveaux documents* 1: xxv; these are the court documents, which are most likely to survive. For monetary units, see Appendix O, below.

48. Liebel, *Pierre Dugua, sieur de Mons*, 327, 336.

49. Ibid., 325, 329, 342, 336.

50. Ibid., 93.

3. HENRI IV AND CHAMPLAIN

1. "Majesté, à laquelle i'estois obligé tant de naissance, que d'vne pension de laquelle elle m'honoroit." Samuel de Champlain, *Les Voyages faits au Grand Fleuve Sainct Laurens par le sieur de Champlain Capitaine ordinaire pour le Roy en al marine, depuis l'année 1608 iusques en 1612* (Paris, 1613) in *Works* ed. Biggar (CWB) 3:315.

2. "Le Roy [et] patrie . . . Dieu et le monde," ibid., 6:99.

3. Ibid., 3:315. For the meaning of *obligé* in the era of Samuel de Champlain, see *Le Grand Robert de la langue française*, 6:2050–52, s.v., "obliger." The first example is "la loi naturelle, la loi divine nous oblige à honorer père et mere; natural and divine law obliges us to honor our father and mother." The second meaning is "assujettir par une obligation d'ordre moral; to subject oneself by an obligation of a moral order." Third, fourth and fifth meanings of "obliger" are: "assujettir par une obligation d'ordre juridique; to subject oneself by an obligation of a judicial order"; "mettre quelqu'un dans la nécessité de (faire quelque chose); to put someone under a necessity of doing something"; and "attacher quelqu'un par une obligation; to attach someone by an obligation."

4. "Bail de Jacques Hersan et Marie Camaret," March 15, 1619, Le Blant and Baudry, eds., *Nouveaux documents sur Champlain et son époque* (Ottawa, 1967), 165.

5. CWB 3:315; Raymonde Litalien and Denis Vaugeois, eds., *Champlain: The Birth of French America* (Montreal, 2004), 364.

6. Marcel Trudel, *Histoire de la Nouvelle-France: Les Vaines Tentatives, 1524–1603* (Montreal and Paris, 1963), 1:255; Hubert Deschamps, *Les Voyages de Samuel Champlain, saintongeais, père du Canada* (Paris, 1951), 4n5.

7. *Life of Mà-Ka-Tai-Me-She-Kià-Kiàk or Black Hawk . . . dictated by himself*, ed. J. B. Patterson (Cincinnati, 1834), new edition, ed. Milo M. Quaife (Chicago, 1916), 24; the best scholarly edition is *Black Hawk, An Autobiography*, ed. Donald Jackson (Urbana, Ill., 1955, 1964, 1990), 41–45, 45n; Gordon M. Sayre, *Les sauvages Américaines* (Chapel Hill, 1997), 64; see conclusion above.

8. David Buisseret, *Henry IV* (London, 1984), 6–7; Pierre de Vaissière, *Henri IV* (Paris, 1925); Irene Mahoney, *Royal Cousin: The Life of Henry IV of France* (New York, 1970); Pierre-Victor Palma-Cuyet, *Chronologie novenaire* [1589–98] and *Chronologie septenaire* [1598–1604], ed. J. A. Buchon (Paris, 1836).

9. For Henri's presence in Saintonge, 1568–72, see Janine Garrison, *Henry IV* (Paris, 1984), "Le Prince de La Rochelle," 46–52; Jean-Pierre Babelon, *Henri IV* (Paris, 1982), 138–58.

10. The *particule de noblesse* and the title "sieur de Champlain" appeared as early as 1595 in pay records of the royal army in Brittany. These documents are in the Archives d'Ille-et-Vilaine C2914 (fonds des États de Bretagne). They were discovered by Arthur de la Borderie, archivist in Rennes, and noted by Jouon de Longrais in *Bulletin et mémoires de la Societé archéologique du département d'Ille-et-Vilaine* 42 (1913), xlvi–xlviii. A modern transcription appears in Le Blant et Baudry, *Nouveaux documents*, 17–19.

11. The particule *de* preceding a patronymic name is often called the *particule de noblesse*, or *particule nobiliare*. It was never explicitly a sign of authentic nobility, but an emblem of rank, status, distinction, or merit that was awarded to others in common usage. In Champlain's era the *particule de noblesse* commonly referred to someone who was thought worthy of respect, usually by rank and status—though not exclusively to people with authentic titles of nobility. In the nineteenth century it was assumed by the bourgeoisie as an instrument of social striving. As Victor Hugo complained in *Les Misérables*, "Le particule, on le sait, n'a aucune significance; it is well known that the particle means nothing at all" (III. iv. 1). See *Le Grand Robert de la langue française* 5: 279, s.v. "particule," II. 2.

    Robert Le Blant observed that Champlain signed himself Champlain, without the "de" word. An exception was his manuscript map of 1607. See Le Blant's "La condition sociale de Samuel Champlain," *Actes du 87e congrès national des Sociétés savantes*, Poitiers, 1962, (n.p., 1963), 669–77. It might be noted that Pierre Dugua, sieur de Mons, signed himself either Pierredugua, or Dugua, or Monts, or Mons, but not de Mons or de Monts. Photographs of his signatures appear in William Inglis Morse, *Pierre Dugua sieur de Mons* (London, 1939), 93ff.

    The title "sieur" was commonly defined as a "titre honorifique pour un homme; an honorific title for a man." In Champlain's world it was given on the same criteria as the *particule de noblesse*. It did not refer exclusively to the nobility, but to men of honor who were thought to be worthy of respect. Only a very small proportion of the men mentioned in Champlain's writings were called "sieur." See *Le Grand Robert de la langue française* 6:436, s.v. "sieur," I–III.

12. CWB 3:315.

13. Babelon, *Henri IV*, 7.

14. See, for example, René de La Croix de Castries, *Henri IV, roi de coeur, roi de France* (Paris, 1970); André Castelot, *Henri IV le passionné* (Paris, 1986); Marcelle Vioux, *Le vert-galant: vie héroique at amoureuse de Henri IV* (Paris, 1935); Francis Bayrou, *Henri IV: le roi libre* (Paris, 1994).

15. Christian Desplat, *Cultures en Béarn* (Librairie des Pyrénées et de Gascogne, 2001), excellent on the persistence of ancient and medieval folkways in the modern world, and the interplay of French and Bearnaise language and culture; Nicolas de Bordenave, *Histoire de Béarn et de Navarre* (Paris, 1873), a fine work of scholarship.

16. Buisseret, *Henri IV*, 1, from Pierre-Victor Palma-Cayet, *Chronologie novenaire contenant l'histoire de la guerre* (Paris, 1608) 1:175.

17. Nancy Lyman Roelker, *Queen of Navarre: Jeanne d'Albret* (Cambridge, Mass., 1968), a classic and charming work; Marquis de Rochambeau, *Lettres d'Antoine de Bourbon et de Jehanne d'Albret* (Paris, 1878); Jeanne d'Albret, *Memoires et poésies de Jeanne d'Albret* (Paris, 1893).

18. Roelker, *Queen of Navarre*, trans. as *Jeanne d'Albret, reine de Navarre* (Paris, 1979).

19. Frederic J. Baumgartner, *Henri II: King of France, 1547–1559* (Durham, N.C., 1988).

20. David Hackett Fischer, *The Great Wave: Price Revolutions and the Rhythm of History* (New York, 1996), 65–102.

21. Barbara B. Diefendorf, *Beneath the Cross: Catholics and Huguenots in Sixteenth-Century Paris* (Oxford, 1991) 50–56; Natalie Zemon Davis, "The Rites of Violence: Religious Riot in Sixteenth-Century France," *Society and Culture in Early Modern France* (Palo Alto, 1976), 152–87; Denis Richet, "Aspects socio-culturels des conflits religieux à Paris dans la seconde moitié du XVIe siècle," *Annales ESC* 32 (1977), 764–89.

22. Sylvia Shannon, "The Political Activity of François de Lorraine, duc de Guise, 1559–1563," (thesis, Boston University, 1988), 344–82 compares four primary sources, two Protestant and two Catholic; Arlette Jouanna et al., *Histoire et dictionnaire des guerres de religion* (Paris, 1998), 106–10.

23. Denis Crouzet, *Les Guerriers de Dieu: La violence au temps des troubles de religion, vers 1520–vers 1610*, 2 vols. (Paris, 1990), a major work; on Sens and Tours, see Jouanna et al., *Guerres de religion*, 117; and on Montbrison, see Robert Knecht, *French Religious Wars 1562–1598* (Botley, 2002), 73–75.

24. Knecht, *The French Religious Wars*, 29–37; a great classic is Pierre de Ronsard, *Discours des misères de ce temps* and its sequel, published in his *Oeuvres complètes* (Paris, 1552).

25. Jouanna et al., *Guerres de religion*, 163–85.

26. Mark Greengrass, *France in the Age of Henri IV: The Struggle for Stability* (New York, 1995), 11.

27. Eliane Vigé and Jimmy Vigé, *Brouage: capitale du sel et patrie de Champlain* (Bordessoules, 1990),42, 44, 49.

28. *Mémoires et autres écrits de Marguerite de Valois, la Reine Margot*, ed. Yves Cazeau (Paris, 1971, 1986), 11–12, 58–59.

29. Another factor was the war in the Netherlands, where the Protestant Dutch were fighting for their freedom from a Spanish Catholic ruler. In August 1572, the French king, Charles IX, gave Admiral de Coligny permission to take a French army into the Netherlands in support of the Dutch. The attempted assassination of de Coligny was an effort by the Catholic party to stop that intervention. A papal envoy reported that "if the Admiral had died from the shot, no others would have been killed." But the admiral survived and the St. Bartholemew

Massacre followed. See Lisa Jardine, *The Awful End of Prince William the Silent* (New York, 2006), 36.

30. Arlette Jouanna, *La Saint-Barthélemy: les mystères d'un crime d'État, 24 août 1572* (Paris, 2007), 160–200.

31. Barbara B. Diefendorf, *Beneath the Cross: Catholics and Huguenots in Sixteenth-Century Paris* (New York, 1991); Philip Benedict, "The Saint Bartholemew's Massacres in the Provinces," *Historical Journal* 21 (1978) 205–25; Greengrass, *France in the Age of Henry IV*, 9.

32. Buisseret, *Henri IV*, 10.

33. Ibid.; Henri IV, *Lettres missives de Henri IV*, 9 vols. (Paris, 1843–76) 1:122.

34. Jean H. Mariéjol, *Henri IV et Louis XIII* (Paris, 1905), 252–53.

35. Michael Wolfe, *The Conversion of Henry IV: Politics, Power, and Religious Belief in Early Modern Times* (Cambridge, 1993), 22.

36. Marcel Trudel, a great historian of New France, raised a Roman Catholic, concluded that Champlain was born Protestant and converted to Catholicism. See Trudel, *Histoire de la Nouvelle-France* 1:235–36; Deschamps, *Les Voyages de Samuel Champlain*, 4–5. A Protestant historian, Samuel Eliot Morison, thought that Champlain was "probably born and certainly brought up a Catholic," but he did not appear to know the evidence. *Samuel de Champlain*, 17. Other scholars, such as Bishop, *Champlain*, 4, and Armstrong, *Champlain*, 4, remained agnostic on these questions.

37. Buisseret, *Henri IV*, 122.

38. Champlain's religious books appear in Robert le Blant, "Inventaire des meubles faisant partie de la communauté entre Samuel Champlain et Hélène Boullé, Nov. 21, 1636," *Revue d'histoire de l'Amérique française* 18 (1965) 595, 603, 599; for Henri's Christian piety see Buisseret, *Henri IV*, 50.

39. Buisseret, *Henri IV*, 50–51, 54.

40. Ibid., 178.

41. Ibid., 12.

42. Knecht, *The French Religious Wars*, 91.

43. Variant estimates of these payments appear in Claude Groulart, *Mémoires ou Voyages par lui faits en Cour* (Paris, 1857); Sully, *Les Oeconomies royales de Sully* ed., David Buisseret and Bernard Barbiche, (Paris, 1970), and an earlier edition, *Les Économies Royales* ed. Michaud and Poujoulat, 2 vols. (Paris, 1837), and manuscript materials in Buisseret, *Henri IV*, 48; Greengrass, *France in the Age of Henri IV*, 87, 393.

44. Buisseret, *Henri IV*, 48–49.

45. Eliane Vigé and Jimmy Vigé, *Brouage, ville d'histoire et place forte* (Saint-Jean-d'Angély, 1989), 34–69.

46. S. Annette Finley-Croswhite, *Henri IV and the Towns: The Pursuit of Legitimacy in French Urban Society, 1589–1610* (Cambridge, 1999), 20–22.

47. Henri IV was quoted as saying, "Si Dieu me donne encore de la vie, je feray qu'il n'y aura point de laboureur en mon Royaume, qui n'ait moyen d'avoir une poule dans son pot." The earliest source I have found for this much quoted saying is Bishop Hardouin de Beaumont de Péréfixe, *Histoire du Roy Henry Le Grand* (1661, revised corrected and expanded by the author, Paris, 1681), annexe, "Recueil de quelques belles actions et paroles mémorables du Roy Henri Le Grand," 528. Péréfixe was a tutor of Louis XIV.

48. Jean-Pierre Babelon, *Demeures parisiens sous Henri IV et Louis XIII* (Paris, 1965); Buisseret, *Henri IV*, 196.

49. Buisseret, *Henri IV*, 139–40.

50. Péréfixe, *Histoire du Roy Henry Le Grand*, annexe, "Recueil de quelques belles actions," 529.

51. Jean-François Labourdette, "L'importance du Traité de Vervins," 15–26.

4. A SOLDIER IN BRITTANY

1. Champlain's Army Pay Records, 1595, Archives de l'Ille-et-Vilaine, Fonds des États de Bretagne, C. 1924, ff. 229, 523–27; Robert Le Blant and René Baudry, eds., *Nouveaux documents sur Champlain et son époque* (Ottawa, 1967), 17–19.

2. For an overview, and a great work of scholarship see Denis Crouzet, *Les guerriers de Dieu: la violence au temps des troubles de religion (vers 1525–vers 1610)*, 2 vols. (Seyssel, 1990); also James B. Collins, "La Guerre de la Ligue et le bien public," in Jean-François Labourdette, Jean-Pierre Poussou, and Marie-Catherine Vignal, eds., *Le Traité de Vervins* (Paris, 2000), 81–96.

3. Louis Grégoire, *La Ligue en Bretagne* (Paris and Nantes, 1856). Major documents are in the second volume of Pierre-Victor Palma-Cayet, *Chronologie novenaire* and *Chronologie septenaire* (Paris 1836); and Henri IV, *Recueil des lettres missives*, 9 vols. (Paris, 1843–76), vols. 4–5.

4. Mark Greengrass, *France in the Age of Henry IV* (2d edition 1984, London, 1995) 86; H. Wacquet, *Mémoires du chanoine Jean Moreau sur les guerres de la ligue en Bretagne* (Quimper, 1960).

5. Champlain's army records are reproduced in Le Blant and Baudry, eds., *Nouveaux documents sur* 1:9–11.

6. For monetary units see Frank C. Spooner, *The International Economy and Monetary Movements in France, 1493–1725* (Cambridge, 1972); John J. McCusker, *Money and Exchange in Europe and America, 1600–1775* (Chapel Hill, 1978), 9–13, 87–97, 280–90, passim; David Hackett Fischer, *The Great Wave: Price Movements in World History* (1996, 2d edition, Oxford, 2000). In general 1 silver écu equalled 3 livres tournois (a money of account), or about 6 English silver shillings in 1619; for monetary values, see Frank C. Spooner. On Champlain's monetary units, see Appendix O below.

7. "Paiement de diverses sommes à Jean Hardy et Samuel Champlain, pour leurs gages dans l'armée royale de Bretagne," March–Dec. 1595, Le Blant and Baudry, eds., *Nouveaux documents* 1:17–19.

8. "A Samuel de Champlain, ayde du Sieur Hardy . . . pour certain voiage secret qu'il a faict important le service du Roy," March–Dec. 1595, in Le Blant and Baudry, eds., *Nouveaux documents* 1:18.

9. This title appeared in pay records for the period from March to December 1595. Before the reference in folio 195 to the secret voyage and service to the king, he appears to have been called Champlain. Thereafter, he was sieur de Champlain. Cf. Le Blant and Baudry, eds., *Nouveaux documents*, 1:17–19.

10. "Au sieur de Champlain la somme de trois escuz pour aller trouver Monsieur le marechal et luy representer quelques chose important le service du Roy," Le Blant and Baudry, eds., *Nouveaux documents*, 1:19. For Saint-Luc see Éliane Vigé and Jimmy Vigé, *Brouage: ville d'histoire et Place forte* (Saint-Jean-d'Angély, 1989), 34–55.

11. Claude de Chastillon, "The Royal Camp of Henri IV at the Siege of La Fère," January 1596,

British Library; David Buisseret, *Henri IV* (London, 1984) plates 8, 9. This engraving gives a good sense of the role of the *Logis du Roy* in active campaigns.

12. Full accounts of the campaign are written by English participants and historians: R. B. Wernham, *After the Armada: Elizabethan England and the Struggle for Western Europe* (Oxford, 1984); J. S. Nolan, "English Operations around Brest, 1594," *Mariner's Mirror* 81 (1995), 259–74; James McDermott, "The Crozon Peninsula, *El Leon*, 1594," *Martin Frobisher, Elizabethan Privateer* (New Haven, 2003), 407–23.

13. For Champlain's presence at Crozon see Arthur le Moyne de la Borderie and Barthélemy Pocquet, *Histoire de Bretagne*, 6 vols., (Rennes, 1905–14), 5:260; Samuel E. Morison, *Champlain: Father of New France* (New York, 1972), 17; Morris Bishop, *Champlain: The Life of Fortitude* (New York, 1948, 1963), 10; Joe C. W. Armstrong, *Champlain* (Toronto, 1987), 22; cf, Narcisse-Eutrope Dionne, *Champlain: fondateur de Québec et père de la Nouvelle France* (Quebec 1981, 1926) 1:8, who has him on the wrong side, fighting for the Catholic League; cf. Champlain himself in Henry Percival Biggar, ed., *The Works of Samuel de Champlain*, 6 vols. and a portfolio of maps and drawings (CWB) (Toronto, 1922–36, reprinted 1971) 1:3.

14. After-action report by English officers, 8 Nov. 1594, Cotton MSS, Caligula E IX, 1, f 211, British Library, as cited in McDermott, *Frobisher*, 480n.

15. Champlain, *Brief Discours*, CWB 1:3; *Voyage* (1612), Ibid., 2:257; *Voyages* (1632), Ibid., 4:156.

16. "Champlain, capitaine d'une compagnie en garnison à Quimper," Le Blant and Baudry, eds., *Nouveaux documents* 1:11.

17. Champlain, *Traitté de la Marine*, CWB 6: xii–xiv.

18. Ibid.

19. See McDermott, *Martin Frobisher*, 407–23.

20. James McDermott, ed., *The Third Voyage of Martin Frobisher to Baffin Island* (London, 2001), 409–17.

21. V. Steffanson, ed., *The Three Voyages of Martin Frobisher*, 2 vols. (London, 1938); McDermott, ed., *The Third Voyage of Martin Frobisher*; Samuel Eliot Morison, *The European Discovery of America: The Northern Voyages, AD 500–1600* (New York, 1971); for Champlain on "Messire Martin Forbichet" see CWB 1:227; 3:300; 6:196.

22. Nancy Lyman Roelker, ed., *The Paris of Henry of Navarre, as seen by Pierre de l'Estoile; Selections from his Mémoires-Journaux* (Cambridge, 1958), 287 (March 1698); extracts are from de l'Estoile, *Mémoires-Journaux* ed. Brunet et al., 12 vols. (Paris, 1875–96).

23. The full text is in Roland Mousnier, *The Assassination of Henri IV*, tr. Joan Spencer (New York, 1973), appendix 4, 316–63.

24. For an overview, see Jean-François Labourdette, "L'importance du Traité de Vervins," in Labourdette, Poussou, and Vignal eds., *Le Traité de Vervins* (Paris, 2000), 15–26.

25. Peter Kruger, "Vervins: le resultat précoce d'une vue systémique des affaires étrangères en Europe," in Labourdette, Poussou, and Vignal eds., *Le Traité de Vervins*, 415–29.

26. David Buisseret, *Henry IV* (London, 1984), 69.

27. Samuel Eliot Morison, *The European Discovery of America: The Southern Voyages, 1492–1616* (New York, 1974), 97–98; Francis G. Davenport, ed., *European Treaties Bearing on the History of the United States and its Dependencies* (Washington, 1914); Luis Weckmann, *Las Bulas Alejandrinas de 1493 y la Teoría Política del Papado Medieval* (Mexico City, 1949).

28. This subject is much confused in the secondary literature, and lines of amity have been understood in many different ways. For a review of the literature see Eric Thierry, "La Paix de Vervins et les ambitions françaises en Amérique," in Labourdette, Poussou, and Vignal, eds., *Le Traité de Vervins*, 373–89; Olive Dickason, *The Myth of the Savage; and the Beginnings of French Colonization in the Americas* (Edmonton, 1984), 139.

29. Thierry, "La Paix de Vervins," 375; quoting David Asseline, *Antiquités et chroniques de la ville de Dieppe* (Dieppe, 1874) 2:149.

30. L. Pauliat, *La politique coloniale sous l'Ancien Régime d'après des documentes empruntés aux archives coloniales du ministre de la marine et des colonies* (Paris, 1887) 177–79; Thierry, "La Paix de Vervins," 375; Carl Bridenbaugh, *No Peace Beyond the Line* (New York and Oxford, 1972), 3.

31. Thierry, "La Paix de Vervins," 375–77. I understand Claude Groulart to testify that Henri IV said in 1600 he was unable to make an agreement in the last treaty for peaceful trade in Brazil, the Indies and other places "beyond the line," and that the Spanish were seizing French ships when found there, and therefore he would do the same to their ships. Cf. Claude Groulart, *Mémoires ou voyages par lui faits en cour* (Paris, 1857).

32. Buisseret, *Henry IV*, 138; also Auguste Poirson, *Histoire du règne de Henri IV*, 4 vols. (Paris, 1865) 2:283–87.

33. Robert Le Blant, "Henri IV et le Canada," *Revue de Pau et du Béarn* 12 (1984–85), 43–57.

34. Yves Cazaux, *Henri IV: les horizons du règne* (Paris, 1986), 284–85; Le Blant, "Henri IV et le Canada," 44.

35. Buisseret, *Henry IV*, 19.

36. Étienne Taillemite, "The Royal Navy in Champlain's Time," in Raymonde Litalien et Denis Vaugeois, eds., *Champlain: The Birth of French America* (Montreal, 2004), 19–23.

37. Bernard Barbiche, "Autour de la visite de Henri IV au Havre en septembre 1603," in Annie Blondel-Loisel, Raymonde Litalien, Jean Paul Barbiche and Claude Briot, eds., *De la Seine au Saint-Laurent avec Champlain* (Paris, 2005), 55–66; Buisseret, *Henri IV*, 88, 103, 108, 157; Jean-Pierre Babelon, *Henri IV* (Paris, 1982), 708, 866, 888.

38. Taillemite, "The Royal Navy in Champlain's Time," 19–23.

39. Ibid., 21–22.

40. Ibid., 19–23.

41. Bernard Barbiche, "Henri IV and the World Overseas: A Decisive Time in the History of New France," in Litalien and Vaugeois, eds., *Champlain*, 24–32.

42. Richard Colebrook Harris, *The Seigneurial System in Early Canada: A Geographical Study* (Madison, 1968), 3; Edmond Lareau, *Histoire du droit canadien* (Montreal, 1888), 1:159–60.

43. Barbiche, "Henri IV and the World Overseas," 30; Sully, *Économies Royales*, 2 vols. (1611–17, 1638) (Paris 1836–37), published in the second series of the *Nouvelle collection des mémoires pour servir à l'histoire de France* 1:516b; David Buisseret, *Sully and the Growth of Centralized Government in France, 1598–1610* (London, 1968), 178.

44. Sully, *Les Oeconomies royales de Sully*, David Buisseret and Bernard Barbiche, eds., (Paris, 1988) 2:257.

45. Barbiche, "Henri IV and the World Overseas," 30.

46. Champlain, CWB 3:302.

5. A SPY IN NEW SPAIN

1. Henry Percival Biggar, ed., *The Works of Samuel de Champlain*, 6 vols. and a portfolio of maps and drawings (CWB), (Toronto, 1922–36, reprinted 1971) 1:63.

2. CWB 1:3. Nearly everything in this Spanish period of Champlain's life has been challenged by skeptics, debunkers, and iconoclasts in the late twentieth century. The text of this chapter centers on the history of what Champlain actually did, with historical evidence on disputed questions in the notes. A historiographical discussion of this literature appears in Appendix C below.

3. In the nineteenth and twentieth centuries, the center of commerce and industry on that southern coast of Brittany shifted to the modern ports of Lorient and Saint-Nazaire. Blavet/Port-Louis preserved much of its sixteenth-century scale and character as a consequence of rapid change in other towns—a pattern that also appears in Brouage, Crozon, Honfleur, and other places that were important in Champlain's early life. When we visited these very attractive small towns, we had the sense of traveling through time.

4. The first point raised by skeptics was whether Champlain served in the Brittany campaign and could have been at Blavet. In 1950, Jean Bruchési suggested that Champlain falsified the record of his military service in Brittany. See "Champlain a-t-il menti?" *Cahiers des Dix* 15 (1950), 39–53. Much evidence has come to light on Champlain's military service, including army pay records kept by treasurer Gabriel Hus, that confirm Champlain's account in the *Brief Discours*. The documents are published in Robert Le Blant and René Baudry, eds., *Nouveaux documents sur Champlain et son époque (1560–1622)* (Ottawa, 1967), I, xxv, 18–21.

5. CWB 1:4.

6. Ibid.

7. Spanish captains were allowed to employ foreigners, "except English and rebel Dutchmen." See L. A. Vigneras, "Le Voyage de Samuel Champlain aux Indes occidentales," *RHAF* 11 (1957), 163–200.

8. For ship-types, see Appendix M. Bonnault argued that Champlain was never in Blavet and invented Captain Provençal out of whole cloth. See Claude de Bonnault, "Encore le Brief discours: Champlain a-t-il été à Blavet en 1598?" *Bulletin des recherches historiques* 60 (1954), 59–64. A major document has been found in Cadiz and published in Joe C. W. Armstrong's *Champlain* (Toronto, 1987), 274–77. It is a will and covenant signed by Champlain and his uncle on June 26, 1601. It clearly establishes their relationship as Champlain described it, and confirms many parts of the *Brief Discours*.

9. Marcel Delafosse, "L'oncle de Champlain," *RHAF* 12 (1958), 208–16; L.-A. Vigneras, "Encore le capitaine provençal," *RHAF* 13 (1959–60), 544–49; Champlain, "Brief Narrative," CWB 1:4; Narcisse-Eutrope Dionne, *Champlain: fondateur de Québec et père de la Nouvelle France* (Quebec, 1891, 1926), 1:14–19; Samuel Eliot Morison, *Samuel de Champlain: Father of New France* (New York, 1972), 18.

10. CWB 1:4. Several scholars have argued that Captain Provençal was not Champlain's uncle. Both men confirmed this relationship in a Spanish affidavit dated June 26, 1601, in the Archivo Historico Provincial in Cádiz, Spain. A copy of this document is in the Public Archives of Canada, and a transcription appears in Joe C. W. Armstrong, "The Testament of Guillermo Elena," *Champlain*, appendix II, 274–78. Cf. Delafosse, "L'oncle de Champlain," 208–16; Vigneras, "Encore le capitaine provençal," 544–49; CWB 1:4, 7–8.

11. CWB 1:7. For evidence from Spanish archives that the *Saint-Julien* was chartered to carry

troops from Blavet to Spain, see Laura Giraudo, "Research Report: A Mission to Spain," and François-Marc Gagnon, "Is the *Brief Discours* by Champlain?" in Raymonde Italien and Denis Vaugeois, eds., *Champlain: The Birth of French America* (Montreal, 2004), 93–97, 86–88; also Vigneras, "Voyage," 168.

12. Gaston de Carné, *Correspondance du duc de Mercoeur* (Rennes, 1899), 2:162.

13. CWB 1:3&n; 2:257&n; 4:156; Governor de la Hottière's charter gave him 40 reals per ton, which would have come to 2,000 reals altogether for the charter of the *Saint-Julien*. Captain Provençal was paid 400 reals to serve as master of the vessel.

14. Vigneras, "Le Voyage de Samuel Champlain." Critics have made much of the fact that the *Brief Discours* garbled the name of Captain General Zubiaur, the Spanish commander of the fleet, sometimes making it Soubriago. Laura Giraudo's study of orthography in the three early manuscripts of the *Brief Discours* finds that the name of the Spanish commander appeared in two of them as Subiaure and Subiaur, very close to the original Zubiaur. Broad variations in orthography were routine; S and Z were used interchangeably in Spanish and French. A Spanish court document in Cadiz reports the name Champlain as Zamplen. See Gagnon, "Is the *Brief Discours* by Champlain?" 86; and Laura Giraudo, "The Manuscripts of the *Brief Discours*," in Litalien and Vaugeois, eds., *Champlain: The Birth of French America*, 67.

15. For the smuggling of illegal cargo in the *Saint-Julien*, and for Zubiaur's involvement, see Giraudo, "Research Report," 95.

16. CWB 1:3–4. Supporting evidence in Spanish archives was found by Giraudo, "Research Report," 93–95.

17. Critics have made much of inconsistencies in chronology between Champlain's *Discours* and Spanish records. Champlain remembered the date of departure from Blavet as "the beginning of the month of August." He estimated the arrival at Cape Finisterre as ten days later, the arrival at Vigo Bay as one day thereafter, the departure from Vigo six days later; doubling Cape St. Vincent three days later; arrival at Cadiz soon after that; stay in Cadiz one month. Spanish records gave the date of August 23, 1598, for the departure from Blavet, August 28 for arrival in Vigo Bay, September 7 for departure from Vigo, September 14 for arrival at Cadiz, and the stay in Cadiz from September 14 to October 12, 1598. Champlain erred in his memory of the date of departure, but thereafter the accounts are consistent, and they are clearly describing the same voyage. The initial error can be explained by the fact that Champlain was writing from memory long after the event, without a journal or a logbook. Cf. CWB 1:5–7; Vigneras, "Voyage," 168; Giraudo, "Research Report," 86; Gagnon, "Is the *Brief Discours* by Champlain?" 86.

18. Zubiaur, Report, Oct. 7, 1598, qtd. in Vigneras, "Voyage," 168.

19. CWB 1:5.

20. Vigneras, "Voyage," 168–69.

21. John Cummins, *Francis Drake, The Lives of a Hero* (New York, 1995, 1997), 164–78; Julian S. Corbett, *Drake and the Tudor Navy*, 2 vols. (London, 1892); Kenneth Andrews, *Drake's Voyages, a Reassessment . . .* (London, 1964).

22. CWB 1:7 and plate. Vigneras observes of Champlain's plans of Spanish cities that "the two plans are accurate [*exactes*] and appear to be the work of someone who had actually been there." See Vigneras, "Voyage," 170.

23. Vigneras, "Voyage," 169, found in Spanish records confirmation that *Saint-Julien* remained

at Cadiz from September 14 to October 12, and moved to Sanlucar, just as Champlain wrote.

24. On the accuracy of Champlain's plan see Vigneras, "Voyage," 170.

25. A full account that confirms Champlain's references to these events is Richard T. Spence, *The Privateering Earl: George Clifford, 3rd Earl of Cumberland, 1558–1605*, 141–75.

26. Zubiar's appointments are confirmed in Spanish archives. See Giraudo, "Research Report," 95.

27. Ibid., 95–97. See also Vigneras, "Voyage," 163.

28. For the *patache d'avis*, see CWB 1:8.

29. CWB 1:9; Giraudo, "Research Report," 95.

30. Giraudo, "Research Report," 95.

31. The eight beatitudes in the Sermon on the Mount: "blessed are the poor in spirit, the meek, the pure, the merciful, the peacemakers); blessed are they that mourn, seek righteousness, and blessed are they that are persecuted for righteousness sake."

32. For bizarria see Pablo E. Pérez-Mallaína, *Los hombres del océano. Vida cotidiana de los tripulantes de las flotas de Indias, Siglo XVI* (Seville, 1992); translated by Carla Rahn Phillips as *Spain's Men of the Sea: Daily Life on the Indies Fleets in the Sixteenth-Century* (Baltimore, 1998), 1,152.

33. CWB 1:10.

34. Ibid.

35. For the six clandestine passengers see Vigneras, "Voyage," 174; and Gagnon, "Is the *Brief Discours* by Champlain?" 87.

36. Gagnon, "Is the *Brief Discours* by Champlain?" 87; Vigneras discovered a list of officers aboard the *San Julian*. Champlain was not among them. Don Francisco Coloma also wrote that nobody aboard the *San Julian* had powers of attorney from the owners. Laura Giraudo writes, "The hypothesis advanced by Vigneras to the effect that Champlain undertook the voyage clandestinely or in a subordinate role appears more and more likely." She found more evidence of clandestine passengers aboard the *Saint-Julien*. "Research Report," 95.

    The key to Champlain's status may be found in the language of his own description. Champlain wrote, "mon oncle . . . me commist la charge dudict vaisseau pour esgard à iceluy." CWB 1:10. The operative words are *charge* and *esgard*. *Charge*, in early modern French usage, did not mean "in charge," but a more general and less formal sense of concern. See *Le Grand Robert*, s.v., *charge*, ii, 3–5. *Esgard* came from the verb *esgarder*, to be attentive or to look after something, or to watch over it, or to be concerned about it. It did not necessarily imply power or authority. *Esgard* is rarely used in French today, and does not appear in *Le Grand Robert*, but it was common in early modern French, as in the preface to Pascal's *Pensées*, "l'indifférence à l'esgard de toutes choses"; or Montaigne's essay on cannibals, "esgard aux règles de la raison."

37. Champlain's *Brief Discours* and Spanish records are similar on the departure for the West Indies, but with a difference of dates. Gagnon writes, "the one month gap between the date given by Champlain and the date shown in official documents has yet to be explained" (Gagnon, "Is the *Brief Discours* by Champlain?" 87).

    Champlain wrote that his ship "hoisted sail" for America at the beginning of January, 1599. This may have been the date when the ships began to shift their moorings at Sanlucar, and dropped down the river to join a fleet that was forming inside the bar. According to

Spanish records *San Julian* cleared the bar at the mouth of the Guadalquivir River on February 3, 1599, with river pilot Adrián García aboard. We know this from his very large fee of ten Venetian ducats, which suggests that he may have been aboard the ship for some time, perhaps guiding her downstream from an upriver mooring.

Critics have made much of this discrepancy, but both statements could have been correct. The ships of the fleet had moored in the Guadalquivir River, as much as fifty miles upstream. In the Second World War, convoys smaller than the Spanish treasure fleets took weeks to form up in Halifax harbor. Delays might also have developed as river pilots watched the winds and tides over the treacherous Sanlucar bar. Compare CWB 1:10; Vigneras, "Voyage," 174; Gagnon, "Is the *Brief Discours* by Champlain?" 87.

38. Pérez-Mallaína, *Spain's Men of the Sea*, 8–15.

39. CWB 1:10. Champlain's account and Spanish records were similar on the Atlantic passage, with exactly the same routes from Sanlucar through the Canary Islands to a landfall at La Deseade Island in the West Indies. But again we find a difference of dates. Champlain reckoned that the crossing took 66 days; Spanish records made it forty-five days. The disparity could be explained by the difference in departure dates between Champlain's date of hoisting sail in the river and the Spanish date when the *Saint Julian* crossed the bar. See CWB 1:10–11; Vigneras, "Voyage," 175; Pérez-Mallaína, *Spain's Men of the Sea*, 10–11.

40. CWB 1:10–11; Pérez-Mallaína, *Spain's Men of the Sea*, 10.

41. CWB 1:11; Pérez-Mallaína, *Spain's Men of the Sea*, 10–11; Gagnon, "Is the *Brief Discours* by Champlain?" 87.

42. CWB 1:11. Again we have a disparity of time between Champlain's *Brief Discours* and Spanish records. Champlain reckoned the passage at two months and six days from the *San Julian*'s mooring in the Gaudalquivir River. Spanish sources set the arrival at La Deseada Island at March 18, which would yield a passage of one month and fifteen days. *San Julian* might have left her upstream mooring in January, and waited at the river's mouth for the fleet to form. If so, then Champlain's estimate of his landfall in the West Indies had the same date in mid-March as did the reports in the Spanish archives. Here again Champlain gives the date of first sailing. The Spanish sources give the date of crossing the bar.

43. For troubles aboard the *San Julian*, see Vigneras, "Voyage," 188; Giraudo, "Research Report," 95.

44. Vigneras and Giraudo found evidence that Coloma paired large vessels with small pataches, and that specifically on this voyage *San Julian* was paired with the *Sandoval*. Vigneras also found evidence in Spanish archives that Coloma sailed directly to Puerto Rico and *San Julian* had lagged behind. All of this evidence comes together if we conclude that *San Julian* made repairs in Guadeloupe, that she and *Sandoval* sailed together toward San Juan; when they were near the Virgin Islands the commanders found that *San Julian* could make San Juan on her own, and *Sandoval* was then detached to Margarita Island. Spanish records confirm that the patache *Sandoval* was sent on the annual errand to Margarita Island and that she rejoined the fleet in San Juan. All this is consistent with Champlain's account. Compare CWB 1:12–13, and works cited above by Vigneras, Giraudo, and Gagnon.

45. CWB 1:12.

46. Ibid.

47. Several debunkers have severely chastised Champlain for gross inaccuracy in his sketch-map of Guadeloupe, which they offer as proof that he was never there. It is true that the drawing is inaccurate in its representation of the indented coast of Guadeloupe, which gives the island

its distinctive butterfly shape. Champlain tells us that he was on the other side of the island, and this coast is represented more accurately. The pattern of this error is evidence that he worked from his own observation, rather than other sources. See Vigneras, "Voyage," 176; Gagnon, "Is the *Brief Discours* by Champlain?" 91.

48. This interpretation reconciles Champlain's narrative with evidence found by Vigneras in Spanish archives. Coloma sailed directly to Puerto Rico; *San Julian* lagged behind, and the patache *Sandoval* was sent to Margarita Island. Cf. CWB 1:12–13; Vigneras, "Voyage," 176–77, 189; there is no necessary contradiction here, and strictures in Bishop, *Champlain*, 16–17, are without foundation.

49. CWB 1:13; Gagnon, "Is the *Brief Discours* by Champlain?" 83, 87; R. A. Donkin, *Beyond Price: Pearls and Pearl Fishing: Origins to the Age of Discoveries* (Philadelphia: American Philosophical Society, 1998).

50. CWB 1:12–13; Clyde L. Mackenzie, Jr., Luis Troccoli and Luis B. Leon, "History of the Atlantic Pearl-Oyster, *Pinctata imbricata*, Industry in Venezuela and Colombia, with Biological and Ecological Observations," *Marine Fisheries Review* 65 (2003) 1–20; F[ernando] Cervigon, *Las perlas en la historia de Venezuela* (Caracas, 1998); R. A. Donkin, *Beyond Price: Pearls and Pearl Fishing: Origins to the Age of Discoveries* (Philadelphia: American Philosophical Society, 1998).

51. CWB 1:12–14; Vigneras, "Voyage," 177, 189; cf. Gagnon, "Is the *Brief Discours* by Champlain?" 83, 87, 90–91.

52. CWB 1:14.

53. Ibid. 1:17; Here is another disparity of dates which has been used by iconoclasts to impeach Champlain's *Brief Discours*. Spanish accounts reported that the English privateers had left much earlier; Champlain wrote that some English raiders left only fifteen days before Don Francisco's ships arrived. English records indicate that the Earl of Cumberland left earlier, but his second-in-command, Sir John Berkeley, remained in San Juan to continue the work of destroying the walls of the fortress.

Champlain's account is confirmed by Richard T. Spence, *The Privateering Earl*, 141–75. The best primary account of the English attack is by Dr. John Layfield, an Oxford don who was chaplain to the Earl of Cumberland. His manuscript is in the British Library, Sloane MS 3289, partly published in S. Purchas ed., *Hakluytus Posthumus; or Purchas his pilgrimes* (20 vols., Glasgow, 1905–07), 16: 43–106; the Earl's account is in Purchas 6: 29–42; an account based on interviews by Richard Robinson is in George Williamson, *George, Third Earl of Cumberland (1558–1805)* (Cambridge, 1920), 177–85.

54. CWB 1:15, 18–19, 22.

55. Ibid. 1:18; Vigneras, "Voyage," 177.

56. CWB 1:19–20; Iconoclasts have mocked these reports as fantasies. Champlain may have been describing a grove of Puerto Rican trees called the Benjamin Fig—not *ficus sp.* as Biggar believed, but *ficus benjamina*. Modern studies report that it has "the greatest crown spread of any tree on the island," and "might be more accurately described as a clone formed of many aerial roots grown into stems from interconnected and ever-spreading branches," much as Champlain observed. The largest *ficus benjamina* known to modern botany has a crown of about two hundred feet. A grove of them could have covered a very large area. Cf. CWB 1:19–22 with John K. Francis, *Champion Trees of Puerto Rico* (United States Department of Agriculture, Forest Service, International Institute of Tropical Forestry, Rio Piedras, P.R., 2000?), 1; and John K. Francis and Carol A. Lowe, eds., *Bioecología de Arboles Nativos*

y Exóticos de Puerto Rico y las Indias Occidentales (United States Department of Agriculture, Forest Service, International Institute of Tropical Forestry, Rio Piedras, Puerto Rico, General Technical Report IITF-15, June 2000).

57. Champlain's account of the division of the fleet and the itinerary of his squadron is fully confirmed in Spanish records. Cf. CWB 1:25–31; Vigneras, "Voyage," 179–80.

58. This is Biggar's point, in CWB, 1:31&n; Vigneras compared Champlain's work with Spanish records and concluded that "L'auteur du *Brief Discours* suit avec exactitude l'itinéraire de Joannes Urdayre, et ses croquis de Puerto Plata, Manzanillo, Mosquitos et Monte Christi semblent pris sur le vif ou sont d'excellentes copies." As always Vigneras gave Champlain a sharp elbow at the end! Cf. CWB 1:25–31; Vigneras, "Voyage," 179, and evidence in Spanish records found by Vigneras and Laura Giraudo.

59. Champlain's account of the squadron's track along this coast has been confirmed in Spanish archives; Cf. CWB 1:25–31; and records reported by Vigneras, 179. Vigneras adds, "His sketches of Puerto Plata, Manzanillo, Mosquitos et Monte Christi appear to be taken from life or are excellent copies."

60. Vigneras, "Voyage," 179–80, concludes from his search of Spanish archives that "the version that Champlain gives accords with Spanish sources, except for several small details."

61. Champlain's account differs from Spanish records in several details such as the number of enemy ships (thirteen by Champlain's count, eleven in Spanish records). There was also a difference on the location of the skirmish. The *Brief Discours* puts it on the south side of Cap St. Nicolas; Spanish sources place it at Gonaives. To study the coast is to see that this is a matter of language; the two accounts are fundamentally consistent. Compare CWB 1:26–31, and Vigneras, "Voyage," 179–80.

62. CWB 1:32.

63. CWB 1:23.

64. Champlain's description of the arid coast of southern Cuba with the Sierra Maestra rising behind it is very accurate, as I can testify from having cruised it several times. Cf. CWB 1:32–33.

65. CWB 1:33–34. Critics have argued that Champlain could not have visited the Cayman Islands because the records of the Spanish squadron make no mention of it—the fallacy of negative proof. Champlain wrote that they paused only one day. The Caymans lay directly on their course. Champlain's description of the fauna and flora was accurate. He has been chastised for writing that the Cayman Islands were six or seven in number. Today they are reckoned as three, but with the others as islets. He noted that only three islands had harbors. Cf. Vigneras, "Voyage," 181.

    Champlain's account has the ring of truth in its vivid and idiosyncratic detail. He wrote: "We anchored between the islands, and we remained there one day. I landed on two of them, and saw a very fine and most pleasant harbor. I walked a league inland, through very thick woods, and caught some rabbits, which were very numerous, a few birds, and a lizard as thick as my thigh, grey and the color of dead leaves." He accurately described the flora and fauna, and was fascinated by the deep woods, huge flocks of birds, "very good fruits," and the large Cayman iguanas, which are now protected. He caught a flightless bird as big as a goose and tried to eat it, a big mistake and a very bad taste (fort mauuais goust). It was evidence of Champlain's omnivorous curiosity, and a testament to the authenticity of this experience. CWB 1:33–34.

66. This also finds confirmation in the *West India Pilot*, which advised that "the attention of the mariner is drawn to the fishing grounds pointed out on the chart of the Campeche Bank, which would amply repay a couple of hours' delay by an abundant supply of rock-fish and red snappers." Compare *West India Pilot* (London, 1903), 1:453, quoted in CWB 1:35n.

67. Champlain's account of his visit to Mexico is the largest part of the *Brief Discours*, nearly 40 percent of the work. It was also the most controversial, and has been sharply attacked by hostile critics who argue that Champlain's claim to have landed at Vera Cruz, to have traveled to Mexico City, and then to have visited Panama in a small vessel was either fiction or falsehood (Vigneras, "Voyage," 182–85).

There is indeed a major problem of chronology here. Vigneras found records in Seville that Urdayre's Spanish squadron remained at Vera Cruz for about nine weeks, from May 1 to June 29, 1699. He read Champlain's *Brief Discours* as saying that his ship was there for more than fifteen weeks, perhaps eighteen weeks.

Champlain appears to say that he was two weeks at San Juan de Luz, spent an "entire month" in Mexico, made a voyage of three weeks to Porto Bello in Panama, was a month at Panama, returned to San Juan de Luz with no time given, and remained a period of fifteen days at San Juan de Luz while *San Julian* was careened and repaired yet again. This would appear to make a total of fifteen weeks plus the return from Panama, which Vigneras reckons at four and a half months. From this discrepancy Vigneras concludes that Champlain did not have time to spend one month at Mexico and another at Port-Bello, and that "it is necessary to reject one of these voyages, or perhaps both" (Vigneras, "Voyage," 183; CWB 1:38, 66, 70).

But there are also problems in the analysis of Vigneras. Champlain's count of weeks is not clear in his text, particularly for the trip to Portobello. Vigneras assumes that he was three weeks going there, a month in Panama, and three weeks returning, for a total of eleven or twelve weeks. But it is not certain that these temporal units were separate or overlapping, and Champlain gave no estimate of time for his return voyage.

The distance between Vera Cruz and Portobello was approximately 1,200 nautical miles. At a speed of five knots, each passage would have taken ten days, and Champlain might have been ten days at Portobello, for a total of four or five weeks, or a month overall, or even a little less, not eleven or twelve weeks. Perhaps this was what actually happened.

Champlain's *Discours* and Spanish records used different ways of timekeeping. The Spanish worked from documents and referred to calendar dates. Champlain worked from memory and reckoned time in intervals of weeks and months. He rarely referred to the calendar, and then only with vague references and never exact dates. This clearly caused a bias in time estimates. Throughout the *Discours* Champlain tended to overestimate the length of time intervals in the past, a clear pattern of memory distortion. For example, he remembered the passage from Blavet to Vigo Bay at eleven days; Spanish records showed that the voyage lasted five days. Champlain's memory of the Atlantic crossing from San Lucar to Deseada was sixty-six to seventy days; Spanish records made it forty-five days. The disparity is roughly comparable in estimates of time spent in New Spain.

This pattern of bias appears to have been working in Champlain's memory of the Portobello trip, and time spent at San Juan de Luz. Also, the fifteen days spent careening the *San Julian* at San Juan de Luz could well have overlapped with his passage from Portobello.

When we correct for a bias in Champlain's inflated overestimates of time intervals, and if some of those intervals may have overlapped, it is possible that he could have made trips both to Mexico City and Portobello during the nine weeks when his squadron was moored at San Juan de Luz.

Gagnon suggests another interpretative possibility, that Champlain included events that he witnessed, and happenings that were experienced by his shipmates. Gagnon suggests that we watch his pronouns carefully. Sometimes he spoke of "I" and sometimes of "we," to mean voyages not only by himself but by others in his squadron. I believe that this is correct and important as a general way of reading Champlain's text. But it does not apply to the Mexican and the Portobello voyage, because both were cast in the first person singular. Champlain tells us in no uncertain terms that he was there. Cf. Gagnon, "Is the *Brief Discours* by Champlain?" 91.

68. CWB 1:36.

69. Ibid. 1:36–37.

70. Gagnon, "Is the *Brief Discours* by Champlain?" 91; CWB 1:66; Records in Spanish archives establish that Urdayre ordered *San Julian*'s captain to go to Mexico City, and they report the length of the journey at thirty-nine days, very similar to Champlain's estimate. Here is strong supporting evidence that Champlain did go to Mexico City, as he claimed. Vigneras was not persuaded, but his own research in Spanish archives strongly supports Champlain's account, even if it does not explicitly mention his name.

71. CWB 1:39–41.

72. Ibid.1:56.

73. Ibid. 1:54.

74. CWB 1:60; Vigneras is exactly right when he notes the caution in Champlain's statements, which hostile readers missed. Compare Vigneras, "Voyage," 185.

75. CWB 1:63–65.

76. Ibid. 1:43.

77. Ibid. 1:63.

78. Ibid.

79. On these points his critics were correct and Champlain was mistaken. But these problems of accuracy on specific points of fact do not impeach the authenticity of the document.

80. CWB 1:66–67.

81. Ibid. 1:70.

82. Ibid. 1:69.

83. Ibid. 1:70–71. Champlain's account is confirmed in Spanish records of payment to seamen who did the repair work, June 20, 1599, see Giraudo, "Research Report," 26; citing AWI Contracción 2965. Confirmation for the careenage at San Juan de Luz also appears in Spanish records; but chronology is again a problem.

84. CWB 1:71.

85. Spanish records confirm that the ship was separated from the squadron, severely damaged, and by luck reached Havana.

86. Champlain's account and Spanish records are consistent on the separation of the *San Julian* from Urdayre's squadron, on reports that she was almost lost, and on the later arrival of Coloma. Vigneras, "Voyage," 188.

87. Giraudo, "Research Report," 95.

88. CWB 1:73.

89. Ibid. 1:77.

90. Ibid. 1:77–79.

91. On problems of chronology in this part of Champlain's travels, see Morris Bishop, *Champlain: The Life of Fortitude* (New York, 1948, 1963), 343–44. Note that Coloma was back by February 1600; Champlain tells us that he returned two years and two months after his departure, which would have been March or April 1601.

92. Testament of Guillermo Elena, June 26, 1601; Armstrong, *Champlain*, 275.

93. Ibid.

94. CWB 1:208.

95. Ibid. 1:68.

96. *Voyages* (1632), in CWB 3:314; note the interlocking with the narrative of the West Indies and the connection with the king.

97. *Voyages* (1632); CWB 3:315.

98. CWB 4:362.

6. GEOGRAPHER IN THE LOUVRE

1. Henry Percival Biggar, ed., *The Works of Samuel de Champlain*, 6 vols. and a portfolio of maps and drawings (CWB), (Toronto, 1922–36, reprinted 1971) 3:294–95.

2. Philippe Erlanger, *La vie quotidienne sous Henri IV* (Paris, 1958, 1977), 91–92; for Champlain's presence at court, CWB 3:314–16.

3. Quoted in Erlanger, *La vie quotidienne*, 92.

4. For the composition of the royal household in 1602, see a contemporary list in the British Public Record Office, "Officiers de la couronne," PRO SP 78/44 folio 404; this and other sources are cited in David Buisseret, *Henri IV* (London, 1984), 94–105. Social historians have done much interesting analytic work on the courts of Louis XIV, XV, and XVI as communities. See Emmanuel Le Roy Ladurie, *Saint-Simon and the Court of Louis XIV* (Chicago, 2001); William R. Newton, *L'espace du roi: la cour de France au Château de Versailles, 1682–1789* (Paris, 1999); and Newton, *La petite Cour: services et serviteurs à la Cour de Versailles* (Paris, 2006). The court of Henri IV was smaller than that of Louis XIV, but similar in many aspects of its structure and function.

5. Louis Batiffol. *Le Louvre sous Henri IV et Louis XIII: La vie de la cour de France au XVIIe siècle* (Paris, 1930), 13; Michel Carmona, *Le Louvre et les Tuileries: huit siècles d'histoire* (Paris, 2004), 75–80.

6. Jean-Pierre Babelon, *Henri IV* (Paris, 1982), 814–17; Babelon, "Les travaux de Henri IV au Louvre et aux Tuileries," *Paris et Île de France Mémoires* 29 (1978) 55–130; Batiffol, *Le Louvre sous Henri IV et Louis XIII*; Jacques Thuillier, "Peinture et politique: une théorie de la galerie royale sous Henri IV," *Études d'art français offertes à Charles Sterling* (Paris, 1975); Michel Carmona, *Le Louvre et les Tuileries*, 71–108.

7. Buisseret, *Henri IV*, 94; Bertrand de Jouvenel, *Du Pouvoir: Histoire naturelle de sa croissance* (Geneva, 1945; Paris, 1972); translated by J. F. Huntington as *On Power: The Natural History of Its Growth* (Boston, 1962).

8. Buisseret, *Henri IV*, 94–95.

9. Keith Thomas has some wonderful unpublished work on the theme of fashion and change in the early modern era.

10. Buisseret, *Henri IV*, 94, 96; citing contemporary lists in the Bibliothèque nationale de

France, Collection Clairambault, 837 folio 3225–3349; AN KK 151, 152, 153; also "Officiers de la Couronne," PRO SP 78/44 folio 404 British National Archives.

11. David Buisseret, in *The Mapmaker's Quest: Depicting New Worlds in Renaissance Europe* (Oxford, 2003), 64, 67, 116, 131, 139, passim. This is an excellent and deeply learned work by an expert on early cartography and a biographer of Henri IV. It is critically important for an understanding of Champlain's career, and for the depth of Henri IV's activity in supporting geography and cartography. It also describes the king's large staff of expert geographers and cartographers such as Claude de Chastillon and Pierre Fougeu, and surveyors and instrument makers such as Philippe Danfrie at the Louvre.

12. Marc Lescarbot referred to Champlain as "géographe du Roy" in his *Histoire de la Nouvelle France* 2d edition, revised, corrected, and augmented (Paris, 1611), 612; John Carter Brown Library. Marcel Trudel was skeptical, and wrote: "Était-il *géographe du roi*, comme le saluera Lescarbot dans un sonnet de 1607? Nulle part Champlain ne porte ce titre et personne autre que Lescarbot ne le lui donne; rien n'établit que Champlain, tout en agissant en géographe, ait occupé le poste officiel de géographe du roi." Cf. Marcel Trudel, *Histoire de la Nouvelle-France* (Montreal, 1963) 1:258. The phrase does not appear in Lescarbot's sonnet but it is in the second edition of his history of New France, as cited above.

    Trudel is correct as to an official title of *the* Royal Geographer, but Buisseret reports that many geographers, cartographers, and experts in related sciences were employed by the king, with apartments in the Louvre. We have evidence that Champlain was receiving an annual pension from the king of 600 livres a year and that he was at the Louvre in this period, and Champlain himself wrote that the king wished to keep him "about his person." Buisseret observes that "the King was a great patron of Samuel de Champlain who would soon be compiling his astonishing maps of North America." See David Buisseret, *The Mapmaker's Quest: Depicting New Worlds in Renaissance Europe* (Oxford, 2003), 64, 92–95. From this I conclude that Trudel was correct in his statement that Champlain was not the only official *géographe du roi* under Henri IV, but Buisseret and Lescarbot are correct in describing him as one of many *géographes du roi* who worked in the basement of the Grande Galerie of the Louvre.

13. A biographical sketch of Champlain in the *Biographie Saintonge*, 1852, reported that Champlain had worked as an *armateur* in Dieppe during these years; see also Morris Bishop, *Champlain: A Life of Fortitude* (New York, 1948, 1963), 37.

14. CWB 3:260.

15. Guilheume Allene [sic], Agreement, Nov 7, 1570, folios 709–10, Archives départementales de la Charente-Maritime; reproduced in Pauline Arsenault, "Acadia in Champlain's New France: From Arcadia to China," Litalien and Vaugeois eds., *Champlain: The Birth of French America* (Montreal 2004), 114–20.

16. Samuel E. Morison, *Samuel de Champlain: Father of New France* (New York, 1972), 24–25.

17. Marine archaeologists have raised some of these sixteenth-century boats from coastal waters off Labrador. They are remarkably similar to the whaleboats of Nantucket and New Bedford in the nineteenth century. See James A. Tuck and Robert Grenier, *Red Bay, Labrador, World Whaling Capital A.D., 1550–1600* (St. John's, Newfoundland, 1989), 36–37.

18. CWB 1:463, 3:415; Lescarbot, *New France* 2:362; Cartier had similar encounters with Basque fishermen as early as 1534 and 1535. See also Tuck and Grenier, *Red Bay, Labrador*, 2–3.

19. Robert Le Blant and René Baudry, *Nouveaux documents sur Champlain et son époque* (Ottawa, 1967), xxvii.

20. René Bélanger, *Les Basques dans l'estuaire du Saint-Laurent, 1535–1635* (Montreal, 1971); Laurier Turgeon, "Pêcheurs basques et indiens des côtes du Saint-Laurent au XVIe siècle: Perspectives de recherches," *Études canadiennes/Canadian Studies* 13 (1982), 9–14; Turgeon, "Pêches basques en Atlantique Nord (XVIIe–XVIIIe siècles): étude d'économie maritime" (Bordeaux, thèse de doctorat, 1982) and many essays by Selma Barkham, including "The Basques: Filling a Gap in Our History between Jacques Cartier and Champlain," *Canadian Historical Journal* 96 (1978), 8–19; "The Documentary Evidence for Basque Whaling Ships in the Strait of Belle Isle," in G. M. Story, ed., *Early European Settlement and Exploitation in Atlantic Canada: Selected papers* (St. John's, Nfld., 1982), 53–95; "The Basque Whaling Establishment in Labrador, 1536–1632: A Summary," *Arctic* 37 (1984), 515–19; "A Note on the Strait of Belle Isle during the Period of Basque Contact with Indians and Inuit," *Études/Inuit/Studies* 4 (1980), 51–58.

21. Peter Bakker, "A Basque Etymology for the Word 'Iroquois,'" *Man in the Northeast* 40 (1990), 89–93; idem, "The Language of the Coast Tribes is Half Basque: A Basque-Amerindian Pidgin in Use between Europeans and Native Americans in North America, ca. 1540–ca. 1640," *Anthropological Linguistics* 31 (1989), 117–41; G. M. Day, "Iroquois, An Etymology," *Ethnohistory* 15 (1968) 389–402; and I. Goddard, "Synonymy," in B. G. Trigger ed., *Handbook of North American Indians, Northeast* (Washington, 1978) 15:319–21.

22. CWB 1:228.

23. Ibid. 3:261.

24. Ramsay Cook, ed., *The Voyages of Jacques Cartier* (Toronto, 1993), xxv–xli, passim; Gustave Lanctot, *A History of Canada* (Toronto, 1963), 55.

25. For Cartier's kidnapping of Donnacona and his sons, see Cook, ed., *The Voyages of Jacques Cartier*, xxxviii–xxxix. See also Roland Tremblay, *Les Iroquoiens du Saint-Laurent: peuple du maïs* (Montreal, 2006), 100–11.

26. Cook, ed., *The Voyages of Jacques Cartier*, xli, with much more on the mistrust of Cartier.

27. CWB 6:193; 3:298–99; 1:227; H. P. Biggar, ed., *The Voyages of Jacques Cartier* (Ottawa, 1924); *A Collection of Documents relating to Jacques Cartier and the Sieur de Roberval* (Ottawa, 1930); Lanctot, *Canada*, 1:52–75.

28. CWB 3:264.

29. Ibid. 3:265–66.

30. Ibid. 3:268–69.

31. Ibid. 3:290–91.

32. Ibid. 3:275.

33. Ibid. 3:289–91.

34. Marq de Villiers and Sheila Hirtle, *Sable Island* (New York, 2004), 2–10, 123–33.

35. Joseph de Ber, ed., "Un document inédit sur l'île de Sable et le Marquis de la Roche," *RHAF* 2 (1948–49) 199–213; Lescarbot, *New France*, 2:398–405; Dionne, *Samuel Champlain*, appendix, 354–60.

36. Lescarbot, *New France*, 194–95; Lanctot, *Canada*; Trudel, *Histoire de la Nouvelle-France* 1: 231–33; Bishop, "The Marquis de la Roche and Sable Island," in *Champlain*, 347–49; Gustave Lanctot, "l'Établissement du Marquis de La Roche à l'Île de Sable," *Rapport de la*

Société historique du Canada, 1933, in *Annual Report of the Canadian Historical Association* (1933), 33–37; Charles Bréard and Paul Bréard, *Documents relatifs à la Marine Normande et à ses armements aux XVIIe et XVIIIe siècles* (Rouen, 1889), 79–83.

37. CWB 3:302–04.

38. This Pierre de Chauvin should not be confused with Captain Pierre Chauvin de la Pierre (var. Chavin) of Dieppe, whom Champlain appointed acting commander of Quebec in 1609–10. For Dieppe and North America, and a discussion of the two Chauvins, see Pierre Ickowicz and Raymonde Litalien, *Dieppe-Canada: cinq cents ans d'histoire commune* (Dieppe, 2004), 14ff.

39. CWB 3:311.

40. Ibid. 3:308.

41. Ibid. 3:305–12.

42. Ibid. 3:310; Bréard and Bréard, *Documents relatifs à la Marine Normande*, 65–92.

43. CWB 3:293–94.

44. Ibid. 2:294–95.

45. Ibid. 3:302–04.

46. H. P. Biggar, *The Early Trading Companies of New France* (1901, 1937, Clifton, N.J., 1972), 45–49.

47. CWB 1:229; 3:312–18; 6:194.

48. Ibid. 3:313.

49. Ibid. 3:313–14.

50. Ibid. 3:315.

51. Ibid. 3:316.

7. TADOUSSAC

1. Alain Beaulieu, "The Birth of the Franco-American Alliance," in Raymonde Litalien and Denis Vaugeois, eds., *Champlain: The Birth of French America* (Montreal, 2004), 160.

2. CWB 3:315–16.

3. CWB 5:92–93, 198; 3:316; Morris Bishop, *Champlain: A Life of Fortitude* (New York, 1948, 1963), 38; Samuel E. Morison, *Samuel de Champlain: Father of New France* (New York, 1972), 23.

4. D'Aumont to Henri IV, July 3, 1594, Robert Le Blant and René Baudry, *Nouveaux documents sur Champlain et son époque* (Ottawa, 1967),15–16.

5. CWB 3:305.

6. Ibid. 4:363.

7. Bishop, *Champlain*, 39; Joe C. W. Armstrong, *Champlain* (Toronto, 1987), 39; CWB 1:98.

8. Details of the ships appear in *actes notariés*, Feb. 18, 24, Mar. 10, 12, 1603, Charles Bréard and Paul Bréard, *La Marine normande et ses armements aux XVIe et XVIIe siècles pour le Canada, l'Afrique, les Antilles, le Brésil et les Indes* (Rouen, 1889), 99–101.

9. Ibid.

10. For a discussion of Champlain's purposes, see Alain Beaulieu and Réal Ouellet, eds., *Des Sauvages* (Montreal 2002), 36–37.

11. CWB 3:316. For the shipment of prefabricated boats, see William A. Baker, *The Mayflower and Other Colonial Vessels* (London, 1983), 65–74. A description of shallops "transported in

portions" can be found in Captain John Smith's account of the first voyage to Virginia, and in *Mourt's Relation*, a journal recounting the Pilgrims' venture at Plymouth.

12. CWB 1:92.

13. Ibid.

14. CWB 1:92–94; Morison, *Samuel de Champlain*, 27.

15. Ibid. 3:316.

16. Ibid. 1:105–06. Some historians believe that this first encampment was very small, and that the larger group gathered in response to the French arrival. But Champlain tells us explicitly: "They were 1,000 people—men, women and children. The place at St. Matthew's Point where they first camped, is very pleasant."

17. Eleanor Leacock, "Seventeenth-Century Montagnais Social Relations and Values," and Edward S. Rogers and Eleanor Leacock, "Montagnais-Legaspi," in June Helm, ed., *Handbook of North American Indians 6: Subarctic* (Washington, 1981), 169–89, 190–95; notes and materials in the Canadian Museum of Civilization, Hull, Quebec; conversations with Martin Gagnon, ethnographer and historian of the Montagnais nation at the Innu Cultural Centre, Essipit Reserve.

18. CWB 1:103. Champlain always called them nations, not tribes, and recorded their names as "Montagnes, Estechemins & Algoumekins." Some scholars have raised a question: were the three nations all present, or was this merely a gathering of Montagnais? Alain Beaulieu concludes that all three were there. I absolutely agree, on the basis of Champlain's language, on the numbers cited in two passages, on the location of the meeting in relation to their homelands, and the description of the tabagie. Cf. Beaulieu, "The Birth of the Franco-American Alliance," 15–62.

19. Camil Girard and Édith Gagné, "Première alliance interculturelle. Rencontre entre Montagnais et Français à Tadoussac en 1603," *Recherches Amérindiennes au Québec* 25 (1995), 3–14.

20. Was Anadabijou a name or a title? Some of Champlain's passages imply that it was a title; others, that it was a name. For a discussion, see Beaulieu, "The Birth of the Franco-American Alliance," 15–62. For the length of the lodge see CWB 1:101, where Champlain writes that "they had eight or ten kettles full of meats in the midst of the said lodge, and they were set some six paces apart, each on its own fire." CWB 1:101; see also Victor Tremblay, "Anadabijou," *Saguenayensia*, Sept.–Oct. 1959, 98–101.

21. CWB 1:99–101.

22. Ibid. 1:101.

23. Ibid. 1:104.

24. Ibid. 1:104.

25. Ibid. 1:108–09, 118.

26. Ibid. 1:109–11.

27. Ibid. 1:110.

28. Historians have come to different conclusions on the nature of this event. Early writers thought of it as an understanding on the fur trade and exploration. Benjamin Sulte in 1882 may have been the first to describe it as an alliance between the French and the Indians. The Abbé Tremblay thought of it as more than an alliance and called it a "traité." Marcel Trudel described it as an "entente," or understanding rather than a *traité* or formal alliance. Olive Patricia Dickason thought of it as "une alliance selon le ritual amérindien" and that Champlain also had this idea of it. I believe that this interpretation is correct. This informal en-

tente, anchored in Indian rituals, proved to be more durable in that form than many formal treaties or pacts that were reduced to writing in a formal document of consent on a European model. For a discussion see Girard and Gagné, "Première alliance interculturelle," 5–9.

29. Marcel Trudel, *Histoire de la Nouvelle-France: Les Vaines Tentatives, 1524–1603* (Montreal, 1963), 260–61; Beaulieu and Ouellet, in their excellent edition of Champlain's *Des Sauvages,* 11–60. My wife, Judy, and I learned much in conversation on August 7, 2007, with Jacques Martin in his home near Pointe aux Alouettes (also called Pointe Saint-Mathieu) on the Saguenay River. Martin knows intimately the place, the people, and the event. He lives the dream of Champlain and Anadabijou, as do we, and is devoted to the preservation of its memory, and he showed us some of the artifacts that he has found in the area.

30. Marcel Trudel, "Bâtir une Nouvelle-France plutôt sur l'axe Tadoussac-Baie d'Hudson?" *Mythes et réalités dans l'histoire du Québec* (Montreal, 2001), 39–47.

31. Ibid., 39–48.

32. Champlain's soundings appeared in his map, "Port de Tadoussac," reproduced in CWB 2:19 facing page; also CWB 2:16–19; 1:96–97, 121–24; by the evidence of soundings in the twentieth century, the Saguenay River is not as deep in our time as in Champlain's. Rivermen told us that sediment as much as 500 feet deep has accumulated near the river's mouth.

33. Ibid., 2:16–19; Pierre Béland, *Beluga: A Farewell to Whales* (New York, 1996), 32–49.

34. CWB 1:96–97.

35. Ibid. 2:19.

36. Ibid. 2:18.

37. Trudel, "L'axe Tadoussac," 41.

38. CWB 1:124.

39. CWB (1632) 3:316.

40. CWB 1:137.

41. Ibid. 1:127.

42. Ibid. 1:129.

43. Ibid. 1:131–32.

44. Ibid. 1:137.

45. Ibid. 1:135.

46. Ibid. 1:138, 140–41.

47. Ibid. 1:149; 3:316–17.

48. Ibid. 1:151.

49. Ibid. 1:151.

50. Ibid. 1:152.

51. Ibid. 1:156.

52. Ibid. 1:153–56.

53. Ibid. 1:180–85; Carl O. Sauer, *Northern Mists* (Berkeley, 1970), 78.

54. Morison, *Samuel de Champlain*, 32.

55. Ibid.

56. Samuel de Champlain, *Des Savvages, ov, Voyage de Samvel Champlain, de Brovage, fait en la France nouvelle en l'an mil six cens trois* (Paris, chez Clavde de Monstr'oeil, tenant sa boutique en la Cour du Palais, au nom de Jésus, avec privilege dv Roi, 1603). A modern edition, edited by Alain Beaulieu et Réal Ouellet is published by Les Messageries (Montreal, 1993). A bilingual edition in French and English is in Champlain, *Works*, CWB 1:81–189.

57. Alain Rey et al., eds. *Le Grand Robert de la langue française*, 6 vols. (Paris 2001) 6:213ff, s.v.

"sauvage." For discussion see Peter N. Moogk, *La Nouvelle France: The Making of French Canada, A Cultural History* (East Lansing, 2000), 17ff; also Gervais Carpin, *Histoire d'un mot: l'ethnonyme Canadien de 1535 à 1691* (Sillery, 1995), chapter 2, "Le canadien nommant Le 'Sauvage,' "25–66; and Olive Patricia Dickason, *The Myth of the Savage and the Beginnings of French Colonialism in the Americas* (Edmonton, 1984).

58. CWB 1:110.

59. Ibid. 3:81ff, 91n; 169–72; 4:267, 275, 335.

60. Marc Lescarbot, *History of New France*, 3 vols. (Toronto, 1907) 1:32–33; CWB 1:308.

61. CWB 1:110.

62. Ibid.1:120.

63. Ibid.1:111, 117.

64. Ibid.1:111.

65. Ibid.1:111.

66. Ibid. 3:222; Bruce Trigger wrote of Champlain: "He failed completely to understand the consensual nature of native political arrangements, because he viewed all power as being delegated from above, he did not comprehend that Indian leaders could not decide matters." Trigger, *Natives and Newcomers: Canada's "Heroic Age" Reconsidered* (Montreal, 1985, 1994), 198–99. This is mistaken. Champlain repeatedly noted that chiefs had very little authority in the European sense. He repeated these observations from 1603 to the end of his life, and organized many approaches to the Indians around an understanding of the more consensual Indian polities.

67. CWB 1:119.

68. Ibid. 3:13.

69. Ibid. 3:17.

8. SAINTE-CROIX

1. Henry Percival Biggar, ed., *The Works of Samuel de Champlain*, 6 vols. and a portfolio of maps and drawings (CWB), (Toronto, 1922–36, reprinted 1971) 1:307.

2. CWB 3:317.

3. The "special account" and manuscript map that Champlain gave Henri IV in 1603 have not been found. Probably the special account was a detailed report on the tabagie at Tadoussac, and prospects for settlement in the St. Lawrence Valley. It would have been very different from *Des Sauvages*. Champlain had been explicitly ordered to submit such a document by de Chaste and the king himself (CWB 3:318).

   The map probably centered on the St. Lawrence River. Champlain wrote later, "I made a very exact map of what I saw, which I had engraved in 1604, which since then has been published with the account of my first voyages [in 1612]." No map engraved by Champlain in 1604 has been found. His map of 1612 centers on his observations in the St. Lawrence Valley and on reports that the Indians had given him about the Great Lakes. It also includes much additional information about Acadia and Norumbega that Champlain obtained on his coastal voyages of 1604–06. The 1612 map was likely based on the 1603 manuscript map and the 1604 engraving, with additions from the subsequent voyages. Cf. CWB 3:411, 318 and discussion in C. E. Heidenreich's excellent *Explorations and Mapping of Samuel de Champlain, 1602–1632* (Toronto, 1976), 2–4; Cartographica monograph 17; also published as a beiheft to *Canadian Cartographer* 13 (1976).

4. CWB 3:318.

5. Jean Liebel, *Pierre Dugua, sieur de Mons, fondateur de Québec* (Quebec, 1999), 75, citing a manuscript in the Bibliothèque nationale de France, n. acq. fr. 9281 folio 2 recto; see also Guy Binot, *Pierre Dugua de Mons* (Royan, 2004), 66–70. Some of the major documents were first published as *Commissions du Roy et de Monseigneur l'Admiral au sieur de Monts, pour l'habitation ès terres de Lacadie, Canada, & autres endroits en la nouvelle France. Ensemble les défenses premières et secondes à tous autres de traffiquer avec les Sauvages desdites terres. Avec la verification en la Cour de Parlement à Paris* (Paris, 1605; facsimile published in Bar Harbor, Maine, 1915); also *Collection de manuscrits contenant lettres, mémoires, et autres documents historiques relatifs à la Nouvelle France, recueillis aux Archives de la Province de Québec ou copiés à l'étranger* 4 vols. (Quebec, 1883), 1:40–49. These and other primary materials on de Mons' appointment also appear in Binot, *Pierre Dugua de Mons* (Royan, 2004), 247–55; also William Inglis Morse, ed., *Pierre du Gua, sieur de Monts: Records Colonial and 'Saintongeois,'* (London, 1939), 4–13.

6. Binot, *Pierre Dugua de Mons*, 60.

7. CWB 1:231.

8. For Champlain's association with these three men—Pierre Jeannin (1540–1622?), Nicolas Brûlart, marquis de Sillery (1544–1624), and Charles II de Cossé-Brissac (ca. 1550–1621)—see CWB 1:3; 2:243, 257; on the men themselves, also see Pierre Saumaise, *Éloge sur la vie de Pierre Janin* (Dijon, 1623); Henri Ballande, "*Rebelle et conseiller de trois souverains: le président Jeannin (1542–1643)*" (Paris, 1981); L. E. Bois, *Le Chevalier Noël Brûlart de Sillery, Étude Biographique* nouvelle édition corrigée (Québec, 1871); the entire text of the latter book is online in OurRoots/NosRacines.ca; this was the son of Nicolas Brûlart de Sillery; see also Pierre Cossé, *Les Brissac et l'histoire* (Grasset, 1973); and Cossé, *Les Brissac* (Farquelle, 1952).

9. CWB 3:320.

10. CWB 3:320–21; Guy Binot, another man of Saintonge, observed that de Mons was drawn to Acadia as "plus méridional, située sur la même latitude que sa Saintonge natale." Cf. *Pierre Dugua de Mons*, 65.

11. Samuel E. Morison, *Samuel de Champlain: Father of New France* (New York, 1972), 35.

12. Elizabeth Jones, *Gentlemen and Jesuits: Quests for Glory and Adventure in the Early Days of New France* (Toronto, 1986), 19.

13. Ernest H. Wilkins, "Arcadia in America," *APS Proceedings* 101 (1957) 4–30; Carl O. Sauer, *Seventeenth Century North America* (Berkeley, 1980), 77; Andrew H. Clark, *Acadia: The Geography of Nova Scotia to 1760* (Madison, 1968), 71n.

14. The commission is published in Morse, ed., *Pierre Du Gua, sieur de Monts*, 4–6.

15. De Mons, "Articles proposed Nov. 6, 1603," in *Collection de manuscrits contenant lettres, mémoires et autres documents historiques relatifs à la Nouvelle-France,* 1:40–43.

16. Reply to Articles proposed Nov. 6, 1603, Ibid.1:40–43.

17. "Commission of 8 Nov. 160–3"; "Remonstrances par le sieur de Mons, 18 déc. 1603, Bibliothèque Nationale, Dupuy vol. 318, 107–108r; for discussion, Binot, *Pierre Dugua de Mons*, 65–67; Liebel, *Pierre Dugua, sieur de Mons*, 78–83; Marcel Trudel, *Histoire de la Nouvelle-France* (Montreal, 1963) 2: 9–11.

18. Binot, *Pierre Dugua de Mons*, 68.

19. Walter Isaacson and Evan Thomas, *The Wise Men* (New York, 1986). In the huge literature

on the American founding fathers, nobody has brought out the linkage between their hard experience and high ideals. To these two generations one might add the circles that formed around Elizabeth I in England and Henri IV in France.

20. Documents dated 17 January and 25 January, 1604, in Henri Harrisse, *Notes pour servir à l'histoire, à la bibliographie, et à la cartographie de la Nouvelle-France et des pays adjacents, 1545–1700* (Paris, 1872), 280–82; and Édouard Gosselin, *Nouvelles glanes historiques normandes puisées exclusivement dans des documents inédits* (Rouen, 1873), 21–23; Trudel, *Histoire de la Nouvelle-France* 2:14.

21. "The Two Monopolies of Monts," H. P. Biggar, *The Early Trading Companies of New France* (1937, rpt. Clifton, N.J., 1937), 51–55; Trudel, *Histoire de la Nouvelle-France* 2:14–15; Contract of Feb. 19, 1604, in Gosselin, *Nouvelles glanes*, 24–29; Binot, *Pierre Dugua de Mons*, 81–82; Liebel, *Pierre Dugua, sieur de Mons*, 85–93; "Association de Samuel Georges et Jean Macain à la compagnie de Pierre du Gua, sieur de Mons," Feb. 10, 1604, and related documents of the same date, in Robert Le Blant et René Baudry, eds., *Nouveaux documents sur Champlain et son époque* (Ottawa, 1967) 1:80–85.

22. CWB 3:323.

23. Liebel, *Pierre Dugua, sieur de Mons*, 105; Trudel, *Histoire de la Nouvelle-France* 2:63, 465, 486; Marc Lescarbot, *History of New France* (Toronto, 1907), 3:231.

24. Adrien Huguet, *Jean de Poutrincourt, Fondateur de Port-Royal en Acadie; Vice-Roi du Canada, 1557–1615: campagnes, voyages et aventures d'un colonisateur sous Henri IV* (Amiens and Paris, 1932), 154–72. The title is inaccurate; Poutrincourt was never viceroy of Canada or New France, but this book is still the most comprehensive study of Poutrincourt.

25. Lescarbot, *History of New France* 2:27, 228; Champlain, CWB 1:234, 277, 391; Trudel, *Histoire de la Nouvelle-France* 2:24. This Boullay or Boullet should not be confused with Eustache Boullé, the future brother-in-law of Champlain, who was prominent in later voyages. Cf. Biggar, who is mistaken in CWB 1:247n; and Trudel, *Histoire de la Nouvelle-France* 2:24n, who puts it right.

26. Charles Bréard and Paul Bréard, *Documents relatifs à la Marine Normande et à ses armements aux XVIe et XVIIe siècles* (Rouen, 1889), 56, 102; CWB 1:230, 276n, 363; Lescarbot, *History of New France* 2:227, 253; Liebel, *Pierre Dugua, sieur de Mons* (n.p., 1999), 123.

27. The most complete list appears on Champlain's sketch of the Isle Sainte-Croix. Scattered references in Champlain and Lescarbot. For the sieur Ralluau see CWB 1:239 passim.

28. Trudel, *Histoire de la Nouvelle-France* 2:24; CWB 1:246–47.

29. Liebel, *Pierre Dugua, sieur de Mons*, 98.

30. CWB 1:233; 3:321.

31. Trudel, *Histoire de la Nouvelle-France* 2:34, 36.

32. A procuration of Pierre du Gua [sieur de Monts] for Mathieu de Coste, described as "nègre" or "naigre." De Monts had contracted for his services with Nicolas de Bauquemare, merchant of Rouen; see Declaration of Nicolas de Bauquemare for le nègre Mathieu de Coste for services "de Canada Cadie et ailleurs . . . Canada, Acadie, et Nouvelle France"; Le Blant and Baudry, eds., *Nouveaux documents*, 105–06, 194, 195, 203, 212, 235, 388. For his kidnapping and ransom see Morse, ed., *Pierre du Gua, Sieur de Mons*, 51; and Le Blant and Baudry, *Nouveaux documents* 1:196. Morison garbled the name as "d'Acosta" and wrote contemptuously that he "had somehow managed to learn the Indian languages and . . . caused his master so much trouble," (p. xxvi).

33. CWB 1:253–54, 275; Lescarbot, *History of New France* 2:232, 242–44, 247; 3:45, 130.

34. Trudel, *Histoire de la Nouvelle-France* 2:25; CWB 3:327; Gabriel Sagard, *Histoire du Canada* (1636) 1:9.

35. Liebel, *Pierre Dugua, sieur de Mons*, 103.

36. Jean Liebel found much primary material in the manuscript port records of Honfleur and other records in the departmental archives of Calvados, 8E 6517 folio 6Or; 6566 folio 149r; 6666, folio 106v, 184v,r; 6517 folio 302r; 335r; 5520 folio 318, 342; 6666 f. 184v, 185r, 196r, 197v, T96v; 6517, f335r, 107v, 184v recto; all in *Pierre Dugua sieur de Mons*, 95–108. He also found a source for the relationship of tonnage to length in Père Fournier, S.J. *Hydrographie, contenant la théorie et la pratique de toutes les parties de la navigation* (Paris, 1643), a chapter on "Architecture navale," 16–43.

37. Liebel, *Pierre Dugua, sieur de Mons*, 100.

38. CWB 1:238–39; Liebel, *Pierre Dugua, sieur de Mons*, 127.

39. At least four accounts of this voyage survive: one in Champlain's *Voyages* published in 1613, CWB 1:234–36; another in Champlain's Voyages of 1632, CWB 3:321–25; a third by Lescarbot (who was not aboard, but talked with Poutrincourt and others) in *History of New France* 2:227–31; and an anonymous essay in *Le Mercure François*, volume for 1608 (1611) 294; reprinted in *Transactions of the Royal Society of Canada* 8 (1902) 2:172. See also new material in Liebel, *Pierre Dugua, sieur de Mons*, 108–12.

   Champlain wrote in his first account that the date of departure was April 7, 1604. Lescarbot and the *Mercure François* made it March 7. Champlain's editor, H. P. Biggar, believed that Lescarbot and the *Mercure François* were correct and Champlain was mistaken, a judgment repeated by other scholars. But Champlain was right about the date and Lescarbot was mistaken. Evidence has turned up in court records that merchants were still signing on passengers as late as March 17, 1604, and that *Don-de-Dieu* was still at Honfleur until 24 March, then sailed on that date for Le Havre and joined *La Bonne-Renommée* which had been there since at least March 17, 1604. See Liebel, *Pierre Dugua, sieur de Mons*, 98, 104.

40. Lescarbot, *History of New France* 2:301.

41. Lescarbot, *History of New France* 2:228.

42. CWB 1:234; 3:321.

43. CWB 1:236n; Nicolas Denys, *The Description and Natural History of the Coasts of North America (Acadia)*, ed. William F. Ganong (Toronto, 1908), 147n, a bilingual edition published by the Champlain Society.

44. CWB 1:235; 3:322. Biggar did not believe that it could be so, but Champlain had made even faster crossings. In 1615 he sailed from Honfleur on April 24 (he wrote August by mistake) and reached Tadoussac on May 24. He did it again in 1618, from Honfleur on May 24 to Tadoussac on June 24. See Liebel, *Pierre Dugua, sieur de Mons*, 110.

45. CWB. The chart was published at Paris in 1613. It is reprinted with a modern chart in CWB I:236.f.

46. Sheila Chambers et al., *Historic LaHave River Valley: Images of Our Past* (Halifax, 2004); Joan Dawson, "History," www.fortpointmuseum.com/history.asp.

47. Silas Tertius Rand, *Legends of the Micmacs, Wellesley Philological Publications* (New York and London, 1894), 225–26; cf Nicolas Denys, *Acadia*, 323. The 400th Anniversary celebrations at Sainte–Croix sponsored with the endorsement of the National Park Service in 2004 asserted that Mi'kmaq Indians thought Champlain's ships were great white birds. This is complete humbug. The long history of maritime activity on the North Atlantic coast has left

archaeological evidence. Peter Pope writes that "translucent chert from Ramah Bay in northern Labrador has a wide distribution in pre-contact sites along the eastern littoral of North America as far south as Long Island Sound." Cf. Peter Pope, *The Many Landfalls of John Cabot* (Toronto, 1997), 152.

48. CWB 1:237. Champlain's estimate of five leagues from La Hève to Rossignol (today called Liverpool) was mistaken; eight leagues would be more accurate. A similar account is in Lescarbot, 2:229. A third account by Pont-Gravé, dated 24 Oct. 1604, is in Bréard and Bréard, *Documents relatifs à la Marine Normande*. All confirm the accuracy of Champlain's accounts. Owners of the seized ship brought suit, and after four years of litigation a settlement was reached. De Mons and his associates, "moved by pity and compassion," made a gift of 900 livres but kept the furs. For the litigation that followed in France, and its outcome, see "Procuration donnée par les bourgeois du navire La Levrette. . . ." March 26, 1608, and "Transaction de Pierre Dugua, Samuel Georges et leurs associés, avec les bourgeois havrais du navire *La Levrette*," April 4, 1608, in Le Blant and Baudry, eds., *Nouveaux documents*, 1:166–67, 169–72. For more detail about *La Levrette*, see Liebel, *Pierre Dugua, sieur de Monts*, 112–13. He estimates a figure of 500 livres for the payment to Rossignol and the owners of *Levrette*, which differs from other sources.

49. A version of this oral tradition was published in Mike Parker, *Guides to the North Woods: Hunting and Fishing Tales from Nova Scotia 1860–1960* (Halifax, 1990), 95–96, from which these quotations are taken.

50. We know this story from a happy conjunction of sources. Oral legends of the Mi'kmaq and *Métis* people of Acadia interlock perfectly with the narratives of Champlain, Marc Lescarbot, François Pont-Gravé, and French court documents. These elements came together four centuries later, August 22, 2004, when we heard the legends again from Matthew Verge on a beautiful late summer day in the harbor where they took place. Many thanks to Matthew Verge for lending a copy of Mike Parker's book, and for taking the time to talk with us on our visit to Liverpool in the summer of 2004.

51. CWB 1:237–38, 251, 3:332; 6:233; Lescarbot, *History of New France* 2:229.

52. CWB 1:239.

53. Ibid. 1:239–40.

54. Ibid. 1:241–43.

55. Ibid. 1:243.

56. Ibid. 1:247–49.

57. Ibid. 1:250–51.

58. For Jean Ralluau, see CWB 1:239, 267, 280, 388, 456; Trudel, *Histoire de la Nouvelle-France* 1:22, 26, 30, 52, 70, 174, 482; Le Blant et Baudry, eds., *Nouveaux documents* 1: xii, xxiv, 212, 225, 317–18, passim.

59. CWB 1:255n.

60. Ibid. 1:256.

61. Ibid. 1:256.

62. Ibid. 1: 258–59.

63. Ibid. 1:261–63.

64. Ibid. 1:265–68.

65. Ibid. 1:269.

66. Still a leading study is William F. Ganong, *Champlain's Island* (1902, expanded edition, Saint John, 2003), 122–139, 74–77; it examines the eyewitness accounts by Champlain and

Lescarbot who visited the island shortly after it was abandoned. Ganong's research confirms the accuracy of both accounts. Another study is Edwin A. Garrett IV, "L'île Sainte-Croix–St. Croix Island," ms., 2007, with thanks to the author for a copy of his manuscript.

67. CWB 1:302.

68. Champlain tells us that they reached the Saint John River on June 24, 1604, St. John's Day. They sailed through the reversing falls but "not farther," which required two tides, then explored islands to the south, went hunting, then continued south to the Sainte-Croix River, and up the river to Sainte-Croix. This would have required at least two days after June 24, perhaps three or four. On that basis, we might estimate the date of arrival at Sainte-Croix as between June 26 and June 28. The date of June 24, 1604, given for the "choice of Ste. Croix," in the excellent chronology of Litalien and Vaugeois, *Champlain*, 365, is not possible. Morison's date of "mid-June" is mistaken in *Champlain*, 41. Liebel has it about right at June 26, 1604, in *Pierre Dugua, sieur de Monts*, 121.

69. CWB 1:275.

70. Ibid. 1:277.

71. Ibid. 1:274–75.

72. Ibid. 1:277; Lescarbot, *History of New France* 2:255; Liebel, *Pierre Dugua, sieur de Mons*, 124; Ganong, *Champlain's Island*, 90.

73. CWB 1:277–78; Lescarbot, *History of New France* 2:255; Liebel, *Pierre Dugua, sieur de Mons*, 124; Ganong, *Champlain's Island*, 64–78.

74. CWB 1:275–77; Lescarbot, *History of New France* 2:255.

75. Ganong writes from close study of the island, "the engraver probably used a crude though approximately accurate sketch by Champlain, and from this drew his attractive picture." CWB 1:275–79. A survey of archaeology done on Sainte-Croix Island appears in Gretchen Fearn Faulkner, "A History of Archeological Investigation on St. Croix," unpub. paper, University of Maine, 1982; a copy is in the library of the Acadia National Park, Bar Harbor, Maine.

    The first major project was done as early as 1796–97 by Loyalist settlers in New Brunswick, who wanted to determine that this was in fact the Sainte-Croix River and that their land grants were safe north of the river. Thomas Wright, surveyor general of Prince Edward Island, made a survey of the island and found that the foundations of the settlement closely matched plans and descriptions that Champlain had published. For a discussion see Ganong, *Champlain's Island*, 122–39, 74–77.

    Many amateur digs followed in the nineteenth century, and also several projects by professional archaeologists in the twentieth century. One project, led by Wendell Hadlock, was described in his "Narrative Report on Preliminary Exploration at St. Croix Island, Dec. 4, 1950," and see also J. C. Harrington, "Preliminary Archeological Excavations at St. Croix Island, Maine," January 30, 1951.

    Another study followed in the late 1960s. Its leader, Jacob W. Gruber, reported his results in "The French Settlement on St. Croix Island, Maine, Excavations for the National Park Service, 1968–69," ms. report, 1970; and "Champlain's Dead: The Cemetery at St. Croix," Department of Anthropology, Temple University, Philadelphia, Pa.

    More work was done in the 1990s. See Thomas A. J. Crist, "Biocultural Response to Scurvy: An Example from Ste. Croix Island, New France, 1604–05," unpub. paper, 1995; and Eric S. Johnson "Archeological Overview and Assessment of the Saint Croix Island International Historic Site, Calais, Maine," University of Massachusetts Archeological Service, Amherst, Mass., 1996.

The largest project was a set of re-excavations and analyses in 2003–05, led by Dr. Steven Pendry and Lee Terzis. Their results are in process of publication at the time of this writing. Each of these studies was progressively more refined, but the ground was also increasingly more disturbed. The reports and many physical artifacts are in the Library of Acadia National Park, Bar Harbor, Maine; and at the North Atlantic Regional Office of the National Park Service, in Boston, Massachusetts.

76. Jean Grove, *The Little Ice Age* (Routledge, 1988), a work of scholarship; Brian Fagan, *Little Ice Age*, is a lively essay; annual climate series have been constructed by Hal Fritts at the University of Arizona.

77. Thomas A. J. Crist, Marcella H. Sorg, Robert Larocque, and Molly H. Crist, "Champlain's Cemetery: Skeletal Analysis of the First Acadians, Saint Croix Island International Historic Site, Calais, Maine," prepared for the United States National Park Service, Acadia National Park, Bar Harbor, Maine; ms. Utica College, Utica, N.Y., 2005.

78. The most striking evidence are CT scans of a French colonist, performed by Dr. John Benson, director of medical imaging at Mount Desert Hospital, Bar Harbor, Maine, June 26, 2003. The results were reported by Dr. Benson in a paper presented to the Radiological Society of North America, Nov. 29, 2004. Films and reports are on file in the library of Acadia National Park, Mount Desert Island, Maine. The autopsied skull was reexcavated by a group led by Dr. Steven Pendry in June 2003, and analyzed by a joint Canadian-American team of forensic anthropologists led by Dr. Thomas Crist and Dr. Molly Crist of Utica College, Dr. Marcella Sorg, Maine State Forensic Anthropologist, and Physical Anthropologist Dr. Robert Larocque of Université Laval, Quebec. See Thomas A. Crist and Marcella H. Sorg, "'We Opened several of them to determine the Causes of their Illness:' Samuel de Champlain and the New World's First Adult Autopsy, L'île Sainte Croix, 1604–1605," paper presented to the annual meeting of the American Academy of Forensic Sciences, Dallas, Texas, 2004.

79. Kenneth J. Carpenter, *The History of Scurvy and Vitamin C* (Cambridge, 1986), 11.

80. Champlain counted thirty-five dead; Lescarbot reported thirty-six deaths. Cf. CWB 1:204–05; Lescarbot, *History of New France*, 2:258; Pierre Biard, Relations of 1616, *Jesuit Relations*, 3:52–53.

81. Kenneth J. Carpenter, *The History of Scurvy and Vitamin C* (Cambridge, 1986), 230–33 reviews the evidence on this question, both from experiments by polar explorers such as Stefansson, and from nutritional studies of ascorbic acid in fresh meat in Eskimo diet, as well as in other sources available in North America such as licorice root, mountain sorrel, and angelica.

82. Paul Gafferel, *Histoire du Brésil français au seizième siècle* (Paris, 1878), with original documents; Trudel, *Histoire de la Nouvelle-France* 1, 180–92; 2:2, 3, 31, 33.

9. NORUMBEGA

1. Marcel Trudel, *Histoire de la Nouvelle France* (Montreal, 1963) 2:62.

2. Henry Percival Biggar, ed., *The Works of Samuel de Champlain*, 6 vols. and a portfolio of maps and drawings (CWB), (Toronto, 1922–36, reprinted 1971) 1:280.

3. CWB 1:280; for her probable length see Jean Liebel, *Pierre Dugua, sieur de Mons* (n.p., 1999), 127; also Père Fournier, *Hydrographie contenant la théorie et la pratique de toutes les parties de la navigation* (Paris, 1643), 11. The French text of 1628 that defined a *patache* as a "petit navire de guerre préposé à la surveillance des côtes" is quoted in Alain Rey et al. eds., *Le Grand Robert* (Paris, 2001) 5:333; Samuel Eliot Morison, *Samuel de Champlain: Father of New France* (New York, 1972) defines a patache erroneously by her rig, as a square-rigged ketch. Contemporary drawings suggest that her hull design was very different from that of the larger navires and smaller shallops, which typically had bluff bows, a broad beam, a lee board, and a large degree of "tumble home" that was much favored in the early seventeenth century. For a discussion of these ship-types, see appendix M.

4. CWB 1:428.

5. Some drawings of these small craft show a two-masted rig, with a small foremast and a larger mainmast; others have a mainmast and mizzen. The foremast was rigged with a sail that Champlain called *bourcet* or lugsail, an irregular quadrilateral bent on a diagonal yard. When coming about, the leading edge of the yard would be "dipped" and brought to the lee side of the mast. Cf. CWB 1:377; Howard I. Chapelle, *American Small Craft: Their Design, Development and Construction* (New York, 1951), 284–85; maps and drawings in Allan Forbes and Paul Cadman, *France and England* (Boston: 1925–29) 3:11–12.

6. CWB 1:280; 390.

7. Ibid. 2:437, 276; for Champlain on spares, see his *Traitté de la Marine* in CWB 6:253–348.

8. On other voyages Champlain sailed with a small *barque du port* of five to eight tons, in company or on a towline. See CWB 1:276–78; see appendix M on Champlain's ships and small craft.

9. CWB 1:280. For helpful guides that confirm the accuracy of Champlain's account see Hank and Jan Taft with Curtis Rindlaub, *A Cruising Guide to the Maine Coast* 3rd edition revised and expanded (1988, Peaks Island, Maine, 1996); also James L. Bildner, *A Visual Cruising Guide to the Maine Coast* (New York, 2006), which usefully combines chart segments with aerial photographs. Another useful tool are satellite images of the Maine coast, easily accessible on Google mapping programs, with maps and satellite photographs linked.

10. CWB 1:281.

11. Carl O. Sauer, *Seventeenth Century America* (Berkeley, 1980), 78; Kenny Taylor, *Puffins* (Stillwater, Minn., 1999), 26.

12. Morison thought that Champlain's *Isles Rangées* were Cross, Libby's, Head Harbor, Steel Harbor, and Great Wass islands. I take them to be the small islets south of Roque Island, which are even more regular. Compare Morison, *Champlain*, 46, with Google Satellite maps, s.v. "Roque Island."

13. Many writers assert that Champlain spent the night somewhere near Schoodic. Biggar believed that he slept on Heron Island on the west side of Schoodic. Morison wrote that Champlain "put in at one of the little harbors (Birch, Wonsqueak, or Prospect)" and spent the night on the east side of Schoodic. This is not what Champlain wrote, and his narrative is our only guide. Champlain's French text tells us very plainly that he left the Sainte-Croix River on September 5, sailed southwest 25 leagues (probably about 75 nautical miles or 86 statute miles), and "this same day, *ce mesme jour*," reached the island he named Mount Desert. Champlain's account indicates that he did not stay the night on Schoodic; Morison,

Biggar, and Slafter (*Champlain's Voyages* [Boston, 1878–82]) are mistaken. Cf. CWB 1:282; Morison, *Champlain*, 46; Biggar, in CWB 1:282n.

14. CWB 2:282–83.

15. In 1608, when he explored the valley of the Saguenay River, he wrote: "Il y a quelques isles dedans icelle riuiere qui sont *fort desertes*, n'estas que rochers, couuertes de petits sapins & bruieres; there are several islets in this river which are *very barren*, nothing but rocks covered with small spruce and briars." John Squair translates *désertes* here as barren; CWB 2:17.

    Another example from the same passage: "Toute la terre que i'y ay veuë ne sont que montaignes & premontoires de rochers, la pluspart couuerts de sapins et boulleaux, terre fort mal plaisante, tant d'un costé que d'autre; enfin ce sont de *vrais déserts*, inhabités d'animaux & oyseaux; the country on both sides of the river is nothing but mountains and rocky promontories, for the most part covered with spruce and birch, a very unpleasant place, on both sides of the river, in short they are a *real wilderness*, uninhabited by animals and birds" CWB 2:17. Note that the French *habité* means "inhabited" in English; *inhabité* means "uninhabited." Here is another linguistic "false friend" where the same cognate has opposite meanings in English and French—at once the despair and delight of a translator.

16. CWB 1:282.

17. For the run of twenty-five leagues, see CWB 1:281; at sea Champlain tended to use Spanish leagues of three nautical miles; see appendix N.

18. "Peregrine Falcons in Acadia," U.S. National Park Service, 1999; Candace Savage, *Peregrin Falcons* (San Francisco, 1994); J. T. Harris, *The Peregrine Falcon in Greenland* (Columbia, Mo., 1981); A. C. Bent, *Life Histories of North American Birds of Prey* (1937, New York, 1961).

19. CWB 1:282.

20. Champlain does not identify the cove in his narrative. Some islanders think that he might have run into Salisbury Cove, or Cromwell Harbor, or possibly Compass Harbor, but Otter Cove would have been closer and more convenient for careening his patache and more consistent with the text. Morison agrees in *Champlain*, 46.

21. Today's Frenchman Bay should not be confused with Champlain's Baie Françoise (or Française), which was his name for the Bay of Fundy.

22. Morison's account is mistaken, as are other works that follow him. Cf. Morison, *Champlain*, 47; and CWB 1:283–84.

23. Ibid. 1:286.

24. Ibid. 1:290.

25. Ibid. 1:291.

26. Ibid. 1:290.

27. Lucien Campeau, "Bonaventure, enfant montagnais," *Monumenta Novae Franciae* 2:662, 120, 248, 480, 602; CWB 1:289–96, 352–61.

28. CWB 1:294; Pierre Biard, in "Relation de la Nouvelle France," *Relations des Jesuites* IV; Colin Calloway, ed., *Dawnland Encounters: Indians and Europeans in Northern New England* (Hanover, N.H., 1991).

29. CWB 1:294–95. Champlain was not the first Christian to sail up the Penobscot River. The Portuguese explorer Estevan Gómez went there in 1525 and left an inscription on a map, "no gold." Gómez explored the coast of North America, found nothing of value, and to turn a profit captured a shipload of Indians in hope of selling them as slaves in Europe. He acted

against the explicit orders of Charles V, and Spanish authorities forced him to free the few Indians who survived his treatment. Gómez also sailed with Magellan's squadron in another ship, organized a mutiny, murdered his captain, and deserted the expedition. Fortunately for Champlain, the Indians of the Penobscot Valley did not see much of Gómez, and appear to have forgotten about him by 1604. Cf. Morison, *European Discovery of America: The Northern Voyages* (New York, 1971), 326–31.

30. CWB 1:295. On the location of the meeting, most historians defer to the judgment of Fannie Eckstrom, a gifted scholar who knew the ground, and a rigorous critic with very high standards of accuracy. She wrote: "The statements of many historians and near historians are so full of errors and so contradictory that it is useless to cite them as evidence, [and] needless to demolish them as errors." Fannie Hardy Eckstrom, *Old John Neptune and other Maine Indian Shamans* (1945, rpt. Portland, 1980), 76.

31. CWB 1:294–96; *The Maine Atlas and Gazetteer* 25th edition (Yarmouth, 2002), maps 23, 77. On the west side of the Penobscot River was the large grove of oaks that attracted Champlain. On the east bank of the river was the handsome stand of white pines in what is now the town of Brewer. Local historians believe that the meeting place took place at the junction of the two rivers, near the intersection of Oak Street and Washington Street in Bangor.

32. CWB 1:296.

33. Ibid. 1:297; cf. *Maine Atlas and Gazetteer*, plate 23.

34. US Route 1 runs very close to the water's edge through this area from Moose Point to Belfast Bridge.

35. CWB 1:284n; Samuel E. Morison, *Northern Voyages* (New York, 1971), 67, 464–70, 488–89; Sigmund Diamond, "Norumbega: New England Xanadu," *American Neptune* 11 (1951), 95–107.

36. CWB 1:297–99.

37. Ibid. 1:299.

38. Ibid. 1:300.

39. Ibid. 1:298. On the ethnic identity of these people, a helpful work of high importance is Bruce J. Bourque, "Ethnicity on the Maritime Peninsula, 1600–1759," *Ethnohistory* 36 (1989), 257–84; also Dean R. Snow, "The Ethnohistoric Baseline of the Eastern Abenake," *Ethnohistory* 23 (1976), 291–306. Still very helpful are the works of Fannie Eckstrom, especially "The Indians of Maine," in Louis C. Hatch ed., *Maine: A History* (New York, 1919), 43–64; Jeanne Patten Whitten, *Fannie Hardy Eckstrom: A Descriptive Bibliography of her Writings, Published and Unpublished* (Orono, 1976), 38–52.

40. CWB 1:311–12, 362; Sauer, *Seventeenth Century America*, 80.

41. James L. Bildner, *A Visual Cruising Guide to the Maine Coast* (Camden, Me., 2006), 224–25.

42. CWB 1:312; Morison, *Champlain*, 56.

43. Morison asserts that he sailed from Crow Island and, "without stopping he passed outside Mount Desert and Isle au Haut and anchored in a harbor near Bedabedec." This cannot be correct, as Champlain tells us that they were thirteen days and nights getting from Sainte-Croix to Bedabedec. In between, the only places that Champlain mentioned were Crow Island, Mount Desert and "one of the islands at the mouth of the Kennebec River." Query: where did they spend thirteen nights along this coast from June 18 to July 1, 1605? I think it probable that they stayed at least several days at each of these places including Mount Desert Island, perhaps on the island itself. Cf. CWB 1:312; Morison, *Champlain*, 56.

44. Champlain always called the Penobscot the Nurembega. CWB 1:312–23; for sailing times, see Joe C. W. Armstrong, *Champlain* (Toronto, 1987), 59.

45. CWB 1:314–15.

46. Edmund Slafter and the Abbé C.-H. Laverdière worked out Champlain's route. It was mapped by Henry Biggar and confirmed by Morison, who sailed it in a small boat. CWB 1:315; Morison, *Champlain*, 56–59; Edmund F. Slafter, ed., *Champlain's Voyages* (Boston, 1878–82).

47. CWB 1:316.

48. Ibid. 1:317–20; Taft and Rindlaub, *Cruising Guide to the Maine Coast*, 107–110.

49. CWB 1:325; Champlain's Almouchiquois were Lescarbot's and Biard's Armouchiquois; cf. Marc Lescarbot, *History of New France* (Toronto, 1907) 2:308, 325, 3:144; Pierre Biard, "Relation de la Nouvelle France. Écrite en 1614," *Relations des Jesuites* 3:208–09; John Smith, *Complete Works* (Chapel Hill, 1986) 1:328, 2:407. For a general discussion of ethnic groups in this part of Maine, see Bruce J. Bourque, *Twelve Thousand Years: American Indians in Maine* (Lincoln, Neb., 2001), 103–26; Bruce Bourque and Ruth Whitehead, "Trade and Alliances in the Contact Period," *Norumbega: American Beginnings*, ed. Emerson W. Baker et al. (Lincoln, Neb., 1994), 327–41.

50. CWB 1:327; Bourque, *Twelve Thousand Years,* 106; Howard S. Russell, *Indian New England before the Mayflower* (Hanover, 1980), 133–64.

51. CWB 1:330.

52. Ibid. 1:333.

53. Ibid. 1:335.

54. Ibid. 1:335.

55. Ibid. 1:337.

56. Ibid. 1:337–38; Lescarbot, *History of New France* 3:95; S. F. Cook, *The Indian Population of New England in the Seventeenth Century* (Berkeley, 1976), 29–35; William S. Simmons, *Spirit of the New England Tribes: Indian History and Folklore* (Hanover, 1986), 15–16; Kathleen Bragdon, *Native People of Southern New England, 1500–1650* (Norman, Oklahoma, 1996), 20–23.

57. CWB 1:340–41.

58. Ibid. 1:345.

59. Ibid. 1:348–49.

60. Ibid. 1:341–56; Cook, *The Indian Population*, 40–41.

61. CWB 1:351; Sauer, *Seventeenth Century America*, 83.

62. Ibid. 1:351–52; Sauer, *Seventeenth Century America*, 80–82.

63. CWB 1:354.

64. Lescarbot, *History of New France* 2:277–78; CWB 1:354–55.

65. CWB 1:355.

66. Ibid. 1:357.

67. George Rosier, "The Voyage of George Waymouth, 1605," rpt. in Charles Herbert Levermore, ed., *Forerunners and Competitors of the Pilgrims and Puritans* 2 vols. (New York, 1912) 1:335; CWB 1:365.

68. Levermore, ed., *Forerunners of the Pilgrims and Puritans* 1:63–64, 67.

69. Lescarbot, *History of New France*, 2:253.

70. Ibid. 2:322; CWB 1:393.

71. CWB 1:394.

72. Ibid. 1:363, 395; Lescarbot, *History of New France* 2:324.

73. For this custom in the Pacific Northwest see Helen Codere, *Fighting with Property* (New York, 1950); Gordon MacGregor, *Warriors without Weapons* (Chicago, 1946).

74. CWB 1:395–96; Lescarbot, *History of New France*, 2:323–24. Both accounts are in fundamental agreement. Lescarbot was not present, but appears to have worked from an eyewitness account by Poutrincourt.

75. CWB 1:398; Lescarbot, *History of New France* 2:324–25; 2:327.

76. CWB 1:399–400.

77. Lescarbot, *History of New France* 2:328; CWB 1:402.

78. CWB 1:413–14; Cook, *The Indian Population of New England*, 40–45; Frank G. Speck, *Territorial Subdivisions and Boundaries of the Wampanoag, Massachusetts, and Nauset Indians*, Museum of the American Indian Publications Misc. Series 7 (1928), 1–152; Bragdon, *Native People of Southern New England*, 24.

79. CWB 1:417.

80. Ibid. 2:416.

81. Ibid. 1:418.

82. A contrasting example of Champlain's cross-raising later appeared in his exploration of the Upper Ottawa Valley. See below, 310.

83. CWB 1:422.

84. Ibid. 1:422; Lescarbot, *History of New France* 2:330–37.

85. Morison, *Champlain*, 82; CWB 1:421–22; Lescarbot, *History of New France* 2:330–37.

10. PORT-ROYAL

1. Marc Lescarbot, *Histoire de la Nouvelle-France* third edition, 3 vols., Paris, 1617; and ed. Edwin Tross 3 vols. (Paris, 1866); tr. as *The History of New France*, tr. W. L. Grant, ed. H. P. Biggar, 3 vols. (Toronto, 1907), 1:32–33.

2. Marc Lescarbot, *Une lettre inédite de Lescarbot publiée avec une notice biographique sur l'auteur*, ed. G. Marcel (Paris, 1885), 7; Éric Thierry, *Marc Lescarbot (vers 1570–1641). Un homme de plume au service de la Nouvelle-France* (Paris, 2001), 124.

3. Lescarbot, *History of New France* 2:344; Champlain, in Henry Percival Biggar, ed., *The Works of Samuel de Champlain*, 6 vols. and a portfolio of maps and drawings (CWB), (Toronto, 1922–36, reprinted 1971) 1:367.

4. CWB 1:267, 269–70.

5. Charles Bréard and Paul Bréard, *Documents relatifs à la Marine Normande et à ses armements aux XVIe et XVIIe siècles* (Rouen, 1889), 146, 200–06.

6. Nicolas-Claude de Fabri, seigneur de Peiresc, "Observations de Peiresc sur les curiosités rapportées d'Acadie par Pierre du Gua, sieur de Mons," Nov. 26, 1605 and March 13, 1606; Robert Le Blant and René Baudry, eds., *Nouveaux documents sur Champlain et son époque*, (Ottawa, 1967), 102–06; also Journal of Jehan Herouard, royal physician, ed. A.-Léo Leymarie, "Le Canada pendant la jeunesse de Louis XIII," *Nova Francia* 1 (1925), 161–70, at 169; Guy Binot, *Pierre Dugua de Mons, Gentilhomme Royannais* (Royan, 2004), 110; Elizabeth Jones, *Gentlemen and Jesuits: Quests for Glory and Adventure in the Early Days of New France* (Toronto, 1986), 63–64, 266–67; Marcel Trudel, *Histoire de la Nouvelle-France: Le comptoir, 1604–1627* (Montreal, 1966) 2:50.

7. CWB 1:277; 370; Trudel, *Histoire de la Nouvelle-France* 2:24, 34, 36, 50, 481, 485.

8. CWB 1:370.

9. M. A. MacDonald, *Fortune and La Tour: The Civil War in Acadia* (Halifax, 2000), 4.

10. CWB 1:373, 376; the result of early archaeology on the site appear in Ganong's plate on page 373.

11. CWB 1:376.

12. An elaborate reconstruction was erected on a different site.

13. Lescarbot, *History of New France* 2:281.

14. Ibid. 2:316.

15. CWB 1:371.

16. Ibid. 1:373. On the gazebo or cabinet, see Samuel E. Morison, *Samuel de Champlain: Father of New France* (New York, 1972), 72.

17. CWB 1:261–62; 169–70, 180–84.

18. CWB 1:375; Lescarbot, *History of New France* 2:280–85.

19. CWB 1:376.

20. Ibid. 1:375–76, 449, 303–06; 2:29–63; 3:264–65; 5:213; 6:181; Kenneth J. Carpenter, *The History of Scurvy and Vitamin C* (Cambridge, 1986), 229–33; Stephen R. Bown, *Scurvy* (New York, 2003), 32.

21. Lescarbot, *History of New France* 2:344.

22. Adrien Huguet, *Jean de Poutrincourt, fondateur de Port-Royal en Acadie, Vice-Roi du Canada, 1557–1615): campagnes, voyages et aventures d'un colonisateur sous Henri IV* (Amiens and Paris, 1932), 3–138, is a very full and helpful account of Poutrincourt's origins and early life.

23. Huguet, *Jean de Poutrincourt*, 112–13, 297–98. His family had a long interest in America. One of Poutrincourt's cousins had married into a Spanish Basque family and attempted to found a colony in America. After it failed he put his animals ashore on Sable Island, where their offspring remained for centuries.

24. Lescarbot, *History of New France* 2:484–86. The second passage was drawn by Lescarbot from Psalms, 45:7. The English translation of these passages by W. L. Grant in the Champlain Society's edition of *The History of New France by Marc Lescarbot*, 3 vols. (Toronto, 1911) 2:286–87, is not correct; the French text appears in the same edition, 2:531. For excellent discussions see Éric Thierry, *Marc Lescarbot*, 71–112; and Bernard Émont, *Marc Lescarbot: mythes et rêves fondateurs de La Nouvelle-France* (Paris, 2002), esp. 216–56, 289–300; and Louis-Martin, *Marc Lescarbot: Le Chantre de l'Acadie* (Quebec, 1997).

25. Lescarbot, *History of New France* 2:288. The full text of "Adieu à la France" appears in idem., 2:532–35; it might be compared with subsequent works, "Adieu aux François," August 25, 1606, and "Adieu à la Nouvelle France," July 30 1607, in idem., 3:470–72, 480–89.

26. Lescarbot, *History of New France* 2:531; 3:333; CWB 1:279; for a review of the evidence see Trudel, *Histoire de la Nouvelle-France* 2:29; and Le Blant and Baudry, *Nouveaux documents*, 163, 237, 276, 344, 368, 242–43. Poutrincourt appeared in legal records as master of "the seigneury of Port Royal and adjacent lands."

27. On the La Tours, for a celebration see Azarie Couillard-Després, *Charles de Saint-Étienne de la Tour, gouverneur, lieutenant-général en Acadie, et son temps, 1593–1666* (Arthabaska, 1930). For an execration, see Lauvrière, "Deux Traitres d'Acadie et leur victime: les La Tour père et fils et Charles d'Aulnay-Charnisay," *Canada français* 19 (1931–32), 14–33, 83–105, 168–79, 233–38, 317–43; also published in Paris, 1932. For a refutation, see Azarie Couillard-Després, *Charles de Saint-Étienne de la Tour, gouverneur en Acadie, 1593–1666, au tribunal*

de l'histoire (n.d.). An excellent work is M. A. MacDonald, *Fortune and La Tour: The Civil War in Acadia* (Halifax, 2000).

28. CWB 1:422n; Jones, *Gentlemen and Jesuits*, 74.

29. This Captain du Boullay should not be confused with Eustache Boullé or Boulay, who would be Champlain's future son-in-law and his comrade in Quebec, ca. 1618–29; see DCB s.v., "Eustache Boullé"; and Trudel, *Histoire de la Nouvelle France* 2:24, 26, 34, 36, 49, 273, 471, 495.

30. The journeyman carpenters were Jehan Pussot, and Simon Barguin from Rheims, and Guillaume Richard from Lusignan in Poitou. Three journeymen woodcutters signed on for one year and were paid 100 livres: Antoine Esnault from Montdidier in Picardy, Michel Destrez from Magny en Vexin, and Michel Genson from Troyes in Champagne.

31. Lescarbot, *History of New France* 2:289.

32. Ibid. 2:288.

33. Trudel, *Histoire de la Nouvelle France* 2:63, 465, 486.

34. Lescarbot in *History of New France* 2:330, 333, 350; Jones, *Gentlemen and Jesuits*, 75; Richardson, ed., *The Theatre of Neptune*, xxii; Champlain CWB 1:209, 422; Trudel, *Histoire de la Nouvelle France* 2:474, 486.

35. Marc Lescarbot, *La Conversion des Sauvages qui one esté baptisés en la Novvelle France, avec un bref récit du voyage du Sieur De Povtrincovrt* (Paris, n.d. [1610] rpt. in *The Jesuit Relations and Allied Documents* (New York, 1959) 1:102–03.

36. *Mercure françois* 1:296; Trudel, *Histoire de la Nouvelle-France* 2:63; CWB 1:439–40 with a map by Biggar on its probable location. Lescarbot, *History of New France* 2:347, noted that it was "much admired by the Indians." For its location today, see Brenda Dunn, *A History of Port-Royal/Annapolis Royal (1605–1800)*, (Halifax, 2004), 6; MacDonald, *Fortune and La Tour*, 199.

37. Trudel, *Histoire de la Nouvelle-France* 2:54–56; Jones, 146.

38. Lescarbot, *History of New France*; Trudel, *Histoire de la Nouvelle-France* 2:62; Jones, *Gentlemen and Jesuits*, 146.

39. Lescarbot, *History of New France* 2:317, 3:246–49.

40. Ibid. 2:320.

41. Ibid. 2:320.

42. Ibid. 2:321.

43. Ibid. 2:320–21.

44. See above p. 197.

45. Here again we have multiple sources for this event. Champlain made brief reference to it in CWB 1:438, and Lescarbot, the author of the work, did the same in his *History of New France*, 2:341; Lescarbot also included the script in an appendix to his history, called "The Muses of New France," idem 3:473–79. It was frequently reprinted in 1611, 1612, 1617, and 1618. In the twentieth century it appeared in the Champlain Society's edition of Lescarbot's works. Complete bilingual texts in French and English were carefully edited by Harriette Taber Richardson, ed., *The Theatre of Neptune in New France* (Boston, 1927). Another English translation followed in Eugene and Renate Benson, "Marc Lescarbot and the Theatre of Neptune," *Canadian Drama* 15 (1989) 84–85, rpt. in Anton Wagner, *Canada's Lost Plays* (Toronto, 1982). All of these texts are reproduced with a learned introduction by Jerry Wasserman, *Spectacle of Empire: Marc Lescarbot's Theatre of Neptune in New France*, 400th Anniversary Edition (Vancouver, 2006).

46. Trudel in *Histoire de la Nouvelle France* 2:63, citing Bibliothèque nationale de France, National Archives of France, 9.269.193v.

47. Don B. Wilmeth and Christopher Bigsby, eds., *The Cambridge History of American Theatre* (New York, 1998) 1:22–23.

48. Compare texts by Lescarbot and Benson in Wasserman, *Spectacle of Empire*, 73–81. Richardson's text is more contemptuous of the Indians. Lescarbot's first Indian's speech begins:

> De la part des peuples sauvages
> Qui environnent ces païs
> Nous rendre les homages
> Deuz aux sacrées Fleur de Lis

Richardson translated it thus:

> In the name of peoples uncouth
> Whose homeland is bound by the seas,
> We come to give our vows in truth
> Unto the sacred Fleur-de-lis

The Bensons rendered it more accurately and less pejoratively:

> On behalf of the Indian people,
> Who inhabit these countries
> We come to render homage
> To the sacred fleur-de-lis.

49. Wasserman, *Spectacle of Empire*, 23; Lescarbot, *History of New France* 2:344, 352; Canadian iconoclasts and debunkers have interpreted the play in the opposite way. A group in Montreal condemned the *Theatre of Neptune* as "an extremely racist play . . . designed to subjugate the First Nations through the appropriation of their identities, collective voices, and lands." They tried to produce what they described as a "subversive, deconstructive counterperformance" called *Sinking Neptune*; Wasserman, *Spectacle of Empire,* 14.

50. Thomas E. Warner, "European Musical Activities in North America before 1620," *Musical Quarterly* 70 (1984), 77–95.

51. Lescarbot, *History of New France* 2:346.

52. CWB 1:451; 2:353. This was not Gaston, the third son of Henri IV, but his older brother, who was born at Fontainebleau April 16, 1607, and died in 1611.

53. CWB 1:447–48; Lescarbot agreed that he was the founder. See *History of New France* 2:342–43; Éric Thierry, "A Creation of Champlain's: The Order of Good Cheer," in Raymonde Italien et Denis Vaugeois, eds., *Champlain: The Birth of French America* (Montreal, 2004), 135–42.

54. CWB 1:448.

55. Lescarbot, *History of New France* 2:342n. Ganong, Grant, and Biggar explain that the rue aux Ours was "the street of the rôtisseurs, or sellers of cooked meat." It is a very old street and exists in the IIIe Arondissement, off the rue St. Martin. In medieval Paris it was called in

Latin *vitus ubi coquntur anseres*, "the street where geese are cooked." In the early modern era, it also became a street of *pelletiers* or furriers, who had strong ties to New France. Cf. Jacques Hillairet, ed., *Dictionnaire historique des rues de Paris* 2 vols. (10th edition, Paris, 1957–61) and supplement (4th edition, 1972); 2:207, s.v. "Ours."

56. *History of New France* 2:342–43.

57. Ibid. 2:343.

58. Michael Salter, "L'Ordre de Bon Temps: A Functional Analysis," *Journal of Sport History* 3 (1976), 2.

59. This information is drawn from rosters in Trudel, *Histoire de la Nouvelle-France: Le Comptoir, 1604–1627* (Montreal, 1966), 465–500, which lists settlers who wintered over in New France from 1606 to 1627. For Addenin, see Éric Thierry, "Creation of Champlain's," 135–42, 142n; Lescarbot, *History of New France* 3:231n.

60. Lescarbot, *History of New France* 2:344.

61. For Champlain's perception of the Abenaquioit see CWB 1:321, 6:12, 43–45 for Canadien 2:57, 6:26, 39 for Etchemin 1:103–20, 292–98, 308–09; 4:370–76; 5:313–18; 6:42, 44; for Souriquois 1:384, 444–58; 2:53–57, 6:307. He divided the Etchemin into smaller groups, mainly by the river valleys where they lived and traded: the Penobscot, the Kennebec (which he called the Norumbega), and the Saint John River. To observe Champlain working in the role of peacemaker is to discover more evidence of error in the writings of academic iconoclasts who argue that he tried to play off one Indian nation against another. His repeated words and acts were the reverse. Champlain always regarded continued hostilities among the Indians as a mortal threat to his design for New France, and he was more effective than any colonial leader in discouraging it.

62. Pierre Biard writes that the young man "made his confession upon the shores of the sea in the presence of all the Savages, who were greatly astonished at thus seeing him upon his knees so long before me. Then he took communion in a most exemplary manner, at which can say tears came into my eyes, and not unto mine alone. The devil was confounded at this act; so he straightaway planned trouble for us this afternoon; but thank God through the justice and goodness of M. de Poutrincourt, harmony was everywhere restored." Cf. Biard in *Jesuit Relations* 1:171.

63. MacDonald, *Fortune and La Tour*, 6.

64. On Bessabes, see CWB 1:284, 296, 442–45, 457–58; 3:360–61; on Secoudon, CWB 1: 267, 374–75, 381–82, 393–94, 436–42; on Sasinou, CWB 1:316, 319, 364–65, 457–58; 3:366, 368.

65. Biard, *Jesuit Relations* 1:167.

66. Lescarbot, *History of New France* 2:354; Lucien Campeau in *Dictionary of Canadian Biography*, s.v., "Membertou, Henri."

67. Lescarbot, *History of New France* 2:354.

68. Ibid. 2:350–51.

69. Ibid. 2:359.

70. Marc Lescarbot, *La Conversion des Savvages* 1:51–113.

71. Lescarbot, *History of New France* 3:37 records a baptismal register that differs in small details and order from the other list. See also *Extrait dv Registre de Bapteme de l'Église dv Port Royal en la Nouvelle France Le iour Sainct Iehan Baptiste* 24. de juin [1610] a record of the baptisms of Sagamore Membertou and his large family on St. John's Day, 1610, by Jesse Fleche. The original is in the John Carter Brown library, Providence, Rhode Island. It is also published in

Jesuit Relations 1:108–13; it is an interesting source for the structure of a Mi'kmaq family in the early seventeenth century.

72. Lescarbot, *History of New France* 3:40.

73. Champlain, CWB 1:384.

74. CWB 1:457, 458n, 451, 442. An account of this war also appears in *The Relation of a Voyage to Sagadahoc*, 1607; CWB 1:458n.

75. CWB 1:444.

76. Lescarbot, *History of New France* 3:184.

77. CWB 1:449; Lescarbot, *History of New France* 2:347, 571.

78. Lescarbot, *History of New France* 2:347.

79. CWB 1:450.

80. Ibid. 1:450.

81. Ibid. 1:454.

82. Ibid. 1:456–58.

83. Ibid. 1:466, 1:468–69; Lescarbot, *History of New France* 2: 364–65; Nicolas Denys, *The Description and Natural History of the Coasts of North America (Acadia),* ed. Willima F. Ganong (Toronto, 1908), 164.

84. Lescarbot, *History of New France* 2:237–38.

11. QUEBEC

1. Henry Percival Biggar, ed., *The Works of Samuel de Champlain,* 6 vols. and a portfolio of maps and drawings (CWB), (Toronto, 1922–36, reprinted 1971) 3:326.

2. Marc Lescarbot, *History of New France* (Toronto, 1907) 2:365–66.

3. Ibid. 2:366–67.

4. Champlain, CWB 2:3; De Mons' address in Paris on October 17, 1607, appears in a "procuration de Pierre du Gua pour s'opposer à l'enlèvement par Samuel Georges des pelleteries rapportées au cours de l'année 1607," in Robert Le Blant et René Baudry, eds., *Nouveaux documents sur Champlain et son époque* (Ottawa, 1967), 144–45.

5. Samuel de Champlain, "Descr[i]psion des costs p[or]ts, rades, Illes de la nouuele france faict selon son vray meridien Avec la declinaison de le[y]ment de plussiers endrois selon que le sieur de Castelfranc le demontre en son liure de la mecometrie de le[y]mant faict et observe par le Sr de Champlain, 1607," The date is written over 1606. Map Division, Library of Congress. Modern images rarely do it justice. The original is very delicate and refined, in a fluent and graceful style. Modern reproductions are more coarse and have a strong yellow-shift that does not appear in the original.

6. David Buisseret, *The Mapmaker's Quest: Depicting New Worlds in Renaissance Europe* (Oxford, 2003), 94–95, 106.

7. Guillaume de Nautonier, sieur de Castelfranc, *Mécometrie de Leymant, cest a dire la manière de mesurier des longitudes par le moyen de l'eyment* (Toulouse, 1603). For a discussion see C. E. Heidenreich, *Cartographica: Explorations and Mapping of Samuel de Champlain, 1603–1632* (Toronto, 1976), 55–59. Champlain appears to have used Nautonier's work not to calculate longitude, but to assist him in orienting his map to true north.

8. CWB 2:18; Henry Percival Biggar, *Early Trading Companies: A Contribution to the History of Commerce and Discovery in North America* (Toronto, 1901, 1937; rpt. Clifton N.J., 1972), 63–64.

9. CWB 3:324.

10. "Interrogatoire de Pierre du Gua . . ." April 2, 1612, in Le Blant and Baudry, eds., *Nouveaux documents*, 213–14; see also Jean Liebel, *Pierre Dugua, sieur de Mons, fondateur de Québec* (Paris, 1999), 210.

11. Sully appears to have accumulated a fortune of 5 to 6 million livres, small by comparison with that of Richelieu (20 million) or Mazarin (38 million), but still very large. Cf. Liebel, *Pierre Dugua sieur de Mons*, 210; Bernard Barbiche and Ségolène de Dainville-Barbiche, *Sully, L'homme et ses fidèles* (Paris, 1997), 305–09, 397–99; Joseph Bergin, *Cardinal Richelieu: Power and the Pursuit of Wealth* (New Haven, 1985), 243; and Claude Dulong, *La fortune de Mazarin* (Paris, 1990), 133.

12. William L. Riordan, *Plunkitt of Tammany Hall: A Series of Very Plain Talks on Very Practical Politics* (1906; New York, 1993), chap. 1.

13. Maximilian de Béthune, duc de Sully to President Jeannin, n.d., Bibliothèque Nationale, Coll. Colbert Cinq Cents, vol. 203, folio 236; as cited in Biggar, *Early Trading Companies*, 64.

14. Marcel Trudel, *Histoire de la Nouvelle-France* (Montreal, 1966) 2:66–67; CWB 3:326; Lescarbot, *History of New France* 2:351.

15. Champlain's scathing judgments of Boyer were confirmed by Lescarbot. Cf. CWB 4:343–46, 363, 366–70; 5:56; and Lescarbot, *History of New France* 2:318–19.

16. In the early twentieth century Biggar found these cases in the Archives Municipales of Saint-Malo, series EE 4, 138. He summarized them in *Early Trading Companies*, 69. Some of this material was lost in the Second World War.

17. CWB 3:325–27.

18. CWB 2:4.

19. Lescarbot, "A Samvel Champlein, Sonnet," *LNAF*, 3:404.

20. CWB 2:4.

21. CWB 4:33; Champlain always believed that the revocation of the Sieur de Mons' commission in 1607 cost the French dearly in North America. Looking back, he wrote, "Had these matters been properly directed . . . the English and Dutch would then not have the places that they stole from us, and where they settled at our expense." CWB 3:328.

22. Commission from Henri IV to the Sieur de Monts, Paris, Jan. 7, 1608; rpt. in CWB 2:5–9; 4:32, Arthur Giry, *Manuel de diplomatique* (Paris, 1894, 1925), 628, 759, 771–74, cited in Biggar, *Early Trading Companies*, 51–68.

23. Liebel, *Pierre Dugua, sieur de Mons*, 214–25.

24. Robert Le Blant, "La première bataille pour Québec en 1608," *Bulletin philologique et historique* (jusqu'a 1610), année 1971 (Paris, 1977), 113–25. This excellent essay has put our knowledge of the founding of Quebec on a new empirical base. Also helpful are documents in Le Blant and Baudry, *Nouveaux documents*, 158–80; Liebel found more materials in the Departmental Archives of Calvados, some of which are available on microfilm at Library and Archives Canada in Ottawa; see *Pierre Dugua, sieur de Mons*, 221–26; also still helpful is Charles Bréard and Paul Bréard, *Documents relatifs à la Marine Normande . . . XVIe et XVIIe siècles* (Rouen, 1889), 106–13.

25. The numbers are those of Le Blant in "Première bataille," 115.

26. Le Blant, "Première bataille," 116–17; Liebel, *Pierre Dugua, sieur de Mons*, 232.

27. CWB 4:31; 2:24–25.

28. Ibid. 4:28.

29. Ibid. 4:31.

30. Ibid. 4:31; Similar arguments with different emphases were made to religious leaders, investors, settlers, de Mons, and the king himself.

31. Champlain in CWB 4:31–32. This dual design was missed in earlier studies, and it does not appear in Champlain's writings. It has emerged with increasing clarity from more recent research in France by Liebel and Le Blant. See Liebel, *Pierre Dugua, sieur de Mons*, 222–23; Le Blant, "Première bataille," 119–21; Lescarbot, *History of New France* 3:303.

32. CWB 4:32.

33. Champlain, CWB 3:1–14.

34. Le Blant and Baudry, *Nouveaux documents*, 154–61; Trudel, *Histoire de la Nouvelle-France* 2:152–53, 486–87; Liebel, *Pierre Dugua, sieur de Mons*, 230–31; John A. Dickinson, "Champlain, Administrator," in Litalian and Vaugeois, eds., *Champlain: The Birth of French America* (Montreal, 2004), 211–17.

35. Contracts survive for Jean Duval and Antoine Notay, smiths; Robert Dieu and Antoine Audry, sawyers of planks; Lucas Louriot, Jean Pernet, and Antoine Cavallier, carpenters; Martin Béguin, gardener; Nicolas du Val, Lyevin Lefranc, François Jouan, and Marc Balleny, carpenters; Mathieu Billoteau dit La Taille, tailor; Pierre Linot, woodcutter; Clément Morel and Guillaume Morel, laborers; François Bailly and Jean Loireau, masons. The manuscripts are in the French National Archives, Minutier XV 18 (registre de Cuvillyer). Richard Cuvillier was a notary in the Châtelet at Paris who executed these documents. Four of these contracts have been reprinted in Le Blant and Baudry, eds., *Nouveaux documents* 1:154–61; The surgeon Bonnerme and the boys are mentioned in Champlain's writings, CWB 2:31–32, 59; 136–42 passim; 4:118; 5:128.

36. CWB 2:4–8,11–14, 32–34; 4:8, 19; Trudel, *Histoire de la Nouvelle-France* 2:152–53, 158, 469, 479; Le Blant and Baudry, eds., *Nouveaux documents*, 1:95, 151.

37. Champlain, CWB 3:327.

38. Ibid. 4:28.

39. For preparations and departures see Champlain's accounts in CWB 2:4, 8–9; and 4:32, 37. The best study is Le Blant, "Première bataille," part II, "Les trois navires du Lieutenant-Général de Mons," 119–21.

40. Older works identify this ship as the *Don-de-Dieu*, which appears in the *registres de tabellionage* for the port of Honfleur, 1574–1670, as recorded in Bréard and Bréard, eds., *Documents relatifs à la Marine Normande*, 112, with an entry on April 4, 1608, for the "navire nommé le Don-de-Dieu, de 160 tonneaux, icelluy navire estant présent de présent en ce port et havre prest à faire le voyage de Canada à la conduite de Henry Couillard." It was outfitted by Gilles Beuzelin, merchant of Rouen. This conclusion appears in Trudel, *Histoire de la Nouvelle-France* 2:152 and Samuel E. Morison, *Champlain: Father of New France* (New York, 1972), 103, but the *Don-de-Dieu* of circa 150, 180 or 200 tons cannot be the ship in which Champlain sailed. This *Don-de-Dieu* did depart from Honfleur for America in the spring of 1608, but not until the period from April 30 to May 7, 1608, and her captain, Henri Couillart or Couillard, also went to Brouage and La Rochelle in search of a cargo of salt for the fishing trade (Le Blant, "La première bataille," 119–20). A further complication is that her captain and part owner, Henri Couillard, had been engaged in litigation with de Mons shortly before the voyage; see Le Blant et Baudry, *Nouveaux documents*, 69, 70, 131, 139.

Liebel agrees that Champlain could not have embarked in the *Don-de-Dieu*, and suggests that he may have sailed in little *Levrette*, which appeared in other records as outfitted in December 1607 for the cod fisheries off Newfoundland in 1608. She appeared again in entries of March, 1608, as bound for Canada with Pierre Chauvin, Izaac Levasseur, and François Longin (or Tongin) on board. Chauvin would be one of Champlain's officers in Quebec, but there is no evidence of Champlain's presence on board. If this vessel was Rossignol's *La Levrette*, she was too small to carry the passengers and cargo of "the things necessary and proper for a settlement" that Champlain described. (Liebel, *Pierre Dugua, sieur de Mons*, 233n, citing a manuscript in the Department Archives of Calvados, 8E6521, folios 158, 169, 281, 284, 289, 318, 349, 353, 381).

41. *Liepvre* in some accounts.

42. Bréard and Bréard, *Documents relatifs à la Marine Normande*, 111; Le Blant and Baudry, eds., *Nouveaux documents*, 92, 94; Trudel, *Histoire de la Nouvelle-France* 2:152–53; Liebel, *Pierre Dugua, sieur de Mons*, 231–33; Le Blant, "La première bataille," 119.

43. Lescarbot, *History of New France* 2:367–68; Trudel, *Histoire de la Nouvelle-France* 2:152.

44. Le Blant, "Première bataille," 115–16; Liebel, *Pierre Dugua, sieur de Mons*, 232–33.

45. Paul Laramée and Marie-José Auclair, *La Gaspésie: ses paysages, son histoire, ses gens, ses attraits* (Montreal, 2003), 233–48.

46. Champlain called him Darache. Le Blant identified him from documents in the Departmental Archives of les Pyrénées-Atlantiques, and summarized his findings in "Première bataille," 125.

47. Marcel Trudel writes that Pont-Gravé "made a habit of hunting contraband traders, which he did in a very aggressive way." In 1604, he had arrested four Basque vessels in Acadia and seized their goods. He did it again in 1606. On other occasions Pont-Gravé seized furs belonging to a member of the De Mons' Company, which compelled the sieur de Mons to pay damages. Trudel, *Histoire de la Nouvelle-France* 2:153n, 66–67; Lescarbot, *History of New France* 2:526.

48. Champlain CWB 2:12.

49. Ibid. 2:12–13.

50. Ibid. 2:13–14, with much supporting documentation in Le Blant, "Première bataille," 122–25.

51. Champlain, CWB 2:17.

52. Le Blant, "Première bataille," 120–21; Le Blant and Baudry, *Nouveaux documents*, 151, 162; Trudel, *Histoire de la Nouvelle-France* 1:86–88; *Mercure François* 1:297 recto; Biard, "Relation" (1616), *Jesuit Relations* 3:162–64; Liebel, *Pierre Dugua, sieur de Mons*, 224, 278.

53. Lescarbot, *Histoire de la Nouvelle-France* 3:36.

54. Ibid. 2:325, 368–69; Lucien Campeau, *Monumenta Novae Franciae* (Quebec, 1967), 1:120, 566, 568, 604–66, 661.

55. CWB 2:22.

56. Ibid. 2:23.

57. Champlain's measurements appear to have been inaccurate. He estimated that the island was six leagues long, with a breadth of a league and a half, smaller than its present size. Montmorency Falls appeared to him "nearly twenty-five fathoms [150 feet] high." It is today 265 feet.

58. CWB 2:23.

59. Ibid. 2:24.

60. Ibid. 2:25.

61. Trudel, *Histoire de la Nouvelle-France* 2:157.

62. Gustave Lanctot, *A History of Canada: From its Origins to the Royal Régime* (Toronto, 1963), 1:103. Much archaeology has been done in Quebec, and here again it confirms the accuracy of Champlain's written accounts. For excavations in what is now the Place Royale in Quebec's old town, see Françoise Niellon and Marcel Moussette, *Le site de l'habitation de Champlain à Québec: étude de la collection archéologique (1976–1980)* (Quebec, 1985), 26–78. Many artifacts were discovered, including what may have been Champlain's writing set and a rich trove of other materials, some of which are now on display in the Historical Center at the Place Royale. Other helpful works are Norman Clermont, Claude Chapdelaine, and Jacques Guimont, *L'occupation historique et préhistorique de Place Royale* (Quebec, 1992); and also Camille Lapointe, Béatrice Chassé, and Hélène de Carufel, *Aux origines de la vie québécoise* (Quebec 1983, revised edition, 1994). These are merely three of more than 100 archaeological reports of very high quality that have been published by the 62.2279 Ministry of Culture and Communications in their series "Les Publications de Québec, Collection Patrimoines."

63. Trudel, *Histoire de la Nouvelle-France* 2:157.

64. Champlain, CWB 2:44.

65. Ibid. 2:52.

66. Ibid. 2:60–61.

67. Ibid. 2:52.

68. Ibid. 2:17.

69. See above, 196–97.

70. Champlain CWB 2:25–34; evidence to confirm Champlain's account of this episode appears in Lescarbot, *History of New France* 2:334, 3:6, 303–04; Le Blant and Baudry, eds., *Nouveaux documents*, xxvi, 118, 154; Campeau, *Monumenta Novae Franciae* 1:90; Trudel, *Histoire de la Nouvelle-France* 2:157–58.

71. Champlain, CWB 2:26.

72. Ibid. 2:34.

73. Ibid. 2:34.

74. Ibid. 2:35.

75. Trudel, *Histoire de la Nouvelle-France* 2:157.

76. Champlain, CWB 2:45.

77. Ibid. 4:53.

78. Ibid. 2:69.

79. Ibid. 2:69.

80. Ibid. 2:52–53.

81. Ibid. 4:50; for the history and culture of the Montagnais nation, who now call themselves Innu, we learned much from Martin Gagnon, ethnographer and historian at the Innu Cultural Centre on the Essipit Reservation east of Tadoussac on the St. Lawrence River. For published materials there is Peter Armitage, *The Innu (The Montagnais Nagaspi)* (New York, 1991). The Innu now have a publishing program for work in their own language. A very attractive book on the cultural legends of a hunting people is An-mani Saint-Onge André and Guilaine Saint-Pierre Bertrand, *An-mani utipatshimunissima*, published by the Institut Culturel et Éducatif Montagnais (Sept Îles, Quebec, 1996).

82. CWB 2:44–45; 4:50.

83. Ibid. 4:53.

84. Eleanor Leacock, *The Montagnais "Hunting Territory" and the Fur Trade*, American Anthropological Association Memoirs 78 (1954), 1–9.

85. CWB 4:61.

86. Ibid. 2:46.

87. Ibid. 4:57–58.

88. Ibid. 4:52, 55, 60.

89. Ibid. 2:53.

90. Ibid. 2:63; Kenneth J. Carpenter, *The History of Scurvy and Vitamin C* (Cambridge, 1986), 10–11, 153 passim.

12. IROQUOIA

1. Henry Percival Biggar, ed., *The Works of Samuel de Champlain*, 6 vols. and a portfolio of maps and drawings (CWB), (Toronto, 1922–36, reprinted 1971) 5:74–78.

2. Captain Claude Godet des Maretz appears as Des Marais in Champlain's writings (CWB 2:63, 73, 78, 80, 110, 116, 143; 5:97; Trudel, *Histoire de la Nouvelle-France* 2:161n, 167, 473. He should not be confused with his son François Godet des Maretz, who was left at Quebec in Pont-Gravé's place in 1629. See CWB 6:32; Trudel, idem, 2:315, 473, 499. Claude's brother was Jean Godet du Parc, who took command at Quebec when Champlain was away. This Percheron family was important in the early history of Quebec, more so than suggested by its historiography. Champlain trusted them and they strongly supported him. (Trudel, idem, 2:103, 173, 238, 245, 487, 489. For the pilot Jean Routier (Champlain's La Routte), see CWB 2:73; Trudel, idem, 2:161n, 169, 483.

3. CWB 2:63.

4. CWB 2:108, Trudel, *Histoire de la Nouvelle-France* 2:485.

5. CWB 2:64.

6. In the mid-twentieth century, some historians explained endemic warfare among the Indians as a response to the arrival of Europeans that brought about subsequent trade rivalries, political conflicts, cultural disintegration, and demographic crisis. See George T. Hunt, *The Wars of the Iroquois* (Madison, 1940); and Francis Jennings, *The Invasion of America: Indians, Colonialism and the Cant of Conquest* (Chapel Hill, 1975).

    Even Indian torture and scalping have been attributed to Europeans. For an incisive review of this literature see James Axtell, "The Unkindest Cut, or Who Invented Scalping? A Case Study," and "Scalping: The Ethnohistory of a Moral Question," in *The European and the Indian: Essays in the Ethnohistory of Colonial North America* (Oxford, 1981), 16–35, 207–41. Axtell was among the first to demonstrate the value for historical scholarship of research in ethnography, archaeology, and historical linguistics. For a discussion of assumptions that Indians were "generally peaceful" before Europeans arrived, see Lawrence H. Keeley, *War Before Civilization* (New York, 1996) 30–31; and for a general review of the literature see William Engelbrecht, *Iroquoia: The Development of a Native World* (Syracuse, 2003), 6–8, 41–46, passim.

7. James W. Bradley, *Evolution of the Onondaga Iroquois: Accommodating Change, 1500–1655* (Syracuse, 1987), 108; Dean R. Snow, Charles Gehring, and William A. Starna, eds., *In Mohawk Country: Early Narratives about a Native People* (Syracuse, 1996); Charles T. Gehring and William A. Starna, eds., *A Journey into Mohawk Country and Oneida Country, 1634–1635* (Syracuse, 1988, 1991).

8. CWB 2:143.

9. CWB 2:63–64, 67–70. Others suggested a different motive. Marc Lescarbot wrote in 1610,

"Champlain wishing to see the country of the Iroquois, to prevent the Indians from seizing the fort in his absence, persuaded them to go with him to make war." See Lescarbot's *La Conversion des Savvages* (Paris, 1610) rpt. in *Jesuit Relations*, 1:49–113, at page 103. There is no evidence to support this hypothesis. Champlain had good relations with the Indians who lived near the settlement, and did not express fear that they would take Quebec. His campaign left most Laurentian warriors in the valley.

10. Bruce Trigger, *Natives and Newcomers: Canada's "Heroic Age" Reconsidered* (Montreal, 1985, 1994), 186; Fenton, *The Great Law and the Longhouse: A Political History of the Iroquois Federacy* (Norman, Okla., 1998), 245.

11. CWB 2:64.

12. Ibid. 2:64.

13. Ibid. 2:65.

14. Ibid. 2:65; 1:130–31.

15. Ibid. 2:68.

16. For Ochasteguin, see CWB 2:68–71, 186; 3:73; 4:67–70, 136–50, 260; for Iroquet, see CWB 2:69–104, 4:67–103; also Trigger, *Children of Aetentsic*, 246–49 passim.

17. For discussion of *orenda*, see William Engelbrecht, *Iroquoia*, 4–6, 145–46; Hope L. Isaacs, "*Orenda* and the Concept of Power among the Tonawanda Seneca," in Raymond D. Fogelson and Richard Adams, eds., *The Anthropology of Power: Ethnographic Studies from Asia, Oceana, and the New World* (New York, 1977), 168–73.

18. The same thing happened when Dutch explorer Harmen van den Bogaert visited the Mohawk in 1634. Bogaert was asked again and again to fire his gun. A historian writes, "From the Iroquois perspective, *Orenda* can reside in an object, and clearly guns had power." See Harmen Meyndertsz van den Bogaert, "A Journey into Mohawk and Oneida Country, 1634–1635," in Dean R. Snow, Charles T. Gehring, and William Sarna, eds., *In Mohawk Country: Early Narratives about a Native People* (Syracuse, 1996), 1–13; Engelbrecht, *Iroquoia*, 4–6, 145–46.

19. CWB 2:70–71; Trigger, *Natives and Newcomers*, 175.

20. Ibid. 2:71–72; for canoe types see appendix M below.

21. Ibid. 2:72–73.

22. Ibid. 2:73.

23. Ibid. 2:73–74, 76–77, 1:136.

24. Champlain called his opponents the Iroquois. Scholars agree that in this campaign he was fighting one nation in the Iroquois League: the Mohawk. The French would later call them *agnier*. Champlain referred to other Iroquois nations by their particular names (or in most cases the names given to them by the Huron). But he used Iroquois both for the Mohawk and for the entire League.

25. CWB 2:76; Fenton, *The Great Law and the Longhouse*, 53, 54, 57, 473, passim; Engelbrecht, *Iroquoia*, 124–30. On the Mohawk see Snow, Gehring, and Starna, eds., *In Mohawk Country*.

26. CWB 2:76–78.

27. Ibid. 2:78–79.

28. Ibid. 2:80; Lescarbot wrote in 1612 that Champlain was "accompagné d'un homme et d'un lacquais du sieur de Monts; Champlain was accompanied by a man and by a servant of the sieur de Mons." See Marc Lescarbot, *Histoire de la Nouvelle France* 2d edition, revue, corrigée et augmentée par l'auteur (Paris, 1612), 626. A copy of this very rare work is in the John

Carter Brown Library, Providence. This passage appears only in the second edition, and also in the reprint of Lescarbot's *Histoire de la Nouvelle-France* (Tross, ed.) 3:600. Lescarbot did not include it in his first edition, and removed it from the third. This "servant of de Mons" was probably François Addenin, who was identified as a "domestique du sieur de Mons" and was also a crack shot who was a hunter of game in Port-Royal. He may also have been the French soldier who was ordered by Henri IV to accompany de Mons as a bodyguard. His name was spelled both as Addenin and Admarin. See Lescarbot, *History of New France* 3:231; Trudel, *Histoire de la Nouvelle-France*, 2:63, 461, 486, 162. The other man cannot be identified, but was also a skilled arquebusier. Lescarbot's reference to Addenin (who is not named by Champlain) means that he had a source other than Champlain's works. Thus we have two accounts of the campaign against the Mohawks, one by Lescarbot, the first in print; and the other by Champlain. Lescarbot confirms Champlain's accounts.

29. Marc Lescarbot, *La Conversion des Savvages* (Paris, 1610), *Jesuit Relations*, 1:104.

30. CWB 2:84.

31. Ibid. 2:85. For a helpful study of this campaign in the context of military history, see Fred Anderson and Andrew Cayton, *The Dominion of War; Empire and Liberty in North America, 1500–2000* (New York, 2005), 1–53.

32. Dates are a problem here. Champlain tells us that he left the rapids on the River of the Iroquois on "le 2. Juillet." This date was an error. Close readers agree that it must have been July 12. They camped that night at "an island three miles long," probably Sainte-Thérèse Island. The following day, July 13, they went up the river as far as the entrance to the lake. There they camped again, and "on the following day we entered the Lake." That would be July 14, 1609. Cf. CWB 2:82–90. For the naming of the lake see Trudel, *Histoire de la Nouvelle-France* 2:162.

33. Guy Omeron Coolidge, *The French Occupation of the Champlain Valley from 1609 to 1759* (1938; Flieschmanns, N.Y., 1999), 8–15.

34. CWB 2:90; Coolidge, *French Occupation*, 11.

35. CWB 2:94. On the importance of the moon, I follow an excellent unpublished manuscript by Robert Pell-Dechame, one of the best discussions of the battle that I have read. A copy is in the library at Fort Ticonderoga. This hypothesis is confirmed by NASA's lunar calendars. See http://sunearth.gsfc.nasa.gov; also http://eclipse.gsfc.nasa.gov/phase/phasecat.html.

36. CWB 2:89, 94.

37. Ibid.

38. CWB 2:95; Engelbrecht, *Iroquoia*, 48; Anthony F. C. Wallace, "Dreams and the Wishes of the Soul: A Type of Psychoanalytic Theory among the Seventeenth Century Iroquoians," *American Anthropologist* 60 (1958), 234–48.

39. For Champlain's probable meaning of *cap*, see the definition as a "pointe de terre souvent élevée qui s'avance dans la mer" in Alain Rey et al., eds., *Le Grand Robert la langue française*, new expanded edition, 6 vols. (Paris, 2001) 1:1893, s.v., "cap." The location of Champlain's *cap* is the subject of controversy. Most historians agree that it was at Ticonderoga. For the evidence see appendix J below.

40. In the nineteenth century, the *rivière la chute* was made into a millrace. In the late twentieth part of it became an attractive park in the town of Ticonderoga.

41. Robert Louis Stevenson wrote a gothic poem about Ticonderoga and its "strange outlandish name" that "sings in the sleeping ear," with songs of death for many a Scot and Englishman and French and Indian too. Cf. his "Ticonderoga, A Legend of the West Highlands."

42. Much archaeology has been done on this site. See William A. Ritchie, *The Archaeology of New York State* (New York, 1980); John H. Bailey, "A Rock Shelter at Fort Ticonderoga," *Bulletin of the Champlain Valley Historical Society* 1 (1937), 5–16; also Dechame, unpub. ms., cites other archaeological studies and Mohawk legends.

43. CWB 2:95.

44. An example of an Iroquoian elm boat survives today in the Peabody-Essex Museum, adorned with diagonal red stripes. That motif was repeated in the paddles and fishing equipment. See William N. Fenton and Ernest Dodge, "An Elm Bark Canoe in the Peabody Museum of Salem," *American Neptune* 9 (1949), 185–206; for an early account, Baron de Lahontan, *New Voyages to North-America* ed. Reuben G. Thwaites (1703; 2 vols., New York, 1970) 1:80; see also Engelbrecht, *Iroquoia*, 141–42; for canoes from five nations—Inuit, Montagnais, Têtes de Boule, Ottawa, and Algonquin—see Olive Patricia Dickason, *The Myth of the Savage* (Edmonton, 1984), 89, from Bécard de Granville, *Les raretés des Indes*, LAC C-33287.

45. Champlain, CWB 2:96; Lescarbot, *History of New France* 3:12–13.

46. CWB 2:96–97.

47. Ibid. 2:97n. These passages follow the original French rather than the published English translation in Biggar.

48. Iconoclasts and debunkers have asserted that our only account of the battle is from Champlain himself. This is not correct. The first account was published not by Champlain but by Marc Lescarbot in his *Histoire de la Nouvelle-France* (Paris, 1609), and his *La Conversion des Sauvages qui ont esté baptizés en la Nouvelle France, cette année 1610* (Paris, 1610, rpt. in *Jesuit Relations* 1:49–113). These works were in print three years before Champlain published his first account. They agree on most important facts, including the first shot, but also add details that are not in Champlain's accounts. Lescarbot also published other editions of the *Histoire de la Nouvelle-France* (1611, 1612, and 1618), with added details that vary from one edition to the next. We were able to study these variant editions in the superb collections of the John Carter Brown Library at Providence, R. I. They also confirm the main lines of Champlain's testimony and add details that are not in Champlain's account. They reveal that at least one of Lescarbot's sources other than Champlain must have been an arquebusier who was with Champlain. These accounts were published while other participants were still alive. Even after Lescarbot had his falling out with Champlain, he continued to confirm and support Champlain's account.

49. A key to these events was Champlain's weapon, an *arquebuse à rouet* or wheel lock arquebus, not a matchlock musket as many historians have mistakenly believed. For details and discussion see appendix L below.

50. Lescarbot, *Conversion des Sauvages, Jesuit Relations* 1:105.

51. Some scholars believe that the battle took place on the sandy beach. Champlain's drawing and the course of events indicate that it happened on a clearing above the beach, probably near the present Pavilion at Ticonderoga. Had the battle happened on the beach, Champlain's arquebusiers would not have had a clear shot from the woods.

52. CWB 2:98; Lescarbot, *Conversion des Sauvages, Jesuit Relations* 1:105.

53. CWB 2:99. Lescarbot's account differs from Champlain's in some details, asserting that Champlain loaded with two balls, not four as Champlain wrote. See Lescarbot, *Histoire de la Nouvelle-France* (Paris, 1609), and his *La Conversion des Sauvages* 1:51–113.

Lescarbot later wrote other accounts of the battle in subsequent editions of his *Histoire de la Nouvelle-France* (1611, 1612, 1618). Here he added more information not in Champlain's account about the weather, and the identity of one of the two arquebusiers who joined the fight in support of Champlain. See above, note 47.

54. CWB 2:101.

55. Ibid. 2:100.

56. The latitude of Ticonderoga is 43 degrees 50 minutes north. Crown Point is 43 degrees 55 minutes.

57. CWB 2:94; 1:284.

58. The timing is crucial to the question of whether the battle was fought at Ticonderoga or Crown Point. Champlain had only three hours for exploring after the battle. See appendix J below.

59. CWB 2:94. This problem of time and distance is decisive in determining the location of the battle at Ticonderoga. It could not have happened at Crown Point. A discussion of the evidence appears in appendix J below.

60. CWB 2:101; on Hudson, see Samuel Purchas, *Purchas, His Pilgrims* (1613) 3:567–609.

61. CWB 2:105.

62. Ibid. 2:101.

63. Ibid. 2:102.

64. Ibid. 2:103.

65. Ibid. 2:101–05.

66. Nathaniel Knowles, "The Torture of Captives by the Indians of Eastern North America," *American Philosophical Society Proceedings* 82 (1940), 151–225; Thomas S. Abler, "Iroquoian Cannibalism: Fact not Fiction," *Ethnohistory* 27 (1980), 309–16. For archaeological evidence of cannibalism see James A. Tuck, *Onondaga Iroquois Prehistory: A Study in Settlement Archaeology* (Syracuse, 1971), 113–14.

67. For example, Daniel Richter, *The Ordeal of the Long House: The Peoples of the Iroquois League in the Era of European Colonization* (North Carolina, 1993); Roger M. Carpenter, *The Renewed, The Destroyed, and the Remade: The Three Thought Worlds of the Iroquois and the Huron, 1609–1650* (East Lansing, Mich., 2004), 22, 25, 26.

68. CWB 2:105.

69. Ibid.

70. Ibid. 2:106.

71. New France was a family enterprise, and kin relations were complex. Jean Godet du Parc was the brother of Captain Claude Godet des Maretz, son-in-law of Pont-Gravé; and uncle of François Godet des Maretz. The Godets belonged to a noble family in Perche. See Trudel, *Histoire de la Nouvelle-France* 2:167, 472.

72. "laquelle sa Majesté eut pour agréable." CWB 2:109–10.

73. Samuel E. Morison, *Samuel de Champlain: Father of New France* (New York,1972), 231–33; Daniel Boorstin, *The Image: A Guide to Pseudo-Events* (New York, 1961, 1972) is a history of this intellectual revolution that separates Champlain's world from ours. To Boorstin's analysis one might add French materials such as the comte de Mirabeau's writings on language which argued, ca. 1776, that words are things, with an existence independent from the other things that they purport to describe.

74. CWB 2:109.

75. Ibid. 2:110; Gustave Lanctot, *A History of Canada: From its Origins to the Royal Régime* (Toronto, 1963) 1:106.

76. CWB 2:110.

77. Ibid. 2:112.

78. Ibid. 2:117; Lanctot 1:106.

79. CWB 2:118.

80. Ibid. 2:121.

81. Ibid. 2:118–19.

82. Ibid. 2:123.

83. CWB 2:125. The new moon was June 21, 1610. See National Aeronautics and Space Administration, *Six Millennium Catalog of Phases of the Moon*, online at http://sunearth.gsfc.nasa.gov; see also http://eclipse.gsfc.nasa.gov/phase/phasecat.html, a helpful reconstruction of the lunar calendar.

84. CWB 2:126.

85. Champlain was in low swampy ground at the junction of three rivers: the St. Lawrence, the Yamaska, and the Richelieu, which he called the Rivière des Iroquois in 1610. He was moving through a huge area of wetlands that is now the Lac Saint-Pierre Biosphere Reserve. It holds 40 percent of the St. Lawrence wetlands and is home to hundreds of species of birds, including the largest heron colony in North America. It is still overrun by huge swarms of mosquitoes.

86. CWB 2:127–28; 4:105–18.

87. Ibid. 2:128. Champlain wrote that they went about "une lieue & demi" from the St. Lawrence River. The location of the Mohawk barricade was on the southeast bank of the Richelieu River, about three miles from the St. Lawrence River, at a cape which came to be called *cap de victoire* or the *cap du massacre*. The Huron called it Onthrandéen. It is now within the city of Sorel-Tracy. See Abbé A. Couillard Després, *Histoire de Sorel, de ses origines à nos jours* (Montreal, 1926), 12, 21–24. Biggar in CWB 4:105 was mistaken about its location, and he confused Champlain's references to the Richelieu and the St. Lawrence rivers. Historians who have it right are Trudel in *Histoire de la Nouvelle-France* 2:171; and Morison, *Champlain*, 120–21.

88. CWB 2:128.

89. Ibid. 2:130.

90. Ibid. 2:130–33.

91. Ibid. 2:131.

92. Ibid. 2:132.

93. Ibid. 2:131–34; 4:112–13.

94. Ibid. 2:134.

95. Ibid. 2:136.

96. Ibid. 2:137. For a thoughtful discussion, see Elisabeth Tooker, *Ethnographie des Hurons, 1615–1649* (Montreal, 1987, 1997), 32–40. This excellent work was first published in English as "An Ethnography of the Huron Indians, 1615–1649," *Bureau of American Ethnology Bulletin* 190 (Washington, 1964).

97. William N. Fenton, *The Great Law and the Long House*, 243–44.

98. For the high estimate, see Léo-Paul Desrosiers, *Iroquoisie* (Montreal, 1947) 47; for lower ones, see Trudel, *Histoire de la Nouvelle-France* 2:164, 171. For the population of the Mohawks, ca. 1600, estimates by Snow and Starna range from 8,110 to 10,570. Engelbrecht thinks that those estimates are "generous," and Trigger reckoned the population was "probably no more than 5,000." Cf. Dean R. Snow and William Starna, "Sixteenth-Century Depopulation: A View from the Mohawk Valley," *American Anthropologist* 91 (1989), 142–49;

Engelbrecht, *Iroquoia*, 125; Bruce G. Trigger, *Children of Aataentsic: A History of the Huron People to 1660* (1976, new edition, Montreal, 1987), 260.

99. Trigger, *Natives and Newcomers*, 176–77; Trigger, *The Children of Aataentsic*, 260–61. Other factors were expanding trade with the Dutch in the Hudson Valley to the south and collisions in the Ottawa Valley.

13. MARIE DE MEDICI

1. Henry Percival Biggar, ed., *The Works of Samuel de Champlain*, 6 vols. and a portfolio of maps and drawings (CWB), (Toronto, 1922–36, reprinted 1971) 2:144–45; 3:15.

2. Ibid. 2:117, 147.

3. CWB 2:145.

4. CWB 2:144–45.

5. Marcel Trudel, *Histoire de la Nouvelle-France* vol. 2: *Le Comptoir, 1604–1627* (Montreal, 1966) 2:167; CWB 4:34.

6. CWB 2:146–48. Claude Godet des Maretz was a captain in the King's Marine. Lescarbot described him as a "jeune gentilehomme." He came from Perche and married Jeanne, daughter of Francois Gravé du Pont. Also active in New France were his son, François Godet des Maretz, born at Honfleur in 1616 and his brother Jean Godet du Parc. They would play important roles in Quebec for many years—in 1609, 1610, 1611, 1613, 1616–17, and 1623. Godet du Parc commanded there in 1610–11, and again in 1616–17. See CWB 2: 63, 143, 117, 146n, 305; 3:603, 182, 167, 273, 473, 486–87; 5:97; Trudel, *Histoire de la Nouvelle-France* 2:161, 167, 473, passim.

7. CWB 2:154.

8. Ibid. 2:154.

9. Victor-L. Tapié, *France in the Age of Louis XIII and Richelieu* (Paris, 1952, 1957, tr. Cambridge, 1974, 1984), 4.

10. Joe C. W. Armstrong, *Champlain* (Toronto, 1987), 268.

11. Tapié, *France in the Age of Louis XIII*, 65.

12. Ibid., 49; Gustave Lanctot, *History of Canada*, 1:107.

13. Champlain's pension was awarded by Henri IV, canceled under the queen regent, revived by Louis XIII, canceled by Richelieu, and revived once more by Louis XIII. He also received various *salaires* as lieutenant, mostly paid by commercial companies. Cf. Morison, *Champlain*, 208; Robert Le Blant et René Baudry, eds., *Nouveaux documents sur Champlain et son époque* (Ottawa, 1967), 1:17, 253, 259, 316, 412.

14. CWB 3:15.

15. Ibid. 3:15.

16. Champlain's account, ibid. 2:257; 4:156.

17. Lescarbot, *History of New France* 1:11, 2:335.

18. Champlain's account, CWB 2:257; 4:156.

19. Robert Le Blant, "La Famille Boullé, 1586–1639; 1. Nicolas Boullé," *RHAF* 17 (1963), 55–69; idem, "L'ascension sociale d'un huissier: Nicolas Boullé," *Bulletin philologique et historique* (1969) 819–36; also Le Blant and Baudry, *Nouveaux documents* 1:16n, 108, 330, 398, 401.

20. Le Blant, "L'ascension sociale d'un huissier"; idem, "La famille Boullé."

21. Documents on the terms of the marriage, including the marriage contract, were brought to-

gether by E. Cathelineau in *Nova Francia* 5 (1930),142–55; Trudel, *Histoire de la Nouvelle-France* 2:174; Abbé C.-H. Laverdière, ed., *Oeuvres de Champlain publiées sous le patronage de l'Université Laval* (Quebec, 1946), 372, 1445–47.

22. Marriage Contract 27 Dec. 1610, Archives nationales de France, Paris, series Y, vol. 150, 293ff. The text is published in CWB 2:315–24.

23. CWB 3:23.

24. Buisseret, *Henri IV* (London, 1984), 122.

25. Madame de Guercheville (ca. 1570–1632) was born Antoinette de Pons, the daughter of the comte de Marenne. She was married at a very early age to the Comte de La Roche Guyon, who left her a widow with an infant son in 1586, when she was about sixteen. After his death she withdrew to the country estate of La Roche Guyon in Normandy. In 1594 she remarried and became the wife of Charles du Plessis, marquis de Liancourt and comte de Beaumont-sur-Oise. She and her two husbands had great wealth and were figures of high eminence at court. See Lucien Campeau in *Monumenta Novae Franciae* 1:679–80; Trudel in *Histoire de la Nouvelle-France* 2:95–96; Adrian Huguet, *Jean de Poutrincourt (fondateur de Port-Royal en Acadie . . .)* (Amiens and Paris, 1932), 292–95; Herouard, "Journal," in *Le Canada pendant la jeunesse de Louis XIII,* ed. A-Léo Leymarie, *Nova Francia* 1:161–65.

26. The story was told by the Abbé de Choisy and written by Francis Parkman, *Pioneers of France in the New World* (1865, revised edition with corrections, 1885; rpt. Boston, 1901), 290–91. Parkman's sources are given as *Mémoires de l'Abbé de Choisy,* book xii; *Biographie générale* and *Biographie universelle,* and *Les amours du Grand Alcandre* [a Catholic pejorative for Henry IV]; *Collection Petitot,* 63:515; Morison, *Champlain,* 148.

27. Parkman, *Pioneers of New France,* 290–91.

28. Pierre-François-Xavier de Charlevoix, *Histoire de l'établissement des progrès et de la décadence du christianisme . . .* (Rouen,1713), 1:122; Parkman, *Pioneers of New France,* 202; primary documents appear in the *Factum du procès entre Jean de Biencourt, Sr. de Poutrincourt et les Pères Biard et Massé, Jésuites* (1614, ed. Gabriel Marcel [Paris, 1887]), which includes letters between Madame de Guercheville and Henri IV's Jesuit confessor, Pierre Coton.

29. Association des Jésuites au trafique du Canada, contract dated Jan. 20, 1611, in Parkman, *Pioneers of New France,* 294.

30. Other islanders have located Saint-Sauveur in different places, but Jesuit Point is the most likely, in the judgment of this historian.

31. Champlain included an account of this disaster in his *Voyages*; CWB 4:2–34; the fullest accounts are those of Father Pierre Biard in reports to his superiors, *Jesuit Relations,* 2: 4–285; and in materials collected by Lucien Campeau from archives in Rome, and published in *Monumenta Novae Franciae* 1:3–638, which go beyond what is available in the *Jesuit Relations.*

32. CWB 4:28; Lescarbot, *History of New France* 3:47, 48–49n.

14. TRANSATLANTIC TRIALS

1. Henry Percival Biggar, ed., *The Works of Samuel de Champlain*, 6 vols. and a portfolio of maps and drawings (CWB), (Toronto, 1922–36, reprinted 1971) 2:242.

2. Elsie McLeod, "Savignon," *DCB*, s.v. "Savignon"; Marcel Trudel, "Nicolas Vignau," *DCB*, s.v. "Vignau"; Marcel Trudel, *Histoire de la Nouvelle-France* (Montreal, 1966) 2:174–75.

3. For Thomas Le Gendre, see Charles Bréard and Paul Bréard, *Documents relatifs à la Marine*

Normande . . . aux XVIe et XVIIe siècles (Rouen, 1889), 115–16; for Lucas Le Gendre, see Robert Le Blant et René Baudry, eds., *Nouveaux documents sur Champlain et son époque* (Ottawa, 1967), xiii, xiv, 224, 256, 289, passim; for others aboard, see Trudel, *Histoire de la Nouvelle-France* 2:274.

4. CWB 2:157.
5. Ibid. 2:158–59.
6. Ibid. 2:160.
7. Ibid. 2:161.
8. Ibid. 2:161.
9. Ibid. 2:167.
10. Ibid. 2:157; 168; Samuel E. Morison, *Champlain: Father of New France* (New York, 1972), 124–25.
11. CWB 2:171.
12. Consul Willshire Butterfield, *History of Brûlé's Discoveries and Explorations* (Cleveland, 1898), 18–25.
13. CWB 2:173.
14. Ibid. 2:175.
15. Ibid. 2:176. For earlier inhabitants see Roland Tremblay, *Les Iroquiens du Saint-Laurent: peuple du maïs* (Montreal, 2006), 99–130.
16. CWB 2:178–79; Trudel, *Histoire de la Nouvelle-France* 2:174–76.
17. It appears on Champlain's map dated 1612, reproduced in Laverdière, ed., *Oeuvres de Champlain publiées sous le patronage de l'Université Laval* (Quebec, 1879), 3: endpages; Trudel, *Histoire de la Nouvelle-France* 2:177.
18. CWB 2:179.
19. Ibid. 2:181.
20. Ibid. 2:185.
21. Ibid. 2:184–85. On the naming of the rapids compare Trudel in *Histoire de la Nouvelle-France* 2:176; it would have been typical of Champlain to have had both purposes that Trudel considers.
22. CWB 2:187–88.
23. Ibid. 2:188–89.
24. Ibid. 192.
25. Ibid. 2:196–97; compare Bruce Trigger, *Natives and Newcomers: Canada's "Heroic Age" Reconsidered* (Montreal, 1985), 195–97, which represents the Huron as strongly supportive of the traders and suspicious of Champlain. Trigger also asserted that Champlain tried to undercut the traders in his dealings with the Huron. This was the opposite of what happened. The Huron were deeply suspicious of the traders, and complained about them to Champlain. He in turn tried to defend them.
26. CWB 2:204.
27. Ibid. 2:204.
28. Ibid. 2:205.
29. Ibid. 2:206–12.
30. Ibid. 2:213
31. Ibid. 2:214.
32. Ibid. 2:242–43; N.-E. Dionne, *Champlain: fondateur de Québec et père de la Nouvelle-France*, 2 vols. (Quebec, 1891, 1906) 1:303–05; Jean Liebel, *Pierre Dugua, sieur de Mons, fondateur*

de Québec (Paris, 1999), 280–85; William Inglis Morse, *Pierre Du Gua, Sieur de Monts* (London, 1939), 52.

33. CWB 2:215.

34. Ibid. 2:243.

35. Ibid. 2:243; for the young king in 1611–12, see A. Lloyd Moote, *Louis XIII, the Just* (Berkeley, 1889), 39–60; and Jehan Herouard, *Journal sur l'enfance et la jeunesse de Louis XIII*, 2 vols. (Paris, 1868).

36. Gustave Lanctot, *A History of Canada: From its Origins to the Royal Régime* (Toronto, 1963), 107.

37. CWB 2:243–44, 4:208–09; 5:143; Lanctot, *History of Canada*, 106.

38. For the centrality of Champlain's role, see Henry Percival Biggar, *Early Trading Companies: A Contribution to the History of Commerce and Discovery in North America* (Toronto, 1901, 1937; rpt. Clifton N.J., 1972), 86; Biggar writes that Soissons was "proposed by Champlain," and "at Champlain's request the vice-regency and the monopoly were then transferred to Soissons' nephew, the young Condé. Trudel agrees in *Histoire de la Nouvelle-France* 2:188.

39. Louis XIII to Condé, Nov. 13, 1612; a copy was found in the archives of the Parlement of Rouen by Biggar, *Early Trading Companies*, 195–96; the right to license trade appears to have been limited to the St. Lawrence and did not include Acadia; see Lescarbot, *History of New France* (Toronto, 1907) 3:335; Trudel, *Histoire de la Nouvelle-France* 2:188–89.

40. Morison, *Champlain*, 137.

41. Lanctot, *History of Canada*, 107.

42. CWB 2:244–47.

43. Little is known about Quebec in the period from the fall of 1611 to the spring of 1613. We do not know the names or numbers of those who lived there. Probably the commander continued to be Jean Godet du Parc, who had that title in 1613 and 1616. See Trudel's reconstruction of the habitants each winter in *Histoire de la Nouvelle-France* 2:488–89.

44. CWB 2:257–58.

45. Ibid. 2:258.

46. Ibid. 2:249–50.

47. Ibid. 2:251.

48. Ibid. 2:251, 255.

49. Ibid. 2:252.

50. Ibid. 2:252.

51. Ibid. 2:252–54.

52. Ibid. 2:255.

53. Ibid. 2:255–56.

54. Ibid. 2:261.

55. Ibid. 2:263.

56. Ibid. 2:262–64.

57. These Algonquin were known also as the Kinounchepirini. They lived near the Ottawa River south of Allumette Island. See notes in Laverdière, *Oeuvres de Champlain* and also Biggar's commentary in CWB 2:264–65.

58. CWB 2:271–72.

59. Ibid. 2:274–75. For Champlain's astrolabe, see H. Scadding, *The Astrolabe of Samuel Champlain* (Toronto, 1880); C. MacNamara, "Champlain's Astrolabe," *Canadian Field Naturalist*

33 (1919), 103–09; Jean-Pierre Chrestien, "Champlain's Astrolabe," Litalien and Vaugeois, eds., *Champlain: The Birth of French America* (Montreal, 2004), 351–53.

60. CWB 2:276.

61. Ibid. 2:274–76.

62. Ibid. 2:278.

63. Ibid. 2:297.

64. CWB 2:255–58, 287–305, 307. Other scholars have suggested that Vignau was an innocent victim of Tessoüat, and that the Kichesperini Algonquin wanted to keep Champlain from making contact with the Nipissing. This may be true, but Champlain had deep doubts about Vignau long before he talked with Tessoüat. Compare Trigger, *Natives and Newcomers*, 179; CWB 2:255.

65. Trudel, *Histoire de la Nouvelle-France* 2:206.

66. The major documents dated Nov. 14, 15, and 20, 1613, are in the Bibliothèque nationale de France, Paris, NAF, 9269, and are cited by Trudel, *Histoire de la Nouvelle-France* 2:206n; also the Letters Patent, Dec. 14, 1613, were read ca. 1901, by Biggar in the Archives of the Parlement de Rouen, and are quoted in *Early Trading Companies of New France*, 94; see also Trudel, idem, 2:205–06; Morison, *Champlain*, 147; Laverdière, *Oeuvres de Champlain*, 3:326; Robert Le Blant and Marcel Delafosse, "Les Rochelais dans la vallée du Saint Laurent (1599–1618)," *RHAF* 3 (1956), 333–63.

67. CWB 3:23; Biggar, *Early Trading Companies*, 96–97.

68. Biggar, *Early Trading Companies*, 94.

69. Morison, *Champlain,* 133.

70. C. E. Heidenreich, *Explorations and Mapping of Samuel de Champlain, 1603–1632* (Toronto, 1976), 79–82.

71. For an excellent discussion see Denis Vaugeois, "Seeking Champlain," *The Beaver*, special 400th anniversary Collector's Issue, (Winnipeg, 2008), 34; Raymonde Litalien, Jean-François Palomino, and Denis Vaugeois, *Mapping a Continent: Historical Atlas of North America, 1492–1814* (Montreal, 2007), 82–89, 111–13; and Litalien and Vaugeois, eds., *Champlain*, 294, 301, 319–20.

72. CWB 2:222–23; Morison, *Champlain*, 134; Heidenreich, *Explorations and Mapping*, 104.

73. Ibid. 3:16; Trudel, *Histoire de la Nouvelle-France* 2:210; Gabriel Sagard, *Histoire du Canada . . . depuis l'an 1615* (ed. Tross, 1865) 1:24–42.

74. CWB 3:17.

75. Ibid. 3:18.

76. "furtivement absentée et desrobée," in "Exhérédation de Hélène Boullé. . . ." Jan. 10, 1614; "testament de Marguerite Alix," Feb. 14, 1614; and "Revocation" May 23, 1636, in Le Blant and Baudry eds., *Nouveaux documents*, 330–35.

77. Champlain, "Testament," ANF Minutier central, Minutes de Fleffé 62:138; reproduced in the Digital ArchivesCanadaFrance.com; see also Robert Le Blant, "Le Testament de Samuel Champlain," *RHAF* 17 (1963), 269–86.

15. HURONIA

1. Henry Percival Biggar, ed., *The Works of Samuel de Champlain*, 6 vols. and a portfolio of maps and drawings (CWB), (Toronto, 1922–36, reprinted 1971) 3:65.

2. Ibid. 3:23.

3. Ibid. 3:22.

4. Alain Rey et al., eds., *Le Grand Robert de la langue française* (Paris, 2001) 5:977, s.v. "porte-parole," meanings 1 and especially 2: "a person who transmits words and thoughts from one group to another, and mediates among them."

5. CWB 3:23.

6. Charles Bréard and Paul Bréard, *Documents relatifs à la Marine Normande et ses armements aux XVIe et XVIIe siècles* (Rouen, 1889), 124, 127–28 passim; CWB 3:24.

7. Ibid., 127–28.

8. CWB 3:24.

9. For further discussion, see David Hackett Fischer, *Liberty and Freedom* (New York and Oxford, 2006), 1–13, 712, 714, 716–24.

10. CWB 3:23–24.

11. Genesis: 39. William Tyndale's translation in the Tyndale Bible, quoted in R. H. Tawney, *Religion and the Rise of Capitalism* (1926, N.Y., 1954), 164. In the King James version it becomes "And the Lord was with Joseph, and he was a prosperous man."

12. CWB 3:24–25.

13. Ibid. 3:27.

14. Ibid. 3:26.

15. Ibid. 3:27.

16. Ibid.

17. Ibid. 3:31.

18. Ibid.

19. Ibid. 3:31–32.

20. Ibid.

21. Ibid. 3:32, 35.

22. Ibid. 3:34; Chrestien Le Clercq, *Premier établissement de la foy dans la Nouvelle-France*, 2 vols. (Paris, 1691) 1:62–65.

23. CWB 3:35.

24. C. E. Heidenreich, *Explorations and Mapping of Samuel de Champlain, 1603–1632* (Toronto, 1976), 23.

25. CWB 3:34–36.

26. Ibid. 3:38–39.

27. Ibid. 3:45–46.

28. Ibid. 3:43–45.

29. Ibid. 3:48.

30. Ibid. 3:51.

31. Ibid. 3:48–56; Gabriel Sagard, *The Long Journey to the Country of the Hurons* (Paris, 1632, ed. Wrong, 1939), 76; C. E. Heidenreich, *Huronia: A History and Geography of the Huron Indians (1600–1650)* (Toronto, 1971), 34–36.

32. CWB 3:50–53; the fullest study is Heidenreich, *Huronia*, 168–99.

33. CWB 3:49–50; Sagard, *Long Journey*, 150; Heidenreich, *Huronia*, 79–80.

34. CWB 3:53.

35. The name that Champlain used—Entouhonoron or Antouhonoron—derived from Onontaeerhonon, the Huron name for the Onondaga; CWB 3:54–55; 4:244n, 283; 5:230; 6:249–50; Morris Bishop, *Champlain: The Life of Fortitude* (New York, 1948, 1963), 356; James W. Bradley, *Evolution of the Onondaga Iroquois: Accommodating Change, 1500–1650*

(Syracuse, 1987); James A. Tuck, *Onondaga Iroquois Prehistory: A Study in Settlement Archae-ology* (Syracuse, 1990); Dennis Connors, *Onondaga: Portrait of a Native People* (Syracuse, 1986). For another view, entirely mistaken, of the Onondaga as "a beaten people . . . on the defensive deep in their own forests," see George Hunt, *The Wars of the Iroquois* (1940, Madison, Wisc., 1960), 24, 161.

36. Champlain and Sagard left eyewitness accounts of Cahiagué. Archaeologists have added much detail about this extraordinary place from excavations at the Warminster site, which many but not all scholars believe to have been Cahiagué. Cf. CWB 3:49, 53, 56, 94; 4:240, 244, 247; Sagard, *Long Journey*, 92; T. F. McIlwraith, "Archaeological Work in Huronia, 1946: Excavations near Warminster," *CHR* 27 (1946), 394–401; idem, "On the Location of Cahiagué," *TRSC* ser. 3, 41 (1947) ii: 99–102.11; J. N. Emerson, "Cahiagué," mimeo (Orillia: University of Toronto Archaeological Field School, 1961); J. G. Cruickshank and C. E. Heidenreich, "Pedological Investigations at the Huron Indian Village of Cahiagué," *Canadian Geographer* 13 (1969), 34–46; Bruce Trigger, *Children of Aataentsic: A History of the Huron People to 1660* (Montreal, 1976, 1987 ed.), 302–5; W. R. Fitzgerald, "Is the Warminster Site Champlain's Cahiagué?" *Ontario Archaeology* 45 (1986), 3–7. Some archaeologists believe that Champlain may have doubled the number of lodges, but by their estimate it was still a very large town, with as many as 3,000 inhabitants. If Champlain was right (and he may well have been), the population could have been as large as 6,000.

37. CWB 3:5; Le Jeune, "Relation" (1636), *Jesuit Relations* 9:260–61.

38. CWB 3:55.

39. Marcel Trudel, *Histoire de la Nouvelle-France* (Montreal, 1963–79) 2:219.

40. CWB 3:61.

41. Ibid. 3:61.

42. Ibid. 3:62.

43. Ibid. 3:59–62. Champlain's account of the march is clear in a general way, but doubtful in some of its details. A reconstruction and map of Champlain's route appears in Elizabeth Metz, *Sainte Marie among the Iroquois*, 3rd edition (Syracuse, 1995), 41. The best account is in Bishop, *Champlain*, 230–32. Samuel E. Morison, *Samuel de Champlain: Father of New France* (New York, 1972), 155–57, tried to follow the route by air but was mistaken in Champlain's destination. Still useful is O. H. Marshall, "Champlain's Expedition of 1615," *Historical Writings of the late Orasmus H. Marshall* (Albany, 1887), 101ff.

44. CWB 3:63.

45. Bishop, *Champlain*, 231–32; James W. Bradley, *Evolution of the Onondaga Iroquois: Accommodating Change (1500–1655)* (Syracuse, 1987), 113.

46. CWB 3:65.

47. Le Jeune, "Relation" (1636) 9:258–61, Champlain did not mention this episode in his account, but Le Jeune made a record of it, and observed that "they have some reason or rather excuse for treating their enemies this way, for the Iroquois are still more rabid when they get hold of them." He added, "These proud spirits . . . will not submit to any yoke."

48. On the fort's location, historians have long disagreed. The best archaeological evidence now points to Lake Onondaga. For details and discussion see appendix K.

49. CWB 3:67.

50. Ibid. 3:73.

51. Ibid. 3:72–73; 4:260.

52. Ibid. 3:73–75; Trudel, *Histoire de la Nouvelle-France* 2:219, 222.

53. CWB 3:76.

54. Ibid. 3:72; O. H. Marshall, "Champlain's Expedition of 1615," 43–66.

55. Trudel, *Histoire de la Nouvelle-France* 2:222–23.

56. Bruce Trigger, *Natives and Newcomers: Canada's "Heroic Age" Reconsidered* (Montreal, 1985), 309.

57. José António Brandao, *Your Fyre Shall Burn No More: Iroquois Policy toward New France and its Native Allies to 1701* (1997, Lincoln, Neb., 2000), 93–98.

58. William N. Fenton, *The Great Law and the Longhouse: A Political History of the Iroquois Federacy* (Norman, Okla., 1998), 243–44.

59. CWB 3:76–77.

60. Ibid. 3:78–79.

61. Ibid. 3:80–81.

62. Ibid. 3:114.

63. Elisabeth Tooker, *Ethnographie des Hurons, 1615–1649* (Montreal, 1987), 4–7, and much more, in a very interesting three-way comparison with Sagard.

64. CWB 3:81–83.

65. Ibid. 3:83–91.

66. Ibid. 3:81–83, 91–95.

67. Ibid. 3:115–16.

68. Ibid. 3:106, 109.

69. Ibid. 3:47, 138–40; Trigger, *Children of Aataentsic*, 300, 367–68, 388, 718–19.

70. CWB 3:136.

71. Le Jeune, "Relation" (1634), *Jesuit Relations* 6:228–35.

72. CWB 3:52; 145.

73. Ibid. 3:148–49.

74. Ibid. 3:143.

75. Ibid. 3:52.

76. Ibid. 3:142.

77. Ibid. 3:137.

16. THE COURT OF LOUIS XIII

1. Henry Percival Biggar, ed., *The Works of Samuel de Champlain*, 6 vols. and a portfolio of maps and drawings (CWB), (Toronto, 1922–36, reprinted 1971) 4:339.

2. Ibid. 3:173–75; 4:338; other accounts in Gabriel Sagard, *Histoire du Canada et voyages que les Frères Mineurs recollects y ont faicts pour la conversion des infidèles depuis l'an 1615* (first edition Paris, 1636; reprint edition, Tross 1866), 1:44; Chrestien Le Clercq, *Premier établissement de la foy dans la Nouvelle-France*, 2 vols. (Paris, 1691)1:101; Marcel Trudel, *Histoire de la Nouvelle-France*, vol. 2 (Montreal, 1966) 2:238.

3. CWB 4:339; Trudel, *Histoire de la Nouvelle-France* 2:238–39; le duc d'Aumale, *Histoire des princes de Condé pendant les XVIe et XVIIe siècles* 8 vols. (Paris, 1855–96) 2:222–348; 3:483–664.

4. Champlain writes that this "certain personage" applied to the sieur de Beaumont, master of requests, who was a friend of the maréchal de Thémines. Thémines advised him to ask for the

post of "King's lieutenant in New France, during the detention of my Lord the Prince [of Condé]. And this he obtained from the Queen Mother, the Regent." Cf. CWB 4:340; and Trudel's interpretation, HNF 2:240–41.

5. CWB 4:340, 345.

6. Adrian Huguet, Jean de Poutrincourt (fondateur de Port-Royal en Acadie, Vice-Roi du Canada, 1557–1615): campagnes, voyages et aventures d'un colonisateur sous Henri IV (Amiens and Paris, 1932), 427–44, with a manuscript account of the fight at Méry-sur-Seine, 513–20.

7. Victor-Louis Tapié, France in the Age of Louis XIII and Richelieu (Paris, 1952, 1957, tr. Cambridge, 1974, 1984), 77.

8. D'Aumale, Histoire des princes de Condé, 2:222–348; 3:483–664; A. Lloyd Moote, Louis XIII, the Just (Berkeley, 1989), 86–87.

9. Tapié, France in the Age of Louis XIII, 77.

10. Ibid., 91.

11. Moote, Louis XIII, 187–89, 283, 282.

12. CWB 4:345; Trudel, Histoire de la Nouvelle-France 2:241.

13. Trudel, Histoire de la Nouvelle-France 2:241; Henry Percival Biggar, The Early Trading Companies of New France: A Contribution to the History of Commerce and Discovery in North America (Toronto, 1901, 1937; rpt. Clifton, N.J., 1972), 107.

14. CWB 4:342.

15. Ibid. 4:340–41.

16. Ibid. 4:342.

17. Ibid. 4:343.

18. Ibid. 4:344.

19. Ibid.

20. Captain Morel had commanded Bonne-Renommée on the voyage of 1604; see Lescarbot, History of New France 2:227; CWB 1:234n.

21. Some historians, including Morris Bishop, doubted that Champlain went to New France at all in 1617 but missed several of Champlain's clear statements to that effect. For primary evidence see CWB 3:209–10; 4:343–45; Le Clercq, Premier établissement de la foy, 1:104–05; Sagard, Histoire du Canada, 1:34–41; for discussion see Trudel, Histoire de la Nouvelle-France 2:241n.

22. Trudel, Histoire de la Nouvelle-France 2:242.

23. Charles Bréard and Paul Bréard, Documents relatifs à la Marine Normande et ses armements aux XVIIe et XVIIIe siècles pour le Canada, l'Afrique, les Antilles, le Brésil et les Indes (Rouen, 1889),129; Le Clercq, Premier établissement de la foy, 1:105. On Hébert's emigration with his family, Lucien Campeau makes it April 11, 1617. I think it was March 11 of the same year, but he may be correct, in which case Champlain's departure is misdated in his Voyages. Cf. Monumenta Novae Franciae 1:670.

24. Trudel, Histoire de la Nouvelle-France 2:474, 468.

25. All this comes not only from Champlain's account but from the Récollet fathers and from the family itself. The fullest account is Le Caron, Au Roy sur la Nouvelle France (pamphlet n.p. 1626); also Le Clerq, Premier établissement de la foy 1:104–05; and Sagard, Histoire du Canada 1:45–46.

26. Trudel, Histoire de la Nouvelle-France 2:502–03.

27. Ibid. 2:234–36, 324–27, 489–91.

28. Ibid. 2:103, 167, 173, 238, 245, 273, passim; in Champlain's works he appears as Sieur Du Parc, 2:117, 146–47; 3:182.

29. CWB 4:344.

30. Contract for employment of Isabel Terrier signed by Samuel de Champlain, Richard Terrier, Hélène Boullé, and two others. Étienne Charavay, *Documents inédits sur Samuel de Champlain* (Paris, 1875), 4–5; rpt. in CWB 2:324–25.

31. CWB 2:339.

32. Ibid. 2:341.

33. Champlain to the Chamber of Commerce, n.d. ca. 1617–18; text in CWB 2:339–45.

34. CWB 2:326.

35. Ibid. 2:326–37.

36. Ibid. 2:327.

37. Ibid. 2:329.

38. Ibid. 2:329.

39. Champlain to the King and Lords of his Council, text in CWB 2:326–39.

40. CWB 4:365.

41. "De Par le Roy, March 12, 1618," signed Louis, and below, "Potier." CWB 4:365.

42. CWB 3:177–78.

43. Ibid. 3:203–11.

44. Ibid. 3:180, 203.

45. Ibid. 3:181–213.

46. Ibid. 3:181.

47. Ibid. 3:191.

48. Ibid. 2:201.

49. Ibid. 3:191.

50. Ibid. 3:210.

51. Ibid. 3:213.

52. Ibid. 3:208.

53. Ibid. 4:227.

54. Ibid. 4:227, 210–11.

55. Ibid. 3:229–30.

56. This new address appears in legal documents dated March 15, 1619, Feb. 23, 1620, in Robert Le Blant and René Baudry, *Nouveaux documents sur Champlain et son époque (1560–1662)* (Ottawa, 1967) 1:374, 397; earlier, Champlain had lived on the rue du Marché in the Marais-Temple area, which was closer to Louvre. See Moote, *Louis XIII*, 282; CWB 5:138.

57. François Moureau, "Les Amérindiens dans le ballets de Cour à l'époque de Champlain," Litalien and Vaugeois, eds., *Champlain: The Birth of French America* (Montreal, 2004), 43; Paul Lacroix, *Ballets et mascarades de Cour sous Henri IV et Louis XIII*, 6 vols. (Geneva, 1868–70) spans the period from 1581 to 1652. Wonderful images are reproduced in Litalien and Vaugeois, *Champlain*.

58. Moureau, "Les Amérindiens dans les Ballets de Cour," 43–49.

59. Ibid. 43.

60. Ibid. 45.

61. Ibid. 41.

62. CWB 3:5–6.

63. Ibid. 4:3.

64. Ibid. 3:4.
65. Samuel E. Morison, *Samuel de Champlain: Father of New France* (New York, 1972), 174.
66. CWB 4:350.
67. Ibid. 4:350–51.
68. Ibid. 4:351.
69. Ibid. 4:352.
70. Ibid. 4:357.
71. Ibid.
72. Ibid. 4:361.
73. Ibid. 4:363.
74. Ibid. 4:366.
75. Ibid.
76. Ibid.

17. A FRAMEWORK FOR NEW FRANCE

1. Louis [XIII] to Champlain, May 7, 1620, signed Louis and Brûlart, rpt. in Henry Percival Biggar, ed., *The Works of Samuel de Champlain*, 6 vols. and a portfolio of maps and drawings (CWB), (Toronto, 1922–36, reprinted 1971) 4:370–71.
2. CWB 5:60, 72.
3. For the purposes of Louis XIII, see A. Lloyd Moote, *Louis XIII, the Just* (Berkeley, 1989), xi, 13–15, passim.
4. Marcel Trudel, *Histoire de la Nouvelle-France* (Montreal, 1966) 2:264; *Mercure François* (1619) 6:334–40.
5. Champlain, CWB 4:367–68; Trudel found the record of the sale for 10,000 écus or crowns, plus another thousand for interest. *Histoire de la Nouvelle-France* 2:264; citing Bibliothèque nationale Fonds français 16738, soc 143:4. Viceroy Montmorency is not to be confused with Admiral Charles de Montmorency, to whom Champlain dedicated his first book and for whom he named Montmorency Falls.
6. CWB 4:367.
7. Much tertiary writing about New France variously asserts that the office of intendant was "created during the 1630s by Cardinal Richelieu," or that "the first intendant of New France was Jean Talon, appointed in 1665." Both these statements are mistaken. Intendants were well established in France before Richelieu, and the first intendant for New France was Jean-Jacques Dolu, in 1620. Cf. W. B. Munro, "The Office of Intendant in New France: A Study in French Colonial Policy," *AHR* 12 (1906), 15–38.
8. CWB 4:369; Trudel, *Histoire de la Nouvelle-France* 2:265–67, with citations to commissions and articles in the Bibliothèque nationale.
9. CWB 4:369–70.
10. CWB 4:370.
11. Louis XIII to Champlain, May 7, 1620, signed by both the king and Brûlart, May 7, 1620; text in CWB 4:370–71.
12. On Isabelle Terrier see Trudel, *Histoire de la Nouvelle-France* 2:242, 262, 267, 483n, 492–95. For Champlain's manservant see his reference to the "Frenchman who had been my servant," a young man who was sent to live among the Indians upriver, and died there. CWB 5:123.
13. Chrestien Le Clercq, *Premier établissement de la foy dans la Nouvelle-France*, 2 vols. (Paris,

1691), 1:162; Gabriel Sagard, *Histoire du Canada et voyages que les Frères Mineurs recollects y ont faicts pour la conversion des infidèles depuis l'an 1615* (first edition Paris, 1636; reprint ed., Tross 1866), 1:68; Trudel, *Histoire de la Nouvelle-France* 2:267; CWB 5:1–3, 11.

14. CWB 5:1–3.

15. For Champlain's departure and arrival in New France, see CWB 5:2; I see no reason to correct Champlain's explicit date of departure from May to June, as Biggar does. Champlain wrote elsewhere that the king wrote him a letter dated May 7, 1620, "on my departure." CWB 4:370. For the ship, see Charles Bréard and Paul Bréard, *Documents relatifs à la Marine Normande et ses armements aux XVIIe et XVIIIe siècles pour le Canada, l'Afrique, les Antilles, le Brésil et les Indes* (Rouen, 1889), 130.

16. CWB 5:5–7.

17. John A. Dickinson, "Champlain, Administrator," in Raymonde Litalien and Denis Vaugeois, eds., *Champlain: The Birth of French America* (Montreal, 2004), 211; for the soldiers see CWB 5:11.

18. CWB 5:7.

19. Ibid. 5:5.

20. Ibid. 5:8.

21. "La meffiance est la mère de seureté." CWB 5:90–91.

22. "Il faut porter sa considération plus avant." CWB 5:8.

23. CWB 5:8.

24. Ibid. 5:111.

25. Ibid. 5:3.

26. Trudel, *Histoire de la Nouvelle-France* 2:267.

27. Francis Parkman, *Pioneers of France in the New World* (1865, revised edition with corrections, 1885; rpt. Boston, 1901), 431; *Extraits des Chroniques de l'Ordre des Ursulines, Journal de Québec,* 10 March 1855.

28. *Chroniques de l'Ordre des Ursulines,* quoted in N.-E. Dionne, *Champlain: Founder of Quebec, Father of New France* (Toronto, 1962), 2:395–403, appendix I; Morris Bishop, *Champlain: The Life of Fortitude* (New York, 1948, 1963), 282; Samuel E. Morison, *Samuel de Champlain: Father of New France* (New York, 1972),179; Dominique Deslandres, "Samuel de Champlain and Religion," in Litalien and Vaugeois, *Champlain*, 198.

29. Litalien and Vaugeois, *Champlain*, 198; Nicole Fyfe-Martel, *Hélène de Champlain*, 2 vols. (Quebec, 2003) 1:11–12.

30. CWB 4:368.

31. He increased Champlain's salary to 200 Crowns. See CWB 4:368; 5:6, 7, 11, 13, 15, 37, 39, 84; 6:35a; appendix I, 5:399; Trudel, *Histoire de la Nouvelle-France* 2:274, 277, 283, 288, 290, 301. Much information about Dolu appears in Robert Le Blant and René Beaudry, *Nouveaux documents sur Champlain et son époque (1560–1662)* (Ottawa, 1967) 1:407, 415, 417, 423, 426, 427, 430, 432, 444, 464. For monetary values, see appendix O below.

32. CWB 5:9–10.

33. Ibid. 1:10.

34. Ibid. 5:127.

35. Dickinson, "Champlain, Administrator," 215.

36. CWB 5:123, 126.

37. Ibid. 5:116, 127, 131–34.

38. Trudel, *Histoire de la Nouvelle-France* 2:280–81.

39. Ibid. 2:281. See also Sagard, *Histoire du Canada* 1:845–89; Le Clercq 1:176; in attendance were Champlain himself, commissioner Baptiste Guers, the Récollet fathers, Louis Hébert, Gilbert Courseron, Eustache Boullé, Olivier Le Tardif, and others. The company's officers, including Champlain's old friend Pont-Gravé and Captain Raymond de Ralde, did not attend.

40. Lanctot, *Canada*, 1:117–19; Trudel, *Histoire de la Nouvelle-France* 2:280–83. For the members of the assembly see Sagard, *Histoire du Canada* 1:84–89; Le Clercq, *Premier établissement* 1:176.

41. CWB 5:55.

42. Ibid. 5:56.

43. Dickinson, "Champlain, Administrator," 212.

44. CWB 5:15–16, 39.

45. Ibid. 5:86.

46. Ibid. 5:207.

47. Charles Lalement to Jérôme Lalement, Aug. 1, 1626, *Jesuit Relations*, ed. Reuben Gold Thwaites (Cleveland, 1896–1901) 4:210; Jean-Paul de Lagrave, *La liberté d'expression en Nouvelle-France (1608–1760)* (Montreal, 1975).

48. CWB 5:108, 5:100–01, 108; Trudel, *Histoire de la Nouvelle-France* 2:481, 465–85 passim.

49. CWB 5:12, 124–25.

50. Ibid. 5:125.

51. Ibid. 5:98.

52. Ibid. 5:61; Bruce Trigger, *Natives and Newcomers: Canada's "Heroic Age" Reconsidered* (Montreal, 1985, 1994), is mistaken on this point.

53. Others knew him as Mahigan Aticq Ouche. See CWB 5:60–71, 73–80, 82, 215–45, 257, 412; Trudel, *Histoire de la Nouvelle-France*, 2:358n, 360n, 370; Sagard, *Histoire du Canada*, 3:623.

54. CWB 5:73, 75–80.

55. Ibid. 5:80.

56. Ibid. 5: 117, 130.

57. Ibid. 5:118.

58. Ibid. 5:131.

59. Ibid. 5:133. Others believe that there was a formal agreement for a general peace with all the Iroquois, and a solemn ceremony in 1624. The source is Le Clercq, *Premier établissment de la foy* 1:286. Le Clercq was writing on the basis of conversations in New France fifty years later. He also asserted that the Iroquois in thirty canoes launched a major assault on Quebec in 1622 and were beaten off. He said that he had heard this story from Guillemette Hébert many years after the fact. No other source confirms the attack or a formal peace treaty. Champlain made no mention of it, nor did Sagard or the Jesuits. Trudel wrote, correctly in my judgment, that Le Clercq's informant "may well have confused or exaggerated the facts; the silence of Champlain and of Sagard appears to us much more convincing." Trudel, *Histoire de la Nouvelle-France* 2:369; Bruce Trigger, "The Mohawk-Mahican War (1624–28): The Establishment of a Pattern," *CHR* 52 (1971), 276–86, is in error.

60. CWB 5:103.

61. Ibid. 5:23.

62. Ibid. 5:91–92.

63. Ibid. 5:110–12.

64. Ibid. 5:113–15.

65. Ibid. 5:110, 112.

66. Ibid. 5:113, 119–20.

67. This stone was found long afterward, but was lost to a fire in 1854.

68. CWB 5:120, 116; Marcel Trudel, "Champlain," *DCB*.

69. CWB 5:134.

70. Ibid. 5:136.

71. Ibid. 5:136–37.

72. Ibid. 5:137; Sagard, *Histoire du Canada*, 38–39.

73. CWB 5:137–38.

18. THE CARDINAL'S RING

1. Commission to Monsieur de Champlain, 1625; text reproduced in Henry Percival Biggar, ed., *The Works of Samuel de Champlain*, 6 vols. and a portfolio of maps and drawings (CWB), (Toronto, 1922–36, reprinted 1971) 5:143.

2. Gabriel Sagard, *Histoire du Canada et voyages que les Frères Mineurs recollects y ont faicts pour la conversion des infidèles depuis l'an 1615* (Paris, 1636; reprinted by the Librarie Tross in four vols., Paris, 1866) 4:830.

3. Joe C. W. Armstrong, *Champlain* (Toronto, 1987), 213.

4. CWB 5:138.

5. For a discussion, see Victor-L. Tapié, *France in the Age of Louis XIII and Richelieu* (1952, tr. C. M. Lockie, Cambridge, 1974, 1988), 129.

6. Michel Carmona, *La France de Richelieu* (Paris, 1984), chap. 9, "Richelieu et les femmes," 331–36; Tapié, *France in the Age of Louis XIII*, 135, 119, 137, 232, 286, 425; Joseph Bergin, *Cardinal Richelieu: Power and the Pursuit of Wealth* (New Haven, 1985), 39, 260, 288, passim.

7. For Richelieu's life the two classic works are Carl Burckhardt, *Richelieu*, 4 vols. (Munich, 1933–67); English translation, 3 vols. (London, 1970–71); and Gabriel Hanotaux with the duc de La Force, *Histoire du Cardinal de Richelieu*, 6 vols. (Paris, 1893–1947). Brief biographies include C. V. Wedgwood, *Richelieu and the French Monarchy* (London, 1949); Michel Carmona, *Richelieu: l'ambition et le pouvoir* (Paris, 1983); and *La France de Richelieu* (Paris, 1984). For the Richelieu family see Maximin Deloche, *Les Richelieu* (Paris, 1923).

8. "Il aimait les femmes et craignait le scandale." Tapié, *France in the Age of Louis XIII*, 130.

9. Richelieu made a habit of secrecy in public and private affairs. He wrote, "Secrecy is the first essential in affairs of state." He advised others, "Never write a letter, and never destroy one."

10. "Il faut écouter beaucoup et parler peu pour bien agir au gouvernement," in Richelieu, "Maximes et papiers d'état," ed. Gabriel Hanotaux, *Mélanges historiques* III (Paris, 1880), 705–822. See also Louis André ed., *Testament politique du Cardinal de Richelieu* (Paris, 1947). For Richelieu's relations with Louis XIII see Louis Battifol, *Richelieu et le roi Louis XIII: les véritables rapports du souverain et de son ministre* (Paris, 1934); Richard Bonney, *Political Change in France under Richelieu and Mazarin, 1624–1661* (Oxford, 1978); and Orest Ranum, *Richelieu and the Councilors of Louis XIII* (Oxford, 1963). For the private fortune that Richelieu extracted from public office see the excellent work of Joseph Bergin, *Cardinal Richelieu: Power and the Pursuit of Wealth* (New Haven, 1985), 243–63.

11. G. Fagniez, *Père Joseph et Richelieu*, 2 vols. (Paris, 1894); Tapié, *France in the Age of Louis XIII*, 130, 137–39.

12. Bergin, *Cardinal Richelieu*, 264; Tapié, *France in the Age of Louis XIII*, 137.

13. "Savoir dissimuler est le savoir des rois"; "Pour tromper un rival, l'artifice est permis; on peut tout emploier contre ses ennemis." Richelieu, "Maximes et papiers d'état," 705–822.

14. "Qu'on me donne six lignes écrites de la main du plus honnête homme, j'y trouverai de quoi le faire pendre." But this is a paraphrase of Quintilian, and I can find no source closer to Richelieu than Françoise Bertaut's *Mémoires pour servir à l'histoire d'Anne d'Autriche*.

15. Bergin, *Cardinal Richelieu*, 264; Tapié, *France in the Age of Louis XIII,* 137.

16. Tapié, *France in the Age of Louis XIII*, 140.

17. Richelieu, *Testament politique*, 179–99. Selections are translated in Henry Bertram Hill, *The Political Testament of Cardinal Richelieu* (Madison, Wisc., 1961). A more recent edition of the *Testament politique* is edited by Françoise Hildesheimer (Paris, 1995). See also Hanotaux, "Maximes et papiers d'état," 705–822.

18. Tapié, *France in the Age of Louis XIII*, 140.

19. A. Lloyd Moote, *Louis XIII, the Just*, 182, 212; on Richelieu's jealousy of Montmorency see Louis Vaunois, *Vie de Louis XIII* (Paris, 1961), 462–63.

20. CWB 5:139.

21. Procuration dated April 29, 1625, copy in Library and Archives Canada, MG3 series 19, 1. His name appears variously in different documents. In Champlain's Commission it was Ventadour. Other sources make it Vantadour, Lévy-Vantadour, Lévis-Ventadour, or Lévis-Vantadour.

22. A short biography appears in Lucien Campeau, *Monumenta Novae Franciae* (Quebec, 1967) 2:839–40, s.v. "Lévis"; other materials are in Marcel Trudel, *Histoire de la Nouvelle-France* (Montreal, 1966) 2:291–313, 433–53, passim.

23. Trudel, *Histoire de la Nouvelle-France* 2:298; Campeau, *Monumenta* 2:839.

24. Ventadour, Commission to Samuel de Champlain, Feb. 15, 1625, full text rpt in CWB, 5:142–49.

25. Many documents are printed in Campeau, *Monumenta* 2:839ff.

26. Ventadour, Commission to Samuel de Champlain.

27. CWB 5:142–43.

28. On Boullé, see Robert Le Blant, "La famille Boullé, 1586–1639," *RHAF* 17 (1963), 55–69; CWB 5:152, 1:247n, 5:2–3, 218–20, 317 passim; on Ensign Destouches, CWB 5:152, 135; Trudel, *Histoire de la Nouvelle-France* 2:299, 307, 314, 470, 498.

29. CWB 5:142.

30. Ibid. 5:139.

31. Robert Le Blant and René Baudry, eds., *Nouveaux documents sur Champlain et son époque,* vol. 1 (1560–1662) (Ottawa, 1967), 75, 419n.

32. CWB 5:150–51.

33. Ibid. 5:150.

34. Ibid. 5:152; Trudel, *Histoire de la Nouvelle-France* 2:276.

35. Charles Lalement to Champlain, July 28, 1625; Charles Lalement to the Reverend Father Provincial of the Récollet fathers, July 28, 1625, Charles Lalement to Father Mutio Vitelleschi, General of the Society of Jesus, Rome, August 1, 1625; Charles Lalement to his brother Jérôme Lalement, August 1, 1626, published at Paris, 1627; all in *Jesuit Relations* 4:161–227; Joseph Le Caron, *Au Roy sur La Nouvelle France* (n.p. [Paris] 1626); I have used a photocopy in LAC; another copy in the Bibliothèque nationale de France is published in Campeau, *Monumenta* 2:99–120.

36. *Jesuit Relations* 4:193, 178, 179.

37. Ibid. 4:179, 199.

38. Ibid. 4:195, 199.

39. Ibid.

40. Ibid. 4:171.

41. Ibid. 4:207.

42. Joseph Le Caron, *Advis Au Roy sur les Affaires de la Nouvelle France* (Paris, 1626). This very rare pamphlet is in the Bibliothèque nationale de France; I used a photocopy in the Library and Archives of Canada, Ottawa. It is reprinted in Campeau, *Monumenta* 2:99–120. For discussion pro and con of Le Caron's argument see Trudel, *Histoire de la Nouvelle-France* 2:302–04 (con) and Father Campeau's introduction, *Monumenta* 2:99–102 (pro).

43. *Jesuit Relations* 4:171.

44. CWB 5:142.

45. Ibid. 5:145.

46. *Jesuit Relations* 5:153–55; CWB 5:153–54, 194–95; Trudel, *Histoire de la Nouvelle-France*, 2:307n; Gabriel Sagard, *Histoire du Canada* (1636, ed Tross, 1865) 3:791.

47. CWB 5:155.

48. Ibid. 5:156.

49. Ibid. 5:200.

50. Ibid. 5:237.

51. Ibid. 2:21; 4:45.

52. Ibid. 5:110, 202; A lively, rigorous, and graceful report by a leading historian and archaeologist is Jacques Guimont, *La Petite-ferme du Cap Tourmente: de la ferme de Champlain aux grandes volées d'oies* (Quebec, 1996), 31.

53. CWB 5:202–03.

54. Guimont, *La Petite-ferme*, 52; Léo-Guy de Repentigny, *La ferme d'en bas du Cap Tourmente: La petite ferme et la Réserve nationale de faune du cap Tourmente: occupation humaine des origines à 1763* (Quebec, 1989); and cf. CWB 5:203.

55. Guimont, *La Petite-ferme*, 51–52, 56–58; CWB 5:202.

56. CWB 5:213, 236, 241; Guimont, *La Petite-ferme*, 51.

57. CWB 5:241; Abbé C.-H. Laverdière, *Oeuvres de Champlain* (Quebec, 1870), 1134; Sagard, *Histoire du Canada* 3:813–21. One of the victims was a laborer named Dumoulin; the other a servant named Henri, who served the widow Hébert.

58. For primary sources, CWB 5:257–59; confirmed by Sagard 3:813–21; for secondary analysis, Trudel, *Histoire de la Nouvelle-France* 2:360n.

59. Two accounts of this event survive, by Champlain and by Sagard. Both agree in every important way, and each adds details not in the other. See CWB 5:249–50, 6:52, 60, 62, 70, 104–24, 144; Sagard, *Histoire du Canada*, 4:829–30, 909–11. For discussions see Marcel Trudel, "Charity, Esperance, Foi," in *BCD/DBC*, s.v. "Charity," and Trudel, *Esclavage au Canada français: Histoire et conditions de l'esclavage* (Quebec, 1960), 8. Champlain misdated the offer from the Montagnais as Jan. 2, 1628; it was Feb. 2, 1628.

60. For Champlain's repeated efforts to maintain peace with the Iroquois see CWB 5:72–80, 131–32, 208–09, 214–32.

61. CWB 5:195, 308.

62. Moote, *Louis XIII*, 46, 57, 121.

63. CWB 5:194–95.

64. "Articles accordez par le Roy, à la Compagnie du Canada, April 29, 1627," article 2; in Blanchet et al., *Collection de documents relatifs à l'histoire de La Nouvelle France*, 1:65. The operative sentence reads: "Sans toutefois qu'il soit loisible aux dits associez et aultres, faire passer aucun estranger ès dits lieux, ainsy peupler la dite colonie de naturels François Catholiques [without it, however, being permissible for the said associates and others to transport any foreigner to the said places, so as to populate the colony with native-born French Catholics]." Marcel Trudel concludes: "La situation en 1627 n'est pas différente de celle d'avant: c'est une Nouvelle-France catholique que les protestants Chauvin de Tonnetuit, Du Gua de Monts, et de Caën avaient mission d'établir, comme c'est une Nouvelle-France catholique que l'on attend des Cent-Associés, mais les huguenots n'en sont exclus [the situation in 1627 was not very different from what preceded it. Just as it was a Catholic New France that Protestants Chauvin de Tonnetuit, Du Gua de Monts and de Caen had a mission to establish, it was a Catholic New France that was expected from the Cent-Associés, but Huguenots were not excluded]" (my translation) *Histoire de la Nouvelle-France* 3.1:13. I believe that Trudel is correct in his interpretation.

65. CWB 5:194.

66. "Qu'on ne leur deuoit oster ceste liberté."

67. CWB 5:195.

68. Ibid. 5:194–95. Some historians have interpreted this event differently. Samuel E. Morison judged Champlain's policy as "cynical," a miscomprehension. Compare his *Samuel de Champlain: Father of New France* (New York, 1972), 186.

69. Henri Percival Biggar, *The Early Trading Companies of New France: A Contribution to the History of Commerce and Discovery in North America* (Toronto, 1901, 1937; rpt. Clifton, N.J., 1972), 134.

70. Marcel Trudel, "La seigneurie des cent-associés," *Histoire de la Nouvelle-France* 3.1: 1–22; Lucien Campeau, *Les finances publiques de la Nouvelle France sous les Cent-Associés, 1632–1665* (Montreal, 1975); Robert Le Blant, "Les débuts difficiles de la Compagnie de la Nouvelle-France: l'affaire Langlois," *RHAF* 22 (1968), 25–34. The major documents are in a large and little-used collection of photostat copies of originals in the Ministry of Foreign Affairs at the Quai d'Orsay, the Ministry of Marine, and the Bibliothèque nationale, made early in the twentieth century, in manuscript Division, LC; some are published without attribution in J. Blanchet et al. eds., *Collection de manuscrits contenant Lettres, mémoires et autres documents historique recueillis aux archives de la province de Québec ou copiés à l'étranger* (Quebec, 1883) 1:62–85.

71. A list of the hundred original investors and the 102 others who invested after 1628 appears in Trudel, *Histoire de la Nouvelle-France* 3.1: 415–37.

72. The powers of the company are published as "Articles accordez par le Roy, à la Compagnie de Canada, 29 April 1628," in Blanchet et al., *Collection de documents relatifs a l'histoire de la Nouvelle France,* 64–72; also in the manuscript division, Library of Congress. For the composition of the Board, see Trudel, *Histoire de la Nouvelle-France* 3.1: 7–8n.

73. Trudel's very helpful "tableau des hivernements, 1604–1628," is in *Histoire de la Nouvelle-France* 2:428, and 485–500.

19. NEW FRANCE LOST

1. "Il ne faut pas négliger de se loger fortement, aussi bien en temps de paix, que de guerre, pour se maintenir aux accidents qui peuvent arriver, c'est ce que ie conseille à tous entrepreneurs de rechercher lieu pour dormir en seureté; one must not neglect to situate oneself in a strong place, in times of peace and in war, to protect oneself against accidents that might occur. The advice I give to all adventurers is this: seek a place where you can sleep in safety." Champlain, *Voyages* (1632), in Henry Percival Biggar, ed., *The Works of Samuel de Champlain*, 6 vols. and a portfolio of maps and drawings (CWB) 6:176.

2. A book mindful of these comparisons is J. H. Elliott, *The Count-Duke of Olivares: The Statesman in an Age of Decline* (New Haven, 1986), 146, 181–82, 220–24, 659, passim; also Victor-L. Tapié, *France in the Age of Louis XIII and Richelieu* (1952, Cambridge, 1974, 1984), 141; Roger Lockyer, *Buckingham: The Life and Political Career of George Villiers, First Duke of Buckingham, 1592–1628* (London, 1981, 1984).

3. The text of the marriage contract is reprinted in Henri Carré, *Henriette de France, reine d'Angleterre, 1609–1669* (Paris, 1947), 21–24.

4. Tapié, *France in the Age of Louis XIII*, 198; F. de Vaux de Folletier, *Le siège de La Rochelle* (Paris, 1931).

5. CWB 6:158.

6. Ibid. 6:86, 130. For the Kirke family, see Maurice Duteurtre, "Jarvis Kirke et ses cinq fils," in Pierre Ickowicz and Raymonde Litalien, eds., *Dieppe-Canada: cinq cents ans d'histoire commune* (Dieppe, 2004), 44–46. On the Scottish colony in Dieppe see Pope, *Fish into Wine*, 132–44, drawing on much new material from British archives; also Charles de la Roncière, *Histoire de la Marine française* (Paris, 1934), 4:634.

7. CWB 5:272–73.

8. Arrêt du conseil d'État, 26 Jan. 1628 Bibliothèque nationale, Fonds français, 16 738:147; see also: Archives nationales, serie E 95A:95, as cited by Marcel Trudel, *Histoire de la Nouvelle-France* (Montreal, 1966) 3.1: 30n.

9. Trudel, *Histoire de la Nouvelle-France* 3.1:30; CWB 5:287; Gabriel Sagard, *Histoire du Canada* (1636, ed. Tross, 1865) 4:838, 852.

10. Champlain, CWB 5:273; Trudel, *Histoire de la Nouvelle-France* 3.1:32; Sagard, *Histoire du Canada* 4:832, 838; Henry Kirke, *The First English Conquest of Canada* (London, 1871).

11. CWB 5:267.

12. CWB 5:268.

13. La Fourière, also called La Ferrière, Forière, Fourière, and Foyrière, was a Montagnais leader, also called Erouachy or Esrouachit. Cf. CWB 5:258–266, 268, 305–17, and 3:190–91; 6:6–25; Trudel, *Histoire de la Nouvelle-France* 2: 258n, 325, 356, 372, 403.

14. CWB 5:273; Trudel, *Histoire de la Nouvelle-France* 3.1:32–34.

15. CWB 5:275. See Jacques Guimont, *La Petite-ferme du cap Tourmente: de la ferme de Champlain aux grandes volées d'oies.* (Quebec, 1996). Guimont writes that Farmer Pivert survived to make a report to Champlain, and he appears to have returned to the site. Afterward, the farm was abandoned for a time, and then recovered. A larger farm was built there for the seminary of Quebec, and farmed for more than three centuries. It became part of the Canadian National Parks system in 1969. Today it is a wildlife refuge and a center for nature studies. No historical exhibits were available when we visited there in the summer of 2007.

16. Sagard, *Histoire du Canada* 4:834.

17. Ibid. 4:834.

18. CWB 5:285: Guimont, *La Petite-ferme*, 61–64; Guy de Repentigny, *La Ferme d'en bas du cap Tourmente: La petite ferme et la Réserve nationale de faune du cap Tourmente: occupation humaine des origines à 1763* (Quebec, 1989).

19. CWB 6:22.

20. CWB 5:277.

21. CWB 5:277–79; Sagard, *Histoire du Canada* 4:837.

22. David Kirke to Champlain, July 18, 1628 O.S.; July 8, 1628 N.S. The text is reproduced by Champlain in CWB 5:279–80; and in Sagard 4:838–39 (copied from Champlain). In that year, Britain still used the old-style Julian calendar. The French had shifted to the new style of the Gregorian calendar. (See appendix P.) These and other documents are reprinted in Abbé C.-H. Laverdière, *Oeuvres de Champlain*, 3:13, 16.

23. CWB 5:282–85.

24. Ibid. 5:286; other documents are reproduced from Catholic archives in Lucien Campeau, *Monumenta Novae Franciae* (Quebec, 1967) 2:201–03.

25. CWB 5:286.

26. Ibid. 5:287.

27. Sagard, *Histoire du Canada*, 4:863, 852; Champlain, CWB 5:287.

28. The French *commis* Thierry Deschamps heard the sounds of battle when he was at St. Barnabé Island, opposite the site of today's Rimouski. See CWB 5:291.

29. Sagard, *Histoire du Canada* 4:863.

30. CWB 6:131.

31. Ibid. 6:2.

32. The date of July 18 is given in Sagard 4:852; Trudel dates the meeting of the two fleets to July 17, with the battle following on July 18.

33. CWB 6:28.

34. Ibid. 6:29.

35. Trudel, *Histoire de la Nouvelle-France* 3.1:34; citing Henry Kirke, *The First English Conquest of Canada*, 65, 16, 206–08; also Léon Pouliot, "Que penser des frères Kirke?" *BRH* 44 (1938), 321–35.

36. This discovery was announced by Dr. James Tuck and archaeologist Barry Gaulton. See "Archaeologists Strike Gold," *Memorial University Research Report* (2004–05), www.mun.ca/research/2005).

37. CWB 5:293.

38. Ibid. 5:236; Trudel, *Histoire de la Nouvelle-France* 2:428.

39. CWB 5:296.

40. Ibid. 6:48.

41. Ibid. 5:297.

42. Ibid. 5:298.

43. Ibid. 5:300–01.

44. Sagard, *Histoire du Canada* 4:885.

45. Sagard, *Histoire du Canada* 4:853; CWB 5:326.

46. Ibid. 6:40.

47. CWB 6:51, 5:300–04; Trudel, *Histoire de la Nouvelle-France* 3.1: 34; Sagard, *Histoire du Canada* 4:885.

48. Ibid. 6:48–49; Sagard, *Histoire du Canada* 4:854.

49. CWB 6:50.

50. Ibid. 5:298, 321, 266; 6:48; Sagard, *Histoire du Canada* 4:854; Trudel, *Histoire de la Nouvelle-France* 3.1:34.

51. CWB 5:299.

52. Ibid. 6:41.

53. Ibid. 6:47.

54. Ibid. 6:45–46.

55. Ibid. 6:27–28.

56. Ibid. 6:42. Choumina's brother was called Ouagabemat by Champlain, Neogabinat by Sagard, and Onagabemat by scholars.

57. Ibid. 6:43–45.

58. Ibid. 6:50.

59. The documents appear in the British *Calendar of State Papers, Colonial,* 5, no. 2; rpt. Kirke, *English Conquest of Canada,* appendix D; Henry Percival Biggar, *The Early Trading Companies of New France: A Contribution to the History of Commerce and Discovery in North America* (Toronto, 1901, 1937; rpt. Clifton, N.J., 1972), 143.

60. CWB 6:53.

61. Louis and Thomas Kirke to Champlain July 19, 1629; CWB 6:53–54.

62. Champlain to Louis and Thomas Kirke, July 19, 1629; CWB 6:54–55.

63. "Articles which are to be granted by the Sieur Kirke, at present commanding the English vessels lying off Quebec, to the sieur Champlain and Dupont, 19 July 1629"; text in CWB 6:56.

64. CWB 6:59–61.

65. Ibid. 6:62.

66. Ibid. 6:63.

67. Ibid. 6:69.

68. Ibid. 6:63, 69.

69. Ibid. 6:67.

70. Ibid. 6:71.

71. Ibid. 6:70.

72. Ibid. 6:74.

73. Ibid. 6:69.

74. Ibid.

75. Ibid. 6:81–82.

76. Ibid. 5: 52, 60, 62, 70, 104–24, 144; Sagard, *Histoire du Canada* 4:908–11.

77. CWB 6:143; Champlain, "alloüettes, pluuiers, courlieux, bécassines." Biggar translates the first as snipes; citing Ganong, *The Identity of the Animals and Plants, etc.* 202, 205; I make it larks.

78. CWB 6:143.

79. Ibid. 6:86–87.

20. NEW FRANCE REGAINED

1. Champlain, *Voyages* (1632), in Henry Percival Biggar, ed., *The Works of Samuel de Champlain,* 6 vols. and a portfolio of maps and drawings (CWB), (Toronto, 1922–36, reprinted 1971) 6:69.

2. Gabriel Sagard, *Histoire du Canada* (1636, ed. Tross, 1865) 4:911; CWB 4:144.

3. CWB 6:144.

4. Champlain, *Traitté de la Marine*, CWB 6:144–45.

5. CWB 6:145; Victor-L. Tapié, *France in the Age of Louis XIII and Richelieu* (1952, tr. C. M. Lockie, Cambridge, 1974, 1988), 253–55.

6. CWB 6:126–27; Marcel Trudel, *Histoire de la Nouvelle-France* (Montreal, 1966) 3.1: 41, 46, 49; Lucien Campeau, *Monumenta Novae Franciae* (Quebec, 1967) 2:58, 59.

7. CWB 6:145.

8. Ibid. 6:146.

9. Ibid. 6:147–48.

10. Ibid. 6:146–49.

11. Ibid. 6:148–49.

12. Ibid. 6:147.

13. Ibid. 6:150; Henri Carré, *Henriette de France, reine d'Angleterre, 1609–1669* (Paris, 1947), includes the marriage contract, 21–24; See also Charles I to Sir Isaac Wake, English ambassador in France, June 12, 1631, reprinted in N.-E. Dionne, *Champlain, Founder of Quebec, Father of New France* (Toronto, 1962) 2:526–30, Pièces Justificatifs, 13.

14. CWB 6:149.

15. Ibid. 6:151.

16. "Ie m'acheminay à Paris" suggests a journey by land; CWB 6:107.

17. CWB 6:69.

18. Ibid.

19. Trudel, *Histoire de la Nouvelle-France* 3.1: 19–21, 50, 417, 433, 439; M. A. MacDonald, *Fortune and la Tour: The Civil War in Acadia* (Halifax, 2000), 66–70.

20. CWB 6:168.

21. Ibid.

22. Ibid.; documents in C.-H. Laverdière, *Oeuvres de Champlain* (Quebec, 1870).

23. CWB 6:151–522.

24. Ibid. 6:169.

25. Ibid.

26. Ibid. 6:169.

27. Trudel, *Histoire de la Nouvelle-France* 3.1:47; CWB 6:170–71.

28. *Mercure François*, reprinted by Campeau in his *Monumenta Novae Franciae* 2:350–97; 3:403–04.

29. Champlain, "carte de la nouvelle france . . . 1632," legend.

30. CWB 6:224–52.

31. Trudel, *Histoire de la Nouvelle-France* 3.1: 55–60; Robert Le Blant, "Les Compagnies du Cap-Breton (1629–1647) *RHAF* 16 (1962), 81–94.

32. Charles Daniel, "Narrative of the Voyage Made by Captain [Charles] Daniel of Dieppe to New France in the present year 1629" (1629); reprinted as *Voyage à la Nouvelle France du Capitaine Charles Daniel de Dieppe* (Rouen, 1881), and also in CWB 6:153–61. Daniel's account confirms the accuracy of Champlain's writings on this subject.

33. CWB 6:157; Daniel, "Narrative."

34. CWB 6:159; Daniel, "Narrative."

35. CWB 6:161; Daniel, "Narrative."

36. "There was in 1631, a second sub-contracting company founded in Normandy and interested in Cape Breton . . . the expedition being directed by Samuel de Champlain." Trudel, *Histoire de la Nouvelle-France* 3.1:58, 62, 120; Lucien Campeau, "Le dernier voyage de Champlain, 1633," MSRC ser. 4, 10 (1972) 81–101; *Mercure François* (1633), 19:806.

37. Libert, Daniel, and Desportes were all members of the Hundred Associates. Trudel, *Histoire de la Nouvelle-France* 3.1:60.

38. Campeau, "Le dernier Voyage de Champlain," 81–101; *Mercure François* 19:806–08; Trudel, *Histoire de la Nouvelle-France* 3.1:58–60, 62.

39. No previous biographer of Champlain was aware of this voyage. There is no doubt that it took place, but no certainty that Champlain led it. Even so, both Campeau and Trudel make a case for its high probability. Compare Lucien Campeau, "Le dernier voyage de Champlain, 1633," 80–101; and Trudel, *Histoire de la Nouvelle-France* 3.1:58–60. The primary evidence appears in an anonymous relation of the voyage in 1632, published in *Mercure François* 19 (1633), 80. The leader who remained in the fort was the sieur de Remercier; two Jesuits in residence were Antoine Daniel and Ambrose Davost.

40. CWB 6:173; Trudel, *Histoire de la Nouvelle France* 3.1:47 citing "Extrait de l'état général des dettes passives de la Compagnie de la Nouvelle-France 5 Feb. 1642; Robert Le Blant, "La Compagnie de la Nouvelle France et la restitution de l'Acadie," *Revue d'histoire des colonies* 42, 146 (1955), 77–80; Lucien Campeau, *Les finances publiques de la Nouvelle-France, sous les Cent-Associés, 1632–1635* (Montreal, 1975), 31–33.

41. CWB 6:175–78, 181; Nicolas Denys, *The Description and Natural History of the Coasts of North America (Acadia)* ed. William F. Ganong, 131–37, 477–79.

42. Trudel, *Histoire de la Nouvelle-France* 3.1:64, 70, passim; citing documents in the archives de la Charente Maritime BB 188 30–31v; Denys, *Acadia*, 474, 476, 479. Trudel identifies the ships that traded with the La Tour settlements: *Cheval Blanc* (120 tons); *Renard Noir* (220 tons); *Saint-luc* (90 tons); *Saint-Jean* (100 tons); *Pigeon blanc* (200 tons); *Saint-Pierre*; this from Delafosse in *RHAF* 4.4 (March 1951), 485; Trudel, *Histoire de la Nouvelle-France* 3.1:60.

43. MacDonald, *Fortune and La Tour*, 50–51; CWB 6:171–72, 198–99; Trudel, *Histoire de la Nouvelle-France* 3.1:428.

44. CWB 5:165, 212, 280; Trudel, *Histoire de la Nouvelle-France* 2:311; W. F. Ganong, "A History of Miscou," *Acadiensis* 6 (1906), 79–94; idem, "The History of Miscou and Shippegan," revised and enlarged from the author's notes by Susan Brittain, *New Brunswick Historical Studies* 5 (Saint John, N.B., 1946) 42–45; Denys, *Acadia*, 201; Robert Le Blant, "La Premiere Compagnie de Miscou, (1635–1645)," *RHAF* 17 (1963), 269–81; N.-E. Dionne, "Miscou, hommes de mer et hommes de Dieu," *Le Canada Français* 2 (1889), 432–77, 514–31.

45. Trudel, *Histoire de la Nouvelle-France* 3.1: 60.

46. Marcel Hamelin, "Thierry Desdames," DCB, s.v., "Desdames"; Champlain CWB 5: 88, 94–96, 322–25; 6: 40, 95; Dionne, "Miscou, hommes de mer et hommmes de Dieu" 2:445–47; Ganong, *History of Miscou and Shippegan*, NBHS 5 (Saint John, N.B., 1946), 44–45.

47. Trudel, *Histoire de la Nouvelle-France* 3.1:20–21, 60, 80, 388; Robert Le Blant, "Inventaire des meubles faisant partie de la communauté entre Samuel Champlain et Hélène Boullé, 21 Nov 1636," *RHAF* 18 (1965), 601.

48. Trudel, "Émery de Caën," *DCB*.

49. Declaration of Razilly, May 12, 1632, LAC, C11 A, 2, I:49 cited in Trudel, *Histoire de la Nouvelle-France* 3.1:121; see also Joe C. W. Armstrong, *Champlain* (Toronto, 1987), 259.

50. Trudel, *Histoire de la Nouvelle-France* 3.1:121; Champlain to Richelieu, August 15, 1633, and August 18, 1634, rpt. in CWB 6:375–78, appendices 6, 7.

21. REALIZING THE DREAM

1. Paul Le Jeune, "Relation de ce qui s'est passé en la Nouvelle France en l'année 1633 . . ." (Paris, 1634), *Jesuit Relations*, ed. Reuben Gold Thwaites (Cleveland, 1896–1901) 5:253.

2. Ibid. 6:103.

3. "Mémoire et instruction baillés au Sieur de Champlain par les Directeurs de la Nouvelle-France, Paris, Feb. 4, 1633; and "Supplément d'Instructions . . . , Dieppe, March 17, 1633; *Mercure François* 19 (1633) 809–11; Lucien Campeau, *Monumenta Nova Franciae* (Quebec, 1967) 2:340–41, 359–60.

4. This was probably the family of Jacques Panis and his wife, Marie Pouchet (or Pousset), with their daughters Isebeau and Marie. Both girls would marry in Quebec six years later, on Sept. 3 and 12, 1639. See Campeau's note in *Monumenta* 2:354n.

5. [Champlain], "Relation du voyage du sieur de Champlain en Canada," *Mercure François* 19 (1636), 803–67, 803–06; rpt in Campeau, *Monumenta* 2:350–97; Le Jeune, "Relation" (1634) 5:220; Marcel Trudel, *Histoire de la Nouvelle-France* (Montreal,1979) 3.1: 121–22.

6. For Champlain as "nostre Gouverneur," see *Jesuit Relations* 9:207.

7. [Champlain], "Relation du Voyage," *Mercure François* 19 (1636), 803–67; Campeau, *Monumenta* 2: 353; for Jacquinot see Campeau, *Monumenta* 1:671–2.

8. [Champlain], "Relation du Voyage," *Mercure François* 19:804.

9. Ibid. 19:805; Campeau, *Monumenta* 2:355.

10. Campeau, *Monumenta* 2:805. Here is further evidence that Champlain was present at Ste. Anne in 1632.

11. Samuel E. Morison, *Samuel de Champlain: Father of New France* (New York, 1978), 216.

12. Le Jeune, "Relation" (1633), *Jesuit Relations* 5:83–85.

13. Ibid. 5:201.

14. Ibid. 5:202, 6:72–74; Marcel Trudel, *Histoire de la Nouvelle-France* (Montreal, 1979) 3.1:121–22; John A. Dickinson, "Champlain, Administrator," in Litalien and Vaugeois, eds., *Champlain and the Birth of French America* (Montreal, 2004), 212.

15. Le Jeune, "Relation" (1634), *Jesuit Relations* 6:103–05.

16. Ibid. 6:105.

17. Ibid. 5:211–13 (1632–33).

18. Champlain, *Traitté de la Marine*, Henry Percival Biggar, ed., *The Works of Samuel de Champlain*, 6 vols. and a portfolio of maps and drawings (CWB), (Toronto, 1922–36, reprinted 1971) 6:259–60.

19. Samuel Eliot Morison, *The Founding of Harvard College* (Cambridge, 1935), 416–18, includes a short history of the Jesuit College of Quebec with an argument that "the answer to this question as to which college was 'first' depends on one's definition of a college." Morison concocted a unique definition by which Harvard "may justly be called the first college" north of Mexico. By any reasonable definition, the Jesuit College was first.

20. Morison, *Champlain*, 216–17.

21. Le Jeune, "Relation," 1634, *Jesuit Relations* 6:103.

22. Ibid.

23. Le Jeune, "Relation," 1635, *Jesuit Relations* 8:18; Champlain to Richelieu, Aug. 18, 1634, CWB 6:378–79; Champlain in *Mercure François* 19:821, 833; rpt in Campeau, *Monumenta* 2:367.

24. [Champlain], "Relation du Voyage," *Mercure François* 19:803–67, at 828–38; rpt in Campeau, *Monumenta* 2:350–97, at 372–78. The murderer was still in confinement when this account was written.

25. Ibid. 2:375.

26. Ibid. 2:378.

27. Le Jeune, "Relation," 1633, *Jesuit Relations* 5:221.

28. Ibid. 5:203, 288n; Chrestien Le Clercq, *Premier Établissement de la foy dans la Nouvelle-France*, 2 vols. (1691), ed. John Gilmary Shea (New York, 1881) 1:161–74; C.-H. Laverdière, *Oeuvres de Champlain* (Quebec, 1870), 1042, 1113, 1228.

29. Le Jeune, "Relation" (1633), *Jesuit Relations* 5:144–45, 178–95.

30. Ibid. 5:123.

31. Ibid. 5:203 (May 24, 1633).

32. Morison, *Champlain*, 217.

33. Le Jeune, "Relation" (1633), *Jesuit Relations* 5:205.

34. Ibid. 5:203–05, 207, 209–11.

35. [Champlain], "Relation du Voyage," *Mercure François* 18:56–73, rpt. in Campeau, *Monumenta* 2:380–81.

36. One chronology indicates that 500 to 700 Huron came to Quebec after Champlain had sent Louys de Saincte Foy (called by the Indians Amantacha) to the Huron to ask them to come and trade. See [Champlain], "Relation du Voyage," *Mercure François* 19:893–67, rpt. in Campeau, *Monumenta* 2: 350–97.

37. Le Jeune, "Relation," 1633, *Jesuit Relations* 5:243; [Champlain], "Relation du Voyage," *Mercure François* 19:803–867, rpt. in Campeau, *Monumenta* 2:383. The same passage appears in the accounts of Champlain and Le Jeune, but they turned the same observation in different ways. Champlain delighted in the richness and diversity of Indian customs. Father Le Jeune complained about it. He commented: "Oh how weak is the spirit of man! For over 4,000 years he has been seeking to ornament and beautiful himself, and all the nations of the world have not yet been able to agree as to what is true beauty and adornment." This passage was removed by Champlain.

38. Le Jeune, "Relation," 1633, *Jesuit Relations* 5:247.

39. Le Jeune's account is in *Jesuit Relations* 5:249; Champlain's account appears in [Champlain], "Relation du Voyage," *Mercure François* 19:803–67, rpt. in Campeau, *Monumenta* 2:383.

40. Le Jeune, "Relation," 1633, *Jesuit Relations* 5:253.

41. Ibid.

42. Ibid.5:257.

43. Ibid. 5:107.

44. Ibid. 5: 212–15; [Champlain], "Relation du Voyage," *Mercure François* 19:821, rpt in Campeau, *Monumenta* 3:366–69; CWB 6:376; Trudel, *Histoire de la Nouvelle-France* 3.1:126–27.

45. Champlain to Richelieu, Aug. 15, 1633, CWB 6:375–77; photocopies of these manuscripts from the Ministry of Foreign Affairs are in the manuscript division, Library of Congress.

46. Champlain, "Relation du Voyage," 1633, rpt. in Campeau, *Monumenta* 2:381–82.

47. In this force of "cent hommes," Champlain enumerated approximately 120 men. "Relation du Voyage," 1633, *Mercure François* 19:841–44, rpt in Campeau, *Monumenta* 2:381–82.

48. Ibid.

49. Ibid.

50. Champlain to Richelieu, Aug. 15, 1633; CWB 6:375–77.

51. Ibid.

52. Champlain to Richelieu Aug. 15, 1633, Archives of the Ministry of Foreign Affairs, Library of Congress; original text in Champlain, CWB 6: 375–77; English translation in N.-E. Dionne, *Champlain, Fondateur du Québec et père de la Nouvelle France*, ed. Flenley (Quebec, 1891, 1926), 246–49.

53. Champlain to Richelieu, Aug. 18, 1634, in CWB 6: 378–79.

54. Michel Carmona, *La France de Richelieu* (Paris, 1984), 187.

22. THE PEOPLING OF QUEBEC

1. Marcel Trudel, *Histoire de la Nouvelle-France* (Montreal, 1979) 3.1:130.

2. "This is the only French family settled in Canada," he wrote. Paul Le Jeune, "Relation de ce qui est passé en la Nouvelle France en l'année 1633 . . ." (Paris, 1634), *Jesuit Relations*, ed. Reuben Gold Thwaites (Cleveland, 1896–1901) 5:40–44. Champlain had helped other families to settle before 1625: Abraham Martin, his wife Marguerite Langlois, and several children; Pierre Desportes and Françoise Langlois; and Nicolas Pivert, his wife Marguerite Lesage, and an anonymous niece. They appear to have left the colony after the British conquest, and returned in 1632. A few other married couples may have been at Quebec in 1632, but if so their numbers were small and Le Jeune did not recognize them as "families." Cf. Trudel, *Histoire de la Nouvelle-France* 2:491–500; 3.1:33, 53.

3. Madeleine Jurgens, "Recherches sur Louis Hébert et sa famille," *Mémoires de la Société généalogique canadienne-française* 8 (1957), 106–12, 135–45; 11 (1960), 24–31; Azarie Couillard-Després, *La premiere famille française au Canada et Louis Hébert: premier colon canadien et sa famille* (Lille, 1913; Montreal, 1918); Champlain, CWB 1:402; 3:203–05; 5:326–27, 6:48, 62, 70–74, 184; Marc Lescarbot, *History of New France*, 3 vols. (Toronto, 1907) 2:209, 234, 328, 331; 3:246; Gabriel Sagard, *Histoire du Canada et voyages que les frères mineurs recollects y ont faicts pour la conversion des infidèles depuis l'an 1615* (first edition, Paris, 1636; reprint edition, Tross 1866) 1:53, 83, 158–59; Chrestien Le Clercq, *Premier établissement de la foy dans la Nouvelle-France*, 2 vols. (1691), ed. John Gilmary Shea (New York, 1881) 1:164–67, 281; *Jesuit Relations* 5:41–43.

4. Le Jeune, "Relation" (1632), *Jesuit Relations* 5:41.

5. Ibid.

6. Ibid.

7. Trudel, *Histoire de la Nouvelle-France* 2:485; 3.1:123, 130, 141. Estimates based on Trudel's numbers for immigrant ships.

8. Trudel was able to identify by name nine or eleven immigrants in 1633, 46 in 1634, 43 in 1635, and 98 in 1636; *Histoire de la Nouvelle-France* 3:123, 130, 141.

9. Hubert Charbonneau et al., *Naissance d'une population: les Français établis au Canada au XVIIe siècle* (Montreal and Paris, 1987), 15; translated as *The First French Canadians: Pioneers in the St. Lawrence Valley* (Newark, Del., 1993), 32–37; Henri Bunle, *Mouvements migra-*

toires entre la France et l'étranger (Paris, 1943); Marcel Trudel, *Catalogue des immigrants, 1632–1662* (Montreal, 1983); Lucien Campeau, *Les Cent-Associés et le peuplement de la Nouvelle-France, 1633–1663* (Montreal, 1974).

Deep change is a model of historical change. It begins with the assumption that the world is always changing, but not always in the same way. To measure rates of change empirically is to find evidence of distinct "change-regimes," which were often highly dynamic, but also stable in their dynamism, sometimes for long periods. These change regimes invariably break down sooner or later in moments of "deep change," and are followed by another change regime, which then breaks down again, and is succeeded by a third, and so on.

For this model of deep change see David Hackett Fischer, *Price Revolutions and the Rhythm of History* (Oxford and New York, 1996); and a work in progress, tentatively called "Deep Change: The Rhythm of American History."

10. In 1633 Champlain brought with him the family of Jacques Panis and his wife, Marie Pouchet, (or Pusset) and their daughters Isabeau, or Isabel, and Marie, aged thirteen and six. Both would marry in Quebec within a few years. Another daughter was born to Guillemette Hébert-Couillard in 1632–33. Also back in Quebec by the fall of 1633 were: the family of Abraham Martin with his wife, Marguerite Langlois, and daughters Anne, Marguerite, and Hélène; Pierre Desportes with his wife, Françoise Langlois (sister of Marguerite), and their daughters Hélène; and Nicolas Pivert with his wife, Marguerite Lesage. They had arrived in New France as early as 1629, perhaps earlier (Champlain, CWB 5:329), but had returned to France after the English conquest. They were not in Quebec when Le Jeune arrived in 1632, but were back by the fall of 1633. See Campeau, *Les Cent-Associés et le peuplement de la Nouvelle-France,* 18n; Lucien Campeau, *Monumenta Novae Franciae* (Quebec, 1967) 2: 354n.

11. These generalizations derive from two generations of historical demography by the rigorous method of "family reconstitution," which was invented in France at the Institut National d'études démographiques, founded by Louis Henri. That center sponsored a pioneering study on New France: Jacques Henripin, *La population Canadienne au début du XVIIIe siècle* (Paris, 1954), which produced results mainly for the period from 1660 to 1760. In a much larger effort, teams of Canadian historical demographers greatly broadened the population under careful study. They extended the inquiry backward in time to the beginning of settlement with the results noted below. See Hubert Charbonneau et al., *Naissance d'une population: les Français établis au Canada au XVIIe siècle* (Montreal and Paris, 1987). This very important volume has appeared in an English translation as Hubert Charbonneau et al., *The First French Canadians: Pioneers in the St. Lawrence Valley* (Newark, Del., 1993).

12. Hubert Charbonneau et al., *Naissance d'une population,* table 81, pp. 107–25; also striking is the fact that this proportion changed very little from the mid-eighteenth to the mid-twentieth century.

13. Articles accordez par le Roi, à la Compagnie de Canada, April 29, 1627, article 2; in Blanchet et al., *Collection de manuscrits contenant letters, mémoires et autres documents relatifs à l'histoire de La Nouvelle France,* 4 vols. (Quebec, 1828–88) 1:65.

14. Henry B. M. Best, "Abraham Martin, *dit* L'Écossais or Master Abraham," DCB, s.v. "Martin"; Lucien Campeau, biographical sketch of Abraham Martin in *Monumenta* 2:842; Trudel, in *Histoire de la Nouvelle-France* 2:263, 491–97 passim.

15. "Le premier enfant françois né en Amérique," 1621, in Blanchet et al., *Collection de Documents* 1:65.

16. Campeau, *Monumenta* 2:842.

17. Ibid.

18. Robert Le Blant, "Le testament de Samuel de Champlain, 17 novembre 1635," *RHAF* 17 (1963), 269–86.

19. J. M. LeMoine, *The Scot in New France, an Ethnological Study* (Montreal, 1881); R.-B. Casgrain, "La fontaine d'Abraham Martin et le site de son habitation," RSC *Transactions* 2 ser 9 (1903), 145–65; B. C. Roy, "Abraham Martin dit L'Écossais et les plaines d'Abraham," *BRH* 34 (1928), 568–70; Léon Roy, "La première canadienne-française," *BRH* 48 (1942), 205–08; idem, "Anne Martin, épouse de Jean Côté," *BRH* 49 (1943), 203–04.

     A revisionist argument appears in Jacques Mathieu and Eugen Kedl, *The Plains of Abraham: The Search for the Ideal* (Quebec, 1993), 25–32, which seeks to minimize the connection of the Plains of Abraham to Abraham Martin with "historical and geographical and moral [!] arguments." It insists that Martin "never possessed or lived on the parcels of land that carry his name" and "did nothing remarkable that would have justified lending his name to this site," and "died in relative dishonor for having forfeited his honor with a sixteen-year-old seductress in 1649." I take a different view.

20. Don Thomson, *Men and Meridians: The History of Surveying and Mapping in Canada* (Ottawa, n.d.) 1:36–38. Notarial acts wrote of the "côte d'Abraham" at an early date. Some of Martin's land was sold to the Ursuline Order in 1675 and is thought to have included the ground on which their convent was erected.

21. Trudel in *Histoire de la Nouvelle-France* 3.1:130.

22. The terms of Giffard's grant appear in Harris, 22, 55, 108, 119; N.-E. Dionne, *Champlain, Founder of Quebec, Father of New France* (Toronto, 1962) 2:336–37.

23. Trudel, *Histoire de la Nouvelle-France* 3.1:131; Le Jeune, "Relation" (1634), *Jesuit Relations* 7:213.

24. Champlain to Richelieu, Aug. 18, 1634, photocopy in the Library of Congress, from the original in the Archives of the Ministry of Foreign Affairs, Paris; French text in CWB 6: 378–79.

25. "l'homme providentiel sur qui reposait la confiance de toutes les familles." Dionne, *Champlain*, 2:346.

26. Grants, confirmations, and title deeds are published in *Pièces et documents relatifs à la tenure seigneuriale*, 2 vols. (Quebec, 1852–54); the Héberts' confirmation is 2:373.

27. Historians have called these survey lines a *rhumb de vent* or rhumb line. This is an incorrect adaptation of a usage in navigation, but may have had deep roots in a culture that applied many maritime terms to terrestrial purposes.

28. Richard Colebrook Harris, *The Seigneurial System in Early Canada* (Madison, 1968), 23; Honorius Provost, "Robert Giffard de Moncel," *DCB*; Campeau, *Monumenta* 2:824–25; Joseph Besnard, "Les diverses professions de Robert Giffard," *Nova Francia* 4 (1929) 322–29; T. E. Giroux, *Robert Giffard, seigneur colonisateur . . .* (Quebec, 1934).

29. Peter Moogk, *La Nouvelle France: The Making of French Canada: A Cultural History* (East Lansing, 2000), 486.

30. Samuel Eliot Morison, *The Story of Mount Desert Island* (Boston, 1960, 1988), 19–21.

31. Estimates vary between 56 and 68 percent of colonists in Quebec.

32. Many studies have replicated this result. See Archange Godbout, "Nos hérédités provinciales françaises," *Les Archives de Folklore* 1 (1946), 26–40; Hubert Charbonneau et al., *Naissance d'une population*, 46; Trudel, *Histoire de la Nouvelle-France* 3.2: 11–56, passim; Leslie Choquette, *Frenchmen into Peasants: Modernity and Tradition in the People of French Canada*

(Cambridge, Mass., 1997); tr. as *De Français à paysans: modernité et tradition dans le peuplement du Canada français* (Quebec, 2001); Gervais Carpin, *Le Réseau du Canada: étude du mode migratoire de la France vers la Nouvelle-France (1628–1662)* (Quebec and Paris, 2001); Peter N. Moogk, *La Nouvelle France*, 87–120.

33. Sources for what follows include Philippe Barbeau, *Le choc des patois en Nouvelle-France: Essai sur l'histoire de la francisation au Canada* (Montreal, 1984); Raymond Mougeon and Édouard Beniak, *Les origines du français québécois* (Quebec, 1994); Lionel Meney, *Dictionnaire québécois français* (Montreal, 1999); Jean-Marcel Léard, *Grammaire québécoise d'aujourd'hui comprendre de québécismes* (Montreal, 1995).

34. J. S. Tassie, "The Use of Sacrilege in the Speech of French Canada," *American Speech* 36 (1961), 34–40. Statements by several linguists that this pattern of profanity first appeared in the 1830s are mistaken. For common use of blasphemy and sacrilege, including the punishment for repeated offenders in seventeenth-century France, see Philip Riley, *A Lust for Virtue: Louis XIV's Attack on Sin in Seventeenth Century France* (Greenwood, 2001), 124–25. The persistence of this old speechway in modern Quebec is a theme of a hilarious bilingual comedy *Bon Cop, Bad Cop* (2006), which won top film honors in 2007. It is about two police detectives from the Ontario Provincial Police and the Sûreté de Quebec who are ordered to work together. Much of humor was about the meeting of two cultures, and in particular about the bewilderment of the Ontario policeman at his Quebec colleague who muttered such imprecations as "Tabarnak" and "Câlisse."

35. Moogk, *La Nouvelle France*, 146.

36. Michel Lessard and Huguette Marquis, *Encyclopédie de la maison Québécoise* (Montreal and Brussels, 1972), 35, 70–74, 488, passim.

37. Ibid., 35.

38. For a list of all clergy in Quebec from 1604 to 1629 see Trudel, *Histoire de la Nouvelle-France* 2:460–62. On the arrivals in 1633–34 see also *Histoire de la Nouvelle-France* 3.1:123n. For the six Jesuit missions from Cape Breton to Lake Huron see *Jesuit Relations* 7:3. The arrivals of a further seven Jesuits in 1636 are also documented in Trudel 3.1:134n.

39. G.-É. Giguere, *Oeuvres de Champlain* (Montreal, 1973) 1:409.

40. Pierre Biard, "Relation de la Nouvelle France. Écrite en 1614," *Relations des Jésuites,* IV, 100), Lyon (1616); reproduced in *Jesuit Relations* 3:104; Bruce Trigger, *Children of Aataentsic: A History of the Huron People to 1660* (1976, new edition, Montreal, 1987), 269.

41. Robert Laroque, "Les agents pathogènes, des envahisseurs clandestins," in Litalien and Vaugeois, eds., *Champlain: The Birth of French America* (Quebec, 2004), 266–75.

23. THE CRADLE OF ACADIA

1. Denys, *Acadia*, 146n, 124n; for statistical data see the U.S. Bureau of the Census, *1990 Census of Population, Supplementary Reports, Detailed Ancestry Groups* (1990 CP-S-1-2); Canadian estimates are diverse.

2. M. A. MacDonald, *Fortune and La Tour: The Civil War in Acadia* (1983, rpt. Halifax, 2000) is a very graceful book on its subject, and a first-class work of historical scholarship. Brenda Dunn, *A History of Port-Royal/Annapolis Royal, 1605–1800* (Halifax, 2004), 1–45, is an excellent history of the principal settlement, with much primary research.

3. For the Compagnie de Razilly see Marcel Trudel, *Histoire de la Nouvelle-France* (Montreal, 1979) 2:52–54.

4. Pierre Castagnos, *Richelieu face à la mer* (Rennes, 1989), 78–80.

5. Joan Dawson, *Isaac de Razilly, 1587–1635: Founder of LaHave* (LaHave, Nova Scotia,1982); George Macbeath, "Isaac de Razilly," *DCB* (Toronto, 1966) 1:567–69; Michel-Gustave de Rasilly, *Généalogie de la famille de Rasilly* (Laval, 1903); Léon Deschamps, *Un colonisateur au temps de Richelieu: Isaac de Razilly* (Paris, 1887).

6. CWB 6:219–20.

7. Isaac de Razilly, Mémoire du chevalier de Razilly, Nov. 26, 1626, published by Léon Deschamps as a "memoire inédit," in the *Revue de Géographie* 19 (1886) 374–83; the original is lost; a manuscript copy is in the Bibliothèque Sainte-Geneviève, Paris.

8. Razilly was admitted to the Hundred Associates by François Bertrand as its forty-third member, on January 9, 1628; Champlain was enrolled by his wife Hélène Boullé as the fifty-second member, on January 14, 1628. See Trudel, "La Seigneurie des Cent-Associés," appendix A, *Histoire de la Nouvelle-France* 3.1: 419–20. For Razilly and Richelieu see Castagnos, *Richelieu face à la mer*, 20; and Trudel, *Histoire de la Nouvelle-France* 2:433; 3.1:4–6. Lucien Campeau, *Monumenta Novae Francia* (Quebec, 1967) 2:852–53, takes another approach, minimizing the role of Razilly's memoir and maximizing the role of religious leaders, both Récollet and Jesuit.

9. Razilly, Declaration, May 12, 1632, cited in Trudel, *Histoire de la Nouvelle-France* 3.1: 121; Joe C. W. Armstrong, *Champlain* (Toronto: 1987), 259.

10. CWB 6:219–20.

11. See above, 161.

12. René Baudry, "Charles D'Aulnay et la Compagnie de la Nouvelle-France," *RHAF* 11 (1957), 218–41; Trudel, *Histoire de la Nouvelle-France* 3.1:53.

13. René Baudry, "Quelques documents nouveaux sur Nicolas Denys," *RHAF* 9 (1955), 14–30; Denys, *Acadia.*

14. Joan Dawson, "Colonists or Birds of Passage? A Glimpse of the Inhabitants of LaHave, 1632–1636," *NSHR* 9 (1989), 42–61.

15. Robert Le Blant, "La Compagnie de la Nouvelle-France et la Restitution de l'Acadie (1627–1636)," *Revue d'Histoire des Colonies*, 126 (1955) 71–93; Trudel, *Histoire de la Nouvelle-France* 3.1:54.

16. Denys, *Acadia*, 147.

17. Ibid.

18. Ibid., 149; Brenda Dunn, *A History of Port-Royal/Annapolis Royal, 1605–1800* (Halifax, 2004), 13.

19. A historical museum stands today on Fort Point, with many treasures and some manuscripts that tell the story of this founding.

20. Marcel Delafosse, "La Rochelle et le Canada au XVIIe siècle," *RHAF* 4 (1951), 469–511. Delafosse lists ships sailing from 1632.

21. Azarie Couillard-Després, "Aux sources de l'histoire de l'Acadie," *MSRC* 3rd ser. 27 (1933) 63–81; Candide de Nant, *Pages glorieuses de l'épopée: une mission Capucine en Acadie* (Montreal, 1927), 91.

22. John G. Reid, *Maine and New Scotland: Marginal Colonies in the Seventeenth Century* (Toronto, 1981); MacDonald, *Fortune and la Tour:* 46–47.

23. John G. Reid, "The Scots Crown and the Restitution of Port Royal, 1629–1632," *Acadiensis* 6 (1977), 106–77; Dunn, *Port-Royal/Annapolis Royal*, 15, citing Brigitta Wallace, "The Scots

Fort: A Reassessment of its Location," mss, Parks Canada Atlantic Service Centre, 1994, not seen.

24. Dunn, *Port-Royal/Annapolis Royal*, 15–16; Dawson, "Colonists or Birds of Passage," 42–61.

25. Razilly to Marc Lescarbot, Aug. 16, 1634, BN 13,343:349–50; a copy was in the Fort Port Museum, LaHave, when we visited there.

26. Denys, *Acadia*, 149–52.

27. George MacBeath, "Jean Thomas," and "Bernard Marot," DCB; René Baudry, "Nicolas Le Creux du Breuil," DCB; Candide de Nant, *Pages glorieuses* (Montreal, 1927).

28. Geneviève Massignon, *Les parlers français d'Acadie*, 2 vols. (Paris, n.p. [1962?]) 1:19.

29. Denys, *Acadia*, 124, 146–52; the historian is Ganong, *Acadia*, 124n.

30. Massignon, *Les parlers français d'Acadie* 1:19; a parish study by Rameau de Saint-Père is in *Une colonie féodale en Amérique: 1604–1881*, 2 vols. (Paris and Montreal, 1889) 2:322.

31. The best study is a *grand thèse* at the Sorbonne by Geneviève Massignon, a linguistic historian who was interested in the roots of Acadian and Quebec speech. She examined the origins of the Acadian population in census data of 1671, 1707, and 1938 and compared her results with evidence for Quebec and the St. Lawrence Valley. See Massignon, *Les parlers français d'Acadie*, 1:42–75, with a summary on pp. 74–75.

32. Massignon, *Les parlers français d'Acadie* 2:741; Yves Cormier, *Dictionnaire du français acadien* (Quebec, 1999), with an excellent bibliography, 381–426; see also Louise Péonnet et al., *Atlas linguistique du vocabulaire maritime acadien* (Quebec, 1998); Pascal Poirier, *Glossaire* (1953, 1977, 1993); idem, *Le parler franco-acadien et ses origines* (Quebec, 1928).

33. Cormier, *Dictionniare ue français acadien*, 30.

34. These examples are drawn from Cormier, *Dictionnaire du français acadien*; Poirier, *Glossaire*; and Poirer, *Le parler franco-acadien et ses origines* (Quebec, 1928).

35. A comparative table comes from the careful work of Geneviève Massignon, *Les Parlers Français d'Acadie* 2:741.

36. Andrew Hill Clark, *Acadia: The Geography of Nova Scotia to 1760* (Madison, 1968), 158; Yves Cormier, *Les aboiteaux en Acadie: hier et aujourd'hui* (Moncton, 1990),19; Françoise Marie Perrot, "Relation de la Provence d'Acadie," LAC; on tidal meadows see Denis, *Acadia*, 118.

37. Denys, *Acadia*, 138–39.

38. Dunn, *Port-Royal/Annapolis Royal*, 17.

39. Cormier, *Les aboiteaux en Acadie*, 30–31.

40. Denys, *Acadia*, 123.

41. Clark, *Acadia,* 360.

42. Bernard V. LeBlanc and Ronnie-Gilles LeBlanc, "La culture matérielle traditionelle en Acadie," in *L'Acadie des Maritimes* ed. Jean Daigle (Moncton, 1993), 601–48, with an excellent essay on vernacular architecture, 627–42. For primary accounts of early Acadian buildings see Champlain, CWB 1:373; Marc Lescarbot, *History of New France*, 3 vols. (Toronto, 1907), 2:514; Gargas, "Mon Séjour de l'Acadie, 1687–88," in William Inglis Morse ed., *Acadiensia Nova, 1598–1779* (London, 1935) 1:179; Baron de Lahontan, *New Voyages to North America* ed. R. G. Thwaites (1905) 1:330–32; accounts of Meneval in 1688, Clark, *Acadia*, 138; Sieur de Dièreville, *Relation du Voyage de Port Royal de l'Acadie, 1699–1700* (Toronto, Champlain Society, 1993).

For archaeological evidence see Andrée Crépeau and Brenda Dunn, *The Melanson Settle-*

ment: An Acadian Farming Community (ca. 1664–1755), Canadian Parks Research Bulletin 250 (Ottawa, 1986); David J. Christianson, *Bellisle 1983: Excavations of a Pre-Expulsion Acadian Site, Curatorial Report 48* (Halifax, Nova Scotia Museum, 1984); Marc C. Lavoie, *Bellisle Nova Scotia, 1680–1755: Acadian Material Life and Economy, Curatorial Report 65* (Halifax, Nova Scotia Museum, 1988).

    For a general discussion see Clarence Lebreton, *The Acadians in the Maritimes* (Moncton, 1982); Naomi Griffiths, *The Acadians: Creation of a People* (Toronto, 1973); Rameau de Saint-Père, *Une colonie féodale*; J. Rodolphe Bourque, *Social and Architectural Aspects of Acadians in New Brunswick* (Fredericton, 1971).

43. For the *maison madrier* see the description of the house of Louis Allain, in LeBlanc and Le-Blanc, "La culture matérielle," 630.

44. Peter Moogk, *La Nouvelle France: The Making of French Canada: A Cultural History* (East Lansing, 2000), 270.

45. On hydraulic systems and power see Karl A. Wittfogel, *Oriental Despotism* (New Haven, 1957, 1963).

46. Moogk, *La Nouvelle France*, 270.

47. Clark, *Acadia*, 387.

48. Massignon, *Les parlers français* 1:31, 36.

49. Clark, *Acadia,* 361, 89, 95, 128, 377, passim.

24. TROIS-RIVIÈRES

1. Paul Le Jeune, "Relation de ce qui s'est passé en la Nouvelle France en l'année 1633 . . ." (Paris, 1634), *Jesuit Relations*, ed. Reuben Gold Thwaites (Cleveland, 1896–1901) 5:211.

2. Alexander Ross, *The Red River Settlement: Its Rise, Progress and Present State* (London, 1856), 252.

3. Le Jeune, "Relation" (1634), *Jesuit Relations* 5:206; [Champlain], "Relation du Voyage du Sieur de Champlain en Canada," 1633, *Mercure François* 19 (1633), 803–67 at 838; rpt. in Lucien Campeau, *Monumenta Novae Franciae* (Quebec, 1967) 2: 350–97.

4. *Jesuit Relations* 7:225.

5. Marcel Trudel, *Histoire de la Nouvelle-France* (Montreal,1979) 3.1:130, 136, 137, 138.

6. DCB, "Laviolette"; *Jesuit Relations* 4: 261, 2:52; Benjamin Sulte, *Histoire des Canadiens-Français, 1608–1880, 8 vols.* (Montreal, 1882–84) 2: 48–54; idem, *Histoire de la ville des Trois-Rivières* (Montreal, 1870); *Album de l'histoire des Trois-Rivières* (Montreal, 1881); Campeau, *Monumenta* 2:66, 731.

7. The word had been brought to France by soldiers in the Crusades, and later by diplomats whom Francis had sent to Suleiman the Magnificent. Its Arabic and Akkadian origins are stressed in *Le Grand Robert*, s.v., "truchement," and Alain Rey et al., *Dictionnaire historique de la langue française* (2006), s.v., "truchement." For a variant theory of the Turkish root, see Jean-Benoît Nadeau and Julie Barlow, *The Story of French* (New York, 2006), 100.

8. More than two dozen French *truchements* appear by name in this chapter, and several dozen more in other descriptions quoted below, plus many Indian interpreters.

9. "Commençoit à se licentier en la vie des Anglois [*sic*]." This was Champlain's comment on an Indian *truchement*, Louis le Sauvage. CWB 6:101–02.

10. Campeau, "Bruslé," in *Monumenta* 2:808–09, which corrects earlier writing on the basis of new research. See also Bruce Trigger, *Natives and Newcomers: Canada's "Heroic Age" Reconsid-*

ered (Montreal, 1985, 1994), 177, 182, 194–997, 202, 246, 320, 326, 331, along with much material on Brûlé and the Indians. Indispensable are Champlain's accounts in CWB 2:138–42; 3:36, 213; 4:213–66; 5:100n; 6:98–102, and passim; also materials in *Jesuit Relations*; Consul Willshire Butterfield, *History of Brulé's Discoveries and Explorations, 1610–1626* (Cleveland, 1898), 12–19, has been superseded by new research, but its appended documents are still very useful.

11. CWB 2:139, 142; Bruce G. Trigger, *Children of Aataentsic: A History of the Huron People to 1660* (Montreal, 1976, 1987), 261–62. Trigger writes, "Champlain did not explain, and probably never knew why Iroquet and Ochasteguin arranged this complicated exchange." (262). Champlain's account, with its explicit references to Iroquet, the "Algoumequins," "the tribe of the Ochateguins, and the negotiations among them, suggests that he understood very well the complexity of these relationships. Cf. Trigger, *Children of Aataentsic*, 262; CWB 2:142.

12. CWB 2:188; 3:213. Part of this description is from Morris Bishop, *Champlain: The Life of Fortitude*, 175.

13. CWB 3: 36, 53, 58, 213–26. For the trip to Lake Superior see Gabriel Sagard, *Le Grand voyage au pays des Huron* (Paris, 1632) and Campeau, *Monumenta* 2:808–09; Conrad E. Heidenreich, "Explorations and Mapping of Champlain, 1603–1632," *Cartographica* (1976), 27–28; Trigger thinks that they passed through the Neutral Nation, keeping clear of the Iroquois. They had to pass through the country of the Iroquois, had a fight on the way, won it, and reached the village of Carantoüan with its eight hundred warriors well fortified with "high and strong palisades, firmly tied and joined together." They were too late and missed Champlain by two days. They then returned and Brûlé had to stay there for the autumn and winter. He employed himself in exploring the country, visiting the tribes and territories near the place, and making his way along a river [Susquehanna?] with "many powerful and warlike tribes." He followed the river "to the sea, past islands and coasts near them, which were inhabited by several tribes and numerous savage peoples, who nevertheless are well disposed and love the French nation above all others."

14. CWB 3:225.

15. CWB 5: 97, 100, 132.

16. Campeau, *Monumenta*, 808–09.

17. CWB 5:128; André Vachon, *DCB*, s.v. "Marsolet"; *Jesuit Relations* 4:206–14; 5:112.

18. CWB 5:63; 1:108.

19. CWB 6:99–100.

20. Ibid.

21. Trigger favors the political hypothesis on very little evidence, and suspects Captain Aenons, of whom more in the appendix, Historiography. See *Children of Aataentsic*, 473–76.

22. Gabriel Sagard, *Histoire du Canada et voyages que les frères mineurs recollects y ont faicts pour la conversion des infidèles depuis l'an 1615* (Paris, 1636; rpt. Librairie Tross, 4 vols. Paris, 1866), 368–70, 397–404, 621–29, 1228, 1249.

23. Le Jeune, "Relation" 1633, *Jesuit Relations* 4:206–14, 5:112.

24. For biographies see Émile Ducharme, "Olivier le Tardif," ASGCF Mémoires 12 (1961), 4–20; Amédée Gosselin, "Olivier le Tardif, juge-prévôt de Beaupré," RSCT, ser. 3, 17 (1923) 1–16; Marcel Trudel, *DCB*, s.v. "Le Tardif"; Chrestien Le Clercq, *Premier établissement de la foy dans la Nouvelle-France*, 2 vols. (1691), ed. John Gilmary Shea (New York, 1881) 1:161–74; C.-H. Laverdière, *Oeuvres de Champlain* (Quebec, 1870), 1042, 1113, 1228;

Campeau, *Monumenta* 2:838; Trudel, *Histoire de la Nouvelle-France* 3.1: 122; *Jesuit Relations* 5: 288n.

25. *Jesuit Relations* 5:202; CWB 5: 95, 209; 6:62–63, May 10, 1623, Aug. 25, 1626.

26. Le Jeune, "Relation" (1633), *Jesuit Relations* 5:203, 288; Campeau, *Monumenta* 2:452; Campeau, "Olivier Letardif," *Monumenta* 2:838; Le Clercq, *Premier établissement* 1:161–74.

27. Trudel, *Histoire de la Nouvelle-France* 2:149; 3.1:49, 117, 122, 149, 151, 160, 163, 178, 182–83, 191, 194.

28. René Blémus, *Jean Nicollet en Nouvelle France: un Normand à la découverte des Grands Lacs canadiens (1598–1642)* (Cherbourg, 1988), 120–25.

29. On Nicollet's arrival in New France, conflicting dates appear in the sources. Barthélemy Vimont wrote that Nicollet came to New France in the year 1618 . . . was sent to winter with the island Algonquins, in order to learn their language," and "tarried with them two years" (*Jesuit Relations* 23:276–78). But a legal document survives in which Jean Nicollet, son of Thomas Nicollet, was present when a piece of land was sold at Hainneville near Cherbourg on May 10, 1619 (Nicollet Mss, LAC.) Trudel concludes that Nicollet's "definitive arrival in Canada could not have been before 1619." It is also possible that Nicollet could have come earlier to New France and returned briefly in 1619. See also *Jesuit Relations* 8: 247, 257, 267, 295; 23:274–82; Sagard, *Histoire du Canada* (1866), 194.

30. Vimont in *Jesuit Relations* 23:276–78.

31. On January 18, 1642, Madeleine-Euphrosine was the godmother of an Indian at the Ursulines in Quebec. On November 21, 1642, she married Jean Leblanc, dit Lecourt, and had at least five children. On February 22, 1663, she remarried Elie Dusceau dit Lafleur, and had four more children. See Marcel Trudel, "Jean Nicollet dans le Lac Supérieur et non dans le Lac Michigan," *RHAF* 34 (1980) 186n.

32. [Champlain], "Relation du Voyage," *Mercure François* 19 (1633) 803–67; rpt. in Campeau, *Monumenta* 2:370; see Campeau's note, 370n.

33. Champlain wrote: "On June 20, a shallop arrived from Sainte-Croix which gave us news of the arrival of forty canoes, which were the Bésérévis [his name for the Nipissing], and with them a French interpreter whom the Sieur de Caën had sent the previous year [1632] to encourage the Indians to come for trade, and he asked the sieur de Champlain to come quickly to Sainte-Croix, desiring to see him. He immediately ordered a shallop to be prepared, in which he embarked and arrived the same day at Sainte-Croix." This text is from Champlain's own account, in his "Relation du Voyage," 370. The French interpreter is not named. Campeau concluded that "this interpreter was most probably Jean Nicollet (370n). This document has not been discussed in the controversy over Nicollet's great journey that followed.

34. For Nicollet's presence in Quebec see [Champlain] "Relation du Voyage," 372, 387n; confirmed also in Le Jeune's "Relation" (1633); also in Campeau, *Monumenta*, 405, 460.

35. In the *Jesuit Relations* they were also called Ouinipigous. The Ottawa told Champlain that the Puan could be reached by following the north shore of Lake Huron. For a discussion, see Heidenreich, *Explorations and Mapping of Champlain*, 95.

36. They are so labeled in a version of Champlain's 1616 map, as completed by Pierre Duval in 1653 and reproduced in Heidenreich, *Explorations and Mapping of Samuel de Champlain*, plates 85, 114; plates 6, 9.

37. Champlain's map of 1632 locates the Puan on the north shore of Lake Superior. Marcel Tru-

del, a Canadian historian, shares that view. See Marcel Trudel, "Jean Nicollet dans le Lac Supérieur," 188–89.

38. Most scholars agree that Nicollet made this journey and that it was an extremely important event in the history of New France and North America. But they are not of one mind about the details of Nicollet's trip. One interpretation was worked out by John Gilmary Shea, *Discovery and Exploration of the Mississippi Valley* (New York, 1953) and developed by Benjamin Sulte, *Mélanges d'Histoire et de Littérature* (Ottawa, 1876); and Consul W. Butterfield, *History of the Discovery of the North-West by John Nicolet* (Cincinnati, 1881). Shea believed that Nicollet went west to Lake Michigan, found his way to Green Bay and the Fox River, and met the Winnebago people in what is now Wisconsin. Historians with strong ties to Minnesota and Michigan insist that this account is mistaken and that Nicollet journeyed to their states. Also at issue are questions about when Nicollet made the journey, who sent him, whom he met, and what the consequences have been. See Clifford P. Wilson, "Where did Nicollet Go?" *Minnesota History* 27 (1946), 216–20; and Harry Dever, "The Nicolet Myth," *Michigan History* 50 (1966) 318–22; Trudel developed these ideas in "Jean Nicollet dans le Lac Supérieur et non dans le Lac Michigan," 183–96; on line at www.uwgb.edu/wisfrench/library/articles/nicolet.htm. A helpful overview of the subject is published in Jerrold C. Rodesch, "Jean Nicolet," *Voyageur: The Historical Review of Brown County and Northeast Wisconsin* (Spring 1984), 4–8.

Another generation of interpretation appears in Robert L. Hall, "Rethinking Jean Nicollet's Route to the Ho-Chucks in 1634," and Michael McCafferty, "Where did Jean Nicollet meet the Winnebago in 1634? A Critique of Robert L. Hall's 'Rethinking Nicollet's Route' " *Ontario History* 96 (2004), 170–82; with corrections in *Ontario History* 96 (2005).

My judgment is that Trudel and others are correct about the early part of Nicollet's journey, but that linguistic evidence confirms a visit to the country of the Winnebago. It is also possible that he followed the north shore of Lake Huron to its apex, crossed by canoe to the other side of the lake at its narrow neck, visited Lake Michigan as far as the Winnebago country, and than returned north to Sault Ste. Marie and explored part of the shore of Lake Superior. This interpretation may give the optimal fit to the evidence. If so, warring local historians of Michigan, Minnesota, Wisconsin, and Illinois may each have a part of the answer, and they could dwell together in peace and truth on the basis of a third hypothesis.

39. Vimont, in *Jesuit Relations* 23:275–79.

40. CWB 2:217.

41. Benjamin Sulte, "Les interprètes du temps de Champlain," RSCT ser 1, 1 (1882–83), 53.

42. CWB 2: 201–3, 205–06.

43. DCB, s.v. "Hertel"; *Jesuit Relations* 4: 24; 8:37; 9:33.

44. Ibid. 9:33, 57, 305; C.-H. Laverdière, *Oeuvres de Champlain* (Quebec, 1870) 6:58.

45. Campeau, *Monumenta* 2:141.

46. Trudel, *Histoire de la Nouvelle-France* 3.1:xxxvi, 44, 160, 176, 190; Campeau, *Monumenta* 2:108n.

47. Trudel, *Histoire de la Nouvelle-France* 3.1:40; CWB 1: 108; 6:108.

48. Trudel, *Histoire de la Nouvelle-France* 3.1:23.

49. Campeau, *Monumenta* 2: 825, 168, 172, 174; Sagard, *Histoire du Canada* (Tross) 4:880–92; Trudel, *Histoire de la Nouvelle-France* 3.1:22.

50. Trudel, *Histoire de la Nouvelle-France* 3.1: 137, 160, 176.

51. For a lively survey, see Georges-Hébert Germain, *Les Coureurs des Bois: La Saga des Indiens Blancs* (Quebec, 2003).

52. Alexander Ross, *The Fur Hunters of the Far West* (1885, Norman, Okla., 2001).

53. Jean-Benoît Nadeau and Julie Barlow, *The Story of French* (New York, 2006), 102–103.

54. Mitford Mathews, *Dictionary of Americanisms* (Chicago, 1951), s.v., "ozark."

55. Donna Evans, "On Coexistence and Convergence of Two Phonological Systems in Michif," (North Dakota,1982); Peter Bakker, *A Language of our Own: The Genesis of Michif, the Mixed Cree-French Language of the Canadian Métis* (New York, 1997).

56. *Jesuit Relations* 35:213.

57. *Dictionnaire historique de la langue française*, s.v. "métis"; Jennifer S. H. Brown, "Métis, Half-breeds, and Other Real People: Changing Cultures and Categories," *The History Teacher* 27 (1993), 20.

58. Terms such as *half-breed, métis,* and *métif* began to appear with increasing frequency in the travel literature (Jacqueline Peterson, 39). The French called them "bois-brûlé" or burned wood, from the Chippewa *wisahkotewan niniwak*, "men partly burned" (Verne Dusenberry, "Waiting for a Day that Never Comes: Dispossessed Métis of Montana," in Jacqueline Peterson and Jennifer S. Brown, *The New Peoples: Being and Becoming Métis in North America* [n.p., Montana, 1958], 120).

59. Duke Redbird, *We are Métis: A Métis View of the Development of a Native Canadian People* (Willowdale, 1980), 53; quoted in Brown, "Métis, Halfbreeds," 24.

60. Dusenberry, "Dispossessed Métis," 121.

61. Brown, "Métis, Halfbreeds," 24.

62. Alexander Ross, quoted in Bob Beal and Rod Macleod, *Prairie Fire* (Toronto, 1994), 17; Marcel Giraud, *Le Métis canadien: son rôle dans l'histoire des provinces de l'ouest* (1945), tr. George Woodcock (Edmonton, 1986); Jacqueline Peterson, "The People in Between: Indian-White Marriage and the Genesis of a Métis Society and Culture in the Great Lakes Region, 1680–1830," Ph.D. dissertation, Univ. of Illinois, Chicago, 1980); Jennifer S. H. Brown, "People of Myth, People of History: A Look at Recent Writings on the Métis," *Acadiensis* 17 (1987), 150–62; films: Christine Welsh, *Women in the Shadows* (NFB, 1992).

63. Peterson and Brown, *The New Peoples: Being and Becoming Métis in North America* (Winnipeg, 1985), 7.

25. CHAMPLAIN'S LAST LABOR

1. Paul Le Jeune, "Relation de ce qui est passé en la Nouvelle France en l'année 1635 . . ." (Paris, 1636), *Jesuit Relations*, ed. Reuben Gold Thwaites (Cleveland, 1896–1901) 9:206–09.

2. Charles de la Morandière, *Histoire de la pêche française de la morue dans l'Amérique septentrionale,* 3 vols. (Paris, 1962–66) 1:277–315, 248.

3. Gabriel Sagard, *Histoire du Canada et voyages que les frères mineurs recollects y ont faicts pour la conversion des infidèles depuis l'an 1615* (Paris, 1636; rpt. Librairie Tross, 4 vols. (Paris, 1866) 4:830.

4. Benjamin Sulte, *Histoire des Canadiens-Français, 1608–1880*, 8 vols. (Montreal, 1882–84) 2:59, 107; Marcel Trudel, *Histoire de la Nouvelle-France* (Montreal, 1979) 3.1:142, n. 64.

5. Ibid. 3.1:141.

6. Le Jeune, "Relation" (1636), *Jesuit Relations* 9:208–09.

7. Ibid. 9:209.

8. Robert Le Blant, ed., "Inventaire des Meubles faisant partie de la Communauté entre Samuel Champlain et Hélène Boullé," *RHAF* 18 (1965), 599.

9. Le Jeune, "Relation" (1636), *Jesuit Relations* 9:208–09.

10. Ibid. 9:207–08.

11. Ibid. 9:208–09.

12. Trudel, *Histoire de la Nouvelle-France* 3.1:130, 142–46, 333, 446–47.

13. Lucien Campeau, *Monumenta Novae Franciae* (Quebec, 1967) 2:818; Trudel, *Histoire de la Nouvelle-France* 3.1: 122, 141, 147, 163; R. Douvelle, *DCB*, s.v. "Derré de Gand."

14. Campeau, *Monumenta* 2:815–16, 824–25, 835.

15. Trudel, *Histoire de la Nouvelle-France* 3.1:133n.

16. A. Godbout, "Poisson," *Mémoires de la Societé généalogique canadienne-française* 3.3: 183–91.

17. Campeau, "Bonaventure, enfant montagnais," *Monumenta* 2:803.

18. Trudel, *Histoire de la Nouvelle-France* 3.1: xxvii, 132.

19. What follows is from the text of the will, which was discovered in the French National Archives in 1959. It is published in Robert Le Blant, "Le Testament de Samuel Champlain, 17 novembre 1635," *RHAF* 17 (1963), 269–86.

20. David Hackett Fischer, *The Great Wave: Price Revolutions and the Rhythm of History* (Oxford and New York, 1996); data reported in figure 0.01.

21. A partial inventory appears in Robert Le Blant, ed., "Inventaire des meubles," 594–603; see also idem, "Le triste veuvage d'Hélène Boullé," *RHAF* 18 (1965), 425–37. This evidence, as M. A. MacDonald observes, "reveals a modest financial situation, attesting to the honour and integrity of the great explorer." I agree. M. A. MacDonald, *Robert Le Blant, Seminal Researcher and Historian of Early New France: A Commented Bibliography* (Saint John, N.B., 1986), 23.

22. A. Ledoux, "Abraham Martin, Français ou Écossais?" *Mémoires de la Societé généalogique canadienne-française*, 27, 162–64.

23. Trudel, *Histoire de la Nouvelle-France* 3.1: 122, 141, 147; Le Jeune, "Relation" (1635), *Jesuit Relations* 7:302–03; Campeau in *Monumenta* 2:818.

24. Samuel E. Morison, *Samuel de Champlain: Father of New France* (New York, 1972), 224.

25. *Jesuit Relations* 9:206–07.

26. Ibid.

27. Paul Bouchart d'Orval, *Le mystère du tombeau de Champlain* (Quebec, 1951); Silvio Dumas, *La Chapelle Champlain et Notre-Dame de la Recouvrance* (Quebec, 1958). Research projects carried out in the 1980s yielded no results.

28. Le Blant, "Le Triste Veuvage d'Hélène Boullé," 425–37.

29. Robert Le Blant, "L'Annulation du Testament de Champlain," *Revue d'Histoire des Colonies* 131–32 (1950), 203–31.

30. Trudel, *Histoire de la Nouvelle-France* 3.1: 142–43.

31. J. E. Roy, "M. de Montmagny," *Nouvelle-France* 5 (1906), 105–21, 161–73, 417–28, 520–30; Jean Hamelin, *DCB*, s.v. "Charles Huault de Montmagny"; Morison, *Champlain*, 225.

32. Morison, *Champlain*, 225.

33. Alain Rey, *Dictionnaire historique de la langue française*, 3 vols., rev. edition, Paris, 2006), s.v., "devoir," "service."

CONCLUSION

1. Morris Bishop, *Champlain: The Life of Fortitude* (New York, 1948), 341.
2. For a biography of Black Hawk see Roger L. Nichols, *Black Hawk and the Warrior's Path* (Wheeling, Ill., 1992); a history of his nation is William T. Hagan, *The Sac and Fox Indians* (Norman, Okla., 1958); for the Black Hawk War of 1831–32, see Ellen M. Whitney, ed., *The Black Hawk War, 1831–1832*, 3 vols. (Springfield, 1970) with a helpful introduction by Anthony F. C. Wallace.
3. J. B. Patterson, *Life of Ma-Ka-Tai-Me-She-Kia-Kiak or Black Hawk . . . Dictated by Himself* (Rock Island, Ill., 1833), with certificate of authenticity by Antoine LeClaire, "U.S. Interpreter for the Sacs and Foxes." Other editions followed in Boston, New York, Philadelphia, Baltimore, and Mobile. The first scholars' edition was edited by Milo Milton Quaife and published in the Lakeside Classics (Chicago, 1916). The best scholarly edition is Donald Jackson, ed., *Black Hawk: An Autobiography* (Urbana, 1995). Two centuries later, *The Autobiography of Black Hawk* is still in print, and much cherished as a major work of American literature. The text of the first edition is posted on line as part of the Abraham Lincoln Historical Digitization project. Black Hawk's warning appears on the dedication page. For a literary analysis see Mark Wallace, "Black Hawk's *An Autobiography*: The Production and Use of an Indian Voice," *American Indian Quarterly* 18 (1994), 481–94.

   A hostile critic named Thomas Ford alleged that the book was a fraud concocted by a "halfbreed Indian interpreter." LeClaire was a *Métis*, with a French Canadian father and a Potawatomi mother. He learned French, English, and "a dozen Indian languages," and his name appears on many Indian treaties. He became a leading citizen of Iowa with a fortune of half a million dollars, was a founder of the town of Davenport, had his portrait put on the Iowa State Bank's five-dollar bill, and was celebrated for his character. Winfield Scott wrote that "he has been faithful to both sides, to the Americans as well as to the Sac and Fox." See Charles Snyder, "Antoine LeClaire, the First Proprietor of Davenport," *Annals of Iowa* 3rd series, 23 (1941–42) 79–117. The critic Ford appears not to have read the book. Recent study by Donald Jackson confirms its authenticity.
4. *Black Hawk: An Autobiography*, ed. Jackson, dedication page.
5. The dates are uncertain, as in much oral history. Black Hawk (1767–1838) was translated as calling his ancestor his "great grandfather," but said that Na-Nà-Ma-Kee's meeting with the "white father" happened "a long time" before "the British overpowered the French" in 1759, and at a time when Black Hawk's ancestors were "people who had never yet seen a white man." The word that LeClaire translated as "great grandfather" may have been more accurately rendered as "forefather." Probably Na-Nà-Ma-Kee would have been Black Hawk's great-great-great-great-grandfather, six generations removed. It is known that in the early seventeenth century the Sauk nation lived with other Algonquin people in the Upper St. Lawrence Valley, that they were at war with the French by the beginning of the eighteenth century, and moved many times to Wisconsin, then to Iowa, back to Wisconsin and to Illinois.
6. Na-Nà-Ma-Kee's story was an oral tradition, and it grew through the years by a process of accretion. Some of its elements were added later: for example the story mentions that among the white man's gift to Na-nà-ma-kee were guns. Champlain did not give Indians guns, and often opposed the gift or sale of guns to Indians by Dutch and English traders. There is no evidence that Champlain gave medals to the Indians, a practice that became more common in the eighteenth and nineteenth centuries.

But most elements of the story point directly to Champlain and only to Champlain. Among them are the assertion that this white man was a Frenchman, that he had a special relationship with the king of France, that he was in the St. Lawrence Valley, that he was the first white man Na-Nà-Ma-Kee's people had ever seen, that he was a soldier and a "great and brave general," that he exchanged goods and presents more to establish trust and build a relationship than for a commercial purpose, which followed later; that he was an honest and honorable man who kept his word and treated the Indians with respect. No other French explorer matched this description of an encounter that happened "a long time" before "the British overpowered the French" in the eighteenth century, and at a time when Black Hawk's ancestors "had never yet seen a white man."

Champlain repeatedly mentioned that in his early travels up the St. Lawrence Valley he met nations who had never before seen a European. Further, the substance of this oral history is true to the area in which Champlain traveled, and also to the way in which he worked with the Algonquin nations of the St. Lawrence Valley.

Two American historians have studied Black Hawk's autobiography. Both conclude that Na-Nà-Ma-Kee's white man was Champlain. See Donald Jackson, ed., *Black Hawk: An Autobiography* (Urbana, Ill., 1955, 1964, 1990), 45n; and Gordon M. Sayre, *Les sauvages américaines* (Chapel Hill, 1997), 64, a monograph on Indian images in American literature. No biographer of Champlain or historian of New France appears to have been familiar with Black Hawk's autobiography.

7. Fred Anderson and Andrew Cayton, *The Dominion of War: Empire and Liberty in North America, 1500–2000* (New York, 2005), 41; for more Indian memories of first encounters, see Sylvie Vincent et al., *Traditions et récits sur l'arrivée des Européens en Amérique*, published in *Recherches amérindiennes au Québec* 22.2–3 (Automne 1992) 1–180. Especially helpful in that collection is Denys Delage, "Les Premiers Contacts," 101–16.

8. Perry Miller, *Roger Williams: His Contribution to the American Tradition* (New York, 1962), 49–73; Ola Elizabeth Winslow, *John Eliot, "Apostle to the Indians"* (Boston, 1968); 71–159; Henry W. Bowden and James P. Ronda, eds., *John Eliot's Indian Dialogues* (Westport, Conn., 1980); Lewis Hanke, *The Spanish Struggle for Justice in the Conquest of America* (1949, rpt. Boston, 1965) 20–22, passim.

9. Ramsay Cook, ed., *The Voyages of Jacques Cartier* (Toronto, 1993), xxv-xli, passim.

10. It is most accessible in a bilingual edition, edited by H. P. Biggar in his edition of Champlain's major works, sponsored by the Champlain Society, CWB 6: 253–346.

11. See appendix E below.

12. CWB 6: 297, 295, 314, 279, 269–70.

13. CWB 6:257–68.

14. CWB 6:261.

MEMORIES OF CHAMPLAIN

1. Gérard Malchelosse, *Trois-Rivières d'autrefois: études éparses et inédites de Benjamin Sulte* (Montreal, 1934); qtd. in Denis Martin, "Discovering the Face of Samuel de Champlain," in Raymonde Litalien and Denis Vaugeois, eds., *Champlain: la naissance de l'Amérique française* (Quebec, 2004); tr. as *Champlain: The Birth of French America* (Montreal, 2004), 358.

2. For a short but very thoughtful survey of the literature, see Raymonde Litalien, "Historiography of Samuel Champlain," in Litalien and Vaugeois, eds., *Champlain*, 11–16. General

studies of Canadian historiography include: H.-A. Scott, *Nos anciens historiographes et autres études d'histoire canadienne* (Quebec, 1930); Serge Gagnon, *Le Québec et ses historiens* (Quebec, 1978), of which portions are translated in two volumes as *Quebec and Its Historians: 1840–1920* (Montreal, 1982) and *Quebec and Its Historians: The Twentieth Century* (Montreal, 1985); and "The Historiography of New France, 1960–1974," *Journal of Canadian Studies* 13 (1978), 80–99. Also useful are D. A. Muise, *Approaches to the Native History of Canada* (Ottawa, 1977); Bruce G. Trigger, "The Indian Image in Canadian History," in *Natives and Newcomers: Canada's "Heroic Age" Reconsidered* (Montreal and Kingston, 1985, 1986, 1994), 3–49.

3. Marc Lescarbot, *Histoire de la Nouvelle-France*, published in Paris in 1609 with English translations in the same year and German in 1613; other French editions followed in 1611, 1612, 1617, and 1618; also, Marc Lescarbot, *History of New France*, 3 vols. (Toronto, Champlain Society, 1907), edited by H. P. Biggar with a translation by Oxford linguist W. L. Grant; *La Conversion des Sauvages* (Paris, 1610), rpt. in *Jesuit Relations* 1:49–113; and *Relation dernière de ce qui s'est passé au voyage du sieur de Poutrincourt en la Nouvelle France depuis 20 mois ença* (Paris, 1912) rpt. in *Jesuit Relations* 1, 119–91. See Éric Thierry, *Marc Lescarbot (vers 1570–1641): un homme de plume au service de la Nouvelle-France* (Paris, 2001); idem, "Champlain and Lescarbot: An Impossible Friendship," in Litalien and Vaugeois, eds., *Champlain*, 121–34; Bernard Émont, *Marc Lescarbot: Mythes et rêves fondateurs de la Nouvelle France* (Paris, Budapest, and Turin, 2002); Louis-Martin Tard, *Marc Lescarbot: le chantre de l'Acadie* (Quebec, 1997); H. P. Biggar, "The French Hakluyt: Marc Lescarbot of Vervins," *AHR* 6 (1901), 671–92.

4. Marc Lescarbot, *Les Muses de la Nouvelle-France* (Paris, 1618), 49. The first publication includes a note, "Fait aux iles de Câpseau en la Nouvelle-France."

5. W. L. Grant, in Lescarbot, *New France* 2:27.

6. Champlain in Henry Percival Biggar, ed., *The Works of Samuel de Champlain* 6 vols. and a portfolio of maps and drawings (CWB), (Toronto, 1922–36, reprinted 1971) 1:452; Lescarbot, *New France* 2:169–70, 172; 1:30, 104; 2: 76, 83–84, 99, 108, 110–11, 141, 168, 172–76, 179, 234, 241, 359; 3:6, 34.

7. Lescarbot, *New France* 2:117, 22, 233, 342; 3: 6, 9–15, 17, 24–27, 28–29.

8. Charles Daniel, *Voyage à la Nouvelle France du Capitaine Charles Daniel de Dieppe* (n.p., 1629; rpt. Rouen, 1881; CWB 6:153–61. Pierre Victor Palma Cayet, *Chronologie Septenaire* (Paris, 1605), 415–24, included passages from Champlain's *Des Sauvages*. Jacques-Auguste de Thou's *Histoire universelle depuis 1543 jusq'en 1607* was published first in a Latin edition and later in a French translation (Paris, 1739). For an example of periodical literature see *Le Mercure François* 19 (1633), 802–67.

9. Le Jeune, "Relation, 1636," *Jesuit Relations* 9: 218–83; Morris Bishop, *Champlain: The Life of Fortitude* (New York, 1948), 341.

10. Gordon M. Sayre, *Les sauvages américaines* (Chapel Hill, 1997), 64; see Conclusion, above.

11. For some of these Montagnais stories see Sylvie Vincent, "L'arrivée des chercheurs de terres: récits et dires des Montagnais de la Moyenne et de la Basse Côte-Nord," *Recherches amérindiennes au Québec* 22:2–3 (1992),19–29.

12. Le Jeune, "Relation, 1637," *Jesuit Relations* 12:86–87; 13:147; for Captain Aenon see Bruce Trigger, *The Children of Aataentsic: A History of the Huron People to 1660* (1976; new edition, Montreal, 1987), 474; and *Jesuit Relations* 20:19.

13. Bishop, *Champlain: The Life of Fortitude*, 340.

14. Ibid. 341.
15. David Knowles, *Great Historical Enterprises: Problems in Monastic History* (London, 1963), 3–62.
16. Gabriel Sagard, *Le Grand Voyage du pays des Hurons* (Paris, 1632), new edition (Tross, Paris, 1865); an English translation appeared as *The Long Journey to the Country of the Hurons*, tr. H. H. Langton, ed., George M. Wrong (Toronto, 1939). A scholarly edition with a French text was established by Réal Ouellet, and an introduction and notes by Réal Ouellet and Jack Warwick (Quebec, 1990); idem, *Histoire du Canada* (Paris, 1636; rpt. Tross, Paris, 1866), in four duodecimo volumes, still the edition of choice. It has not been translated into English or reprinted in a modern scholarly edition.
17. Gilbert Chinard, *L'Amérique et le rêve exotique dans la littérature française au XVIIe et XVIIIe siècle* (Paris 1913); Bishop, *Champlain: The Life of Fortitude*, 259.
18. Chrestien Le Clercq, *Nouvelle relation de la Gaspésie* (Paris, 1691); and *Premier établissement de la foy dans la Nouvelle-France* (Paris, 1691), in at least two other editions with variant titles. Both were published in English translations as *First Establishment of the Faith in New France*, ed. J. G. Shea, 2 vols. (New York, 1881); and *New Relation of Gaspesia with the Customs and Religions of the Gaspesian Indians*, vol. 5 in the publications of the Champlain Society, ed. W. F. Ganong (Toronto, 1910).
19. Le Clercq, *Premier établissement*, 114–15, 129, 150–53, 158–59.
20. Champlain to Louis XIII, Sieur de Montmorency, Chancellor de Sillery and the Sieur de Villemenon, 25 August 1622, BN ms 16738, fol 143; cited in H. P. Biggar, *Early Trading Companies of New France, A Contribution to the History of Commerce and Discovery in North America* (Toronto, 1901, 1937; rpt. Clifton, N.J., 1972), 279–80.
21. Pierre-Francis-Xavier de Charlevoix, *Histoire de l'établissement, des progrès, et de la décadence du christianisme dans l'Empire du Japon*, 3 vols. (Rouen, 1713).
22. Pierre-Francis-Xavier de Charlevoix, *Histoire et description générale de la Nouvelle-France* with *Journal historique*, 3 vols, in quarto, six volumes in duodecimo (Paris, 1744); an excellent modern scholarly edition of the *Travels* is *Charlevoix: Journal d'un voyage fait par ordre du roi dans l'Amérique septentrionale* ed. Pierre Berthiaume, 2 vols. (Montreal, 1994). English translations include *History and General Description of New France*, tr. John Gilmary Shea, 6 vols. (New York, 1866–1872, rpt. Chicago, 1962); and Louise Phelps Kellogg, *Journal of a Voyage to North America*, 2 vols. (Chicago, 1923); David M. Hayne, "Charlevoix," *DCB/DBC*.
23. Charlevoix, *Journal d'un Voyage*, ed. Berthiaume, 1:317–18, 364–65; 2:89, passim.
24. Ibid. 2:89.
25. Ibid. 1:215, 244, 251, 453–54]; idem, *History and General Description of New France*, ed. Shea, 2:12, 90.
26. Charlevoix, *Journal d'un Voyage*, ed. Berthiaume, 2:32.
27. Cadwallader Colden, *History of the Five Indian Nations* (1727, 1747, rpt., 1866; Ithaca, 1958), chap. 1, 1–6.
28. Ibid., 6.
29. Jean le Rond d'Alembert and Denis Diderot, *Encyclopédie ou dictionnaire raisonné des sciences, des arts, et des métiers* (Paris, 1751), s.v., "Québec."
30. Portrait of Samuel de Champlain, anonymous *sanguine* of unknown provenance and date, Archives nationales du Québec, reproduced in Alain Beaulieu et Réal Ouellet, eds., Samuel de Champlain, *Des Sauvages* (Montreal, 1993), 10.

31. François-Xavier Garneau, *Histoire du Canada, depuis sa découverte jusqu'à nos jours*; my set is the second edition, corrected and enlarged, 3 vols. (Quebec, 1852).

32. Ibid. 1:121.

33. Ibid. 1:120.

34. Ibid. 1:121.

35. Ibid. 1:120.

36. Andrew Bell, *History of Canada . . . translated from Histoire du Canada of F.-X. Garneau, Esq.*, 3 vols. (Montreal, 1860) 1:iv; 1:120, 128.

37. Marcel Trudel, *Memoirs of a Less Travelled Road* (translation of *Mémoires d'un autre siècle*) (1987, Montreal, 2002), 152.

38. Francis Parkman, *Pioneers of France in the New World* (1865, revised edition with corrections, 1885; rpt. Boston, 1901), 186–87.

39. Ibid. xix.

40. Ibid. 280, 438.

41. Ibid. 185, 255.

42. Ibid. 243, 255.

43. Ibid. 464.

44. Ibid. xxv.

45. Parkman's notes and collected materials are in the manuscript collections of the Massachusetts Historical Society.

46. Gagnon, *Quebec and Its Historians,* 45–66.

47. Ibid. 54–55.

48. Parkman, *Pioneers*, 244.

49. Abbé Auguste Gosselin, "Le vrai monument de Champlain: ses oeuvres éditées par Laverdière," *Mémoires de la Societé Royale du Canada* 1 (1908), 3–23.

50. Philéas Gagnon, *Essai de bibliographie canadienne* (Quebec, 1895) 1:103.

51. Gosselin, "Le vrai monument de Champlain," qtd. in Ronald Rudin, *Founding Fathers: The Celebration of Champlain and Laval in the Streets of Quebec, 1878–1908* (Toronto, 2003), 56.

52. For a short biography of Ducornet, see Emmanuel Bénézit, *Dictionnaire critique et documentaire des peintres, sculpteurs, dessinateurs et graveurs* (Paris, 1999).

53. "Samuel de Champlain, governor general of Canada," lithograph, 1854, attributed to Louis-César-Joseph Ducornet (1806–56); Litalien and Vaugeois, eds., *Champlain*, 356.

54. Litalien and Vaugeois, eds., *Champlain*, 357.

55. Samuel de Champlain, steel-plate engraving by J. A. O'Neil, ca. 1866; reproduced in Litalien and Vaugeois, eds., *Champlain*, 357; O'Neil's engraving appeared as the frontispiece in John Gilmary Shea's edition of Charlevoix's *History and General Description of New France* published in the United States that year.

56. Victor-Hugo Paltsits, "A Critical Examination of Champlain's Portrait," *Acadiensis* 4 (1904), 306–11; rpt. in *Bulletin des Recherches Historiques* 38 (1932), 755–59.

57. H. P. Biggar, "The Portrait of Champlain," *CHR* 1 (1920), 379–80; Bishop, *Champlain*, 6n; Joe C. W. Armstrong, *Champlain* (Toronto, 1987), 20–21; Jean Liebel, "Les faux portraits de Champlain," *Vie des arts* 28 (1983), 112; Martin, "The Face of Champlain," 354–62.

58. Martin, "The Face of Champlain," 359; Trudel, *Champlain*, 15.

59. "What did Champlain really look like?" www.champlainsoc.ca.

60. Martin, "The Face of Champlain," 357.

61. Narcisse-Eutrope Dionne, *Champlain, fondateur de Québec et père de la Nouvelle-France*, 2 vols. (Quebec, 1891). An abridged edition would later be published in English as *Champlain, Founder of Quebec, Father of New France* (Toronto, 1962); Trudel, *Memoirs*, 152–53, passim.

62. Abbé Henri-Raymond Casgrain, *Champlain, sa vie et son caractère* (Quebec, 1898); Gabriel Gravier, *Vie de Samuel de Champlain, fondateur de la Nouvelle-France* (Paris, 1900), 363.

63. Many of Sulte's articles were brought together in his *Mélanges littéraires* and *Mélanges historiques*, which ran to 23 volumes (1918–34). More accessible was his *Histoire populaire du Canada, d'après les documents français et américains*. An excellent study of his work appears in Gagnon, *Quebec and Its Historians*, 67–110, 103–04.

64. John Bach McMaster, *The History of the People of the United States*, 9 vols. (New York, 1883–1927).

65. Gagnon, *Quebec and Its Historians*, 90.

66. Benjamin Sulte, *Histoire des Canadiens-français, 1608–1880*, 8 vols. (Montréal, 1882–84) 2:58; Gagnon, *Quebec and Its Historians*, 74.

67. Sulte, *Histoire des Canadiens-français*, 1:57, 5:35; Gagnon, *Quebec and Its Historians*, 74, 86, 89.

68. Trudel, *Memoirs*, 133.

69. The Champlain Society's website includes essays on the history of the society and on Sir Edmund Walker; http://www.champlainsociety.ca.cs_origins-history.htm. See also Heidenreich's monograph on the publication of Champlain's *Works*.

70. H. P. Biggar, ed., *The Works of Samuel de Champlain*, 6 vols, and a portfolio of maps and drawings (Toronto: Champlain Society, 1922, rpt. University of Toronto Press, 1971).

71. John Squair, *Autobiography of a Teacher of French*, n.p. (Toronto, ca. 1928, published posthumously). Squair also left a manuscript diary and memoir; see www.chass.utoronto.ca/french/dept-of-french/history/chap3a.html.

72. Nicolas Denys, *The Description and Natural History of the Coasts of North America (Acadia)* (Toronto, Champlain Society, 1908); Lescarbot's *History of New France*, 3 vols. (Toronto, Champlain Society, 1907); and Recollet father Gabriel Sagard's *Le Grand Voyage du pays des Hurons* published as *The Long Journey to the Country of the Hurons*, ed., George M. Wrong and tr. by H. H. Langton, now available online in digital editions that are key-word searchable, a great tool for serious scholars: 7 volumes for Champlain himself, now the indispensable source for Champlain; three for his comrade and later enemy. A new edition of Champlain's works is in progress at the society, edited by C. E. Heidenreich.

73. William Francis Ganong, *Sainte Croix (Dochet) Island*, first published in *Transactions of the Royal Society of Canada* in 1902, revised and enlarged by Susan Brittain Ganong (Saint John, 1945 and 1979), reprinted again with new material as *Champlain's Island* (Saint John, 2003).

74. Ganong, *Champlain's Island*, 20.

75. The leading study is Ronald Rudin, *Founding Fathers: The Celebration of Champlain and Laval in the Streets of Quebec, 1878–1908* (Toronto, 2003), esp. 53–102.

76. Patrice Groulx, "In the Shoes of Samuel de Champlain," Litalien and Vaugeois, eds., *Champlain*, 338; David Russell Jack, "Proposed Champlain Memorial at Saint John, N.B.," *Acadiensis* 5 (1901); W. F. Ganong, "A Visitor's Impressions of the Champlain Tercentenary," *Acadiensis* 5 (1905), as cited in Groulx, 378–79.

77. Groulx, "In the Shoes of Champlain," 338–39.

78. Henry Raymond Hill, *The Champlain Tercentenary: First Report of the New York Lake Champlain Tercentenary Commissions* (Albany, 1913). A full set of these materials is in the Research Center at Fort Ticonderoga.

79. The source for this paragraph is Groulx, "In the Shoes of Champlain," 341.

80. Quoted in Gérard Malchelosse, *Trois-Rivières* (1934), 13–14; from Martin, "The Face of Champlain," 358. In practice, it was looser than that. The standard formula combined the costumes of Louis XIII with the characters of Dumas père, and the hair of Napoleon III. The sculptor Hébert added one other element. For the face of Laviolette, he used the features of his friend Benjamin Sulte.

81. Rudin, *Founding Fathers*, 233; quoting Maurice Aguilhon, "La 'statuomanie' et l'histoire," *Ethnologie française* (1978), 145–72.

82. Roger Motus, *Maurice Constantin-Weyer, écrivain de l'Ouest et du Grand Nord* (n.p., 1982).

83. Maurice Constantin-Weyer, *Champlain* (Paris, 1931), iv.

84. Constantine-Weyer, *Champlain*: 11 (courage and humanity); vii (patience); and 113–16 (perseverance).

85. Ibid. vi.

86. Bishop, *Champlain: The Life of Fortitude*, 87.

87. Ibid. 341.

88. Ibid. 87.

89. Hubert Deschamps, *Roi de la Brousse: mémoires d'autres mondes* (Paris, 1975).

90. William B. Cohen, Review, *International Journal of African Historical Studies* 10 (1977), 300–03; compare with a hostile review by Myro Echenberg in *Revue Canadienne des Études Africaines* 11 (1977), 157–59, who suggests that Deschamps was not a democratic socialist but a "romantic reactionary."

91. Hubert Deschamps, *Les voyages de Samuel Champlain, saintongeais, père du Canada* (Paris, 1951).

92. Ibid. 6.

93. Florian de la Horbe, *L'incroyable secret de Champlain*, preface by Hubert Deschamps (Paris, 1958), author's collection.

94. Jean Bruchési, "Champlain a-t-il menti?" *Cahiers des Dix* 15 (1950), 39–53.

95. Claude de Bonnault, "Encore le Brief Discours: [Please check for possible italics] Champlain a-t-il été à Blavet en 1598?" *Bulletin des recherches historiques* 60 (1954), 59–64.

96. Wilson Smith, *Professors and Public Ethics* (Ithaca, 1955).

97. Marcel Trudel, *Histoire de la Nouvelle-France* 3.1:xix: see full citation below (n 115).

98. Raymonde Litalien, "L'inventaire des archives françaises relatives à la Nouvelle-France: bref historique," *Archives* 33 (2001–02), 53–62.

99. M. A. MacDonald, *Robert Le Blant, Seminal Researcher and Historian of Early New France* (Saint John, N.B., 1986).

100. Of particular value for Champlain are the first three volumes in Campeau's great work: *La première mission d'Acadie, 1602–1616*; *Établissement à Québec, 1616–1634* (Rome and Quebec, 1979); and *Fondation de la mission Huronne, 1635–1637*. Other volumes include: 4. *Les grandes épreuves, 1638–1640*; 5. *La bonne nouvelle reçue, 1641–1643*; 6. *Recherche de la paix, 1644–1646*; 7. *Le témoignage du sang, 1647–1650*; 8. *Au bord de la ruine, 1651–1656*.

101. The documents are reproduced in William F. Ganong, *Champlain's Island* (1902, 1946, 1972, Saint John, N.B., 2003). Much unpublished material is available in the archives and library of Acadia National Park, Bar Harbor, Maine.

102. Camille Lapointe, Béatrice Chassé, Héléne de Carufel, *Aux origines de la vie québécoise* (Quebec, 1983, 1987, 1995), 102.

103. Yves Cormier, *Les Aboiteaux en Acadie, Hier et Aujourd'hui* (Moncton, 1990); Alaric Faulkner and Gretchen Faulkner, *The French at Pentagoet, 1635–1674: An Archaeological Portrait of the Acadian Frontier* (Saint John, N.B. and Augusta, Me., 1987, 1988); James A. Tuck and Robert Grenier, *Red Bay, Labrador, World Whaling Capital, 1550–1600* (St. John's, Nfld., 1989, 1990).

104. Gregory M. Pfitzer, *Samuel Eliot Morison's Historical World* (Boston, 1991) surveys Morison's career.

105. Samuel Eliot Morison, *Samuel de Champlain, Father of New France* (Boston, 1972). Other material appears in his *The Story of Mount Desert Island* (Boston, 1960).

106. Morison, *Samuel de Champlain*, 22.

107. Conrad E. Heidenreich, *Huronia: A History and Geography of the Huron Indians, 1600–1650* (Toronto, 1971), 310–11.

108. Conrad E. Heidenreich, *Explorations and Mapping of Samuel de Champlain, 1603–1632* (Toronto, 1976), published by the Geography Department of York University in a series of monographs called Cartographica, monograph 17 (Toronto, 1976), and also as supplement 2 to *Canadian Cartographer* 13 (1976). For quotations see pp. 71, 99, 100.

109. Don W. Thomson, *Men and Meridians: The History of Surveying and Mapping in Canada* (Ottawa, 1966), 35–47. This was an official history by the private secretary to the Minister of Mines and Technical Surveys in Canada. The first volume carried the story to 1867. Champlain was a central figure. See also Paul La Chance, "L'arpenteur-géomètre au Canada français" (Quebec, 1962).

110. Carl O. Sauer, *Seventeenth Century America* (Turtle Island Foundation, 1980), 89–113; Chandra Mukerji, unpublished lecture on Champlain, ecology, and social thought, presented at the College of the Atlantic, Bar Harbor, Maine, 2005.

111. Marcel Trudel, *Mémoires d'un autre siècle* (Montreal, 1987); translated by Jane Brierley as *Memoirs of a Less Travelled Road: A Historian's Life* (Montreal, 2002), 13–32.

112. Trudel, *Memoirs*, 198.

113. Ibid., 205.

114. Gagnon, *Quebec and Its Historians: The Twentieth Century*, 20.

115. Marcel Trudel, *Histoire de la Nouvelle-France: Les Vaines tentatives (1524–1563)* (Montreal and Paris, 1963); *Le Comptoir, 1604–1627* (Montreal, Paris, and Ottawa, 1996); *La Seigneurie des Cent Associés, 1627–1663:1. Les Événements* (Montreal and Paris, 1979); *La Seigneurie des Cent Associés, 1627–1663:2. La Société* (Montreal and Paris, 1983); and *La Guerre de la Conquête, 1754–1760* (Montreal, 1975).

116. Marcel Trudel, *Champlain*, 2d edition revised and enlarged (Montreal and Paris, 1968).

117. Gagnon, *Quebec and its Historians: The Twentieth Century*, 42–43.

118. Trudel, *Champlain* 1:212; Gagnon, *Quebec and Its Historians: The Twentieth Century*, 50–51.

119. Trudel, "Champlain," *DCB*.

120. Louis Henry, *Fécondité des mariages: nouvelle méthode de mesure* (Paris, 1953).

121. Cyprien Tanguay, *Dictionnaire généalogique des familles canadiennes depuis la fondation de la colonie jusqu'à nos jours*, 7 vols. (Montreal, 1871–1890); Jacques Henripin, *La population canadienne au début du XVIIIe siècle: nuptualité-fécondité-mortalité infantile* (Paris, 1954), 112.

122. Hubert Charbonneau, André Guillemette, Jacques Lagre, Bertrand Desjardins, Yves Landry, François Bault, Real Bates, and Mario Boleda, *Naissance d'une population; les Francais établis au Canada au XVIIe siècle* (Montreal and Paris, 1987); tr. by Paola Colozzo as *The First French Canadians: Pioneers in the St. Lawrence Valley* (Newark, Del., 1993).

123. H. P. Biggar, *The Early Trading Companies of New France*, 274–81, passim.

124. Harold Innis, *The Fur Trade in Canada: An Introduction to Canadian Economic History* (revised edition Toronto, 1956); idem, *The Cod Fisheries: The History of an International Economy* (revised edition, Toronto, 1956); idem, *Essays in Canadian Economic History* (Toronto, 1956); Melville Watkins, "A Staple Theory of Economic Growth," *Canadian Journal of Economics and Political Science* 29 (1963), 141–58; for its refinement and application to other economies see Marc W. Egnal, *New World Economies* (Oxford, 1998).

125. Egnal, *New World Economies*, 131, 212–13n; John Hare et al., *Histoire de la Ville de Québec, 1608–1871* (Montreal, 1987), 327; Louise Dechêne, *Habitants and Merchants in Seventeenth-Century Montreal* (Montreal, 1992), 292.

126. Lewis Henry Morgan, *League of the Ho-dé-no-sau-nee, or Iroquois* (Rochester, 1851).

127. George Hunt, *The Wars of the Iroquois* (Chicago, 1940), 184–85.

128. Denis Delâge, *Le pays renversé: Amérindiens et Européens en Amérique du Nord-est, 1600–1664* (Montreal, 1985); tr. by Jane Brierley as *Bitter Feast: Amerindians and Europeans in Northeastern North America, 1600–1664* (Vancouver, 1993).

129. Ibid. 333.

130. Ibid. 96, 84, x.

131. Cf. Denys Delâge, "Uneasy Allies," *The Beaver* Feb.-March 2008, 14–21.

132. Bruce Trigger, *The Children of Aataentsic: A History of the Huron People to 1660* (Montreal, 1976).

133. Ibid. 246–330.

134. Bruce Trigger, "Champlain Judged by His Indian Policy: A Different View of Early Canadian History," *Anthropologica* 13 (1971), 85–114; idem, *Natives and Newcomers*.

135. Trigger, *Children of Aataentsic*, 274.

136. To discuss a few points at issue:

    Trigger is mistaken that Champlain and the Récollets did not understand the ways of the Indians, and that they "did not possess such knowledge or have the motivation to obtain it" (*Natives and Newcomers*, 317). One could debate the question of understanding, but as to motivation, the Recollets and Champlain wrote often and at great length of their deep interest in the ways of the Indians, repeatedly described their sustained efforts to learn and understand, and left long accounts of Indian ways.

    Trigger's assertion that Champlain (increasingly through time) thought of the Indians not as individuals but as instruments of his purposes is also inaccurate. Champlain often wrote of his relations with individual Indians. This trend grew stronger through time, both in his relations with Indian leaders and his Christian *caritas* for three young Indian girls, the Montagnais boy Bonaventure and also many others.

    Trigger's argument that a major change occurred in Champlain in 1612 is not supported by the evidence. Virtually all of Champlain's attitudes and judgments were the same before and after that date, and his actions too, in regard to making alliances with the Indians, working closely with them, and establishing strong rapport. An exception is the trouble that he had later with the Montagnais, but the rule is strong and consistent.

    Trigger argues that Champlain and the Recollets "undermined relations between the

French and Montagnais by their high handed ethnocentric treatment of native peoples," and did so specifically in trying to persuade the Montagnais to "settle down and become farmers," and even "to become French." This was a misunderstanding of Champlain. He was moved by the sufferings of the Montagnais and their starvation in late winter and early spring. He urged that they add farming to hunting, as the Algonquin, Huron, and Iroquois did. He was not asking them to become French, but advised those in the southern end of their territory to provide for themselves much as other Indian nations did. This policy had some success.

Champlain is accused by Trigger of imposing French ideas of justice on the Indians after several murders of Frenchmen by Montagnais. What actually happened was the opposite. Champlain worked very hard to frame processes of justice that both Indians and Europeans would accept as legitimate.

Trigger writes that Champlain "failed completely to understand the consensual nature of native political arrangements. Because he viewed all power as being delegated from above, he did not comprehend that Indian leaders could not decide matters but had to secure individual consent from their followers" (*Natives and Newcomers*, 199). This statement is the reverse of what Champlain repeatedly observed—that Indian leaders had little control over their followers. He made that observation after his first meeting with the Montagnais in 1603, again with the Algonquin, and once more with the Huron, frequently commenting at length on the leaders' lack of power and authority. When preparing his last campaign against the central Iroquois, Champlain visited almost every village in Huronia, persuading the local leaders and warriors to join him. Trigger misread the evidence as to how that happened and why. He also missed Champlain's driving purpose.

Trigger writes: "In general, Champlain appears to have been extremely ethnocentric and inflexible. Since neither of these characteristics would have been particularly helpful when it came to interacting with Indians, it is likely that Champlain's early successes were the result more of the situation than of the man. It also appears that he pursued the Indian policies that he or his employers had formulated with less understanding of their ways, and less sympathy, than the majority of historians have imagined."

There is some truth in these statements. It is true that Champlain wrote that the Indians had neither faith nor law, and many ethnohistorians have convicted him of ethnocentrism on the basis of these passages. But it should be noted that Champlain was well aware of Indian spiritual beliefs and legal customs. He described them in detail. But he believed that Indians lived mainly by an idea of law as *lex talionis*, and justice as a process that punished one wrong by the commission of another. He believed that they had no idea of law as a system of universal rights and protections against wrong, and in that sense had no law.

He also thought that Indian spiritual beliefs were not a universal religion such as Christianity. Champlain believed that nations could live in peace with one another with mutual respect and forbearance only on the basis of universal ethical and religious beliefs that recognized the humanity of all people. Secular social scientists reject this way of thinking as ethnocentric, and some ways it was so. But it transcended its ethnocentrism in its aspirations to universal justice, faith, truth, and law. In short, ethnocentric in some ways, yes, but Champlain's attitudes were grounded in ideas of universal justice, faith, and peace. Trigger missed the heart of this man.

137. René Lévesque, *Memoirs* (Toronto, 1986), 65.
138. Armstrong, *Champlain*, xvi.

139. Pierre Berton, *My Country* (Toronto, 1976), 65.

140. Caroline Montel-Glénisson, *Champlain au Canada; les aventures d'un gentilhomme explorateur* (Quebec, 2004), with illustrations by Michel Glénisson.

141. Hundreds of essays, many of very high quality, appear in Raymonde Litalien and Denis Vaugeois, ed. *Champlain; la Naissance de l'Amérique française* (Quebec, 2004); *Champlain and the Birth of French America* (Montreal, 2004); Mickaël Augeron and Dominique Guillemet, *Champlain, ou les portes du Nouveau Monde: Cinq siècles d'échanges entre le Centre-Ouest français et l'Amérique du Nord, XVIe–XXe siècles* (Ligugé, Éditions Geste, 2004); Annie Blondel-Loisel and Raymonde Litalien, in collaboration with Jean Paul Barbiche and Claude Briot, *De la Seine au Saint Laurent avec Champlain* (Paris, 2005); Pierre Icowicz and Raymonde Litalien, eds., *Dieppe-Canada: cinq cents ans d'Histoire commune* (Paris and Dieppe, 2004); Bertrand Guillet and Louise Pothier, eds., *France/Nouvelle-France: naissance d'un peuple français en Amérique* (Montreal and Paris, 2005); James Kelly and Barbara Clarke Smith, eds., *Jamestown-Quebec-Santa Fe: Three North American Beginnings* (Washington and New York, 2007).

A. CHAMPLAIN'S BIRTH DATE

1. Marcel Trudel, *Histoire de la Nouvelle-France, Les Vaines Tentatives, 1524–1603* (Montreal and Paris, 1963) 1:255; A.-L. Leymarie, "Inédit sur le fondateur de Québec," *Nova Francia* 1 (1925), 80–85.

2. Morris Bishop, *Champlain: The Life of Fortitude* (New York, 1948), 343.

3. Laverdière, *Champlain*, 1:x.

4. Ibid. 1:x–xii.

5. Bishop, *Champlain: The Life of Fortitude*, 344.

6. Narcisse-Eutrope Dionne, *Champlain, Fondateur de Québec et Pére de la Nouvelle-France*, 2 vols., (Quebec, 1891) 1:4; Marcel Trudel, *Histoire de la Nouvelle-France* (Montreal and Paris, 1963), 1:255; Samuel Eliot Morison, *Samuel de Champlain, Father of New France* (New York, 1972), 16.

7. Jean Liebel, "Ou a vieilli Champlain," *Revue d'histoire de l'Amérique Française* 32 (1978), 229–37.

8. Ibid. 233.

9. Ibid.

10. Raymonde Litalien and Denis Vaugeois, eds., *Champlain: la naissance de l'Amérique française* (Quebec, 2004); tr. as *Champlain and the Birth of French America* (Montreal, 2004), 37, 121.

11. The army records are reproduced in Robert Le Blant and René Baudry, *Nouveaux documents sur Champlain et son époque* (Ottawa, 1967) 1:17–19; for Crozon, see above, pp. 63–65.

12. *The voyages of the Sieur de Champlain of Saintonge. . . .* (Paris, 1913), preface; CWB, 1:209–10.

13. "Après avoir passé trente huict ans de mon âge à faire plusieurs voyages sur mer." CWB 6:255.

14. CWB 4:363.

15. John A. Williamson, *Antisubmarine Warrior in the Pacific* (Tuscaloosa, Al., 2005), 127.

16. Bishop, *Champlain: The Life of Fortitude*, 344.

B. CHAMPLAIN'S VOYAGES: A CHRONOLOGY

1. Chronologies of Champlain's voyages have been compiled by C.-H. Laverdière; by N.-E. Dionne in a list entitled "Affrètement de Navires, 1605–1615," 1:288–95, and "1616–1625" 2:389–92; Samuel E. Morison, *Champlain: The Founder of New France* (New York, 1972), 231–33; Raymonde Litalien and Denis Vaugeois, eds., *Champlain: The Birth of French America* (Montreal, 2004), 364–71; Jean Glénisson, *La France d'Amérique: Voyages de Samuel Champlain* (Paris, 1994), 48–53. No two of these lists are the same. Morison's list included four voyages that never happened and missed two that did. He erroneously reported that Champlain made twenty-nine Atlantic crossings from 1599 to 1635.

   This list returns to primary sources, mainly to Champlain's own writings, and after 1632 to materials in Marcel Trudel's *Histoire de la Nouvelle-France*, Lucien Campeau's *Monumenta Novae Franciae*, and the *Jesuit Relations*. It also incorporates specialized studies by Trudel, Campeau, and students of Champlain's West Indian Voyages.

C. CHAMPLAIN'S *BRIEF DISCOURS*: PROBLEMS OF ACCURACY AND AUTHENTICITY

1. For a discussion see Laura Giraudo, "Les manuscripts du Brief Discours," in Raymonde Litalien et Denis Vaugeois, eds., *Champlain: The Birth of French America* (Quebec, 2004), 63–82; an earlier inquiry in the mid-nineteenth century that confirms this provenance appears in Francis Parkman, *Pioneers of France in the New World* (1865, revised edition with corrections, 1885; rpt. Boston, 1901), 243.

2. These materials appear in Champlain, *Narrative of a Voyage to the West Indies and Mexico in the Years 1599–1602*, trans. Alice Wilmere, ed. Norton Shaw (London: Hakluyt Society, 1859, 1880); Charles-Honoré Laverdière, ed., *Oeuvres de Champlain*, 2nd edition, 6 vols. in 4 (Quebec, 1870), 1, 10, 25, 26, 32, 35, 47, 48; H. P. Biggar, ed., *The Works of Samuel de Champlain*, 6 vols. and a portfolio of maps and drawings (CWB) (Toronto, 1922–36, reprinted 1971) 1: 5, 18, 46, 54, 60, 69, 77, 80.

3. See N.-E. Dionne, *Samuel de Champlain: fondateur de Québec at père de la Nouvelle France*, 2 vols. (Quebec, 1891); Gabriel Gravier, *Vie de Samuel de Champlain: fondateur de la Nouvelle-France* (Paris, 1900); L'Abbé H. R. Casgrain, *Champlain: sa vie et son caractère* (Paris 1900).

4. Parkman, *Pioneers*, 242–43.

5. Morris Bishop, *Champlain: The Life of Fortitude* (New York, 1948), 22.

6. Jean Bruchési, "Champlain a-t-il menti?" *Cahiers des Dix* 15 (1950), 39–53.

7. See Claude de Bonnault, "Encore le Brief discours: Champlain a-t-il été à Blavet en 1598?" *Bulletin des recherches historiques* 60 (1954), 59–64; idem, "Les archives d'Espagne et le Canada: Rapport sur une mission dans les archives d'Espagne," *Rapport de l'Archiviste de la province de Québec* 1951–52, 1952–53; also idem, "Champlain et les Espagnols," essay in the René Baudry Collection, Library and Archives Canada.

8. Hubert Deschamps, *Les voyages de Samuel Champlain, saintongeais, père du Canada* (Paris, 1951), 5.

9. See Jacques Rousseau, "Samuel de Champlain, botaniste mexicain et antillais," *Cahiers des Dix* 16 (1951), 39–61.

10. CWB 1:22; L. A. Vigneras, "Le Voyage de Samuel Champlain aux Indes occidentales," *RHAF* 11 (1957), 177, 187, 189.

11. See Vigneras, "Le Voyage de Samuel Champlain," 163–200.

12. See Morris Bishop, "Champlain's Veracity: A Defence of the *Brief Discours*," *Queen's Quarterly* 66 (1959), 127–34.

13. See Samuel Eliot Morison, *Samuel de Champlain, Father of New France* (Boston, 1972), 277.

14. Compare Marcel Trudel, *Histoire de la Nouvelle-France: Les Vaines Tentatives, 1524–1603* (Montreal and Paris, 1963) 1:257–58.

15. Jean Liebel, "On a vieilli Champlain," *RHAF* 32 (1978), 229–37, 232.

16. Compare Codignola, "Samuel de Champlain et les mystères de son voyage au Indes occidentales, 1599–1601: l'état de la recherche et quelques routes à suivre," in Cecilia Rizza, ed., "La découverte de nouveaux mondes: aventure et voyages imaginaires au XVIIe siècle," in *Actes du XXIIe colloque du centre méridional de rencontres sur le XVIIe siècle, Gênes 23–25 January, 1992* (Fasano, 1993), 56–58; also Luca Codignola, "Le prétendu voyage de Samuel de Champlain aux Indes occidentales, 1599–1601," in Madeline Frédéric et Serge Jasumain eds., *Actes du séminaire de Bruxelles: la relation de voyage: un document historique et littéraire* (Brussels, 1999).

17. Joe C. W. Armstrong, *Champlain* (Toronto, 1987), 274–78, 32–34; CWB 1:79.

18. Armstrong, *Champlain*, 274–78.

19. Ibid., 32–34; cf. Champlain in CWB 1:79.

20. Laura Giraudo's results are published as "Rapport de recherche: une mission en Espagne," and "Les manuscrits du Brief Discours," both in Raymonde Litalien et Denis Vaugeois, eds., *Champlain: The Birth of French America* (Quebec, 2004), 63–82, 93–97.

21. See François-Marc Gagnon, "Le Brief Discours est-il de Champlain?" in Litalien et Vaugeois, eds., *Champlain*, 83–92.

22. See "Champlain's Voyage accounts, Interview with Jean Glénisson," interview by Raymonde Italien, revised and authorized by Jean Glénisson, in Litalien and Vaugeois, eds., *Champlain*, 280.

23. CWB 1:1–2.

D. CHAMPLAIN'S PUBLISHED WRITINGS: A QUESTION OF AUTHORSHIP

1. Charles-Honoré Laverdière, ed., *Oeuvres de Champlain*, 2nd edition, 6 vols. in 4 (Quebec, 1870) 5: v–vi; Morris Bishop, *Champlain: The Life of Fortitude* (New York, 1948), 324; and Le Blant, who agreed with Laverdière.

2. H. P. Biggar, *Early Trading Companies of New France, A Contribution to the History of Commerce and Discovery in North America* (Toronto, 1901, 1937; rpt. Clifton, N.J., 1972), 279.

3. Ibid.

4. Ibid. 276, 179.

E. CHAMPLAIN'S *TRAITTÉ DE LA MARINE*: AN ESSAY ON LEADERSHIP

1. H. P. Biggar, ed., *The Works of Samuel de Champlain*, 6 vols. and a portfolio of maps and drawings (CWB) (Toronto, 1922–36, reprinted 1971) 6: 253–346.

2. Morris Bishop, *Champlain: The Life of Fortitude* (New York, 1948), 324.

3. Joe C. W. Armstrong, *Champlain* (Toronto, 1987), 253.

4. Samuel Eliot Morison, *Samuel de Champlain, Father of New France* (New York, 1972), 236–67.

5. D. W. Waters, *The Art of Navigation in England in Elizabethan and Early Stuart Times* (New Haven, 1958), 625–28.

6. Ibid., 232n; CWB 6:322.

7. That is, west of the Zuider Zee.

8. John Smith, *An Accidence, or The Path-way to Experience. Necessary for all Young Sea-men* (London, 1626) and its sequel, *A Sea Grammar, with the Plaine Exposition of Smith's Accidence for Young Seamen, Enlarged* (London, 1627), reprinted in Philip L. Barbour, ed., *The Complete Works of Captain John Smith (1580–1631)*, 3 vols. (Chapel Hill, 1986) 3: 3–121. This editor of Smith's work observes unkindly that his *Accidence* is "little more than an omnium gatherum of names for the appurtenances and people that make up a ship and her crew." Barbour 3:7.

9. CWB 6:255–56.

10. Ibid.

11. Ibid. 6:257–58.

12. Ibid. 6:267.

13. Ibid. 6:258, 262.

14. Ibid. 6:259–60.

15. Ibid. 6: 267, 282.

16. Ibid. 6:259, 262–63.

17. Ibid. 6:297.

18. Ibid. 6:312, 264, 268.

19. Ibid. 6:269–70.

20. Ibid. 6:270.

21. Ibid. 6:268.

22. Ibid. 6:261.

23. Ibid. 4:362.

24. Alain Rey et al., eds., *Le Grand Robert de la langue française*, 6 vols. (Paris 2001), s.v. "honnête" II, 1.

F. ANOTHER SELF-PORTRAIT?

1. Cf. Marcel Trudel, *Histoire de la Nouvelle-France: La Seigneurie des Cent-Associés, 1627–1663* (Montreal, 1975) 3.1:35; idem, "La carte de Champlain en 1632; ses sources et son originalité," *Cartologica* (1978), 51; François-Marc Gagnon, *Premiers peintres de la Nouvelle-France*, 2 vols. (Quebec, 1976) 2:25–26; Martin, "Samuel de Champlain à visage découvert," in Litalien and Vaugeois, eds., *Champlain: The Birth of French America* (Montreal, 2004), 360–62.

2. They are to be found in Samuel de Champlain, "Descr[i]psion des costs p[or]ts, rades, Illes de la nouuele france faict selon son vray meridien Avec la declinaison de le[y]ment de plussiers endrois selon que le sieur de Castelfranc le demontre en son liure de la mecometrie de le[y]mant faict et observe par le Sr de Champlain, 1607," Map Division, Library of Congress.

G. CHAMPLAIN'S SUPERIORS: VICEROYS AND GENERALS OF NEW FRANCE

1. Leading studies include Jean Liebel, *Pierre Dugua, sieur de Mons, fondateur de Québec* (Paris, 1999); Jean-Yves Grenon, *Pierre Dugua de Mons, fondateur de l'Acadie (1604–05); Co-Fondateur de Québec (1608)* (Annapolis Royal, 2000); Guy Binot, *Pierre Dugua de Mons* (Royan, 2004); William Inglis Morse, *Pierre de Gua, Sieur de Monts* (London, 1939).

2. See Henry Percival Biggar, ed., *The Works of Samuel de Champlain*, 6 vols. and a portfolio of maps and drawings (CWB), (Toronto, 1922–36, reprinted 1971) 2:243–44; 4:208–16; 5:143; Lucien Campeau, *Monumenta Novae Franciae* (Quebec, 1967) 1:665; Marcel Trudel, *Histoire de la Nouvelle-France*, vol. 2: *Le Comptoir, 1604–1627* (Montreal, 1966), 186–88; Docteur Cabanès, *Les Condé: grandeur et dégénérescence d'une famille princière*, 2 vols. (Paris, n.d., [1932]).

3. For sources see CWB 2:239, 245; 3:15–20; 4:216–18, 339, 344–46; 367–70; Trudel, *Histoire de la Nouvelle-France* 2:18–89; 452; Lucien Campeau, *Mercure François*, 4:228; Cabanès, *Les Condé*; Robert Le Blant, "La famille Boullé, 1586–1639," *RHAF* 17 (1963), 55–69.

4. See CWB 4:340–42, 344–47, 367; Trudel, *Histoire de la Nouvelle-France* 2: 240–41, 452.

5. See CWB 4:367–70; Trudel, *Histoire de la Nouvelle-France* 2: 264–65, 297, 452; Campeau, *Monumenta Novae Franciae* 1:678, with a correction in 2:248.

6. See CWB 5:139–52; Trudel, *Histoire de la Nouvelle-France* 2:296–99.

7. Sources on Richelieu and New France include Campeau, *Monumenta Novae Franciae* 2:850–51 passim; Trudel, *Histoire de la Nouvelle-France* 2:306, 432–34; Pierre Castagnos, *Richelieu face à la mer* (Rennes, 1989), 72–76, 125–27; Michel Carmona, *La France de Richelieu* (Paris, 1984), 185–93; CWB 3:235–38, 5:288, 6:147, 153, 167–71, 214, 219–20.

H. TRADING COMPANIES AND MONOPOLIES IN
NEW FRANCE DURING CHAMPLAIN'S ERA, 1588–1635

1. Sources: H. P. Biggar, *The Early Trading Companies of New France* (Toronto, 1901, 1937; rpt. Clifton, N.J., 1972) is still useful for the period from 1588 to 1632. Very helpful for the later period are two monographs by Lucien Campeau, *Les finances publiques de la Nouvelle-France sous les Cent-Associés, 1632–1665* (Montreal, 1975) and *Les Cent-Associés et le peuplement de la Nouvelle France (1633–1663)* (Montreal, 1974). For the entire period, and especially for the subsidiary companies, the best work is Marcel Trudel, *Histoire de la Nouvelle-France, III: La Seigneurie des Cent-Associés*, 2 vols. (Montreal, 1979, 1983).

I. INDIAN NATIONS IN CHAMPLAIN'S WORLD, 1603–35

1. Henry Percival Biggar, ed., *The Works of Samuel de Champlain*, 6 vols. and a portfolio of maps and drawings (CWB), (Toronto, 1922–36, reprinted 1971) 1:123; 2:18.

2. Lescarbot wrote that "the tribes of Gaspé and of Chaleur Bay who are near the 48th parallel of latitude to the south of the great river (St. Lawrence), call themselves Canadaquoa (as they pronounce it), that is to say, Canadaquois as we say" (*Histoire de la Nouvelle-France* 2:25; Champlain called them Canadiens, and wrote that their customs were the same as those of the Etchemin and Sourquois.

3. CWB 3:55.
4. CWB 6:249.

J. THE BATTLE WITH THE MOHAWK IN 1609: WHERE DID IT HAPPEN?

1. Cf. Carte de la nouvelle France, augmentée . . . ," 1632 in the folio of maps attached to the Biggar edition; the key is in Henry Percival Biggar, ed., *The Works of Samuel de Champlain*, 6 vols. and a portfolio of maps and drawings (CWB), (Toronto, 1922–36, reprinted 1971) 6:240.
2. CWB 2:93.
3. Guy Omeron Coolidge, *The French Occupation of the Champlain Valley, from 1609 to 1759* (New York, 1938, 1940), 12; and in *Proceedings of the Vermont Historical Society* 6 (1938), 143–53; Joe C. W. Armstrong, *Champlain* (Toronto, 1987), 298–99, and New York's bicentennial leaders, who put up a monument to Champlain at Crown Point. The case for Ticonderoga appears in S. H. P. Pell, "Was Champlain a Liar?" *Bulletin of the Fort Ticonderoga Museum* 5 (1939) 5–8. Morris Bishop discussed the evidence in his *Champlain: The Life of Fortitude* (New York, 1948), appendix E, "The Site of the Battle of 1609," 353–54, Marcel Trudel, *Histoire de la Nouvelle-France*, vol. 2: *Le Comptoir, 1604–1627* (Montreal, 1966), 164; Samuel Eliot Morison, *Samuel de Champlain, Father of New France* (New York, 1972), 110; and Robert Pell-Duchame's excellent ms. history. A few local historians continue to support the claims of the Crown Point site, which cannot be correct.

K. THE ATTACK ON THE IROQUOIS FORT, 1615:
WHICH FORT? WHAT NATION?

1. Francis Parkman, *Pioneers of France in the New World* (1865, revised edition with corrections, 1885; rpt. Boston, 1901), 413n.
2. Samuel Eliot Morison, *Samuel de Champlain, Father of New France* (New York, 1972), 156–58; Bruce Trigger, *Natives and Newcomers: Canada's "Heroic Age" Reconsidered* (Montreal and Kingston, 1985, 1986, 1994), 309; Louise W. Murray, ed., *Selected Manuscripts of General John S. Clark relating to the Aboriginal History of the Susquehanna* (Athens, Ohio, 1931); A. G. Zeller, *The Champlain-Iroquois Battle of 1615* (New York, 1962).
3. Peter Pratt, *Archaeology of the Oneida Indians*, Occasional Publications in Northeastern Anthropology no. 1 (Rindge, N.H., 1976), viii–ix; idem, "A Perspective on Oneida Archaeology," in Robert E. Funk and Charles F. Hayes III, eds., *Current Perspectives on Northeastern Archaeology: Essays in Honor of William A Ritchie: Researches and Transactions of the New York State Archaeological Association* 17 (1977) no. 1:51–69; Daniel H. Weiskotten, "The Real Battle of Nichols Pond," 1998.
4. Conversation with Peter Pratt, 2007; William Engelbrecht, *Iroquoia; The Development of a Native World* (Syracuse, 2003), 147; cf. O. H. Marshall, "Champlain's Expedition of 1615," *Historical Writings of the late Orasmus H. Marshall* (Albany, 1887), 43–66.

L. CHAMPLAIN'S FAVORED FIREARM: THE *ARQUEBUSE À ROUET*

1. Cf. Samuel Eliot Morison, *Samuel de Champlain, Father of New France* (New York, 1972), 282; Fred Anderson and Andrew Cayton, *Dominion of War: Empire and Liberty in North America, 1500–2000* (New York, 2005), 16.
2. Russel Bouchard, *Les armes à feu en Nouvelle-France* (Sillery, Quebec, 1999), 102–06.
3. M. A. O. Paulin-Desormeaux, *Nouveau manuel complet de l'armurier du fourbisseur et de l'arquebusier*, nouvelle édition, 2 vols. (Paris, 1852, rpt. Paris, 1977), 1:11–14, 184–93; author's collection.
4. Lisa Jardine, *The Awful End of William the Silent: The First Assassination of a Head of State with a Handgun* (London, 2005).

M. CHAMPLAIN'S SHIPS AND BOATS

1. R. R. Palmer and Jacques Godechot, "Le Problème de l'Atlantique du XVIIIe et XXe siècle," *Relazione del X Congresso Internationale di Scienze Storiche, Roma 4–11 Settembre 1955* (Florence, 1955) 5: 175–239. This little-read paper, which led to the vogue for Atlantic history in the late twentieth century, is in the Library of Congress.
2. Frederic C. Lane, "Tonnages, Medieval and Modern," *Economic History Review*, n.s., 17 (1964), 213–33.
3. William A. Baker, *Colonial Vessels: Some Seventeenth Century Ship Designs* (Barre, Mass., 1962), 25–27.
4. Père Fournier, *Hydrographie, contenant la théorie et la pratique de toutes les parties de la navigation* (Paris, 1643), 49; Jean Liebel, *Pierre Dugua, sieur de Mons, fondateur de Québec* (Paris, 1999), 99, 100; Charles Bréard and Paul Bréard, *Documents relatifs à la Marine Normande et à ses armements aux XXVIe et XVIIe siècles* (Rouen, 1889), 2.
5. Carla Rahn Phillips, *Six Galleons for the King of Spain: Imperial Defense in the Early Seventeenth Century* (Baltimore, 1986), 228.
6. Henry Percival Biggar, ed., *The Works of Samuel de Champlain*, 6 vols. and a portfolio of maps and drawings (CWB), (Toronto, 1922–36, reprinted 1971) 1:6–8; Laura Giraudo, "Research Report: A Mission in Spain," in Raymonde Litalien and Denis Vaugeois, eds., *Champlain: The Birth of French America* (Montreal, 2004), 96; L. A. Vigneras, "Le voyage de Samuel de Champlain aux Indes Occidentales," *RHAF* (1959–60), 167, 188; Morison, *European Discovery of America, The Southern Voyages, 1492–1616* (New York, 1974), 149, 114.
7. Carla Rahn Phillips, *Six Galleons for the King of Spain: Imperial Defense in the Early Seventeenth Century* (Baltimore, 1986), 33–34, 41–46, 71–72, 78–79, 229–33; Timothy Walton, *The Spanish Treasure Fleets* (Sarasota, 1994), 57–64; Pablo E. Pérez-Mallaína, *Spain's Men of the Sea; Daily Life on the Indies Fleets in the Sixteenth Century*, 8, 30, 134–35; Angus Konstam, *The Spanish Galleon, 1530–1690* (Wellingborough, 2004), 4–16.
8. CWB 3:24; Liebel, *Pierre Dugua, sieur de Mons*, 98–100, found highly variable estimates of tonnage, some of which referred to different ships of the same name. For other examples and discussion see CWB 1:388n, 456n; 6:153; Marcel Trudel, *Histoire de la Nouvelle-France*, vol. 2: *Le Comptoir, 1604–1627* (Montreal, 1966), 206, 417; Samuel E. Morison, *Samuel de Champlain: Father of New France* (New York, 1972), 5, 8, 10, 77, 89, 94, 97–98, 186, 214, 238; Bréard and Bréard, *Documents relatifs à la Marine Normande*, 41–134.

9. Liebel, *Pierre Dugua, sieur de Mons,* 20; Père Fournier, S.J., *Hydrographie contenant la théorie et la pratique de toutes les parties de la navigation* (Paris, 1643),16–43, 423.

10. Bréard and Bréard, *Documents relatifs à la Marine Normande,* 2.

11. CWB 6:155.

12. Bréard and Bréard, *Documents relatifs à la Marine Normande,* 2.

13. Ibid. 2, 153.

14. William A. Baker, "A Colonial Bark, circa 1640," in Baker, *Colonial Vessels: Some Seventeenth Century Ship Designs,*78–110.

15. CWB 1:401; Baker, *Colonial Vessels,* 82.

16. Ibid. 1:377.

17. Ibid. 6:61.

18. Quoted in Alain Rey et al. eds., *Le Grand Robert de la langue française,* 6 vols. (Paris, 2001) 5:333.

19. CWB 1:428.

20. Ibid. 6:61.

21. Ibid. 1:276–78; 3:203; Biggar mistakenly translates Champlain's "barque" as a "long boat" or "pinnace."

22. Google images, www.famsf.org/image base.

23. See CWB 1:428.

24. CWB 3:316.

25. James Tuck and Robert Grenier, *Red Bay, Labrador* (St. John's, Nfld., 1989), 36–38.

26. The best primary account is Nicolas Denys, *Description and Natural History of the Coasts of North America (Acadia)* (Toronto, 1908), 295–301, 273–74, 302–05 drawing facing 311.

27. Champlain CWB 4:39 also 1:104–05, 338–39, 339n; 2:14–15; 3:384–85.

28. Ibid. 3:37.

29. An early drawing of canoes used by the Montagnais, Têtes de Boule, Ottawa, and Algonquin nations appears in Olive Patricia Dickason, *The Myth of the Savage* (Edmonton, 1984), 89, from Bécard de Granville, *Les Raretés des Indes* LAC C–33287.

30. See William N. Fenton and Ernest Dodge, "An Elm Bark Canoe in the Peabody Museum of Salem," *American Neptune* 9 (1949), 185–206; for an early account, Baron de Lahontan, *New Voyages to North-America* ed. Reuben G. Thwaites, 2 vols. (1703; New York, 1970) 1:80; see also William Engelbrecht, *Iroquoia: The Development of a Native World* (Syracuse, 2003), 141–42. An excellent general work is Edwin Tappan Adney and Howard I. Chapelle, *The Bark Canoes and Skin Boats of North America* (Washington, 1964), 7–174.

31. CWB 1:337; Carl O. Sauer, *Seventeenth Century America* (Berkeley, 1980), 81.

32. The leading studies are E. Y. Arima, *Inuit Kayaks in Canada: A Review of Historical Records and Construction,* Canadian Ethnology service paper no. 110 (Ottawa, 1987), 235 pages; and Adney and Chapelle, *Bark Canoes and Skin Boats of North America,* 175–211.

33. See Adney and Chapelle, *Bark Canoes and Skin Boats of North America,* 219–20.

N. CHAMPLAIN'S WEIGHTS AND MEASURES

1. Marcel Trudel, *Introduction to New France* (Toronto and Montreal, 1968), 221.

2. Jean Liebel, *Pierre Dugua, sieur de Mons, fondateur de Québec* (Paris, 1999), 12.

3. Conrad E. Heidenreich, *Explorations and Mapping of Samuel de Champlain, 1603–1632* (Toronto, 1976), 46, and see generally, 43–50.

4. Henry Percival Biggar, ed., *The Works of Samuel de Champlain*, 6 vols. and a portfolio of maps and drawings (CWB), (Toronto, 1922–36, reprinted 1971) 1:200; Samuel E. Morison, *Samuel de Champlain: Father of New France* (New York, 1972), xiii.

5. Heidenreich, *Explorations and Mapping*, 43–49.

O. CHAMPLAIN'S MONEY

1. Sources include John J. McCusker, *Money and Exchange in Europe and America, 1600–1775: A Handbook* (Chapel Hill, 1978), 87–97; Frank C. Spooner, *The International Economy and Monetary Movements in France, 1493–1725* (Cambridge, 1972); David Hackett Fischer, *The Great Wave: Price Revolutions and the Rhythm of History* (New York, 1996); for archaeological evidence see Françoise Niellon and Marcel Moussette, *Le site de l'habitation de Champlain à Québec: étude de la collection archéologique* (Quebec, 1981), 139–44.

2. The original contracts executed by sieur de Mons, 17–22 Feb., 1608, appear in Robert Le Blant and René Baudry, eds., *Nouveaux documents sur Champlain et son époque, vol. 1* (1560–1662) (Ottawa, 1967), 154–59.

P. CHAMPLAIN'S CALENDARS

1. Sources include Marcel Trudel, *Introduction to New France* (Toronto and Montreal, 1968), 221–24; Don W. Thomson, *Men and Meridians: the History of Surveying and Mapping in Canada* (Ottawa, 1966) 1:47; James Pritchard, *In Search of Empire: The French in the Americas, 1670–1730* (Cambridge, 2004).

2. Henry Percival Biggar, ed., *The Works of Samuel de Champlain,* 6 vols. and a portfolio of maps and drawings (Toronto, 1922–36, reprinted 1971) 5:282.

BIBLIOGRAPHY

Biographers of Samuel Champlain and historians of early New France routinely begin their works with a litany of complaint about their sources. Most of Champlain's manuscripts and papers have disappeared. We know that he tried to preserve them, and Marc Lescarbot used them as a source for his history of New France. On his deathbed, Champlain asked Father Charles Lalement and François Derre de Gand to gather his papers and send them to his wife, Hélène, in Paris. Both men probably did as they were asked, but then the trail goes cold, and Champlain's papers have vanished without a trace. Scattered manuscripts have survived mostly in court files, financial records, and government archives.

This problem was not specific to Champlain. The same thing happened to the papers of Aymar de Chaste, the sieur de Mons, Pont-Gravé, Lescarbot, Razilly, and most major figures in the early history of New France. In the late twentieth century, the great Canadian historian Marcel Trudel searched high and low in France for manuscripts on Champlain and New France. He also went looking for the records of commercial companies, especially the Company of New France, which had been in public archives in the mid-nineteenth century. Trudel concluded that they were destroyed by the Communards of 1871, who hauled them out of the Châtelet with many other papers and made a bonfire in the streets of Paris. For the historical period before 1627, he complained of an extreme "pauvreté de documentation," and a "grande pénurie d'information." Trudel wrote that in the course of his research in France he "rarely found an unpublished manuscript" of any importance. He observed that the condition of French sources for the early seventeenth century is very different from the eighteenth, and even the sixteenth (*Histoire de la Nouvelle-France*, 1:x; 2:xxiii; 3.1:xix).

A leading American historian had a similar experience. Samuel Eliot Morison collected Champlain material through much of his busy career. He looked for published sources in France, and wrote in frustration, "Search the French literature of the reigns of Henry IV and Louis XIII and you will find very, very few references to Canada, and those mostly ironical, and even fewer to Champlain" (Morison, *Champlain*, 188).

Even so, many manuscripts and imprints have survived, and in the course of the twentieth century they have become more accessible to historians. Archivists in the United States, France, and especially in Canada have made a sustained effort to find manuscripts relating to America in European archives. Early leaders were H. P. Biggar, who worked in British and French archives; Claude de Bonnault, an archivist trained in the French École des Chartes, and more recently Raymonde Litalien, who has played a major role. In many years of labor, Canadian archivists began by compiling inventories, then ordered manual transcriptions in the early twentieth century. After 1945, microfilm projects copied more than 2.5 million pages of records on New France. In 1988, the emphasis began to shift toward digital databases and electronic texts. Since 1999, these materials have been coming online in websites sponsored by Library and Archives Canada in Ottawa.

UNPUBLISHED MANUSCRIPTS: THE LIBRARY OF CONGRESS

In the United States, the Manuscript Division of the Library of Congress has a collection of manuscript materials copied from French government archives. The copies were made in the early twentieth century, of materials relating to American history. A large proportion are large bundles of photostats. Useful for this inquiry were copies of manuscripts from the Ministry of Foreign Affairs, and the Ministry of Marine and Colonies from the period from 1604 to 1635. Much of this material touches on the career of Champlain. It includes royal edicts of Henri IV and Louis XIII for New France, as well as charters, letters patent, and other official documents from the Royal Council. Also in these records are documents on the loss of New France and its recovery. Richelieu's instructions to the de Caëns are there, and memoirs on trade in New France. Also in this material are scattered records of the Company of New France.

The Geography and Map Division of the Library of Congress has Champlain's manuscript draft of his map of New France dated 1607/08. This is the only manuscript of his cartography and art that is known to survive. It has often been reproduced, but rarely with accuracy. The best published image is in the Map Division's *Geography and Maps: An Illustrated Guide* (Washington, 1996, 28). Any serious student of Champlain must see the original of this manuscript to form an accurate understanding of his work.

UNPUBLISHED MANUSCRIPTS: THE JOHN CARTER BROWN LIBRARY

The founder and namesake of this extraordinary library had a particular interest in Champlain, and assembled one of the finest collections of imprints in the world. The library owns not only all the major works of Champlain and Lescarbot, but also nearly all variant printings in the early seventeenth centuries. This is of particular importance for Lescarbot's history of New France, as he added new materials that make a difference to what we know of Champlain's world.

The John Carter Brown Library also has the best of three known manuscript copies of Champlain's *Brief Discours*, with the largest set of Champlain's many color illustrations, in what may be original manuscripts, or copies contemporary with Champlain.

UNPUBLISHED MANUSCRIPTS: LIBRARY AND ARCHIVES CANADA

Many collections here are useful for a student of Champlain's career, and include copies of manuscripts in archives scattered widely throughout France. For many years, this material was extremely difficult of access for historians. After many years of work by Canadian and French archivists, this material is now coming available on microfilm in Canada and increasingly online—a process that has only begun. In Ottawa, we worked in the following collections:

Bibliothèque nationale de France, Département des Imprimés; thirty-five documents on New France;

Archives nationales de France, Documents concernant la Nouvelle-France, 1532–1759; six bobbins of microfilm;

Amirauté de France, Juridictions spéciales, 1572–1666;

Materials on the Compagnie de Caën, the Compagnie de Montmorency, and the Compagnie de la Nouvelle-France;

Fonds des Archives départementales de la Charente-Maritime, 1599–1787: sixty bobbins of microfilm;

Fonds des Archives départementales du Calvados, 1568–1791: ten bobbins of microfilm;

Fonds des Archives municipales de Honfleur: 1 document;

Fonds de la Compagnie de la Nouvelle-France, 1627–1635: fifty-seven pages.

UNPUBLISHED MANUSCRIPTS ON THE WEB

A resource of growing importance to researchers in this field is the Gallica Project, founded in 2004 by James H. Billington and Jean-Noël Jeanneney, leaders of the Library of Congress in Washington and the Bibliothèque nationale de France in Paris. It is a bilingual website called "Gallica, La France en Amérique," and includes much material from the Bibliothèque nationale on "the French presence in North America." Materials encompass a very large array of manuscripts, imprints, maps, prints, designs, stamps, and other genres of primary sources. They are organized around historical themes. One is "exploration and colonisation of the continent," and has much material on Champlain. For example, Champlain's petition to Louis XIII in 1630 is available on this site.

Materials in most cases can be downloaded and printed for purposes of research without charge, but application must be made for reproduction of maps and prints. The website includes links for that purpose. Web addresses have changed since the founding of this site, but it is accessible through the Library of Congress's website by searching for Gallica, or FranceAmérique. This project is part of a larger program at the Library of Congress called Global Gateway, which seeks to form collaborative web-projects among all National Libraries in the entire world.

Another important website is ArchivesCanadaFrance, founded in 2004 by the combined efforts of Library and Archives Canada, the Archives de France, and the Canadian Embassy in Paris. Its purpose is to make freely available on the web a large quantity of manuscripts and other materials. It reproduces records of the "central administration" in Paris that pertain to North America, from ministries of Finance, Marine, and the Colonies. Also it includes admiralty records for Bayonne, Brouage, Guyenne, Honfleur, and La Rochelle, as well as notorial and tabellionage archives of La Rochelle, Rochefort, and Saint-Jean-de-Luz. Archival materials from Quebec and private papers are also part of this vast enterprise.

A recent keyword search of this material turned up only three documents for Samuel Champlain himself: his account of the capture of Quebec in 1629, his last will and testament in 1635, and one other item. More material relates indirectly to Champlain's career. Most of what is here refers to events after Champlain's time. This immense project is very much a work in progress. Finding aids and search engines are still in process of development. This great archival effort promises to revolutionize the relationship between scholars and sources for the history of New France.

PUBLISHED MANUSCRIPTS FROM FRENCH ARCHIVES

An effort of another kind was made by a very able French archivist with a particular interest in Champlain. Robert Le Blant was a lawyer, jurist, and councillor of the French Court of Appeal at Douai, and a highly skilled archivist who knew well the complex ways of French institutions. He searched many French provincial and national archives, and found a trove of materials that had eluded earlier students of Champlain. Le Blant and René Baudry published his findings in historical journals, and also in a larger work called *Nouveaux documents sur Champlain et son époque.* The first volume, covering the period from 1560 to 1622, was printed by the then Public Archives of Canada in 1967. A second volume from 1622 to 1635 was promised but not published. A careful bibliography of Le Blant's work is M. A. MacDonald, *Robert le Blant: Seminal researcher and Historian of Early New France* (Saint John, New Brunswick, 1986). Of Le Blant's many publications through half a century, the following are relevant to Champlain.

Le Blant, Robert, and René Baudry. *Nouveaux documents sur Champlain et son époque*, vol. 1 (1560–1622) (Ottawa, 1967), publishes 196 documents relating to directly or indirectly to Champlain, mostly legal and financial records.

Le Blant, Robert. "Les trois mariages d'une acadienne: Anne d'Entremont (1694–1718)." *Nova Francia* 7 (1932) 210–29.

———. "Une sédition basque à Terre-Neuve en 1690." *Revue historique et archéologique de Béarn et du Pays basque* (1932) 56–57.

———. *Une figure légendaire de l'histoire acadienne:le baron de Saint-Castin* (Paris, 1934).

———. *Histoire de la Nouvelle-France: les sources narratives du début du XVIIIe siècle et Le Recueil de Gédéon de Catalogne* (Paris, 1940).

———. "Les études historiques sur la colonie française d'Acadie, 1603–1713." *Revue d'histoire des colonies* 122 (1948) 84–113.

———. "L'annulation du testament de Champlain." *Revue d'histoire des colonies*, 131 and 132 (1950), 203–31.

———. "La Compagnie de la Nouvelle-France et la restitution de l'Acadie (1627–1633)." *Revue d'histoire des colonies,* 126 (1955) 71–93.

———. "Les arrêts du parlement de Rouen du 25 juin et les premières compagnies du Canada." *Revue des Sociétés savantes de Haute Normandie* 3 (1956) 41–55.

———. "Notes sur les découvreurs français. . . ." *Revue d'histoire de l'Amérique française* 11 (1957–58) 413–35; 563–74.

———. "Nouveaux documents additionnels aux trois voyages de Champlain (1560–1651)." *Bulletin philologique et historique jusqu'à 1610* (1959) 369–380.

———. "Du nouveau sur les La Tour." *Mémoires de la Société généalogique canadienne-française* 11 (1960), 21–25.

———. "Les compagnies du Cap Breton (1629–1647)." *Revue d'histoire de l'Amérique française* 16 (1961) 81–94.

———. "Les écrits attribués à Jacques Cartier." *Revue d'histoire de l'Amérique française* 15 (1961) 90–103.

———. "Les plus anciens contrats de travail pour le Canada (1606–1608)." *Bulletin philologique et historique* (1961) 309–17.

———. "Le commerce compliqué des fourrures canadiennes au début du 17e siècle." *Revue d'histoire de l'Amérique française* 16 (1962) 53–66.

———. "L'ascension sociale d'auvergnats Parisiens au XVIIe siècle: Les Chanut (1545–1703)." *Actes du 88e congrès des Sociétés savantes*, Clermont-Ferrand, 1963, Section d'Histoire moderne et contemporaine, 695–707.

———. "La condition sociale de Samuel Champlain." *Actes du 87e congrès national des Sociétés savantes*, Poitiers, 1962, Section d'Histoire moderne et contemporaine, Imprimerie nationale (1963) 669–77.

———. "La famille Boullé (1586–1639)." *Revue d'histoire de l'Amérique française* 17 (1963) 55–69.

———. "La première compagnie de Miscou (1635–1645)." *Revue d'histoire de l'Amérique française* 17 (1963) 363–70.

———. "Le Testament de Samuel Champlain, 17 novembre 1635." *Revue d'histoire de l'Amérique française* 17 (1963) 269–81.

———. "Le triste veuvage d'Hélène Boullé." *Revue d'histoire de l'Amérique française* 18 (1964) 425–37.

————, ed., "Inventaire des biens communs entre Samuel de Champlain et Hélène Boullé, 21 novembre 1636." *Revue d'histoire de l'Amérique française* 18 (1965) 594–603.

————. "Un compagnon blaisois de Samuel Champlain: Jean Ralluau (5 janvier 1576–après 1er janvier 1628), *Revue d'histoire de l'Amérique française* 19 (1966) 503–12.

————. "La pêche et le périple des morues du Saint-Laurent." *Revue philologique et historique* (1966) 259–71.

————. "Les prémices de la fondation de Québec." *Revue d'histoire de l'Amérique française* 22 (1966) 44–55.

————. "Marchands tourangeaux à Paris au début du XVIIe siècle." *Bulletin philologique et historique* (1968), 907–23.

————. "Les débuts difficiles de la compagnie de la Nouvelle-France: l'affaire Langlois (1628–1632)." *Revue d'histoire de l'Amérique française* 22 (1968) 323–34.

————. "L'ascension sociale d'un huissier: Nicolas Boullé (fin XVI–début XVIIe siècle)." *Bulletin philologique et historique* (1969) 819–36.

————. "Jean de Lauson et Marie Gaudard, leur appartenance à une structure sociale." *Revue d'histoire de l'Amérique française* 23 (1969) 110–21.

————. "La première bataille pour Québec en 1608," *Bulletin philologique et historique* 2 (1971) 113–25.

————. "L'ascension sociale d'un aventurier champenois: Claude Turgis (XVIe–XVIIe siècle)." *Revue d'histoire de l'Amérique française* 26 (1972) 53–66.

————. "Documents inédits sur Guillaume Decaen, Protestant Normand au Canada sous le Cardinal de Richelieu." *Congrès des Sociétés savantes de Caen*, 1980, Section d'Histoire moderne, 1 (1980) 445–60; not seen.

————. "Henri IV et le Canada." *Revue de Pau et du Béarn*, 12 (1984–85) 43–57.

Le Blant, Robert, and Marcel Delafosse. "L'avitaillement du Port-Royal d'Acadie par Charles de Biencourt et les marchands Rochelais (1615–1618)." *Revue d'histoire des colonies*, 155 (1958) 563–74.

————. "Les Rochelais dans la vallée du Saint-Laurent (1599–1618)." *Revue d'histoire de l'Amérique française* 10 (1956) 333–63.

PUBLISHED PRIMARY MATERIALS: CHAMPLAIN'S MAJOR WRITINGS

These are the most important sources for any study of Champlain. First editions were as follows:

Des Savvages ov, Voyage De Samvel Champlain, De Brovage, fait en la France Nouuelle, l'an mil six cens trois (A Paris, Chez Clavde De Monstr'oeil, tenant sa boutique en la Cour du palais, au nom de Iesus. Avec Privilege Dv Roy. 1603) (licensed November 13, 1603).

Les Voyages Dv Sievr De Champlain, Xaintongeois, capitaine ordinaire pour le Roy, en la Marine. Divisez En Devx Livres (A Paris, Chez Iean Berjon, rue S. Jean de Beauuais, au Cheual volant, & en sa boutique au Palais, à la gallerie des prisonniers M.DC.XIII. Avec Privilege Dv Roy) (licensed January 9, 1613).

Voyages Et Descovvertures Faites En La Novvelle France, depuis l'année 1615. iusques à la fin de l'année 1618. Par le Sieur de Champlain, Cappitaine ordinaire pour le Roy en la Mer du Ponant (A Paris, Chez Clavde Collet, au Palais, en la gallerie de prisonniers. M.DC.XIX (licensed March 18, 1619).

Les Voyages De La Novvelle France Occidentale, Dicte Canada, Faits Par Le Sr De Champlain Xainc-

tongeois, Capitaine pour le Roy en la Marine du Ponant, & toutes les Descouuertes qu'il faites en ce
païs depuis l'an 1603 iusques en l'an 1629 (A Paris. Ches Clavde Collet au Palais, en la Gallerie
de prisonniers, à l'Estoille d'Or. M.DC.XXXII (no license printed).
Traitté De La Marine Et Dv Devoir D'vn Bon Marinier. Par le Sievr De Champlain [1632], bound
and published with the *Voyages* of 1632.

The first scholarly edition of these works was C.-H. Laverdière, ed., *Oeuvres de Champlain, publiées*
sous le patronage de l'Université Laval 6 vols. in quarto. Other bindings vary (Quebec, 1870). A facsimile edition was published by Éditions du Jour in 3 vols. (Montreal, 1973). Laverdière's *Cham-*
plain is still very useful for its commentary and editorial apparatus. See also Abbé Auguste Gosselin,
"Le vrai monument de Champlain: ses oeuvres éditées par Laverdière." *Mémoires de la Societé Roy-*
ale du Canada 1 (1908) 3–23.

A modern bilingual edition of Champlain's major published works, with texts in old French
and English, is Henry Percival Biggar et al., ed. *The Works of Samuel de Champlain* 6 vols.
(Toronto: Champlain Society, 1922–35; rpt. University of Toronto Press, 1971). Vol. 1 was translated and edited by H. H. Langton and W. F. Ganong; vol. 2 by John Squair; vol. 3 by H. H. Langton and W. F. Ganong; vol. 4 by H. H. Langton; vol. 5 by W. D. LeSueur; and vol. 6 by W. D. Le
Sueur and H. H. Langton. It is available online, on the website of the Champlain Society, in a digital edition that is keyword searchable, a great tool for serious scholars.

The Champlain Society is sponsoring a new translation of Champlain's works by an editorial
team headed by Conrad Heidenreich. The first volume is promised for 2008.

Many editions of selected works or individual works have been published: Passages from Champlain's *Des Sauvages* were reprinted in Pierre Victor Palma Cayet, *Chronologie Septenaire* (Paris,
1605), 415–24. Excerpts also appeared in Jacques-Auguste de Thou's *Histoire universelle depuis 1543*
jusqu'en 1607, published first in a Latin edition and later in a French translation (Paris, 1739).

Shaw, Norton, ed., Alice Wilmere, trans. *Narrative of a Voyage to the West Indies and Mexico in the*
     Years 1599–1602. This was the first published edition of Champlain's ms. *Brief Discours* on his
     travels in the Spanish empire (London: Hakluyt Society, 1859, 1880).
Slafter, Edmund F., ed. *Voyages of Samuel de Champlain* 3 vols. Publications of the Prince Society
     (Boston, 1878–81).
Grant, W. L. ed., *Voyages of Samuel de Champlain, 1604–1618.* Issued in J. F. Jameson's *Original*
     Narratives series (New York, 1907, 1952, 1959); includes the *Voyages* of 1613 and 1619.
Deschamps, Hubert. *Les voyages de Samuel de Champlain: Saintongeais, père du Canada* (Paris,
     1951, 1952).
Trudel, Marcel, ed. *Champlain, textes choisis par M. Trudel.* Collection Fides (Montreal, 1956).
Beaulieu, Alain, et Réal Ouellet, eds. *Champlain, Des Sauvages* (Montreal, 1993). The best edition
     of this work with an excellent introduction of sixty-three pages and full editorial apparatus. It
     adds many documents relevant to the 1603 expedition.
Glénisson, Jean, ed. *La France d'Amérique: Voyages de Samuel Champlain* (Paris, 1994); a one-
     volume edition, handsomely presented.

Helpful assessments appear in Raymonde Litalien, "Champlain's Voyage accounts: Interview
with Jean Glénisson." Revised and authorized by Jean Glénisson, in Raymonde Litalien and Denis
Vaugeois, eds., *Champlain: The Birth of French America* (Montreal, 2004), 280.

CHAMPLAIN'S MAPS AND CHARTS

Champlain's titles in his own vagrant orthography are as follows, with sites and dates after C. E. Heidenreich, *Explorations and Mapping of Samuel Champlain* (Toronto, 1976), 110–14.

CHARTS OF RIVERS AND HARBORS

Port de La Heue (La Have River, Nova Scotia), May 1604

Por du Ross ÿ nol (Liverpool, Nova Scotia), May 1604

port au mouton (Port Mouton, Nova Scotia), May 1604

port Royal (Annapolis Basin, Nova Scotia), June 1604

Port des mines (Advocate Harbor, Nova Scotia), June 1604

R. St. Jehan (Saint John River, New Brunswick), June 1604

Isle de sainte Croix (St. Croix Island, Maine) July? 1604

qui ni be quy (Kennebec River, Maine), July 1605

Chauacoit R (Saco River, Maine), July 1605

Port St Louis (Plymouth Harbor, Massachusetts), July 1605

Malle-Barre (Nauset Harbor, Massachusetts), July 1605

Le Beau-port (Gloucester, Massachusetts), September 1606

port fortuné (Stage Harbor, Massachusetts), October 1606

port de tadoucac (Tadoussac, Quebec), July 1603, June 1608

Quebec (Quebec City, Quebec), 1608

le grand sault st.louis (Montreal, Lachine), 1608, June 1611

LARGE MAPS AND CHARTS OF NEW FRANCE

"Descr[i]psion des costs p[or]ts, rades, Illes de la nouuele france faict selon son vray meridien Avec la declinaison de le[y]ment de plussiers endrois selon que le sieur de Castelfranc le demontre en son liure de la mecometrie de le[y]mant faict et observe par le Sr de Champlain, 1606, 1607." Manuscript Map Division, Library of Congress.

Carte Geographiqve De La Novvelle Franse Faictte Par Le Sievr De Champlain Saint Tongois Cappitaine Povr Le Roi En La Marine, faict len 1612.

Carte geographique de la Nouelle franse en sonvraymordia [1612?].

Carte geographique de la Nouelle franse en son vraymeridiein faicte par le Sr. Champlain Cappine por le Roy en la marine—1613.

[La Nouvelle-France] faict par Sr. de Champlain 1616. A proof of a map that Champlain did not publish, John Carter Brown Library.

Carte de la nouuelle france, augmentée depuis la derniere seruant a la nauigation faicte en son vray Meridien, pa le Sr de Champlain Captaine pour le Roy en la Marine lequel depuis l'an 1603 jusques en l'année, 1629; a descouuert plusieurs costes, terres, lacs, riuieres, et Nations de sauuages, par cy deuant incognuës, comme il se voit en ses relations quil faict Imprimer en 1632. ou il se uoit cette marque ce sont habitations qu'ont faict les françois. Faict l'an 1632 par le Sieur de Champlain. (Two states of this map exist with the same date.) See also Marcel Trudel, "La carte de Champlain en 1632: ses sources et son originalité." *Cartologica* (1978).

CHAMPLAIN'S OTHER PUBLISHED PAPERS AND DOCUMENTS

Charavay, Étienne. *Documents inédits sur Samuel de Champlain, fondateur de Québec, Extrait de la Revue des documents historiques* (Paris, 1875).

Louis Audiat, *Brouage et Champlain, 1578–1667, Documents inédits* (Paris, 1879).

Champlain to Louis XIII, Sieur de Montmorency, Chancellor de Sillery and the Sieur de Ville-menon, 25 August 1622, Bibliothèque nationale de France, ms 16738, fol 143. In Biggar, H. P. *Early Trading Companies of New France* (Toronto, 1901), 279–80.

"La minute notariée du contrat de mariage de Champlain" [Dec. 27, 1610, registered January 11, 1611], ed. Emmanuel de Cathelineau, *Nova Francia* 5 (1930) 142–55. Also in Biggar, H. P. ed., *The Works of Samuel de Champlain,* 6 vols. (Toronto, 1922–36, rpt. 1971) (CWB) 2:315–24, 4:372–73.

Champlain, Samuel, and Helene Boullé, "Contrat d'engagement d'Ysabelle Terrier: agreement to hire a servant, July 27, 1617," In Biggar, CWB 2:324–26; N.-E. Dionne, *Champlain: fondateur de Québec* 2:510–11.

"Au Roy et à nos seigneurs de son conseil" [Petition to the King and Lords of His Council], Feb. 1618. In Biggar, CWB 2:326–29. First printed by Louis Audiat in *Archives historiques de la Saintonge et d l'Aunis* 6:381; and also in Audiat, *Brouage et Champlain*, 26–28.

Champlain, "De l'utilité que le roi peut tirer de la Nouvelle-France." n.d., [Feb. 1618], Audiat, *Brouage et Champlain*, 29–35.

Champlain, "Plaise à messieurs de la chambre du commerce." Paris, Feb. 1618. In Biggar, CWB 2:339–46; and also Audiat, *Champlain et Brouage*, 35–38.

"Extrait des Lettres de la Chambre du Commerce sur la requête . . . et supplique au roi en sa faveur," Paris, Feb. 9, 1618. Ibid.

Receipt for Champlain's salary, Dec. 24, 1618. In Biggar, CWB 2:330.

Champlain et al. "Articles de la commission en assemblée générale de Français residant au Canada et remise au P. georges le Baillif, Recolet, envoyé en France pour fair connaître au roi les plaintes et les désirs des habitants," Aug. 18, 1621. In Dionne, *Champlain: fondateur de Québec* 2:513–15. Champlain's signature is the first of twelve; it is followed by "Tres humbles remtrances et memoires," 516–18.

Champlain, *Documents, 1625–26.* "Inédit sur le fondateur de Québec." Ed. A. Léo-Leymarie, *Nova Francia* 1 (1925) 80–85.

"Commission du Roy à Champlain," April 27, 1628. In Dionne, *Champlain: fondateur de Québec* 2: 523–24.

"Commission à Champlain des Intendant et Directeurs de la Compagnie de la Nouvelle-France," March 21, 1629. In Dionne, *Champlain: fondateur de Québec* 2:525–26.

Account of the voyages of 1608, vol. for 1608, printed in 1611. Page 294. Rpt. in *Transactions of the Royal Society of Canada* 8 (1902) ii, 172.

Champlain, Correspondence and Depositions Concerning the Seizure of Quebec, 1629–32. In C.-H. Laverdière, *Oeuvres de Champlain*, Pièces justificatives, documents, 1–30.

Champlain, "Contrats de vente de 1630." Ed. M. Delafosse. *Revue d'histoire de l'Amérique française* 9 (1963) 282–86.

Champlain, *Mémoire en Requête de Champlain pour la Continuation du paiement de sa Pension,* ca. 1630. Ed. Gabriel Marcel (Paris, Tross, 1886); copy in New York Public Library.

Champlain, "Contrat de Donation Mutuelle entre Champlain et Hélène Boullé," Feb. 13, 1632. In Dionne, *Champlain: fondateur de Québec* 2:239–40.

"Mémoir et instruction baillés au Sieur de Champlain par les Directeurs de la Nouvelle-France," Paris, Feb. 4, 1633; "Supplément d'Instructions au Sieur de Champlain par les directeurs de la Nouvelle France . . . ," Dieppe March 17, 1633; *Mercure François* 19 (1633) 809–11; L. Campeau, *Monumenta Novae Franciae* 2:340–41, 359–60.

Champlain, "Relation du Voyage de sieur de Champlain en Canada" (1633). *Mercure François* 803–67; rpt. in Campeau, *Monumenta Novae Franciae* 2:350–402.

Champlain, Samuel de, to Richelieu, Aug. 15, 1633. *Archives du Ministère des affaires étrangères.* Original text in Biggar, CWB 6:375–77; and Dionne, *Champlain: fondateur de Québec* 2:246–49.

Champlain, Lettre au Cardinal Richelieu, Aug. 18, 1634. Ms. Photocopy, *Library of Congress.* From the original in the *Archives of the Ministry of Foreign Affairs, Paris*; Library of Congress Transcripts; French text in Biggar, CWB 6:378–79.

Champlain, "Lettre au Cardinal de Richelieu," Aug. 15, 1635. In Dionne, *Champlain: fondateur de Québec* 2:537–39.

Champlain, "Testament," Nov. 17, 1635. *Revue d'histoire de l'Amérique française* 17 (1963) 282–86; partial inventory, "l'inventaire des meubles qui faisaient partie de la communauté de biens entre Champlain et Hélène Boullé, ibid., 18 (1965) 594–603.

PUBLISHED WORKS OF MARC LESCARBOT

Histoire de la Nouvelle-France, published at Paris in 1609 with English translations in the same year and another in German in 1613; French editions were reprinted in 1611, 1612, 1617, and 1618. Later French printings added new material useful for the career of Champlain. Nearly all variant editions are in the John Carter Brown Library.

Lescarbot, Marc. *Histoire de la Nouvelle-France.* Ed. Edwin Tross, 3 vols. (Paris, 1866).

————. *History of New France,* 3 vols. (Toronto, 1907). Ed. H. P. Biggar with a translation by Oxford linguist W. L. Grant.

————. *Histoire de la Nouvelle-France.* Ed. W. L. Grant and H. P. Biggar, 3 vols. (Toronto, 1914); *La Conversion des Savvages qui ont esté baptisés en la Novvelle France, avec un bref récit du voyage du Sieur De Povtrincovrt* (Paris, n.d. [1610]), rpt. in Reuben Gold Thwaites, ed., *The Jesuit Relations and Allied Documents* 1:49–113.

————. *Relation dernière de ce qui s'est passé au voyage du sieur de Poutrincourt en la Nouvelle-France depuis 20 mois en ça* (Paris, 1912); rpt. *Jesuit Relations* 1:119–91.

————. *La Conversion des Sauvages* (1610; rpt. 1612).

————. *Les Muses de la Nouvelle-France* (Paris, 1618).

PUBLISHED PRIMARY RECORDS AND WORKS OF OTHER INDIVIDUALS

Albret, Jeanne d'. *Mémoires et Poésies de Jeanne d'Albret* (Paris, 1893).

Avaux, comte d'. *Correspondance inédite du comte d'Avaux avec son père (1627–1642),* Ed. A. Boppe (Paris, 1887).

Barbour, Philip L., ed. *The Complete Works of Captain John Smith (1580–1631)* 3 vols. (Chapel Hill, 1986).

Bertrand, le sieur, Lettre missive, touchant la conversion et baptesme du grand Sagamos de la nouvelle France . . . a letter to his brother le sieur de la Troncheraie, June 28, 1610 (Paris,

Regnoul, 1610); rpt. in *Jesuit Relations* 1:118–23); copy of the original in the New York Public Library.

Bideau, Michel, ed. *Jacques Cartier: Relations* (Montreal, 1986).

[Black Hawk] Jackson, Donald, ed. *Black Hawk: An Autobiography* (Urbana, Ill., 1990). Patterson, J. B., ed., *Life of Mà-Ka-Tai-Me-She-Kia-Kiàk or Black Hawk . . . Dictated by Himself* (Rock Island, Ill., 1833), with certificate of authenticity by Antoine LeClaire, U.S. interpreter for the Sac and Fox nations. Other editions followed in Boston, New York, Philadelphia, Baltimore, and Mobile. The first modern edition was edited by Milo Milton Quaife and published in the Lakeside Classics (Chicago, 1916) as the *Life of Mà-Ka-Tai-Me-She-Kia-Kiàk or Black Hawk . . . Dictated by Himself.* Ed. J. B. Patterson (Cincinnati, 1834); new edition, ed. Milo M. Quaife (Chicago, 1916).

[Bogaert] Gehring, Charles T., and William Sterna, eds. *A Journey into Mohawk and Oneida Country, 1634–35: The Journal of Harmen Meynderts van den Bogaert* (Syracuse, 1988).

[Bourbon, Antoine de] Rochambeau, marquis de. *Lettres d'Antoine de Bourbon et Jeanne d'Albret* (Paris, 1877).

Bueil, Honorat de, seigneur de Racan. *Oeuvres complètes* (Paris, 1857).

Cartier, Jacques. *The Voyages of Jacques Cartier.* Published from the originals with translations, notes, and appendices by H. P. Biggar (Ottawa, 1924); *A Collection of Documents relating to Jacques Cartier and the Sieur de Roberval,* ed. H. P. Biggar (Ottawa, 1930); *The Voyages of Jacques Cartier,* ed. Ramsay Cook (Toronto, 1993).

Colden, Cadwallader. *History of the Five Indian Nations* (1727, 1747; rpt., 1866; Ithaca, N.Y., 1958).

Charlevoix, Pierre-Francis-Xavier de. *Histoire et description générale de la Nouvelle France,* with *Journal historique,* 3 vols. in quarto, 6 vols. in duodecimo (Paris, 1744). An excellent modern scholarly edition of the *Voyages* is *Charlevoix, Journal d'un Voyage fait par ordre du roi dans l'Amérique septentrionale,* ed. Pierre Berthiaume, 2 vols. (Montreal, 1994). English translations include: *History and General Description of New France,* trans. John Gilmary Shea 6 vols. (New York, 1866–1872, rpt. Chicago, 1962); and Louise Phelps Kellogg, *Journal of a Voyage to North America* 2 vols. (Chicago, 1923).

Charlevoix, Pierre-Francis-Xavier de. *Histoire de l'établissement des progrès et de la décadence du christianisme dans l'Empire du Japon* 3 vols. (Rouen, 1713).

Daniel, Charles. *Voyage à la Nouvelle France du Capitaine Charles Daniel de Dieppe* (1629; rpt. Rouen, 1881); CWB 6: 153–61. For an example of periodical literature see *Le Mercure François* 19 (1633) 802–67.

Davis, John. *The Seaman's Secrets* (London, 1607). In Albert Hastings Markham, ed., *The Voyages and Works of John Davis, the Navigator.* Hakluyt Society, series 1, vol. 54 (London, 1880).

Denys, Nicolas. *Histoire Naturelle des Peuples, des Animaux, des Arbres et Plantes de l'Amerique Septentrionale, & de ses divers Climats. Avec une Description exacte de la Pesche des Moluës, tant sur le Grand Banc qu'à la Coste; & de tout ce qui s'y pratique de plus particulier, &c* (Paris, 1672). Another copy in the Public Records Office bears the date of May 10, 1687. A Dutch translation appeared in 1688, with additional text and engravings not in the French edition. A bilingual English and French edition is *The Description and Natural History of the Coasts of North America (Acadia)* ed. William F. Ganong, with much editorial commentary (Toronto, 1908).

[De Coste, Mathieu] "Declaration of Nicolas de Bauquemare, par laquelle il reconnaît avoir engagé le nègre Mathieu de Coste pour des services de Canada, Cadie et ailleurs; Canada, Acadie, et Nouvelle-France." In Le Blant and Baudry, eds. *Nouveaux documents*, 105–06, 194, 195, 203, 212, 235, 388.

[Elena, Guillermo] Testament of Guillermo Elena, 26 June 1601. Original in the Archivo Historico Provincial, Cádiz; copy in Library and Archives Canada, Ottawa; an English translation of the Spanish original is published in Joe C. W. Armstrong, *Champlain* (Toronto, 1987), appendix 2, 274–78.

Estoile, Pierre de l'. *Mémoires-Journaux* 12 vols. Ed. Brunet (Paris, 1875–96).

———. *The Paris of Henry of Navarre, as seen by Pierre de l'Estoile: Selections from his Mémoires-Journaux (1574–1611)*. Trans. and ed. by Nancy Lyman Roelker (Cambridge, 1958).

Fiefmelin, André Magé de. *Les Oeuvres du Sieur Fiefmelin* (Poitiers, 1601).

Gargas, M. de. "Mon Séjour de l'Acadie, 1687–88," in William Inglis Morse, ed., *Acadiensia Nova, 1598–1779* (London, 1935).

Giffard, Robert. Marriage contract. *Bulletin des Recherches Historiques* 9 (1903), 267–70.

———. "Concession à Robert Giffard, Sr. de Beaufort," signed Bras-de-Fer Châteaufort, Jan. 15, 1634, N.-E. Dionne, *Champlain: fondateur de Québec*, 535–37.

Mercoeur, duc de. *Correspondance du duc de Mercoeur*. Ed. Gaston de Carné (Rennes, 1899).

Henri IV, *Recueil des Lettres missives de Henri IV*. Ed. M. F. Guessard, 9 vols. (Paris, 1843–76). The major source. A survey of many other published materials appears in Bernard Barbiche, ed., *Lettres de Henri IV. . . .* (Rome, 1968). A definitive modern scholars' edition of the scattered writings of Henri IV would be a major contribution to our understanding of a great leader in modern history.

Herouard, Jean. *Journal*. Published as "Le Canada pendant la jeunesse de Louis XIII." Ed., A.-Léo Laymarie, *Nova Francia,* 1 (1925), 161–70.

Juet, Robert, "The Voyage of the *Half Moon* from 4 April to 7 November 1609." In Robert M. Lunny, ed. *Collection of the New Jersey Historical Society* 12 (Newark, N.J., [1609] 1959).

Lahontan, Baron de. *New Voyages to North America*. Ed. Reuben G. Thwaites (1703; 2 vols., New York, 1970); *Oeuvres complètes*. Réal Ouellet and Alain Beaulieu, eds., 2 vols. (Montreal, 1990); the best edition.

La Tour, Charles Turgis de Saint-Étienne de. Letter to Louis XIII, July 25, 1627. In Trudel, *Histoire de la Nouvelle-France* 2:270.

Lauson, Jean de. Lettre à Richelieu, 30 juin 1627. Archives du Ministère des Affaires étrangères de France. *Mémoires et documents, France,* vol. 785: 178r. VI 4 (March 1953) 517–35.

Layfield, Dr. John. Account of travels in the Spanish Empire, ca. 1599. In S. Purchas, ed., *Hakluytus Posthumous; or Purchas His Pilgrimes . . .* 20 vols. (Glasgow, 1905–07) 16:43–106.

[Mons, var. Monts, Montz]

W. I. Morse ed. *Pierre du Gua, Sieur de Monts, Colonial and Saintongeais* (London, 1939). Other letters from de Mons are published in Biggar, CWB; Le Caron, *Au Roy*; Lescarbot, *New France* and *Documents relatifs à la Nouvelle-France*.

Pieresc, Nicolas-Claude de Babri, seigneur de Peiresc. "Observations de Peiresc sur les curiosités rapportées d'Acadie par Pierre du Gua, sieur de Mons," 26 Nov. 1605 and 13 March 1606. In Le Blant and Baudry, eds., *Nouveaux Documents sur Champlain*, 102–06.

———. *Journal*. Publié par F.-W. Gravit as "Un document inédit sur le Canada." *Revue de l'Université Laval* 1, 4 (1946) 282–88.

Razilly, Isaac de, "Lettre de Razilly à Lescarbot, 16 août, 1634," *Bibliothèque nationale de France,* Fonds français, 13,423:349–50. Copies of this document are available in LAC and Fort Point Museum, La Have, Nova Scotia.

———. "Memoir du chevalier de Razilly, Nov. 26, 1626." Published by Léon Deschamps as a "mémoire inédit." *Revue de Géographie* (1886) 374–83, 453–64. The original is lost; a manuscript copy is in the *Bibliothèque Sainte-Geneviève* (Paris).

[La Roche] Le Ber, Joseph. "Un document inédit sur l'Ile de Sable et le marquis de la Roche." *Revue d'histoire de l'Amérique française* 2 (1948) 199–213.

[Thevet] Schlesinger, R., and A. P. Stabler, eds. *André Thevet's North America: A Sixteenth-Century View* (Montreal, 1986).

Sully, duc de. *Les Économies Royales* 2 vols. (1611–17, Paris 1836–37). The best edition is edited by David Buisseret and Bernard Barbiche; 2 vols. (Paris, 1970, 1988).

———. *Mémoires du duc de Sully.* Nouvelle édition (Paris, 1822).

[Valois], *Mémoires de Marguerite de Valois.* Ed. M. F. Guessard (Paris, 1842).

OFFICIAL RECORDS

Bréard, Charles, and Philippe Barrey, eds. *Documents relatifs à la Marine Normande aux XVe et XVIe siècles* (Rouen, 1906).

Bréard, Charles, and Paul Bréard. *Documents relatifs à la Marine Normande et à ses armements aux XVIe et XVIIe siècles pour le Canada, l'Afrique, les Antilles, le Brésil et les Indes* (Rouen, 1889).

Bois, Monique. *Inventaire des documents relatifs au Canada de 1522 à 1604 dans les tabellionages de Rouen et du Havre conservés aux archives départementales Seine-Maritime* (Paris and Ottawa, 1990).

Calendar of State Papers, Colonial Series, 1574–1660 [. . .] Edited by W. Noël Sainsbury [. . .] (London, 1860).

Calendar of State Papers, Colonial Series, America and West Indies, 1675–1676. Also Addenda, 1574–1674 [. . .] Edited by W. Noël Sainsbury [. . .] (London, 1893).

Bonnault, Claude de. "Les archives d'Espagne et le Canada. Rapport sur une mission dans les archives d'Espagne." Rapport de l'archiviste de la Province de Québec (Quebec, 1951–52 and 1952–53).

Brodhead, John Romeyn. *Documents Relative to the Colonial History of the State of New York: Procured in Holland, England and France by John Romeyn Brodhead* [. . .] Edited by E. B. O'Callaghan.(Albany, 1853–87).

Collection de manuscrits contenant lettres, mémoires et autres documents historiques relatifs à la Nouvelle-France, recueillis aux Archives de la Province de Québec ou copiés à l'étranger (Quebec, 1879–88).

Pièces et documents relatifs à la tenure seigneuriale, demandés par une adresse de l'Assemblée législative, 1851 2 vols. (Quebec, 1852).

Conseil Supérieur de Québec, *Complément des ordonnances et jugements des gouverneurs et intendants du Canada* (Quebec, 1856).

Gosselin, Édouard. *Nouvelles glanes historiques normandes puisées exclusivement dans des documents inédits* (Rouen, 1873).

RELIGIOUS RECORDS: JESUITS

The Jesuit Relations and Allied Documents 73 volumes (Cleveland, 1896–1901, rpt. New York, 1959) is a bilingual edition of reports by Jesuits to their superiors, with many other documents. The English translations in this bilingual work, originally compiled and edited by the American historian Reuben Gold Thwaites, must be checked against the original, and used with great caution. Most helpful for a student of Champlain are relations by Pierre Biard, Charles Lalement, Énemond Massé, Paul Le Jeune, in particular: Biard, "Relation, 1614," *Jesuit Relations* 3:83; 4:7–167; "Relation, 1616," "Relation,1633," *Jesuit Relations* 5:83–85; "Relation, 1636," *Jesuit Relations* 9: 218–83; Le Jeune, "Relation, 1637," *Jesuit Relations* 12:86–87, 13:147; Biard, Pierre, s.j., "Relation de la Nouvelle France. Écrite en 1614," *Relations des Jésuites,* 4:100 (Lyon, 1616), rpt in *Jesuit Relations* 3:21–283, 4:7–167.

Also of high value is another compilation by Jesuit scholar Lucien Campeau, who devoted his career to a great historical project that he called *Monumenta Novae Franciae.* Campeau conceived this as a subseries of the Jesuits' *Monumenta Historica Societatis Jesu.* His purpose was to publish all major documents relating to the Jesuits in Canada and Acadia, with another series to follow for the Illinois country and Louisiana. He intended it to supersede the large bilingual collection of Jesuit Relations by Thwaites. For a discussion of strengths and weaknesses, see "Memories of Champlain," above.

Of particular value for Champlain are the first three volumes in Campeau's great work: *La première mission d'Acadie, 1602–1616; Établissement à Québec, 1616–1634* (Rome and Quebec, 1979); and *Fondation de la mission huronne, 1635–1637.* Other volumes consist of: vol. 4, *Les grandes épreuves, 1638–1640*; vol. 5, *La bonne nouvelle reçue, 1641–1643*; vol. 6, *Recherche de la paix, 1644–1646*; vol. 7, *Le témoignage du sang, 1647–1650; vol. 8, Au bord de la ruine, 1651–1656.*

Also very useful are the private letters of Jesuit father Charles Lalement, separately published:

"Lettre à Champlain, 28 juill. 1625, écrite de Québec," in Gabriel Sagard, *Histoire* (ed. Tross) 3:789. Reproduced in Gabriel Sagard, *Histoire du Canada,* 4:170.

"Lettre au Provincial des Récollets, 28 juill. 1625, écrite de Québec," in Sagard, *Histoire du Canada* 3:789. Reproduced according to Sagard's text in *Jesuit Relations* 4:172–75.

"Lettre à son frère Jérôme, August 1, 1626, écrite de Québec," publiée à Paris en 1627. *Mercure François* 13:12–34, 4:185–227.

"Lettre au Général des Jésuites, August 1626, écrite de Québec," *Jesuit Relations* 4:176–83.

Extrait dv Registre de Bapteme de l'Eglise dv Port Royal en la Nouvelle France Le iour Sainct Iehan Baptiste 24. de juin [1610]: a record of the baptisms of Sagamore Membertou and his large family on St. John's Day, 1610, by Jesse Fleche. The original is in the John Carter Brown library; published in *Jesuit Relations* 1:108–13; also an interesting source for the structure of a Mi'kmaq family in the early seventeenth century.

RELIGIOUS RECORDS: RÉCOLLETS

Récollet relations and other documents have not been collected as systematically as those of the Jesuits, but some individual works are of high importance.

Le Baillif, Georges. *Plainte de la nouvelle France dicte Canada* (Paris?, n.d.). Photocopy in Library and Archives Canada, Ottawa.

Le Caron, Joseph. *Au Roy sur La Nouvelle France* (Paris, 1626). Photocopy in Library and Archives Canada, Ottawa.

Le Clercq, Chrestien. *Nouvelle relation de la Gaspesia* (Paris, 1691): *New Relation of Gaspesia with the Customs and Religions of the Gaspesian Indians.* Vol. 5 in the publications of the Champlain Society, W. F. Ganong, ed., (Toronto, 1910).

———. *Premier établissement de la foy dans la Nouvelle-France* (Paris, 1691) in at least two other editions with variant titles. Published in English translation as *First Establishment of the Faith in New France*, ed. J. G. Shea, 2 vols. (New York, 1881).

Sagard, Gabriel. *Le grand voyage du pays des Hurons* (Paris, 1632); new edition (Paris, Tross, 1865). An English translation appeared as *The Long Journey to the Country of the Hurons*, tr. H. H. Langton, ed. George M. Wrong (Toronto, Champlain Society, 1939); available online in digital editions that are keyword searchable. A modern French edition appeared as *Le grand voyage du pays des Hurons,* with an introduction by Marcel Trudel. *Cahiers du Québec,* "Documents d'histoire" series (Montreal, 1976). It has appeared also in a scholarly edition with a French text established by Réal Ouellet, introduction and notes by Réal Ouellet and Jack Warwick (Quebec, 1990).

———. *Histoire du Canada et voyages que les frères mineurs recollects y ont faicts pour la conversion des infidèles: depuis l'an 1615* (first edition, Paris, 1636); reprinted in four duodecimo volumes, still the edition of choice. It has not been translated into English or reprinted in a modern scholarly edition.

RELIGIOUS RECORDS: URSULINES

"Chroniques de l'Ordre des Ursulines." In Dionne, *Champlain: fondateur de Québec* 2:395–403, appendix I.

"Extraits des Chroniques de l'Ordre des Ursulines," *Journal de Québec*, 10 March, 1855.

ORAL HISTORY OF INDIAN NATIONS

GENERAL WORKS

Vincent, Sylvie, ed. "Traditions et récits sur l'arrivée des Européens en Amérique." *Recherches amérindiennes au Québec* 22, 2–3 (autumn, 1992); a collection of twenty essays and interviews.

ALGONQUIN

Jackson, Donald, ed. *Black Hawk: An Autobiography* (Urbana, Ill., 1995, 1964, 1990) (Sac and Fox).

Brasser, T. J. C. "Group Identification along a Moving Frontier." *Verhandlungen des XXXVIII Internationalen Amerikanistenkongresses* (Munich, 1871) 2:261–65.

HURON

Le Jeune, Paul. "Relation, 1636," *Jesuit Relations* 9:218–83; Le Jeune, "Relation, 1637," *Jesuit Relations* 12:86–87, 13:147.

IROQUOIA

Pratt, Peter P. *Archaeology of the Oneida Iroquois* (George's Mills, N.H., 1976).
———. "A Perspective on Oneida Archaeology." In Robert E. Funk and Charles F. Hayes III, eds. *Current Perspectives on Northeastern Archaeology: Essays in Honor of William A. Ritchie.* New York State Archaeological Association 17 (1977) 1:51–69.
———. *Archaeology of the Oneida Indians*, Occasional Publications in *Northeastern Anthropology* 1 (Rindge, N.H., 1976), viii–ix.

MI'KMAQ

Porter, Mike. *Guides to the North Woods* (Halifax, 1990).
Rand, Silas Tertius. *Legends of the Micmacs* (New York, 1894).

MONTAGNAIS

Vincent, Sylvie. "L'arrivée des chercheurs de terres: récits et dires des Montagnais de la Moyenne et de la Basse Côte-Nord," *Recherches amérindiennes au Québec* 22:2–3 (1992) 19–29.

WINNEBAGO

Lurie, Nancy O. "Winnebago Protohistory." In Sigmund Diamond, ed. *Culture in History: Essays in Honor of Paul Radin* (New York, 1960), 790–808.

WYANDOT

Clarke, Peter Dooyentate. *Origin and Traditional History of the Wyandots* (Toronto, 1870).

ARCHAEOLOGY AND MATERIAL CULTURE

MONTAGNAIS

Moreau, Jean Français. "Objets amérindiens et européens au Saguenay-Lac-Saint-Jean. La portée des transferts culturels en fôret boréale." In Michel Fortin, ed., *L'archéologie et la rencontre de deux mondes* (Quebec, 1992) 103–31.
———. "Indices archéologiques de transferts culturels par la voie du Québec central." In Laurier Turgeon, Denys Delâge, and Réal Ouellet, eds. *Transferts culturels et métissages: Amérique/ Europe XVIe–XXe siècles* (Quebec and Paris, 1996), 209–42.
Clermont, Norman, and Pierre Corbeil, *Pointe-du-Buisson: une expérience archéologique* (Melocheville, 1995).

HURON

McIlwraith, T. F. "On the Location of Cahiagué," *Transactions of the Royal Society of Canada,* ser. 3, 41 (1947) ii: 99–102.11.
———. "Archaeological Work in Huronia, 1946: Excavations near Warminster," *Canadian Historical Review* 27 (1946) 394–401.
Fitzgerald, William. "Chronology to Cultural Process: Lower Great Lakes Archaeology, 1500–1650," Ph.D. dissertation, Department of Anthropology, McGill University, Montreal (1990).

FISHING AND WHALING STATIONS

Tuck, James A. and Robert Grenier. *Red Bay, Labrador: World Whaling Capital, 1550–1600* (St. John's, Nfld., 1989, 1990).
Fitzgerald, William, et al. "Late Sixteenth-Century Basque Banded Copper Kettles," *Historical Archaeology* 27 (1993) 1.

SAGUENAY RIVER AND TADOUSSAC

Lapointe, Camille. *Le Site de Chicoutimi: un établissement commercial sur la route des fourrures du Saguenay-Lac-Saint-Jean* (Quebec, 1985).

ACADIA

Yves Cormier. *Les aboiteaux en Acadie, hier et aujourd'hui* (Moncton, 1990).

NORUMBEGA

Faulkner, Alaric, and Gretchen Fearon Faulkner. *The French at Pentagoet, 1635–1674: An Archaeological Portrait of the Acadian Frontier* (Saint John, N.B., and Augusta, Me., 1987, 1988).

CAP TOURMENTE

Guimont, Jacques. *La Petite-ferme du Cap Tourmente* (Quebec, 1996); Léo-Guy de Repentigny, *La Ferme d'en bas du Cap Tourmente: de la ferme de Champlain aux grandes volées d'oies* (Quebec, Environnement Canada, Conservation et protection, 1989).

QUEBEC

Niellon, François, and Marcel Moussette. *L'habitation de Champlain* (Quebec, 1981).
Lapointe, Camille, Béatrice Chassé, and Hélène de Carufel. *Aux origines de la vie québecoise* (Quebec, 1983, 1987, 1995).
Clermont, Norman, Claude Chapdelaine, and Jacques Guimont. *L'occupation historique et préhistorique de Place Royal* (Quebec, 1992).

ICONOGRAPHY AND VISUAL MATERIALS

"Portrait of Samuel de Champlain," anonymous *sanguine* of unknown provenance and date, Archives nationales du Québec. Reproduced in Alain Beaulieu et Réal Ouellet, eds. *Samuel de Champlain: Des Sauvages* (Montreal, 1993).

"Samuel de Champlain, governor general of Canada," lithograph, 1854. Attributed to Louis-César-Joseph Ducornet (1806–56); Litalien and Vaugeois, *Champlain: The Birth of French America,* 356. For a short biography of Ducornet by Emmanuel Bénézit, see *Dictionnaire critique et documentaire des peintres, sculpteurs, dessinateurs et graveurs* (Paris, 1999).

"Samuel de Champlain," steel-plate engraving by J. A. O'Neil, ca. 1866. Reproduced in Litalien and Vaugeois, *Champlain: The Birth of French America,* 357.

"Messire Michael Particelli Chevallie [sic]," by Balthasar Moncornet, engraving, 1654, Bibliothèque nationale de France, C56240; Samuel de Champlain, lithograph attributed to Louis-César-Joseph Ducornet, 1854, Musée National des Beaux-Arts du Québec; "Samuel de Champlain," steel engraving by J. A. O'Neil, after a painting by Théophile Hamel, frontispiece to J. G. Shea, ed. *History and General Description of New France* by Pierre-François-Xavier de Charlevoix, 1864, CA C14305; "Samuel de Champlain," frontispiece in C.-H. Laverdière, *Oeuvres de Champlain,* 1870, CA 13204; C14305.

Paltsits, Victor-Hugo. "A Critical Examination of Champlain's Portrait," *Acadiensis* 4 (1904) 3:611; rpt. in *Bulletin des Recherches Historiques* 38 (1932), 755–59; Biggar, Henry Percival. "The Portrait of Champlain," *Canadian Historical Review* 1 (1920), 379–80; Bishop, Morris. *Champlain: The Life of Fortitude,* 6n; Armstrong, Joe C. W. *Champlain,* 20–21; Liebel, Jean. "Les faux portraits de Champlain," *Vie des arts* 28 (1983), 112; Martin, Denis. "Discovering the Face of Samuel de Champlain," in Litalien and Vaugeois eds. *Champlain,* 354–62.

"Champlain," engraving by Eugène Ronjat, ca. 1870. Illustration in Sulte, *Histoire des Canadiens Français* (1882), Litalien and Vaugeois, eds. *Champlain,* 261.

Gagnon, François-Marc. *Premiers peintres de la Nouvelle-France* 2 vols.(Quebec, 1976) 2:25–26; Martin, Denis. "Samuel de Champlain à visage découvert," in Litalien and Vaugeois, eds. *Champlain,* 360–62.

FRENCH MASQUES AND BALLETS DE COUR

Moreau, François. "Les Amérindiens dans le ballets de cour à l'époque de Champlain," in Litalien and Vaugeois, *Champlain: The Birth of French America*; citing Paul Lacroix, *Ballets et mascarades de cour sous Henri IV et Louis XIII* 6 vols. (Geneva, 1868–1870) 2:158.

WORKS OF CARTOGRAPHY AND NAVIGATION IN CHAMPLAIN'S ERA

Medina, Pedro de. *Arte de Navegar* (Seville, 1545). It was translated by John Frampton as *The Arte of Navigation . . . made by Master Peter de Medina* (London, 1581).

Wagenaer, Lucas Janszoon. *T'eerste Deel Vande Spieghel der Zeevaerdt vandde navigatie der Westersche Zee: The First Part of Mirror of the Navigation for Sailing the Western Sea.* Translated into English as *The Mariner's Mirror.*

Nautonier, Guillaume de. *The Mecographie of Ye Loadstone* (Toulouse, 1603).

John Davis, *The Seaman's Secrets* (London, 1607). In Albert Hastings Markham, ed., *The Voyages and Works of John Davis, the Navigator*. Publications of the Hakluyt Society, ser. 1, vol. 54 (London, 1880).

Mainwaring, Sir Henry. "The Seaman's Dictionary." In G. E. Mainwaring and W. G. Perrin, eds. *The Life and Works of Sir Henry Mainwaring* (vols. 54 and 56 in the publications of the Navy Records Society, London, 1920, 1922).

John Smith, *An Accidence, or The Path-way to Experience. Necessary for all Young Sea-men* (London, 1626) and its sequel, *A Sea Grammar, with the Plaine Exposition of Smith's Accidence for Young Seamen, Enlarged* (London, 1627), reprinted in Philip L. Barbour, ed., *The Complete Works of Captain John Smith (1580–1631)* 3 vols. (Chapel Hill, 1986) 3:3–121.

DICTIONARIES, GLOSSARIES OF CHAMPLAIN'S ERA

Anon., *Lexique du patois Charentais*, http://membres.lycos.fr/xaintong/patois.htm.

Académie francaise, *Dictionnaire de l'Académie française* (Paris, 1635).

Aubin, *Dictionnaire de Marine contenant les termes de la navigation et de l'architecture navale* (Amsterdam, 1702).

Cotgrave, Randle. *Dictionarie of the French and English Tongues* (London, 1611).

Guillet, sieur de. *Dictionaire du gentilhomme* (Hague, 1686).

Huguet, E. *Dictionnaire de la langue française du seizième siècle* (Paris, 1961).

Mainwaring, Henry. *The Seaman's Dictionary, or Nomenclator Navalis* (ca. 1620).

MODERN DICTIONARIES ON HISTORICAL PRINCIPLES
AND STUDIES IN HISTORICAL LINGUISTICS

Léard, Jean-Marcel. *Grammaire québécoise d'aujourdhui: comprendre les québécismes* (Montreal, 1995).

Massignon, Geneviève. *Les parlers français d'Acadie* 2 vols. (Paris, n.d. [1962?]).

Mathews, Mitford. *Dictionary of Americanisms on Historical Principles* (Chicago, 1956).

Morissoneau, Christian. *Le langage géographique de Cartier et de Champlain* (Quebec, 1978).

Musset, Georges, Marcel Pellisson, and Charles Vigon. *Glossaire des patois et des parlers de l'Aunis et de la Saintonge* 2 vols. (La Rochelle, 1922).

"Michif Language," en.wikipedia.org/wiki/Michif_language.

Rey, Alain, et al., eds. *Le Grand Robert de la langue française* 6 vols. (Paris, 2001).

Rey, Alain. *Dictionnaire historique de la langue française* 3 vols. rev. edition (Paris, 2006).

Xaintonge, editors, "Le grand lexique du patois charentais," in six livrets, *Xaintonge*, journal hors serie 1–6 (May 2003–December 2006).

BIOGRAPHICAL AND GENEALOGICAL DICTIONARIES
AND ENCYCLOPEDIAS

The *Dictionary of Canadian Biography/ Dictionnaire Biographique du Canada* was founded in 1959 with the object of providing critical biographies of all major figures in Canadian history. The project expanded in 1961 to a joint Anglo-French enterprise directed jointly by George W. Brown at the University of Toronto Press and Marcel Trudel at Université Laval. The first volume was published in 1966. The first series, through 1900, was completed in 1990. A second series, for Canadians who lived in the twentieth century, is complete through 1920. A web edition includes additions and corrections.

D'Alembert, Jean le Rond, and Denis Diderot. *Encyclopédie, ou Dictionnaire Raisonné des Sciences, des Arts, et des Métiers* (Paris, 1751), s.v., "Québec."

Tanguay, Cyprien, *Dictionnaire généalogique des familles canadiennes depuis la fondation de la colonie jusqu'à nos jours* 7 vols. (Montreal, 1871–90).

PALEOGRAPHY

Audisio, Gabriel, and Isabelle Rambaud, *Lire le français d'hier: manuel de paléographie moderne XVe–XVIIIe siècle*, 3rd edition (Paris, 2005); an excellent guide to handwriting in Champlain's era.

Hector, L. C. *The Handwriting of English Documents* (London, 1958, 1966).

SECONDARY SOURCES

Abler, Thomas S. "Iroquoian Cannibalism: Fact or Fiction." *Ethnohistory* 27 (1980), 309–16.

Adney, Edwin Tappan and Howard I. Chapelle. *Bark Canoes and Skin Boats of North America* (Washington, 1964).

Anderson, Fred, and Andrew Cayton. *The Dominion of War: Empire and Liberty in North America, 1500–2000.* Chapter 1, "Champlain's Legacy: The Transformation of Seventeenth-Century North America" (New York, 2005).

Andrews, Kenneth. *Drake's Voyages: A Reassessment of Their Place in Elizabethan Maritime Expansion* (London, 1964).

Anonymous. *Chronologie septenaire de l'histoire de la paix entre les Roys de France et d'Espagne* [. . .] (Paris, 1612).

———. "Lutte originale de Champlain contre le scorbut: 'l'Ordre de Bon Temps,' " *Vie médicale au Canada français* 1 (1972); not seen.

Anquez, Leonce. *Historie des assemblées politiques des Réformés de France* (Paris, 1959).

Arima, E. Y. *Inuit Kayaks in Canada: A Review of Historical Record and Construction.* Canadian Ethnology service paper no. 110 (Ottawa, National Museums of Canada, 1987).

Armstrong, Joe C. W. *Champlain* (Toronto, 1987); includes "The Testament of Guillermo Elena," appendix II, 274–78.

———. *From Sea unto Sea: Art and Discovery Maps of Canada* (Scarborough, Ont., 1982).

Arsenault, Pauline. "Acadia in Champlain's New France: From Arcadia to China." In Raymonde Litalien and Denis Vaugeois, eds., *Champlain: The Birth of French America* (Montreal, 2004).

Asseline, David. *Antiquités et chroniques de la ville de Dieppe* (Dieppe, 1874).

Audiat, Louis. *Samuel de Champlain de Brouage, fondateur de Quebec, 1567–1635* (Saintes and La Rochelle, 1893); includes material from local histories.

Augeron, Mickaël, and Dominique Guillemet, eds. *Champlain, ou les portes du Nouveau Monde: cinq siècles d'échanges entre le Centre–Ouest français et l'Amérique du Nord, XVIe–XXe siècles* (Geste, 2004).

Aumale, duc d'. *Histoire des princes de Condé pendant les XVIe et XVIIe siècles* 8 vols. (Paris, 1855–96).

———. *Histoire des princes de Condé* (Paris, 1863–64).

Axtell, James. *The Invasion Within: The Conquest of Cultures in Colonial North America* (New York, 1985).

Babelon, Jean-Pierre. *Demeures parisiens sous Henri IV et Louis XIII* (Paris, 1965).

———. *Henri IV* (Paris, 1982).

Bachman, Van Cleaf. *Peltries or Plantations: The Economic Policies of the Dutch West India Company in New Netherland, 1623–1639* (Baltimore, 1909).

Bailey, Alfred G. *The Conflict of European and Eastern Algonkian Culture, 1594–1700* (Toronto, 1937, 1969, 1976).

Baker, Emerson et al. *American Beginnings: Exploration, Culture, and Cartography in the Land of Norumbega* (Lincoln, Neb., 1994).

Baker, William A. *Colonial Vessels: Some Seventeenth-Century Ship Designs* (Barre, Mass., 1962).

———. *The Mayflower and Other Colonial Vessels* (London, 1983).

Bakker, Peter. "A Basque Etymology for the Word 'Iroquois.'" *Man in the Northeast* 40 (1990), 89–93.

———. *Language of Our Own: The Genesis of Michif, the Mixed Cree-French Language of the Canadian Métis* (New York, 1997).

———. "The Language of the Coast Tribes in Half Basque," *Anthropological Linguistics* 3–4 (1989), 117–47.

Barbeau, Marius. *Huron and Wyandot Mythology* (Ottawa, 1915).

Barbeau, Philippe. *Le choc des patois en Nouvelle-France: essai sur l'histoire de la francisation au Canada* (Montreal, 1984).

Barbiche, Bernard. "Henri IV and the World Overseas: A Decisive Time in the History of New France." In Raymonde Litalien et Denis Vaugeois, eds., *Champlain: The Birth of French America* (Montreal, 2004).

Barkham, Selma Huxley. "The Basques: Filling a Gap in Our History between Jacques Cartier and Champlain." *Canadian Geographical Journal* 96 (1978), 8–19.

———. *The Basque Coast of Newfoundland* (n.p., 1989).

———. "The Documentary Evidence for Basque Whaling Ships in the Strait of Belle Isle." In G. M. Story, ed. *Early European Settlement and Exploitation in Atlantic Canada: Selected Papers* (St. John's, Nfld., 1982).

———. "The Basque Whaling Establishment in Labrador, 1536–1632: A Summary." *Arctic* 37 (1984), 515–19.

———. "A Note on the Strait of Belle Isle during the Period of Basque Contact with Indians and Inuit." *Études/Inuit/Studies* 4 (1980), 51–58.

Batiffol, Louis. *Le Louvre sous Henri IV et Louis XIII: la vie de la cour de France au XVIIe siècle* (Paris, 1930).

Baudry, René. "Charles d'Aulnay et la Compagnie de la Nouvelle-France." *Revue d'histoire de l'Amérique française* 11 (1957), 218–41.

———. "Madame de Champlain," *Les Cahiers de Dix* 33 (1968), 12–53.

———. "Nicolas Le Creux du Breuil." Ibid.

Baumgartner, Frederic. *Henri II, King of France, 1547–1559* (Durham, N.C., 1996).

Baxter, James Phinney. "Samuel de Champlain." *Acadiensis* 4 (1904).

Bayrou, François. *Henri IV: le roi libre* (Paris, 1994).

Beal, Bob, and Rod Macleod. *Prairie Fire* (Toronto, 1884, 1994).

Beaulieu, Alain. "The Birth of the Franco-American Alliance." In Raymonde Litalien and Denis Vaugeois, eds., *Champlain: The Birth of French America* (Montreal, 2004).

Beaulieu, Alain, and Réal Ouellet, eds. *Des Sauvages* (Montreal, 1993).

Bélanger, René. *Les Basques dans l'estuaire du Saint-Laurent, 1535–1635* (Montreal, 1971).

Benedict, Philip. "The Saint Bartholemew's Massacres in the Provinces." *Historical Journal* 21 (1978) 205–25.

Benes, Peter, and Jane Montague Benes, eds. *Algonkians of New England: Past and Present* (Boston, 1993).

Bent, C. *Life Histories of North American Birds of Prey* (1937; New York, 1961).

Berger de Xivrey, M., ed. *Recueil des lettres missives de Henri IV* (Paris, 1858).

Bergier, J. F. *Une Histoire du Sel* (Fribourg, 1982).

Bergin, Joseph. *Cardinal Richelieu: Power and the Pursuit of Wealth* (New Haven, 1985).

Berthiaume, Pierre. "Gabriel Sagard: le grand voyage du pays des Hurons." *Lettres québécoises* (Nov. 1977), 39–41.

Berton, Pierre. *My Country* (Toronto, 1990).

Besnard, Joseph. "Les diverses professions de Robert Giffard." *Nova Francia* 4 (1929), 322–29.

Bideau, Michel. "L'Indien de Champlain: objet ethnologique ou sujet de colonisation." In Gilles Thérien ed., *Les figures de l'Indien* (Montreal, 1988 and 1995).

———. "Des Sauvages: une singularité narrative." *Études françaises* 22 (1986), 35–45.

Biggar, Henry Percival. "The Death of Poutrincourt," *Revue canadienne* 18 (1882).

———. "The Death of Poutrincourt." *Canadian Historical Review* 1 (1920), 195–201.

———. *The Early Trading Companies of New France: A Contribution to the History of Commerce and Discovery in North America* (Toronto, 1901, 1937; rpt. Clifton, N.J., 1972).

———. "The French Hakluyt: Marc Lescarbot of Vervins." *American Historical Review* 6 (1901), 671–92.

———. "The Portrait of Champlain." *Canadian Historical Review* 1 (1920), 379–80.

Bildner, James L. *A Visual Cruising Guide to the Maine Coast* (Camden, Me., 2006).

Binot, Guy. *Pierre Dugua de Mons, gentilhomme royannais, premier colonisateur du Canada, lieutenant général de la Nouvelle-France de 1603 à 1612* (Royan, 2004).

Bishop, Morris. *Champlain: The Life of Fortitude* (New York, 1948, 1963).

———. "Champlain's Veracity: A Defence of the *Brief Discours*." *Queen's Quarterly* 66 (1959), 127–34.

———. "The Marquis de la Roche and Sable Island." In *Champlain: A Life of Fortitude* (New York, 1948, 1963), 347–49.

Blémus, René. *Jean Nicollet en Nouvelle-France: Un Normand à la découverte des grands lacs canadiens (1598–1642)* (Cherbourg, 1988).

Blondel-Loisel, Annie, and Raymonde Litalien, eds., in collaboration with Jean Paul Barbiche and Claude Briot, *De la Seine au Saint Laurent avec Champlain* (Paris, 2005).

Bonnault, Claude de. "Champlain et les Espagnols." Essay in the René Baudry Collection, Library and Archives Canada.

———. "Encore le Brief Discours: Champlain a-t-il été à Blavet en 1598?" *Bulletin des recherches historiques* 60 (1954), 59–64.

Bonnault, Claude de, and L.-A. Vigneras. "Le Voyage de Samuel Champlain aux Indes occidentales." *Revue d'histoire de l'Amérique française* XI (1957), 163–200.

Bordenave, Nicolas de. *Histoire de Béarn et de Navarre* (Paris, 1873).

Bordonove, Georges. *Henri IV le Grand* (Paris, 1891).

Bouchard Russel. *Les armes à feu en Nouvelle-France* (Sillery, Quebec, 1999).

———. *Le dernier des Montagnais: de la préhistoire au début du XVIIIe siècle* (Chicoutimi-Nord, 1995).

Bouchet, Marie-Claude. *Pierre Dugua de Mons* (Royan, 1999).

Boulanger, Georges. "Samuel de Champlain, instaurateur de la langue française en Amérique du Nord." *Concorde* (Quebec [Quebec City's monthly magazine], n.d.), 6.

Bourque, Bruce. *Diversity and Complexity in Prehistoric Maritime Societies: A Gulf of Maine Perspective* (New York, 1995).

———. "Ethnicity on the Maritime Peninsula, 1600–1759." *Ethnohistory* 36 (1989) 257–84.

———. *Twelve Thousand Years: American Indians in Maine* (Lincoln, Neb., 2001).

Bourque, J. Rodolphe. *Social and Architectural Aspects of Acadians in New Brunswick* (Fredericton, 1971).

Bridenbaugh, Carl. *No Peace Beyond the Line* (New York and Oxford, 1972).

Bradley, James, and S. Terry Childs. "Basque Earrings and Panther's Tails: The Form of Cross-Cultural Contact in Sixteenth-Century Iroquoia." In Robert M. Ehrenreich, ed., *Metals in Society: Theory beyond Analysis* (Philadelphia, 1991).

Bragdon, Kathleen J. *Native People of Southern New England* (Norman, Okla., 1996).

Brandão, José António. *Your Fyre Shall Burn No More: Iroquois Policy toward New France and Its Native Allies to 1701* (1997, Lincoln, Neb., 2000).

Bréard, Charles. *Le vieux Honfleur et ses marin: biographies et récits maritimes* (Rouen, 1897).

Brooks, R. C. "A Problem of Provenance: A Technical Analysis of the 'Champlain' Astrolabe," *Cartographica* 36 (1999), 1–16.

Brown, Jennifer S. H. "People of Myth, People of History: A Look at Recent Writings on the Métis." *Acadiensis* 17 (1987) 150–62.

———. "Métis, Halfbreeds, and Other Real People: Changing Cultures and Categories." *The History Teacher* 27 (1993) 20.

Brown, Stephen R. *Scurvy* (New York, 2003).

Bruchési, Jean. "Champlain a-t-il menti? [Champlain: Was He a Liar?] *Cahiers des Dix,* 15 (1950) 39–53; rpt. as "Champlain aurait-il menti?"

Brunelle, Gayle K. *The New World Merchants of Rouen, 1559–1630* (Kirksville, Mo., 1950).

Buisseret, David. *Henry IV* (London, 1984).

———. *Sully and the Growth of Centralized Government in France, 1598–1610* (London, 1968).

———. *The Mapmaker's Quest: Depicting New Worlds in Renaissance Europe* (Oxford, 2003).

Bull, Stephen. *An Historical Guide to Armes and Armour* (New York, 1991).

Bunle, Henri. *Mouvements migratoires entre la France et l'étranger* (Paris, 1943).

Bures, Maurice. *Le type saintongeais* (Paris, 1908; Le Croît Vif, 1991).

Burley, David V. "Proto-Historic Ecological Effects of the Fur Trade on Micmac Culture in Northeastern New Brunswick." *Ethnohistory* 38 (1981) 3:203–16.

Burnet, M., and D. O. White. *Natural History of Infectious Disease* (Cambridge, 1972).

Butterfield, Consul Willshire. *History of the Discovery of the Northwest by John Nicolet* (Cincinnati, 1881).

———. *History of Brulé's Discoveries and Explorations, 1610–1626* (Cleveland, 1898).

Cabanès, (Docteur). *Les Condé: Grandeur et dégénérescence d'une famille princière* 2 vols. (Paris, n.d., [1932]).

Caesar, Julius. *The Gallic Wars* (London, 1970).

Callame, Bernard, and Isabelle Delavaud. *Brouage et son marais: pour une meilleure connaissance des marais littoraux en Charente-Maritime* (Saintes, 1996).

Calloway, Colin, ed., *Dawnland Encounters: Indians and Europeans in Northern New England* (Hanover, 1991).

Campeau, Lucien. *Les finances publiques de la Nouvelle-France, sous les Cent-Associés, 1632–1635* (Montreal, 1975).

———. "Bonaventure, enfant montagnais." *Monumenta Novae Franciae* 2:803 (Quebec, 1967).

———. *Les Cent-Associés et le Peuplement de la Nouvelle-France (1633–1663)* (Montreal, 1974).

———. "Les Jésuites ont-ils retouché les écrits de Champlain?" *Revue d'Histoire de l'Amérique française* 5 (1951) 3:340–61.

———. *Les Cent-Associés et le peuplement de la Nouvelle-France, 1633–63* (Montreal, 1974).

———. *Les finances publiques de la Nouvelle-France sous les Cent-Associés, 1632–1665* (Montreal, 1975).

———. "Autour de la relation du Père Pierre Biard." *Revue d'histoire de l'Amérique française* 6 (1953) 517–35.

———. *Catastrophe démographique sur les Grands Lacs: les premiers habitants du Québec* (Montreal, 1986).

———. "La grande crise de 1612 à Port-Royal." *Lettres du Bas-Canada* 15 (1961) 7–27.

———. "La première mission des Jésuites en Nouvelle-France." *Lettres du Bas-Canada* 15 (1961), 129–57.

———. "Notre-Dame-des-Anges." *Lettres du Bas-Canada* 8 (1954) 77–107.

Carmona, Michel. *La France de Richelieu* (Paris, 1984).

———. *Le Louvre et les Tuileries: huit siècles d'histoire* (Paris, 2004).

———. *Marie de Médicis* (Brussels, 1984).

Caron, Ivanhoe. *Liste des prêtres et religieux qui ont exercé le saint Ministère en Canada (1604 à 1629), Bulletin des recherches historiques* 47 (1941) 76–78.

Carpenter, Kenneth J. *The History of Scurvy and Vitamin C* (Cambridge, 1986).

Carpenter, Roger M. *The Renewed, the Destroyed, and the Remade: The Three Thought Worlds of the Iroquois and the Huron, 1609–1650* (East Lansing, Michigan, 2004).

Carpin, Garvais. *Histoire d'un mot: l'ethnonyme Canadien de 1535 à 1691* (Sillery, Quebec, 1995).

———. *Le réseau du Canada: Étude du mode migratoire de la France vers la Nouvelle-France (1628–1662)* (Quebec and Paris, 2001).

Casgrain, Henri-Raymond: *Champlain: sa vie et son caractère* (Quebec, 1898; Paris, 1900).

Castagnos, Pierre. *Richelieu face à la mer* (Rennes, 1989).

Castelot, André. *Henri IV, le passionné* (Paris, 1986).

Castries, *Henri IV, roi de coeur roi de France* (Paris, 1970).

Cell, Gillian T. *Newfoundland Discovered: English Attempts at Colonisation, 1610–1630* (London, 1982).

Cervigon, F[ernando]. *Las perlas en la historia de Venezuela* (Caracas, 1998).

Chabot, M.-E. "Boullé, Hélène." In George Williams Brown (ed.), *Dictionary of Canadian Biography/Dictionnaire biographique du Canada* vol. 1 (Sainte Foy, 1966). Also available in web text.

Chapelle, Howard I. *American Small Craft: Their Design, Development, and Construction* (New York, 1951).

Charbonneau, Hubert, et al. *Naissance d'une population: les Francais établis au Canada au XVIIe siècle* (Montreal and Paris, 1987); tr. by Paola Colozzo as *The First French Canadians: Pioneers in the St. Lawrence Valley* (Newark, Del., 1993).

Chinard, Gilbert. *L'Amérique et la rêve exotique dans la littérature française au XVIIe et XVIIIe siècles* (Paris, 1913).

Chartier, Roger et al. *L'éducation en France du XVIe au XVIIIe siècles* (Paris, 1976).

Choisy, Abbé de. *Mémoires de l'Abbé de Choisy*. Ed. by Georges Mongrédien; Book xii: *Biographie générale, Biographie universelle,* and *Les Amours du Grand Alcandre* [a Catholic pejorative for Henry IV] (Paris, 1966, 2000).

Choquette, Leslie. *Frenchmen into Peasants: Modernity and Tradition in the People of French Canada* (Cambridge, Mass., 1997); tr. as *De Français à paysans: modernité et tradition dans le peuplement du Canada français* (Quebec, 2001).

Christianson, David J. "Belleisle 1983: Excavations of a Pre-Expulsion Acadian Site," *Curatorial Report 48* (Halifax, 1984).

Christou, Marie-Françoise, "Les ballets-mascarades des Fêtes de la Forêt de Saint-Germain et de la Douairière de Billebahaut et l'oeuvre de Daniel Rabel." *Revue d'histoire du théâtre* 1 (1961).

Clark, Andrew H. *Acadia: The Geography of Nova Scotia to 1760* (Madison, 1968).

Clément, Daniel, ed. *The Algonquins* (Hull, 1996).

Codignola, Luca. "Le prétendu voyage de Samuel de Champlain aux Indes occidentales, 1599–1601." In Madeline Frédéric et Serge Jasumain, eds., *La relation de voyage: un document historique et littéraire.* Actes du séminaire de Bruxelles (Brussels, 1999), 61–80.

Codignola, Luca. "Samuel de Champlain et les mystères de son voyage au Indes occidentales, 1599–1601: l'état de la recherche et quelques routes à suivre." In Cecilia Rizza, ed., *La découverte de nouveaux mondes: aventure et voyages imaginaires au XVIIe siècle.* Actes du XXIIe Colloque du Centre Méridional de Rencontres sur le XVIIe siècle, Gênes 23–25 January, 1992 (Fasano, 1993).

Colden, Cadwallader. *History of the Five Indian Nations* (1727, 1747); rpt., 1866 (Ithaca, 1958).

Constantin-Weyer, M. *Champlain* (Paris, 1931).

Cook, Peter. "Vivre comme frères: Le rôle du registre fraternel dans les premières alliances franco-amérindiennes au Canada (vers 1580–1650)," *Recherches amérindiennes au Québec* 31 (2001), 55–65.

Coolidge, Guy Omeron. *The French Occupation of the Champlain Valley from 1609 to 1759* (1938, Flieschmanns, N.Y., 1999).

Corbett, Julian S. *Drake and the Tudor Navy,* 2 vols. (London, 1892).

Couillard-Després, Azarie. *La premiere famille française au Canada;* and *Louis Hébert: premier colon canadien et sa famille* (Lille, 1913; Montreal, 1918).

———. *Charles de Saint-Étienne de La Tour, gouverneur, lieutenant-général en Acadie, et son temps, 1593–1666* (Arthabaska, 1930).

Crépeau, André, and Brenda Dunn. "The Melanson Settlement: An Acadian Farming Community (ca. 1664–1755)," Canadian Parks Research Bulletin 250 (Ottawa, 1986).

Cruickshank, J. G., and C. E. Heidenreich. "Pedological Investigations at the Huron Indian Village of Cahiagué." *Canadian Geographer* 13 (1969) 34–46.

Crouse, N. M. *Contributions of the Canadian Jesuits to the Geographic Knowledge of New France, 1632–75* (Ithaca, 1924).

Cummins, John. *Francis Drake: The Lives of a Hero* (New York, 1995, 1997).

Daeffler, Michael. "La peintre et l'archéologue." In Annie Blondel-Loisel and Raymonde Litalien et al., eds. *De la Seine au Saint-Laurent avec Champlain* (Paris, 2005), 103–15.

Davenport, Francis G., ed. *European Treaties Bearing on the History of the United States and Its Dependencies* (Washington, 1914).

Davis, Natalie Zemon. "The Rites of Violence and Religious Riots in Sixteenth-Century France." *Past and Present* 59 (1973); rpt in *Society and Culture in early Modern France* (Palo Alto, 1976).

Dawson, Joan. *Isaac de Razilly, 1587–1635: Founder of La Hève* (La Have, Nova Scotia, 1982).

Day, G. M. "Iroquois, An Etymology." *Ethnohistory* 15 (1968), 389–402.

De Bry, Théodore. *Théâtre du Nouveau Monde: les grands voyages de Théodore de Bry.* Ed. Marc Bouyer and Jean-Paul Duviols (Paris, 1992).

Dechêne, Louise. *Habitants and Merchants in Seventeenth-Century Montreal* (Montreal, 1992).

Delafosse, Marcel. "L'oncle de Champlain." *Revue d'histoire de l'Amérique française* 12 (1958) 208–16.

Delafosse, Marcel, and Claude Laveau. *Le Commerce du sel de Brouage aux XVIIe et XVIIIe siècles*; published as *Cahiers des Annales*, 17 (Paris, 1960) 13–26.

Delâge, Denys. *Le pays renversé: Amérindiens et Européens en Amérique du Nordest, 1600–1664* (Montreal, 1985); tr. by Jane Brierley as *Bitter Feast; Amerindians and Europeans in Northeastern North America, 1600–1664* (Vancouver, 1993).

———. "Le premiers contacts." In Sylvie Vincent, ed., "Traditions et récits sur l'arrivée des Européens en Amérique." *Recherches amérindiennes au Québec* 22 (1992), 101–16.

———. "Les influences amérindiennes sur la culture matérielle des colons de la Nouvelle France." In Michel Fortin, ed., *L'archéologie et la rencontre de deux mondes* (Quebec, 1992), 173–203.

Dennis, Matthew. *Cultivating a Landscape of Peace: Iroquois-European Encounters in Seventeenth-Century America* (Ithaca, 1993, 1995).

De Repentigny, Léo-Guy. *La Ferme d'en bas du Cap Tourmente* (Quebec, 1989).

Deschamps, Hubert. *Les Voyages de Samuel Champlain: Saintongeais, père du Canada* (Paris, 1951); includes a biographical essay.

———. "Pierre de Mons: fondateur de l'Acadie et du Canada." *Revue d'histoire des colonies françaises* (1956).

———. *Roi de la brousse: mémoires d'autres mondes* (Paris, 1975).

Deschamps, Léon. "Un colonisateur du temps de Richelieu. Isaac de Razilly: Biographie. Mémoire inédit." *Revue de géographie* (Oct. 1886), not seen.

———. *Un Colonisateur au temps de Richelieu: Isaac de Razilly* (Paris, 1887).

Deslandres, Dominique. *Croire et faire croire* (Paris, 2003).

Desplat, Christian. *Cultures en Béarn* (Librairie des Pyrénées et de Gascogne, 2001).

Desrosiers, Léo-Paul. *Iroquoisie 1534–1632* (Montreal, 1947); new edition with a preface by Denis Vaugeois and introduction by Alain Beaulieu (Quebec, 1998).

Dever, Harry. "The Nicolet Myth." *Michigan History* 50 (1966), 318–22.

Dickason, Olive Patricia. *Canada's First Nations: A History of Founding Peoples from Earliest Times* (Toronto, 1992).

———. *The Myth of the Savage* (Edmonton, 1984).

———. *The Myth of the Savage and the Beginnings of French Colonization in the Americas* (Edmonton, 1984).

Dickinson, John A. "La guerre Iroquoise et la mortalité en Nouvelle France, 1608–1666," *Revue d'histoire de l'Amérique française* 35 (1982), 31–54.

———. "The Pre-contact Huron Population: A Reappraisal." *Ontario History* 72 (1980) 173–79.

———. "Champlain, Administrator." In Litalien and Vaugeois, eds., *Champlain: The Birth of French America* (Montreal, 2004) 211–17.

Diefendorf, Barbara B. *Beneath the Cross: Catholics and Huguenots in Sixteenth-Century Paris* (Oxford, 1991).

Dièreville, Simon. *Relation du Voyage de Port Royal de l'Acadie, 1699–1700* (Amsterdam, 1710).

Dionne, Narcisse-Eutrope. *Champlain: fondateur de Québec et père de la Nouvelle-France,* 2 vols. (Quebec, 1891, 1926). An abridged edition was published in English as *Champlain: Founder of Quebec, Father of New France* (Toronto, 1962).

———. "Le plus grand des Souriquois." *Revue canadienne* 26 (1890) 577–86.

———. "Le sauvage Pastedechouan en France." *Bulletin des recherches historiques* 13 (1907) 120–24.

———. "Les Indiens en France." *Revue canadienne* 26 (1890) 641–58.

———. "Miscou, hommes de mer et hommes de Dieu." *Canada français* 2 (1889) 432–77, 514–31.

Doiron, Normand. "Sainte-Croix: le nom et le lieu." *Études canadiennes/Canadian Studies* (1984) 17.

Donkin, R. A. *Beyond Price: Pearls and Pearl Fishing: Origins to the Age of Discoveries* (Philadelphia, 1998).

Doughty, A. G. "Le drapeau de la Nouvelle-France." *Mémoires de la Société royale du Canada* 20 (1926) I:43–46.

Doyan, Pierre-Simon. "L'iconographie botanique en Amérique française du XVIIe au milieu du XVIIIe siècle." Ph.D. dissertation, History Department, Université de Montréal (1993).

Drouin, Alice. *Les marais salants en Aunis et Saintonge jusqu'en 1789* (Royan, 1999).

Duccini, Hélène. *Concini; Grandeur et misère du favori de Marie de Médicis* (Paris, 1991).

Ducharlet, Émile. *Samuel Champlain, enfant de Brouage.* Comité du mémorial des origines de la Nouvelle-France, Brouage, et La Lucarne ovale (2002).

———. "Olivier le Tardif." *ASGCF Mémoires* 12 (1961) 4–20.

Dumas, G.-M. "Le Ballif, Georges." In George Williams Brown (ed.), *DCB/DBC* Online: http://www.biographi.ca/EN/index.html.

Dumas, Silvio. *La Chapelle Champlain et Notre-Dame-de-Recouvrance* (Quebec, 1958).

Dunn, Brenda. *A History of Port Royal/Annapolis Royal, 1605–1800* (Halifax, 2004).

Durand, Yves. *L'Ordre du monde: idéal politique et valeurs sociales en France du XVIe–XVIIIe siècle* (Paris, 2001).

Eccles, W. J. "Samuel de Champlain: Father of New France." *American Historical Review* 78, 4 (1973) 1147–48.

Eckstrom, Fannie Hardy. *Old John Neptune and Other Maine Indian Shamans* (1945; rpt Portland, 1980).

Egnal, Mark. *New World Economies* (Oxford, 1998).

Emerson, N. "Cahiagué." Mimeo: University of Toronto Archaeological Field School (Orillia, 1961).

Émont, Bernard. *Marc Lescarbot: mythes et rêves fondateurs de la Nouvelle France* (Paris, Budapest, and Turin, 2002).

Engelbrecht, William. *Iroquoia: The Development of a Native World* (Syracuse, 2003).

Erlanger, Philippe. *La vie quotidienne sous Henri IV* (Paris, 1958, 1977).

Evans, Donna. "On Coexistence and Convergence of two Phonological systems in Michif." Work Papers of the Summer Institute of Linguistics, University of North Dakota Session, 26, 158–73.

Fagnez, Gustave. *L'économie sociale de la France sous Henri IV (1589–1610)* (Geneva, 1975).

Fenton, William N., and Ernest Dodge. "An Elm Bark Canoe in the Peabody Museum of Salem." *American Neptune* 9 (1949) 185–206.

Fenton, William N. *The Great Law and the Long House: A Political History of the Iroquois Confederacy* (Norman, Okla., 1998).

Ferland, Abbé J. B.-A. *Cours d'histoire du Canada* 2 vols. (Quebec, 1861–65).

ffoulkes, Charles. *The Armourer and His Craft* (London, 1912).

Finley-Croswhite, S. Annette. *Henri IV and the Towns: The Pursuit of Legitimacy in French Urban Society, 1589–1610* (Cambridge, 1999).

Fiquet, Nathalie, and François-Yves Le Blanc. *Brouage, ville royale, et les villages du golfe de Saintonge* (Chauray-Niort, 1997).

Fiquet, Nathalie. "Brouage in the Time of Champlain: A New Town Open to the World." In Raymonde Litalien and Denis Vaugeois, eds., *Champlain: The Birth of French America* (Montreal, 2004), 35, 33–42.

Fischer, David Hackett. *Albion's Seed: Four British Folkways in America* (New York and Oxford, 1989).

———. "Forenames and the Family in New England: An Exercise in Historical Onomastics." In Robert M. Taylor, Jr. and Ralph J. Crandall, *Generations and Change: Genealogical Perspectives in Social History* (Macon, Ga., 1986).

———. *The Great Wave: Price Revolutions and the Rhythm of History* (New York, 1996; 4th printing, New York, 2006).

———. *Liberty and Freedom* (New York and Oxford, 2006).

Fisher, Roger. *L'art de restaurer une maison paysanne* (Paris, 1966).

Fitzgerald, W. R. "Is the Warminster Site Champlain's Cahiagué?" *Ontario Archaeology* 45 (1986) 3–7.

Forbes, Allan, and Paul Cadman. *France and New England,* 3 vols. (Boston, 1925–29).

Fortier, Loftus M. *Champlain's Order of Good Cheer and some Brief Notes Relating to Its Founder* (Toronto, 1928).

Fortin, Jean. *Montagnais de la Côte Nord* (Quebec, 1992).

Fournier, Georges, s.j. *Hydrographie, contenant la théorie et la pratique de toutes les parties de la navigation* (Paris, 1643, 1667).

Francis, John K. *Champion Trees of Puerto Rico* (United States Department of Agriculture, Forest Service, International Institute of Tropical Forestry, Rio Piedras, Puerto Rico, 2001).

Francis, John K., and Carol A. Lowe, eds. "Bioecología de Arboles Nativos y Exóticos de Puerto Rico y las Indias Occidentales." United States Department of Agriculture, Forest Service, International Institute of Tropical Forestry, Rio Piedras, Puerto Rico, General Technical Report IITF-15 (June, 2000).

Frati, Lodovico. "Samuel Champlain et son voyage aux Indes occidentales." *Bulletin de la Société de géographie de Québec* 19 (1925), not seen.

Gagnon, François-Marc. "De la bonne manière de faire la guerre. Analyse de quatre gravures dans les Œuvres de Champlain." *Études littéraires* 10 (1977) 1–2.

———. "Is the *Brief Discours* by Champlain?" In Raymonde Litalien and Denis Vaugeois, eds. *Champlain: The Birth of French America* (2004), 83–92; draws on the author's *"Le Brief Discours* est-il de Champlain?" *Cahiers d'histoire* 4 (1983).

Gagnon, François-Marc. "L'iconographie indienne." In Daniel Drouin, ed., *Louis-Philippe Hébert* (Montreal, 2001).

———. *Ces hommes dits sauvages* (Montreal, 1984).

———. *Premiers peintres de la Nouvelle-France* 2 vols. (Quebec, 1976).

Gagnon, Philéas. *Essai de bibliographie canadienne* (Quebec City, 1895).

———. *Essai d'une bibliographie canadienne* (Quebec, 1895).

———. "Notes bibliographiques sur les écrits de Champlain, manuscrits et imprimés." *Bulletin de la Société de géographie de Québec* 3 (1908) 55–77.

Gagnon, Serge. *Le Québec et ses historiens* (Quebec, 1978), of which portions are translated as *Quebec and Its Historians, 1840–1920* (Montreal, 1982); and *Quebec and Its Historians: The Twentieth Century* (Montreal, 1985).

———. "The Historiography of New France, 1960–1974." *Journal of Canadian Studies* 13 (1978) 80–99.

Ganong, William Francis. "Champlain's Narrative of the Exploration and First Settlement of Acadia." *Acadiensis* 5 (1904) 4.

———. "Crucial Maps in the Early Cartography and Place Nomenclature of the Atlantic Coast of Canada." *Transactions of the Royal Society of Canada*, sec. 2, vol. 25 (1931); also published as *Crucial Maps in the Early Cartography and Place-Nomenclature of the Atlantic Coast of Canada* (Toronto, 1964).

———. "Ste. Croix (Dochet) Island." *Transactions of the Royal Society of Canada* (1902); revised and republished by Susan Brittain Ganong (Saint John, N.B., 1945) and reprinted in 1979, and again reprinted as *Champlain's Island* with a new foreword and preface (Saint John, N.B., 2003).

———. "The Identity of the Animals and Plants Mentioned by the Early Voyagers to Eastern Canada and Newfoundland." *Proceedings and Transactions of the Royal Society of Canada* (1903) 3.

———. "The History of Miscou and Shippegan," revised and enlarged from the author's notes by Susan Brittain, *New Brunswick Historical Studies* 5 (Saint John, N.B., 1946), 42–45. Ganong also wrote on the natural history of the island in *Bulletin of the Natural History Society of New Brunswick* 5:449–64; "La première compagnie de Miscou, 1635–45," *Revue d'histoire de l'Amérique française* 363.

———. "A Visitor's Impressions of the Champlain Tercentenary." *Acadiensis* 5 (1904), 15–23.

Garneau, François-Xavier. *Histoire du Canada, depuis sa découverte jusqu'à nos jours*; second edition, corrected and enlarged, 3 vols. (Quebec, 1852); and Andrew Bell, *History of Canada from the Time of Its Discovery till the Union Year (1840–1) translated from Histoire du Canada of F.-X. Garneau, Esq.* 3 vols. (Montreal, 1860).

Garrisson, Janine. *L'Edit de Nantes et sa révocation: histoire d'une intolérance* (Paris, 1985).

———. *Henry IV* (Paris, 1984) 46–52.

Gellner, Ernest. *Nation and Nationalism* (Oxford, 1983).

Gilbert, Roger Paul. *De l'arquebuse à la bure* (Montreal, 1999).

Girard, Camil, and Mathieu D'Avignon. "Champlain et les Montagnais (Innus): alliances, diplomatie et justice. Ingérence et déférence. 1600–1635." Actes du colloque D'Amérique et d'Atlantique (Tadoussac, 2000).

Girard, Camil, and Édith Gagné. "Première alliance interculturelle: rencontre entre Montagnais et Français à Tadoussac en 1603." *Recherches Amérindiennes au Québec* 25 (1995) 3–14.

Girard, Camil, and Normand Perron, *Histoire du Saguenay-Lac-Saint-Jean* (Quebec, 1995).

Giraud, Marcel. *Le Métis canadien: son rôle dans l'histoire des provinces de l'ouest* (1945); tr. by George Woodcock as *The Metis in the Canadian West* (Edmonton, 1986).

Giraudo, Laura. "Research Report: A Mission to Spain." In Raymonde Litalien et Denis Vaugeois, eds. *Champlain: The Birth of French America* (Montreal, 2004), 63–82.

———. "The Manuscripts of the *Brief Discours.*" In Raymonde Litalien et Denis Vaugeois, eds. *Champlain: The Birth of French America* (Montreal, 2004), 93–97.

Giroux, T.-E. *Robert Giffard, seigneur colonisateur au tribunal de l'histoire* (Quebec, 1934).

Glénisson, Caroline Montel. *Champlain: la découverte du Canada* (n.p., 2004).

———. *Un tour de France canadien: guide des noms et des lieux aux sources de la Nouvelle-France* (Montreal, 1979).

Glénisson, Jean. *La France d'Amérique: voyages de Samuel Champlain* (Paris, 1994).

———. "Champlain's Voyage Accounts: Interview with Jean Glénisson." In Raymonde Litalien et Denis Vaugeois, eds. *Champlain: The Birth of French America* (Montreal, 2004) 179–283.

———. "Samuel Champlain et François Gravé, sieur du Pont, remontent le Saint-Laurent." In Henri-Alexandre Wallon, *Célébrations nationales* (Paris, 2003).

Godbout, Archance. "Poisson." *Mémoires de la Societé généalogique canadienne-française* 3, 183–191.

———. "Nos hérédités provinciales françaises." *Les archives de folklore* 1 (1946) 26–40.

Goddard, Ives. "Synonymy." In B. G. Trigger, ed., *Handbook of North American Indians*, vol. 15: *Northeast* (Washington, 1978).

Gosselin, Abbé Auguste. "Le vrai monument de Champlain: ses Oeuvres éditées par Laverdière." *Mémoires de la Societé Royale du Canada* 1 (1908) 3–23.

Gosselin, Amédée. "Champlain, Sa jeunesse. Voyage aux Indes occidentales." *Bulletin de la Société de géographie de Québec* 3 (1908) 2.

———. "Olivier le tardif, juge-prévôt de Beaupré." *RSCT*, ser. 3, 17 (1923) 1–16.

Gravier, Gabriel. *Vie de Samuel de Champlain, fondateur de la Nouvelle-France* (Paris, 1900).

Gravit, Francis W. "Un document inédit sur le Canada; Raretés rapportées du Nouveau Monde par M. de Monts," *Revue de l'Université de Laval* 4 (1946), 282–88.

Greenblatt, Stephen. *Marvelous Possessions: The Wonder of the New World* (Chicago, 1991).

Greengrass, Mark. *France in the Age of Henry IV* (1984, London; 2d edition, 1995).

Grelle, Maxime le. *Brouage-Quebec: foi de pionniers* (St. Jean-d'Angély, 1980).

Grenon, Jean-Yves. *Dugua de Mons: fondateur de l'Acadie (1604–05), co-fondateur de Québec (1608)* (first published in French, 1997, 1999); *Pierre Dugua de Mons, Founder of Acadia (1604–05), Cofounder of Quebec (1608)* (bilingual edition, Annapolis Royal, Peninsular Press, 2000).

Griffiths, Naomi. *The Acadians: Creation of a People* (Toronto, 1973).

Groulart, Claude. *Mémoires, ou voyages par lui faits en cour* (Paris, 1838).

Goubert, Jean-Pierre. *La conquête de l'eau* (Paris, 1986).

Guillet, Bertrand, and Louise Pothier, eds. *France, Nouvelle-France: naissance d'un peuple français en Amérique* (Montreal and Paris, 2005).

Guimont, Jacques. *La Petite-ferme du Cap Tourmente: de la ferme de Champlain aux grandes volées d'oies* (Quebec, 1996).

Hagan, William T. *The Sac and Fox Indians* (Norman, Okla., 1958).

Hall, Robert L. "Rethinking Jean Nicollet's route to the Ho-Chucks in 1634"; and Michael McCafferty, "Where did Jean Nicollet meet the Winnebago in 1634? A Critique of Robert L. Hall's 'Rethinking Jean Nicollet's Route . . . '" *Ontario History* 96 (2004) 170–82; with corrections in ibid. (2005).

Hamelin, Jean. "Charles Huault de Montmagny." DCB/DBC Online http:www.biograph.ca/EN/Index.html.

Hare, John, et al. *Histoire de la Ville de Quebec, 1608–1871* (Montreal, 1987).

Harrington, Faith. "We Tooke Great Store of Cod-fish: Fishing Ships and First Settlements on the

Coast of New England, 1600–1630." In W. Baker et al., eds. *American Beginnings: Exploration, Culture, and Cartography in the Land of Norumbega* (Lincoln, Neb., 1993).

Harris, J. T. *The Peregrine Falcon in Greenland* (Columbia, Mo., 1981).

Harris, Richard Colebrook. *The Seigneurial System in Early Canada: A Geographical Study* (Madison, 1968).

———. *Historical Atlas of Canada: From the Beginning to 1800* (Toronto, 1987).

Harrisse, Henry. *Découverte et évolution cartographique de Terre-Neuve et des pays circonvoisins 1497–1501–1769* (Paris, 1900).

———. *Notes pour servir à l'histoire, à la bibliographie et à la cartographie de la Nouvelle-France et des pays adjacents, 1545–1700* (Paris, 1872).

Hayne, David M. "Charlevoix," *DCB/DBC* Online http://www.biographi.ca/EN/index.html.

Heidenreich, Conrad E. "An Analysis of Champlain's Maps in Terms of his Estimates of Distance, Latitude and Longitude." *Revue de l'Université d'Ottawa/University of Ottawa Quarterly* 48 (1978) 1–2, 11–45.

———. "The Beginning of French Exploration out of the St. Lawrence Valley: Motives, Methods, and Changing Attitudes towards Native People." In Germaine Warkentin and Carolyn Podruchny, eds., *Decentring the Renaissance: Canada and Europe in Multidisciplinary Perspective 1500–1700* (Toronto, 2001), 236–51.

———. "Estimates of Distance Employed on 17th and Early 19th Century Maps of Canada." *Canadian Cartographer* 12 (1975) 121–37.

———. *Explorations and Mapping of Samuel de Champlain, 1603–1632* (Toronto, 1976).

———. "Explorations and Mapping of Samuel de Champlain 1603–1632." *Cartographica* (1976) 17.

———. *Huronia* (Toronto, 1971).

Heidenreich, Conrad E., and Edward H. Dahl. "The Two States of Champlain's *Carte Geographique*," *Canadian Cartographer* 16 (1979), 1–16.

Henripin, Jacques. *La population canadienne au début du XVIIIe siècle: nuptualité-fecondité-mortalité infantile* (Paris, 1954).

Henry, Louis. *Fécondité des mariages: nouvelle méthode de mesure* (Paris, 1953).

Henzeli, Victor Egon. *Missionary Linguistics in New France: A Study of Seventeenth and Eighteenth Century Description of American Indian Languages* (Paris, 1989).

Hill, Henry Raymond. "The Champlain Tercentenary," First report of the New York Lake Champlain Tercentenary Commissions (Albany, 1913).

Hodgen, Margaret T. *Early Anthropology in the Sixteenth and Seventeenth Centuries* (Philadelphia, 1964).

Hollingsworth, Michael. *The History of the Village of the Small Huts* (Winnipeg,1985).

Hudak, Heather. *Samuel de Champlain* (Discovering Canada) (Calgary, 2005).

Hugolin, Marie-Lemay. *L'établissement des Récollets de la province de Saint-Denis à Plaisance en l'île de Terre-Neuve* (Quebec, 1911).

Huguet, Adrian. *Jean de Poutrincourt: fondateur de Port-Royal en Acadie, Vice-Roi du Canada, 1557–1615; Campagnes, voyages et aventures d'un colonisateur sous Henri IV* (Amiens and Paris, 1932).

———. "Jean de Poutrincourt: fondateur de Port-Royal en Acadie, vice-roi du Canada." *Mémoires de la Société des Antiquaires de Picardie* 44 (Amiens and Paris, 1932).

Humphreys, John. *Plaisance: Problems of Settlement at this Newfoundland Outpost of New France, 1660–1690* (Ottawa, 1970).

Hunt, George T. *The Wars of the Iroquois: A Study in Intertribal Trade Relations* (Madison, 1960).

Huvet-Martinet, Micheline. *L'Aventure du Sel* (Rennes, 1995).

Innis, Harold. *Essays in Canadian Economic History* (Toronto, 1956).

———. *The Cod Fisheries: The History of an International Economy*; revised edition (Toronto, 1956).

———. *The Fur Trade in Canada: An Introduction to Canadian Economic History*; revised edition (Toronto, 1956).

Isaacs, Hope L. "*Orenda* and the Concept of Power among the Tonawanda Seneca." In Raymond D. Fogelson and Richard Adams, eds., *The Anthropology of Power: Ethnographic Studies from Asia, Oceana, and the New World* (New York, 1977), 168–73.

Jack, David Russell. "Proposed Champlain Memorial at Saint John, N.B." *Acadiensis* 5 (1901).

Jaenen, Cornelius J. "The Meeting of the French and Amerindians in the Seventeenth Century." In J. M. Bumsted, ed., *Interpreting Canada's Past*: vol. 1, *Before Confederation* (Toronto, 1986).

———. *Friend and Foe* (Toronto, 1976).

———. *The Role of the Church in New France* (Toronto, 1976).

Jamet, Dom Albert, ed. *Les Annales de l'Hôtel-Dieu de Québec, 1636–1716* (Quebec, 1984).

Jannini, Aniel. "La ricezione dei Voyages di Champlain nelle storiografia letteraria." *Scritti sulla Nouvelle-France nel seicento* (Bari and Paris, 1984), 27–29.

Jardine, Lisa. *The Awful End of William the Silent: The First Assassination of a Head of State with a Handgun* (London, 2005).

Jeffreys, Charles W. *The Reconstruction of the Port Royal Habitation of 1605–13* (n.p., n.d.).

Jenness, Diamond. *The Indians of Canada* (n.p., 1932).

Johnson, Hugh. *The World Atlas of Wine* (New York, 1971, 1977).

Johnson, Laurence, and Charles A. Martijn. "Les Malécotes et la traite des fourrures." *Recherches amérindiennes au Québec* 24 (1994) 3.

Johnston, A. J. B. *Mathieu Da Costa et les débuts du Canada: possibilités et probabilités* (Halifax, 1991).

Jones, Elizabeth. *Gentlemen and Jesuits: Quests for Glory and Adventure in the Early Days of New France* (Toronto, 1986).

Jourin, Michel Mollat du. "Les marais salants charentais: carrefour du commerce internationale (XIIe–XVIe siècles." *Annales de l'université francophone d'été Saintonge-Québec* (1979).

Julien-Laferrière, l'abbé L. *L'art en Saintonge et en Aunis* (Toulouse, 1879).

Jurgens, Madeleine. "Recherches sur Louis Hébert et sa famille." *Mémoires de la Société généalogique canadienne-française* 8 (1957) 106–12, 135–45; 11 (1960) 24–31.

Jurgens, Olga. "Brûlé, Étienne." In George Williams Brown, ed., *DCB/DBC* Online: http://www.biographi.ca/EN/index.html.

Kelly, James, and Barbara Clarke Smith, eds. *Jamestown-Quebec-Santa Fe: Three North American Beginnings* (Washington and New York, 2007).

Kirke, H. *The First English Conquest of Canada* (London, [1871] 1908).

Knowles, David. *Great Historical Enterprises: Problems in Monastic History* (London, 1963).

Knowles, Nathaniel. "The Torture of Captives by the Indians of Eastern North America." *American Philosophical Society Proceedings* 82 (1940) 151–225.

Konstam, Angus. *The Spanish Galleon, 1530–1690* (Wellingborough, 2004).

Krech, Shepard, III. *The Ecological Indian: Myth and History* (New York, 1999).

Kruger, Peter. "Vervins: le résultat précoce d'une vue systémique des affaires étrangères en Europe."

In Jean–François Labourdette, Jean-Pierre Poussou, and Marie-Catherine Vignal, eds., *Le Traité de Vervins* (Paris, 2000), 415–29.

Kupp, T. J. "Quelques aspects de la dissolution de la compagnie de M. de Monts, 1607. Brève étude de l'influence du commerce hollandais sur les premiers efforts concertés au XVIIe siècle en vue de coloniser le Canada." *Revue d'histoire de l'Amérique française* 23 (1970) 3.

La Horbe, Florian de. *L'incroyable secret de Champlain* (Paris, 1959).

Labourdette, Jean-François. "L'importance du traité de Vervins dans l'histoire de l'Europe." In Jean-François Labourdette, Jean-Pierre Poussou, and Marie-Catherine Vignal, eds., *Le traité de Vervins* (Paris, 2000), 14–26.

Lachance, André. *La justice criminelle du roi au Canada au XVIIIe siècle* (Quebec, 1978).

Lacroix, Paul. *Ballets et mascarades de cour sous Henri IV et Louis XIII* 6 vols. (Geneva, 1868–70).

Ladurie, Emmanuel Le Roy, *Histoire du Languedoc* (Paris, 1962; 6th edition, 2000).

———. *Times of Feast, Times of Famine: A History of Climate since the Year 1000* (New York, 1971).

———. *L'état royal: de Louis XI à Henri IV 1460–1610* (Paris, 1987).

Lainey, Jonathan C. *La "Monnaie des Sauvages": les colliers de wampum d'hier à aujourdhui* (Sillery and Paris, 2004).

Lake Champlain Tercentenary Commission of Vermont. *The Tercentenary Celebrations of the Discovery of Lake Champlain and Vermont* (Montpelier, 1910).

Lanctot, Gustave. "L'établissement du Marquis de La Roche à l'île de Sable." Rapport de la Société historique du Canada, 1933, in *Annual Report of the Canadian Historical Association* (1933) 33–37.

———. "L'administration de la Nouvelle-France" (Paris, 1929).

Lane, Frederic C. "Tonnages, Medieval and Modern." *Economic History Review* 17 (1964) 213–33.

Lareau, Edmond. *Histoire du droit canadien* (Montreal, 1888).

Larocque, Robert. "Le rôle de la contagion dans la conquête des Amériques: importance exagérée attribuée aux agents infectieux." *Recherches amérindiennes au Québec* 18 (1988) 1.

———. "Secret Invaders: Pathogenic Agents and the Aboriginals in Champlain's Time." In Raymonde Litalien et Denis Vaugeois, eds. *Champlain: The Birth of French America* (Montreal, 2004), 266–75.

Latourelle, René, s.j. *Étude sur les écrits de saint Jean de Brébeuf* (Montréal, 1952); vols. 9 and 10 of *Studia Collegii Maximi Immaculatae Conceptionis*.

———. *Brébeuf* (Montreal, 1958).

Lavoie, Marc C. "Report," Curatorial Report 65 (Halifax, Nova Scotia Museum, 1988).

Lebel, François, and Jean-Marie Lebel. "Le roman-feuilleton du tombeau de Champlain," *Cap-aux-diamants* 4 (1988) 45–88.

LeBlanc, Bernard V., and Ronnie-Gilles LeBlanc. "La culture matérielle traditionelle en Acadie." In Jean Daigle, ed., *L'Acadie des Maritimes* (Moncton, 1993), 601–48.

Le Bras, Yvon. *L'Amérindien dans les Relations du Père Lejeune, 1632–1641* (Sainte-Foy, 1994).

Lebreton, Clarence. *Acadians in the Maritimes* (n.p., n.d.).

Ledoux, Albert H. "Abraham Martin, Français ou Écossais?" *Mémoires de la Société généalogique canadienne-française* 27 (1976) 162–64.

Lemay, Hugoin, o.f.m. "Le Père Nicolas Viel, récollet, fut-il assassiné?" (Montreal, 1936).

Lemay, Hugolin, o.f.m. *Notes bibliographiques pour server à l'histoire des Récollets du Canada.* Vol. 1: *Les écrits imprimés laissés par les Récollets*; vol. 2: *Le Père Nicolas Viel,* 28 (Montreal, 1932).

———. "L'œuvre manuscrite ou imprimée des Récollets de la Mission du Canada." *Mémoires de la Société Royale du Canada* ser. 3, vol. 30 (1936).

Lessard, Michel, and Huguette Marquis. *Encyclopédie de la maison québécoise* (Montreal and Brussels, 1972).

Lessard, Michel, Huguette Marquis, and Abbé A. Couillard-Després. *Histoire de la Seigneurie de Saint-Ours, 1330–1785* (Quebec, 1915).

Levermore, Charles Herbert. *Forerunners and Competitors of the Pilgrims and Puritans* (New York, 1912).

Lévesque, Jean. "Représentation de l'autre et progande coloniale dans les récits de John Smith en Virginie et de Samuel de Champlain en Nouvelle-France (1615–1618)." *Canadian Folklore/ Folklore canadien* 17 (1995) 1.

Lévesque, René. *Memoirs* (Toronto, 1995).

Leymairie, A.-Léo. "Le Canada pendant la jeunesse de Louis XIII." *Nova Francia,* I (1925) 161–70.

Liebel, Jean. "On a vieilli Champlain." *Revue d'histoire de l'Amérique française* 32 (1978) 229–37.

———. *Pierre Dugua, sieur de Mons: fondateur de Québec* (Le Croît Vif, Paris, 1999).

Litalien, Raymonde. "Historiography of Samuel Champlain." In Raymonde Litalien and Denis Vaugeois, eds., *Champlain: The Birth of French America* (Montreal, 2004) 11–16.

———. *Le rôle des Saintongeais dans la découverte du Canada* (Jonzac, 1990).

Litalien, Raymonde, and Denis Vaugeois, eds. *Champlain: la naissance de l'Amérique française* (Quebec and Paris, 2004); translated as *Champlain: The Birth of French America* (Montreal, 2004).

Lourde, Michel, et al. *Chauvin Trading Post, Tadoussac* (Tadoussac, 1970).

MacBeath, George. "Isaac de Razilly," "Bernard Marot," and "Jean Thomas." *DCB/DBC* Online: http://www.biographi.ca/EN/index.html.

MacDonald, M. A. *Fortune and La Tour: The Civil War in Acadia* (Halifax, 2000).

———. *Robert Le Blant: Seminal Researcher and Historian of Early New France* (Saint John, N.B., 1986).

Mackenzie, Clyde L. Jr., Luis Troccoli, and Luis B. Leon. "History of the Atlantic Pearl-Oyster, *Pinctata imbricata*, Industry in Venezuela and Colombia, with Biological and Ecological Observations." *Marine Fisheries Review* 65 (2003) 1–20.

MacNamara, Charles. "Champlain's Astrolabe," *The Canadian Field-Naturalist* 33 (1919) 103–09.

Mahoney, Irene. *Royal Cousin: The Life of Henry IV of France* (New York, 1970).

Maillet, Antonine, and Rita Scalabrini. *L'Acadie pour quasiment rien. Guide historique, touristique et humoristique d'Acadie* (Montreal, 1973).

Mainwaring, Sir Henry. "The Seaman's Dictionary." In G. E. Mainwaring and W. G. Perrin, eds., *The Life and Works of Sir Henry Mainwaring,* vols. 54 and 56 in the publications of the Navy Records Society (London, 1920, 1922).

Malchelosse, Gerard. *Trois Rivières d'autrefois: études éparses et inédites de Benjamin Sulte* (Montreal, 1934).

Mannion, John, ed. *The Peopling of Newfoundland: Essays in Historical Geography* (St. John's, Nfld., 1977).

Marcel, Gabriel, ed. *Mémoire en requête de Champlain pour la continuation du paiement de sa pension* (Paris, 1886).

Mariéjol, Jean H. *Henri IV et Louis XIII* (Paris, 1905).

Marot, Jean (1463–1526). "D'avoir esgard à l'Honneur," *Oeuvres* (Paris, 1536).

Marshall, O. H. "Champlain's Expedition of 1615." *Historical Writings of the late Orsamus H. Marshall* (Albany, 1887).

Martijn, Charles A., ed. *Les Micmacs et la mer* (Montreal, 1986).

Martin, Denis. "Discovering the Face of Samuel de Champlain." In Raymonde Litalien and Denis Vaugeois, eds., *Champlain: The Birth of French America* (Quebec, 2004), 360–62.

Martinière, G. "Henri IV et la France équinoxiale." In *Henri IV, le roi et la reconstruction du royaume. Actes du colloque de Pau-Nérac, 14–17 septembre 1989* (Pau, 1990).

McCusker, John J. *Money and Exchange in Europe and America, 1600–1775* (Chapel Hill, 1978).

———. *Money and Exchange in Europe and America, 1600–1775: A Handbook* (Chapel Hill, 1978).

McDermott, James. *Martin Frobisher, Elizabethan Privateer* (New Haven, 2001).

———. *The Third Voyage of Martin Frobisher to Baffin Island* (London, 2001).

McGhee, Robert. *Canada Rediscovered* (Montreal, 1991).

McGowan, Margaret. *L'Art du ballet de cour en France (1581–1643)* (Paris, 1978).

McMaster, John Bach. *The History of the People of the United States,* 9 vols. (New York, 1883–1927).

Mechling, William H. *Malecite Tales.* Department of Mines. Geological Survey Branch, Memoir 49 (Ottawa, 1914).

Medina, Pedro de. *Arte de Navegar* (Seville, 1545); tr. by John Frampton as *The Arte of navigation . . . made by Master Peter de Medina* (London, 1581).

Mémoire rédigé par les Récollets en 1637. Bibliothèque nationale de France (Nouv. Acq. Franç., 9,269: 51r–53r). In Pierre Margry, *Découvertes et établissements des Français dans l'ouest et dans le sud de l'Amérique septentrionale* 1:3–18.

Meney, Lionel. *Dictionnaire québécois français* (Montreal, 1999).

Metz, Elizabeth. *Sainte Marie among the Iroquois: A Living History Museum of the French and the Iroquois at Onondaga in the 17th Century* (Syracuse, 1995).

Michaud, Joseph François and Jean Joseph François. *Histoire &c., abrégée à l'Usage de la Jeunesse* 2 vols. (Paris, 1838); and manuscript materials in Buisseret, *Henri IV.*

Migliore, Sam. "Viral Infections among the Huron: An Ecological Approach." *Nexus* (1983–84).

Moogk, Peter N. *La Nouvelle France: The Making of French Canada: A Cultural History* (East Lansing, 2000).

Morandière, Charles de la. *Histoire de la pêche française de la morue dans l'Amérique septentrionale* 3 vols. (Paris, 1962–66).

Moureau, François. "American Aboriginals in the *Ballets de Cour* in Champlain's Time." In Raymonde Litalien and Denis Vaugeois, eds., *Champlain: The Birth of French America* (Montreal, 2004) 43–49.

Morison, Samuel Eliot. *Samuel de Champlain: Father of New France* (New York, 1972).

———. *The Great Explorers: The European Discovery of America* (New York, 1978).

———. *The European Discovery of America: The Southern Voyages, 1492–1616* (New York, 1974); *The Northern Voyages* (New York, 1971).

———. *Portuguese Voyages to America in the Fifteenth Century* (Cambridge, 1940).

———. *The Story of Mount Desert Island* (Boston, 1960, 1988).

Morisset, Gérard. *L'architecture en Nouvelle-France* (Quebec, 1949).

Morissonneau, Christian. *Le langage géographique de Cartier et de Champlain. Choronymie, vocabulaire et perception* (Quebec, 1978).

Morris, E. P. *The Fore and Aft Rig in America* (New York, 1970).

Morrison, Alvin H., and Thomas H. Goetz. "Membertou's Raid on the Chouacoet 'Almouchiquois': The Micmac Sack of Saco in 1607." *Papers of the Sixth Algonquian Conference* (Ottawa, 1974).

Morse, William Inglis. *Pierre du Gua, Sieur de Monts* (London, 1939).

Motus, Roger. *Maurice Constantin–Weyer: écrivain de l'ouest et du grand nord* (n.p., 1982).

Mougeon, Raymond, and Édouard Beniak. *Les origines du français québécois* (Quebec, 1994).

Mousnier, Roland. *The Assassination of Henri IV;* tr. by Joan Spencer (New York, 1973).

Moussette, Marcel. "Un héros sans visage: Champlain et l'archéologie." *Les Cahiers des Dix* (2000) 54.

Muchembled, Robert. *L'Invention de l'homme moderne. Culture et sensibilités en France du XVe au XVIII siècle* (Paris, 1994).

Muise, D. A. *Approaches to the Native History of Canada* (Ottawa, National Museum of Man, 1977).

Mukerji, Chandra. "Champlain as Gardener." Lecture, College of the Atlantic (Bar Harbor, 2005).

Munro, W. B. "The Office of Intendant in New France: A Study in French Colonial Policy." *American Historical Review* 12 (1906) 15–38.

Murray, Louise W., ed. *Selected Manuscripts of General John S. Clark relating to the Aboriginal History of the Susquehanna* (Athens, Ohio, 1931).

Nadeau, Jean-Benoît, and Julie Barlow. *The Story of French* (New York, 2006).

Nant, Candide de. *Pages glorieuses de l'épopée canadienne: une mission Capucine en Acadie* (Montreal, 1927).

Neel, J. V. et al. "Notes on the Effects of Measles and Measles Vaccine in a Virgin-soil Population of South America." *American Journal of Epidemiology* 91 (1970) 4.

New York Lake Champlain Tercentenary Commission. "Report on the Champlain Tercentenary" (Albany, 1911).

Nichols, Roger L. *Black Hawk and the Warrior's Path* (Wheeling, Ill., 1992).

Novelli, Novella. "Discours de Champlain pour un établissement permanent." In *Scritti sulla Nouvelle-France nel Seicento* (Bari and Paris, 1984).

Oakeshott, E. Ewart. *The Sword in the Age of Chivalry* (New York, 1964).

O'Meara, Maureen F. "Converting the Otherness of Membertou: The Patriarchal Discourse of Champlain, Lescarbot, and Biard." *L'espirit créateur* 30 (1990), 51–58.

Orval, Paul Bouchart d'. *Le Mystère du Tombeau de Champlain* (Quebec, 1951).

Ouellet, Réal. *Rhétorique et conquête missionnaire: le Jesuite Paul Lejeune* (Quebec, 1993).

Ouellet, Yves. *Tadoussac, The Magnificent Bay* (Laval, 2000).

Palmer, R. R., and Jacques Godechot. "Le Problème de l'Atlantique du XVIIIe et XXe siècle." *Relazione del X Congresso Internationale di Scienze Storiche, Roma 4–11 Settembre 1955* (Florence, 1955) 5:175–239.

Paltsits, Victor Hugo. "A Critical Examination of Champlain's Portraits." *Acadiensis* 4 (1904) 3–4:306–11.

———. "A Fictitious Portrait of Sieur de Monts." *Acadiensis* 4 (1904) 3–4: 303–05.

Parkman, Francis. *Pioneers of France in the New World* (Boston, 1865, revised edition with corrections, 1885; rpt. Boston, 1901).

Pascal, Blaise. *Pensées* (Oxford, 1999).

Pauliat, Louis. *La politique coloniale sous l'Ancien Régime d'aprés des documentes empruntes aux archives coloniales du ministre de la marine et des colonies* (Paris, 1887).

Paulin-Desormeaux, M. A. O. *Nouveau manuel complet de l'armurier du fourbisseur et de l'arquebusier*; nouvelle édition, 2 vols. (Paris, 1852; rpt. Paris, 1977).

Pell, S. H. P. "Was Champlain a Liar?" *Bulletin of the Fort Ticonderoga Museum* 5 (1939) 5–8.

Pepy, L. "Brouage et ses marais." *Revue Géographique des Pyrénées et du Sud-Ouest* 6 (1935) 281–323.

Péréfixe, Hardouin [de Beaumont] de. *Histoire du Roy Henry le Grand* (Paris, 1681); annexe, "Recueil de quelques belles actions et paroles mémorables du Roy Henry Le Grand" (Paris, 1749) 529.

Pérez-Mallaína, Pablo E. *Spain's Men of the Sea: Daily Life on the Indies Fleets in the Sixteenth Century* (Baltimore, 1998).

Perrot, Françoise-Marie. "Relation de la Provence d'Acadie," n.p., n.d., in *Library and Archives Canada*.

Peterson, Jacqueline, and Jennifer S. H. Brown. *The New Peoples: Being and Becoming Métis in North America* (n.p., 1985).

Peterson, Harold. *Arms and Armor in Colonial America, 1526–1783* (Harrisburg, Pa., 1956).

Peterson, Jacqueline. "The People In Between: Indian-White Marriage and the Genesis of a Métis Society and Culture in the Great Lakes Region, 1680–1830." Dissertation (Univ. of Illinois, 1980).

Phillips, Carla Rahn. *Six Galleons for the King of Spain: Imperial defense in the Early Sixteenth century* (Baltimore, 1986).

Picard, François. *Chronologie de Tadoussac* (Tadoussac, 1983).

Plan of a *chaloupe biscayenne*, collections of the Fine Arts Museums of San Francisco [Google images, www.famsf.org/image base].

Platter, Thomas. *Le Voyage de Thomas Platter*. Emmanuel Le Roy Ladurie, ed. (Paris, 2000).

Pocquet, Barthélemy. *Histoire de Bretagne* (Rennes, 1896–1914).

Poirson, Auguste. *Histoire du règne de Henri IV* 4 vols. (Paris, 1865).

Poli, Oscar de. "Samuel de Champlain. Notes et documents." In *Annuaire du Conseil héraldique de France* (Paris, 1895).

Pope, Peter E. *The Many Landfalls of John Cabot* (Toronto, 1997).

Porter, Mike. *Guides to the North Woods* (Halifax, 1990).

Pouliot, Léon. "Que penser des frères Kirke?" *Bulletin des recherches historiques* 44 (1938) 321–35.

Pritchard, James. *In Search of Empire: The French in the Americas, 1670–1730* (Cambridge, 2004).

Provost, Honorious. "Robert Giffard de Moncel," *DCB/DBC* Online: http://www.biographi.ca/EN/index.html; Campeau *MNF* 2:824–25.

———. "La Chaudière et l'Etchemin." *Revue de l'université Laval* 2 (1947–48) 114–21.

Prowse, D. W. *History of Newfoundland* (1895, Boulder, 2002).

Quinn, David Beers. *England and the Discovery of America, 1481–1620* (New York, 1974).

———. *North America from the Earliest Discovery to the First Settlements: The Norse Voyages to 1612* (New York, 1977).

Rainguet, Pierre Damien. *Biographie saintongeaise ou dictionnaire historique de tous les personnages* (Saintes, 1851).

Rameau de Saint-Père, François-Edme. *Une colonie féodale en Amérique (1604–1881)*, 2 vols. (Paris and Montreal, 1889).

Rasilly, Michel-Gustave de. *Généalogie de la famille de Rasilly* (Laval, 1903).

Redbird, Duke. *We Are Métis: A Métis View of the Development of a Native Canadian People* (Willowdale, 1980).

Reid, John G. "The Scots Crown and the Restitution of Port Royal, 1629–1632." *Acadiensis* 6 (1977) 106–77.

———. *Maine and New Scotland: Marginal Colonies in the Seventeenth Century* (Toronto, 1981).

Richet, Denis. "Aspects socio-culturels des conflits religieux à Paris dans la seconde moitié du XVIe siècle," *Annales ESC* 32 (1977), 764–89.

Richter, Daniel K. *The Ordeal of the Longhouse: The Peoples of the Iroquois League in the Era of European Colonization* (Chapel Hill, 1992).

Rodesch, Jerrold C. "Jean Nicolet." *Voyageur: The Historical Review of Brown County and Northeast Wisconsin* (Spring, 1984) 4–8.

Rodrigues, M. G. *Le père du Canada, Pierre Dugua* (1994); not seen.

Roelker, Nancy Roelker. *Queen of Navarre, Jeanne d'Albret* (Cambridge, 1968).

Rosier, James. *The Voyage of George Waymouth, 1605. Narrative by James Rosier.* Publié dans le precedent, I: 308–351.

Ross, Alexander. *The Fur Hunters of the Far West* (1855, Norman, Okla., 1956).

———. *The Red River Settlement: Its Rise, Progress and Present State* (London, 1856).

Rousseau, Jacques. "Samuel de Champlain, botaniste mexicain et antillais." *Cahiers des Dix* 16 (1951) 39–61.

———. "Le Canada aborigène dans le contexte historique," *Revue d'histoire de l'Amérique française*, 18, 1 (1964) 39–63.

———. "Les premiers Canadiens." *Cahiers des Dix* 25 (1960) 9–64.

Roy, J. Edmond. "M. de Montmagny," *Nouvelle-France* 5 (1906) 105–21, 161–73, 417–28, 520–30.

———. "La Cartographie et l'Arpentage sous le régime français." *Bulletin Recherches Historiques* 1 (1895) 17.

Roy, Régis. "Guillaume de Caën." *Bulletin des recherches historiques* 32 (1926) 531.

———. "M. de Chaste," *Bulletin de recherches historiques* 7 (1921), 214–15.

Rudin, Ronald. *Founding Fathers: The Celebration of Champlain and Laval in the Streets of Quebec, 1878–1908* (Toronto, 2003).

Rumrill, Donald. "The Mohawk Glass Trade Bead Chronology: ca. 1560–1785," *Beads* (n.d.) 3:5–45.

Russell, A. J. *On Champlain's Astrolabe, lost on the 7th June, 1613, and Found in August, 1867: Considered in solution of an obscurity in his journal of his first voyage up the Ottawa; and the great antiquity of astrolabes, and origin of their graduation* (Montreal, 1879).

Russell, Howard S. *Indian New England before the Mayflower* (Hanover, 1980)

Saintonge, Jacques. *Nos Ancêtres* 3 vols. cit; http://membres.lycos.fr/saintonge/surnommes.htm.

Salisbury, Neal. *Manitou and Providence: Indians, Europeans, and the Making of New England, 1500–1643* (New York, 1982).

Salone, Émile. *La colonisation de la Nouvelle-France* (Trois-Rivières, 1970).

Salter, Michael A. "L'Ordre de Bon Temps: A Functional Analysis." *Journal of Sport History* 3 (1976), 111–19.

Sauer, Carl O. *Seventeenth Century North America* (Berkeley, 1980).

Saunders, R. M. "The First Introduction of European Plants and Animals into Canada." *Canadian Historical Review* (1935) 16.

Savard, Rémi. *L'Algonquin Tessouat et la fondation de Montréal* (Quebec, 1996).

Savage, Candace. *Peregrin Falcons* (San Francisco, 1994).

Sayles, Hilary M. J. "Chronological List of Emblem Books." *Studies in Seventeenth-Century Imagery* (Rome, 1974) 17.

Sayre, Gordon M. *Les sauvages américaines* (Chapel Hill, 1997).

Scott, H.-A. *Nos anciens historiographes et autres études d'histoire canadienne* (Quebec, 1930).

Seed, Patricia. *American Pentimento: The Invention of Indians and the Pursuit of Riches* (Minneapolis, 2001).

———. *Ceremonies of Possession: Europe's Conquest of the New World, 1492–1640* (Cambridge, 1995).

Seguin, Marc. *Histoire de l'Aunis et de la Saintonge: Le début des temps modernes, 1480–1610* (Poiteau, 2005).

Shea, John Gilmary. *Discovery and Exploration of the Mississippi Valley* (New York, 1953).

Simmons, William S. *Spirit of the Indian Tribes: Indian History and Folklore, 1620–1984* (Hanover, 1986).

Smith, Nicholas B. "Notes on the Malecite of Woodstoek, New Brunswick." *Anthropologica* 5 (1957), 1–39.

Snow, Dean R. "The Ethnohistoric Baseline of the eastern Abenaki," *Ethnohistory* 23 (1976) 291–306.

Snow, Dean R., and K. M. Lanphear. "European Contact and Indian Depopulation in the Northeast: The Timing of the First Epidemics." *Ethnohistory* 35 (1988), 15–39.

———. "Mohawk Demography and the Effects of Exogenous Epidemics on American Indian Populations." *Journal of Anthropological Archaeology* 15(1996), 160–82.

Snow, Dean R., and William Starna. "Sixteenth-Century Depopulation: A View from the Mohawk Valley." *American Anthropologist* 91:142–49.

Societe d'ethnologie et de folklore du Centre Ouest. *Patois Charentes* (n.p., 1994).

Soissons, Charles de Bourbon de. "Commission à Champlain, 15 oct. 1612." In Champlain, *Œuvres* (éd. Biggar). IV: 209–16.

Spence, Richard T. *The Privateering Earl: George Clifford, 3rd Earl of Cumberland, 1558–1603* (Far Thrupp Stroud, UK, 1995).

Spiess, A. E., and B. D. Spiess, "New England Pandemic of 1616–1622: Cause and Archaeological Implication." *Man in the Northeast* (1987), 34.

Spooner, Frank C. *The International Economy and Monetary Movements in France, 1493–1725* (Cambridge, 1972).

Squair, John. *Autobiography of a Teacher of French* (Toronto, 1928).

Stefansson, Sigurdir. *Terrarum Hyperboream, Of the Northern Lands* (n.p., circa 1590).

Steffansson, V., ed. *The Three Voyages of Martin Frobisher* 2 vols. (London, 1938).

Stewart, F. "Seasonal Movements of Indians in Acadia as Evidenced by Historical Documents and Vertebrate Faunal Remains from Archeological Sites." *Man in the Northeast* (1989) 38.

Stewart, George. "The Flag of Champlain and Its History." *Acadiensis*, 4 (1904) 221–24.

Stimson, A. *The Mariner's Astrolabe: A Survey of Known, Surviving Sea Astrolabes* (Utrecht, 1988).

Sulte, Benjamin. *Histoire des Canadiens-Français, 1608–1880* 8 vols. (Montreal, 1882–84).

———. *Histoire populaire du Canada, d'après les documents français et américains* (Philadelphia, Chicago, Toronto, 1901).

———. *Mélanges historiques* 21 vols. (Montreal, 1918–34).

———. *Mélanges d'histoire et de littérature* (Ottawa, 1876).

———. "Etienne Brûlé." *Mémoires de la Société royale du Canada* 1 (1907) 97–126.

———. "Québec, de 1620 à 1632." *Bulletin des recherches historiques* 5 (1899) 292–304, 324–40.

———. *Chronique Trifluvienne* (1879, Montreal, 1981).

———. *Histoire de la ville des Trois-Rivières* (1870, Montreal, 1981).

———. *Album de l'histoire des Trois-Rivières* (1881, Montreal, 1981).

Taft, Hank, and Jan Taft. *A Cruising Guide to the Maine Coast* 3rd edition (Peaks Island, Me., 1996).

Taillemite, Étienne. "The Royal Navy in Champlain's time." In Raymonde Litalien et Denis Vaugeois, eds., *Champlain: The Birth of French America* (Quebec, 2004) 19–23.

———. *Louis XVI ou le navigateur immobile* (Paris, 2002).

Tapié, Victor-L. *France in the Age of Louis XIII and Richelieu* (Paris, 1952, 1957; tr. Cambridge, 1974, 1984).

Tard, Louis-Martin. *Marc Lescarbot: le chantre de l'Acadie* (Quebec, 1997).

Tawney, R. H. *Religion and the Rise of Capitalism* (1926, N.Y., 1954).

Thérien, Gilles. "*Memoria* as the Place of Fabrication of the New World." In Germaine Warkentin and Carolyn Podruchny, eds., *Decentring the Renaissance: Canada and Europe in a Multidisciplinary Perspective 1500–1700* (Toronto, 2001), 68–84.

Therrien, Jean-Marie. *Parole et pouvoir: figure du chef amérindien en Nouvelle-France* (Montreal, 1986).

Théry, Chantal. "Un Jésuite et un Récollet parmi les femmes: Paul Le Jeune et Gabriel Sagard chez les sauvages du Canada." *Les Jésuites parmi les hommes aux XVIe et XVIIe siècles.* Actes du colloque de Clermont-Ferrand, publiés par G. et G. Demerson, B. Dompnier et A. Regond, Association des publications de la Faculté des lettres et sciences humaines de Clermont-Ferrand (1987) 105–13.

Thierry, Éric. "La Paix de Vervins et les ambitions françaises en Amérique." In Jean-François Labourdette, Jean Pierre Poussou, and Marie-Catherine Vignal, eds., *Le Traité de Vervins* (Paris, 2000) 373–89.

———. "Champlain and Lescarbot: An Impossible Friendship." In Raymonde Litalien et Denis Vaugeois, eds., *Champlain: The Birth of French America* (Quebec, 2004) 121–34.

———. *Marc Lescarbot (vers 1570–1641). Un homme de plume au service de la Nouvelle-France* (Paris, 2001).

Thomas, Gerald. *The Two Traditions: The Art of Storytelling amongst French Newfoundlanders* (St. John's, Nfld., 1993).

Thomson, Don W. *Men and Meridians: The History of Surveying and Mapping in Canada* (Ottawa, Queen's Printer, 1966–69).

Tooker, Elisabeth. *Ethnographie des Hurons, 1615–1649* (Montreal, 1987).

———. *The Indians of the Northeast: A Critical Bibliography* (1978).

Tremblay, Roland. *Les Iroquiens du Saint-Laurent: peuple du maïs* (Montreal, 2006).

Trigger, Bruce G. "Champlain Judged by His Indian Policy: A Different View of Early Canadian History." *Anthropologica* 13 (1971) 85–114.

———. *The Children of Aataentsic: A History of the Huron People to 1660* (1976, new edition, Montreal, 1987).

———. *Natives and Newcomers: Canada's "Heroic Age" Reconsidered* (Montreal, 1985, 1994).

———. *Les Indiens, la fourrure et les Blancs: Français et Amérindiens en Amérique du Nord* (Montreal and Paris, 1990).

———. "Ontario Native People and the Epidemics of 1634–1640." In S. Krech, III, ed., *Indians, Animals and the Fur Trade: A Critique of Keepers of the Game* (Athens, Ga., 1981).

Trudel, Marcel. *Histoire de la Nouvelle-France,* vol. 1: *Les vaines tentatives 1524–1603* (Montreal, 1963).

———. *Histoire de la Nouvelle-France,* vol. 2: *Le Comptoir, 1604–1627* (Montreal, 1966).

———. *Histoire de la Nouvelle-France,* vol. 3.1: *La Seigneurie des Cent-Associés, Les Événements* (Montreal, 1979).

———. *Histoire de la Nouvelle-France,* vol. 3.2: *La Seigneurie des Cent-Associés, La Societé* (Montreal, 1979).

———. *Initiation à la Nouvelle-France* (1968); tr. as *Introduction to New France* (Toronto and Montreal, 1983).

———. "Champlain, Samuel de," "De Caën, Guillaume," "Gravé Du Pont, François," "Lejeune, Olivier," and "Vignau, Nicolas de." In George Williams Brown, ed., *DCB/DBC* Online http://www.biographi.ca/EN/index.html.

———. "Jean Nicollet dans le Lac Supérieur et non dans le Lac Michigan." *Revue d'histoire de l'Amérique francaise* 34, 2 (1980) 183–96.

———. "La carte de Champlain en 1632: ses sources et son originalité." *Cartologica* 51 (1978), 1–20.

———. *Catalogue des immigrants, 1632–1662* (Montreal, 1983).

———. *Champlain* (Montreal, 1956); 2d edition revised and enlarged (Montreal and Paris, 1968).

———. *Mémoires d'un autre siècle* (Montreal, 1987); tr. by Jane Brierley as *Memoirs of a Less Travelled Road* (Montreal, 2002).

Tuck, James A. *Onondaga Iroquois Prehistory: A Study in Settlement Archaeology* (Syracuse, 1971).

Tuck, James, and Barry Gaulton. "Archaeologists Strike Gold," Memorial University Research Report (2004–05) www.mun.ca/research/2005.

Tuck, James A., and Robert Grenier. *Red Bay, Labrador: World Whaling Capital, A.D. 1550–1600* (St. John's, Nfld., 1989).

Turgeon, Laurier. "Basque-Amerindian Trade in the Saint Lawrence during the Sixteenth Century: New Documents, New Perspectives." *Man in the Northeast* 40 (1990), 81–88.

———. "Bordeaux and the Newfoundland Trade during the Sixteenth Century." *International Journal of Maritime History* 9 (1997), 1–28.

———. "French Beads in France and Northeastern North America During the Sixteenth Century." *Historical Archaeology* 35 (2001), 58–81.

———. "French Fishers, Fur Traders, and Amerindians during the Sixteenth Century: History and Archeology." *William and Mary Quarterly* 60 (1998), 585–610.

———. "Pêcheurs basques et indiens des côtes du Saint-Laurent au XVIe siècle: perspectives de recherches." *Études canadiennes/Canadian Studies* 13 (1982) 9–14.

———. "Pour redécouvrir notre XVIe siècle: les pêches à Terre-Neuve d'après les archives notariales de Bordeaux." *Revue d'histoire de l'Amérique française* 39 (1986), 523–49.

———. *Pêches basques en Atlantique Nord* (XVIIe–XVIIIe siècle: *Étude d'Économie Maritime* (Bordeaux, thèse de doctorat, 1982).

U.S. National Park Service, *Peregrine Falcons in Acadia* (1999).

Vaissière, Pierre de. *Henri IV* (Paris, 1925).

Valois, Noël. *Inventaire des arrêts du Conseil d'État. Règne de Henri IV* (Paris, 1893).

Vaugeois, Denis, ed. *Les Hurons de Lorette* (Sillery, 1996).

Vaugeois, Denis. "Champlain et Dupont-Gravé: Un Formidable Tandem." *Cap-aux-Diamants* 92 (2008), 10–15.

Vaugeois, Denis, and Raymonde Litalien eds. *Champlain: La Naissance de l'Amérique française* (Quebec, 2004); English translation, *Champlain: The Birth of French America* (Montreal, 2004).

Vaugeois, Denis, Raymonde Litalien, and Jean-Francois Palomino, eds. *Mapping A Continent: Historical Atlas of North America, 1492–1814* (Montreal, 2007).

Vaux de Foletier, François de. *Le Siège de la Rochelle* (La Rochelle, 1978).

Velázquez Gáztelu, Juan Pedro. *Estado Maritimo de Sanlúcar de Barrameda* (*ASEHA*, [1774] 1998).

Vigé, Éliane, and Jimmy Vigé, *Brouage: capitale du sel et patrie de Champlain* (Bordessoules, 1990).

———. *Brouage, capitale du sel et patrie de Champlain* (Saint-Jean-d'Angély: Bordessoules, 1990).

———. *Brouage: ville d'histoire et place forte* (Saint-Jean-d'Angély, 1989).

Vigneras, L. A. "Le Voyage de Samuel Champlain aux Indes occidentales." *Revue d'histoire de l'Amérique française* 11 (1957) 163–200.

———. "Encore le capitaine provençal." *Revue d'histoire de l'Amérique française* 13 (1959–60) 544–49.

Villeneuve, Gaby. *Tadoussac . . . Là, où commence l'histoire* (Tadoussac, post-1998).

Vimont, Barthélemy. *Jesuit Relations* 23:276–78.

Vincent, J.-B. "Un port français oublié: Brouage la ville morte raconté par les documents." *Revue maritime* (Aug.–Oct. 1912).

Vincent, Sylvie. "La tradition orale montagnaise, comment l'interroger?" *Cahiers de Clio* 70 (1982), 5–26.

Viola, Herman J., and Carolyn Margolis. *Seeds of Change* (Washington, DC, 1991).

Vioux, Marcelle. *Le vert-galant, vie héroique et amoureuse de Henri IV* (Paris, 1935).

Wacquet, H. *Mémoires du chanoine Jean Moreau sur les guerres de la ligue en Bretagne* (Quimper, 1960).

Wagenaer, Lucas Janszoon. *T'eerste Deel Vande Spieghel der Zeevaerdt vandde navigatie der Westersche Zee,* The First Part of the Mirror of the Navigation for Sailing the Western Sea [that is, west of the Zuider Zee] (Leyden, 1584).

Wallace, Anthony F. C. "Dreams and the Wishes of the Soul: A Type of Psychoanalytic Theory among the Seventeenth Century Iroquoians." *American Anthropologist* 60 (1958) 234–48.

Wallace, Brigitta. "The Scots Fort: A Reassessment of its Location," mss., Parks Canada Atlantic Service Centre, 1994; not seen.

Wallace, Mark. "Black Hawk's *An Autobiography*: The Production and Use of an Indian Voice." *American Indian Quarterly* 18 (1994) 481–94.

Walton, Timothy. *The Spanish Treasure Fleets* (Sarasota, 1994).

Warwick, Jack. "Humanisme chrétien et bons sauvages." *XVIIe siècle* (Paris, 1972) 25–49.

Waters, D. W. *The Sea or Mariner's Astrolabe*. Coimbra, Junta de Investigaçoes Do Ultramar (Agrupamento de Estudos de Cartographia Antiga, 1966).

———. *The Art of Navigation in England in Elizabethan and Early Stuart Times* (New Haven, 1958).

Watkins, Melville. "A Staple Theory of Economic Growth." *Canadian Journal of Economics and Political Science* 29 (1963) 141–58.

Weckmann, Luis. *Las bulas alejandrinas de 1493 y la teoría política del papado medieval* (Mexico City, 1949).

Weiskotten, Daniel H. "The Real Battle of Nichols Pond"; unpublished paper, 1998.

Welsh, Christine. Film. *Women in the Shadows* (1992).

Whitehead, Ruth Holmes. "Nova Scotia: The Protohistoric Period, 1500–1630," Curatorial Report 75, Nova Scotia Museum (Halifax, 1993).

———. "Navigation des Micmacs le long de la côte Atlantique." In Charles Martjin, ed., *Les Micmacs et la mer* (Montreal, 1986).

Whitney, Ellen M., ed. *The Black Hawk War, 1831–1832,* 3 vols. (Springfield, 1970).

Wilcox, R. Turner. *The Mode in Furs: The History of Furred Costumes* (New York, 1948).

———. *The Mode in Hats and Headdress* (New York, 1948).

Wilkins, Ernest H. "Arcadia in America," *American Philosophical Society Proceedings* 101 (1957) 4–30.

Wilson, Clifford P. "Where did Nicollet Go?" *Minnesota History* 27 (1946) 216–20.

Wiseman, Frederick M. *The Voice of the Dawn: An Autohistory of the Abenaki Nation.*

Wolfe, Michael. *The Conversion of Henry IV: Politics, Power and Religious Belief in Early Modern Times* (Cambridge, 1993).

Wright, Gordon K. *The Neutral Nations* (Rochester, N.Y., 1963).

Xaintonge. An entire issue of Journal 2 (Oct.–Nov. 1997), 1–32, is devoted to the subject of "La Cagouille: l'emblème des Charentais," with essays on "Légendes et croyances," "Coutumes et traditions de la race Cagouillarde," "Des Cagouilles sur les églises," etc.

Zeller, A. G. *The Champlain-Iroquois Battle of 1615* (New York, 1962).

MAP SOURCES

MAPS BY SAMUEL CHAMPLAIN AND JOHN SMITH

SOURCES FOR MAPS BY JEFFREY WARD

PAGE

17   Brouage and the Biscay Coast: Plan of Brouage, c. 1570, manuscript, Public Record Office, London; Christophe Tassin "Plan de Brouage, 1634," in Nathalie Fiquet et al., *L'Art de se défendre* (Brouage, 1999), 26; Nathalie Fiquet and François-Yves Leblanc, *Les Arsenals de Richelieu: Brouage, Brest, Le Havre, vers l'Arsenal Idéal* (Brouage, 2003), 8, 18; Nathalie Fiquet and François-Yves Le Blanc, *Brouage, Ville Royale et les villages du golfe de Saintonge* (Chauray-Niort, 1997), 76–78; Nicholas Chereau, *Visite Historique de Brouage* (n.p., 2002), 31–32.

33   Saintonge: Marc Seguin, *Histoire de l'Aunis et de la Saintonge* (Ligugé, 2005), 12, 21, 52; "Le grand lexique du patois charentais," by the editors of the journal *Xaintonge*, hors serie 1–6 (May 2003–December 2006); Raymonde Doussinet, "Xaintonge, L'Aire d'Expression du Patois Saintongeais," *Xaintonge* (Oct.–Nov. 1996), 1.

53   Wars of Religion in France: Robert Knecht, *The French Religious Wars* (Botley, 2002), 14, 19, 42, 55; Arlette Jouanna et al., *Histoire et Dictionnaire des Guerres de Religion* (Paris, 1998), 368; Denis Crouzet, *Les Guerriers de Dieu; La Violence au temps des troubles de religion, vers 1520–vers 1610,* 2 vols. (Paris, 1990); James McDermott, *Martin Frobisher, Elizabethan Privateer* (New Haven, 2003), 407–23; J. S. Nolan, "English Operations Around Brest, 1594," *Mariner's Mirror* 81 (1995) 259–74.

87   Champlain in New Spain: Champlain, "Brief Discours," in *Works,* ed. Biggar, 1:3–80; François-Marc Gagnon, "Le Brief Discours . . . ," Litalien and Vaugeois, eds., *Champlain,* 83.

113 Failed French Settlements in North America before Champlain: Ramsay Cook, ed., *The Voyages of Jacques Cartier* (Toronto, 1993), xxv–xli; Mark de Villiers and Sheila Hirtle, *Sable Island* (New York, 2004), 2–10, 123–33.

120 French Seaports and American Fisheries: Mickaël Augeron and Dominique Guillemet eds., *Champlain ou les portes de Nouveau Monde* (n.p., 2004), 23, passim; voyages tabulated from data in Charles De La Morandière, *Histoire de la Pêche Française de la Morue dans l'Amérique Septentrionale,* 3 vols. (Paris, 1962–66), 1:248, 277–315.

135 Indian Nations, 1603–35: Daniel Clément, ed., *The Algonquins* (Hull, 1996); Bruce G. Trigger, *Children of Aataentsic* (Montreal, 1976, 1987); Conrad Heidenreich, *Huronia* (Toronto, 1971), map 24; Gordon K. Wright, *The Neutral Nations* (Rochester, N.Y., 1963); Frederick M. Wiseman, *The Voice of the Dawn; An Autohistory of the Abenaki Nation;* Kathleen J. Bragdon, *Native People of Southern New England* (Norman, 1996), 243; Howard S. Russell, *Indian New England before the* Mayflower (Hanover, 1980), 19–29; R. Cole Harris ed., *Historical Atlas of Canada* (Toronto, 1987) 1: plate 33, 35; Christian Morissoneau, in Litalien and Vaugeois, *Champlain* (Montreal, 2004), 162; "Le Canada faict par Sr de Champlain, 1616," his best ethnographic map, survives only in an unfinished printer's proof (1619) ms. John Carter Brown Library.

151 Explorations of Acadia: Champlain, *Works,* ed. Biggar, 1:234–74; Elizabeth Jones, *Gentlemen and Jesuits* (Toronto, 1986), xiv; Trudel, *Histoire de la Nouvelle France,* 3:32, 42.

175 Exploring the Rivers of Maine; Champlain, *Works,* ed. Biggar, 1:313–21; W. F. Ganong, "Kennebec River and Approaches," in Morison, *Champlain,* 56–59.

185 Norumbega, Cruises on the Coast of Maine: Champlain, *Works,* ed. Biggar, 1:280–300, 311–66, 392–438.

237   The St. Lawrence Valley: Champlain, *Works,* ed. Biggar, vols. 2–4; Trudel, *Histoire de la Nouvelle France,* 3.1:31.

264   Lake Champlain and the River of the Iroquois: Champlain, *Works,* ed. Biggar, 2:76–101, 122–38.

307   Explorations in the Ottawa Valley: Champlain, *Works,* 2:259–302; J. L. Morris, "Plan shewing Route Taken by Champlain through Muskrat Lake . . . ," Ibid., 2: 273.

326   Huronia and the Onondaga Country: Champlain, *Works,* 3:45–79, 4:239–70; Trigger, *Children of Aataentsic* (Montreal, 1976, 1987), 302; Conrad Heidenreich, *Huronia* (Toronto, 1971); R. Cole Harris, *Historical Atlas of Canada* (Toronto, 1987), 1:34; Trudel, *Histoire de la Nouvelle France,* 3.1:201.

473   Peopling of Quebec: Marcel Trudel, *Histoire de la Nouvelle France,* 2:247, 420, 427; 3.1:27, 125; 3.2 11–56; Archange Godbout, "Nos hérédités provinciales françaises *Les Archives de Folklore* 1 (1946) 26–40; Hubert Charbonneau et al., *Naissance d'une population,* 46; Gervais Carpin, *Le Réseau du Canada; Étude du mode migratoire de la France vers la Nouvelle-France (1628–1662)* (Quebec and Paris, 2001); Peter N. Moogk, *La Nouvelle France* (East Lansing, Michigan, 2002), 87–120.

481   Cradle of Acadia: Geneviéve Massignon, *Parlers Français d'Acadie,* 2 vols. (Paris, 1962), 1:42–75; Cormier, *Les Aboiteaux en Acadie* (Moncton, 1990), 19; A. J. B. Johnston and W. P. Ker, *Grand-Pré: Heart of Acadie* (Halifax, 2004), 18.

497   Travels of Champlain's Interpreters: Champlain, *Works,* ed. Biggar, 2:138–42; 3:36, 213; 4:213–266; 5:95, 100n, 202, 209, 6:62–63, 98–102; and [Champlain], "Relation du Voyage," in Lucien Campeau, ed., *Monumenta Novae Franciae,* 2:452, 808–09; Paul Le Jeune, Relation (1633), in *Jesuit Relations,* 5:202, 203, 288; Harris, ed., *Historical Atlas of Canada,* 1: plate 36.

ART CREDITS

125   Jacques Gomboust, Honfleur before 1670 © Musée de la Marine, Honfleur

129   Morse, "Isle Percée," *Acadiensa Nova* (London, 1935), 1:35; Photo Library and Archives Canada, Acc. 1997–2–2

130   De Bry, Whalers at Tadoussac, 1592 © Visual Arts Library (London)/Alamy

143   Champlain, Des Sauvages, 1603 title page Courtesy of the John Carter Brown Library at Brown University

146   Franz Hals, Descartes, 1649, Louvre © Erich Lessing/Art Resource, NY

147   Montaigne, late 16th century, Musée Condé, Chantilly, © Lauros/Giraudon/The Bridgeman Art Library International

149   Pierre Dugua de Mons, Bust, Annapolis Royal, photo by J. Y. Grenon © Scott Leslie/ www.scottleslie.com / www.photographersdirect.com

153   "Defenses du Roi," Henri IV's Grant of Monopoly to de Mons, Dec. 18, 1603, Archives Nationales d'Outre Mer, France. (CIIA I fol.48–50v)

156   Poutrincourt or his cousin, Informations Musée Galliera

159   Mi'kmaq rock drawings of European vessels, History Collection, Nova Scotia Museum

169   Champlain's Settlement Plan on Sainte-Croix Island, 1604, Library of Congress

172   Skull of Autopsied Settler, CT Scan, Mt. Desert Island Hospital; Benson, Sorg & Hunter: Multidetector Computerized Tomography (MDCT) Analysis of Skeletal Remains of Members of Samuel de Champlain's 1604 Settlement on Isle de Ste. Croix, RSNA, 2004

183   Champlain, Etchemin Indian, *Voyages* (1619) © Rare Books Division, The New York Public Library, Astor, Lenox and Tilden Foundations

184   Champlain, Almouchiquoise woman, Carte géographique de la nouvelle Franse, 1612, detail, The Newberry Library

191   Champlain, fight between de Mons' crew and Nauset Indians, 1605, Library of Congress

198   Champlain, fight between Poutrincourt's crew and Indians at Port Fortune, 1606, Library of Congress

199   De Bry, English explorer Bartholomew Gosnold on the New England coast, ca. 1602, British Library, London/© HIP/Art Resource, New York

204   Champlain, Habitation at Port-Royal, *Voyages* (1613), Library of Congress

213   C. W. Jeffreys, The Theatre of Neptune at Port-Royal, *Picture Gallery of Canadian History*, 1942, Courtesy of the National Gallery of Canada

215   C. W. Jeffreys, Order of Good Cheer. Library and Archives Canada, acc. 1996–282–3, item 00003, C-013986

219   Emmanuel Nivon, Membertou's Gourd, 1610, Stewart Museum, Montreal, Canada, acc. 1976.58.1

228   Fontainebleau, 2006, photo © Judith Fischer

231   Henri Chatelaine, Beavers, 1719, Smithsonian Museum of Natural History, image courtesy of Donald A. Heald Rare Books, Prints & Maps, New York

232   Abraham Bosse, Beaver Hats, 1605–1630, Library and Archives Canada, acc. 1937–043, item 00001, C-002947

246   Champlain, First Habitation at Quebec, 1610, *Voyages,* 1613, Library of Congress

250   Champlain, Montagnais man and woman, Library of Congress LAC-MNC 6327

·

COLOR PLATES

B-1   Catlin, Mandan Dance © Smithsonian Museum of American History, Washington, DC / Art Resource, NY

B-2   St. Croix Island aerial photo, ca. 2004, National Park Service, Acadia National Park, Bar Harbor, Maine

B-3   Francis Back, "Settlement at Port Royal, 1603," photo H. Foster, 1997 © Canadian Museum of Civilization, image S97–9646

B-4   Indians Fishing (*Codex Canadiensis,* Oklahoma), Courtesy of the Gilcrease Museum of Tulsa, OK. Reproduced with the permission of the Museum

B-5   Mi'kmaq Warriors (*Codex Canadiensis,* Oklahoma), Courtesy of the Gilcrease Museum of Tulsa, OK. Reproduced with the permission of the Museum

B-6   Francis Back, "Trading Scene at Quebec (1628)," Photo © Canadian Museum of Civilization, Francis Back Collection, photo H. Foster, 1996, image no. S96–25083

B-7   Rubens, "Henri IV, Louis XIII, and Marie de Medici," © Peter Willi/SuperStock

B-8   (bottom left) Pierre Jeannin © Bibliothèque Nationale de France

B-8   (top right) Brulart de Sillery © Musée National du Château de Pau, Pau, France/ Réunion des Musées Nationaux/Art Resource, NY

B-8   (top left) Brissac © Bibliothèque Nationale de France

B-9   Philippe de Champaigne, Richelieu, Triple Portrait, National Gallery, London, © Image Asset Management Ltd./SuperStock

B-10   *La Consideratio de la Mort,* 1600, © Bibliothèque Nationale de France

ACKNOWLEDGMENTS

This book had its beginning on Mount Desert Island in Maine, where everybody knows Samuel Champlain. In 1604, he gave the island its name, and a large part of its identity. For the 400th anniversary of his first visit, I was asked to give a lecture at the College of the Atlantic by two friends and fellow islanders, Steve Katona and Ed Blair. That invitation was the beginning of this book. It would not have happened without them.

In the work itself, many people have had a hand. I have a debt of fifty years to the great libraries of Massachusetts, and to the staffs past and present of the American Antiquarian Society, the Boston Public Library, the Bostonian Society, the Brandeis Libraries, the Harvard Libraries, and the Massachusetts Historical Society.

Important for this project was the New York Public Library, for its collections of French and Canadian journals, monographs, conference reports, and for finding aids which indexed individual articles in a unique way. At Baltimore's Peabody Institute Library long ago, I began to learn about Champlain in conversations with Lloyd Brown, a scholar of early cartography who was director of the library when I was a stack boy, discovering the camaraderie of bookmen.

At Princeton in 1955–56 my first extended research in this field was a junior paper on French maritime history in the early modern era. My advisor was Elmer Beller, a scholar's scholar of 17th-century Europe. He set a high standard for his students. At Johns Hopkins I studied with Frederic Lane, who combined an unrivalled command of sources in early modern maritime history with active experience of maritime affairs.

In the Manuscript Division of the Library of Congress, my old friend Jeffrey Flannery helped me use its large collection of manuscript materials on Champlain and New France from the archives of French ministries and the Bibliothèque National. The staff of the Map Division also allowed me to work closely with Champlain's only surviving manuscript map.

It was a pleasure to visit the Virginia Historical Society in Richmond and talk with my friend and colleague and coauthor James C. Kelly and also with Barbara Clarke Smith of the Smithsonian, while they were working on their Champlain project. And at the Newberry Library in Chicago some years ago, Frederick Hoxie invited me to meetings with leaders of about thirty Indian nations. Those discussions had a major impact on this inquiry.

At the John Carter Brown Library in Providence, director Ted Widmer and his staff helped me use a great collection of early imprints, which include all of Champlain's first editions, nearly all variant printings of Marc Lescarbot's books, and a manuscript copy of Champlain's *Brief Discours* with its luminous watercolors that must be seen in the original.

Also important for this inquiry was the research center at Fort Ticonderoga, New York, where director Nick Westbrook and his staff guided us through their holdings of imprints, maps, and papers. With Nick and Ann McCarty, Judy and I launched two canoes on Lake Champlain and followed the route he and his allies took past Willow Point, Sandy Beach, the promontory of Ticonderoga, and the Chute from Lake George.

On Lake Onondaga near Syracuse, New York, the staff at Sainte Marie among the Iroquois enlightened us on the Onondaga nation. Archaeologist Peter P. Pratt, of the State University of New

York at Oswego, told me about his field work on Onondaga villages in a brief but helpful phone conversation, which guided us on visits to sites in Madison County.

The archives of Acadia National Park in Bar Harbor hold manuscript records of archaeological projects on Sainte-Croix Island. We are grateful to Stephen Pendry, the Park Service's senior archaeologist in Boston, who directed the most recent projects and took an interest in ours. Thanks go to Paul Haertel and Sheridan Steele, superintendents of Acadia National Park, for their encouragement and support. In Calais, Maine, the new visitor center sponsored jointly by the National Park Service and Parcs Canada holds artifacts on the Sainte-Croix settlement. A Maine fisherman took us up the Saint Croix River in his boat. On the coast of Maine, Ed Blair, who got us working on this project, also took us exploring in his boat, following Champlain's wake so closely that we came very near the same ledge that holed Champlain's patache off Otter Cliffs. Through the years we have sailed the coast with our friends Colin and Virginia Steele and Richard and Jo Goeselt, and visited every harbor that Champlain mapped.

At the Library and Archives of Canada in Ottawa, we were fortunate to meet archivist George De Zwaan, who guided us through the vast holdings of that great treasure house, with its trove of manuscript material from many French archives, copies of rare French imprints, and scarce secondary writings. On several visits to the great Museum of Civilization in Hull, across the river from Ottawa, we found Champlain artifacts, and excellent materials on Indian nations and on Métis cultures.

In Quebec's Center of Historical Interpretation in Place Royale we found the results of archaeology on Champlain's habitation and other sites. Also helpful was the old Musée de l'Amérique Française and the new Museum of Civilization in Quebec. In the parks of the province of Quebec, we rented a canoe and explored some of the rivers and rapids. We also studied the site at Cap Tourmente, now preserved as an environmental center, and the Wendake-Wendat Huron Reserve, where he studied the traditions of the Huron nation, and also were given a memorable lunch such as Champlain shared with his friends in Huronia. In Tadoussac the staff of the Chauvin Trading Post Interpretation Center and Museum showed us through their collections, added to our manuscript materials, and gave us a memorable lunch of marinated seal meat.

Judy and I explored the lower St. Lawrence and the mouth of the Saguenay River by zodiac boat and Tadoussac harbor by kayak. Highlights of our travel in the lower St. Lawrence Valley east of Tadoussac were two visits to the Essipit Innu Reserve, where historian Martin Gagnon welcomed us, showed us through his excellent center at Miles Bay, introduced us to a trove of materials, and greatly deepened our knowledge of the history of the Innu nation (Champlain's Montagnais). We learned much from a meeting with Jacques Martin in his home near Tadoussac crossing about the tabagie of 1603, of which he has great knowledge.

At Nova Scotia's Port Royal National Historic Site and in Annapolis Royale we learned much from listening to Wayne and Alan Melanson, identical twins and leading experts on the early history of Acadia. Also very informative was the site of the early 17th-century Melanson farm, where major work has been done on Acadian aboiteaux. A visit to Université Sainte Anne was enlightening for the persistence of francophone culture in Acadia, as was the major center of interpretation for Acadian culture at Grand Pré.

On the Atlantic coast of Nova Scotia, the Fort Point Museum at La Have has copies of rare manuscript material and many artifacts. At Liverpool Harbor (Champlain's Port Rossignol), Matthew Verge helped us in a major way on the oral history of the Mi'kmaq. In Lunenberg, the fascinating Museum of the Atlantic Fisheries is an important center for research and interpretation of its subject. We are grateful to its very hospitable staff, and to the crew of the schooner *Blue Nose*.

In the province of New Brunswick, we explored the coastal sites and rivers that Champlain had visited from Saint Croix to the St. John River and the Bay of Fundy. We much enjoyed a visit to the New Brunswick Museum in St. John, a center of scholarship and interpretation.

On our travels in France we tried to visit all places of known importance to Champlain, and everywhere we met the kindness of strangers. We remember with thanks the staff at the Champlain House in Brouage, and also at the Brouage Visitor Center, the La Rochelle museum, the naval base of Rochefort, where we stayed while we explored the area, and the historical museum at Royan. We are grateful to the Vicomte and Vicomtesse de Kerdaniel for giving us a place to stay in Brittany, where we also visited the Marine Museum in Blavet/Port Louis, historic sites in Crozon, Quimper, Blavet-Port-Louis. In Normandy we remember with thanks the staff of the Musée Marine in Honfleur. In Paris our base was the hotel Jeux de Pomme, a converted 16th-century tennis court on which Champlain may have played. It was in easy reach of Champlain's Paris: Louvre, the Musee Carnevalet, which holds many treasures, the church where he was married, and the Marais-Temple district, where he lived. Thanks go to the staffs of the French Maritime Museum in Paris and its branches in Rochefort and Port-Louis, and to the staffs of the Chateau Chenoncaex, and the Palace at Fontainebleau. For particular items we are grateful to the many libraries and museums that appear in the illustration credits.

As the book took shape, my agents Andrew Wylie and Scott Moyers were close collaborators. Before they tried to sell the book, Scott drew on his skill as an editor to tighten its structure. Andrew offered many suggestions, and both of them helped it in many ways. I formed high respect for their professionalism and complete integrity, and as we worked together, Scott and Andrew became colleagues and friends.

They arranged simultaneous publication by two great houses. Simon & Schuster in the United States has had great success in reaching a large public with serious works of history. It was a privilege to have the benefit of their experience and the encouragement of publisher David Rosenthal. It was a genuine pleasure to work with senior editor Bob Bender and to have the support of his professional skill and long experience in the field. He found the time to line-edit the manuscript, and I came to rely very much on his judgment.

The firm of Knopf Canada preserves the purposes of Alfred Knopf as a living tradition and publishes beautiful books of very high quality. Its founder and publisher, Louise Dennys, was my Canadian muse. She was a source of encouragement, support, sound judgment, and wise advice. It was pleasure to work with her, and with a first-class team that she has put together. The line-editing in Canada was done by Rosemary Shipton with the skill and attention that she has brought to so many books. Jane McWhinney was a superb copy editor who improved my errant English, cleaned up my French, and did it all with patience, intelligence, and grace.

The two presses divided tasks between them and worked pleasantly together. We had no major problems of coordination—which was due to Bob, Louise, and especially to our excellent traffic editor, Deirdre Molina, who was a gracious and good humored taskmistress.

For the new maps in the book, it was a great pleasure to work once again with Jeffrey Ward, the best historical cartographer in the business. His work uniquely combines creativity and rigor in a professional and collegial way.

The many contemporary images in the book are used not just as illustrations, but as artifacts, evidence, and interpretations. The enormous labor of bringing them together was done by four teams. In Maine and Massachusetts, Judy and I worked together to compile a preliminary list, and Judy also created digital scans and did photography in France. In New York, Bob Bender and Johanna Li played a major role. In the Knopf offices Michelle MacAleese and her colleagues in Toronto gathered many Canadian materials. Most important was the brilliant team of Alexandra Truitt and Jerry Marshall in Salem, New York. They drew on a vast network, found many new images, collected high resolution scans, obtained permissions, and coordinated our efforts.

In scholarship, I have a major debt to three men I have never met: Henry Percival Biggar and Charles-Honoré Laverdière, who established the French texts of Champlain's work, and especially to Marcel Trudel, one of the truly great historians in our time. His many books and most of all the five volumes of his *Histoire de la Nouvelle France* (1963–83), have been vital to this inquiry. An indispensable new book is *Champlain: la naissance de l'Amérique française* (2004, also in an English edition), edited by Raymonde Litalien and Denis Vaugeois. They have carried the subject to a new level of rigor and seriousness.

Denis Vaugeois also took time from his own work to read a draft of my book in manuscript. He made many suggestions for improvement and gave me the benefit of his knowledge with a generosity that he has shown to many Champlain scholars throughout the world. I am grateful for his help.

Thanks go to Eric Thierry, one of the most distinguished Champlain scholars in France, who wrote to me about his excellent new book, *La France de Henri IV en Amérique du Nord*. I very much appreciate his kindness in sharing his work with me.

My Brandeis friend and colleague in French history Paul Jankowski was a source of advice failing assistance and advice. A friend of many years, John Demos offered wise counsel. Dona Delorenzo and Judy Brown kept things running and made the office an oasis of happiness and calm in academe. My superb Brandeis students were also my teachers. And our very able president, Jehuda Reinharz, has been a colleague and friend for many years.

In Boston the Consul General of France, François Gauthier, and his gracious wife, Françoise, actively supported the book in many ways. Both are trained historians with an abiding interest in Champlain. They followed his travels as we have done, and in their work and lives they keep alive Champlain's spirit of amitié and concorde.

This book was a family project. My brother, Miles, helped with the Dutch translation. Susanna Fischer saw several drafts and offered helpful suggestions, and Erik helped us with computers at a critical moment. Anne and Fred Turner were a source of unfailing encouragement, as also were John Fischer and Ann Fischer, William Fischer and Kirstin Fischer. The next generation were our inspiration: Althea Turner, Mathew Mueller, Eliza Fischer, Kevin Fischer, Samuel Fischer, and Natalie Fischer. My wife, Judy, took time from her work to be a partner in the project. We traveled together, she helped in the archives, gathered images, edited the text, and much more. My father, John, was once again my most trusted advisor. This book is dedicated to him, with the gratitude of all his growing family for the gift of his wisdom and judgment.

D.H.F.
Blasted Ledge, Mount Desert Island, Maine
June 23, 2008

INDEX